ON THE ROAD

YOUR COMPLETE DESTINATION GUIDE
In-depth reviews, detailed listings
and insider tips

Nevada
p54

Utah
p386

Southwestern
Colorado
p354

Arizona
p106

New Mexico
p234

SURVIVAL GUIDE

VITAL PRACTICAL INFORMATION TO
HELP YOU HAVE A SMOOTH TRIP

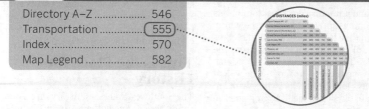

DISTANCES (miles)

THIS EDITION WRITTEN AND RESEARCHED BY

Amy C Balfour, Michael Benanav, Sarah Chandler,
Lisa Dunford, Carolyn McCarthy

welcome to Southwest USA

The Great Outdoors

Beauty and adventure don't just join hands in the Southwest. They crank up the white-water, unleash the single track, add blooms to the trail and drape a sunset across the red rocks. Then they smile and say, 'Come in.' This captivating mix of scenery and possibility lures travelers who want to rejuvenate physically, mentally and spiritually. The big draw is the Grand Canyon, a two-billion-year-old wonder that shares its geologic treasures with a healthy dose of fun. Next door in Utah, the red rocks will nourish your soul while thrashing your bike. In southern Colorado ice climbing and mountain biking never looked so pretty. Tamp down the adrenaline in New Mexico

with a scenic drive, an art walk or a lazy slide down a shimmery dune. And Vegas? Your willpower may be the only thing exercised, but chasing the neon lights will certainly add verve to your vacation.

This is the Place for History

The Southwest wears its history on its big, sandy sleeve. Ancient cultures left behind cliff dwellings and petroglyphs while their descendants live on in reservations and pueblos. Navajos and Apaches arrived next, followed by Spanish conquistadors. Next up? The missionaries, who left a string of stunning missions in their wake. Mormon religious refugees arrived with

The Southwest is America's playground, luring adventurers and artists with the promise of red-rock landscapes, the legends of shoot-'em-up cowboys and the kicky delights of a green chile stew.

(left) The Mittens, Monument Valley
(below) Cactus blooms

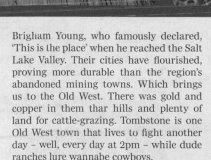

Brigham Young, who famously declared, 'This is the place' when he reached the Salt Lake Valley. Their cities have flourished, proving more durable than the region's abandoned mining towns. Which brings us to the Old West. There was gold and copper in them thar hills and plenty of land for cattle-grazing. Tombstone is one Old West town that lives to fight another day – well, every day at 2pm – while dude ranches lure wannabe cowboys.

Multicultural Meanderings

It's the multicultural mix – Native American, Hispanic, Anglo – that makes a trip to the Southwest unique. There are 19 Native American pueblos in New Mexico, and the Navajo Reservation alone covers more than 27,000 sq miles. Monument Valley and Canyon de Chelly, two of the most striking geologic features in the Southwest, are protected as sacred places. Tribal traditions and imagery influence art across the region. The Spanish and Mexican cultures are also a part of daily life, from the food to the language to the headlines about illegal immigration. In Utah 58% of the population identifies as Mormon, and the religion's stringent disapproval of 'vices' keeps the state on an even keel. So savor the cultural differences – and start with that green chile stew.

❯ Southwest USA

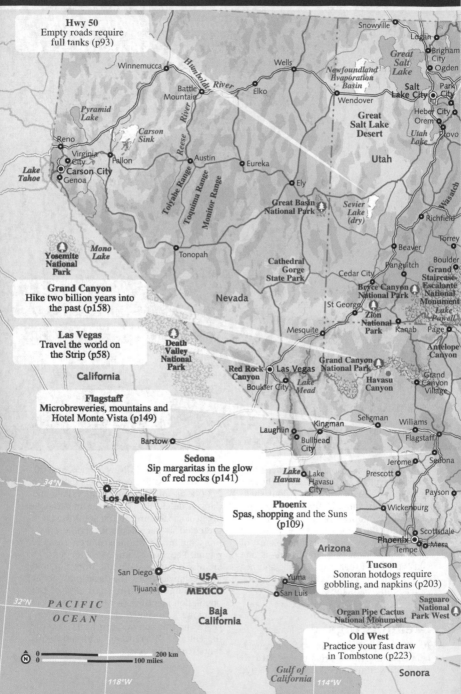

Hwy 50
Empty roads require full tanks (p93)

Grand Canyon
Hike two billion years into the past (p158)

Las Vegas
Travel the world on the Strip (p58)

Flagstaff
Microbreweries, mountains and Hotel Monte Vista (p149)

Sedona
Sip margaritas in the glow of red rocks (p141)

Phoenix
Spas, shopping and the Suns (p109)

Tucson
Sonoran hotdogs require gobbling, and napkins (p203)

Old West
Practice your fast draw in Tombstone (p223)

Snowville
Logan
Brigham City
Ogden
Great Salt Lake
Salt Lake City
Park City
Heber City
Orem
Provo
Utah Lake
Great Salt Lake Desert
Wendover
Newfoundland Evaporation Basin
Wells
Elko
Winnemucca
Battle Mountain
Humboldt River
Reese River
Austin
Eureka
Ely
Utah
Richfield
Torrey
Wasatch
Beaver
Boulder
Panguitch
Grand Staircase-Escalante National Monument
Lake Powell
Cedar City
Bryce Canyon National Park
St George
Zion National Park
Kanab
Page
Mesquite
Antelope Canyon
Great Basin National Park
Sevier Lake (dry)
Pyramid Lake
Reno
Virginia City
Fallon
Carson Sink
Carson City
Genoa
Lake Tahoe
Tojabe Range
Toquima Range
Monitor Range
Tonopah
Nevada
Cathedral Gorge State Park
Yosemite National Park
Mono Lake
Death Valley National Park
Red Rock Canyon
Las Vegas
Boulder City
Lake Mead
Grand Canyon National Park
Havasu Canyon
Grand Canyon Village
California
Kingman
Seligman
Williams
Laughlin
Bullhead City
Flagstaff
Barstow
Jerome
Sedona
Prescott
Lake Havasu
Lake Havasu City
Payson
Los Angeles
Wickenburg
Scottsdale
Phoenix
Mesa
Tempe
Arizona
San Diego
Tijuana
USA
MEXICO
Yuma
San Luis
Tucson
PACIFIC OCEAN
Baja California
Organ Pipe Cactus National Monument
Saguaro National Park West
Gulf of California
Sonora
34°N
32°N
118°W
114°W
0   200 km
0   100 miles
N

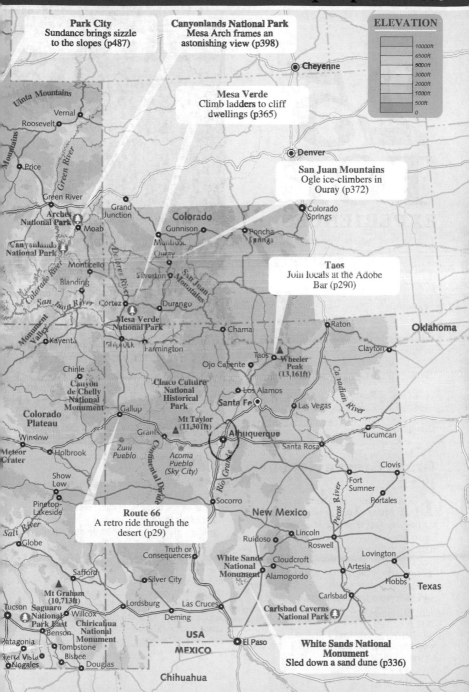

ELEVATION

10000ft
6500ft
5000ft
3000ft
2000ft
1000ft
500ft
0

Park City
Sundance brings sizzle
to the slopes (p487)

Canyonlands National Park
Mesa Arch frames an
astonishing view (p398)

Mesa Verde
Climb ladders to cliff
dwellings (p365)

San Juan Mountains
Ogle ice-climbers in
Ouray (p372)

Taos
Join locals at the Adobe
Bar (p290)

Route 66
A retro ride through the
desert (p29)

**White Sands National
Monument**
Sled down a sand dune (p336)

25 TOP EXPERIENCES

Grand Canyon National Park

1 Go ahead, don't hold back. Let out that 'Whoa!' as you peek over the edge for the very first time. The sheer immensity of the canyon is what grabs you first: it's a two-billion-year-old rip across the landscape that reveals the Earth's geologic secrets with commanding authority. But it's Mother Nature's artistic touches – from sun-dappled ridges and crimson buttes to lush oases and a ribbon-like river – that hold your attention and demand your return. As Theodore Roosevelt said, this natural wonder is 'unparalleled throughout the rest of the world.'

Sedona

2 The beauty of the red rocks hits you on an elemental level. Yes, the jeep tours, crystal shops and chichi galleries add to the fun, but it's the crimson buttes – strange yet familiar – that make Sedona unique. Soak up the beauty by hiking to Airport Mesa, bicycling beneath Bell Rock or sliding across Oak Creek. New Agers may tell you to seek out the vortexes, which allegedly radiate the Earth's power. The science may be hard to confirm, but even non-believers can appreciate the sacred nature of this breathtaking tableau.

RALPH HOPKINS/LONELY PLANET IMAGES ©

CHEYENNE ROUSE/LONELY PLANET IMAGES ©

Las Vegas

3 Just as you awaken from your in-flight nap – rested, content, ready for red-rock inspiration – here comes Vegas shaking her thing on the horizon like a showgirl looking for trouble. As you leave the airport and glide beneath the neon of the Strip, she puts on a dazzling show: dancing fountains, a spewing volcano, the Eiffel Tower. But she saves her most dangerous charms for the gambling dens – seductive lairs where the fresh-pumped air and bright colors share one goal: separating you from your money. Step away if you can for fine restaurants, Cirque du Soleil and a shark-filled reef.

Old West Towns of Arizona

4 If you judge an Old West town by the quality of its nickname, then Jerome, once known as the Wickedest Town in the West, and Tombstone, the Town Too Tough to Die, are the most fascinating spots in Arizona. While Bisbee's moniker – Queen of the Copper Camps – isn't quite as intriguing, the town shares key traits with the others: a rough-and-tumble mining past, a remote location capping a scenic drive, and a quirky cast of entrepreneurial citizens putting their spin on galleries, B&Bs and restaurants. Pardner, they're truly the best of the West. Bisbee

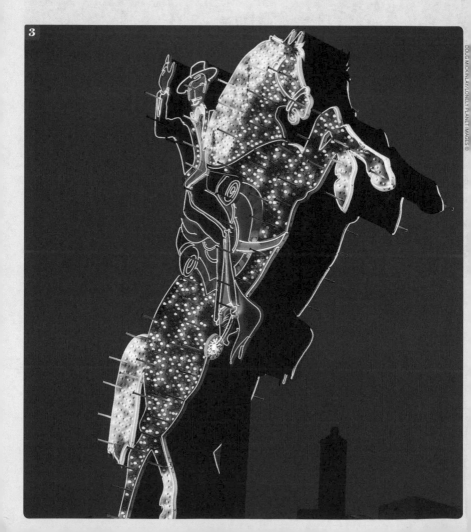

3

Santa Fe

5 Santa Fe may be celebrating her 400th birthday, but she's kicking up her stylish heels like a teenager. On Friday night, art lovers flock to Canyon Rd to gab with artists, sip wine and explore more than 100 galleries. Art and history partner up within the city's consortium of museums, with international crafts, Native American art, world-class collections and a new history museum competing for attention. And oh, the food and the shopping. With that crystal-blue sky as a backdrop, dining and shopping on the Plaza isn't just satisfying, it's sublime.

Route 66

6 As you step up to the counter at the Snow Cap Drive-In in Seligman, Arizona, you know a prank is coming – a squirt of fake mustard or ridiculously incorrect change. And though it's all a bit hokey, you'd be disappointed if the owner forgot to 'get you'. It's these kitschy, down-home touches that make the Mother Road so memorable. Begging burros, the Wigwam Motel, the neon signs of Tucumcari – you gotta have something to break up the scrubby Southwest plains. We'll take a squirt of fake mustard over a mass-consumption McBurger every time.

Angels Landing (Zion)

7 The climb to Angels Landing in Zion National Park may be the best day-hike in North America. The 2.2-mile trail crosses the Virgin River, hugs a towering cliffside, squeezes through a narrow canyon, snakes up Walter's Wiggles then traverses a razor-thin ridge – where steel chains and the encouraging words of strangers are your only reliable friends. Your reward after the final scramble to the 5790-ft summit? A lofty view of Zion Canyon. The hike encapsulates what's best about the park: beauty, adventure and the shared community of travelers who love the outdoors.

Moab

8 The Slickrock Trail won't kick my butt, dude, no way. I'm fit, I'm ready, I'm – ow! I'm flat on my back. That rock just ate my bike, bro. Awesome! Oh yes, the bike-thrashing, 12.7-mile Slickrock Trail is the signature ride in this gnarly gateway town, and with a trail that tough, you gotta have the appropriate backup: a sunrise java joint, a cool indie bookstore, outdoor shops and a post-ride brewery that smells of beer and adventure. Moab scores on all points.

Mesa Verde National Park

9 You don't just walk into the past at Mesa Verde, the site of 600 ancient cliff dwellings. You scramble up 10ft ladders, scale a 60ft rock face and crawl 12ft through a tunnel. Yes, it's interactive exploring at its most low-tech, but it's also one of the most exhilarating adventures in the Southwest. It's also a place to puzzle out the archaeological and cultural clues left by its former inhabitants – Ancestral Puebloans who vacated the site in AD 1300 for reasons still not fully understood.

Flagstaff

10 Flagstaff is finally the perfect mountain town. For years this outdoorsy mecca – think hiking, biking, skiing and star-gazing – fell short of perfection due to the persistent blare of passing trains, up to 125 daily. Today, the horns have been silenced and Grand Canyon travelers can finally enjoy a decent night's sleep. Well-rested? Stay longer to walk the vibrant downtown, loaded with ecofriendly eateries, indie coffee shops, convivial breweries and atmospheric hotels. It's a liberal-minded, energetic place fueled by students at North Arizona University – and it's ready to share the fun.

Monument Valley & Navajo Nation

11 'May I walk in beauty' is the final line of a famous Navajo prayer. Beauty comes in many forms on the Navajo's sprawling reservation but makes its most famous appearance at Monument Valley, a majestic cluster of rugged buttes and stubborn spires. Beauty swoops in on the wings of birds at Canyon de Chelly, a lush valley where farmers till the land near age-old cliff dwellings. Elsewhere, beauty is in the connections, from the docent explaining Navajo clans to the cafe waiter offering a welcoming smile. *Canyon de Chelly*

Taos

12 The grab bag of celebrities who are crazy for Taos is as eclectic as the town itself. In the 1840s, mountain man Kit Carson chose Taos as the end of the trail. Today, outdoorsy types hike and ski in the surrounding mountains while history buffs wander Carson's home and the Taos Pueblo. Georgia O'Keeffe and DH Lawrence led the artists' charge, and now more than 80 galleries line the streets. Carl Jung and Dennis Hopper? Maybe they came for the quirky individualism, seen today in the wonderfully eccentric Adobe Bar and the off-the-grid Earthship community. *Earthship community*

Carlsbad Caverns National Park

13 As the elevator drops, it's hard to comprehend the ranger's words. Wait, what? We're plunging the length of the Empire State Building? I'm not sure that's such a great idea. But then the doors open. Hey, there's a subterranean village down here. A snack bar, water fountains, restrooms and, most impressive, the 255ft-high Big Room where geologic wonders line a 2-mile path. But you're not the only one thinking it's cool – 250,000 Mexican free-tailed bats roost here from April to October, swooping out to feed at sunset.

Georgia O'Keeffe Country

14 O'Keeffe's cow-skull paintings and mesa-filled landscapes are gateway drugs for New Mexico – one look will have you hankering for arid landscapes framed by brilliant blues. What drew the state's patron artist? As she explained, 'It's something that's in the air, it's different. The sky is different. The wind is different.' Travelers can experience this uniqueness with a stroll through Santa Fe, stopping by the Georgia O'Keeffe Museum for background and a close-up view of her paintings. From there, the best stops include Abiquiú and the atmospheric Ghost Ranch where the views are superb.

Tucson

15 Like so many Arizonan towns, Tucson sprawls. Yet it still manages to feel like a cohesive whole. From the pedestrian-friendly anchor of 4th Ave, you can walk past indie clothing boutiques and live music clubs that balance cowboy rock with East Coast punk, stopping to eat the original chimichanga and see a show at a Gothy burlesque club. With wheels, you can follow the saguaros to their namesake park then catch a sunset at Gates Pass. Conclude with a Sonoran hotdog, a festival of delicious excess that celebrates the city's muticultural heritage.

White Sands National Monument

16 Frisbee on the dunes, colorful umbrellas in the sand, kids riding wind-blown swells – the only thing missing at this beach is the water. But you don't really mind its absence, not with 275 sq miles of gypsum draping the landscape with a hypnotic whiteness that rolls and rises across the southern New Mexico horizon. A 16-mile scenic drive loops past one-of-a-kind views, but to best get a handle on the place, full immersion is key: buy a disc at the gift store, trudge to the top of a dune, run a few steps and...wheee!

Salt Lake City

17 The 2002 Winter Olympics dropped the world at the door, and Salt Lake City is riding the momentum. Outdoorsy tourists and new residents are swooping in for world-class hiking, climbing and skiing, and they're infusing this Mormon enclave with rebel spirit. For decades, the populace was like its streets: orderly and square, with the Mormon influence keeping change at bay. But no more. It's a post-Olympic world with bustling brewpubs, eclectic restaurants and a flourishing arts scene.

Phoenix

18 Sometimes you just have to ask: what about me? Phoenix answers that question with a stylish grin. Golfers have their pick of more than 200 courses. Posh resorts cater to families, honeymooners and even dear old Fido. The spas are just as decadent, offering aquatic massages, citrusy facials and healing desert-clay wraps. Add in world-class museums, patio-dining extraordinaire, chichi shopping and more than 300 days of sunshine, and it's easy to condone a little selfishness.

Arches & Canyonlands National Parks

19 More than 2500 arches cluster within 116 miles at Arches, a cauldron of geologic wonders that includes a balanced rock, a swath of giant fins and one span that's so photogenic it's emblazoned on Utah license plates. Just north is equally stunning Canyonlands, a maze of plateaus, mesas and canyons as forbidding as it is beautiful. How best to understand the subtle power of the landscape? As eco-warrior Edward Abbey said in *Desert Solitaire*, 'you can't see anything from the car.' So get out, breathe in, walk forward.

Bryce National Park

20 At sunrise and sunset, the golden-red spires of Utah's smallest national park shimmer like trees in a magical stone forest – a hypnotic, Tolkien-esque place that is surely inhabited by nimble elves and mischievous sprites. The otherworldly feeling continues as you navigate the maze of crumbly hoodoos beside the 1.4-mile Navajo Loop trail, which drops 521ft from Sunset Point. Geologically, the park is magical too; the spires are the limestone edges of the Paunsaugunt Plateau – eroded by rain, shaped by freezing water.

Park City

21 Park City, how'd you get to be so cool? Sure, you hosted events in the 2002 Winter Olympics, and you're home to the US Ski Team, but it's not just the snow sports. There's the Sundance Film Festival, which draws enough glitterati to keep the world abuzz. We're also digging the stylish restaurants; they serve fine cuisine but never take themselves too seriously. Maybe that's the key – it's a world-class destination comfortable with its small-town roots.

Pueblos

22 Nineteen Native American pueblos are scattered across New Mexico. These adobe villages – often rising several stories above the ground – offer a glimpse into the distinct cultures of some of America's longest running communities. Not all are tourist attractions, but several offer unique experiences that may be among your most memorable in the Southwest. Marvel at the mesa-top views at Acoma, shop for jewelry at Zuni and immerse yourself in history at the Taos Pueblo – where the fry bread at Tewa's makes a tasty distraction.

CHEYENNE ROUSE/LONELY PLANET IMAGES ©

ANN CECIL/LONELY PLANET IMAGES ©

STEPHEN SAKS/LONELY PLANET IMAGES ©

ED DARACK/SCIENCE FACTION/CORBIS ©

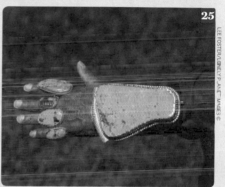

LEE FOSTER/LONELY PLANET IMAGES ©

Hwy 50: The Loneliest Road in America

23 You say you want to drop off the grid? Are you sure? Test your resolve on this desolate strip of pavement that stretches across the white-hot belly of Nevada. The highway passes through a poetic assortment of tumbleweed towns following the route of the Overland Stagecoach, the Pony Express and the first transcontinental telephone line. Today, it looks like the backdrop for a David Lynch film, with scrappy ghost towns, hardscrabble saloons, singing sand dunes and ancient petroglyphs – keeping things more than a little off-kilter.

San Juan Mountains

24 Adventure lovers, welcome home. The San Juans are a steep, rugged playground renowned for mountain biking, hut-to-hut hiking and high-octane skiing. But it's not all about amped-up thrills in the towns lining US 550, also known as the San Juan Byway (or the Million Dollar Highway between Ouray and Silverton). Both glitzy and gritty, secluded Telluride draws travelers to its outdoor festivals while Ouray lures 'em in with hot springs and ice climbing. In summer, a historic train chugs into Silverton daily from Durango. Leaf-peepers, start your engines for the yellow-aspen shimmer in the fall.

Native American Art

25 Native American art is not stuck in the past. While designs often have a ceremonial purpose or religious significance, the baskets, rugs and jewelry that are crafted today often put a fresh spin on the ancient traditions – in Phoenix's Heard Museum, dedicated to Southwest cultures, you'll even see pottery emblazed with a Harry Potter theme. From Hopi kachina dolls and Navajo rugs to Zuni jewelry and the baskets of the White Mountain Apaches, art is a window into the heart of the native Southwest peoples.

need to know

When to Go

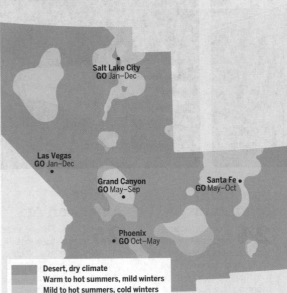

Salt Lake City
GO Jan–Dec

Las Vegas
GO Jan–Dec

Grand Canyon
GO May–Sep

Santa Fe
GO May–Oct

Phoenix
GO Oct–May

Desert, dry climate
Warm to hot summers, mild winters
Mild to hot summers, cold winters

High Season
(Jun–Aug, Nov–Feb)

» Enjoy warm temperatures and sunny skies in New Mexico, Utah and northern Arizona.

» In winter, hit the slopes in Utah, New Mexico and Colorado or giddy-up at Arizona dude ranches.

Shoulder Season (Mar–May, Sep–Oct)

» In fall, check out colorful aspens and cottonwoods in southern Colorado and northern New Mexico.

» Cooler temperatures and lighter crowds on the Grand Canyon South Rim.

Low Season
(Nov–Feb, Jun–Aug)

» National parks in northern Arizona and Utah clear out as the snow arrives.

» In summer, locals flee the heat in southern Arizona.

Your Daily Budget

Budget less than
$100

» Campgrounds and hostels: $20-40

» Taquerias, sidewalk vendors, supermarkets for self-caterers

» Share a rental car; split cost of park vehicle entry fees

Midrange
$100–250

» Mom-and-pop motels, low-priced chains: $50-90

» Diners, good local restaurants

» Visit museums, theme parks, national and state parks

Top end over
$250

» Boutique hotels, B&Bs, resorts, national park lodges: $120-650

» Upscale restaurants

» Hire an outdoor outfitter; take a guided tour; book ahead for top performances

Money

» ATMs widely available in cities and towns, but less prevalent on Native American land. Credit cards accepted in most hotels and restaurants.

Visas

» Generally not required for stays up to 90 days for countries included in the Visa Waiver Program.

Cell Phones

» Local SIM cards can be used in unlocked European and Australian phones. Cell phone reception can be non-existent in remote or mountainous areas.

Driving/ Transportation

» Best option for exploring is a car. Amtrak and Greyhound buses typically do not stop in national parks or small towns.

Websites

» **National Park Service** (www.nps.gov) Current information about national parks.

» **Lonely Planet** (www.lonelyplanet.com/usa/southwest) Summaries, travel news, links and traveler forum.

» **Recreation.gov** (www.recreation.gov) Camping reservations on federally managed lands.

» **American Southwest** (www.americansouthwest.net) Comprehensive site for national parks and natural landscapes.

» **Grand Canyon Association** (www.grandcanyon.org) Online bookstore with helpful links.

Exchange Rates

Australia	A$1	$1.04
Canada	C$1	$1.02
Europe	€1	$1.43
Japan	¥100	$1.28
Mexico	10 pesos	$.83
New Zealand	NZ$1	$.84
UK	£1	$1.64

For current exchange rates see www.xe.com.

Important Numbers

Country code	☏1
International access code	☏011
Emergency	☏911
National sexual assault hotline	☏800-656-4673
Statewide road conditions	☏511

Arriving in the Southwest

» **McCarran International Airport, Las Vegas, NV**

» Shuttles – $7 to the Strip; take exit door 9 to Bell Trans

» Taxis – $10-15 to the Strip; 30 min in heavy traffic

» **Sky Harbor International Airport, Phoenix, AZ**

» Shuttles – $14 to downtown, $20 to Old Town Scottsdale

» Taxis – $17-19 to downtown, $24 to Old Town Scottsdale

Time

Most of the Southwest is on Mountain Time, which is seven hours behind Greenwich Mean Time. Nevada is one hour behind Mountain Time, on Pacific Time.

Daylight saving time currently begins in mid-March, when clocks are put forward one hour, and ends in early November, when clocks are turned back one hour.

Arizona does not use daylight saving time, so during that period it's one hour behind the other Southwestern states. The Navajo Reservation, which lies in Arizona, New Mexico and Utah, *does* use daylight-saving time (ie the whole reservation is on the same time zone). The small Hopi Reservation, which is surrounded by the Navajo Reservation in Arizona, follows the rest of Arizona. At hotels and restaurants on the Utah and Arizona border, you're likely to see two clocks on the wall – one for each state.

if you like...

Green Chile

Green chile is to New Mexico what breath is to life – essential. Chiles are picked green, roasted in special barrel-shaped contraptions then sold at roadside stands statewide in September and October.

Hatch The soil and water in this town 40 miles north of Las Cruces are perfect for chile-growing, earning it the nickname 'Chile Capital of the World.' Read more on p335.

Green chile cheeseburgers Restaurants across the state boast about the tastiness of their green chile-topped burgers. Our favorites are Sparky's Burgers (p335) and the Owl Bar Café (p325).

Chile Pepper Institute Part of the Chile Pepper Breeding and Genetics Program at NMSU, the institute has chile-filled demonstration gardens (p333).

Horseman's Haven Serving the HOTTEST green chile in Santa Fe, this horse bites (p275)!

Red or green? This is New Mexico's official state question. It's typically asked by waiters wondering whether to serve your dish with red or green chile.

Wine & Microbrews

Whether it's après-ski in Park City, post-ride brews in Durango or wine sipping after shopping in Sedona and Jerome, it just feels right to celebrate your adventures – and the scenery – with a post-workout toast. And with brewpubs, microbreweries and wineries scattered across the region, celebrating is not hard to do.

Polygamy Porter Lip-smacking Utah microbrew with a catchy slogan: 'Why drink just one?' Try one, or two, at the Wasatch Brew Pub (p494).

Beaver Street Brewery The perfect brewery: darn good food, friendly service, convivial patrons and beer that goes down smooth (p155).

Verde Valley Wine Country Home to an up-and-coming Arizona wine trail that winds past wineries and vineyards in Cottonwood, Jerome and Cornville (p139).

Durango, CO This knobby-tired mountain town hosts the San Juan Brewfest (p361).

Napoleon's More than 100 types of champagne? *Mais oui* at this 19th-century French theme bar (p80).

Hiking

As you descend the South Kaibab Trail past 2 billion years of geologic history, it's easy to feel insignificant. Until you hike back up and your pain becomes rather, well, significant. The Southwest is a rambler's paradise, with scenery to satisfy every type of craving: mountain, riparian, desert and red rock.

Grand Canyon Trails The Rim Trail offers inspiring views, but to really appreciate the age and immensity of the canyon you've got to hike into its depths (p163).

Santa Fe National Forest Nearly 1000 miles of trail twist through forests and meadows in the forest's Pecos Wilderness (p311).

Zion National Park Slot canyons, hidden pools and lofty scrambles make this stunner Utah's top national park for hiking (p447).

Piestewa Peak Stroll past saguaros and scale a 2608ft peak in the scrubby heart of Phoenix (p117).

Red Rock Country Hike to vortexes in Sedona (p141), hoodoos in Bryce Canyon (p435) and slender spans in Arches (p415) and Canyonlands (p398) National Parks.

JOHN HAY/LONELY PLANET IMAGES ©

» Chile wreath

Small Towns

The small towns of the Southwest may have been settled by ornery miners, greedy cattle barons and single-minded Mormon refugees, but today these places have adjusted comfortably into welcoming artist communities and outdoorsy outposts that typically offer a warm hello.

Bisbee One-time mining town merges artsy, grungy and quirky with thoroughly engaging flair (p225).

Torrey Mecca for outdoor lovers headed into Capital Reef National Park. Also has a bad movie festival, pioneer buildings and the fantastic Café Diablo (p425).

Billy the Kid Highway Named for the outlaw, this scenic byway swoops past shoot-'em-up Lincoln, Smokey the Bear's El Capitan and woodsy Ruidoso (p343).

Ouray Hooray for you-ray, and sometimes ooh-ray, an ice climber's paradise in winter and a haven for hikers in summer that's plunked beside the Million Dollar Hwy (p378).

Wickenburg Channels the 1890s with an ice cream parlor, an Old West museum, home-cooked breakfast joints and several range-riding dude ranches (p130).

Film Locations

From glowing red buttes to scrubby desert plains to the twinkling lights of Vegas, the landscape glows with undeniable cinematic appeal. It's simultaneously a place of refuge, unknown dangers and breathtaking beauty. In other words, it's catnip to movie directors looking to drop their heroes into inspirational settings.

Monument Valley Stride John Wayne–tall beneath the iconic red monoliths that starred in seven of the Duke's beloved Westerns (p188).

Las Vegas Bad boys and their hi-jinks brought Sin City back to the big screen in *Oceans Eleven* and *The Hangover* (p65).

Moab & around Directors of *Thelma & Louise* and *127 Hours* shot their most dramatic scenes in nearby parks (p410).

Butch Cassidy & The Sundance Kid Cassidy roamed southwestern Utah; Grafton ghost town is the site of the movie's bicycle scene (p427).

Very Large Array 27 giant antenna dishes look to the stars in extraterrestrial-themed movies like *Contact* and *Cocoon* (p325).

Kitsch & Offbeat

There's a lot of empty space in the Southwest, and this empty space draws the weird out of people. And we mean that as a compliment. Dinosaur sculptures. Museums of the bizarre. Festivals that spotlight cannibals and desert creativity. Perhaps the bumper sticker we saw in Jerome says it best: 'We're all here because we're not all there.'

Route 66 This two-lane ode to Americana is dotted with wacky roadside attractions, especially in western Arizona (p198).

Burning Man A temporary city in the Nevada desert attracts 55,000 for a week of self-expression and blowing sand (p103).

Roswell, NM Did a UFO crash outside Roswell in 1947? Museums and a UFO festival explore whether the truth is out there (p345).

Ogden Eccles Dinosaur Park Roadside dinosaurs at their kitschy, animatronic best (p495).

Wacky museums The death mask of John Dillinger (p227), mummified bobcats (p31) and Doc Holliday's card table (p224) keep things kitschy in Arizona.

» Stegosaurus replica, Dinosaur National Monument (p502)

Art

Cranes etched on rocks. Georgia O'Keeffe's cow skulls. Black-and-white photographs by Ansel Adams. The Southwest has inspired self-expression in all its forms. Today, former mining towns have re-emerged as artists' communities, and you'll find galleries and studios lining 1800s-era main streets. For artists and shoppers alike, northern New Mexico reigns supreme.

Santa Fe Sidewalk artisans, chichi galleries and sprawling museums are framed by crisp skies and the Sangre de Cristos (p255).

Heard Museum The art, craftsmanship and culture of Southwestern tribes earn the spotlight at this engaging Phoenix museum (p110).

Abiquiú & the Ghost Ranch Captivating red rock landscapes that Georgia O'Keeffe claimed as her own (p285).

Bellagio Gallery of Fine Art Art? On the Las Vegas Strip? You betcha, and the exhibits here draw from top museums and collections (p59).

Jerome This former mining town lures weekend warriors with artist cooperatives, an art walk and one-of-a-kind gift shops (p136).

Historic Sights

Across the Southwest, dinosaurs left their footprints, ancient civilizations left their cliff dwellings and outlaws and sheriffs left behind enough legends to fill hundreds of books. Many of these sights have barely changed over the centuries, making it easy to visualize how history unfolded, sometimes just a few steps away.

Dinosaur National Monument Touch a 150-million-year-old fossil at one of the largest dinosaur fossil beds in North America, discovered in 1909 (p502).

Mesa Verde Climb up to cliff dwelling that housed Ancestral Puebloans more than 700 years ago (p365).

Virginia City Site of the Comstock Lode, which begat an 1859 silver rush (p102).

Picacho Peak State Park On April 15, 1862 this desolate place witnessed the westernmost battle of the Civil War (p216).

Golden Spike National Historic Site Union Pacific Railroad and Central Pacific Railroad met here on May 10, 1869, completing the transcontinental railroad (p481).

Water Adventures

Water adventures? In a land of deserts, red rocks and cacti? Thank the big dams like Hoover, Glen Canyon and Parker for the region's big lakes and all their splashy activities. Elsewhere, hurtle over whitewater, paddle over ripples, slide through a plastic tube or simply sip a cocktail beside a Sin City pool – there's something here to fit your speed.

Grand Canyon Rafting the Colorado through the Big Ditch is the Southwest's most thrilling, iconic expedition (p166).

Pools & theme parks Las Vegas pools are playgrounds for adults (p73); Phoenix water parks are the ideal splash grounds for the kiddies (p120).

Big lakes Water-skiers zip across Lake Mead (p90) and house-boaters putter below crimson rocks on Lake Powell (p420).

Moab rivers The Colorado and Green Rivers win Most Well-Rounded, offering rafting, canoeing and kayaking (p406).

Fly fishing McPhee Lake in Dolores, CO has the best catch ratio in the Southwest (p372).

If you like...spooky stories
The Jerome Grand Hotel
in Jerome offers guests a
ghost tour of the hotel, which
used to be a hospital for
miners (p137).

Old West

The legend of the Wild West has always been America's grandest tale, capturing the imagination of writers, singers, filmmakers and travelers around the world. At atmospheric sites across the region, you can compare the truth to the myth.

Lincoln Billy the Kid's old stomping – and shooting – ground during the Lincoln County War (p343).

Tombstone Famous for the Gunfight at the OK Corral, this dusty town is also home to Boothill Cemetery and the Bird Cage Theater (p223).

Whiskey Row This block of Victorian-era saloons has survived fires and filmmakers (p132).

Kanab Hundreds of Westerns were filmed near this rugged Mormon outpost known as Utah's Little Hollywood (p443).

Steam train Channel the Old West on the steam-driven train that's chugged between Durango and Silverton for 125 years (p360).

Spas & Resorts

When it comes to lavish resorts, the Southwest serves up everything except an oceanfront view. But what Phoenix and Santa Fe lack in beachfront property, they make up for with world-class shopping, dining, art and pampering.

Truth or Consequences Built over Rio Grande–adjacent hot springs, the bathtubs and pools here bubble-up with soothing, hydro-healing warmth (p326).

Ten Thousand Waves The soaking tubs at this intimate Japanese spa are tucked on a woodsy hillside (p263).

Phoenix & Scottsdale Honeymooners, families, golfers – there's a resort for every type of traveler within a few miles of Camelback Rd (p118).

Las Vegas Many four- and five-star hotels – Encore, Bellagio, Wynn – offer resort-like amenities (p72).

Sheraton Wild Horse Pass Resort & Spa On the Gila Indian Reservation, this resort embraces its Native American heritage with style (p121).

Different Cultures

Cowboys and miners showed up late for the party, following on the heels of several vibrant cultures that had already laid claim to the region. Descendants of these early inhabitants (Native Americans, Spanish and Mexican settlers, and Mormons) live in the region today, giving the Southwest a multicultural flair evident in its art, food and festivals.

Hopi Reservation The past and present merge atop the Hopi's long-inhabited mesas, the center of their spiritual world (p192).

Temple Square Trace the history of Mormon pioneers and their leaders on a 10-acre block in Salt Lake City (p466).

National Hispanic Cultural Center Galleries and a stage spotlight Hispanic arts (p243).

Pueblos Multi-level adobe villages, some dating back centuries, are home to a diverse array of Native American tribes in northern New Mexico (p251).

Canyon de Chelly Learn about the history and traditions of the Navajo on a guided tour into this remote but stunning canyon (p190).

If you like...souvenir shops
The kitsch-tastic Bonanza Gift Shop in Las Vegas might just be heaven (p86).

If you like...outlandish rock formations
Make the drive to the Bisti Badlands in northwestern New Mexico and wander past the multicolored hoodoos and balanced rocks (p316).

Geology

The Southwest's geologic story starts with oceans, sediment and uplift, continues with a continental collision and more oceans, then ends with wind, water and erosion.

Grand Canyon A 277-mile river cuts through two-billion-year-old rock whose geologic secrets are layered and revealed within a mile-high stack (p532).

Chiricahua National Monument A rugged wonderland of rock chiseled by rain and wind into pinnacles, bridges and balanced rocks (p228).

Sand dunes The white and chalky gypsum dunes at White Sands National Monument are, simply put, mesmerizing (p336).

Arches National Park Sweeping arcs of sandstone create windows on the snowy peaks and desert landscapes (p415).

Caverns Head to Carlsbad Caverns for an 800ft plunge to a subterranean wonderland (p350) or step into the pristine confines of Kartchner Caverns for an educational tour (p229).

Wildlife

You'd be surprised how much wildlife you can see from the confines of your car – roadrunners, coyotes, elk, maybe a condor. But really, how much fun is that? As descendants of hunting nomads isn't it in our genes to scan the horizon for signs of life?

Bird-watching Southern Arizona is the place to be in April, May and September for migrating birds attracted to its riparian forests (p220).

Valles Caldera National Preserve Dormant crater of a super-volcano is now home to New Mexico's largest elk herd (p283).

Gila National Forest Javelina, bear and trout live in this remote and rugged corner of New Mexico (p330).

California Condors This prehistoric bird, recently on the verge of extinction, is making a comeback near the Vermilion Cliffs (p181)

Arizona-Sonora Desert Museum Education-minded wildlife repository spotlights desert denizens (p207).

Shopping

High quality Native American jewelry and crafts make shopping in the Southwest unique. The stunning landscapes here attract artists galore, and their paintings make for wonderful gifts. There's also plenty of upscale shopping for those who seek it, but remember to save five dollars for that kitschy key chain from Route 66.

Trading Posts Scattered across the southwest, these were the first go-to shops for Native American crafts (p192).

Scottsdale Honey, Manolo up: we don't have *malls* in Scottsdale, we have borgatas, commons and fashion squares (p126).

Santa Fe boutiques Eclectic specialty stores dot downtown and 100+ galleries hug Canyon Road (p278 and p264).

The Strip Over-the-top goes over-the-top at Vegas' newest designer-label malls: Crystal's at City Center and the Shoppes at Palazzo (p85).

Singing Wind Bookshop Destination indie bookstore has everything you'll ever want to read about the Southwest, and a whole lot more (p230).

month by month

Top Events

1 **Sundance Film Festival**, January

2 **Cactus League**, March

3 **Telluride Bluegrass Festival**, June

4 **Burning Man**, September

5 **Balloon Festival**, October

January

Start the New Year swooshing down mountain slopes in New Mexico, Utah and yes, even Arizona. Artsy events like film festivals and poetry readings will turn your mind from the cold. Snowbirds keep warm in Phoenix and Yuma.

Cowboy Poetry

Wranglers and ropers gather in Elko, NV for a week of poetry readings and folklore performances. Started in 1985, this event has inspired cowboy poetry gatherings across the region.

Ice Climbing

Billed as 'The Biggest Ice Festival in North America,' this mid-January party offers chills and thrills with four days of climbing competitions, clinics and microbrew beer – all in Ouray, CO.

Sundance Film Festival

Hollywood moves to Park City in late January when aspiring filmmakers, actors and industry buffs gather for a week of cutting-edge films.

February

Wintery sports not your thing? Hit an urban center for indoor distractions like shopping, gallery hopping or attending the symphony. If your family wants to rope and ride on a dude ranch, now is the time to finalize reservations in southern Arizona.

Tucson Gem & Mineral Show

At the largest mineral and gem show in the US, held the second full weekend in February, about 250 dealers sell jewelry, fossils, crafts and lots and lots of rocks. Lectures, seminars and a silent auction round out the weekend.

ARTfeast

Eat, drink and be merry while gallery hopping in Santa Fe, NM during this weekend-long festival in late February that comes at just the right time – the fashion shows and wine tastings do a good deal to temper the late-winter cold.

March

March is spring break season in the US. Hordes of rowdy college students descend on Arizona's lakes while families head to the region's national parks. Lodging prices may jump in response. Skiers will want to enjoy their last runs in Telluride.

Spring Training

Major league baseball fans have it good in March and early April. That's when Arizona hosts the preseason Cactus League, when some of the best pro teams play ball in Phoenix and Tucson.

Wildflower Viewing

Depending on rainfall, spring is wildflower season in the desert. Check www.desertusa.com for wildflower bloom reports at your favorite national and state parks.

April

Birders flock (sorry) to nature preserves across the region to scan for migrating favorites.

Spring is also the season for outdoor art and music festivals. Runners might consider the Salt Lake City marathon.

Native American Powwow

More than 3000 Native American dancers and singers from the US and Canada come together at the Gathering of Nations Powwow to compete in late April in Albuquerque, NM. There's also an Indian market with more than 800 artists and craftsmen.

Route 66 Fun Run

Classic cars, not joggers, 'run' down Route 66 between Seligman and Golden Shores in western Arizona in late April. Roadster enthusiasts can check out the cars, vans and buses at the Powerhouse Visitor Center parking lot in Kingman on Saturday afternoon.

May

As the school year winds down, May is a good time to enjoy pleasant weather and lighter crowds at the Grand Canyon and other national parks. Southern Arizona starts to heat up, so get that shopping spree done before Phoenix starts to melt. Memorial Day weekend marks the start of summer fun.

Cinco de Mayo

Mexico's 1862 victory over the French in the Battle of Puebla is celebrated on May 5 with parades, dances, music, arts and crafts and street fairs. And lots of Mexican beer.

(above) Blooming cactus flowers along Camino del Diablo in the Sonoran Desert
(below) 'Aliens' at the UFO Festival, Roswell (p28)

(above) Art installation at the Burning Man festival (p28)
(below) Albuquerque's International Balloon Festival in full swing (p28)

June

⭐ Utah Shakespearean Festival

Head to Cedar City for a dramatic 'Shakesperience' with performances, literary seminars and educational backstage tours from mid-June to October. 2011 marked its 50th anniversary.

☆ Bluegrass in the Mountains

In mid-June enjoy the high lonesome sounds of bluegrass in the mountain-flanked beauty of Telluride. Favorites like Old Crow Medicine Show, Sam Bush and Emmylou Harris keep festivarians happy.

July

Summer is in full swing, with annual 4th of July celebrations reminding us that the season is almost halfway over. If you've always wanted to luxuriate in a fancy Phoenix spa, now's your chance. The 100+ heat drives away tourists, so it's a fantastic time to score awesome deals. Mountain bikers can hit the trails at ski resorts in Utah and Colorado.

⭐ Independence Day

Cities and towns across the region celebrate America's birth with rodeos, music, parades and fireworks on the 4th of July. For something different, drive Route 66 to Oatman for the 4th of July sidewalk egg fry.

UFO Festival

Held over the 4th of July weekend, this festival beams down on Roswell, NM with an otherworldly costume parade, guest speakers and workshops. There's even an Alien Battle of the Bands.

Spanish Market

This weekend festival draws huge crowds to Santa Fe in late July. The main event is the acclaimed juried show when traditional Spanish Colonial arts – from small religious devotionals like *retablos* to *bultos* to handcrafted furniture and metalwork – are shown.

August

This is the month to check out Native American culture, with arts fairs, markets and ceremonial gatherings in several cities and towns. Popular parks like the Grand Canyon will likely be booked up, so try for cancellations or grab your tents and water jugs for dispersed camping in nearby national forests and on the Bureau of Land Management (BLM) acreage.

Navajo Festival of Arts & Culture

Artists, dancers and storytellers share the customs and history of the Diné in Flagstaff on a weekend in early August.

Santa Fe Indian Market

Only the best get approved to show their work at Santa Fe's most famous festival, held the third week of August on the historic plaza, that includes a world-famous juried show where more than 1100 artists from 100 tribes and pueblos exhibit.

August Doin's – World's Oldest Continuous Rodeo

Steer wrestling and barrel racing are on tap in Payson, where the annual rodeo has been held for 127 continuous years.

September

It's back to school for the kiddies, which means lighter crowds at the national parks. Fall is a particularly nice time for an overnight hike to the bottom of the Grand Canyon. Leaf-peepers may want to start planning fall drives in northern mountains.

Burning Man

In 2011 an estimated 54,000 people attended this outdoor celebration of self-expression known for its elaborate art displays, barter system, blowing sand and final burning of the man. This temporary city rises in the Nevada desert before Labor Day.

Navajo Nation Fair

The country's largest Native American Fair, with a rodeo, a parade, dances, songs, arts, crafts and food, is held in early September in Window Rock, AZ.

Beer Tasting

Mountain bikers, microbrews, an outdoorsy town and a late-August weekend. The only thing missing is a beer festi- oh wait, there is one. The San Juan Brewfest in Durango serves samples of more than 60 beers.

October

Shimmering aspens lure road trippers to Colorado and northern New Mexico for the annual fall show. Keep an eye out for goblins, ghouls and ghost tours as Halloween makes its annual peek-a-boo appearance on October 31.

Sedona Arts Festival

This fine-art show overflows with jewelry, ceramics, glass and sculptures in early October. More than 150 artists exhibit their art at Sedona's Red Rock High School.

International Balloon Festival

The world's biggest gathering of hot-air balloons, with daily mass lift-offs in early October that invoke childlike awe in Albuquerque, NM.

December

It's Christmas season in the Southwest, which means nativity pageants and holiday lights displays. It's also high season at resorts across the region, from Phoenix to ski resort towns.

Festival of Lights

Some 6000 luminaries twinkle in Tlaquepaque Arts & Crafts Village in Sedona with Santa Claus and a mariachi band.

Route 66 & Scenic Drives

Buckle Up

Route 66
758 to 882 miles (depending on segments driven)
A classic journey through small town America, with a side of kitsch.

Hwy 84/89A: Wickenburg to Sedona
120 miles
The Old West meets the New West on this drive past dude ranches, mining towns, art galleries and stylish wineries.

Billy the Kid Highway
84 miles
This outlaw loop shoots through Billy the Kid's old stomping grounds.

Kayenta-Monument Valley Scenic Road
40 miles
Star in your own western on an iconic drive past cinematic red rocks in Navajo Country.

Highway 50: The Loneliest Road
320 miles
An off-the-grid ramble mixing the quirky, historic and dry lonesome in tumbleweed Nevada.

Million Dollar Highway
25 miles
There's gold in them thar mountain views, but don't squint too hard or you might run off the ro-whoa!

High Road to Taos
85 miles
Drive into your own landscape painting on this picturesque mountain romp between Santa Fe and Taos.

The Southwest is chock-full of picturesque drives and we've dedicated a chapter to the very best. From Route 66 to the Million Dollar Highway to the Loneliest Road in America, we've got a drive for every corner of the region.

For more drives in a particular region, check the destination chapters.

Route 66

'Get your kitsch on Route 66' might be a better slogan for the scrubby stretch of Mother Road running through Arizona and New Mexico. Begging burros. Lumbering dinosaurs. A wigwam motel. It's a bit offbeat, but all the folk along the way sure seem glad that you're stopping by.

Why Go?

History, scenery and the open road. This alluring combination is what makes a road trip on Route 66 so fun. From Topock, Arizona, heading east, highlights include the begging burros of Oatman, the Route 66 Museum in Kingman and an eclectic general store in tiny Hackberry. Kitsch roars its dinosaury head at Grand Canyon Caverns, luring you 21 stories underground for a tour and even an overnight stay. Burma-Shave signs spout amusing advice on the way to Seligman, a funny little village that greets travelers with retro motels, a roadkill cafe and a squirt of fake mustard at the Snow Cap Drive-In.

Route 66 & Scenic Drives

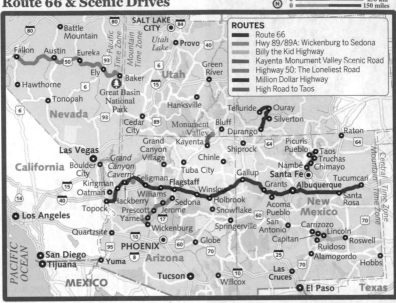

ROUTES
- Route 66
- Hwy 89/89A: Wickenburg to Sedona
- Billy the Kid Highway
- Kayenta Monument Valley Scenic Road
- Highway 50: The Loneliest Road
- Million Dollar Highway
- High Road to Taos

Next up is Williams, a railroad town lined with courtyard motels and brimming with small-town charm. Route 66 runs parallel to the train tracks through Flagstaff, passing the wonderful Museum Club, a cabinlike roadhouse where everyone's having fun. From here, must-sees include Meteor Crater and the 'Take it Easy' town of **Winslow** where there's a girl, my Lord, in a flatbed Ford... Snap a photo of the famous corner then savor a spectacular dinner in the Turquoise Room at La Posada hotel. Finish Arizona in kitschy style with a snooze in a concrete teepee in Holbrook.

In New Mexico, look for the 1937 El Rancho hotel (John Wayne slept here!) in Gallup then slurp green-chile stew at Albuquerque's beloved eatery, Frontier. Route 66 runs uninterrupted through Gallup, passing the restored 1926 Spanish Colonial El Morro Theatre. Next up? Santa Rosa's scuba-ready Blue Hole and the neon signs of Tucumcari, comforting reminders of civilization as dusk falls over the lonesome plains.

When to Go

The best time to travel Route 66 is from May to September, when the weather is warm and you'll be able to take advantage of more open-air activities.

The Route (882 miles)

This journey starts in Topock, Arizona then continues northeast to Kingman. After crossing I-40, Route 66 travels east and cuts through Flagstaff, Winslow and Holbrook. In New Mexico, it passes through Gallup and Grants before entering Albuquerque, Santa Rosa and Tucumcari.

Time

If you're racing down the Mother Road, this trip will take about two days because the route is primarily two-lane and there are lots of stoplights in the cities. If you have some time, it's best explored over the course of a week.

Hwy 89 & 89A: Wickenburg to Sedona

Hwy 89 and its sidekick Hwy 89A are familiar to Arizona road-trippers because they cross some of the most scenic and distinct regions in the center of the state. The section described here travels from Wickenburg over the Weaver and Mingus Mountains before rolling into Sedona.

Why Go?

This is our favorite drive in Arizona. It may not be the prettiest or the wildest, but the trip is infused with a palpable sense of the Old West, like you've slipped through the swinging doors of history. But the route's not stuck in the 19th century – far from it. Weekend art walks, a burgeoning wine trail, stylish indie shops and top-notch restaurants all add some 21st-century spark. For those interested in cowboy history, Wickenburg and its dude ranches are a good place to spend some time. Hwy 89 leaves town via Hwy 93 and soon tackles the Weaver Mountains, climbing 2500ft in 4 miles. The road levels out at mountain-topping Yarnell, 'where the desert breeze meets the mountain air,' then swoops easily past grassy buttes and grazing cattle in the Peeples Valley. From here, highlights include Prescott's Whiskey Row, towering Thumb Butte and the unusual boulders at Granite Dells.

Follow Hwy 89A to Jerome and hold on tight. This serpentine section of road brooks no distraction, clinging tight to the side of Mingus Mountain. If you dare, glance east for stunning views of the Verde Valley. The zigzagging reaches epic proportions in Jerome, a former mining town cleaved into the side of Cleopatra Hill. Pull over for art galleries, tasting rooms, quirky inns and an unusually high number of ghosts. Hwy 89A then drops into Clarkdale, Tuzigoot National Monument and Old Town Cottonwood. On the way to the red rocks of Sedona and Oak Creek Canyon, detour to wineries on Page Springs Rd or loop into town via the Red Rock Loop Rd past Cathedral Rock.

When to Go

This route is best traveled in spring, summer and fall to avoid winter snow – although you might see a few flakes in the mountains in April. In the dead of summer, you won't want to linger in low-lying, toasty Wickenburg.

The Route (120 miles)

From Wickenburg, follow Hwy 93 to Hwy 89 then drive north to Prescott. North of town pick up Hwy 89A, following it to Sedona.

Time

This trip takes about a half-day to drive without stopping, assuming you don't get stuck behind a slow-moving recreational

---

ROADSIDE ODDITIES: ROUTE 66

» Grand Canyon Caverns tour & underground motel room A guided tour 21 stories below the earth's surface loops past mummified bobcats, civil-defense supplies and a $700 motel room.

» Burma-Shave signs Red-and-white ads from a bygone era line the roadside, offering tongue-in-cheek advice for life.

» Seligman's Snow Cap Drive-In Juan Delgadillo opened this prankish burger joint and ice-creamery in 1953.

» Meteor Crater A fiery rock slammed into the earth 50,000 years ago, leaving a 550ft-deep pockmark that's nearly 1 mile across.

» Holbrook's Wigwam Motel Concrete wigwams will flash you back to the 1950s with retro hickory log-pole furniture.

---

vehicle. To fully enjoy the scenery and the towns, give yourself four to five days.

Billy the Kid Highway

Named for the controversial outlaw famous for his role in the Lincoln County War, the Billy the Kid National Scenic Byway loops around his old stomping grounds in the rugged mountains of Lincoln National Forest in central New Mexico.

Why Go?

This mountain-hugging loop provides a cool respite from the heat and hustle-bustle of Roswell and Alamogordo. For a primer on Billy the Kid, also known as William Bonney, the best place to start is Lincoln, population 50 (see also p344). This one-road hamlet was the focal point of the Lincoln County war, a bloody rivalry between two competing merchants and their gangs in the late 1870s. Billy took an active role in the conflict and evidence of his involvement can be seen today at the courthouse: a bullet hole in the wall left after he shot his way to freedom during a jailbreak. From here, you can visit Smokey the Bear's grave in Capitan, hike up Sierra Blanca Peak, or take in a bit of horse racing at

HOTEL & MOTEL

EL RANCHO

HOME OF THE MOVIE STARS

RESTAURANT
STEAKS • BBQ RIBS

Armand WORLD FAMOUS
Ortega's INDIAN STORE

HISTORIC
HOTEL

» (above) El Rancho Hotel and Motel
(p319), a National Historic Landmark
on Route 66
» (left) Hairpin bend on Million Dollar
Highway (p34)

JOHN ELK III/LONELY PLANET IMAGES ©

Ruidoso Downs. End with dinner at Rickshaw, serving the best Asian food in the region.

When to Go

Although there's skiing in the area in winter, the best time for a scenic drive is during summer, when average temperatures hover between 77°F and 82°F (25°C and 28°C). It's also a pleasant time to enjoy hiking and fly-fishing in the surrounding national forest.

The Route (84 miles)

From Roswell, follow Hwy 70 west to Hwy 380, following it through Hondo, Lincoln and Capitan before looping south on Hwy 48 to Ruidoso then take Hwy 70 east to close the loop at Hondo.

Detour

For art galleries, antique shops and a few members of the herd of Painted Burros – a mulish spin on the colorful painted cows in New York and Chicago – head to tiny Carrizozo sitting 20 miles west of Capitan on Hwy 360. Curious kids will enjoy a short hike through a lava field at Valley of Fires Recreation Area.

Time

If you're not stopping, this route should take about half a day. To see the sights, including Carrizozo, allow three days.

Kayenta-Monument Valley Scenic Road

One of the cool things about road-tripping to Monument Valley – and there are many – is that the place isn't easy to reach. Upon arrival, you can't help but feel a special sense of accomplishment, that you're in on a secret that's saved only for the most worthy of travelers.

Why Go?

From a distance, the rugged sandstone formations of Monument Valley look like a prehistoric fortress, a huddled mass of red and gold protecting ancient secrets. But as you approach, individual buttes and craggy formations break from the pack, drawing you closer with sun-reflected beauty and unusual shapes. Up close they're downright hypnotic, an alluring mix of familiar and elusive. Yes, we've seen them in the John Ford Westerns, but the big screen doesn't quite capture the changing patterns of light, the imposing height, or the strangeness of the angles and forms.

The closest town to Monument Valley is Kayenta, a cluster of gas stations, motels and restaurants at the junction of Hwys 160 and 163. The Burger King there has a small exhibit on the Navajo Code Talkers. Like Monument Valley, Kayenta is part of the sprawling Navajo Reservation; at 27,000 sq miles it's the country's largest reservation. Hwy 163 leads to the entrance of the Monument Valley Navajo Tribal Park and the 17-mile drive that loops around the major formations. Goulding's Lodge is across from the entrance, on the other side of Hwy 163 (Harry Goulding opened a trading post here in 1925 and enticed director John Ford to the area) and there's a small movie-themed museum on the grounds.

The Monument Valley loop ($5) is a dusty, bumpy dirt road that winds beneath the sandstone formations, most named for the objects or animals they resemble, from the Mittens to Elephant Butte. Budget about an hour and a half for the drive. SUVs will find the drive easy, compact cars may have to drive more carefully. A new addition to the landscape is the View Hotel, which blends in well with the surrounding rocks.

When to Go

Temperatures remain comfortable April through November, reaching the low-to-mid 90s (or low 30s in Celsius) in July and August. With average lows in the 20s (around -6°C) in December and January, winter can be a bit chilly!

The Route (40 miles)

From Tuba City, Arizona, take Hwy 160 northeast to Kayenta. Follow Hwy 163 north 22 miles to the park entrance.

Time

This trip can be done in a day, but to spend some time exploring the area, allow two to three days.

Highway 50: The Loneliest Road

Stretching east from Fallon, Nevada, to Great Basin National Park and the Nevada state line, remote Highway 50 follows some of America's most iconic routes – the Pony

Express, the Overland Stagecoach and the Lincoln Highway – across the heart of the state.

Why Go?

Why would you drive the Loneliest Road in America? As mountaineer George Mallory said about Everest: 'Because it's there.' And yes, Mallory disappeared while attempting the feat, but the lesson still applies. You drive Highway 50 because something might just...happen. So take the blue pill Neo, wake up from your slumber and point your ride toward Fallon, a former pioneer town now home to the US Navy's TOPGUN fighter-pilot school. From here, listen for the singing dunes at Sand Mountain Recreation Area then pull over and hike to the ruins of a Pony Express station – the FedEx office of its day.

Just east of Austin (population 340 last we checked) look for petroglyphs, then yell 'Eureka!' for the tiny town that coughed up $40 million in silver in the 1800s. Then check out the beehive-shaped buildings at Ward Charcoal Ovens State Park near Ely, where charcoal was created to use in the silver smelters. End at Great Basin National Park, gaining 4000ft in elevation on the 12-mile Wheeler Peak Scenic Drive and earning expansive views of the Great Basin Desert.

HISTORY OF ROUTE 66

Built in 1926, Route 66 stretched from Chicago to Los Angeles, linking a ribbon of small towns and country byways as it rolled across eight states. The road gained notoriety during the Great Depression, when migrant farmers followed it west from the Dust Bowl across the Great Plains. It's nickname, 'Mother Road', first appeared in John Steinbeck's novel about the era, *The Grapes of Wrath*. Things got a little more fun after World War II, when newfound prosperity prompted Americans to get behind the wheel and explore. Sadly, just as things got going, the Feds rolled out the interstate system, which eventually caused the Mother Road's demise. The very last town on Route 66 to be bypassed by an interstate was Arizona's very own Williams, in 1984.

When To Go

Your best bet is summer. Sections of the road get hit with snow and rain in winter and early spring; in a few towns the road requires 4WD and chains during the worst conditions.

The Route (320 miles)

From Fallon, Nevada – about 75 miles east of Lake Tahoe – follow Hwy 50 east to Austin, Eureka, Ely and then Great Basin National National Park, bordering Utah.

Time

The Loneliest Road can be driven in less than a day but to check out a few sites and the national park, allow for two or three.

Million Dollar Highway

Stretching between old Colorado mining towns Ouray and Silverton is one of the most gorgeous alpine drives in the US. Part of the 236-mile San Juan Skyway, this section of US 550 is known as the Million Dollar Highway, most likely because its roadbed is filled with ore.

Why Go?

Twenty-five miles of smooth, buttery pavement twists over three mountain passes, serving up views of Victorian homes, snow-capped peaks, mineshaft head-frames and a gorge lined with rock. But the allure isn't just the beauty – there is also the thrill of driving. Hairpin turns, occasional rock slides and narrow, mountain-hugging pavement flip this Sunday afternoon drive into a NASCAR-worthy adventure.

Charming Ouray sits at nearly 7800ft, surrounded by lofty peaks. It also fronts the Uncompahgre Gorge, a steep, rocky canyon famous for its ice climbing. While here, take a hike or soak in the town's hot springs. From Ouray, the Million Dollar Highway – completed in 1884 after three years of construction – hugs the side of the gorge, twisting past old mines that pock the mountainsides. Stay vigilant for the masochistic, spandex-clad cyclists pumping over the passes on the ribbon-thin road. In Silverton, step away from the car and enjoy the aspen-covered mountains or watch the steam-powered Durango & Silverton Narrow Gauge Railroad chug into town.

When to Go

In winter, Red Mountain Pass south of Ouray may close if there is too much snow; at other times you may need chains. You might even see snow on the ground in summer, though it likely won't be on the road.

The Route (25 miles)

From Ouray, follow Hwy 550 south to Silverton.

Detour

The drive between Ouray and Telluride is 50 miles – if you take the paved route. If you're feeling adventurous (and have the right vehicle) consider the 16-mile road over Imogene Pass. On this old mining road you'll cross streams, pass through alpine meadows, negotiate one of the state's highest passes, and even drive by the old mine itself. But we should mention one thing: this 'shortcut' takes three hours. Still game?

Time

Travel time depends on who's traveling in front of you and weather conditions, but at a minimum allow yourself half a day to drive it. If you have time, spend two to three days exploring the region.

High Road to Taos

This picturesque byway in northern New Mexico links Santa Fe to Taos, rippling through a series of adobe villages and mountain-flanked vistas in and around the Truchas Peaks.

Why Go?

Santa Fe and Taos are well-known artists' communities, lovely places brimming with galleries, studios and museums that are framed by turquoise skies and lofty moun-tains. Two cities this stunning should be linked by an artistically pleasing byway. The High Road to Taos, a wandering route that climbs into the mountains, obliges.

In Nambé, hike to waterfalls or simply meditate at Lake Nambé. From here, the road leads north to picturesque Chimayo. Ponder the crutches left in the Santuario de Chimayo (the 'Lourdes of America') or admire fine weaving and wood carving in family-run galleries. Near Truchas, a village of galleries and century-old adobes, you'll find the High Road Marketplace. This cooperative on SR 676 sells a variety of artwork by area artists.

Further up Hwy 76, original paintings and carvings remain in good condition inside the Church of San José de Gracia, considered one of the finest surviving 18th-century churches in the USA. Next is the Picuris Pueblo, once one of the most powerful pueblos in the region. This ride ends at Penasco, a gateway to the Pecos Wilderness that's also the engagingly experimental Penasco Theatre. From here, follow Hwy 75 and 518 to Taos.

When to Go

Catch blooms in spring, the high season in summer and changing leaves in the fall. With the mountains on this route, winter is not the best time to visit.

The Route (85 miles)

From Santa Fe, take 84/285 west to Pojoaque and turn right on Hwy 503, toward Nambé. From Hwy 503, take Hwy 76 to Hwy 75 to Hwy 518.

Time

You can spend a half day enjoying just the scenery, or two days checking out the history and galleries as well.

itineraries

Whether you've got six days or 60, these itineraries provide a starting point for the trip of a lifetime. Want more inspiration? Head online to lonelyplanet .com/thorntree to chat with other travelers.

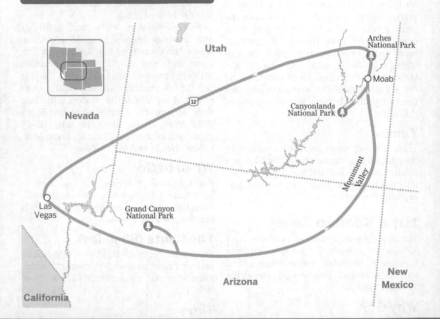

Two Weeks

Vegas, Grand Canyon & Southern Utah Loop

> If you only have time for a short loop, this tour offers a taste of the Southwest's most famous city, canyon and scenery. Start in **Las Vegas** and dedicate a few days to traveling the world on the Strip. When you've soaked up enough decadence, head east to canyon country – **Grand Canyon** country, that is. You'll want a couple of days to explore America's most famous park. For a once-in-a-lifetime experience, descend into the South Rim chasm on the back of a mule and spend the night at Phantom Ranch on the canyon floor.

From the Grand Canyon head northeast through **Monument Valley**, with scenery straight out of a Hollywood Western, to the national parks in Utah's southeast corner – they're some of the most visually stunning in the country. Hike the shape-shifting slot canyons of **Canyonlands National Park**, watch the sun set in **Arches National Park**, or mountain-bike sick slickrock outside **Moab**. Then drive one of the most spectacular stretches of pavement, **Hwy 12**, west until it hooks up with I-15 and takes you back to Las Vegas.

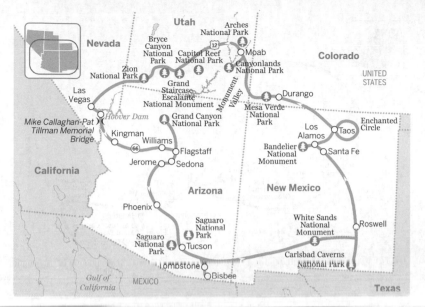

Throw a pair of cowboy boots, hiking boots and comfy walking shoes into the saddle-bag, pardner, and get ready to ride. Suspend judgments and roll the dice for two days on the **Las Vegas Strip** before crossing the new **Mike Callaghan-Pat Tillman Memorial Bridge** – be sure to ogle **Hoover Dam** – as you swoop into Arizona. Next up is **Route 66**, which chases trains and Burma-Shave signs as it unfurls between **Kingman** and **Williams**. Funky **Flagstaff** is a welcoming spot to regroup before venturing into the **Grand Canyon National Park**, where a hike is always a must-do. After three days in the park, end the week among the red rocks of **Sedona**.

Heading south, get in touch with your shabby-chic side in **Jerome** before driving into **Phoenix** for two days of shopping and museum hopping. Mellow out on 4th Avenue, **Tucson**, then study the cacti at **Saguaro National Park**. Fancy yourself a gunslinger in **Tombstone** before ending the week with a two-day stay in charming **Bisbee**.

Next up is New Mexico, where you can sled down sand dunes in the remote **White Sands National Monument**. Spend a day exploring the caves at **Carlsbad Caverns National Park** then head north to **Roswell** to ponder its UFO mysteries. Plan to spend two days in **Santa Fe**, a foodie haven and a magnet for art fiends. Atomic-age secrets are revealed at nearby **Los Alamos**, which are an interesting contrast to the laid-back musings of the hippies and ski bums just north in **Taos**. Drive the luscious **Enchanted Circle** then chill out with a microbrew and bike ride in **Durango**. Next up? Pondering the past inside the amazing cliff dwellings at **Mesa Verde National Park**. You'll be equally amazed by the towering red buttes at **Monument Valley**.

For the most stunning wilderness in the US, spend your last week in Utah's national parks, including **Canyonlands National Park** and **Arches National Park**, for which **Moab** serves as a staging area. From Moab follow **Hwy 12** back to Las Vegas, stopping at **Capitol Reef National Park**, **Grand Staircase-Escalante National Monument**, the spires of **Bryce Canyon National Park** and the sheer red rock walls at **Zion National Park** along the way.

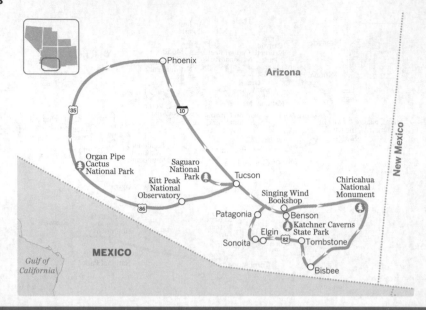

Ten to 12 Days
Southern Arizona

This crazy-eight loop starts in **Phoenix**, where the multitude of posh spas, top museums and upscale dining and shopping options on offer will have you primed for exploring. Escape the urban crush with a long drive south on **Hwy 85** to the lonely but rejuvenating **Organ Pipe Cactus National Park**. Hike, explore and relax for two days. From there, take Hwy 85 north to Hwy 86. Follow this lonely two-lane road east to lofty **Kitt Peak National Observatory**, site of 24 optical telescopes – the largest collection in the world. Take a tour or reserve a spot for nighttime stargazing.

Just northeast, laid-back **Tucson** is a pleasant place to chill out for a day or two. Indie shops line 4th Ave, and Congress St is the place to catch live music. Stop and smell the cacti in **Saguaro National Park** before spending the night in **Benson**, a good launchpad for the pristine **Kartchner Caverns** and the gloriously eclectic **Singing Wind Bookshop**. Wander the odd rock formations at **Chiricahua National Monument** then loop south on Hwys 191 and 181 for eye-catching galleries, great restaurants and an interesting mine tour in **Bisbee**. And you can't drive this far south without swinging by **Tombstone** for a reenactment of Wyatt and Doc's shootout with the Clantons. From Tombstone, Hwy 82 unfurls across sweeping grasslands, the horizon interrupted by scenic mountain ranges (known in these parts as sky islands).

Enjoy a day of wine-tasting in the villages of **Sonoita** and **Elgin** capped off with a slice of Elvis-inspired pizza in **Patagonia**. Close the loop with a swing back through Tucson on I-10 West, grabbing a Sonoran dog for the drive back to Phoenix.

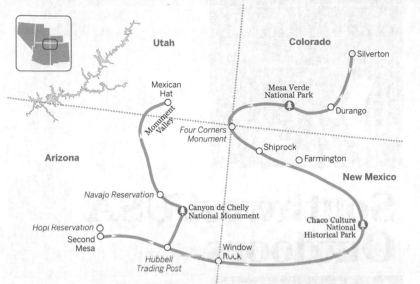

Four Corners/Native American Journey

Start in **Durango** and spend a day exploring the historic mining town. The next day, ride the narrow-gauge railway to **Silverton** and quaff a beer at a Durango microbrewery on your return. Climb ladders into the haunting ruins at **Mesa Verde National Park** before heading to Arizona, stopping on the way at the recently revamped **Four Corners Monument** – check out that snazzy new plaza – to snap a cheesy picture with your hands and feet in four different states.

As you head into New Mexico, ogle **Shiprock**, a stunning, ragged red-rock formation. Spend the night at a motel in nearby **Farmington** or enjoy a snooze inside Kokopelli's Cave, a B&B room 70ft underground – complete with hot tub. A dusty, rutted drive leads to the isolated **Chaco Culture National Historical Park**, an amazing architectural sight. Stay near **Window Rock**, the capital of the **Navajo Reservation**, and be sure to check out the namesake rock. The old-world **Hubbell Trading Post** was the reservation's lifeline when it was established in the 1870s. Detour (65 miles each way) to **Second Mesa**, the heart of the **Hopi Reservation**, where you will find artisans and the Hopi Cultural Center.

Next up? The relatively verdant **Canyon de Chelly National Monument**, an inhabited, cultivated canyon with hogans and sheep herds. Remember to breathe as you approach the out-of-this-world beautiful **Monument Valley**. Drive the 17-mile loop around the towering buttes then spend the night at the adjacent View Hotel, you'll want to spend time – a lot of time – gaping at the monuments from your balcony. Finish the trip with a drive north to **Mexican Hat** in Utah – trust us, you can't miss it.

Southwest USA Outdoors

Best Short Hikes to Big Views

South Kaibab Trail to Cedar Ridge South Rim, Grand Canyon National Park

Bright Angel Point Trail North Rim, Grand Canyon National Park

Angels Landing Zion National Park

Mesa Arch Trail, Canyonlands National Park

Spider Rock Overlook Canyon de Chelly National Monument

Best Wildlife Watching

Birds Patagonia-Sonoita Creek Preserve and Ramsey Canyon Preserve, Arizona

Elk Jemez Trail, Valles Caldera, New Mexico

Eagles Mesa Canyon near Durango, Colorado

Bears Gila National Forest, New Mexico and southern Colorado mountains

California condors Zion National Park and Vermilion Cliffs area, Arizona

Best Water Activities

Splashing Beneath Havasu Falls, Havasupai Reservation, Arizona

Tubing On the Virgin River, Springdale, Utah

One-day rafting trip On the Rio Grande near Taos, New Mexico or the Colorado and Green Rivers in Moab, Utah

Multi-day rafting trip On the Colorado River through Grand Canyon National Park

Fly fishing Dolores, Colorado

The Southwest earns its reputation as the USA's land of adventure with a dizzying array of outdoor landscapes begging to be explored. Plunging canyons, lofty peaks, prickly deserts and red rock formations galore – with this embarrassment of riches it's hard to know where to start. Our advice? Pick one small pocket of the Southwest and get to know it well, rather than crisscrossing the region in search of the next best thing. Many of the towns and parks here are multisport destinations, and you get a different perspective depending on whether you travel by foot, bike, raft or skis.

Hiking
Planning

It's always hiking season somewhere in the Southwest. When temperatures hit the 100s (about 40°C) in Phoenix, cooler mountain trails beckon in Utah and New Mexico. When highland paths are blanketed in snow, southern Arizona provides balmy weather. Parks near St George in southwestern Utah offer pleasant hiking possibilities well into midwinter. Of course, hardy and experienced backpackers can always don cross-country skis or snowshoes and head out for beautiful wintertime mountain treks.

More and more people venture further from their cars and into the wilds these days, so logistics isn't the only reason for careful planning. Some places cap the number of backpackers due to ecological sensitivity or limited facilities. Reservations are essential in highly visited areas such as the Grand Canyon (p158) and during the busy spring and fall months in more seasonal areas like Canyonlands National Park (p398). Consider going to the less heavily visited Bryce Canyon National Park (p435) or Bureau of Land Management (BLM) lands and state parks, for a backpacking trip during busy months. Not only are they less restrictive than the national parks, but usually you can just show up and head out.

Backcountry areas are fragile and cannot support an inundation of human activity, especially when insensitive and careless. The key is to minimize your impact, leaving no trace of your visit and taking nothing but photographs and memories. To avoid erosion and damage, stay on main trails.

Safety

The climate is partly responsible for the epic nature of the Southwestern landscape. The weather is extraordinary in its unpredictability and sheer, pummeling force – from blazing sun to blinding blizzards and deadly flash floods. When there's too much water – the amounts necessary to scour slot canyons smooth – drownings can occur. Too little water combined with unforgiving heat leads to crippling dehydration (see p550). A gallon (3.8L) of water per person per day is the recommended minimum in hot weather. Sun protection (brimmed hats, dark glasses and sunblock) is vital to a desert hiker. Know your limitations, pace yourself accordingly and be realistic about your abilities and interests.

Solo travelers should always let someone know where they are going and how long they plan to be gone. At the very least, use sign-in boards at trailheads or ranger stations. Travelers looking for hiking companions can inquire or post notices at ranger stations, outdoors stores, campgrounds and hostels.

Mountain Biking & Cycling

As with hiking and backpacking, perfect cycling weather can be found at any time of year in different parts of the Southwest. Southern Arizona is a perfect winter destination; Tucson (p203), considered a bicycle-friendly city, has many bike lanes and parks with bike trails. In spring and fall, Utah's

Moab (p403) is an incredibly popular destination for mountain bikers who want to spin their wheels on scenic slickrock trails.

In southern Colorado, the area around Durango has numerous trails (see p360) as do Crested Butte (p383) and the Four Corners area (see p371). Hut-to-hut biking is also available in the San Juans (see p377).

Local bike shops in all major and many minor cities rent bikes and provide maps and information. Visitor information offices and chambers of commerce usually have brochures with detailed trail maps. See p558 for info on rules, costs and so on.

The following are some additional choice mountain-biking spots.

Black Canyon of the Gunnison National Park

A dark, narrow gash above the Gunnison River leads down a 2000ft-deep chasm that's as eerie as it is spectacular. Head to the 6-mile-long South Rim Rd, which takes you to 11 overlooks. To challenge your senses, cycle along the smooth pavement running parallel to the rim.

The nearest town to this area is Montrose. For more info contact **Black Canyon of the Gunnison National Park** (☏970-249-1915; www.nps.gov/blca; 7-day admission per vehicle $15). See also p382.

Carson National Forest

Carson contains an enormous network of mountain-bike and multiuse trails between Taos, Angel Fire and Picuris Peak. The nearest town is Taos (p290), where you can rent bikes from **Gearing Up Bicycle Shop** (Map p294; ☏575-751-0365; www.gearingupbikes.com; 129 Paseo del Pueblo Sur; ⊙9am-6:30pm) for $35 per day. For more info contact Carson National Forest (☏575-758-6200; www.fs.fed .us/r3/carson).

Kaibab National Forest

One of the premier mountain biking destinations in Arizona is the 800-plus-mile Arizona Trail. A popular section that's great for families is the Tusayan Bike Trail System (p174). East of the town of Tusayan it's a pretty easy ride mostly on an old logging road that cuts through the Kaibab National Forest to the South Rim of the Grand Canyon. If you ride or walk the trail into the park, you've got to pay the $12 entrance fee that's good for seven days. For more info contact the Tusayan Ranger Station (☏928-638-2443; www.fs.fed.us/r3/kai).

NATIONAL PARKS & MONUMENTS

PARK	FEATURES	ACTIVITIES	PAGE
Arches NP	sandstone arches, diverse geologic formations	hiking, camping, scenic drives	415
Black Canyon of the Gunnison NP	rugged deep canyon, ancient rocks	rock climbing, rafting, hiking, horseback riding	382
Bosque del Apache NWR	cottonwood forest along Rio Grande, abundant cranes & geese each winter	birding	324
Bryce Canyon NP	eroded hillsides, red & orange hoodoos & pillars	camping, hiking, scenic drives, stargazing, cross-country skiing	435
Canyon de Chelly NM	ancient cliff dwellings, canyons, cliffs	hiking and backpacking (guided only), horseback riding, scenic overlooks	189
Canyonlands NP	sandstone formations at confluence of Green & Colorado Rivers	rafting, camping, mountain biking, backpacking	398
Capitol Reef NP	buckled sandstone cliffs along the Waterpocket Fold	mountain biking, hiking, camping, wilderness, solitude	421
Carlsbad Caverns NP	underground cave system, limestone formations, bat flight in evening	ranger-led walks, spelunking (experienced only), backpacking	350
Dinosaur NM	fossil beds along Yampa & Green Rivers, dinosaur fossils & exhibits	hiking, scenic drives, camping, rafting	502
Grand Canyon NP	canyon scenery, geologic record, remote wilderness, condors	rafting, hiking, camping, mountain biking, road cycling	158
Grand Staircase-Escalante NM	desert wilderness, mountains, canyons, wildlife	mountain biking, hiking, camping, solitude	431
Great Basin NP	desert mountains, canyons, wildlife, fall colors	hiking, camping	95
Mesa Verde NP	Ancestral Puebloan sites	hiking, cross-country skiing	365
Monument Valley Navajo Tribal Park	desert basin with sandstone pillars & buttes	scenic drive, guided tours, horseback riding	188
Natural Bridges NM	premier examples of stone architecture	hiking, camping, sightseeing	396
Organ Pipe Cactus NM	Sonoran Desert, cactus bloom May & Jun	cactus viewing, scenic drives, mountain biking	217
Petrified Forest NP	Painted Desert, fossilized logs	scenic drives, backcountry hiking	232
Red Rock Canyon NCA	unique geologic features close to Las Vegas, waterfalls	scenic drives, hiking, rock climbing	88
Saguaro NP	desert slopes, giant saguaro, wildflowers, Gila woodpeckers, wildlife	cactus viewing, hiking, camping	208
San Pedro Riparian NCA	40 miles of protected river habitats	birding, picnicking, fishing, horseback riding	222
Sunset Crater Volcano NM	dramatic volcanic landscape	hiking, sightseeing	157
White Sands NM	white sand dunes, specially adapted plants & animals	scenic drives, limited hiking, moonlight bicycle tours, range of walks	336
Zion NP	sandstone canyons, high mesas	hiking, camping, scenic drives, backpacking, rock climbing	447

NP – National Park; NM – National Monument; NCA – National Conservation Area; NWR – National Wildlife Refuge

Moab

Bikers from around the world come to pedal the steep slickrock trails and challenging 4WD roads winding through woods and into canyon country around Moab (p403). The legendary Slickrock Trail is for experts only. This 12.7-mile, half-day loop will kick your butt. Intermediate riders can learn to ride slickrock on Klondike Bluffs Trail, a 15.6-mile round-trip that passes dinosaur tracks. For a family-friendly ride, try the 8-mile Bar-M Loop.

Full-suspension bikes start at around $43 a day at **Rim Cyclery** (Map p404; 435-259-5333; www.rimcyclery.com; 94 W 100 N, Moab) – check out its museum.

Visit www.go-utah.com/Moab/Biking and www.discovermoab.com/biking.htm for excellent Moab biking info. Both have loads of easy-to-access pictures, ratings and descriptions about specific trails.

Snow Sports

All five states offer snow sports on some level. Yes, you can even ski in Arizona. Southwestern Colorado is riddled with fabulous ski resorts, while the Lake Tahoe area reigns in Nevada. In New Mexico head to the steeps at Taos and in Utah the resorts outside Salt Lake City – they were worthy of hosting the Winter Olympic Games!

Downhill Skiing & Snowboarding

Endless vistas, blood-curdling chutes, sweet glades and ricocheting half-pipes: downhill skiing and boarding are epic, whether you're hitting fancy resorts or local haunts. The season lasts from late November to April, depending on where you are.

Salt Lake City and nearby towns hosted the 2002 Winter Olympics, and have rip-roaring routes to test your metal edges. Slopes are not crowded at Snowbasin (p496), where the Olympic downhill races were held. The terrain here is, in turns, gentle and ultra-yikes. Nearby Alta (p484) is the quintessential Utah ski experience: unpretentious and packed with powder fields, gullies, chutes and glades.

New Mexico's Taos Ski Valley (p303) is easily one of the most challenging mountains in the US, while the Santa Fe ski area (p263), just 15 miles outside town, allows you the chance to ski in the morning and shop Canyon Rd galleries come afternoon.

In Colorado you'll want to head to Telluride (p372) or Crested Butte (p383). For extreme skiing, try Silverton (p380). All three are wonderfully laid-back old mining towns turned ski towns, offering the opportunity to ride some of the best powder in the state by day, then chill in some of the coolest old saloons at night. For something completely local and low-key, check out family-run Wolf Creek (p359). For more details about where to ride powder in the state visit www.coloradoski.com. The website lists 'ski and stay' specials and provides resort details and snow reports.

The Lake Tahoe area, straddling the Nevada–California border, is home to nearly a dozen ski and snowboard resorts. See p104 for more.

And then there's Arizona. Yes, you can ski. The snow isn't anything to write home about, but the novelty value may be. Head to the Arizona Snowbowl (p153) outside Flagstaff.

Ski areas generally have full resort amenities, including lessons and equipment rentals (although renting in nearby towns can be cheaper). Got kids? Don't leave them at home when you can stash them at ski school for a day. For 'ski, fly and stay' deals check out web consolidators and the ski areas' own websites.

Cross-Country & Backcountry Skiing

Backcountry and telemark skiing are joining cross-country skiing and snowshoeing as alternative ways to explore the untamed Southwestern terrain.

A must-ski for cross-country aficionados? Utah's serene Soldier Hollow (p498), which was the Nordic course used in the 2002 Winter Olympics. It's accessible to all skill levels.

The North and South Rims of the Grand Canyon both boast cross-country trails. The North Rim is much more remote. On the south side, you'll find several trails of easy

FLASH FLOODS: A DEADLY DESERT DANGER

Flash floods, which occur when large amounts of rain fall suddenly and quickly, are most common during the 'monsoon months' from mid-July to early September, but heavy precipitation in late winter can also cause these floods. They occur with little warning and reach a raging peak in minutes. Rainfall occurring miles away is funnelled from the surrounding mountains into a normally dry wash or canyon and a wall of water several feet high can appear seemingly out of nowhere. There are rarely warning signs – perhaps you'll see some distant rain clouds – but if you see a flash flood coming, the only recommendation is to reach higher ground as quickly as possible.

Floods carry a battering mixture of rocks and trees and can be extremely dangerous. A swiftly moving wall of water is much stronger than it appears; at only a foot high, it will easily knock over a strong adult. A 2ft-high flood sweeps away vehicles.

Heed local warnings and weather forecasts, especially during the monsoon season. Avoid camping in sandy washes and canyon bottoms, which are the likeliest spots for flash floods. Campers and hikers are not the only potential victims; every year foolhardy drivers driving across flooded roads are swept away. Flash floods usually subside fairly quickly. A road that is closed will often be passable later on the same day.

to medium difficulty groomed and signed within the Kaibab National Forest (p174).

The San Juan Hut Systems (see p377) consist of a great series of shelters along a 60-mile route in Colorado from Telluride to Ouray – the scenery is fantastic.

Rock Climbing

If Dr Seuss had designed a rock-climbing playground, it would look a lot like the Southwest: a surreal landscape filled with enormous blobs, spires, blobs on spires and soaring cliffs. While southern Utah seems to have the market cornered on rock climbing, the rest of the region isn't too shabby when it comes to the vertical scene. Just keep an eye on the thermometer – those rocks can really sizzle during summer. Help keep climbing spaces open by respecting access restrictions, whether they are set by landowners harried by loud louts or because of endangered, cliff-dwelling birds that need space and silence during nesting season.

Southwestern Utah's Snow Canyon State Park (p465) offers more than 150 bolted and sport routes. Zion Canyon has some of the most famous big-wall climbs in the country, including Moonlight Buttress, Prodigal Son, Touchstone and Space Shot. In southeastern Utah, Moab (p403) and Indian Creek (p401) make awesome destinations.

Otherwise, make a swift approach to central Arizona's Granite Mountain Wilderness, which attracts rock climbers in warmer months. Pack your rack for the rocky reaches of Taos Ski Valley (p303) or pack your picks

for the Ouray Ice Park (p379), where a 2-mile stretch of the Uncompahgre Gorge has become world renowned for its sublime ice formations. **Chicks with Picks** (✍970-316-1403, office 970-626-4424; www.chickswith picks.net; 163 County Rd 12; prices vary) makes it easy for women to get involved too.

Caving & Canyoneering

Much of the Southwest's most stunning beauty is out of sight, sitting below the earth's surface in serpentine corridors of stone that make up miles of canyons and caves. Visit Carlsbad Caverns National Park (p350) and not only will you feel swallowed whole by the planet, you'll be amply rewarded with a bejeweled trove of glistening, colorful formations.

Canyoneering adventures vary from pleasant day hikes to multiday technical climbing excursions. Longer trips may involve technical rock climbing, swimming

TOP SPOTS FOR WHITE-WATER RAFTING

Grand Canyon National Park (p166) Arizona

Cataract Canyon (p406) Moab, Utah

Westwater Canyon (p406) Moab, Utah

Taos Box (p265) Pilar, New Mexico

Animas River (p361) Durango, Colorado

> **DIVING**
>
> If you're into diving, check out **Blue Hole** (www.santarosanm.org) near Santa Rosa, NM. It has an 81ft-deep artsesian well; blue water leads into a 131ft-long submerged cavern.

across pools, shooting down waterfalls and camping. Many experienced canyoneers bring inflatable mattresses to float their backpacks and sleep on.

Arizona and Utah offer some of the best canyoneering anywhere. The first canyoneers in the huge gashes of the Colorado Plateau were Native Americans, whose abandoned cliff dwellings and artifacts mark their passage. See for yourself at the many-fingered Canyon de Chelly (p189), which is accessible with a Navajo guide intimately familiar with its deep mazes.

The Grand Canyon (p158) is the mother of all canyoneering experiences, attracting thousands to its jaw-dropping vistas.

Then there are slot canyons, hundreds of feet deep and only a few feet wide. These must be negotiated during dry months because of the risk of deadly flash floods. Always check with the appropriate rangers for weather and safety information. The Paria Canyon (p446), carved by a tributary of the Colorado River on the Arizona Utah border, includes the amazing Buckskin Gulch, a 12-mile-long canyon, hundreds of feet deep and only 15ft wide for most of its length. Perhaps the best-known (though now highly commercialized) slot canyon is Antelope Canyon (p183), near Lake Powell. You can also drive through magical Oak Creek Canyon (p148), with dramatic red, orange and white cliffs sweetened with aromatic pine. A nimbus of giant cottonwoods crowd the creek.

Zion National Park (p447) offers dozens of canyoneering experiences for day hikers and extreme adventurers, with weeping rocks, tiny grottoes, hanging gardens and majestic, towering walls.

Water Sports

Water in the desert? You betcha. In fact, few places in the US offer as much watery diversity as the Southwest. Bronco-busting rivers share the territory with enormous lakes and sweet trickles that open into great escapes.

Boating

Near the California–Arizona state line, a series of dammed lakes on the lower Colorado River is thronged with boaters year-round. Area marinas rent canoes, fishing boats, speedboats, water-skiing boats, jet skis and windsurfers. On the biggest lakes – especially Arizona's Lake Powell (p189) in the Glen Canyon National Recreation Area near the Grand Canyon and Lake Mead (p89) in the Lake Mead National Recreation Area near Las Vegas – houseboat rentals sleep six to 12 people and allow exploration of remote areas difficult to reach on foot.

The thrill of speed mixed with alcohol makes popular houseboat areas dangerous for kayakers and canoeists. If you're renting a big rig, take the same care with alcohol as you would when driving a car. Travel at a speed that is safe based on the conditions, which include the amount of traffic on the water and the likelihood of underwater hazards (more common when water levels drop). Carbon monoxide emitted by houseboat engines is a recently recognized

HORSEBACK RIDING

WHERE	WHAT	INFORMATION
Southern AZ dude ranches	cowboy up in Old West country; most ranches closed in summer due to the heat	www.azdra.com
Grand Canyon South Rim, AZ	low-key trips through Kaibab National Forest; campfire ride	www.apachestables.com
Santa Fe, NM	themed trail rides; sunsets	www.bishopslodge.com
Telluride, CO	all-season rides in the hills	www.ridewithroudy.com
Durango, CO	day rides and overnight camping in the Weminuche Wilderness	www.vallecitolakeoutfitter.com

RANKING RAPIDS

White-water rapids are rated on a class scale of I to V, with Class V being the wildest and Class I being nearly flat water. Most beginner trips take rafters on Class III rivers, which means you'll experience big rolling waves and some bumps along the way, but nothing super technical. In Class IV water you can expect to find short drops, big holes (meaning giant waves) and stronger undertows, making it a bit rougher if you get thrown off the boat. Class V rapids are the baddest of all and should only be attempted by strong swimmers with previous white-water experience – you should expect to be thrown out of the boat and perhaps sucked under for a few moments. You'll need to know what to do and not panic.

Tip: if you do get thrown, float through the rapid, lying on your back – your life vest will keep you afloat. Point your feet downriver and keep your toes up. Protect your head and neck with your arms (don't leave them loose or they can get caught in rocks).

Of course the difficulty of the rafting will depend a lot on the kind of trip you're on – it's much harder to kayak a Class V rapid than it is to ride it out in a motorized pontoon boat or even in a boat being oared by a professional. If you aren't a world-class kayaker, but want more interaction beyond being rowed down the river, try a paddle trip. On these, each person in the boat paddles, following the directions shouted by the experienced guide at the helm of the ship.

The I to V class system applies to all Southwestern rivers except for a portion of one. The part of the Colorado River running through the Grand Canyon is just too wild to play by traditional rules and requires its own scale system – from Class I to Class X – to classify its 160-plus rapids. Many of the Grand's rapids are ranked Class V or higher; two merit a perfect 10.

threat. Colorless and odorless, the deadly gas is heavier than air and gathers at water level, creating dangerous conditions for swimmers and boaters. In recent years, several swimmers have drowned after being overcome by carbon monoxide.

Swimming & Tubing

Most lakes and many reservoirs in the Southwest allow swimmers. The exception will be high-traffic areas of the bigger lakes, where swimming is very dangerous due to the number of motorboats. It's not unusual to see locals swimming in rivers during the hot summer months, and tubing on creeks throughout the Southwest is popular. If you happen to see a bunch of people riding down a creek, and wish to join, just ask where they go for their tires – where there's tubing in this region there is usually an entrepreneur renting tubes from a van in the nearest parking lot. Swimming in lakes and rivers is generally free but if you are in a state or national park, or on a reservoir you may have to pay an entrance fee to enter the property itself.

Golfing

With more than 300 golf courses, Arizona is ranked the number-one golf destination in North America by the International Associ-ation of Golf Tour Operators. The state has some of the top golf resorts in the country, with the best ones designed by famous pros. Just about every sizable town in Arizona has a course and the bigger cities have dozens, a few of which are listed in this book. The Phoenix area alone has about 200.

In many desert areas, golf courses are viewed as welcome grassy amenities that also bring in tourist dollars, but this comes at a high price – the courses need lots of water, and conservationists decry the use of this most precious of desert resources for en-tertainment. In 2010 about 15% of the state's courses were considered at-risk because of a dip in tourism, increased competition and higher costs for water and labor.

Golf is also expensive for players. Some courses don't allow golfers to walk from hole to hole. A round of 18 holes on the best courses, often in upscale resorts that special-ize in golf vacations, can cost hundreds of dollars (including use of a golf cart) during the balmy days of a southern Arizona win-ter. In the heat of summer, rates can drop to under $100 for the same resort. If you don't have that kind of money, try the public city courses where rounds are more reasonable. Several Phoenix city courses charge less than $50 for 18 holes in winter.

Travel with Children

Best Regions for Kids

Arizona

Outdoorsy families can hike Grand Canyon trails and ponder the cacti outside Tucson. Water parks lure kiddies to Phoenix, while dude ranches, ghost towns and cliff dwellings are only a scenic drive away.

New Mexico

Swoop up a mountain on the Sandia Peak Tramway, drop into Carlsbad Caverns or scramble to the Gila Cliff Dwellings.

Utah

National parks in Utah sprawl across swaths of red rock country, offering fantastic hiking, biking and rafting. In the mountains, skis, alpine slides or snow tubes are equally fun.

Southwestern Colorado

Chug through the San Juans on a historic steam train, relax in Ouray's hot springs or take your pick of adventures – hiking, fishing, skiing – in low-key Telluride.

Las Vegas & Nevada

Children are not allowed in the gaming areas, but roller coasters and animal exhibits cater to the kiddies. For outdoor adventure, head to Great Basin National Park or Valley of Fire State Park.

Southwest USA for Kids

The Southwest is a great place to travel with kids. Yes, the long drives, unforgiving desert landscapes and oppressive summer heat can be daunting, but the rewards for families far outweigh the challenges. These rewards can be found in the most mundane of activities – an afternoon splashing in a creek in New Mexico's Jemez Mountains (p283), picnicking on the edge of the Grand Canyon in Kaibab National Forest (p174), watching an old Western on the big screen at Parry Lodge's Old Barn Playhouse (p444) in Kanab, UT. To make it even more enticing, the region's geology, human history and wildlife, accessible in concrete ways at every turn, make the Southwest as educational as it is fun – kids learn without even trying.

Lodging

Most hotels and motels offer cribs and rollaway beds, sometimes for a minimal fee. Ask about bed configurations, suites, adjoining rooms and rooms with microwaves or refrigerators. While many hotels allow children to stay free with adults, some can charge as much as $90 extra per night – always ask.

Full-scale resorts with kids' programs, lovely grounds, full service and in-house babysitting can be found throughout the region, but particularly in Phoenix and, to a lesser degree, Tucson. There are far fewer resorts in New Mexico – try Bishop's Lodge Resort & Spa (p272) in Santa Fe and the

Native American–owned Hyatt Tamaya (p252), on the Santa Ana Pueblo, just north of Albuquerque. For the real Western-immersion cowboy experience, complete with trail rides through the chamisa, cattle wrangling and beans 'n' corn bread round the fire, consider a stay at a dude ranch, such as the Flying E Ranch (p131) in Wickenburg, AZ.

If it's late, you're tired and you don't want any surprises, head to a chain motel. Hilton perches at the high end of the scale, while Motel 6 and Super 8, usually the least expensive, offer minimal services, and Best Western is notoriously inconsistent. Your best bets are Holiday Inn Express and Fairfield Inn & Suites.

Finally, even the most novice campers will find beautiful campsites in national and state forests and parks throughout the region to be perfect for car-camping. You can't beat the flexibility and price, and kids love it.

Dining

While the Southwest offers the usual fast-food suspects, you may find yourself driving mile after mile, hour after hour without a neon-lit fast-food joint anywhere. Be prepared with snacks and, if appropriate, a cooler packed with picnic items. Many lodgings offer free breakfast.

Don't sacrifice a good meal or attractive ambience because you have kids. All but a handful of upscale restaurants welcome families and many provide crayons and children's menus. To avoid the dilemma of yet another fried meal, ubiquitous on kids' menus, simply ask for small adaptations to the standard menu, such as grilled chicken with no sauce, a side of steamed vegetables or rice with soy sauce.

Children's Highlights
Outdoor Adventure

» Explore Grand Canyon National Park in Arizona.

» Ride the range at a Wickenburg dude ranch in southern Arizona.

» Chug into the San Juan Mountains on the Durango & Silverton Narrow Gauge Railroad in Colorado.

» Ride horses at Ghost Ranch in New Mexico.

» Ski the slopes at Wolf Mountain in Utah.

Theme Parks & Museums

» Relive the rootin', tootin' Old West with gold panning, burro rides and shoot-outs at Rawhide Western Town & Steakhouse in Mesa, AZ.

» Take in coyotes, cacti and demos at the Arizona-Sonora Desert Museum.

» Check out the Hall of Jurassic Supergiants at the Museum of Natural History & Science in Albuquerque, AZ.

» Visit with local artists and scientists at the Santa Fe Children's Museum in New Mexico.

» Have fun at Thanksgiving Point in Salt Lake City, UT, which has 55 acres of gardens, a petting farm, a movie theater and golf.

Wacky Attractions

» Get close to the begging burros that loiter in the middle of downtown Oatman, AZ.

» Marvel at the fake dinosaurs and mummified bobcats at Grand Canyon Caverns in Arizona – Route 66 kitsch at its best.

» Gaze at the world's most comprehensive collection of rattlesnake species at the Rattlesnake Museum in Albuquerque, AZ.

» Discover the truth, and lots of wild theories, at the International UFO Museum & Research Center in Roswell, NM.

» Visit Mexican Hat in Utah – hey, that rock looks like a sombrero!

Native American Sites

» Climb four ladders to a ceremonial cave that combines education with adventure at Bandelier National Monument in New Mexico.

» Explore ancient living history inside Taos Pueblo, NM, a multistory pueblo village dating to the 1400s.

» Discover Acoma Pueblo in New Mexico, also known as Sky City, which sits atop a mesa 7000ft above sea level.

» Climb into cliff dwellings in Mesa Verde National Park in southwestern Colorado for hands-on learning at its best.

» Match the names to the butte – Mittens, Eagle Rock – at Monument Valley Navajo Tribal Park in Arizona.

Transportation
Car Seat Laws

Child restraint laws vary by state and are subject to change. The requirements should be checked before departure. Currently, Arizona law states that children under the age of five must be properly secured in a child-restraint device. Children five to eight years old are not required to use safety seats, but a federal car-safety board has asked the state to consider tightening its requirements. The website for the Arizona Governor's office (www.azgohs.gov /transportation-safety) provides booster-seat specifics. Children between five and 15 must wear a seatbelt if sitting in the front seat.

In Colorado, infants under the age of one year and weighing less than 20lbs must be in a rear-facing infant seat, children aged one to three years and between 20lbs and 40lbs must be in a car seat and four- to seven-year-olds must use a booster. Nevada requires children five and under, and those weighing less than 80lbs, to use a booster. In New Mexico, infants under one year must be restrained in a rear-facing infant seat, children aged one to four or weighing less than 40lbs must use a car seat, and five- and six-year-olds and kids weighing less than 60lbs must use a booster. Utah law requires children under eight years old or shorter than 57in to sit in a car seat or booster; children who are not yet eight but are 57in or taller can use the car seat belt alone.

Most car-rental agencies rent rear-facing car seats (for infants under one), forward-facing seats (from one to four years old or up to a certain height/weight) and boosters for $11 per day, but you must reserve these in advance. Clarify the type of seat when you make the reservation as each is suitable for specified ages and weights only.

Flying

Children under two fly free on most airlines when sitting on a parent's lap. Remember to bring a copy of your child's birth certificate – if the airline asks for it and you don't have it, you won't be able to board. Ask about children's fares, and reserve seats together in advance. Other passengers have no obligation to switch seats and sometimes have no qualms about refusing to do so. Southwest Airlines' open seating policy helps avoid this.

Planning
Planning Ahead

Perhaps the most difficult part of a family trip to this region will be deciding where to go and avoiding the temptation to squeeze in too much. Distances are deceptive and any one state could easily fill the standard two-week family vacation. Choose a handful of primary destinations, such as major cities, national parks and centers for outdoor recreation, to serve as the backbone of your trip. Then sit down with the map and connect these dots with a flexible driving plan.

HELPFUL RESOURCES FOR FAMILIES

GrandCanyon.org (www.grandcanyon .org) Excellent listing of regionally focused children's books.

Kids in Vegas (www.kidsinvegas.com) A complete listing of kid friendly places in Las Vegas.

Family Travel Files (www.thefamily travelfiles.com) Ready-made vacation ideas, destination profiles and travel tips.

Kids.gov (www.kids.gov) Eclectic, enormous national resource; download songs and activities, or even link to the CIA Kids' Page.

For all-around information and advice, check out Lonely Planet's *Travel with Children*. For outdoor advice, read *Kids in the Wild: A Family Guide to Outdoor Recreation* by Cindy Ross and Todd Gladfelter, and Alice Cary's *Parents' Guide to Hiking & Camping*.

Book rooms at the major destinations and make advance reservations for horseback rides, rafting trips, scenic train rides and educational programs or camps, but allow a couple of days between each to follow your fancy.

Throughout this book, we've used the child-friendly icon (🏠) to indicate attractions and sleeping and eating options that are geared toward families. This helps make planning your trip a cinch.

What to Bring

If you plan on hiking, you'll want a front baby carrier or a backpack with a built-in shade top. These can be purchased or rented from outfitters throughout the region (see listings in regional chapters). Older kids need sturdy shoes and, for playing in streams, water sandals.

Other things you'll want to include are towels, rain gear, a snuggly fleece or heavy sweater (even in summer, desert nights can be cold – if you're camping, bring hats) and bug repellent. To avoid children's angst at sleeping in new places and to minimize concerns about bed configurations, bring a Pack N Play – or a similar travel playpen/bed – for infants and sleeping bags for older children.

regions at a glance

Scenic as a road trip may be, we don't advise spending the *whole* trip in the car. Las Vegas is decidedly offbeat and works best for travelers interested in nightlife, dining and adult-oriented fun. Arizona offers nightlife and culture in Phoenix, but the state earns bragging rights at the Grand Canyon. Its mining towns and Native American sites are also a draw, attracting cultural explorers to the deserts and mountains. New Mexico unfurls the red carpet for artists, but its chile-infused cuisine and Pueblo culture lure crowds too. Peak baggers and cyclists love Colorado's lofty San Juan Mountains, while Mesa Verde wins praise from history buffs. Utah closes the book with swooping red-rock style and delicate natural grace.

Las Vegas & Nevada

Nightlife ✓✓✓
Dining ✓✓✓
Offbeat ✓✓

Casinos
The flashy casinos on the Las Vegas Strip are self-contained party caves where you can hold 'em, fold 'em, sip cocktails, shake your booty and watch contortionists and comedians.

Cornucopias
In Vegas, food is about both quantity and quality. Stretch your budget and your waistline at the ubiquitous buffets or dine like royalty at a chef-driven sanctuary.

Out There
From Hwy 50 (the Loneliest Rd) to Hwy 375 (the Extraterrestrial Hwy), Nevada is wild and wacky. Caravan to the Black Rock Desert in September for Burning Man, a conflagration of self-expression.

p54

Arizona

Culture ✓✓
Adventure ✓✓✓
Scenery ✓✓✓

Native Americans
The history and art of the Native American tribes make Arizona unique. From craftwork to cliff dwellings to sprawling reservations, tribal traditions flourish across the state.

Hiking & Rafting
Want to take it easy? Hike a desert interpretative trail or kayak a man-made lake. To ramp it up, head to canyon country to clamber over red rocks or swoosh over white-capped rapids.

Canyons & Arches
After the continents collided, Mother Nature got involved with the decorating. Crumbly hoodoos, swooping spans, glowing buttes and crimson ridges – got batteries for the camera?

p106

New Mexico

Art✓✓✓
Culture✓✓✓
Food✓✓

Santa Fe
Vendors on the Plaza. The galleries of Canyon Rd. Studio tours. The Georgia O'Keeffe Museum. The city itself is a living work of art, framed by mountains and crisp blue skies.

Pueblos
Nineteen Native American pueblos are clustered in the western and north-central regions of the state. They share similarities, but their histories, customs and craftwork are distinctly fascinating.

Red & Green
New Mexican food comes with a chile-infused twist. Red, green – they're not just for salsas but are an integral part of the whole. Pinto beans. Posole. *Carne adobada* (marinated pork chunks). Isn't this why you're here?

p234

Southwestern Colorado

Adventure✓✓✓
Scenery✓✓✓
History✓✓

Tracks & Racks
You got stuff? Skis, snowboards, bikes, fishing poles? Then start unpacking. The San Juan Mountains are a primo place to empty your stuff racks and dirty up your gear.

Peaks & Ponderosas
When it comes to alpine scenery in the US, few places are more sublime than the San Juan Skyway: craggy peaks, steep canyons and glorious meadows. Just don't drive off the road.

Holes in the Rock
The Mesa Verde cliff dwellings offer a fascinating glimpse into the lives of the ancient Puebloans. Up in the San Juan Mountains, the mining past is recalled in Victorian homes and the abandoned claims.

p354

Utah

Outdoors✓✓✓
Ancient Sites✓✓
History✓✓

Romping Room
When it comes to all-natural play-grounds, Utah takes the lead. From tightly run national parks to empty Bureau of Land Management (BLM) expanses, the place is ready-made for adventure – usually with a sandstone backdrop.

Rock On
Dinosaurs roamed the earth and trilobites swam the seas, leaving footprints and fossils as calling cards. Elsewhere, cliff dwellings and rock art remind us we weren't the first inhabitants.

Mormons
The Mormons arrived in the 1840s, building temples, streets, farms and communities. Get some background at Temple Square in Salt Lake City, then explore.

p386

Every listing is recommended by our authors, and their favourite places are listed first

Look out for these icons:

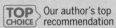 Our author's top recommendation

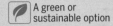 A green or sustainable option

 No payment required

See the Index for a full list of destinations covered in this book.

On the Road

Las Vegas & Nevada

Includes »

Best Places to Eat

» Wicked Spoon Buffet
(p77)

» DOCG Enoteca (p75)

» L'Atelier de Joël Robuchon
(p76)

» Firefly (p78)

» Old Granite Street Eatery
(p100)

Best Places to Stay

» Encore (p72)

» Hard Rock (p74)

» Golden Nugget (p74)

» Peppermill (p100)

» Tropicana (p72)

Why Go?

Ski boots, high heels, flip flops, golf cleats, cowboy boots: when you come to Nevada, none of these would look out of place. Mysterious and misunderstood, Nevada's a paradox, which makes packing tricky. Expect thrills aplenty, whether you're a nightclub aficionado, an adventure junkie, a kitsch connoisseur or a conspiracy theorist.

If you're in the mood for extremes, you're in the right place. Rural brothels and hole-in-the wall casinos sit side-by-side with Mormon churches and Basque cowboy culture. The Wild West lives on in old silver mining towns, while Vegas offers up its own brand of modern day lawlessness. Piercing blue lakes and snowy mountains in the Reno–Tahoe area seem a world away from the open vistas of Great Basin and the lonely curves of Highway 50, where fighter jets whiz overhead at the speed of light...or was that an alien ship?

Whether Nevada delights, excites, intrigues or confounds you (and possibly all at once!) you just can't say it's not interesting.

When to Go
Las Vegas

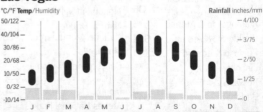

Apr–May
Southern parts of the state are balmy by day and pleasantly cool at night.

Dec
Las Vegas deals in excess, and they don't go more buck wild than at Christmas.

Jun–Aug
Yes, it's hot. Yet low season in Vegas means awesome hotel deals.

Vegas Planning

Planning a Vegas trip can be strangely counterintuitive, because Vegas refuses to play by the rules of most cities. First off: though parking is widely free, it's not time or cost-effective to rent a car unless you'll be doing a lot of day trips. Stick to taxis, walking and the good bus/monorail system while you're exploring the city. Dinner reservations are often necessary; note that many high-end restaurants, bars and nightclubs enforce a dress code.

DON'T MISS

Even if late nights, gambling and neon aren't your style, cut loose and cruise Las Vegas' infamous **Strip** for at least a day or two: chill out poolside at a 4-star resort, hit the clubs, and splurge on steak and martinis in Rat Pack style. While you're there, don't miss a **Cirque du Soleil show**.

In a state known for lovably bizarre small towns, the prize for the most unique is a toss-up between **Virginia City**, where the gold rush and the Wild West live on, or spirited **Elko**, with its Basque restaurants and cowboy poetry festival.

For unmatched outdoor bliss, **Lake Tahoe** offers fairytale ski slopes come winter and pristine summer beaches. If untamed wilderness strikes your fancy, you'll want to get lost in the vast **Great Basin National Park** or brave the eerily deserted **US Hwy 50**, nicknamed the 'Loneliest Road in America.'

Finally, the hottest place in Nevada is also home to one of the Southwest's most unique yearly events: the **Burning Man** festival, where iconoclasts, rebels, artists, soul-seekers and the irrepressibly curious celebrate and create in the shimmering heat of the Black Rock Desert.

Tips for Drivers

» Most drivers speed across Nevada on interstate highways I-80 or I-15.

» It takes less than two hours to drive 125 miles from Primm, on the California state line, to Mesquite near the Utah border via I-15; the best overnight stop along this route is Las Vegas.

» When driving across the state on I-80, Winnemucca and Elko are the most interesting places to pull off for a night's sleep.

» Note that US Hwy 95 may be the quickest route between Las Vegas and Reno, but it's still a full day's drive without much to see or do along the way.

» For road conditions, call ☑877-687-6237 or visit www.nvroads.com.

TIME ZONE

Nevada is in the Pacific Time Zone.

Fast Facts

» Nevada population: 2.7 million

» Area: 109,800 sq miles

» Sales tax: 6.85%

» Las Vegas to Grand Canyon, AZ: 275 miles, 4½ hours

Resources

» Nevada Commission on Tourism (☑800-638-2328; www.travelnevada.com)

» Las Vegas Convention & Visitors Authority (www.visitlasvegas.com)

» VEGAS.com (www.vegas.com)

» Cheapo Vegas (www.cheapovegas.com)

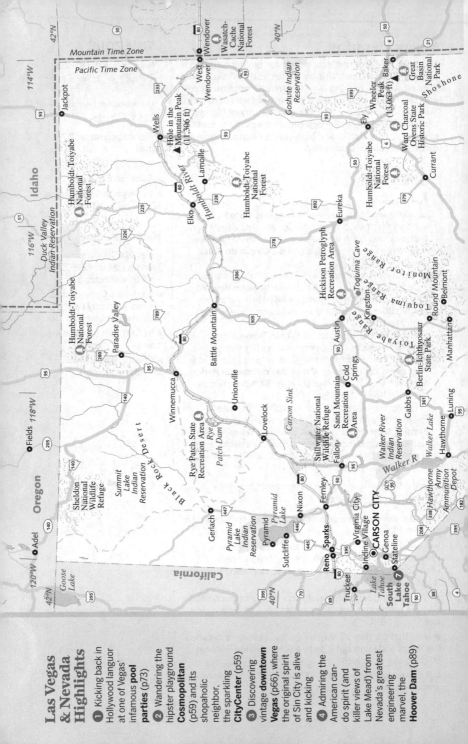

Las Vegas & Nevada Highlights

1 Kicking back in Hollywood languor at one of Vegas' infamous **pool parties** (p73)

2 Wandering the hipster playground **Cosmopolitan** (p59) and its shopaholic neighbor, the sparkling **CityCenter** (p59)

3 Discovering vintage **downtown Vegas** (p66), where the original spirit of Sin City is alive and kicking

4 Admiring the American can-do spirit (and killer views of Lake Mead) from Nevada's greatest engineering marvel, the **Hoover Dam** (p89)

History

What history, you ask. Looking around, you are to be forgiven. Unlike the rest of the ruin-laden Southwest, traces of early history are scarce in the Silver State.

Contrary to Hollywood legend, there was much more at the dusty crossroads than a gambling parlor and some tumbleweeds the day mobster Ben 'Bugsy' Siegel rolled in and erected a glamorous tropical-themed casino, the Flamingo, under the searing sun.

In 1855, Mormon missionaries built and then abandoned a fort in the Las Vegas valley, where a natural-springs oasis flowed. In 1859, the richest vein of silver ever discovered in the USA, the Comstock Lode, was struck at Virginia City, which became the most notorious boomtown in the West. President Abraham Lincoln ratified Nevada as a state in 1864.

After the completion of the railroad, Las Vegas finally boomed in the 1920s. Gambling dens, brothels and saloons soon sprang up beside the tracks, especially in Las Vegas' infamous Block 16 red-light district, which survived Nevada's bans on gambling and the supposedly 'dry' years of Prohibition.

The legalization of gambling in 1931, and the sudden lessening of the divorce residency requirement to six weeks, guaranteed an influx of jet-setting divorcees and taxable tourist dollars that carried Vegas through the Great Depression. WWII brought a huge air-force base and big aerospace bucks, plus a paved highway to Los Angeles. Soon after, the Cold War justified the Nevada Test Site. Monthly aboveground atomic blasts shattered casino windows in Las Vegas, while the city's official 'Miss Atomic Bomb' beauty queen graced tourism campaigns.

A building spree sparked by the Flamingo in 1946 led to mob-backed tycoons upping the glitz ante at every turn. Big-name entertainers, like Frank Sinatra, Liberace and Sammy Davis Jr, arrived on stage at the same time as topless French showgirls in the 'Fabulous Fifties.'

Since then, Sin City continues to exist chiefly to satisfy the desires of visitors. Once North America's fastest-growing metropolitan area, the recent housing crisis hit residents here especially hard. Now among the glittering lights of the Strip, you'll spot unlit, vacant condominium towers that speak to a need for economic revival. Yet Vegas has always been a boom or bust kind of place, and if history is any judge, the city will double-down and resume its winning streak in no time.

Nevada Scenic Routes

For those who love wild and lonely places, almost all of Nevada's back roads are scenic routes. Nicknamed the 'Loneliest Road in America,' famous Hwy 50 bisects the state. Request the *Hwy 50 Survival Guide* from the **Nevada Commission on Tourism** (☏800-638-2328; www.travelnevada.com) to find out how to get a free souvenir pin and a signed certificate from the governor.

Plenty of shorter scenic routes abound in Nevada. The Las Vegas Strip is the USA's only nighttime scenic byway. Around Las Vegas, Red Rock Canyon, the Valley of Fire, Lake Mead and the Spring Mountains all have scenic drives, too. Lesser-known routes around Nevada include the Ruby Mountains outside Elko; stairway-to-heaven Angel Lake Rd via Wells; and, near Reno, the Pyramid Lake Scenic Byway and the Mt Rose Hwy, which winds down to Lake Tahoe.

LAS VEGAS

It's three in the morning in a smoky casino when you spot an Elvis lookalike sauntering by arm-in-arm with a glittering showgirl just as a bride in a long white dress shrieks 'Blackjack!'

Vegas, baby: it's the only place in the world where you can spend the night partying in Ancient Rome, wake up in Paris and brunch under the Eiffel Tower, bump into Superman on the way to dinner in New York, watch an erupting volcano at sunset and get married in a Pink Cadillac at midnight. Take a free craps lesson or double down with the high rollers, browse couture or tacky souvenirs, sip a neon 3ft-high margarita or a frozen vodka martini set on a bar made of ice. Vegas' landscape is a constantly shifting paradox, a volatile cocktail of dueling forces: sophistication and smut, risk and reward, boom and bust. Sound schizophrenic? That's all part of its charm.

Head downtown to explore Vegas' nostalgic beginnings and its cultural renaissance of vintage shops and cocktail bars where local culture thrives. Explore east and west of the Strip to find intriguing museums celebrating Vegas' neon, atomic-fueled past, and discover local restaurants that give celebrity chefs a run for their money.

Despite the city's recent economic downturn, this spirited city never stops. If you can imagine the kind of vacation – or life – you want, it's already a reality here. Welcome to the dream factory: just don't expect to get much sleep.

To get your bearings: the Strip, aka Las Vegas Blvd, is the center of gravity in Sin City. Roughly four miles long, Circus Circus Las Vegas caps the north end of the Strip and Mandalay Bay is on the south end near the airport. Whether walking or driving, distances on the Strip are deceiving.

Downtown, the original town center at the north end of Las Vegas Blvd, is incredibly compact and can be explored with a minimum of fuss. Its main drag is fun-loving Fremont St.

McCarran International Airport is southeast of the Strip, off I-215. For local transportation, see p87.

◎ Sights

The action in Vegas centers on casinos, but there are some unique museums along with thrill rides and amusements guaranteed to get your adrenaline pumping.

THE STRIP

Ever more spectacular, the world-famous (or rather, infamous) Strip is constantly reinventing itself. As the cliché goes, it's an adult Disneyland, dealing nonstop excitement. Every megaresort is an attraction in its own right, with plenty on offer besides gambling. Open for business 24/7/365 is the unwritten rule at casino hotels.

Major tourist areas are safe. However, Las Vegas Blvd between downtown and the Strip gets shabby, along with a desolate area along Las Vegas Blvd known as the 'Naked City'.

TOP **Cosmopolitan** CASINO
CHOICE
(Map p60; www.cosmopolitanlasvegas.com; 3708 Las Vegas Blvd S) Hipsters who have long thought they were too cool for Vegas finally have a place to go where they don't need irony to endure – much less enjoy – the aesthetics. Like the new Hollywood 'IT' girl, the Cosmo looks good at all times. Expect a steady stream of ingénues and entourages, plus regular folks who enjoy contemporary design. With a focus on pure fun, it avoids utter pretension, despite the constant wink-wink, retro moments: the Art-o-Matics (vintage cigarette machines hawking local art rather than nicotine), and possibly the best buffet in town, the **Wicked Spoon**. The va-va-va-voom casino lives up to the hotel's name, and the hotel bars – from a James Bond-esque lounge to a live music joint where soul singers belt it out on a stage that's practically on top of the bar – are some of the best in town.

TOP **Encore** CASINO
CHOICE
(Map p60; www.encorelasvegas.com; 3121 Las Vegas Blvd S) A slice of the French Riviera in Las Vegas – and classy enough to entice any of the Riviera's regulars – Steve Wynn has upped the wow factor, and the skyline, yet again with the Encore. Filled with indoor flower gardens, a butterfly motif and a dramatically luxe casino with scarlet chandeliers, it's an oasis of bright beauty. **Botero**, the restaurant headed by Mark LoRusso, is centered on a large sculpture by Fernando Botero himself. Don't miss the elegant Baccarat room with its jeweled peacocks, or the stunning casino bar. Come summertime, the **Encore Beach Club** (www.encorebeachclub.com) throws one of the hottest pool parties in town.

Bellagio CASINO
(Map p60; www.bellagio.com; 3600 Las Vegas Blvd S) Fans of eye-popping luxury, along with movie buffs who liked *Ocean's Eleven* (several key scenes were shot here) won't want to miss Steve Wynn's Vegas' original opulent pleasure palazzo. Inspired by a lakeside Italian village, the Bellagio is now a classic fixture of the strip, perhaps best known for its dazzling choreographed dancing fountain show that takes place every 15 to 30 minutes during the afternoon and evening. Other highlights include the dreamy pool area, a swish shopping concourse, a European-style casino and the **Bellagio Gallery of Fine Art** (adult/student $17/12; ⊙10am-6pm Sun-Tue & Thu, to 7pm Wed, Fri & Sat). Don't miss the hotel lobby's showpiece: a Dale Chihuly sculpture composed of 2000 hand-blown glass flowers in vibrant colors. Check out the **Bellagio Conservatory & Botanical Gardens** (admission free; ⊙daily) which features gorgeously ostentatious floral designs that change seasonally.

CityCenter SHOPPING CENTER
(Map p60; www.citycenter.com; 3780 Las Vegas Blvd S) Just when you thought you'd seen it all on the Strip, where themed hotels compete to outdo each other, comes the CityCenter, which beats the competition by not competing at all. We've seen this symbiotic relationship before (think giant hotel anchored by a mall 'concept') but the way this

The Strip

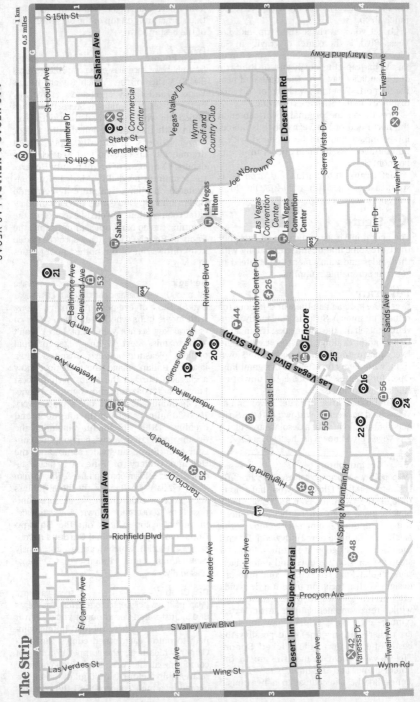

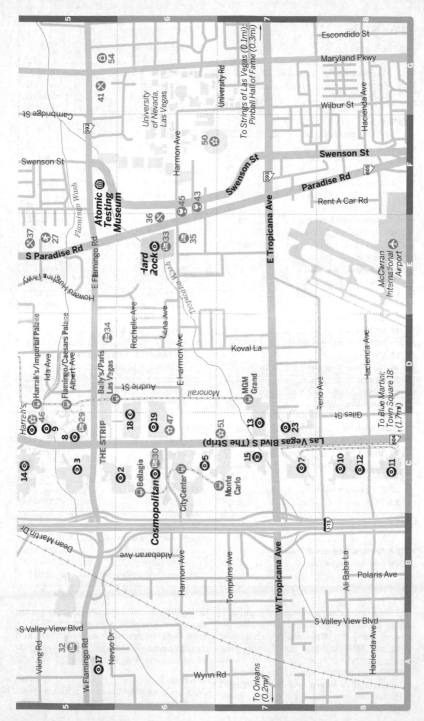

The Strip

LEED-certified complex places a small galaxy of hyper-modern, chichi hotels in orbit around the glitzy **Crystals** (www.crystalslasvegas.com; 3750 Las Vegas Blvd S) shopping center is a first.

The uber-upscale spread includes the subdued, stylish **Vdara** (www.vdara.com; 2600 W Harmon Ave), the hush-hush opulent **Mandarin Oriental** (www.mandarinoriental.com; 3752 Las Vegas Blvd) and the dramatic architectural showpiece **Aria** (www.arialasvegas.com; 3730 Las Vegas Blvd), whose sophisticated wood and chrome casino provides a fitting backdrop for its visually stunning restaurants.

Venetian   CASINO
(Map p60; www.venetian.com; 3355 Las Vegas Blvd S) In a city filled with spectacles, the

Drinking

Entertainment

Shopping

Venetian is surely one of the most spectacular. This facsimile of a doge's palace, inspired by the splendor of Italy's most romantic city, features roaming mimes and minstrels in period costume, hand-painted ceiling frescoes and full-scale reproductions of the Italian port's famous landmarks. Flowing canals, vibrant piazzas and stone walkways attempt to capture the spirit of La Serenissima Repubblica, reputedly the home of the world's first casino. Take a **gondola ride** (adult/private $16/64) outdoors or stroll through the atmospheric **Grand Canal Shoppes.**

Palazzo CASINO
(Map p60; www.palazzo.com; 3325 Las Vegas Blvd S) The Venetian's pretty but less interesting kid sister, the Palazzo may be younger but she's hardly the scintillating life of the

party. The decor exploits a variation on the Italian theme to a somewhat predictable effect, and despite the caliber of the **Shops at Palazzo** and the star-studded dining – including exhilarating ventures by culinary heavyweights Charlie Trotter, Emeril Legasse and Wolfgang Puck – the luxurious casino area somehow exudes a lackluster brand of excitement.

Caesars Palace CASINO
(Map p60; www.caesars.com; 3570 Las Vegas Blvd S) If you want to glimpse a vision of the pre-Bellagio version of quintessential four-star Las Vegas, Caesar's is your first stop. When it debuted in 1966, this Greco-Roman fantasyland captured the world's attention with its full-size marble reproductions of classical statuary and its cocktail waitresses clothed as goddesses. Bar girls continue to roam the gaming areas in skimpy togas, and faux-ancient Muses guard the high-roller rooms. The Colosseum showroom hosts mega-concerts featuring international icons like chanteuse Celine Dion. Don't skip a stroll through the curious mix of haute couture and cheesy Roman spectacle at the **Forum Shops**.

Mirage CASINO
(Map p60; www.mirage.com; 3400 Las Vegas Blvd S) With a tropical setting replete with a huge atrium filled with jungle foliage and soothing cascades, the Mirage captures the imagination. Circling the atrium is a vast Polynesian-themed casino, which places gaming areas under separate roofs to evoke intimacy, including a popular high-limit poker room. Don't miss the 20,000-gallon saltwater aquarium, with 60 species of critters hailing from Fiji to the Red Sea (including puffer fish, tangs and pygmy sharks), in the hotel registration area. Out front in the lagoon, a fiery faux volcano erupts hourly after dark until midnight.

New York-New York CASINO
(Map p60; www.nynyhotelcasino.com; 3790 Las Vegas Blvd S) Give me your tired, huddled (over a Wheel of Fortune slot machine) masses. The frenetic mini-megapolis New York-New York features scaled-down replicas of the Brooklyn Bridge and the Statue of Liberty, with a Coney Island-style roller coaster wrapped around the exterior. Claustrophobes beware: this Disneyfied version of the Big Apple can get even more crowded than the real deal. Eateries and a handful of fun bars – from dueling pianos to perfectly poured Irish pints – hide behind colorful facades from Greenwich Village and Times Sq. Upstairs, kids dig the **Coney Island Emporium arcade**.

Paris-Las Vegas CASINO
(Map p60; www.parislv.com; 3655 Las Vegas Blvd S) Adorned with fake Francophone signs like 'Le Buffet,' Paris-Las Vegas is a Gallic caricature that strives – with admirable effort – to capture the essence of the grande dame by re-creating her landmarks. Cut-rate likenesses of the Hotel de Ville, Opéra, Arc de Triomphe, Champs-Élysées and even the River Seine adorn the property. Check out the new **Chateau Beer Gardens**, where a mediocre beer list is redeemed by gorgeous views from the terrace.

Of course, the signature attraction is the **Eiffel Tower Experience** (Map p60; ☑702-946-7000; adult/child from $10.50/7.50; ☺10am-1am, weather permitting). Ascend in a glass elevator to the observation deck for panoramic views of the Strip, notably the Bellagio's dancing fountains.

Circus Circus CASINO
(Map p60; www.circuscircus.com; 2880 Las Vegas Blvd S) From the outside, Circus Circus looks bedraggled and pretty cheesy – and it *is*. Yet let's be honest: kids go crazy for this stuff. Suspended above the casino is the Circus Circus **Midway**, where acrobats, contortionists and trapeze artists freely perform daily every 30 minutes until midnight. The revolving carousel of the Horse-a-Round Bar, made infamous by gonzo journalist Hunter S Thompson's *Fear and Loathing in Las Vegas,* has views of the stage and can feel hallucinogenic even to those who are completely sober. Cheap beers, cheap eats and cheap thrills like 24-hour beer pong rule **Slots A' Fun**, just a drunken stumble away. Out back of the casino hotel, kids will dig the indoor amusement park, **Adventuredome** (www.adventuredome.com; day pass over/under 48in tall $27/17, per ride $5-8; ☺hr vary).

Excalibur CASINO
(Map p60; www.excalibur.com; 3850 Las Vegas Blvd S) Faux drawbridges and Arthurian legends aside, the medieval caricature castle known as Excalibur epitomizes gaudy Vegas. Down on the Fantasy Faire Midway are buried ye-olde carnival games, with joystick joys and motion-simulator ridefilms hiding in the Wizard's Arcade. The dinner show, **Tournament of Kings**, is more of a demolition derby with more hooves than a flashy Vegas production.

Flamingo
CASINO

(Map p60; www.flamingolasvegas.com; 3555 Las Vegas Blvd S) Back in 1946, the Flamingo was the talk of the town. Its original owners – all members of the New York mafia – shelled out millions to build this unprecedented tropical gaming oasis in the desert. Today, it isn't quite what it was back when its janitorial staff wore tuxedos; think more *Miami Vice*, less *Bugsy*. Drop by during the madhouse afternoon happy hours to sling back massive margaritas. Out back is a wildlife habitat with magnificent gardens where Chilean flamingos and African penguins wander, and 15 acres of meandering pools and waterfalls filled with swans and exotic birds.

Luxor
CASINO

(Map p60; www.luxor.com; 3900 Las Vegas Blvd S) Only a faint echo of Egypt's splendid ancient city, the landmark Luxor has a 40-billion-candlepower beacon visible to astronauts in outer space that shoots up out of its jet-black pyramid. Out front are a 10-story crouching sphinx and a sandstone obelisk etched with hieroglyphics. The interior is adorned with huge Egyptian statues and an audacious replica of the Great Temple of Ramses II. The confusingly laid out casino has a sub-par spread of table games and slot machines.

Mandalay Bay
CASINO

(Map p60; www.mandalaybay.com; 3950 Las Vegas Blvd S) Almost everything at 'M Bay' is a spectacle, if you know where to look. There's a constellation of star chefs' restaurants, the sky-high **Mix** lounge atop **THEhotel**, where couples escape to **THEbathhouse** spa. High-stakes gamblers will appreciate the classy casino and cutthroat poker room, while those who prefer observing the survival of the fittest in nature will appreciate Bay's **Shark Reef** (Map p60; ☏702-632-4555; adult/child $18/12; ☉10am-8pm Sun-Thu, 10am-10pm Fri & Sat), a walk-through aquarium that's home to thousands of submarine beasties. M-Bay is connected to Luxor by the eclectic **Mandalay Place** (Map p60) shopping mall.

Wynn Las Vegas
CASINO

(Map p60; www.wynnlasvegas.com; 3131 Las Vegas Blvd S) Steve Wynn's signature (literally, his name is written in script across the top, punctuated by a period) casino hotel stands on the site of the imploded 1950s-era Desert Inn. The curvaceous, copper-toned 50-story tower exudes secrecy – the entrance is obscured from the Strip by an artificial mountain of greenery. Inside, the resort comes alive with vibrant colors, inlaid flower mosaics, natural-light windows, lush foliage and waterfalls. The sprawling casino is always crowded, especially the cutthroat poker room. Acclaimed director Franco Dragone created Wynn's dreamy production show, *La Rêve*, in a specially constructed theater-in-the-round, where a million-gallon pool doubles as the stage.

MGM Grand
CASINO

(Map p60; www.mgmgrand.com; 3799 Las Vegas Blvd S) With a sprawling 5000 rooms, gaming areas equal in size to four football fields and a slew of fancy restaurants, the MGM is easy to get lost in. Owned by movie mogul Metro Goldwyn Mayer, the shimmering emerald-green 'City of Entertainment' co-opts themes from classic Hollywood movies. The casino consists of one gigantic circular room with an ornate domed ceiling and replicated 1930s glamour. Out front, it's hard to miss the USA's largest bronze statue, a 100,000lb lion. Popular attractions include a **lion habitat**.

TI (Treasure Island)
CASINO

(Map p60; www.treasureisland.com; 3300 Las Vegas Blvd S) Yo, ho, whoa: although traces of the original swashbuckling skull-and-crossbones theme linger at this casino hotel, TI's shift from family-friendly to bawdy and oh-so naughty epitomizes Vegas' efforts to put the 'sin' back in 'casino.' One-armed Playboy bandits have replaced the playful pirates, plastic doubloons and chests full o'booty. Several times nightly, the spiced-up and totally cheesy **Sirens of TI** show stages a mock sea battle between sultry temptresses and renegade freebooters.

Tropicana
CASINO

(Map p60; www.troplv.com; 3801 Las Vegas Blvd S) As once-celebrated retro properties go under, the Tropicana –keeping the Strip tropical vibe going since 1953 – just got (surprise!) cool again. The massive renovation shows,

VEGAS ON FILM

» *Casino*, Martin Scorsese

» *Ocean's Eleven*, Steven Soderbergh

» *Leaving Las Vegas*, Mike Figgis

» *Fear and Loathing in Las Vegas*, Terry Gilliam

» *The Hangover*, Todd Phillips

LAS VEGAS IN...

One Day

Cruise the Strip, then hit the megaresorts like the **Venetian** and the **Encore** for a taste of high-roller action. Ride the double-decker Deuce bus or the monorail between casinos, with stops for noshing and shopping. Head to the **Bellagio** at sunset to watch the fountain show. After dinner at a star chef's **restaurant**, catch a late Cirque Du Soleil **show**, then party till dawn at **Tryst** or **Marquee**.

Two Days

Shake off the Rabelaisian fête of the night before at a brunch **buffet**. Indulge at a **spa** or chill poolside at your hotel before rolling west to **Red Rock Canyon** for sunset. On the way back to town, enjoy a casual dinner at local faves **Firefly** or **Ferraro's**, then head for cocktails at **Mix** to admire the skyline views before hitting a hot new ultralounge like the **Gold Lounge**.

Three Days

Spend the morning **shopping** and the afternoon at one of Vegas' quirky attractions, such as the **Pinball Hall of Fame** and the **Atomic Testing Museum**. Head downtown after dark to see where it all began. Visit the trippy **Fremont Street Experience** and the al-fresco **Neon Museum**, before testing your blackjack luck at the **Golden Nugget**. After midnight, let it ride on the Strip one last time, grabbing a bite or a nightcap at the Peppermill's **Fireside Lounge** before sunrise. Still have energy? The after-hours party at **Drai's** rages till past dawn.

Four Days

Better not push your luck.

from the airy casino to the lush, relaxing gardens and pool area with its with their newly unveiled **Nikki Beach Club**. Nope, this isn't your father's Tropicana – although he'll probably enjoy it too. The happy hour under illuminated palm trees on **Café Nikki** (www.nikkibeachlasvegas.com/cafe-nikki) wooden deck is one of our favorite sunset secrets.

Stratosphere CASINO
(Map p60; www.stratospherehotel.com; 2000 Las Vegas Blvd S) Standing over 100 stories, the three-legged Stratosphere is the tallest observation tower in the US. While the casino recently received a much-needed remodel, skip it and head straight to the elevators. Atop the tapered **tower** (adult/child $16/10; ☺10am-1am Sun-Thu, to 2am Fri & Sat) is a revolving restaurant, a circular bar and indoor and outdoor viewing decks offering the most spectacular 360-degree panoramas in town. To get there, ride the USA's fastest elevators, which ascend 108 floors in 37 ear-popping seconds. Up top, queue for adrenaline-pumping **thrill rides** (per ride $12-13, all rides incl elevator $28-34; ☺10am-1am Sun-Thu, to 2am Fri & Sat).

Planet Hollywood CASINO
(Map p60; www.planethollywoodresort.com; 3667 Las Vegas Blvd S) Lest you mistake that Planet Hollywood is to Hollywood what the Hard Rock is to rock and roll, two steps into the casino will instantly clear up the difference. We're not sure what the inordinate number of scantily clad women gyrating on poles above the table games have to do with the movies, but if that's your thing, plunk down your cash on blackjack in the Pleasure Pit. The coolest movie stuff actually hangs in some of the most inconspicuous places, like by the elevators or in the hallways: go figure.

Imperial Palace CASINO
(Map p60; ☎702-731-3311; www.imperialpalace.com; 3535 Las Vegas Blvd S; admission free; ☺24hr) The blue neon-roofed pagoda facade and faux-Far East theme are unbelievably hokey, but the zany atmosphere inside the casino is quite all right. Elvis fans, rejoice: the King never leaves the building.

DOWNTOWN

Think Vegas doesn't have real grit or soul? Come downtown and think again. The original spirit of Las Vegas looms large here.

Serious gamblers, colorful locals and rowdy tourists come to play $5 blackjack and drink giant daiquiris amid the swirling neon and open air shows on Fremont St. Expect a retro feel, cheaper drinks and lower table limits.

Note that the areas between downtown and the Strip and Fremont St east of downtown can be rather unsavory.

TOP CHOICE Neon Museum MUSEUM
(Map p68; ☎702-387-6366; www.neonmuseum.org; 821 Las Vegas Blvd N; displays free, guided tours $15; ☉displays 24hr, guided tours noon & 2pm Tue-Sat) Experience the outdoor displays through a fascinating walking tour ($15) of the newly unveiled Neon Boneyard Park, where irreplaceable vintage neon signs – the original art form of Las Vegas – spend their retirement. At press time, the museum was expanding their digs and hoped to add a self-guided component in 2012; until then, be sure to reserve your tour at least one to two weeks in advance.

Stroll around downtown come evening (when the neon comes out to play) to discover the free, self-guided component of the 'museum.' You'll find delightful al fresco galleries of restored vintage neon signs, including sparkling genie lamps, glowing martini glasses and 1940s motel marquees. The biggest assemblages are found at the on the 3rd St cul-de-sac just north of Fremont St.

Downtown Arts District ARTS
On the **First Friday** (www.firstfriday-lasvegas.org) of each month, a carnival of 10,000 art lovers, hipsters, indie musicians and hangers-on descend on Las Vegas' downtown arts district. These giant monthly block parties feature gallery openings, performance art, live bands and tattoo artists. The action revolves around the **Arts Factory** (Map p68; ☎702-676-1111; 101-109 E Charleston Blvd), **Commerce Street Studios** (Map p68; 1551 S Commerce St) and the **Funk House** (Map p68; 1228 S Casino Center Blvd). Check the website for shuttle bus info.

Fremont Street Experience PLAZA
(Map p68; www.vegasexperience.com; Fremont St, btwn Main St & Las Vegas Blvd; ☉hourly 7pm- midnight) Streaking down the center of Vegas' historic Glitter Gulch gambling district, this five-block pedestrian mall is topped by an arched steel canopy. Hourly from dusk until midnight, the 1400ft-long canopy turns on a six-minute light-and-sound show enhanced by 550,000 watts of wraparound sound and 12.5 million synchronized LEDs. The shows are ridiculously cheesy, but mesmerizing enough to stop passersby in their tracks, especially drunks.

El Cortez CASINO
(Map p68; www.elcortezhotelcasino.com; 600 Fremont St) Downtown and in the mood for blackjack? Head to the deliciously retro El Cortez, Vegas' oldest continuously operating casino. Going strong since 1941, it's one of the only joints in town where the slots are the real thing. If you hit the jackpot, you'll enjoy the clatter of actual coins – none of that newfangled paper ticket nonsense. For an all-out retro evening, duck into the **Flame Steakhouse** (www.elcortez.com; 1 E Fremont St; mains $10-26; ☉dinner) and you'll swear Bugsy Siegel himself might wander in. The coral dining room is the color of a Hollywood starlet's handbag and the menu (Steak Diane, wedge salad) is straight out of 1941.

GAMBLER'S SURVIVAL GUIDE

» The house always wins – eventually. Except for poker, all casino games pit the player against the house, which always has a statistical edge. Think of gambling only as entertainment – for which you do pay a fee.

» Always sign up for free player clubs at the casinos – they're located at the information desk on the casino floor.

» On a budget? Drink free cocktails while you're gambling, and hit the buffets at lunch – you'll probably not need to eat much the rest of the day.

» Take advantage of the introductory lessons in poker, blackjack and craps offered at some casinos.

» Don't be afraid to ask the dealer for advice on strategy or odds.

» If you're winning, it's polite to give your dealer a 'toke' (tip).

» As for the famous saying, 'what happens in Vegas stays in Vegas,' it's often true – especially in regard to your cash.

Downtown Las Vegas

Golden Nugget
CASINO
(Map p68; www.goldennugget.com; 129 E Fremont St) Downtown's royal jewel has serious panache, thanks in part to gorgeous Dale Chihuly-inspired glasswork everywhere you look. No brass or cut glass was spared inside the swanky (and lively) casino, known for its nonsmoking poker room; the RUSH Lounge, where live local bands play; and some of downtowns' best restaurants. Don't miss the gigantic 61lb Hand of Faith, the world's largest gold nugget, around the corner from the hotel lobby.

Main Street Station
CASINO
(Map p68; www.mainstreetcasino.com; 200 N Main St) This surprisingly elegant neo-Victorian casino hotel is adorned throughout with notable *objets d'histoire* under its pressed tin ceilings and elegant ceiling fans. Pick up a free *Guide to Artifacts, Antiques & Artworks* pamphlet from the hotel registration desk, then look for the art-nouveau chandelier from a Parisian opera house and a graffiti-covered chunk of the Berlin Wall.

Binion's
CASINO
(Map p68; www.binions.com; 128 E Fremont St) This old-school casino hotel is best known for its 'zero limit' betting policy and for being the birthplace of the World Series of Poker. While its heyday is over, it's a perfect place for beginners to learn blackjack at the low-limit ($2 and up) tables.

Viva Las Vegas Wedding Chapel
CHAPEL
(Map p68; ☑702-384-0771, 800-574-4450; www .vivalasvegasweddings.com; 1205 Las Vegas Blvd S; wedding packages from $201; ☺hr vary) Even if you're not contemplating tying the knot, it's worth a peek inside this little assembly-line wedding chapel of loooovvvee to see if anyone is getting married. The public is welcome to attend the themed weddings: kitschy as all get-out, too, they range from Elvis' 'Blue Hawaii' and 'Pink Caddy' to

Downtown Las Vegas

'James Bond,' 'Gangster' and 'Dracula's Tomb' themes.

OFF THE STRIP

TOP CHOICE **Atomic Testing Museum**   MUSEUM
(www.atomictestingmuseum.org; 755 E Flamingo Rd; adult/child $14/11; ⊙10am-5pm Mon-Sat, noon-5pm Sun) Recalling an era when the word 'atomic' conjured modernity and mystery, the Smithsonian-run Atomic Testing Museum remains an intriguing testament to the period when the fantastical – and destructive – power of nuclear energy was tested just outside of Las Vegas. After visiting the museum, it's almost possible to imagine that during the atomic heyday of the 1950s, gamblers and tourists picnicked on downtown casino rooftops while mushroom clouds rose on the horizon. Don't skip the deafening Ground Zero Theater, which mimics a concrete test bunker.

TOP CHOICE **Hard Rock**   CASINO
(Map p60; www.hardrockhotel.com; 4455 Paradise Rd) Beloved by SoCal visitors, this très-hip casino hotel is home to one of the world's most impressive collections of rock and roll memorabilia, including Jim Morrison's handwritten lyrics to one of the Door's greatest hits, Madonna's cone bra and leather jackets from a who's who of famous rock stars. **The Joint** concert hall,

Vanity Nightclub and **Rehab summer pool parties** attract a pimped-out, sex-charged crowd flush with celebrities.

Springs Preserve   NATURE PRESERVE
(www.springspreserve.org; 333 S Valley View Blvd; adult/child $19/11, admission to gardens & trails by donation; ⊙10am-6pm, trails close at dusk, 🅿) On the site of the natural springs (which ran dry in 1962) that fed *las vegas* ('the meadows'), where southern Paiutes and Spanish Trail traders camped, and later Mormon missionaries and Western pioneers settled the valley, this educational complex is an incredible trip through historical, cultural and biological time. The touchstone is the Desert Living Center, demonstrating sustainable architectural design and everyday eco-conscious living.

Palms   CASINO
(Map p60; www.palms.com; 4321 W Flamingo Rd) Equal parts sexy and downright sleazy, the Palms attracts notorious celebrities and gossip standbys (think Britney Spears) as well as a younger, mostly local crowd. While critics claim the Palms' glory days are waning, others rave that its restaurants and nightclubs remain some of the hottest in town. Highlights at the Palms include a 14-screen movie theater with IMAX capabilities and a 1200-seat showroom, the **Pearl**. PS: Don't take the elevator to the **Playboy**

Club expecting debauchery à la Hef's mansion: while a few bunny-eared, surgically enhanced ladies deal blackjack in a stylishly appointed lounge full of mostly men, the sexiest thing about it is the stunning skyline view.

🏃 Activities

Cue Club
POOL

(Map p60; www.lvcueclub.com; Commercial Center, 953 E Sahara Ave; per hr $10.50; ⊘24hr) Swim with the pool sharks at Vegas' largest billiard hall.

Pole Position Raceway
SPORTS

(www.polepositionraceway.com; 4175 S Arville St, off W Flamingo Rd; membership $5, race from $20; ⊘11am-10pm Sun-Thu; 11am-midnight Fri & Sat) Dreamed up by Nascar and Supercross champs and modeled on Formula 1 road courses, this European-style raceway boasts the USA's fastest indoor go-karts (up to 45mph).

Richard Petty Driving Experience
SPORTS

(www.1800bepetty.com; Las Vegas Motor Speedway, 7000 Las Vegas Blvd N, off I-15 exit 54; rides from $149; ⊘hr vary) If you've got a need for speed, this driving experience is your chance to ride shotgun during a Nascar-style qualifying run.

Royal Links
GOLF

(☎888-427-6688; www.royallinksgolfclub.com; 5995 E Vegas Valley Dr; green fees $75-275) Inspired by the British Open's famous greens. Tiger Woods set the record here, scoring 67.

Tournament Players Clubs Las Vegas
GOLF

(☎702-256-2500; www.tpc.com; 9851 Canyon Run Dr; green fees $119-235) A PGA tour stop, the naturalistic, minimal-irrigation Canyons course is also an Audubon-certified cooperative sanctuary.

Spas & Gyms

The Strip's spas are perfect for pampering. Day-use fees ($20 to $45) are usually waived with a treatment (minimum $75). Most spas have fitness centers; workout attire and gym shoes are required.

TOP CHOICE Qua Baths & Spa
SPA

(Map p60; ☎866-782-0655; www.harrahs.com /qua; Caesars Palace, 3570 Las Vegas Blvd S; ⊘6am-8pm) Social spa going is encouraged in the tea lounge, herbal steam room and arctic ice room, where dry-ice snowflakes fall. Among the many over-the-top spas in Vegas, this one remains a favorite for its

unique atmosphere and ability to provide a blissful state of calm that's a rarity anywhere on the Strip.

THEbathhouse
SPA

(Map p60; ☎877-632-9636; www.mandalaybay .com; THEhotel at Mandalay Bay, 3950 Las Vegas Blvd S; ⊘6am-9:30pm) A multimillion-dollar minimalist temple, it offers 'aromapothecary' massage oils, ayurvedic herbal baths and plunge pools.

The Spa & Salon at Encore
SPA

(Map p60; ☎702-770-3900; www.wynnlasvegas .com; Encore Las Vegas, 3131 Las Vegas Blvd S; ⊘5:30am-10pm) One of the newest spas in town, with an already legendary reputation among spa addicts.

🏂 Courses

Blue Sky Yoga
YOGA

(Map p68; www.blueskyyogalv.com; 101 E Charleston Blvd; suggested donation $12; ⊘hr vary) Drop-in classes for all levels in Jivamukti, Vinyasa and Kundalini styles.

Stripper 101
DANCE

(Map p60; ☎702-260-7200; www.stripper101 .com; Planet Hollywood, 3667 Las Vegas Blvd S; tickets from $40; ⊘hr vary) In a cabaret setting complete with strobe lights, cocktails and feather boas, these (non-nude) pole-dancing classes are popular with bachelorettes.

👉 Tours

It's easy enough to tour the Strip on your own via monorail or bus or on foot, but these companies offer more unique experiences. Check online for frequent promotions.

Haunted Vegas Tours
TOUR

(Map p60; ☎702-339-8744; www.hauntedvegas tours.com; Royal Resort, 99 Convention Center Dr; 2½hr show & tour $66) A campy sideshow begins a tell-all bus tour visiting Bugsy at the Flamingo casino hotel, creepy Liberace's cafe, the 'Motel of Death' and more.

Papillon Grand Canyon Helicopters
TOUR

(Map p60; ☎702-736-7243, 888-635-7272; www .papillon.com; McCarran Executive Terminal, 275 E Tropicana Ave) Flightseeing tour operator offers luxury Grand Canyon tours. Its 10-minute 'Neon Nights Express' jetcopter flyover of the Strip (adult/child from $69/49) is popular.

Vegas Mob Tour
TOUR

(Map p60; ☎702-339-8744; www.vegasmobtour .com; Royal Resort, 99 Convention Center Dr; 2½hr

LAS VEGAS FOR CHILDREN

Few places in Vegas actually bill themselves as family-friendly. State law prohibits anyone under 21 from loitering in gaming areas. The only casino hotels on the Strip that cater to children are Circus Circus and Excalibur. That said, there are still plenty of things to see and do with youngsters. Don't miss Mandalay Bay's Shark Reef. Teenagers may be most entranced by sassy pool scenes.

Coney Island Emporium (Map p60; www.coneyislandemporium.com; New York-New York, 3790 Las Vegas Blvd S; games from 50¢, roller coaster $14, all-day pass $25; ☉11am-11pm Sun-Thu, 10:30am-midnight Fri & Sat; ▣) The highlight of NY-NY's gargantuan video arcade and amusement center is the roller coaster, a four-minute high-octane ride with stomach-dropping dipsy-dos and stellar Strip views.

MGM Grand Lion Habitat (Map p60; www.mgmgrand.com; MGM Grand, 3799 Las Vegas Blvd S; admission free; ☉11am-7pm; ▣) Inside the casino, this glass-walled habitat showcases up to six magnificent felines daily, all descendants of the movie company's original mascot. The kid-friendly, tropical-themed Rainforest Cafe is nearby.

Pinball Hall of Fame (off Map p60; www.pinballmuseum.org; 1610 E Tropicana Ave; admission free, games 25-50¢; ☉11am-11pm Sun-Thu, to midnight Fri & Sat; ▣) Next to a discount cinema east of the Strip, this interactive museum is more fun than any slot machines. Picture 200 plus vintage pinball, video arcade and carnival sideshow games dating from the 1950s to the '90s.

College of Southern Nevada Planetarium (☏702-651-4759; www.csn.edu/planetarium; 3200 E Cheyenne Ave, east of I-15 exit 4b; adult/child $6/4; ☉shows usually 6pm & 7:30pm Fri, 3:30pm, 6pm & 7:30pm Sat; ▣) Young scientists will love the multimedia shows and 'skywatch' astronomy programs at this small planetarium. Show up early to get a seat (no latecomers allowed). Weather permitting, the observatory telescopes open for public viewing after the late show.

tour & film $66) Nighttime bus tour delves into the mafia underworld of Sin City's past, including celebrity scandals, mobster assassinations and other dirty laundry.

Festivals & Events

For more information about special events, contact the LVCVA (p87).

Chinese New Year CULTURAL
(www.lvchinatown.com) Lunar new year celebrations in January/February.

Nascar Weekend EXTREME SPORTS
(www.nascar.com) Rabid race fans descend on the Las Vegas Motor Speedway in early March.

St Patrick's Day CULTURAL
Fremont St throws a party and parade every March 17.

UNLVino FOOD & DRINK
(www.unlvino.com) Not-for-profit wine tasting extravaganza in mid-April.

Viva Las Vegas MUSIC
(www.vivalasvegas.net) Ultimate rockabilly weekend downtown in mid-April.

Helldorado Days CULTURAL
(www.elkshelldorado.com) Historic Old West hoedown, rodeo and barbecue near Fremont St in May.

World Series of Golf GOLF
(www.worldseriesofgolf.com) Ingeniously combines golf with high-stakes poker in mid-May.

World Series of Poker CASINO
(www.worldseriesofpoker.com) High rollers, casino dealers, Hollywood celebs and internet stars vie for millions from early June to mid-July.

National Finals Rodeo RODEO
(www.nfrexperience.com) Ten days of cowboys at the Thomas & Mack Center in December.

New Year's Eve CULTURAL
The Strip sees the biggest crush of humanity this side of Times Sq.

Sleeping

Pricewise, Vegas hotels are feast or famine: the awesome deal you got yesterday? It might triple for Friday's Lady Gaga concert.

TOP POKER HOTSPOTS

With the rules of Texas Hold 'em a frequent conversation starter these days, it's obvious poker is the hottest game in town.

» **Wynn Las Vegas** (p65) Vegas' most posh poker room

» **Bellagio** (p59) World Poker Tour stop

» **Golden Nugget** (p68) Classy carpet joint with nonsmoking tables

» **Hard Rock** (p69) Poker Lounge with bottle service, iPod docking stations and free lessons lure in the young and the hip

Then again, bargains in summer, midweek, and *after* holidays can be shockingly good – even at luxe properties. If you arrive midweek, rooms go for up to 50% less than on weekends. Note that the best deals are often found via hotel websites – which usually feature calendars listing day-by-day room rates – rather than through discount travel websites. Travelzoo.com is a good website to find current deals.

Don't be surprised when you find a 'resort' fee of $5 up to $25 per night on your bill. Valet (tip at least $2) and self-parking are free.

THE STRIP
While few places on the Strip offer rock-bottom budget accommodations, you can still snag surprisingly reasonable deals, especially at some of the older properties. Families on a budget are in luck: the cheapest tend to be the most child-friendly.

TOP CHOICE Encore CASINO HOTEL $$$
(Map p60; 702-770-8000; www.encorelasvegas.com; 3121 Las Vegas Blvd S; r $199-850; P※@⊛≋) Classy and playful more than overblown and opulent – even people cheering at the roulette table clap with a little more elegance. The rooms are studies in subdued luxury.

Tropicana CASINO HOTEL $
(Map p60; 702-739-2222; www.troplv.com; 3801 Las Vegas Blvd S; r from $40, ste from $140; P※@⊛≋) A recent multi-million dollar renovation has made 'the Trop' one of our new faves on the Strip. We like how the 1950s spirit lingers in the casino, while the amenities and design are utterly contemporary. The earth-toned, breezily tropical rooms and bi-level Jacuzzi suites are steals, and the pool area is a hidden delight.

Venetian CASINO HOTEL $$$
(Map p60; 702-414-1000, 877-883-6423; www.venetian.com; 3355 Las Vegas Blvd S; ste $199-1000; P※@⊛≋) The 700-sq-ft 'standard' suites are anything but. In fact, they're among the Strip's largest and most luxurious, with oversized Italian marble baths and sunken living rooms.

Mandalay Bay CASINO HOTEL $$$
(Map p60; 702-632-7777, 877-632-7800; www.mandalaybay.com; 3950 Las Vegas Blvd S; r $100-380; P※@⊛≋) The ornately appointed rooms have a South Seas theme, and amenities include floor-to-ceiling windows and luxurious bathrooms. Swimmers will swoon over the sprawling pool complex, with a sand-and-surf beach. Or check into **THEhotel** (Map p60; 702-632-7777; www.mandalaybay.com; Mandalay Bay, 3950 Las Vegas Blvd S; ste $120-540; @⊛≋), Mandalay's all-suite hotel, decked out with wet bars, plasma-screen TVs and deep soaking tubs.

Bellagio CASINO HOTEL $$$
(Map p60; 702-693-7111, 888-987-6667; www.bellagio.com; 3600 Las Vegas Blvd S; r $169-570; P※@⊛≋) Once the belle of the ball, the nouveau-riche Bellagio is still lavishly and artistically designed. Do rooms look small? That's because bathrooms are oversized. Luxurious lake-view suites front the resort's dancing fountains.

Caesars Palace CASINO HOTEL $$
(Map p60; 866-227-5938; www.caesarspalace.com; 3570 Las Vegas Blvd S; r from $99; P※@≋) Send away the centurions and decamp in style – Caesars' standard rooms are some of the most luxurious you will find in town.

Wynn Las Vegas CASINO HOTEL $$$
(Map p60; 702-770-7100, 877-321-9966; www.wynnlasvegas.com; 3131 Las Vegas Blvd S; r $199-515, ste from $289; P※@⊛≋) Deluxe five-diamond resort rooms are bigger than some studio apartments, with high-thread-count linens, flat-screen high-definition TVs, Turkish towels and lots of little luxuries. Salon suites enjoy floor-to-ceiling windows and VIP check-in.

Bill's Gamblin' Hall & Saloon CASINO HOTEL $$
(Map p60; ☎702-737-2100, 866-245-5745; www.billslasvegas.com; 3595 Las Vegas Blvd S; r $70-200; P❄@📶) The mid-Strip's worst-kept budget secret sports plasma TVs, Victorian decor and a rollicking fun casino with low-limit blackjack tables for beginners. Guests may use the pool next door at the Flamingo without charge.

Cosmopolitan CASINO HOTEL $$$
(Map p60; ☎702-698-7000; www.cosmopolitanlasvegas.com; 3708 Las Vegas Blvd S; r 200-400; P❄@📶🏊) Are the too-cool-for-school, hip rooms worth the price tag, especially when the service falls short of flawless? The indie set seems to think so. The rooms are impressive exercises in mod design, but the real delight of staying here is to stumble out of your room at 1am to play some pool in the upper lobbies before going on a mission to find the 'secret' pizza joint.

Mirage CASINO HOTEL $$
(Map p60; ☎702-791-7111, 800-374-9000; www.mirage.com; 3400 Las Vegas Blvd S; r $80-699; P❄@📶🏊) Don't expect your room to evoke an erupting volcano: gone is the four-star hotel's original tropical theme, replaced by chic, contemporary rooms. Expect bold color palettes, plush patterned rugs, plasma-screen TVs and stereos with iPod docks.

New York-New York CASINO HOTEL $$
(Map p60; ☎702-740-6969, 866-815-4365; www.nynyhotelcasino.com; 3790 Las Vegas Blvd S; r $70-480; P❄@📶🏊) The cheapest digs are rather tiny (just what one would expect in NYC), but pay more for a stylish Park Ave Deluxe and you'll have plenty of legroom. Avoid noisy lower-level rooms facing the roller coaster.

Paris-Las Vegas CASINO HOTEL $$
(Map p60; ☎702-946-7000, 877-603-4386; www.parislasvegas.com; 3655 Las Vegas Blvd S; r from $80; P❄@🏊) Nice rooms with a nod to classic French design; the newer Red Rooms are a study in sumptuous class.

MGM Grand CASINO HOTEL $$
(Map p60; ☎702-891-7777, 800-929-1111; www.mgmgrand.com; 3799 Las Vegas Blvd S; r $80-500, ste from $150; P❄@📶🏊👪) There's plenty to choose from at the world's largest hotel (5000-plus rooms), but is bigger better? That depends, but top-drawer restaurants, a sprawling pool complex and a monorail station always make it a good bet – if you can find your room. Standard rooms have blah decor, so stay in the minimalist-modern West Wing instead.

Planet Hollywood CASINO HOTEL $$
(Map p60; ☎702-785-5555, 866-919-7472; www.planethollywoodresort.com; 3667 Las Vegas Blvd S; r $69-369; P❄@📶🏊) Though not a standout in any category, Planet Hollywood remains one of the better midrange deals on the Strip. Skip the all-suite PH Towers Westgate and stay in the better value main tower instead. Each spacious, purple-accented room is themed after a specific movie (we spent the night with a 1990s Hugh Grant flop). Despite its sexy moniker, the 'Pleasure Pool' is fairly blah. Rooms with a view of the

COOL POOLS

» **Hard Rock** (p74) Seasonal swim-up blackjack and Tahitian-style cabanas at the beautifully landscaped and uber-hip Beach Club, a constant throbbing (literally, there are underwater speakers!) meat-market party, especially during summer-only 'Rehab' pool parties.

» **Mirage** (p73) Lush tropical pool is a sight to behold, with waterfalls tumbling off cliffs, deep grottos and palm-tree studded islands for sun bathing. Feeling flirty? Check out the topless Bare lounge.

» **Mandalay Bay** (p72) Splash around an artificial sand-and-surf beach built from imported California sand and boasting a wave pool, lazy-river ride, casino and DJ-driven topless Moorea Beach Club.

» **Caesars Palace** (p72) Corinthian columns, overflowing fountains, magnificent palms and marble-inlaid pools make the Garden of the Gods Oasis divine. Goddesses proffer frozen grapes in summer, including at the topless Venus pool lounge.

» **Golden Nugget** (p74) Downtown's best pool offers lots of fun and zero attitude. Play poolside blackjack, or sip on a daiquiri in the Jacuzzi and watch the sharks frolic in the nearby aquarium.

Bellagio fountain are a worthy splurge: the vantage point couldn't be better.

TI (Treasure Island)
CASINO HOTEL $$

(Map p60; ☑702-894-7111, 800-288-7206; www .treasureisland.com; 3300 Las Vegas Blvd S; r $90-390; P✴@☎☳) The micro rooms here feel deceptively expansive, thanks to floor-to-ceiling windows, airy earth tones, and soaking tubs. Rooms facing the strip overlook the cheesy-sexy pirate ship battle, an eye-rolling spectacle that best represents the way that TI has rebranded itself as towards grown up and cheeky rather than family-friendly.

DOWNTOWN
Avoid rent-by-the-hour fleapits by sticking close to the Fremont Street Experience.

TOP CHOICE El Cortez Cabana Suites
BOUTIQUE HOTEL $$

(Map p68; ☑800-634-6703; www.eccabana.com; 651 E Ogden Ave; ste $45-150; P✴@☎) You probably won't recognize this sparkling little boutique hotel for its brief movie cameo in Scorcese's *Casino* (hint: Sharon Stone was murdered here) and that's a good thing, because a massive makeover has transformed it into a vintage oasis downtown. Mod suites decked out in mint green include iPod docking stations, big flatscreen TVs and fab retro tiled bathrooms. There's a free fitness room and the funkiest old school casino in town – the El Cortez – is right across the street.

Golden Nugget
CASINO HOTEL $$

(Map p68; ☑702-385-7111, 800-846-5336; www .goldennugget.com; 129 E Fremont; r $59-229; P✴@☎☳) Looking like a million bucks, this casino hotel has set the downtown benchmark for extravagance since opening in 1946. Ample standard rooms sport half-canopy beds and marble everywhere. Outside by the lavish pool area, a three-story water slide plunges through a 200,000-gallon shark tank.

Main Street Station
CASINO HOTEL $$

(Map p68; ☑702-387-1896, 800-713-8933; www .mainstreetcasino.com; 200 N Main St; r $40-120; P✴☎) For a more intimate experience, try this 17-floor hotel tower with marble-tile foyers and Victorian sconces in the hallways. Bright, cheery hotel rooms with plantation shutters and comfy beds are as handsome as the casino.

California
CASINO HOTEL $$

(Map p68; ☑702-385-1222, 800-634-6255; www .thecal.com; 12 E Ogden Ave; r $39-145, ste $139-239; P✴☎☎☳) Tropical flair and a rooftop pool make it popular with visitors from Hawaii. Airy rooms have white plantation shutters, mahogany furnishings and mini-fridges.

EAST OF THE STRIP
Don't get stuck at chain cheapies near the airport or the city's convention center.

TOP CHOICE Hard Rock
CASINO HOTEL $$$

(Map p60; ☑702-693-5000, 800-473-7625; www .hardrockhotel.com; 4455 Paradise Rd; r $69-450; P✴@☎☳) Everything about this boutique hotel spells stardom. French doors reveal skyline and palm tree views, and brightly colored Euro-minimalist rooms feature souped-up stereos and plasma-screen TVs. While we dig the jukeboxes in the HRH All-Suite Tower, the standard rooms are nearly as cool. The hottest action revolves around the lush Beach Club.

Rumor
BOUTIQUE HOTEL $

(Map p60; ☑877-997-8667; www.rumorvegas .com; 455 E Harmon Ave; ste from $69; P✴@☎☎☳) Across from the Hard Rock, Rumor features a carefree, Miami-cool atmosphere with fun happy hours and DJ nights in the lobby. Its airy suites overlook a palm-shaded courtyard pool area dotted with daybeds and hammocks perfect for lounging.

Platinum Hotel
BOUTIQUE HOTEL $$

(Map p60; ☑702-365-5000, 877-211-9211; www .theplatinumhotel.com; 211 E Flamingo Rd; r from $129; P✴@☎☳) Just off the Strip, the coolly modern rooms at this spiffy, non-gaming property are comfortable and full of nice touches – many have fireplaces and they all have kitchens and Jacuzzi tubs.

WEST OF THE STRIP
Some off-strip hotels may provide free shuttles to the Strip.

TOP CHOICE Artisan Hotel
BOUTIQUE HOTEL $$

(Map p60; ☑800-554-4092; www.artisanhotel .com; 1501 W Sahara Ave; r $40-129; P✴☎☎☳☀) A Gothic baroque fantasy with a decadent dash of rock and roll, each suite is themed around the work of a different artist. Yet with one of Vegas' best after parties raging on weekend nights downstairs (a fave with the local alternative set), you may not spend much time in your room. The libidinous, mysterious vibe here isn't for everyone, but if you like it, you'll love it.

Orleans CASINO HOTEL $$

(☑702-365-7111, 800-675-3267; www.orleanscasino .com; 4500 W Tropicana Ave; r $50-175; P❋@☎ ❀♨) Tastefully appointed French-provincial rooms are good-value 'petite suites.' There's a free-access fitness center for guests in the spa, on-site childcare, a movie theater, a bowling alley and a live-music pub.

Palms CASINO HOTEL $$$

(Map p60; ☑702-942-7777, 866-942-7770; www .palms.com; 4321 W Flamingo Rd; r $99-459, ste from $149; P❋@☎♨) Britney Spears spent her *first* wedding night here. Standard rooms are generous, as are tech-savvy amenities. Request an upper floor to score a Strip view. Playpen suites are tailored for bachelor and bachelorette parties, or escape to the high-rise Palms Place.

GREATER LAS VEGAS

Most of these hotels offer free Strip shuttles.

Sam's Town CASINO HOTELS $

(☑702-456-7777, 800-897-8696; www.samstownlv com; 5111 Boulder Hwy, east of I-515/US Hwy 93/US Hwy 95 exit 69; r $40-275; P❋@☎♨) Ranchers, locals and RVers flock to this Wild West casino hotel, which neopunk band the Killers named their sophomore album after. Townn-sized rooms face a kitschy indoor garden or the city's neon lights.

South Point CASINO HOTELS $$$

(☑702-796-7111, 866-791-7626; www.southpoint casino.com; 9777 Las Vegas Blvd S; r $70-300; @☎ ❀♨) Popular with cowboys for its equestrian center, this budget-deluxe casino hotel is a short drive south of the Strip, near the outlet mall. With rooms this big and beds this divine, who needs a suite? Perks include a spa, a cineplex and a bowling center.

Red Rock Resort RESORT $$$

(☑702-797-7878; www.redrocklasvegas.com; 11011 W Charleston Blvd; r $110-625; P❋@☎♨) Red Rock touts itself as the first off-Strip billion-dollar gaming resort, and most people who stay here eschew the Strip forever more. For adventurous types who want the best of Vegas' urban jungle and its vast outdoor desert playground, this stylish place rocks. There's free transportation between the Strip, and outings to the nearby Red Rocks State Park and beyond. Rooms are well appointed and comfy. Check out the PBA-tour **bowling alley**, with 72 lanes and VIP suites with bottle service.

✖ Eating

Sin City is an unmatched culinary adventure. As celebrity chefs take up residence in nearly every casino, stakes are high, and there are many overhyped eating gambles.

Make reservations for more expensive restaurants as far in advance as possible, especially if you're here on a weekend. The dress code at most upscale eateries is business casual. At the most famous places, jackets and ties are preferred for men. For an unvarnished local view of the Vegas dining scene, check out the blog Eating Las Vegas (www.eatinglv.com).

THE STRIP

Strip casino restaurants alone could be fodder for an entire book; here are some favorites, but the choice seems nearly infinite. Look for the newest celebrity chefs' restaurants at the Palazzo resort, the CityCenter and the Cosmopolitan.

For a good range of budget options, head to New York-New York, where Greenwich Village bursts with tasty, budget-saving options.

TOP CHOICE Sage AMERICAN $$$

(Map p60; ☑702-590-8690; Aria, www.arialas vegas.com; 3730 Las Vegas Blvd S; mains $26-42; ☺5pm-11pm Mon-Sat) Acclaimed Chicago chef Shawn McClain meditates on the seasonally sublime with global inspiration and artisanal, farm-to-table ingredients in one of Vegas' most drop-dead gorgeous dining rooms. Lounge at the eggplant velvet banquettes underneath the giant scrims of Impressionist paintings, or head to the stunning bar to sip on inspired seasonal cocktails doctored with housemade liqueurs.

TOP CHOICE Social House JAPANESE $$$

(Map p60; ☑702-736-1122; www.socialhouselv .com; Crystals Mall, CityCenter, 3720 Las Vegas Blvd S; mains $24-44, tasting menu $95; ☺5pm-10pm Mon-Thu, noon-11pm Fri & Sat, noon-10pm Sun) Nibble on creative dishes inspired by Japanese street food in one of the Strip's most serene yet sultry dining rooms. Watermarked scrolls, wooden screens and loads of dramatic red and black conjure visions of Imperial Japan, while the sushi and steaks are totally contemporary.

DOCG Enoteca ITALIAN $$$

(Map p60; ☑702-893-2001; Cosmopolitan, 3708 Las Vegas Blvd S; mains $15-27; ☺5:30pm-11pm) Among the Cosmopolitan's alluring dining options, this is one of the least glitzy – but most authentic – options. That's not to say it isn't loads of fun. Order up to-die-for fresh pasta or a wood-fired pizza in the stylish *enoteca* (wine shop) inspired room that feels like you've joined a festive dinner party. Or head next door to sexy **Scarpetta**, which offers a more intimate, upscale experience by the same fantastic chef, Scott Conant.

Jean Philippe Patisserie   FRENCH $$
(Map p60; www.ariavegas.com; Aria; 3730 Las Vegas Blvd S; items $3-12; ⊘6am-midnight; 🐾) Step out of the Aria's mod casino buzz into this fantastical Alice in Wonderland land of sugar and spice (along with coffee, gelato and killer almond brioche). Indulge in creative takes on classic desserts like éclairs and Napoleons in flavors that promise to satisfy even the most hard-to-impress pastry connoisseur.

Hash House a Go Go   AMERICAN $$$
(www.hashhouseagogo; Imperial Palace; 3535 Las Vegas Blvd; mains $12-29; ⊘7am-11pm, to 2am Fri & Sat; 🐾) Fill up on this SoCal import's 'twisted farm food,' which has to be seen to be believed. The pancakes are as big as tractor tires, while farm-egg scrambles and house-made hashes could knock over a cow.

Joël Robuchon   FRENCH $$$
(Map p60; ☑702-891-7925; MGM Grand, 3799 Las Vegas Blvd S; menu per person $120-420; ⊘5:30-10pm Sun-Thu, to 10:30pm Fri & Sat) A once-in-a-lifetime culinary experience; block off a solid three hours and get ready to eat your way through the multicourse seasonal menu of traditional French fare. But we secretly dig next-door **L'Atelier de Joël Robuchon** even more, where you can belly up to the sexy scarlet and black lacquer bar for a slightly more economical but still wow-inducing meal.

Mesa Grill   SOUTHWESTERN $$$
(Map p60; ☑702-731-7731; www.mesagrill.com/las-vegas-restaurant; Caesar's Palace, 3750 Las Vegas Blvd S; mains $15-36; ⊘5pm-11pm daily, 11am-2:30pm Mon-Fri, 10:30am-3pm Sat & Sun) While New York star chef Bobby Flay doesn't cook on the premises, his bold signature menu of Southwestern fusion fare lives up to the hype.

Mon Ami Gabi   FRENCH $$$
(Map p60; ☑702-944-4224; www.monamigabi.com; Paris-Las Vegas, 3655 Las Vegas Blvd S; mains $12-28; ⊘7am-midnight) No, this charming

French brasserie doesn't live up to culinary heavyweights like Bouchon, and it's not trying to. Come for solid classics like friendly service and alfresco brunches on one of the Strip's nicest outdoor patios.

'wichcraft   SANDWICH SHOP $
(Map p60; www.mgmgrand.com; MGM Grand, 3799 Las Vegas Blvd S; sandwiches $8-11; ⊘10am-5pm; 🐾) This designy little sandwich shop, the brainchild of celebrity chef Tom Colicchio, is one of the best places to taste gourmet on a budget. Think grilled cheddar with smoked ham and baked apples.

Olives   MEDITERRANEAN $$$
(Map p60; ☑702-693-8181; www.bellagio.com; Bellagio, 3600 Las Vegas Blvd S; mains $16-52; ⊘11am-3pm, 5pm-10:30pm) Bostonian chef Todd English dishes up homage to the life-giving fruit. Flatbread pizzas, house-made pastas and flame-licked meats get top billing, and patio tables overlook Lake Como. Or try his rollicking new CityCenter venture, **Todd English PUB** (Map p60; www.toddenglish pub.com; Crystals, 3720 Las Vegas Blvd S; mains $13-24; ⊘lunch & dinner) a strangely fun cross between a British pub and a frat party, with creative sliders, English pub classics and an interesting promotion: if you drink your beer in less than seven seconds, it's on the house.

Fiamma   ITALIAN $$$
(Map p60; ☑702-891-7600; www.mgmgrand.com; MGM Grand, 3799 Las Vegas Blvd S; meals $50-60; ⊘5:30-10pm Sun & Mon, to 10:30pm Tue-Thu, to 11pm Fri & Sat) With its gorgeous woodwork and good happy hour, Fiamma is a top-tier dining experience you won't be paying off for the next decade. You haven't had spaghetti until you've had Fiamma's take on it, made with Kobe beef meatballs.

Seablue   SEAFOOD $$$
(Map p60; ☑702-891-3486; www.michaelmina.net; MGM Grand, 3799 Las Vegas Blvd S; mains $19-45; ⊘cafe lunch & dinner, restaurant dinner) Anything from Nantucket Bay scallops to Manila clams comes raw, fried, steamed or roasted out of two exhibition kitchens. Create your own farm fresh salads, or come for the shrimp and oyster happy hour from 5:30pm to 7:30pm.

Wolfgang Puck
Pizzeria & Cucina   MEDITERRANEAN, PIZZERIA $$$
(Map p60; www.wolfgangpuck.com; Aria; 3720 Las Vegas Blvd S; mains $10-26; ⊘11:30am-10pm, to

WORTHY INDULGENCES: BEST BUFFETS

The adage 'you get what you pay for' was never truer: most large casino hotels in Nevada lay on all-you-can-eat buffets, but look before you buy. Not all buffets are created equal. No host should stop you from perusing the offerings before putting down your money.

On the Strip, expect to pay $8 to $20 for a breakfast buffet, $15 to $25 for lunch and $20 to $40 or more for dinner or weekend champagne brunch. If you're insanely hungry, go for broke and try the 24-hour **Buffet of Buffets** (www.caesars.com/buffets; $49.99, or $44.99 if you sign up for the Total Rewards Players Club) pass, which gives you 24-hour access to seven buffets.

Vegas' best buffets, all of which are open for three round meals a day (unless otherwise noted), include the following:

» **Wicked Spoon Buffet** (www.cosmopolitanlasvegas.com; The Cosmopolitan, 3655 Las Vegas Blvd S)

» **Le Village Buffet** (www.parislv.com; Paris-Las Vegas, 3655 Las Vegas Blvd S)

» **Spice Market Buffet** (Planet Hollywood, 3667 Las Vegas Blvd S)

» **Golden Nugget** (Map p68; www.goldennugget.com; 129 E Fremont St)

» **Sterling Brunch at Bally's** (☑702-967-7999; Bally's, 3645 Las Vegas Blvd S; ☺Sun)

» **The Buffet** (☑702 693 7111; www.bellagio.com; Bellagio, 3600 Las Vegas Blvd S)

» **Sunday Gospel Brunch** (☑702-632-7600; www.hob.com; House of Blues, Mandalay Bay, 3708 Las Vegas Blvd S)

11pm Fri & Sat) Dig into crispy, creative pizzas and Cal-Italian classics on the primo terrace upstairs at the Crystals Mall.

Bouchon
FRENCH $$$
(Map p60; www.bouchonbistro.com; The Venetian, 3355 Las Vegas Blvd S; breakfast & lunch $12-25, dinner $19-37; ☺7am-10pm) Thomas Keller's rendition of a Lyonnaise bistro features French classics in a lovely poolside dining room. Come for the extensive raw bar and leisurely, decadent breakfasts.

Society Café
CAFE $$$
(www.wynnlasvegas.com; Encore, 3121 Las Vegas Blvd S; mains $14-30; ☺7am-midnight Sun-Thu, 7am-1am Fri & Sat) A slice of reasonably priced culinary heaven in the midst of Encore's loveliness.

Payard Bistro
FRENCH, DESSERTS $$$
(Map p60; ☑702-731-7292; Caesars Palace, 3570 Las Vegas Blvd S; breakfast & lunch $16-25, prix-fixe dinner $45-60; ☺6:30am-11pm, dinner Wed-Sun) Operated by third-generation chocolatier Françoise Payard, this exquisite place offers fresh takes on bistro classics and outrageously indulgent dessert-only dinner menus. Take-out pastry and espresso bar.

Stripburger
BURGERS $
(Map p60; www.stripburger.com; Fashion Show, 3200 Las Vegas Blvd S; items $4-10; ☺11:30am-1am Sun-Thu, to 2am Fri & Sat; ✋) On a bustling (read: loud) corner outside the mall, a silver diner-in-the-round serves up all-natural beef, chicken, tuna and veggie burgers, with stupendous cheese fries, thick milkshakes and gigantic cocktails.

DOWNTOWN
Fremont St is the neon-illuminated land of cheap and bountiful buffets, retro cafes and authentic ethnic hideaways.

Lillie's Asian Cuisine
TOP CHOICE / ASIAN $$$
(Map p68; www.goldennugget.com; Golden Nugget, 129 E Fremont St; mains $19-35; ☺dinner Mon & Thu-Sun) For sheer fun, this is one of downtown's top eating experiences. Amid blood-red light sculptures and walls of water flowing over glass, hibachi chefs dazzle with flashing knife tricks. Sit around an illuminated marble table and take your pick from seafood, steak and veggies, lit aflame as you watch.

Florida Café
CUBAN $$
(Map p68; www.floridacafecuban.com; Howard Johnson's, 1401 Las Vegas Blvd S; mains $9-18; ☺7am-10pm) Among a spirited local scene with live music some nights, enjoy authentic shredded steak and seasoned chicken with yellow rice. Café con leche, flan and batidos (tropical shakes) are superb.

CHEAP EATS FOR LOSERS

Lucky streak on the downswing? Seeking solace in the form of comfort food at 3am, but are down to the last roulette bet in your pocket? Join the club.

» 24-hour omelets at the **Peppermill**

» $1.99 shrimp cocktail at **Golden Gate**

» Old fashioned cheeseburgers and malts at vintage diner **Tiffany's Cafe**

» $4.99 steak and eggs at **Mr. Lucky's**

» The cheap and tasty buffet at **Main Street Station**

» Everything on the menu is half price during happy hour (4pm to 8pm) at **Blue Martini**

» Locals are in on the tastiest late-night dining deal in Vegas: happy hour antipasti at **Ferraro's** from 10pm to 2am (and 4pm to 7pm) Monday to Friday

» Half off all food (and drinks!) on Tuesdays to 1am, plus other days between 5pm and 7pm at **Paymon's Mediterranean Cafe**

Triple George Grill   SUPPER CLUB $$$

(Map p68; ☎702-384-2761; www.triplegeorgegrill.com; 201 N 3rd St; lunch $10-27, dinner $13-37; ⏰11am-10pm Mon-Fri, 4pm-10pm Sat) Inspired by San Francisco's legendary Tattage Grill, this art-decoish joint feels like Sinatra himself might have breezed in post-concert for a filet mignon. Against a swinging 1940s soundtrack, sip a stiff martini at the mile-long bar, or head next door to the vintage **Sidebar** for a cigar.

Aloha Specialties   HAWAIIAN $

(Map p68; Hotel California; mains $4-8, cash only; ⏰9am-9pm, to 10pm Fri & Sat) The local secret that even Hawaii transplants crave: think fried mahi mahi, giant teriyaki rice bowls and creamy coconut pudding. Where else in Vegas can you get Spam for breakfast?

Second Street Grill   STEAK $$$

(Map p68; ☎702-385-3232; Fremont, 200 E Fremont St; mains $19-35; ⏰dinner Mon & Thu-Sun) At this unabashedly rococo gem, chef Rachel Bern flies in the seafood fresh from Hawaii. You can score a 16oz T-bone steak with all the trimmings for under 20 bucks, too.

Golden Gate   SEAFOOD $

(Map p68; ☎702-385-1906; 1 E Fremont St; ⏰11am-3am) Famous $1.99 shrimp cocktails (supersize 'em for $3.99).

Grotto   ITALIAN $$$

(Map p68; ☎702-385-7111; Golden Nugget, 129 E Fremont St; mains $13-30; ⏰11:30am-10:30pm Sun-Thu, to 11:30pm Fri & Sat) A convivial spot to nosh on housemade pastas with a unique shark tank view. On a blackjack run and forgot dinner? Wood-fired pizzas and 200 wines are available at the bar until 1am.

EAST & WEST OF THE STRIP

Pan-Asian delights and several food trucks – part of Vegas' new craze – await around the Spring Mountain Rd strip malls of Chinatown.

TOP CHOICE Ferraro's   ITALIAN $$$

(Map p60; www.ferraroslasvegas.com, 4480 Paradise Rd; mains $10-39; ⏰11:30am-2am weekdays, 4pm-2am Sat & Sun) The photos on the wall offer testimony to the fact that locals have been flocking to classy, family-owned Ferraro's for 85 years to devour savory Italian classics. These days, the fireplace patio and the amazing late night happy hour draw an eclectic crowd full of industry and foodie types at the friendly bar. To-die-for housemade pastas compete for attention with legendary osso buco, and a killer antipasti menu served till midnight.

TOP CHOICE Firefly   TAPAS $$

(Map p60; www.fireflylv.com; 3900 Paradise Rd; small dishes $4-10, large dishes $11-20; ⏰11:30am-2am Sun-Thu, to 3am Fri & Sat) Locals seem to agree on one thing about the Vegas food scene: a meal at Firefly can be twice as much fun as an overdone Strip restaurant, and half the price. Is that why it's always hopping? Nosh on traditional Spanish tapas, while the bartender pours sangria and flavor-infused mojitos.

Luv-It Frozen Custard   ICE CREAM $

(☎702-384-6452; 505 E Oakey Blvd; items $2.50-6; ⏰1-10pm Sun-Thu, 1-11pm Fri & Sat; ♿) A local mecca since 1973, Luv-It's handmade concoctions are creamier than ice cream. Flavors change daily, so you'll be tempted to go back. Try the Luv-It special (strawberries, salted pecans, cherry) or a double-thick milkshake. Cash only.

Pink Taco

MEXICAN $$

(Map p60; www.hardrockhotel.com; Hard Rock, 4455 Paradise Rd; mains $8-24; ☺7am-11am Mon-Thu, to 3am Fri & Sat) Whether it's the 99¢ taco and margarita happy hour, the leafy poolside patio or the friendly rock and roll clientele, Pink Taco always feels like a worthwhile party.

Paymon's Mediterranean Café

MEDITERRANEAN $$

(Map p60; www.paymons.com; 4147 S Maryland Pkwy; mains $8-20; ☺11am-1am Sun-Thu, to 3am Fri & Sat; ☝) One of the city's few veggie spots serves baked eggplant with fresh garlic, baba ganoush, tabbouleh and hummus. The adjacent Hookah Lounge is a tranquil by day, too-much-fun by night spot to chill with a water pipe and fig-flavored cocktail.

Lotus of Siam

THAI $$$

(Map p60; www.saipinchutima.com; 953 E Sahara Ave; mains $8.95-28.95; ☺11:30am-2pm Mon-Fri, 5:30-9:30pm Mon-Thu, 5:30-10pm Fr & Sat) The top Thai restaurant in the US? According to *Gourmet Magazine*, this is it. One bite of simple pad Thai – or any of the exotic northern Thai dishes – nearly proves it.

Alizé

FRENCH $$$

(Map p60; ☎702-951-7000; Palms, 4321 W Flamingo Rd; mains $36-68; ☺dinner) André Rochat's top-drawer gourmet room is

named after a gentle Mediterranean trade wind. The panoramic floor-to-ceiling views (enjoyed by every table) are stunning, just like the haute French cuisine. A huge wine-bottle tower dominates the room.

Veggie Delight

VEGETARIAN $

(Map p60; www.veggiedelight.biz; 3504 Wynn Rd; items $3-10; ☺11am-9pm; ☝) Buddhist-owned, Vietnamese-flavored vegetarian/vegan kitchen mixing up chakra color-coded Chinese herbal tonics.

Harrie's Bagelmania

BAKERY, DELI $

(Map p60; ☎702-369-3322; 855 E Twain Ave; items from $1.50, mains $4-8; ☺6:30am-3pm; ☝) Best bagels in Vegas? Even New Yorkers swear by this Kosher deli and bakery, with fantastic breakfast sandwiches.

Mr. Lucky's

AMERICAN $$

(Map p60; www.hardrockhotel.com; Hard Rock, 4455 Paradise Rd; mains $5-16; ☺24hr; ☝) If curing your hangover with a 'Rehab breakfast' while a giant portrait of Jim Morrison stares down at you amid the glow of vintage motel signs appeals, this joint's for you.

 Drinking

For those who want to mingle with the locals and drink for free, check out **SpyOnVegas** (www.spyonvegas.com).

BLOODY GOOD STEAKS

Vegas caters to all kinds of steak lovers, whether you like it rare or well done, celebrity or local, retro or mod, and your background music Frank Sinatra or Lady Gaga.

» **STK** (Map p60; ☎702-698-7990; www.stkhouse.com; Cosmopolitan, 3950 Las Vegas Blvd S; mains $22-69; ☺dinner) Vegas' uber-stylish new 'Not Your Daddy's' steakhouse, flush with fashionistas, high rollers and hipsters, rocks a club vibe with DJs that you'll love or hate.

» **Golden Steer** (Map p60; ☎702-384-4470; www.goldensteersteakhouselasvegas.com; 308 W Sahara; mains $30-55; ☺11:30am-4:30pm Mon-Fri, 5pm-11pm daily) A fabulously retro steakhouse where the Rat Pack once dined. The steak and the tableside Caesar salad are perfectly good, but you're here to soak up the old Vegas vibe and your waiter's salty tales.

» **Stripsteak** (Map p60; ☎702-632-7414; www.mandalaybay.com; Mandalay Bay, 3950 Las Vegas Blvd S; mains $25-72; ☺5:30-11pm) Famed seafood chef Michael Mina has dived into the competitive world of Vegas steakhouses. An exceptional menu of Angus and Kobe beef delightfully detours from tradition.

» **Victorian Room** (Map p60; www.billslasvegas.com; Bill's Gamblin' Hall & Saloon, 3595 Las Vegas Blvd S; mains $8-25; ☺24hr) A hokey old-fashioned San Francisco theme belies one of the best deals in sit-down restaurants in Las Vegas. The rib-eye or steak and eggs specials are delicious around the clock.

» **N9NE** (Map p60; ☎702-933-9900; Palms, 4321 W Flamingo Rd; mains $26-43; ☺dinner) At this hip steakhouse heavy with celebs, a dramatic dining room centers on a champagne and caviar bar. Chicago-style aged steaks and chops keep coming, along with everything from oysters Rockefeller to Pacific sashimi.

THE STRIP

One of Vegas' dark secrets: the Strip is packed with over-the-top ultralounges where wannabe fashionistas sip overpriced mojitos and poseur DJs spin mediocre Top-40 mashups. Head to these places instead to avoid the deadly combination of alcohol and boredom.

⌜TOP⌟ La Cave
CHOICE
WINE BAR

(Map p60; www.wynnlasvegas.com; Wynn; 3131 Las Vegas Blvd S) This inspired wine and tapas bar is a hidden Strip gem that gets raves from regulars and newbies alike in every category: wine, food, service, value and ambiance.

⌜TOP⌟ Chandelier Bar
CHOICE
BAR

(Map p60; www.cosmopolitanlasvegas.com; Cosmopolitan, 3709 Las Vegas Blvd S) In a city full of lavish hotel lobby bars, this one pulls out the stops. Kick back with the cosmopolitan hipsters and enjoy the curiously thrilling feeling that you're tipsy inside a giant crystal chandelier.

Parasol Up – Parasol Down
BAR, CAFE

(Map p60; www.wynnlasvegas.com; Wynn, 3131 Las Vegas Blvd S) Unwind with a fresh fruit mojito by the soothing waterfall at the Wynn to experience one of Vegas' most successful versions of paradise.

Gold Lounge
LOUNGE, NIGHTCLUB

(Map p60; www.arialasvegas.com; Aria, 3930 Las Vegas Blvd S) A fitting homage to Elvis, you won't find watered-down Top 40 at this luxe ultralounge done up like a 1970s-era playboy's rec room, but you will find gold, gold and more gold. Make a toast in front of the giant portrait of the King himself.

Mix
LOUNGE

(Map p60; www.mandalaybay.com;64th fl, THEhotel at Mandalay Bay, 3950 Las Vegas Blvd S; cover after 10pm $20-25) THE place to grab sunset cocktails. The glassed-in elevator has amazing views, and that's before you even glimpse the mod interior design and soaring balcony. This is the best bathroom view we've seen – anywhere.

Red Square
BAR

(Map p60; www.mandalaybay.com; Mandalay Bay, 3950 Las Vegas Blvd S) Heaps of Russian caviar, a solid ice bar and over 200 frozen vodkas, infusions and cocktails. Don a Russian army coat to sip vodka in the subzero vault.

Mandarin Bar & Tea Lounge
LOUNGE

(Map p60; www.mandarianoriental.com; Mandarin Oriental, 3752 Las Vegas Blvd S) With panoramic Strip views from the hotel's 23rd floor lobby, this sophisticated lounge serves exotic teas by day and champagne by night.

LAVO
LOUNGE, NIGHTCLUB

(www.palazzo.com; Palazzo, 3325 Las Vegas Blvd S) One of the sexiest new restaurant-lounge-nightclub combos for the see-and-be-seen set, LAVO's terrace is the place to be at happy hour. Sip a Bellini in the dramatically lit bar or stay to dance among reclining Renaissance nudes in the club upstairs.

Napoleon's
THEME BAR

(Map p60; Paris-Las Vegas, 3655 Las Vegas Blvd S; ⊙4pm-2am) Be whisked away to a never-neverland of 19th-century France, with over-stuffed sofas and over 100 types of bubbly, including vintage Dom Perignon.

O'Sheas
BAR

(www.osheaslasvegas.com; 3555 Las Vegas Blvd S; drinks from $2; ⊙24hr) Luckily for the thirsty among us, O'Sheas has a 24-hour happy hour and 'bottle service' that gets you a bottle of Jack Daniel's or Smirnoff vodka and a mixer for $45.

DOWNTOWN

Want to chill out with the locals? Head to one of these go-to favorites, and watch for new bastions of hipness as they open up along Fremont St.

⌜TOP⌟ Fireside Lounge
CHOICE
COCKTAIL BAR

(Map p68; www.peppermilllasvegas.com; Peppermill, 2985 Las Vegas Blvd S; ⊙24hr) The Strip's most unlikely romantic hideaway is inside the **Peppermill**, a retro coffee shop serving giant omelets, pancakes and pie to the just married, the freshly divorced and the hungover. Courting couples flock here for the low lighting, sunken fire pit and cozy nooks built for supping on multi-strawed tiki drinks and for acting out your most inadvisable 'what happens in Vegas, stays in Vegas' moments.

Beauty Bar
COCKTAIL BAR

(Map p68; www.beautybar.com; 517 E Fremont St; cover $5-10; ⊙10pm-4am) At the salvaged innards of a 1950s New Jersey beauty salon, swill a cocktail while you get a makeover demo or chill out with the hip DJs and live local bands. Then walk around the

EMERGENCY ARTS

A coffee shop, an art gallery, working studios and a de facto community center of sorts, all under one roof and right smack downtown? The **Emergency Arts** (Map p68; www .emergencyartslv.com; 520 Fremont St) building, also home to the **Beat Coffeehouse** (www.thebeatlasvegas.com; sandwiches $6-7; ☺7am-midnight Mon-Fri, 9am-midnight Sat, 9am-3pm Sun) is a friendly bastion of laid-back cool, with strong coffee and fresh baguette sandwiches against a soundtrack of vintage vinyl spinning on old turntables. It's also home to the retro-fabulous **Burlesque Hall of Fame** (www.burlesquehall.com; admission free; ☺noon-6pm Fri & Sat, to 3pm Sun). If you're aching to meet some savvy locals who know their way around town, this is your hangout spot. After 7pm they serve beer and wine, and the space transforms into a 21+ venue.

corner to the **Downtown Cocktail Room**, a low-lit speakeasy owned by the friendly young entrepreneurs who run the **Beat Coffeehouse**.

Triple 7 Restaurant & Microbrewery   MICROBREWERY
(Map p68; www.mainstcasino.com; Main St Station; 200 N Main St; cover $5-10; ☺24hr) Sports fans, tourists and a crusty crowd of gamblers flock to this gargantuan brew pub for excellent happy hour and graveyard specials including decent sushi and microbrews on tap.

OFF THE STRIP

TOP CHOICE Double Down Saloon   BAR
(Map p60; www.doubledownsaloon.com; 4640 Paradise Rd; no cover; ☺24hr) You can't get more punk rock than a dive whose tangy, blood-red house drink is named 'Ass Juice' and where happy hour means everything in the bar is two bucks. (Ass Juice and a Twinkie for $5; one of Vegas' bizarrely badass bargains.) Killer jukebox, cash only.

Blue Martini   COCKTAIL BAR
(Map p60; www.bluemartinilounge.com; Town Square; 6593 Las Vegas Blvd S) Want to meet an actual Vegas local? (Yes, they do exist.) This is Vegas' friendliest, best-deal happy hour and possibly the perfect antidote to the fear that you could while away your evenings drinking overpriced martinis with tourists.

Frankie's Tiki Room   THEME BAR
(www.frankiestikiroom.com; 1712 W Charleston Blvd; average drinks $8; ☺24hr) At the only round-the-clock tiki bar in the US, the drinks are rated in strength by skulls and the top tiki sculptors and painters in the world

have their work on display. After a couple of mai tais in the dim light you might be transported to the South Seas.

ghostbar   ULTRA LOUNGE
(Map p60; www.n9negroup.com; 55th fl, Palms, 4321 W Flamingo Rd; cover $10-25; ☺8pm-4am) Sure, these days the crowd is thicker with celeb wannabes rather than actual celebs, but this sky-high ultra lounge gets packed nonetheless (and who can tell the difference between the average B-lister and her lookalikes, anyway?) Join hoochie mamas and guys living out their *Entourage* fantasies on the balcony to take in the admittedly stunning panoramic skyline views.

Hofbräuhaus   BEER HALL
(Map p60; www.hofbrauhauslasvegas.com; 4510 Paradise Rd; ☺11am-11pm Sun-Thu, to midnight Fri & Sat) This Bavarian beer hall and garden is a replica of the original in Munich. Celebrate Oktoberfest year-round with premium imported suds, trademark *gemütlichkeit* (congeniality), fair *fräuleins* and live oompah bands nightly.

☆ Entertainment

Las Vegas has no shortage of entertainment on any given night, and **Ticketmaster** (☎702-474-4000; www.ticketmaster.com) sells tickets for pretty much everything except nightclubs.

Nightclubs

Little expense has been spared to bring clubs inside casino hotels on par with NYC and LA in the area of wildly extravagant hangouts. Most are open 10pm to 4am later in the week; cover charges average $20 to $40. For Clubbing FAQs, including how to get on the all-important 'list,' see p84.

VEGAS HAPPY HOURS

When the slots have eaten up all of your cash, you might not want to lay down 15 bucks for that pomegranate mojito, even if the ice is hand-crushed and served by a bronzed model in a satin corset. If that's the case, head to one of these happy hours, which feature half-price or discounted drinks, usually in the early evening hours. Contrary to what overpriced bars want you to believe, they do exist in Vegas. Here are a few of the best:

» **Double Down Saloon** (p81)
» **Blue Martini** (p81)
» **Triple 7 Brewery** (p81)
» **LAVO** (p80)
» **Café Nikki** (p65)
» **Firefly** (p78)
» **Frankie's Tiki Room** (p81)

TOP CHOICE **Tryst** CLUB
(Map p60; www.trystlasvegas.com; Wynn; 3131 Las Vegas Blvd S) All gimmicks aside, the flowing waterfall makes this place ridiculously (and literally) cool. Blood red booths, and plenty of space to dance ensure that you can have a killer time even without splurging for bottle service.

Marquee CLUB
(Map p60; www.cosmopolitanlasvegas.com; Cosmopolitan, 3708 Las Vegas Blvd) When someone asks where the coolest club in Vegas is these days, Marquee is lately the undisputed answer. Celebrities (we spotted Macy Gray as we danced through the crowd), an outdoor beach club, hot DJs and that certain *je ne sais quoi* that makes a club worth waiting in line for.

Surrender CLUB
(Map p60; www.surrendernightclub.com; Encore; 3121 Las Vegas Blvd S) Even the club-averse admit that this is an audaciously gorgeous place to hang out for an evening, with its saffron-colored silk walls, mustard banquettes and a bright yellow patent leather entrance. Play blackjack by the pool at night or join one of the raging daytime pool parties. Surrender Your Wednesdays is one of the best club nights in town, with plenty of in-the-know locals.

XS CLUB
(Map p60; Encore; www.xslasvegas.com; 3131 Las Vegas Blvd S) The only club where we've seen club goers jump in the pool to dance (and not be thrown out by the bouncers), XS is an up-and-coming Vegas favorite with a more diverse crowd (read: you won't feel outta place if you're over 30) than most. Dress up or you won't get in.

Drai's CLUB
(Map p60; Bill's Gamblin' Hall & Saloon; www.drais.net; 3595 Las Vegas Blvd S; ⊙1am-8am Thu-Mon) Feel ready for an after-hours scene straight outta Hollywood? Things don't really get going until 4am, when DJs spinning progressive discs keep the cool kids content. Critics say it's full of cooler-than-thou scenesters; fans say it's the best afterparty in town, especially on Industry Mondays. Dress to kill.

Krāve GAY CLUB
(Map p60; www.kravelasvegas.com; Miracle Mile Shops, 3663 Las Vegas Blvd S; ⊙nightly) Drawing a mixed crowd, it's the hottest gay nightclub in town, and the only one on the Strip. A glam warehouse-sized dance space is packed wall-to-wall with hard bodies and VIP cabanas.

Stoney's Rockin' Country LIVE MUSIC
(www.stoneysrockincountry.com; 9151 Las Vegas Blvd S; cover after 8pm Fri & Sat $10; ⊙7pm-5am Tue-Sat) An off-Strip place worth the trip. Friday and Saturday has all-you-can-drink draft beer specials and free line dancing lessons from 7:30pm to 8:30pm. Bikini bull-riding, anyone?

Moon CLUB
(Map p60; www.n9negroup.com; 53rd fl, Fantasy Tower, Palms, 4321 W Flamingo Rd) Stylishly outfitted like a nightclub in outer space, the retractable roof opens for dancing under the stars. Admission includes entry to the only **Playboy Club** in the world, a surprisingly chic and intimate affair whose skyline views are decidedly more eye-popping and dramatic than the, ah, views offered by the surgically-enhanced, bunny-eared blackjack dealers.

Tao CLUB
(Map p60; www.taolasvegas.co; Venetian, 3355 Las Vegas Blvd S) Some Vegas clubbing aficionados claim that Tao, like a Top 40 hit that's maxed out on radio play, has reached a been-there-done-that saturation point. Newbies however, still gush at the decadent

details and libidinous vibe: from the giant gold Buddha to the near-naked go-go girls languidly caressing themselves in rose petal-strewn bathtubs.

Live Music

Contact these live-music venues directly for ticket prices and show times.

House of Blues
LIVE MUSIC

(Map p60; ☎702-632-7600; www.hob.com; Mandalay Bay, 3950 Las Vegas Blvd S) Blues is the tip of the hog at this Mississippi Delta juke joint, showcasing modern rock, pop and soul.

Joint
LIVE MUSIC

(Map p60; ☎702-693-5066; www.hardrockhotel .com; Hard Rock, 4455 Paradise Rd) Concerts at this intimate venue (capacity 1400) feel like private shows, even when the Killers or Coldplay are in town.

Pearl
LIVE MUSIC

(Map p60; ☎702-944-3200; www.palms.com; Palms, 4321 W Flamingo Rd) Modern rock acts like Gwen Stefani and Morrissey have burned up the stage at this 2500-seat concert hall with brilliant acoustics.

Sand Dollar Blues Lounge
LIVE MUSIC

(Map p60; ☎702-871-6651; 3355 Spring Mountain Rd, enter off Polaris Ave; cover $5-10) Dive bar with live blues nightly after 10pm.

Production Shows & Comedy

Some say it's a crime to leave town without seeing a show. But choose wisely: plenty of casino stage shows are fairly lame productions with jacked-up prices. The shows we've listed are all established and well-reviewed. In general, you can't go wrong with Cirque du Soleil: the production values, creativity, talent and sheer entertainment value justify the sometimes eye-popping prices.

If you're a comedy fan, check out who's headlining at the Hilton, Flamingo, Caesars Palace and Golden Nugget casino hotels.

You can buy same-day discount tickets for a variety of shows at **Tix 4 Tonight** (☎877-849-4868; www.tix4tonight.com; Fashion Show, 3200 Las Vegas Blvd S; ⏰11am-8pm), with additional locations on the Strip and downtown, or from **Tickets 2Nite** (Map p60; ☎702-939-2222; www.tickets2nite.com; Showcase Mall, 3785 Las Vegas Blvd S; ⏰11am-9pm).

TOP CHOICE LOVE
PERFORMING ARTS

(Map p60; ☎702-792-7777, 800-963-9634; www .cirquedusoleil.com; Mirage, 3400 Las Vegas Blvd S; tickets $99-150; ⏰7pm & 9:30pm Thu-Mon;

⏹) Another smash hit from Cirque du Soleil, which has a dizzying number of shows on the Strip, LOVE psychedelically fuses the musical legacy of the Beatles with the troupe's aerial acrobatics.

TOP CHOICE Steel Panther
LIVE MUSIC

(☎702-617-7777; www.greenvalleyranchresort. com; Green Valley Resort, 2300 Paseo Verde Pkwy, Henderson; admission free; ⏰11pm-late Thu) A hair-metal tribute band makes fun of the audience, themselves and the 1980s with sight gags, one-liners and many a drug and sex reference.

Phantom
PERFORMING ARTS

(Map p60; ☎702-414-9000, 866-641-7469; www .venetian.com; Venetian, 3355 Las Vegas Blvd S; tickets $69-158; ⏰7pm Mon-Sat, 9:30pm Mon & Sat; ⏹) A $40-million, gorgeous theater mimics the 19th-century Parisian opera house where Andrew Lloyd Webber's musical story takes place. Expect pyrotechnics, an onstage lake and chandelier tricks to wow even musical haters. If the show isn't sold out, ask for a free seat upgrade.

Crazy Horse Paris
CABARET

(Map p60; ☎702-891-7777, 800-880-0880; www .mgmgrand.com; MGM Grand, 3799 Las Vegas Blvd S, tickets $51-61; ⏰8pm & 10.30pm Wed-Mon) Za, za, zoom. The 100% red room's intimate bordello feel oozes sex appeal. Onstage, balletic dancers straight from Paris' Crazy Horse Saloon perform provocative cabaret numbers.

O
PERFORMING ARTS

(Map p60; ☎702-796-9999; www.cirquedusoleil .com; tickets $99-200) Still a favorite is Cirque du Soleil's aquatic show, O, performed at the Bellagio.

Zumanity
PERFORMING ARTS

(Map p60; ☎702-740-6815; www.cirquedusoleil .com; tickets $69-129) A sensual and sexy adult-only show at New York-New York.

Kà
PERFORMING ARTS

(Map p60; ☎702-891-7777, 877-880-0880; www .ka.com; MGM Grand, 3799 Las Vegas Blvd S; adult $69-150, child $35-75; ⏰7pm & 9:30pm Tue-Sat; ⏹) Cirque du Soleil's sensuous story of imperial twins takes place on moving platforms elevating a frenzy of martial arts-inspired performances.

Improv
COMEDY

(Map p60; ☎702-369-5223; www.harrahs.com; Harrah's, 3475 Las Vegas Blvd S; admission $29;

VEGAS CLUBBING 101

Brave the velvet rope – or skip it altogether – with these nightlife survival tips culled from Vegas doormen, VIP hosts and concierges.

» Avoid waiting in that long line by booking ahead with the club VIP host. Most bigger clubs have someone working the door during the late afternoon and early evening hours. Stop by in the late afternoon or early evening to get on the list.

» Always be polite and friendly with club staff. Being 'assertive' (aka pushy) usually backfires, possibly leaving you at the back of the line…all night.

» Do dress well. Most clubs have a dress code, and will generally not let in men wearing sneakers, baggy clothes or athletic wear. What's acceptable for a Saturday night outing in the rest of the US may not pass muster here.

» Ask the concierge of your hotel for clubbing suggestions – he or she will almost always have free passes for clubs, or be able to make you reservations with the VIP host.

» Cover charges vary wildly depending on the night, if you have a reservation, and your gender (yep, it's sexist – clubs aim for more women than men). While men usually have to pay a cover charge of between $20 and $40 at the hotter clubs, men who have female friends in their company will have an easier time getting to the front of the line.

» If you hit blackjack at the high-roller table or just want to splurge, think about bottle service: yes, it's expensive (starting at around $300 to $400 and upwards for a bottle, including mixers, plus tax and tip) but it usually waives cover charge (and waiting in line) for your group, plus you get a table.

» Friday and Saturday nights invariably mean crowds and high cover charges, but don't overlook other less-crowded but equally cool weeknights where locals come for special themes, DJs or promotions. Remember, in Vegas it's a 24/7 party: why not go clubbing on Tuesday? (Check hours in advance, however: most clubs go dark between two to four nights a week).

⊘8:30pm & 10:30pm Tue-Sun) NYC's well-established showcase spotlights touring stand-up headliners *du jour*.

Cinemas

Check **Fandango** (☑800-326-3264; www .fandango.com) for show times and more theater locations.

Las Vegas 5 Drive-In   CINEMA
(☑702-646-3565; 4150 W Carey Ave, off N Rancho Dr; adult/child $6/free; ⊘gates open 6:30pm or 7pm;) Old-fashioned place screens up to five double-features daily.

Town Square 18   CINEMA
(www.mytownsquarevegas.com; Town Square, 6587 Las Vegas Blvd S; adult/child $10/6.25) Swanky off-Strip cineplex offers digital projection and XL stadium seating.

Sports

Although Vegas doesn't have any professional sports franchises, it's a sports-savvy town. You can wager on just about anything at most casinos' race and sports books.

For auto racing, including Nascar, Indy racing, drag and dirt-track races, check out the mega-popular **Las Vegas Motor Speedway** (www.lvms.com; 7000 Las Vegas Blvd N, off I-15 exit 54).

World-class boxing draws fans from all over the globe to Las Vegas. The biggest and most popular venues include the **Mandalay Bay Events Center** (☑877-632-7800; www .mandalaybay.com; Mandalay, 3950 Las Vegas Blvd S), **MGM Grand Garden** (Map p60; ☑877-880-0880; www.mgmgrand.com; MGM Grand, 3799 Las Vegas Blvd S) and the **Thomas & Mack Center** (Map p60; ☑702-739-3267, 866-388-3267; www.unlvtickets.com; UNLV campus, S Swenson St at Tropicana Ave) among others.

Strip Clubs

Prostitution may be illegal, but plenty of places offer the illusion of sex on demand. R-rated lap dances cost from $20, while X-rated ones take place in the VIP rooms (bottle service required). Unescorted women are usually not welcome at popular strip clubs, including the following.

Spearmint Rhino
STRIP CLUB
(www.spearmintrhinolv.com; 3344 S Highland Dr; cover $30; ⊘24hr) Fall in love, if only for two minutes (the length of an average lap dance, that is). Strip club connoisseurs rave about the Rhino.

Treasures
STRIP CLUB
(Map p60; www.treasureslasvegas.com; 2801 Westwood Dr; cover $30; ⊘24hr) Treasures gets raves as much for its four-star steaks as it does for its faux-baroque interior and glam dancers. Good happy hour from 4pm to 8pm with cheap beer and a free buffet.

🔒 Shopping
The Strip has the highest-octane shopping action, with the full gamut of both chain and designer stores. Downtown is the center of vintage and retro inspired cool. Cruise west of the Strip for XXX adult goods and trashy lingerie. East of the Strip, near UNLV, Maryland Parkway is chock-a-block with hip, bargain-basement shops catering to college students.

Shopping Malls & Arcades
Most casino shopping malls and arcades are open from 10am until 11pm Sunday through Thursday, until midnight Friday and Saturday.

Crystals
MALL
(Map p60; www.crystalsatcitycenter.com; 3720 Las Vegas Blvd S) If you're on a first name basis with Stella (McCartney), Donna (Karan), Gianni (Versace) or Nanette (Lepore), you'll feel right at home in Vegas' newest shopping extravaganza.

Forum Shops
MALL
(Map p60; www.caesarspalace.com; 3570 Las Vegas Blvd S) Franklins fly out of Fendi bags faster at Caesars' fancifully gaudy re-creation of an ancient Roman market, housing 160 catwalk designer emporia.

Grand Canal Shoppes
MALL
(Map p60; www.thegrandcanalshoppes.com; Venetian, 3355 Las Vegas Blvd S) Living statues and mezzo-sopranos stroll along the cobblestone walkways of this Italianate indoor mall, winding past 85 upscale shops like BCBG, Burberry, Godiva, Jimmy Choo and Sephora.

Shoppes at the Palazzo
MALL
(Map p60; www.theshoppesatthepalazzo.com; Palazzo, 3327 Las Vegas Blvd S). Next door to Grand Canal, Palazzo is anchored by Barneys New York. Over 80 international designers, from Tory Burch to Jimmy Choo, flaunt their goodies.

Wynn Esplanade
MALL
(Map p60; www.wynnlasvegas.com; 3131 Las Vegas Blvd S) Wynn has lured high-end retailers like Oscar de la Renta, Jean-Paul Gaultier, Chanel and Manolo Blahnik to a giant concourse of consumer bliss.

Miracle Mile Shops
MALL
(Map p60; www.miraclemileshopslv.com; Planet Hollywood, 3663 Las Vegas Blvd S) A staggering 1.5 miles long; get a tattoo, drink and rock star duds.

Fashion Show Mall
MALL
(Map p60; www.thefashionshow.com; 3200 Las Vegas Blvd S) Nevada's biggest and flashiest mall.

Las Vegas Premium Outlets
MALL
(Map p68; www.premiumoutlets.com; 875 S Grand Central Pkwy) Discount-shopping outlet mall features high end names such as Armani Exchange, Calvin Klein, Dolce & Gabbana, Guess and Max Studio, alongside casual everyday brands like Levi's.

Not Just Antiques Mart
ANTIQUES
(Map p68; www.notjustantiquesmart.com; 1422 Western Ave; ⊘10:30am-5:30pm Mon-Sat) It's a one-stop antique-shopping extravaganza in the downtown arts district. Look for art-deco estate jewelry, casino memorabilia and vintage tiki ware.

Clothing & Jewelry

⬛TOP CHOICE Attic
VINTAGE
(Map p68; www.atticvintage.com; 1018 S Main St; ⊘10am-6pm, closed Sun) Be mesmerized by fabulous hats and wigs, hippie-chic clubwear and lounge-lizard furnishings at Vegas' best vintage store.

Buffalo Exchange
USED CLOTHING
(Map p60; www.buffaloexchange.com; 4110 S Maryland Pkwy; ⊘10am-8pm Mon-Sat, 11am-7pm Sun) Trade in your nearly new garb for cash or credit at this savvy secondhand chain. They've combed through dingy thrift-store stuff and culled only the best 1940s to '80s vintage fashions, clubwear and designer duds.

Fred Leighton: Rare Collectible Jewels
JEWELRY
(Map p60; www.fredleighton.com; Via Bellagio, 3600 Las Vegas Blvd S; ⊘10am-midnight) Many

---

WANT MORE?

For in-depth information, reviews and recommendations at your fingertips, head to the Apple App Store to purchase Lonely Planet's *Las Vegas City Guide* iPhone app.

Academy Awards night adornments are on loan from the world's most prestigious collection of antique jewelry.

Weird & Wonderful

TOP CHOICE **Bonanza Gift Shop** SOUVENIRS
(Map p60; www.worldslargestgiftshop.com; 2460 Las Vegas Blvd S; ☺8am-midnight) If it's not the 'World's Largest Gift Shop,' it's damn close. The amazing kitsch selection of over-priced souvenirs includes entire aisles of dice clocks, snow globes, tacky T-shirts and shot glasses. If you're seeking R (or X) rated gifts, check out the adult-only annexe of the store, where grown adults can be spotted blushing and giggling as they peruse candy underwear and naughty games.

Gamblers General Store SOUVENIRS
(Map p68; www.gamblersgeneralstore.com; 800 S Main St; ☺9am-6pm) It boasts one of the largest inventories of slot machines in Nevada, with new models and beautiful vintage machines, plus loads of souvenir gambling paraphernalia.

Strings of Las Vegas ACCESSORIES
(www.stringsvegas.com; 4970 Arville St; ☺noon-8pm Mon-Sat) All those hard-working sexy women and beefy guys obviously don't have time to make their own G-strings and tasseled undies. This industrial strip-mall warehouse outfits them from head to toe, with almost nothing in between.

Houdini's Magic Shop QUIRKY
(Map p60; www.houdini.com; Forum Shops, 3500 Las Vegas Blvd S) The legendary escape artist's legacy lives on at this shop packed with gags, pranks, magic tricks and authentic Houdini memorabilia. Magicians perform, and each purchase includes a free private lesson.

Zia Records MUSIC
(off Map p60; www.ziarecords.com; 4225 S Eastern Ave; ☺10am-midnight) You can dig up a demo by Vegas' next breakout band (who needs the Killers anyway?) at this shop, which calls itself the 'last real record store.' Live in-store performances go off on a stage, with a warning sign: 'No moshing allowed.'

Bauman's Rare Books BOOKS
(Map p60; www.baumanrarebooks.com; Shoppes at the Palazzo, 3327 Las Vegas Blvd S; ☺10am-11pm) Book lovers won't want to miss browsing Bauman's, where rare first editions of books like *The Great Gatsby* and *Huckleberry Finn* sit side-by-side with historical documents signed by US presidents and historic figures.

ℹ Information

Emergency
Gamblers Anonymous (☎702-385-7732; www.gamblersanonymous.com) Assistance with gambling concerns.
Police (www.lvmpd.com; ☎702-828-3111)
Rape Crisis Hotline (☎702-366-1640)

Internet Access
Wi-fi is available in most hotel rooms (about $10 to $25 per day, sometimes included in the 'resort fee') and there are internet kiosks with attached printers in most hotel lobbies. Free wi-fi hotspots are found at some chain coffee shops, casual restaurants and off-Strip at the airport and convention center. If you didn't bring your laptop, try:
FedEx Kinko's (www.fedexkinkos.com)
Downtown (☎702-383-7022; 830 S 4th St; per min 10-30¢; ☺7am-9pm Mon-Fri, 9am-5pm Sat); East of the Strip (☎702-951-2400; 395 Hughes Center Dr; per min 10-30¢; ☺24hr)

Media
The conservative daily *Las Vegas Review-Journal* (www.lvrj.com) is Nevada's largest newspaper, publishing Friday's *Neon* entertainment guide. Free alternative tabloid weeklies include *Las Vegas Weekly* (www.lasvegasweekly.com), with good restaurant and entertainment listings, and *Las Vegas CityLife* (www.lasvegascitylife.com). Available in hotel rooms and at the airport, free tourist magazines like *Las Vegas Magazine + Showbiz Weekly* and *What's On* contain valuable discount coupons and listings of attractions, entertainment, nightlife, dining and more.

Medical Services
Harmon Medical Center (☎702-796-1116; www.harmonmedicalcenter.com; 150 E Harmon Ave; ☺24hr) Discounts for uninsured patients; limited translation services.
Sunrise Hospital & Medical Center (☎702-731-8000; www.sunrisehospital.com; 3186 S Maryland Pkwy)
University Medical Center (☎702-383-2000, emergency 702-383-2661; www.umcsn.com; 1800 W Charleston Blvd; ☺24hr) Nevada's most advanced trauma center.

Walgreens The Strip (☑702-739-9645; 3765 Las Vegas Blvd S; ☺24hr); Downtown (☑702-385-1284; 495 E Fremont St; ☺24hr) Call for prescription pharmacy hours.

Money

Every casino and bank and most convenience stores have ATMs. Fees imposed by casinos for foreign-currency exchange and ATM transactions (which usually carry a $5 fee) are much higher than at banks.

American Express (☑702-739-8474; Fashion Show, 3200 Las Vegas Blvd S; ☺10am-9pm Mon-Fri, to 8pm Sat, noon-6pm Sun) Changes currencies at competitive rates.

TIPPING Dealers expect to be tipped (or 'toked') only by winning players, typically with a side bet that the dealer collects if the bet wins. Buffet meals are self-serve, but leave a couple of dollars per person for the waitstaff who bring your drinks and clean your table. Valet parking is usually free, but tip at least $2 when the car keys are handed back to you.

Post

Post office Downtown (Map p68; www.usps .com; 201 Las Vegas Blvd S ☺8:30am-5pm Mon-Fri); Strip Station (Map p60; www.usps .com; 3100 S Industrial Rd; ☺8:30am-5pm Mon-Fri)

Tourist Information

Las Vegas Visitor Information Center OR **Las Vegas Convention & Visitors Authority** (LVCVA; Map p60; ☑702-892-0711, 877-847-4858; www.visitlasvegas.com; 3150 Paradise Rd; ☺8am-5pm) Helpful hotline (6am to 9pm), and an office with free local calls, internet access and maps galore.

Websites

Cheapo Vegas (www.cheapovegas.com) Good for a run-down of casinos with low table limits and their insider's guide to cheap eating.

Only Vegas (www.visitlasvegas.com) The city's official tourism site.

Raw Vegas (www.rawvegas.tv) Programing 24/7, from daily news to reality vlogs.

Las Vegas.com (www.lasvegas.com) Travel services.

Lasvegaskids.net (www.lasvegaskids.net) The lowdown on what's up for the wee ones.

Vegas.com (www.vegas.com) Travel information with booking service.

Getting There & Away

Air

Las Vegas has direct flights (including many cheap deals) from most US cities, as well as some Canadian, Mexican, European and Asian gateways. During peak periods (eg holidays, weekends), vacation packages including airfare and accommodations can be fair deals.

Near the South Strip, **McCarran International Airport** (LAS; Map p60; ☑702-261-5211; www .mccarran.com; 5757 Wayne Newton Blvd; ☎) offers free internet access; ATMs, currency-exchange booths and a bank; a post office; a 24-hour fitness center (day pass $10) and a kids' play area. Left-luggage lockers are unavailable post-September 11. Most domestic airlines use Terminal 1; international, charter and some domestic flights use Terminal 2. A free, wheelchair-accessible tram links outlying gates. Short-term metered parking costs 25¢ per 10 minutes.

Bus & Train

Long-distance Greyhound buses arrive at a downtown **bus station** (Map p68; ☑702-384-9561; Plaza, 200 S Main St). Amtrak's California Zephyr follows I-80 across northern Nevada, stopping in Reno, Winnemucca and Elko en route to Chicago from San Francisco Bay. The nearest Amtrak station to Las Vegas, however, is in Kingman, AZ. Greyhound may provide connecting Thruway motor coach service to Las Vegas ($27 to $34, 2¾ to four hours).

Car & Motorcycle

The main roads into and out of Las Vegas are I-15 and US Hwy 95. US Hwy 93 leads southeast from downtown to Hoover Dam; I-215 goes by McCarran International Airport. It's a 165-mile drive (2½ hours) to Utah's Zion National Park, 275 miles (4½ hours) to Arizona's Grand Canyon Village and 270 miles (four hours) to Los Angeles. Along the I-15 corridor to/from California, Highway Radio (98.1FM, 99.5FM) broadcasts traffic updates every 30 minutes.

For car rental companies and policies, see p559.

Getting Around

Gridlock along the Strip makes navigating the city's core a chore. The best way to get around is on foot, along with the occasional air-con taxi, monorail or bus ride.

To/From the Airport

Shuttle service remains the fastest affordable option. **Bell Trans** (☑702-739-7990; www.bell -trans.com) operates shuttles ($7) between the airport and the Strip. Fares to downtown or off Strip destinations are slightly higher. At the airport, exit door 9 near baggage claim to find the Bell Trans booth.

Taxi fares to Strip hotels – 30 minutes in heavy traffic – run $10 to $15 (to downtown, average $20), cash only. Fare gouging ('long-hauling') through the airport connector tunnel is common; ask your driver to use surface streets instead.

If you're traveling light, CAT bus No 109 ($2, 30 to 60 minutes) runs downtown 24/7. Between 5am and 2am, CAT bus 108 ($2, 40 to 55 minutes) also heads downtown, stopping at the Las Vegas Convention Center, Hilton and Sahara monorail stations.

Car & Motorcycle

RENTAL

Trying to decide whether to rent a car in Vegas? The biggest pro: all of the attractions in Vegas have free self-parking and valet parking available. The biggest cons: car rentals in Las Vegas are more expensive than elsewhere in the Southwest, and using a car to navigate the Strip (especially in the evening) will certainly transport you to Venice, Paris or New York– but not in the way you'd imagined.

Hertz (☑800-654-3131; www.hertz.com) rents cars at the McCarran International Airport. Booking ahead is essential on weekends, with the airport usually being cheaper than the Strip or downtown.

TRAFFIC

Traffic often snarls, especially during morning and afternoon rush hours and at night on weekends around the Strip. Work out in advance which cross street will bring you closest to your destination and try to utilize alternate routes like Industrial Rd and Paradise Rd. Tune to 970AM for traffic updates. If you're too drunk to drive, call **Designated Drivers** (☑702-456-7433; ☺24hr) to pick you up and drive your car back to your hotel; fees vary, depending on mileage.

Public Transportation

The fast, frequent **monorail** (www.lvmonorail.com; 1-/2-ride ticket $5/9, 24/72hr pass $12/28, child under 6 free; ☺7am-2am Mon-Thu, to 3am Fri-Sun) stops at the MGM Grand, Bally's/Paris-Las Vegas, Flamingo/Caesars Palace, Harrah's/Imperial Palace, Las Vegas Convention Center and Las Vegas Hilton stations. A discounted six-ride ticket ($20) can be used by multiple riders.

Citizens Area Transit (CAT; ☑702-228-7433, 800-228-3911; www.catride.com; 24hr pass $5; ☺most routes 5am-2am) operates dozens of local bus lines (one-way fare $2) and double-decker the **'Deuce'** buses (2-hour/24-hour pass $5/7), which run 24/7 along the Strip to and from downtown. Cash only (exact change required).

Many off-Strip hotels and resorts offer guests free shuttle buses or trams to/from and around the Strip: ask your concierge what your hotel offers.

Taxi

It's illegal to hail a cab on the street. Taxi stands are found at casino hotels and malls. A 4.5-mile lift from one end of the Strip to the other runs $12 to $16, plus tip. Fares (cash only) are metered: flagfall is $3.30, plus $2.60 per mile and 20¢ per minute while waiting. By law, the maximum number of passengers is five, and all companies must have at least one wheelchair-accessible van. Call **Desert Cab** (☑702-386-9102), **Western Cab** (☑702-736-8000) or **Yellow/Checker/Star** (☑702-873-2000).

AROUND LAS VEGAS

You might be surprised to discover geologic treasures in Nevada's amazing wind- and water-carved landscape, all within a short drive of surreal facsimiles of Ancient Rome and belle-époque Paris. While Las Vegas may be the antithesis of a naturalist's vision of America, it's certainly close to some spectacular outdoor attractions. For iconic desert landscapes, Red Rock Canyon and Valley of Fire State Park are just outside the city limits. Straddling the Arizona–Nevada state line are Hoover Dam, just outside Boulder City, and the cool oasis of Lake Mead National Recreation Area.

☞ Tours

Hoover Dam package deals can save ticketing and transportation headaches, while adventure outfitters ease logistical hassles for many outdoor excursions. Some tours include free pick-ups and drop-offs from Strip casino hotels. Check free Vegas magazines for deals.

Black Canyon River Adventures   RAFTING
(☑702-294-1414, 800-455-3490; www.blackcanyon adventures.com; Hacienda Hotel & Casino, off US Hwy 93, Boulder City; adult/child $88/54) Motor-assisted Colorado River raft floats launch beneath Hoover Dam, with stops for swimming and lunch.

Desert Adventures   KAYAKING, HIKING
(☑702-293-5026; www.kayaklasvegas.com; 1647 Nevada Hwy, Suite A, Boulder City; trips from $149) With Lake Mead and Hoover Dam just a few hours' drive away, would-be river rats should check out Desert Adventures for lots of half-, full- and multiday kayaking adventures. Hiking, horseback and mountain-bike trips, too.

Red Rock Canyon

The startling contrast between Las Vegas' artificial neon glow and the awesome natural forces in this **national conservation area** (www.redrockcanyonlv.org; day-use per car/bicycle $7/3; ☺scenic loop 6am-dusk) can't be exaggerated. Created about 65 million years ago, the canyon is more like a valley, with a steep, rugged red rock escarpment rising 3000ft on its western edge, dramatic evidence of tectonic-plate collisions.

A 13-mile, one-way scenic drive passes some of the canyon's most striking features, where you can access hiking trails and rock-climbing routes, or simply be mesmerized by the vistas. Stop at the **visitor center** (☑702-515-5350; ☺8:30am-4:30pm), for its natural-history exhibits and information on hiking trails, rock-climbing routes and 4WD routes. **Red Rock Canyon Interpretive Association** (☑702-515-5361/5367; www.redrockcanyonlv.org) operates the nonprofit bookstore there and organizes activities, including birding and wildflower walks (advance reservations may be required).

Call ahead to reserve guided horseback tours led by **Cowboy Trail Rides** (☑702-387-2457; www.cowboytrailrides.com; off Hwy 159; tours $69-339; ⊞). Mountain biking is allowed only on paved roads, not dirt trails. Rent bikes at **Las Vegas Cyclery** (☑702-596-2953; www.lasvegascyclery.com; 8221 W Charleston Blvd; per day from $30; ☺10am-6pm Mon-Fri, 9am-6pm Sat, 10am-4pm Sun) in suburban Summerlin.

To get here from the Strip, take I-15 south, exit at Blue Diamond Rd (NV Hwy 160), and drive westward, veering right onto NV Hwy 159. On the return trip, keep driving east on Hwy 159, which becomes Charleston Blvd. About 2 miles east of the visitor center off NV Hwy 159 is a **campground** (☑702-515-5350; tent & RV sites $15; ☺Sep-May), offering first-come, first-served sites with water and vault toilets.

Spring Mountain Ranch State Park

South of Red Rock Canyon's scenic loop drive, a side road leaves Hwy 159 and enters the petite **Spring Mountain Ranch State Park** (☑702-875-4141; entry $9; ☺8am-dusk, visitor center 10am-4pm), abutting the cliffs of the Wilson Range. The ranch was established in the 1860s and has had various owners including the eccentric billionaire Howard Hughes. Popular with picnicking families on weekends, today it's a verdant place, with white fences and an old red ranch house, which has historical exhibits. Call for schedules of guided ranch tours, moonlight canyon hikes and outdoor summer theater performances.

MOVING ON?

For tips, recommendations and reviews, head to shop.lonelyplanet.com to purchase a downloadable PDF of the Palm Springs and the Desert chapter from Lonely Planet's *California* guide.

Lake Mead & Hoover Dam

Even those who challenge, or at least question, the USA's commitment to damming the US West have to marvel at the engineering and architecture of the Hoover Dam. Set amid the almost unbearably dry Mohave Desert, the dam towers over Black Canyon and provides electricity for the entire region.

Hoover Dam created Lake Mead, which boasts 700 miles of shoreline, while Davis Dam created the much smaller Lake Mohave, which straddles the Arizona border. Black Canyon, the stretch of the Colorado River just below Hoover Dam, links the two lakes. All three bodies of water are included in the Lake Mead National Recreation Area, created in 1964.

◉ Sights

Hoover Dam HISTORIC SITE
(☑information 702-293-8321, reservations 702-992-7990, 866-998-3427; www.usbr.gov/lc/hoover dam; US Hwy 93; admission $8, incl power-plant tour adult/child $11/9, all-inclusive tour $30; ☺9am-5pm, to 6pm in summer, last ticket sold 45min before closing) A statue of bronze winged figures stands atop Hoover Dam, memorializing those who built the massive 726ft concrete structure, one of the world's tallest dams. Originally named Boulder Dam, this New Deal public works project, completed ahead of schedule and under budget in 1936, was the Colorado River's first major dam. Thousands of men and their families, eager for work in the height of the Depression, came to Black Canyon and worked in excruciating conditions – dangling hundreds of feet above the canyon in 120°F (about 50°C) desert heat. Hundreds lost their lives.

Today, guided tours begin at the visitor center, where a video screening features original footage of the construction. Then take an elevator ride 50 stories below to view the dam's massive power generators,

WORTH A TRIP

VALLEY OF FIRE STATE PARK

A masterpiece of desert scenery filled with psychedelically shaped sandstone outcroppings, this **park** (www.parks.nv.gov/vf.htm; admission $10) on the north edge of Lake Mead wows. It's amazing that this fantasyland of wondrous shapes carved in psychedelic sandstone by the erosive forces of wind and water is also a relaxing escape that's only 55 miles from Vegas.

Hwy 169 runs right past the **visitor center** (☏702-397-2088; ☺8:30am-4:30pm), which offers information on hiking, and excellent desert-life exhibits. sells books and maps, and has information about ranger-led activities like guided hikes and stargazing.

Take the winding scenic side road out to **White Domes**, an 11-mile round-trip. En route you'll pass **Rainbow Vista**, followed by the turn-off to **Fire Canyon** and **Silica Dome** (incidentally, where Captain Kirk perished in *Star Trek: Generations*).

Spring and fall are the best times to visit; daytime summer temperatures typically exceed 100°F (more than 37°C). The valley is at its most fiery at dawn and dusk, so consider grabbing a first-come, first-served site in the campgrounds (tent/RV sites $20/30). The fastest way here from Las Vegas is to drive I-15 north to NV Hwy 169, taking about an hour.

---

each of which alone could power a city of 100,000 people. Parking at the site costs $7.

Hoover Dam Museum   MUSEUM
(☏702-294-1988; www.bcmha.org; Boulder Dam Hotel, 1305 Arizona St, Boulder City; adult/child $2/1; ☺10am-5pm Mon-Sat; ⛟) You'll enjoy the dam tour more if you stop at this small but engagingly hands-on museum first. It's upstairs at the historic Boulder Dam Hotel, where Bette Davis, FDR and Howard Hughes once slept. Exhibits focus on Depression-era America and the tough living conditions endured by the people who came to build the dam. A 20-minute film features historic footage of the project.

Mike O'Callaghan-Pat Tillman Memorial Bridge   BRIDGE
Featuring a pedestrian walkway with perfect views upstream of Hoover Dam, this bridge is definitely not recommended for anyone with vertigo. Mike O'Callaghan was governor of Nevada from 1971 to 1979. NFL star Pat Tillman was a safety for the Arizona Cardinals when he enlisted as a US Army Ranger in 2002. He was slain by friendly fire during a battle in Afghanistan in 2004, and top army commanders, who promoted the fabrication that he'd been killed by enemy forces, covered up the circumstances surrounding his death.

🏃 Activities

For motorized float trips and guided kayaking tours launching below Hoover Dam, see p88. Popular year-round activities in Lake Mead National Recreation Area (☏702-293-8906; www.nps.gov/lame; 7-day entry pass individual/car $5/10; ☺24hr) include swimming, fishing, boating, waterskiing and kayaking. The splendid scenic drive winds north along Lakeshore Dr and Northshore Rd, passing viewpoints, hiking and birding trailheads, beaches and bays, and full-service marinas.

Don't overlook a simple stroll around charming, serene Boulder City, the only casino-free town in Nevada. Originally erected to house workers constructing the Hoover Dam, casinos were outlawed to prevent distractions from their monumental task.

Fish Vegas   FISHING
(☏702-293-6294; www.fishvegas.com; guided tours 1-2 people from $300) Chartered fishing trips on Lake Mead. Go online for Cap'n Mike's monthly fishing reports and news.

Lake Mead Cruises   BOAT TOUR
(☏702-293-6180;www.lakemeadcruises.com;90min midday cruise per adult/child $24/12; ☺noon & 2pm) Kid-friendly tours, along with lunch and brunch cruises, on triple-decker, air-con, Mississippi-style paddle wheelers depart from Hemenway Harbor.

Hiking

While most visitors come to Lake Mead for the water, there are a handful of hiking trails, too, most of which are short. At Grapevine Canyon near Lake Mohave, for instance, a quarter-mile jaunt takes you to a petroglyph panel, but if you want you can boulder-hop further up the gorge, which cups a ribbon-like stream trickling down from a spring. Longer routes include a 3.7-mile trail along a historic railway line with five tunnels that links the Alan Bible Visitor Center to Hoover Dam. The most challenging hike in the park follows a 3-mile trail down 800ft to a set of hot springs in a slot off Black Canyon. This one's not recommended in summer.

🛌 Sleeping

Cottonwood Cove Motel   MOTEL **$$**
(☎702-297-1464; www.cottonwoodcoveresort.com; r $65-115) On Lake Mohave, this motel has rooms with sliding glass doors overlooking a swimming beach.

NPS Campgrounds   CAMPGROUNDS **$**
(☎702-293-8906; tent & RV sites $10) It's first-come, first-served at these campgrounds found on Lake Mead at Boulder Beach, Callville Bay, Echo Bay and Las Vegas Bay.

Boulder Dam Hotel   HOTEL **$$**
(www.boulderdamhotel.com; ☎702-293-3093; r $61-140; ✳️🐾) For a peaceful night's sleep worlds away from the madding crowds and neon of Vegas, this gracious Dutch Colonial-style hotel has welcomed illustrious guests since 1933. Relax with a cocktail at the art-deco jazz lounge onsite.

🍴 Eating

Milo's   WINE BAR **$$**
(www.miloswinebar.com; 538 Nevada Way; dishes $4.50-13; ⏲️11am-10pm Sun-Thu, to midnight Fri & Sat) In downtown Boulder City, Milo's serves fresh sandwiches, salads and gourmet cheese plates at sidewalk tables outside the wine bar.

Le Bistro Café   ITALIAN **$$**
(☎702-293-7070; 1312 Nevada Hwy; mains $12-18; ⏲️dinner) Order home-cooked classic Italian pasta dishes and meatier fare, with tiramisu afterward.

You'll find only basic restaurants at the Temple Bar, Boulder Beach and Echo Bay marinas on Lake Mead, and at Cottonwood Cove and Katherine Landing on Lake Mohave. Other lakeshore marinas have convenience stores for snacks and drinks.

ℹ️ Information

Boulder City (☎702-294-1252; 100 Nevada Hwy, off US Hwy 93; ⏲️8am-4:30pm) Near Hoover Dam.
Alan Bible Visitor Center (☎702-293-8990; Lakeshore Scenic Dr, off US Hwy 93; ⏲️8am-4:30pm) In Nevada, 5 miles west of Hoover Dam. Excellent source of information on area recreation and desert life.
Katherine Landing Ranger Station (☎928-754-3272; off AZ Hwy 68, Bullhead City; ⏲️8:30am-4pm) In Arizona, 3 miles north of Davis Dam.

ℹ️ Getting There & Away

From the Strip, take I-15 south to I-215 east to I-515/US 93 and 95 and continue over Railroad Pass, staying on US Hwy 93 past Boulder City. As you approach the dam, park in the multilevel parking lot ($7, cash only; open 8am to 6pm) before you reach the visitor center. Or continue over the Arizona state line and park for free on the roadside (if you can find a space), then walk back over the top of the dam to the visitor center.

Mt Charleston

Up in the Humboldt-Toiyabe National Forest, the Spring Mountains form the western boundary of the Las Vegas valley, with higher rainfall, lower temperatures and fragrant pine, juniper and mahogany forests.

Just past the NV Hwy 158 turn-off and campground, the **information station** (☎702-872-5486; www.fs.fed.us/r4/htnf; Kyle Canyon Rd; ⏲️hours vary) has free trail guides, brochures and outdoor activity information.

The village of Mt Charleston gives access to several hikes, including the demanding 16.6-mile round-trip **South Loop Trail** up Charleston Peak (elevation 11,918ft), starting from Cathedral Rock picnic area. The easier, 2.8-mile round-trip **Cathedral Rock Trail** offers canyon views.

Mt Charleston Lodge (☎702-872-5408, 800-955-1314; www.mtcharlestonlodge.com; 1200 Old Park Rd; cabins $108-295; 🐾) has a chalet-style **dining room** (mains $11-24; ⏲️8am-9pm Sun-Thu, 8am-10pm Fri & Sat) and rustic, romantic log cabins with fireplaces, whirlpool tubs and private decks.

Heading back downhill, turn left onto Hwy 158, a curvy alpine road that passes even more trailheads and **campgrounds** (☎reservations 518-885-3639, 877-444-6777; www.recreation.gov; tent & RV sites $15-25; ⏲️mid-May–Oct, some year-round). At NV Hwy 156 (Lee Canyon Rd), turn either right to return to US Hwy 95 or left to reach **Las Vegas Ski & Snowboard Resort** (☎702-385-2754; snow report 702-593-9500; www.skilasvegas.com; half-day pass adult/child $50/30; ⏲️usually mid-Nov–Apr; 🐾), which has four lifts, 11 trails (longest run 3000ft) and a half-pipe and terrain park for snowboarding.

PIONEER SALOON

Seven miles west of Jean, near the California border, have a mini Wild West adventure in the almost ghost town of Goodsprings where the tin-roofed **Pioneer Saloon** (☑702-874-9362; ☺11am-late) dates from 1913. Riddled with bullet holes, it still serves up cold beers atop an antique cherrywood bar. Admire the vintage poker table and movie-star memorabilia.

Mesquite

Just over an hour's drive northeast of Las Vegas via I-15, **Mesquite** (☑877-637-7848; www.visitmesquite.com) is another Nevada border town stuffed full of casino hotels, all banking on slot machine-starved visitors from Utah and Arizona. Escape the casinos by overnighting at the **Falcon Ridge Hotel** (☑702-346-2200; www.falconridgehotel.com; 1030 W Pioneer Blvd; d $70-119; ☞☒), down the street from **Sushi Masa** (☑702-346-3434; 155 Pioneer Blvd; mains $6-18; ☺10am-10pm) where even Californians rave about the sushi lovingly crafted by the talented Japanese chef.

GREAT BASIN

Geographically speaking, nearly all of Nevada lies in the Great Basin – a high desert characterized by rugged mountain ranges and broad valleys that extends into Utah and California. Far from Nevada's major cities, this land is largely empty, textured only by peaks covered by snow in winter. It's big country out here – wild, remote and quiet. Anyone seeking the 'Great American Road Trip' will savor the atmospheric small towns and quirky diversions tucked away along these lonely highways. Each of the main routes used by drivers to cut across the state is described here, covering interesting places to stop along the way, plus some unusual detours.

Along Hwy 95

US Hwy 95 runs vaguely north–south through western Nevada. Although it's hardly a direct route, it's the fastest way to get from Las Vegas to Reno – and still, it's a full day's drive of 450 miles, so get an early start. The highway zigzags to avoid mountain ranges and passes through old mining centers that are not much more than ghost towns today.

BEATTY

It's another hour's drive northwest to broken-down Beatty, the northeastern gateway to Death Valley National Park. The **chamber of commerce** (☑775-553-2424, 866-736-3716; www.beattynevada.org; 119 Main St; ☺9:30am-2:30pm Tue-Sat) is downtown. Four miles west of town, off NV Hwy 374, is the mining ghost town of **Rhyolite** (www.rhyolitesite.com; donation appreciated; ☺24hr), where you can see a 1906 'bottle house' and the skeletal remains of a three-story bank. Next door, the bizarre **Goldwell Open Air Museum** (☑702-870-9946; www.goldwellmuseum.org; admission free; ☺24hr) stars Belgian artist Albert Szukalski's spooky *The Last Supper*. Five miles north of town, past the sign for Angel's Ladies brothel, **Bailey's Hot Springs** (☑775-553-2395; entry $5, tent/RV sites $15/18; ☺8am-8pm) offers private mineral pools at a 1906 former railroad depot.

GOLDFIELD & TONOPAH

Another hour's drive further north, Goldfield became Nevada's biggest boomtown after gold was struck here in 1902. A few precious historic structures survive today, including the Goldfield Hotel; a restored firehouse, now a museum; and the county courthouse, with its Tiffany lamps. Another survivor, the rough-and-tumble **Santa Fe Saloon** (☑775-485-3431; 925 N 5th Ave; ☺hours vary) is a hoary watering hole.

WHAT THE...? NEVADA TEST SITE

About 65 miles northwest of Las Vegas, starkly scenic US Hwy 95 rounds the Spring Mountains and passes a side road signposted 'To Mercury.' Behind barbed wire lies the **Nevada Test Site**, where over 900 atmospheric and underground nuclear explosions were detonated between 1951 and 1992. Free public bus tours (☑702-295-0944; www.nv.doe.gov/nts/tours.htm) depart monthly, usually from Las Vegas' Atomic Testing Museum, but you must apply for reservations months in advance.

WORTH A TRIP

AREA 51 & THE EXTRATERRESTRIAL HWY

Die-hard UFO fans and conspiracy theorists won't want to miss the way-out-there trip to Area 51, where some believe secret government research into reverse-engineering alien technology takes place.

Coming from Tonopah, drive east along US Hwy 6 for 50 miles, then follow NV Hwy 375, aka the 'Extraterrestrial Hwy,' for another hour to the roadside pit-stop of Rachel. Have burgers and beer at the **Little A'le'Inn** (775-729-2515; www.littlealeinn.com; 1 Old Mill Rd, Alamo; meals from $5, RV sites with hookups $12, r $50-140; 8am-10pm).

Sky-watchers gather further east at the 29-mile marker on the south side of Hwy 375.

Almost 30 miles further north, huge mine headframes loom above **Tonopah**, a historic silver-mining town that clings to its remaining population in a bereft yet beautiful setting. The **Central Nevada Museum** (775-482-9676; 1900 Logan Field Rd; admission free; 9am-5pm Tue-Sat) has a good collection of Shoshone baskets, early photographs, mining relics and mortician's instruments. The **Tonopah Historic Mining Park** (775-482-9274; www.tonopahhistoricminingpark.com; 520 McCulloch Ave; admission free, walking tours adult/child $5/4; 9am-5pm daily Apr-Sep, 10am-4pm Wed-Sun Oct-Mar) lets you explore an underground tunnel and peer into old silver-mine shafts. At night, it's dark enough for **stargazing** (www.tonopahstartrails.com).

HAWTHORNE

The desert surrounding Hawthorne is oddly dotted with concrete bunkers storing millions of tons of explosives from a WWII-era military ammunition depot bizarrely turned into a golf course. Hungry yet? Locals adore **Maggie's Restaurant & Bakery** (775-945-3908; 785 E St; meals $5-15; 7am-8:30pm).

Heading north, Hwy 95 traces the shrinking shoreline of **Walker Lake State Recreation Area** (775-867-3001; www.parks.travel nevada.com; admission free; 24hr), a popular picnicking, swimming, boating and fishing spot that's evaporating fast. Alt-US Hwy 95 is the scenic route to Reno, joining I-80 westbound at Fernley.

Along Hwy 93

US Hwy 93 is the oft-deserted route from Las Vegas to Great Basin National Park, a 300-mile trip taking over five hours. Expect to pass by mining ghost towns and wide open rangeland populated by more head of cattle than humans.

PAHRANAGAT VALLEY

North of I-15, US Hwy 93 parallels the eastern edge of the Desert National Wildlife Range, where bighorn sheep can be spotted. About 90 miles outside of Las Vegas, the road runs by **Pahranagat National Wildlife Refuge** (775-725-3417; www.fws.gov /desertcomplex/pahranagat; admission free; 24hr), where spring-fed lakes surrounded by cottonwoods are a major stopover for migratory birds, and a public rest area provides a good stopover for a bathroom break and a shaded picnic lunch.

CALIENTE

Past Alamo and Ash Springs, US Hwy 93 leads to a junction, where you turn east through some desolate countryside to Caliente, a former railroad town with a Mission-style 1923 railway depot that makes for a cool photo op. Locals rave about **Pioneer Pizza** (775-726-3215; 127 N Spring St; mains $10-17; dinner). South of town via NV Hwy 317, **Rainbow Canyon** is known for its colorful cliffs and petroglyphs.

East of US Hwy 395, take a backcountry drive along NV Hwy 372 to **Spring Valley State Park** (775-962-5102;www.parks.travel nevada.com; entry $7, tent & RV sites $17) or **Echo Canyon State Park** (775-962-5103; www .parks.travelnevada.com; entry $7, tent & RV sites $17), both offering boating and fishing on artificial reservoirs.

NORTH TO HWY 50 & I-80

US Hwy 93 continues north for 80 miles to US Hwy 50, heading east to Great Basin National Park or west to Ely.

Along Hwy 50

The nickname says it all: on the 'Loneliest Road in America' barren, brown desert hills collide with big blue skies. The highway goes on forever, crossing solitary terrain.

CATHEDRAL GORGE STATE PARK

Awe, then *ahhh*: this is one of our favorite state **parks** (☎775-728-4460; ww.parks.nv.gov/cg.htm entry $4, tent & RV sites $10; ⊙visitor center 9am-4pm), not just in Nevada, but in the whole USA. Fifteen miles north of Caliente, just past the turn-off to Panaca, **Cathedral Gorge State Park** really does feel like you've stepped into a magnificent, many-spired cathedral, albeit one whose dome is a view of the sky. Miller Point Overlook has sweeping views, with several easy hikes into narrow side canyons. Sleep under the stars at the first-come, first-served **campsites** ($17) set amid badlands-style cliffs.

Towns are few and far between, with the only sounds being the whisper of wind or the rattle-and-hum of a truck engine. Once part of the coast-to-coast Lincoln Hwy, US Hwy 50 follows the route of the Overland Stagecoach, the Pony Express and the first transcontinental telegraph line.

FALLON

Look up into the sky and you might spot an F-16 flying over Fallon, home of the US Navy's TOPGUN fighter-pilot school. Dragsters and classic hot rods compete at the **Top Gun Raceway** (☎775-423-0223; www.top gunraceway.com; tickets $8-65) between March and November.

Besides the usual pioneer relics, the **Churchill County Museum & Archives** (☎775-423-3677; www.ccmuseum.org; 1050 S Maine St; admission free; ⊙10am-5pm Mon-Sat, closes 1hr earlier Dec-Feb) also displays an interesting replica of a Paiute hut and sponsors twice-monthly guided tours ($1) of Hidden Cave. The cave is near **Grimes Point Archaeological Area** (☎775-885-6000; www .blm.gov/nv; admission free; ⊙24hr; 🚻), about 10 miles east of Fallon, where a marked trail leads past boulders covered by Native American petroglyphs. Northeast of town, off Stillwater Rd (NV Hwy 166), **Stillwater National Wildlife Refuge** (☎775-428-6452; www.fws.gov/stillwater; admission free; ⊙24hr) is a haven for over 280 species of birds, best seen during the **Spring Wings Festival** (www.springwings.org) in mid-May.

SAND MOUNTAIN RECREATION AREA

About 25 miles southeast of Fallon off US Hwy 50, this **recreation area** (☎775-885-6000; www.blm.gov/nv; admission free; ⊙24hr) boasts sand dunes that 'sing,' occasionally producing a low-pitched boom. The best time to hear it is on a hot, dry evening when the dunes are not covered with screeching off-road vehicles and whooping sandboarders. Pony Express station ruins have been excavated at the small Sand Springs Desert Study Area. Designated campsites with vault toilets (no water) are free.

COLD SPRINGS

Midway between Fallon and Austin, there's a historical marker on the south side of the highway. There a windswept 1½-mile walking path leads to the haunting ruins of **Cold Springs Pony Express Station**, built in 1860 but quickly replaced by a stagecoach stop and then the transcontinental telegraph line. It's just about the best place on US Hwy 50 to be carried away by the romance of the Old West. In fact, the mountain vistas alone are worth stopping for, at least to stretch your legs.

AUSTIN

Although it looks pretty interesting after hours of uninterrupted basin-and-range driving, there's not much to this mid-19th-century boomtown – really, just a few frontier churches and atmospherically decrepit buildings along the short main street.

What most people come to Austin for is to play outdoors. Mountain biking is insanely popular; the **chamber of commerce** (☎775-964-2200; www.austinnevada.com; 122 Main St; ⊙9am-noon Mon-Thu) can recommend routes. The **USDA Forest Service Austin Ranger District office** (☎775-964-2671; www.fs.fed.us /htnf; 100 Midas Canyon Rd, off US Hwy 50; ⊙7:30am-4:30pm Mon-Fri) has info on camping, hiking trails and scenic drives, including the trip to **Toquima Cave**, where you can see rock art by ancient Shoshones.

Inside a former hotel moved here in pieces from Virginia City in 1863, the **International Cafe & Saloon** (www.international cafeandsaloon.com; 59 Main St; meals $4-11; ⊙6am-8pm) is one of Nevada's oldest buildings. The **Toiyabe Cafe** (☎775-964-2301; 150 Main St; items $3-10; ⊙6am-2pm Oct-Apr, 6am-9pm May-Sep) is known for its breakfasts.

North of US Hwy 50 at Hickison Summit, about 24 miles east of Austin, **Hickison**

Petroglyph Recreation Area (☎775-635-4000; www.blm.gov/nv; admission & camping free; ⊙24hr; ☎) has panoramic lookout points; a self-guided, ADA-accessible trail for viewing the petroglyphs; and a primitive campground (vault toilets, no water).

EUREKA

Eureka! In the late 19th century, $40 million worth of silver was extracted from the hills around Eureka. Pride of place goes to the **county courthouse** (☎775-237-5540; 10 S Main St; admission free; ⊙8am-5pm Mon-Fri), with its handsome pressed-tin ceilings and walk-in vaults, and the beautifully restored **opera house** (☎775-237-6006; 31 S Main St), also dating from 1880, which hosts an art gallery and summer folk-music concerts. The **Eureka Sentinel Museum** (☎775-237-5010; 10 S Bateman St; admission free; ⊙10am-6pm Tue-Sat Nov-Apr, 10am-6pm daily May-Oct) displays yesteryear newspaper technology and some colorful examples of period reportage. Budget motels and cafes line Main St.

ELY

The biggest town for miles around, Ely deserves an overnight stop. Its old downtown has beautiful regional history murals and awesome vintage neon signs.

East of downtown's gambling strip, marked by the 1929 Hotel Nevada and Jailhouse Casino, the **White Pine County Tourism & Recreation Board** (☎775-289-3720; www.elynevada.net; 150 Sixth St; ⊙8am-5pm Mon-Fri) provides visitor information on zany town events like Cocktails and Cannons and the annual Bathtub Races. Ask about the mysterious **Ghost Train** and the **Ely Renaissance Village** (www.ely renaissance.com; 150 Sixth St; ⊙10am-4pm Sat, Jul-Sep) a collection of 1908 period homes built by settlers from France, Slovakia, China, Italy and Greece.

Ely was established as a mining town in the 1860s, but the railroad didn't arrive until 1907. The interesting **East Ely Railroad Depot Museum** (www.museums.nevadaculture.org; 1100 Ave A; adult/child $2/free; ⊙8am-4:30pm, Wed-Sat) inhabits the historic depot. There the **Nevada Northern Railway** (☎775-289-2085, 866-407-8326; www.nevada northernrailway.net; adult/child from $24/15; ⊙Apr-Dec) offers excursion rides on trains pulled by historic steam engines.

Off US Hwy 93 south of town via sign-posted dirt roads, **Ward Charcoal Ovens**

State Historic Park (☎775-728-4460; http://parks.nv.gov/ww.htm; entry $7, tent & RV sites $14, yurt $20) protects a half-dozen beehive-shaped structures dating from 1876 that were once used to make charcoal to supply the silver smelters.

Kitsch lovers will dig the **Hotel Nevada** (☎775-289-6665, 888-406-3055; www.hotelnevada .com; 501 Aultman St; r $35-125; ❊☎@) with clean rooms above a funky old casino with a bar that defines the term 'local color.' In the morning, stop by the **cafe** (mains $6-20; ⊙24 hr) for giant cinnamon rolls, steak and eggs, and Starbucks coffee.

Ely's casinos have mostly ho-hum eateries, some open 24 hours. The **Silver State Restaurant** (☎775-289-8866; 1204 Aultman St; meals from $6; ⊙6am-9pm) is an authentic diner-style coffee shop, where the waitresses call you 'hun' and comfort food is the only thing on the menu (cash only). **La Fiesta** (☎775-289-4114; 700 Ave H; mains $9-20; ⊙11am-9pm; ☎) serves up deliciously cheesy enchiladas and good frozen margaritas.

GREAT BASIN NATIONAL PARK

Near the Nevada–Utah border, this uncrowded **national park** (☎775-234-7331; www.nps.gov/grba; admission free; ⊙24hr) encompasses 13,063ft Wheeler Peak, rising abruptly from the desert, creating an awesome range of life zones and landscapes within a very compact area. The peak's narrow, twisting scenic drive is open only during summer, usually from June through October. Hiking trails near the summit take in superb country made up of glacial lakes, groves of ancient bristlecone pines (some over 5000 years old) and even a permanent ice field. The summit trail is an 8.2-mile round-trip trek, with a vertical ascent of nearly 3000ft.

Back below, the main park **visitor center** (⊙8am-4:30pm, extended hr summer) sells tickets for guided tours ($4 to $10) of **Lehman Caves**, which are brimming with limestone formations. The temperature inside is a constant 50°F (10°C), so bring a sweater.

The park's four developed **campgrounds** (tent & RV sites $12) are open during summer; only Lower Lehman Creek is available year-round. Next to the visitor center, a simple cafe stays open from May through October. The nearby village of Baker has a gas station, a basic restaurant and sparse accommodations.

Along I-80

I-80 is the old fur trappers' route, following the Humboldt River from northeast Nevada to Lovelock, near Reno. It's also one of the earliest emigrant trails to California. Transcontinental railroad tracks reached Reno in 1868 and crossed the state within a year. By the 1920s, the Victory Hwy traveled the same route, which later became the interstate. Although not always the most direct route across Nevada, I-80 skirts many of the Great Basin's steep mountain ranges. Overnight stops in the Basque-flavored country around Elko or Winnemucca will give you a true taste of cowboy life.

LOVELOCK

Couples in love who want to leave a piece of their romance in Nevada would be advised to stop by the quiet small town of Lovelock, a 90-minute drive northeast of Reno. Behind the **Pershing County Courthouse** (☑775-273-7213; 400 S Main St; ☺8am-5pm Mon-Fri), inspired by Rome's pantheon, you can symbolically lock your passion on a chain for all eternity in **Love Lock Plaza** (www.loverslock .com). At the 1874 **Marzen House** (☑775-273-4949; 25 Marzen Lane; admission free; ☺1:30-4pm May-Oct), a small historical museum displays mementos of local sweetheart Edna Purviance, Charlie Chaplin's leading lady. A country-style diner, the **Cowpoke Cafe** (☑775-273-2444; 995 Cornell Ave; meals from $5; ☺6am-8pm Mon, Wed & Thu, to 8pm Tue & Fri, 7am-3pm Sat, 8am-3pm Sun) serves from-scratch buffalo burgers, brisket sandwiches and homemade desserts like red velvet cake.

UNIONVILLE & AROUND

This rural late-19th-century ghost town's big claim to fame is that Mark Twain tried his hand (albeit unsuccessfully) at silver mining here. Take a stroll by the writer's old cabin and the Buena Vista schoolhouse, pioneer cemetery and old-fashioned covered bridge. Further west along I-80, **Rye Patch State Recreation Area** (☑775-538-7321; www.parks.nov.gov; entry $7, tent & RV sites $14) offers swimming, fishing and boating.

WINNEMUCCA

Winnemucca has been a travelers' stop since the days of the Emigrant Trail. Even Butch Cassidy dropped by to rob a bank. Named after a Paiute chief, the biggest town on this stretch of I-80 is also a center for the state's Basque community, descended from 19th-century immigrant shepherds.

Unassuming Winnemucca boasts a vintage downtown full of antique shops and a number of Basque restaurants, in keeping with the town's fascinating Basque heritage. Get information on the town's annual June **Basque Festival** at the **Winnemucca Visitors Center & Chamber of Commerce** (☑775-623-5071; www.winnemucca.nv.us; 50 W Winnemucca Blvd; ☺8am-noon, 1-5pm Mon-Fri, 9am-noon Sat, 11am-4pm Sun), along with a self-guided downtown walking tour brochure and information on horseback riding at local ranches. Wannabe cowboys and cowgirls should check out the **Buckaroo Hall of Fame** – full of cowboy art and folklore – while taxidermy fans will want to check out the big game museum in the lobby.

North of the river in a former church, the **Humboldt County Museum** (www.humboldt museum.com; cnr Jungo Rd & Maple Ave; admission free; ☺10am-noon Mon-Fri, 1-4pm Mon-Sat) shows off antique cars, farming implements and beautiful Paiute baskets.

East of town, off Highland Dr at the end of Kluncy Canyon Rd, the **Bloody Shins Trails** are part of a burgeoning mountain biking trail system. Stop by the **BLM Winnemucca Field Office** (☑775-623-1500; www .blm.nv.gov; 5100 E Winnemucca Blvd; ☺7:30am-4:30pm Mon-Fri) for more information.

Winnemucca's main drag has abundant motels and a few casino hotels with 24-hour restaurants. Family-owned **Town House Motel** (☑775-623-3620, 800-243-3620; www .townhouse-motel.com; 375 Monroe St; r $70-80; ☎) has tidy budget rooms equipped with microwaves and mini-fridges, while the **Winnemucca Inn** (☑775-623-2565; www.winnemuccainn .com; 741 W Winnemucca Blvd; r from $80; ❋☎@❄☝) offers spacious, well-equipped rooms with a bustling casino, 24 hour restaurant and children's arcade.

Don't miss a stop at the **Griddle** (www .thegriddlecom; 460 W Winnemucca Blvd; mains $4-12; ☺breakfast & lunch daily, dinner Thu-Sat) one of Nevada's best retro cafes, serving up fantastic breakfasts, diner classics and homemade desserts since 1948. Locals also adore the **Third Street Bistro** (☑775-623-0800; 45 E Winnemucca Blvd; mains $7-10; ☺7am-2pm Mon-Sat) for its homebaked goods, tasty soups and excellent Philly cheesesteaks in a genteel atmosphere. Those making Winnemucca a full overnight trip should seriously plan their evening around dinner at the **Martin Hotel** (www

WHAT THE...? THE MINESHAFT

While sultry – or, more often, seedy – establishments employing scantily clad women are practically as commonplace across Nevada as casinos themselves, there's one consolation that even the flesh-wary can count on: that it's the employees, not the customers, who you might vie in various states of undress. Not so at Winnemucca's **The Mineshaft Bar** (www.themineshaftbar.com; 44 W Railroad St; ⊘24hr) which bills itself as 'Nevada's only clothes-optional bar.' You know it's a serious dive when its website features the competing slogans 'Hard Rock Music for Hard Rock Miners,' and 'Where T and A is A-OK.' Weekend nights aren't for the faint of heart or the easily offended: think metal bands, wet t-shirt contests and girl-on-girl kissing contests.

.themartinhotel.com; 94 W Railroad St; multi-course dinner $17-32; ⊘11:30am-2pm Mon-Fri, 4-9pm nightly; 🐾), where ranchers, locals and weary travelers have come since 1898 to enjoy family-style Basque meals under pressed-tin ceilings.

To fuel up for what will likely be a long drive in any direction, delightful **Delizioso Global Coffee** (☎775-625-1000; 508a W Winnemucca Blvd; items $2-5; ⊘5am-5pm Mon-Fri, 6am-1pm Sat; 🛜) offers creative espresso drinks like the 'Winnemocha' and fresh scones amid a fanciful forest-like interior.

About 50 miles north of town, the Santa Rosa Mountains offer rugged scenery, hiking trails and camping in the **Humboldt-Toiyabe National Forest**.

ELKO

Though small, Elko is the largest town in rural Nevada and a center of cowboy culture, with a calendar of Western cultural events and a museum big on buckaroos, stagecoaches and the Pony Express. The other cultural influence is Basque; in fact, Basque shepherds and Old West cattlemen had some violent conflicts over grazing rights in the late 19th century. The **visitor center** (☎775-738-4091, 800-248-3556; www.elkocva.com; 1405 Idaho St; ⊘hr vary) is inside a historic ranch house.

The **Northeastern Nevada Museum** (☎775-738-3418; www.museumelko.org; 1515 Idaho Ave; adult/child $5/1; ⊘9am-5pm Mon-Sat, 1-5pm Sun) has excellent displays on pioneer life, Pony Express riders, Basque settlers and modern mining techniques. Free monthly tours of the nearby Newmont gold mine usually start here; call ☎775-778-4068 for reservations. Aspiring cowboys and cowgirls should visit the **Western Folklife Center & Wiegland Gallery** (www.westernfolklife.org; 501 Railroad St; admission free; ⊘10:30am-5:30pm Tue-Fri), which hosts the remarkably popular **Cowboy Poetry Gathering** in January. The

National Basque Festival (www.elkobasque.com) is held around July 4, with games, traditional dancing and even Elko's own 'Running of the Bulls.'

South of Elko, the **Ruby Mountains** (www.rubymountains.org) are a superbly rugged range, nicknamed Nevada's alps for their prominent peaks, glacial lakes and alpine vegetation. The village of **Lamoille** has basic food and lodging, and one of the most photographed rural churches in the USA. Just before the village, Lamoille Canyon Rd branches south, following the forested canyon for 12 miles past cliffs, waterfalls and other glacial sculptures to the Ruby Crest trailhead at 8800ft.

A popular overnight stop for truckers and travelers, Elko has over 2000 rooms that fill up fast, especially on weekends. Chain motels and hotels line Idaho St, particularly east of downtown. Of the chains, we like the comfy **Hilton Garden Inn** (☎775-777-1200; www.hiltongardeninn.com; 736 Idaho St; r $90-160; P🅿❋🛜♿✉🐾), while the best budget choice is the locally run **Thunderbird Motel** (☎775-738-7115; www.thunderbirdmotelelko.com; 345 Idaho St; r incl breakfast $59-69; P🅿❋🛜✉🐾).

For decent pizza and local Nevada beer, sidle up to the bar at the **Stray Dog Pub & Café** (☎775-753-4888; 374 5th St; mains $7-12; ⊘dinner 3-9pm Mon-Sat, bar open late, closed Sun), decked out with old bikes and surfboards. If you've never sampled Basque food, the best place in town for your inaugural experience is the **Star Hotel** (www.elkostarhotel.com; 246 Silver St; mains $15-32; ⊘lunch Mon-Fri, dinner Mon-Sat), a family-style supper club located in a 1910 boardinghouse for Basque sheepherders. The irrepressibly curious will not want to miss a peek behind the restaurant, where Elko's small 'red light' district of legal brothels sits, including 'Inez's Dancing and Diddling,' perhaps the most bizarrely-named business – tawdry or not – in the state.

MOVING ON?

For tips, recommendations and reviews, head to shop.lonelyplanet.com to purchase a downloadable PDF of the California chapter from Lonely Planet's *USA* guide.

Serving up strong espresso from the crack of dawn through the afternoon, **Cowboy Joe** (☎775-753-5612; 376 5th St; items $2-6; ☺6am-5pm Mon-Fri, 5:30am-3pm Sat, 7am-noon Sun; ☎) is a great little small-town coffeehouse with an eponymous signature drink that will keep you going till Reno.

WELLS

Sports fans should know that heavyweight boxer Jack Dempsey started his career here, as a bouncer in the local bars. After strolling around the rough-edged **Front Street historic district** today, you can imagine how tough that job must've been. The **Trail of the '49ers Interpretive Center** (☎775-752-3540; www.wellsnevada.com; 395 S 6th St; ☺hr vary) tells the story of mid-19th-century pioneers on the Emigrant Trail to California.

Southwest of town, scenic byway NV Hwy 231 heads into the mountains, climbing alongside sagebrush, piñon pine and aspen trees past two **campgrounds** (☎877-444-6777; www.recreation.gov; tent sites $12-22; ☺Jun-Oct). After 12 miles, the road stops at cobalt-blue **Angel Lake** (8378ft), a glacial cirque beautifully embedded in the East Humboldt Range. Along NV Hwy 232, further south of Wells, a large natural window near the top of **Hole in the Mountain Peak** (11,306ft) is visible from the road.

WEST WENDOVER

If you just can't make it to Salt Lake City tonight, stop in West Wendover, where ginormous **casino hotels** (☎800-537-0207; www.wendoverfun.com; r $55-140) with 24-hour restaurants line Wendover Blvd. Over on the Utah side, **Historic Wendover Airfield** (www.wendoverairbase.com; 345 Airport Apron, Wendover; admission by donation; ☺8am-6pm) is a top-secret WWII-era USAF base, where the Enola Gay crew trained for dropping the atomic bomb on Japan. The **Bonneville Speed Museum** (☎775-664-3138; 1000 E Wendover Blvd, Wendover; adult/child $2/1; ☺10am-6pm Jun-Nov) documents attempts to set land speed records on the nearby Bonneville Salt Flats, where 'Speed Week' time trials in the third full week of August draw huge crowds every year.

RENO-TAHOE AREA

A vast sagebrush steppe, the western corner of the state is carved by mountain ranges and parched valleys. It's also the place where modern Nevada began. It was the site of the state's first trading post, pioneer farms and the famous Comstock silver lode, which spawned Virginia City, financed the Union during the Civil War and earned Nevada its statehood. Today, Reno and the state capital, Carson City, have little of the Wild West rawness still extant in the Black Rock Desert, reached via Pyramid Lake. For pampering all-seasons getaways, it's a short drive up to emerald Lake Tahoe, right on the California border.

Reno

A soothingly schizophrenic city of big-time gambling and top-notch outdoor adventures, Reno resists pigeonholing. the 'Biggest Little City in the World' has something to raise the pulse of adrenaline junkies, hardcore gamblers and city people craving easy access to wide open spaces.

◉ Sights

National Automobile Museum   MUSEUM
(☎775-333-9300; www.automuseum.org; 10 S Lake St; adult/child $10/4; ☺9:30am-5:30pm Mon-Sat, 10am-4pm Sun; ☜) Stylized street scenes illustrate a century's worth of automobile history at this engaging car museum. The collection is enormous and impressive, with one-of-a-kind vehicles including James Dean's 1949 Mercury from *Rebel Without a Cause,* a 1938 Phantom Corsair and a 24-karat gold-plated DeLorean, and rotating exhibits bringing in all kinds of souped-up or fabulously retro rides.

Nevada Museum of Art   MUSEUM
(☎775-329-3333; www.nevadaart.org; 160 W Liberty St; adult/child $10/1; ☺10am-5pm Wed-Sun, 10am-8pm Thu) In a sparkling building inspired by the geologic formations of the Black Rock Desert north of town, a floating staircase leads to galleries showcasing temporary exhibits and images related to the American West. Great cafe for postcultural refueling.

University of Nevada, Reno UNIVERSITY
Pop into the flying saucer-shaped **Fleischmann Planetarium & Science Center** (775 784 4811; http://planetarium.unr.nevada.edu; 1650 N Virginia St; admission free; noon-5pm Mon & Tue, noon-9pm Fri, 10am-9pm Sat, 10am-5pm Sun) for a window on the universe during star shows and feature presentations (adult/child $6/4). Nearby is the **Nevada Historical Society Museum** (775-688-1190; www.museums.nevadaculture.org; 1650 N Virginia St; adult/child $4/free; 10am-5pm Wed-Sat), which includes permanent exhibits on neon signs, local Native American culture and the presence of the federal government.

VIRGINIA ST
Wedged between the I-80 and the Truckee River, downtown's N Virginia St is casino central. South of the river it continues as S Virginia St. All of the following hotel casinos are open 24 hours.

Circus Circus CASINO
(www.circusreno.com; 500 N Sierra St) The most family-friendly of the bunch, it has free circus acts to entertain kids beneath a giant, candy-striped big top, which also harbors a gazillion carnival and video games that look awfully similar to slot machines.

Silver Legacy CASINO
(www.silverlegacyreno.com; 407 N Virginia St) A Victorian-themed place, it's easily recognized by its white landmark dome, where a giant mock mining rig periodically erupts into a fairly tame sound-and-light spectacle.

Eldorado CASINO
(www.eldoradoreno.com; 345 N Virginia St) The Eldorado has a kitschy Fountain of Fortune that probably has Italian sculptor Bernini spinning in his grave.

Harrah's CASINO
(www.harrahsreno.com; 219 N Center St) Founded by Nevada gambling pioneer William Harrah in 1946, it's still one of the biggest and most popular casinos in town.

Peppermill CASINO
(www.peppermillreno.com; 2707 S Virginia St) About 2 miles south of downtown, this place dazzles with a 17-story Tuscan-style tower.

Atlantis CASINO
(www.atlantiscasino.com; 3800 S Virginia St) Now more classy than zany, with an extensive spa, the remodeled casino retains a few tropical flourishes like indoor waterfalls and palm trees.

Activities
Reno is a 30- to 60-minute drive from Tahoe ski resorts, and many hotels and casinos offer special stay and ski packages.

Truckee River Whitewater Park WATER SPORTS
Mere steps from the casinos, the park's Class II and III rapids are gentle enough for kids riding inner tubes, yet sufficiently challenging for professional freestyle kayakers. Two courses wrap around Wingfield Park, a small river island that hosts free concerts in summertime. **Tahoe Whitewater Tours** (775-787-5000; www.gowhitewater.com) and **Wild Sierra Adventures** (866-323-8928; www.wildsierra.com) offer kayak trips and lessons.

Historic Reno Preservation Society WALKING TOUR
(775-747-4478; www.historicreno.org; tours $10) Dig deeper with a walking or biking tour highlighting subjects including architecture, politics and literary history.

Festivals & Events
Reno River Festival SPORTS
(www.renoriverfestival.com) The world's top freestyle kayakers compete in a mad paddling dash through Whitewater Park in mid-May. Free music concerts as well.

WORTH A TRIP

PYRAMID LAKE
A piercingly blue expanse in an otherwise barren landscape 25 miles north of Reno on the Paiute Indian Reservation, Pyramid Lake is a stunning standalone sight, with shores lined with beaches and eye-catching tufa formations. Nearer its east side, iconic pyramidlike Anaho Island is a bird sanctuary for American white pelicans. Popular for camping and fishing, the area offers permits for **camping** (primitive campsites per vehicle per night $9) and **fishing** (per person $9) at outdoor suppliers and CVS drugstore locations in Reno, as well as at the **ranger station** (775-476-1155; www.pyramidlake.us; 8am-6pm) on SR 445 in Sutcliffe.

RENO AREA TRAILS

For extensive information on regional hiking and biking trails, including the Mt Rose summit trail and the Tahoe-Pyramid Bikeway, download the **Truckee Meadows Trails guide** (www.reno.gov/Index.aspx?page=291).

Tour de Nez   SPORTS
(www.tourdenez.com) Called the 'coolest bike race in America,' the Tour de Nez brings together pros and amateurs for five days of races and partying in July.

Hot August Nights   CULTURAL
(www.hotaugustnights.net) Catch the *American Graffiti* vibe during this seven-day celebration of hot rods and rock and roll in early August. Hotel rates skyrocket to their peak.

🛏 Sleeping

Lodging rates vary widely depending on the day of the week and local events. Sunday through Thursday are generally the best; Friday is somewhat more expensive and Saturday can be as much as triple the midweek rate.

In the summer months, there's gorgeous high altitude camping at **Mt Rose** (☎877-444-6777; www.recreation.gov; Hwy 431; RV & tent sites $16).

TOP CHOICE **Peppermill**   CASINO HOTEL $$
(☎775-826-2121, 866-821-9996; www.peppermill reno.com; 2707 S Virginia St; r Sun-Thu $50-140; Fri & Sat $70-200; P✳@🛜≋) Now awash in Vegas-style opulence, the popular Peppermill boasts Tuscan-themed rooms in its newest 600-room tower, and has almost completed a plush remodel of its older rooms. The three sparkling pools (one indoor) are dreamy, with a full spa on hand. Geothermal energy powers the resort's hot water and heat.

Sands Regency   CASINO HOTEL $
(☎775-348-2200, 866-386-7829; www.sands regency.com; 345 N Arlington Ave; r Sun-Thu/Fri & Sat from $29/89; P✳🛜≋≋) With some of the largest standard digs in town, rooms here are decked out in a cheerful tropical palette of upbeat blues, reds and greens – a visual relief from standard-issue motel decor. The 17th-floor gym and Jacuzzi are perfectly positioned to capture your eyes with drop-

dead panoramic mountain views. Empress Tower rooms are best.

Wildflower Village   MOTEL $$
(☎775-747-8848; www.wildflowervillage.com; 4395 W 4th St; r $50-75, B&B $100-125; P✳@🛜) Perhaps more of a state of mind than a motel, this artists colony on the west edge of town has a tumbledown yet creative vibe. Individual murals decorate the facade of each room, and you can hear the freight trains rumble on by.

🍴 Eating

Reno's dining scene goes far beyond the casino buffets.

TOP CHOICE **Old Granite Street Eatery**   AMERICAN $$
(☎775-622-3222; 243 S Sierra St; dishes $9-24; ⊙11am-10pm Mon-Thu, 11am-midnight Fri, 10am-midnight Sat, 10am-4pm Sun) A lovely well-lighted place for organic and local comfort food, old-school artisanal cocktails and seasonal craft beers, this antique-strewn hotspot enchants diners with its stately wooden bar, water served in old liquor bottles and its lengthy seasonal menu. Forgot to make a reservation? Check out the iconic rooster and pig murals and wait for seats at a community table fashioned from a barn door.

Pneumatic Diner   VEGETARIAN $
(501 W 1st St, 2nd fl; dishes $6-9; ⊙noon-10pm Mon, 11am-10pm Tue-Thu, 11am-11pm Fri & Sat, 8am-10pm Sun; 🖋) Consume a garden of vegetarian delights under salvaged neon lights. This groovy little place near the river has meatless and vegan comfort food and desserts to tickle your inner two-year-old, like the ice-cream laden Cookie Bomb. It's attached to the Truckee River Terrace apartment complex; use the Ralston St entrance.

Silver Peak Restaurant & Brewery   PUB $$
(124 Wonder St; mains lunch $8-10, dinner $9-21; ⊙11am-midnight) Casual and pretense-free, this place hums with the chatter of happy locals settling in for a night of microbrews and great eats, from pizza with roasted chicken to shrimp pasta and filet mignon.

Peg's Glorified Ham & Eggs   DINER $
(420 S Sierra St; dishes $7-10; ⊙6:30am-2pm; 🖋) Locally regarded as the best breakfast in town, Peg's offers tasty grill food that's not too greasy.

🍷 Drinking

Jungle Java & Jungle Vino　　CAFE, WINE BAR
(www.javajunglevino.com; 246 W 1st St; ⊙6am-midnight; 🛜) A side-by-side coffee shop and wine bar with a cool mosaic floor and an internet cafe all rolled into one. The wine bar has weekly tastings, while the cafe serves breakfast bagels and lunchtime sandwiches ($8) and puts on diverse music shows.

Imperial Bar & Lounge　　BAR
(150 N Arlington Ave; ⊙11am-2am Thu-Sat, to midnight Sun-Wed) A classy bar inhabiting a relic of the past, this building was once an old bank, and in the middle of the wood floor you can see cement where the vault once stood. Sandwiches and pizzas go with 16 beers on tap and a buzzing weekend scene.

St James Infirmary　　BAR
(445 California Ave) With an eclectic menu of 120 bottled varieties and 18 on tap, beer aficionados will short circuit with delight. Red lights blush over black-and-white retro banquettes and a wall of movie and music stills, and it hosts sporadic events including jazz and bluegrass performances.

☆ Entertainment

The free weekly *Reno News & Review* (www .newsreview.com) is your best source for listings.

Edge　　CLUB
(www.edgeofreno.com; Peppermill, 2707 S Virginia St; admission $10-20; ⊙Thu-Sun) The Peppermill reels in the nighthounds with a big glitzy dance club, where go-go dancers, smoke machines and laser lights may cause sensory overload. If so, step outside to the view lounge patio and relax in front of cozy fire pits.

Knitting Factory　　LIVE MUSIC
(☑775-323-5648; http://re.knittingfactory.com; 211 N Virginia St) This mid-sized venue opened in 2010, filling a gap in Reno's music scene with mainstream and indie favorites.

ℹ Information

An **information center** sits near the baggage claim at Reno-Tahoe Airport, which also has free wi-fi.

Java Jungle (246 W 1st St; per hr $2; ⊙6am-midnight; 🛜) Great riverfront cafe with a few computers and free wi-fi.

Reno-Sparks Convention & Visitors Authority (☑800-367-7366; www.visitrenotahoe.com; 2nd fl, Reno Town Mall, 4001 S Virginia St; ⊙8am-5pm Mon-Fri)

ℹ Getting There & Away

About 5 miles southeast of downtown, the **Reno-Tahoe International Airport** (RNO; www .renoairport.com; 🛜) is served by most major airlines.

The **North Lake Tahoe Express** (☑866-216-5222; www.northlaketahoeexpress.com) operates a shuttle ($40, six to eight daily, 3:30am to midnight) to and from the airport to multiple North Shore Lake Tahoe locations including Truckee, Squaw Valley and Incline Village. Reserve in advance.

To reach South Lake Tahoe (weekdays only), take the wi-fi-equipped **RTC Intercity bus** (www.rtcwashoe.com) to the Nevada DOT stop in Carson City ($4, five per weekday, one hour) and then the **BlueGo** (www.bluego.org) 21X bus ($2 with RTC Intercity transfer, seven to eight daily, one hour) to the Stateline Transit Center.

Greyhound (☑775-322-2970; www.greyhound .com; 155 Stevenson St) buses run daily service to Truckee, Sacramento and San Francisco ($34, five to seven hours), as does the once daily westbound California Zephyr route operated by **Amtrak** (☑775-329-8638, 800-872-7245; 280 N Center St). The train is slower and more expensive, but also more scenic and comfortable, with a bus connection from Emeryville for passengers to San Francisco ($46, 7½ hours).

DOWN & DIRTY NEVADA

Prostitution is illegal only in Clark and Washoe Counties (including Las Vegas and Reno), yet illegal prostitution runs rampant (*especially* in Las Vegas) under the guise of strip clubs, escort services and massage parlors. Remember that not only is paying for sex through these seemingly innocuous channels illegal and punishable by law, but anyone who does so may be contributing to Nevada's sex trafficking problem. The human trafficking of women and girls is an international epidemic that is unfortunately growing in the United States.

Legalized, heavily regulated brothels are found in Nevada's more rural counties. Don't expect a romantic Old West bordello, though; most are just a few doublewide trailers behind a scary barbed-wire fence on the side of a lonesome highway.

ℹ Getting Around

The casino hotels offer frequent free airport shuttles for their guests (and don't ask to see reservations).

The local **RTC Ride buses** (☑775-348-7433; www.rtcwashoe.com; per ride/all day $2/4) blanket the city, and most routes converge at the RTC 4th St Station downtown. Useful routes include the RTC Rapid line for S Virginia St, 11 for Sparks and 19 for the airport. The free Sierra Spirit bus loops around all major downtown landmarks – including the casinos and the university – every 15 minutes from 7am to 7pm.

Carson City

Is this the most underrated town in Nevada? We're going to double down and say that it is. An easy drive from Reno or Lake Tahoe, it's a perfect stop for lunch and a stroll around the quiet, old-fashioned downtown. Expect handsome antique buildings and pleasant tree-lined streets centered around the **1870 Nevada State Capitol** (cnr Musser & Carson; admission free) where the governor's door is always open – you'll just have to charm your way past his assistant. Note the silver dome, which fittingly symbolizes Nevada's 'Silver State' status.

US Hwy 395 from Reno becomes the town's main drag, called Carson St. Look for the Cactus Jack neon sign letting you know you've reached downtown. About a mile further south, the **Carson City Convention & Visitors Bureau** (☑775-687-7410, 800-638-2321; www.visitcarsoncity.com; 1900 S Carson St; ⊕9am-4pm Mon-Fri, to 3pm Sat & Sun) has information about mountain-biking trails and hands out a historical walking-tour map of the Kit Carson Trail, with interesting podcasts that you can download online.

Several historic attractions and museums are worth visiting. Housed inside the 1869 US Mint building, the **Nevada State Museum** (www.nevadaculture.org; 600 N Carson St; adult/child $8/free; ⊕8:30am-4:30pm Wed-Sat) puts on rotating exhibits of Native American, frontier and mining history. Train buffs shouldn't miss the **Nevada State Railroad Museum** (☑775-687-6953; 2180 S Carson St; adult/child $6/free; ⊕8:30am-4:30pm), displaying some 65 train cars and locomotives, most pre-dating 1900. For made-in-Nevada artisan crafts, shop at the **Brewery Arts Center** (☑775-883-1976; www.breweryarts.org; 449 W King St; ⊕10am-4pm Mon-Sat).

Lunch, sip and linger at fetching, art-filled **Comma Coffee** (www.commacoffee.com; 312 S Carson St; dishes $5-9; ⊕7am-6pm Mon & Wed-Thu, to 10pm Tue & Fri & Sat; 🛜🖶🎵) where eavesdropping is always interesting: the next table over might be Nevada lobbyists discussing a new bill over lattes or wine. Nosh on English pub classics in red velvet booths at the **Firkin and Fox** (www.thefirkinandfox.com; 310 S Carson St; mains $10-19; ⊕11am-midnight Sun-Thu, to 2am Fri & Sat) downtown in the historic St Charles Hotel. Or spend the evening at the town's friendly, locally owned microbrewery, **High Sierra Brewing Company** (www.highsierrabrewco.com; 302 N Carson St; mains $8-20; ⊕11am-midnight Sun-Thu, to 2am Fri & Sat), for great local beer and eclectic international dishes on the patio or near the stage, where nationally touring musicians perform some nights.

Virginia City

Twenty-five miles south of Reno, this national historic landmark is the site where the legendary Comstock Lode was struck, sparking a silver bonanza that began in 1859 and stands as one of the world's richest strikes. During the 1860s gold rush, Virginia City was a high-flying, rip-roaring Wild West boomtown. Newspaperman Samuel Clemens, alias Mark Twain, spent some time in this raucous place during its heyday and vividly captured the Wild West shenanigans in a book called *Roughing It*.

Sure, Virginia City can feel a bit like a high-elevation theme park, but it's still fun to visit. The high-elevation town is a bona

---

WHET YOUR WHISTLE

Drink like an old-time miner at one of the many Victorian-era watering holes that line C street. We like the longtime family-run **Bucket of Blood Saloon** (www.bucketofblood saloonvc.com; 1 S C St; ⊕2-7pm) which serves up beer and 'bar rules' at its antique wooden bar ('If the bartender doesn't laugh, you are not funny') and the **Palace Restaurant & Saloon** (www.palacerestaurant1875.com; 1 S C St; mains $6-10; ⊕hr vary) which is full of town memorabilia and serves up tasty breakfasts and lunches.

GREAT BALLS OF FIRE!

For one week at the end of August, **Burning Man** (www.burningman.com; admission $210-320) explodes onto the sunbaked Black Rock Desert, and Nevada sprouts a third major population center – Black Rock City. An experiential art party (and alternative universe) that climaxes in the immolation of a towering stick figure, Burning Man is a whirlwind of outlandish theme camps, dust-caked bicycles, bizarre bartering, costume-enhanced nudity and a general relinquishment of inhibitions.

fide National Historic Landmark, with a main street of Victorian buildings, wooden sidewalks and historic saloons. The main drag is C St; check out the **visitor center** (775-847-4386, 800-718-7587; www.virginiacity-nv.org; 86 S C St; 10am-4pm) inside the historic Crystal Bar. Nearby is the **Mark Twain Bookstore** (www.marktwainbooks.com; 111 S C St; hours vary).

The cheesy, old-fashioned **Way It Was Museum** (775-847-0766; 113 N C St; adult/child $3/free; 10am-6pm) offers historical background on mining the lode. Stop by the **Mackay Mansion** (775-847-0173; 129 D St; admission $3; 10am-6pm) to see how the mining elite once lived.

From May through October, the **Virginia & Truckee Railroad** (775-847-0380; www.virginiatruckee.com; F & Washington Sts; 35min narrated tour adult/child $9/5;) offers vintage steam-train excursions.

A mile south of town via NV Hwy 342, the **Gold Hill Hotel & Saloon** (775-847-0111; www.goldhillhotel.net; 1540 Main St; r $55-225;) claims to be Nevada's oldest hotel, and feels like it, with a breezy, old-fashioned charm and atmospheric bar boasting a great wine and spirits selection. Some rooms have fireplaces and views of the Sierras.

Inside a 1870s boarding house, **Sugarloaf Mountain Motel** (775-847-0551; 430 S C St; r $60-100) is cozily historical and gets raves for hosts Jim and Michelle's friendly hospitality. The renovated rooms at **Silverland Inn & Suites** (; 775-847-4484; www.silverlandusa.com; 100 N E St; r $89-169;) will appeal to those who prefer more modern (if nondescript) digs along with a sunny pool and hot tub area with mountain views.

Locals agree that the best food in Virginia City is probably at **Cafe del Rio** (www.cafedelriovc.com; 394 S C St; mains $9-15; 4:30-8pm Wed & Thu, 11:30-8pm Fri & Sat, 10am-2pm Sun), serving a nice blend of *nuevo* Mexican and Southwest cuisine, including brunch. For gorgeous 100-mile views of the surrounding valleys, sip a

strong coffee or have an ice-cream cone on the back porch of the **Comstock Creamery** (775-847-7744; 171 S C St; mains $4-8) where the friendly owners also serve up eight different kinds of burgers.

Genoa

This pretty village at the edge of Carson Valley, beneath the Sierra Nevada mountains, was the first European settlement at the western edge of the former Utah Territory. The **Genoa Saloon** claims to be the oldest bar in the state (since 1863), and it certainly looks the part. The **Genoa Courthouse Museum** (775-782-4325; 2304 Main St; adult/child $3/2; 10am-4:30pm May-Oct) contains the original jail and a collection of woven Washo baskets. It's free to wander through the early settlement of **Mormon Station State Historic Park** (775-782-2590; museum $1; 10am-4pm Wed-Sun). About 2 miles south of town, off NV Hwy 206, **David Walley's Hot Springs & Spa** (775-782-8155; www.davidwalleys-resort.com; 2001 Foothill Rd; pools, sauna & work-out room day pass $20; 7am-10pm) offers a respite from traveling Nevada's dusty roads.

Black Rock Desert

North of Pyramid Lake, NV Hwy 447 continues straight as an arrow for about 60 miles to the dusty railway town of Gerlach, with a gas station, a motel, a cafe and a few bars. Its motto is 'Where the pavement ends, the West begins.' **Bruno's Country Club** (775-557-2220; 445 Main St; meals $6-15; hr vary) for its famous for its meaty ravioli in cheese sauce. Outside Gerlach, world land-speed records have been set on the dry, mud-cracked *playas* of the **Black Rock Desert** (775-557-2900; www.blackrockfriends.org). Although most people only visit during the Burning Man festival, this vast wilderness is primed for outdoor adventures year-round.

Lake Tahoe

Shimmering in myriad blues and greens, Lake Tahoe is the nation's second-deepest lake. Driving around its spellbinding 72-mile scenic shoreline gives you quite a workout behind the wheel. The north shore is quiet and upscale; the west shore, rugged and old-timey; the east shore, undeveloped; and the south shore, busy and tacky with aging motels and flashy casinos. The horned peaks surrounding the lake, which straddles the California–Nevada state line, are four-seasons playgrounds.

Tahoe gets packed in summer, on winter weekends and holidays, when reservations are essential. **Lake Tahoe Visitors Authority** (☎800-288-2463; www.tahoesouth.com) and **North Lake Tahoe Visitors' Bureaus** (☎888-434-1262; www.gotahoenorth.com) can help with accommodations and tourist information. There's camping in **state parks** (☎reservations 800-444-7275; www.reserveamerica.com) and on **USFS lands** (☎reservations 877-444-6777; www.recreation.gov).

SOUTH LAKE TAHOE & WEST SHORE

With retro motels and eateries lining busy Hwy 50, South Lake Tahoe gets crowded. Gambling at Stateline's casino hotels, just across the Nevada border, attracts thousands, as does the world-class ski resort of **Heavenly** (☎775-586-7000; www.skiheavenly.com; 3860 Saddle Rd; ⊕). In summer, a trip up Heavenly's gondola (adult/child $32/20) guarantees fabulous views of the lake and **Desolation Wilderness** (www.fs.fed.us/r5/ltbmu). This starkly beautiful landscape of raw granite peaks, glacier-carved valleys and alpine lakes is a favorite with hikers. Get maps, information and overnight **wilderness permits** (per adult $5-10; www.recreation.gov) from the **USFS Taylor Creek Visitor Center** (☎530-543-2674; Hwy 89; ⊕daily May-Oct, hr vary). It's 3 miles north of the 'Y' intersection of Hwys 50/89, at **Tallac Historic Site** (tour $5; ⊕10am-4:30pm mid-Jun-Sep, Fri & Sat only late May–mid-Jun), which preserves early 20th-century vacation estates. **Lake Tahoe**

WANT MORE?

For further information head to shop.lonelyplanet.com to purchase a downloadable PDF of the Lake Tahoe chapter from Lonely Planet's *California* guide.

Cruises (☎800-238-2463; www.zephyrcove.com; adult/child from $39/15) ply the 'Big Blue' year-round. Back on shore, vegetarian-friendly **Sprouts** (3123 Harrison Ave; mains $6-10; ⊕8am-9pm; ☑) is a delish natural-foods cafe.

Hwy 89 threads northwest along the thickly forested west shore to **Emerald Bay State Park** (www.parks.ca.gov; per car $8, campsites $35; ⊕late May-Sep), where granite cliffs and pine trees frame a fjordlike inlet, truly sparkling green. A steep 1-mile trail leads down to **Vikingsholm Castle** (tours adult/child $5/3; ⊕10:30am-4:30pm). From this 1920s Scandinavian-style mansion, the 4.5-mile **Rubicon Trail** ribbons north along the lakeshore past an old lighthouse and petite coves to **DL Bliss State Park** (www.parks.ca.gov; entry per car $8, campsites $35-45; ⊕late May-Sep), offering sandy beaches. Further north, **Tahoma Meadows B&B Cottages** (☎530-525-1553, 866-525-1533; www.tahomameadows.com; 6821 W Lake Blvd, Tahoma; d incl breakfast $109-269) rents darling country cabins (pet fee $20).

NORTH & EAST SHORES

The north shore's commercial hub, **Tahoe City** is great for grabbing supplies and renting outdoor gear. It's not far from **Squaw Valley USA** (☎530-583-6985; www.squaw.com; off Hwy 89; ⊕), a megasized ski resort that hosted the 1960 Winter Olympics. Après-ski crowds gather for beer 'n' burgers at woodsy **Bridgetender Tavern** (www.tahoebridgetender.com; 65 W Lake Blvd; mains $8-12; ⊕11am-12am, to midnight Fri & Sat) back in town, or fuel up on French toast and eggs Benedict at downhome **Fire Sign Cafe** (1785 W Lake Blvd; dishes $6-12; ⊕7am-3pm).

In summer, swim or kayak at **Tahoe Vista** or **Kings Beach**. Spend a night at **Franciscan Lakeside Lodge** (☎530-546-6300, 800-564-6754; www.franciscanlodge.com; 6944 N Lake Blvd, Tahoe Vista; d $80-265; ⊕✉☑⊕), where simple cabins, cottages and suites have kitchenettes. East of Kings Beach, which has cheap, filling lakeshore eateries, Hwy 28 barrels into Nevada. Try your luck at the gambling tables or catch a live-music show at the **Crystal Bay Club Casino** (☎775-831-0512; www.crystalbaycasino.com; 14 Hwy 28). But for more happening bars and bistros, drive further to **Incline Village**.

With pristine beaches, lakes and miles of multiuse trails, **Lake Tahoe-Nevada State Park** (http://parks.nv.gov/lt.htm; per car $7-12) is the east shore's biggest draw. Summer crowds splash in the turquoise waters of **Sand Harbor**. The 15-mile **Flume Trail** ([☎]775-749-5349; www.theflumetrail.com; trailhead bike rental $45-65, shuttle $5-10), a mountain biker's holy grail, starts further south at **Spooner Lake**.

TRUCKEE & AROUND

North of Lake Tahoe off I-80, Truckee is not in fact a truck stop but a thriving mountain town, with organic-coffee shops, trendy boutiques and dining in downtown's historical district. Ski bunnies have several area resorts to pick from, including glam **Northstar-at-Tahoe** ([☎]800-466-6784; www.northstarattahoe.com; off Hwy 267; [⛷]); kid-friendly **Sugar Bowl** ([☎]530-426-9000; www.sugarbowl.com; off Hwy 40; [⛷]), cofounded by Walt Disney; and **Royal Gorge** ([☎]530-426-3871; www.royalgorge.com; off I-80; [⛷]), paradise for cross-country skiers.

West of Hwy 89, Donner Summit is where the infamous Donner Party became trapped during the fierce winter of 1846–47. Led astray by their guidebook, less than half survived – by cannibalizing their dead friends. The grisly tale is chronicled at the museum inside **Donner Memorial State Park** (www.parks.ca.gov; Donner Pass Rd; entry per car $8, campsites $35; [⊙]museum 9am-4pm daily year-round, campground mid-May–mid-Sep), where **Donner Lake** is popular with swimmers and windsurfers.

Eco-conscious **Cedar House Sport Hotel** ([☎]530-582-5655, 866-582-5655; www.cedarhousesporthotel.com; 10918 Brockway Rd; r incl breakfast $170-270; [⊛]) is green building-certified, and has an outdoor hot tub and stylishly modern boutique rooms (pet fee $50). For live jazz and wine, **Moody's Bistro & Lounge** ([☎]530-587-8688; www.moodysbistro.com; 10007 Bridge St; dinner mains $18-40; [⊙]11:30am-9:30pm

Sun-Thu, to 10pm Fri & Sat) sources locally ranched meats and seasonal produce. Down pints of 'Donner Party Porter' at **Fifty Fifty Brewing Co** (www.fiftyfiftybrewing.com; 11197 Brockway Rd) across the tracks.

[ⓘ] Getting There & Around

To/From the Airport

South Tahoe Express ([☎]866-898-2463; www.southtahoe express.com) runs frequent shuttles from Nevada's **Reno-Tahoe International Airport** to Stateline (adult/child one way $27/15). **North Lake Tahoe Express** ([☎]866-216-5222; www.northlaketahoeexpress.com) connects Reno's airport with Truckee, Squaw Valley and north-shore towns (one way/round-trip $40/75).

Bus & Train

Truckee's **Amtrak depot** (10065 Donner Pass Rd) has daily trains to Sacramento ($37, 4½ hours) and Reno ($16, 1¼ hours) and twice daily Greyhound buses to Reno ($18, one hour), Sacramento ($42, 2½ hours) and San Francisco ($40, six hours). Amtrak Thruway buses connect Sacramento with South Lake Tahoe ($34, three hours)

Tahoe Area Regional Transit (TART; [☎]800-736-6365; www.laketahoetransit.com; s-ride/24hr pass $1.75/3.50) runs local buses to Truckee and around the north and west shores. South Lake Tahoe is served by **BlueGO** ([☎]530-541-7149; www.bluego.org; s-ride/day pass $2/6), which operates a summer-only trolley up the west shore to Tahoma, connecting with TART.

Car

Tire chains are often required in winter on I-80, US 50, Hwy 89 and Mt Rose Hwy, any or all of which may close during and after snowstorms.

Arizona

Includes »

Best Places to Stay

» El Tovar (p169)
» Grand Canyon Lodge (p180)
» Motor Lodge (p134)
» Boulders (p120)
» View Hotel (p189)

Best Places to Eat

» Elote Cafe (p146)
» Poco (p227)
» 15.Quince Grill & Cantina (p138)
» El Tovar Dining Room (p170)
» Cafe Poca Cosa (p212)

Why Go?

Arizona makes you wish your life was set to music. Cowboy songs in Monument Valley. The Eagles in Winslow. Anything produced by T Bone Burnett on a dusty mining road. And for the Grand Canyon? A fist-pumping 'We Will Rock You,' of course. Arizona, you see, is made for road trips. It has its gorgeous, iconic sites, but it's the road that breathes life into a trip. Take Route 66 into Flagstaff for a dose of mom-and-pop friendliness. Channel the state's mining past on a twisting drive through rugged Jerome. Reflect on Native American history as you drive below a mesa-top Hopi village.

Political controversies – such as immigration reform and budget slashing – have grabbed headlines recently, but these hot-button issues need perspective. Politicians are temporary. But the sunset beauty of the Grand Canyon, the saguaro-dotted deserts of Tucson and the red rocks of Sedona... they're here for the duration and hoping you'll stop by, regardless of the politics.

When to Go

Phoenix

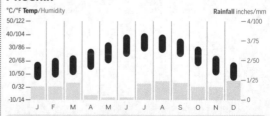

Jan–Mar	Jun–Aug	Sep & Oct
Visit spas in southern Arizona. Cross-country ski in Kaibab National Forest.	High season for exploring the Grand Canyon, Monument Valley and Sedona.	Hike down to Phantom Ranch from the Grand Canyon's South Rim.

Arizona Planning

Although the summer months (June to early September) are a popular time to visit Grand Canyon National Park, it's the opposite in the southern part of the state where the heat can be unbearable at that time of year. Save trips to Phoenix and southern Arizona for the spring. A good rule of thumb is to gauge the climate by the altitude. The lower you are, the hotter and drier it will be.

For Grand Canyon trips, make reservations for lodging, overnight mule rides and white-water rafting a year in advance, particularly if you plan to visit in summer.

DON'T MISS

Grand Canyon Visitor Center on the South Rim has been revamped. Read the interpretive exhibits for background then stroll to Mather Point on the new, pedestrian-friendly plaza. You'll also find bike rentals and the introductory film *Grand Canyon: A Journey of Wonder.* On the Rim Trail, just west of the Yavapai Geology Museum & Observation Station, look for the new **Trail of Time** display.

In summer, save time and gas by prepurchasing your ticket and hopping on the new **Tusayan shuttle**, which runs from the National Geographic Visitor Center in Tusayan to the Grand Canyon Visitor Center in the park.

The California condor isn't new, but the gnarly bird with the 9ft wingspan remains a popular topic of conversation at the park. To learn more about this prehistoric scavenger, attend a ranger-led **Condor Talk**, held daily on both rims during the busy seasons (March to October South Rim, mid-May to mid-October North Rim).

Tips for Drivers

» The main east–west highway across northern Arizona is the 400-mile stretch of I-40, which roughly follows the path of Historic Route 66. It's the interstate to take if you're headed for the Grand Canyon or the Navajo Reservation. I-10 enters western Arizona at Blythe and travels about 400 miles to New Mexico via Phoenix and Tucson.

» South of Phoenix, the I-8 coming west from Yuma joins the I-10. The I-8 is the most southerly approach from California, and it's a lonely highway indeed.

» Cell phone reception, FM radio, lodging and gas are almost nonexistent along I-8 between Yuma and Gila Bend.

» Phoenix Sky Harbor International Airport (p127) and Las Vegas' McCarran International Airport (p87) are major gateways, but Tucson also receives its share of flights.

» Greyhound and Amtrak do not typically stop at national parks in Arizona, nor do city buses and trains.

» For more information on transportation throughout the Southwest, see p557.

(p127) ... (p87) ... see p557.

TIME ZONE

Arizona is on Mountain Time (seven hours behind GMT) but is the only Western state not to observe daylight saving time from spring to fall. The exception is the Navajo Reservation, which – in keeping with those parts of the reservation located in Utah and New Mexico – does observe daylight saving time. The small Hopi Reservation, which it surrounds, follows Arizona.

Fast Facts

» Population: 6.39 million
» Area: 113,635 sq miles
» Sales tax: 6.6%
» Phoenix to Grand Canyon Village: 235 miles, 3½ hours
» Phoenix to Tucson: 116 miles, 1¾ hours
» Kingman to Holbrook: 240 miles, 3¼ hours

Resources

» Arizona Department of Transportation: www.az511 .gov
» Arizona Heritage Traveler: www.arizonaheritage traveler.org
» Arizona Office of Tourism: www.arizonaguide.com

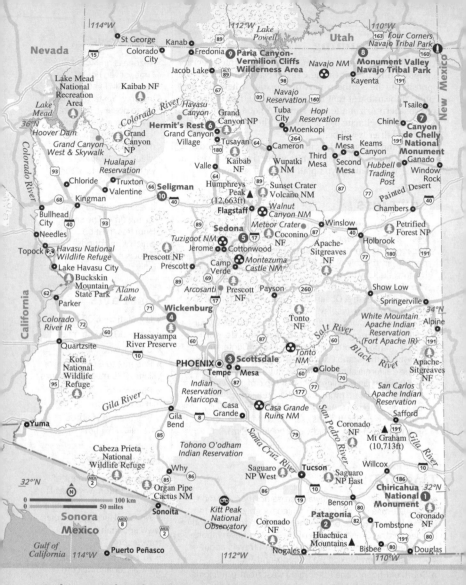

Arizona Highlights

1 Wander past towering formations at **Chiricahua National Monument** (p228)

2 Swoop in for birdwatching and wine tasting in **Patagonia** (p219)

3 Pamper yourself with spa treatments, upscale shopping and patio dining in **Scottsdale** (p114)

4 Cowboy up for a dude ranch ride in **Wickenburg** (p130)

5 Commune beside a vortex in **Sedona** (p141)

6 Bike the Greenway and the road to **Hermit's Rest** at Grand Canyon National Park (p161)

7 Walk in beauty at **Canyon de Chelly National Monument** (p189)

8 Revel in the surreal beauty of the towering buttes in **Monument Valley Navajo Tribal Park** (p188)

9 Hide your Chihuahua; California condors with 9ft wingspans nest in the **Vermilion Cliffs** (p181)

10 Embrace the kitsch of Route 66 in **Seligman** (p198)

History

Native American tribes inhabited Arizona for centuries before Spanish explorer Francisco Vásquez de Coronado led an expedition from Mexico City in 1540. Settlers and missionaries followed in his wake, and by the mid-19th century the US controlled Arizona. The Indian Wars, in which the US Army battled Native Americans to protect settlers and claim land for the government, officially ended in 1886 with the surrender of Apache warrior Geronimo.

Railroad and mining expansion grew and people started arriving in ever larger numbers. After President Theodore Roosevelt visited Arizona in 1903 he supported the damming of its rivers to provide year-round water for irrigation and drinking, thus paving the way to statehood: in 1912 Arizona became the last of the 48 contiguous US states to be admitted to the Union.

The state shares a 250 mile border with Mexico and an estimated 250,000 immigrants crossed it illegally in 2009. After the mysterious murder of a popular rancher near the border in 2010, the legislature passed a law requiring police officers to ask for identification from anyone they suspect of being in the country illegally. This controversial law, known as SB 1070, is winding its way through the federal court system.

Arizona Scenic Routes

Dozens of scenic roads crisscross the state. Some of Arizona's best drives are included in monthly magazine *Arizona Highways* (www.arizhwys.com), created in 1925 to cover them all and still going strong. For additional ideas, see www.byways.org and www.arizonascenicroads.com.

Grand Canyon North Rim Parkway (Hwy 67) Runs from Jacob Lake south to the North Rim via the pine, fir and aspen of Kaibab National Forest (p182).

Historic Route 66 from Topock to Seligman The longest uninterrupted remaining stretch of original Mother Road (p29).

Wickenburg to Sedona (Hwy 89A) Tremendous views of the Mogollon Rim and a grand welcome to Red Rock Country (p30).

Monument Valley (Hwy 163) Stupendous drive past crimson monoliths rising abruptly from the barren desert floor northeast of Kayenta (p33).

Oak Creek Canyon (Hwy 89A) Winds northeast from Sedona through dizzyingly narrow walls and dramatic rock cliffs before climbing up to Flagstaff (p148).

Sky Island Parkway Traverses ecozones equivalent to a trip from Mexico to Canada as it corkscrews up to Mt Lemmon (9157ft), northeast of Tucson (p210).

Vermilion Cliffs to Fredonia (Hwy 89A) Climbs through the remote Arizona Strip from fiery red Vermilion Cliffs up the forested Kaibab Plateau (p182).

GREATER PHOENIX

It's hard to put a label on Phoenix. Just when you've dismissed it as a faux-dobe wasteland of cookie-cutter subdivisions, bland shopping malls and water-gobbling golf courses, you're pulled short by a golden sunset setting the urban peaks aglow. Or a stubborn desert bloom determined to make a go of it in the dry, scrubby heat. Or maybe it's the mom and pop breakfast joint drawing crowds and thumbing its nose at the ubiquitous chains that dominate the landscape.

It's these little markers of hope – or defiance – that let travelers know there's more substance here than initially meets the eye. The catch? You've got to pull off the interstate and get out of the car to appreciate them. And with more than 300 days of sunshine a year – hence the nickname 'Valley of the Sun' – this isn't a disagreeable proposition (except in June, July and August when the mercury tops 100°F, or about 40°C).

Culturally, Phoenix offers an opera, a symphony, several theaters, and two of the state's finest museums: the Heard Museum and the Phoenix Art Museum. The Desert Botanical Garden is a stunning introduction to the region's flora and fauna. For sports fans, there are local teams in the national football, baseball and ice hockey leagues, and the area is dotted with more than 200 golf courses.

Greater Phoenix – also referred to as the Valley – may be vast and amorphous, but the areas of visitor interest are limited to three or four communities. Phoenix is the largest city and combines a businesslike demeanor with a burgeoning cultural scene and top-notch sports facilities. Southeast of here, student-flavored Tempe (tem-*pee*) is a lively district hugging 2-mile-long Tempe Town

Greater Phoenix

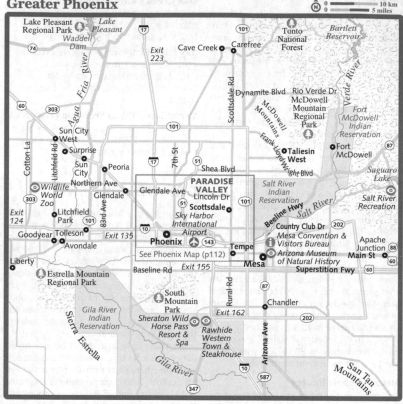

Lake. Further east it segues smoothly into ho-hum Mesa, which has a couple of interesting museums. North of Phoenix, Paradise Valley and Scottsdale are both ritzy enclaves. While the former is mostly residential, Scottsdale is known for its cutesy old town, galleries and lavish resorts.

◉ Sights

Since the Phoenix area is so spread out, attractions are broken down by community. Opening hours change seasonally for many of the area's museums and restaurants, with earlier hours in summer.

PHOENIX

At first glance, Downtown Phoenix appears to be all buttoned-up business and bureaucracy (the state capitol is here), but there's actually plenty of partying going on in its cultural venues, sports stadiums, bars and restaurants. There's even a small alternative art scene.

TOP CHOICE Heard Museum   MUSEUM
(Map p112; ☎602-252-8848; www.heard.org; 2301 N Central Ave; adult/child 6-12/student/senior $15/7.50/7.50/13.50; ◷9:30am-5pm Mon-Sat, 11am-5pm Sun; ⌖) This extraordinary museum is a magical mystery tour through the history, life, arts and culture of Native American tribes in the Southwest. It emphasizes quality over quantity and is one of the best museums of its kind in America.

There are rooms of ethnographic displays, art galleries, a get-creative kids exhibit and an unrivaled Hopi kachina gallery (many of the pieces were a gift from Barry Goldwater). Most disturbing is the Boarding School Experience gallery about the controversial federal policy of removing Native American children from their families and sending them to remote boarding schools in order to 'Americanize' them. Overall, allow two to three hours to explore, and keep a lookout for unexpected treasures – like the

Harry Potter bowl tucked in among more traditional pottery in the Native People in the Southwest gallery. Guided tours run at noon, 2pm or 3pm at no extra charge. Also check out the busy events schedule and the superb gift shop.

Selections from the Heard's vast collection are also displayed at the **Heard Museum North** (480-488-9817; 32633 N Scottsdale Rd; adult/child 6-12/student/senior $6/2/2/4; 10am-5pm Mon-Sat, 11am-5pm Sun) in Scottsdale.

Parking at both locations is free. Valley Metro light-rail stops beside the downtown museum at Encanto/Central Ave.

Desert Botanical Garden   GARDENS
(Map p112; 480-941-1225; www.dbg.org; 1201 N Galvin Pkwy; adult/child/student/senior $18/8/10/15; 8am-8pm Oct-Apr, 7am-8pm May-Sep) This inspirational garden is a refreshing place to reconnect with nature and it offers a great introduction to desert plant life. Looping trails lead past an astonishing variety of desert denizens, arranged by theme (including a desert wildflower loop and a Sonoran Desert nature loop). It's pretty dazzling year round, but the flowering season of March to May is the busiest and most colorful time to visit. Another highlight is December's nighttime luminarias, when plants are draped in miles of twinkling lights.

Pueblo Grande Museum & Archaeological Park   MUSEUM
(Map p112; 602-495-0901; www.pueblogrande.com; 4619 E Washington St; adult/child 6-17/senior $6/5/3; 9am-4:45pm Mon-Sat, 1-4:45pm Sun) The juxtaposition of the ancient and modern makes this former Hohokam village memorable. Don't be surprised if a plane glides into view as you squint across ancient sightlines built into an age-old astronomy chamber. Excavations at the site, which is tucked between Phoenix and Tempe, have yielded many clues about the daily lives of an ancient people famous for building such a well-engineered 1000-mile network of irrigation canals that some modern canals follow their paths. Study this fascinating culture at the small museum then stroll past the park's excavations, which include a ball court, a ceremonial platform and a section of the original canals.

Phoenix Art Museum   MUSEUM
(Map p116; 602-257-1222; www.phxart.org; 1625 N Central Ave; adult/child 6-17/student/senior $10/4/8/8, free Wed 3-9pm; 10am-9pm Wed, 10am-5pm Thu-Sat, noon-5pm Sun;) The Phoenix Art Museum is Arizona's premier repository of fine art. Galleries include works by Claude Monet, Diego Rivera and Georgia O'Keeffe. The striking landscapes in the Western American gallery will get you in the mind-set for adventure. Take kids to the ingeniously crafted miniature period rooms in the Thorne Rooms, borrow a family audio guide or a KidPack, or visit the PhxArtKids Gallery (see www.phxartkids.org).

Grown-ups might want to join the free guided tours at noon, 1pm and 2pm. The museum's contemporary Arcadia Farms

PHOENIX IN...

One Day

Before the day heats up, hike to the top of **Piestewa Peak** then replenish your fuel supplies at **Matt's Big Breakfast**. Afterward, head to the **Heard Museum** for a primer on Southwestern tribal history, art and culture. If it's not too hot, take a prickly postprandial stroll through the exquisite **Desert Botanical Garden**; otherwise, steer toward your hotel pool or **Wet 'n' Wild Phoenix** to relax and cool off. Wrap up the day with a sunset cocktail on the slopes of Camelback Mountain at **Edge Bar** before reporting to dinner at **Dick's Hideaway** or **Chelsea's Kitchen**.

Two Days

On day two, head to **Taliesin West** to learn about the fertile mind of architectural great Frank Lloyd Wright, then grab a gourmet sandwich at the **Herb Box** before browsing the galleries and souvenir shops of **Old Town Scottsdale**. In the afternoon hit the pool and, if you've got one, see a masseuse back at your hotel ahead of getting all dressed up for a gourmet dinner at **Kai Restaurant**. Families might prefer an Old West afternoon of cowboys and shoot 'em ups at **Rawhide** followed by casual Mexican cuisine at **Tee Pee**.

Phoenix

Exit 206

Piestewa Peak/ Dreamy Draw Recreation Area

9

Northern Ave

35th Ave

31st Ave

N Central Ave

Piestewa Peak (2608ft)

51

P

Glendale Ave

Black Canyon Hwy

Acoma Dr

Maryland Ave

21st Ave

23rd Ave

19th Ave

12th St

Bethany Home Rd

21

Missouri Ave

24th St

7th St

16th St

11

34

24

Exit 203

Camelback Rd

20

Campbell Ave

15th Ave

7th Ave

31

25

20th St

Highland Ave

60

Exit 208

27th Ave

Grand Ave

Indian School Rd

33

28th St

13

Central Ave

Osborn Rd

Thomas Rd

Encanto Golf Courses

Encanto Park

Encanto Blvd

22

18

Grand Canal

Heard Museum

37

Oak St

32

Exit 200

McDowell Rd

Grand Ave

7th Ave

1st Ave

7th St

McDowell Rd
Exit 147

Papago Fwy

10

17

Roosevelt St

10

Van Buren St

16th St

Jefferson St

Washington St

See Central Phoenix Map (p116)

16th St

Sky Harbor Blvd

17th Ave

Buckeye Rd

7th St

Exit 194/ 150

Durango St

Maricopa Fwy

19th Ave

7th Ave

16th St

Salt River

Broadway Rd

Café is a great place to grab a meal, and it's not only for museum-goers.

Heritage & Science Park
PLAZA

Tune out the surrounding skyscrapers and imagine thundering hooves and creaking stagecoaches as you amble around **Historic Heritage Square** (Map p116; ☎602-262-5029; http://phoenix.gov/PARKS/heritage.html; 115 N 6th St), a cluster of stately Victorians. Join a tour of the 1895 **Rosson House** (Map p116; www .rossonhousemuseum.org; tours adult/child/senior

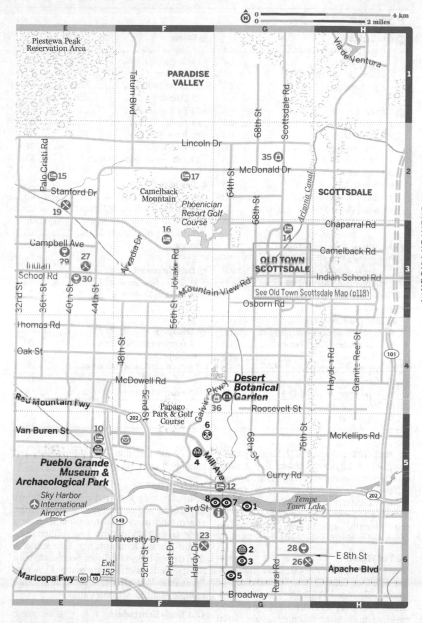

See Old Town Scottsdale Map (p118)

$7.50/4/6; ⊕10am-4pm Wed-Sat, noon-4pm Sun) or take the tots to the **Arizona Doll & Toy Museum** (Map p116; ☎602-253-9337; cnr 7th & Monroe Sts; adult/child $3/1; ⊕10am-4pm Tue-Sat, noon-4pm Sun Sep-Jul; ⊞) in the nearby 1901 Stevens House. The 1912 schoolroom with

antique dolls squeezed behind the wooden desks is adorable. Star Wars figurines and GI Joe keep things from getting too frou-frou.

Too quaint? Make a beeline to the **Arizona Science Center** (Map p116; ☎602-716-2000; www.azscience.org; 600 E Washington

Phoenix

St; adult/child 3-17/senior; $12/10/10; ⊙10am-5pm; ⊡), a high-tech, interactive temple of discovery where kids can slide through a stomach or investigate kinetic energy before winding down at the five-story **IMAX Theatre** (adult/child 3-17/senior $14/12/11) or the recently overhauled **Planetarium** (general admission plus adult/child/senior $8/8/7).

Hall of Flame MUSEUM
(Map p112; ☑602-275-3473; www.hallofflame .org; 6101 E Van Buren St, Phoenix; adult/child 3-5/ student 6-17/senior $6/1.50/4/5; ⊙9am-5pm Mon-Sat, noon-4pm Sun; ⊡) There are more than 90 restored firefighting machines and related paraphernalia from 1725 onward. The National Firefighting Hall of Heroes lists the names of American firefighters killed on the job since 1981. There's also a tribute to the firefighters and police officers who died during the attack on September 11, 2001. Kids can don firefighting gear and clamber on one of the fire trucks.

SCOTTSDALE
Scottsdale sparkles with self-confidence, her glossy allure fuelled by good looks, charm and money. Distractions include a pedestrian-friendly downtown, chic hotels and a vibrant food and nightlife scene. A free trolley links Old Town Scottsdale with Scottsdale Fashion Square mall via the new Scottsdale Waterfront, a retail and office complex on the Arizona Canal.

Old Town Scottsdale NEIGHBORHOOD
Tucked among the glitzy malls and chichi bistros is Old Town Scottsdale, a tiny Wild West-themed enclave filled with cutesy buildings, covered sidewalks and stores hawking mass-produced 'Indian' jewelry and Western art. One building with genuine history is the 1909 Little Red School House,

now home of the **Scottsdale Historical Museum** (Map p118; ☎480-945-4499; www .scottsdalemuseum.com; 7333 E Scottsdale Mall; admission free; ⊙10am-5pm Wed-Sun Oct-May, 10am-2pm Wed-Sun Jun & Sep), where low-key exhibits highlight Scottsdale's history. Old Town is centered on Main St and Brown Ave.

In a cleverly adapted ex-movie theater, the **Scottsdale Museum of Contemporary Arts** (Map p118; ☎480-874-4666; www.smoca.org; 7374 E 2nd St; adult/child/student $7/free/5, free on Thu; ⊙10am-5pm Tue-Wed & Fri & Sat, 10am-8pm Thu, noon-5pm Sun, closed Wed Sep-May) showcases global art, architecture and design, including James Turrell's otherworldly Knight Rise skyspace in the sculpture garden. The museum is across from the local performing arts center.

Taliesin West　　　　ARCHITECTURE
(Map p110; ☎480-860-2700; www.franklloyd wright.org, 12621 Frank Lloyd Wright Blvd, ⊙9am-5pm) Frank Lloyd Wright was one of the seminal American architects of the 20th century. Taliesin West was his desert home and studio, built between 1938 and 1940. Still home to an architecture school and open to the public for guided tours, it's a prime example of organic architecture with buildings incorporating elements and structures found in surrounding nature. During the popular **Insights Tour** (adult/child 4-12/ student/senior $32/17/28/28; ⊙half-hourly 9am-4pm Nov-mid Apr, hourly 9am-4pm mid-Apr-Oct), a docent lead visitors to Wright's office with its slanted canvas roof, the grand stone-walled living room where you can sit on original Wright-designed furniture, and the half-sunken Cabaret Theater. This informative tour feels much quicker than its 90 minutes. Shorter and longer tours are also available.

Cosanti　　　　ARCHITECTURE
(☎480-948-6145; www.arcosanti.org; 6433 E Doubletree Ranch Rd; donation appreciated; ⊙9am-5pm Mon-Sat, 11am-5pm Sun) The home and studio of Wright student Paolo Soleri, this unusual complex of cast-concrete structures served as a stepping stone for Soleri's experimental Arcosanti village, 65 miles north (p128). Cosanti is also where Soleri's signature bronze and ceramic bells are crafted. You're free to walk around, see the bells poured (usually between 10:30am and 12:30pm weekdays) and browse the gift shop. Located about 9 miles south of Taliesin West.

TEMPE
Sandwiched between downtown Phoenix and Mesa, just south of Scottsdale, Tempe is a fun and energetic district enlivened by the 58,000 students of **Arizona State University** (ASU; www.asu.edu). Founded in 1885, the vast campus is home to Sun Devil Stadium, performance venues, galleries and museums.

ASU Art Museum　　　　MUSEUM
(Map p112; ☎480-965-2787; http://asuartmuseum .asu.edu/http; cnr Mill Ave & 10th St; admission free; ⊙11am-5pm Wed-Sat year-round, to 8pm Tue) This airy, contemporary gallery space has eye-catching art and intriguing exhibits. Architecture fans can tour the circular **Gammage Auditorium** (Map p112; ☎480-965-3434 box office; 480-965-6912 tours; www .asugammage.com; cnr Mill Ave & Apache Blvd; admission free, tickets from $20; ⊙1-4pm Mon-Fri Oct-May), Frank Lloyd Wright's last major building. A popular performance venue, it stages primarily Broadway-style musicals and shows.

DON'T MISS

ART WALKS

It may not have the mystique of Santa Fe or the cachet of New York, but Phoenix has almost imperceptibly worked its way up the ladder of art cities that matter. Scottsdale in particular teems with galleries laden with everything from epic Western oil paintings to cutting-edge sculpture and moody Southwestern landscapes. Every Thursday evening some 100 of them keep their doors open until 9pm for **Art Walk** (www.scottsdalegalleries .com), which centers on Marshall Way and Main St.

The vibe is edgier and the setting more urban during **First Fridays** (www.artlinkphoenix .com; ⊙6-10pm), which draws up to 20,000 people to the streets of downtown Phoenix on the first Friday of every month, primarily for art but also for music, poetry slams and other events. Stop by the Central Phoenix Library for a brochure, map and shuttle-bus schedule before joining the fun.

Central Phoenix

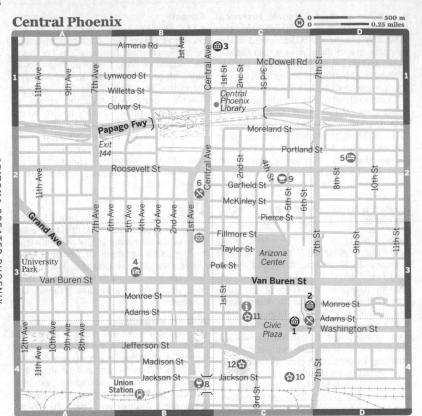

Mill Ave   NEIGHBORHOOD
(Map p112) Situated along the campus' western edge, Mill Ave is Tempe's main drag and lined with restaurants, bars and a mix of national chains and indie boutiques. It's a fine place to browse for old vinyl records and vintage dresses. For cool metro and mountain views, huff it up for half a mile to the top of **'A' Mountain**, so-called because of the giant letter 'A' painted there by ASU students, but officially known as Tempe Butte or Hayden Butte. The trailhead is on E 3rd St, near Mill Ave.

Mill Ave spills into **Tempe Town Lake** (www.tempe.gov/lake), a 2-mile-long recreational pond created by reclaiming the long-dry Salt River in the 1990s. Have a picnic at **Tempe Beach Park** and watch kids letting off steam at the waterfalls, rock slides and shallow pools of the ingenious **Splash Playground** (admission free; ⊙May-Sep; 🖈). There's no swimming in the lake, but **Tempe Town**

Lake Boat Rentals (☑480-517-4050; http://boats4rent.com; 72 W Rio Salado Pkwy; pedalboats/kayaks/16ft pontoon for 2hr $25/40/130) rents human-powered and motorized watercraft. Free outdoor concerts and festivals bring crowds to the park on weekends. The lakeshore has the shiny new lakefront **Tempe Center for the Arts** (www.tempe.gov/tca).

To get around downtown Tempe on weekdays, use the free **Orbit bus** (www.tempe.gov /tim/Bus/Orbit.htm; 6am-10pm Mon-Fri, 8am-10pm Sat, 8am-7pm Sun) that runs along Mill Ave and around the university every 15 minutes Monday to Saturday and every 30 minutes on Sunday.

MESA
Founded by Mormons in 1877, low-key Mesa is one of the fastest-growing cities in the nation and the third-largest city in Arizona with a population of nearly 500,000.

Central Phoenix

Arizona Museum of Natural History

MUSEUM

(Map p110; ☎480-644-2230; www.azmnh.org; 53 N MacDonald St; adult/child 3-12/student/senior $10/6/8/9; ☺10am-5pm Tue-Fri, 11am-5pm Sat, 1-5pm Sun; 👶) Even if you're not staying in Mesa, this museum is worth a trip, especially if your kids are into dinosaurs (and aren't they all?). In addition to the multi-level Dinosaur Mountain, there are loads of life-size casts of the giant beasts plus a touchable apatosaurus thighbone. Other exhibits highlight Arizona's colorful past, from a prehistoric Hohokam village to an eight-cell territorial jail.

Rawhide Western Town & Steakhouse

THEME PARK

(Map p110; ☎480-502-5600; www.rawhide.com; 5700 W N Loop Rd, Chandler; admission free, per attraction or show $5, unlimited day pass $15; ☺5-9pm Wed-Fri, noon-9:30pm Sat, noon-8:30pm Sun, varies seasonally; 👶) Every 'howdy' sounds sincere at this re-created 1880s frontier town located about 20 miles south of Mesa on the Gila River Indian Reservation. Test your mettle on a mechanical bull or a stubborn burro, ride a cutesy train, pan for gold, and join in all sorts of other hokey-but-fun

shenanigans. The steakhouse has rattlesnake and Rocky Mountain oysters (bull testicles) for adventurous eaters and mesquite-grilled slabs of beef for everyone else.

🏃 Activities

In Phoenix, taking a walk on the wild side feels like a micro-vacation from the urban bustle. Find maps and trail descriptions for Piestewa Peak and South Mountain Park at http://phoenix.gov/recreation/rec/index .html.

Both parks described below have trails designated for mountain bikers.

Piestewa Peak/Dreamy Draw Recreation Area

HIKING

(Map p112; ☎602-261-8318; Squaw Peak Dr, Phoenix; ☺5am-11pm, but last entry at 6:59pm) Dotted with saguaros, ocotillos and other local cacti, this convenient park was previously known as Squaw Peak. It was renamed for local Native American soldier Lori Piestewa who was killed in Iraq in 2003. Be fore warned: the trek to the 2608ft summit is hugely popular and the park can get jammed on winter weekends. Parking lots northeast of Lincoln Dr between 22nd and 24th Sts fill early. Dogs are allowed on some trails.

South Mountain Park

HIKING

(Map p110; ☎602-262-7393; 10919 Central Ave, Phoenix; ☺5am-11pm, but last entry at 6:59pm) At 25 sq miles, this local favorite is larger than Manhattan. The 51-mile trail network (leashed dogs allowed) dips through canyons, over grassy hills and past granite walls, offering city views and access to Native American petroglyphs.

Cactus Adventures

BIKING

(☎480-688-9170; www.cactusadventures.com; 4747 Elliot Rd, Suite 21; half-day rental from $30; ☺9am-7pm Mon-Sat, 9am-5pm Sun) A quarter-mile pedal from South Mountain Park, Cactus Adventures rents bikes and offers guided hiking and biking tours.

Ponderosa Stables

HORSEBACK RIDING

(☎602-268-1261; www.ponderosastablesaz.com; 10215 S Central Ave, Phoenix; 1/2hr rides $33/55; ☺8am-4pm Mon-Sat, 9am-4pm Sun Oct-May, shorter hours Jun-Sep) This outfitter leads rides through South Mountain Park. Reservations required for most trips.

Salt River Recreation

TUBING

(Map p110; ☎480-984-3305; www.saltrivertubing .com; 1320 N Bush Hwy; tubes & shuttle $15, cash

Old Town Scottsdale

only; ⏰9am-6:30pm May-late Sep; 🚶) Floating down the Salt River in an inner tube is loads of fun and a great way to cool down on a hot summer day. On this trip, you'll take the Lower Salt River through the stark Tonto National Forest. The launch is in northeast Mesa, about 15 miles north of Hwy 60 on Power Rd. Floats are two, three or five hours long, including the shuttle-bus ride back. Kids must be at least 4ft tall and at least eight years old.

🎊 Festivals & Events

The most popular event in Phoenix is the **Fiesta Bowl football game** (📞480-350-0911; www.fiestabowl.org; 1 Cardinals Dr, Glendale) held in early January at the University of Phoenix Stadium. It's preceded by one of the largest parades in the Southwest.

The **Arizona State Fair** (www.azstatefair .com; 1826 W McDowell Rd) lures folks to the Arizona State Fairgrounds the last two weeks of October and first week of November with a rodeo, livestock displays, a pie-eating contest and concerts.

🛏 Sleeping

Greater Phoenix is well stocked with hotels and resorts, but you won't find many B&Bs, cozy inns or charming mom-and-pops'. Locals know that prices plummet in summer, and you'll see plenty of Valley residents taking advantage of super-low prices at their favorite resorts when the mercury rises.

PHOENIX

Royal Palms Resort & Spa RESORT $$$
(Map p112; 📞602-840-3610; www.royalpalms resortandspa.com; 5200 E Camelback Rd; r $329-429, ste from $366; 🅿❄@🛜🏊🐾) This posh boutique resort at the base of Camelback Mountain was once the winter retreat of New York industrialist Delos Cook. Today, it's a hushed and elegant place, dotted with Spanish Colonial villas, flower-lined

Old Town Scottsdale

walkways and palms imported from Egypt. Pets can go Pavlovian for soft beds, personalized biscuits and walking services. The $28 daily resort fee covers parking, wi-fi, the fitness center and gratuities.

Arizona Biltmore Resort & Spa RESORT **$$$**
(Map p112; ☎602-955-6600, 800-950-0086; www.arizonabiltmore.com; 2400 E Missouri Ave; r $300-459, ste from $489; P❄@☎❄⚓) With architecture inspired by Frank Lloyd Wright, the Biltmore is perfect for connecting to the magic of yesterday: when Irving Berlin penned 'White Christmas' in his suite and Marilyn Monroe splashed around in the pool. It boasts more than 700 discerning units, two golf courses, several pools, a spa, a kids' club and more luxe touches. Unfortunately wi-fi can be spotty beyond the lobby and the main pool. Daily resort fee is $28.

Clarendon Hotel HOTEL **$$**
(Map p112; ☎602-252-7363; www.theclarendon.net; 401 W Clarendon Ave; r $160-199; P❄@☎⚓❄) This upbeat indie hotel has a finger-snapping, minimalist cool that manages to be both welcoming and hip. In the standard rooms look for 42-inch flat-screen TVs, artsy prints and dark custom furniture. Unwind in the Oasis pool with its glass waterwall, then ride up to the breezy skydeck for citywide views. Only bummer? The $20 daily fee

covering wi-fi, parking and phone calls. Pets are $50 per stay.

Aloft Phoenix-Airport HOTEL **$$**
(Map p112; ☎602-275-6300; www.aloftphoenixairport.com; 4450 E Washington St; r $129-160; P❄@☎❄) Rooms blend a pop-art sensibility with the cleanest rounded edges of modern design. The hotel is near Tempe and across the street from the Pueblo Grand Museum. No extra fee for pets.

HI Phoenix Hostel HOSTEL **$**
(Map p116; ☎602-254-9803; www.hiusa.org/phoenix; 1026 N 9th St; dm $20-23, d $35-50; ❄@☎) This is the kind of hostel that makes you fall back in love with backpacking. It's a veritable UN of half-mad guests with fun owners who know Phoenix and want to enjoy it with you. The 14-bed hostel sits in a working-class residential neighborhood and has relaxing garden nooks. Check-in is from 8am to 10am and 5pm to 10pm. Closed in July and August.

Budget Lodge Downtown MOTEL **$**
(Map p116; ☎602-254-7247; www.blphx.com; 402 W Van Buren St; r incl breakfast $50-55; P❄☎) The Budget Lodge doesn't have time for sassiness or charisma. It's got a job to do, and it does it well: providing a clean, low-cost place to sleep. Rooms have a microwave and fridge.

SCOTTSDALE

TOP CHOICE ▷ Boulders RESORT **$$$**
(☎480-488-900; www.theboulders.com; 34631 N Tom Darlington Dr, Carefree; casitas $350-850, villas $1050-1250; P❄@☎❄) Tensions evaporate the moment you arrive at this desert oasis that blends nearly imperceptibly into a landscape of natural rock formations – and that's before you've put in a session at the massage table or steam room at the ultraposh on-site Golden Door Spa. Basically, everything here is calculated to take the edge off travel, making it a perfect destination for recovering from jet lag or rediscovering your significant other. For extra privacy book an individual casita, to which you will be whisked on a golf cart past the 18-hole Jay Morris-designed championship golf course. Daily resort fee is $30. Weekend rates can drop as low as $139 in summer.

TOP CHOICE ▷ Hotel Valley Ho BOUTIQUE HOTEL **$$$**
(Map p118; ☎480-248-2000; www.hotelvalleyho.com; 6850 E Main St; r $289-339, ste $399-439;

PHOENIX FOR CHILDREN

Phoenix is a great family town with plenty to keep the tykes occupied. If your child loves animals, head to **Phoenix Zoo** (Map p112; ☑602-273-1341; www.phoenixzoo.org; 455 N Galvin Pkwy, Phoenix; adult/child $18/9; ☉9am-5pm early Jan-May, 7am-2pm Jun-Aug, 9am-5pm Sep & Oct, 9am-4pm Nov-early Jan; ⓜ). A wide variety of animals, including some rare ones, are housed in several distinct and natural-looking environments. Watch the giraffes nibble on a lofty lunch from the overlook beside the African savanna, then walk through Monkey Village – those squirrel monkeys are pretty darn cute.

If that's too tame, make the trip out to the private **Wildlife World Zoo** (Map p110; ☑623-935-9453; www.wildlifeworld.com; 16501 W Northern Ave, Litchfield Park; adult/child $28/15, aquarium only/aquarium after 5pm $17/9; ☉zoo 9am-6pm, aquarium 9am-9pm; ⓜ) 35 miles northwest of downtown Phoenix. View exotic creatures, many of them endangered, and predators like crocodiles and piranhas in the aquarium.

Older kids will likely get more out of **Castles N' Coasters** (☑602-997-7575; www.castlesncoasters.com; 9445 E Metro Pkwy, Phoenix; unlimited rides Sat & Sun $21, activities individually priced Mon-Fri; ☉hours vary; ⓜ), a big amusement park by the Metrocenter Mall about 20 miles northwest of downtown, near exit 207 off I-17. From chickens to bravehearts, there's a coaster (or ride) for everyone.

To cool off in summer, **Wet 'n' Wild Phoenix** (☑623-201-2000; www.wetnwildphoenix.com; 4243 W Pinnacle Peak Rd, Glendale; over/under 48in tall $35/28, senior $28; ☉10am-6pm Sun-Wed, 10am-10pm Thu-Sat, 11am-7pm Sun Jun-Jul, varies May, Aug & Sep; ⓜ) has pools, tube slides, wave pools, waterfalls, floating rivers and other splash zones. It's located in Glendale, 2 miles west of I-17 at exit 217, about 30 miles northwest of downtown Phoenix.

P✷@⊚☒⛱) Everything's swell at the Valley Ho, where midcentury modern gets a 21st-century twist. This jazzy joint once bedded Bing Crosby, Natalie Wood and Janet Leigh, and today it's a top pick for movie stars filming on location in Phoenix. Bebop music, upbeat staff and eye-magnets like the 'ice fireplace' recapture the Rat Pack-era vibe, and the theme travels well to the balconied rooms. Don't ignore the VH Spa, whose expert staff put the 'treat' in treatments. Pets stay free, but wi-fi is $10 per day.

Sanctuary on Camelback Mountain
RESORT $$$

(Map p112; ☑480-948-2100; www.sanctuaryon camelback.com; 5700 E McDonald Dr; r $419-629, houses $1800-3500; P✷@⊚☒) Draped across the northern slopes of Camelback Mountain, this luxe resort feels like a hideaway of the gods. Mountain suites, spa casitas, private homes – no matter your choice, you will feel pampered, protected and deserving. Lodgings are decorated with the beautiful warm tones of the desert and outfitted with whatever amenities your craving heart desires. Make sure you enjoy a cocktail at Edge Bar, Sanctuary's swank outdoor watering hole with sweeping views of the Valley. Daily resort fee $18.

Hermosa Inn
BOUTIQUE HOTEL $$$

(Map p112; ☑602-955-8614; www.hermosainn.com; 5532 N Palo Cristi Rd; r & casitas $289-449; P✷⊚☒⛱) The signage is discreet but the flowers are not at this gorgeous retreat. The 34 rooms and casitas give off soothing vibes thanks to Spanish Colonial decor that makes perfect use of color and proportion. There's an excellent restaurant on site. Pets OK and no extra fee.

FireSky Resort & Spa
RESORT $$$

(Map p112; ☑480-945-7666; www.fireskyresort.com; 4925 N Scottsdale Rd; r $275-330; ✷@⊚☒) This all-inclusive resort is certainly plush, but it feels less stuffy than some of its highfalutin neighbors. The vibe from the lobby to the rooms in this cozy Kimpton property is a blend of classic elegance, Sonoran desert aesthetics and modern amenities.

Hotel Indigo Scottsdale
HOTEL $$

(Map p118; ☑480-941-9400; www.scottsdalehip hotel.com; 4415 N Civic Center Plaza; r $174-184, ste $204-224; P✷@⊚☒⛱) Sleek, spacious rooms are adorned with a wall-sized desert photo, and the sumptuous bedding is perfect hangover prevention after a night of cavorting. Other hot-spot trappings include outdoor fire pits, club music in the lobby, fancy toiletries and plasma TVs. Dogs welcome at no extra charge.

Sleep Inn
HOTEL **$**

(☎480-998-9211; www.sleepinnscottsdale.com; 16630 N Scottsdale Rd; r incl breakfast $99-114; P ❄@🛜🏊) It's part of a chain, but this Sleep Inn wins points for its extensive complimentary breakfast, afternoon cookies, friendly staff and proximity to Taliesin West. There's also a laundry and free 24hr hotel shuttle that runs within five miles of the hotel. Pets $20 per night.

TEMPE

TOP CHOICE Sheraton Wild Horse Pass Resort & Spa
RESORT **$$$**

(Map p110; ☎602-225-0100; www.wildhorsepass resort.com; 5594 W Wild Horse Pass Blvd, Chandler; r $239-579; P❄@🛜🏊) At sunset, scan the lonely horizon for the eponymous wild horses silhouetted against the South Mountains. Owned by the Gila River tribe and nestled on their sweeping reservation south of Tempe, this 500-room resort is a stunning alchemy of luxury and Native American traditions. The domed lobby is a mural-festooned roundhouse and rooms reflect the traditions of local tribes. The spa offers Bahn (Blue Coyote) wraps and a Pima Medicine massage. The award-winning Kai Restaurant (p123) serves indigenous Southwestern cuisine. That, plus two 18-hole golf courses, an equestrian center, tennis courts, sumptuous rooms and a waterslide modeled after Hohokam ruins round out the appeal. Wi-fi is available in the lobby.

Best Western Inn of Tempe
HOTEL **$**

(Map p112; ☎480 784 2233; www.innoftempe. com; 670 N Scottsdale Rd; r incl breakfast $75-90; P❄@🛜🏊) This well-kept, accommodating contender sits right next to the busy 202 freeway but within walking distance from Tempe Town Lake. ASU and lively Mill Ave are within staggering distance. Perks include a free airport shuttle that also runs to stops within three miles of the hotel.

InnSuites
MOTEL **$$**

(☎480-897-7900; www.innsuites.com/tempe; 1651 W Baseline Rd; r incl breakfast $109-179; P❄@🛜🏊) Shopaholics: this property sits right across from the Arizona Mills mall, and there's plenty of space in your Southwest-styled room to store your loot. Airport shuttle available from 6am to 10pm.

✖ Eating

Phoenix has the biggest selection of restaurants in the Southwest. Reservations are recommended at the more fashionable places. And yes, our picks are heavy on Mexican restaurants, but isn't that part of the reason you're here?

PHOENIX

TOP CHOICE Matt's Big Breakfast
BREAKFAST **$**

(Map p116; ☎602-254-1074; 801 N 1st St, at McKinley St; mains $5-8; ⏱6:30am-2:30pm Tue-Sun) First, a warning: even on weekdays lines are often out the door. There are no reservations, so sign your name on the clipboard and expect a 20-minute wait (and bring quarters for the meter). The upside? Best. Breakfast. Ever. Every regular menu item is great but daily specials – such as eggs scrambled with peppers and chorizo into fluffy-spicy-ohmygoodness on a bed of mouthwatering crispy home fries – are supremely yummy. A true Phoenix institution.

TOP CHOICE Dick's Hideaway
NEW MEXICAN **$$**

(Map p112; ☎602-241-1881; http://richardsonsnm .com; 6008 N 16th St; breakfast $8-16, lunch $12-16, dinner $17-37; ⏱7am-midnight) A mysterious stranger at a bar in Bisbee recommended this pocket-sized ode to New Mexican cuisine, and boy are we glad he did. Grab a small table beside the bar or settle in at the communal table in the side room and prepare for hearty servings of savory, chile-slothered New Mexican fare, from enchiladas to tamales to rellenos. We especially like the Hideaway for breakfast, when the Bloody Marys arrive with a shot of beer. A tip: the unmarked entrance is between the towering shrubs.

Durant's
STEAKHOUSE **$$**

(Map p112; ☎602-264-5967; 2611 N Central Ave; most mains $17-34; ⏱lunch & dinner) This dark and manly place is a gloriously old-school steak house. You will get steak. It will be big and juicy. There will be a potato. The ambiance is awesome too: red velvet cozy booths and the sense that the Rat Pack is going to waltz in at any minute.

Pizzeria Bianco
PIZZERIA **$$**

(Map p116; ☎602-258-8300; 623 E Adams St; pizza $12-16; ⏱11am-10pm Tue-Sat) James Beard-winner Chris Bianco may have stepped back from the ovens at his famous downtown pizza joint (allergies are to blame), but the thin-crust gourmet pies remain as tasty as ever. The tiny restaurant is now open for lunch, good news for travelers exploring the adjacent Heritage Square.

Barrio Café
MEXICAN $$

(Map p112; ☎602-636-0240; 2814 N 16th St; mains $11-26, brunch $10-15; ☺lunch Tue-Fri & Sun, dinner Tue-Sun) Barrio's T-shirts are emblazoned with *comida chingona*, which translates as 'fucking good food'. Crude, maybe. To the point, definitely. Barrio makes Mexican food at its most creative: how many menus featuring guacamole spiked with pomegranate seeds or goat-milk-caramel-filled churros have you seen?

Da Vang
VIETNAMESE $

(Map p112; ☎602-242-3575; 4538 N 19th Ave; most mains $6-13; ☺8am-8pm) Gosh dang, da Vang, how'd you get so good? Our favorite Vietnamese in the Valley is served in a Spartan dining room; it's as if the plainness of the location is in direct proportion to the awesomeness of the food. The *pho* is fantastic, and you'd be remiss not to try some of the lovely 'dry' rice noodle dishes.

Tee Pee Mexican Food
MEXICAN $

(Map p112; ☎602-956-0178; www.teepeemexicanfood.com; 4144 E Indian School Rd; mains $8-11; ☺11am-10pm Mon-Sat, to 9pm Sun) If you're at all snobby about Mexican food, you will not be happy at Tee Pee. If, however, you like piping-hot plates piled high with cheesy, messy, American-style Mexican food, with a side of friendly service, then grab a booth at this 40-year-old Phoenix fave. George W Bush ate here in 2004 and ordered two enchiladas, rice and beans – now called the Presidential Special. Dig in!

Arcadia Farms Café
AMERICAN $$

(Map p116; ☎602-257-2191; 1625 N Central Ave; mains $11-15; ☺10am-8:30pm Wed, 10am-4pm Thu-Sat, 10:30am-4pm Sun) Hmm, the smoked-salmon club? Or the wild mushroom, spinach and goat-cheese tart? Perhaps the strawberry chicken salad on baby greens? The problem with this chic bistro, tucked inside the Phoenix Art Museum (p111), is that everything sounds delectable. This welcoming eatery uses only seasonal organic ingredients for its light yet satisfying dishes. And for ladies who lunch, there's always the peach Bellini.

Chelsea's Kitchen
AMERICAN $$

(Map p112; ☎602-957-2555; 5040 N 40th St; lunch $10-17, dinner $10-27; ☺lunch & dinner daily, brunch Sun) Kick up the wardrobe for this see-and-be-seen eatery (you will get a once-over); but then again, looking nice just feels right. Brick walls, lofty industrial ceiling, leather booths: this casual place wouldn't be out of place in New York's Chelsea. The cuisine, however, is distinctly Western-inspired. Burgers, salads and tacos make appearances, but we're partial to the organic meats tanned to juicy perfection in the hardwood rotisserie. There's a nice patio too.

Noca
AMERICAN $$$

(Map p112; ☎602-956-6622; 3118 E Camelback Rd; mains $20-33; ☺lunch & dinner Tue-Sun, open Mon Dec-Mar) Short for north of Camelback, Noca is where foodies go to die content. The restaurant serves New American fare using American ingredients in the style of classical innovator French Laundry. The tasting menu costs $50, but a better deal is the $27 multi-course simple Sunday suppers.

Pane Bianco
SANDWICHES $

(Map p112; ☎602-234-2100; 4404 N Central Ave; sandwiches $8; ☺11am-8pm Mon-Sat) Part of the Pizzeria Bianco empire, Pane Bianco is one of the best spots in town for an artisan sandwich. You can't eat inside but there are picnic tables just out the door.

SCOTTSDALE

Fresh Mint
VIETNAMESE $

(☎480-443-2556; www.freshmint.us.com; 13802 N Scottsdale Rd; mains $6-14; ☺11am-9pm Mon-Sat; ☝) What? Never had kosher Vietnamese vegan? Us too, but there's always a first time – and if it tastes anything like the food at Fresh Mint, you'll want to get more. If you're skeptical of soy chicken and tofu (served many ways; we like it in the lemongrass curry) we understand, but we respectfully submit that this stuff is as tasty as any bacon cheeseburger.

Oregano's
PIZZERIA $$

(Map p118; ☎480-970-1860; 3622 N Scottsdale Rd; mains $6-15, pizza $9-23; ☺11am-10pm) This outpost of the popular local pizza chain earns its kudos: savory, Chicago-style pies, welcoming service and a patio near-to-bursting with happy people. Not up for pizza? Try one of the hearty pastas. At the Old Town location the hostess stand is beside the patio out back. Everybody loves the Pizza Cookie.

Herb Box
AMERICAN $$

(Map p118; ☎480-289-6160; www.theherbbox.com; 7134 E Stetson Dr; lunch $10-15, dinner $14-25; ☺lunch daily, dinner Mon-Sat) It's not just about sparkle and air kisses at this chichi bistro in the heart of Old Town's Southbridge. It's also about fresh, regional ingredients, artful presentation and attentive service. For a light, healthy, ever-so-stylish lunch (steak salad, turkey avocado wrap, pear-gorgonzola flatbread), settle in on the patio and toast your good fortune – with an organic chamomile citrus tea, of course.

Mastro's Ocean Club SEAFOOD $$$
(☏480-443-8555; www.mastrosrestaurants.com; 15045 N Kierland Blvd; mains $30-50; ☻dinner) Mastro's is gunning for the title of best seafood in the Valley of the Sun, and we think it may deserve the crown. The allure of the restaurant, part of an upscale chain, is in its incredibly rich, decadent take on everything that swims under the waves. The restaurant is located in Kierland Commons.

Sugar Bowl ICE CREAM $
(Map p118; ☏480-946-0051; 4005 N Scottsdale Rd; ice cream under $5, mains $6-9; ☻11am-10pm Sun-Thu, 11am-midnight Fri & Sat; ▦) Get your ice cream fix at this pink-and-white Valley institution. Also serves a whole menu of sandwiches and salads.

Cowboy Ciao AMERICAN $$
(Map p118; ☏480-946-3111; www.cowboyciao.com; 7133 E Stetson Dr; lunch $13-15, dinner $15-35, ☻lunch & dinner) At this mood-lit cantina dishes are a veritable cauldron of textures and flavors. The elk loin, for instance, is paired with crunchy hazelnut pesto, creamy mushroom risotto and a rich cabernet demi-glace. Sometimes it works, sometimes it's too complex for comfort.

TEMPE
⟨TOP CHOICE⟩ Kai Restaurant NATIVE AMERICAN $$$
(☏602-225-0100; www.wildhorsepassresort.com; 5594 W Wild Horse Pass Blvd, Chandler; mains $40-49, 8-course tasting menu $200; ☻dinner Tue-Sat) Native American cuisine soars to new heights at Kai, enhanced and transformed by traditional crops grown along the Gila River. Dinners are like fine tapestries – with such dishes as pecan-crusted Colorado lamb with native seeds mole or caramelized red mullet with cereal of chia seeds – striking just the right balance between adventure and comfort. Service is unobtrusive yet flawless, the wine list handpicked and the room decorated with Native American art. Dress nicely (no shorts or hats). It's at the Sheraton Wild Horse Pass Resort & Spa on the Gila River Indian Reservation.

⟨TOP CHOICE⟩ Essence CAFE $
(Map p112; ☏480-966-2745; 825 W University Dr; breakfast $5-7, lunch $8-9, ☻7am-3pm Mon-Fri, 8am-3pm Sat, closed Sun). The iced caramel coffee at this breezy box of deliciousness may be the best drink on the planet. Essence has the chic allure of a French bistro but the service is friendly and, on our visit, fairly quick. Look for French toast and egg dishes at breakfast, and salads, gourmet sandwiches and a few Mediterranean specialties at lunch. The eco-minded cafe strives to serve organic, locally grown fare.

Pita Jungle MIDDLE EASTERN $
(Map p112; ☏480-804-0234; 1250 E Apache Blvd; dishes $6-15; ☻10:30am-10pm; ✏) One bite and you're hooked by the tangy hummus, crispy falafel and chicken shawarma at this upbeat, funky industrial joint – a local chain – that's on the radar of tousled students.

MESA
Landmark AMERICAN $$
(☏480-962-4652; 809 W Main St; lunch $8-13, dinner $10-25; ☻lunch & dinner, closes 7pm Sun) If you worship at the culinary altar of steak and prime rib, you'll want to make the pilgrimage to this converted 1908 Mormon church that's been a family-owned local mainstay for decades. Lighter eaters, meanwhile, have an entire 'Salad Room' with over 100 items for grazing (lunch/dinner $11/15).

Drinking
Posh watering holes are found in the most unlikely of spots in the Phoenix area, even amid chain stores in strip malls. Scottsdale has the greatest concentration of trendy bars and clubs as well as a convivial line-up of patios on Scottsdale Rd in Old Town; Tempe attracts the student crowd.

Cafes
Lux Coffeebar COFFEE $
(Map p112; www.luxcoffee.com; 4400 N Central Ave ☻7am-10pm; ☏) Bowie's 'Rebel, Rebel' may be spilling from the speakers but we're not convinced that the hipsters tapping away on their MacBooks in porkpie hats are going to be breaking too many rules. But hey, the staff schmoozes just fine, the espresso is organic and the vibe is welcoming, so it's all good.

Bars
⟨TOP CHOICE⟩ Postino Winecafé Arcadia WINE BAR $$
(Map p112; www.postinowinecafe.com; 3939 E Campbell Ave, at 40th St, Phoenix; ☻11am-11pm

Mon-Thu, 11am-midnight Fri & Sat, 11am-10pm Sun) Your mood will improve the moment you step into this convivial, indoor-outdoor wine bar. It's a perfect gathering spot for friends ready to enjoy the good life – but solos will do fine too. Highlights include the misting patio, rave-worthy bruschetta, and $5 wines by the glass between 11am and 5pm. This spot used to be the home of the Arcade Post Office.

Vig   BAR $

(Map p112; 4041 N 40th St, Scottsdale; ☉11am-1am, bar until 2am) Ignore the imposing Soviet-style exterior and step inside. The Vig is where the smart set – stylish, well-scrubbed, happy – comes to knock back a few cocktails. Sleek booths, a dark bar, a bustling patio, an upbeat vibe: be careful or you might find yourself tossing your hair and flashing your tan like the rest of 'em. Park in the grocery store lot across the street in designated Vig spots.

Edge Bar   BAR $

(Map p112; 5700 E McDonald Dr, Sanctuary on Camelback Mountain, Paradise Valley) Enjoy a sunset 'on the edge' at this stylish cocktail bar perched on the side of Camelback Mountain. No room outside? The equally posh, big-windowed Jade Bar should do just fine. Both are within the plush confines of Sanctuary on Camelback Mountain. Free valet.

Rusty Spur Saloon   BAR $

(Map p118; ☎480-425-7787; 7245 E Main St, Scottsdale; ☉11am-2am) Nobody's putting on airs at this fun-lovin', pack-'em-in-tight country bar where the grizzled Budweiser crowd gathers for cheap drinks and twangy country bands. It's in an old bank building that closed during the Depression; the vault now holds liquor instead of greenbacks – except for the dollar bills hanging from the ceiling. Pardner, we kinda like this place.

Alice Cooperstown   SPORTS BAR $

(Map p116; www.alicecooperstown.com; 101 E Jackson St, Phoenix; ☉11am-9pm Mon-Thu, 11am-10pm Fri, noon-10pm Sat) This beer hall really is the original shock rocker's (and Phoenix resident's) baby. Cooperstown is a play on Alice Cooper's name and the real location of the Baseball Hall of Fame. On game days it floods with giddy sports lovers toasting their teams. For music fans, rock-and-roll memorabilia covers the walls.

Four Peaks Brewing Company   BREWERY $

(Map p112; ☎480-303-9967; www.fourpeaks.com; 1340 E 8th St, Tempe; ☉11am-2am Mon-Sat, 10am-2am Sun) Beer lovers rejoice: you're in for a treat at this quintessential neighborhood brewpub in a cool Mission Revival-style building.

Greasewood Flat   BAR $

(☎480-585-9430; www.greasewoodflat.net; 27375 N Alma School Pkwy, Scottsdale; ☉11am-11pm) At this beer-garden-sized outdoor pub and ex-stagecoach stop, rough-and-tumble types – cowboys, bikers, preppy golfers – gather around the smoky barbecue and knock back the whisky. Cash only.

Lost Leaf   BAR $

(Map p116; www.lostleaf.org; 914 N 5th St, Phoenix; ☉5pm-2am) Yeah, it's an average-sized house from the outside. But inside? Pop-art paintings, cozy wood furnishings, an intimate patio for smoking and a beer menu that made us snap a salute in respect. Live music nightly.

Nightclubs & Live Music

Char's Has the Blues   BLUES $

(Map p112; ☎602-230-0205; www.charshasthe blues.com; 4631 N 7th Ave, Phoenix; no cover Mon-Thu, cover Fri-Sun; ☉8pm-1am Sun-Wed, 7:30pm-1am Thu-Sat) Dark and intimate – but very welcoming – this blues cottage packs 'em in with solid acts most nights of the week, but somehow still manages to feel like a well-kept secret.

Rhythm Room   LIVE MUSIC $-$$

(Map p112; ☎602-265-4842; www.rhythmroom .com; 1019 E Indian School Rd, Phoenix) Some of the Valley's best live acts take the stage at this small venue, where you feel like you're in the front row of every gig. It tends to attract more local and regional talent than big names, which suits us just fine. Check the calendar for show start times.

BS West   GAY $

(Map p118; ☎480-945-9028; www.bswest.com; 7125 E 5th Ave, Scottsdale; ☉2pm-2am) A high-energy gay video bar and dance club in the Old Town Scottsdale area, this place has pool tables and a small dance floor, and hosts karaoke on Sunday. Most agree that when it comes to the Valley's gay clubs, this is the place to be; the boys are hot, the music is loud and the straight interlopers, while present, haven't overwhelmed the dance floor.

CACTUS LEAGUE SPRING TRAINING

Before the start of the major league baseball season, teams spend March in Arizona (Cactus League) and Florida (Grapefruit League) auditioning new players, practicing and playing games. Tickets are cheaper (from $6 to $8 depending on the venue), the seats better, the lines shorter and the games more relaxed. Check www.cactusleague .com for schedules and links to tickets.

Crown Room   DJ $
(Map p118; ☎480-423-0117; 1019 E Indian School Rd, Phoenix; ☺9pm-2am Sun, Mon & Wed, 8pm-2am Thu-Sat) Combine Scottsdale's sophistication with its sun-kissed, carefree sexuality and you get the Crown: a thumping nightclub so cool it wears sunglasses in the dark. The Crown isn't just a meat market, but it is very much a place to see and be seen.

☆ Entertainment

The entertainment scene in Phoenix is lively and multifaceted, if not particularly edgy. You can hobnob with high society at the opera or symphony, mingle with the moneyed at a chic nightclub, or let your hair down at a punk concert in a local dive. Spectator sports are huge.

These publications will help you plug into the local scene in no time:

Arizona Republic Calendar (www.azcentral .com/thingstodo/events) The Thursday edition of this major daily newspaper includes a special section with entertainment listings.

Phoenix New Times (www.phoenixnewtimes .com) This free, alternative weekly is published on Thursday and available citywide.

Performing Arts
The following are the most acclaimed venues and companies in Phoenix. Not much goes on during summer.

Phoenix Symphony   SYMPHONY
(Map p116; ☎administration 602-495-1117, box office 602-495-1999; www.phoenixsymphony.org; 75 N 2nd St & 1 N 1st St) Arizona's only full-time professional orchestra plays classics and pops, mostly at **Symphony Hall** (Map p116) and sometimes at its 1st St outpost, from September to May.

Arizona Opera   OPERA
(Map p116; ☎602-266-7464; www.azopera.com; 75 N 2nd St) The state ensemble produces five operas per season, usually big-ticket favorites such as Mozart's *Magic Flute* and Verdi's *La Traviata*. Performances are at Symphony Hall.

Phoenix Theatre   PERFORMING ARTS
(Map p112; ☎602-254-2151; www.phoenixtheatre .com; 100 E McDowell Rd) The city's main dramatic group puts on a good mix of mainstream and edgier performances. The attached Cookie Company does children's shows.

Gammage Auditorium   PERFORMING ARTS
(☎480-965-3434; www.asugammage.com; 1200 S Forest Ave, Tempe) At the ASU Tempe campus, this venue presents crowd-pleasing plays and musicals.

Sports
Phoenix has some of the nation's top professional teams, and tickets for the best games sell out fast. Many of the following teams play at the **US Airways Center** (Map p116).

Arizona Cardinals   FOOTBALL
(☎602-379-0101; www.azcardinals.com; 1 Cardinals Dr, Glendale) In 2006 this National Football League (NFL) team moved from Tempe to the brand-new and architecturally distinguished University of Phoenix Stadium in the western Valley city of Glendale. The season runs from fall to spring.

Arizona Diamondbacks   BASEBALL
(☎602 462 6500; www.arizona.diamondbacks.mlb .com; 201 E Jefferson St, Phoenix) This major-league baseball team won the World Series in 2001 and plays at **Chase Field** (Map p116) in downtown Phoenix.

Phoenix Coyotes   HOCKEY
(☎480-563-7825; www.phoenixcoyotes.com; 9400 Maryland Ave, Glendale) Hosted by the **Jobing .com Arena**, this National Hockey League (NHL) team plays from October to March.

Phoenix Mercury   BASKETBALL
(☎602-252-9622; www.wnba.com/mercury; 201 E Jefferson St, Phoenix) The women's 2007 National Basketball Association (NBA) winners play professional basketball from June to September at the US Airways Center.

Phoenix Suns   BASKETBALL
(☎602-379-7900; www.nba.com/suns; 201 E Jefferson St, Phoenix) The NBA Suns play at the US Airways Center from December to April.

Shopping

The Valley of the Sun is also the Valley of the consumer. From western wear to arts and crafts and Native Americana, it's easy to find a souvenir. Mall culture is also huge. **Old Town Scottsdale** is known for its art galleries and Southwestern crafts shops. **Mill Ave** in Tempe has a nice mix of indie and chain boutiques.

Bookstores

Bookmans   BOOKS
(602-433-0255; www.bookmans.com; 8034 N 19th Ave; 9am-10pm;) The bibliophile's indie mecca, with a neighborhood vibe, events and aisle after aisle of new and used books, mags and music. Free wi-fi.

Changing Hands   BOOKS
(480-730-0205; www.changinghands.com; 6428 S McClintock Dr, Tempe; 10am-9pm Mon-Fri, 9am-9pm Sat, 10am-6pm Sun) *Publisher Weekly*'s 2007 Bookstore of the Year has used, new, hard-to-find and out-of-print books and magazines, plus lots of events.

Malls

Biltmore Fashion Park   MALL
(Map p112; www.shopbiltmore.com; 2502 E Camelback Rd, at 24th St, Phoenix) This exclusive mall preens on Camelback just south of the Arizona Biltmore.

Kierland Commons   MALL
(www.kierlandcommons.com; 15205 N Kierland Blvd, Scottsdale) This new outdoor mall in northern Scottsdale is pulling in crowds.

Scottsdale Fashion Square   MALL
(Map p118; www.fashionsquare.com; 7014 E Camelback, at Scottsdale Rd, Scottsdale) From Abercrombie & Fitch to Z Tejas Grill, this upscale mall has chains, department stores and restaurants.

Borgata   MALL
(Map p112; www.borgata.com; 6166 N Scottsdale Rd, Scottsdale) One of the fancier outdoor malls, with lots of boutiques and galleries, it was designed to look like a medieval Italian town.

Museum Shops

For unique gifts, some of the best finds are in the shops attached to Phoenix's best museums. You do not need to pay admission to the museum to access the shops (but you're missing out).

Heard Museum Shop   ARTS & CRAFTS
(Map p112; www.heardmuseumshop.com; 2301 N Central Ave, Phoenix; 9:30am-5pm, from 11am Sun) The museum store at the Heard Museum has one of the finest collections of Native American original arts and crafts in the world. Their kachina collection alone is mind-boggling. Jewelry, pottery, Native American books and a wide array of fine arts are also on offer.

**Garden Shop at the
Desert Botanical Garden**   GARDENING
(Map p112; www.dbg.org; 1201 N Galvin Pkwy; 9am-5pm) Plant your own desert garden with a starter cactus from this indoor-outdoor gift shop. Eye-catching Southwestern cards, loads of cactus jellies and desert-minded gardening books are also on sale.

Information

Emergency

Police (602-262-6151; http://phoenix.gov/police; 620 W Washington St, Phoenix)

Internet Access

Burton Barr Central Library (602-262-4636; www.phoenixpubliclibrary.org; 1221 N Central Ave, Phoenix; 9am-5pm Mon, 11am-9pm Tue-Thu, 9am-5pm Fri & Sat, 1-5pm Sun;) Free internet; see website for additional locations.

Medical Services

Both hospitals have 24-hour emergency rooms.
Banner Good Samaritan Medical Center (602-839-2000; www.bannerhealth.com; 1111 E McDowell Rd, Phoenix)
St Joseph's Hospital & Medical Center (602-406-3000; www.stjosephs-phx.org; 350 W Thomas Rd)

Post

Downtown post office (602-253-9648; 522 N Central Ave, Phoenix; 9am-5:30pm Mon-Fri)

Telephone

Greater Phoenix has three telephone area codes: 480, 602 and 623. You need to dial the area code even if you're in it.

Tourist Information

Downtown Phoenix Visitor Information Center (602-452-6282, 877-225-5749; www.visitphoenix.com; 125 N 2nd St, Suite 120; 8am-5pm Mon-Fri) The Valley's most complete source of tourist information.
Mesa Convention & Visitors Bureau (480-827-4700, 800-283-6372; www.mesacvb.com; 120 N Center St; 8am-5pm Mon-Fri)
Scottsdale Convention & Visitors Bureau (480-421-1004, 800-782-1117; www.scottsdalecvb.com; 4343 N Scottsdale Rd, Suite 170;

⊙8am-5pm Mon-Fri) Inside the Galleria Corporate Center.

Tempe Convention & Visitors Bureau (✆480-894-8158, 800-283-6734; www.tempecvb.com; 51 W 3rd St, Suite 105; ⊙8:30am-5pm Mon-Fri)

Websites

Lonely Planet (www.lonelyplanet.com/usa /southwest/phoenix) Planning advice, author recommendations, traveler reviews and insider tips.

❶ Getting There & Away

Sky Harbor International Airport (✆602-273-3300; http://skyharbor.com; 🛜) is 3 miles southeast of downtown Phoenix and served by 17 airlines, including United, American, Delta and British Airways. Its three terminals (Terminals 2, 3 and 4; Terminal 1 was demolished in 1990) and the parking lots are linked by the free 24-hr Airport Shuttle Bus.

Greyhound (✆602-389-4200; www.greyhound .com; 2115 E Buckeye Rd) runs buses to Tucson ($20-27, two hours, eight daily), Flagstaff ($32-42, three hours, five daily), Albuquerque ($71-89, 10 hours, five daily) and Los Angeles ($42-64, 7½ hours, 10 daily). Valley Metro's No 13 buses link the airport and the Greyhound station.

❶ Getting Around

To/From the Airport

All international car-rental companies have offices at the airport.

The citywide door-to-door shuttle service provided by **Super Shuttle** (✆602-244-9000, 800-258-3826; www.supershuttle.com) costs about $14 to downtown Phoenix, $16 to Tempe, $21 to Mesa and $20 to Old Town Scottsdale.

Three taxi companies serve the airport: **AAA/Yellow Cab** (✆480-888-8888), **Apache** (✆480-557-7000) and **Mayflower** (✆602-955-1355). The charge is $5 for the first mile and $2 for each additional mile; from the airport there's a $1 surcharge and $15 minimum fare. Expect to pay $17 to $19 to downtown.

A free shuttle (look for the silver and black bus) provides the 15-minute connection to the 44th St/Washington light-rail station; from here it's a 35-minute ride in the light-rail to downtown. The PHX Sky Train is scheduled to replace the shuttle in late 2013. Bus route 13 also connects airport to town for the same fare.

Car & Motorcycle

The network of freeways, most of them built in the last 15 years, is starting to rival Los Angeles and so is the intensity of its traffic. Always pad your sightseeing day for traffic jams. The I-10 and US 60 are the main east–west thoroughfares, while the I-17 and SR 51 are the major north–south arteries. Loops 101 and 202 link most of the suburbs. Parking is plentiful outside of the downtown area.

Public Transportation

Valley Metro (✆602-253-5000; www.valley metro.org) operates buses all over the Valley and a 20-mile light-rail line linking north Phoenix with downtown Phoenix, Tempe/ASU and downtown Mesa. Fares for both light-rail and bus are $1.75 per ride (no transfers) or $3.50 for a day pass. Buses run daily at intermittent times. **FLASH buses** (www.tempe.gov/tim/ bus/flash.htm) operate daily around ASU and downtown Tempe, while the **Scottsdale Trolley** (www.scottsdaleaz.gov/trolley) loops around downtown Scottsdale, both at no charge.

CENTRAL ARIZONA

Much of the area north of Phoenix lies on the Colorado Plateau and is cool, wooded and mountainous. It's draped with the most diverse and scenic quilt of sites and attractions in all of Arizona. You can clamber around a volcano, channel your inner goddess on a vortex, taste wine in a former mining town, hike through sweet-smelling canyons, schuss down alpine slopes, admire 1000-year-old Native American dwellings and delve into Old West and pioneer history. The main hub, Flagstaff, is a lively and delightful college town and gateway to the Grand Canyon South Rim. Summer, spring and fall are the best times to visit.

You can make the trip between Phoenix and Flagstaff in just over two hours if you put the pedal to the metal on I-17, which provides a straight 145-mile shot between the two cities. Opt for one of the more leisurely routes along Hwys 87 or 89, though, and you'll be rewarded with beautiful scenery and intriguing sites along the way.

Verde Valley & Around

ROCK SPRINGS CAFÉ

A slice of fresh pie from **Rock Springs Café** (✆623-374-5794; www.rockspringscafe.com; 35769 S Old Black Cyn Hwy; slice of pie $4.29, mains $7-18; ⊙breakfast, lunch & dinner) shouldn't be missed. Only problem? This Old West eatery, off exit 242, will drive you crazy with choices – apple crumble, blueberry, rhubarb, banana cream – all sitting pretty in a cooler in the dining room. Heartier grub includes burgers, steaks and fried catfish. The attached **Farmers Market** sells produce, hot sauce, beef jerky and cactus arrangements. On the first Saturday of the month, roll in for **Hogs N Heat** (☺1-11pm) when the barbecue smokers fire up out back. This party draws Harley riders and, well, everybody within sniffin' distance.

ARCOSANTI

Two miles east of I-17 exit 262 (Cordes Junction; 65 miles north of Phoenix), **Arcosanti** (☑928-632-7135; www.arcosanti.org; suggested donation for tours $10; ☺tours 10am-4pm) is an architectural experiment in urban living that's been a work in progress since 1970. The brainchild of groundbreaking architect and urban planner Paolo Soleri, it is based on Soleri's concept of 'arcology', which seeks to create communities in harmony with their natural surroundings, minimizing the use of energy, raw materials and land. If and when it is finished, Arcosanti will be a self-sufficient village for 5000 people with futuristic living spaces, large-scale greenhouses and solar energy.

Hour-long tours take you around the site and provide background about the project's history and design philosophy. A **gift shop** sells the famous bronze bells cast at the foundry in Cosanti (p115), near Phoenix. Tours start on the hour beginning at 10am, with no tour at noon.

CAMP VERDE & FORT VERDE STATE HISTORIC PARK

Camp Verde was founded in 1865 as a farming settlement only to be co-opted soon after by the US Army, who built a fort to prevent Native American raids on Anglo settlers. Tonto Apache chief Chalipun surrendered here in April 1873. Today, the town's **Fort Verde State Historic Park** (☑928-567-3275; http://az stateparks.com/Parks/FOVE/index.html; 125 E Hollamon St; adult/child $4/2; ☺9am-5pm Thu-Mon), operating on a five-day schedule, offers an authentic snapshot of frontier life in the late 19th century. Exploring the well-preserved fort, you'll see the officers' and doctor's quarters, the parade grounds and displays about military life and the Indian Wars. Take exit 287 off I-17, go south on Hwy 260, turn left at Finnie Flat Rd and left again at Hollamon St.

Mediocre chain motels cluster near exit 287.

MONTEZUMA CASTLE NATIONAL MONUMENT

Like nearby Tuzigoot (p141), **Montezuma Castle** (☑928-567-3322; www.nps.gov /moca; adult/child $5/free, combination pass with Tuzigoot National Monument $8; ☺8am-6pm Jun-Aug, 8am-5pm Sep-May) is a stunningly well-preserved 1000-year-old Sinagua cliff dwelling. The name refers to the splendid castlelike location high on a cliff; early explorers thought the five-story-high pueblo was Aztec and hence dubbed it Montezuma. A **museum** interprets the archaeology of thesite, which can be spotted from a short self-guiding, wheelchair-accessible trail. Entrance into the 'castle' itself is prohibited, but there's a virtual tour on the website. Access the monument from I-17 exit 289, drive east for half a mile, then turn left on Montezuma Castle Rd.

Montezuma Well (☑928-567-4521; admission free; ☺8am-6pm Jun-Aug, 8am-5pm Sep-May) is a natural limestone sinkhole 470ft wide, surrounded by both Sinaguan and Hohokam dwellings. Water from the well was used for irrigation by the Native Americans and is still used today by residents of nearby Rimrock. Access is from I-17 exit 293, 4 miles north of the Montezuma Castle exit. Follow the signs for another 4 miles through McGuireville and Rimrock.

Hwy 87: Payson & Mogollon Rim

A considerably more scenic route takes you northeast out of Phoenix on Hwy 87 (the Beeline Hwy) to Payson, just below the sheer cliffs of the Mogollon Rim. From here, hook northwest on Hwy 260 via Pine and Strawberry to the I-17. Then you can either head straight up north for the quick 55-mile trip to Flagstaff or take the more circuitous and slower 60-mile drive continuing on Hwy 260 to Cottonwood, and from there north to Sedona and Oak Creek Canyon before reaching Flagstaff.

PAYSON & THE MOGOLLON RIM

Founded by gold miners in 1882, Payson's real riches turned out to be above the ground. Vast pine forests fed a booming timber industry; ranchers ran cattle along the Mogollon Rim and down to the Tonto Basin; and wild game was plentiful. Frontier life here captivated Western author Zane Grey, who kept a cabin outside town. Today, Payson is a recreational and retirement destination for Phoenix citizens. The biggest attractions are hunting and fishing in the forests, lakes and streams around the Rim.

⊙ Sights

Rim Country Museum   MUSEUM
(☑928-474-3483; www.rimcountrymuseums.com;
700 Green Valley Pkwy; adult/child/student/senior
$5/free/3/4; ☺10am-4pm Wed-Mon, 1-4pm Sun)
This lakeside museum is the only real sight
in Payson, with exhibits that illustrate the
native, pioneer and resource-extraction
history of the region. Highlights include
a replica of a blacksmith shop and a walk-
through of the Zane Grey Cabin, faithfully
rebuilt here after the author's original homestead burned in the 1990 Dude Fire. You can
only check out the museum on a guided tour
which, at about 1½ hours, seems a bit long,
especially for kids.

Tonto Natural Bridge State Park   PARK
(☑928-476-4202; www.azstateparks.com; off I lwy
87; adult/child $5/2; ☺8am-6pm daily Jun-Aug,
open Thu-Mon Sep-May) Long ago, 11 miles
north of Payson, a curious thing happened
as Pine Creek flowed downhill – it ran smack
into a massive dam of calcium carbonate.
As creeks will, it gradually cut its way
through, carving out the world's largest
natural travertine bridge, which is 183ft
high and spans a 150ft-wide canyon. You
can walk over it and view it from multiple
angles, and there are steep trails down into
the canyon for close-ups.

The park entrance is 3 miles off Hwy 87;
the final stretch of the access road is precipitous and winding, and an adventure in itself.
Heavy snow may close the park in winter.
Website updated daily.

✱✿ Festivals

Payson hosts a dizzying variety of events,
from dog shows to doll sales, including the
World's Oldest Continuous Rodeo, held
every August since 1884. Arizona's **Old Time
Fiddlers Contest** is in late September.
Visit www.paysonrimcountry.com for more
details about these and other events.

🛏 Sleeping

Payson is surrounded by Tonto National
Forest, so it's easy to find spots to camp
for free along forest roads. If you're looking for basic facilities like toilets and
drinking water, there are a few established
USFS **campgrounds** (campsite $14-16; ☺Apr-
Oct) spread along Hwy 260, 15 to 21 miles
east of town. Hotel rates in Payson vary
depending on demand, so you might
find yourself paying $20 more or less

depending on the day or the season. Chain
motels are scattered along Beeline Hwy
and Hwy 260.

Houston Mesa Campground   CAMPGROUND $
(☑928-468-7135; RV no hookups & tent sites both
$20; ☺Feb-Nov) Two miles north of Payson
along Hwy 87, this USFS campground has
showers and a short nature trail through
a mixed juniper and pine forest. Some
sites available by reservation, see www
.recreation.gov.

Majestic Mountain Inn   MOTEL $$
(☑928-474-0185; www.majesticmountaininn.com;
602 E Hwy 260; r $80-136; ❋@🌐🏊) Set among
landscaped pines and grassy lawns, this is
easily the nicest lodging in Payson – and a
good value one, too. The two-story property
is more of a motel than a lodge-like inn,
but the luxury rooms have double-sided
gas fireplaces, sloped wooden ceilings and
spa tubs.

Super 8   MOTEL $
(☑928-474-5241; www.super8.com; 809 Hwy
260 E; r incl breakfast $85-155; ❋🌐🏊) It's a
chain, but rooms have a bit of sleek style
and come with a flat-screen TV, microwave
and refrigerator. Top it off with a help-
ful front desk and continental breakfast,
and you've got a nice base for regional
adventure.

✗ Eating & Drinking

Gerardo's Italian Bistro   ITALIAN $$
(☑928-468-6500; www.gerardosbistro.com; 512
N Beeline Hwy; lunch $7-16, dinner $12-18; ☺lunch
& dinner Tue-Sun) This award-winning
bistro is helmed by Italian-trained chef
Gerardo Moceri who, judging by the family photos on the wall, looks like he might
have red sauce flowing in his veins. Belly-
stuffing dishes zing with freshness; even
our exacting lasagna critic says 'bravo!'

Buffalo Bar & Grill   AMERICAN $$
(☑928-474-3900; 311 S Beeline Hwy; mains $8-16;
☺10am-1am) So this is where everybody is.
A fun, casual pub; it has a pool table, kids'
menu and live music a couple of nights
a week.

Beeline Cafe   DINER $
(☑928-474-9960; 815 S Beeline Hwy; mains $4-
13; ☺5am-9pm) This home-style restaurant
could be called the beehive, mornings are
so busy with locals swarming in for massive
breakfasts. Cash only.

WHAT THE...?

One of the most famous alien abductions ever reported supposedly occurred in the Apache-Sitgreaves National Forest, not far from Show Low. In 1975 Travis Walton, a member of a logging crew, vanished from the forest for five days. He claimed to have been taken into a flying saucer before being deposited back on Earth at the gas station in Heber. Witnesses – who were fellow loggers and not your typical New Age believers – corroborated the story of the UFO and of Walton's mysterious disappearance. The incident became national news and was the basis for the 1993 movie *Fire in the Sky*. Walton did fail a polygraph test but he never wavered in his insistence that he was telling the truth.

Information

Hwy 87 is known as Beeline Hwy through Payson. The town of Payson maintains a very helpful website about area activities and attractions at www.paysonrimcountry.com.

Hospital (☑928-474-3222; www.payson hospital.com; 807 S Ponderosa)

Post office (☑928-474-2972; 100 W Frontier St; ☺8:30am-4pm Mon-Fri, 9am-noon Sat)

Tonto National Forest Payson Ranger Station (☑928-474-7900; 1009 E Hwy 260; ☺8am-noon, 1-4:30pm Mon-Fri) All the info you need about the forest.

Visitor center (☑928-474-4515; www .rimcountrychamber.com; 100 W Main at Hwy 87; ☺9am-5pm Mon-Fri, 10am-2pm Sat) At the chamber of commerce; there are plenty of brochures about local activities and events.

Getting There & Away

White Mountain Passenger Lines (☑928-537-4539; www.wmlines.com) runs shuttles Monday to Saturday from Phoenix ($35) and Show Low ($35).

NORTH ON HWY 89

The longest but most rewarding route from Phoenix to Flagstaff is via Hwys 89/89A (Alt 89), which follows a sight-packed old stagecoach route. For a summary of one of the most scenic sections of this road trip, from Wickenburg to Sedona, see p30.

The rest of this section is structured following this route.

Wickenburg

Wickenburg looks like it fell out of the sky – directly from the 1890s. Downtown streets are flanked by Old West storefronts, historic buildings and several life-size statues of the prospectors and cowboys who brought this place to life in the 1800s. In later years, once the mining and ranching played out, guest ranches began to flourish, drawing people in search of the romance of the open range. Today, the one-time 'dude ranch capital of the world' still hosts weekend wranglers, but it has also evolved (quietly and discreetly) into a 'rehab capital' for A-listers. The town, located 60 miles northwest of Phoenix via Hwy 60, is pleasant anytime but summer, when temperatures can top 110°F (43°C).

Sights & Activities

The small downtown is dotted with statues of the town's founders as well as a few colorful characters. One of the latter was George Sayers, a 'bibulous reprobate' who was once chained to the town's **Jail Tree** on Tegner St in the late 1800s.

Desert Caballeros Western Museum   MUSEUM
(☑928-684-2272; www.westernmuseum.org; 21 N Frontier St; adult/child/senior $7.50/free/6; ☺10am-5pm Mon-Sat, noon-4pm Sun, closed Mon Jun-Aug) The Spirit of the Cowboy collection examines the raw materials behind the cowboy myth, showcasing bridles and saddles, bits and spurs, and even some angora woolies. Hopi kachina dolls, colorful Arizona minerals and eye-catching art by Western artists, including Charles M Russell and Frederic Remington, are additional highlights. The annual Cowgirl Up! exhibit and sale in March and April is a fun tribute to an eclectic array of Western women artists.

Hassayampa River Preserve   NATURE RESERVE
(☑928-684-2772; www.nature.org; admission $5; ☺7-11am Fri-Sun mid-May–mid-Sep, 8am-5pm Wed-Sun mid-Sep–mid-May) The Hassayampa River normally runs underground, but just outside downtown it shows off its crystalline shimmer. Managed by the Nature Conservancy, this is one of the few

riparian habitats remaining in Arizona and a great place for birders to go gaga for the 280 or so feathered resident and migrating species. It's on the west side of Hwy 60, 3 miles south of town.

Vulture Mine
MINE

(☏602-859-2743; Vulture Mine Rd; admission $10; ⊙8am-4pm winter, to 2pm summer) Town founder Henry Wickenburg discovered gold nuggets here in 1863. The mine itself spat out gold until 1942, but today it's a crusty ghost town, one that recently spooked the hosts of the Travel Channel's *Ghost Adventures*. A self-guided tour winds past the main shaft, the blacksmith shop and the Hanging Tree where 18 miners were strung up for stealing chunks of gold-filled ore, an illegal practice known as high-grading. Decaying buildings and mine shafts here may not be safe for young children. Pets on leashes are OK. No credit cards. Head west on Hwy 60, turn left onto Vulture Mine Rd and follow it for 12 miles. It may be worth calling first to confirm opening hours because they occasionally change.

🛏 Sleeping

Dude ranches typically close for the summer in southern Arizona.

TOP CHOICE Flying E Ranch
DUDE RANCH $$

(☏928-684-2690; www.flyingeranch.com; 2801 W Wickenburg Way; s $192-263, d $308-392; ⊙Nov-Apr; ⊛🐕) This down-home working cattle ranch on 20,000 acres in the Hassayampa Valley is a big hit with families. Rooms are Western-themed and rates include activities and three family-style meals daily. It's open to guests from November to April, with two- or three-night minimum stays. Two-hour horseback rides cost $40. There's no bar; BYOB. Wi-fi available in certain areas.

Wickenburg Inn
HOTEL $

(☏928-684-5461; www.wickenburginn.com; 850 E Wickenburg Way, N Tegner St; r incl breakfast $82-92; ⊛@🐕🛜⊛) Lost? Get your bearings with a quick look at the giant map painted on the lobby wall inside this welcoming motel. Colorful prints, comfy chairs and granite countertops add oomph to mid-size rooms. The extensive continental breakfast is outstanding, and the sausage gravy is some of the best we tasted in Arizona. Small pets OK; $15 per day per pet.

Rancho de los Caballeros
DUDE RANCH $$$

(☏928-684-5484; www.ranchodeloscaballeros.com; 1551 S Vulture Mine Rd; r include breakfast $465-625; ⊙Oct–mid-May; ⊛⊛🐕) With an 18-hole championship golf course, exclusive spa, special kids' program and fine dining, this sprawling ranch feels more *Dallas* than *Bonanza*. The lovely main lodge – with flagstone floor, brightly painted furniture and copper fireplace – gives way to cozy rooms decked out stylishly with Native American rugs and handcrafted furniture. Dinner is a dress-up affair, but afterwards you can cut loose in the saloon with nightly cowboy music. Open to guests October to early-May.

🍴 Eating & Drinking

TOP CHOICE Horseshoe Cafe
DINER $

(☏928-684-7377; 207 E Wickenburg Way; mains under $10; ⊙5am-9pm Mon & Tue, to 1pm Wed & Thu, to 2pm Fri-Sun) If you judge the quality of a restaurant by the number of cowboy hats in the dining room, then this charming place has got to be the best eatery in town. It's gussied up with chaps, a saddle or two and, of course, some horseshoes. The service is super welcoming, and the biscuit with a side of gravy is lick-the-platter good.

Anita's Cocina
MEXICAN $$

(☏928-684-5777; 57 N Valentine St; mains $7-16; ⊙7am-9pm) In the heart of downtown, this happenin' hacienda is a perfect spot for winding down south-of-the-border style. Think margaritas, burritos, combo platters and a heaping basket of free chips with hot or mild salsa (or both). Good for groups and families, but solos will be just fine. Sports fans will find games on the many flat-screen TVs.

Screamer's Drive-In
AMERICAN $

(☏928-684-9056; 1151 W Wickenburg Way; dishes $3-6; ⊙6am-8pm Mon-Sat, 10:30am-8pm Sun) If you've got a hankering for a big and juicy green chile burger with a side of crispy fries and a shake, this '50s-style diner (not really a drive-in) will steer you toward contentment. Indoor and outdoor seating.

Hog Trough Smokehouse BBQ
BARBECUE $

(www.hogtroughbbq.com; 169 E Wickenburg Way; mains $5-16; ⊙11am-8pm daily Sep-May, 11am-8pm Wed, Thu & Sun, to 9pm Fri & Sat) Not sure we love the name but... oink-oink, the pulled pork sure is tasty.

Pony Espresso
CAFE $

(223 E Wickenburg Way; pastries under $3, mains $5-8; ⊙8am-6pm; 🛜) This funky, friendly little

coffee shop also serves scones, brownies and sandwiches.

ⓘ Information

Chamber of Commerce (☎928-684-5479; www.outwickenburgway.org; 216 N Frontier St; ◉9am-5pm Mon-Fri, 10am-2pm Sat & Sun) Inside an 1895 Santa Fe Railroad depot; offers local info and a walking tour of downtown.

Wickenburg Community Hospital (☎928-684-5421; www.wickhosp.com; 520 Rose Ln) 24hr emergency room.

ⓘ Getting There & Away

Wickenburg is about equidistant (60 miles) from Phoenix and Prescott off Hwy 60. There is no bus service. Coming from Kingman and the I-40 you can reach it via Hwy 93, which runs a lonely 105 miles to Wickenburg. It's dubbed Joshua Tree Forest Pkwy because pretty much the only living things growing here are those spiny bushes that are a member of the lily family – but it's a gorgeous drive nonetheless.

Prescott

Fire raged through Whiskey Row in downtown Prescott (press-kit) on July 14, 1900. Quick-thinking locals managed to save the town's most prized possession: the 24ft-long Brunswick Bar that anchored the Palace Saloon. After lugging the solid oak bar across the street onto Courthouse Plaza, they grabbed their drinks and continued the party.

Prescott's cooperative spirit lives on, infusing the historic downtown and mountain-flanked surroundings with a welcoming vibe. This easy-to-explore city, which served as Arizona's first territorial capital, also charms visitors with its eye-catching Victorian buildings, breezy sidewalk cafes, tree-lined central plaza and burgeoning arts scene. But it's not all artsy gentility and Victorian airs. Whiskey Row hasn't changed much from the 1800s, and there's always a party within its scrappy saloons.

Prescott also offers some of Arizona's best outdoor scenery. Hikers, cyclists and campers in search of memorable views don't have to travel far from downtown to find them. The boulder-strewn Granite Dells rise to the north, while in the west the landmark Thumb Butte sticks out like the tall kid in your third-grade picture. To the south, the pine-draped Bradshaw Mountains form part of the Prescott National Forest.

◉ Sights

Historic Downtown   NEIGHBORHOOD

Montezuma St west of Courthouse Plaza was once the infamous **Whiskey Row**, where 40 drinking establishments supplied suds to rough-hewn cowboys, miners and wastrels. A devastating 1900 fire destroyed 25 saloons, five hotels and the red-light district, but several early buildings remain. Many are still bars, mixed in with boutiques, galleries and restaurants. Take a stroll through the infamous **Palace Saloon**, rebuilt in 1901. A museum's worth of photographs and artifacts (including the fire-surviving Brunswick Bar) are scattered throughout the bar and restaurant. A scene from the Steve McQueen movie *Junior Bonner* was filmed here, and a mural honoring the film covers an inside wall.

The columned **County Courthouse** anchoring the elm-shaded plaza dates from 1916 and is particularly pretty when sporting its lavish Christmas decorations. **Cortez St**, which runs east of the plaza, is a hive of antique and collectible stores, as well as home to **Ogg's Hogan** (☎928-443-9856; 111 N Cortez St), with its excellent selection of Native American crafts and jewelry, mostly from Arizona tribes.

Buildings east and south of the plaza escaped the 1900 fire. Some are Victorian houses built by East Coast settlers and are markedly different from adobe Southwestern buildings. Look for the fanciest digs on Union St; No 217 is the ancestral Goldwater family mansion (yes, of Barry Goldwater fame).

Sharlot Hall Museum   MUSEUM

(☎928-445-3122; www.sharlot.org; 415 W Gurley St; adult/child $5/free; ◉10am-5pm Mon-Sat, noon-4pm Sun May-Sep, 10am-4pm Mon-Sat, noon-4pm Sun Oct-Apr) Although Prescott's most important museum is named for its 1928 founder, pioneer woman Sharlot Hall (1870-1943), it's actually a general historical museum highlighting Prescott's period as territorial capital. A small exhibit in the lobby commemorates Miss Hall, who distinguished herself first as a poet and activist before becoming Territorial Historian. In 1924, she traveled to Washington DC to represent Arizona in the Electoral College dressed in a copper mesh overcoat – currently in the display case – provided by a local mine. There would be no mistaking that Arizona was the 'Copper State!'

WHISKEY ROW TO GALLERY ROW

There's still plenty of drinkin' and dancin' going on in Whiskey Row's fine historic saloons, but more recently the infamous strip has taken on a second life as Gallery Row. Standouts include **Arts Prescott Gallery** (☎928-776-7717; www.artsprescott.com; 134 S Montezuma St), a collective of 24 local artists working in all media, including painting, pottery, illustration and jewelry. Prices are quite reasonable. Deeper pockets are required at **Van Gogh's Ear** (☎928-776-1080; www.vgegallery.com; 156 S Montezuma St), where you can snap up John Lutes' ethereal glass bowls, Dale O'Dell's stunning photographs or works by three dozen other nationally known artists making their home in the Prescott area. A great time to sample Prescott's growing gallery scene is during the monthly **4th Friday Art Walk** (www.artthe4th.com).

The most interesting of the nine buildings making up this museum campus is the 1864 **Governor's Mansion**, a big log cabin where Hall lived in the attic until her death. It's filled with a hodgepodge of memorabilia from guns to opium pipes and letters. The **Sharlot Hall Building** next door is the main exhibit hall. Small but informative displays cover the area's historical highlights. Outside, the Rose Garden pays homage to Arizona's pioneer women.

Phippen Museum   MUSEUM
(☎928-778-1385; www.phippenartmuseum.org; 4701 Hwy 89; adult/student/senior $7/free/5; ☺10am-4pm Tue-Sat, 1-4pm Sun) The Phippen, located 7 miles north of Prescott en route to Jerome, is named after cowboy artist George Phippen and hosts changing exhibits of celebrated Western artists, along with contemporary art depicting the American West. At press time, the museum was wrapping up a major expansion. On Memorial Day weekend the museum hosts the Western Art Show & Sale at Courthouse Plaza.

Smoki Museum   MUSEUM
(☎928-445-1230; www.smokimuseum.org; 147 N Arizona St; adult/child/student/senior $5/free/3/4; ☺10am-4pm Mon-Sat, 1-4pm Sun) This pueblo-style museum displays Southwestern Native American objects – baskets, pottery, kachina dolls – dating from prehistoric times to the present. One surprising exhibit addresses the true origins of the 'Smoki' tribe. The tribe was a philanthropic society created by white Prescottonians to raise money for the city's rodeo. The group's annual Hopi Snake Dance was considered a religious mockery by local tribes and was discontinued in 1990. Today, the museum works with area tribes to instill understanding and respect for the region's indigenous cultures. The correct pronunciation is 'smoke-eye.'

🏃 Activities

Prescott sits in the middle of the Prescott National Forest, a 1.2 million acre playground well stocked with mountains, lakes and ponderosa pines. The **Prescott National Forest Office** has information about local hikes, drives, picnic areas and campgrounds. Be aware that a $5 day-use fee is required – and payable – at many area trailheads. Intra-agency passes, including the America the Beautiful pass, cover this fee. You can buy passes at the Forest Service office but, for basic questions, the busy folks here ask that travelers first check out the website for answers.

If you only have time for a short hike, get a moderate workout and nice views of the town and mountains on the 1.75-mile **Thumb Butte trail**. The trailhead is about 3.5 miles west of downtown Prescott on Gurley St, which changes to Thumb Butte Rd. Leashed dogs are OK.

There are five lakes within a short drive of town. The dazzling **Lynx Lake**, 4 miles east of Prescott on Hwy 69 then 3 miles south on Walker Rd, offers fishing, hiking and camping. The most scenic lake for our money is **Watson Lake**, where the eerily eroded rock piles of the Granite Dells are reflected in the crystalline stillness. About 4 miles north of town, off Hwy 89, the city-run **Watson Lake Park** is great for boating, picnicking and bouldering, as well as **summer tent camping** (www.cityofprescott.net; camping $15, parking $2 ☺Thu-Mon nights Apr-Sep).

North of town, the **Granite Mountain Wilderness** attracts rock climbers in the warmer months.

For two rugged, off-the-main-road drives past some of the area's old mining sites, pick up the Forest Service's *Bradshaw Mountains' Motor Tour* pamphlet. High clearance vehicles are suggested for this tour.

✯✯ Festivals & Events

Prescott has a packed year-round events calendar. See www.visit-prescott.com for the full scoop.

Territorial Days Arts & Crafts Show   ART
(☎928-445-2000; www.prescott.org) Arts, crafts, demonstrations, performances; in June.

World's Oldest Rodeo   RODEO
(www.worldsoldestrodeo.com) Bronco busting (since 1888), a parade and an arts-and-crafts fair the week before July 4.

🛏 Sleeping

Don't expect many lodging bargains in Prescott. Check out www.prescottbb.com for links to area B&Bs and inns.

Free dispersed camping is permitted at designated sites next to several fire roads in Prescott National Forest. The Forest Service also manages nine fee-based campgrounds with spots available on a first-come, first-served basis. See www.fs.fed.us/r3/prescott for details.

TOP CHOICE Motor Lodge   BUNGALOW $$
(☎928-717-0157; www.themotorlodge.com; 503 S Montezuma St; r $89-139; ❄🐾🛜) Open the fridge upon arrival and you'll find two Fat Tire beers. This sudsy welcome is one of many personal touches at the Motor Lodge, where 12 snazzy bungalows are horseshoed around a central driveway. This hospitality, along with whimsical prints and stylish but comfy bedding, makes the Motor Lodge one of the finest budget choices we've seen. Rooms and bathrooms can be on the small side, but many have kitchens and porches for extra space. The lime-green bungalows, built as summer cabins in the early 1900s, are within cycling distance of downtown.

Rocamadour B&B   B&B $$
(☎928-771-1933, www.prescottbb.com/inns/10 .html; 3386 N Hwy 89; r $149-219; ❄🛜) The enchanting Rocamadour – meaning 'lover of rocks' in old French – is a 10-acre haven for wildlife nestled among the boulders of the Granite Dells. The three-room B&B is a great place for road-weary travelers to relax, and guests can access city-managed trails near the Dells that link up with other trail systems. Owners Mike and Twyla managed a chateau hotel in France, and they've brought back elegant furniture and a healthy dose of *savoir vivre*. Breakfasts are gourmet affairs.

Hotel Vendome   HISTORIC INN $$
(☎928-776-0900; www.vendomehotel.com; 230 S Cortez St; r $99-139, d $159-199, rate incl breakfast; ❄@🐾🛜) This dapper two-story inn, dating from 1917, charms guests with lace curtains, old-fashioned quilts and a few bathrooms with clawfoot tubs. If you ask, the welcoming hosts might even tell you about the ghost.

Hassayampa Inn   HISTORIC HOTEL $$
(☎928-778-9434; www.hassayampainn.com; 122 E Gurley St; r incl breakfast $139-209; ❄🛜🛜) One of Arizona's most elegant hotels when it opened in 1927, today the restored inn has many original furnishings, hand-painted wall decorations and a lovely dining room. The 67 rooms vary, but all include rich linens and sturdy dark-wood furniture. It has an on-site restaurant, the Peacock Room & Bar. Pets under 45lbs are allowed for an extra $10 per night.

Hotel St Michael   HOTEL $
(☎928-776-1999; www.stmichaelhotel.com; 205 W Gurley St; r $89-99, ste $99-119, rate incl breakfast; 🛜) Gargoyles, ghosts and a 1925 elevator keep things refreshingly offbeat at this Victorian-era hotel in the heart of downtown. The no-frills, old-fashioned rooms, which include three family units, are within staggering distance of Whiskey Row. Rate includes a cooked-to-order breakfast in the downstairs bistro from 7am until 9am.

Apache Lodge   MOTEL $
(☎928-445-1422, www.apachelodge.com; 1130 E Gurley St; s/d $67/79; ❄🛜) The well-worn Apache won't impress domestic divas, but for everyone else, the accommodating service, wallet-friendly price and awesome communal coffee-machine should be enough of a draw.

Point of Rocks RV Park   CAMPGROUND $
(☎928-445-9018; www.pointofrockscampground .com; 3025 N Hwy 89; RV sites $28; 🛜🛜) Commercial campground tucked among beautiful granite boulders behind Watson Lake. Most sites are level, tree-shaded and have full hookups. No tent sites.

✕ Eating

TOP CHOICE Iron Springs Cafe   CAFE $$
(☎928-443-8848; www.ironspringscafe.com; 1501 Iron Springs Rd; lunch $8-11, dinner $8-20; ⊗8am-7pm Wed-Sat, 9am-2pm Sun) Cajun and Southwestern specialties chug into this former train station, all of them packed tight on a one-page menu that's loaded with savory, often spicy, palate pleasers. From the n'awlins muffaletta with sliced ham, salami and mortadella, to the black-and-blue steak with bluecheese butter, it all sounds delicious. Train decor, colorful blankets and easy-bantering waitstaff enliven three tiny rooms. The green chile pork stew has an addictively spicy kick. Recently started serving breakfast.

TOP CHOICE Lone Spur Cafe   BREAKFAST $
(☎928-445-8202; 106 W Gurley St; mains $7-16; ⊗8am-2pm) Mornin' cowboy there's just one rule at the Lone Spur Cafe: always order the biscuit with sausage gravy as your side dish at breakfast. Never the toast. You can't count calories at a place this good, and the sausage gravy will knock your hat off. Even better, portions are huge and there are three bottles of hot sauce on every table. Decor includes stuffed mounts, cowboy gear and a chandelier made out of antlers. Waitstaff are super-nice.

Raven Café   CAFE $$
(☎928-717-0009; 142 N Cortez St; breakfast $5-9, lunch & dinner $8-18; ⊗7:30am-11pm Mon-Fri, 7:30am-midnight Sat, 8am-3pm Sun; ⊛✏) This may be the closest you'll get to skinny jeans in Prescott: a cool, loftlike spot that changes its stripes from daytime coffee hangout to after-dark pub with live music and 30 beers on tap. The mostly organic menu offers a mix of sandwiches, burgers, salads and a few 'big plates' – and lots of vegetarian options, too.

Peacock Room & Bar   FINE DINING $$
(☎928-777-9563; www.hassayampainn.com; 122 E Gurley St; breakfast $7-12, lunch $9-16, dinner $16-31; ⊗breakfast, lunch & dinner) The stuffily stylish dining room at the Hassayampa Inn is famous for its classic American dinners, but we like it best before noon. Huevos rancheros (a Mexican fried-egg dish with chile sauce and cheese) should get your day off to a scrumptious start. Unwind with after work cocktails at the bar, which hums with sweet live jazz Wednesday to Saturday evenings.

Bill's Pizza   PIZZERIA $
(www.billspizzaprescott.com; 107 S Cortez St; slice $2.50, pizza $7-21; ⊗11am-9pm Mon-Thu, 11am-10pm Fri & Sat, noon-6pm Sun) The name of this downtown pizza joint doesn't arouse much excitement, but that's OK – the creativity has been left for the six sauces and 36 toppings that can be slathered over your thin-crusted gourmet pizza. Local art, microbrews and feta-loaded salads round out the appeal.

Prescott Brewing Company   AMERICAN $$
(www.prescottbrewingcomany.com; 130 W Gurley St; mains $9-20; ⊗lunch & dinner; ⊕) This popular brewpub, across from Courthouse Plaza, works well for families. Bangers and mash, fish tacos and pizzas are on the menu; Lodgepole Light, Pine Tar Stout and Willow Wheat are on tap.

🍸 Drinking & Entertainment

Prescott is not afraid to have a good time. The chamber of commerce prints its own 'Prescott Pub Crawl' handout, and there's live music at clubs downtown every night of the week. For a saloon crawl, there's no better place than historic Whiskey Row.

Palace Saloon   BAR
(☎928-541-1996; 120 S Montezuma St; mains $8-20; ⊗lunch & dinner) Kick open the swinging doors and time-warp to 19th-century Whiskey Row days, back when the Earp brothers would knock 'em back with Doc Holliday at the huge Brunswick Bar.

Matt's Saloon   HONKY-TONK
(☎928-778-9914; 112 S Montezuma St) This dark bar is similar in appearance to the Palace but has, in fact, only been around since the 1960s. Buck Owens and Waylon Jennings used to perform live back then, and today it's still Prescott's kickiest two-stepping place.

Cupper's   COFFEE SHOP
(www.cupperscoffee.com; 226 S Cortez St; ⊗7am-5pm Mon-Sat, 8am-4pm Sun; ⊛) An inviting coffee shop brewing up business inside a Victorian-style cottage. Surf the net while savoring a tasty hunk of blueberry bread with a Mexican mocha (dark chocolate with cinnamon).

Bird Cage Saloon   BAR
(☎928-771-1913; 148 Whiskey Row; ⊗10am-2am) Dive bar filled with stuffed birds and motorcycle riders.

ℹ Information

Police (☎928-777-1988; 222 S Marina St)
Post office Downtown (101 W Goodwin St; ⊘8:30am-5pm Mon-Fri), Miller Valley Rd (442 Miller Valley Rd, 8:30am-5pm Mon-Fr, 10am-2pm Sat)
Prescott National Forest office (☎928-443-8000; www.fs.fed.us/r3/prescott; 344 S Cortez St; ⊘8am-4:30pm Mon-Fri) Info on camping, hiking and more in the surrounding national forest.
Tourist office (☎928-445-2000, 800-266-7534; www.visit-prescott.com; 117 W Goodwin St; ⊘9am-5pm Mon-Fri, 10am-2pm Sat & Sun) Information and brochures galore, including a handy walking tour pamphlet ($1) of historical Prescott.
Yavapai Regional Medical Center (☎928-445-2700; www.yrmc.org; 1003 Willow Creek Rd; ⊘24hr emergency room)

ℹ Getting There & Away

Prescott's tiny **airport** (www.cityofprescott.net) is about 9 miles north of town on Hwy 89 and is served by Great Lakes Airlines with daily flights to and from Denver and Ontario, CA.

Prescott Transit Authority (☎928-445-5470; www.prescotttransit.com; 820 E Sheldon St) Runs buses to/from Phoenix airport (one-way adult/child $28/15, two hours, 16 daily) and Flagstaff ($22, 1½ hours, daily). Also offers a local taxi service. **Shuttle U** (☎800-304-6114; www.shuttleu.com; 1505 W Whipple St) runs the same route on an almost identical schedule (one-way adult/child $36/20, 2¼ hours, 16 daily).

Jerome

It's hard to describe Jerome without using the phrase 'precariously perched.' This stubborn hamlet, which enjoys one of the most spectacular views in Arizona, is wedged into steep Cleopatra Hill. Jerome was the home of the fertile United Verde Mine, nicknamed the 'Billion Dollar Copper Camp.' It was also dubbed the 'Wickedest Town in the West,' and teemed with brothels, saloons and opium dens.

When the mines petered out in 1953, Jerome's population plummeted from 15,000 to just 50 stalwarts practically overnight. Then came the '60s, and scores of hippies with an eye for the town's latent charm. They snapped up crumbling buildings for pennies, more or less restored them and, along the way, injected a dose of artistic spirit that survives to this day inside the numerous galleries scattered across town. A groovy joie de vivre permeates the place, and at times it seems every shop and restaurant is playing a hug-your-neighbor folk song from the 1960s or '70s.

Quaint as it is, the most memorable aspect of Jerome is its panoramic views of the Verde Valley embracing the fiery red rocks of Sedona and culminating in the snowy San Francisco Peaks. Sunsets? Ridiculously romantic, trust us.

More than 1.2 million visitors – most of them day-trippers and weekend-warrior bikers – spill into Jerome each year, but the tiny town doesn't feel like a tourist trap. It's far from over-gentrified; as one bumper sticker plastered on a downtown business put it: 'We're all here because we're not all there.'

To experience Jerome's true magic, spend the night. Who knows, you might even see a ghost. This is, after all, 'Arizona's ghost capital.'

⊙ Sights

If you're interested in the town's unique history, take an hour to stroll past some of Jerome's most historic buildings. Start at the corner of Main St and Jerome Ave at the **Connor Hotel**, the town's first solid stone lodging. From there, a leg-stretching climb leads to the **Jerome Grand Hotel**, the onetime home of the United Verde Hospital. This sturdy facility served miners and the community between 1927 and 1951. Known for its ghosts, it's actually a relaxing place to enjoy expansive views of the crimson-gold rocks of Sedona and the Verde Valley.

Heading back downhill, consider the fact that there are 88 miles of tunnel under your feet. Combine these tunnels with steep hills and periodic dynamiting, and it's easy to see why buildings in Jerome regularly collapsed, caught fire or migrated downhill. The **Sliding Jail**, southeast of the visitor center, has moved 225ft from its original 1927 location.

Jerome State Historic Park   MUSEUM
(☎928-634-5381; www.pr.state.az.us; adult/child 7-13 $5/2; 8:30am-5pm Thu-Mon) Recently reopened after extensive structural repairs, this state park preserves the 1916 mansion of eccentric mining mogul Jimmy 'Rawhide' Douglas. Exhibits offer insight into the town's mining heyday. Just outside the entrance, at the **Audrey Headframe Park** (admission free; ⊘8am-5pm daily), stand on a glass platform and look down into

Jerome

⊙ 0 — 100 m
ⓝ 0 — 0.05 miles

a 1900ft mining shaft dating from 1918. The shaft is longer than the Empire State Building by 650ft!

Mine Museum
MUSEUM

(☑928-634-5477; www.jeromehistoricalsociety.com; 200 Main St; adult/child/senior $2/free/1; ⊙museum 9am-5pm, gift shop until 5:30pm) Two halves of a 4-ton flywheel mark the entryway to this small but informative museum that highlights Jerome's hardscrabble past. Displays include a claustrophobic mining cage, a Chinese laundry machine and a wall dedicated to an old-school sheriff who gunned down three vigilantes on Main St then went home and ate lunch – without mentioning to his wife what had happened.

Gold King Mine
GHOST TOWN

(☑928-634-0053; adult/child/senior $5/3/4; ⊙9am-5pm; ⛬) Kids and antique-car buffs will most appreciate the rambling, slightly kitschy attractions at this miniature ghost town a mile north of Jerome via Perkinsville Rd. Walk among rusting mining equipment and an impressive stash of old autos, trucks, service vehicles and chickens. Don't shriek if owner Don Robertson, the spitting image of a white-bearded, 19th-century prospector, pops out from behind a truck to say hello.

🛏 Sleeping

Historic hotels, cozy inns and a few B&Bs are your choices in Jerome, and you won't find a single national chain. In fact, most accommodations are as charmingly eccentric as the town itself. (And many are home to a ghost or two.)

Jerome Grand Hotel
HOTEL $$

(☑928-634-8200; www.jeromegrandhotel.com; 200 Hill St; r $120-205, ste $270-460; ✳🖗) This former hospital looks like the perfect setting for a sequel to *The Shining*. Built in 1926 for the mining community, this sturdy fortress plays up its unusual history. The halls are filled with relics of the past, from incinerator chutes to patient call lights. There's even a key-operated Otis elevator. Rooms are more traditionally furnished, with a nod to the Victorian era. Spend an extra few dollars for a valley-side room; they're brighter and offer better views. For $20 hotel guests can join the evening ghost tour of the premises. Enjoy a fine meal and a dazzling valley panorama at the attached Asylum Restaurant.

Connor Hotel
HISTORIC HOTEL $$

(928-634-5006; www.connorhotel.com; 164 Main St; r $90-165;) The 12 restored rooms at this rambling 1898 haunt convincingly capture the Victorian period, with such touches as pedestal sinks, flowery wallpaper and a pressed-tin ceiling. It's above the popular Spirit Room Bar, which has live music on weekends; rooms one to four get most of the bar noise and allow smoking. Enter through the gift shop.

Mile High Inn
B&B $$

(928-634-5094; www.jeromemilehighinn.com; 309 Main St; r $85-130;) Rooms are dapper and a bit pert at this snug B&B, which once had a stint as a bordello. The seven newly remodeled rooms have unusual furnishings, and the ghost of the former madam supposedly haunts the room dubbed Lariat & Lace. A full breakfast is served at the downstairs restaurant. Four rooms have shared bathrooms.

Ghost City B&B
B&B $$

(928-634-4678; www.ghostcityinn.com; 541 Main St; r $105-155,) In an 1898 building, this B&B is owned by Jerome's police chief Allen Muma and his wife Jackie. Each room has a different theme, from the cowboy-inspired Western room to the more girly Verde Valley room with an antique brass bed and killer views.

✗ Eating

Jerome is a gourmand's delight, and you'll probably be happy at any of the restaurants in town. Enjoy!

TOP CHOICE 15.Quince Grill & Cantina
NEW MEXICAN $$

(928-634-7087; www.15quincejerome.com; 363 Main St; mains $8-17; 11am-8pm Mon & Wed, 11am-9pm Tue, Thu & Fri, 8am-9pm Sat, 8am-8pm Sun) Even the quesadillas have personality at 15.Quince, a cozy cantina in the heart of downtown. Energized by bold colors, upbeat music, amiable waitstaff and Grand Canyon beer, it's a festive spot for gathering after a long day of road tripping. New Mexican-style dishes are the house specialty, and the joint's known for its chile sauces. A smattering of low-heat salads, sandwiches and burgers are available for the timid.

Flatiron Café
CAFE $

(928-634-2733; www.flatironcafejerome.com; 416 Main St; breakfast $7-13, lunch $9-13; 7am-3pm Wed-Mon) This captivating cafe may be tiny but it packs a big, delicious punch. Savor a cheesy scrambled-egg-and-salmon quesadilla at breakfast or a walnut-and-cranberry chicken salad sandwich at lunch. Order at the counter then grab one of three inside tables, or head across the street to the small patio. The mocha latte gets rave reviews.

Grapes
AMERICAN $$

(928-639-8477; www.grapesjerome.com; 111 Main St; lunch & dinner $9-17; 11am-9pm Mon-Fri, 8am-9pm Sat & Sun) Wine newbies and grape connoisseurs are equally happy at this breezy, brick-walled bistro that serves ahi tuna burgers, a Tuscan berry salad with feta, and 10 different gourmet pizzas. Wine selections come with a bin number, and these numbers are helpfully paired with food listings on the menu. From 5pm to 9pm on weekdays all wines by the glass are $5.

Asylum Restaurant
AMERICAN $$$

(928-639-3197; www.theasylum.biz; 200 Hill St; lunch $9-15, dinner $21-32; lunch & dinner) Deep-red walls, lazily twirling fans, gilded artwork and views, views, views make this venerable dining room at the Jerome Grand Hotel one of the state's top picks for fine dining. Order the roasted butternut-squash soup with cinnamon-lime crème and the prickly-pear barbecue pork tenderloin, and you'll see what we mean. Superb wine list too. We've heard Senator John McCain loves it here.

Haunted Hamburger
BURGERS $$

(928-634-0554; 410 N Clark St; mains $8-21; 11am-9pm) Perched high on a hill and often packed, this patty-and-bun joint is definitely a candidate for 'burger king' of the town.

♀ Drinking

The bar at Asylum Restaurant is a genteel place for a cocktail and the views are stunning, but if you want to let your hair down, head to the **Spirit Room Bar** (928-634-8809; www.spiritroom.com; 166 Main St; 11am-1am). Whether you sip a pint at the bar, shoot pool, strike up a conversation with (friendly) Harley riders or study the bordello scene mural, you'll have a fine time at this dark, old-time saloon. There's live music on weekend afternoons and an open-mic night on Wednesday.

VERDE VALLEY WINE TRAIL

Several new vineyards, wineries and tasting rooms have opened along Hwy 89A and I-17, bringing a dash of style and energy to the area. Bringing star power is Maynard James Keenan, lead singer of the band Tool and owner of Caduceus Cellars and Merkin Vineyards. His 2010 documentary *Blood into Vine* takes a no-holds-barred look at the wine industry.

In Cottonwood, start with a drive or a float to Verde River-adjacent **Alcantara Vineyards** (www.alcantaravineyard.com; 7500 E Alcantara Way) then stroll through Old Town where two new tasting rooms, **Arizona Stronghold** (www.azstronghold.com; 1023 N Main St) and **Pillsbury Wine Company** (www.pillsburywine.com; 1012 N Main S) sit across from each other on Main St.

In Jerome there's a tasting room on every level of town, starting with **Bitter Creek Winery/Jerome Gallery** (www.bittercreekwinery.com; 240 Hull Ave) near the visitor center. From there, stroll up to Keenan's **Caduceus Cellars** (www.caduceus.org; 158 Main St; ⊙11am-6pm Sun-Thu, until 8pm Sun) then finish up with a final climb to **Jerome Winery** (☑928-639-9067; 403 Clark St; ⊙11am-5pm Mon-Thu, 11am-8pm Sat, 11am-4pm Sun Jun-Aug, slightly shorter hours rest of the year), a wine shop with an inviting patio, more valley views and your pick of 19 different sips.

Three wineries with tasting rooms hug a short, scrubby stretch of Page Springs Rd east of Cornville: bistro-housing **Page Springs Cellars** (www.pagespringscellars.com; 1500 N Page Springs Rd), the welcoming **Oak Creek Vineyards** (www.oakcreekvineyards .net; 1555 N Page Springs Rd), and the mellow-rock-playing **Javelina Leap Vineyard** (www.javelinaleapwinery.com; 1565 Page Springs Rd).

Leave the driving to others with **Sedona Adventure Tours** (www.sedonaadventure tours.com), or **Arizona Grape Escapes** (www.arizonagrapeescapes.com), which leaves from Phoenix. For a wine-trail map and more details about the wineries, visit www.vvwine trail.com.

ARIZONA JEROME

New wine-tasting rooms have opened in and around Jerome, adding another level of fun.

 Shopping

In the downtown business district, galleries are mixed in with souvenir shops

TOP CHOICE Jerome Artists Cooperative Gallery ARTS & CRAFTS
(☑928-639-4276; www.jeromeartistscoop.com; 502 N Main St; ⊙10am-6pm) Need a gift? At this bright and scenic gallery more than 30 local artists work in pottery, painting, jewelry and other media, before selling their creations at very fair prices.

Nellie Bly SPECIALTY
(☑928-634-0255; www.nbscopes.com; 136 Main St) This cool place is an Aladdin's cave of kaleidoscopes in all shapes and sizes. Also sells art glass.

Downhill, the **Old Jerome High School** harbors seven artist studios and galleries. Many are open to the public most days, but the best time to visit them all is during the **Jerome Art Walk** (www.jeromeartwalk.com) on the first Saturday of the month from 5pm to 8pm. During the 26-gallery art walk, a free shuttle runs between the high school, galleries downtown and the Jerome Grand Hotel. Some galleries have openings, live music and refreshments.

 Information

Remember the board game Chutes & Ladders? There's a similar concept at work in Jerome. The town is essentially stacked up the side of Cleopatra Hill, on three distinct levels. Hwy 89A twists tightly between the different levels and splits into two one-way streets (Hull Ave and Main St) at the Y-intersection in front of the Flatiron Café. On crowded weekends grab a parking spot as soon as you can, then walk through town.

Chamber of Commerce (☑928-634-2900; www.jeromechamber.com; Hull Ave, Hwy 89A north after the Flatiron Café split; ⊙11am-3pm) Offers tourist information.

Police (☑928-634-8992; www.jeromepd.org; 305 Main St) Visit the website just for the music!

Post office (☑928-634-8241; 120 Main St; ⊙8am-noon, 12:30-2:45pm Mon-Fri)

❶ Getting There & Away

To reach Jerome from Prescott follow Hwy 89A north for 34 miles. The drive is slow and windy, and not recommended for large trailers.

Cottonwood

Cottonwood doesn't get the respect it deserves. Yes, it's afflicted with a bit of cookie cutter sprawl, but its walkable Old Town district buzzes with new restaurants, two stylish wine-tasting rooms and an eclectic array of indie shops. Cottonwood is also a cheap and convenient base for regional exploring. Located in the Verde Valley, it's only 16 miles from Sedona and 9 miles from Jerome. The main approach is via Hwy 89A, a faceless, busy thoroughfare.

For information, head to the helpful **chamber of commerce** (☎928-634-7593; www.cottonwoodchamberaz.com; 1010 S Main St; ⊙9am-5pm Mon-Fri, 9am-1pm Sat & Sun) at the intersection of Hwy 89A and Hwy 260. For a list of shops and restaurants in Old Town, visit www.oldtown.org.

⊙ Sights

Dead Horse Ranch State Park   PARK
(☎928-634-5283; www.azstateparks.com; 675 Dead Horse Ranch Rd; day use per vehicle $7, tent/RV site/cabins from $15/25/55) The Verde River runs past this 423-acre park which offers picnicking, fishing, multi-use trails (for bikes, horses and hikers) and a playground. Overnighters can choose between cabins or campsites, some with hookups, and enjoy hot showers. Camping reservations are now available online, as well as by phone (☎520-586-2283; ⊙8am-5pm). Bird-watchers will want to make the short trek to the bird-watching stand at **Tavasci Marsh** to train their binoculars on the least bittern, the Yuma clapper rail and the belted kingfisher. For the horse-lover, **Trail Horse Adventures** (☎928-634-5276; www.trailhorseadventures.com; rides $64-125) will saddle you up for rides lasting one to 2½ hours. There's also a three-hour lunch ride.

🛏 Sleeping

Cottonwood is the land of motels, mostly of the chain variety, but prices are as low as you'll find in the area.

View Motel   MOTEL $
(☎928-634-7581; www.theviewmotel.com; 818 S Main St; r $59-75; ❋🐾🍽️♿🐾) Professionally run, this motel delivers the views its name promises. It's an older property and the furniture is back-to-basics, but rooms are very clean and come with a refrigerator and microwave. A few have kitchenettes. Dogs are $10 per night.

Little Daisy Motel   MOTEL $
(☎928-634-7865; www.littledaisy.com; 34 S Main St; r $56-61, house $125; ❋🐾🐾) Named after a local mine, this motel won't spoil you with frilly extras or fancy furnishings, but it's a good choice if all you want is a solid night's sleep. A two-bedroom house is available for up to four people. Dogs OK ($10 per night), but no felines or ferrets allowed.

Pines Motel   MOTEL $
(☎928-634-9975; www.azpinesmotel.com; 920 S Camino Real; r $85-94; ❋@🐾🐾🐾) This two-story motel, also on a hill with nice views, offers mini-suites with kitchenettes, in addition to standard king and queen units. Pets are $20 the first night, then $5 each night after that.

🍴 Eating & Drinking

Old Town is packed tight with good cafes and restaurants. For more information on its wine tasting rooms, see p139.

Crema Coffee
& Creamery   COFFEE SHOP, SANDWICHES $
(www.cremacoffeeandcreamery.com; 917 N Main St; breakfast under $6, lunch $6-9; ⊙7am-4pm Mon-Fri, 8am-4pm Sat & Sun; 🐾) The patio is a pleasant place to surf the web while nibbling a fresh-from-the-oven blueberry scone (try to visit at 8:30am). Salads and gourmet sandwiches are available for lunch, and there's also yummy gelato.

Nic's Italian Steak
& Crab House   STEAKHOUSE, SEAFOOD $$$
(☎928-634-9626; www.nicsaz.com; 925 N Main St; lunch $8-14, dinner $11-31; ⊙lunch, dinner) You wouldn't really expect an old Chicago vibe – dark, cozy, woodsy – in Cottonwood, but this joint gets it right. Same goes for the grilled steaks, even better when smothered in mushrooms and onions. This place draws a crowd.

Tavern Grille   AMERICAN $$
(www.taverngrille.net; 914 N Main St; mains $9-24; ⊙11am-9pm) The folks behind Nic's also own the patio-fronted Tavern Grille across the street. Inside, booths, flat-screen TVs and a convivial happy-hour crowd surround a

CLARKDALE: THE TRAIN & TUZIGOOT

Clarkdale is a former mining town with two star attractions. On the **Verde Canyon Railroad** (☑928-639-0010, 800-293-7245; www.verdecanyonrr.com; 300 N Broadway; coach adult/child/senior $55/35/50, 1st class all passengers $80) vintage FP7 engines pull climate-controlled passenger cars on leisurely four-hour narrated round trips into the splendid canyon north of Cottonwood Pass, traveling through roadless wilderness with views of red-tinged rock cliffs, riparian areas, Native American sites, wildlife and, from December to April, bald eagles. Monthly schedules are posted on the website. An adults-only wine trip, the Grape Train, is offered in the summer. Reservations are recommended for all trips.

Draped across a ridge about 2 miles east of Clarkdale, **Tuzigoot National Monument** (☑928-634-5564; www.nps.gov/tuzi; adult/child $5/free, combination ticket with Montezuma Castle National Monument $8/free; ☉8am-6pm Jun-Aug, 8am-5pm Sep-May), a Sinaguan pueblo like nearby Montezuma, is believed to have been inhabited from AD 1000 to 1400. At its peak, as many as 250 people may have lived in its 110 rooms. A short, steep trail (not suitable for wheelchairs) winds in and around the structure's limestone walls. A short climb to the roof leads to panoramic views of the Verde River Valley and Mingus Mountain. A half-mile round-trip trail leads to an overlook with views of the bird-attracting Tavasci Marsh.

large central bar. Upscale pub grub includes Southwestern sourdough burgers and Cajun-blackened halibut.

Blazin' M Ranch AMERICAN $$
(☑928-634-0334, 800-937-8643; www.blazinm.com; 1875 Mabery Ranch Rd; adult/child/senior $35/25/33; ☉site opens at 5pm; 🏮) Near Dead Horse Ranch State Park, here you can yee-haw with the rest of them at chuckwagon suppers paired with rootin' tootin' cowboy entertainment. Kids big and small love it. Call for dates and reservations.

Orion Bread Company BAKERY $
(www.orionbread.com; 1028 N Main St; loaves & pastries under $6, sandwiches $7-8; ☉7am-5pm; 🦅) Stop by for preservative-free loaves, baked goods, sandwiches (between 11am and 3pm) and coffee.

Bing's Burger Station BURGERS $
(www.bingsburgers.com; 794 N Main St; mains $4-7; ☉11am-7pm Tue-Sat) Fuel up on burgers '50s-style at this spiffy diner fronted by gas pumps and a cherry red Plymouth (the place used to be a service station, natch). Shakes and malts sold too.

Sedona

Sedona's a stunner, but it's intensely spiritual as well – some even say sacred. Nestled amid alien-looking red sandstone formations at the south end of the 16-mile gorge that is Oak Creek Canyon, Sedona attracts spiritual seekers, artists and healers, and day-trippers from Phoenix trying to escape the oppressive heat. Many New Age types believe that this area is the center of vortexes (not 'vortices' here in Sedona) that radiate the Earth's power, and Sedona's combination of scenic beauty and mysticism draws throngs of tourists year-round. You'll find all sorts of alternative medicines and practices, and the surrounding canyons offer excellent hiking and mountain biking.

The town itself bustles with art galleries and expensive gourmet restaurants. In summer the traffic and the crowds can be heavy. The town's main drag is Hwy 89A. Sedona's navigational center is the roundabout at the intersection of Hwys 89A and 179, known as the Y. Northeast of the Y is Uptown Sedona, the pedestrian center where you'll find most of Sedona's hotels, boutiques and restaurants. Turning south at the Y will take you to Tlaquepaque Village; from here you can cross over Oak Creek and continue down to the Village, where you'll find more shopping, restaurants and hotels. West of the Y is West Sedona, where strip malls line the highway and lead to Red Rock State Park.

⊙ Sights
Scenic Drives
In town, the short drive up paved **Airport Rd** opens up to panoramic views of the

Sedona

valley. At sunset, the rocks blaze a psychedelic red and orange that'll have you burning up the pixels in your camera. Airport Mesa is the closest vortex to town.

Any time is a good time to drive the winding 7-mile **Red Rock Loop Rd**, which is all paved except one short section and gives access to Red Rock State Park as well as Red Rock Crossing/Crescent Moon Picnic Area (day-use $8). A small army of photographers usually gather at the crossing at sunset to record the dramatic light show unfolding on iconic **Cathedral Rock**, another vortex. There's also swimming in Oak Creek. Access is via Upper Red Rock Loop Rd off Hwy 89A, 4 miles west of the Y.

For a breathtaking loop, follow Dry Creek Rd to **Boynton Pass Rd**, turn left, then left again at Forest Rd 525. It's mostly paved but there are some lumpy, unpaved sections. The route passes two of the most memorable rock formations, Vultee Arch and Devil's Bridge. Extend this trip by turning right on FR 525 and taking in the Palatki ruins.

Red Rock State Park   PARK
(📞928-282-6907; www.azstateparks.com/Parks/
RERO; 4050 Red Rock Loop Rd; per car/bicycle or
pedestrian $10/3; ⊙8am-5pm) Not to be confused with Slide Rock State Park, this low-key

park includes an environmental education center, a **visitor center** (⊙9am-5pm), picnic areas and 5 miles of well-marked trails in a riparian habitat amid gorgeous scenery. Ranger-led activities include nature walks, bird walks and full-moon hikes during the warmer months.

FREE **Chapel of the Holy Cross**
& Buddhist Stuppas   RELIGIOUS
(📞928-282-4069; www.chapeloftheholycross.com;
780 Chapel Rd; ⊙9am-5pm Mon-Sat, 10am-5pm
Sun) Situated between spectacular, statuesque red-rock columns 3 miles south of town, this modern, nondenominational chapel was built in 1956 by Marguerite Brunwig Staude in the tradition of Frank Lloyd Wright. There are no services, but even if you're not affiliated with any religion, the soaring chapel and the perch it occupies may move you as it did its architect. There are no restrooms on the site.

Another example of sacred architecture can be admired across town in the West Sedona hills at the **Amitabha Stupa** (📞928-300-4435; www.stupas.org), a consecrated Buddhist shrine set quite stunningly amid piñon and juniper pine and the ubiquitous rocks. There's a smaller stupa further down and an entire park is being planned. Heading along

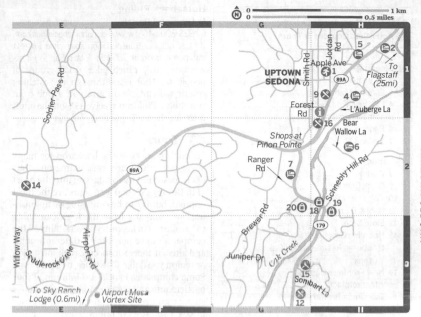

Hwy 89A west from the Y, turn right on Andante Dr, left on Pueblo Dr, then head up the gated trail on your right.

Palatki Heritage Site

RUINS

(☎928-282-3854; www.fs.fed.us/r3/coconino; admission free, Red Rock Pass required; ☉9:30am-3pm) Thousand-year-old Sinagua cliff dwellings and rock art are good-enough reasons to brave the 9-mile dirt road leading to this enchantingly located archaeological site on the edge of the wilderness. There's a small visitor center and two easy trails suitable for strollers but not for wheelchairs. With only limited parking, reservations are required. No pets. True ruin groupies should ask here about exploring the **Honanki Ruins**, a further 3 miles north.

To get to the site, follow Hwy 89A west of the Y for about 10 miles, then hook a right on FR 525 (Red Canyon Rd, a dirt road) and follow it 8 miles north to the parking lot.

🏃 Activities

Hiking and **mountain-biking** trails crisscross the surrounding red-rock country and the woods and meadows of green Oak Creek Canyon. Available at the visitor centers and ranger stations, the free Red Rock Country recreation guide describes hiking and biking trails for all skill levels and includes a map of scenic drives. One popular hiking trail in Oak Creek Canyon is the **West Fork Trail**, which follows the creek for 7 miles – the canyon walls rise more than 200ft in places. Wander up as far as you want, splash around and turn back when you've had enough. The trailhead lies about 3 miles north of Slide Rock, in the Call of the Canyon Recreation Area.

Rent bikes at the **Fat Tire Bike Shop** (☎928-852-0014; www.thefattire.com; 325 Jordan Rd; per day $75; ☉9am-5pm Mon-Sat). They also do group rides several days a week; call the shop for more info.

Oak Creek holds several good swimming holes. If Slide Rock is too crowded, check out **Grasshopper Point** ($8 per car) a few miles south. Southwest of town you can splash around and enjoy splendid views of Cathedral Rock at **Red Rock Crossing**, a USFS picnic area along a pretty stretch of Oak Creek; look for the turnoff about 2 miles west of the hospital on Hwy 89A.

For an easy hike that leads almost immediately to gorgeous views, check out Airport Mesa. From Hwy 89A, follow Airport Dr about half a mile up the side of the mesa to a parking turnout on your left. From here, the short **Yavapai Loop Trail** leads to an awe-inspiring view of Courthouse Butte

Sedona

and, after a brief scramble, a sweeping 360-degree panorama of the city and its flanking red rocks. This is one of Sedona's vortex sites. Try to start this hike in the morning – before 8:30am, when the parking lot starts to fill. There's a Red Rock Pass machine in the parking lot. The Yavapai Loop Trail links onto the longer **Airport Loop Trail**.

Another stunningly beautiful place to hike is through the red rock of **Boynton Canyon**, an area that exudes spiritual energy and where some have reported experiencing the antics of such energetic spirits (who may not necessarily want them trekking through)! Look for the rock formation known as **Kachina Woman** and try not to be moved. Boynton Canyon is about 5 miles north of Hwy 89A up Dry Creek Rd; get an early start to avoid crowds.

Horseback Riding

M Diamond Ranch   HORSEBACK RIDING
(☏928-300-6466; www.sedonahorsebackrides.com; 1hr trail ride incl transportation adult/child $70/50, trail ride & cookout $85-115; ☺Mon-Sat; ⊞) This working cattle ranch takes small groups of people on trail rides through eye-catching countryside. Staff will give you a ride from your hotel. Children receive 15% off the adult price for the trail ride and cookout.

☞ Tours

Sedona's scenery is the backdrop for many a rugged adventure, and numerous tour operators stand by to take you into the heart of it. Bumpy off-road jeep tours are the most popular, but it can be confusing distinguishing one company from the next. One thing to check is backcountry accessibility – the companies have permits for different routes and sites. If there's a specific rock formation or region you'd like to explore, be sure to ask. Some companies expect a minimum of four participants and charge more per person for smaller groups. Many offer discounted tour prices if you reserve online.

A Day in the West   JEEP
(☏928-282-4320; www.adayinthewest.com) Those rootin' tootin' cowboys strolling through Uptown are most likely guides for this Western-themed jeep tour company. It offers a combo jeep tour/horseback ride with Western-style dinner and show (adult/child $149/129). Also leads a jeep and winery trip ($99) and several backcountry-only trips (adult $45 to $75, child $35 to $60).

Earth Wisdom Jeep Tours   SPIRITUAL
(☏928-282-4714; www.earthwisdomtours.com; 293 N Hwy 89A; tours $49-98) Groovy jeep tours with a metaphysical bent and Native American focus, with journeys to vortexes and sacred Native American sites.

Evening Sky Tours   ASTRONOMY
(☏928-203-0006; www.eveningskytours.com) View planets, stars, galaxies and nebula with the naked eye and through large Dobsonian telescopes. Ninety-minute tours cost $50 to $60, depending on group size. Kids are $25.

Northern Light Balloon Expeditions   BALLOON
(☏928-282-2274; www.northernlightballoon.com) Spend about one hour floating in the air at sunrise ($195 per person) then enjoy a champagne picnic back on solid ground.

RED ROCK PASS

If you want to park anywhere in the forest surrounding Sedona, you'll need to buy a Red Rock Pass, which is available at the ranger station, visitor centers and vending machines at some trailheads and picnic areas. Passes cost $5 per day or $15 per week (and $20 per year) and must be displayed in the windshield of your car. You don't need a pass if you're just stopping briefly for a photograph or to enjoy a viewpoint, or if you have an America the Beautiful pass ($80). With the latter, place it in the windshield with your signature facing out. You can also swing by a visitor center for a hangtag – the passes have been known to melt! For additional details see www.redrockcountry.org. Passes are not valid at other fee areas, including state parks, national monuments and the day-use areas of Banjo Bill, Crescent Moon, Call of the Canyon and Grasshopper Point; these four day-use areas charge $8 to $10 per vehicle.

Pink Jeep Tours　　　　　　　　JEEP
(☑928-282-5000; www.pinkjeep.com; 204 N Hwy 89A) This company must be doing something right because it recently celebrated its 50th anniversary. The company runs 13 different thrilling and funny, if bone-rattling, off-road tours lasting from about two hours (adult/child $55/42) to four hours ($167/144). Tours to the Grand Canyon are also offered.

Red Rock Jeep Tours　　　　　　JEEP
(☑928-282-6667; www.redrockjeep.com; 270 N Hwy 89A) Guides in cowboy garb take you on mild to wild jeep adventures; this is the only company going out to the historic Soldier Pass Trail (adult/child $69/55), used by General George Crook during his campaign against the Apaches. Also offers a vortex tour (adult/child $109/75).

Sedona Adventure Tours　　　　RIVER
(☑928-204-6440; www.sedonaadventuretours.com; 2020 Contractors Rd; 🐾) Specializes in river trips, with a funyak trip down the Verde River and a 'Water to Wine' float to Alcantara Vineyard. Water to Wine tours range from $85 to $172. Funyak and inner-tube rentals too.

Sedona Trolley　　　　　　　SCENIC
(☑928-282-4211; www.sedonatrolley.com; 276 N Hwy 89A; adult/child $12/6, both tours $22/11; ⊙9am-5pm, may vary seasonally) Choose from two narrated tours, both lasting 55 minutes and departing on the hour. 'Sedona Highlights' covers Tlaquepaque Village and the Chapel of the Holy Cross, while 'Seven Canyons Scenic' runs to West Sedona and Boynton Canyon.

✦ Festivals & Events

Sedona Arts Festival　　ARTS & CRAFTS
(☑928-282-1177; www.sedonaartsfestival.org) Fine arts, crafts and non-stop entertainment in early October.

Sedona International Film Festival　FILM
(☑928-282-1177; www.sedonafilmfestival.com) Usually takes place during the month of February, but screenings and events occur throughout the year.

🛏 Sleeping

Sedona is rich with beautiful B&Bs, creekside cabins and full-service resorts. Rates at chain motels range from $75 to $130, reasonable by Sedona standards. For lodging in Oak Creek Canyon, see (p149).

Apart from camping, tiny Sedona doesn't have many options for the budget traveler.

Rancho Sedona RV Park　　CAMPING
(☑928-282-7255, 888-641-4261; www.ranchosedona.com; 135 Bear Wallow Ln; RV sites $31-63) Offers a laundry, showers and 30 RV sites, most with full hookups.

TOP CHOICE ✎ Briar Patch Inn　CABIN $$$
(☑928-282-2342; www.briarpatchinn.com; 3190 N Hwy 89A; cottages $219-395; 🐾🐾) Nestled in nine wooded acres along Oak Creek, this lovely inn offers 19 log cottages with southwestern decor and Native American art. All cottages include patios, many have fireplaces, and several lie beside the burbling creek. In summer, a hearty buffet breakfast is served on a stone patio that overlooks the creek and is accompanied by live chamber music (Wednesday to Sunday). There's a two-night minimum on weekends and it's best to book at least a few months ahead.

L'Auberge de Sedona　　RESORT $$$
(☑928-282-1661; www.lauberge.com; 301 L'Auberge Ln; ❄🐾🐾) Situated creekside in Uptown Sedona, the red-rock backdrop looms within reaching distance. With well-appointed cabins amid the green lawns, luxuries

VORTEX PRIMER

Several vortexes (swirling energy centers where the Earth's power is said to be strongly felt) are located around Sedona, which is one of the reasons it has become a mecca of spiritual seekers and New-Age types. The four best-known vortexes are in Sedona's Red Rock Mountains. These include **Bell Rock**, near the Village of Oak Creek, **Cathedral Rock**, near Red Rock Crossing, **Airport Mesa**, along Airport Rd, and **Boynton Canyon**. Local maps show these four main sites, although some individuals claim that others exist. Stop by the Sedona Chamber of Commerce Visitor Center to find out about different tours.

include Jacuzzis, wine and cheese every evening and free yoga classes daily –and even a gift bag for your dog, who is most welcome here ($35 to $50 fee applies).

Cozy Cactus
B&B $$
(☎928-284-0082; www.cozycactus.com; 80 Canyon Circle Dr, Village of Oak Creek; r $165-325; ❄@�()) This five-room B&B, run by Carrie, Mark and black lab Margi, works well for adventure-loving types ready to enjoy the great outdoors. The Southwest-style abode bumps up against a National Forest trail and is just around the bend from cyclist-friendly Bell Rock Pathway. Post-adventuring, get comfy beside the firepit on the back patio for wildlife watching and stargazing. Breakfasts alternate between savory and sweet (huevos rancheros; apple-pie French toast) and come with fruit and Mark's famous muffins.

Lantern Light Inn
B&B $$-$$$
(☎928-282-3419; www.lanternlightinn.com; 3085 W Hwy Alt 89; r $139-195, ste $195-309; @�()) The lovely couple running this small inn in West Sedona put you right at ease in their comfortable antique-filled rooms. Rooms range from small and cozy, overlooking the back deck and garden, to the huge guesthouse in back (breakfast not included), but all feel comfortably overstuffed. There's a common room (more of a family library with musical instruments) that can be used for meetings. Credit cards not accepted.

Sky Ranch Lodge
MOTEL $-$$
(☎928-282-6400; www.skyranchlodge.com; Airport Rd; r $80-164, cottages $194; ❄�()❄) At the top of Airport Rd, with spectacular views of the town and surrounding country, this lodge offers spacious motel rooms, six landscaped acres, and a pool and hot tub. Rates vary according to type of bed and your view. Some include balconies,

fireplaces, kitchenettes and/or refrigerators; also available are cottages with vaulted ceilings.

La Vista Motel
MOTEL $
(☎928-282-7301; www.lavistamotel.com; 500 N Hwy Alt 89; r $66-90, s $90-100; ❄�()) Right on the side of the highway leading into Oak Creek Canyon, this friendly, family-run motel has clean rooms and suites. Some suites are decked out with full kitchens, porches, tile floors, sofas, refrigerators and bathtubs.

Sedona Motel
MOTEL $
(☎928-282-7187; www.thesedonamotel.com; 218 Hwy 179; r $79-89; ❄) Directly south of the Y, this friendly little motel offers big value within walking distance of Tlaquepaque and Uptown Sedona. Rooms are basic but clean, but the fantastic red rock views may be all the luxury you need.

Matterhorn Inn
MOTEL $$
(☎928-282-7176; www.matterhorninn.com; 230 Apple Ave; r $150; ❄�()❄) All rooms at this friendly, central motel include refrigerators and have balconies or patios overlooking Uptown Sedona and Oak Creek.

✕ Eating

TOP CHOICE Elote Cafe
MEXICAN $$
(☎928-203-0105; www.elotecafe.com; King's Ransom Hotel, 771 Hwy 179; mains $17-22; ⊙5pm-late Tue-Sat) Some of the best, most authentic Mexican food you'll find in the region. Serves unusually traditional dishes you won't find elsewhere, like the fire-roasted corn with lime and cotija cheese, or the tender, smoky pork cheeks. Reservations are not accepted, so if you want to eat at a reasonable hour, line up by 4:30pm or resign yourself to waiting with a white sangria.

L'Auberge Restaurant on Oak Creek
AMERICAN $$$

(☎928-282-1661; www.lauberge.com; 301 L'Auberge Lane; mains $34-52; ⊙7am-9pm Mon-Sat, 9am-2pm & 5:30-9pm Sun) Featuring refined American cuisine with a French accent, the menu at L'Auberge changes seasonally (you might find ramps and morels in the spring, and roast duck and beets in the fall). The creekside spot is a local favorite for celebrating special occasions in elegant environs, with a select wine list to complement your meal.

Dahl & DiLuca Ristorante
ITALIAN $$$

(☎928-282-5219; www.dahlanddiluca.com; 2321 Hwy 89A; mains $13-33; ⊙5-10pm) Though this lovely Italian place fits perfectly into the groove and color scheme of Sedona, at the same time it feels like the kind of place you'd find in a small Italian seaside town. It's a bustling, welcoming spot serving excellent, authentic Italian food.

Heartline Café
AMERICAN $$

(☎928-282-0785; www.heartlinecafe.com; 1600-1610 W Hwy 89A; mains $18-28; ⊙8am-4pm & 5-9.30pm) This restaurant's name refers to a Zuni Native American symbol for good health and long life, and indeed the imaginative menu offers fresh and clean gourmet victuals. A cozy ambience and creative, seasonal menu make it a long-running favorite. Nowadays, the Heartline Gourmet Express next door serves breakfast and lunch.

Oak Creek Brewery & Grill
PUB

(☎928-282-3300; www.oakcreekpub.com; 336 Hwy 179; beers $5.75; ⊙11:30am-9pm; ☎) At Tlaquepaque Village, this spacious brewery serves a full menu that includes upmarket pub-style dishes like crab cakes and 'fire-kissed' pizzas.

Shugrue's Hillside Grill
AMERICAN $$-$$$

(☎928-282-5300; www.jamrestaurants.com; Hillside Plaza, 671 Hwy 179; mains $15-38; ⊙11am-3pm Mon-Fri, 9am-3pm Sat & Sun, 5-9pm daily) Promising panoramic views, an outdoor deck from which to enjoy them and consistently excellent food, this restaurant is a great choice for an upscale meal. If it's too chilly to sit outside, don't fret – the walls are mostly glass, so you can still enjoy the scenery. The menu offers everything from steak to ravioli, but it is best known for its wide variety of well-prepared seafood.

Coffee Pot Restaurant
BREAKFAST $

(☎928-282-6626; www.coffeepotsedona.com; 2050 W Hwy Alt 89; mains $4-11; ⊙6am-2pm; ☎) This has been the go-to breakfast and lunch joint for decades. It's always busy and service can be slow, but it's friendly, the meals are reasonably priced and the selection is huge – 101 types of omelets, for a start. (Jelly, peanut butter and banana omelet, anyone?)

Sedona Memories
DELI $

(☎928-282-0032; 321 Jordan Rd; mains $7; ⊙10am-2pm Mon-Fri) This tiny local spot assembles gigantic sandwiches on slabs of homemade bread (which they don't sell seperately). There are several vegetarian options, and you can nosh on their quiet porch. Cash only.

Black Cow Café
ICE CREAM $

(☎928-203-9868; 229 N Hwy 89A; ice creams $4-5; ⊙10:30am-9pm) Many claim the Black Cow has the best ice cream in town. It also does sandwiches and soup.

Pick up groceries and healthy picnic components at **New Frontiers Natural Marketplace** (Native American ☎928-282-6311; 1420 W Hwy 89A; mains $4-10; ⊙8am-9pm Mon-Sat, to 8pm Sun; ☎) or stop by for smoothies, vegetarian salads or panini from the deli. Another good Arizona grocery chain is **Bashas'** (☎928-282-5351; 160 Coffee Pot Dr; ⊙6am-11pm).

Drinking & Entertainment

Check the listings at *Sedona Red Rock News* (www.redrocknews.com) for current local entertainment.

Heart of Sedona
CAFE

(☎928-282-5777; 1370 W Hwy 89A; coffee $2-5; ⊙6am-11pm; ☎) Offering a pleasant outdoor patio with good views, this coffee shop is the best spot for a jolt of caffeine and a pastry while you check your email on their free wi-fi network.

Oak Creek Brewery & Grill
BREWERY

(☎928-282-3300; www.oakcreekpub.com; 336 Hwy 179; beers $5.75; ⊙11:30am-9pm; ☎) Wash the pub food down with a house brew – we're partial to the Oak Creek Amber.

Oak Creek Brewing Company
BREWERY

(www.oakcreekbrew.com; 2050 Yavapai Dr) In West Sedona, with a limited menu, has bands on the weekend.

Shopping

Shopping is a big draw in Sedona, and visitors will find everything from expensive boutiques to T-shirt shops. Uptown along Hwy 89A is the place to go souvenir hunting.

Tlaquepaque Village MALL
(☎928-282-4838; www.tlaq.com; ◷10am-5pm) Just south of Hwy 89A on Hwy 179, this is a series of Mexican-style interconnected plazas that is home to dozens of high-end art galleries, shops and restaurants. It's easy to lose a couple of hours meandering the lovely maze here.

Garland's Navajo Rugs HANDICRAFTS
(☎928-282-4070; www.garlandsrugs.com; 411 Hwy 179; ◷10am-5pm) This 35-year-old institution offers the area's best selection of rugs, and also sells other Native American crafts. It's an interesting shop to visit even if you don't plan on buying anything – it displays naturally dyed yarns with their botanical sources of color, as well as bios of the weavers and descriptions of how many hours it takes to create a handwoven rug.

Center for the New Age NEW AGE
(☎928-282-5910; 313 Hwy 179; ◷8:30am-8:30pm) On Hwy 179 across the street from Tlaquepaque Village is this interesting purveyor of New Age books and gifts. Come here for a vortex guide.

Information

Police station (☎928-282-3100; www.sedonaaz.gov; 100 Roadrunner Dr; ◷emergency 24hr)

Post office (☎928-282-3511; 190 W Hwy 89A; ◷8:45am-5pm Mon-Fri, 9am-1pm Sat)

Sedona Chamber of Commerce Visitor Center (☎928-282-7722, 800-288-7336; www.visitsedona.com; 331 Forest Rd; ◷8:30am-5pm Mon-Sat, 9am-3pm Sun) Located in Uptown Sedona, pick up free maps, brochures and get last-minute hotel bookings.

USFS South Gateway Visitor Center (☎928-203-7500; www.redrockcountry.org; 8379 Hwy 179; ◷8am-5pm) Get a Red Rock Pass here, as well as hiking guides, maps and local national forest information. It's just south of the Village at Oak Creek.

Verde Valley Medical Center (☎928-204-3000; www.verdevalleymedicalcenter.com; 3700 W Hwy 89A; ◷24hr)

Getting There & Away

While scenic flights depart from Sedona, the closest commercial airport is Phoenix (two hours) or Flagstaff (30 minutes).

Ace Express (☎928-649-2720, 800-336-2239; www.acexshuttle.com; one way/round-trip $60/99) Door-to-door shuttle service running between Sedona and Phoenix Sky Harbor.

Amtrak (☎800-872-7245; www.amtrak.com) Stops in Flagstaff, about 40 miles north of Sedona.

Greyhound (☎800-231-2222; www.greyhound.com) Stops in Flagstaff.

Sedona-Phoenix Shuttle (☎928-282-2066, 800-448-7988; www.sedona-phoenix-shuttle.com; one way/round-trip $50/90) Runs between Phoenix Sky Harbor and Sedona eight times daily; call to make reservations.

Getting Around

Barlow Jeep Rentals (☎928-282-8700, 800-928-5337; www.barlowjeeprentals.com; 3009 W Hwy 89A; ◷9am-6pm)

Bob's Taxi (☎928-282-1234) Local cab service.

Enterprise (☎928-282-2052; www.enterprise.com; 2090 W Hwy 89A; ◷8am-6pm Mon-Fri, 9am-noon Sat) Rental cars available here.

Oak Creek Canyon

Hwy 89A from Sedona into Oak Creek Canyon is a surreally scenic drive that won't soon be forgotten. The canyon is at its narrowest here, and the crimson, orange and golden cliffs at their most dramatic. Pine and sycamore cling to the canyon sides and the air smells sweet and romantic. Giant cottonwoods clump along the creek, providing a scenic shady backdrop for trout-fishing and swimming, and turn a dramatic golden in fall. Unfortunately, traffic can be brutal in summer.

Sights & Activities

About 2 miles into the drive north from Sedona, **Grasshopper Point** (day-use $8) is a great swimming hole. Another splash zone awaits a further 5 miles north at **Slide Rock State Park** (☎928-282-3034; www.azstateparks.com/Parks/SLRO; 6871 N Hwy 89A; per car Memorial Day-Labor Day $20, Sep-May $10; ◷8am-7pm Memorial Day-Labor Day, 8am-5pm Sep-May), a historic homestead and apple farm along Oak Creek. Short trails ramble past old cabins, farming equipment and an apple orchard, but the park's biggest draw is the fun rock slides. Picture people swooshing down the creek through rock-lined chutes and over water-covered rock 'slides'. It's an all-natural waterpark. Unfortunately, water quality can be an issue, but it's tested daily; call the hotline on ☑602-542-0202. This park gets jam-packed in summer, so come early or late in the day to avoid the worst congestion.

About 13 miles into the canyon, the road embarks on a dramatic zigzag climb, covering 700ft in 2.3 miles. Pull into **Oak Creek Vista** and whip out your camera to capture the canyon from a bird's-eye perspective. A small visitor center is open seasonally, and there's a year-round Native American arts and crafts market.

Beyond here, the highway flattens out and reaches I-17 and Flagstaff in about 8 miles.

🛏 Sleeping

Camping

Dispersed camping is not permitted in Red Rock Canyon. The **USFS** (☑928-282-4119, 877-444-6777; www.recreation.gov) runs the following campgrounds along Hwy 89A in Oak Creek Canyon (none with hookups). All are nestled in the woods just off the road. It costs $20 to camp, but you don't need a Red Rock Pass. Reservations are accepted for all campgrounds but Pine Flat East.

Manzanita Eighteen sites; open year-round; 6 miles north of town.

Cave Springs Eighty-two sites; showers; 11.5 miles north.

Pine Flat East and Pine Flat West Fifty-seven sites; 12.5 miles north.

Lodging

Garland's Oak Creek Lodge LODGE $$$
(☑928-282-3343; www.garlandslodge.com; Hwy 89A; cabins $180-295; ⊙closed Sun & mid-Nov–Apr 1; 🔊) Set back from Oak Creek on eight secluded acres with broad lawns, woods and an apple orchard, this lodge offers nicely appointed Western log cabins, many with fireplaces. Rates include a full hot breakfast, 4pm tea and a superb gourmet dinner. Catering to guests who crave peace and quiet amid verdant surroundings, Garland's is 8 miles north of Sedona and is often booked up a year in advance. If you can't stay overnight, booking dinner is a delicious alternative; there are sometimes a few spots are available for nonguests.

Junipine Resort LODGE $$-$$$
(☑928-282-3375; www.junipine.com; 8351 N Hwy 89A; creekhouses $135-400; @🔊🔊🔊) In the Oak Creek Canyon woodland, 8 miles north of Sedona, this resort offers lovely, spacious one- and two-bedroom creekhouses. All have kitchens, living/dining rooms, wood-burning stoves and decks – and some even have lofts. The on-site restaurant serves great food as well as microbrews and wine.

Slide Rock Lodge MOTEL $$
(☑928-282-3531; www.sliderocklodge.com; 6401 N Hwy 89A; r $99-149, ste $179; ✴) This log-cabin longhouse has rooms along the canyon wall that tend toward the simple and rustic. Some rooms have fireplaces, all are clean and there's a large grassy area outside to relax and grill. The atmosphere is friendly, quiet and conducive to a laid-back stay.

Flagstaff

Flagstaff's laid-back charms are countless, from its pedestrian-friendly historic downtown crammed with eclectic vernacular architecture and vintage neon, to its high-altitude pursuits like skiing and hiking. Buskers play bluegrass on street corners while bike culture flourishes. Locals are a happy, athletic bunch, skewing more toward granola than gunslinger. Northern Arizona University (NAU) gives Flag its college-town flavor, while its railroad history still figures firmly in the town's identity. Throw in a healthy appreciation for craft beer, freshly-roasted coffee beans and an all-around good time and you have the makings of a town you want to slow down and savor.

Approaching Flagstaff from the east, I-40 parallels Old Route 66. Their paths diverge at Enterprise Rd: I-40 veers southwest, while Old Route 66 curls northwest, hugging the railroad tracks, and is the main drag through the historic downtown. NAU sits between downtown and I-40. From downtown, I-17 heads south toward Phoenix, splitting off at Hwy 89A (also known as Alt 89), a spectacularly scenic winding road through Oak Creek Canyon to Sedona. Hwy 180 is the most direct route northwest to Tusayan and the South Rim (80 miles), while Hwy 89 beelines north to Cameron (59 miles), where it meets Hwy 64 heading west to the canyon's East Entrance.

Flagstaff

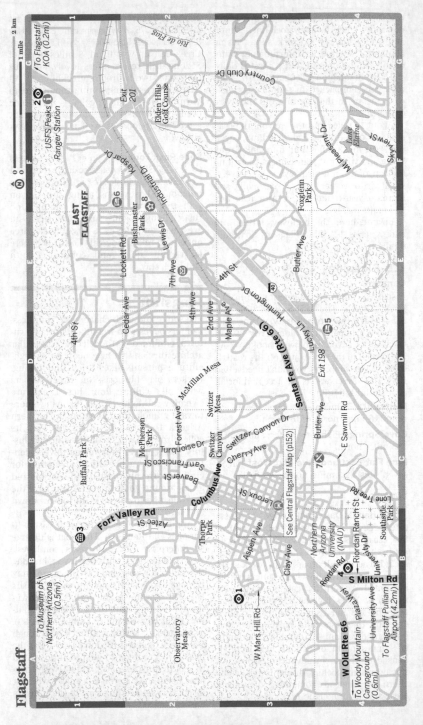

EAST FLAGSTAFF

To Flagstaff KOA (0.2mi)

Rio de Flag

Exit 201

Elden Hills Golf Course

Country Club Dr

USFS Peaks Ranger Station

2

Kaspar Dr

Industrial Dr

Bushmaster Park

Lewis Dr

Lockett Rd

6

8

Lake Elaine

Mt Pleasant Dr

Foxglenn Park

Skyview St

4th St

7th Ave

4th Ave

Cedar Ave

2nd Ave

Maple Ave

4th St

Huntington Dr

Santa Fe Ave (Rte 66)

Butler Ave

Butler Ave

Lucky Ln

Exit 198

5

4

McMillan Mesa

Switzer Mesa

Switzer Canyon

Switzer Canyon Dr

Cherry Ave

Forest Ave

Turquoise Dr

McPherson Park

San Francisco St

Beaver St

Columbus Ave

Buffalo Park

Fort Valley Rd

Aztec St

Thorpe Park

Leroux St

See Central Flagstaff Map (p152)

Northern Arizona University (NAU)

Riordan Ranch St

University Dr

Lone Tree Rd

E Sawmill Rd

Butler Ave

7

Southside Park

3

To Museum of Northern Arizona (0.5mi)

Observatory Mesa

W Mars Hill Rd

1

Aspen Ave

Clay Ave

W Old Rte 66

Riordan Rd

S Milton Rd

University Ave

University Way

Plaza

To Woody Mountain Campground (0.6mi)

To Flagstaff Pulliam Airport (4.2mi)

2 km
1 mile

0
0

Flagstaff

◉ Sights

With its wonderful mix of cultural sites, historic downtown and access to outdoorsy pursuits, it's hard not to fall for Flagstaff.

Museum of Northern Arizona MUSEUM
(off Map p150; ☎928-774-5213; www.musnaz.org; 3101 N Fort Valley Rd; adult/child/senior $7/4/6; ◷9am-5pm) This small but excellent museum features exhibits on local Native American archaeology, history and culture, as well as geology, biology and the arts. Don't miss the extensive collection of Hopi kachina (also spelled katsina, p524) dolls and a wonderful variety of Native American basketry and ceramics.

Riordan Mansion State Historic Park HISTORIC SITE
(Map p150; ☎928-779-4395; www.azstateparks.com/Parks/RIMA; 409 W Riordan Rd; adult/child $7/3; ◷9:30am-5pm May-Oct, 10:30am-5pm Nov-Apr) Having made a fortune from their Arizona Lumber Company, brothers Michael and Timothy Riordan had the house built in 1904. The Craftsman-style design was the brainchild of architect Charles Whittlesey, who also designed El Tovar on the South Rim. The exterior features hand-split wooden shingles, log-slab siding and rustic stone. Filled with Edison, Stickley, Tiffany and Steinway furniture, the interior is a shrine to Arts and Crafts. Visitors are welcome to walk the grounds and picnic, but entrance to the house is by guided tour only. Tours leave daily and on the hour; advance reservations are accepted.

Lowell Observatory OBSERVATORY
(Map p150; ☎928-774-3358; www.lowell.edu; 1400 W Mars Hill Rd; adult/child $6/3; ◷9am-5pm Mar-Oct, noon-5pm Nov-Feb, call for evening hours) This national historic landmark was built in 1894 by Percival Lowell. The observatory has witnessed many important discoveries, the most famous of which was the first sighting of Pluto – in 1930 through the 1896 24-inch Clark Telescope. In the '60s NASA used the Clark telescope to map the moon. Weather permitting, visitors can stargaze through the telescope; check the website for the evening schedule. The short, paved Pluto Walk climbs through a scale model of our solar system, providing descriptions of each planet. You can stroll the grounds and museum on your own, but the only way to see the telescopes and lovely observatories is on a tour (on the hour from 10am to 4pm in summer; on the hour from 1pm to 4pm in winter).

Arboretum GARDENS
(☎928-774-1442; 4001 S Woody Mountain Rd; www.thearb.org; adult/child $7/3; ◷9am-5pm Apr-Oct; ♿) The Arboretum is a lovely spot to rejuvenate your spirit and enjoy a picnic. Two short wood-chip trails enfold a meadow and wind beneath ponderosa pines, passing an herb garden, native plants, vegetables and wildflowers. The Arboretum offers tours (11am, 1pm and 3pm), as well as a summer adventure program for children aged four to 12. From Route 66 west of Milton Ave, follow Woody Mountain Rd 3.8 miles south – most of this stretch is unpaved but it should be driveable for most cars.

Pioneer Museum MUSEUM
(Map p150; ☎928-774-6272; www.arizonahistoricalsociety.org/museums/flagstaff.asp; 2340 N Fort Valley Rd; adult/child $5/free; ◷9am-5pm Mon-Sat) Housed in the old 1908 hospital, this museum preserves Flagstaff's early history in photographs and an eclectic mix of memorabilia, including a piece of luggage recovered from Bessie and Glenn Hyde's ill-fated honeymoon trip down the Grand Canyon's Colorado River in 1928.

🏃 Activities
Hiking & Biking
Ask at the USFS ranger stations for maps and information about the scores of hiking and mountain-biking trails in and around Flagstaff. Another useful resource is *Flagstaff Hikes: 97 Day Hikes Around Flagstaff*,

Central Flagstaff

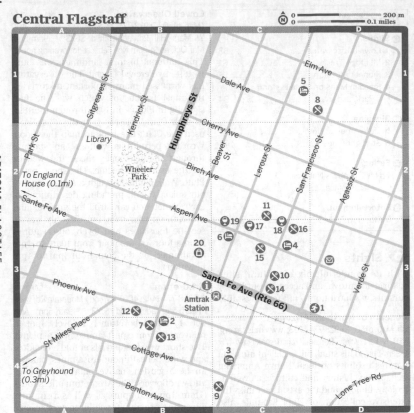

by Richard and Sherry Mangum (Hexagon Press, 2007); available at the visitor center and Babbitt's Backcountry Outfitter, among other places.

Consider tackling the steep, 3-mile one-way hike up 9299ft **Mt Elden** to the ranger station at the top of the peak's tower, which has stairs you can climb to the ranger's lookout. Arizona Snowbowl offers several trails, including the strenuous 4.5-mile one-way hike up 12,633ft **Humphreys Peak**, the highest point in Arizona; wear decent boots as sections of the trail cross crumbly volcanic rock. In summer, ride the scenic **chairlift** (adult/child $12/8; ⊗10am-4pm Fri-Sun, Mon hols Memorial Day-Labor Day) at Arizona Snowbowl to 11,500ft, where you can hike, attend ranger talks and take in the desert and mountain views. Children under eight ride for free.

There's also a beautiful stretch of the Arizona Trail running through the area. If you head toward Walnut Canyon (p158), you'll see a turnoff on the right leading to the **Walnut Canyon Trailhead**. Drive 1.7 miles down the graded dirt road and you'll come to the trailhead. There are no restrooms, no water, no nothin' – come prepared with a map and supplies if you want to do the Fisher Point Trail (6.7 miles one way) or hike up to Marshall Lake (13.4 miles one way).

For an inside track on the local mountain-biking scene, check out the super-friendly gearheads at **Absolute Bikes** (Map p152; ☏928-779-5969; www.absolutebikes.net; 202 E Rte 66; bike rentals per day from $40; ⊗9am-7pm Mon-Fri, 10am-6pm Sat, 10am-4pm Sun). Though Flagstaff is blessed with several excellent bike shops, this is the only one that offers rentals.

Central Flagstaff

Other Activities

If you can't guess by glancing around at the townsfolk, Flagstaff is full of active citizens. So there's no shortage of outdoor stores and places to buy or rent camping, cycling and skiing equipment. For ski rentals, swing by **Peace Surplus** (Map p152; 14 W Rte 66).

Arizona Snowbowl SKIING
(☎928-779-1951; www.arizonasnowbowl.com; Hwy 180 & Snowbowl Rd; lift ticket adult/child $49/26; ☺9am-4pm) About 7 miles north of downtown, AZ Snowbowl is small but lofty, with four lifts that service 30 ski runs between 9200ft and 11,500ft.

Flagstaff Nordic Center SKIING
(☎928-220-0550; www.flagstaffnordiccenter.com; Mile Marker 232, Hwy 180; weekend/weekday from $16/10; ☺9am-4pm weather permitting) Fifteen miles north of Flagstaff, the Nordic Center offers 30 groomed trails for cross-country

skiing, as well as lessons, rentals and food. Past the Nordic Center off Hwy 180 you'll find plenty of USFS cross-country skiing pullouts, where you can park and ski for free.

Northern Arizona Trail Rides HORSEBACK RIDING
(☎928-225-1538; www.northernarizonaridingstables.com; 9215 Old Munds Hwy; 1/1½/2hr rides $35/55/75) On your way to the Grand Canyon but have an extra day in Flagstaff? Try this friendly company for a short ride. Reservations are helpful, but they may be able to fit you in last minute – call 'em and see!

🛏 Sleeping

Dozens of nondescript, independent motels, with rates ranging from $30 to $50, line Old Route 66 and the railroad tracks east of downtown (exit 198 off I-40). Check the room before you pay – some are much worse than others. For the money, you're far better off at one of the hostels or historic hotels downtown.

Chain motels and hotels line Milton Rd, Beulah Blvd and Forest Meadows St, clustering around exit 198 off I-40.

CAMPING

Free dispersed camping is permitted in the national forest surrounding Flagstaff. Also check out p149 for information about USFS campgrounds in Oak Creek Canyon, 15 to 30 miles south of town.

Woody Mountain Campground CAMPGROUND
(off Map p150; ☎928-774-7727, 800-732-7986; www.woodymountaincampground.com; 2727 W Rte 66; tent/RV sites $20/$30; ☺Mar-Oct; @🗢⛽) Has 146 sites, playground and coin laundry; off I-40 at exit 191.

Flagstaff KOA CAMPGROUND
(off Map p150; ☎928-526-9926, 800-562-3524; www.flagstaffkoa.com; 5803 N Hwy 89; tent sites $26-33, RV sites $33-44; ☺year-round; 🗢) This big campground lies a mile north of I-40 off exit 201, 5 miles northeast of downtown. A path leads from the campground to trails at Mt Elden.

LODGING

TOP CHOICE Inn at 410 B&B $$-$$$
(Map p152; ☎928-774-0088; www.inn410.com; 410 N Leroux St; r $125-200; 🅿@) This elegant and fully renovated 1894 house offers nine spacious, beautifully decorated and themed bedrooms, each with a refrigerator and

private bathroom. Many rooms have four-poster beds and views of the garden or the San Francisco Peaks. A short stroll from downtown, the inn has a shady garden with fruit trees and a cozy dining room, where the full gourmet breakfast and afternoon snacks are served.

England House
B&B $$

(off Map p152; ☎928-214-7350; www.englandhousebandb.com; 614 W Santa Fe Ave; r $129-199; ✳@🅰) This Flagstaff B&B has a distinctive stone exterior made of local Moenkopi and Coconino sandstones. Even more elegant is the meticulously designed interior, from the original stamped-tin ceilings to the carefully curated antique French furniture. Gourmet meals are healthy and delicious.

Starlight Pines
B&B $$

(Map p150; ☎928-527-1912; www.starlightpinesbb.com; 3380 E Lockett Rd; r $135-189; ✳@🅰) Starlight Pines has four spacious rooms in a Victorian-style house, each decorated with Tiffany-style lamps, antique clawfoot tubs, Stickley chairs and other lovely touches. Your hosts, Michael and Richard, are as welcoming and warm as the house itself and are happy to give travel advice on the canyon and local attractions.

Comfi Cottages
BUNGALOW $$

(☎928-774-0731; www.comficottages.com; cottages $140-285; 🅰🚼🐾) These bungalows, which are spread out in residential areas around town, are all less than a mile from the historic district. Most were built in the 1920s and '30s and have a homey feel to them, with wood floors, Craftsman-style kitchens and little lawns. Cabinets are filled with breakfast foods, and each cottage includes a TV, VCR, telephone, bicycles, tennis rackets, a BBQ grill, a picnic table and picnic baskets.

Arizona Mountain Inn
CABIN $$-$$$

(☎928-774-8959; www.arizonamountaininn.com; 4200 Lake Mary Rd; cabins $130-230; 🚼🐾) With cute cabins tucked here and there in a peaceful, sun-dappled pine grove, this place brings to mind a magical village in a book about hobbits and wood nymphs. Hobbits aside, the sturdy but stylish cabins here come with porches, kitchens, grills and wood-burning fireplaces. They don't have TVs or wi-fi. There are three B&B-style rooms inside the adjacent inn, and guests there enjoy an extended continental breakfast. Dogs OK for a small fee.

Grand Canyon International Hostel
HOSTEL $

(Map p152; ☎928-779-9421; www.grandcanyonhostel.com; 19½ S San Francisco St; dm $18-20, r with shared bath $36-43, both incl breakfast; ✳@🅰) Housed in a historic building with hardwood floors and Southwestern decor, this bright, homey hostel offers private rooms or dorms with a four-person maximum. It has a slightly more mellow feel than the DuBeau, which is owned by the same proprietors. The kitchens are spotless, and there's a TV room with a video library.

DuBeau Hostel
HOSTEL $

(Map p152; ☎928-774-6731; www.grandcanyonhostel.com; 19 W Phoenix Ave; dm $21-24, r $46-66, both incl breakfast; ✳@🅰🚼) This independent hostel offers the same friendly service and clean, well-run accommodations as the Grand Canyon International Hostel. There are also laundry facilities and bright kitchens. Convivial common areas include a non-smoking lounge with a fireplace, as well as a jukebox, foosball and pool table – it's a bit livelier over here.

Weatherford Hotel
HOTEL $-$$

(Map p152; ☎928-779-1919; www.weatherfordhotel.com; 23 N Leroux St; r with shared bath $49-79, r with private bath $89-139; ✳🅰) This historic three-story brick hotel offers 11 charmingly decorated rooms with a turn-of-the-20th-century feel. Three of the rooms are newly renovated and incorporate modern amenities such as TVs, phones and air-conditioning. Since the Weatherford's three bars often feature live music, it can get noisy; if you need silence for sleeping, consider staying elsewhere. If you do stay, note that there's a 2am curfew.

Hotel Monte Vista
HOTEL $-$$

(Map p152; ☎928-779-6971; www.hotelmontevista.com; 100 N San Francisco St; d $65-130, ste $120-175; 🅰) A huge, old-fashioned neon sign towers over this allegedly haunted 1926 hotel, hinting at what's inside: feather lampshades, vintage furniture, bold colors and eclectic decor. Rooms are named for the movie stars who slept in them, such as the Humphrey Bogart room, with dramatic black walls, yellow ceiling and gold-satin bedding. Several resident ghosts supposedly make regular appearances. Though lacking in high-end amenities, the Monte Vista's appeal comes from all of its glorious funkiness.

Little America Hotel
MOTEL $$

(Map p150; ☎928-779-7900; http://flagstaff.little america.com; 2515 E Butler Ave; r $119-159, ste $269-349; ❋➔❋⊞) When you reach the Sinclair truck stop, don't drive away thinking you have the wrong place. A little further down the side-driveway is a sprawling boutique-style motel with spacious rooms, immaculately decorated in French Provincial style and furnished with goose-down bedding, refrigerators and large bathrooms.

✖ Eating

TOP CHOICE Criollo Latin Kitchen
FUSION $$

(Map p152; ☎928-774-0541; www.criollolatin kitchen.com; 16 N San Francisco St; mains $13-30; ⊙11am-10pm Mon-Thu, 11am-11pm Fri, 9am-11pm Sat, 9am-2pm & 4-10pm Sun) This Latin fusion spot has a romantic, industrial setting for cozy cocktail dates and delectable late night small plates, but the blue-corn blueberry pancakes make a strong argument for showing up for brunch on weekends. The food is sourced locally and sustainably whenever possible, and the wine list is divine.

Diablo Burger
BURGERS $

(Map p152, www.diabloburger.com, 120 N Leroux St; mains under $12; ⊙11am-9pm Mon-Wed, 11am-10pm Thu-Sat) The beef maestros at this gourmet burger joint are so proud of their creations they sear the DB brand onto the English-muffin bun. The cheddar-topped Blake gives a nod to New Mexico with Hatch chile mayo and roasted green chiles. Diablo uses locally produced ingredients and includes a 'terroir-ist's manifesto' on the menu. The place is tiny, four tables inside and a few bar seats (they serve microbrews, wine and milkshakes), so come early. Cash only.

Beaver Street Brewery
BREWPUB $$

(Map p152; www.beaverstreetbrewery.com; 11 S Beaver St; lunch $8-10, dinner $10-12; ⊙11am-11pm Sun-Thu, 11am-midnight Fri & Sat) This place packs them all in – families, river guides, ski bums and businesspeople. The menu is typical brewpub fare, with delicious pizzas, burgers and salads, and there's usually five handmade beers on tap, like its Railhead Red Ale or R&R Oatmeal Stout, plus some seasonal brews. Serious drinkers can walk next door to play pool at the 21-and-over Brews & Cues. Nightly dinner specials run between $13 and $16.

Macy's
CAFE $

(Map p152; www.macyscoffee.net; 14 S Beaver St; mains $3-7; ⊙6am-8pm Mon-Wed, to 10pm Thu-Sun; ☞🖉) The delicious house-roasted coffee at this Flagstaff institution has kept the city buzzing for over 30 years now. The vegetarian menu includes many vegan choices, along with traditional cafe grub like pastries, steamed eggs, bagels, yogurt and granola. A coin laundry is sandwiched between here and La Bellavia, so you can pop in a load and relax with your latte and book. Macy's is cash only.

Pato Thai Cuisine
THAI $$

(Map p152; ☎928-213-1825; www.patothai.com; 104 N San Francisco St; mains $7-14; ⊙11am-9:30pm Mon-Sat, noon-8:30pm Sun) Pato Thai welcomes guests into a warmly-hued dining room redolent with galangal, Thai basil and lemongrass. The attractive environs are matched by well executed, authentic Thai cuisine with a few Chinese dishes thrown in for good measure. The spiciness level is adjusted to your taste (err on the mild side).

Fratelli Pizza
PIZZERIA $$

(Map p152; www.fratellipizza.net; 119 W Phoenix; mains $10-20, slices $2.50; ⊙10:30am-9pm Sun-Thu, to midnight Fri & Sat) Consistently voted Flagstaff's best pizza joint, Fratelli still pulls them in with its handmade, stone oven-baked pizza. Sauce choices include red, BBQ, pesto and white, and toppings range from standard pepperoni to grilled chicken, walnuts, artichoke hearts and cucumber.

MartAnne's Burrito Palace
MEXICAN $

(Map p152; 10 N San Francisco St; mains $7-10; ⊙7:30am-2pm Mon-Fri, 8:30am-1pm Sun) For those about to diet, we salute you. For those about to dig into a *fratelliquile*, a pork-and-scrambled-eggs burrito smothered in green chile, green onions and cheese, we embrace you and call you friend. For we, too, understand the power of its goodness. MartAnne's, a snug hole-in-the-wall with sassy Day of the Dead decor, checkered floors and bright coffee mugs, is locally beloved. Cash only.

La Bellavia
BREAKFAST $

(Map p152; 18 S Beaver St; mains $4-9; ⊙6:30am-2pm) Be prepared to wait in line at this popular, cash-only breakfast spot. The seven-grain French toast with bananas, apples or blueberries is excellent; or try one of their egg dishes, such as eggs sardo, with sautéed spinach and artichoke hearts. Lunch includes a grilled portobello-mushroom sandwich and a grilled salmon salad, as well as standard options like grilled cheese, burgers and a tuna melt.

Brix
AMERICAN $$$

(Map p152; ☎928-213-1021; www.brixflagstaff.com; 413 N San Francisco St; mains $23-34; ☺11am-2pm & 5-9pm Mon-Fri, 5-9pm Sat) Situated in a renovated brick carriage house, Brix brings a breath of fresh, unpretentious sophistication to Flagstaff's dining scene. The menu varies seasonally, using to delicious advantage what is fresh and ripe, and sometimes organic, for classics like salade Niçoise and roasted rack of lamb. Reservations are highly recommended.

Café Olé
MEXICAN $-$$

(Map p152; ☎928-774-8272; 119 S San Francisco St; mains $6-12; ☺11am-3pm & 5-8pm Tue-Sat; ☎) Food at this bright and friendly family-run place veers towards New Mexican-style, featuring green and red chile sauce.

Mountain Oasis
INTERNATIONAL $$

(Map p152; ☎928-214-9270; 11 E Aspen; mains $9-19; ☺11am-9pm; ✐) Vegetarians and vegans will find a bunch of options on this internationally spiced menu. Tasty specialties include the TBLT (tempeh bacon, lettuce and tomato), and Thai veggies and tofu with peanut sauce and brown rice. Steak and chicken are also featured on the menu at this relaxed, plant-filled oasis.

For groceries, **Bashas'** (☎928-774-3882; www.bashas.com; 2700 S Woodlands Village Blvd; ☺5am-11pm) is a good local chain supermarket with a respectable selection of organic foods. Our favorite health-food market is **New Frontiers Natural Marketplace** (Map p150; ☎928-774-5747; 320 S Cambridge Lane; mains $4-10; ☺8am-9pm Mon-Sat, 8am-8pm Sun; ✐) good for cobbling together healthy picnics.

Drinking

Pay 'n Take
BAR

(Map p152; www.payntake.com; 12 W Aspen Ave; ☺7am-10pm Mon-Wed, 7am-1am Thu-Sat, 9am-10pm Sun; ☎) This kickback spot has a great bar where you can enjoy a beer or a coffee. Help yourself to whatever you'd like from the wall refrigerators, and take it to one of the small tables inside or on the back patio. You can even have pizza delivered or bring takeout. Free wi-fi.

Cuvee 928
WINE BAR

(Map p152; ☎928-214-9463; www.cuvee928winebar.com; 6 W Aspen Ave, Suite 110; ☺11:30am-9pm Mon-Tue, to 10pm Wed-Sat) This wine bar on Heritage Square makes a pleasant venue for people-watching as well as wine tasting. It has a relaxed but upscale ambience, well-rounded menu and full bar.

Late for the Train
COFFEE SHOP

(Map p152; www.lateforthetrain.com; 107 N San Francisco St; mains $2-6; ☺6am-6pm Sun-Thu, 6am-9pm Fri & Sat; ☎) Beans are roasted in-house, so the coffee and espresso drinks are some of the best in town. But on those really frigid winter days, try the habanero hot cocoa.

☆ Entertainment

Flagstaff hosts all sorts of festivals and music programs; call the visitor center or log on to its website for details. On summer weekends, people gather on blankets for fun evenings at Heritage Square. Live music starts at 6:30pm, followed at 9pm by a kid-friendly movie projected on an adjacent building.

Pick up free local rag *Flagstaff Live!* or check out www.flaglive.com for current shows and happenings around town.

Charly's Pub & Grill
LIVE MUSIC

(Map p152; ☎928-779-1919; www.weatherfordhotel.com; 23 N Leroux St; ☺8am-10pm) This restaurant at the Weatherford Hotel has regular live music. Its fireplace and brick walls provide a cozy setting for the blues, jazz and folk played here. Head upstairs to stroll the wraparound verandah outside the popular third-floor Zane Grey Ballroom, which overlooks the historic district. Inside, check out the 1882 bar, fireplace and original Thomas Moran painting.

Monte Vista Cocktail Lounge
MUSIC

(Map p152; ☎928-779-6971; www.hotelmontevista.com; Hotel Monte Vista, 100 N San Francisco St; ☺from 4pm) In the Hotel Monte Vista; this hopping lounge hosts DJs most nights, and on weekends welcomes diverse bands, from country to hip-hop to rock.

Museum Club
BAR

(Map p150; ☎928-526-9434; www.themuseumclub.com; 3404 E Rte 66; ☺11am-2am Mon-Sat, to 9pm Sun) Housed in a 1931 taxidermy museum (hence its nickname, 'the zoo'), this log cabin-style club has been a roadhouse since 1936. Today, its Route 66 vibe, country music and spacious wooden dance floor attract a lively crowd.

ℹ Information

Coconino National Forest Supervisor's Office (☎928-527-3600; www.fs.fed.us/r3/coconino; 1824 S Thompson St; ☺8am-4:30pm Mon-Fri) For information on hiking, biking and camping in the surrounding national forest.

Flagstaff Medical Center (☎928-779-3366; www.flagstaffmedicalcenter.com; 1200 N Beaver St; ☺emergency 24hr)

Police station (☎928-779-3646; 911 E Sawmill Rd; ☺emergency 24hr)

Post office (☎928-714-9302; 104 N Agassiz St; ☺9am-5pm Mon-Fri, to 1pm Sat)

USFS Flagstaff Ranger Station (☎928-526-0866; 5075 N Hwy 89; ☺8am-4:30pm Mon-Fri) Provides information on the Mt Elden, Humphreys Peak and O'Leary Peak areas north of Flagstaff.

Visitor center (☎928-774-9541, 800-379-0065; www.flagstaffarizona.org; 1 E Rte 66; ☺8am-5pm Mon-Sat, 9am-4pm Sun) Inside the Amtrak station, the visitor center has a great Flagstaff Discovery map and tons of information on things to do.

ℹ Getting There & Away

Flagstaff Pulliam Airport is 4 miles south of town off I-17. **US Airways** (☎800-428-4322; www.usairways.com) offers several daily flights from Phoenix Sky Harbor International Airport.

Greyhound (☎928-774-4573, 800-231-2222; www.greyhound.com; 399 S Malpais Ln) stops in Flagstaff en route to/from Albuquerque, Las Vegas, Los Angeles and Phoenix. **Arizona Shuttle** (☎928-226-8060, 877-226-8060; www.arizonashuttle.com) has shuttles that run to the park, Williams and Phoenix Sky Harbor Airport.

Operated by **Amtrak** (☎928-774-8679, 800-872-7245; www.amtrak.com; 1 E Rte 66; ☺3am-10:45pm), the Southwest Chief stops at Flagstaff on its daily run between Chicago and Los Angeles.

ℹ Getting Around

Mountain Line Transit (☎928-779-6624; www.mountainline.az.gov; adult/child $1.25/0.60) services six fixed bus routes daily; pick up a user-friendly map at the visitor center. Those with disabilities can use the company's on-call VanGo service.

If you need a taxi, call **A Friendly Cab** (☎928-774-4444) or **Sun Taxi** (☎928-779-1111). Several major car-rental agencies operate from the airport and downtown; see p560.

Around Flagstaff

CAMERON

A tiny, windswept community 32 miles east of the park's East Entrance and 54 miles north of Flagstaff, Cameron sits on the western edge of the Navajo Reservation. There's not much to it; in fact, the town basically comprises just the **Cameron Trading Post & Motel** (☎928-679-2231; www.camerontradingpost.com; RV sites $15, r $99-109, ste $149-179; ❄☎). In the early 1900s Hopis and Navajos came to the trading post to barter wool, blankets and livestock for flour, sugar and other goods. Today visitors can browse a large selection of quality Native American crafts, including Navajo rugs, basketry, jewelry and pottery, and plenty of kitschy knickknacks.

Spacious rooms, many with balconies, feature hand-carved furniture and a Southwestern motif. RV sites offer hookups, and you can dine at **Cameron Trading Post Dining Room** (☎928-679-2231; mains $9-23; ☺6am-10pm), a good place to try the Navajo taco (fried dough with whole beans, ground beef, chile and cheese).

SUNSET CRATER VOLCANO NATIONAL MONUMENT

Covered by a single $5 entrance fee (valid for seven days), both Sunset Crater Volcano and Wupatki National Monument lie along Park Loop Rd 545, a well-marked 36-mile loop that heads east off Hwy 89 about 12 miles north of Flagstaff, then rejoins the highway 26 miles north of Flagstaff.

In AD 1064 a volcano erupted on this spot, spewing ash over 800 sq miles, spawning the Kana-A lava flow and leaving behind 8029ft **Sunset Crater**. The eruption forced farmers to vacate lands they had cultivated for 400 years; subsequent eruptions continued for more than 200 years. The **visitor center** (☎928-526-0502; www.nps.gov/sucr; admission $5; ☺visitor center 8am-5pm May-Oct, 9am-5pm Nov-Apr, monument sunrise-sunset) houses a seismograph and other exhibits pertaining to volcanology, while viewpoints and a 1-mile interpretive trail through the **Bonito lava flow** (formed c 1180) grant visitors a firsthand look at volcanic features; a shorter 0.3-mile loop is wheelchair accessible. You can also climb **Lenox Crater** (7024ft), a 1-mile round-trip that climbs 300ft. More ambitious hikers and mountain-bikers can ascend **O'Leary**

Peak (8965ft; 8 miles round-trip), the only way to peer down into Sunset Crater (aside from scenic flights).

Across from the visitor center, the USFS-run **Bonito Campground** (☑928-526-0866; tent & RV sites $18; ☺May–mid-Oct) provides running water and restrooms but no showers or hookups.

WUPATKI NATIONAL MONUMENT

The first eruptions here enriched the surrounding soil, and ancestors of today's Hopi, Zuni and Navajo people returned to farm the land in the early 1100s. By 1180 thousands were living here in advanced multistory buildings, but by 1250 their pueblos stood abandoned. About 2700 of these structures lie within **Wupatki National Monument** (☑928-679-2365; www .nps.gov/wupa; admission $5; ☺9am-5pm), though only a few are open to the public. A short self-guided tour of the largest dwelling, **Wupatki Pueblo**, begins behind the visitor center. **Lamaki**, **Citadel** and **Nalakihu Pueblos** sit within a half-mile of the loop road just north of the visitor center, and a 2.5-mile road veers west from the center to **Wukoki Pueblo**, the best preserved of the buildings. In April and October rangers lead visitors on a 16-mile round-trip weekend backpacking tour ($50; supply your own food and gear) of **Crack-in-Rock Pueblo** and nearby petroglyphs. Chosen by lottery, only 13 people may join each tour; apply two months in advance via the website or in writing.

WALNUT CANYON NATIONAL MONUMENT

The Sinagua cliff dwellings at **Walnut Canyon** (☑928-526-3367; www.nps.gov/waca; admission $5, valid for 7 days; ☺8am-5pm May-Oct, 9am-5pm Nov-Apr) are set in the nearly vertical walls of a small limestone butte amid this forested canyon. The mile-long **Island Trail** steeply descends 185ft (more than 200 stairs), passing 25 rooms built under the natural overhangs of the curvaceous butte. A shorter, wheelchair-accessible **Rim Trail** affords several views of the cliff dwelling from across the canyon. Even if you're not all that interested in the mysterious Sinagua people, whose origins are unknown and whose site abandonments are still not understood today, Walnut Canyon itself is a beautiful place to visit, not so far from Flagstaff.

GRAND CANYON REGION

No matter how much you read about the Grand Canyon or how many photographs you've seen, nothing really prepares you for the sight of it. One of the world's seven natural wonders, it's so startlingly familiar and iconic you can't take your eyes off it. The canyon's immensity, the sheer intensity of light and shadow at sunrise or sunset, even its very age, scream for superlatives.

At about two billion years old – half of Earth's total life span – the layer of Vishnu Schist at the bottom of the canyon is some of the oldest exposed rock on the planet. And the means by which it was exposed is of course the living, mighty Colorado River, which continues to carve its way 277 miles through the canyon as it has for the past six million years.

The three rims of the Grand Canyon offer quite different experiences and, as they lie hundreds of miles and hours of driving apart, they're rarely visited on the same trip. Summer is when most of the visitors arrive (4.38 million in 2010), and 90% of them only visit the South Rim, which offers easy-access viewpoints, historic buildings, Native American ruins and excellent infrastructure. If it's solitude you seek, make a beeline for the remote North Rim (p178). Though it has fewer and less-dramatic viewpoints, its charms are no less abundant: at 8200ft elevation (1000ft higher than the South Rim), its cooler temperatures support wildflower meadows and tall, thick stands of aspen and spruce.

Run by the Hualapai Nation and not part of Grand Canyon National Park, Grand Canyon West (p178) is famous for its Sky-walk, the controversial glass bridge jutting out over the rim that debuted in 2007. Critics consider the Skywalk sacrilege and a harbinger of unwise development on the fragile West Rim, but most agree that its construction will be a much needed financial shot in the arm for the casino-less Hualapai Nation to keep their tribe afloat.

Grand Canyon National Park – South Rim

If you don't mind bumping elbows with other travelers, you'll be fine on the South Rim. This is particularly true in summer when camera-toting day-trippers converge en masse, clogging its roads and easiest

Grand Canyon Region

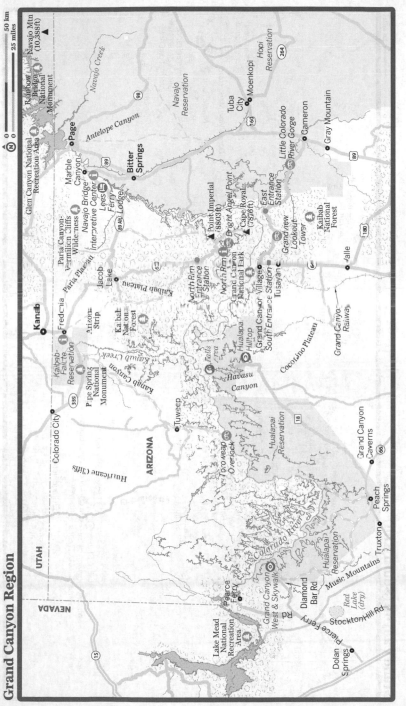

0 50 km
0 25 miles

UTAH
NEVADA
ARIZONA

Lake Mead National Recreation Area

Rainbow Bridge National Monument

Navajo Mtn (10,388ft)

Glen Canyon National Recreation Area

Page

Navajo Creek

Antelope Canyon

Navajo Reservation

Hopi Reservation

264

Moenkopi

Tuba City

160

Gray Mountain

Cameron

Little Colorado River Gorge

89

180

Kaibab National Forest

Valle

Grandview Lookout Tower

East Entrance Station

Cape Royal (7876ft)

Bright Angel Point

Point Imperial 8803ft

Grand Canyon National Park

North Rim

North Rim Entrance Station

Kaibab Plateau

Jacob Lake

67

Grand Canyon Village

South Entrance Station

Tusayan

Grand Canyon Railway

Cocolino Plateau

Coconino Plateau

Hualapai
Hilltop

Falls Area

Havasu Canyon

Kanab Creek

Kaibab National Forest

Arizona Strip

Fredonia

Kanab

Kaibab Paiute Reservation

Pipe Spring National Monument

335

Colorado City

Hurricane Cliffs

Kanab Canyon

Tuweep

Toroweap Overlook

18

Hualapai Reservation

Grand Canyon Caverns

66

Peach Springs

Truxton

Music Mountains

Grand Canyon West & Skywalk

Diamond Bar Rd

Colorado River

Hualapai Reservation

Pearce Ferry

Pierce Ferry Rd

Red Lake (dry)

Stockton Hill Rd

Dolan Springs

15

Marble Canyon

Lees Ferry

Lodge

89Alt

89

Bitter Springs

Paria Canyon-Vermilion Cliffs Wilderness

Navajo Bridge Interpretive Center

Paria Plateau

67

98

Grand Canyon (South Rim)

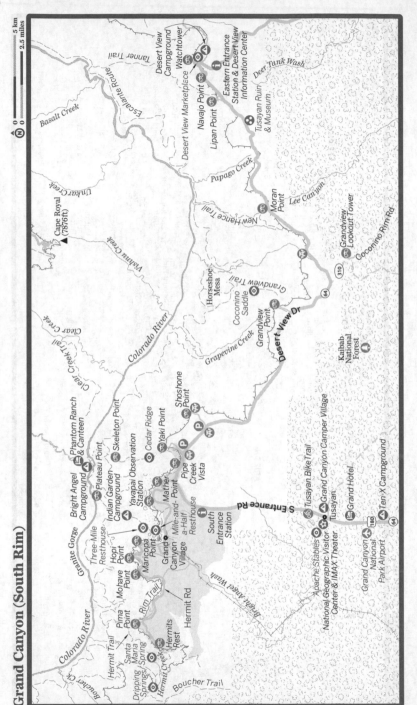

trails. Why is this rim so popular? Easy access is the most obvious reason: it's a mere 60 miles north of the I-40. Abundant infrastructure is another. This is where you'll find an entire village worth of lodging, restaurants, bookstores, libraries, a supermarket and a deli. Shuttles ply two scenic drives, and the flat and paved Rim Trail allows the mobility-impaired and stroller-pushing parents to take in the dramatic, sweeping canyon views.

If you want to venture into the inner gorge you'll have several trails to choose from – or you can just let a mule do the walking. Several museums and historic stone buildings illuminate the park's human history, and rangers lead a host of daily programs on subjects from geology to resurgent condors.

Though the accessibility of the South Rim means sharing your experience with others, there are many ways to commune with the canyon and its wildlife, and enjoy its sublime beauty, one on one. Escaping the crowds can be as easy as taking a day hike below the rim or merely tramping a hundred yards away from a scenic overlook.

Most visitors arrive via the **South Entrance**, 80 miles northwest of Flagstaff on Hwy 64/180. Avoid summer wait times of 30 minutes or more by prepaying your park ticket at the National Geographic Visitor Center in Tusayan (p172), which allows you to cruise smugly through in a special lane. Or arrive at the East Entrance instead. In summer, if you've bought your ticket or have a park pass, you can now hop on the park's Tusayan shuttle at the IMAX Theater in Tusayan and disembark at the Grand Canyon Visitor Center.

A few miles north of the South Entrance, **Grand Canyon Village** (or simply the Village) is the primary hub of activity. Here you'll find lodges, restaurants, two of the three developed campgrounds, backcountry office, visitor center, medical clinic, bank, grocery store, shuttles and other services. Coin-operated showers and laundry facilities are located next to Mather Campground.

West of the Village, **Hermit Rd** follows the rim for 8 miles, ending at Hermit's Rest. Seven pullouts along the way offer spectacular views; from those at Mohave and Hopi Points you can spot three Colorado River rapids. Interpretive signs explain the canyon's features and geology. From March to November the road is closed to private vehicles and accessible only by tour or free shuttle bus.

In the opposite direction, **Desert View Dr** meanders 25 miles to the **East Entrance** on Hwy 64, passing some of the park's finest viewpoints, picnic areas, the Tusayan Ruin & Museum and the Watchtower. A camp ground, snack bar, small information center and general store are in Desert View, right by the entrance. Also here is the park's only gas station, which offers 24-hour pay-at-the-pump service from April to September. Gas stations in Tusayan are closer to the Village and open year-round.

Climate

On average, temperatures are 20°F (about 11°C) cooler on the South Rim than at the bottom of the Grand Canyon. In summer,

GETTING STARTED

Park admission is $25 per vehicle, or $12 per person if arriving on foot or by bicycle; it's valid for seven days at both rims. Bus and train passengers may pay a lesser fee or have it included in the tour price. Upon entering, you'll be given a map and *The Guide*, an incredibly useful newspaper thick with additional maps, the latest park news and information on ranger programs, hikes and park services. It also lists current opening hours of restaurants and businesses.

The Grand Canyon Visitor Center should be your first stop. Recently remodeled, it offers a number of new interpretive exhibits inside the main visitor center building and on the adjacent plaza. In the attached theater, watch the new film *Grand Canyon: Journey of Wonder*, a 20-minute introduction to the park's geology, history and plant and animal life. Take note that you can no longer pull over on the side of the road after entering the park and dash to Mather Point. Traffic is directed away from the rim, passing several new parking lots on its way into Grand Canyon Village. Instead, walk on the new plaza out to Mather Point – where the views are still as amazing.

Likewise, head to **Lonely Planet** (www.lonelyplanet.com/usa/grand-canyon-national-park) for planning advice, author recommendations, traveler reviews and insider tips.

GRAND CANYON SOUTH RIM IN...

One Day

Catch a predawn shuttle to see the sun come up at **Yaki Point**, then head back to the Village for coffee and pastries at the **Deli at Marketplace**. Swing by the **Grand Canyon Visitor Center**, stroll the **Rim Trail** from Mather Point to **Yavapai Observation Station** and the **Trail of Time** exhibit, then make a beeline to **El Tovar Dining Room** to beat the lunchtime crowds. In the afternoon, catch the shuttle to **Hermit's Rest** and hike about 10 minutes down the **Hermit Trail** to look for ancient fossil beds, then catch the sunset at **Hopi Point**.

Two Days

Follow the one-day itinerary, capping the day with dinner in the elegant **Arizona Room** and an overnight stay in the Village (book well ahead). The morning of day two, hike into the canyon on the **South Kaibab Trail**, stopping at **Cedar Ridge** for a picnic. Wrap up your Grand Canyon adventure with a drive east along **Desert View Dr**, stopping at viewpoints, the **Tusayan Ruin & Museum** and the **Watchtower**.

---

expect highs in the 80s and lows around 50°F (highs in the 30s and lows around 10°C). Weather is cooler and more changeable in fall, and snow and freezing overnight temperatures are likely by November. January has average overnight lows in the teens (-10°C to -7°C) and daytime highs around 40°F (4°C) Winter weather can be beautifully clear, but be prepared for snowstorms that can cause havoc.

The inner canyon is much drier, with about eight inches of rain annually, around half that of the South Rim. During summer, temperatures inside the canyon soar above 100°F (40°C) almost daily, often accompanied by strong hot winds. Even in midwinter, the mercury rarely drops to freezing, with average temperatures hovering between 37°F and 58°F (3°C and 14°C).

⊙ Sights

The Grand Canyon's natural splendor is of course the prime draw, but to enrich your trip it pays to visit the park's cultural and architectural sites. Some of the most important buildings were designed by noted architect Mary Jane Colter to complement the landscape and reflect the local culture. Unless otherwise noted, sights are in the Village and they are free.

Yavapai Geology Museum & Observation Station
MUSEUM

(Map p164; ⊗8am-7pm) Views don't get much better than those unfolding behind the plate-glass windows of this little stone building at Yavapai Point, where handy panels identify and explain the various formations before you. Another reason to swing by is the superb geology display that'll deepen your understanding of the canyon's multilayered geological palimpsest. From here, check out the new **Trail of Time** exhibit just west of the Rim Trail. This interpretive display traces the history of the canyon's formation, and every meter equals one million years of geologic history.

Kolb Studio
GALLERY

(Map p164; ⊗8am-7pm) Photographers Ellsworth and Emery Kolb arrived at the Grand Canyon from Pennsylvania in 1902 and made a living photographing parties going down the Bright Angel Trail. Because there was not enough water on the rim to process the film, they had to run 4.5 miles down the trail to a spring at Indian Garden, develop the film and race back up in order to have the pictures ready when the party returned. Eventually, they built a small studio on the edge of the rim, which has since been expanded and now holds a small bookstore and an art gallery with changing exhibits.

Lookout Studio
HISTORIC BUILDING

(Map p164; ⊗8am-sunset) Like Mary Colter's other canyon buildings, Lookout Studio was modeled after stone dwellings of the Southwest Pueblo Native Americans. Made of rough-cut Kaibab limestone, with a roof that mirrors the lines of the rim, the studio blends into its natural surroundings. Inside, you'll find a small souvenir shop and a tiny back porch that offers spectacular canyon views. There's also a stone stairway snaking below Lookout Studio towards another terrace, which is the site of the popular ranger-led Condor Talks.

Hopi House ARCHITECTURE

(Map p164; ⊘8am-8pm) A beautiful Colter-designed stone building, Hopi House has been offering high-quality Native American jewelry, basketwork, pottery and other crafts since its 1904 opening. The structure was built by the Hopi from native stone and wood, inspired by traditional dwellings on their reservation.

Tusayan Ruin & Museum MUSEUM

(⊘9am-5pm) Near the East Entrance, 22 miles east of the Village, you'll come across what's left of the nearly 900-year-old Ancestral Puebloan settlement of Tusayan. Only partially excavated to minimize erosion damage, it's less impressive than other such ruins in the Southwest but still interesting and worth a look. A small musuem displays pottery, jewelry and 4000-year-old twig animal figurines.

Watchtower ARCHITECTURE

Scramble to the top of Colter's stone tower at Desert View and pat yourself on the back for having reached the highest spot on the rim (7522ft). Unparalleled views take in not only the canyon and the Colorado River but also the San Francisco Peaks, the Navajo Reservation and the Painted Desert. The Hopi Room has festive murals depicting the snake legend, a Hopi wedding and other scenes.

🏃 Activities

Hiking

To truly experience the majesty of the canyon, hit the trail. It may look daunting, but there are options for all levels of skill and fitness. Though summer is the most popular season for day hikes – despite oppressively hot 100°F (40°C) plus temperatures below the rim – experienced canyon hikers know that it's much more pleasant to hike in the spring and fall, when there are also significantly fewer visitors.

The easiest and most popular is the **Rim Trail**, which is quite literally a walk in the park. It connects a series of scenic points and historical sights over 13 miles from Pipe Creek Vista to Hermit's Rest. The section of the Rim Trail between Pipe Creek Vista and Maricopa Point is paved, and mostly wheelchair accessible. It's possible to catch a shuttle bus to a viewpoint, walk a stretch,

then catch the next shuttle back or onward. The 3 miles or so winding through the Village are usually packed, but crowds thin out further west.

Heading down into the canyon means negotiating supersteep switchbacks. The most popular is the **Bright Angel Trail**, which is wide, well graded and easy to follow. Starting in the Village, right by Kolb Studio, it's a heavily trafficked route that's equally attractive to first-time canyon hikers, seasoned pros and mule trains. But the din doesn't lessen the sheer beauty. The steep and scenic 7.8-mile descent to the Colorado River is punctuated with four logical turn-around spots, including two resthouses offering shade and water. The first resthouse is about 1.5 miles down the trail, the second is 3 miles. Day hikers and first-timers should strongly consider turning around at one of them or otherwise hitting the trail at dawn to safely make the longer hikes to Indian Garden or Plateau Point (9.2 and 12.2 miles round-trip, respectively). Hiking to the Colorado River for the day is not an option.

One of the park's prettiest trails, the **South Kaibab Trail** combines stunning scenery and adventurous hiking with every step. The only corridor trail to follow a ridgeline, the red-dirt path allows for unobstructed 360-degree views. It's steep, rough and wholly exposed, which is why rangers discourage all but the shortest of day hikes during summer. A good place to turn around is **Cedar Ridge**, reached after about an hour. It's a dazzling spot, particularly at sunrise, when the deep ruddy umbers and reds of each canyon fold seem to glow from within. During the rest of the year, the trek to **Skeleton Point**, 1.5 miles beyond Cedar Ridge, makes for a fine hike – though the climb back up is a beast in any season. The South Kaibab Trailhead is 4.5 miles east of the Village on Yaki Point Rd and can only be reached by shuttle or the Hikers' Express leaving from Bright Angel Lodge around dawn (stopping at the Backcountry Information Center).

One of the steepest trails in the park, dropping 1200ft in the first 0.75 miles, **Grandview Trail** is also one of the finest and most popular hikes. The pay-off is an up-close look at one of the inner canyon's sagebrush-tufted mesas and a spectacular sense of solitude. While rangers don't recommend the trek to **Horseshoe Mesa** (3 miles, four to six

Grand Canyon Village

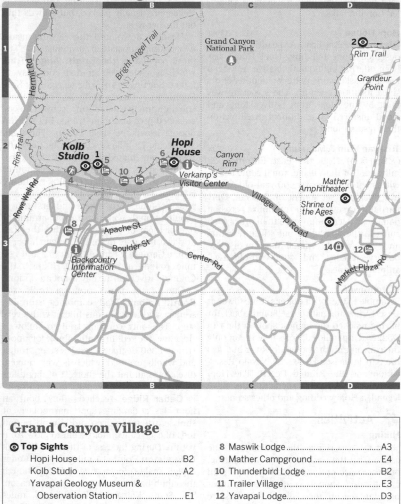

Grand Canyon Village

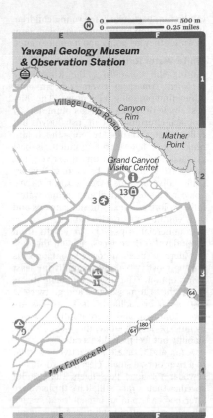

or to **Dripping Springs** via a spur trail (6.5 miles round-trip). The upper section of the Hermit is well shaded in the morning, making it a cool option in summer. The trailhead is at the end of its namesake road, 8 miles west of the Village. Although the road is only accessible via shuttle bus during the summer peak season, overnight backpackers are permitted to park near the trailhead year-round.

Biking

Cyclists have limited options inside the park, as bicycles are only allowed on paved roads and the Greenway Trail. The multi-use Greenway Trail, open to cyclists as well as pedestrians and wheelchairs, stretches about 13 miles from Hermit's Rest all the way to the South Kaibab Trailhead.

Hermit Rd offers a scenic ride west to Hermit's Rest, about 16 miles round-trip from the village. Shuttles ply this road every 10 to 15 minutes between March and November (the rest of the year, traffic is minimal). They are not permitted to pass cyclists, so for the first 4 miles you'll have to pull over each time one drives by. However, starting from the Abyss, a completed section of the Greenway Trail diverges from the road and continues separately all the way to Hermit's Rest.

Alternatively, you could ride out to the East Entrance along Desert View Dr, a 50-mile round-trip from the village. The route is largely shuttle-free but sees a lot of car traffic in summer. Just off Desert View Dr, the 1-mile dirt road to Shoshone Point is an easy, nearly level ride that ends at this secluded panoramic vista, one of the few places to escape South Rim crowds.

Bright Angel Bicycles   BICYCLE RENTAL
(Map p164; ☎928-814-8704; www.bikegrand canyon.com; full-day adult/child $35/25; ⊙8am-6pm May-Sep, 10am-4:30pm Mar-Apr & Oct-Nov, weather permitting) Renting 'comfort cruiser' bikes on the South Rim, the friendly folks here custom-fit each bike to the individual. Rates include helmet and bicycle-lock rental; child trailers also available.

Mule Rides

Due to erosion concerns, the National Park Service (NPS) has limited inner-canyon mule rides to those traveling all the way to Phantom Ranch. Rather than going below the rim, three-hour day trips ($119) now take riders along the rim, through the ponderosa and piñon-and-juniper forest to the

hours) in summer (there's no water on the very exposed trail, and the climb out is a doozy), it's not overly long and certainly doable for strong hikers strapped with a hydration system and hiking early or late in the day. For a shorter but still rewarding option, hike as far as **Coconino Saddle**. Though it's only 1.5 miles round-trip, it packs a quick and precipitous punch as you plunge 1600ft in less than a mile. With the exception of a few short level sections, the Grandview is a rugged, narrow and rocky trail. The trailhead is at Grandview Point, 12 miles east of the Village on Desert View Dr.

The wild **Hermit Trail** descends into pretty Hermit Canyon via a cool spring. It's a rocky trip down, but if you set out early and take it slow, it offers a wonderfully serene hike and glimpses into secluded corners. Day hikers should steer towards **Santa Maria Spring** (5 miles round-trip)

TOP FIVE OVERLOOKS

Mohave Point For a look at the river and three rapids.

Hopi Point Catch huge sunset views.

Lipan Point Creeks, palisades, rapids and sunrises.

Desert View Climb to the top of the Watchtower and wave down at the river.

Yaki Point A favorite point to watch the sunrise warm the canyon's features.

Abyss overlook. Riders dismount to enjoy the view and a snack before heading back to the village.

Overnight trips (one/two people $482/850) and two-night trips (one/two people $701/1170) still follow the Bright Angel Trail to the river, travel east on the River Trail and cross the river on the Kaibab Suspension Bridge. Riders spend the night at Phantom Ranch. It's a 5½-hour, 10-mile trip to Phantom Ranch, and the return trip up the 8-mile South Kaibab Trail is an hour shorter. Overnight trips include dorm accommodations and all meals at Phantom.

Riders must be at least 4ft 7in tall, speak fluent English and weigh no more than 200lbs fully clothed. Personal backpacks, waist packs, purses or bags of any kind are not allowed on the mules. Anything that could possibly fall off and injure someone in the canyon below will be kept for you until you return. For complete regulations and more information, consult the Xanterra website below.

Mule trips are popular and fill up quickly; to book a trip more than 24 hours and up to 13 months in advance, call **Xanterra** (☎888-297-2757, 303-297-2757; www.grandcanyonlodges .com/mule-rides-716.html). If you arrive at the park and want to join a mule trip the following day, ask about availability at the transportation desk at Bright Angel Lodge (your chances are much better during the off season). If the trips are booked, join a waiting list, cross your fingers and show up at the lodge at 6:15am on the day of the trip and hope there's been a cancellation. Or make tracks to the other side of the canyon: mule rides on the North Rim (p178) are usually available the day before the trip.

If you're not planning a mule trip, just watching the wranglers prepare the mules

can be fun, particularly for young children. In summer stop by the mule corral at 8am; in winter they get going about an hour later.

White-Water Rafting

Rafting the Colorado – the King Kong of North American rivers – is an epic, adrenaline-pumping adventure. The biggest single drop at Lava Falls plummets 37 stomach-churning feet in just 300yd. But roller-coaster thrills are only the beginning. The canyon's true grandeur is best grasped looking up from the river, not down from the rim. Its human history comes alive in ruins, wrecks and rock art. You can hike to mystical grottos and waterfalls, explore ethereally lit slot canyons and view wildlife in its native habitat.

Commercial trips vary in length from three days to three weeks and in the type of watercraft used. Motorized pontoon rafts are the most stable and generally the least scary option. The huge inflatable boats seat eight to 16 passengers and go twice as fast as oar or paddle boats. Oar boats are more common, and more exciting. Rowed by an experienced guide, they provide good stability but feel more like a raft.

A fun and intimate alternative is to float in a river dory, a small, elegant hard-shelled rowboat for four passengers that's a lot speedier than a raft. Still, if it's thrills you're after, book a trip in an inflatable raft, which has you, your raft-rat shipmates and a guide paddling all at once.

At night you'll be camping under stars on sandy beaches (gear provided). It's not as primitive as it sounds – guides are legendary not only for their white-water acumen but also for their culinary skills.

It takes about two or three weeks to run the entire 279 miles of river through the canyon. Shorter sections of around 100 miles take four to nine days. Prices listed here are just a sampling of what each company offers.

Arizona Raft Adventures RAFTING
(☎928-786-7238, 800-786-7238; www.azraft.com; 6-day Upper Canyon hybrid trips/paddle trips $1940/2040, 10-day Full Canyon motor trips $2830) This multigenerational family-run outfit offers paddle, oar, hybrid (with opportunities for both paddling and floating) and motor trips.

Arizona River Runners RAFTING
(☎602-867-4866, 800-477-7238; www.raftarizona .com; 6-day Upper Canyon oar trips $1795, 12-day

Full Canyon motor trips $2695) Have been at their game since 1970, offering oar-powered and motorized trips.

SOARS   RAFTING
(☎209-736-4677, 800-346-6277; www.oars.com; 6-day Upper Canyon oar trips $2608, 15-day Full Canyon dory trips $5010) One of the best outfitters out there, OARS offers oar, paddle and dory trips, and offers the option of carbon-offsetting your trip.

Wilderness River Adventures   RAFTING
(☎928-645-3296, 800-992-8022; www.river adventures.com; 6-day Full Canyon motor trips $2135, 12-day Full Canyon oar trips $3520) Also offers hybrid trips that give rafters the chance to paddle or float as on an oar-powered trip.

Ranger-Led Activities
Rangers are fonts of information, which they happily share in free programs. Their talks cover everything from fossils to birds to Native Americans, while their hikes deepen your understanding of the canyon's geology and history. *The Guide* newspaper and the displays outside Grand Canyon Visitor Center list the latest offerings.

☞ Tours
Coach Tours
First-time visitors can keep the overwhelm factor at bay by joining a narrated bus tour. Tours travel west to Hermit's Rest (two hours, $26) and east to Desert View (about four hours, $45; combination tour $58), stopping at key viewpoints. Sunrise and sunset tours are also available. Stop by the

BACKCOUNTRY ACCESS

Most overnight backpacking trips go from the South Rim to the river and then return, because South Rim-to-North Rim trips involve a tedious four- to five-hour shuttle ride. Most people spend two nights below the rim – either two nights at Bright Angel Campground or Indian Garden Campground, or one night at each. If you do arrange a shuttle you could add a night at Cottonwood Campground on the way up to the North Rim. If your time is limited, a one-night trip is also rewarding. If you prefer a bed to a sleeping bag, make reservations at the canyon-bottom Phantom Ranch (p169) at least a year in advance.

Overnight hikes require a **backcountry permit**. The park issued 13,616 backcountry permits in 2009, but demand far exceeds available slots. If you're caught camping in the backcountry without a permit, expect a hefty fine and possible court appearance.

Permits cost $10, plus an additional $5 per person per night, and are required for all backcountry use unless you've got a reservation at Phantom Ranch. The fee is nonrefundable and payable by check or credit card. Reservations are accepted in person or by mail or fax (☎928-638-2125) beginning the first day of the month, four months prior to the planned trip (ie on May 1, request a date in September). Permits faxed on the first day of the month before 5pm are considered first when assigning permits, though not necessarily in the order received (they are randomly assigned a computer-generated number). Be sure to list your second and third choices on the form to improve your odds of snagging a spot. Backcountry rangers read all notes on the forms and will try to meet your order of preference. Faxing your request is the best way to go. You cannot email your permit request.

For detailed instructions and to download the permit request form, go to the park's website (www.nps.gov/grca/planyourvisit/backcountry.htm) and click on the Backcountry Permit Quicklink. Alternatively, contact the **Backcountry Information Center** (☎928-638-7875; fax 928-638-2125; ☺8am-noon & 1-5pm Mon-Fri) and ask them to mail you the form. If you arrive without a permit, hightail it to the center, near Maswik Lodge, and get on the waiting list. You must show up daily at 8am to remain on the list, but you'll likely hear your name called in one to four days, depending on the season and itinerary. For safety reasons, you will not be granted a permit for the day you show up at the office; the earliest would be for the next day.

Email backcountry questions – but not your permit request – to the office at grca_bic@nps.gov. Staff are very helpful.

transportation desk at any lodge, or ask the El Tovar concierge for the latest schedule and tickets. Kids under 16 ride for free.

Flyovers

At press time, more than 300 flyovers of the Grand Canyon were departing daily from Tusayan and Las Vegas. However, the NPS and the Federal Aviation Administration were inviting public comments on a draft environmental impact report in June 2011, which may have implications for the number or existence of scenic flyovers at Grand Canyon National Park. Flights have already been restricted in number, altitude and routes to reduce noise pollution affecting the experience of other visitors and wildlife.

Contact the following companies for specific rates, as each offers several options.

Grand Canyon Airlines (☎866-235-9422, 928-638-2359; www.grandcanyonairlines.com)

Grand Canyon Helicopters (☎928-638-2764, 702-835-8477; www.grandcanyonhelicopters az.com)

Maverick Helicopters (☎888-261-4414; www.maverickhelicopter.com)

Papillon Grand Canyon Helicopters (☎888-635-7272, 702-736-7243; www.papillon .com)

Scenic Airlines (☎866-235-9422; www.scenic .com)

🛏 Sleeping

Pitch a tent in one of three campgrounds or enjoy a solid roof in one of the six hotels ranging from no-frill motels to luxurious lodges. **Xanterra** (☎303-297-2757, 888-297-2757; www.grandcanyonlodges.com) operates all park lodges, as well as Trailer Village. Reservations are accepted up to 13 months in advance and should be made as early as possible. For same-day bookings call the **South Rim Switchboard** (☎928-638-2631). Summer rates we've quoted below usually drop by 10% or 20% in winter. Children under 16 stay free, but cribs and cots are $10 per day.

If everything in the park is booked up, consider Tusayan (7 miles south; p172), Valle (30 miles south; p173) or Williams (60 miles south; p174). Campers can pitch a tent for free in the surrounding Kaibab National Forest (p174).

Camping

The **National Park Service** (☎877-444-6777, international 518-885-3639; www.recreation.gov)

operates Mather and Desert View Campgrounds. Reservations for Mather are accepted up to six months in advance, up until the day before your arrival. From mid-November through February sites at Mather Campground are first-come, first-served.

Desert View Campground   CAMPGROUND $
(Map p160; campsites $12; ⊙May–mid-Oct) In a piñon-juniper forest near the East Entrance, this first-come, first-served campground is quieter than Mather Campground in the Village, with nicely spread-out sites that ensure a bit of privacy. The best time to secure a spot is midmorning, when people are breaking camp. Facilities include toilets and drinking water, but no showers or hookups.

Mather Campground   CAMPGROUND $
(Map p164; www.recreation.gov; Grand Canyon Village; campsites $18; ⊙year-round) Sites are shaded and fairly well dispersed, and the flat ground offers a comfy platform for your tent. You'll find pay showers, laundry facilities, drinking water, toilets, grills and a small general store; a full grocery store is a short walk away. Reservations are accepted from March through mid-November; the rest of the year it's first-come, first-served. Walk or bike in for $6 sites. No hookups.

Trailer Village   CAMPGROUND $
(Map p164; ☎888-297-2757, same-day reservations 928-638-2631; www.xanterra.com; Grand Canyon Village; campsites $32; ⊙year-round) As the name implies, this is basically a trailer park with RVs lined up tightly at paved pull-through sites amid a rather barren, dry patch of ground. Check for spots with trees on the far north side. You'll find picnic tables and barbecue grills, but showers are a quarter-mile away at Mather Campground.

Stays at any of the three campgrounds below the rim require a backcountry overnight permit (see p167). **Indian Garden Campground** has 15 sites and is 4.6 miles down the Bright Angel Trail, while **Bright Angel Campground** is on the canyon floor near Phantom Ranch, some 9.3 miles via the Bright Angel Trail. Both are ranger-staffed and have water and toilets. **Cottonwood Campground** is halfway up the North Kaibab Trail to the North Rim, about 16.6 miles from the South Rim; see p191.

Lodges

With the exception of Phantom Ranch, which sits on the canyon floor, all of the lodges listed below are located in Grand Canyon Village. All lodges are booked through **Xanterra** (📞303-297-2757, 888-297-2757; www.grandcanyonlodges.com). Advance reservations are highly recommended. For same-day reservations or to reach any lodge, call the **South Rim Switchboard** (📞928-638-2631).

🔺TOP CHOICE El Tovar · LODGE $$-$$$

(Map p164; d $178-273, ste $335-426; ☉year-round; ❄️📶) Yup, Albert Einstein slept here and so did Teddy Roosevelt, and despite a recent renovation, this rambling 1905 wooden lodge hasn't lost a lick of its genteel historic patina. Even if you're not checking into one of the 78 rooms, swing by the hotel for its replica Remington bronzes, stained glass and exposed beams or to admire the stunning canyon views from its wide porches, martini in hand. Standard rooms are on the small side, so those in need of elbow room should go for the deluxe.

Phantom Ranch · CABIN $

(Map p160; dm $43;☉year-round; ❄️) It ain't luxury, but after a day on the trail, even a bunk is likely to feel heavenly. These are spread across cozy private cabins sleeping four to 10, and single-sex dorms outfitted for 10 people. Rates include bedding, soap, shampoo and towels, but meals are extra (breakfast/dinner from $21/27) and must be reserved when booking your bunk. You're free to bring your own food and stove. Snacks, limited supplies, beer and wine are also sold. Without a reservation, try showing up at the Bright Angel Lodge transportation desk before 6am and hope to snag a canceled bunk.

Bright Angel Lodge & Cabins · LODGE $$

(Map p164 d without/with private bath $81/92, cabins $113-178; ☉year-round; ❄️@📶) This 1935 log-and-stone lodge on the ledge delivers historic charm by the bucketload and has the nicest rooms on the South Rim (except for those at El Tovar). Public spaces, though, are busy and less elegant. If you're economizing, get a basic double (no TV – just a bed, desk and sink) with shared bathrooms down the hall. Cabins are brighter, airier and have tasteful Western character; the most expensive have rim views.

Maswik Lodge · LODGE $$

(Map p164; d South/North $92/173, cabins $92; ☉year-round; ❄️@📶) Maswik is comprised of 16 modern two-story buildings set in the woods; rooms are of the standard motel variety. Rooms at Maswik North feature private patios, air-con, cable TV, high ceilings and forest views, while those at Maswik South are smaller, with fewer amenities and more forgettable views. The cramped cabins are available only in the summer.

Kachina & Thunderbird Lodges · LODGE $$

(Map p164; d streetside/rimside $173/184; ☉year-round; ❄️) Beside the Rim Trail between El Tovar and Bright Angel, these institutional-looking lodges offer standard motel-style

GRAND CANYON FOR CHILDREN

The **Junior Ranger** program for kids from four to 14 is popular. Pick up an activity book at the visitor center, fulfill the requirements and attend a ranger program – then get sworn in as a junior ranger and receive a certificate and badge.

Aspiring naturalists aged nine to 14 can borrow a **Discovery Pack** containing binoculars, a magnifying glass, field guides and other tools. Kids attend a 90-minute ranger-led program before heading off with their families to complete the activities in their field journal. Completion earns a Discovery Pack patch.

Active types can earn the Dynamic Earth patch by joining a ranger-led **Adventure Hike**, either down the Hermit Trail for close-ups of fossils or to Pima Point to learn about the canyon's geological mysteries.

In the **Way Cool Stuff for Kids** and **Kids Rock!** programs, which are geared to kids aged six to 12, rangers use hands-on activities to teach kids about ecology and wildlife. For example, the ranger builds a forest with the children, who pretend to be trees, grasses, bees and other plants and animals.

Little ones get in on the fun during **Story Time Adventure** held on the rim-facing porch of El Tovar.

rooms with two queen beds, full bath and TV. It's worth spending a little for the rimside rooms, some with partial canyon views.

Yavapai Lodge
LODGE $$

(Map p164; d West/East $114/163; ☺Apr-Oct; ❄🖘) Yavapai Lodge lies more than a mile from the traffic and chaos of the central village, but is still within walking distance of the grocery store, post office and bank in Market Plaza. The lodgings are stretched out amid a peaceful piñon and juniper forest, yet you can pull your car right up to your door. Rooms in Yavapai East are in six air-conditioned, two-story buildings, while rooms in Yavapai West are spread out in 10 single-story buildings without air-conditioning. These are basic, clean motel rooms with tubs, showers and TVs.

✖ Eating & Drinking

Grand Canyon Village has all the eating options you need, whether it's picking up picnic parts at Canyon Village Marketplace, an après-hike ice cream cone at Bright Angel Fountain, or a sit-down celebratory dinner at El Tovar Dining Room. Hours listed here are for the summer and may vary in slower seasons.

All South Rim bars close at 11pm, and drinks are prohibited along the rim itself.

TOP CHOICE El Tovar Dining Room
INTERNATIONAL $$-$$$

(Map p164; El Tovar; ☑928-638-2631, ext 6432; mains $18-31; ☺6:30-11am, 11:30am-2pm & 5-10pm) The memorable surroundings feature darkwood tables set with china and white linen, and huge picture windows with views of the rim and canyon beyond. The service is excellent, the menu creative, the portions big and the food very good. Breakfast options include fresh-squeezed orange juice, El Tovar's pancake trio (buttermilk, blue cornmeal and buckwheat pancakes with pine nut butter and prickly pear syrup) and cornmeal-encrusted trout with two eggs. Lunch and dinner menus are equally creative.

Reservations are required for dinner. To avoid lunchtime crowds, eat before the Grand Canyon Railway train arrives at 12:15pm. The adjacent cocktail lounge is busy for afternoon cocktails and after-dinner drinks.

🍽 Arizona Room
AMERICAN $$-$$$

(Map p164; Bright Angel Lodge; mains $8-28; ☺11:30am-3pm Mar-Oct & 4:30-10pm Mar-Dec)

Antler chandeliers hang from the ceiling and picture windows overlook a small lawn, the rim walk and the canyon. Try to get on the waitlist when doors open at 4:30pm, because by 4:40pm you may have an hour's wait – reservations are not accepted. Mains include steak, chicken and fish dishes, while appetizers include such creative options as pulled pork quesadillas.

Phantom Ranch Canteen
AMERICAN $$$

(Map p160; Phantom Ranch; mains $27-42; ☺5am & 6:30am breakfast seatings, 5pm & 6:30pm dinner seatings) On the canyon floor, Phantom Ranch offers family-style meals on a set menu: hearty stew, steaks and vegetarian chili, as well as hearty breakfasts and sack lunches for the trail. You must make meal reservations before your descent, ideally when you reserve your accommodations. The canteen is open to the public for cold lemonade and packaged snacks between 8am and 4pm, and for beer, wine and hot drinks from 8pm to 10pm.

Bright Angel Restaurant
AMERICAN $$

(Map p164; Bright Angel Lodge; mains $10-26; ☺6:30am-10pm; 🖩) Menu offerings include burgers, fajitas, salads and pasta. Families with small children gravitate here so it can get loud, and the harried staff provide the most perfunctory service of the three waitstaffed restaurants on the South Rim. Reservations not accepted.

The dark, windowless bar off the hallway doesn't offer much in the way of character, but it's a cozy spot for a beer or espresso.

Canyon View Deli
CAFETERIA $

(Map p164; ☑928-631-2262; Market Plaza; mains $4-7; ☺7am-8pm) This counter in the village grocery store is the best place to find fresh-made sandwiches and premade salads. Breakfast burritos, doughnuts and coffee are available in the morning.

Maswik Cafeteria
CAFETERIA $

(Map p164; Maswik Lodge; mains $4-10; ☺6am-10pm) Though fairly predictable, the food encompasses a nice variety and isn't too greasy. The various food stations serve burgers, sandwiches, fried chicken, Mexican food and even Vietnamese *pho*. The adjoining Maswik Pizza Pub serves beer and shows sporting events on TV.

Canyon Café
CAFETERIA $

(Map p164; Yavapai Lodge; mains $4-10; ☺6am-10pm) At Yavapai Lodge, this cafe has the same sort of food and setup as at Maswik Cafeteria, and you can get boxed lunches to go. Hours vary seasonally.

Bright Angel Fountain
FAST FOOD $

(Map p164; ☑928-638-2631; Bright Angel Lodge; mains $2-5; ☺10am-8pm) On the rim at Bright Angel Lodge, this cafeteria-style fountain serves hot dogs, premade sandwiches, ice cream, fruit, juice and bottled water. Cash only.

Hermit's Rest Snack Bar
FAST FOOD $

(Map p160; ☑928-638-2351; Hermit's Rest; mains $2-5; ☺9am-5pm) This walk-up window outside Hermit's Rest is basically a human-powered vending machine, and is cash-only.

🔒 Shopping

Books & More
BOOKS

(☺8am-8pm Jun-Aug, vary rest of the year) Located across the plaza from the Grand Canyon Visitor Center, Books & More has an extensive collection of books about the canyon. You'll also find canyon prints and T-shirts

Canyon Village Marketplace
MARKET

(Map p164; ☑928-631-2262; Market Plaza; ☺8am-8pm) The biggest source for supplies on either rim, this market offers everything you'd expect from your local grocery store, including a fair selection of organic items and over-the-counter medications. Prices and selection are better outside the park.

Desert View Marketplace
MARKET

(Map p160; ☑928-638-2393; Desert View; ☺9am-5pm) At the East Entrance, this general store sells simple groceries and souvenirs. There's also a snack bar nearby.

ℹ️ Information

Almost all services on the South Rim are in Grand Canyon Village, easily accessible via the blue Village Route shuttles. On the east side, **Market Plaza** includes the grocery/deli/outdoor shop **Canyon Village Marketplace** (☑928-631-2262; ☺8am-8pm), **Chase Bank** (☑928-638-2437; ☺9am-5pm Mon-Thu, 9am-6pm Fri) with a 24-hour ATM, and a **post office** (☑928-638-2512; ☺9am-4:30pm Mon-Fri, 11am-1pm Sat) where stamps are available via a vending machine from 5am to 10pm. The main visitor center is **Grand Canyon Visitor Center** (☑928-638-7644; ☺7:30am-6:30pm), just behind Mather Point.

Limited hours go into effect between October and March. If you have questions, NPS rangers and the people who staff the hotels, restaurants and services are typically helpful and friendly.

Internet Access
Grand Canyon Community Library (☑928-638-2718; per 50min $3; ☺10:30am-5pm Mon-Fri) Just behind the garage, this little brown building houses the community library and several terminals providing internet access; hours vary seasonally, so call ahead.

Park Headquarters Library (☺8am-noon & 1-4:30pm Mon-Thu & alternate Fri) At the back of the courtyard at Park Headquarters, the small library offers free internet access (when someone's staffing it).

Tourist Information
Backcountry Information Center (☑fax 928-638-7875; ☺8am-noon & 1-5pm) Located near Maswik Lodge, this is the place to get waitlisted for a backcountry permit if you haven't reserved one ahead of time.

Bright Angel, Yavapai & Maswik Transportation Desks (☑928-638-2631, ext 6015; ☺8am-5pm) In the lobbies of Bright Angel, Yavapai and Maswik Lodges, these service desks can book bus tours and same- or next-day mule trips. They can also answer questions about horseback rides, scenic flights and smooth-water float trips. Bright Angel can arrange last-minute lodgings at Phantom Ranch, if available.

Desert View Information Center (☑928-638-7893; ☺9am-5pm) This staffed information center also offers books and maps.

El Tovar (☺8am-5pm) This hotel's helpful concierge can answer questions, arrange same- or next-day bus tours and sell stamps.

Grand Canyon Visitor Center (☑928-638-7644; ☺8am-5pm) Three hundred yards behind Mather Point, this is the main visitor center, encompassing the theater and a bookstore. Outside the visitor center, bulletin boards and kiosks display information on ranger programs, the weather, tours and hikes. Inside is a ranger-staffed information desk and a lecture hall, where rangers offer daily talks on a variety of subjects.

Tusayan Ruin & Museum (☑928-638-2305; ☺9am-5pm) Three miles west of Desert View, this museum features exhibits on the park's indigenous people and has a ranger-staffed information desk.

Verkamp's Visitor Center (☺8am-7pm) Next to Hopi House, also features a display about the building's history.

ℹ️ Getting Around

Though the park can seem overwhelming when you first arrive, it's actually quite easy to navigate, especially when you leave it to shuttle drivers. *The Guide* contains a color coded shuttle-route map in the centerfold.

Car

Note that from March through November, cars are not allowed on Hermit Rd, which heads west from the village to Hermit's Rest.

Shuttle

Free shuttle buses ply three routes along the South Rim. In the pre-dawn hours, shuttles run every half-hour or so and typically begin running about an hour before sunrise; check *The Guide* for current sunrise and sunset information. From early morning until after sunset, buses run every 15 minutes.

The red **Hermit's Rest Route** runs west along Hermit Rd from March through November, during which time the road is closed to private vehicles.

The blue **Village Route** provides year-round transportation between the Grand Canyon Visitor Center, Yavapai Point, Market Plaza, the Backcountry Information Center, hotels, restaurants, campgrounds and parking lots.

The green **Kaibab Trail Route** provides service to and from the Yavapai Geology Museum, Mather Point, Grand Canyon Visitor Center, Pipe Creek Vista, South Kaibab Trailhead and Yaki Point. South Kaibab Trailhead and Yaki Point are on a spur road off Desert View Dr that is closed to cars year-round.

The early-bird **Hikers' Express** shuttle leaves daily from Bright Angel Lodge, stopping at the Backcountry Information Center before heading to the South Kaibab Trailhead. Check the guide for seasonal departure times.

The purple **Tusayan Route** (summer only) runs between Tusayan and the Grand Canyon Visitor Center. Stops include the airport and the IMAX Theater. You must purchase a park permit prior to boarding. Park permits are for sale in Tusayan at the National Geographic Visitor Center next to the IMAX.

Taxi

Grand Canyon South Rim Taxi Service (☏928-638-2822) offers taxi service to and from Tusayan and within the park. Service is available 24 hours, but there are only a couple of taxis, so you may have to wait.

Tusayan

The friendly little town of Tusayan, situated 1 mile south of the park's South Entrance along Hwy 64, is basically a half-mile strip of hotels and restaurants. The National Geographic Visitor Center & IMAX Theater is a good place to regroup– and buy your park tickets – before arriving at the South Entrance. In summer, you can catch the Tusayan shuttle from here into the park .

As you drive into Tusayan from the south, you'll pass the airport. The southernmost hotels are the Best Western Grand Canyon Squire Inn on your left and the Grand Hotel on your right. In quick succession are Seven Mile Lodge, Red Feather Lodge and the National Geographic Visitor Center & IMAX Theater, all bordering the west side of Hwy 64. We Cook Pizza & Pasta and Sophie's Mexican Kitchen are across Hwy 64, just south of Grand Canyon Camper Village.

🛏 Sleeping

Some of these motels offer a touch more character than you'd find at most other American roadside motels, but don't expect anything particularly memorable.

Grand Hotel   HOTEL $$-$$$

(Map p160; ☏928-638-3333; www.grandcanyon grandhotel.com; d $190-220; ❄@🛜🛎) The distinct Western motif in this hotel's open public spaces gives this newish hotel an old look, and it works. Relatively large, comfortable rooms are filled with pleasing Mission-style furniture, and the ones in back face the woods. You may catch Navajo dance performances in the evening (schedule varies), and nightly live country music draws locals and visitors from around 10:30pm.

Ten-X Campground   CAMPGROUND $

(Map p160; ☏928-638-7851; sites per vehicle $10; ☺May-Sep) Woodsy and peaceful, this first-come, first-served USFS campground 2 miles south of Tusayan has 70 sites and can fill up early in the summer. You'll find large sites, picnic tables, fire rings and BBQ grills (the campground host sells firewood), water and toilets, but no showers.

Seven Mile Lodge   MOTEL $

(☏928-638-2291; d $90; ❄🛜) This simple, friendly motel doesn't take reservations, but you can show up as early as 9am to see if there are any vacancies; rooms are usually filled by early afternoon in the summer.

Best Western Grand Canyon
Squire Inn   HOTEL $$$

(☏928-638-2681; www.grandcanyonsquire.com; d $260; ❄@🛜🛎♿) Rooms range from standard doubles in a two-story 1973 annex, sans elevator, to spacious interior rooms in the main hotel, with elevator. Amenities include a restaurant, popular sports bar, bowling alley, pool tables, fitness center, coin laundry and seasonal outdoor pool.

Red Feather Lodge MOTEL $$-$$$
(📞928-638-2414; www.redfeatherlodge.com; d
$140-170; ❄@🛜🏊♿) This motel offers well-
kept rooms in two buildings, as well as a
fitness center and an outdoor pool. The
three-story hotel features elevators and
interior doors; the older two-story motor
lodge offers outside entrances and stairs.

Grand Canyon
Camper Village CAMPGROUND $
(📞928-638-2887; www.grandcanyoncampervillage
.com; tent sites $25, RV sites $35-50; 🛜♿) A mile
south of the park on Hwy 67, this private
campground has a ton of sites, many with
no shade or natural surroundings, but there
are toilets and pay showers. Full hookups
are available.

Eating
Considering the number of annual tourists that pass through Tusayan, the village
manages to retain a sort of old-fashioned,
roadside-hub pace. There's an OK variety
of eateries to choose from, but as yet no
one has established a notable culinary
presence.

Sophie's Mexican Kitchen MEXICAN $$
(📞928-638-1105; mains $10-16; ⏰11am-9pm;
♿) Festooned with colorful *papel picado*
(cut paper banners), this cheery restaurant
offers Mexican food like street-style tacos,
fajitas and a few vegetarian options.

RP's Stage Stop CAFE $
(mains $3-7, ⏰7am-8pm, 🐕) The only place in
Tusayan to grab an espresso drink and pick
up a sandwich for your picnic lunch; also
a good spot to find wi-fi if you don't have
access where you're staying.

We Cook Pizza & Pasta PIZZERIA $$
(📞928-638-2278; mains $10-29; ⏰11am-10pm;
♿) This cavernous, busy pizza joint is
the kind of place where you order, take a
number, and unceremoniously chow down
at one of the big tables. The pizza isn't
particularly compelling, but it's good and
no-nonsense, just like its name.

Coronado Room AMERICAN $$-$$$
(📞928-638-2681; mains $13-30; ⏰5-10pm; ♿)
The Best Western Grand Squire Inn serves
the classiest cuisine around. Wild game such
as venison, elk and bison figure prominently,
but tamer options like chicken and crab
cakes are equally good.

PARK PASSES

Park passes are available at the National
Geographic Visitor Center when a ranger
is on duty.

⭐ Entertainment
Nightlife in Tusayan is mostly limited to
the popular sports bar in the Best Western
Grand Canyon Squire Inn, which also
features live music nightly and Navajo dance
performances on some weekend evenings.

National Geographic Visitor Center
& IMAX Theater THEATER
(Map p160; 📞928-638-2468; www.explorethe
canyon.com; adult/child $13/10; ⏰8am-10pm Apr-
Oct, 10am-8pm Nov-Mar) Hourly, on the half-
hour, the IMAX theater here screens the
terrific 34-minute film *Grand Canyon – The
Hidden Secrets.* With exhilarating river-
running scenes and virtual-reality drops off
canyon rims, the film plunges you into the
history and geology of the canyon through
the eyes of ancient Native Americans, John
Wesley Powell and a soaring eagle.

The IMAX experience affords you a safer,
cheaper alternative to a canyon flyover, but
if you do have your heart set on a helicopter
ride, you'll also find **Grand Canyon National
Park Airport** (Map p160) conveniently located
in Tusayan.

Valle
About 25 miles south of the park, Valle
marks the intersection of Hwy 64 to Williams and Hwy 180 to Flagstaff. There isn't
much to it apart from a couple of curiosities,
as well as a gas station, minimart and rooms
next door at the **Grand Canyon Inn** (📞800-
635-9203, 928-635-9203; www.grand-canyon-inn
.com; d $120; ❄🛜🏊). This family-run motel
offers standard motel rooms, a restaurant
(open 7:30am to 2pm and 6pm to 9pm) and
a heated outdoor pool.

Flintstones Bedrock City AMUSEMENT PARK
(📞928-635-2600; admission $6; ⏰7am-9pm Mar-
Oct) You probably won't want to stay at the
barren windswept campground (tent/RV
sites $12/16), but kids and fans of camp (the
kitsch kind) will love this slightly spooky,
well-worn roadside attraction. Built in 1972,
it features a constant loop of Flintstones
episodes in the tiny concrete movie theater,

a Flintmobile that circles a volcano and a clutch of Bedrock-style buildings. The gift shop and basic diner are straight out of a David Lynch film.

Planes of Fame Air Museum   MUSEUM
(☑928-635-1000;   www.planesoffame.org;   cnr Hwys 64 & 180; adult/child/under 5 $6.95/1.95/ free; ☺9am-5pm) This air museum has a collection of over 150 vintage airplanes on display, most of them fully functional and in immaculate condition. Aviation enthusiasts will find it fascinating.

Kaibab National Forest

No canyon views, but no crowds either. Divided by the Grand Canyon into two distinct ecosystems, this 1.6-million-acre **forest** (www.fs.fed.us/r3/kai) offers a peaceful escape from the park madness. Thick stands of ponderosa dominate the higher elevations, while piñon and juniper create a fragrant backdrop further down. Sightings of elk, mule, deer, turkeys, coyotes and even mountain lions and black bears are all possible.

Hwy 64/180 slices through 60 miles of forest between the South Rim and Williams, offering access to outdoor recreation at its finest. There's a ranger station in Tusayan (☑928-638-2443), but the best place to pick up maps and information is at the visitor center in Williams.

There are literally hundreds of miles of **hiking trails** to explore, and dogs are allowed off-leash as long as they don't bother anyone. **Mountain biking** is possible after the snowmelt, roughly between April and November. A popular, moderate ride is along the Tusayan Bike Trail, actually an old logging road. The trailhead is 0.3 miles north of Tusayan on the west side of Hwy 64/180. It's 16 miles from the trailhead to the Grandview Lookout Tower,an 80ft-high fire tower with fabulous views. If you don't want to ride all that way, three interconnected loops offer 3-, 8- and 9-mile round-trips. From the lookout you can continue on the easy and still-evolving 24-mile Arizona Trail. In the winter the USFS maintains 21 miles of **cross-country skiing** trails.

Apache Stables (☑928-638-2891; www .apachestables.com; Moqui Dr/Forest Service Rd 328; 1/2hr ride $49/89, trail & wagon ride $59) offers horseback rides through the forest (no canyon views). You can also ride your pony on a one-hour evening trek to a campfire and return by wagon or go both ways by wagon. Either way, you must bring your own food (think hot dogs and marshmallows) and drinks. The stables are about 1 mile north of Tusayan on Moqui Dr (Forest Service Rd 328) off Hwy 64/180.

There's free backcountry camping throughout the forest as well as seven first-come, first-served developed campgrounds, including Ten X Campground.

Williams

A pretty slow spot by day, Williams comes to life in the evening when the Grand Canyon Railway train returns with passengers from the South Rim... and then closes down again on the early side. It's a friendly town and caters to canyon tourists. Route 66 passes through the main historic district as a one-way street headed east; Railroad Ave parallels the tracks and Route 66, and heads one-way west.

◉ Sights & Activities

There are plenty of opportunities for **hiking** and **biking** in nearby Kaibab, Coconino and Prescott National Forests.

Grand Canyon Railway   HISTORIC RAILWAY
(☑800-843-8724;   www.thetrain.com;   Railway Depot, 233 N Grand Canyon Blvd, round-trip adult/child from $70/40; ⊞) Following a 9:30am **Wild West show** by the tracks, this historic train departs for its two-hour ride to the South Rim. If you're only visiting the rim for the day, this is a fun and hassle-free way to travel. You can leave the car behind and enjoy the park by foot, shuttle or tour bus.

Bearizona   WILDLIFE PARK
(☑928-635-2289; www.bearizona.com; 1500 E Rte 66; adult/child/under 4 $16/8/free; ☺8am-5pm Mar-Nov) Established in 2010, this awesomely named drive-through wildlife park is inhabited by indigenous North American fauna. Visitors drive themselves along a road that winds through various fenced enclosures over 160 acres, where they can see roaming gray wolves, bison, bighorn sheep and black bears up close.

🛏 Sleeping

Camping

Free dispersed camping is allowed in the national forest provided you refrain from camping in meadows, within a quarter-mile of the highway or any surface water, or within a half-mile of any developed campground.

Three pleasant USFS campgrounds near Williams offer year-round camping without hookups. Swimming is not allowed in any of the lakes. Contact the visitor center or the Williams Ranger Station for information.

Kaibab Lake Campground　　CAMPGROUND $
(tent & RV sites $18-30) Four miles northeast of town; take exit 165 off I-40 and go north 2 miles on Hwy 64.

Circle Pines KOA　　CAMPGROUND $
(☑928-635-2626, 800-562-9379; www.circlepines koa.com; 1000 Circle Pines Rd; tent/RV sites $26/45, cabins $52-228; 🛜🐕🏠🏊) Amid 27 acres of ponderosa-pine forest, a half-mile north of I-40 (take exit 167), Circle Pines is open year-round and offers plenty of activities for children and adults alike.

Lodging

[TOP CHOICE] Red Garter Bed & Bakery　　B&B $$
(☑928-635-1484; www.redgarter.com; 137 W Railroad Ave; d $120-145; 🐕🏊) Up until the 1940s, gambling and girls were the draw at this 1897 bordello-turned-B&B across from the tracks. Nowadays, the place trades on its historic charm and reputation for hauntings. Of the four restored rooms, the suite was once reserved for the house's 'best gals,' who would lean out the window to flag down customers. Rates include a 'continental-plus' breakfast with freshly-baked pastries. Sociable innkeeper John Holst knows the area well and is happy to get out a map.

Grand Canyon Hotel　　BOUTIQUE HOTEL $
(☑928-635-1419; www.thegrandcanyonhotel.com; 145 W Rte 66; dm $28, d with shared bath $60, d with private bath $70-125; 🐕@🛜) This charming spot is just what the town needed – a European-style hotel in a historic 1889 building right on Route 66. There's air-con in interior rooms, but in the exterior rooms you can get a good breeze going with the window open and ceiling fan whirring. Private rooms are individually themed and decorated.

Lodge on Route 66　　MOTEL $$-$$$
(☑928-635-4534; www.thelodgeonroute66.com; 200 E Rte 66; r $85-100, ste $135-185; 🐕🛜) The

Lodge is a beautifully designed blend of a Route 66 motel with low-key Southwestern style (ie no Kokopelli motif). Sturdy dark-wood furniture and wrought-iron accents give an elegant feel to this upmarket motel. Standard rooms are on the cramped side, with the big beds and little else taking up most of the available space, but roomier suites feature kitchenettes. Continental breakfast included.

Canyon Motel & RV Park　　MOTEL $-$$
(☑928-635-9371; www.thecanyonmotel.com; 1900 E Rodeo Rd; RV sites $35-38, cottages $74-78, train cars $78-160; 🐕🐕🐕🏠) Stone cottages and rooms in two railroad cabooses and a former Grand Canyon Railway coach car offer a quirky alternative to a standard motel. Kids love the cozy train cars, which sport bunk beds and private decks. Cottages feature wood floors and kitchenettes.

FireLight B&B　　B&B $$-$$$
(☑928-635-0200; www.firelightbedandbreakfast .com; 175 W Meade Ave; r $160-175, ste $250; 🐕🛜) Four well-appointed and tastefully decorated rooms in this Tudor-style motel have their own fireplaces. A gourmet breakfast is served every morning by your hosts Debi (the interior designer) and Eric; this romantic spot is adults only.

Grand Canyon Railway Hotel　　HOTEL $$
(☑928-635-4010; www.thetrain.com; 235 N Grand Canyon Blvd; d $190; 🐕🐕🛜) This sprawling hotel caters primarily to Grand Canyon Railway passengers (railway packages also available). The Southwestern-style rooms are what you'd expect at any standard hotel. A restaurant, lounge and coffee house cover the dining and drinking bases.

🍴 Eating & Drinking

American Flyer Coffee Company　　CAFE $
(www.americanflyercoffeeco.com; 326 W Rte 66; mains $2-6; ⏰7am-2pm Sun-Thu & 7am-6pm Fri & Sat; 🛜) This extremely friendly cafe/bike-repair shop offers wi-fi access, freshly-baked pastries and healthy items like salads and wraps along with its excellent house-roasted coffee.

Pancho McGillicuddy's Mexican Cantina　　MEXICAN $
(☑928-635-4150; www.vivapanchos.com; 141 W Railroad Ave; mains $9-10; ⏰11am-10pm) This bustling place serves up perfectly decent Mexican food to hungry passengers. The

restaurant is housed in an 1893 tavern and has a lively bar serving local microbrews on tap.

Pine Country Restaurant AMERICAN $

(☏928-635-9718; www.pinecountryrestaurant. com; 107 N Grand Canyon Blvd; mains $9-22; ☺6am-9pm) This family restaurant offers reasonably priced American basics and gigantic pies. Though the menu offers few surprises, the price is right. Just across the street from the visitor center, it has wide windows and plenty of room to relax in a home-style setting.

Dara Thai Cafe THAI $

(☏928-635-2201; 145 W Rte 66, Suite C; mains $8-12; ☺11am-2pm & 5-9pm Mon-Sat; ☑) Dara Thai offers a lighter alternative to meat-heavy menus elsewhere in town. Lots of choice for vegetarians, and all dishes are prepared to your specified spiciness. Despite its address, the front door is found along S 2nd St.

Red Raven Restaurant AMERICAN $$

(☏928-635-4980; www.redravenrestaurant.com; 135 W Rte 66; mains $10-22; ☺11am-2pm & 5-9pm Tue-Sun) White tablecloths and candlelight set the mood at the family-run Red Raven, delivering the most upscale dining experience you'll find in Williams.

Cruisers Café 66 AMERICAN $$

(www.cruisers66.com; 233 W Rte 66; mains $10-20; ☺3-10pm) Housed in an old Route 66 gas tation and decorated with vintage gas pumps and old-fashioned Coke ads, this cafe is a fun place for kids. Expect barbecue fare, such as burgers, spicy wings, pulled-pork sandwiches and mesquite-grilled ribs (cooked on the outdoor patio).

World Famous Sultana Bar BAR $

(301 W Rte 66; ☺10-2am) Expect the once-over when you walk in, as this place seems to spook most tourists. But if you like the sort of bar that's kitted out with dusty taxidermied animals, crusty locals and a jukebox, stop by for a beer and a game of pool.

ⓘ Information

Police station (☏928-635-4461; 501 W Rte 66; ☺9am-5pm Mon-Fri)

Post office (☏928-635-4572; 120 S 1st St; ☺9am-5pm Mon-Fri, to noon Sat)

Visitor center (☏928-635-4061, 800-863-0546; www.williamschamber.com; 200 W Railroad Ave; ☺8am-5pm) Inside the historic

train depot; offers a small bookstore with titles on the canyon, Kaibab National Forest and other areas of interest.

Williams Health Care Center (☏928-635-4441; 301 S 7th St; ☺8am-8pm)

Williams Ranger Station (☏928-635-5600; 742 S Clover Rd; ☺8am-4pm Mon-Fri) You'll find USFS rangers at both the visitor center and here.

ⓘ Getting There & Around

Amtrak (☏800-872-7245; www.amtrak.com; 233 N Grand Canyon Blvd) Trains stop at Grand Canyon Railway Depot.

Arizona Shuttle (☏928-225-2290, 800-563-1980; www.arizonashuttle.com) Offers three shuttles a day to the canyon (per person $22) and to Flagstaff (per person $19).

Havasupai Reservation

One of the Grand Canyon's true treasures is Havasu Canyon, a hidden valley with four stunning, spring-fed waterfalls and inviting azure swimming holes in the heart of the 185,000-acre Havasupai Reservation. Parts of the canyon floor, as well as the rock underneath the waterfalls and pools, are made up of limestone deposited by flowing water. These limestone deposits are known as travertine, which gives the famous blue-green water its otherworldly hue.

Because the falls lie 10 miles below the rim, most trips are combined with a stay at either Havasupai Lodge in Supai or at the nearby campground. Supai is the only village within the Grand Canyon, situated 8 miles below the rim. The Havasupai Reservation lies south of the Colorado River and west of the park's South Rim. From Hualapai Hilltop, a three- to four-hour drive from the South Rim, a well-maintained trail leads to Supai, waterfalls and the Colorado River. For detailed information on traveling into Havasu Canyon, see www.havasupai -nsn.gov/tourism.html.

Before heading down to Supai, you *must* have reservations to camp or stay in the lodge. Do not try to hike down and back in one day – not only is it dangerous, but it doesn't allow enough time to see the waterfalls.

About a mile beyond Supai are the newly-formed (and as yet unofficially-named) **New Navajo Falls** and **Rock Falls** and their blue pools below. The new falls developed above the former Navajo Falls, which was completely destroyed in a major flash flood in

2008. After crossing two bridges, you will reach beautiful **Havasu Falls**; this waterfall drops 100ft into a sparkling blue pool surrounded by cottonwoods and is a popular swimming hole. Havasu Campground sits a quarter-mile beyond Havasu Falls. Just beyond the campground, the trail passes **Mooney Falls**, which tumbles 200ft down into another blue-green swimming hole. To get to the swimming hole, you must climb through two tunnels and descend a very steep trail – chains provide welcome handholds, but this trail is not for the faint of heart. Carefully pick your way down, keeping in mind that these falls were named for prospector DW James Mooney, who fell to his death here. After a picnic and a swim, continue about 2 miles to **Beaver Falls**. The Colorado River is 5 miles beyond. It's generally recommended that you don't attempt to hike to the river and, in fact, the reservation actively discourages this.

🛏 Sleeping & Eating

It is essential that you make reservations in advance; if you hike in without a reservation, you will not be allowed to stay in Supai and will have to hike 8 miles back up to your car at Hualapai Hilltop.

Havasu Campground   CAMPGROUND $
(📞928-448-2121, 928-448-2141, 928-448-2180; Havasupai Tourist Enterprise, PO Box 160, Supai, AZ 86435; per night per person $17) Two miles past Supai, the campground stretches three-quarters of a mile along the creek between Havasu and Mooney Falls. Sites have picnic tables and the campground features several composting toilets, as well as drinking water at Fern Spring. Fires are not permitted but gas stoves are allowed.

Havasupai Lodge   LODGE $$
(📞928-448-2111, 928-448-2101; PO Box 159, Supai, AZ 86435; r $145; ❄) The only lodging in Supai offers motel rooms, all with canyon views, two double beds, air-conditioning and private showers. There are no TVs or telephones. Reservations are essential.

The Sinyella Store (⏰7am-7pm) is the first shop you'll see as you walk through the village. In Supai, the **Havasupai Tribal Cafe** (📞928-448-2981; ⏰6am-6pm) serves breakfast, lunch and dinner daily, and the **Havasupai Trading Post** (📞928-448-2951; ⏰6am-6pm) sells basic but expensive groceries and snacks.

ℹ Information

Havasupai Tourist Enterprise (📞928-448-2141, 928-448-2237; www.havasupai-nsn.gov; PO Box 160, Supai, AZ 86435; adult/child $35/free; ⏰5:30am-7pm) Visitors pay an entry fee and $5 environmental care fee when they arrive in Supai.

The local **post office** is the only one in the country still delivering its mail by mule, and mail sent from here bears a special postmark to prove it.

There's also a small **emergency clinic** (📞928-448-2641) in Supai.

Liquor, recreational drugs, pets and nude swimming are not allowed, nor are trail bikes allowed below Hualapai Hilltop.

ℹ Getting There & Around

Seven miles east of Peach Springs on historic Route 66, a signed turnoff leads to the 62-mile paved road ending at Hualapai Hilltop. Here you'll find the parking area, stables and the trailhead into the canyon – but no services.

Don't let place names confuse you: Hualapai Hilltop is on the Havasupai Reservation, not the Hualapai Reservation, as one might think.

Helicopter

On Sunday, Monday, Thursday and Friday from mid-March through mid-October, a helicopter ($85 one way) shuttles between Hualapai Hilltop and Supai from 10am to 1pm. Advance reservations are not accepted; show up at the parking lot and sign up. However, service is prioritized for tribal members and those offering services and deliveries to the reservation. Call Havasupai Tourist Enterprise before you arrive to be sure the helicopter is running.

Horse & Mule

If you don't want to hike to Supai, you can ride a **horse** (round-trip to lodge/campground $120/187). It's about half that price if you hike in and ride out, or vice versa. You can also arrange for a **packhorse** or **mule** (round-trip $85) to carry your pack into and out of the canyon.

Horses and mules depart Hualapai Hilltop at 10am year-round. Call the lodge or campground (wherever you'll be staying) in advance to arrange a ride.

Hualapai Reservation & Skywalk

Home to the much-hyped Skywalk, the Hualapai Reservation borders many miles of the Colorado River northeast of Kingman, covering the southwest rim of the canyon and bordering the Havasupai Reservation to the east and Lake Mead National Recreation Area to the west.

In 1988 the Hualapai Nation opened Grand Canyon West, which is *not* part of Grand Canyon National Park. Though the views here are lovely, they're not as sublime as those on the South Rim – but the unveiling of the glass bridge known as the Grand Canyon Skywalk in 2007 added a completely novel way to view the canyon.

Sights & Activities

GRAND CANYON WEST

Nowadays, the only way to visit **Grand Canyon West** (928-769-2636, 888-868-9378; www.grandcanyonwest.com; per person $43-87; 7am-7pm Apr-Sep, 8am-5pm Oct-Mar), the section of the west rim overseen by the Hualapai Nation, is to purchase a package tour. A hop-on, hop-off shuttle travels the loop road to scenic points along the rim. Tours can include lunch, horse-drawn wagon rides from an ersatz Western town and informal Native American performances.

All but the cheapest packages include admission to the **Grand Canyon Skywalk**, the horseshoe-shaped glass bridge cantilevered 4000ft above the canyon floor. Jutting out almost 70ft over the canyon, the Skywalk allows visitors to see the canyon through the glass walkway. Would-be visitors to the Skywalk are required to purchase a package tour, which makes the experience a pricey prospect.

PEACH SPRINGS

The tribal capital of the Hualapai Reservation is tiny Peach Springs, also a jumping-off point for the only one-day rafting excursions on the Colorado River. Grand Canyon West is about 55 miles northwest of here via what locals have dubbed 'Buck-and-Doe-Rd.' It's beautiful, but don't even think about taking it without a 4WD.

If you plan to travel off Route 66 on the Hualapai Reservation, you need to buy a permit ($16 plus tax, per person) at the **Hualapai Office of Tourism** (928-769-2219) at the Hualapai Lodge. This is also where you arrange raft trips operated by **Hualapai River Runners** (928-769-2219; 928-769-2636; http://grandcanyonwest.com; Mar-Oct). Packages ($328) include transportation from the lodge to the river at Diamond Creek via a bone-jarring 22-mile track (the only road anywhere to the bottom of the canyon), the motorized-raft trip to Pierce Ferry

landing, a helicopter ride out of the canyon and the bus ride back to Peach Springs.

The modern **Hualapai Lodge** (928-769-2230; 900 Rte 66; d $110;) is the only place to stay in Peach Springs and, oddly, has a saltwater swimming pool and hot tub. The attached **Diamond Creek Restaurant** (mains $7-13; breakfast, lunch, dinner) serves American standards. Lodging/rafting packages are available.

Getting There & Around

At the time of writing, 12 of the 21 miles of Diamond Bar Rd to Grand Canyon West were paved, and the middle 9 miles were being graded regularly. Call the Hualapai Lodge to check road conditions before heading out, especially if it's been raining, as the road may be impassable. If you don't want to drive, use the **park-and-ride service** (702-260-6506; per person round-trip $15) that departs from Meadview, Arizona; advance reservations required.

To get to Grand Canyon West from Kingman, fill up your gas tank and drive north on Hwy 93 for approximately 26 miles. Then head northeast along the paved Pierce Ferry Rd for about another 30 miles, before turning onto Diamond Bar Rd for the final 21-mile stretch. Directions from other towns are detailed on the Grand Canyon West website: www.grandcanyonwest .com.

Grand Canyon National Park – North Rim

On the Grand Canyon's North Rim, solitude reigns supreme. There are no shuttles or bus tours, no museums, shopping centers, schools or garages. In fact, there isn't much of anything here beyond a classic rimside national park lodge, a campground, a motel, a general store and miles of trails carving through sunny meadows thick with wildflowers, willowy aspen and towering ponderosa pines. Amid these forested roads and trails, what you'll find is peace, room to breathe and a less fettered Grand Canyon experience.

At 8200ft, the North Rim is about 10°F (6°C) cooler than the south – even on summer evenings you'll need a sweater. The lodge and all services are closed from mid-October through mid-May. Rambo types can cross-country ski in and stay at the campground (p180).

Park admission is $25 per vehicle or $12 per person if arriving on foot or by bicycle; it's valid for seven days at both rims. Upon

GRAND CANYON NORTH RIM IN...

One Day

Arrive at the rim as early as possible and get your first eyeful of the canyon from **Bright Angel Point**. If you didn't bring a picnic, grab a sandwich at **Deli in the Pines**, then spend the rest of the morning hiking through meadows and aspen on the **Widforss Trail**. In the afternoon drive out to **Point Imperial**, soak up the view, then backtrack and head out on **Cape Royal** road. Return to **Grand Canyon Lodge** to relax in a rough-hewn rocker on the verandah before pointing the wheels back north.

Two Days

Follow the one-day itinerary, wrapping the day up with dinner and a good night's sleep at the **Grand Canyon Lodge**. On day two, hike down the **North Kaibab Trail** as far as **Roaring Springs** for a picnic with a side of stunning views. Chill your feet in a cool pool before making the trek back to the top. Don't have buns of steel? Let a mule do the walking.

entering, you'll be given a map and *The Guide*. The entrance to the North Rim is 24 miles south of Jacob Lake on Hwy 67. From here, it's another 20 miles to the Grand Canyon Lodge.

⊙ Sights & Activities

Hiking & Backpacking

The short and easy paved trail (0.3 miles) to **Bright Angel Point** is a canyon must. Beginning from the back porch of the Grand Canyon Lodge, it goes to a narrow finger of an overlook with unfettered views of the mesas, buttes, spires and temples of Bright Angel Canyon. That's the South Rim, 11 miles away, and beyond it the San Francisco Peaks near Flagstaff.

The 1.5-mile **Transept Trail**, a rocky dirt path with moderate inclines, meanders north from the lodge through aspens to the North Rim Campground. The winding **Widforss Trail** follows the rim for five miles with views of canyon, meadows and woods, finishing at Widforss Point. The trailhead is 1 mile west of Hwy 67, or 2.7 miles north of the lodge.

The steep and difficult 14-mile **North Kaibab Trail** is the only maintained rim-to-river trail and connects with trails to the South Rim near Phantom Ranch. The trailhead is 2 miles north of Grand Canyon Lodge. There's a parking lot, but it's often full soon after daylight. An informal **hikers' shuttle** departs around 5:45am and 7:10am, but you need to sign up the night before.

If you just want to get a taste of inner-canyon hiking, walk 0.75 miles down to **Coconino Overlook** or 2 miles to the **Supai Tunnel**. More ambitious day-hikers can continue another 2 miles to the waterfall of **Roaring Springs**, which is also a popular mule-ride destination. Take the short detour to the left, where you'll find picnic tables and a pool to cool your feet. Seasonal water is available at the restrooms.

If you wish to continue to the river, plan on camping overnight (backcountry permit required, see p167) at Cottonwood Campground (p191), some 2 miles beyond Roaring Springs. It's a beautiful spot with seasonal drinking water, pit toilets, a phone and a ranger station, but the 11 campsites are not shaded.

From the campground, it's a gentle downhill walk along Bright Angel Creek to the Colorado River. Phantom Ranch and the Bright Angel Campground are 7 and 7.5 miles respectively below Cottonwood.

Rangers suggest three nights as a minimum to enjoy a rim-to-river-to-rim hike, staying at Cottonwood on the first and third nights and Bright Angel on the second. Faster trips would be an endurance slog and not much fun.

Hiking from the North Rim to the South Rim requires a ride on the Trans-Canyon Shuttle to get you back.

Mule Rides

Canyon Trail Rides   HORSEBACK RIDING
(☑435-679-8665; www.canyonrides.com; ⊙mid-May–mid-Oct) You can make reservations anytime for the upcoming year but, unlike mule trips on the South Rim, you can usually book a trip upon your arrival at the

park; just duck inside the lodge to the **Mule Desk** (📞928-638-9875; ⏱7am-5pm). Mule rides from the North Rim don't go into the canyon as far as the Colorado River, but the half-day trip gives a taste of life below the rim.

One Hour Rim of the Grand Canyon
(7 year age limit, 220lb weight limit; $40; ⏱several departures daily) Wooded ride to an overlook.

Half-Day Trip to Uncle Jim's Point
(10 year age limit, 220lb weight limit; $75; ⏱7:30am & 12:30pm) Follow the Ken Patrick Trail through the woods.

Half-Day Canyon Mule Trip to Supai Tunnel (10 year age limit, 200lb weight limit; $75; ⏱7:30am & 12:30pm) Descend 1450ft into the canyon along the North Kaibab Trail.

Cross-Country Skiing

Once the first heavy snowfall closes Hwy 67 into the park (as early as late October or as late as January), you can cross-country ski the 44 miles to the rim and camp at the campground (no water, pit toilets). Camping is permitted elsewhere with a backcountry permit, available from rangers year-round. You can ski any of the rim trails, though none are groomed. The closest ski rental is in Flagstaff.

Scenic Drives

Driving on the North Rim involves miles of slow, twisty roads through dense stands of evergreens and aspen to get to the most spectacular overlooks. From Grand Canyon Lodge, drive north for about 3 miles, then take the signed turn east to Cape Royal and Point Imperial and continue for 5 miles to a fork in the road called the Y.

From the Y it's another 15 miles south to **Cape Royal** (7876ft) past overlooks, picnic tables and an Ancestral Puebloan site. A 0.6-mile paved path, lined with piñon, cliffrose and interpretive signs, leads from the parking lot to a natural arch and Cape Royal Point, arguably the best view from this side of the canyon.

Point Imperial, the park's highest overlook at 8803ft, is reached by following Point Imperial Rd from the Y for an easy 3 miles. Expansive views include Nankoweap Creek, the Vermilion Cliffs, the Painted Desert and the Little Colorado River.

The dirt roads to **Point Sublime** (34 miles round-trip; an appropriately named 270-degree overlook) and **Toroweap** (122 miles round-trip; a sheer-drop view of the

Colorado River 3000ft below) are rough, require high-clearance vehicles and are not recommended for 2WDs. While they certainly offer amazing views, they require navigating treacherous roads and if your goal is absolute solitude, you might be disappointed. The dirt road to Point Sublime starts about 1 mile west of Hwy 67, 2.7 miles north of Grand Canyon Lodge (look for the Widforss Trail sign). It should take about two hours to drive the 17 miles each way. Toroweap is reached via BLM Rd 109, a rough dirt road heading south off Hwy 389, 9 miles west of Fredonia. The one-way trip is 61 miles and should take at least two hours.

🛏 Sleeping

Accommodations on the North Rim are limited to one lodge and one campground.

North Rim Campground   CAMPGROUND $
(📞877-444-6777, 928-638-7814; www.recreation .gov; sites $18-25; 🐾) This campground, 1.5 miles north of the lodge, offers shaded sites on level ground blanketed in pine needles. Sites 11, 14, 15, 16 and 18 overlook the Transept (a side canyon) and cost $25. There's water, a store, a snack bar, coin-op showers and laundry facilities, but no hookups. Reservations are accepted up to six months in advance.

Grand Canyon Lodge   LODGE $$
(📞928-638-2611 for same-day reservation, 877-386-4383 for reservations up to 12 months in advance, 480-337-1320 for reservations from outside the USA; www.foreverlodging.com; r $116, cabins $121-187 for 2, $10 for each additional guest over 15; ⏱mid-May–mid-Oct; 🛜🐾) Walk through the front door of Grand Canyon Lodge into the lofty sunroom and there, framed by picture windows, is the canyon in all its glory. Rooms are not in the lodge itself, but in rustic cabins sleeping up to five people. The nicest are the bright and spacious Western cabins, made of logs and buffered by trees and grass. Reserve far in advance; children under 16 sleep free. About 0.5 miles up the road are 40 simple motel rooms, each with a queen bed.

If these two options are fully booked, try snagging a room at the **Kaibab Lodge** (📞928-638-2389; www.kaibablodge.com; Hwy 67, 18 miles north of North Rim; r $140-150, cabins $85-180; ⏱mid-May–mid-Oct; 🛜🐾), on Hwy 67 about 6 miles north of the park entrance;

it also has a restaurant. Nearby is the first-come, first-served **DeMotte Campground** (Hwy 67, 16 miles north of North Rim; per site for first vehicle $17, for second $8; ⊙mid-May–mid-Oct; 🐾) with 38 primitive sites. None have hookups. It usually fills up between noon and 3pm.

There's also free dispersed camping in the surrounding Kaibab National Forest. Otherwise, you'll find more options another 60 miles north in Kanab, Utah (p444).

🍴 Eating & Drinking

Visitors can contact the restaurants through the North Rim Switchboard (📞928-638-2612, 928-638-2611). With a day's notice, the Lodge Dining Room will prepare a sack lunch ($11) ready for pick-up at 6:30am for those wanting to picnic on the trail.

TOP CHOICE Grand Canyon Lodge
Dining Room AMERICAN $$
(📞928-645-6865, call btwn Jan 1 & Apr 15 for next season; mains $12-24; ⊙6:30-10am, 11:30am-2:30pm, 4:45-9:45pm, mid-May–mid-Oct) Although seats beside the window are wonderful, views from the dining room are so huge, it really doesn't matter where you sit. While the solid menu includes buffalo steak and several vegetarian options, don't expect culinary memories. Make reservations in advance of your arrival to guarantee a spot for dinner (reservations are not accepted for breakfast or lunch).

Rough Rider Saloon BAR $
(snacks $2-5; ⊙5:30-10:30am & 11:30am-11pm, mid-May–mid-Oct) If you're an early riser stop at this small saloon on the boardwalk beside the lodge for an espresso, a fresh-made cinnamon roll and a banana. Starting at 11:30am the saloon serves beer, wine and mixed drinks, as well as hot dogs and Anasazi chile. Teddy Roosevelt memorabilia lines the walls, honoring his role in the history of the park. This is the only bar in the lodge, so if you want to enjoy a cocktail on the sun porch or in your room, pick it up here.

Grand Canyon Cookout
Experience AMERICAN $$
(adult $30-35, child $12-22, no charge for children under 6; ⊙6-7:45pm Jun-Sep; 🐾) Chow down on barbecued meat, skillet cornbread and southwestern baked beans all served buffet style, with a side of Western songs and cheesy jokes.

Deli in the Pines CAFETERIA $
(mains $4-8; ⊙7am-9pm, mid-May–mid-Oct) This small cafeteria adjacent to the Lodge serves surprisingly good food, although the menu is limited to sandwiches, pizza and other more simple items.

ℹ Information

At the Lodge you'll find a restaurant, deli, saloon, postal window and gift shop, as well as the **North Rim Visitor Center** (📞928-638-7864; www.nps.gov/grca; ⊙8am-6pm). About a mile up the road, next to the campground, are laundry facilities, fee showers, a gas station, a **general store** (⊙7am-7pm) and the **North Rim Backcountry Office** (📞928-638-7875; ⊙1-5pm). To contact the Grand Canyon Lodge front desk, saloon, gift shop, gas station or general store, call the **North Rim Switchboard** (📞928-638-2612). The closest ATM is in Jacob Lake.

ℹ Getting There & Around

The only access road to the Grand Canyon North Rim is Hwy 67, which closes with the first snowfall and reopens in spring after the snowmelt (exact dates vary).

Although only 11 miles from the South Rim as the crow flies, it's a grueling 215-mile, four- to five-hour drive on winding desert roads between here and Grand Canyon Village. You can drive yourself or take the **Trans-Canyon Shuttle** (📞928-638-2820; one way/round-trip $70/130, no credit cards), which departs from Grand Canyon Lodge at 7am daily to arrive at the South Rim at 11:30am. Reserve at least two weeks in advance.

Arizona Strip

Wedged between the Grand Canyon and Utah, the Arizona Strip is one of the state's most remote and sparsely populated regions. Only about 3000 people live here, in relative isolation, many of them members of the Fundamentalist Church of Latter-Day Saints (FLDS), who defy US law by practicing polygamy.

Only one major paved road – Hwy 89A – traverses the Arizona Strip. It crosses the Colorado River at Marble Canyon before getting sandwiched by the crimson-hued Vermilion Cliffs to the north and House Rock Valley to the south. Scan the skies for California condors, an endangered species recently reintroduced to the area. Desert scrub gives way to piñon and juniper as the highway climbs up the Kaibab Plateau to enter the Kaibab National Forest. At Jacob

PIPE SPRING NATIONAL MONUMENT

Fourteen miles southwest of Fredonia on Hwy 389, **Pipe Spring** (☑928-643-7105; www
.nps.gov/pisp; adult/child $5/free; ◷7am-5pm Jun-Aug, 8am-5pm Sep-May) is quite literally
an oasis in the desert. Visitors can experience the Old West amid cabins and corrals, an
orchard, ponds and a garden. In summer, rangers and costumed volunteers re-enact
various pioneer tasks. Tours (on the hour and half-hour) let you peek inside the stone
Winsor Castle (◷8am-4:30pm Jun-Aug, 9am-4pm Sep-May), and there's also a small
museum (◷7am-5pm Jun-Aug, 8am-5pm Sep-May) that examines the turbulent history of
local Paiutes and Mormon settlers.

Lake, it meets with Hwy 67 to the Grand
Canyon North Rim. Past Jacob Lake, as the
road drops back down, you get stupendous
views across southern Utah.

MARBLE CANYON & LEES FERRY

About 14 miles past the Hwy 89/89A fork,
Hwy 89A crosses the Navajo Bridge over the
Colorado River at Marble Canyon. Actually,
there are two bridges: a modern one for
motorists that opened in 1995, and a historical one from 1929. Walking across the
latter you'll enjoy fabulous views down
Marble Canyon to the northeast lip of the
Grand Canyon. The **Navajo Bridge Interpretive Center** (◷9am-5pm, May–Oct) on
the west bank has good background info
about the bridges, as well as the area and
its natural wonders. Keep an eye out for
California condors!

Just past the bridge, a paved 6-mile road
veers off to the fly-fishing mecca of Lees
Ferry. Sitting on a sweeping bend of the
Colorado River, it's in the far southwestern
corner of Glen Canyon National Recreation
Area (p183) and a premier put-in spot for
Grand Canyon rafters. Fishing here requires
an Arizona fishing license, available at local
fly shops and outfitters such as **Marble Canyon Outfitters** (☑928-645-2781; www.leesferry
flyfishing.com; inside Marble Canyon Lodge, Alt 89).

Lees Ferry was named for John D Lee,
the leader of the 1857 Mountain Meadows
Massacre, in which 120 emigrants from
Arkansas were brutally murdered by
Mormon and Paiute forces. To escape prosecution, Lee moved his wives and children to
this remote outpost, where they lived at the
Lonely Dell Ranch and operated the only
ferry service for many miles around. Lee
was tracked down and executed in 1877, but
the ferry service continued until the Navajo
Bridge opened in 1929. You can walk around
Lonely Dell Ranch and have a picnic amid
the stone house and the log cabins.

On a small hill, **Lees Ferry Campground** (campsites $12) has 54 riverview
sites along with drinking water and toilets,
but no hookups. Public coin showers are
available at **Marble Canyon Lodge** (☑928-
355-2225; www.marblecanyoncompany.com; Alt
89, Marble Canyon, 0.4 miles west of Navajo
Bridge; s/d/apt $70/80/140; ◷restaurant 6am-
10pm; 🕸), which has simple rooms, and deli
sandwiches to go.

Another option is the rustic but comfortable **Lees Ferry Lodge** (☑928-355-2231; www
.vermilioncliffs.com; Alt 89, Marble Canyon,
3.5 miles west of Navajo Bridge; s/d $64/74;
◷6:30am-9pm; 🐾), which has 10 rooms
plus a restaurant and bar with 100 international beers (unless somebody finished
off a few brands the night before). It's one
of those bars where you're never quite sure
who's going to roar off the highway and
stomp through the door – but they'll surely
have an interesting story.

JACOB LAKE

From Marble Canyon, Hwy 89A climbs
5000ft over 40 miles to the Kaibab National
Forest and the oddly lakeless outpost of
Jacob Lake. All you find is a motel with a
restaurant, a gas station and the USFS
Kaibab Plateau Visitor Center (☑928-643-
7298; intersection of Hwys 89A & 67; ◷8am-5pm,
Jun–Sep). From here Hwy 67 runs south for
44 miles past meadows, aspen and ponderosa pine to the Grand Canyon North Rim.
The only facilities between Jacob Lake and
the rim are the Kaibab Lodge, North Rim
Country Store and DeMotte Campground,
about 18 miles south.

Camping is free in the national forest or
you can try **Jacob Lake Inn** (☑928-643-7232;
www.jacoblake.com; intersection of Hwys 89A &
67, 44 miles north of North Rim; r $119-138, cabins
$89-103; ◷6:30am-9pm mid-May–mid-Oct, 8am-
8pm mid-Oct–mid-May; 🐾🕸), which has no-
frills cabins with tiny bathrooms, well-worn

motel rooms and spacious doubles in the modern hotel-style building. There's also a **restaurant** (⊙6:30am-9pm, varies seasonally) with a great bakery and ice cream counter. Try the Cookie in a Cloud, a cakey cookie topped with marshmallow and chocolate.

Kaibab Lodge Camper Village (☑928-643-7804; www.kaibabcampervillage.com; tent/RV sites $17/35; ⊙mid-May–mid-Oct), a mile south of Jacob's Lake, has more than 100 sites for tents and RVs.

Page & Glen Canyon National Recreation Area

An enormous lake tucked into a landlocked swath of desert? You can guess how popular it is to play in the spangly waters of **Lake Powell**. The country's second-largest reservoir and part of the **Glen Canyon National Recreation Area** (☑928-608-6200; www.nps.gov/glca; 7-day pass per vehicle $15) was created by the construction of Glen Canyon Dam in 1963. To house the scores of workers an entire town was built from scratch near the dam. Now a modern town with hotels, restaurants and supermarkets, Page is a handy base for lake visitors.

Straddling the Utah-Arizona border, the 186-mile-long lake has 1960 miles of empty shoreline set amid striking red-rock formations, sharply cut canyons and dramatic desert scenery. Lake Powell is famous for its houseboating, which appeals to families and college students alike. Though hundreds of houseboats ply its waters at any given time, it's possible to explore its secluded inlets, bays, coves and beaches for days with hardly seeing anyone at all.

The gateway to Lake Powell is the small town of Page (population 6800), which sits right next to Glen Canyon Dam in the far southwest corner of the recreation area. Hwy 89 (called N Lake Powell Blvd in town) forms the main strip.

Aramark (☑800-528-6154; www.lakepowell.com) runs five of the lake's six marinas, including the often frenetic **Wahweap Marina** (☑928-645-2433), 6 miles north of Page. The only other marina on the Arizona side is the much more peaceful **Antelope Point Marina** (☑928-645-5900, ext 5), which opened in 2007 on the Navajo Reservation about 8 miles east of Page. Marinas have stores, restaurants and other services, and rent boats, kayaks, jet skis and water skis.

◉ Sights

Antelope Canyon　　　　　　　　　CANYON
(www.navajonationparks.org/htm/antelopecanyon.htm) Unearthly in its beauty, Antelope Canyon is a popular slot canyon on the Navajo Reservation a few miles east of Page and open to tourists by Navajo-led tour only. Wind and water have carved sandstone into an astonishingly sensuous temple of nature where light and shadow play hide and seek. Less than a city block long (about a quarter-mile), its symphony of shapes and textures are a photographer's dream. Lighting conditions are best around mid-morning between April and September, but the other months bring smaller crowds and a more intimate experience.

Four tour companies offer trips into upper Antelope Canyon; **Antelope Slot Canyon Tours** (☑928-645-5594; www.antelopeslotcanyon.com; 55 S Lake Powell Blvd), owned by Chief Tsotsie, is recommended. The 90-minute sightseeing tour costs $29, while the 2½-hour photographic tour is $46; both include the $6 Navajo Permit Fee. The company also offers tours to lesser-known Cathedral Canyon.

John Wesley Powell Museum　　　MUSEUM
(☑928-645-9496; www.powellmuseum.org; 64 N Lake Powell Blvd; admission $5; ⊙9am-5pm mid-Feb–mid-Dec) In 1869, one-armed John Wesley Powell led the first Colorado River expedition through the Grand Canyon. This small museum displays memorabilia of early river runners, including a model of Powell's boat, with photos and illustrations of his excursions.

Glen Canyon Dam　　　　　　　　　　DAM
At 710ft tall, Glen Canyon Dam is the nation's second-highest concrete arch dam – only Hoover Dam is higher, by 16ft. Guided 45-minute tours departing from the **Carl Hayden Visitor Center** (☑928-608-6404; tours adult/child $5/2.50; ⊙8am-5pm Mar–mid-May, Sep & Oct, 8am-6pm mid-May–Aug) take you deep inside the dam via elevators. Tours run every half-hour from 8:30am to 4pm in summer (less frequently the rest of the year). Displays and videos in the visitor center tell the story of the dam's construction and offer technical facts on water flow, generator output etc.

Rainbow Bridge National Monument　PARK
(☑928-608-6404; www.nps.gov/rabr; admission $4) On the south shore of Lake Powell,

ℹ NEED A LIFT?

The main town in the Arizona Strip is postage-stamp-sized Fredonia, some 30 miles northwest of Jacob Lake. Fredonia has the **Kaibab National Forest District Headquarters** (☏928-643-7395; 430 S Main St; ⊙8am-5pm Mon-Fri), where you can pick up info on hiking and camping in the forest. Fredonia also has a service station, **Judd Auto Service** (☏928-643-7726, 623 S Main St; ⊙seasonal variation), which provides towing as well as tire repair and simple mechanical work.

about 50 miles by water from Wahweap Marina, Rainbow Bridge is the largest natural bridge in the world, at 290ft high and 275ft wide. A sacred Navajo site, it resembles the graceful arc of a rainbow. Most visitors arrive by boat, but experienced backpackers can also drive along dirt roads to access two unmaintained trails (each 28 miles round-trip) on the Navajo Reservation. Tribal permits are required. Check with the **Navajo Parks & Recreation Department** (☏928-871-6647; www.navajonationparks.org) on how to obtain one.

🏃 Activities

Boating & Cruises

Marinas rent kayaks (in peak season, June to August, per day single/double $26/32), 19ft powerboats ($375), wakeboards ($41), kneeboards ($27) and other toys. From Wahweap Marina, **Aramark** (☏800-528-6154; www.lakepowell.com) offers boat cruises to Rainbow Bridge (April to October all day adult/child $124/84; mid-June to October half-day $81/50). Because of low water levels, seeing the arches is no longer possible from the boat but involves a 2-mile round-trip hike. Dinner cruises, sunset cruises and trips to Navajo Canyon (adult/child $59/35) and the waterside of Antelope Canyon ($38/23) are also offered.

Hiking & Mountain Biking

Ask at the Carl Hayden Visitor Center at Glen Canyon Dam for information and maps of the area's many hiking and mountain-biking trails. **Lakeside Bikes** (☏928-645-2266; 12 N Lake Powell Blvd) rents mountain bikes for $25 per day.

The most popular hike is the 1.5-mile round-trip trek to the overlook at

Horseshoe Bend, where the river wraps around a dramatic stone outcropping to form a perfect U. Though it's short, the sandy, shadeless trail and moderate incline can be a slog. Toddlers should be secured safely in a backpack, as there are no guardrails at the viewpoint. The trailhead is south of Page off Hwy 89, across from mile marker 541.

The 15-mile **Rimview Trail**, a mix of sand, slickrock and other terrain, bypasses the town and offers views of the surrounding desert and Lake Powell. While there are several access points (pick up a brochure from the museum or chamber of commerce), a popular starting point is behind Lake View School at the end of N Navajo Dr.

🛏 Sleeping

You can camp anywhere along the Lake Powell shoreline for free, as long as you have a portable toilet or toilet facilities on your boat.

Courtyard by Marriott   HOTEL $$
(☏928-645-5000; 600 Clubhouse Dr; r $150-160, children under 18 free; ✳@🛜🌊) Surrounded by a golf course away from the strip's noise and traffic, with attractive, spacious rooms and a quiet garden courtyard with a large pool, this hotel is a peaceful alternative to other chain hotels. It has a bar and a restaurant, but you'd be better off going elsewhere for a meal.

Lake Powell Resort   RESORT $$
(☏928-645-2433; www.lakepowell.com; 100 Lake Shore Dr; r $170-190, ste $250-280, children under 18 free; ✳🛜🌊🐾) This bustling resort on the shores of Lake Powell offers beautiful views and a lovely little pool perched in the rocks above the lake, but it is impersonal and frenetic. Rates for lake-view rooms with tiny patios are well worth the extra money. In the lobby you can book boat tours and arrange boat rental. Wi-fi is available in the lobby only.

Debbie's Hide a Way   MOTEL $$
(☏928-645-1224; www.debbieshideaway.com; 117 8th Ave; ste $129-199; ✳@🛜) The owners encourage you to feel right at home – throw a steak on the grill, leaf through one of several hundred books that line bookshelves, or just hang out with other guests among the rose and fruit trees. All accommodation is in basic suites, rates include up to seven people, and there are free laundry facilities.

Lone Rock Beach CAMPGROUND $

(sites $18; 😈) Everyone here just pulls up next to the water and sets up house. It's a popular spot with college revelers, and can be busy and loud late into the night during the weekends. Escape to the dunes or the far edges of the lot if you're looking for quiet. There are bathrooms and outdoor cold showers.

✖ Eating & Drinking

Unless otherwise noted, the following restaurants stretch along Dam Plaza, a back-to-back strip mall in the Safeway parking lot at the corner of Lake Powell Blvd and Navajo Dr. Starbucks is inside the Safeway.

Bean's Coffee CAFE $

(644f N Navajo Dr; mains $5-11; ☺6:30am-6pm Mon-Fri, 7am-6pm Sat, 8am-2pm Sun; @🛜) While the coffee runs weak, this tiny cafe serves good breakfast burritos and sandwiches – try the tasty cashew chicken as a picnic lunch to go.

Slackers BURGERS $

(810 N Navajo Dr; mains $6-12; ☺11am-9pm Mon-Fri) A chalkboard menu includes excellent burgers (though no kick to the green chile) and hot or cold sub sandwiches. Count on long lunch lines, or call to order in advance. Picnic tables offer shaded outdoor strip-mall seating. Connects to **Big Dipper Ice-Cream & Yogurt** where, strangely, there's a DVD player with a selection of movies to pop in at your pleasure.

Blue Buddha Sushi Lounge SUSHI $$

(810 N Navajo; mains $14-26; ☺5-10pm Mon-Sat, to 9pm Sun, closed Mon & Sun Oct-May) With cold sake and a relaxing blue-hued modern decor, this ultra-cool hideaway hits the spot after a hot and dusty day in the Arizona desert. Beyond sushi, there's a limited menu including teriyaki chicken and blackened tuna.

Dam Bar & Grille AMERICAN $$

(644 N Navajo Dr; mains $8-18; ☺11am-10pm) Raft guides recommend the dependable pub fare, including steak, pasta and ribs. There's a microbrewery feel here, and the patio is pleasant on summer evenings, despite the strip-mall view.

Ranch House Grille DINER $

(819 N Navajo Dr; mains $6-13; ☺6am-3pm) There's not much ambiance but the food is good, the portions huge and the service fast. This is your best bet for breakfast. To get

here from the dam, turn left off of N Lake Powell Blvd onto N Navajo Dr.

Jadi Tooh AMERICAN $$

(Antelope Point Marina; mains $12-23; ☺11am-10pm) A 'floating restaurant' with solid food at the Navajo-owned marina provides a peaceful respite from the bustling strip of Page, which is 8 miles southwest. Come for the relative quiet and the view.

Rainbow Room AMERICAN $$

(📞928-645-2433; Lake Powell Resort, 100 Lake Shore Dr; ☺6-10am, 11am-2pm & 4-11pm) Perched above Lake Powell, picture windows frame dramatic red-rock formations against blue water. Your best bet is to eat elsewhere and come to the bar here for a beautiful sunset drink.

ℹ Information

The Glen Canyon National Recreation Area entrance fee, good for up to seven days, is $15 per vehicle or $7 per individual entering on foot or bicycle.

Emergency

National Park Service 24-hour Dispatch Center (📞928-608-6300)

Police station (📞928-645-2463; 808 Coppermine Rd)

Marinas

Marinas (except for Dangling Rope and Hite) rent boats, host rangers and small supply stores, and sell fuel. **Aramark** (📞800-528-6154; www.lakepowell.com) runs all the marinas except for Antelope Point, which is on Navajo land.

Antelope Point (📞928-645-5900) Peaceful Navajo-owned marina, 8 miles northeast of Page.

Bullfrog (📞435-684-3000) Connects to Halls Crossing marina by 30-minute ferry. On Lake Powell's west shore, 290 miles from Page.

Medical Services

Page Hospital (📞928-645-2424; Vista Ave at N Navajo Dr)

Pharmacy (📞928-645-8155; 650 Elm St; 9am-8pm Mon-Fri, 9am-6pm Sat, 10am-4pm Sun) Inside the Safeway Food & Drug.

Post

Post office (📞928-645-2571; 44 6th Ave; ☺8:30am-5pm Mon-Fri)

Tourist Information

In addition to Bullfrog Visitor Center and Carl Hayden Visitor Center, there is a third GCNRA Visitor Center 39 miles southwest of Page at Navajo Bridge in Marble Canyon.

Bullfrog Visitor Center (☎435-684-7423; ⊗9am-5pm Wed-Sun, May-Oct) On the lake's north shore, this is a drive of more than 200 miles from Page.

Carl Hayden Visitor Center (☎928-608-6404; www.nps.gov/glca; ⊗8am-7pm Memorial Day-Labor Day, to 4pm rest of the year) A well-stocked bookstore and the best source of regional information in Page. It's located at Glen Canyon Dam on Hwy 89, 2 miles north of Page.

❶ Getting There & Away

Great Lakes Airline (☎928-645-1355, 800-554-5111; www.flygreatlakes.com) offers flights between Page Municipal Airport and Phoenix. Page sits 125 northwest of the North Rim.

Car rental is available through **Avis** (☎928-645-9347, 800-331-1212).

NAVAJO RESERVATION

The mission statement on the Navajo Parks & Recreation website includes a famous Navajo poem that ends with the phrase 'May I walk in beauty.' This request is easily granted at many spots on the Navajo Reservation in northeastern Arizona. At 27,000 sq miles the reservation is the country's largest, spilling over into the neighboring states of Utah, Colorado and New Mexico. Most of this land is as flat as a calm sea and barren, until – all of a sudden – Monument Valley's crimson red buttes rise before you or you come face-to-face with ancient history at the cliff dwellings at Canyon de Chelly and Navajo National Monuments. Elsewhere, you can walk in dinosaur tracks or be mesmerized by the shifting light of hauntingly beautiful Antelope Canyon.

While it's true that this remote northeastern corner of the state embraces some of Arizona's most photogenic and iconic landscapes, there's also plenty of evidence of the poverty, depression and alcoholism that affect Native American communities to this day. You'll see it in rusting, ramshackle trailers, or in crumbling social services buildings in small nowhere towns, or in the paucity of stores and businesses.

Many Navajo rely on the tourist economy for survival. You can help keep their heritage alive by staying on reservation land, purchasing their crafts or trying their foods, such as the ubiquitous Navajo taco.

For historic background on the Navajo, see p524. Tips on reservation etiquette can be found on p527.

❶ Information

Unlike Arizona, the Navajo Reservation observes daylight saving time. The single best source of information for the entire reservation is the **Navajo Tourism Office** (☎928-871-6436; www.discovernavajo.com). Contact the **Navajo Parks & Recreation Department** (☎928-871-6647; www.navajonationparks.org) for general information about permits for hiking ($5 per day) and camping ($5-15), which are required. For a list of park offices selling permits, visit www.navajonationparks.org/permits.htm.

Pick up a copy of the *Navajo Times* (www.navajotimes.com) for the latest Navajo news. Tune your radio to AM 660 KTNN for a mix of news and Native American music.

Keep in mind that due to historical and present-day problems, alcohol is illegal here.

❶ Getting There & Around

You really need your own wheels to properly explore this sprawling land. Gas stations are scarce and fuel prices are higher than outside the reservation.

The only public transportation is provided by the **Navajo Transit System** (☎928-729-4002, 866-243-6260; www.navajotransit.com), but services are geared towards local, not tourist, needs. It operates daily buses on seven routes, including one that goes from Tuba City to Window Rock via the Hopi Reservation. There are also services between Kayenta, near Monument Valley, to Window Rock via Chinle and Tsaile near Canyon de Chelly; and from Window Rock to Gallup in New Mexico. Every route costs only $2.

Tuba City & Moenkopi

Hwy 160 splits these contiguous towns in two: to the northwest, Tuba City is the largest single community in the Navajo Nation, with a handful more folks than Shiprock, New Mexico. To the southeast is the village of Moenkopi, a small Hopi island surrounded by Navajo land. Moenkopi has got a gas station, a new 24hr Denny's and one of the best hotels on either reservation – but doesn't have much else.

Tuba City is named for 19th-century Hopi chief Tuve (or Toova), who welcomed a group of Mormons down from Utah to build a village of their own next to Moenkopi. The best reason to stop on this side of Hwy 160 is the Navajo cultural museum.

Open since June 2007, the **Explore Navajo Interactive Museum** (☎928-640-0684; www .explorenavajo.com/go2/navajo_museum.cfm; cnr Main St & Moenave Rd; adult/child/senior $9/6/7; ☉10am-6pm Mon-Sat, noon-6pm Sun) is a perfect, if pricey, introductory stop for your reservation explorations and will deepen your understanding of the land, its people and their traditions. You'll learn why the Navajo call themselves the 'People of the Fourth World,' the difference between male and female hogans (traditional homes of the Navajo) and what the Long Walk was all about. Aspects of contemporary life, such as education, the role of the elders, the significance of clans and the popularity of rodeo, are also addressed.

Next door, and included in your entry fee, is a small museum about the Navajo Code Talkers, with a display explaining how the famously uncrackable code was designed.

Visits wrap up in the historic **Tuba Trading Post**, which dates back to the 1880s and sells authentic Native American arts and crafts.

🛏 Sleeping & Eating

Tuba City/Moenkopi is a convenient place to stay before or after a trip through the Hopi Reservation to the east.

Moenkopi Legacy Inn & Suites HOTEL $$
(☎928-283-4500; www.experiencehopi.com; junction Hwys 160 & 264; r $139, ste $159-199, incl breakfast; ⚉❄@⬤) Open since April 2010, this place brings a new level of luxury to town. The exterior is a stylized version of traditional Hopi village architecture, and the lobby, with a soaring ceiling supported by pine pillars, is stunning. Rooms have marble and granite baths and, best of all, reproductions of historic photographs from the Hopi archives at Northern Arizona University. Ask for a room with a balcony facing the inner courtyard. The continental breakfast is hearty, with eggs, potatoes and sausage as well as oatmeal and cereal.

Quality Inn HOTEL $$
(☎928-283-4545; www.explorenavajo.com; cnr Main St & Moenave Rd; r $108-112, ste $153, incl breakfast; ❄@⬤⚉) Comfortable, modern and well maintained, the Quality Inn has been a long time stand-by, and it still holds up. Room rates include breakfast at the popular **Hogan Restaurant** (cnr Main St & Moenave Rd; mains $6-14; ☉breakfast, lunch & dinner) next door, which has an extensive menu of Southwestern, Navajo and American dishes. Smoking rooms available. Pets $10 per night.

Kate's Café DINER $
(cnr Main St & Edgewater Dr; mains $7-13; ☉breakfast, lunch & dinner) Don't be put off by the booth with the posterior-eating hole in the seat, just sit on the other side. This ain't haute cuisine, but it serves up decent, locally popular diner grub.

For a latte and web-surfing, swing by **Hogan Espresso & More** (cnr Main St & Moenave Rd; ☉7am-7pm Mon-Fri, 9am-7pm Sat & Sun).

Navajo National Monument

The sublimely well-preserved Ancestral Puebloan cliff dwellings of Betatkin and Keet Seel are protected as the **Navajo National Monument** (☎928-672-2700; www .nps.gov/nava; Hwy 564; admission free; ☉8am-6pm Jun–mid-Sep, 9am-5pm mid-Sep–May) and can only be reached on foot. It's no walk in the park, but there's truly something magical about approaching these ancient stone villages in relative solitude. The site is administered by the National Park Service, which controls access and maintains a visitor center 9 miles north of Hwy 160 at the end of paved Hwy 564. For a distant glimpse of Betatkin, follow the easy Sandal Trail about half a mile from the center. There's a free campground, **Sunset View**, with 31 first-come, first-served sites, and water nearby.

Betatkin, which translates as 'ledge house,' is reached on a ranger-led 2.5-mile hike (one-way) departing from the visitor center daily at 8:15am and 10am between June and September. Groups are limited to 25 people. Ranger availability and weather permitting, there's also a tour at 10am on weekends during the other months; be sure to phone ahead. Carry plenty of water; it's a tough slog back up to the canyon rim.

The 8.5-mile trail (one-way) to the astonishingly beautiful **Keet Seel** is steep, strenuous and involves crossing sand gullies and shallow streams, but it's well worth the effort. The trail is open from late May to early September and requires a backcountry permit reservable up to five months in advance. Call early since daily access is limited to 20 people; alternatively show up early on the day and hope for cancelations. You hike on your own but are met at the pueblo by a ranger who will take you on a tour. Because the hike is strenuous, most visitors stay at the primitive campground down in the canyon, which has composting toilets but no drinking water.

Kayenta

A top contender for stray-dog capital of Arizona, Kayenta is a cluster of businesses and mobile homes around the junction of Hwys 160 and 163. It's only draw is being the closest town to Monument Valley, some 20 miles away. It has gas stations, motels, restaurants, a supermarket and an ATM.

The Burger King near the junction has a well-meaning but minimal exhibit on the Navajo Code Talkers. **Roland's Navajoland Tours** (☑928-697-3524) and **Sacred Monument Tours** (☑435-727-3218; www.monument valley.net) offer vehicle, hiking and horseback-riding tours through Monument Valley.

🛏 Sleeping & Eating

A dearth of options sends prices sky-high in summer when demand at the three main motels exceeds capacity. Rates drop by nearly half in the slower seasons.

Kayenta Monument Valley Inn   MOTEL **$$**
(☑928-697-3221; www.kayentamonumentvalley inn.com; junction Hwys 160 & 163; r $229-249; ❋@🛜🏊) Formerly the Holiday Inn, this two-story motel doesn't look like much from the outside, but the rooms flash a little modern style with big-screen TVs and cool chocolate-and-black accents. The front desk is helpful, and there's a restaurant on-site.

Wetherill Inn   MOTEL **$$**
(☑928-697-3231; www.wetherill-inn.com; 1000 Main St/Hwy 63; r incl breakfast $132; ❋@🛜🏊) This motel has 54 standard-issue rooms huedin appealing earth tones. All have refrigerators and flat-screen TVs. Other amenities include an indoor pool and a laundry.

Hampton Inn   HOTEL **$$**
(☑928-697-3170; www.hamptoninn.com; junction Hwys 160 & 163; r incl breakfast from $189; ❋🛜🏊🐾). The decor is Native American, and there's an outdoor pool perfect for chilling out in after a day on the dusty roads. For

weekends in summer book well in advance. Kids under 18 stay free and pets are OK.

Golden Sands Cafe   CAFE **$$**
(☑928-697-3684; Hwy 163; mains $7-19; ⊙breakfast, lunch, dinner) Behind the Wetherill Inn is this friendly roadhouse with authentic Old West touches and a casual menu of American and Navajo dishes, including sandwiches with frybread and Navajo tacos.

Monument Valley Navajo Tribal Park

Like a classic movie star, Monument Valley has a face known around the world. Her fiery red spindles, sheer-walled mesas and grand buttes have starred in films and commercials, and have been featured in magazine ads and picture books. Monument Valley's epic beauty is heightened by the drab landscape surrounding it. One minute you're in the middle of sand, rocks and infinite sky, then suddenly you're transported to a fantasyland of crimson sandstone towers soaring up to 1200ft skyward.

Long before the land became part of the Navajo Reservation, the valley was home to Ancestral Puebloans, who abruptly abandoned the site some 700 years ago. When the Navajo arrived a few centuries ago, they called it Valley Between the Rocks. Today, Monument Valley straddles the Arizona-Utah border and is traversed by Hwy 163.

The most famous formations are conveniently visible from the rough 17-mile dirt road looping through **Monument Valley Navajo Tribal Park** (☑435-727-5874; www .navajonationparks.org/htm/monumentvalley.htm; adult/child $5/free; ⊙visitor center 6am-8pm May-Sep, 8am-5pm Oct-Apr, scenic drive 6am-8:30pm May-Sep, 8am-4:30pm Oct-Apr). It's usually possible to drive it in your own vehicle, even standard passenger cars, but expect a dusty, bumpy ride. There are multiple overlooks where you can get out and snap away or browse for trinkets and jewelry offered by Navajo vendors. Most of the formations were named for what they look like: the Mittens, Eagle Rock, Bear and Rabbit, and Elephant Butte. Budget at least 1½ hours for the drive, which starts from the visitor center at the end of a 4-mile paved road off Hwy 163 near Goulding's Lodge. There's also a restaurant, gift shop, tour desk and the new View Hotel. National Park passes are not accepted for admission into the park.

The only way to get off the road and into the backcountry is by taking a Navajo-led tour on foot, on horseback or by vehicle. You'll see rock art, natural arches, and coves such as the otherworldly Ear of the Wind, a bowl-shaped wall with a nearly circular opening at the top. Guides shower you with details about life on the reservation, movie trivia and whatever else comes to mind. Guides have booths set up in the parking lot at the visitor center; they're pretty easy-going, so don't worry about high-pressure sales. Tours leave frequently in summer, less so in winter, with rates starting at $60 for a 90-minute motorized trip. Outfitters in Kayenta and at Goulding's Lodge also offer tours. If you want to have things set up in advance, check out the list of guides on the tribal park's website.

The only hiking trail you are allowed to take without a guide is the **Wildcat Trail**, a 3.2-mile loop trail around the West Mitten formation. The trailhead is at the picnic area, about a half-mile north of the visitor center

🛏️ Sleeping & Eating

They built the View Hotel on the site of the old Mitten Campground, but you can still camp on a dusty patch of ground about a quarter mile north of the hotel. The only facilities are port-o-potties, but hey, you've got the view. It's $10 for up to five people, then an extra $10 for every five additional people.

TOP CHOICE View Hotel HOTEL $$
(☑435-727-5555; www.monumentvalleyview.com; Hwy 163; r $219-229, ste $299-319; ✳@) Probably the most aptly named hotel in Arizona, with Southwestern-themed rooms that are nice but nothing compared to their balconies. You'll never turn the TV on, at least while it's light outside. Rooms that end in numbers higher than 15 (like, say, 216) have unobstructed panoramas of the valley below; the best are on the third floor (and cost $20 more). The restaurant (mains $13 to $23) serves three OK meals a day in a dining room with floor-to-ceiling windows and an outdoor patio. Wi-fi available in the lobby only.

Goulding's Lodge MOTEL $$
(☑435-727-3231; www.gouldings.com; r $185-205; ✳🍴🏊🐾) This historic hotel a few miles west of Monument Valley has 62 modern rooms, most with views of the megaliths in the distance. The style is standard Southwestern, and each has a DVD player so you

can watch one of the many movies shot here, available for rent ($5) in the lobby. The hotel's **Stagecoach Dining Room** (mains $8-27; ⊙6:30am–9:30pm Utah time, shorter hours in winter) is a replica of a film set built for John Ford's 1949 Western *She Wore a Yellow Ribbon*. Get some roughage from the salad bar before cutting into the steaks or popular Navajo tacos. At lunchtime it often swarms with coach tourists. Pets cost $20 per pet per night.

Goulding's Camp Park CAMPGROUND $
(☑435-727-3235; www.gouldings.com; tent sites $25, RV sites $25-44, cabins $79; 🍴🏊) Tucked snugly between red sandstone walls with a shot of the Mittens out of the mouth of the canyon, this is a particularly scenic full-service campground that includes a store, pool and laundry. The three pre-fab cabins can sleep up to six people (if some of them are small).

Canyon De Chelly National Monument

It's a near soundless world, this remote and beautiful multipronged Canyon de Chelly (pronounced d-*shay*), far removed from time and space. Inhabited for 5000 years, it shelters prehistoric rock art and 1000-year-old Ancestral Puebloan dwellings built into alcoves.

Today, **Canyon de Chelly** (☑928-674-5500; www.nps.gov/cach; Chinle; admission free) is private Navajo land administered by the NPS. The name itself is a corruption of the Navajo word *tsegi*, which means 'rock canyon.' The Navajo arrived in the canyon in the 1700s, using it for farming and as a stronghold and retreat for their raids on other tribes and Spanish settlers. But if these cliffs could talk, they'd also tell stories of great violence and tragedy. In 1805, Spanish soldiers killed scores of Navajo hiding deep in the canyon in what is now called Massacre Cave. In 1864, the US Army – led by Kit Carson – drove thousands of Navajos into the canyon and starved them into surrendering, then forced the survivors to march 300 miles – the Long Walk – to Fort Sumner in New Mexico. Four years later, the Navajos were allowed to return.

Today, about 80 Navajo families still raise animals and grow corn, squash and beans on the land, allowing a glimpse of traditional life. Only enter hogans with a guide and don't take photographs without permission.

The mouth of the canyon is about 3 miles east of **Chinle**, where services include a gas station, supermarket, bank with ATM, motels and fast-food outlets.

◉ Sights & Activities

If you only have time for one trip, make it the **South Rim Drive**, which runs along the main canyon and has the most dramatic vistas. The 16-mile road passes six viewpoints before dead-ending at the spectacular **Spider Rock Overlook**, with views of the 800ft freestanding tower atop of which lives Spider Woman, an important Navajo god. Start early so that you have Spider Woman all to yourself; the silence here is strangely invigorating as you watch birds soaring between you and the majestic spire. It's easy to see why this is a sacred spot for the Navajo. Budget about two hours for the round-trip, including stops.

For the most part, **North Rim Drive** follows a side canyon called Canyon del Muerto, which has four overlooks. At the first one, **Antelope House Overlook**, you'll have stunning cliff-top views of a natural rock fortress and cliff dwellings. To see the latter, walk to your right from the walled Navajo fortress viewpoint to a second walled overlook. With few walls and no railings, this overlook may not be suited for small children or pets. The North Rim Drive ends at the Massacre Cave Overlook, 15 miles from the visitor center. The road continues 13 miles to the town of **Tsaile** (say-*lee*), where Diné College has an excellent museum, as well as a library and bookstore with a vast selection of books about the Navajo.

Bring binoculars and water, lock your car and don't leave valuables in sight when taking the short walks at each scenic point. The lighting for photography on the north rim is best in early morning and on the south rim in late afternoon.

☞ Tours

Entering the canyon maze is an amazing experience, as walls start at just a few feet but rise dramatically, topping out at about 1000ft. At many stops, Navajo vendors sell jewelry and crafts, usually at prices much lower than at the trading posts. Summer tours can get stifling hot and mosquitoes are plentiful, so bring a hat, sunscreen, water and insect repellent. For a list of approved tour guides, stop by the visitor center or check the park's website: www.nps.gov/cach /planyourvisit/things2do.htm.

Hiking

With one exception, you need a guide in order to hike anywhere in the canyon. Authorized guides are listed on the park website in the 'Plan Your Visit' section. You can also pick up the list at the park visitor center. A backcountry permit is required (but it's free). Expect to pay a guide about $25 per hour with a three-hour minimum. Rangers sometimes lead free half-day hikes in summer.

Otherwise, the steep and stunning **White House Trail** is your only option. Narrow switchbacks drop 550ft down from the White House Overlook on the South Rim Drive, about 6 miles east of the visitor center. It's only 1.25 miles to the stupendous White House Ruin, but coming back up is strenuous, so carry plenty of water and allow at least two hours. In summer, start out early or late in the day to avoid the worst of the heat.

Horseback Riding

Justin's Horse Tours   HORSEBACK RIDING
(☎928-674-5678) Located at the mouth of the canyon, Justin's has horses available year-round for $15 per person per hour, plus $15 an hour for the guide (two-hour minimum).

Totsonii Ranch   HORSEBACK RIDING
(☎928-755-6209; www.totsoniiranch.com) Located about 1¼ miles beyond the end of the pavement on South Rim Drive, this place charges the same as Justin's Horse Tours. The most popular ride is the four-hour round-trip to Spider Rock ($100 per person; two-person minimum). Also offers an overnight trip starting at $350.

Four-Wheel Driving

Numerous companies offer 4WD trips into the canyon. Consider a tour with **Thunderbird Lodge Tours** (☎928-674-5841; www.tbird lodge.com), based at the Thunderbird Lodge. They use Suburbans for small groups or, in summer, open-top heavy-duty 6WD propane-fuelled troop carriers. Locals call these 'shake-n-bake' tours. Half-day trips leave at 9am, 1pm and 2pm and cost $52/40 for adults/children. All-day tours ($83, no discounts) operate from March to November and include a picnic lunch.

Check with the visitor center for additional tour operators. Expect to pay $150 for a three-hour tour for between one and three people.

🛏 Sleeping & Eating

Lodging near the canyon is limited and often booked solid in summer, so plan ahead. All three motels listed here are decidedly – and similarly – average.

Hotels & Motels

Best Western Canyon
de Chelly Inn   MOTEL $$
(☎928-674-5875; www.bestwestern.com; 100 Main St, Chinle; r $109; ❄@🛜♨) In Chinle but still close to the canyon, this two-story property has an indoor pool and sauna. Rooms are slightly larger than average, if a bit un-inspired and dark. The on-site Junction Restaurant serves mediocre Native American and American dishes. The restaurant also shares its menu and dining room with a Pizza Hut, which was churning out the pies during our visit.

Thunderbird Lodge   MOTEL $$
(☎928-674-5841; www.tbirdlodge.com; d $115-171 $66-95; ❄@🛜♨) The closest lodging to the canyon entrance, this all-Navajo-staffed member of the Green Hotels Association has 73 rooms with TV and phone, most of them in a pink adobe lodge. Wi-fi is best in the rooms near the lobby. The cafeteria (mains $5-21; ⊙breakfast, lunch & dinner) serves mediocre American and Navajo food. Pets $30 per visit.

Holiday Inn   HOTEL $$
(☎928-674-5000; www.holidayinnchinle.com; BIA Route 7; r $117-129; ❄@🛜♨) Half a mile west of the visitor center, this adobe-style hotel offers modern rooms, a restaurant and a heated outdoor pool. Their front desk seems to be the friendliest of the bunch.

Campgrounds

Cottonwood Campground   CAMPGROUND $
(campsites free) Near the visitor center, this NPS-run campground has 96 primitive sites on a first-come, first-served basis. Water is available from April to October, and there are restrooms but no hookups or showers. Fewer sites and bathrooms available in winter. At press time, the park service and the Navajo Nation were discussing the implementation of fees at the campground, so be prepared to pay to camp during your visit.

Spider Rock Campground   CAMPGROUND $
(☎928-674-8261; www.spiderrockcampground.com; tent/RV sites $10/15, hogans $29-39; 🛜) This Navajo-run campground 12 miles from the visitor center on South Rim Dr is surrounded by piñon and juniper trees. Wi-fi is $2. No credit cards.

ℹ Information

En route to the canyon you'll pass the visitor center (☎928-674-5500; www.nps.gov/cach; ⊙8am-5pm), which has information about

---

WORTH A TRIP

WINDOW ROCK

The tribal capital of Window Rock sits at the intersection of Hwys 264 and 12, near the New Mexico border. The namesake rock is a nearly circular arch high up on a red sandstone cliff in the northern part of town. At its base is the new **Navajo Veterans Memorial Park** (☎928-871-6647; www.navajonationparks.org/htm/veterans.htm; admission free; ⊙8am-5pm), whose layout is patterned after a medicine wheel.

The sleek and modern **Navajo Nation Museum** (☎928-871-7941; cnr Hwy 264 & Loop Rd; admission by donation; ⊙8am-5pm Mon, 8am-6pm Tue-Fri, 9am-5pm Sat) looks more imposing and interesting than it really is, with temporary shows that are hit or miss. For a superb selection of Navajo jewelry and crafts, swing by **Navajo Arts & Crafts Enterprise** (NACE; ☎928-871-4090; Hwy 264 at Rte 12; ⊙9am-8pm Mon-Sat, noon-6pm Sun) next to the Quality Inn. Established in 1941, NACE is wholly Navajo operated and guarantees the authenticity and quality of its products.

The **Navajo Nation Fair** (www.navajonationfair.com) held in early September is a weeklong blowout with rodeos, the Miss Navajo Nation pageant, song and dance, livestock shows, horse races, a chile cook-off and lots of other events.

Rooms at the **Quality Inn Navajo Nation Capital** (☎928-871-4108; www.qualityinn.com; 48 W Hwy 264; r incl breakfast $78-93; ❄@🛜♨) are nothing fancy, but we liked the Southwestern motif. The hotel's biggest asset, though, is the falling-over-backwards staff. Rates include a filling breakfast in the reasonably priced restaurant serving Navajo, American and Mexican fare all day long.

guides and tours. Scenic drives skirting the canyon's northern and southern rim start nearby. Both are open year-round and, aside from one hiking trail, they are the only way to see the canyon without joining a guided tour.

Ganado & Hubbell Trading Post

Widely respected merchant John Lorenzo Hubbell established this **trading post** (☑928-755-3475; www.nps.gov/hutr; admission free; ☺8am-6pm May-early Sep, 8am-5pm mid-Sep–Apr) in 1878 to supply Navajos returning from Fort Sumner with dry goods and groceries. Now run by the NPS, it still sells food, souvenirs and local crafts. Navajo women often give weaving demonstrations inside the visitor center. Hubbell himself was an avid collector of these woolen artworks as you'll discover on a tour of his house (adult/child $2/free), given at 10am, 11am, 1pm, 2pm and 3pm. Enjoy a free sample of Arbuckle's Ariosa Coffee (www.arbuckle coffee.com) in the visitor center. This smooth and tasty cowboy coffee, which began selling in the 1860s, was easy to transport and prepare on the trail.

The post is in the village of Ganado, about 30 miles south of Chinle/Canyon de Chelly and 40 miles north of the I-40.

HOPI RESERVATION

Scattered across the tops of three rocky, buff-colored mesas and along the valleys below are the villages of the Peaceful Ones, which is what the Hopi call themselves. Their reservation – at the heart of their ancestral territory, though only containing a scant fraction of it – is like a 2410-sq-mile island floating in the Navajo Reservation. To the Hopi, Arizona's oldest and most traditional tribe, this remote terrain is not merely their homeland but also the hub of their spiritual world.

Deeply ingrained in the Hopi way is an ethic of welcoming strangers – they were even nice (for a long time, anyway) to Spanish conquistadors and missionaries. But decades of cultural abuses by visitors, even well-intentioned ones, have led Hopi villages to issue strict guidelines to protect their world. This is not just a matter of cultural survival, it's also about defending what is most deeply sacred to them.

Because of their isolated location, the Hopi have received less outside influence than other tribes and have limited tourist facilities. Aside from ancient Walpi on First Mesa, villages don't hold much intrinsic appeal for visitors. But a tour of the mesas with a knowledgeable guide can open the door to what's truly fascinating about this place: the people, their history and their traditions, which still thrive today. The Hopi are also extremely accomplished artists and craftspeople and it's well worth stopping at several shops along the main highway to peruse handmade baskets, kachina dolls, overlay silver jewelry and pottery.

Eleven of the 12 Hopi villages lie at the base or on the top of three mesas named by early European explorers, rather prosaically, First Mesa, Second Mesa and Third Mesa. They are linked by Hwy 264 along with the non-Hopi village of Keams Canyon. Narrow and often steep roads lead off the highway to the mesa tops. The twelfth village is Moenkopi, about 45 miles to the west, near Tuba City.

For an eclectically refreshing mix of background music, from Native American music to Cajun to blues to honky-tonk, turn your radio dial to KUYI 88.1, Hopi's radio station.

◉ Sights

FIRST MESA
Three villages squat atop this mesa and another village, nontraditional **Polacca**, hugs its base. The road up is steep; if you're here by RV, leave it in Polacca and walk. The first village is **Hano**, which blends imperceptibly into **Sichomovi**, where you'll find the community center at **Ponsi Hall** (☑928-737-2262; ☺8:30am-4pm Apr-Oct, hours fluctuate in winter). From here, local guides lead tours (adult/youth/child $13/10/5) of the tiny village of **Walpi**, preceded by an introduction to Hopi culture and belief systems. The most dramatic of the Hopi enclaves, Walpi dates back to AD 900 and clings like an aerie onto the mesa's narrow end. Sandstone-colored stone houses seem to sprout organically from the cliffs. These days, their only inhabitants are a few older ladies who live without plumbing or electricity, just like in the old days.

Outside Ponsi Hall, local artisans sell pots, kachinas and *piki* (a wafer-thin, dry rolled bread made from blue-corn meal) at fair prices.

It's best to call before visiting to confirm availability of tours, which may not run if there are private rituals scheduled on a particular day.

SECOND MESA

On Second Mesa, some 10 miles west of First Mesa, the **Hopi Cultural Center Restaurant & Inn** (☎928-734-2401; www.hopiculturalcenter.com) is as visitor-oriented as things get. It provides food and lodging, and there's also the small **Hopi Museum** (☎928-734-6650; adult/child $3/1; ⊗8am-5pm Mon-Fri, 9am-3pm Sat), with walls full of historic photographs and simple exhibits that share just enough about the Hopi world to allow you to understand that it's something altogether different from the one you likely inhabit.

Second Mesa has three villages of which the oldest, **Shungopavi**, is famous for its Snake dances, where dancers carry live rattlesnakes in their mouths. **Mishongnovi** and **Sipaulovi** sometimes have Social or Butterfly dances open to the public.

THIRD MESA

The tribal capital of **Kykotsmovi** sits below Third Mesa with **Batavi**, **Hotevila** and **Old Oraibi** up on top. The latter was established around AD 1200 and vies with Acoma Pueblo in New Mexico for the title of the USA's oldest continuously inhabited village. Park next to **Hamana So-O's Arts and Crafts** (☎928-734-9375) and stick your head inside to say hi and let someone know you're going to walk around. The shop itself has some great locally carved kachinas.

☞ Tours

When visiting Hopi country, the tour is the thing. So little about the place or the culture is obvious, even to the most astute outside eye, that visiting the villages with a knowledgeable local guide is really the only way to get a glimpse inside. Some guides include a trip to nearby Dawa Park, where thousands of ancient petroglyphs are etched into the rocks. **Hopi Tours** (☎928-206-7433; www.hopitours.com) are led by Micah Loma'omvaya, a member of the Bear Clan from Shungopavi and an experienced anthropologist and former tribal archaeologist. His engaging tours blend a trove of historical fact with the personal understanding of the Hopi world that comes from living in it. Bertram Tsavadawa of **Ancient Pathways** (☎928-797-8145; www.experiencehopi.com) and Gary Tso of **Left-Handed Hunter Tour Company** (☎928-734-2567; www.experiencehopi.com; lhhunter68@hopi telecom.net) are also recommended. Prices depend on tour length and group size.

★ Festivals & Events

Each village decides whether to allow non-Hopis at ceremonial dances. Some of the Kachina dances, held between January and July, are closed affairs, as are the famous Snake or Flute dances in August. It's much easier to attend Social dances and Butterfly dances, held late August through November. For upcoming festivities, check with the community development offices at each village. Not all public ceremonies are scheduled on a long-term calendar, and you may only hear about one by word of mouth. Be sure to ask while visiting if you're interested.

Kykotsmovi (☎928-734-2474)

Mews Consolidated Villages (☎928-737-2670)

Sichomovi (☎928-734-1258)

Sipaulovi (☎928-737-5426)

Some Hopi events are listed on www.sipaulovihopiinformationcenter.org/events.html. When attending these ceremonies, be respectful. For details on etiquette, see p527.

🛏 Sleeping & Eating

The reservation's only hotel (☎928-734-2401; www.hopiculturalcenter.com/reservations; d mid-Mar–mid-Oct $105, mid-Oct–mid-Mar $85) is part of the Hopi Cultural Center. Reservations are essential, especially in summer when its 30 modern, if bland, rooms usually book out. The **restaurant** (breakfast & lunch $8-12, dinner $8-20; ⊗breakfast, lunch & dinner) is your chance to taste Hopi treats like *noykwivi* (lamb and hominy stew) served with blue-corn fry bread. Less adventurous palates will find the usual American fare – burgers and grilled chicken.

❶ Information

Make your first stop the **Hopi Cultural Center** (☎928-734-2401; www.hopiculturalcenter.com) on Second Mesa to pick up information and get oriented. Information may be also be obtained from the **Hopi Tribe Cultural Preservation Office** (☎928-734-3612; www.nau.edu/~hcpo-p; ⊗8am-5pm Mon-Fri) in Kykotsmovi (Third Mesa). Each village has its own rules for visitors, which are usually posted along the highways, but generally speaking any form of recording, be it camera, video or audiotape, or even sketching, is strictly forbidden. This is partly for religious reasons but also to prevent commercial exploitation by non-Hopis. Alcohol and other drug use is also prohibited.

As with the rest of Arizona (and different from the surrounding Navajo Reservation), the Hopi Reservation does not observe daylight saving time in summer. The climate is harsh – ungodly hot in summer and freezing cold in winter – so come prepared either way.

Hopi prefer cash for most transactions. There's an ATM outside the one store in Polacca. There's a **hospital** (☎928-737-6000) with 24hr emergency care in Polacca. For other emergencies, call the **BIA police** (☎928-738-2233).

Gas is cheaper outside the reservation, but there are filling stations in Keams Canyon and Kykotsmovi.

❶ Getting There & Away

The Hopi mesas are about 50 miles east of Tuba City and 85 miles west of Window Rock via flat and largely uneventful Hwy 264. Three roads enter the reservation from I-40 in the south. Coming from Flagstaff, the closest approach is by heading east on I-10 to Winslow, then cutting north on Hwy 87 (130 miles). From Winslow it's 70 miles via Hwy 87, and from Holbrook 80 miles on Hwy 77. Buses operated by **Navajo Transit System** (☎928-729-4002, 866-243-6260; www.navajotransit.com) pass through on their daily route between Tuba City and Window Rock.

WESTERN ARIZONA

Arizona may not be on the ocean but it does have a 'West Coast.' At least that's what wily marketers have dubbed the 1000-mile stretch of Colorado River that forms the state's boundary with California. After emerging from the Grand Canyon, the river gets tamed by a series of megadams, most famously Hoover Dam (p89). In winter migratory flocks of birds arrive from frigid northern climes. The winged variety seeks out riverside wildlife refuges, while the two-legged 'snowbird' species packs dozens of dusty RV parks, especially in Yuma. Although summers are hellishly hot, the cool Colorado brings in scores of water rats and boaters seeking relief from the heat in such places as Lake Havasu and Laughlin.

Bullhead City & Laughlin

Named for a rock that resembled the head of a snoozing bull, Bullhead City began as a construction camp for Davis Dam, built in the 1940s. The rock was eventually submerged by Lake Mojave, but the town stuck around and survives today, primarily because of the casinos across the Colorado River in Laughlin.

Its sister (but not twin) city, Laughlin, has a little more sizzle and is known by a number of nicknames: 'Vegas on the cheap', the 'un-Vegas,' the 'anti-Sin City.' It's all just fine by this gambling town, founded in 1964 by gaming impresario Don Laughlin, a high-school dropout from Minnesota. The image of good, clean fun (no leggy showgirls, no sleazy types touting escort services) is a winner with the blue-haired set and, increasingly, budget-strapped families looking for an inexpensive getaway.

Skip either town in summer when temperatures often soar to a merciless 120°F (almost 50°C).

🛏 Sleeping

Laughlin's big hotel-casinos are fantastic value, with spacious doubles starting at $30 during midweek and $60 on weekends. Most charge for wi-fi but some don't offer it at all, since they'd rather have you downstairs pulling slots. All are on Casino Dr, which parallels the river.

Aquarius Casino Resort   HOTEL $
(☎702-298-5111; www.aquariuscasinoresort.com; 1900 S Casino Dr, Laughlin; r $70-100, ste $209-329; ❄@🛜🏊) The Aquarius hits the jackpot: chic, welcoming and budget friendly. The new lobby has art deco touches, while rooms are modern with big windows and flat-screen TVs. The Splash Cabaret has free entertainment on Friday and Saturday nights, and the pool and tennis court area is up on a rooftop mezzanine. Wi-fi is $12 per day or free on the casino level at Starbucks.

Golden Nugget   HOTEL $
(☎702-298-7111; www.goldennugget.com/laughlin; 2300 S Casino Dr; r $80-90; ❄@🛜🏊) This cool and inviting place is the casino on which Vegas mogul Steve Wynn cut his teeth back in 1989. The latest owners of this 300-room 'boutique casino' have sunk big bucks into creating an intimate but classy experience with tropical-themed rooms, a palm-tree-flanked riverfront pool and above-average eateries. Rooms can drop as low as $23 during the week. Wi-fi is $10 per day.

Tropicana Express   HOTEL $
(☎702-298-4200; www.tropicanax.com; 2121 S Casino Dr, Laughlin; r $59-80; ❄@🏊🐾) The

1500-room former Ramada Express has rolled into the 21st century without ditching its family-friendly train theme. The new rooms could give Vegas a run for its money with chocolate-brown contemporary furniture, leather headboards and pillow-top mattresses.

✖ Eating & Drinking

All casinos feature multiple restaurants, usually including a buffet, a 24-hour cafe and an upscale steak house, along with bars and lounges. Even employees at other hotels say that Harrah's has the best buffet in town.

Saltgrass Steakhouse   STEAKHOUSE **$$**
(☑702-298-7153; 2300 S Casino Dr, Laughlin; mains $10-33; ☉dinner Mon-Sat, 7am-10pm Sun) Surrender helplessly to your inner carnivore at this river-view Wild West-themed restaurant at the Golden Nugget. The yummy cuts of Angus beef are the way to go, but char-grilled chicken and fish also put in menu appearances.

Earl's Home Cookin'
at the Castle   AMERICAN **$**
(☑928-754-1118; 491 Long Ave, Bullhead City; $5-21; ☉7am-8pm) Folks are friendly inside this turreted mock-castle in Old Bullhead, where the food sure tastes good and the $5.49 breakfast specials are a deal.

Pints Brewery & Sports Bar   BREWERY **$$**
(☑702-298-4000; 2010 S Casino Dr, Laughlin; mains $9-22; ☉lunch Fri-Sun, dinner daily) This buzzy spot inside the Colorado Belle is home to Laughlin's only brewery. The open kitchen prepares wraps, burgers and wood-fired pizzas. Lots of TVs for sports fans.

Loser's Lounge   BAR
(☑702-298-2535; 1650 S Casino Dr, Laughlin; ☉7pm to late) Pictures of General Custer, Robert E. Lee and other famous 'losers' decorate the walls at this at this bar and dance-club fixture at the Riverside Resort. Live bands play chart music.

❶ Information

Remember, Nevada time is one hour behind Arizona in winter, but in the same time zone in summer (Arizona doesn't observe daylight saving time).
Bullhead Area Chamber of Commerce (☑928-754-4121; 1251 Hwy 95; ☉8am-5pm Mon-Fri)

Laughlin Visitor Center (☑702-298-3321; www.visitlaughlin.com; 1555 S Casino Dr; ☉8am-4:30pm Mon-Fri) The visitor center and the chamber of commerce both have area info, including copies of the *Entertainer*, a weekly guide to the Laughlin casino scene.

Post office (990 Hwy 95, cnr 7th St, Bullhead City; ☉10am-2pm Mon-Fri)

❶ Getting There & Away

There are no longer any commercial flights into Bullhead City/Laughlin Airport. Las Vegas' McCarran International Airport is about 100 miles north of town and linked to Laughlin hotels by **River City Shuttle** (☑928-854-5253; www.rivercityshuttle.com) two times daily ($40 one way, 1¾ hours). Ferries go back and forth across the river between Bullhead and Laughlin.

Route 66: Topock To Kingman

Coming from California, Route 66 enters Arizona at Topock, near the 20-mile **Topock Gorge**, a dramatic walled canyon that's one of the prettiest sections of the Colorado River. It's part of the **Havasu National Wildlife Refuge** (☑760-326-3853; www.fws.gov/southwest/refuges/arizona/havasu), a major habitat for migratory and water birds. Look for herons, ducks, geese, blackbirds and other winged creatures as you raft or canoe through the gorge. There are plenty of coves and sandy beaches for picnics and sunning. Companies renting boats include **Jerkwater Canoe & Kayak** (☑928-768-7753; www.jerkwatercanoe.com) in Topock, which launches day trips ($46) from Topock Marina. Rates include boat rental for the 17-mile float from Topock to Castle Rock and the return shuttle.

North of here, in **Golden Shores**, you can refuel on gas and grub before embarking on a rugged 20-mile trip to the terrifically crusty former gold-mining town of **Oatman**, cupped by pinnacles and craggy hills. Since the veins of ore ran dry in 1942, the little settlement has reinvented itself as a movie set and unapologetic Wild West tourist trap, complete with staged gunfights (daily at noon, 1:30pm, 2:15pm and 3:15pm) and gift stores named Fast Fanny's Place and the Classy Ass. And speaking of asses, there are plenty of them (the four-legged kind, that is) roaming the streets and shamelessly begging for food. You can buy hay squares in town. Stupid and endearing, they're descendents from pack animals left behind by the early miners.

Squeezed among the shops is the 1902 **Oatman Hotel**, a surprisingly modest shack (no longer renting rooms) where Clark Gable and Carole Lombard first shagged, presumably, on their wedding night in 1939. Clark apparently returned quite frequently to play cards with the miners in the downstairs saloon, which is awash in one-dollar bills (some $40,000 worth by the barmaid's estimate). At the time of research, the upstairs, where visitors used to be able to peek into the old guest rooms, was closed for renovations. Beyond Oatman, keep your wits about you as the road twists and turns past tumbleweeds, saguaro cacti and falling rocks as it travels over **Sitgreaves Pass** (3523ft) and corkscrews into the rugged Black Mountains before arriving in Kingman.

KINGMAN

Among Route 66 aficionados, Kingman is known as the main hub of the longest uninterrupted stretch of the historic highway, running from Topock to Seligman. Among its early 20th-century buildings you'll find the former Methodist church at 5th and Spring St where Clark Gable and Carole Lombard tied the knot in 1939. Hometown hero Andy Devine had his Hollywood breakthrough as the perpetually befuddled driver of the eponymous *Stagecoach* in John Ford's Oscar-winning 1939 movie.

These days, Kingman feels like a place teetering between decline and revival. The historic Hotel Brunswick closed in 2010 due to hard times but on Beale St, the axis of historic downtown, some new eateries and galleries are sparking optimism.

Route 66 barrels through town as Andy Devine Ave. Parallel to it is up-and-coming Beale St. Supermarkets, gas stations and other businesses line up along northbound Stockton Hill Rd, which is also the road to take for Grand Canyon West.

Sights & Activities

Route 66 Museum MUSEUM
(☎928-753-9889; www.kingmantourism.org; 120 W Andy Devine Ave; adult/child/senior $4/free/3; ⏲9am-5pm) On the second floor of the 1907 powerhouse, which also holds the visitor center, this small but engaging museum has the best historical overview of the Mother Road anywhere along it. Check out that crazy air conditioner on the 1950 Studebaker Champion!

Mohave Museum of History & Arts MUSEUM
(☎928-753-3195; www.mohavemuseum.org; 400 W Beale St; adult/child/senior $4/free/3; ⏲9am-5pm Mon-Fri, 1-5pm Sat) Admission to the Route 66 Museum also gets you into the Mohave Museum, a warren of rooms filled with extraordinarily eclectic stuff. All sorts of regional topics are dealt with, from frontier life to Andy Devine. There's also an entire wall of portraits of American first ladies.

Hualapai Mountain Park PARK
(☎928-681-5700; www.mcparks.com; day use $5) In summer locals climb this nearby mountain for picnics, hiking and wildlife-watching amid cool ponderosa pine and aspen.

Festivals & Events

Historic Route 66 Fun Run CAR SHOW
(☎928-753-5001; www.azrt66.com) Vintage car rally from Seligman to Topock on the first weekend in May.

Andy Devine Days Parade PARADE
(☎928-753-4003; www.kingmantourism.org) Floats and a rodeo in late September.

Sleeping

Kingman has plenty of motels along Andy Devine Ave north and south of the I-40. Rates start at about $32 per double, but the cheapest places are dingy and popular with down-on-their-luck long-term residents. Inspect before committing.

Hampton Inn & Suites HOTEL **$$**
(☎928-692-0200; 1791 Sycamore Ave; www.hamptoninn.com; r incl breakfast $110-139; ❄@🛜🏊) The best of the chains, the Hampton has clean and spacious rooms and is a good choice for families. There's a small outdoor pool for cooling off after a day on the road. Very welcoming.

Hualapai Mountain Park CAMPGROUND **$**
(☎928-681-5700, 877-757-0915; www.mcparks.com; Hualapai Mountain Rd; tent/RV sites $15/25, cabins $70-125) Camp among granite rock formations and ponderosa pine at this pretty county park, some 15 miles south of town.

Hualapai Mountain Resort LODGE **$**
(☎928-757-3545; www.hmresort.net; 4525 Hualapai Mountain Rd; r $79-99, ste $159; 🐾) Think mountain-man chic: chunky wood furniture, bold paintings of wild game, a front porch that's made for elk- and wildlife-watching among the towering pines. The on-site restaurant serves lunch and dinner Wednesday through Sunday and breakfast on weekends.

Travelodge   MOTEL **$**
(📞928-757-1188; www.travelodge.com; 3275 E
Andy Devine Ave; r incl breakfast $51-64; ❄@🛜🏊)
For budget travelers it's got everything you
need: a Route 66-adjacent location, helpful
staff, continental breakfast, a laundry, free
wi-fi and a few rooms under $55.

Hilltop Motel   MOTEL **$**
(📞928-753-2198; www.hilltopmotelaz.com; 1901 E
Andy Devine Ave; s/d $42/46; ❄@🛜🏊) Rooms
here are a bit of a throwback, but well kept.
On Route 66, with nice views and a cool
neon sign.

✖ Eating & Drinking
Cellar Door   WINE BAR **$**
(📞928-753-3885; www.the-cellar-door.com; 414
E Beale St; appetizers under $8; ⏱4-10pm Wed &
Thu, 4pm-midnight Fri & Sat) This new wine bar
offers about 140 wines by the bottle, 30
by the glass, an international selection of
beers and tasty appetizer plates. It's a hot
little spot that embodies the spirit of revival
in Kingman.

Dambar Steakhouse   STEAKHOUSE **$$**
(📞928-753-3523; 1960 E Andy Devine Ave; lunch
$6-11, dinner $10-22; ⏱lunch & dinner; 👶) This
local landmark serves giant steaks in Old
West bad-boy environs while keeping the
kiddies happy with coloring placemats and
crayons. Local characters hang out at the
spit-and-sawdust saloon with cow hide
tablecloths.

Mr D'z Route 66 Diner   DINER **$**
(📞928-718-0066; 105 E Andy Devine Ave; mains
$6-18; ⏱7am-9pm) Get your *American Graf-
fiti* fix at this modern-vintage diner with its
hot-pink and turquoise color scheme and
cool memorabilia. Oprah herself gave the
thumbs up to its cheeseburgers, onion rings
and signature root-beer float when stopping
by in 2006. Breakfast is served all day.

Beale Street Brews   COFFEE SHOP **$**
(418 E Beale St; ⏱7am-5pm Mon-Fri, 7am-4pm Sat
& Sun; 🛜) This cute indie coffee shop draws
local java cognoscenti with its lattes, live
music and poetry nights.

❶ Information
Kingman Regional Medical Center (📞928-
757-2101; www.azkrmc.com; 3269 Stockton
Hill Rd)
Police (📞928-753-2191; 2730 E Andy Devine Ave)
Powerhouse Visitor Center (📞928-753-6106,
866-427-7866; www.kingmantourism.org; 120

W Andy Devine Ave; ⏱8am-5pm). Lots of
information about Route 66 attractions.

❶ Getting There & Away
Great Lakes Airlines (📞800-554-511; www
.flygreatlakes.com) provides the only commercial
flights in and out of Kingman Airport, linking it
daily to Phoenix.

Greyhound (📞928-757-8400; www.greyhound
.com; 3264 E Andy Devine Ave; ⏱ticket office
8am-1pm & 5:30-6pm) runs daily buses to
Phoenix ($61, 5½ hours), Las Vegas ($46, three
hours), Flagstaff ($56, 2½ hours), Los Angeles
($103, 11 hours) and elsewhere. **Amtrak's**
(📞800-872-7245; www.amtrak.com) westbound
Southwest Chief stops at 11:46pm, the eastbound
at 2:33am. There's a train waiting room at the
corner of Andy Devine Ave (Route 66) and 4th
St. It's not a full station and you cannot buy a
ticket here, so book ahead.

Around Kingman
CHLORIDE
The hills surrounding Chloride, some 20
miles northwest of Kingman, once spewed
forth tons of silver, gold, copper and tur-
quoise from as many as 75 mines. These
days, this peaceful semi-ghost town is
inhabited by quirky locals who create
bizarre junk sculptures and proudly dis-
play them outside their ramshackle homes.
You can post a letter in Arizona's oldest
continuously operating post office (since
1862) or snap a picture of yourself behind
bars at the crumbling jail. Up in the hills,
reached via a super-rough 1.5-mile dirt
road, are Roy Purcell's psychedelic rock
murals. If you don't have a 4WD, hike
up or risk a busted axle. Two gunfighting
troupes stage rip-roarin' shoot-'em-ups at
high noon on Saturday between Septem-
ber and June (and on the first and third
Saturday in July and August). One of
them is the ultimate 'guns and roses' – the
world's only all-girl gun-fighting troupe,
the Wild Roses of Chloride.

For maps and information, stop by the
Mine Shaft Market (📞928-565-4888; 4940
Tennessee Ave; ⏱8am-5pm Mon-Sat, 9am-5pm
Sun).

When the sun goes down and the stars
come out, you'll feel the true Wild West
spirit. Bonnie and John operate a few simple
but cozy adobe-walled rooms with squeaking
mattresses at the **Sheps Miners Inn** (📞928-
565-4251; 9827 2nd St; r $35-65). It's right
behind **Yesterdays** (📞928-565-4251; 9827

2nd St; mains $7-20; ◎lunch, dinner daily, breakfast Sat & Sun), their restaurant and Western saloon, with creaky wooden floors, vintage gas pumps and hand-painted murals. It serves hearty American grub, international beers and toe-tapping live music nightly. The only sad part? There's a dish on the menu called 'yesterday's salmon.'

Route 66: Kingman To Williams

Past Kingman, Route 66 arcs north away from the I-40 for 115 dusty miles of original Mother Road through scrubby, lonely landscape. It merges with the I-40 near Seligman, then reappears briefly as Main St in Williams. Gas stations are rare, so make sure you've got enough fuel. The total distance to Williams is 130 miles.

KINGMAN TO PEACH SPRINGS

It's tempting to try to race the train on this lonely stretch of Mother Road where your only other friend is the pavement unfurling for miles ahead. The first opportunity for socializing arises in tiny **Hackberry**, where highway memorialist Robert Waldmire lures passers-by with his much loved **Old Route 66 Visitor Center** (☑928-769-2605; www.hackberrygeneralstore.com; 11255 E Rte 66; admission free; ◎generally 9am-5pm) inside an eccentrically decorated gas station. It's a refreshing spot for a cold drink and souvenirs. Keep going and you'll pass through the blink-and-you'll-miss-them towns of Valentine and Truxton.

For information about Peach Springs, see p178.

GRAND CANYON CAVERNS

Nine miles past Peach Springs, a plaster dinosaur welcomes you to the **Grand Canyon Caverns & Inn** (☑928-422-3223; www.gccaverns.com; Rte 66, Mile 115; 1hr tour adult/child $15/10; ◎9am-5pm Mar-Oct, 10am-4pm Nov-Feb; ❄♿), a cool subterranean retreat from the summer heat. An elevator drops 210ft underground to artificially lit limestone caverns and the skeletal remains of a prehistoric ground sloth. If you've seen other caverns these might not be as impressive, but kids get a kick out of a visit. The 30 to 45-minute short tour is wheelchair accessible. Since 2010, about 100 people have spent the night in the new Cavern Suite ($700), an underground 'room' with two double beds, a sitting area and multicolored lamps. If you ever wanted to live in one of those postapocalyptic sci-fi movies, here's your chance! One of the DVDs on offer is underground horror flick *The Cave* – watch it here only if you're especially twisted.

Up on the surface, **horseback tours** (per 30min/hr $20/35) from the riding stable trot off on trail rides hourly and at sunset. The **restaurant** (mains $10-16; ◎7am-7pm) is nice if you already happen to be here; it has a small playground and serves burgers, sandwiches and fried food. The bar opens at 4pm and closes based on crowd-size. The **campground** (tent/RV sites $15/30) here has over 50 sites carved out of the juniper forest, plus new open-air, roof-free rooms (from $60) on raised platforms for star-gazers. The **Caverns Inn** (r $85-107; ❄♿❄) has rooms that are basic but well kept. There's wi-fi in the lobby. Pets are $5 per day with a refundable $50 deposit.

SELIGMAN

Some 23 miles of road slicing through rolling hills gets you to Seligman – a town that embraces its Route 66 heritage, thanks to the Delgadillo brothers, who for decades have been the Mother Road's biggest boosters. Juan sadly passed away in 2004, but octogenarian Angel and his wife Vilma still run **Angel's Barbershop** (☑928-422-3352; www.route66giftshop.com; 217 E Rte 66). OK, so he doesn't cut hair anymore, but the barber's chair is still there and you can poke around for souvenirs and admire license plates sent in by fans from all over the world. If Angel is around, he's usually happy to regale you with stories about the Dust Bowl era. He's seen it all.

Angel's madcap brother Juan used to rule prankishly supreme over the **Snow Cap Drive-In** (☑928-422-3291; 301 E Rte 66; dishes $3-6; ◎10am-6pm mid-Mar–Nov), a Route 66 institution now kept going by his sons Bob and John. The crazy decor is only the beginning. Wait until you see the menu featuring cheeseburgers with cheese and 'dead chicken!' Beware the fake mustard bottle... They sometimes open at 9am in mid-summer.

Two good restaurants stare each other down from opposite sides of Route 66. For friendly service and good American grub, try **Westside Lilo's Cafe** (415 W Rte 66; mains $5-16; ◎6am-9pm), which also has an outdoor patio. For beer and a few tongue-in-cheek menu items, try the **Roadkill Café & OK Saloon** (502 W Rte 66; breakfast $5-13, lunch $6-17, dinner $15-25; ◎7am-9pm) across the street, which has an all-you-can-eat salad bar, juicy steaks and burgers and, of course, the 'splatter platter.'

The most appealing hotel is **Canyon Lodge** (📞928-422-3255; 114 E Chino Ave; s/d incl breakfast $50/55; 🛜) where each immaculately clean room is decked out in a '50s-inspired theme. We're partial to the Elvis Room, which dukes it out with the John Wayne Room for most popular among guests. For the best neon sign, look no further than the welcoming **Supai Motel** (📞928-422-4153; www.supaimotel.com; 134 W Chino Ave; s/d $48/54; 🛜), a classic courtyard motel offering simple but perfectly fine rooms with refrigerators and microwaves. The Havasu Falls mural is an inspiring way to start the morning.

Lake Havasu City

Lake Havasu City has all the unreal charm of a manufactured community. It also has London Bridge. Yes, that would be the original gracefully arched bridge that spanned the Thames from 1831 until 1967, when it was quite literally falling down (as predicted in the old nursery rhyme) and put up for sale. Robert McCulloch was busy developing a master planned community on Lake Havasu and badly in need of some gimmick to drum up attention for his project. Bingo! McCulloch snapped up London Bridge for a cool $2.46 million, dismantled it into 10,276 slabs and reassembled it in the Arizona desert. The first car rolled across in 1971.

Listed in the *Guinness World Records* as the world's largest antique, London Bridge may be one of Arizona's most incongruous tourist sites, but it's also among its most popular. Day-trippers come by the busload to walk across it and soak up faux British heritage in the kitschy-quaint English Village. The lake itself is the other major draw. Formed in 1938 by the construction of Parker Dam, it's much beloved by water rats, especially students on spring break (roughly March to May) and summer-heat refugees from Phoenix and beyond.

◉ Sights & Activities

Once you've snapped pics of **London Bridge**, you'll find that most of your options are water related. Several companies offer boat tours (from around $20) from English Village. Options include one-hour narrated jaunts, day trips and sunset tours, which can usually be booked on the spot. Several companies along the waterfront in English Village rent jet skis and other watercraft.

London Bridge Beach　　　　　BEACH
(1340 McCulloch Blvd) This sandy strip has palm trees, a sandy beach, playgrounds and a fenced dog park with faux fire hydrant in the middle, all with bridge views. It's off W McCulloch Blvd, behind Island Inn hotel. Nearby is the **Lake Havasu Marina** (📞928-855-2159; www.lakehavasumarina.com; 1100 McCulloch Blvd), which has boat ramps but no rentals.

🛏 Sleeping

Rates fluctuate tremendously from summer weekends to winter weekdays. Local budget and national chain hotels line London Bridge Rd.

Heat　　　　　　　　　BOUTIQUE HOTEL $$
(📞928-854-2833; www.heathotel.com; 1420 McCulloch Blvd; r $139-159; ste $191-256; ❄🛜) The front desk doubles as a bar at Heat, the slickest hotel on Arizona's west coast. Rooms are hip and contemporary, and most have private patios with views of London Bridge. In the 'inferno' rooms, bathtubs fill from the ceiling! An outdoor cocktail lounge overlooking the bridge and the lake feels almost like the deck of a cruise ship.

Windsor Beach Campground　CAMPGROUND $
(📞928-855-2784; www.azstateparks.com; 699 London Bridge Rd; campsite $18) Sleep just steps from the water at this scenic beach and camping area at Lake Havasu State Park. Amenities include showers, boat launch facilities and new hookups. The 1.5-mile Mohave Sunset Trail runs almost the full-length of the park. Day use is $15 per vehicle.

London Bridge Resort　　　　HOTEL $$
(📞928-855-0888; www.londonbridgeresort.com; 1477 Queens Bay Rd; ste $139-269; ❄🐾@🛜🏊) Enjoy flat-screen TVs, new mattresses and rooms with views of London Bridge (of course) at this popular all-suite property, where a replica of a 1762 royal coach greets guest in the lobby. It's a good choice if you want pools, nightclubs, bars and restaurants all under one roof.

Motel 6　　　　　　　　　MOTEL $
(📞928-855-3200; www.motel6.com; 111 London Bridge Rd; r $54-60; ❄🐾🛜🏊) You know the drill: no-frills rooms, scratchy towels, cheap rates.

Lake Havasu City

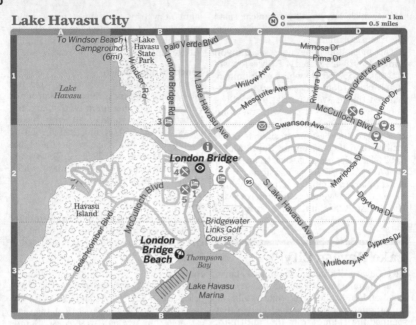

Lake Havasu City

This lakeside location is well-managed and close to London Bridge.

✗ Eating & Drinking

There's no shortage of places to eat and drink in Havasu.

Angelina's Italian Kitchen ITALIAN $$
(☎928-680-3868; 2137 W Acoma Blvd; mains $8-27; ⊘dinner Tue-Sat) If you like your Italian food cooked as if mama was behind the stove, you'll like this very busy hole in the wall on an industrial stretch east of downtown. It's cluttered and some of the patrons may be eccentric, but the home-cooked Italian weaves together pungent flavors like fine tapestry.

Red Onion AMERICAN $
(☎928-505-0302; 2013 N McCulloch Blvd; mains $7-11; ⊘8am-2pm daily, 4-8pm Thu & Fri) A step above a diner, a step below a bistro, the dining room here opens up onto Havasu's 'uptown district.' Try the omelets for a hearty start to your day. Service is friendly, if a bit disorganized.

Javelina Cantina MEXICAN $$
(www.javelinacantina.com; 1420 McCulloch Blvd; mains $11-18; ⊘11am-9pm) The outdoor patio at this busy Mexican restaurant – owned by the folks behind Barley Brothers – has great views of London Bridge.

Wired COFFEE SHOP $
(www.wiredcoffeelhc.com; 2131 N McCulloch Blvd; mains under $6; ⊘5:30am-5:30pm Mon-Fri, 6am-noon Sat & Sun; ☎) If every coffee shop could be this awesome, the world would be a better place. Welcoming staff, scrumptious pastries, free wi-fi, an inviting

interior and fresh coffee – Wired is a great coffee shop. Wraps and sandwiches on sale for lunch. The Death Valley date cookie is tasty.

Barley Brothers   PUB $$
(☎928-505-7837; www.barleybrothers.com; 1425 McCulloch Blvd; mains $10-26; ⊙11am-10pm) It's brews and the views at this busy microbrewery overlooking London Bridge. Steaks, burgers and salads are on the menu, but the place is known for its wood-fired pizzas. Lots of flat-screen TVs for sports fans, and beer drinkers can choose from one of six different microbrews. Biggest drawback? No outdoor patio.

BJ's Tavern   BAR
(2122 N McCulloch Blvd; ⊙6am-2am Mon-Sat) Inside there's a jukebox, pool tables and karaoke, while outdoors is a misted smoking patio.

ⓘ Information
Lake Havasu Post Office (☎928-855-2361; 1750 N McCulloch Blvd; ⊙8.30am-5pm Mon-Fri, 9am-1pm Sat)

Visitor center (☎928-855-5655; www.golakehavasu.com; 420 English Village; ⊙9am-5pm; @ 🛜) Has all the need-to-know info.

ⓘ Getting There & Away
Lake Havasu is on Hwy 95, about 20 miles south of the I-40. There's no public transportation, but **River City Shuttle** (☎928-854-5253; www.rivercityshuttle.com) runs buses to Las Vegas' McCarran International Airport twice daily ($65 one way, 3¼ hours).

Parker

Hugging a 16-mile stretch of the Colorado River known as the Parker Strip, this tiny town south of Lake Havasu is a convenient pit stop for those wanting to explore some of the region's unique riparian parks and preserves. All hell breaks loose in late January/early February when the engines are revved up for the **Best in the Desert Parker 425** (www.bitd.com), an off-road race that lures up to 100,000 speed freaks. Contact the **chamber of commerce** (☎928-669-2174; www.parkertourism.com; 1217 California Ave; ⊙8am-5pm Mon-Fri) for the lowdown.

Parker is 35 miles south of Lake Havasu via Hwy 95.

◉ Sights & Activities
Water-skiing and jet-skiing, fishing, boating and tubing are popular here, and there are plenty of concessionaires along the Parker Strip.

Parker Dam   DAM
Finished in 1938, this mighty dam formed Lake Havasu 15 miles north of town. It may not look it, but it is in fact the world's deepest dam, with 73% of its structural height of 320ft buried beneath the original riverbed. Although the interior of the dam has been off limits to tourists since September 11, 2001, you can drive over it between 5am and 11pm (although the road is too narrow for large RVs).

Buckskin Mountain State Park   PARK
(☎928-667-3231; www.azstateparks.com; 5476 N Hwy 95; admission per vehicle $10) Tucked along a mountain-flanked bend in the Colorado River about 11 miles north of Parker, this park has great family-friendly infrastructure with a playground, swimming beach, basketball court, cafe and grocery store (summer only). **Campsites** (tent & RV sites $30) are now available by reservation online or by phone. Tent campers who want to be close to the water should opt for a covered waterside cabana; those looking for quieter, more scenic desert camping can drive another mile north to the park's **River Island Unit** (☎928-667-3386; sites $25).

🌿 Bill Williams National Wildlife Refuge   PRESERVE
(☎928-667-4144; www.fws.gov/southwest/REFUGES/arizona/billwill.html; 60911 Hwy 95; ⊙8am-4pm Mon-Fri, 10am-2pm Sat & Sun) Abutting Cattail Cove, where the Bill Williams River meets Lake Havasu, is this calm wildlife refuge, which helps protect the unique transition zone between Mohave and Sonoran desert ecosystems. On a finger of land pointing into the lake, there's a 1.4-mile interpretive trail through a botanic garden of native flora, with shaded benches and access to fishing platforms. Endangered birds like to roost in the largest cottonwood/willow grove along the entire length of the Colorado River. Entrance is between Mile 161 and 162.

Colorado River Indian Tribes Museum   MUSEUM
(☎928-669-8970; cnr Mohave Rd & 2nd Ave; admission by donation; ⊙8am-noon, 1-5pm Mon-Fri) Surrounding Parker, the Colorado River

Indian Reservation is inhabited by members of the Mohave, Chemehuevi, Navajo and Hopi tribes. Their stories, along with amazing handicrafts (the basket collection is famous), come to life at this recently expanded museum. Helpful staff will explain the meaning of various designs on the baskets, including the ancient, spirit-focused 'whirlwind' symbol that, unfortunately, became an international symbol of intolerance and hate as the Nazi swastika.

🛏 Sleeping & Eating

There aren't really any great properties in town, but if you must spend the night, the all-purpose, tribal-owned **Blue Water Resort & Casino** (📞928-669-7000; www.blue waterfun.com; 13000 Resort Dr; r $140-150; @🛜 🏊) is probably your best bet. The nicest rooms overlook the river marina. Also OK is the **Budget Inn Motel** (📞928-669-2566; 912 Agency Ave; r $55-65; ❋🛜🏊) which has spacious doubles, some with kitchenettes. Campsites are also available at **Buckskin Mountain State Park** (p201).

For breakfast, try **Coffee Ern's** (1720 S California Ave; meals under $12; ⊙breakfast, lunch & dinner), which stuffs hungry stomachs with home-cooked goodness. They're not going to win any awards for service at **Badenoch's on the Beach** (📞928-669-2681; off Hwy 95; ⊙breakfast, lunch), but who's complaining when the Bloody Marys are $3? This is a booze-and-bikinis kinda place, where people pull in and hop off their watercraft. Order your burger or your patty-melt at the outside counter, grab a seat on the patio (all seating is outside) and consider whether you really need that $2 jello shot. Look for the big Badenoch's sign north of the casino.

Yuma

The territorial prison here was nicknamed the Hellhole of the West based in part on the city's blazing-hot temperatures. Today, the 2007 remake of the 1957 classic *3.10 to Yuma* has again brought recognition to this sprawling city at the confluence of the Gila and Colorado Rivers. It's also the birthplace of farmworker organizer César Chávez and the winter camp of some 70,000 snowbirds craving Yuma's sunny skies, mild temperatures and cheap RV park living. There ain't too much here for the rest of us to ease off the gas pedal, although recent efforts to revitalize the snug historic downtown have met with some success.

◉ Sights

Yuma Territorial Prison State Historic Park   HISTORIC SITE
(📞928-783-4771; www.azstateparks.com; 1 Prison Hill Rd; adult/child/under 7 $5/$2/free; ⊙9am-5pm) Hunkered on a bluff overlooking the Colorado River, this infamous prison is Yuma's star atttraction, and its colorful past is engagingly illuminated in exhibits across the grounds. Between 1876 and 1909, 3069 convicts were incarcerated here for crimes ranging from murder to 'seduction under the promise of marriage.' The small museum is fascinating, with photos and descriptions of individual inmates and their offenses, including a display devoted to the 29 women jailed here. Walking around the yard, behind iron-grille doors and into cells crowded with stacked bunks, you might get retroactively scared straight. Don't miss the Dark Cell, a cave-like room where troublesome prisoners were locked together in a 5ft-high metal cage.

FREE Yuma Quartermaster Depot State Park   HISTORIC SITE
(📞928-329-0471; www.azstateparks.com; 201 N 4th Ave; ⊙9am-5pm) Decades before the jail was built, Yuma became a crucial junction in the military supply lines through the West. Its role in getting gear and victuals to the troops is commemorated at the low-key quartermaster depot, set around a manicured green lawn.

Yuma Art Center   GALLERY
(📞928-329-6607; www.yumafinearts.org; 254 S Main St; ⊙10am-6pm Tue-Thu, 10am-7pm Fri, 10am-5pm Sat) This welcoming downtown spot sells contemporary art in four galleries. It's next to the beautifully restored 1911 Historic Yuma Theater, which hosts concerts and theater from November to March.

🛏 Sleeping & Eating

Yuma has plenty of chain hotels, mostly around exit 2 off the I-8.

Best Western Coronado Motor Hotel   MOTEL $$
(📞928-783-4453; www.bestwestern.com; 233 4th Ave; r incl breakfast $90-110; ❋@🛜🏊🐾) Red-tile roof, bright turquoise doors and newly upgraded rooms with flat-screen TVs – the oldest Best Western in the world doesn't

feel old at all. You also get two swimming pools and a sit-down breakfast. Some rooms have kitchenettes, there are several laundry rooms and kids under 13 stay free.

Yuma Cabaña
MOTEL $

(☎928-783-8311; www.yumacabana.com; 2151 4th Ave; r $40-54, ste $70; ❄✿❄) The hallways are Soviet-bloc institutional, but rooms are cozy, clean and quiet, and the front desk is welcoming and helpful. Some rooms have plush sitting areas and kitchenettes. It's definitely one of the best-value places in town. Pets $6 per day. No wi-fi, but rooms are wired if your laptop is cable-ready.

TOP CHOICE Lutes Casino
AMERICAN $

(☎928-782-2192; www.lutescasino.com; 221 S Main St; mains under $10; ⊙10am-8pm Mon-Thu, 10am-9pm Fri & Sat, 10am-6pm Sun) Lutes is awesome! If you're in town to see the prison, stop here for lunch afterwards. And note that the word casino is misleading – you won't find slots or poker at this 1940s-era hang-out, just a warehouse-big gathering spot filled with attic-like treasures hanging from the ceiling, old-school domino players, movie and advertising memorabilia, a dude playing the piano and a true cross-section of the town. To show you're in the know, order the 'especial' – a burger topped with a sliced hot dog. Antacid not included.

River City Grill
FUSION $$

(☎928-782-7988; www.rivercitygrillyuma.com; 600 W 3rd St; lunch $7-11, dinner $14-26; ⊙lunch Mon-Fri, dinner daily; ✍) Chic, funky and gourmet, with a shaded outdoor patio in back, the River has scrumptious crab cakes and brie-stuffed chicken, as well as mouthwatering vegetarian mains. Come here for a snappy weekday lunch or romantic dinner for two.

Da Boyz Italian Cuisine
ITALIAN $$

(☎928-783-8383; 284 S Main St; dishes $8-18; ⊙lunch & dinner; ✍) We're not crazy about da name, but this stylish downtown Italian eatery with big burgundy booths works well for a variety of travelers: solos, couples and girlfriends on getaways. It's also good family value. Look for filling gourmet pizzas and platters of pasta, plus a decent wine list.

ℹ Information

For maps and information, stop by the **visitor center** (☎928-783-0071; www.visityuma.com; 201 N 4th Ave; ⊙9am-5pm) at its new location beside Yuma Quartermaster Depot State Park.

ℹ Getting There & Away

Yuma Airport (☎928-726-5882; www.yuma internationalairport.com; 2191 32nd St) has flights to Phoenix and Los Angeles. **Greyhound** (☎928-783-4403; 170 E 17 Pl) runs two buses daily to Phoenix ($42-54, 3¾ hours), while Amtrak's *Sunset Limited* stops briefly at **Yuma station** (281 S Gila St) thrice weekly on its run between Los Angeles ($77, six hours) and New Orleans ($138, 41 hours).

SOUTHERN ARIZONA

This is a land of Stetsons and spurs, where cowboy ballads are sung around the campfire and thick steaks sizzle on the grill. It's big country out here, beyond the confines of bustling college-town Tucson, where long, dusty highways slide past rolling vistas and steep, pointy mountain ranges. A place where majestic saguaro cacti, the symbol of the region, stretch out as far as the eye can see. Some of the Wild West's most classic tales were begot in small towns like Tombstone and Bisbee, which still attract tourists by the thousands for their Old West vibe. The desert air is hot, sweet and dry by day, cool and crisp at night. This is a land of stupendous sunsets; a place where coyotes still howl under starry, black-velvet skies.

Tucson

An energetic college town, Tucson (*too-sawn*) is attractive, fun-loving and one of the most culturally invigorating places in the Southwest. Set in a flat valley hemmed in by craggy, odd-shaped mountains, Arizona's second-largest city smoothly blends Native American, Spanish, Mexican and Anglo traditions. Distinct neighborhoods and 19th-century buildings give a rich sense of community and history not found in the more modern and sprawling Phoenix. This is a town rich in Hispanic heritage (more than 40% of the population is Hispanic), so Spanish slides easily off most tongues and high-quality Mexican restaurants abound. The eclectic shops toting vintage garb, scores of funky restaurants and dive bars don't let you forget Tucson is a college town at heart, home turf to the 38,000-strong University of Arizona (UA).

Although it's fun to wander around the colorful historic buildings and peruse the shops, Tucson's best perks are found

Metropolitan Tucson

outside town. Whether you yearn to hike past giant cacti in the beautiful Saguaro National Park, watch the sun set over the rugged Santa Catalina Mountains or check out the world-class Arizona-Sonora Desert Museum, straying beyond the city limits is worth it.

Tucson lies mainly to the north and east of I-10 at its intersection with I-19, which goes to the Mexican border at Nogales. Downtown Tucson and the main historic districts are east of I-10 exit 258 at Congress St/Broadway Blvd, a major west–east thoroughfare. Most west–east thoroughfares are called streets, while most north–south thoroughfares are called avenues (although there is a sprinkling of roads and boulevards). Stone Ave, at its intersection with Congress, forms the zero point for Tucson addresses. Streets are designated west and east, and avenues north and south, from this point.

⊙ Sights & Activities

Most of Tucson's blockbuster sights, including the Saguaro National Park and the Arizona-Sonora Desert Museum, are on the city outskirts. The downtown area and 4th Ave near the university are compact enough for walking. Opening hours for outdoor attractions may change seasonally, typically opening at an earlier hour during the hot summer.

For avid explorers, the Tucson Attractions Passport ($15) may be a ticket to savings. It's available through www.visittucson .org/visitor/attractions/passport or at the visitor center and entitles you to two-for-one tickets and other discounts at dozens of major museums, attractions, tours and parks throughout southern Arizona.

DOWNTOWN TUCSON
Downtown Tucson has a valid claim to being the oldest urban space in Arizona. Although

spates of construction have marred the historical facade, this is still a reasonably walkable city center.

Tucson Museum of Art & Historic Block
MUSEUM

(Map p208; ☎520-624-2333; www.tucsonmuseum ofart.org; 140 Main Ave; adult/child/student/senior $8/free/3/6; ⊙10am-4pm Tue-Sat, noon-4pm Sun) For a small city, Tucson boasts an impressive art museum. There's a respectable collection of Western and contemporary art, and the permanent exhibition of pre-Columbian artifacts will awaken your inner Indiana Jones. A superb gift shop rounds out the works. First Sunday of the month is free.

Presidio Historic District
NEIGHBORHOOD

(www.nps.gov/nr/travel/amsw/sw7.htm) The Tucson Museum of Art is part of this low-key neighborhood, which embraces the site of the original Spanish fort and a ritzy residential area once nicknamed 'Snob Hollow.' This is (per current historical knowledge) one of the oldest inhabited places in North America. The Spanish **Presidio de San Augustín del Tucson** dates back to 1775, but the fort itself was built over a Hohokam site that has been dated to AD 700–900. The original fort is completely gone, although there's a short reconstructed section at the corner of Church Ave and Washington St.

The historical district teems with adobe townhouses and restored 19th-century mansions. Shoppers should steer towards **Old Town Artisans** (Map p208; www.oldtown artisans.com; 201 N Court Ave), a block-long warren of adobe apartments filled with galleries and crafts stores set around a lush and lovely courtyard cafe (this use of an enclosed courtyard comes from Andalucia in southern Spain by way of North Africa). The area is bounded by W 6th St, W Alameda St, N Stone Ave and Granada Ave.

Fox Theatre
HISTORIC BUILDING

(Map p208; ☎520-624-1515; www.foxtucson theatre.org; 17 W Congress St) This renovated art-deco theater on Congress St downtown is a 1930s beauty with fluted golden columns, water fountains and a giant sunburst mural radiating from the ceiling.

Barrio Histórico District/ Barrio Viejo
NEIGHBORHOOD

This compact neighborhood was an important business district in the late 19th century. Today it's home to funky shops and galleries in brightly painted adobe houses. The Barrio centers on 100 S Stone Ave and is bordered by I-10, Stone Ave and Cushing and 17th St.

4th Avenue
NEIGHBORHOOD

(www.fourthavenue.org) Linking historic downtown and the university, lively 4th Ave is a rare breed: a hip yet alt-flavored strip with a neighborhood feel and not a single chain store or restaurant, oops, except for Dairy Queen. The stretch between 9th St and University Blvd is lined with buzzy restaurants, coffee houses, bars, galleries, tattoo parlors, indie boutiques and vintage stores of all stripes.

Under the overpass that crosses 4th Ave and Broadway is the **Tucson Portrait Project** (www.tucsonportraitproject.com), one of our favorite public art projects anywhere. This wall-to-wall mosaic of about 7000 Tucsonian faces is a simple yet powerful testament to the diversity of the city's population.

The best time to visit 4th Ave is during the two annual street fairs held for three days in mid-December and late March or early April. See the 4th Ave website for details.

UNIVERSITY OF ARIZONA
Good university campuses manage to integrate the landscape into the learning space, and the UA campus is no exception. Rather

Tucson

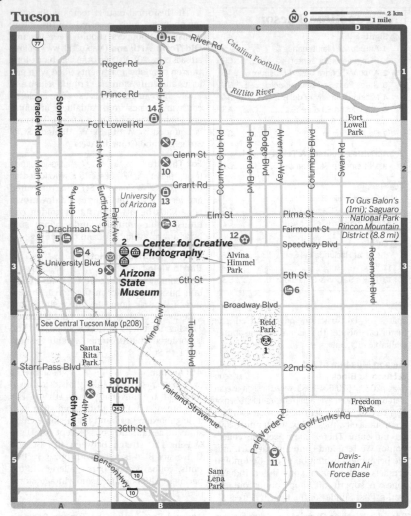

than being a collection of public greens, it seamlessly integrates the desert – although there are some soft lawns for the students to lounge around on. There are several excellent museums on campus.

Arizona State Museum   MUSEUM
(Map p206; ☎520-621-6302; www.statemuseum .arizona.edu; 1013 E University Blvd; adult/child $5/free; ☺10am-5pm Mon-Sat) The oldest and largest anthropology museum in the Southwest provides a fantastic introduction to the history and culture of 10 regional Native American tribes. The main permanent

exhibit about the tribes' cultural history is extensive, but easy to navigate and good for newbies and history buffs alike. These galleries are complemented by much-envied collections of minerals and Navajo textiles. Don't miss the impressive Wall of Pots and take a peek into the climate-controlled Pottery Vault (the museum has more than 20,000 whole vessels).

FREE **Center for Creative
Photography**   MUSEUM
(CCP; Map p206; ☎520-621-7968; www.creative photography.org; 1030 N Olive Rd; donations

Tucson

appreciated; ⏰9am-5pm Mon-Fri, 1-4pm Sat & Sun) The CCP is known for its ever-changing, high-caliber exhibits and for administering the archives of Ansel Adams, perhaps the best-regarded landscape photographer in American history. The museum closes down between exhibits for an extended period, so check the website before visiting.

University of Arizona Museum of Art
MUSEUM

(Map p206; ☎520-621-7567; www.artmuseum .arizona.edu; 1031 Olive Rd; adult/child $5/free; ⏰9am-5pm Tue-Fri, noon-4pm Sat & Sun) Across the road from the CCP, peruse 500 years of European and American paintings and sculpture. The permanent collection features such heavy hitters as Rodin, Matisse, Picasso and Pollock.

AROUND TUCSON

Several of Tucson's best attractions are about 15 miles west of the University. For a scenic, saguaro-dotted drive, follow Speedway Blvd west until it turns into W Gate Pass Rd. As you approach the top of Gates Pass, turn right into the **Gates Pass Scenic Overlook** where you'll have a sweeping view of the west that is especially nice at sunset.

Arizona-Sonora Desert Museum
MUSEUM

(Map p204; ☎520-883-1380; www.desertmuseum .org; 2021 N Kinney Rd; adult/child $14.50/4.50 Sep-May, $12/3 Jun-Aug; ⏰8:30am-5pm Oct-Feb, 7:30am-5pm Mar-May, 7am-4:30pm Jun-Sep, to 10pm Sat Jun-Aug) Home to cacti, coyotes and super-tiny hummingbirds, this ode to the Sonoran desert is one part zoo, one part botanical garden and one part museum – a trifecta that'll keep young and old entertained for easily half a day. All sorts of desert denizens, from precocious coatis to playful prairie dogs, make their home in natural enclosures hemmed in by invisible fences. The grounds are thick with desert plants, and docents are on hand to answer questions and give demonstrations. There are two walk-through aviaries, a mineral exhibit inside a cave (kids love that one), a half-mile desert trail and an underground exhibit with windows into ponds where beavers, otters and ducks frolic. Strollers and wheelchairs are available, and there's

---

WHEN YOU WISH UPON A LOVE TRIANGLE

In Barrio Histórico look for **El Tiradito** (356 S Main Ave), a 'wishing shrine' with a tale of passion and murder behind it. Locals say that in the 19th century a young man fell for his wife's mother. Her husband – his father-in-law – killed the young man. The dead lover was never absolved of his sins, and was thus turned away from the consecrated ground at the nearby Roman Catholic church, so he was buried under the front porch of the house that marks the spot of El Tiradito. Local folks took pity on the young man and began offering prayers and burning candles at the site; over time, El Tiradito became a shrine anyone would pray at to commemorate a lost loved one. The Phoenix New Times ran a story that claimed El Tiradito was the only Catholic shrine in the country dedicated to a sinner buried in unconsecrated ground.

Central Tucson

a gift shop, art gallery, restaurant and cafe. A tip: wear a hat and walking shoes, and remember that the big cats are most active in the morning.

The museum is off Hwy 86, about 12 miles west of Tucson, near the western section of Saguaro National Park.

Saguaro National Park
PARK

(☏520-733-5100; www.nps.gov/sagu; 7-day pass per vehicle/bicycle $10/5; ☉7am-sunset) If you're standing beside a docent at this cacti-filled park, don't refer to the limbs of the saguaro (sah-*wah*-ro) as branches. As the docent will quickly tell you, the mighty saguaro grows *arms*, not lowly branches – a distinction that makes sense when you consider their human-like features. They shake your hand, wave at you or draw a gun on you. They are also the most iconic symbol of the American Southwest, and an entire army of these majestic ribbed sentinels is protected in this national park. Their foot soldiers are

the spidery ocotillo, the fluffy teddy bear cactus, the green-bean-like pencil cholla and hundreds of other plant species.

Saguaros grow slowly, taking about 15 years to reach a foot in height, 50 years to reach 7ft and almost a century before they begin to take on their typical many-armed appearance. The best time to visit is April, when the saguaros begin blossoming with lovely white blooms – Arizona's state flower. By June and July, the flowers give way to ripe red fruit that local Native Americans use for food.

Saguaro National Park is divided into two units separated by 30 miles and the city of Tucson. Both are equally rewarding and it's not necessary to visit them both. Note that trailers longer than 35ft and vehicles wider than 8ft are not permitted on the park's narrow scenic loop roads.

The larger section is the **Rincon Mountain District**, about 15 miles east of downtown. The **visitor center** (Map p204; ☏520-733-5153;

Central Tucson

ARIZONA TUCSON

3693 S Old Spanish Trail; ⊙9am-5pm) has information on day hikes, horseback riding and backcountry camping. The latter requires a permit ($6 per site per day) and must be obtained by noon on the day of your hike. The meandering 8-mile **Cactus Forest Scenic Loop Drive**, a paved road open to cars and bicycles, provides access to picnic areas, trailheads and viewpoints.

Hikers pressed for time should follow the 1-mile round-trip **Freeman Homestead Trail** to a grove of massive saguaro. For a full-fledged desert adventure, head out on the steep and rocky **Tanque Verde Ridge Trail**, which climbs to the summit of Mica Mountain at 8666ft and back in 18 miles (backcountry camping permit required).

West of town, the **Tucson Mountain District** has its own **visitor center** (Map p204; ☏520-733-5158; 2700 N Kinney Rd; ⊙9am-5pm). The **Scenic Bajada Loop Drive** is a 6-mile graded dirt road through cactus forest that begins 1.5 miles north of the visitor center. Two quick, easy and rewarding hikes are the 0.8-mile **Valley View Overlook** (awesome at sunset) and the half-mile **Signal Hill Trail** to scores of ancient petroglyphs. For a more strenuous trek we recommend the 7-mile **King Canyon Trail**, which starts 2 miles south of the visitor center near the Arizona-Sonora Desert Museum. Distances for all three hikes are round-trip.

Old Tucson Studios FILM LOCATION
(Map p204; ☏520-883-0100; www.oldtucson.com; 201 S Kinney Rd; adult/child $17/11; ⊙10am-6pm

Oct-May, 10am-6pm Fri-Sun Jun Sep) Nicknamed 'Hollywood in the Desert,' this old movie set of Tucson in the 1860s was built in 1939 for the filming of *Arizona*. Hundreds of flicks followed, bringing in an entire galaxy of stars, including Clint Eastwood, Harrison Ford and Leonardo DiCaprio. Now a Wild West theme park, it's mostly mom, pop, buddy and sis who are shuffling down its dusty streets. Shootouts, stagecoach rides, saloons, sheriffs and stunts are all part of the hoopla. The studios are a few miles southeast of the Arizona-Sonora Desert Museum off Hwy 86.

Pima Air & Space Museum MUSEUM
(Map p204; ☏520-574-0462; www.pimaair.org; 6000 E Valencia Rd; adult/child/senior & military $13.75/8/11.75 Jun-Oct, $15.50/9/12.75 Nov-May; ⊙9am-5pm, last admission 4pm) An SR-71 Blackbird spy plane, JFK's Air Force One and a massive B-52 bomber are among the stars of this extraordinary private aircraft museum. Allow at least two hours to wander through hangars and around the airfield where more than 300 'birds' trace the evolution of civilian and military aviation. If that's too overwhelming, consider joining the free 50-minute walking tour offered at 10:30am or 11:30am daily (1:30pm & 2:30pm December to April) or shell out an extra $6 for the one-hour tram tour departing at 10am, 11:30am, 1:30pm and 3pm.

Hardcore plane-spotters should call ahead to book space on the 90-minute bus tour of the nearby 309th **Aerospace Maintenance & Regeneration Center** (AMARG; Map p204 adult/child $7/4; ⊘Mon-Fri, departure times vary seasonally) – aka the boneyard – where almost 4000 aircraft are mothballed in the dry desert air. You don't need to pay museum admission to join this tour.

SANTA CATALINA MOUNTAINS

The Santa Catalinas northeast of Tucson are the best-loved and most visited among the region's mountain ranges. You need a Coronado Forest Recreation Pass ($5 per vehicle per day) to park anywhere in the mountain area. It's available at the USFS **Santa Catalina Ranger Station** (Map p204; ☑520-749-8700; www.fs.fed.us/r3/coronado; 5700 N Sabino Canyon Rd; ⊘8am-4:30pm) at the mouth of Sabino Canyon, which also has maps, hiking guides and camping information.

Sabino Canyon (Map p204; www.sabino canyon.com; 5900 N Sabino Canyon Rd), a lush, pretty and shaded mini-gorge, is a favorite year-round destination for both locals and visitors. Narrated hop-on, hop-off tram tours along the **Sabino Canyon Trail** (☑520-749-2861; www.sabinocanyon.com; adult/child $8/4) depart every half hour for a 45-minute, nine-stop loop with access to trailheads and riverside picnic areas. It's nicest in the afternoon, when the sun plays hide and seek against the canyon walls. The last stop is only 3.8 miles from the visitor center, so hikers can listen to the tram driver's narration on the way up then hike back to the visitor center, either on the road or on the lofty but exposed **Telephone Line Trail**. A non-narrated shuttle (adult/child $3/1) provides access to Bear Canyon and the trailhead to Seven Falls, which has picnic sites and swimming but no facilities. From the falls, the trail continues up as high as you want to go.

A great way to escape the summer heat is by following the super-scenic **Sky Island Parkway** (Map p204; officially called Catalina Hwy), which meanders 27 miles from saguaro-dappled desert to pine-covered forest near the top of Mt Lemmon (9157ft), passing through ecosystems equivalent to a journey from Mexico to Canada. Budget at least three hours round-trip. Of the vista points, Babad Do'ag and Aspen are the most rewarding. There is no cost for the drive, but if you plan to explore the forest you must pay for the aforementioned $5 day-use permit, which can be purchased at the Forest Service fee station on the ascent.

In winter, Mt Lemmon has the southernmost **ski area** (Map p204; ☑520-576-1321; 10300 Ski Run Rd, Mt Lemmon; adult/child $37/20; ⊘late Dec-Mar) in the USA. With snow levels rather unpredictable, it's more about the novelty of schussing down the slopes with views of Mexico than having a world-class alpine experience. Rentals, lessons and food are available on the mountain.

✹ Festivals & Events

Tucson knows how to party and keeps a year-round schedule of events. For details check out www.visittucson.org/visitor/events/majorevents.

Fiesta de los Vaqueros RODEO
(Rodeo Week; ☑520-741-2233; www.tucsonrodeo .com) Held the last week of February for over 85 years, the Fiesta brings world-famous cowboys to town and features a spectacular parade with Western-themed floats and buggies, historic horse-drawn coaches, folk dancers and marching bands.

Tucson Folk Festival MUSIC
(www.tkma.org) Held in early May, this music festival with more than 100 local, regional and national performers is put on by the Tucson Kitchen Musicians Association.

Tucson Gem and Mineral Show MINERAL SHOW
(☑520-332-5773; www.tgms.org) This is the most famous event on the city's calendar,

---

TUCSON FOR CHILDREN

A global menagerie including giant anteaters and a Malayan Tiger delights young and old at the small and compact **Reid Park Zoo** (Map p206; ☑520-791-4022; www.tucsonzoo.org; 1100 S Randolph Way; adult/child/senior $7/3/5; ⊘9am-4pm Sep-May, 8am-3pm Jun-Aug; ⊛). Cap a visit with a picnic in the surrounding park, which also has playgrounds and a pond with paddleboat rentals.

Parents also sing the praises of the **Tucson Children's Museum** (Map p208; ☑520-792-9985; www.childrensmuseumtucson.org; 200 S 6th Ave; adult/child $8/6; ⊘9am-8pm Mon, 9am-5pm Tue-Fri, 10am-5pm Sat & Sun Jun-Aug, closed Mon Sep-May; ⊛), which has plenty of engaging, hands-on exhibits – from Dinosaur World to an aquarium.

held on the second full weekend in February. It's the largest of its kind in the world, and an estimated 250 retail dealers who trade in minerals, crafts and fossils take over the Tucson Convention Center.

🛏 Sleeping

Tucson's gamut of lodging options rivals Phoenix for beauty, comfort and location. Rates plummet as much as 50% between June and September, making what would otherwise be a five-star megasplurge an affordable getaway. If it's quaintness you're after, you'll love the old-time mansions resuscitated as B&Bs in the historic downtown district. Chains are abundant along the I-10 and around the airport.

TOP CHOICE Catalina Park Inn　　　　B&R $$
(Map p206; ☎520-792-4541; www.catalinaparkinn.com; 309 E 1st St; r $140-170; ❋@�; ⊙closed Jul & Aug) Style, hospitality and comfort merge seamlessly at this inviting B&B just west of the University of Arizona and 4th Ave. Hosts Mark Hall and Paul Richard have poured their hearts into restoring this 1927 Mediterranean-style villa, and their efforts are on display in each of the six rooms, from the oversized and over-the-top peacock-blue-and-gold Catalina Room to the white and uncluttered East Room with iron canopy bed. The cacti-and-desert garden has lots of little corners for lazy afternoon cat naps.

Arizona Inn　　　　　　　　　　RESORT $$$
(Map p206; ☎520-325-1541, 800 933 1093; www.arizonainn.com; 2200 E Elm St; r $259-333, ste $379-449; ❋@�⛱) The historic feel of this resort provides a definite sense of being one of the aristocracy. The mature gardens and old Arizona grace provide a respite not only from city life but also from the 21st century. Sip coffee on the porch, take high tea in the library, lounge by the small pool or join in a game of croquet, then retire to rooms furnished with antiques. The on-site spa is our favorite in town.

Hacienda del Sol　　　　HISTORIC INN $$$
(Map p204; ☎520-299-1501; www.haciendadelsol.com; 5501 N Hacienda del Sol Rd; r $195-300, ste $355-515; ❋@�⛱) An elite, hilltop girls' school built in the 1920s, this relaxing refuge has artist-designed Southwest-style rooms and teems with unique touches like carved ceiling beams and louvered exterior doors to catch the courtyard breeze. Having been on the radar of Spencer Tracy, Katharine Hepburn and other legends, you'll know you're sleeping with history. Fabulous restaurant, too.

Hotel Congress　　　　HISTORIC HOTEL $$
(Map p208; ☎520-622-8848; www.hotelcongress.com; 311 E Congress St; r $90-120; ❋@�) This beautifully restored 1919 hotel is a bohemian vintage beauty and a beehive of activity, mostly because of its popular cafe, bar and club. Infamous bank robber John Dillinger and his gang were captured here during their 1934 stay when a fire broke out at the hotel. Many rooms have period furnishings, rotary phones and wooden radios – but no TVs. Ask for a room at the far end of the hotel if you're noise-sensitive. Pets are $10 per night.

Flamingo Hotel　　　　　　　　MOTEL $
(Map p206; ☎520-770-1910; www.flamingohoteltucson.com; 1300 N Stone Ave; r incl breakfast $100-105; ❋⛱�⛱) The Flamingo is a top budget option, offering snazzy style, a convenient location near the University and a pretty darn good breakfast. Though recently purchased by the Quality Inn chain, it retains a lot of its great 1950s Rat Pack vibe, and the fact that Elvis slept here doesn't hurt. Rooms come with chic striped bedding, flat-screen plasma TVs, a good sized desk and comfy beds. Pets are $20 per day. One drawback? Wi-fi can be a bit unreliable in the rooms.

Windmill Inn at St Philips Plaza　HOTEL $$
(Map p206; ☎520-577-0007; www.windmillinns.com; 4250 N Campbell Ave; r incl breakfast $120-134; ❋@��⛱) Popular with University of Arizona fans during football season, this modern, efficient and friendly place wins kudos for spacious two-room suites (no charge for kids under 18), free continental breakfast, lending library, heated pool and free bike rentals. We couldn't shake the smell of baby powder, but really, who cares when cookies are served at 4pm?

El Presidio Bed & Breakfast Inn　B&B $$
(Map p208; ☎520-623-6151; www.bbonline.com/az/elpresidio; 297 N Main Ave; ste incl breakfast $125-155; ❋@�) The southern hospitality at this inviting hideaway sets it apart from its peers, and that's without mentioning the stunning, flower-infused central courtyard. Rooms in this 1886 Victorian adobe mansion in the Presidio Historic District reflect the regional history and style – look for fresh flowers, quilted beds and fine china. Each of

ARIZONA TUCSON

the four units has a separate sitting room and two have kitchenettes. Days start with a full breakfast and end with complimentary drinks and snacks.

Desert Trails B&B
B&B $$

(Map p204; ☑520-885-7295; www.deserttrails .com; 12851 E Speedway Blvd; r incl breakfast $130-160, guesthouse $165; ✵⦿▨) Outdoorsy types who want a personable B&B close to Saguaro National Park (Rincon Mountain District) have their answer at Desert Trails on the far eastern fringe of Speedway Blvd. Rooms may not be as chic as those in some of the historic B&Bs in town, but they're welcoming just the same. Even better? Host John Higgins, an avid backpacker, was a fireman for Saguaro National Park for six years and is glad to share his knowledge about the park's trails.

Roadrunner Hostel & Inn
HOSTEL $

(Map p208; ☑520-940-7280; www.roadrunner hostelinn.com; 346 E 12th St; dm/r incl breakfast $20/40; ✵@⦿) Cultural and language barriers melt faster than snow in the desert at this small and friendly hostel within walking distance of 4th Ave. The guest kitchen and TV lounge are convivial spaces and freebies include coffee, tea and a waffle breakfast. The 1900 adobe building once belonged to the sheriff involved in capturing the Dillinger gang at the Hotel Congress in 1934. Closed between noon and 3pm. No credit cards.

Lodge on the Desert
BOUTIQUE HOTEL $$

(Map p206; ☑520-320-2000, www.lodgeonthe desert.com; 306 N Alvernon Way; r $159-249, ste $199-329; @⦿▨✿) Rooms in this gracefully aging 1930s resort are in hacienda-style casitas flanked by cacti and palm trees, and decorated in charmingly modern Southwest style. Many units have beamed ceilings or fireplaces. Dogs are $25 per night per pet.

Gilbert Ray Campground
CAMPGROUND $

(Map p204; ☑520-877-6000; Kinney Rd; tent/RV sites $10/20) Camp among the saguaros at this Pima County campground 13 miles west of downtown. It has 130 first-come, first-served sites along with water, but no showers. There are five tent-only sites. No credit cards.

✖ Eating

Tucson's cuisine scene delivers a flavor-packed punch in everything from family-run 'nosherias' to five-star dining rooms.

Intricately spiced and authentic Mexican and Southwestern fare is king here, and much of it is prepared fresh with regional ingredients.

TOP CHOICE Cafe Poca Cosa
SOUTH AMERICAN $$

(Map p208; ☑520-622-6400; www.cafepocacosa tucson.com; 110 E Pennington St; lunch $13-15, dinner $19-26; ⦿lunch & dinner Tue-Sat) At this award-winning nuevo-Mexican bistro a Spanish-English blackboard menu circulates between tables because dishes change twice daily. It's all freshly prepared, innovative and beautifully presented. The undecided can't go wrong by ordering the Plato Poca Cosa and letting chef Suzana D'avila decide. Great margaritas, too.

🍴 Pasco Kitchen & Lounge
AMERICAN $$

(Map p206; ☑520-882-8013; www.pascokitchen .com; 820 E University Blvd; mains $9-14 ⦿11am-10pm Mon-Wed, 11am-11pm Thu, 11am-1am Fri & Sat, 11am-4pm Sun) The farmers market salad with yard bird is superb at this breezy new eatery near the University. The menu offers fresh, locally sourced comfort food that's prepared with panache and a few tasty twists – think grass-fed all natural burgers topped by braised pork belly and a fried egg, or grits with catfish and fried okra. The owners call it urban farm fare; we call it delicious. Service can be a bit too easygoing, but that may be a first-year kink.

Janos
SOUTHWESTERN $$$

(Map p204; ☑520-615-6100; 3770 E Sunrise Dr; mains $20-50, tasting menu with wine $80; ⦿dinner Mon-Sat) French-trained James Beard Award-winner Janos Wilder is a veritable wizard in creating Southwestern compositions with that certain je ne sais quoi. His dining room at the Westin La Paloma overlooks the entire valley and is perfect for big, long, romantic meals like grilled beef tenderloin with lobster tail and truffled Bordelaise.

Grill at Hacienda del Sol
SOUTHWESTERN $$$

(Map p204; ☑520-529-3500; www.haciendadelsol .com/dining; 5501 N Hacienda del Sol Rd; mains $24-40, Sunday brunch adult/child $35/18; ⦿dinner daily, brunch Sun) The sunset views compete with the smart, grown-up ambience, the Spanish Colonial decor and, of course, the exquisitely composed nouvelle Southwestern cuisine featuring herbs, veggies and fruit grown on site. Oenophiles have an extensive wine list to ponder. Reservations are required.

Mi Nidito

MEXICAN $

(Map p206; 520-622-5081; www.minidito.net; 1813 S 4th Ave; mains $6-13; lunch & dinner Wed-Sun) When it comes to Tucson's two most popular Mexican restaurants, El Charro may have more customers, but Mi Nidito can claim celebrities like Bill Clinton and Enrique Iglesias, plus a somewhat cozier location. Ol' Bill's order at 'My Little Nest' has become the signature president's plate, a heaping mound of Mexican favorites – tacos, tostadas, burritos, enchiladas and more – groaning under melted cheese. Give the prickly pear cactus chili or the *birria* (spicy, shredded beef) a whirl. Solo diners beware – the loudspeaker will boldly announce your name followed by 'party of one' when they're ready for you.

Lovin' Spoonfuls

VEGETARIAN $$

(Map p206; 520-325-7766; 2990 N Campbell Ave; lunch $6-8, dinner $9-11; 9:30am-9pm Mon-Sat, 10am-3pm Sun;) Burgers, country-fried chicken, meatloaf, salads – the menu reads like those at your typical cafe but there's one big difference: no animal products will ever find their way into this vegan haven. Outstandingly creative choices include the cashew-mushroom pâté and the adzuki-bean burger.

Tiny's Saloon & Steakhouse

AMERICAN $

(Map p204; 520-578-7700; 4900 W Ajo Hwy; mains $6-18; 10am-10pm, bar open to midnight Fri;) See that cluster of motorcycles and pick-up trucks in the parking lot? That's your true-blue sign of approval right there. Inside, once your eyes adjust, slide into a booth, nod at the regulars at the bar then order a steerburger with a cold beer. And toast your good fortune. A docent at the Pima Air & Space Museum told us that Tiny's has the best burgers in town, and we think he might be right. Truth be told? For a saloon, Tiny's is actually family friendly – at least during the day – and makes a nice stop after a day at the Arizona-Sonora Desert Museum or Saguaro National Park. Cash only but ATM on-site.

Hub Restaurant & Creamery

AMERICAN $$

(Map p208; 520-207-8201; www.hubdowntown .com; 266 E Congress Ave; lunch $9-17, dinner $9-17 11am-2am) The Hub has injected Congress Ave with industrial-chic style: red brick walls, lofty ceiling, wooden floors and, coolest of all, a walk-up ice-cream stand beside the hostess desk. Upscale comfort food is the name of the game here, from ahi tuna casserole to chicken pot pie, plus a few sandwiches and salads. Even if you don't want a meal, pop in for a kickin' scoop of gourmet ice cream. Choices include salted caramel and bacon scotch.

Yoshimatsu

JAPANESE $

(Map p206; 520-320-1574; 2660 N Campbell Ave; mains $8-17; lunch & dinner;) Billing itself as a healthy Japanese eatery, Yoshimatsu uses mostly organic foods, eschews MSG and offers lots of vegetarian and vegan options. Order a bento box, steamy soup or rice bowl at the counter and eat in the woodsy front tavern, or get table service at the separate and more intimate sushi cafe in back.

Bison Witches

SANDWICHES $

(Map p208; 520-740-1541; www.bisonwitches .com; 326 4th Ave; sandwiches $6-8; food 11am-midnight: bar to 2am) At this funky deli to and bar, everything's made fresh and with healthy ingredients like grilled meats, avocado and sprouts. In addition to sandwiches, there are a few salads on the menu. The back patio is more for the smoking and drinking crowd.

El Charro Café

MEXICAN $$

(Map p208; 520-622-1922; 311 N Court Ave; mains $7-18; lunch & dinner) In this rambling, buzzing hacienda the Flin family has been making innovative Mexican food since 1922. They're particularly famous for the *carne seca*, sundried lean beef that's been reconstituted, shredded and grilled with green chile and onions. The fabulous margaritas pack a Pancho Villa punch.

Gus Balon's

DINER $

(off Map p206; 520-747-7788; 6027 E 22nd St; mains $4-9; 7am-3pm Mon-Sat) Tucson's premier breakfast destination is a great place to fuel up if you're heading off to hike in

ARIZONA TUCSON

HOT DIGGETY DOG

Tucson's signature dish is the Sonoran hotdog, a tasty example of what happens when Mexican ingredients meet American processed meat and penchant for excess. So what is it? A bacon-wrapped hotdog layered with tomatillo salsa, pinto beans, shredded cheese, mayo, ketchup, mustard, chopped tomatoes and onions. We like 'em at **El Guero Canelo** (www.elguero canelo.com; 100 E Congress St).

Saguaro National Park's eastern district. Twenty-four types of pie and the cinnamon rolls are huge.

🍷 Drinking & Entertainment

Bars & Coffee Shops

Nimbus Brewing Company   BREWERY
(Map p206; ☑520-745-9175; www.nimbusbeer.com; 3850 E 44th St; ⊙11am-11pm Mon-Thu, 11am-1am Fri & Sat, 11am-9pm Sun) A cavernous purple warehouse space, here at Nimbus the brewmeisters make ale of every color in the spectrum. No matter what type you prefer, it's likely to be a smooth guzzle. The taproom is at the end of E 44th St, past all the industrial buildings.

Che's Lounge   BAR
(Map p208; ☑520-623-2088; 350 N 4th Ave) Drinkers unite! If everyone's favorite revolutionary heartthrob was still in our midst, he wouldn't have charged a cover either. A slightly skanky but hugely popular watering hole with $1 drafts, a huge wraparound bar and local art gracing the walls, this college hangout rocks with live music Saturday nights.

Surly Wench   BAR
(Map p208; ☑520-882-0009; www.surlywench pub.com; 424 4th Ave) This bat cave of a watering hole is generally packed with pierced pals soaking up $1.50 beer, giving the pinball machine a workout or headbanging to deafening punk, thrash and alt-rock bands. Shows start at 10pm.

Chocolate Iguana   COFFEE SHOP
(Map p208; www.chocolateiguanaon4th.com; 500 N 4th Ave; ⊙8am-10pm Mon-Thu, 7am-10pm Fri, 8am-10pm Sat, 9am-6pm Sun) Chocoholics have their pick of sweets and pastries inside this green-and-purple cottage, while coffee lovers can choose from eight different coffee brews and a long list of specialty drinks. Also sells sandwiches and gifts.

Nightclubs & Live Music

The free *Tucson Weekly* has comprehensive party listings, but for downtown-specific info pick up the *Downtown Tucsonian*, also gratis. Another good source is www.aznightbuzz .com. Congress St in downtown and 4th Ave near the University are both busy party strips.

Club Congress   LIVE MUSIC
(Map p208; ☑520-622-8848; www.hotelcongress .com; 311 E Congress St; cover $7-13) Skinny jeansters, tousled hipsters, aging folkies,

dressed-up hotties – the crowd at Tucson's most-happening club inside the grandly aging Hotel Congress defines the word eclectic. And so does the musical line-up, which usually features the finest local and regional talent. Wanna drink at a bar? Step inside the adjacent **Tap Room**, open since 1919.

Rialto Theatre   LIVE MUSIC
(Map p208; ☑520-740-1000; 318 E Congress St; cover $16-46) This gorgeous 1920 vaudeville and movie theater has been reborn as a top venue for live touring acts. Featuring everything from rock to hip-hop, flamenco to swing, plus the odd comedian; basically anyone too big to play at Club Congress across the street.

Plush   LIVE MUSIC
(Map p208; ☑520-798-1298; www.plushtucson.com; 340 E 6th St; cover $5) Plush is another club to watch when it comes to catching cool bands from LA, Seattle, Chicago and beyond. There's usually a line-up of two or three holding forth in the main room where the light is mellow and the sound is not. Head to the pub-style lounge in front to rest eardrums between sets. At the corner of 4th Ave and 6th St.

IBT's   GAY CLUB
(off Map p208; ☑520-882-3053; 616 N 4th Ave; no cover) At Tucson's most sizzling gay fun house, the theme changes nightly – from drag shows to techno dance mixes to karaoke. Chill on the patio, check out the bods, or sweat it out on the dance floor.

Cinemas & Performing Arts

It's always worth checking out what's on at the deco **Fox Theatre** (Map p208; ☑520-547-3040; www.foxtucsontheatre.org; 17 W Congress St), a gloriously glittery venue for classic and modern movies, music, theater and dance.

For indie, art-house and foreign movies head to **Loft Cinema** (Map p206; ☑520-795-0844; www.loftcinema.com; 3233 E Speedway Blvd).

Check the online calendar for outdoor summer concerts at **St Philips Plaza** (Map p206; www.stphilipsplaza.com; 4280 N Campbell Ave), typically on Friday and Sunday nights.

The **Arizona Opera** (☑520-293-4336; www .azopera.org) and **Tucson Symphony Orchestra** (☑520-792-9155; www.tucsonsymphony.org) perform between October and April at the **Tucson Music Hall** (Map p208; 260 S Church Ave). The **Arizona Theatre Company** (☑520-622-2823; www.arizonatheatre.org), meanwhile, puts on shows from September to April at the **Temple of Music & Art** (Map p208; 330 S Scott Ave), a renovated 1920s building.

Shopping

Old Town Artisans (Map p208; 201 N Court Ave) in the Presidio Historic District is a good destination for quality arts and crafts produced in the Southwest and Mexico. Also recommended is **St Philips Plaza** (Map p206; 4280 N Campbell Ave), where standouts include the **Obsidian Gallery** (www.obsidian -gallery.com) for art and jewelry and **Bahti Indian Arts** (www.bahti.com) for Native American wares.

For fun, eclectic shopping you can't beat 4th Ave, where there's a great cluster of vintage stores between 8th and 7th Sts. **Food Conspiracy Cooperative** (Map p208; 412 4th Ave, sandwiches $8-10) is great for stocking up on organic produce and products, while the **Chocolate Iguana** has an impressive array of chocolate candy, as well as cute gifts.

The special **Native Seeds/SEARCH** (Map p206, www.nativeseeds.org, 3061 N Campbell Ave; 526 4th Ave), which recently moved from 4th Ave, sells rare seeds of crops traditionally grown by Native Americans, along with quality books and crafts.

Bookstores
Antigone Books BOOKS
(Map p208; 411 N 4th Ave; www.antigonebooks.com; 10am-7pm Mon-Thu, 10am-9pm Fri & Sat, noon-5pm Sun) Great indie bookstore with a fun, girl-power focus.

Bookmans BOOKS
(Map p206; www.bookmans.com; 1930 E Grant Rd; 9am-10pm;) Well-stocked Arizona indie chain and locals' hangout.

Information
Emergency
Police (520-791-4444; http://cms3.tucson az.gov; 270 S Stone Ave)

Media
The local mainstream newspapers are the morning *Arizona Daily Star* (http://azstarnet .com) and the afternoon *Tucson Citizen* (http:// tucsoncitizen.com). The free *Tucson Weekly* (www.tucsonweekly.com) is chock-full of great entertainment and restaurant listings. *Tucson Lifestyle* (www.tucsonlifestyle.com) is a glossy monthly mag. Catch National Public Radio (NPR) on 89.1.

Medical Services
Tucson Medical Center (520-327-5461; www.tmcaz.com/TucsonMedicalCenter; 5301 E Grant Rd) 24-hour emergency services.

Post
Post office (520-629-9268; 825 E University Blvd, Suite 111; 8am-5pm Mon-Fri, 9am-12:30pm Sat)

Tourist Information
Coronado National Forest Supervisor's Office (520-388-8300; www.fs.fed.us/r3 /coronado; Federal Bldg, 300 W Congress St; 8am-4:30pm Mon-Fri) Provides information on trekking and camping in Coronado National Forest.

Tucson Convention & Visitors Bureau (520-624-1817, 800-638-8350; www.visit tucson.org; 100 S Church Ave; 9am-5pm Mon-Fri, to 4pm Sat & Sun) Ask for its free *Official Destination Guide.*

Getting There & Away
Tucson International Airport (Map p204; 520-573-8100; www.flytucsonairport.com) is 15 miles south of downtown and served by eight airlines, with nonstop flights to five destinations including Las Vegas, Los Angeles, San Francisco and Atlanta.

Greyhound (520-792-3475; www.grey hound.com; 471 W Congress St) and its partners run up to nine direct buses to Phoenix ($20-27.25, two hours), among other destinations.

The *Sunset Limited* train, operated by **Amtrak** (800-872-7245; www.amtrak.com; 400 E Toole Ave), comes through on its way west to Los Angeles ($62, 10 hours, three weekly) and east to New Orleans ($173, 36 hours, three weekly).

Getting Around
All major car-rental agencies have offices at the airport. **Arizona Stagecoach** (520-889-1000; www.azstagecoach.com) runs shared-ride vans into town for about $29 per person. A taxi from the airport to downtown costs around $25 to $27. Taxi companies include **Yellow Cab** (520-624-6611; www.yellowcabtucson.com) and **Allstate Cab** (520-881-2227).

The **Ronstadt Transit Center** (Map p208; 215 E Congress St, cnr Congress St & 6th Ave) is the main hub for the public **Sun Tran** (520-792-9222; www.suntran.com) buses serving the entire metro area. Fares are $1.50, or $3.50 for a day pass.

Tucson to Phoenix

If you just want to travel between Arizona's two biggest cities quickly, it's a straight 120-mile shot on a not terribly inspiring stretch of the I-10. However, a couple of rewarding side trips await those with curiosity and a little more time on their hands.

Picacho Peak State Park　　　STATE PARK
(☑520-466-3183; http://azstateparks.com; I-10, exit 219; per vehicle $7 mid-Sep–late May; ⊘5am-9pm) Distinctive Picacho Peak (3374ft) sticks out from the flatlands like a desert Matterhorn, about 40 miles northwest of Tucson. The westernmost battle of the American Civil War was fought in this area, with Arizonan Confederate troops killing two or three Union soldiers before retreating to Tucson and dispersing, knowing full well that they would soon be greatly outnumbered. The battle is reenacted every March with much pomp, circumstance and period costumes.

The pretty state park has a **visitor center** (⊘8am-5pm) that acts as a jump-off point for trails onto the mountain. If you're fit, you can walk to the peak of the mountain via a rugged trail that includes cables and catwalks. **Camping** (campsites $25) is available at 85 electric, first-come, first-served sites; suitable for tents or RVs.

Biosphere 2　　　BIOSPHERE
(☑520-838-6200; www.b2science.org; 32540 S Biosphere Rd, Oracle; adult/child/senior $20/13/18; ⊘9am-4pm) Built to be completely sealed off from Biosphere 1 (that would be Earth), Biosphere 2 is a 3-acre campus of glass domes and pyramids containing five ecosystems: tropical ocean, mangrove wetlands, tropical rainforest, savannah and coastal fog desert. In 1991, eight biospherians were sealed inside for a two-year tour of duty from which they emerged thinner but in pretty fair shape. Although this experiment was ostensibly a prototype for self-sustaining space colonies, the privately funded endeavor was engulfed in controversy. Heavy criticism came after the dome leaked gases and was opened to allow a biospherian to emerge for medical treatment. After several changes in ownership, the sci-fi-esque site is now a University of Arizona-run earth science research institute. Public tours take in the biospherians' apartments, farm area and kitchen, the one-million gallon 'tropical ocean' and the 'techno-sphere' that holds the mechanics that made it all possible.

Biosphere 2 is near Oracle, about 30 miles north of Tucson via Hwy 77 (Oracle Rd) or 30 miles east of the I-10 (exit 240, east on Tangerine Rd, then north on Hwy 77). No pets.

Casa Grande Ruins
National Monument　　　NATIONAL MONUMENT
(☑520-723-3172; www.nps.gov/cagr; 1100 W Ruins Dr, Coolidge; adult/child $5/free; ⊘9am-5pm) Built around AD 1350, Casa Grande (Big House) is the country's largest Hohokam structures still standing, with 11 rooms spread across four floors and mud walls several feet thick. Preserved as a national monument it's in reasonably good shape, partly because of the metal awning that's been canopying it since 1932. Although you can't walk inside the crumbling structure, you can peer into its rooms. A few strategically placed windows and doors suggest that the structure may have served as an astronomical observatory. The ball court is one of more than 200 that have been found in major Hohokam villages throughout the region. Experts aren't 100% sure of the purpose of these oval pits, but they may be linked to similar courts used for ball games by the Aztecs.

The visitor center has exhibits about the Hohokam society and Casa Grande itself, including a model of what the place may have originally looked like. Ranger-led 30-minute tours are available between December and April. Call for times.

The ruins are about 70 miles northwest of Tucson. Leave the I-10 at exit 211 and head north on Hwy 87 towards Coolidge and follow the signs. Don't confuse the monument with the modern town of Casa Grande, west of the I-10.

West of Tucson

West of Tucson, Hwy 86 cuts like a machete through the Tohono O'odham Indian Reservation, the second-largest in the country. Although this is one of the driest areas in the Sonora Desert, it's an appealing drive for anyone craving the lonely highway – however, you can expect to see a number of green-and-white border patrol SUVs cruising past. Listen for the sounds of the desert: the howl of a coyote, the rattle of a snake. The skies are big, the land vast and barren. Gas stations, grocery marts and motels are sparse, so plan ahead and carry plenty of water and other necessities.

For details about what to expect if you're stopped by a border patrol agent see p560.

KITT PEAK NATIONAL OBSERVATORY

Dark and clear night skies make remote **Kitt Peak** ([☎]520-318-8726; www.noao.edu/kpno; Hwy 86; admission to visitor center by donation; ⊙9am-3:45pm) a perfect site for one of the world's largest observatories. Just west of Sells, 56 miles southwest of Tucson, this 6875ft-high mountaintop is stacked with two radio and 23 optical telescopes, including one boasting a staggering diameter of 12ft.

There's a visitor center with exhibits and a gift shop, but no food. Guided one-hour **tours** (adult/child $7.75/4 Nov-May, $5.75/3 Jun-Oct; ⊙10am, 11:30am & 1:30pm) take you inside the building housing the telescopes, but alas you don't get to peer through any of them. To catch a glimpse of the universe, sign up for the **Nightly Observing Program** (adult/student/senior $48/44/44; ⊙closed mid-Jul–Aug), a three-hour stargazing session starting at sunset and limited to 46 people. This program books up weeks in advance but you can always check for cancellations when visiting. And dress warmly! It gets cold up there. For this program, children must be at last eight years old.

There's no public transportation to the observatory, but **Adobe Shuttle** ([☎]520-609-0593) runs vans out here from Tucson for $280 for tour people.

ORGAN PIPE CACTUS NATIONAL MONUMENT

If you truly want to get away from it all, you can't get much further off the grid than this huge and exotic **park** ([☎]520-387-6849; www.nps.gov/orpi; Hwy 85; per vehicle $8) along the Mexican border. It's a gorgeous, forbidding land that supports an astonishing number of animals and plants, including 28 species of cacti, first and foremost its namesake organ-pipe. A giant columnar cactus, it differs from the more prevalent saguaro in that its branches radiate from the base. Organ-pipes are common in Mexico but very rare north of the border. The monument is also the only place in the USA to see the senita cactus. Its branches are topped by hairy white tufts, which give it the nickname 'old man's beard.' Animals that have adapted to this arid climate include bighorn sheep, coyotes, kangaroo rats, mountain lions and the piglike javelina. Your best chance of encountering wildlife is in the early morning or evening. Walking around the desert by full moon or flashlight is another good way to catch things

on the prowl, but wear boots and watch where you step.

Winter and early spring, when Mexican gold poppies and purple lupine blanket the barren ground, are the most pleasant seasons to visit. Summers are shimmering hot (above 100°F, or 38°C) and bring monsoon rains between July and September.

The only paved road to and within the monument is Hwy 85, which travels 26 miles south from the hamlet of Why to Lukeville, near the Mexican border. After 22 miles you reach the **Kris Eggle Visitor Center** (⊙8am-5pm), which has information, drinking water, books and exhibits. Ranger-led programs run from January to March.

⊙ Sights & Activities

Two scenic drives are currently open to vehicles and bicycles, both starting near the visitor center. The 21-mile **Ajo Mountain Drive** takes you through a spectacular landscape of steep-sided, jagged cliffs and rock tinged a faintly hellish red. It's a well-maintained but winding and steep gravel road navigable by regular passenger cars (not recommended for RVs over 24ft long). If you prefer to let someone else do the driving, ask at the visitor center about ranger-led van tours available from January to March. The other route is **Puerto Blanco Drive**, of which only the first 5 miles are open, leading to a picnic area and overviews.

Unless it's too hot, the best way to truly experience this martian scenery is on foot. There are several **hiking trails**, ranging from a 200yd paved nature trail to strenuous climbs of over 4 miles. Cross-country hiking is also possible, but bring a topographical map and a compass and know how to use them – a mistake out here can be deadly. Always carry plenty of water, wear a hat and slather yourself in sunscreen.

🛏 Sleeping & Eating

The 208 first-come, first-served sites at **Twin Peaks Campground** (tent/RV sites $12) by the visitor center are often full by noon from mid-January through March. There's drinking water and toilets, but no showers or hookups. Tenters might prefer the scenic, if primitive, **Alamo Canyon Campground** (campsites $8), which requires reservations at the visitor center. There's no backcountry camping because of illegal border crossings.

No food is available at the monument, but there's a restaurant and a small grocery

CROSSING THE BORDER

For more information on crossing the Mexican border, check out p556.

in Lukeville. The closest lodging is in **Ajo**, about 11 miles north of Why, on Hwy 85.

Dangers & Annoyances

Rubbing up against the Mexican border, this remote monument is a popular crossing for undocumented immigrants and drug smugglers, and large sections are closed to the public. A steel fence intended to stop illegal off-road car crossings marks its southern boundary. In 2002, 28-year-old ranger Kris Eggle, for whom the visitor center is named, was killed by drug traffickers while on patrol in the park. Call ahead or check the website for current accessibility.

South of Tucson

From Tucson, the I-19 is a straight 60-mile shot south through the Santa Cruz River Valley to Nogales on the Mexican border. A historical trading route since pre-Hispanic times, the highway is unique in the US because distances are posted in kilometers – when it was built there was a strong push to go metric. Speed limits, however, are posted in miles!

Though not terribly scenic, I-19 is a ribbon of superb cultural sights with a bit of shopping thrown in the mix. It makes an excellent day trip from Tucson. If you don't want to backtrack, follow the much prettier Hwys 82 and 83 to the I-10 for a 150-mile loop.

◉ Sights & Activities

Mission San Xavier del Bac   MISSION
(☑520-294-2624; www.sanxaviermission.org; 1950 W San Xavier Rd; donations appreciated; ☺7am-5pm) The dazzling white towers of this mission rise from the dusty desert floor 8 miles south of Tucson – a mesmerizing mirage just off I-19 that brings an otherworldly glow to the scrubby landscape surrounding it. Nicknamed 'White Dove of the Desert,' the original mission was founded by Jesuit missionary Father Eusebio Kino in 1700 but was mostly destroyed in the Pima uprising of 1751. Its successor was gracefully rebuilt in the late 1700s in a harmonious

blend of Moorish, Byzantine and Mexican Renaissance styles. Carefully restored in the 1990s with the help of experts from the Vatican and still religiously active, it's one of the best-preserved and most beautiful Spanish missions in the country.

Nothing prepares you for the extraordinary splendor behind its thick walls. Your eyes are instantly drawn to the wall-sized carved, painted and gilded retable behind the altar, which tells the story of creation in dizzying detail. In the left transept the faithful line up to caress and pray to a reclining wooden figure of St Francis, the mission's patron saint. Metal votive pins shaped like body parts have been affixed to his blanket, offered in the hope of healing.

A small museum explains the history of the mission and its construction. Native Americans sell fry bread, jewelry and crafts in the parking lot.

From I-19, take exit 92.

Titan Missile Museum   MUSEUM
(☑520-625-7736; www.titanmissilemuseum.org; 1580 W Duval Mine Rd, Suarita; adult/child/senior $9.50/6/8.50; ☺8:45am-5:30pm Nov-Apr, 8:45am-5pm May-Oct) Cold War history comes frighteningly alive in this original Titan II missile site, where a crew stood ready 24/7 to launch a nuclear warhead within seconds of receiving a presidential order. The Titan II was the first liquid-propelled Intercontinental Ballistic Missile (ICBM) that could be fired from below ground and could reach its target – halfway around the world or wherever – in 30 minutes or less. On alert from 1963 to 1986, this is the only one of 54 Titan II missile sites nationwide that has been preserved as a museum. The one-hour tours (last tour is an hour before closing), which are usually led by retired military types, are both creepy and fascinating. After descending 35 feet and walking through several 3-ton blast doors, you enter the Control Room where you experience a simulated launch before seeing the actual (deactivated, of course) 103ft-tall missile still sitting in its launch duct. The tour is wheelchair accessible. Exhibits in the small museum trace the history of the Cold War and related topics.

The museum is 24 miles south of Tucson, off I-19 exit 69.

Tubac   VILLAGE
Tubac, about 45 miles south of Tucson, started as a Spanish fort set up in 1752 to stave off Pima attacks. These days, the

tiny village depends entirely on tourists dropping money for crafts, gifts, jewelry, souvenirs, pottery and paintings peddled in its 100 or so galleries, studios and shops. Compact and lined with prefab, adobe-style buildings, it's an attractive but somewhat sterile place.

Tumacácori National Historic Park MUSEUM
(☎520-398-2341; www.nps.gov/tuma; I-19 exit 29; adult/child $3/free; ☺9am-5pm) Three miles south of Tubac, this pink-and-cream edifice shimmers on the desert like a conquistador's dream. In 1691 Father Eusebio Kino and his cohort arrived at the Tumacácori settlement and quickly founded a mission to convert the local Native Americans. However, repeated Apache raids and the harsh winter of 1848 drove the priests out, leaving the complex to crumble for decades. For self-guided tours of the hauntingly beautiful ruins (ask for the free booklet) start at the visitor center, which also has a few exhibits. Skip the 15-minute video and plunge into the cool church alcoves and thorny gravesites. An impressive mass is held here on Christmas Eve.

Santa Cruz Chili & Spice LANDMARK
(☎520-398-2591; www.santacruzchili.com; 1868 E Frontage Rd; ☺8am-5pm Mon-Fri, from 10am Sat, to 3pm summer) South of the mission, this spice factory has been in business for more than 60 years and sells just about every seasoning under the sun – the stuff to get is its homemade chile pastes. Free samples available too.

Tubac Presidio State Historic Park & Museum MUSEUM
(☎520-398-2252; http://azstateparks.com; 1 Burruel St; adult/child $4/2; ☺9am-5pm) The foundation of the fort is all that's left at this state park, which is within walking distance of Tubac's shops and galleries. The attached museum has some worthwhile exhibits, including Arizona's oldest newspaper-printing press from 1859 and lots of information on the de Anza expedition to California.

🎆 Festivals & Events

Festivals pop off in Tubac all year; check the town's websites for exact dates (www.tubacaz.com, www.tubacarizona.com). The **Tubac Arts & Crafts Festival** is held in early February; **Taste of Tubac** showcases local culinary flair in early April; **Anza Days**, on the third weekend in October, are marked by historical reenactments, including some pretty cool parade ground

maneuvers by faux-Spanish mounted lancers; and in early December the streets light up during **Luminaria**, a Mexican-influenced Christmas tradition.

🛏 Sleeping & Eating

Tubac Country Inn B&B $$
(☎520-398-3178; www.tubaccountryinn.com; 13 Burruel St; r $90-175; ❄@) The decor at this charming five-room inn is best described as Southwest-lite: Navajo prints, Native American baskets and chunky wood furniture. A breakfast basket is delivered to your door in the morning.

Old Tubac Inn AMERICAN $$
(☎520-398-3161; 7 Plaza Rd; dishes $9-21; ☺lunch & dinner) Our favorite place to eat – and drink – in town. It's a combination of cowboy stop and family restaurant, which makes for an interesting vibe. The food is the everywhere-in Arizona mix of beef and Mexican, It cooks up a fine cheeseburger.

Wisdoms Café MEXICAN $$
(☎520-398-2397; www.wisdomscafe.com; 1931 E Frontage Rd; dishes $6.25-16; ☺lunch & dinner) This institution has been satisfying locals since 1944. The Mexican-themed menu heavily touts the signature 'fruit burros' (a fruit-filled crispy tortilla rolled in cinnamon and sugar). We think it executes an excellent take on the enchilada. Located 2 miles south of Tubac.

ℹ Information

There are approximately 100 galleries, art studios and crafts stores in town. As exhibitions and artists constantly rotate it's hard to recommend any one place over the next, but seeing as Tubac is a small village, you can wander all it has to offer very easily on foot.

For more information stop by the **Tubac Welcome Center** (☎520-398-2704; www.tubacaz.com; 2 Tubac Rd; ☺10am-1pm Jun-Sep, to 4pm Oct-May), run by the chamber of commerce.

ℹ Getting There & Away

Tubac is 50 miles south of Tucson off I-19; the main exit into town is exit 34

Patagonia & the Mountain Empire

Sandwiched between the border, the Santa Rita Mountains and the Patagonia Mountains is one of the shiniest hidden gems in the Arizona travel catalogue. In a valley by

ARIZONA PATAGONIA & THE MOUNTAIN EMPIRE

the small town of Patagonia are long vistas of lush, windswept upland grassland; dark, knobby forest mountains; and a crinkle of slow streams. The valleys that furrow across the landscape occupy a special microclimate that is amenable to wine grapes. It may not be the Napa Valley, but who needs 20 chardonnay varietals when you boast a juxtaposition of hard-bitten cowboys and artistic refugees?

Patagonia and smaller Sonoita (and tiny Elgin) sit almost 5000ft above sea level, so the land here is cool and breezy. The first two towns were once important railway stops, but since the line closed in 1962 tourism and the arts have been their bread and butter. The beauty of the montane grasslands was not lost on film scouts; the musical *Oklahoma* and John Wayne's *Red River* were both filmed here.

◉ Sights & Activities

Patagonia Lake State Park   PARK
(☑520-287-6965; http://azstateparks.com/Parks/PALA/index.html; 400 Patagonia Lake Rd; vehicle/bike $10/3; ⊙4am-11pm) A brilliant blue blip dolloped into the mountains, 2.5-mile-long Patagonia Lake was formed by the damming of Sonoita Creek. About 7 miles southwest of Patagonia, the lake is open year-round. At 4050ft above sea level, buffeted by lake and mountain breezes, the air is cool – making this a perfect spot for camping, picnicking, walking, bird-watching, fishing, boating and swimming. The **campsite** (with/without hookups $25/17) makes a fine base for exploring the region.

Patagonia-Sonoita Creek Preserve   PRESERVE
(☑520-394-2400; www.nature.org/arizona; 150 Blue Heaven Rd; admission $5; ⊙6:30am-4pm Wed-Sun Apr-Sep, from 7:30am Oct-Mar) A few gentle trails meander through this enchanting riparian willow forest. Managed by the Nature Conservancy, the preserve supports seven distinct vegetative ecosystems, four endangered species of native fish and more than 300 species of birds, including rarities from Mexico. For bird-watchers, the peak migratory season is April and May, and late August to September. There are guided nature walks offered on Saturday morning at 9am.

Reach the preserve by going northwest on N 4th Ave in Patagonia, then south on Pennsylvania Ave, driving across a small creek and continuing another mile.

Wineries
The Arizona wine industry is starting to attract some notice in the viticulture world. All of the following wineries offer tastings for $7, which is a pretty cheap way to get pleasantly sloshed in some beautiful, sun-kissed hill country.

Callaghan Vineyards   WINERY
(☑520-455-5322; www.callaghanvineyards.com; 336 Elgin Rd; ⊙11am-3pm Fri-Sun) About 20 miles east of Patagonia, Callaghan has traditionally been one of the most highly regarded wineries in the state. To get here, head south on Hwy 83 at the village of Sonoita, then east on Elgin Rd.

BIRD BRAINS

As you drive down Pennsylvania Ave to the Patagonia-Sonoita Creek Preserve, you'll notice **Paton House** (Blue Heaven Rd), just across the first creek crossing, on your left. A chain-link fence surrounds the property, and you'll likely see several cars parked outside. The backyard of the house is decked out with binoculars, birding books and sugar feeders that attract rare hummingbirds, including (according to local birders) the most reliable violet-crowned hummingbird sightings in the USA. It's free and there are no official hours (if the gate to the backyard is closed, that means don't come in), but donations for the feeders are appreciated. William and Marion Paton, the couple who started the bird-watching program, have passed away. The house is currently rented by people who want to maintain their legacy, but there's a chance the status may have changed when you visit.

The famed **Roadside Rest Area** is in a scenic canyon 4.2 miles southwest of Patagonia. It's ostensibly a run-of-the-mill pullout that runs off Hwy 82, which also happens to be one of the most famous birding spots in the state. This is a relatively reliable place to catch the rare rose-throated becard, as well as more common avian fauna such as the canyon wren. Be careful if you stop, as cars may pull over to park at any time.

Canelo Hills Vineyard & Winery
WINERY

(☑520-455-5499; www.canelohillswinery.com; 342 Elgin Rd; ☺11am-4pm Fri-Sun Sep-May, 11am-4pm Sat only Jun-Aug) Almost next door to Callaghan – and sharing the same sweeping views – is Canelo Hills, which does a pretty nice Riesling.

Dos Cabezas Winery
WINERY

(☑520-841-1193; www.doscabezaswinerystore.com; 3248 Hwy 82; ☺10:30am-4:30pm Thu-Sun) This cute, rustically pretty family-run operation is in Sonoita, near the crossroads of Hwys 82 and 83.

🛏 Sleeping

The only really cheap sleeping option is camping at Patagonia Lake State Park. Otherwise, there are some great B&Bs in and around town.

Duquesne House
B&B $$

(☑520-394-2732; www.theduquesnehouse.com; 357 Duquesne Ave, Patagonia; r $125; 🏶) This photogenic, ranch-style B&B was once a boarding house for miners. Today, there are three spacious, eclectically appointed suites with their own distinct garden areas where you can watch the sun set, listen to the birds chirp, smell the rosemary and generally bliss out. On Tuesday and Wednesday the B&B offers a 'Bed, No Bread' special – $110 per night with no breakfast.

🏶 Whisper's Ranch
B&B $$

(☑520-455-9246; www.whispersranch.com; 1490 Hwy 83; r $100-140; 🏶) For a more traditional out West experience get out to Canelo, about 30 miles east of Patagonia, and shack up with the cowboys. Amid rolling hills of oak forest inhabited by bobcats and javelinas, Whisper's is run with green sensibility (water is recycled, for example), and exudes a frontier attitude and energy. The rooms are decidedly rustic-chic; the homemade meals are to die for. **Whisper's Animal Sanctuary** (www.rrheartranch.com), which takes in abused horses, is next door and open for tours.

🍴 Eating & Drinking

Canela Bistro
NEW AMERICAN $$

(☑520-455-5873; www.canelabistro.com; 3252 Hwy 82, Sonoita; mains $16-24; ☺5-9pm Thu, 3-9pm Fri & Sat, 10am-3pm Sun) This bistro offers some of the classiest fare in the Mountain Empire. This is Nouveau American French Laundry-style fare sourced from the Southwest; green chile is made with farm-raised pork while the quiche comes with local red peppers.

Velvet Elvis
PIZZERIA $

(☑520-394-2102; www.velvetelvispizza.com; 29 Naugle Ave, Patagonia; mains $8-26; ☺11:30am-8:30pm Thu-Sun) A velvet Elvis does indeed make an appearance at this gourmet pizza joint in Patagonia, but he keeps things low-key from his perch above the register. Motorcyclists, foreign visitors, date-night couples – everybody visiting the area – rolls in at some point for one of the 13 designer pies. These diet-spoilers will make you feel like Elvis in Vegas: fat and happy.

🌱 Grasslands, A Natural Foods Cafe
CAFE $$

(☑520-455-4770; www.grasslandscafe.com; 3119 Hwy 83, Sonoita; mains $0-10; ☺10am-3pm Thu-Sat, 8am-3pm Sun) Homemade chile-and-cheddar croissants, vegetable pies, organic egg salad, prickly-pear jam and a few German specialties – the hearty fare at this well-run bakery and cafe is locally sourced and organic. It's a great stop for a healthy lunch (lots of vegetarian and gluten-free selections). The chocolate chip cookies are delicious. Cash only.

Gathering Grounds Cafe
COFFEE SHOP $

(☑520-394-2097; 319 McKeown Ave, Patagonia; mains under $5; ☺breakfast & lunch; 🖥) Sip a civilized cup o' Joe, nibble a scone and surf the net.

Wagon Wheel Saloon
BAR $

(www.wagonwheelpatagonia.com; 400 Naugle Ave, Patagonia) Kick it cowboy-style at the Wagon Wheel, where the bar is big, the 'art' is taxidermied and the pool table is ready for action.

ℹ Information

The main road is Hwy 82, the Patagonia Hwy. Patagonia, with about 800 people, is the local center of activity (we use the term loosely). The folks in the **visitor center** (☑520-394-9186, 888-794-0060; www.patagoniaaz.com; 307 McKeown Ave; ☺10am-5pm Mon-Sat, 10am-4pm Sun), in Mariposa Books & More, are friendly and helpful. Sonoita isn't much more than an intersection, and Elgin is just the name for a swath of unincorporated land 20 minutes east of Sonoita. Keep your dial tuned to KPUP 100.5, the awesome local radio station.

ℹ Getting There & Away

Patagonia and the Mountain Empire are connected to the rest of the state by Hwys 82 and 83; the closest major town is Nogales, 20 miles to the southwest.

Sierra Vista & Around

Sierra Vista isn't that exciting, but there are several sites within driving distance that warrant your attention. The **chamber of commerce** (☏520-458-6940; www.sierravista chamber.org, www.visitsierravista.com; 21 E Wilcox Dr; ⊗8am-5pm Mon-Fri, 9am-4pm Sat) serves as a visitor center for the region.

◉ Sights

Ramsey Canyon Preserve   PRESERVE
(☏520-378-2785; www.nature.org; Ramsey Canyon Rd; adult/child $5/free, free 1st Sat of month; ⊗8am-5pm daily, closed Tue & Wed Sep-Feb) A sycamore- and yucca-weaved dome some 5500ft in the sky marks where the Huachuca Mountains meet the Rockies, the Sierra Madres and the Sonoran Desert. This beautiful Nature Conservancy-owned preserve is one of the best hummingbird bagging spots in the USA. Up to 14 species of the little birds flit over the igneous outcrops and a wiry carpeting of trees throughout the year, with especially heavy sightings from April to September. At lower altitudes an incredible diversity of wildlife stalks through the river canyon that geographically defines this area. You can spot coatis, cougars and javelinas, but perhaps the most famous resident is the critically endangered Ramsey Canyon leopard frog, found nowhere else in the world.

Visitation is limited by the 23 parking spots in the visitor center, which is decked out with hummingbird feeders. A very easy 0.7-mile nature-loop trail leaves from here, as well as guided walks on Monday, Thursday and Saturday at 9am, March through October. The reserve is about 11 miles (25 minutes' drive) south of Sierra Vista off Hwy 92. Drive all the way to the very end of Ramsey Canyon Rd, bearing left onto the driveway at the final cul-de-sac.

**San Pedro Riparian National
Conservation Area**   PRESERVE
(☏520-439-6400; www.blm.gov/az/st/en.html; Fry Blvd) About 95% of Arizona's riparian habitat has become victim to overgrazing, logging and development, so what little riverfront ecosystem remains is incredibly important

to the state's ecological health. Some 350 bird species (many endangered), 84 mammal species and nearly 41 species of reptiles and amphibians have been recorded along the 40-mile stretch of the San Pedro River within the conservation area. It's the healthiest riparian ecosystem in the Southwest. Unfortunately it's also become a corridor for drug smuggling from Mexico, so suspicious activity should be reported.

The **visitor center** (⊗9:30am-4:30pm), in the 1930s San Pedro House, is 6 miles east of Sierra Vista on Fry Blvd. From here you can access several hiking trails.

🛏 Sleeping

**⌂TOP
CHOICE Casa de San Pedro B&B**   B&B $$
(☏520-366-1300; http://bedandbirds.com; 8033 S Yell Lane; r $169; ⊛@) This stylish but inviting place feels like the home of your favorite wealthy friend. Ten comfy rooms with Mexican hardwood furnishings are organized around a lovely courtyard and gardens. The common areas are so relaxing, guests might be found snoozing on a couch in the middle of the day! As with many properties in this area, it's maximized for bird-watching fun – it's also the closest accommodations to the San Pedro Riparian National Conservation Area.

Battiste's B&B   B&B $$
(☏520-803-6908; www.battistebedandbirds.com; 4700 E Robert Smith Lane, Hereford; r $150; ☏) This B&B is oriented toward bird-watching, and features cozy rooms arrayed in colorful, Southwestern decor. The owners have counted more than 50 bird species in their backyard alone and each spring host a nesting elf owl that has become a local attraction. Rate reduced to $135 per night if staying multiple nights. Air-conditioning available in one room, the other is fan-cooled.

Sierra Suites   HOTEL $$
(☏520-459-4221; www.sierravistasuites.com; 391 E Fry Blvd; r $99-115; ⊛@☏⊛) The beige brick exterior doesn't inspire much confidence, but once inside, all is quickly forgiven. The airy lobby fronts a customer-oriented hotel that works well for birders and business-people alike. It's also popular with those headed to nearby Fort Huachuca. Enjoy a buffet breakfast, a remodeled weight room and an on-site laundry. Rooms have fridges and microwaves.

✖ Eating

Angelika's German Imports GERMAN $

(📞520-458-5150; 1630 E Fry Blvd; mains $5-13; ⊘10am-5pm Tue-Thu, 10am 8pm Fri, 10am-7pm Sat) Right beside Hwy 92, this cozy place is a takeout sandwich shop, a simple eatery and a small grocery all tucked into one spot. All three sell German specialties. German is spoken here too, but you might just hear, in English, a simple farewell: 'Be careful out there and watch out for the others.' Indeed we will.

Café Sierra CAFE $

(www.sierravistaaz.gov; 2600 E Tacoma; mains under $10; ⊘7am-4pm Mon, 7am-6pm Tue-Thu, 7am-5pm Fri, 10am-5pm Sat; 🛜) Yes, we're recommending an eatery inside the Sierra Vista library. But you know what? This is a nice, low-key spot to surf the net while nibbling a scone and sipping coffee. The chocolate-chip cookies are fantastic. Sandwiches available too.

Tombstone

The grave markers at Boothill Cemetery typically include the cause of death: Murdered. Shot. Killed by Indians. Suicide. One quick stroll around the place tells you everything you need to know about living – or dying – in Tombstone in the late 1800s. How did this godforsaken place come to be? In 1877, despite friends' warnings that all he would find was his own tombstone, prospector Ed Schieffelin braved the dangers of Apache attack and struck it rich. He named the strike Tombstone, and a legend was born. This is the town of the infamous 1881 shootout at the OK Corral, when Wyatt Earp, his brothers Virgil and Morgan and their friend Doc Holliday gunned down outlaws Ike Clanton and Tom and Frank McLaury. The fight so caught people's imaginations, it not only made it into the history books but also onto the silver screen – many times. Watch the 1993 *Tombstone*, starring Kurt Russell and Val Kilmer, to get you in the mood.

Most boomtowns went bust but Tombstone declared itself 'Too Tough to Die.' Tourism was the new silver and as the Old West became en vogue, Tombstone didn't even have to reconstruct its past – by 1962 the entire town was a National Historic Landmark. Yes, it's a tourist trap; but a delightful one and a fun place to find out how the West was truly won.

⊙ Sights

Walking around town is free, but you'll pay to visit most attractions.

OK Corral HISTORIC SITE

(📞520-457-3456; www.ok-corral.com; Allen St btwn 3rd & 4th Sts; admission $10, without gunfight $6; ⊘9am-5pm) Site of the famous gunfight on October 26, 1881, the OK Corral is the heart of both historic and touristic Tombstone. It has models of the gunfighters and other exhibits, including CS Fly's early photography studio and a recreated 'crib,' the kind of room where local prostitutes would service up to 80 guys daily for as little as 25¢ a pop. Fights are reenacted at 2pm (with an additional show at 3:30pm on busy days).

Tickets are also good next door at the kitschy **Tombstone Historama**, a 25-minute presentation of the town's history using animated figures, movies and narration (by Vincent Price). Pick up your free copy of the Tombstone *Epitaph* reporting on the infamous shootout at the historic newspaper office, now the **Tombstone Epitaph Museum** (📞520-457-2211; near cnr 5th & Fremont Sts; admission free; ⊘9:30am-5pm).

The losers of the OK Corral – Ike Clanton and the McLaury brothers – are buried (in row 2), along with other desperados, at **Boothill Graveyard** off Hwy 80 about a quarter-mile north of town. The entrance is via a gift shop but admission, thankfully, is free ($2 for list of specific graves, with location). Some headstones are twistedly poetic. The oft-quoted epitaph for Lester Moore, a Wells Fargo agent, reads:

Here lies Lester Moore

Four slugs from a 44

No less, no more.

Tombstone Courthouse State Historic Park MUSEUM

(📞520-457-3311; http://azstateparks.com/Parks /TOCO/index.html; 223 Toughnut St; adult/child $5/2; ⊘9am-5pm) Seven men were hanged in Tombstone's courthouse courtyard, and today a couple of nooses dangle ominously from the recreated gallows. The story behind their hangings is explained inside this rambling Victorian building, which also displays an eclectic bunch of items relating to the town's history. Check out the tax licenses for prostitutes and the doctor's bullet-removal kit. The exhibits are somewhat different from those at the OK Corral, making it worth a stop.

Bird Cage Theater
HISTORIC SITE

(☑520-457-3421; 517 E Allen St; adult/child/senior \$10/7/9; ☉8am-6pm) Packed tight with antiques and history, the Bird Cage serves as Tombstone's attic. In the 1880s it was a one-stop sin-o-rama. Besides onstage shows, it was a saloon, dance hall, gambling parlor and a home for 'negotiable affections.' The very name derives from the 14 compartments lining the upper floor of the auditorium – like boxes at the opera – where the 'soiled doves' entertained their customers. The entire place is stuffed with dusty old artifacts that bring the period to life, including a faro gambling table used by Doc Holliday, a big black hearse, a fully furnished 'crib' and a creepy 'merman.' And, of course, the theater is haunted.

Rose Tree Museum
MUSEUM

(☑520-457-3326; cnr 4th & Toughnut Sts; adult/child \$5/free; ☉9am-5pm) In April the world's largest rosebush – planted in 1886 – puts on an intoxicating show in the courtyard of this museum, a beautifully restored Victorian home still owned by the Macia family. The inside is brimming with family and town memorabilia, including a 1960 photograph showing the matriarch with Robert Geronimo, son of the Apache chief.

Staged Shootouts
REENACTMENT

These days, lawlessness in Tombstone takes the form of rip roarin' shootouts. Apart from the 2pm show at the OK Corral, there are daily shows at **Helldorado Town** (☑520-457-9035; 339 S 4th St, at Toughnut St). Stop by the chamber of commerce for current times.

✯ Festivals & Events

Tombstone events revolve around weekends of Western hoo-ha with shootouts (of course!), stagecoach rides, fiddling contests, 'vigilette' fashion shows, mock hangings and melodramas. The biggest event is **Helldorado Days** (www.helldoradodays.com; third weekend in October). See the chamber of commerce website for details about other events, which include **Wyatt Earp Days** (Memorial Day weekend), **Vigilante Days** (second weekend in August) and **Rendezvous of the Gunfighters** (Labor Day weekend).

🛏 Sleeping

Properties increase their rates during special events; reservations are recommended at these times.

TOP CHOICE Larian Motel
MOTEL \$

(☑520-457-2272; www.tombstonemotels.com; 410 E Fremont St; r \$70-90; ❋🐾🛜) This one's a rare breed: a motel with soul, thanks to the personalized attention from proprietor Gordon, cute retro rooms named for historical characters (Doc Holliday, Curly Bill, Wyatt Earp) and a high standard of cleanliness. It's also close to the downtown action. Children under 14 stay free.

Tombstone Bordello B&B
B&B \$

(☑520-457-2394; www.tombstonebordello.com; 107 W Allen St; r \$89-99; ❋@🛜) This fascinating place used to be a house of ill-repute, and the names of the rooms – Shady Lady, Fallen Angel – embrace its colorful past. The 10-room B&B, built in 1881, was once owned by Big Nose Kate. The Victorian-style bedrooms (which held up to four working girls) feel very much of the era, so much so that some of the former residents are said to haunt the building.

Best Western Lookout Lodge
MOTEL \$\$

(☑520-457-2223; www.bestwesterntombstone.com; 801 N Hwy 80; r incl breakfast \$98-108; ❋@🛜🐾🏊) On a hill about five minutes from town; this property gets high marks for its spacious rooms overlooking the Dragoon Mountains, pretty gardens and outdoor firepit – and its Ranch 22 restaurant with cooked breakfast included. Pets are \$20 per night, per pet.

Katie's Cozy Cabins
CABIN \$

(☑520-457-3963; www.cabinsintombstone.com; 16 W Allen St; r \$89 Sun-Thu, \$99 Fri & Sat, 2-night minimum on weekend; ❋) Four new cabins sleep up to six people. Upstairs lofts have a double bed, while the rooms below have a couple of bunks.

🍴 Eating

It's a tourist town, so don't expect any culinary flights of fancy. In keeping with its Old West theme, the food is mostly standard American and Mexican.

Longhorn Restaurant
AMERICAN \$\$

(☑520-457-3405; www.thelonghornrestaurant.com; 501 E Allen St; mains \$7-19; ☉7:30am-9pm) The original 'Bucket of Blood Saloon,' this was where Virgil Earp was shot dead from a

2nd-floor window in 1881. Enjoy a cowboy breakfast or spike your cholesterol with a 14oz steak.

The Depot Steak House
STEAKHOUSE **$$**
(☑520-457-3404; 60 S 10th St; mains $8-26; ☺4pm-8:30pm Wed & Thu, 4pm-9:30pm Fri, noon-9:30pm Sat, noon-8:30pm Sun) Pelts, rifles and steer skulls dot the walls of this locals' favorite just north of downtown. The menu is mainly cowboy fare – steaks, ribs and burgers – but there are a few chicken dishes and salads. Service was a bit haphazard on our visit, but the food was fine. For pool and beer, wander through the doorway to **Johnny Ringo's Bar**, named for the legendary outlaw and Wyatt Earp antagonist.

Café Margarita
MEXICAN **$$**
(☑520-457-2277; 131 S 5th St; mains $7-15; ☺11am-8pm) Formerly Nellie Cashman's in the Russ House, this new eatery serves Mexican fare as well as a few Italian dishes. Eat inside or on the patio. Enjoy live music on Friday and Saturday nights. Biggest bummer? No free chips and salsa.

Drinking

There's little more to do in the evening than to go on a pub crawl – or make that a saloon stagger.

Crystal Palace Saloon
BAR
(www.crystalpalacesaloon.com; 436 E Allen St, at 5th St; ☺11am-10pm Sun-Thu, to 1am Fri & Sat) This lively saloon was built in 1879 and has been completely restored. It's a favorite end-of-the-day watering hole with Tombstone's costumed actors or anyone wanting to play outlaw for a night.

Big Nose Kate's
BAR
(www.bignosekates.info; 417 E Allen St; ☺10am-midnight) Full of Wild West character, Doc Holliday's girlfriend's bar features great painted glass, historical photographs and live music in the afternoons. Down in the basement is the room of the Swamper, a janitor who dug a tunnel into the silver mine shaft that ran below the building and helped himself to buckets of nuggets. Or at least so the story goes...

ℹ Information

Police (☑520-457-2244; 315 E Fremont St)
Post office (☑520-457-3479; 100 Haskell St; ☺8:30am-4:30pm)
Tombstone Chamber of Commerce (☑520-457-3929, 888-457-3929; www.tombstone chamber.com; 395 E Allen St, at cnr of 4th St; ☺9am-5pm)

ℹ Getting There & Away

Tombstone is 24 miles south of the I-10 via Hwy 80 (exit 303 towards Benson/Douglas). The Patagonia Hwy (Hwy 82) links up with Hwy 80 about 3 miles north of Tombstone. There is no public transport into town.

Bisbee

At first glance, Bisbee isn't that attractive. Wedged between the steep walls of Tombstone Canyon, its roads are narrow and twisty, the buildings old and fragile, and there's a monstrous open-pit mine gaping toward the heavens at the east end of town. You drove all the way here for this? But then you take a closer look. Those 19th-century buildings are packed tight with classy galleries, splendid restaurants and charming hotels. As for the citizens, well, just settle onto a bar stool at a local watering hole and a chatty local will likely share all of the town's gossip before you order your second drink.

Bisbee built its fortune on ore found in the surrounding Mule Mountains. Between 1880 and 1975, underground and open-pit mines coughed up copper in sumptuous proportions, generating more than $6 billion worth of metals. Business really took off in 1892 when the Phelps Dodge Corporation, which would soon hold a local monopoly, brought in the railroad. By 1910 the population had climbed to 25,000, and with nearly 50 saloons and bordellos crammed along Brewery Gulch, Bisbee quickly gained a reputation as the liveliest city between El Paso and San Francisco.

As the local copper mines began to fizzle in the 1970s, Bisbee began converting itself into a tourist destination. At the same time hippies, artists and counterculture types migrated here and decided to stay. The interweaving of the new creative types and the old miners has produced a welcoming bunch of eccentrics clinging to the mountainside. It's one of the coolest places (weather and attitude) in southern Arizona – and definitely worth the drive.

Hwy 80 runs through the center of town. Most businesses are found in the Historic District (Old Bisbee), along Main St and near the intersection of Howell and Brewery

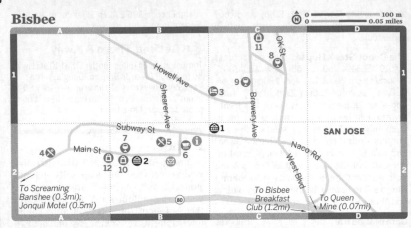

Bisbee

Bisbee

◉ Sights

🛌 Sleeping

🍴 Eating

🍷 Drinking

🛍 Shopping

Aves. Many businesses close from Monday to Wednesday.

◉ Sights & Activities

Walking through Old Bisbee – up winding back alleys, steep staircases and cafe- and shop-lined Main St – is a delight in itself. For sweeping views, walk up OK St above the southern edge of town. A path at the top leads to a hill where locals have built colorful shrines filled with candles, plastic flowers and pictures of the Virgin Mary.

Bisbee Mining & Historical Museum　MUSEUM
(☏520-432-7071; www.bisbeemuseum.org; 5 Copper Queen Plaza; adult/child/senior $7.50/3/6.50; ☺10am-4pm) Located in the 1897 former headquarters of the Phelps Dodge Corporation, this museum is affiliated with the Smithsonian Institution, and it shows. It does an excellent job delineating the town's past, the changing face of mining and the use of copper in our daily lives. You even get to 'drive' a shovel with a dipper larger than most living rooms.

Queen Mine　MINE
(☏520-432-2071; www.queenminetour.com; 478 Dart Rd, off Hwy 80; adult/child $13/5.50; ☺9am-3:30pm; 🚼) Don miners' garb, grab a lantern and ride a mine train 1500ft into one of Bisbee's famous copper mines. In the early 20th century this was the most productive mine in Arizona, famous for producing particularly deep-shaded turquoise rocks known as Bisbee Blue. The tour, which lasts about an hour, is good fun for the kids, but maybe not so much for the claustrophobic.

To see the aftermath of open-pit mining, drive a half-mile south on Hwy 80 to the not-so-truthful 'Scenic View' sign. It's pointing toward the **Lavender Pit**, an immense stair-stepped gash in the ground that produced about 600,000 tons of copper between 1950 and 1974. It's ugly, but it's impressive.

👉 Tours

To get the scoop on the town's turbulent past, join a fun and engaging **walking tour** (http://londonswalkingtour.blogspot.com

/p/history.html) with local historian Michael London, an eccentric bearded character who looks like he's just walked off a movie set. The one-hour tours cost $10 and leave from the visitor center.

Stop by the visitor center for information on jeep tours and ghost walks.

🛌 Sleeping

Bisbee is refreshingly devoid of chain hotels, with most lodging in historic hotels or B&Bs. Weekends often fill early, so come midweek if you don't have a reservation.

TOP CHOICE Shady Dell   QUIRKY $

(📞520-432-3567; www.theshadydell.com; 1 Douglas Rd; rates $50-145) This fun-loving trailer park has a deliciously retro twist: each 'unit' is an original 1950s travel trailer, meticulously restored and outfitted with period accoutrements such as vintage radios (playing '50s songs upon arrival) and record players. All have tiny kitchens, some have toilets, but showers are in the bathhouse. A 1947 Chris Craft yacht and a tiki-themed bus are also available. Units use swamp coolers for cold air.

Jonquil Motel   MOTEL $

(📞520-432-7371; www.thejonquil.com; 317 Tombstone Canyon Rd; r $90-115; ❄️@) The inviting Jonquil is as retro in its styling as anywhere else in Bisbee. In this case, however, the decor is artily done-up roadside motel, not frilly Victorian B&B. We immediately fell for the 60ft mural that wraps around the property, based on the 1928 poem 'Romance Sonámbulo' by Federico García Lorca. The rooms are a bit on the small side, but excellent value for money.

School House Inn   B&B $$

(📞520-432-2996; www.schoolhouseinnbb.com; 818 Tombstone Canyon; r incl breakfast $89-149; 📶) Report to the Principal's Office or get creative in the Art Room. No matter which of the nine darling rooms in this converted 1918 school you choose, you'll be charmed by the detailed decor, the homey comforts, and John (the proprietor). Relax below the 160-year-old live oak on the patio. Rates include a delicious full breakfast.

Copper Queen Hotel   HOTEL $$

(📞520-432-2216; www.copperqueen.com; 11 Howell; r $122-197; ❄️@📶♨️) Howdy pilgrim. Is John Wayne your man? Then reserve yourself Room 109 because the Duke did indeed

sleep here. The Copper Queen is a grand old dame that's welcomed guests since 1902. It's a splendid find with a vibe that merges casual, late-19th-century elegance with modern amenities. Rooms vary in size and comfort.

🍴 Eating

TOP CHOICE Poco   VEGETARIAN $

(📞520-432-3733; 15 Main St (Peddlar's Alley); mains $7.50-10; ⏰11am-8pm Wed-Sun, 🍴) Wow! People were talking about this new courtyard cafe as far away as Patagonia, and it's easy to see why: upbeat and accommodating service, a Mexican-inspired menu (it all sounds good) and mostly organic ingredients that burst with savory goodness. Did we mention it's vegetarian? Trust us: grab a spot in line, order at the counter then settle in on the patio for one of southern Arizona's simplest but tastiest meals. And remember, you can never go wrong with the burritos. Or the cupcakes. Or the... Just go!

Cafe Roka   NEW AMERICAN $$$

(📞520-432-5153; 35 Main St; dinner $15-29; ⏰dinner Thu-Sat) Past the art-nouveau steel door awaits this sensuously lit grown-up spot with innovative American cuisine that is at once smart and satisfying. The four-course dinners include salad, soup, sorbet and a rotating choice of mains. The welcoming central bar is great for solo diners, and if you chat with your neighbors you might just hear some juicy town gossip. Reservations recommended.

Screaming Banshee   PIZZERIA $$

(📞520-432-6788; 2 Copper Queen Plaza; mains $8-18; ⏰lunch & dinner) Fancy a helping of electric mushrooms or a B Hill Burger? Drop by this cozy and casual eatery that welcomes you with warm words, historical photographs and imaginative takes on American standards. Get a side of beer-battered fries to share.

High Desert Market & Café CAFE $

(☑520-432-6775; 203 Tombstone Canyon; mains $5-9; ☺7am-7pm) This cheerful nosh spot serves breakfast along with fresh and custom-made sandwiches and salads opposite the Iron Man, a 1935 socialist-aesthetic statue of a manly, bare-chested miner. Its shelves are stocked with local and imported produce and products.

Bisbee Breakfast Club BREAKFAST $

(www.bisbeebreakfastclub.com; 75a Erie St; mains under $10; ☺7am-3pm) The breakfasts at this longtime favorite seem to have have lost a touch of their wow factor. That being said, this bustling eatery is still the see-and-be-seen spot in town, and the food remains pretty darn yummy.

🍺 Drinking

Old Bisbee Brewing Company BREWERY

(www.oldbisbeebrewingcompany.com; 200 Review Alley) This new watering hole serves up eight lip-smacking brews, including root beer.

St Elmo's BAR

(36 Brewery Ave) This 100-year-old dive is Arizona's oldest bar. Today, a boisterous mix of thirsty locals and tourists keep things hoppin'. The signed beer mugs behind the cash register belong to regulars.

Bisbee Grand Hotel BAR

(www.bisbeegrandhotel.com; 61 Main St) The bar in the bottom of the Grand Hotel in downtown has a cool punk rock meets Old West vibe. In fact, we saw a young buck with a handlebar moustache more kick-ass than Wyatt Earp's. Hipster or cowboy? We weren't 100% sure, but no one seemed to mind either way.

Bisbee Coffee Co COFFEE SHOP

(www.bisbeecoffee.com; 2 Copper Queen Plaza; ☺6:30am-9pm; ☎) This easy-going coffee shop, which sits between the post office and the visitor center, serves java strong enough to get you through a double shift on the tourist track.

🛍 Shopping

You can't walk in Bisbee without tripping on an art gallery. There's a wide range of styles and quality; have a wander up Main St to get a feel for what's out there.

Atalanta Music & Books BOOKS

(☑520-432-9976; 38 Main St) A chaotic whirlwind of used books.

Bisbee Bicycle Brothel BICYCLES

(☑520-432-2922; www.bisbeebicyclebrothel.com; 43 Brewery Ave) The 'best little wheelhouse in Arizona' has vintage bicycles from as far back as the 1940s. You can't rent wheels here, but why rent when you'll be so tempted to own? Sells some pretty awesome T-shirts and assorted Bicycle Brothel gear as well.

Bisbee Stitches Teeny Tiny Toy Store TOYS

(☑520-432-8028; www.bisbeestitches.com; 40 Main St) This delightful little shop sells homemade and hip toys for kids and kids-at-heart.

ℹ Information

Bisbee Visitor Center (☑520-432-3554, 866-224-7233; www.discoverbisbee.com; 2 Copper Canyon Plaza; ☺9am-5pm)

Copper Queen Hospital (☑520-432-5383; www.cqch.org; 101 Cole Ave) 24-hour emergency services.

Police (☑520-432-2261; 1 Hwy 92)

Post office (☑520-432-2052; 6 Main St; ☺7:30am-noon Mon-Fri, 9am-noon Sat)

ℹ Getting There & Away

Bisbee is about 50 miles south of the I-10 (exit 303 towards Benson/Douglas), 25 miles south of Tombstone, and only about 10 miles north of the Mexican border.

Chiricahua National Monument

Cutting an arrow-straight swath south from the I-10 past fields of swaying blond grass, fence-trapped tumbleweeds and the virtual ghost-town of Dos Cabezas, Hwy 186 provides no clue as to the natural treasure hiding in the mountains beyond. Pronounced 'cheery-cow-wha,' **Chiricahua National Monument** (☑520-824-3560; www.nps.gov/chir; Hwy 181; adult/child $5/free) is one of Arizona's most unique and evocative landscapes; a wonderfully rugged yet whimsical wonderland. Rain, thunder and wind have chiseled volcanic rocks into fluted pinnacles, natural bridges, gravity-defying balancing boulders and soaring spires reaching skyward like totem poles carved in stone. The remoteness made Chiricahua a favorite hiding place of Apache warrior Cochise and his men. Today it's attractive to birds and wildlife: bobcats and bears are often sighted on the hiking trails. Also watch for deer, coatis and javelinas.

Past the entrance, the paved **Bonita Canyon Scenic Drive** climbs 8 miles to Massai Point at 6870ft, passing several scenic pullouts and trailheads along the way. RVs longer than 29ft are not allowed beyond the **visitor center** (⊙8am-4:30pm), which is about 2 miles along the road.

To explore in greater depth, lace up your boots and hit the trails. Eighteen miles of hiking trails range from easy, flat 0.2-mile loops to strenuous 7-mile climbs. A hikers' shuttle bus leaves daily from the visitor center at 8:30am, going up to Massai Point for $2. Hikers return by hiking downhill.

If you're short on time, hike the **Echo Canyon Trail** at least half a mile to the Grottoes, an amazing 'cathedral' of giant boulders where you can lie still and enjoy the wind-caressed silence. The most stupendous views are from **Massai Point**, where you'll see thousands of spires positioned on the slopes like some petrified army.

Bonita Campground (campsites $12), near the visitor center, has 22 first-come, first-served sites that often fill by noon. There's water, but no hookups or showers. Wilderness camping is not permitted inside the monument, but there is a USFS **campground** (www.fs.fed.us/r3/coronado) about 5 miles up Pinery Rd, which is near the park entrance station.

The monument is about 37 miles off I-10 at Willcox.

Benson & Around

A railway stop since the late 1800s, Benson is best known as the gateway to the famous Kartchner Caverns, among the largest and most spectacular caves in the USA. This wonderland of spires, shields, pipes, columns, soda straws and other ethereal formations has been five million years in the making, but miraculously wasn't discovered until 1974. In fact, its very location was kept secret for another 25 years in order to prepare for its opening as **Kartchner Caverns State Park** (⊘reservations 520-586-2283, information 520-586-4010; http://azstateparks.com/Parks/KACA/index.html; Hwy 90; park entrance per vehicle/bicycle $6/3, Rotunda Tour adult/child $23/13, Big Room Tour mid-Oct–mid-Apr $23/13; ⊙10am-3pm Mon-Fri Jun-Sep, to 3:40pm Sat & Sun, vary other times of the year). Two 90-minute tours are available, both equally impressive. The Big Room Tour closes to the public around mid-April, when a colony of migrating female cave myotis bats starts arriving from Mexico to roost and give birth to pups in late June. Moms and baby bats hang out until mid-September before flying off to their wintering spot. While a bat nursery, the cave is closed to the public.

The focus here is on education, so there are a number of rules – no purses, no water, no cameras, no touching the walls – to protect the delicate ecosystem. Tours often sell-out far in advance, so make reservations – online or by phone – early. The entrance is 9 miles south of I-10, off Hwy 90, exit 302.

About 15 miles east of Benson, in Dragoon, the private, nonprofit **Amerind Foundation** (⊘520-586-3666; www.amerind.org; 2100 N Amerind Rd; adult/child/senior $8/5/7; ⊙10am-4pm Tue-Sun) exhibits Native American artifacts, history and culture from tribes from Alaska to Argentina, from the Ice Age to today. The Western gallery has exceptional works by such renowned artists as Frederic Remington and William Leigh. It's right off I-10 exit 318.

The complex is near **Texas Canyon** in the **Little Dragoon Mountains**, which is known for its clumps of giant and photogenic granite boulders. For a closer look, swing by the historic **Triangle T Guest Ranch** (⊘520-586-7533; www.azretreatcenter.com; 4190 Dragoon Rd; casitas $149-189, cabins/bunkhouses $225/425; ⊛), where you can arrange horseback rides ($45 per hour), enjoy refreshments in the saloon or spend the night in fairly basic casitas. Tenters ($20) and RVers ($20 to $30) can set up among the rocks.

Campers can also spend the night at the **KOA Campground** (⊘520-586-3977; http://koa.com/campgrounds/benson; 180 W Four Feathers Ln; tent sites $27, RV sites $37-40, cabins $49, lodges $85-135; ⊛⊛). Otherwise, lodging in Benson is mostly about chain motels, which cluster off I-10 exits 302 and 304. One budget option is **Motel 6** (⊘520-586-0066; www.motel6.com; 637 Whetstone Commerce Dr; r $40), which is just off I-10 and almost a straight shot north from Kartchner Caverns via Hwy 90.

Benson isn't exactly the spot to experience a culinary tour de force – with the exception of **Magaly's** (⊘520-720-6530; 675 W 4th St; mains $7-10; ⊙lunch & dinner), a cute

THE BOOKS, MY FRIEND, ARE SINGING IN THE WIND

While you're in Benson, make sure to stop by the **Singing Wind Bookshop** (☑520-586-2425; www.bensonvisitorcenter.com; 700 W Singing Wind Rd; ☉9am-5pm), which is surely one of the great indie bookstores in the Southwest. Winnifred 'Winn' Bundy keeps tens of thousands of titles arranged in lovely literary chaos on a ranch 4 miles north of Benson. There's an excellent selection of Southwestern-themed books, but with this volume of stock there's something for every taste on the shelves. Winn herself is often around; if you get a chance to chat with her, do so and enjoy the company of one of the true great characters of the American West. To get here, enter Benson (likely from I-10). Go north on Occtillo St for about 2.5 miles until you see the sign for Singing Wind Bookshop on your right. It's about half a mile down a dirt road from here. After you enter through the gate, close it behind you.

little hacienda that serves up very good Mexican food. The house red chile is rich and spicy and damn delicious. For quick-and-easy coffee before your next adventure, drive through **Old Benson Ice Cream Stop**, (☑520-586-2050; 102 W 4th St; 6:30am-9pm Sun-Thu, 9:30pm Fri & Sat) beside the railroad tracks. It also sells 44 flavors of soft serve.

Benson is about 50 miles southeast of Tucson and 65 miles northeast of Patagonia. If you're approaching from any direction but the south you'll get here via I-10; if coming from the south, use Hwy 90 or Hwy 80. The main exit into town is exit 303 off I-10. Amtrak's *Sunset Limited* comes through thrice weekly on its run between Los Angeles and New Orleans.

EASTERN ARIZONA

From Flagstaff east to the New Mexico line, the most dominant scenic feature often seems to be the Burlington Northern-Santa Fe Railway freights that run alongside the interstate. But there are some iconic Route 66 sites along here, and a few spots that will surprise you just off the road.

Meteor Crater

The wooly mammoths and ground sloths that slouched around northern Arizona 50,000 years ago must have got quite a nasty surprise when a fiery meteor crashed into their neighborhood, blasting a hole some 550ft deep and nearly 1 mile across. Today the privately owned **crater** (☑928-289-5898; www.meteorcrater.com; adult/child/senior $15/8/14; ☉7am-7pm summer, shorter hours rest of the year) is a major tourist attraction with exhibits about meteorites, crater geology and the Apollo astronauts who used its lunar-like surface to train for their moon missions. You're not allowed to go down into the crater, but there are guided one-hour rim walking tours departing from 9:15am to 2:15pm (free with admission). The crater is about 6 miles off I-40 exit 233, 35 miles east of Flagstaff and 20 miles west of Winslow.

Winslow

'Standing on a corner in Winslow, Arizona...' Sound familiar? Thanks to the Eagles' catchy '70s tune 'Take It Easy', lonesome little Winslow is now a popular stop on the tourist track. In a small **park** (www.standinonthecorner.com; 2nd St & Kinsley Ave) on Route 66 you can pose with a life-size bronze statue of a hitchhiker backed by a charmingly hokey trompe l'oeil mural of that famous girl – oh Lord! – in a flatbed Ford. Up above, a painted eagle poignantly keeps an eye on the action, and sometimes a red antique Ford parks next to the scene. In 2005 a fire gutted the building behind the mural, which was miraculously saved.

◉ Sights & Activities

Homolovi State Park   PARK
(☑928-289-4106; http://azstateparks.com; per vehicle $7; ☉visitor center 8am-5pm) Closed in 2010 during the state budget crisis, this grasslands park beside the Little Colorado River re-opened in 2011 with a shorter name (it was formerly Homolovi Ruins State Park) and a renewed commitment to protect the artifacts and structures within this sacred Hopi ancestral homeland. Before the area

was converted into a park in 1993, bold thieves used backhoes to remove artifacts. Today, short hikes lead to petroglyphs and partly excavated ancient Native American sites. There's a first-come, first-served **campground** (tent & RV sites $25), with electric hookups, water and showers, near the Homolovi ruins. The park is 3 miles northeast of Winslow via Hwy 87 (exit 257).

Lorenzo Hubbell Trading Post　　MUSEUM
(☑928-289-2434; 523 W 2nd St; ⊙9am-5pm Mon-Fri, 9am-3pm Sat) Built in 1917, this trading post was tilting toward ruin until the chamber of commerce renovated it and took possession in 2009. Now it's a beautiful rustic space that's part visitor center, part museum.

🛏 Sleeping & Eating

Winslow is a handy base for the Hopi Reservation (p192), some 60 miles northeast of here. There are plenty of chain hotels and restaurants off I-40 at exit 253.

La Posada　　HISTORIC HOTEL $$
(☑928-289-4366; www.laposada.org; 303 E 2nd St; r $109-169; ❄️🐾) An impressively restored 1930 hacienda designed by star architect du jour Mary Jane Colter, this was the last great railroad hotel built for the Fred Harvey Company along the Santa Fe Railroad. Elaborate tilework, glass-and-tin chandeliers, Navajo rugs and other details accent its palatial Western-style elegance. They go surprisingly well with the splashy canvases of Tina Mion, one of the three preservation-minded artists who bought the rundown place in 1997. The period-styled rooms are named for illustrious former guests, including Albert Einstein, Gary Cooper and Diane Keaton.

TOP CHOICE Turquoise Room　　SOUTHWESTERN $$
(La Posada; breakfast $6-11, lunch $9-13, dinner $17-32; ⊙7am-9pm) Even if you're not staying at La Posada, treat yourself to the best meal between Flagstaff and Albuquerque at its unique restaurant. Dishes have a neo-Southwestern flair, the placemats are handpainted works of art, and there's a children's menu as well. If the fried squash blossoms are on the appetizer menu, toast your good fortune and order up, for the gods have smiled on you today.

❶ Information

The **visitor center** (☑928-289-2434; www.winslowarizona.org; 523 W 2nd St; ⊙9am-5pm Mon-Fri, 9am-3pm Sat year-round, 9am-3pm Sun

mid-Jun–mid-Aug) can be found inside the recently renovated Lorenzo Hubbell Trading Post.

❶ Getting There & Away

Greyhound buses stop at McDonald's at 1616 N Park Dr, but tickets aren't sold here; you can buy them in advance online or from the driver (at their discretion). The *Southwest Chief* stops daily (westbound at 7:50pm, eastbound at 5:39am) at the unstaffed **Amtrak station** (501 E 2nd St). Tickets can be purchased onboard, but are twice as pricey as they are with advance reservations.

Holbrook

In the 1880s Holbrook may have been one of the wickedest towns in the Old West ('too tough for women and churches'), but today this collection of rock shops and gas stations is better known as the Route 66 town with the wacky wigwam motel. It's also a convenient base from which to explore Petrified Forest National Park and its fossilized wood.

For the best selection and quality of petrified wood and other rocks and minerals, stop by **Jim Gray's Petrified Wood Co** (☑928-524-1842; www.petrifiedwoodco.com; cnr Hwys 77 & 180; ⊙7:30am-8pm), an expansive complex about a mile south of town. Polished and primed pieces of the ancient wood for sale here can cost up to $16,000. The smooth and unique coffee tables are hard to resist.

◉ Sights & Activities

Navajo County Historical Museum　　MUSEUM
(☑928-524-6558; 100 E Arizona St; donations appreciated; ⊙8am-5pm Mon-Fri, 8am-4pm Sat & Sun) The 1898 county courthouse is home to an eclectic assortment of historic local exhibits as well as Holbrook's chamber of commerce and visitor center. Each room of the museum highlights a different aspect of Holbrook's history. A creepy highlight is the old county jail, where the windowless cells were still being used as recently as 1976.

🛏 Sleeping & Eating

A full array of chain hotels are spaced along the northern part of Navajo Blvd.

Travelodge　　MOTEL $
(☑928-524-6815; www.travelodge.com; 2418 E Navajo Blvd; r incl breakfast $58-65; ❄️🐾📶🏊) This well-run place is a budget find, and it feels

more like a mom-and-pop than part of a national chain. Spotless standard rooms all come with refrigerators and microwaves. The continental breakfast includes scrambled eggs and sausage. Before you book online, give the manager a call and he might give you a lower rate.

Wigwam Motel MOTEL $
(☑928-524-3048; www.galerie-kokopelli.com /wigwam; 811 W Hopi Dr; r $52-58; ❄) Embrace the schlock of Route 66 at this motel, where each room is its own concrete tipi. Each is outfitted with restored 1950s hickory log-pole furniture and retro TVs.

Joe & Aggie's Cafe MEXICAN, AMERICAN $$
(121 W Hopi Dr; mains $5-15; ⊙6am-8pm Mon-Sat) This Route 66 favorite is a bit uninspired, but its tacos, enchiladas, burgers and chicken-fried steak are fine for anyone looking for dependable grub after a hard day of sightseeing. The salsa served with the free chips has a satisfying kick.

Mesa Italiana ITALIAN $$
(☑928-524-6696; 2318 E Navajo Blvd; mains $11-21; ⊙lunch Mon-Fri, dinner daily) Locals vouch for this place.

❶ Information

For online information, check out www.holbrook chamberofcommerce.com/holbrook.

Police (☑928-524-3991; 120 E Buffalo)

Post office (☑928-524-3311; 100 W Erie; ⊙9am-5pm Mon-Fri, 10am-2pm Sat)

Visitor center (☑928-524-6558; 100 E Arizona St; ⊙8am-5pm Mon-Fri, 8am-4pm Sat & Sun) In the county courthouse.

❶ Getting There & Away

Greyhound (☑928-524-2255) stops at the Circle K at 101 Mission Lane, where you can buy tickets.

Holbrook to New Mexico

East of Holbrook, Route 66 barrels on as I-40 for 70 miles before entering New Mexico just beyond Lupton. The only attraction to break the monotony of the road is the section cutting through the Painted Desert in Petrified Forest National Park.

PETRIFIED FOREST NATIONAL PARK
Forget about green. The 'trees' of the Petrified Forest are fragmented, fossilized logs scattered over a vast area of semidesert

grassland. Sounds boring? Not so! First, many are huge – up to 6ft in diameter – and at least one spans a ravine to form a natural bridge. Second, they're beautiful. Take a closer look and you'll see extravagantly patterned cross-sections of wood shimmering in ethereal pinks, blues and greens. And finally, they're ancient: 225 million years old, making them contemporaries of the first dinosaurs that leapt onto the scene in the Late Triassic period.

The trees arrived via major floods, only to be buried beneath silica-rich volcanic ash before they could decompose. Groundwater dissolved the silica, carried it through the logs and crystallized into solid, sparkly quartz mashed up with iron, carbon, manganese and other minerals. Uplift and erosion eventually exposed the logs. Souvenir hunters filched thousands of tons of petrified wood before Teddy Roosevelt put a stop to the madness and made the forest a national monument in 1906 (it became a national park in 1962). Scavenge some today and you'll be looking at fines and even jail time.

Aside from the logs, the park also encompasses Native American ruins and petroglyphs, plus an especially spectacular section of the Painted Desert north of the I-40.

Petrified Forest National Park (☑928-524-6228; www.nps.gov/pefo; per vehicle $10; ⊙7am-7pm May-Aug, 7am-6pm Mar, Apr & Sep, 8am-5pm Oct-Feb), which straddles the I-40, has an entrance at exit 311 off I-40 in the north and another off Hwy 180 in the south. A 28-mile paved scenic road links the two. To avoid backtracking, westbound travelers should start in the north, eastbound ones in the south.

A video describing how the logs were fossilized runs regularly at the **Painted Desert Visitor Center**, near the north entrance, and the **Rainbow Forest Museum** near the South Entrance. Both have bookstores, park exhibits and rangers that hand out free maps and information pamphlets.

The scenic drive has about 15 pullouts with interpretive signs and some short trails, but there's no need to stop at each and every one in order to appreciate the park. Two trails near the southern entrance provide the best access for close-ups of the petrified logs: the 0.6-mile **Long Logs Trail**, which has the largest concentration, and the 0.4-mile **Giant Logs Trail**, which is entered through the Rainbow Forest Museum and sports the park's largest log.

A highlight in the center section is the 3-mile loop drive out to **Blue Mesa**, where you'll be treated to 360-degree views of spectacular badlands, log falls and logs balancing atop hills with the leathery texture of elephant skin. Nearby, at the bottom of a ravine, hundreds of well-preserved petroglyphs are splashed across **Newspaper Rock** like some prehistoric bulletin board. Hiking down is verboten, but free spotting scopes are set up at the overlook.

There's more rock art at **Puerco Pueblo**, but the real attraction here is the partly excavated 100-room ruins that may have been home to as many as 1200 people in the 13th century.

North of the I-40 you'll have sweeping views of the **Painted Desert**, where nature presents a hauntingly beautiful palette, especially at sunset. The most mesmerizing views are from **Kachina Point** behind the **Painted Desert Inn** (admission free; ⊙9am-5pm year-round), an old adobe turned museum adorned with impressive Hopi murals.

Kachina Point is also the trailhead for wilderness hiking and camping. There are no developed trails, water sources or food, so come prepared. Overnight camping requires a free permit available at the visitor centers.

There are no accommodations within the park and food service is limited to snacks available at the visitor centers. The closest lodging is in Holbrook.

ARIZONA HOLBROOK TO NEW MEXICO

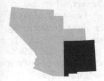

New Mexico

Includes »

Best Places to Eat

- » San Marcos Café (p275)
- » Trading Post Cafe (p299)
- » Ellis Store Country Inn (p344)
- » Pie-O-Neer Café (p325)
- » Coyote Café (p273)

Best Places to Stay

- » Earthships (p293)
- » St James Hotel (p309)
- » Christ in the Desert Monastery (p286)
- » Los Poblanos (p246)
- » La Fonda (p271)

Why Go?

It's called the 'Land Of Enchantment' for a reason. Maybe it's the drama of sunlight and cloud shadow playing out across endlessly rolling juniper-speckled hills; or the traditional mountain villages of horse pastures and adobe homes; or the gentle magnificence of the 13,000-foot Sangre de Cristo range; or the volcanoes, river canyons and vast desert plains spread beneath an even vaster sky. The beauty sneaks up on you, then casts a powerful spell. Mud-brick *santuarios* filled with sacred folk art; ancient and contemporary Indian pueblos; real-life cowboys and legendary outlaws; chile-smothered enchiladas: all add to the distinct vibe of otherness that often makes New Mexico feel like a foreign country.

Maybe the state's indescribable charm is best expressed in the iconic paintings of Georgia O'Keeffe. She herself exclaimed, on her very first visit: 'Well! Well! Well!...This is wonderful! No one told me it was like this.'

But seriously, how could they?

When to Go

Santa Fe

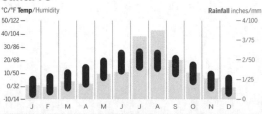

Mid-Aug–mid-Oct	Christmas season	June–mid-Aug
New Mexico at its best: gorgeous weather, wild sunflowers, chile harvest, fiestas.	Ski the Sangres, walk Canyon Rd on Christmas Eve, join in local holiday traditions.	Prime time for outdoor activities. But beware the monsoon storms!

New Mexico Planning

Due to major differences in altitude, when it's comfy in the lower, southern part of the state, it might be freezing in the northern mountains. Likewise, when the weather's perfect in Santa Fe, it's scorching in Carlsbad. If traveling around the state, bring a versatile wardrobe. With rare exception, casual dress is the way to go in New Mexico.

If you're afraid of spicy foods, order your chile (green, red or 'Christmas') on the side – but do try it. If you enjoy hot foods, beware: New Mexican chile is said to have addictive properties!

DON'T MISS

Steeped in traditional Native American and Hispanic cultures, soulful **Santa Fe** has world-class art, gourmet restaurants and great local food, old adobe architecture and famous festivals. An hour-and-a-half north is **Taos**, the famous artist community and hippy haven, known for the nearby historic Pueblo and world-class ski area. These two towns feel like nowhere else in the USA. Both sit beneath the **Sangre de Cristo Mountains**, which are laced with hiking/biking trails and wilderness backpacking routes.

Further south, tiny **Lincoln**, set in a scenic valley along the meandering Rio Bonito, oozes Wild West history as the former stomping grounds of Billy the Kid.

Among the state's most fantastic natural features are **White Sands National Monument** – where you can play among gleaming white dunes that ripple, swell and curl through the Tularosa Basin – and **Carlsbad Caverns National Park**, where you can walk through a massive underground fantasyland of stalagmites and stalactites. Most beautiful of all might be the **Ghost Ranch** area, where you'll find the landscape that so vividly influenced Georgia O'Keeffe.

Tips for Drivers

» New Mexico's main arteries are I-40 – which cuts east–west from Texas to Arizona via Albuquerque – and I-25, running north–south from the Colorado border, through Santa Fe and Albuquerque to Las Cruces. I-40 is occasionally closed in spring due to windstorms; both interstates may close during heavy blizzards in winter.

» Along highways in the south, you'll hit Border Patrol checkpoints with dogs (hint: think twice before bringing your cannabis prescription down from Denver).

» Interstate speed limits are 75mph, while state highways may go to 70mph.

» For road conditions, call 800-432-4269 or visit www.nmroads.com.

Fast Facts

» Population: 2 million

» Area: 121,599 sq miles

» Sales tax: 5-8%

» Albuquerque to Las Cruces: 223 miles, 3½ hours

» Gallup to Tucumcari: 311 miles, 4½ hours

» Santa Fe to Taos: 70 miles, 1½ hours

State Bird

The roadrunner can run nearly 20mph and kills and eats rattlesnakes

Resources

» All About New Mexico: www.psych.nmsu.edu /~linda/chilepg.htm

» New Mexico CultureNet: www.nmcn.org

» New Mexico Department of Tourism: www.new mexico.org

New Mexico Highlights

1 Immerse yourself in art and culture in the iconic state capital, **Santa Fe** (p255)

2 Visit the famous Pueblo, ski fluffy powder and get your mellow on in groovy **Taos** (p290)

3 Hike high peaks and camp beside alpine lakes in the **Pecos Wilderness** (p267)

4 Walk in the bootprints of Billy the Kid in historic **Lincoln** (p343)

5 Explore the underground fantasyland of **Carlsbad Caverns National Park** (p350)

6 Slide down the mesmerizing dunes at **White Sands National Monument** (p336)

7 Get healed at the 'Lourdes of America' – the **Santuario de Chimayo** (p288)

8 Wonder at the mystery of ancient civilization at **Chaco Culture National Historical Park** (p317)

9 Trek through rugged wilderness and climb into cliff dwellings in **Gila National Forest** (p330)

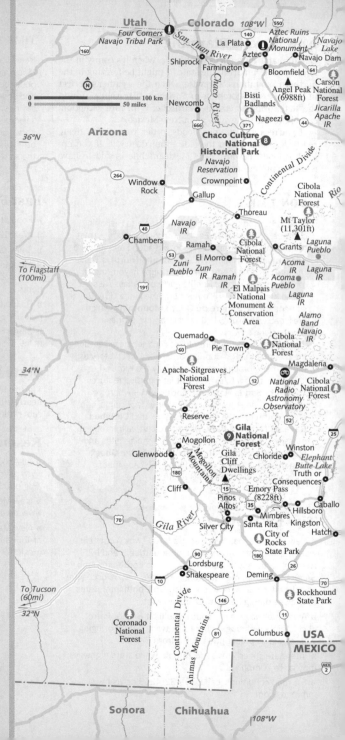

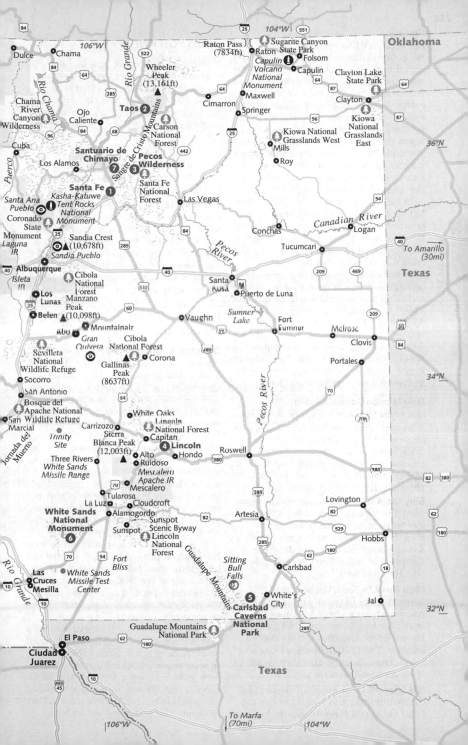

History

People roamed this land as far back as 10,500 BC, but by Francisco Vasquez de Coronado's arrival in the 16th century, Pueblo Indians made up the dominant communities. Santa Fe was established as the Spanish colonial capital around 1610, after which Spanish settlers and farmers fanned out across northern New Mexico and missionaries began their often violent efforts to convert the area's Puebloans to Catholicism. Following a successful revolt in 1680, Native Americans occupied Santa Fe, until 1692 when Don Diego de Vargas recaptured the city.

In 1851 New Mexico became US territory. Native American wars, settlement by cowboys and miners, and trade along the Santa Fe Trail further transformed the region, and the arrival of the railroad in the 1870s created an economic boom.

Painters and writers set up art colonies in Santa Fe and Taos in the early 20th century, and in 1912 New Mexico became the 47th state. A top-secret scientific community descended on Los Alamos in 1943 and developed the atomic bomb. Some say that four years later, aliens crashed outside of Roswell. Maybe that's why New Mexico is now poised to become a leader in space tourism and commercial space flights.

New Mexico Scenic Routes

One of the best ways to explore New Mexico is to travel its scenic highways. Eight have been selected as National Scenic Byways (www.byways.org) – though they are not necessarily the most striking stretches of pavement in the state. Just a few of the most rewarding roads you can drive:

Billy the Kid Scenic Byway (www.billybyway.com) This mountain-and-valley loop in southeastern New Mexico swoops past Billy the Kid's stomping grounds (p343), Smokey Bear's gravesite and the orchard-lined Hondo Valley. From Roswell (p345), take Hwy 380 west.

High Road to Taos The back road between Santa Fe (p255) and Taos (p290) passes through sculpted sandstone desert, fresh pine forests and rural villages with historic adobe churches and horse-filled pastures. The 13,000ft Truchas Peaks soar above. From Santa Fe, take Hwy 84/285 to Hwy 513, then follow the signs.

NM Hwy 96 From Abiquiú Lake to Cuba (p317), this little road wends through the heart of Georgia O'Keeffe country, beneath the distinct profile of Cerro Pedernal, then past Martian-red buttes and sandstone cliffs striped purple, yellow and ivory.

NM Hwy 52 Head west from Truth or Consequences (p326) into the dramatic foothills of the Black Range, past the old mining towns of Winston and Chloride (p328). Continue north, emerging onto the sweeping Plains of San Augustin before reaching the bizarre Very Large Array (p325).

For more scenic drives and the lowdown on **Route 66**, check out p29.

Dangers & Annoyances

Albuquerque sits over 5000ft above sea level, Santa Fe and Taos are at 7000ft and the mountains top 13,000ft – so if you're arriving from sea level, you may feel the altitude. Take it easy for the first day or two, and be sure to drink plenty of water to help get adjusted – a good idea, anyway, considering how arid the state is. Combined with altitude, the 300-plus days of sunshine also make this an easy place to get sunburned. And New Mexico leads the nation in lightning-strike deaths per capita, so be cautious if hiking in exposed areas during monsoon thunderstorms, which can be downright apocalyptic.

If you're into outdoor adventures, your New Mexico plans may hinge on how wet or dry the year has been. Ski areas may have some of the best or worst conditions in the West depending on snowfall; national forests sometimes close completely during severe summer drought.

Back around 1880, Territorial Governor Lew Wallace wrote, 'Every calculation based on experience elsewhere fails in New Mexico.' In many regards, that's still true today. Things here just don't work the way you might expect. That, paired with the entrenched *mañana* mindset, might create some baffling moments. Our advice: just roll with it.

> **DID YOU KNOW?**
>
> New Mexico is the only state with an official state question: 'red or green? – referring to chile, of course! You'll hear it every time you order New Mexican food. Feeling ambivalent? Choose 'Christmas' and try both.

NEW MEXICO

ℹ Getting There & Around

Most travelers fly into Albuquerque International Sunport (ABQ), but a few flights also land in Santa Fe (SAF).

Amtrak offers passenger train service on the Southwest Chief, which runs between Chicago and Los Angeles, stopping in Raton, Las Vegas, Lamy (for Santa Fe), Albuquerque and Gallup. A Native American guide hops aboard between Albuquerque and Gallup to provide insightful commentary. The Sunset Limited stops in Deming on its way from Florida to Los Angeles.

Greyhound buses travel to some New Mexico towns, but service has been cut back in recent years. Some areas in the state now have regional transport systems that connect small villages and larger towns and are either extremely cheap or free. But due to limited public transport options and the long distances, renting a car is the best choice for most visitors. For more information on driving, see Tips for Drivers (p235), New Mexico Scenic Routes and Route 66 & Scenic Drives (p29)

For more information on transportation throughout the Southwest, see p557.

ALBUQUERQUE

This bustling crossroads has an understated charm, one based more on its locals than on any kind of urban sparkle. In New Mexico's largest city, folks are more than happy to share history, highlights and must-try restaurants – making this much more than just the dot on the Route 66 map where Bugs Bunny should have turned left.

Centuries-old adobes line the lively Old Town area, and the shops, restaurants and bars in the hip Nob Hill zone are all within easy walking distance of each other. Good hiking is abundant just outside of town, through evergreen forests or among panels of ancient petroglyphs, while the city's modern museums explore space and nuclear energy. There's a vibrant mix of university students, Native Americans, Hispanics and gays and lesbians. You'll find square dances and yoga classes flyered with equal enthusiasm, and see ranch hands and real-estate brokers chowing down beside each other at hole-in-the-wall *taquerías* (Mexican fastfood restaurants) and retro cafes.

◉ Sights

Central Ave is Albuquerque's main street, passing through Old Town, downtown, the university, Nob Hill and the state fairground. Street addresses often conclude with a directional designation, such as Wyoming NE: the center point is where Central Ave crosses the railroad tracks, just east of downtown. For instance, locations

Greater Albuquerque

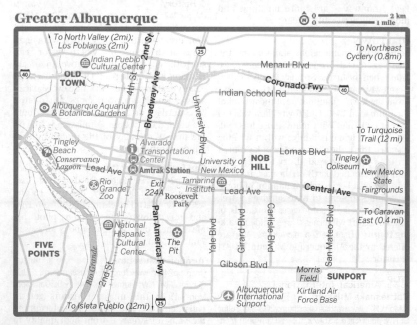

ALBUQUERQUE IN...

One Day

Jump-start your belly with a plate of huevos rancheros from **Frontier**, before heading to the **Indian Pueblo Cultural Center**, where you'll get a head start on a primo Pueblo education.

Next up visit the **BioPark**, which has a zoo, aquarium, botanical gardens and nature trails along the bosk. Head back into town for lunch, grabbing a bite at **Golden Crown Panaderia**, then wander over to **Old Town** for the afternoon. Walk off lunch admiring the **San Felipe de Neri Church**, browsing galleries and catching up on your snake trivia at the **American International Rattlesnake Museum**. Dine outdoors in **Nob Hill**; Albuquerque's grooviest neighborhood is thick with eateries.

Two Days

Wander around the **Petroglyph National Monument**, then head over to **Rudy's Bar-B-Q** for lunch before blowing your mind at the **National Museum of Nuclear Science and History**. Reach the top of **Sandia Crest** before sunset, either by **Tramway** or by scenic road, for expansive views of the Rio Grande Valley. When you get back down, linger over delicious food and wine at the **Slate Street Café & Wine Loft**.

north of Central Ave and east of the tracks would have a NE designation.

Most of Albuquerque's top sites are concentrated in Old Town, a straight shot down Central Ave from Nob Hill and the University of New Mexico (UNM). Some of the best attractions, however – including the Indian Pueblo Cultural Center, Petroglyph National Monument and Sandia Peak Tramway – are more far-flung and most easily accessible by car.

OLD TOWN

Some of the quaint adobe shops lining the alleyways of Old Town have been here since 1706, when the first 15 Spanish families called the newly named Albuquerque their home. From the town's founding until the arrival of the railroad in 1880, Old Town Plaza was the hub of daily life. With many museums, galleries and original buildings within walking distance, this is the city's most popular tourist area. As you walk around, try to keep your mind's eye trained partly on the past. Imagine this area as it began, with a handful of hopeful families grateful to have survived a trek across hundreds, in some cases thousands, of miles of desert wilderness. Free guided **walking tours** (⊙11am Tue-Sun, mid-Apr–mid-Nov) are offered by the Albuquerque Museum of Art & History.

⌐TOP⌐
⌐CHOICE⌐ **American International Rattlesnake Museum** MUSEUM
(Map p242; www.rattlesnakes.com; 202 San Felipe St NW; adult/child $3.50/2.50; ⊙10am-5pm Mon-

Sat, 1-5pm Sun) If you've ever been curious about serpents, this is the museum for you. It's possibly the most interesting museum in town, and you won't find more species of rattlesnake in one place anywhere else in the world. Come here for the lowdown on one of the world's most misunderstood snakes.

Albuquerque Museum of Art & History MUSEUM
(Map p242; www.cabq.gov/museum; 2000 Mountain Rd NW; adult/child $4/1; ⊙9am-5pm Tue-Sun) Conquistador armor and weaponry are highlights at this museum, where visitors can study the city's tricultural Native American, Hispanic and Anglo past. There's also a great gallery featuring the work of New Mexican artists. Family art workshops are offered on Saturdays at 2:30pm, and gallery tours are given daily at 2pm. Admission is free on the first Wednesday of the month and on Sundays until 1pm.

San Felipe de Neri Church CHURCH
(Map p242; www.sanfelipedeneri.org; Old Town Plaza; ⊙7am-5:30pm daily, museum 9:30am-4:30pm Mon-Sat). The church dates from 1793 and is Old Town's most famous photo op. Mass is held daily at 7am; Sunday Mass is at 7am, 10:15am and noon.

Turquoise Museum MUSEUM
(Map p242; www.turquoisemuseum.com; 2107 Central Ave NW; admission $4; ⊙9:30am-3pm Mon-Sat) At this museum visitors get an enlightening crash course in determining the value of stones – from high quality to

fakes. Joe Dan Lowry, the turquoise expert who owns the museum, is as opinionated as he is knowledgeable, so you're in for an interesting time!

Also in the Old Town are **¡Explora!** (p245) children's museum/science center and the New Mexico **Museum of Natural History & Science** (p245).

DOWNTOWN

Albuquerque's small downtown isn't the epicenter for action that it was some decades ago, when Route 66 was a novelty and reason enough to set out from either coast in a big '55 Chevy. City planners and business owners have tried in recent years to restore some of that fab '50s neon while encouraging trendy restaurants, galleries and clubs, with mixed success. On Saturday nights, Central Ave is jammed with 20-somethings cruising in low riders to see and be seen. Note: the area around the Alvarado Transportation Center has a particularly sketchy vibe.

NOB HILL & UNM AREA

A fun and funky place to shop, eat, see art films or get a haircut at a cigar/wine bar, this stretch of Central Ave starts at UNM and runs east to about Carlisle Blvd. Fashion-lovers can browse colorful shops for that unique outfit or accessory; artists will find inspiration and supplies. Even those not looking for anything in particular should find something of interest to muse over. See Shopping, below, for recommended stores.

University of New Mexico MUSEUMS (UNM; Map p239; www.unm.edu; Central Ave NE). There are 8 museums and galleries, along with loads of public art, packed onto the grounds of UNM. This small but peaceful campus is also home to a performing arts center and the **Tamarind Institute** (www .tamarind.unm.edu; ☺9am-5pm Mon-Fri), which helped save the art of lithography from extinction in the 1960s and '70s. The **Maxwell Museum of Anthropology**

NEW MEXICO ALBUQUERQUE

ALBUQUERQUE'S MOUNTAIN: SANDIA CREST

Albuquerqueans always know which way is east thanks to 10,378ft **Sandia Crest**, sacred to Sandia Pueblo and well named for both its wavelike silhouette and the glorious pink (sandia is Spanish for 'watermelon') its granite cliffs glow at sunset. There are three ways to the top.

Beautiful 8-mile (one-way) **La Luz Trail** (FR 444; parking $3) is the most rewarding, rising 3800ft from the desert, past a small waterfall to pine forests and spectacular views. It gets hot, so start early. Take Tramway Blvd east from I-25, then turn left on FR 333 to the trailhead.

Sandia Peak Tramway (p243) is the most extravagant route to the top; ride round-trip or take the tram up then hike down La Luz, walking two more miles on Tramway Trail to your car.

Finally you can drive, via NM 14, making a left onto Sandia Crest Rd (NM 165). The road is lined with trailheads and picnic spots (a daily $3 parking fee covers all of them), and low-impact camping ($3) is allowed by permit throughout Cibola National Forest. The choices are endless, but don't skip the easy 1-mile round-trip to **Sandia Man Cave**, where the oldest human encampment in North America was discovered in 1936. Bring a flashlight. The trailhead is along Hwy 165, north of the spur road to Sandia Crest.

At the top, the **Sandia Crest Visitor Center** (☏505-248-0190; NM 165; ☺10am-sunset in winter, to 7pm in summer) offers nature programs daily; **Sandia Crest House** (dishes $3-8), in the same building, serves burgers and snacks. This is the jumping-off point for the exquisite **Sandia Crest Trail**. With incredible views either way you go, paths lead north along the ridgeline for 11 miles and south along the ridge for 16.

Take the trail 2 miles south, past **Kiwanis Cabin** rock house, to the tram terminal and **High Finance** (☏505-243-9742; www.sandiapeakrestaurants.com; lunch mains $7-15, dinner mains $20-30; ☺11am-9pm), where the food is nothing special but the views are fabulous.

This is also the site of **Sandia Peak Ski Park** (☏505-242-9052; www.sandiapeak.com; lift tickets adult/child $50/40; ☺9am-4pm Dec-Mar & Jun-Sep), a smallish but scenic ski area. In summer, the park has a bike and lift combo for $58 (with $650 deposit) – you get a bike and lift pass to blaze those downhill runs all day long; note that bikes aren't allowed on the tram.

Old Town Albuquerque

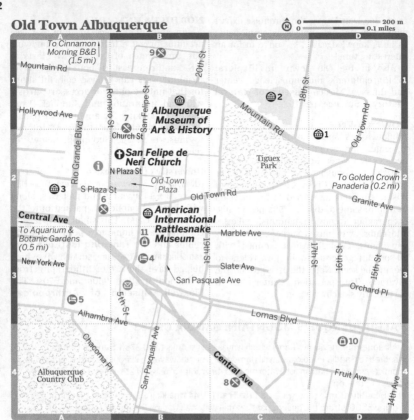

(www.unm.edu/~maxwell; 🕙10am-4pm Tue-Sat) is one of the best of its kind in the country. Visit the **UNM Welcome Center** (Map p239; ☎505-277-1989; 2401 Redondo Dr; 🕙8am-5pm Mon-Fri) for information and maps.

METROPOLITAN ALBUQUERQUE

TOP
CHOICE **Indian Pueblo Cultural Center**   MUSEUM
(Map p239; ☎505-843-7270; www.indianpueblo. org; 2401 12th St NW; adult/child $6/3; 🕙9am-5pm) Operated by the All Indian Pueblo Council, the cultural center is a must-see even on the shortest of Albuquerque itineraries. The history exhibits are fascinating, and the arts wing features the finest examples of each Pueblo's work. The IPCC also houses a large gift shop and retail gallery. Along with serving Pueblo-style cuisine, the on-site **Pueblo Harvest Café** (mains $5-8; 🕙8am-3pm Mon-Fri, to 5pm Sat & Sun; ☎🍴) has weekend art demonstrations, bread-baking demos and dances.

Petroglyph National Monument   ARCHAEOLOGICAL SITE
(www.nps.gov/petr) More than 20,000 petroglyphs are etched on basalt along the edge of an ancient lava field. Stop by the visitor center, on Western Trail at Unser Blvd, to determine which of three viewing trails – in different sections of the park – best suits your interests. **Rinconada Canyon** has the longest trail (2.2 miles round-trip) and is best if you want some solitude; **Boca Negra Canyon** features three short trails; **Piedras Marcadas** has 300 petroglyphs along a 1.5-mile trail. To leave the city behind for great views but no rock art, hit the **Volcanoes Trail**. Note: smash-and-grab thefts have been reported at some trailhead parking lots, so don't leave valuables in your vehicle. The visitor center is 7.5 miles north of Old

Old Town Albuquerque

Town; head west on I-40 across the Rio Grande and take exit 154 north.

Sandia Peak Tramway CABLE CAR
(www.sandiapeak.com, Tramway Blvd, vehicles $1, adult/child $20/12; ⊙9am-8pm Wed-Mon, from 5pm Tue Sep-May, 9am-9pm Jun Aug) Albuquerque's most famous attraction is the world's longest aerial tram, rising 2.7 miles from the desert floor to the top of 10,378ft Sandia Peak. Views are spectacular any time (but sunsets are particularly brilliant). The tramway is in the northeast corner of Albuquerque; take the Tramway Rd exit off I-25.

National Museum of Nuclear Science & History MUSEUM
(www.nuclearmuseum.org; 601 Eubank Blvd SE, adult/child & senior $8/7; ⊙9am-5pm; ⚿) Exhibits here examine the Manhattan Project, the history of arms control and the use of nuclear energy as an alternative energy source. Docents here are retired military, and they're very knowledgeable. There are interactive activities for kids. To get there from Central Ave, turn south on Eubank.

National Hispanic Cultural Center CULTURAL BUILDING
(Map p239; www.nhccnm.org; 1701 4th St SW; adult/child $3/free, admission free Sun; ⊙10am-5pm Tue-Sun) In the historic Barelas neighborhood, this center for Hispanic visual, performing and literary arts has three galleries and the nation's premier Hispanic genealogy library. Each June it hosts the Festival Flamenco.

South Valley & North Valley NEIGHBORHOOD
These traditional agricultural areas near the Rio Grande are characterized by open spaces, small ranches, farms, and *acequias* (traditional irrigation ditches that also mark walking paths). Chickens and horses roam fields between historical adobe and wood-frame houses and newer developments. The 39-sq-mile South Valley is bordered by I-25, I-40 and the West Mesa and volcanic cliffs.

North Valley is more mixed and upscale, with a reputation as affluent, pastoral, quiet and determined to keep it that way. Although it's just 7 miles from downtown Albuquerque, it feels like a world away. This 100-sq-mile area is roughly bordered by I-40, I-25, the Rio Grande and the Bernalillo–Sandoval County line.

Corrales NEIGHBORHOOD
This village, just north of North Valley, was established by Spanish settlers in 1710 but was home to Tewa Indians for centuries before that – they were practicing irrigated agriculture here 1300 years ago. Even more rural than North Valley, Corrales offers splendid strolling through the bosk (riparian woods) and along *acequias*. Take NM 448 north into the village and then drive or walk along any side roads – most are unpaved and will reward with earthy scents as scampering rabbits and quail crisscross your path among 200-year-old adobes and modern replicas. There's also a surprising amount of fine wine being made in these hills.

FREE **Gruet Winery** WINERY
(www.gruetwinery.com; 8400 Pan American Fwy NE; ⊙10am-5pm Mon-Fri, from noon Sat) Gives daily tours at 2pm and free tastings. Off I-40, north of city center.

Casa Rondeña
WINERY

(www.casarodena.com; 733 Chavez Rd NW; ⊙10am-6pm Mon-Sat, from noon Sun) Only gives tours during the area's summer Lavender Festival and charges $5 for tastings. In the Los Ranchos area of the North Valley; turn east off of Rio Grande Blvd to get here.

🏃 Activities

Hiking

Sandia Crest is Albuquerque's outdoor playground, popular for skiing and hiking (see p241). **Elena Gallegos Picnic Area** (Simms Park Rd; weekday/weekend parking $1/2; ⊙7am-7pm mid-Oct–mid-Apr, to 9pm mid-Apr–mid-Oct), in the foothills of the Sandias, is a popular jumping-off point for hiking, running and mountain-biking trails; some are wheelchair-accessible. Go early in the day before the sun gets too hot, or at dusk to take advantage of the panoramic views and watch the city lights begin twinkling below. You might be lucky enough to hear a chorus of howling coyotes at sunset. Follow Simms Park Rd from Tramway Blvd, south of the Sandia Peak Tramway.

Cycling

Cycling is big in Albuquerque, both for beginners and national-level competitors. Get outfitted at **Northeast Cyclery** (off Map p239; ☑505-299-1210; 8305 Menaul NE; rentals per day $25) and head out. Download a useful city map at www.cabq.gov/bike to find dedicated off-road tracks along arroyos. To ride along the Rio Grande, park at the Albuquerque BioPark and follow the riverside trail north or south. (The smell of green chiles roasting at local factories is best appreciated if you head south during autumn; the path is less urban if you head north.)

Walking

Walking the irrigation ditches is a downright local thing to do. Get a decent city map from the visitor center (many hotels also have them) and find the thin blue lines branching out in North Valley from the Rio Grande between Montaño Rd and Paseo del Norte and around Rio Grande Blvd. *Acequias* are bordered by walking paths, a gift to early-morning risers who value cool temperatures in the summer.

Rock Climbing

Rock climbers itching to hit the wall will dig the **Stone Age Climbing Gym** (☑505-341-2016; www.climbstoneage.com; 4201 Yale Blvd NE; day pass $14; ⊙noon-11pm Mon-Fri, 10am-8pm Sat & Sun), offering 12,000 sq ft of professionally designed climbing terrain simulating a variety of real rock features. Classes are offered and you can rent gear. For real rock, there are lots of great routes in the Sandias. To get here, take Comanche Rd exit off I-25

☞ Tours

Story of New Mexico Program
GENERAL

(☑505-277-2527; www.dcereg.com) The UNM Department of Continuing Education offers excellent lectures on all things New Mexico, as well as tours to Santa Fe and events like the Folk Art Market, Indian Market and opera, and gallery tours along the High Road to Taos by top-notch guides. Advance registration is required.

✷ Festivals & Events

Friday's *Albuquerque Journal* (www.abqjournal.com) includes a venue section with an exhaustive listing of festivals and activities. The following are most notable.

Gathering of Nations Powwow
CULTURAL

(www.gatheringofnations.com) Features dance competitions, displays of Native American arts and crafts, and the 'Miss Indian World' contest. Held in late April.

Zia Regional Rodeo
RODEO

(www.nmgra.com) Three days of riding and roping, sponsored by the NM Gay Rodeo Association. Mid-August.

Bernalillo Wine Festival
WINE

(www.newmexicowinefestival.com; admission $12) Locally produced wine, and live music too, staged about 15 minutes north of Albuquerque – a real treat if you're in town in early September.

New Mexico State Fair
RODEO

(www.exponm.com) A biggie rodeo, live music, games and rides; runs for 16 days in September.

International Balloon Fiesta
BALLOON

(www.balloonfiesta.org) The largest balloon festival in the world. You just haven't lived until you've seen a three-story-tall Tony the Tiger land in your hotel courtyard, which is exactly the sort of thing that happens during the nine-day festival, held between the first and second weekends in October.

ALBUQUERQUE FOR CHILDREN

Albuquerque has lots on offer for kids – from hands-on museums to cool hikes.

To give your little one a lesson in astronomy or a chance to check out the latest educational IMAX flick on a five-story-tall screen, visit the New Mexico **Museum of Natural History & Science** (Map p242; www.nmnaturalhistory.org; 1801 Mountain Rd NW; adult/child $7/4; ⊘9am-5pm; ⛶). It also has a number of kid-friendly activities and exhibits – children dig the Hall of Jurassic Supergiants and Dynatheater.

Hands-on science is the focus at **¡Explora!** (Map p242; www.explora.us; 1701 Mountain Rd NW; adult/child $8/4; ⊘10am-6pm Mon-Sat, from noon Sun; ⛶), where kids of all ages learn through playing with bubbles and balls and water and blocks. Most could stay here happily all day.

Adults will get as much out of the **Albuquerque BioPark** (Map p239; www.cabq.gov /biopark; adult/child three parks $12/5, per park $7/3; ⊘9am-5pm; ⛶) as children. When the weather is nice, and you're traveling with family, the place is especially appealing for the combo ticket to three kid-friendly attractions: a zoo, an aquarium and a botanic gardens. It's a good-value way to stay entertained all day. Set on 60 shady acres along the Rio Grande, the park's **Rio Grande Zoo** (Map p239; 903 10th St NW) is home to more than 250 species. There's a lot going on here: sea-lion feedings take place daily at 10:30am and 3:30pm, camel rides are offered in the spring and summer, and an entertaining summertime live animal show happens at 11am and 2pm Wednesday through Sunday. Meanwhile the **Albuquerque Aquarium** (Map p239; 2601 Central Ave NW), 2.5 miles northwest of the zoo, has a 285,000-gallon shark tank.

On the flora side, visit the **Rio Grande Botanic Gardens** (Map p239), next to the aquarium, and let the kids marvel at the 10,000-sq ft glass conservatory filled to the brim with Mediterranean and desert fauna. Special garden events include a **Butterfly Pavilion** from May to September.

Tingley Beach (1800 Tingley Ave SW; admission free; ⊘sunrise-sunset; ⛶) is connected to the aquarium and botanic gardens. This beloved open space includes fishing ponds stocked with rainbow trout, a children's pond and trails. You'll need a fishing license (day pass $12), but fortunately they are sold on-site at the **gift shop** (⊘9am-5pm). A little **train** connects the Zoo, Aquarium/Botanic Gardens and Tingley Beach; it runs approximately every half-hour.

When the kids have had enough learning (or they're hot), **Cliff's Amusement Park** (Map p239; www.cliffsamusementpark.com; 4800 Osuna NE; admission $25; ⊘Apr-Sep; ⛶) is a great reward. The park has about 25 rides, including a roller coaster, water rides, a play area and other traditional favorites. Hours vary.

🛏 Sleeping

Although Albuquerque has about 150 hotels (all full during the International Balloon Fiesta and the Gathering of Nations), it's not exactly swimming in interesting nonmotel lodging.

If you're looking for budget lodgings, inexpensive motels line Central Ave in metropolitan Albuquerque, concentrated around the I-25 on-ramp and east of Nob Hill. You can score a room in the $35 to $45 range, but trust your gut as some are pretty sleazy. The best bets for cheap accommodations are the endless chain motels that hug I-25 and I-40.

OLD TOWN
Böttger Mansion　　B&B $$
(Map p242; ☎505-243-3639, 800-758-3639; www .bottger.com; 110 San Felipe St NW; r incl breakfast $104-179; P❉@☎) A friendly and informative proprietor gives this well-appointed Victorian-era B&B an edge over some tough competition. The eight-bedroom mansion, built in 1912, is a one-minute walk from Old Town Plaza. The honeysuckle-lined courtyard is a favorite with bird-watchers. Famous past guests in the home include Elvis, Janis Joplin and Machine Gun Kelly.

Casas de Sueños　　B&B $$
(Map p242; ☎505-247-4560; www.casasdesuenos .com; 310 Rio Grande Blvd SW; r incl breakfast from $159; ❉@☎❋) This lovely and peaceful place with luscious gardens and a pool has 21 adobe casitas featuring handcrafted furniture and original artwork. Some casitas have a kitchenette, fireplace and/or private

hot tub – a couple are even outside in a private garden.

DOWNTOWN

TOP CHOICE Andaluz
BOUTIQUE HOTEL $$

(☎505-242-9090; www.hotelandaluz.com; 125 2nd St NW; r $140-240; P❄@🖝) Albuquerque's top hotel will wow you with style and attention to detail, from the dazzling lobby – where six arched nooks with tables and couches offer alluring spaces to talk and drink in public-privacy – to the Italian-made hypoallergenic bedding. The restaurant is one of the best in town, and there's a beautiful guest library and a rooftop bar. The hotel is so 'green' you can tour its solar water heating system – the largest in the state. You'll get big discounts booking online. It's one block north of Central Ave in the heart of downtown.

Route 66 Hostel
HOSTEL $

(☎505-247-1813; www.rt66hostel.com; 1012 Central Ave SW; dm $20, r from $25; P❄🖝) With discounts for HI-USA members, this 42-person hostel is clean, fun, cheap and conveniently located between downtown and Old Town. A kitchen and library are available for guest use. Just west of the downtown business district.

Mauger Estate B&B
B&B $$

(☎505-242-8755, 800-719-9189; www.maugerbb .com; 701 Roma Ave NW, cnr 7th St NW; r incl breakfast $99-195, ste $160-205; P🖝❄) This restored Queen Anne mansion (Mauger is pronounced 'major') has comfortable rooms with down comforters, stocked refrigerators and freshly cut flowers. Kids are welcome and there's one dog-friendly room complete with Wild West decor and a small yard ($20 extra).

Hotel Blue
HOTEL $

(☎877-878-4868; www.thehotelblue.com; 717 Central Ave NW; r incl breakfast $60-99; P❄@🖝) Well positioned beside a park on the western edge of downtown, the art-deco 134-room Hotel Blue has Tempur-Pedic beds and a free airport shuttle. Bonus points awarded for the good-size pool and 40in flat-screen TVs.

NOB HILL & UNM AREA

Hiway House
MOTEL $

(☎505-268-3971; www.hiwayhousemotel.com; 3200 Central Ave SE; s/d $35/40; ❄🖝) Hiway was once a prolific Southwest chain, and this was the last one built in the 1950s. Just beyond the heart of the UNM and Nob Hill

neighborhood, it's a 60-room place with the original 1958 neon sign and colonial-style architecture, but has been updated, with wi-fi. Not the cleanest, but an OK budget bet.

METROPOLITAN ALBUQUERQUE

TOP CHOICE Los Poblanos
B&B $$$

(off Map p239; ☎505-344-9297, 866-344-9297; www.lospoblanos.com; 4803 Rio Grande Blvd NW; r $130-360; ❄🖝) This amazing 20-room B&B, set among 25 acres of gardens, lavender fields (blooming mid-June through July) and an organic farm, is a registered National Historic Place. Los Poblanos is a five-minute drive from Old Town and is within walking distance of the Rio Grande and open-space trails. Organic eggs and produce from the farm are served for breakfast, and rooms feature kiva fireplaces.

Cinnamon Morning B&B
B&B $$

(off Map p242; ☎800-214-9481; www.cinnamon morning.com; 2700 Rio Grande Blvd NW; r $109-225; 🖝) This wired B&B near Old Town has four rooms, a two-bedroom guesthouse and an outdoor hot tub. Lots of Southwest charm and common areas make it a relaxing and homey place to slumber.

Casita Chamisa B&B
B&B $$

(☎505-897-4644; www.casitachamisa.com; 850 Chamisal Rd NW; r $105-125; ❄🖝🏊) Accommodations here include a two-bedroom guesthouse equipped with a kitchenette and vibrant greenhouse; a large bedroom in the main house; and a studio with a kitchenette. The friendly host, Arnold Sargeant, offers valuable advice about the area, including the archaeological site where the B&B is located. In the North Valley; turn east on Chamisal Rd from Rio Grande Blvd.

Albuquerque North Bernalillo KOA
CAMPGROUND $

(☎505-867-5227; www.koa.com; 555 S Hill Rd, Bernalillo; tent sites $23-30, RV sites $34-52, cabins $38-48; 🖝🏊) About 15 miles north of the Albuquerque city limits, the better of the city's two KOA franchises has wi-fi and is within easy exploring distance of city attractions. Take exit 240 or 242 off I-25; S Hill Rd is close to the interstate.

✗ Eating

Albuquerque offers the region's widest variety of international cuisines while serving up some good New Mexican grub. However, it's not a foodie destination like

Santa Fe, and many restaurants geared to tourists are less than outstanding. If you're not sure what you want, head to Nob Hill and browse a variety of spots ranging from hip to homey until one catches your eye.

OLD TOWN

The plaza is surrounded by average eateries serving average food at premium prices. Consider walking a few blocks for a better selection.

TOP CHOICE **Golden Crown Panaderia** BAKERY $
(off Map p242; ☑505-243-2424; www.goldencrown.biz; 1103 Mountain Rd NW; mains $5-20; ⊙7am-8pm Tue-Sat, 10am-8pm Sun) Who doesn't love a friendly neighborhood bakery? Especially one with gracious staff, fresh-from-the-oven bread and pizza, fruit-filled empanadas, smooth coffee and the frequent free cookie. Call ahead to reserve a loaf of quick selling green chili bread. Go to their website to check out their 'bread cam'.

Garcia's Kitchen NEW MEXICAN $
(Map p242; 1736 Central Ave SW; mains $6-8; ⊙7am-9pm Sun-Thu, to 10pm Fri & Sat) Part of a small local chain, this place just east of Old Town has some of the best New Mexican food in Albuquerque. The red vinyl booths and eclectic crowd give it a pure local feel. It's a great spot for breakfast.

Church St Cafe NEW MEXICAN $$
(Map p242; 2111 Church St NW; mains $7-15; ⊙8am-4pm Sun-Wed, to 8pm Thu-Sat) The food is good for the plaza area, and the cafe is historic and huge, with a nice patio. Try the Spanish hot chile dip or the veggie fajitas.

Seasons Rotisserie & Grill MODERN AMERICAN $$$
(Map p242; ☑505-766-5100; www.seasonsabq.com; 2031 Mountain Rd NW; lunch $9-16, dinner $17-31; ⊙11:30am-2:30pm Mon-Fri, 5-9:30pm Sun-Thu, 5-10:30pm Fri & Sat) With bright-yellow walls, high ceilings, fresh flowers and a creative menu, this contemporary place provides welcome relief from the usual Old Town atmosphere. Try the house-made raviolis or fresh grilled fishes and meats.

Antiquity STEAKHOUSE $$$
(Map p242; ☑505-247-3545; 112 Romero St NW; mains $17-26; ⊙5-10pm) With just 14 tables in an atmosphere of rustic elegance, Antiquity specializes in steak, seafood and fine wine. The desserts list isn't long, but it doesn't

need to be. This is a favorite of locals and visitors alike.

DOWNTOWN

TOP CHOICE **Slate Street Café & Wine Loft** MODERN AMERICAN $$
(off Map p239; ☑505-243-2210; www.slatestreetcafe.com; 515 Slate St; mains breakfast $6-12, lunch $9-15, dinner $11-27; ⊙7:30am-3pm Mon-Fri, 9am-2pm Sat & Sun, 5-9pm Tue-Sat) This downtown establishment is usually packed with people who come to sample the clever Southwestern/American fare in the cafe and drink merlot in the upstairs wine loft. The wine-tasting menu changes regularly and offers 30 different wines by the bottle from all over the world. It is located off 6th St NW, just north of Lomas Blvd.

Artichoke Café MODERN AMERICAN $$$
(Map p239; ☑505-243-0200; www.artichokecafe.com; 424 Central Ave SE; lunch mains $8-16, dinner mains $19-30; ⊙11am-2:30pm Mon-Fri, 5-9pm daily) Elegant and unpretentious, this popular bistro does creative gourmet cuisine with panache and is always high on foodies' lists of Albuquerque's best. It's on the eastern edge of downtown, between the bus station and I-40.

NOB HILL & UNM AREA

In the grand tradition of university neighborhoods, this is the best area for cheap, healthy and vegetarian meals. But you can also find a number of swanky places to nosh.

Street Food Asia ASIAN $$
(www.streetfoodasiaabq.com; 3422 Central Ave SE; mains $12; ⊙11am-10pm) One of the newest additions to the Nob Hill scene, this restaurant will take you on a culinary tour of the street stalls of Asian capitals, from Beijing to Bangkok to Kuala Lumpur. The concept – and the taste – is fresh and creative. There's even a stir-fry noodle bar.

Frontier NEW MEXICAN $
(www.frontierrestaurant.com; 2400 Central Ave SE; mains $3-8; ⊙5am-1am; ☑🖶) Get in line for enormous cinnamon rolls (made with, like, a stick of butter each!) and some of the best huevos rancheros in town. The food, people-watching and Western art are all outstanding.

Annapurna INDIAN $
(www.chaishoppe.com; 2201 Silver Ave SE; mains $7-12; ⊙7am-9pm Mon-Sat, 10am-8pm Sun; 🕸☑) This awesome vegetarian and vegan cafe has

LITERARY NEW MEXICO

In the year leading up to New Mexico's 2012 centential celebration, the New Mexico Book Co-op polled librarians, authors and the general public to compile a list of the 100 best New Mexico books of all time. Their top 10:

» *Bless Me, Ultima* by Rudolfo Anaya
» *Milagro Beanfield War* by John Nichols
» *A Thief of Time* by Tony Hillerman
» *Death Comes for the Archbishop* by Willa Cather
» *Red Sky at Morning* by Richard Branford
» *Lamy of Santa Fe* by Paul Hordan
» *House Made of Dawn* by N Scott Momaday
» *Ben-Hur: A Tale of the Christ* by Lew Wallace
» *The Rounders* by Max Evans
» *First Blood* by David Morrell

Obviously *Ben-Hur* (which became the epic film starring Charlton Heston) and *First Blood* (the inspiration for Sylvester Stallone's *Rambo* dynasty) are not about New Mexico, but are by authors who have called the state home.

some of the freshest, tastiest healthy food in town, including delicately spiced ayurvedic delights that even carnivores love. Dishes are complemented by authentic Indian (read: *real*) chai.

Il Vicino Pizzeria ITALIAN $
(3403 Central Ave NE; mains $7-9; ⏰11am-11pm, to midnight Fri & Sat) Sure, you can come for simple Italian fare like wood-fired pizza, salads and pasta. But the real bread and butter here is spectacular, award-winning microbrewed beer, including the Wet Mountain IPA and Slow Down Brown.

Flying Star Café AMERICAN $
(3416 Central Ave SE; mains $6-12; ⏰6am-11:30pm; 🛜🅿️♿) This incredibly popular local chain draws flocks with perennial favorites alongside innovative main courses. There's an extensive breakfast menu, sumptuous desserts, free wi-fi and creative, comfortable decor. It's pushed over the top of the groovy scale with organic, free-range and antibiotic-free ingredients.

METROPOLITAN ALBUQUERQUE
The following Albuquerque options are worth the little trek it takes to reach them.

Saigon Far East VIETNAMESE $
(901 San Pedro SE; mains $4-8; ⏰11am-8:30pm Thu-Tue, to 8pm Sun; 🅿️♿) Albuquerque has a bunch of great Southeast Asian restaurants, but this Vietnamese cheapie is our favor-

ite. Don't be deterred by the dodgy-looking exterior. Inside is a friendly, family-run place that's one of the best dining values in town. From Central Ave, head south on San Pedro to the intersection with Kathryn St.

Rudy's Bar-B-Q BARBECUE $
(2321 Carlisle NE; mains $4-16; ⏰10am-10pm; ♿) Mosey on into this barnlike structure filled with long picnic tables and benches, and your nose will tell you you've arrived in the land of serious barbecue. You don't order sandwiches here – you order meat by weight, then add bread. The brisket is so succulent it seems to melt in your mouth. Totally casual, it's great for families. Just north of I-40.

Loyola's Family Restaurant NEW MEXICAN $
(4500 Central Ave SE; mains $6-8; ⏰6am-2pm Tue-Fri, 6am-1pm Sat, 7am-1pm Sun) Pure Route 66 style, baby, Loyola's has been serving fine, no-frills New Mexican fare since before there was even a song about the Mother Road. Some say it has the best chile in town. Just over 500yd east of Nob Hill.

 Drinking

In addition to the places listed here, try the Slate Street Café & Wine Loft downtown for Albuquerque's best wine tasting. Il Vicino Pizzeria has excellent microbrews. Bars are generally open from 4pm to 2am Monday through Saturday, and until midnight on Sunday.

Satellite Coffee
CAFE

(2300 Central Ave SE; ⊘6am-11pm; 🛜🌮) Albuquerque's answer to Starbucks lies in these hip coffee shops – look for plenty of locations around town, including in the UNM and Nob Hill areas – luring lots of laptop-toting regulars. Owned by the same brilliant folks who started the Flying Star.

Kelly's Brewery
BREWERY

(www.kellysbrewpub.com; 3226 Central Ave SE; ⊘8am-midnight) Come to this former Route 66 service station for patio dining, lots of local microbrews and 20-somethings hanging out. You can even mix up your own batch with the help of one of Kelly's brewmasters – but you have to come back two weeks later to bottle it.

Downtown Distillery
BAR

(406 Central Ave SW) Smack in the heart of downtown, the Distillery has a casual crowd, pool and a jukebox, so you can be your own DJ.

Copper Lounge
LOUNGE

(1504 Central Ave SE) Just west of the UNM campus, you'll find a friendly, mixed crowd and daily drink specials at this place, which has a casual patio and a dark lounge area.

☆ Entertainment

For a comprehensive list of Albuquerque's diverse nightspots and a detailed calendar of upcoming events, get *Alibi* (www.alibi .com), a free weekly published every Tuesday. The entertainment sections of Thursday evening's *Albuquerque Tribune* and the Friday and Sunday *Albuquerque Journal* are helpful, too.

Nightclubs & Live Music
Downtown has a great bar scene, and Nob Hill's scene is pretty good, too, because of UNM. The theme seems to be atomic alien.

Caravan East
LIVE MUSIC

(off Map p239; 7605 Central Ave NE) Put on your cowboy boots and 10-gallon hat and hit the dance floor to practice your line dancing and two-stepping at this classic Albuquerque country-and-western music bar. Live bands perform and the ambience is friendly.

El Rey
LIVE MUSIC

(www.elreytheater.com; 620 Central Ave SW, Downtown) A fabulous venue for local and national rock, blues and country acts. Over the years, it's hosted such stars as Ella Fitzgerald, Etta James and Arlo Guthrie.

It also does national poetry slams and occasionally hosts CD launch parties.

Launch Pad
LIVE MUSIC

(www.launchpadrocks.com; 618 Central Ave SW, Downtown) This retro-modern place is the hottest stage for local live music, and still allows smoking inside – wow, now that's old school.

Cinemas

Guild Cinema
CINEMA

(Map p242; www.guildcinema.com; 3405 Central Ave NE, Nob Hill; admission $7) This is the only independently owned, single-screen theater in town, and it always has great indie, avant-garde, Hollywood fringe, political and international features. Stick around when there are discussions following select films.

Performing Arts
Popejoy Hall (www.popejoyhall.com; Central Ave at Cornell St SE) and the historic **KiMo Theater** (www.cabq.gov/kimo; 423 Central Ave NW, Downtown) are the primary places to see big-name national acts, as well as local opera and theater. The **Pit** (Map p239; www.unmtickets.com; 1111 University Blvd SE, UNM Arena) and **Tingley Coliseum** (Map p239; 300 San Pedro NE) also host major events.

The **New Mexico Ballet Company** (www .newmexicoballet.org; tickets $15-20) performs from October to April. The New Mexico Symphony Orchestra folded in April, 2011, but by the time you read this the newly formed **New Mexico Philharmonic** may be playing (www.nmphil.org).

Sports
About those **Albuquerque Isotopes** (www .albuquerquebaseball.com; Isotopes Park, Ave Cesar Chavez & University SE). First of all: yes, the city's baseball team really was named for the episode of *The Simpsons,* 'Hungry, Hungry Homer,' when America's favorite TV dad tried to keep his beloved Springfield Isotopes from moving to Albuquerque. The 'Topes sell more merchandise than any other minor league team. They sometimes win, too.

The **UNM Lobos** (www.golobos.com) have a full roster of teams, but are best known for basketball (men's and women's) and women's volleyball.

🔒 Shopping

The most interesting shops are in Old Town and Nob Hill.

Mariposa Gallery   ARTWORK
(Map p239 ;www.mariposa-gallery.com; 3500 Central Ave SE, Nob Hill) Beautiful and funky arts, crafts and jewelry, mostly by regional artists.

IMEC   JEWELRY
(Map p239; www.imecjewelry.net; 101 Amherst SE, Nob Hill) Around the corner from Mariposa, you'll find more artistic fine jewelry at IMEC.

Palms Trading Post   ARTS & CRAFTS
(Map p242; 1504 Lomas Blvd NW; ⊙9am-5:30pm Mon-Sat) Has Native American crafts and informed salespeople.

Silver Sun   JEWELRY
(Map p242; 116 San Felipe St NW; ⊙9am-4:30pm) A reputable spot for turquoise.

Page One   BOOKS
(www.page1books.com; 11018 Montgomery Blvd NE; ⊙9am-10pm Mon-Sat, to 8pm Sun) A huge and comprehensive selection of books, some secondhand.

❶ Information

Emergency
Police (☑505-764-1600; 400 Roma Ave NW)

Internet Access
Albuquerque is wired. The Old Town Plaza, Sunport, downtown Civic Plaza, Aquarium and Botanic Gardens have free wi-fi, as do Rapid Ride buses.

Internet Resources
Albuquerque Online (www.abqonline.com) Exhaustive listings and links for local businesses.
Albuquerque.com (www.albuquerque.com) Information on attractions, hotels and restaurants.
City of Albuquerque (www.cabq.gov) Public transportation, area attractions and more.

Medical Services
Presbyterian Hospital (☑505-841-1234, emergency 505-841-1111; 1100 Central Ave SE; ⊙24hr emergency)
UNM Hospital (☑505-272-2411; 2211 Lomas Blvd NE; ⊙24hr emergency) Head here if you don't have insurance.

Post
Post office (201 5th St SW)

Tourist information
Albuquerque Convention & Visitors Bureau (☑505-842-9918; www.itsatrip.org; 20 First Plaza; ⊙9am-4pm Mon-Fri) At the corner of 2nd St and Copper Ave.

Old Town Information Center (☑505-243-3215; 303 Romero Ave NW; ⊙10am-5pm Oct-May, to 6pm Jun-Sep)

❶ Getting There & Away

Air
New Mexico's largest airport, the **Albuquerque International Sunport** (☑505-244-7700; www.cabq.gov/airport; 2200 Sunport Blvd SE) is served by multiple airlines and car-rental companies.

Bus
The **Alvarado Transportation Center** (100 1st St SW, cnr Central Ave) is home to **Greyhound** (☑505-243-4435, 800-231-2222; www .greyhound.com; 320 1st St SW), which serves destinations throughout the state and beyond.

Train
Amtrak's Southwest Chief stops at Albuquerque's **Amtrak Station** (☑505-842-9650, 800-872-7245; 320 1st St SW; ticket office ⊙10am-5pm), heading east to Chicago (from $194, 26 hours) or west to Los Angeles (from $101, 16½ hours), once daily in each direction.

A commuter line, the **New Mexico Rail Runner Express** (www.nmrailrunner.com), shares the station, with eight Santa Fe departures (1½ hours; one-way/day pass $7/8) weekdays, four on Saturday and two on Sunday. At the time of writing, plans were being made to reduce weekday service.

❶ Getting Around

To/From the Airport
ABQ Ride bus No 250 provides free service between the Sunport and the downtown area, including the Rail Runner station, four times a day, weekdays only. The **Sunport Shuttle** (☑505-866-4966; www.sunportshuttle.com) runs to local hotels and other destinations; the **Sandia Shuttle** (☑888-775-5696; www.sandia shuttle.com) runs to Santa Fe (one-way/ round-trip $25/45) hourly between 8:45am and 11:45pm.

Bicycle
Contact **Parks & Recreation** (☑505-768-2680; www.cabq.gov/bike) for a free map of the city's elaborate system of bike trails, or visit the website. All ABQ Ride buses are equipped with front-loading bicycle racks.

Bus
ABQ Ride (Map p239; ☑505-243-7433; www .cabq.gov/transit; 100 1st St SW; adult/child $1/35¢; day pass $2) is a public bus system covering most of Albuquerque on weekdays and major tourist spots daily. Maps and schedules

NEW MEXICO'S PUEBLOS

New Mexico is home to 19 Native American pueblos, with the greatest concentration found outside of Santa Fe. For a compelling overview of these communities, stop by Albuquerque's **Indian Pueblo Cultural Center** (p242). Operated by the Puebloans themselves, the museum traces the development of Pueblo cultures, including Spanish influence, and features exhibits of the arts and crafts created in each pueblo.

One unique aspect of New Mexico's pueblos, compared to many other Indian reservations in the rest of the country, is that most are located right where they've been for centuries. While some are populated with descendants of refugees whose pueblos were destroyed by the Spanish, most Pueblo Indians were not radically displaced and have long and deep ties to their lands.

Don't expect all pueblos to be tourist attractions: many offer little for visitors outside of festival weekends. Most are just communities where people live. Many pueblos make money by running casinos (you can gamble on the Indian reservations, but not elsewhere in the state). Note that most casinos don't serve alcohol. Many pueblos charge visitor fees (not for casinos) and photography fees, so check regulations before you start walking around taking pictures.

Our pick of the top three pueblos for visitors:

Taos Pueblo (p302) The most famous pueblo in New Mexico, in a gorgeous spot below Pueblo Peak.

Zuni Pueblo (p320) Less touristy than other Pueblos, with creative jewelry and wild scenery; it's 35 miles outside of Gallup.

Acoma Pueblo (p323) Dramatic mesa-top location; along with Taos Pueblo and Arizona's Hopi villages, it's one of the oldest continually inhabited spots in America.

For more information on etiquette when visiting Indian reservations, see p527. Note that all the Pueblos in this section are mapped on p523. The consortium of pueblos north of Santa Fe is called **Eight Northern Pueblos** (www.enipc.org).

are available on the website; most lines run till 6pm. **Rapid Ride** buses (which run on hybrid diesel engines and have free wi-fi!) service the BioPark, downtown, Nob I Iill, the fairgrounds and Old Town; No 66 goes up and down Central Ave.

Car & Motorcycle

Albuquerque is an easy city to drive around. Streets are wide and there's usually metered or even free parking within blocks, or sometimes steps, from wherever you want to stop.

New Mexico's largest city is also motorcycle friendly: the town has its share of biker bars and you are more likely to hear a 'hog' thundering down the street than not.

Taxi

In general you must call for a taxi, though they do patrol the Sunport, and the Amtrak and bus stations.

Albuquerque Cab (505-883-4888; www.albuquerquecab.com)
Yellow Cab (505-247-8888)

Albuquerque Area Pueblos

There are a number of pueblos north of Albuquerque on the way to Santa Fe.

ISLETA PUEBLO

This **Pueblo** (www.isletapueblo.com), 16 miles south of Albuquerque at I-25 exit 215, is best known for its church, the **San Augustine Mission**. Built in 1613, it's been in constant use since 1692. A few plaza shops sell local pottery, and there's gambling at the flash **Hard Rock Hotel & Casino** (www.hardrockcasinoabq.com; 8am-4am Mon-Thu, 24hr Fri-Sun). On **Saint Augustine's Day** (September 4), ceremonial dancing is open to the public.

SANTA ANA PUEBLO

This **Pueblo** (www.santaana.org; US 150) is *posh*. Really posh. It boasts two great **golf courses** (505-867-9464, 800-851-9469; www.santaanagolf.com; green fees $45-80): the Santa Ana Golf Club, with three nine-hole courses,

WORTH A TRIP

SALINAS PUEBLO MISSIONS

Smack in the center of New Mexico you'll find a mostly empty region of hills and plains. But 350 years ago, the Salinas Valley was one of the busiest places in the Pueblo Indian world. Some 10,000 people lived there, and it bustled with trade between local pueblos, the Rio Grande Valley, Acoma, Zuni, the Spaniards and the Apaches.

Conquistadors arrived in the last years of the 16th century, valuing the Salinas region for the vast quantities of salt available nearby, as well as the chance to convert lots of Indians to Christianity. Impressive churches were built of stone and wood, and what remains of them and the pueblos are preserved within **Salinas Pueblo Missions National Monument** (www.nps.gov/sapu; admission free; ☺9am-5pm, until 6pm in summer). The **visitor center** is in the town of Mountainair, about 1½ hours by car from Albuquerque, but the monument itself is split into three separate sites, each with interpretive trails. **Abo**, off of Hwy 60, 9 miles west of Mountainair, is known for the unusual buttressing of its church, rarely seen in buildings from that period. **Quarai**, 8 miles north of Mountainair along Hwy 55, features the most intact church within the monument. **Gran Quivera**, 25 miles south of Mountainair along Hwy 55, has the most extensively excavated Indian ruins, along with exhibits about Salinas pueblo life. The most scenic way to get to Salinas Pueblo Missions from Albuquerque is to take Hwys 337 and 55 south along the eastern side of the Manzano Mountains.

If you're interested in ancient pottery and up for some off-the-beaten-path adventure, the swath of state land west of Gran Quivera is littered with shards of centuries-old black-on-white ceramics. Just be sure you're not on private property before you go poking around.

and the extravagant Twin Warriors Golf Club, with 18 holes amid waterfalls. **Santa Ana Star Casino** (☎505-867-0000; US 150; ☺8am-4am Sun-Wed, 24hr Thu-Sat) has a staggering buffet, 36 lanes of bowling and live entertainment ranging from Michael Jackson impersonators to Bob Dylan (the real one).

The **Stables at Tamaya** (☎505-771-6037; 2hr trail ride $75 ☺9:30am-3:30pm) offers trail rides and lessons ($75) through the woods, which the pueblo has recently restored. And ancient tradition has survived the modern glitz; there are **Corn Dances** on June 24 and July 26.

The luxurious **Hyatt Tamaya** (☎800-633-7313; www.tamaya.hyatt.com; 1300 Tayuna Trail; r from $159; P@☎☒♠), hidden in the desert landscape with expansive views, has three pools, three restaurants and a small spa.

SANDIA PUEBLO

About 13 miles north of Albuquerque, this **Pueblo** (www.sandiapueblo.nsn.us; I-25 exit 234) was established around the year 1300. It opened one of the first casinos in New Mexico and subsequently used its wealth to successfully lobby for legislation preventing further development of Sandia Crest, the Sandia people's old sacred lands, appropriated by Cibola National Forest. **Sandia Casino** (☎800-526-

9366; www.sandiacasino.com; ☺8am-4am Mon-Thu, 24hr Fri-Sun) boasts an elegant outdoor venue, the Sandia Casino Amphitheater, hosting everything from symphony orchestras to boxing matches to Bill Cosby.

Bien Mur Marketplace (100 Bien Mur Dr NE), across the road from the casino, claims to be the largest Native American–owned trading post in the Southwest, which is probably true. The tribe invites visitors to **Marketfest** (late October), when Native American artists show their work, as well as to corn dances during **Feast Day** (June 13).

ALBUQUERQUE TO SANTA FE

Two main routes connect New Mexico's two major cities: it takes a speedy hour to get from Albuquerque to Santa Fe along the semi-scenic I-25; or about 90 minutes on the much lovelier NM 14, known as the Turquoise Trail.

Along I-25

There are a couple of worthwhile stops off the interstate, including one fantastic place to hike.

CORONADO STATE MONUMENT

At Exit 242, about 1.7 miles west of I-25, you'll find **Coronado State Monument** (www.nmmonuments.org; US 550; adult/under 17yr $3/free, ☺8:30am-5pm Wed-Mon) and the ruins of **Kuaua Pueblo**. It's no Chaco Canyon, but the paintings are considered prime examples of precontact mural art in North America: various Pueblo gods (Kachinas) are depicted as personifications of nature, including the Corn Mother, who gave the Pueblo people corn. The murals have been artfully restored inside the visitor center and underground kiva. There's also a **campground** (tent/RV sites $14/18) with shade shelters and showers.

SAN FELIPE PUEBLO

Though best known for the spectacular **San Felipe Feast Green Corn Dances** (May 1), this conservative Keres-speaking **Pueblo** (I-25 exit 252) now has a couple more claims to fame. The **Casino Hollywood** (www.sanfelipe casino.com; I-25 exit 252; ☺8am-4am Sun-Wed, 24hr Thu-Sat) isn't just for gambling; this themed venue takes full advantage of its location to pull in acts like Los Lobos and Julio Iglesias. The Pueblo opens to the public on May 1 every year. Visitors are also invited to the **San Pedro Feast Day** (June 29) and the **Arts & Crafts Fair** in October.

SANTO DOMINGO PUEBLO

Now officially called **Kewa Pueblo** (Map p266; Hwy 22; ☺8am-dusk), this nongaming pueblo has long been a seat of inter-Pueblo government: the All Indian Pueblo Council still meets here annually. Several galleries and studios at the pueblo abut the plaza in front of the pretty 1886 **Santo Domingo Church**, with murals and frescoes by local artists. The tribe is most famous for *heishi* (shell bead) jewelry, as well as huge **Corn Dances** (August 4) and a wildly popular **Arts & Crafts Fair** in early September.

The Pueblo is on Hwy 22, 6 miles northwest from I-25 exit 259, about halfway between Albuquerque and Santa Fe.

COCHITI PUEBLO

About 10 miles north of Santo Domingo on NM 22, this **Pueblo** (www.pueblodecochiti .org) is known for its arts and crafts, particularly ceremonial bass drums and storyteller dolls. Several stands and shops are usually set up around the plaza and mission (built in 1628); dances open to the public are held on the **Feast Day of San**

Buenaventura (July 14) and other occasions throughout the summer, plus December 25. There's no photography allowed here, but visitors can snap away at the **golf course** (Pueblo de Cochiti Golf Course; ☎505-465-2239; www.golfcochititoday.com; 5200 Cochiti Highway; 9/18 holes $28/57), considered the state's most challenging, or splash in **Cochiti Lake**, favored by swimmers and boaters (no motors allowed).

KASHA-KATUWE TENT ROCKS NATIONAL MONUMENT

The bizarre and beautiful **Kasha-Katuwe Tent Rocks National Monument** (Map p266; www.blm.gov/nm/tentrocks) is a favorite hiking spot for Santa Fe and Albuquerque residents. At this surreal geologic realm, volcanic ash from the ancient Jemez Mountain volcanoes has been sculpted into tipi-like formations and steep-sided, narrow canyons that glow a strange light orange, sometimes with tiger stripes. Hike up a dry riverbed through the piñon-covered desert to the formations, where sandy paths weave through the rocks and canyons. You'll need a couple of hours to drive the desert dirt road to get here and to hike around a bit, but it's well worth it.

Take I-25 exit 264; follow Hwy 16 west to Hwy 22, then right onto Tribal Rte 92. At the time of research, dogs were banned from Tent Rocks.

Turquoise Trail

The Turquoise Trail (Map p266) has been a major trade route since at least 2000 BC, when local artisans began trading Cerrillos turquoise with communities in present-day Mexico. Today it's the scenic back road between Albuquerque and Santa Fe, lined with quirky communities and other diversions. For info, see www.turquoise trail.org.

CEDAR CREST

Located northeast of Albuquerque, on the eastern side of the Sandia Mountains, and just a bit up Sandia Crest Rd (NM 165) from Cedar Crest, the **Tinkertown Museum** (www .tinkertown.com; 121 Sandia Crest Rd; adult/child $3/1; ☺9am-5:30pm Apr-Nov; 🚶) is one of the weirdest museums in New Mexico. Huge, detailed handcarved dioramas of Western towns, circuses and other scenes come alive with a quarter. Woodcarver and wisdom collector Ross J Ward built it and surrounded it with antique toys, 'junque' (aka fancy junk) and suggestions that you eat more mangoes naked.

The nearby **Museum of Archaeology** (22 Calvary Rd; adult/child $3.50/1.50; ⊙noon-7pm Apr-Oct; ⊛), off NM 14, has an 'archaeological site' outdoors (kids dig this) and local Indian artifacts inside. It also runs the adjacent **Turquoise Trail Campground** (☑505-281-2005; www.turquoisetrailcampground .com; tent/RV sites $17.50/27, cabins $36-58), which has hot showers and cool shade. There's national forest access for guests.

MADRID

Madrid (pronounced *maa*-drid) is about 30 miles south of Santa Fe on Hwy 14. A bustling company coal-mining town in the 1920s and '30s, it was all but abandoned after WWII. In the mid-1970s, the company's heirs sold cheap lots to tie-dyed wanderers who have built a thriving arts community with galleries and wacky shops. Though it's become a lot more touristy over the years, beneath the surface its old outlaw heart still beats, remaining a favorite stop on Harley rallies.

There are dozens of galleries and shops in this one-horse town, but pay special attention to The **Crystal Dragon** (www.thecrystal dragon.com; 2891 NM 14), one of Madrid's original galleries, with unique handcrafted jewelry at really reasonable prices; **Seppanen & Daughters Fine Textiles** (www.finetextiles .com; 2879 NM 14), with its tactile and colorful Oaxaca, Navajo and Tibetan rugs; and **Range West** (www.rangewest.com; 2861 NM 14), with its elegant water fountains carved from monolithic granite chunks.

The **Old Coal Mine Museum** (2814 NM 14; adult/child $5/3; ⊙11am-5pm Fri-Mon) preserves plenty of old mining equipment, pretty much right where the miners left it. It also hosts the **Madrid Melodrama & Engine House Theatre** (www.themineshafttavern .com; adult/child $10/4; ⊙3pm Sat & Sun May-Oct), starring a steam locomotive, lots of Wild West desperados, scoundrels and vixens, and stories that leave you feeling good. Admission includes a six-shooter loaded with marshmallows to unload at the villains. At the time of research, the Theatre was closed due to fire-code violations, but will hopefully get those sorted out soon.

Both are attached to the **Mine Shaft Tavern** (www.themineshafttavern.com 2846 NM 14; mains $8-12; ⊙11:30am-7:30pm Sun-Thu, to 9pm Fri & Sat, bar open late daily) to meet locals, listen to live music on weekends and experience the 'longest stand-up bar in New Mexico.' The bar was built in 1946 and has been Madrid's favorite attraction ever since. The sign inside tells you everything you need to know about the place: 'Madrid has no town drunk; we all take turns.'

Mama Lisa's Ghost Town Kitchen (2859 NM 14; snacks $6-10; ⊙11am-4:30pm Fri-Sun) serves good quesadillas and a great red-chile chocolate cake.

Overnight at **Java Junction B&B** (☑505-438-2772; www.java-junction.com; 2855 Hwy 14; ste $89-129; ⊛), which has a charming Victorian suite just upstairs from a cafe where they take their brew seriously.

CERRILLOS

A few miles north of Madrid on Hwy 14, **Cerrillos** still has one foot in the Old West. With unpaved streets threading through an adobe town relatively unchanged since the 1880s, this is the home of the first mine in North America, built to extract turquoise around AD 100.

In a region chock full of artists and galleries, one of the most unique and subtly mind-blowing is the **Thomas Morin Studio** (☑505-474-3147; 8 First St; ⊙10am-4pm Mon-Sat, Apr-Nov), where you can watch the master sculptor work with his current medium of choice: used sandpaper belts. His pieces are absolutely exquisite; even if you're just planning on driving by on Hwy 14, do not miss this gallery. Call ahead if you don't want to leave a visit to chance. If you're on a tight budget, lock your checkbook in the car before going in.

The **Cerrillos Turquoise Mining Museum & Petting Zoo** (17 Waldo St; admission $3; ⊙9am-sunset) packs five rooms with Chinese art, pioneer-era tools, mining equipment dating to 3000 BC, bottles and antiques excavated from an abandoned area hotel, and anything else the owners thought was worth displaying. For $2 more you can feed the goats, llamas and exotic chickens. Hours vary.

Broken Saddle Riding Co (☑505-424-7774; www.brokensaddle.com; off County Rd 57; rides $55-100) offers one- to three-hour horseback rides through juniper-dotted hills and abandoned mines, including a special sunset/moonlight ride. Along the way, you'll learn about local history and geology. Call in advance. Just down the road is **Cerrillos Hills State Park** (www.nmparks.com; per vehicle $5; ⊙sunrise-sunset) where 5 miles of hiking trails link historic mining sites.

SANTA FE

Welcome to 'the city different,' a place that makes its own rules yet never forgets its long and storied past. Walking among the historic adobe neighborhoods, and even around the tourist-filled plaza, there's no denying that Santa Fe has a timeless, earthy soul. Founded around 1610, Santa Fe is the second-oldest city and the oldest state capital in the USA. It's got the oldest public building and throws the oldest annual party in the country (Fiesta). Yet the city is synonymous with contemporary chic, boasting the second-largest art market in the nation, gourmet restaurants, great museums, spas and a world-class opera. It's a beacon of progressive thought and creative culture. The UN named it 'most creative city' in 2005, a fitting honor for a city that is committed to the arts like few other places in the country.

At 7000 feet above sea level, Santa Fe is also the highest state capital in the US.

Sitting at the foot of the Sangre de Cristo range, the city is a fantastic base for hiking, mountain biking, backpacking and skiing. When you come off the trails, you can indulge in chile-smothered local cuisine, then shop for turquoise and silver directly from the Native American jewelers who sell their work around the plaza, visit some of the most unique churches in the country, or simply wander along centuries-old, cottonwood-shaded lanes and fantasize about moving here.

The city is home to a motley crew of characters, including traditional and avant-garde artists, New Age hippie transplants, Spanish families that have called the city home for centuries, undocumented Mexican immigrants, retirees from both coasts, and more than a few Hollywood producers and movie stars. All have come for the relaxed attitude, the space, the unbeatable climate and that certain something that gives Santa Fe a singularly alluring essence.

NEW MEXICO SANTA FE

Greater Santa Fe

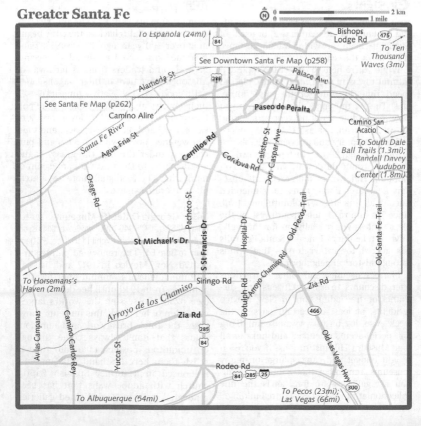

SANTA FE IN...

Two Days

After breakfast at **Cafe Pasqual's**, art up at the **Georgia O'Keeffe Museum**. Stroll around the **plaza**, checking out the Native American jewelry being sold on the sidewalk, on your way to the lovely **St Francis Cathedral**. Have a classic (and cheap) New Mexican lunch at **Tia Sophia's**. Check out the the **Loretto Chapel** on your way over to **Canyon Rd**, stopping at numerous galleries there. For dinner, hit the **Tune Up Café** for casual local dining.

The next morning, chow down at the **Santa Fe Baking Co**. Head over to Museum Hill – don't miss the **Museum of International Folk Art**. Pop into **Harry's Roadhouse** for lunch, then take a scenic drive up **Ski Basin Road**, where there are loads of hiking and biking trails. Have dinner and catch some live flamenco at the city's oldest tavern, **El Farol**. Olé!

Three Days

After two days in town, grab breakfast at the **Tesuque Village Market**, then head on up to **Bandelier National Monument**, to hike in the gorgeous gorges and climb ladders into ancient cliffside kivas. Then it's back to Santa Fe for a dinner of barbecue brisket quesadillas and a Mescal margarita at the Cowgirl Hall of Fame.

⊙ Sights

Most downtown galleries, museums, sights and restaurants are either on or east of Guadalupe St and are within walking distance of the plaza, the center of the action.

While you're here in one of the top-rated cultural towns in the United States, plan to spend time in some of the city's museums. The art museums alone can keep you busy for a while, covering genres including Native American, Spanish Colonial, modern and contemporary, and international folk art.

Most museums are clustered in two locations – around the downtown plaza and on **Museum Hill**, where four excellent museums, a research library and a recommended cafe are all linked by a sculpture-lined trail. Since it's almost 3 miles southwest of the plaza, unless you're really up for the walk, drive or take the M Line – a Santa Fe Trails bus geared toward visitors – that winds through historical neighborhoods.

Many museums and other attractions offer discounts to senior citizens and discounts or free admission to New Mexico residents, at least on certain days of the week. Also, log on to www.museumhill.org for special-events calendars and links to all four Museum Hill institutions. If you're on a tight budget and can't splurge on many museums, remember that Santa Fe's gazillion art galleries are free, as is the fine collection at the State Legislature building.

TOP CHOICE **The Plaza**   PLAZA

(Map p258) Santa Fe's Plaza is the heart of the town, and dates back to the city's beginning over 400 years ago. Between 1822 and 1880 the Plaza served as the end of the Santa Fe Trail, and traders from as far away as Missouri drove here in their wagons laden with goods. Today, Native Americans sell their jewelry and pottery beneath the portico of the Palace of the Governors; kids skateboard and play hackeysack; and tourists weighed down with cameras and purchases wander through the grassy center on their way to the next shop, museum or margarita. The food stalls here are a great place to grab a snack.

TOP CHOICE **Georgia O'Keeffe Museum**   MUSEUM

(Map p258; ☎505-946-1000; www.okeeffemuseum .org; 217 Johnson St; adult/child $10/free; ☉10am-5pm, to 8pm Fri) The renowned painter first visited New Mexico in 1917 and lived in Abiquiú, a village 45 minutes northwest of Santa Fe, from 1949 until her death in 1986 (see p286). Possessing the world's largest collection of her work, this museum showcases the thick brushwork and luminous colors that don't always come through on ubiquitous posters; take your time to relish them here firsthand. The museum is housed in a former Spanish Baptist church with adobe walls that has been renovated to form 10 skylighted galleries.

Tours of O'Keeffe's house an hour away in Abiquiú require advance reservations.

TOP CHOICE **Museums of New Mexico** MUSEUM
(single museum adult/child $8/free, 4-day pass to all 4 museums adult/child $18/free; ⊙10am-5pm Tue-Sun) This is a collection of four very different museums – two of them on Museum Hill and two on the Plaza – which also offers seminars, musical events and a variety of guided tours with historic or artistic focuses, many designed for children. Both the Palace of the Governors and the New Mexico Museum of Art, the two located on the Plaza, are free on Friday from 5pm to 8pm. All the museums have fabulous gift shops.

Museum of International Folk Art
(Map p262; www.internationalfolkart.org; 706 Camino Lejo) On Museum Hill, this museum houses more than 100,000 objects from more than 100 countries and is arguably the best museum in Santa Fe. The exhibits are at once whimsical and mind-blowing, as the world's largest collection of folk art spills across the galleries in festive presentations. There are dolls, masks, toys, garments and entire handmade cities on display. The historical and cultural information is concise and thorough; try to hit the incredible International Folk Art Market, held here each June.

Museum of Indian Arts & Culture
(Map p262; www.indianartsandculture.org; 710 Camino Lejo) This museum opened on Museum Hill in 1987 to display artifacts unearthed by the Laboratory of Anthropology, which must confirm that any proposed building site in New Mexico is not historically significant. Since 1931 it has collected over 50,000 artifacts. Rotating exhibits explore the historical and contemporary lives of the Pueblo, Navajo and Apache cultures. One of the most complete collections of Native American arts anywhere, it's a perfect companion to the nearby Wheelwright Museum.

New Mexico Museum of Art
(Map p258; www.nmartmuseum.org; 107 W Palace Ave) This museum features works by regional artists and sponsors regular gallery talks and slide lectures. It was built in 1918, and the architecture is an excellent example of the original Santa Fe–style adobe. With more than 20,000 pieces – including collections of the Taos Society of Artists, Santa Fe

Society of Artists and other legendary collectives – it's a who's who of the geniuses who put this dusty town's art scene on a par with those of Paris and New York.

Palace of the Governors
(Map p258; 505-476-5100; www.nmhistory museum.org; 105 W Palace Ave) This is one of the oldest public buildings in the country. Built in 1610 by Spanish officials, it housed thousands of villagers when the Indians revolted in 1680 and was home to the territorial governors after 1846. It displays a handful of regional relics, but most of its holdings are now shown in an adjacent exhibition space called the **New Mexico History Museum** (113 Lincoln Ave), a glossy, 96,000-sq-ft expansion that opened in 2009. Volunteers lead free, highly recommended palace tours throughout the day; call for exact times.

St Francis Cathedral CHURCH
(Map p258; www.cbsfa.org; 131 Cathedral Pl, ⊙8:30am-5pm, Mass 7am & 5:15pm Mon-Sat, 8am, 10am, noon & 5:15pm Sun) Jean Baptiste Lamy was sent to Santa Fe by the pope with orders to tame the Wild Western outpost town through culture and religion. Convinced that the town needed a focal point for religious life, he began construction of this cathedral in 1869. Lamy's story was the inspiration for Willa Cather's classic *Death Comes for the Archbishop*. Inside the cathedral is a small chapel, housing the oldest Madonna statue in North America. Carved in Mexico, the statue was brought to Santa Fe in 1625, but when the Indians revolted in 1680, the villagers took it into exile with them. When Don Diego de Vargas retook the city in 1692, he brought it back, and legend has it that its extraordinary powers are responsible for the reconquest of the city.

Loretto Chapel CHURCH
(Map p258; www.lorettochapel.com; 207 Old Santa Fe Trail; admission $3; ⊙9am-5pm Mon-Sat, 10:30am-5pm Sun) The Gothic chapel is modeled on Sainte Chapelle in Paris, and was built between 1873 and 1878 for the Sisters of Loretto, the first nuns to come to New Mexico. Sainte Chapelle has a circular stone staircase, but when the Loretto Chapel was being constructed, no local stonemasons were skilled enough to build one and the young architect didn't know how to design one of wood. The nuns prayed for help and a mysterious traveling carpenter, whom the nuns believed afterward to be St Joseph,

Downtown Santa Fe

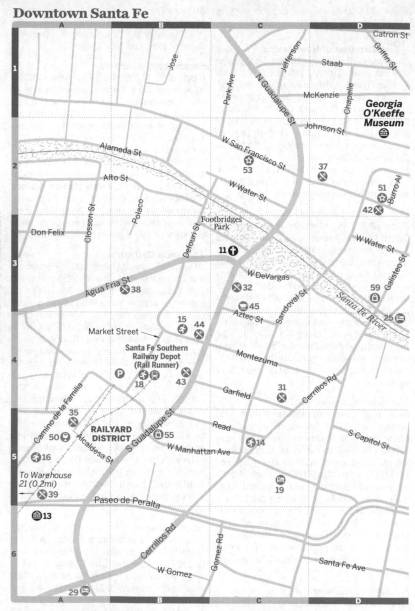

arrived. He built what is known as the Miraculous Staircase, a wooden spiral staircase with two complete 360-degree turns and no central or visible support. He left without charging for his labors and his identity remains unknown.

Today the chapel is a museum popular with tourists who come to snap photos of **St Joseph's Miraculous Staircase** and check out the intricate stations of the cross lining the aisle to the very Catholic main altar. The gift shop is packed with Catholic kitsch.

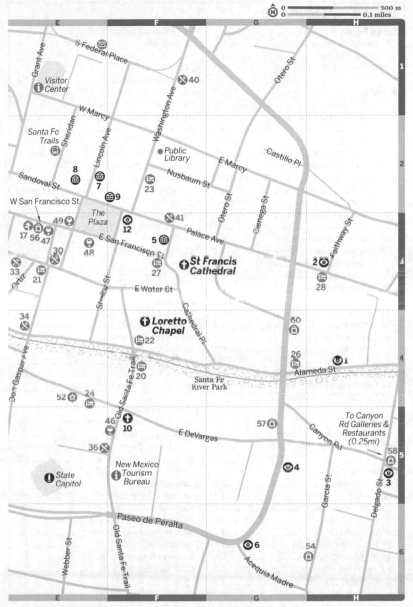

The chapel is one of the top places to get married in Santa Fe (it's nondenominational). After the ceremonies (which are not open to the public) the newlyweds are often led across the plaza to the tunes and dancing of a colorfully costumed mariachi band, a true Santa Fe tradition.

San Miguel Mission CHURCH
(Map p258; 401 Old Santa Fe Trail; admission $1; ⏰9am-5pm Mon-Sat, 10am-4pm Sun, Mass 5pm

Downtown Santa Fe

Sun) The original construction of this mission was started in 1625, and it served as a mission church for the Spanish settlers' Tlaxcalan Indian servants, who had been brought from Mexico. Though considered the oldest church in the United States, much of the original building was destroyed during the Pueblo Revolt of 1680; it was rebuilt in 1710, with new walls added to what remained. The mix of Spanish and Indian artwork inside is well worth a peek!

FREE Santuario de Guadalupe   CHURCH
(Map p258; 100 Guadalupe St; ⊙9am-4pm Mon-Sat) The adobe church is the oldest extant shrine to Our Lady of Guadalupe, the patroness of Mexico. It was constructed between 1776 and 1796, with several additions and renovations since. The oil-on-canvas Spanish baroque *retablo* (altar painting) inside the chapel was painted in Mexico in 1783 by José de Alzíbar. For the trip to Santa Fe, the painting had to be taken apart and transported up the Camino Real in pieces on mule back. This is just one of the many cultural treasures housed here, including the Santa Fe Archdiocese's collection of *santos* – wood-carved portraits of saints, for which New Mexican artisans are famous.

Museum of Contemporary Native Arts   MUSEUM
(Map p258; www.iaia.edu/museum; 108 Cathedral Pl; adult/child $10/free; ⊙10am-5pm Mon & Wed-Sat, noon-5pm Sun, closed Tue) Primarily showing work by the students and faculty of the esteemed Institute of American Indian Arts, this place also has the finest contemporary offerings of Native American artists from tribes across the US. It's an excellent place to see cutting-edge art and understand its role in modern Native American culture.

FREE Wheelwright Museum of the American Indian   MUSEUM
(Map p262; www.wheelwright.org; 704 Camino Lejo; ⊙10am-5pm Mon-Sat, 1-5pm Sun) In 1937 Mary Cabot established this museum, part of Museum Hill, to showcase Navajo ceremonial art. While its strength continues to be Navajo exhibits, it now includes contemporary Native American art and historical artifacts, too. The gift store has an extensive selection of books and crafts.

FREE State Capitol   MUSEUM
(Map p258; ☑505-986-4589; cnr Paseo de Peralta & Old Santa Fe Trail; ⊙7am-6pm Mon-Fri, 9am-5pm Sat in summer, guided tours by appt) Locally referred to as the Roundhouse, the State Capitol is the center of New Mexico's government and was designed after the state symbol, the Zia sign. It also has one of the best (free) art collections in New Mexico. You can walk through by yourself, or call the number above or email Christal Branch (christal.branch@nmlegis.gov) to set up a guided tour.

LA VILLA REAL DE LA SANTA FÉ DE SAN FRANCISCO DE ASIS

When a tiny settlement at the base of the Sangre de Cristo Mountains was made the capital of New Mexico in 1610, the newly appointed Spanish governor named it *La Villa Real de Santa Fé* – The Royal Town of Holy Faith. For many years after its founding, it was known simply as 'La Villa.' Sometime during your stay, you may hear that the city's original name was actually *La Villa Real de la Santa Fé de San Francisco de Asís* – The Royal Town of the Holy Faith of St. Francis of Assisi. But the exhaustively researched *Place Names of New Mexico* disagrees. Its author, Robert Julyan, suggests the St. Francis part was tacked on in more modern times, thanks to 'tourist romanticism.'

Rancho de las Golondrinas   MUSEUM
(Map p266; www.golondrinas.org; 334 Los Pinos Rd, La Cienega; adult/child $6/free; ⊙10am-4pm Wed-Sun Jun-Sep; ⊕) The 'Ranch of the Swallows' has been around nearly as long as the city of Santa Fe. It was built as a stop along the Camino Real; now it's a 200-acre living museum, carefully reconstructed and populated with historical re-enactors. You can watch bread being baked in an *horno* (traditional adobe oven), visit the blacksmith, the molasses mill or traditional crafts workshops. There are orchards, vineyards and livestock. Festivals are held throughout the summer. This is one of the best places to learn something about the history of the area while the kids are having a blast. To get there, take I-25 south to exit 276, then follow the signs.

SITE Santa Fe   MUSEUM
(Map p258; www.sitesantafe.org; 1606 Paseo de Peralta; adult/child $10/free; ⊙10am-5pm Thu & Sat, 10am-7pm Fri, noon-5pm Sun, tours Fri, 2pm Sat & Sun) An enormous, whitewashed space, the 8000-sq-ft SITE Santa Fe is a nonprofit art museum dedicated to presenting world-class contemporary art to the community. From radical installation pieces to cutting-edge multimedia exhibitions, this hybrid museum-gallery takes art to the next level. It also hosts wine-splashed openings, artist

Santa Fe

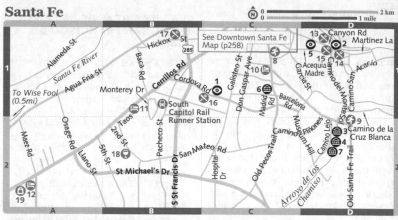

See Downtown Santa Fe Map (p258)

Santa Fe

talks, movie screenings and performances of all kinds. Admission is free on Fridays.

Shidoni Foundry GARDENS, GALLERY
(Map p266; www.shidoni.com; 1508 Bishop's Lodge Rd, Tesuque; ⊙10am-5pm Mon-Sat;) Five miles north of Santa Fe in Tesuque, Shidoni has an 8-acre grassy sculpture garden, a great place for a picnic or for the kids to run around among some funky artwork. There's also an indoor gallery and an on-site glassblowing studio. Every Saturday you can watch 2000°F molten bronze being poured into ceramic shell molds, one of several steps in the complex lost-wax casting technique ($2).

🏃 Activities

Although Santa Fe's museums, churches, galleries and shops are top-notch, visitors do not live by art appreciation alone. Get thee to the great outdoors. The best one-stop spot to peruse your options is the **Public Lands Information Center**, which is inconveniently located south of town off of Hwy 14. If you don't feel like schlepping out there, the folks at Santa Fe's gear shops – like **Sangre de Cristo Mountain Works** (Map p258; ✆505-984-8221; www.sdcmountainworks.com; 328 S Guadalupe St; ⊙10am-7pm Mon-Fri, 10am-6pm Sat, noon-5pm Sun) – know a ton about the area; their website is also packed with details about where to hike, climb, bike and camp.

Before you head out for any strenuous activities, remember the elevations you're dealing with; make sure you've taken time to acclimatize and watch for signs of altitude sickness if you're going high. Weather changes rapidly in the mountains, and summer storms are frequent, especially in the afternoons, so keep an eye on the sky and hike prepared. Most trails are usually closed by snow in winter, and higher trails may be closed through May.

The best area overview map for trails and outdoor action is the Santa Fe/Bandelier/Los Alamos map published by Sky Terrain.

Skiing

Though downhill gets most of the attention around here, there are also numerous cross-country ski trails in both the Sangre de Cristo and Jemez Mountains.

Ski Santa Fe   SKIING
(Map p266; ☎505-982-4429, snow report 505-983-9155; www.skisantafe.com; lift ticket adult/child $63/43; ☉9am-4pm late Nov-Apr) Often overlooked for its more famous cousin outside of Taos, the Santa Fe ski area boasts the same fluffy powder (though usually a little less of it), with an even higher base elevation (10,350ft) and higher chairlift service (12,075ft). Briefly admire the awesome desert and mountain vistas, then fly down powder glade shoots, steep bump runs or long groomers. The resort caters to families and expert skiers alike with its varied terrain. The quality and length of the ski season can vary wildly from year to year depending on how much snow the mountain gets, and when it falls (you can almost always count on a good storm in late March).

On autumn weekends, the chairlift takes passengers up through the shimmering golden foliage of the aspen forest (one-way/round-trip $7/10, small children free); there's also an extensive system of hiking trails off of the parking lot. To get there, take Hwy 475 – known first as Artist Rd, then Hyde Park Rd, then Ski Basin Rd – from just north of the plaza.

Though the ski area rents gear, lots of people prefer to pick up skis, poles, boots and boards at **Cottam's** (Map p266; ☎505-982-0495; www.cottamsskishops.com; 740 Hyde Park Rd) On the way to the slopes, it has reasonable prices on gear packages (from adult/child $22/16) and also rents snowshoes ($13.50). Reserve online and get a discount.

Mountain Biking

Some of the best intermediate single track in New Mexico is found on the **North and South Dale Ball Trail System**, which encompasses more than 20 miles of paved and

---

TOP FIVE SPAS

Many Santa Fe spas offer spectacular natural settings, mountain views and world-class pampering. Below are our top choices.

Absolute Nirvana Spa & Tea Room (Map p258; ☎505-983-7942; www.absolutenirvana .com; 106 Faithway St; ☉10am-6pm Sun-Thu, to 8pm Fri & Sat) Rose-petal baths and sumptuous Indonesian- and Thai-style massage ($105 to $190 per treatment) await you here.

Avanyu Spa (Map p258; ☎505-986-0000; www.laposada.rockresorts.com; 330 E Palace Ave; ☉7am-8pm) Choose from a range of sophisticated therapies, including craniosacral, reiki, polarity and shiatsu ($135 to $200), at this swanky spot within the La Posada Hotel.

Body (Map p262; ☎505-986-0362; www.bodyofsantafe.com; 333 Cordova Rd; ☉7am-9pm) Aimed at local clientele, Body offers high-quality massages with fewer frills for less money ($80). Drop your kids at the supervised play room ($6 per hour) while you de-stress.

Encantado Resort (☎877-262-4666; www.encantadoresort.com; 198 State Rd 592, Tesuque; ☉9am-9pm) Everything from ayurvedic treatments ($155 to $300) to acupuncture ($150) to crystal chakra balancing ($245) – oh, and traditional massage ($150) and facials ($165 to $225).

Ten Thousand Waves (off Map p255; ☎505-982-9304; www.tenthousandwaves.com; 3451 Hyde Park Rd; communal tubs $19, private tubs per person $29-49; ☉2-10:30pm Tue, 9am-10:30pm Wed-Mon Jul-Oct, reduced hours Nov-Jun) This gorgeous Japanese spa offers a host of attractive public and private outdoor soaking tubs, kitted out in a smooth Zen style with cold plunges and saunas. A host of treatments – from prenatal, hot stone and Thai massages to herbal wraps – are offered. Massages start at $99.

CANYON RD & AROUND: SANTA FE GALLERY-HOPPING

Once a footpath used by Pueblo Indians, then the main street through a Spanish farming community, Santa Fe's most famous art avenue, **Canyon Rd** (www.canyonroadarts.com), began its current incarnation in the 1920s, when artists led by Los Cinco Pintores (a group of five painters who fell in love with New Mexico's landscape) moved in to take advantage of the cheap rent.

Today Canyon Rd is a must-see attraction. More than 100 of Santa Fe's 300-plus galleries are found here, and it has become the epicenter of the city's vibrant art scene, with everything from rare Indian antiquities to Santa Fe School masterpieces to wild contemporary work. Gallery-hopping can seem a bit overwhelming, so we'd suggest not worrying and just wandering. Exhibitions are constantly changing, so have a peek in the window; you'll quickly tell what you like and don't like.

Friday nights are particularly fun: that's when the galleries put on glittering openings, starting around 5pm. Not only are these great social events, but you can also browse while nibbling on cheese, sipping Chardonnay or sparkling cider and chatting with the artists.

Below is just a sampling of our Canyon Rd (and around) favorites. For more, pick up a handy, free *Santa Fe & Canyon Road Walking Map* or check out the Santa Fe Gallery Association's website, www.santafegalleries.net. More galleries are concentrated around the Railyard and along Lincoln Ave just north of the Plaza.

Adobe Gallery (Map p262; www.adobegallery.com; 729 Canyon Rd) This gallery includes pieces by the 'Five Matriarchs' of the Pueblo pottery renaissance: Maria Martinez, Margaret Tofoya, Maria Nampeyo, Lucy Lewis and Helen Cordero, among many other famed Southwestern Indian artisans.

Chalk Farm Gallery (Map p262; www.chalkfarmgallery.com; 558 Canyon Rd) This gallery is filled with irresistibly fantastical pieces – mostly paintings, but also sculpture, kaleidoscopes and fine-art furniture.

Economos/Hampton Galleries (Map p258; 500 Canyon Rd) Museums come here to purchase fantastic examples of ancient Native American art, pre-Columbian Mexican pieces and much, much more, all crammed onto two huge floors swirling with history.

GF Contemporary (Map p262; www.gfcontemporary.com; 707 Canyon Rd) Contemporary paintings and mixed-media creations lure with thought-provoking content and presentation.

Marc Navarro Gallery (Map p258; 520 Canyon Rd) Collectors come here to find antique Spanish and Mexican silver pieces, including jewelry studded with onyx and amethyst.

---

unpaved bike and hiking trails with fabulous views of mountains and deserts. Trails vary in length and difficulty – the **South Dale Ball Trails** (off Map p255) are the most challenging. To get to the south trails, follow Upper Canyon Rd north to the well-signed parking lot at Cerro Gordo Rd – there is a great **dog park** across the street. The ride from this parking lot is a favorite, but beware it starts with a super-long, hard and rocky single-track climb, followed by a series of harrowing switchbacks. You'll be rewarded richly, however, with loads of supreme isolation and outstanding views.

The **Winsor Trail** (No 254; Map p266) is one of the most popular intermediate bike routes in the state. The scenery – particularly in the fall – is outstanding. The trail wends through Hyde State Park and Santa Fe National Forest, and serves as the spine of several other multi-use trails, including the bike-friendly Chamisa Loops. The downhill ride on the Winsor from up near the ski area is unforgettable!

For something less alpine, race the trains on the **Santa Fe Rail Trail**. Beginning at the Santa Fe Southern Railway Depot, this 15-mile trail follows the rail line clear to Lamy. The trail is unpaved until you hit Agua Fria St, then paved the rest of the way, though mountain bikers can take a dirt turnoff at the intersection with US 285 to avoid following CR 33 into Lamy.

For bike rental and repair, and more route info, see the kind gentlemen at **Mellow Velo**

Morning Star Gallery (off Map p258; www.morningstargallery.com; 513 Canyon Rd) Of all the Canyon Rd shops dealing Indian antiquities, this remains the best: weavings, jewelry, beadwork, kachina dolls and even a few original ledger drawings are just some of the stars at this stunning gallery, which specializes in pre-WWII Plains Indian ephemera. Some artifacts here are finer than those in most museums – like the 1775 Powhoge ceramic storage jar that sold for $225,000 and the 1860 Nez Perce war shirt that went for $220,000.

Pushkin Gallery (Map p262; www.pushkingallery.com; 550 Canyon Rd) Owned by the family of poet Alexander Pushkin, this gallery shows Russian masters including Nikolai Timkov and Vasily Golubev, who are outshone by newcomer Alexy Smirnov Vókressensky. Museum-quality Orthodox icons and lacquer boxes are also on display.

The following galleries are off Canyon Rd but worth visiting for their unique mediums and creations:

78th St Gallery (Map p258; ☎505-820-0250; www.78thstreetgallery.com; 357 E. Alameda St) Open by appointment only, this gallery just off Canyon Rd features unique paintings by local and international artists that focus on color, movement and spirit. Also check the website.

Gerald Peters Gallery (Map p258; www.gpgallery.com; 1011 Paseo de Peralta) Santa Fe's preeminent restaurant and real-estate tycoon Gerald Peters' gallery, two blocks from Canyon Rd, carries a collection of fine art that few museums can touch, with all the Southwest masters: Nicolai Fechin, Charles Russell, Edward Borein, Woody Gwyn and many more. The back room has treasures the Museum of Fine Arts can't even afford.

Shiprock (Map p258; www.shiprocktrading.com; 53 Old Santa Fe Trail, on Plaza) In a second-floor loft at the northeast corner of the Plaza, Shiprock has an extraordinary collection of Navajo rugs. Run by a fifth-generation Indian country trader, the vintage pieces are the real deal.

Nedra Matteucci Galleries (Map p258; www.matteucci.com; 1075 Paseo de Peralta) Works by the Taos Society (p296) are on display at this top gallery, which shows the best work of Joseph Henry Sharp, Ernest Blumenschein and the rest of the gang. Don't miss the beautiful gardens out back, which have monumental sculptures in stone and bronze, including work by Vietnam Women's Memorial designer Glenna Goodacre.

(Map p262; ☎505-982-8986; www.mellowvelo.com; 621 Old Santa Fe Trail; rentals per day from $35; ⏱9am-5:30pm Mon-Sat). Their website also has a really useful page with trail maps.

Rafting

The two rivers worth running near Santa Fe are the **Rio Grande** – for white-water thrills – and the **Rio Chama** – which is mellower, but better for multiday trips and arguably more scenic.

As soon as it's marginally warm enough, rafting outfits head to the Rio Grande to crash through rapids on the renowned Class V **Taos Box**, which traverses 16 miles of spectacular wilderness gorge. It's fantastically fun but not for the faint of heart, and commercial companies require passengers to be at least 12 years old. Flows in this stretch of the river are usually too low to boat beyond early summer.

Less extreme but still exciting is the Class III **Racecourse**, also on the Rio Grande. It's fine for kids over six or seven (depending on the company), and the put-in is much closer to Santa Fe than the launch point for the Box. The season here usually runs from May to October, depending on water levels. This is also a classic playground for kayakers.

The Rio Chama has a few Class III rapids, but most of it is fairly flat, making it a fantastic choice for families, especially if you were wondering how you were going to get your kids or lazy spouse out into the backcountry for a couple of nights. Parts of the canyon are sublime.

Santa Fe & Around

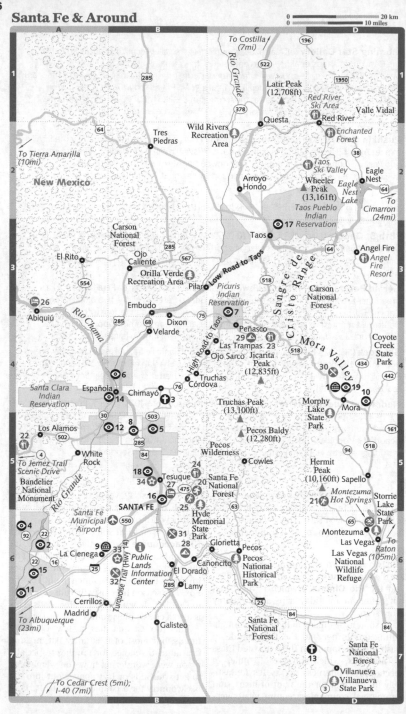

Santa Fe & Around

Outfitters offer a number of variations on the above themes, so check in with them for all the options. Some reliable companies:

Santa Fe Rafting Co   RAFTING
(☎888-988-4914; www.santaferafting.com; per person Taos Box $110-120; Racecourse $65; 3-day Chama $595) Pickup from Santa Fe or meet at the river.

New Wave Rafting Co   RAFTING
(☎800-984-1444; www.newwaverafting.com; per person Taos Box $116; Racecourse adult/child $57/50; 3-day Chama $525) Now based near Pilar; meet at or near the river.

Kokopelli Rafting Adventures   RAFTING
(☎800-879-9035; www.kokopelliraft.com; per person Taos Box $110-120; Racecourse adult/child $53/42; 3-day Chama $449) Pickup from Santa Fe or meet near the river.

Horseback Riding

No Western fantasy is complete without hopping into a saddle, and there's some great riding to be done around Santa Fe. The **Stables at Bishop's Lodge** (Map p266; ☎505-819-4013; www.bishopslodge.com; 1297 Bishop's Lodge Rd; ◷8am-5pm; ☀) has a long menu of themed trail rides to choose from, including a sunset ride on Tuesdays and Thurdays.

Other highly recommended scenic rides are further from town, like those offered down in Cerrillos by Broken Saddle (p254) and at Ghost Ranch (p285), near Abiquiú.

If you're looking for lessons – Western or English – head a half-hour north to Española, where you'll find the affable Erlene Seybold-Smythe, one of the best instructors and horse trainers in the area, at **Roy-El Morgan Farm** (☎505-753-3696; www.roy-elmorgans.com; 1302 McCurdy Rd, Española; ☀), a champion Morgan facility.

Hiking & Backpacking

Some of the best hiking and backpacking in New Mexico is right outside of Santa Fe, in **Santa Fe National Forest**. The heart of the national forest is the undeveloped **Pecos Wilderness**, with nearly 1000 miles of trails leading through spruce and aspen forest, across grassy alpine meadows, and up to several peaks surpassing 12,000ft. The quickest way to get above treeline is to drive

TOP FIVE SANTA FE DAY HIKES

There are a ton of trails around Santa Fe. Whether you're looking for all-day adventure or just a relaxing stroll through a special landscape, you'll find it. Trailheads for all the hikes in this list are within an hour's drive from the Plaza. The first two hikes start from the ski basin parking lot, beginning along the same trail.

Backcountry trails at Bandelier National Monument (see p284) are also suberb.

Raven's Ridge (Map p266) No trail has better views than this one. After hiking the first steep mile of the Upper Winsor Trail, Raven's Ridge cuts east, more or less following the Pecos Wilderness boundary high above treeline to the top of Lake Peak (12,409ft). You can see forever from up here. Make a loop by hiking back down the ski slopes to the parking lot. It's a strenuous hike at substantial elevation, but well worth it if your body can take it. About 4 miles round trip.

Upper Winsor to Puerto Nambe After the first mile or so of steep switchbacks, the trail mellows out, essentially contouring around forested slopes with a moderate uphill section toward the end. Puerto Nambe (11,050ft) is a huge and beautiful meadow in the saddle between Santa Fe Baldy (12,622ft) to the north and Penitente Peak (12,249ft) to the south. It's a great place for picnic. The round-trip is about 10 miles.

Aspen Vista The premier path for immersing yourself in the magic of the fall foliage, this trail lives up to its name. The first mile or so is supereasy, gaining little elevation and following an old dirt road. It gets a little more difficult as you go along. Just go as far as you want, then turn back. The trailhead is at about 10,000ft, along the road to the ski basin; it's marked 'Trail No 150'. Mountain bikers love this one too.

Tent Rocks For something surreal, Kasha-Katuwe Tent Rocks National Monument (p253) has a couple of short trails that meander through a geologic wonderland. The Cave Loop is 1.2 miles long; Veterans Memorial is a mile-long loop that's wheelchair accessible; the Canyon Trail round-trip is about 3 miles. Located 40 miles southwest of Santa Fe.

Valles Caldera A couple of remarkable trails circle small peaks in a massive basin that's really the crater of an ancient supervolcano. Elevations are between 9000ft and 10,000ft. This one pushes the one-hour drive time right to the edge, and is much closer to Los Alamos. You must call Valles Caldera National Preserve (see p283) in advance to reserve a hiking permit.

to the ski basin, hop on the Winsor Trail, and trudge up the switchbacks. For more on the Pecos Wilderness, see p289. For top day hikes in the area, see box.

The most immediately accessible hiking trails are on the city's **Dale Ball Trail System**, just east of downtown. Also close to downtown, the **Randall Davey Audubon Center** (off Map p255; ☎505-983-4609; www.nm.audubon.org; 1800 Upper Canyon Rd; trail use $2; ☺9am-4pm Mon-Fri, to 2pm Sat) offers a few trails, including the 3-mile **Bear Canyon Trail**. Free guided bird walks are given each Saturday at 8:30am.

Fishing

New Mexico's most outstanding fishing holes are better accessed from Taos and the Enchanted Circle, but there are plenty of opportunities out of Santa Fe, including Abiquiú and Nambé Lakes and the Rio Chama. You'll need a license (one-day/five-day $12/24). For gear, fly-fishing lessons and guided trips around northern NM, look no further than **High Desert Angler** (Map p258 ☎505-988-7688; www.highdesertangler.com; 460 Cerrillos Rd; ☺8am-6pm Mon-Sat, 11am-4pm Sun mid-May–mid-Sep, 10am-6pm Mon-Sat, 11am-4pm Sun mid-Sep–mid-May)

Courses

Santa Fe School of Cooking   COOKING (Map p258; ☎505-983-4511; www.santafeschoolofcooking.com; Plaza Mercado) If you develop a love for New Mexican cuisine, try cooking lessons at this cooking school which specializes in Southwestern cuisine. Classes are three hours long and cost between $60 and $80, including the meal.

Santa Fe Workshops
PHOTOGRAPHY

(Map p262; 505-983-1400; www.santafe workshops.com; Mt Carmel Rd; courses $1075-1700) Develop your inner Ansel Adams awareness at these legendary weeklong traditional photography and digital imagery workshops. Course fees do not include meals and lodging.

Santa Fe Clay
CERAMICS

(Map p258; 505-984-1122; www.santafeclay .com; 545 Camino de la Familia) During summer, this premier ceramics gallery offers an array of four-day clay workshops ($525), taught by master potters. In winter and spring, weekend workshops are occasionally held. Though courses go way beyond throwing pots, most are open to aspiring ceramic artists of all levels.

Wise Fool
CIRCUS

(off Map p262; 505-992-2588; www.wisefool newmexico.org; 2778-D Agua Fria St) Ever want to learn the arts of trapeze, juggling, or just plain clowning around? Wise Fool has drop-in classes ($20) and multiday intensives for adults ($175), plus weeklong summer camps for kids ($100).

☞ Tours

Several companies offer walking and bus tours of Santa Fe and northern New Mexico Others organize guided trips to the pueblos, as well as air tours and biking, hiking, rafting and horseback-riding trips.

Santa Fe Southern Railway
SCENIC

(Map p258; 505-989-8600; www.sfsr.com; 410 S Guadalupe St) Offers several scenic rides using the old spur line. The most popular run, a four-hour day trip (adult $32 to $45, child $18 to $32) on Friday (11am) or Saturday (noon), takes you past the Galisteo Basin and to the fairly ghostly town of Lamy. Several other themed trips are offered on other days. Note that the old downtown depot will no longer be home to the railway, but trains will still leave from behind it and tickets will be sold on the platform.

A Well-Born Guide/Have PhD, Will Travel
WALKING

(505-988-8022; www.swguides.com; tours from $22) If the name doesn't lure you in, then the tours will. Run by Stefanie Beninato, an informative local historian who has a knack for good storytelling, these lively trips receive excellent feedback from past participants. Stefanie offers a variety of themed hikes and walks around Santa Fe that focus on everything from bars and former brothels to ghosts, architecture and, of course, art. Multiday trips around New Mexico are also offered.

Seven Directions
GENERAL

(877-992-6128; www.sevendirections.com) Specializes in French-, Italian- and Spanish-language tours of the city and the state.

NEW MEXICO SANTA FE

LOCAL MAGIC: CHRISTMAS EVE ON CANYON RD

On the night before Christmas, Santa Fe is an ethereal site. The city's thousands of adobe buildings glow a warm yellow from the lights of thousands of *farolitos* – real candles nestled in greased brown paper bags – lining streets, entranceways and even the roofs of the adobe homes and shops.

Walking down Santa Fe's most famous gallery avenue, Canyon Rd, on Christmas Eve is a uniquely Santa Fe experience, and in our book a magical must. There's something overwhelmingly graceful and elegant about the taste of the frosty air, the look of miles of glowing pathways of tiny candles and comradely quiet, the way the night sky meets softly lit gallery windows filled with fine art.

The magic comes partly from the intoxicating sights and scents of small piñon and cedarwood bonfires that line the road, offering guiding light and unforgettable memories. Partly it's a few equestrians prancing on horseback, jingle bells jingling, clackity-clacking along the narrow street, evoking memories of early Santa Feans who led their burros up the 'Road of the Canyon' to gather firewood in mountain forests. Partly it's the silhouettes of 250-year-old adobes softly lit by rows of twinkling *farolitos*.

Dress warmly and arrive early – say, by 6pm – if you want to beat the crowds. As night falls, the streets fill with human revelers and their canine friends, all giddy with the Christmas spirit. Small groups of carolers sing remarkably in tune. Join them, then pop into a gallery for a cup of spiced cider and a quick perusal of post-communist Russian art to warm up.

Pink Lady Tours   WALKING
([telephone]505-699-4147; www.wildwackytours.com) Walking tours of Santa Fe, with the guide who strives for the most laughs per minute.

Loretto Line   HISTORICAL
([telephone]505-983-3701; www.toursofsantafe.com) Cruise around in an open-air tram and learn about the history and culture of Santa Fe from experienced guides.

✦♣ Festivals & Events

The **Santa Fe Visitors Bureau** (www.santafe.org) provides an excellent list of events, musical and theatrical productions and museum shows. Some of the biggies:

ARTfeast   ART
(www.artfeast.com) Eat your way around Santa Fe's galleries during this weekend-long festival in late February that incorporates art, food, wine and fashion and benefits art programs for Santa Fe children.

Pride on the Plaza   GAY PRIDE
(www.santafehra.org) Drag queens, parades, floats, a film festival, music, comedy and more; area bars and restaurants throw special bashes for a full week in mid-June, here in the city ranked 'second gayest in America' by the *Advocate* magazine.

Rodeo de Santa Fe   CULTURAL
(www.rodeodesantafe.org; adult/child from $17/10) For more than half a century, wranglers, ranchers and cowpokes, along with plenty of rhinestone cowpersons, have been gathering to watch those bucking broncos, clowns in barrels, lasso tricks and fancy shooting. A pre-rodeo parade takes it all downtown. Held in late June.

[TOP CHOICE] International Folk Art Market   CULTURAL
(www.folkartmarket.org) The largest folk art market in the world brings over 130 artists from 50 countries around the world to the Folk Art Museum for a festive weekend of craft shopping and cultural events in early July. Things get off to a fun start with a free World Music concert at the Railyard.

[TOP CHOICE] Spanish Market   CULTURAL
(www.spanishcolonial.org) Traditional Spanish Colonial arts, from *retablos* and *bultos* to handcrafted furniture and metalwork, make this juried show in late July an artistic extravaganza, second only to the Indian Market. Another Spanish Market is held in early December at the Sweeny Convention Center.

SANTA FE FOR CHILDREN

Check 'Pasatiempo,' the Friday arts and entertainment section of the *Santa Fe New Mexican*, for its 'Bring the Kids' column, which has a rundown on area events for children. Also look for the free local newspaper, *New Mexico Kids*, published six times a year, for great day-by-day event calendars.

The **Santa Fe Children's Museum** (Map p262; www.santafechildrensmuseum.org; 1050 Old Pecos Trail; admission $9, $5 on Sun; ⊙10am-6pm Tue-Sat, noon-5pm Sun; [icon]) features hands-on exhibits on science and art for young children, but adults will enjoy it as well. The museum runs daily two-hour programs, led by local scientists, artists and teachers, that tackle subjects like solar energy and printmaking.

The amazing **Museum of International Folk Art** (p257) has a fantastic big indoor play area with books, Lego and other toys. It is perfect rainy-day entertainment for your little one.

If you're traveling with a budding thespian, check out the backstage tours of the **Santa Fe Opera** (p277) during opera season. They're interesting, and free for folks under 17.

Most restaurants, except those that are seriously upscale, are happy to host your kids, and most have special menus – but only the **Cowgirl Hall of Fame** (p275) has a playground *and* a full bar. One of Santa Fe's top breakfast spots, **Cafe Pasqual's** (p273), is also very child-friendly.

If you want to get out on your own, **Magical Happenings Babysitting** ([telephone]505-982-9327) can have sitters stay with your kids in your hotel room; it's $18 an hour for one child or $20 an hour for two, with a four-hour minimum, and reservations should be made in advance, particularly during the high season.

TOP CHOICE Santa Fe Indian Market   CULTURAL
(www.swaia.org) Only the best get approved to show their work at this world-famous juried show (held the weekend after the third Thursday in August), where more than 1000 artists from 100 tribes and Pueblos exhibit. As if that's not enough, 100,000 visitors converge on the Plaza, at open studios, gallery shows and the Native Cinema Showcase. Get there Friday or Saturday to see pieces competing for the prestigious top prizes (they get snapped up by collectors), but wait until Sunday if you want to try bargaining.

TOP CHOICE Santa Fe Fiesta   CULTURAL
(www.santafefiesta.org) Two weeks of events in early September celebrate the September 4, 1692, resettlement of Santa Fe, including concerts, a carnival, a candlelight procession and the kids' favorite – the Pet Parade. Everything kicks off with the bizarrely pagan and slightly terrifying torching of Zozobra – a 50-foot-tall effigy of Old Man Gloom – as the mob gathered in Fort Marcy Park shouts 'Burn him!'

Wine & Chile Fiesta   FOOD
(www.santafewineandchile.org) It's a gourmet's fantasy fiesta, with wine tastings and fine cuisine; dinner events sell out early. Late September.

🛏 Sleeping

Rates vary from week to week and day to day. Generally, January and February offer the lowest rates – cut by as much as 50% from what's listed here. September, October, March and April generally have midrange rates. In December and during the summer (particularly during Indian Market in August and on opera nights), expect to pay premium prices. Make reservations well in advance. Remember: prices do not include taxes and other add-ons of 11% to 15%.

Many agencies can help with reservations, including **Santa Fe Stay** (📞800-995-2272; www.santafestay.com), specializing in home stays, ranch resorts and casitas.

Most of the low-budget and national chain options line Cerrillos Rd between I-25 and downtown.

When it comes to luxury accommodations, Santa Fe has more than its share of intimate hotels and posh B&Bs ready to cater to your every whim. Book through an internet consolidator for the best rates.

Santa Fe National Forest and Hyde State Park are the best places around for car camping. Stop by the Public Lands Information Center for maps and detailed information.

DOWNTOWN SANTA FE

TOP CHOICE La Fonda   HISTORIC HOTEL $$$
(Map p258; 📞800-523-5002; www.lafondasantafe.com; 100 E San Francisco St; r/ste from $140/260; P🐾@🛜🏊) Staff artist Ernest Martinez has been painting thousands of windows and other fixtures since 1954, giving La Fonda its unique folk-art character. Claiming to be the original 'Inn at the end of the Santa Fe Trail,' here since 1610, the hotel also features Southwest murals and paintings commissioned in the 1920s and '30s. The top-floor luxury suites in the Terrace are lovely, and sunset views from the rooftop Bell Tower Bar are the best in town.

TOP CHOICE El Paradero   B&B $$
(Map p258; 📞505-988-1177; www.elparadero.com; 220 W Manhattan Ave; r $125-200; P🐾@🛜) Just a few blocks from the Plaza, this 200-year-old adobe B&B is one of Santa Fe's oldest inns. Each room is unique and loaded with character; our favorite is No 6. The full breakfasts satisfy. The owners also offer an off-site casita ($350) that sleeps six, with a gorgeous Southwestern-style kitchen and peaceful garden.

TOP CHOICE Inn of the Five Graces   BOUTIQUE HOTEL $$$
(Map p258; 📞505-992-0957; www.fivegraces.com; 150 E DeVargas St; ste $340-900; P🐾🛜) Much more than an ordinary luxury getaway, this one-of-a-kind exquisite, exclusive gem offers an upscale gypsy-style escape. Sumptuous suites are decorated in a lavish Persian/Indian/Asian fusion theme, complete with fireplaces, beautifully tiled kitchenettes and a courtyard behind river-rock walls. They also rent the Luminaria House (per night $2500), with two master bedrooms, five fireplaces and all the luxury you'd expect for the price.

Inn on the Alameda   HOTEL $$
(Map p258; 📞888-984-2121; www.innonthealameda.com; 303 E Alameda St; r $125-245; P🐾@🛜🏊) Handmade furniture, kiva fireplaces, luxe linens, elegant breakfasts and afternoon wine-and-cheese receptions bring B&B-style elegance to a pleasantly efficient hotel. The staff can also arrange

cooking classes, fly-fishing, outdoor adventures and more, all with local experts. The inn is perfectly positioned between Canyon Rd and the Plaza. Small dogs are welcome for an extra $30 per night.

La Posada de Santa Fe LUXURY HOTEL $$$
(Map p258; ☎505-986-0000; www.laposada.rock resorts.com; 330 E Palace Ave; r from $200; P☀@☂☀) Your every need is catered to on this beautiful, shady, 6-acre property a few blocks from the Plaza. Elegantly furnished adobe casitas are outfitted with gas fireplaces. More historical (and smaller) rooms, some with views, are located in the Staab House. On-site Avanyu Spa (see p263) is deservedly fabulous, while the cigar-friendly Staab House Lounge (open 11:30am to 11pm) is a local favorite for its leather-chaired ambience and single-malt scotch.

Inn of the Anasazi LUXURY HOTEL $$$
(Map p258; ☎800-688-8100; www.innofthe anasazi.com; 113 Washington Ave; r $200-525; P☀@☂) Ancient blends seamlessly with ultramodern in this elegant, Navajo-themed property half a block off the Plaza. Details are meticulously attended to. The interior waterfall has been named one of the 'thousand things to see before you die' – though we're not sure why – on one of those lists that declare those kinds of things.

Inn & Spa at Loretto LUXURY HOTEL $$$
(Map p258; ☎505-988-5531; www.hotelloretto .com; 211 Old Santa Fe Trail; r from $180; ☀@☂☀) Modeled after the Taos Pueblo, this gorgeous old hotel has large, luxurious rooms with a Native American theme that includes local art hanging on dark-red walls. Modern amenities include iPod docking stations and huge flat-screen TVs. In-room minibars feature small oxygen tanks, in case you need a quick boost. Have a drink in the lobby bar and look up at the ceiling – each panel is hand-painted.

Hotel St Francis HISTORIC HOTEL $$
(Map p258; ☎505-983-5700; www.hotelstfrancis .com; 210 Don Gaspar Ave; r $120-300; P☀@☂☀) Recently renovated, the St. Francis has traded some of its faded charm for modern upgrades. All in all, it's retained its historic ambience, blending luxurious touches with a nicely underplayed Spanish missionary theme.

Inn of the Governors HOTEL $$
(Map p258; ☎505-982-4333; www.innofthe governors.com; 101 W Alameda St; r from $130;

P☀@☂☀) You can't beat the location, just blocks from the Plaza. Rooms are elegantly decorated with kiva fireplaces, warm-hued bedspreads and Southwestern-style doors and windows. It's an intimate place to slumber. Don't miss the adjoining Del Charro Saloon, with some of the cheapest eats downtown.

Garrett's Desert Inn HOTEL $$
(Map p258; ☎505-982-1851; www.garrettsdesert inn.com; 311 Old Santa Fe Trail; r $80-170; P☀ ☂☀☀) An old motor court–style place, Garrett's has been popular with travelers for half a century now. Rooms are in good shape, and the location is great. The heated pool is a plus. Families can book into one of the large suites and pets stay free.

CERRILLOS RD & METRO SANTA FE

⬛TOP CHOICE Ten Thousand Waves
Japanese Resort & Spa RESORT $$$
(off Map p255; ☎505-982-9304; www.tenthousand waves.com; 3451 Hyde Park Rd; r $200-270; P☀☂☀) This Japanese spa 4 miles from the Plaza features 13 gorgeous, Zen-inspired freestanding guest houses. Most come with fireplaces and either a deck or courtyard, and all are within walking distance of the mountainside hot tubs and massage cabins. Make reservations two months in advance. Pets are welcomed with custom-size beds, bones and treats!

Bishop's Lodge Resort & Spa RESORT $$$
(Map p266; ☎800-419-0492; www.bishopslodge .com; 1297 Bishops Lodge Rd; r from $160; P☀@☂☀☀) Come play (upscale) cowgirl on 450 acres of almost untouched piñon wilderness just 3 miles from the Plaza. This family-friendly destination resort has huge, luxurious rooms and casitas, many with patios, kitchenettes, fireplaces and more. From yoga classes at its spa to a magnificent outdoor pool overlooking the mountains to horseback riding through the mountains, there truly is something for everyone. The on-site restaurant, Las Fuentes, has a lavish Sunday brunch that has been voted best in Santa Fe. Free shuttles take you downtown.

Inn of the Turquoise Bear B&B $$
(Map p262; ☎800-396-4104; www.turquoisebear .com; 342 E Buena Vista St; r $110-245; P☀☂☀) Visitors enjoy the quiet now, but this expansive adobe palace, built by local legend Witter Bynner and partner Robert Hunt, was once home to legendary parties hosting

Thornton Wilder, Robert Oppenheimer, Edna St Vincent Millay, Robert Frost and many, many others. It's now a B&B surrounded by an acre of sculpted gardens, combining authentic ambience and modern amenities.

Sage Inn
HOTEL $$
(Map p258; ☎505-982-5952; www.santafesageinn .com; 725 Cerrillos Rd; r $78-125; P ❄ @ 🛜 🏊 👭 🐾) With more appeal than a chain hotel but not as much as boutique accommodations, the Sage Inn is a nice compromise in terms of quality, service and location. It's modern and clean and a good place for budget-minded families. There's a guest laundromat, pets are OK ($25), and it's right next to Whole Foods.

Silver Saddle Motel
MOTEL $
(Map p262; ☎505-471-7663; www.silversaddle motelllc.com; 2810 Cerrillos Rd; r from $45; P ❄ @ 🛜) Some rooms here have attractively tiled kitchenettes, and all have shady wooden arcades outside and comfortable cowboy inspired decor inside. For a bit of kitsch, request the Kenny Rogers or Wyatt Earp rooms. This is the best budget value in town; rates include continental breakfast.

Santa Fe International Hostel
HOSTEL $
(Map p262; ☎505-988-1153; www.hostelsantafe .com; 1412 Cerrillos Rd; dm $18, r $25-35; P @ 🛜) If you're looking for a true-blue old hippie hostel, you can't beat this experience in communal living – including the refrigerator full of free, donated food. It's not the cleanest place in Santa Fe, but it's definitely the cheapest, and there's usually an interesting array of other travelers to meet. Rooms are simple but big, with metal beds with tired mattresses and fading but freshly washed linens. Rooms facing the main road are a bit noisy. They take cash only, and short daily chores are required.

Rancheros de Santa Fe Campground
CAMPGROUND $
(Map p266; ☎505-466-3482; www.rancheros.com; 736 Old Las Vegas Hwy; tent/RV sites $23/39; 🕐Mar-Oct; 🛜 🏊 👭) Eight miles southeast of the Plaza, off exit 290 from I-25 North, Rancheros has nice views, a convenience store and free wireless internet. Plus, its sites are shady and big. Enjoy hot showers, cheap morning coffee and evening movies.

✗ Eating

Food is another art form in Santa Fe, and some restaurants are as world-class as the galleries. From spicy, traditional Southwest favorites to cutting-edge cuisine, it's all here. Reservations are always recommended for the more expensive venues, especially during summer and ski season. All Santa Fe restaurants and bars are nonsmoking.

Check for current reviews in the *Santa Fe Reporter,* which often has coupons for area eateries, or the free monthly *Local Flavor,* with reviews and news about area restaurants.

THE PLAZA & CANYON RD
If you're on a budget downtown, one of the cheapest and tastiest places to eat lunch or an early dinner is at the takeaway, city-licensed stalls on the Plaza lawn. The beef fajitas with fresh guacamole is our favorite. Tacos and burritos are also offered.

TOP CHOICE Coyote Café
MODERN SOUTHWESTERN $$$
(Map p258; ☎505-983-1615; www.coyotecafe.com; 132 Water St; mains $28-56; 🕐5:30-9pm) Serious foodies return year after year for stellar interpretations of New Mexico cuisine. Now in the capable hands of chef Eric DiStefano, the menu at Santa Fe's most celebrated restaurant changes frequently, featuring creative interpretations of wild game, seafood and steaks. Delish margaritas come in a rainbow of flavors. For more affordable and casual options from the same kitchen, eat upstairs on the roof at the **Coyote Cantina** (mains $7-18; 🕐11:30am-9pm Apr Oct; 🖉), which also serves lunch.

TOP CHOICE El Farol
TAPAS, SPANISH $$$
(Map p262; ☎505-983-9912; www.elfarolsf.com; 808 Canyon Rd; lunch mains $8-18, dinner mains $25 50; 🕐11:30am-late; 🖉👭) This popular restaurant and bar, set in a rustically authentic adobe, has live music nightly. Although El Farol does excellent steaks, most people come to sample the extensive list of tapas ($8). The flamenco dinner show (most nights 6:30pm, $25) is lively and perfect for birthdays or special occasions. Kids will also dig it.

TOP CHOICE Cafe Pasqual's
INTERNATIONAL $$$
(Map p258; ☎505-983-9340; www.pasquals.com; 121 Don Gaspar Ave; breakfast & lunch mains $8-15, dinner mains $20-40; 🕐7am-3pm & 5:30-9pm; 🖉👭) Make reservations for dinner if you'd like, but definitely wait in line to enjoy the famous breakfasts. We highly recommend *huevos motuleños,* made with eggs and black beans, sautéed bananas, feta cheese

and more; *tamale dulce*, a sweet corn tamale with fruit, beans and Mexican chocolate; or the enormous Durango ham-and-cheese omelet. They're all served up in a festive, if crowded, interior. Grab a seat faster by sitting at the community table, where tourists and locals mix it up daily.

Guadalupe Cafe
NEW MEXICAN $$

(Map p258; 442 Old Santa Fe Trail; mains $8-15; ⊘7am-2pm & 5-9pm Tue-Fri, 8am-2pm & 5-9pm Sat; 8am-2pm Sun) With a few dining rooms spread around a cozy old house, and an inviting outdoor patio, this reliable restaurant goes beyond the usual list of New Mexican specialties (try the chicken breast *rellenos*). Breakfasts are hearty and the salads are immense.

Tia Sophia's
NEW MEXICAN $

(Map p258; 210 W San Francisco St; mains $7-10; ⊘7am-2pm Mon-Sat; 🖋🕯) Local artists and visiting celebrities outnumber tourists at this longstanding Santa Fe favorite that's always packed. Breakfast is the meal of choice, with fantastic burritos and other Southwestern dishes. Lunch is pretty damn tasty too; try the perfectly prepared *chile rellenos*. The shelf of kids' books helps little ones pass the time.

Geronimo
MODERN AMERICAN $$$

(Map p262; ✆505-982-1500; 724 Canyon Rd; mains $28-44; ⊘5:45-10pm Mon-Thu, to 11pm Fri & Sat) Housed in a 1756 adobe, Geronimo is among the finest and most romantic restaurants in town. The short but diverse menu currently includes honey-grilled prawns with fiery sweet chile and peppery elk tenderloin with applewood-smoked bacon.

SantaCafé
MODERN SOUTHWESTERN $$$

(Map p258; ✆505-984-1788; www.santacafe.com; 231 Washington Ave; lunch mains $11-15, dinner mains $19-33; ⊘11:30am-2pm Mon-Sat, 5:30-9pm daily; 🖋) Chef David Sellars is practically an international celebrity because of dishes like roasted poblano *chile rellenos* with three-mushroom quinoa and chipotle cream ($19). Housed in an 1850s adobe built by the infamous Padre Gallegos, Santacafé also has the best courtyard in town for summertime dining. Lunch is a deal, the wine list flawless and the dining room historical. In short, perfection.

Compound
MODERN AMERICAN $$$

(Map p262; ✆505-982-4353; www.compound restaurant.com; 635 Canyon Rd; lunch mains $12-20, dinner mains $28-34; ⊘noon-2pm Mon-Sat,

6-9pm daily) A longtime local foodie favorite, the Compound features the contemporary American creations of Mark Kiffin, recognized by the James Beard Foundation as the Best Chef of the Southwest in 2005. The acclaimed seasonal menu draws on the elegant flavors of Southwestern and Mediterranean cooking. Ingredients are always fresh, and the presentation perfect. Come when there's reason to celebrate: the wine list includes several top-notch champagnes.

Del Charro Saloon
PUB $

(Map p258; Inn of the Governors, 101 W Alameda St; mains under $6; ⊘11:30am-midnight) Attached to Inn of the Governors, this popular pub is an atmospheric place with copper-topped tables, lots of vegetation and a blazing fire in the winter. In summer the patio opens up and tables spill onto the sidewalk. It serves giant, inexpensive margaritas and delicious pub grub well into the night.

French Pastry Shop
CREPERIE $

(Map p258; La Fonda Hotel, 100 E San Francisco St; mains $6-9; ⊘6:30am-5pm) Serving delicious French bistro food inside La Fonda hotel, including crepes – filled with everything from ham and cheese to strawberries and cream – along with a host of quiches, sandwiches, cappuccinos and, of course, pastries.

Il Vicino
ITALIAN $

(Map p258; www.ilvicino.com/santafe; 321 W San Francisco St; mains $6-9; ⊘11am-10pm Sun-Thu, until 11pm Fri & Sat; 🕯) For a break from chile, come to Il Vicino, where you'll find brick-oven pizzas, pastas and salads a quick walk from the Plaza.

Shed
NEW MEXICAN $$

(Map p258; www.sfshed.com; 113½ E Palace Ave; lunch mains $8-11, dinner mains $11-17; ⊘11am-2:30pm & 5:30-9pm Mon-Sat; 🕯) Superconvenient to the Plaza and with a fun ambience. The food, however, is seriously overrated, aiming straight for the perceived middle-of-the-road tourist palate. There's a nice patio.

GUADALUPE ST AREA

Off the Plaza but easily walkable from there, this funky little neighborhood is home to some quirky dining and drinking options frequented by Santa Fe's young and hip crowd.

TOP CHOICE Santa Fe Farmers Market
MARKET $

(Map p258; ✆505-983-4098; Paseo de Peralta, 55yd west of Guadalupe St; ⊘7am-noon Sat &

Tue Apr-Nov; 🛒👪) Local produce, much of it heirloom and organic, is on sale at these spacious digs, alongside homemade goodies, inexpensive food, natural body products and arts and crafts.

Ristra
MODERN AMERICAN $$$
(Map p258; 🖉505-982-8608; www.ristrarestaurant.com; 548 Agua Fria St; mains $20-40; ⊗11:30am-2:30pm & 5:30-9:30pm Tue-Sat) Ristra attracts a regular clientele who come for its casual intimacy and excellent food. The contemporary-American menu is influenced by the flavors of France and the Southwest, and changes seasonally. The steaks here are always fantastic, the wine list is lengthy and there are plenty of bottles of bubbly to toast those special occasions.

Cowgirl Hall of Fame
BARBECUE $$
(Map p258; www.cowgirlsantafe.com; 319 S Guadalupe St; mains $8-18; ⊗11am-midnight Mon-Fri, 10am midnight Sat, 10am 11pm Sun; 👪) A fun place for all ages, thanks to the great playground in the back, wacky Western-style feminist flair, outside patio and live music, this restaurant has fabulous food and awesome margaritas. Everything is tasty, but the Cowgirl is known for its barbecue brisket – order it in a quesadilla with green chile. After dark, order smoky mescal margaritas and play a game of pool in the new billiard room.

Zia Diner
AMERICAN $
(Map p258; 366 S Guadalupe St; mains $6-12; ⊗11am 10pm; 👪) Voted Best Comfort Food by locals, this cozy diner is known for its meatloaf, buffalo burgers and yummy homemade pies. Have a beer and watch pink-haired hipsters and graying progressives coo over their blue-plate specials (served weekdays only). It's one of the few places open late on Sundays.

Tomasita's
NEW MEXICAN $$
(Map p258; 🖉505-983-5721; 500 S Guadalupe St; mains $7-15; ⊗11am-10pm Mon-Sat; 👪) Sure it's touristy, but it's good! The menu sticks to traditional New Mexican fare like burritos and enchiladas, and there are huge blue-plate specials. It's a raucous place, good for families hauling exuberant kids. Prepare to wait; the restaurant is always packed.

Cleopatra Cafe
MIDDLE EASTERN $
(Map p258; Design Center, 418 Cerrillos Rd; mains $5-12; ⊗6am-8pm Mon-Sat, to 6pm Sun; 🛜) Makes up for lack of ambience with taste and value: big platters of delicious kebabs, hummus, falafel and other Middle Eastern favorites.

Raaga
INDIAN $$
(Map p258; www.raagacuisine.com; 544 Agua Fria St; mains $13-18; ⊗11:30am-2pm & 5-9:30pm, to 10pm Fri & Sat; 🖉) An awesome new Indian restaurant with delicious curries, biryanis and tandoori specialties. Only one flaw: the chai is lame.

Flying Star Café
AMERICAN $
(Map p258; www.flyingstarcafe.com; 500 Market St; mains $7-13; ⊗7am-9pm Sun-Thu, to 10pm Fri & Sat; 🛜👪) The Santa Fe branch of this casual, Albuquerque-based diner chain, located at the Railyard, has quickly become a local favorite, especially for families with kids.

METRO SANTA FE
Some of the best places to eat aren't right in the center of town. These are worth traveling for.

TOP CHOICE San Marcos Café
NEW MEXICAN $
(Map p266; 🖉505-471-9298; www.sanmarcosfeed.com; 3877 Hwy 14; mains $7-10; ⊗8am-2pm; 👪) About 10 minutes' drive south on Hwy 14, this country-style cafe is well worth the trip. Aside from the down-home feeling and the best red chile you'll ever taste, turkeys and peacocks strut and squabble outside and the whole place is connected to a feed store, giving it some genuine Western soul. The pastries and desserts – especially the bourbon apple pie – sate any sweet tooth. Make reservations on weekends.

Tune-Up Café
INTERNATIONAL $$
(Map p262; www.tuneupcafe.com; 1115 Hickox St; mains $7-14; ⊗7am-10pm Mon-Fri, from 8am Sat & Sun; 👪) Santa Fe's newest favorite restaurant is casual, busy and does food right. The chef, from El Salvador, adds a few twists to classic New Mexican and American dishes while also serving fantastic Salvadoran *pupusas* (stuffed corn tortillas), huevos and other specialties. The molé colorado enchiladas and the fish tacos are exceptional.

Horseman's Haven
NEW MEXICAN $
(off Map p255; 4354 Cerrillos Rd; mains $6-12; ⊗8am-8pm Mon-Sat, 8:30am-2pm Sun; 👪) Hands down, the hottest green chile in town! (The timid should order it on the side). Service is friendly and fast, and their enormous 3D burrito might be the only thing you need to eat all day.

RAILYARD RENAISSANCE

After years of municipal wrangling over how to develop the dormant **Railyard District** (www.railyardsantafe.com), its grand opening was held in 2008. It's already come into its own as a lively multi-use area that merges with the Guadalupe St District. Aside from the welcoming drinking joints & restaurants here, such as **Second Street Brewery** and **Flying Star Café**, it's also home to the **Santa Fe Farmers Market**. One end is devoted to a park with gardens, a few things to climb and play on and an outdoor performance space; it's no Tuileries, but if it's good enough for pot-smoking high school kids, it's good enough for us.

The Railyard is also making a real play at being the epicenter of Santa Fe's contemporary art scene, with 10 galleries and SITE Santa Fe. A few you won't want to miss:

Santa Fe Clay (Map p258; www.santafeclay.com; 545 Camino de la Familia) Fine art ceramics that range from innovative functionality to cutting-edge sculpture.

Tai Gallery (Map p258; www.taigallery.com; 1601B Paseo de Peralta) Featuring fine bamboo crafts by Japanese masters, along with work by Japanese photographers and textile arts from around the world.

LewAllen Galleries (Map p258; www.lewallengalleries.com; 1613 Paseo de Peralta) Probably the most prominent modern contemporary art gallery in town, LewAllen also shows Modernist masters.

Harry's Roadhouse AMERICAN, NEW MEXICAN $ (Map p266; ☎505-989-4629; www.harrysroadhousesantafe.com; 96 Old Las Vegas Hwy; mains breakfast $5-8, lunch $7-11, dinner $9-16; ⊗7am-10pm; ⊛) This longtime favorite on the southern edge of town feels like a rambling cottage. And, seriously, *everything* is good here. Especially the desserts! The mood is casual, it's family-friendly and has a full bar. If you're with six or more, call for reservations.

Santa Fe Baking Company AMERICAN $ (Map p262; www.santafebakingcompanycafe.com; 504 W Cordova Rd; mains $5-11; ⊗6am-8pm Mon-Sat, to 7pm Sun; ⊛⊿⊛) A bustling cafe serving burgers, sandwiches and big breakfast platters all day. There's also a full-on smoothie bar. This is a great spot to get a glimpse of the human melting pot that is Santa Fe. Need proof? The local radio station, KSFR, broadcasts a talk show from here each weekday morning.

Bobcat Bite BURGERS $ (Map p266; www.bobcatbite.com; 420 Old Las Vegas Hwy; mains $6-23; ⊗11am-7:50pm Wed-Sat, 11am-5pm Sun) Often voted as serving the Best Burger in Santa Fe by locals, this relaxed roadhouse beneath the neon really does an outstanding green chile cheeseburger ($7). The steaks are pretty darn good too.

Tesuque Village Market CAFE $$ (www.tesuquevillagemarket.com; 138 Tesuque Village Rd, Tesuque; mains $8-20; ⊗7am-9pm) Once hole-in-the-wall, now country-hip, this is a hot spot on weekend mornings for folks heading to or from the Tesuque Flea Market. If you're hungry and in a hurry, grab a hand-held burrito and take it with you – the breakfast burritos will start your day right, and the *carne adovada* is some of the best anywhere. Take Bishops Lodge Rd or Hwy 285 north to Exit 168.

 Drinking

Bars

Talk to 10 residents and you'll get 10 different opinions about where to find the best margarita. You'll just have to sample the lot to decide for yourself.

Evangelo's
BAR
(Map p258; 200 W San Francisco St) Everyone is welcome in this casual, rowdy joint owned by the Klonis family since 1971 (ask owner/bartender Nick about his father's unusual fame). Drop in, put on some Patsy Cline and grab a draft beer – it's the perfect escape from Plaza culture.

Second Street Brewery
BREWERY
(www.secondstreetbrewery.com) Railyard (Map p258; Railyard); 2nd Street (Map p262; 1814 2nd St) Santa Fe's favorite brewery is the perfect spot to stop for a pint after a long hike. It serves handcrafted English-style beers – brewed on the premises – and also offers a hearty selection of better-than-average pub

grub. Sit outside on the big patio or inside the brewery. There's live music nightly. We like the newer Railyard location better than the original.

Bell Tower Bar
BAR

(Map p258; 100 E San Francisco St; ☺5pm-sunset Mon-Thu, from 2pm Fri-Sun May-Oct) In summer this bar atop La Fonda hotel is the premier spot to catch one of those patented New Mexican sunsets while sipping a killer margarita. After dark, retire to the hotel's lobby Fiesta Bar for live country and folk music.

Dragon Room Bar
BAR

(Map p258; 406 Old Santa Fe Trail) This 300-year-old adobe is a consistent top fave for locals and Hollywood-famous visitors alike. Drop by for a signature Black Dragon margarita. Visit after 9pm on Tuesday, Thursday or Saturday if you want it served with live music (flamenco guitar, Latin jazz and the like).

Ore House
BAR

(Map p258; 50 Lincoln Ave) We think this place makes the best fresh lime (no sweet and sour) margarita in town, and with more than 40 different types to choose from, there's bound to be a margarita for everyone. Choose from the seats on the heated balcony overlooking the Plaza or a table inside. The steaks here make it worth staying for dinner.

Marble Brewery Tap Room
PUB

(Map p258; 60 E San Francisco St) With microbrews on tap and an espresso bar, this upstairs place covers both ends of the legal substance spectrum. An outdoor patio overlooks the Plaza, a leather couched lounge has big flat-screens to watch whatever game is on, and they serve pizza.

Cafes

Aztec Cafe
CAFE

(Map p258; www.azteccafe.com; 317 Aztec St; ☺7am-7pm Mon-Sat, from 8am Sun, closes daily at 6pm in winter; 🛜) Our pick for best local coffeehouse, the Aztec welcomes all kinds to its low-key indoor art space and outdoor patio.

Tea House
CAFE

(Map p262; www.teahousesantafe.com; 821 Canyon Rd; ☺8am-7pm; 🛜) If you're feeling ambivalent, prepare for a dilemma when confronted with the list of 150 types of tea. They have coffee, too, and breakfast and lunch. A perfect stop when you're done with the galleries on Canyon Rd.

☆ Entertainment

Performing Arts

Patrons from the world's most glittering cities are drawn to Santa Fe in July and August because of opera, chamber music, performance and visual arts, an area in which Santa Fe holds its own against anywhere on the globe. The opera may be the belle of the ball – clad in sparkling denim – but there are lots of other highbrow and lowbrow happenings every week. Let the searchable, exhaustive online **Events Calendar** (www.santafe.com/calendar) become your new best friend. Plan ahead to score coveted seats, lodging and gourmet meals.

⌜TOP⌝ Santa Fe Opera
⌞CHOICE⌟
OPERA

(Map p266; ☏505-986-5900; www.santafeopera .org; Hwy 84/285, Tesuqu; ☺late Jun–late Aug) Many come to Santa Fe for this and this alone: the theater is an architectural marvel, with nearly 360-degree views of wind-carved sandstone wilderness crowned with sunsets and moonrises, and at center stage the world's finest talent performs Western civilization's masterworks. It's still the Wild West, though; you can even wear jeans – just try *that* in New York City.

Gala festivities begin two hours before the curtain rises, when the ritual tailgate party is rendered glamorous in true Santa Fe style right in the parking lot. Bring your own caviar and brie, make reservations for the buffet dinner and lecture or a picnic dinner, or have your own private caterer – several customize the menu to the opera's theme – pour the champagne. **Prelude Talks**, free to all ticket holders, are offered in Stieren Orchestra Hall one hour and two hours before curtain to accommodate various dining schedules. Shuttles run to and from the event from Santa Fe and Albuquerque; reserve through the opera box office.

Youth Night at the Opera offers families a chance to watch dress rehearsals a few nights each summer, for bargain rates; one precedes the run of each of the season's operas – with brief talks aimed at audience members ages 6 to 22. **Backstage tours** (adult/child $5/free; ☺9am Mon-Fri Jun-Aug) offer opportunities to poke around the sets, costume and storage areas.

Lensic Performing Arts Theater
PERFORMING ARTS

(Map p258; ☏505-984-1370; www.lensic.com; 211 W San Francisco St) A beautifully renovated

NEW MEXICO SANTA FE

1930 movie house, the theater hosts a weekly classic film series and eight different performance groups, including the Santa Fe Symphony Orchestra & Chorus.

Santa Fe Playhouse
THEATER

(Map p258; ☎505-988-4262; www.santafeplayhouse.org; 142 E De Vargas St; ⊙8pm Thu-Sat, 2pm Sun) The state's oldest theater company performs avant-garde and traditional theater and musical comedy. On Sunday, admission is as much as you can afford.

Santa Fe Chamber Music Festival
CLASSICAL MUSIC

(☎505-982-1890; www.sfcmf.org; ⊙Jul & Aug) This is the other big cultural event, known for filling elegant venues like the Lensic with Brahms, Mozart and other classical masters. It's not just world-class acts like violinist Pinchas Zukerman and pianist Yuja Wang defining the season; top-notch jazz, world music and New Music virtuosos round out the menu.

Santa Fe Desert Chorale
LIVE MUSIC

(☎505-988-2282, 800-244-4011; www.desertchorale.org) Twenty lauded professional singers from around the country come together in July, August and the winter holidays to perform everything from Gregorian chants and gospel to Renaissance madrigals and modern love songs at venues like St Francis Cathedral and Loretto Chapel.

Live Music & Dance Clubs

La Fonda and the Inn & Spa at Loretto are just two of many hotel bars offering live music most nights. Check the *Santa Fe Reporter* and the 'Pasatiempo' section of Friday's *New Mexican* for a thorough listing of what's going on in Santa Fe – clubs here change faster than the seasons.

TOP CHOICE El Farol
TRADITIONAL DANCE, LIVE MUSIC

(Map p262; www.elfarolsf.com; 808 Canyon Rd) Aside from the Flamenco dinner shows, there's a regular Latin soul show and other entertainment.

Santa Fe Brewing Co
LIVE MUSIC

(Map p266; www.santafebrewing.com; 35 Fire Pl) One of Santa Fe's best venues for out-of-town bands, especially reggae masters. Enjoy a handcrafted microbrew, from pilsner to porter to stout. Out on Hwy 14, just south of town.

Vanessie of Santa Fe
CABARET

(Map p258; 434 W San Francisco St) You don't really come to Vanessie for the food, though there's nothing wrong with it. No, the attraction here is the piano bar, featuring blow-dried lounge singers who bring Neil Diamond and Barry Manilow classics to life in their own special way.

Warehouse 21
LIVE MUSIC

(off Map p258; www.warehouse21.org; 1614 Paseo de Peralta) This all-ages club and arts center in a 3500-sq-ft warehouse is the perfect alcohol-free venue for edgy local bands, plus a fair number of nationally known acts, or for just showing off the latest in multihued hairstyles.

 Shopping

Besides the Native American jewelry sold directly by the artists under the Plaza *portales*, there are enough shops for you

---

ⓘ TOP TIP: SHOPPING FOR NATIVE AMERICAN ART IN SANTA FE

The best place for shopping is the under the *portales* (overhangs) in front of the Palace of Governors. This is where Indians come – some from as far as 200 miles away – to sell their gorgeous handmade jewelry. It's a tradition that began in the 1880s, when Tesuque artisans began meeting the train with all manner of wares. Today up to 1200 members, representing almost every New Mexican tribe, draw lots for the 76 spaces under the vigas each morning. Those lucky enough to procure the desirable spots display their work – bracelets, pendants, fetishes (small statues) and thick engraved silver wedding bands – on colorful woven blankets. The classic turquoise and silver jewelry is the most popular, but you'll find many other regional stones in a rainbow of colors. The artists are generally happy to tell you the story behind each piece in his or her open-air gallery – and most are one-of-a-kinds. Not only are the prices better here than in a store but the money goes directly back to the source: the artist. It's best not to barter, unless it's suggested, as the artists may find this insulting.

to spend weeks browsing and buying in Santa Fe. Many venues are gallery-and-shop combos. The focus is mainly on art, from Native American jewelry to wild contemporary paintings. For the gallery lowdown, see p264.

Seret & Sons
HANDICRAFTS

(Map p258; www.seretandsons.com; 224 Galisteo St) Feel like you've stepped into an Asian or Arabian bazaar at this giant art-and-sculpture warehouse. It has a vast and fascinating collection of fine carpets, giant stone elephants, Tibetan furniture, pillars and solid teak doors. Of course getting all this home takes a bit of effort (or shipping money), but it's a fun just to browse too.

Kowboyz
CLOTHING

(Map p258; www.kowboyz.com; 345 W Manhattan Ave) This secondhand shop has everything you need to cowboy up. Shirts are a great deal at $10 each; the amazing selection of boots, however, demands top dollar. Movie costumers looking for authentic Western wear often come in here.

Nambé Foundry Outlet
HOMEWARES

(Map p258; www.nambe.com; 104 W San Francisco St) A unique metal alloy that contains no silver, lead or pewter (but looks like silver) was discovered in 1951 to the north of Santa Fe, near Nambé. Fashioned into gleaming and elegant pieces, Nambéware designs are individually sand-cast and have become an essential element of Santa Fe style. Another, larger outlet (924 Paseo de Peralta) is near the start of Canyon Rd.

Nathalie
CLOTHING

(Map p258; www.nathaliesantafe.com; 503 Canyon Rd; ⊙10am-6pm Mon-Sat) Come here for exquisite cowboy and cowgirl gear, including gemstone-studded gun holsters, handmade leather, denim couture and lingerie for that saloon girl with a heart of gold. The Spanish Colonial antiques are stunning.

Tesuque Flea Market
MARKET

(Map p266; www.pueblooftesuquefleamarket; US Hwy 84/285; ⊙8am-4pm Fri-Sun Mar-Nov) An outdoor market a few minutes' drive north of Santa Fe at Tesuque Pueblo, it has everything from high-quality rugs, turquoise rings and clothing to the best used (read: broken-in) cowboy boots in the state. Nowadays, most booths are like small shops; there aren't many individuals left who come to sell funky junk.

Jackalope
HANDICRAFTS

(Map p262; www.jackalope.com; 2820 Cerrillos Rd; ⊙10am-6pm) Essential pieces of Southwest decor can be yours for a song. Start with a cow skull like the ones Georgia O'Keeffe made famous, snap up a kiva ladder, add some colorful pottery and Navajo pot holders and you'll be set. Don't leave without watching live prairie dogs frolic in their 'village.'

Travel Bug
MAPS

(Map p258; www.mapsofnewmexico.com; 839 Paseo de Peralta; ⊙7:30am-5:30pm Mon-Sat, 11am-4pm Sun; @⊗) This shop has one of the most complete selections of travel books and maps you'll find anywhere; you can even have topo maps printed on demand on waterproof paper. Local travelers, including some authors and photographers, give slide shows about their adventures Saturdays at 5pm. There's also a coffee bar, wi-fi and computer terminals.

Garcia Street Books
BOOKS

(Map p258; www.garciastreetbooks.com; 376 Garcia St; ⊙9:30am-6pm) Scavengers are rewarded with excellent bargains as well as the town's best selection of art books, and such rarities as the wood engraving prints of Willard Clark.

ℹ Information

EMERGENCY Police (☑505-955-5000; 2515 Camino Entrada)

INTERNET ACCESS Travel Bug (☑505-992-0418; 839 Paseo de Peralta; @⊗) Free wi-fi and internet from on-site terminals.

MEDICAL SERVICES St Vincent's Hospital (☑505-983-3361; 455 St Michael's Dr) Has 24-hour emergency care.

Walgreens (☑505-982-4643; 1096 S St Francis Dr) A 24-hour pharmacy.

MONEY It's a tourist town, and all-too-convenient ATMs are everywhere. **Wells Fargo** (☑505-984-0424; 241 Washington Ave) changes foreign currency.

POST Post office (120 S Federal Pl)

TOURIST INFORMATION New Mexico Tourism Bureau (Map p258; ☑505-827-7440; www.newmexico.org; 491 Old Santa Fe Trail; ⊙8am-5pm;@) Housed in the historic 1878 Lamy Building (site of the state's first private college), this friendly place is very helpful.

Public Lands Information Center (Map p266; ☑505-438-7542; www.publiclands.org; 1474 Rodeo Rd; ⊙8:30am-4:30pm Mon-Fri) This place is very helpful, with maps and information on public lands throughout New Mexico.

Visitor Center (Map p258; ☑505-955-6200, 800-777-2489; www.santafe.org; 201 W Marcy St; ☺8am-5pm Mon-Fri) Conveniently located at the Sweeny Convention Center.

WEBSITES Lonely Planet (www.lonelyplanet .com/usa/santa-fe) Planning advice, author recommendations, traveler reviews and insider tips.

❶ Getting There & Around

American Eagle (☑800-433-7300; www.aa .com) flies in and out of **Santa Fe Municipal Airport** (SAF; Map p266; ☑505-955-2900; wwwsantafenm.gov; 121 Aviation Dr), with three daily flights to/from Dallas (DFW) and one daily flight to/from Los Angeles (LAX).

If you're flying into Albuquerque, **Sandia Shuttle Express** (☑505-242-0302; www.sandia shuttle.com) runs between Santa Fe and the Albuquerque Sunport ($27); make advance reservations. **North Central Regional Transit** (www.ncrtd.org) provides free shuttle bus service from downtown Santa Fe to Española, where you can transfer to shuttles to Taos, Los Alamos, Ojo Caliente and other northern destinations. Downtown pick-up/drop-off is by the Santa Fe Trails bus stop on Sheridan St, a block northwest of the Plaza. There's also an **express shuttle** (www.taosexpress.com; one-way $10; ☺Fri-Sun) to Taos on weekends from the corner of Guadalupe & Montezuma Sts, by the Railyard. **Santa Fe Trails** (Map p258; ☑505-955-2001; www.santafenm.gov; one-way adult/ senior & child $1/50¢, day pass $2/1) provides local bus service.

The **Rail Runner** (www.nmrailrunner.com) commuter train has multiple daily departures for Albuquerque – with connections to the airport and the zoo. The trip takes about 1½ hours. Board at the Railyard or the South Capital Station. **Amtrak** (☑800-872-7245; www.amtrak .com) services Lamy station, from where buses continue 17 miles to Santa Fe.

If you need a taxi, call **Capital City Cab** (☑505-438-0000).

Despite these options, most visitors will want to have their own car.

AROUND SANTA FE

Don't get too comfortable in Santa Fe, because there's plenty to explore nearby. Whichever direction you head, you'll be traveling through some of New Mexico's finest scenery, from pine forests to rainbow-colored canyons, from mesa lands to mountain views. This area also offers the state's best hot-spring resort, streams made for fly-fishing, endless hiking trails, and museums celebrating everything from Pueblo crafts to the building of the atom bomb. Small towns reveal unexpected treasures – from beautiful old adobe churches to fabulous local restaurants to art studios where the artists and artisans create and sell their work.

Pecos

When the Spanish arrived, they found a five-story pueblo with almost 700 rooms that was an important center for trade between the Pueblo Indians of the Rio Grande and the Plains Indians to the east. The Spaniards completed a church in 1625, but it was destroyed in the Pueblo Revolt of the 1680s. The remains of the rebuilt mission, completed in 1717, are the major attraction. The Pueblo itself declined, and in 1838 the 17 remaining inhabitants moved to Jemez Pueblo (see p283).

At the **Pecos National Historical Park Visitor Center** (☑505-757-6414; www.nps.gov /peco; adult/child $3/free; ☺8am-5pm), a museum and short film explain more about the area's history. From Santa Fe, take I-25 north for about 25 miles and follow signs.

Tesuque Pueblo

Nine miles north of Santa Fe along Hwy 285/84 is **Tesuque Pueblo**, whose members played a major role in the Pueblo Revolt of 1680. Today, the reservation encompasses more than 17,000 acres of spectacular landscape, including sections of the Santa Fe National Forest. If driving through on the highway, look for the aptly named **Camel Rock** on the west side of the road, more or less opposite **Camel Rock Casino** (www .camelrockcasino.com; ☺8am-2am Mon-Thu, 24 hrs Fri-Sun). **San Diego Feast Day** (November 12) features dancing; the Deer and Buffalo dances in December are known for their costumes and attention to ritual detail. The flea market held here is well worth checking out (see p279).

Pojoaque Pueblo

Although this Pueblo's history predates the Spaniards, a smallpox epidemic in the late 19th century killed many inhabitants and forced the survivors to evacuate. No old buildings remain. The few survivors intermarried with other Pueblo people and Hispanics, and their descendants now number about 300 (most people who live on the Pueblo's land are not Native American). In 1932, a handful of people returned to the Pueblo and they have since worked to rebuild their people's traditions, crafts and culture.

The **Poeh Cultural Center & Museum** (www.poehcenter.com; ⊘10am-4pm Mon-Sat), on the east side of Hwy 84/285, features exhibits on the history and culture of the Tewa-speaking people. Next door, check out the large selection of top-quality crafts from the Tewa Pueblos at the **visitor center** (☑505-455-9023; 96 Cities of Gold Rd). The Pueblo also runs the giant **Buffalo Thunder Resort** (☑505-455-5555; www.buffalothunderresort.com; r from $190; ❋@⊛⚛⛲), with luxurious rooms and suites, four 9-hole golf courses, a spa and casino.

The Pueblo public buildings are 16 miles north of Santa Fe on the east side of Hwy 84/285, just south of Hwy 502. The annual **Virgin de Guadalupe Feast Day** on December 12 is celebrated with ceremonial dancing.

San Ildefonso Pueblo

Eight miles west of Pojoaque along Hwy 502, this ancient **Pueblo** (☑505-455-3549; per vehicle $4, camera/video/sketching permits $10/20/25; ⊘8am-5pm) was the home of Maria Martinez, who in 1919, along with her husband, Julian, revived a distinctive traditional black-on-black pottery style. Her work, now valued at tens of thousands of dollars, has become world famous and is considered by collectors to be some of the best pottery ever produced.

Several exceptional potters (including Maria's direct descendants) work in the Pueblo, and many different styles are produced, but black-on-black remains the hallmark of San Ildefonso. Several gift shops and studios, including the **Maria Poveka Martinez Museum** (admission free; ⊘8am-4pm Mon-Fri) sell the Pueblo's pottery. The **Pueblo Museum**, with exhibits on the Pueblo's history and culture and a small store, is next to the visitor center.

Visitors are welcome to **Feast Day** (January 23) and **corn dances**, which are held throughout the summer.

NEW MEXICO SAN ILDEFONSO PUEBLO

WORTH A TRIP

STUDIO TOURS

In case you need more reasons to explore the region around Santa Fe, check out any of the many studio tours held throughout the year. Artists along the various routes open up their homes and personal studios to the public and show their work; often the houses themselves are as interesting as the artwork. Most tours feature locally cooked foods to sample, too. For a complete statewide list, visit www.newmexico.org. Among the best:

Dixon Studio Tour (www.dixonarts.org) New Mexico's original studio tour is still going strong; it's held the first weekend in November in scenic Dixon (p289), one hour north of Santa Fe.

Galisteo Studio Tour (www.galisteostudiotour.org) Held in the historic abobe village of Galisteo, 25 minutes south of Santa Fe, in mid-October.

High Road Art Tour (www.highroadnewmexico.com) From Chimayo to Truchas to Peñasco plus villages between and beyond, the High Road to Taos (p287) opens its doors the last two weekends in September.

Abiquiú Studio Tour (www.abiquiustudiotour.org) In Georgia O'Keeffe's former home town along the lovely Chama River, the Abiquiú (p285) tour runs on Columbus Day weekend. It's 50 minutes from Santa Fe.

Eldorado Studio Tour (www.eldoradostudiotour.org) Over 100 artists show in this Santa Fe–style suburb, just 10 minutes from town, in mid-May.

For an art-themed excursion further afield, head south to the **Lincoln County Art Loop** (www.artloop.org) studio tour, held the first weekend after July 4, which links towns throughout the beautiful Lincoln area (p343).

Santa Clara Pueblo

The Pueblo entrance is 1.3 miles southwest of Española on Hwy 30. Several galleries and private homes sell intricately carved black pottery, but stop first at **Singing Water Gallery** (☑505-753-9663; www.singing water.com; Hwy 30; ⊙11:30am-5pm), right outside the main Pueblo. In addition to representing 213 of some 450 Santa Clara potters, owners Joe and Nora Baca also offer tours of the Pueblo on weekends ($12), pottery demonstrations ($30) and classes, and can arrange feast meals ($15) with 48 hours' notice.

On the reservation at the entrance to Santa Clara Canyon, 5.7 miles west of Hwy 30 and southwest of Española, are the **Puye Cliff Dwellings** (☑888-320-5008; www .puyecliffs.com; tours adult/child $20/18; ⊙hourly 9am-5pm May-Sep, 10am-2pm Oct-Apr) where you can visit ancestral Puebloan cliffside and mesa-top ruins abandoned sometime around 1500.

Santa Clara Feast Day (August 12) and **St Anthony's Feast Day** (June 13) feature the Harvest and Blue Corn Dances. Both are open to the public; the **governor's office** (Hwy 30; ⊙8am-4:30pm Mon-Fri) issues photo and video permits ($5).

Los Alamos

The top-secret Manhattan Project sprang to life in Los Alamos in 1943, turning a sleepy mesa-top village into a busy laboratory of secluded brainiacs. Here, in the 'town that didn't exist,' the first atomic bomb was developed in almost total secrecy. Humanity can trace some of its greatest achievements and greatest fears directly to this little town. Los Alamos National Laboratory still develops weapons, but it's also at the cutting edge of other scientific discoveries, including mapping the human genome and making mind-boggling supercomputing advances.

The Lab dominates everything here and gives Los Alamos County the highest concentration of PhDs per capita in the US, along with the highest per-capita income in the state. You only have to be here for five minutes before realizing it's a place unto itself that feels very little like anywhere else around. It's in a beautiful spot atop a series of mesas and hugged by national forest, much of which unfortunately burned in the 48,000-acre Cerro Grande fire of 2000, leaving the hills behind town eerily barren.

More of the surrounding forest was ablaze in 2011, as the fire around Las Conchas scorched over 150,000 acres – the largest ever recorded in New Mexico. Fortunately, the fire narrowly missed the Lab.

⊙ Sights & Activities

Entering from the east on Hwy 502, Central Ave is the main axis and is where you'll find most places of interest. To connect to Hwy 4, heading to Bandelier National Monument or into the Jemez Mountains, head west on Trinity, Central or Canyon, then take Hwy 501 south for 5 miles.

Most of the town's sights are related to the atomic bomb project. Outside of town, there's some good **rock climbing** (with plenty of top-roping), including the **Overlook** and the **Playground** in the basalt cliffs east of Los Alamos.

TOP CHOICE **Bradbury Science Museum** MUSEUM
(www.lanl.gov/museum; 1350 Central Ave; admission free; ⊙10am-5pm Tue-Sat, from 1pm Sun & Mon) You can't actually visit the Los Alamos National Laboratory, where the first atomic bomb was conceived, but the Bradbury Science Museum has compelling displays on bomb development and atomic history, along with medical and computer sciences. There's even a room where you can twist your brain into a pretzel with hands-on problem-solving games. Pop into the **Otowi Station Museum Shop and Bookstore** next door for a great selection of science-y books, gifts and toys.

FREE **Los Alamos Historical Museum** MUSEUM
(www.losalamoshistory.org; 1050 Bathtub Row; ⊙10am-4pm Mon-Fri, from 11am Sat, from 1pm Sun) Pop-culture artifacts from the atomic age are on display at the interesting Los Alamos Historical Museum. It also features exhibits on the social history of life 'on the hill' during the secret project. Pick up one of the self-guided downtown walking-tour pamphlets.

Pajarito Mountain Ski Area SKIING, MOUNTAIN BIKING
(www.skipajarito.com; lift tickets adult/child $57/ 34; ⊙Fri-Sun Dec-Mar) Ever wanted to ski down the rim of a volcano? Look no further: this ski area, 7 miles west of downtown, has 40 runs – from easy groomers to challenging mogul steeps – plus a terrain park for snowboarders.

SCENIC DRIVE: JEMEZ MOUNTAIN TRAIL

To the west of Los Alamos, Hwy 4 twists and curves through the heart of the Jemez Mountains, on a sublime scenic drive that's made even better by all the places to stop.

At the time of writing, **Las Conchas Trail** (between mile markers 36 & 37) was closed due to fire damage. It's a lovely place to hike and there's some great rock climbing along the path, so we hope it reopens soon (call ☎575-834-7235 for current conditions).

A few miles further along, you'll enter the **Valles Caldera National Preserve** (☎866-382-5537; www.vallescaldera.gov; permits adult/child $10/5), which is basically what the crater of a dormant supervolcano looks like 1,250,000 years after it first blows. (The explosion was so massive that chunks were thrown as far away as Kansas.) The 89,000-acre bowl – home to New Mexico's largest elk herd – is simply breathtaking, with vast meadows from which hills rise like pine-covered islands. Though there are two trails on the edge of the preserve with free, open hiking, you should make reservations for the limited number of permits given out to hike within the caldera on any given day. Access to those trailheads is only possible by shuttle bus from the visitor center. If you want to gape at the lay of the land but aren't up for high-altitude exertion, take a van tour. It's also possible to bike, ride horseback, fish, hunt, and cross-country ski here. There's an information center in Jemez Springs.

Continuing along Hwy 4, there are a number of natural hot springs to hike into. One of the most accessible is **Spence Hot Springs**, between Miles 24 and 25. The temperature's about perfect, and the inevitable weird naked guy adds authenticity to the experience.

The pretty village of **Jemez Springs** (www.jemezsprings.org) was built around a cluster of springs, as was the ruined pueblo at the small **Jemez State Monument** (www.nm monuments.org; NM 4; adult/child $3/free; ⊗8:30am-5pm Wed-Sun). You can experience the waters yourself at rustic **Jemez Springs Bath House** (☎575-829-3303; 62 Jemez Springs Plaza; per hr $17; ⊗10am-7pm), which has private tubs, massages and more. In winter, bliss out in the hot-spring pools – bathing suits required; sorry, weird naked guy – at **Bodhi Manda Zen Center** (☎575-829-3854; www.bmzc.org; $10 suggested donation; ⊗9am-5pm Tue-Sat). At other times they run intensive Zen meditation programs – see their website for details.

Eat at **Los Ojos Restaurant & Saloon** (www.losojossaloon.com; Hwy 4; mains $5-11; ⊗11am-9:30pm Mon-Fri, from 8am Sat & Sun, bar open late; ✅), which has a surprising variety of vegetarian fare considering the number of animal heads on the walls. And if you're not traveling with kids or pets, stay at **Cañon del Rio B&B** (☎575-829-4377; www.canondelrio.com; $140-150; 🗎🖳), which has gorgeous canyon views, a pool, hot tub and day spa, killer breakfasts and terrific hosts.

Ten miles south of Jemez Springs, the **Walatowa Visitor Center** (7413 Hwy 4; ⊗8am-5pm) at **Jemez Pueblo** houses the small, sort-of-interesting **Museum of Pueblo Culture** (admission free). If you're into wine, take a little detour to **Ponderosa Valley Winery** (www.ponderosawinery.com; 3171 Hwy 290; ⊗10am-5pm Tue-Sat, from noon Sun) for a bottle of late-harvest riesling or pinot noir, before emerging onto Hwy 550, between Bernalillo and Cuba. From there, continue on to Albuquerque, back to Santa Fe, or up towards Chaco Canyon and the Four Corners.

The area is open daily around Christmas and New Year's. In summer, lifts run on weekends ($25) for some serious mountain-biking action, including courses with jump ramps and log rides.

FREE **Art Center at Fuller Lodge**   MUSEUM
(www.fullerlodgeartcenter.org; 2132 Central Ave; ⊗10am-4pm Mon-Sat) The Art Center mounts mixed-media shows of local and national artists. Fuller Lodge, built in 1928 to serve as the dining hall for the local boys' school, was purchased by the US government for the Manhattan Project. Inside are two small but good museums.

🛏 Sleeping

Adobe Pines B&B   B&B $
(☎505-661-8828; www.losalamoslodging.com; 1601 Loma Linda Dr; s/d $87/94; 🌐🖳) Adobe Pines offers five distinct rooms in an adobe

building. Each is a little different. Try the 2nd-floor East Room, which comes with a king-size bed, private sitting area and a balcony to enjoy the city lights by evening or Jemez Mountains by day. The Sun Room has plate-glass doors, a wooden four-poster bed and white linens, giving it airy appeal.

Best Western Hilltop House Hotel HOTEL $$
(☑505-662-1118; www.bestwesternlasalamos.com; 400 Trinity Dr; r incl breakfast from $86; ❀@ ☂❀❀) This is the nicest hotel in Los Alamos. Guests are greeted with a welcome drink in the hotel lounge, and rooms are spacious and recently upgraded, with lots of amenities. There is a workout room and spa on-site, plus an indoor heated pool.

✗ Eating

Hill Diner DINER $$
(1315 Trinity Dr; mains $8-15; ⊘11am-8pm) Those craving some home-cooked American classics, like chicken-fried steak and white country gravy, won't be disappointed by the array of American diner fare served daily at this popular place. There are good salads and other veggie options, too.

Blue Window Bistro AMERICAN $$
(labluewindowbistro.com; 813 Central Ave; lunch mains $10-12, dinner mains $10-27; ⊘11am-2:30pm & 5-8:30pm Mon-Sat; 9:30am-2:30pm Sun, closed Sat lunch) On the north side of the shopping center, this brightly colored cafe offers lunchtime gyros and poached salmon, and dinners like Southwestern chicken and double-cut pork chops.

Central Avenue Grill FUSION $$
(1789 Central Ave; mains $10-26; ⊘11am-8:30pm Mon-Sat) For a more upscale and contemporary setting, try this spot, with high ceilings and big windows that open onto downtown Los Alamos. It serves satisfying if rather pricey dishes like shrimp fajitas, green-curry chicken and Asian-spiced salmon.

❶ Information

Chamber of Commerce (☑505-662-8105, 800-444-0707; www.visit.losalamos.com; 109 Central Park Sq; ⊘9am-5pm Mon-Fri, 9am-4pm Sat, 10am-3pm Sun)
Hospital (☑505-662-4201; 3917 West Rd; ⊘24hr)
Post office (1808 Central Ave)

Bandelier National Monument

The sublime, peach-colored cliffs of Frijoles Canyon are pocked with caves and alcoves that were home to Ancestral Puebloans until the mid-1500s. Today, they're the main attraction at **Bandelier National Monument** (www.nps.gov/band; per vehicle $12; ⊘8am-6pm summer, 9am-5:30pm spring & fall, 9am-4:30pm winter). This is one of the most popular day trips from Santa Fe, rewarding whether you're interested in ancient Southwestern cultures or just want to walk among pines and watch the light glowing off the canyon walls. The **Ceremonial Cave**, 140ft above the ground and reached by climbing four ladders, is a highlight of a visit. The more adventurous can strike out on rugged trails that traverse 50 sq miles of canyon and mesa wilderness dotted with archaeological sites; backpackers should pick up a free backcountry permit from the visitor center.

The park, 12 miles from Los Alamos, has a good **bookstore** that sells trail maps and guidebooks.

Juniper Campground (campsites $12), set among the pines near the monument entrance, has about 100 campsites, drinking water, toilets, picnic tables and fire grates, but no showers or hookups.

13 miles north of the visitor center on Hwy 4 (about 20 minutes closer to Santa Fe by road), Bandelier's satellite site, **Tsankawi** (admission free) is less impressive than Frijoles Canyon but still nice, with a 1.5-mile loop trail that cuts across a mesa top and winds down a cliffside past a few small caves. Views of the Sangres are full on.

Española

Founded by conquistador Don Juan de Oñate in 1598, Española (www.espanolaonline .com) is at a major fork in the road between Santa Fe and points north, including Taos, Ojo Caliente, and Abiquiú. There's not much to appeal to visitors here, unless you're in search of a Super Wal-Mart or the best chicken-guacamole tacos on the planet.

It's still known as the 'Low Rider Capital of the World' and you're sure to see some seriously pimped-up rides cruising through Española on summer weekend nights, but there are far fewer on the streets these days than when it first claimed its title. For some of the craziest stories you'll ever read, pick up a copy of the *Rio Grande Sun*, the local paper; be sure to check out the police blotter.

Just north of Española is **Ohkay Owingeh Pueblo**, which was visited in 1598 by Juan de Oñate, who named it San Gabriel and made it the short-lived first capital of New Mexico. The **Oke Oweenge Crafts Cooperative** (☎505-852-2372; Hwy 74; ◎9am-4:30pm Mon-Sat) has a good selection of traditional red pottery, seed jewelry, weavings and drums. Public events include the **Basket Dance** (January), **Deer Dance** (February), **Corn Dance** (June 13), **San Juan Feast Day** (June 23–24) and a series of Catholic and traditional dances and ceremonies from December 24 to 26.

📛 Sleeping & Eating

There's no compelling reason to stay in Española, unless it happens to be convenient for you for some reason.

Santa Claran   CASINO HOTEL $$
(☎877-505-4949; www.santaclaran.com; 460 N Riverside Dr; r from $100; ✳◉⊛) Run by Santa Clara Pueblo, this is Española's nicest and most reliable hotel. The pueblo theme throughout adds some character. Even better than the casino is the 24-lane bowling center on the ground floor.

TOP CHOICE **El Parasol**   NEW MEXICAN $
(☎www.elparasol.com; 603 Santa Cruz Rd; mains $2-5; ◎7am-9pm) As local as it gets. Line up outside of this tiny trailer that's the somehow more delicious offspring of the fancy-ish El Paragua Restaurant next door. The chicken-guacamole tacos are a handful of greasy goodness (order at least two) and the *carne adovada* (pork in red chile) is the real deal. Though it's begun opening other branches, this is the original and best, and the only one where you're supposed to hang out in the shaded parking lot to eat your order.

❶ Getting There & Away

The town sits at the junction of US 84/285 (Santa Fe Hwy/S Riverside Dr), leading southeast to Santa Fe; NM 30 (Los Alamos Ave), running southwest to Santa Clara Pueblo, Los Alamos and Bandelier; US 84 (Oñate St), heading northwest to Abiquiú and Ghost Ranch; NM 76 (Santa Cruz Rd; High Road to Taos), the back road to Taos,

going through Chimayo; and N Riverside Dr/NM 68, heading north out of town as the Low Road to Taos.

Abiquiú

The tiny community of Abiquiú (sounds like barbeque), on Hwy 84 about 45 minutes' drive northwest of Santa Fe, is famous because the renowned artist Georgia O'Keeffe lived and painted here. With the Rio Chama flowing through farmland, and spectacular rock formations, the ethereal landscape continues to attract artists, and many live and work here.

◉ Sights & Activities

Georgia O'Keeffe Home   HOUSE
(☎505-946-1083; www.okeeffemuseum.org; tours $35-45; ◎Tue, Thu & Fri mid-Mar–Nov, Sat Jun-Oct) Georgia O'Keeffe died in 1986, at age 98, and the Spanish Colonial adobe house she restored is open for limited visits. One-hour tours are often booked months in advance, so plan ahead.

Ghost Ranch   OUTDOORS, MUSEUM
(☎505-685-4333; www.ghostranch.org; US Hwy 84; ⚐) Set amid the colorful canyonlands that were obviously inspirational for O'Keeffe, Ghost Ranch is now an education and retreat center run by the Presbyterian Church. Hiking trails – including the 4-mile round-trip trek into **Box Canyon** and the popular 3-mile round-trip to **Chimney Rock** – are open to the public, as is **Piedra Lumbre Visitor Center** (◎9am-5pm Tue Sun, closed Dec–mid-Mar), with displays about the area's natural history. The **Ruth Hall Museum of Paleontology** (◎9am-5pm Mon-Sat, 1-5pm Sun) features exhibits on the trove of dinosaurs found right at Ghost Ranch. **Horseback riding** (adult/child from $40/20) is offered for riders of all levels, and for kids as young as four. Fun factoid: scenes from *City Slickers* were filmed here.

Christ in the Desert Monastery   MONASTERY
(www.christdesert.org; ◎9:15am-5pm) Day visitors are welcome at this ecosustainable Benedictine monastery, in a secluded geological wonderland, for a one-of-a-kind spiritual-architectural experience. Take Forest Service Rd 151, a dirt road off of Hwy 84, just south of Echo Amphitheater and 5 miles north of Ghost Ranch, and drive 13 beautiful miles. Do not attempt this road if it's muddy.

GEORGIA O'KEEFFE

Although classically trained as a painter at art institutes in Chicago and New York, Georgia O'Keeffe was always uncomfortable with traditional European style. For four years after finishing school, she did not paint, and instead taught drawing and did graphic design.

However, after studying with Arthur Wesley Dow, who shared her distaste for the provincial, O'Keeffe began developing her own style. She drew abstract shapes with charcoal, representing dreams and visions, and eventually returned to oils and water-colors. These first works caught the eye of her future husband and patron, photographer Alfred Stieglitz, in 1916.

In 1929 she visited Taos' Mabel Dodge Luhan Ranch and returned to paint 'The Lawrence Tree,' which still presides over the **DH Lawrence Ranch** (p304). O'Keeffe tackled the subject of the San Francisco de Asis Church in Ranchos de Taos, painted by so many artists before her, in a way that had never been considered: only a fragment of the mission wall, contrasted against the blue of the sky.

It was no wonder O'Keeffe loved New Mexico's expansive skies, so similar to her paintings' negative spaces. As she spent more time here, landscapes and fields of blue permeated her paintings. During desert treks, she collected the smooth white bones of animals, subjects she placed against that sky in some of her most identifiable New Mexico works.

Telltale scrub marks and bristle impressions divulge how O'Keeffe blended and mixed her vibrant colors on the canvas itself. This is in direct contrast to photographs of her work, which convey a false, airbrush-like smoothness. At the **Georgia O'Keeffe Museum** (p256), you can experience her work firsthand.

Dar Al Islam Mosque   MOSQUE
(www.daralislam.org) Muslims worship at this adobe mosque that welcomes visitors. From Hwy 84, take Hwy 554 (southeast of Abiquiú) towards El Rito, cross the Rio Chama, take your first left on to County Rd 155 and follow it for 3 miles. The mosque is up a dirt road on the right.

Surrounded by red rock and high-desert terrain, **Abiquiú Lake & Dam** (Hwy 84; ⊙dawn-dusk) is a beautiful swimming spot.

🛏 Sleeping & Eating

⭐TOP CHOICE Christ in the Desert
Monastery   MONASTERY **$**
(www.christdesert.org; off US Rte 84; r incl board suggested donation $50-75) When you really want to get away from it all, head west from US Hwy 84 onto the rough dirt Forest Service Rd 151, then follow it along the meandering Rio Chama for 13 inspirational miles to this isolated Benedictine monastery. Rates for the simple rooms, plus outrageous trails and peace and quiet, include vegetarian meals served without conversation. Chores are requested (not required) and include minding the gift shop or tending the garden.

Ghost Ranch   HOSTEL **$**
(☑505-685-4333; www.ghostranch.org; US Hwy 84; tent/RV sites $19/22, dm incl board $50, r with shared/private bath incl breakfast from $50/80) A friendly place to stay in an unbeatable setting, with lots to do (see above).

Abiquiú Inn   HOTEL **$$**
(☑505-685-4378, 800-447-5621; www.abiquiuinn.com; US Hwy 84; RV sites $18, r $140-200, 4-person casitas $189) An area institution, this sprawling collection of shaded faux-dobes is peaceful and lovely; some spacious rooms have kitchenettes. The on-site **Cafe Abiquiú** (breakfast mains under $10, lunch & dinner mains $10-20; ⊙7am-9pm) is the best restaurant around. Specialties include chipotle honey-glazed salmon and fresh trout tacos.

Bode's General Store   DELI **$**
(www.bodes.com; US Hwy 84; mains $5-12; ⊙6:30am-7pm Mon-Sat, to 6pm Sun; 🛜) The hub of Abiquiú, Bode's (pronounced Boh-dees) has been around since 1919. This is the place to buy everything from artsy postcards to fishing lures to saddle blankets. Grab a sandwich or tamale at the deli and hang out with the locals.

❶ Getting There & Away

Abiquiú is on Hwy 84, about 50 minutes' drive northwest of Santa Fe. It is best reached by private vehicle.

Ojo Caliente

At 140 years old, **Ojo Caliente Mineral Springs Resort & Spa** (☑505-583-2233, 800-222-9162; www.ojospa.com; 50 Los Baños Rd; r $139-169, cottages $179-209, ste $229-349; ✽✆) is one of the country's oldest health resorts – and Pueblo Indians were using the springs long before then! Fifty miles north of Santa Fe on Hwy 285, the newly renovated resort has 10 soaking pools with several combinations of minerals (shared/private pools from $18/40). Hit the sauna and steam room before indulging in one of the superpampering **spa treatments** (massages $89-149, wraps $12-90, facials from $59, luxury packages from $125), a yoga class in a yurt, or hiking along one of the trails. If you're staying at the resort, admission to the pools is free. In addition to pleasant, if nothing-special, historic hotel rooms, the resort has added 12 plush, boldly colored suites with kiva fireplaces and private soaking tubs, and 11 New Mexican–style cottages.

The on-site **Artesian Restaurant** (breakfast mains $5-10, lunch mains $9-12, dinner mains $11-28; ☺7:30am-10:30am, 11:30am-2:30pm & 5-9pm Sun-Thu, to 9:30pm Fri & Sat) prepares organic and local ingredients with aplomb.

Other accommodations within walking distance of the springs include the slightly cheaper **Inn at Ojo** (☑505-583-9131; www.ojocaliente.com; Los Baños Dr; s/d $85/115; ✽✆), which is run by a former Los Alamos physicist, his wife and their daughter. It's a personable spot where rooms are decorated with 19th-century wardrobes.

For eats, try the **Mesa Vista Café** (Hwy 285; dishes $4-7; ☺8am-9pm; ✐), serving New Mexican diner food with lots of veggie options and a recommended red chile cheeseburger.

Ojo Caliente is about 50 miles north of Santa Fe on Hwy 285. It's a pretty drive.

Twelve miles south of Ojo Caliente is one of New Mexico's top lodging and dining experiences, **Rancho de San Juan** (☑505-753-6818; www.ranchodesanjuan.com; 34020 Hwy 285; half-board r/casita from $450/700; ✽✆). Set among 225 strikingly scenic acres, this little gem features first-class rooms, a spa, great service and a spectacular setting for dining on New Mexican classics at two nightly settings. Even if you can't afford to stay, it's worth coming to eat (prix fixe menu $85). Considered the number-one restaurant in New Mexico by many, Rancho de San Juan is so good that locals drive from Santa Fe just to dine. The meals are specially prepared but are planned in advance, so call a week ahead with any special dietary requirements. At the time of research, they were in the process of selling their liquor license, so their impressive wine list may no longer exist by the time you read this (and dinner prices will have dropped).

High Road To Taos

Go on, take the high road. One of two routes between Santa Fe and Taos, the famous High Road isn't necessarily any prettier (although beauty is relative here; both are gorgeous) than the faster Low Road, but it's got a special rural mountain feeling that is classic northern New Mexico. The road winds through river valleys, skirts sandstone cliffs and traverses high pine forests, all beneath the gaze of the 13,000-ft Truchas Peaks. Villages along this route are filled with old adobe houses with pitched tin roofs. Massive firewood piles rise next to rusting, disassembled pick-up trucks in yards surrounded by grassy horse pastures. Many of these towns are home to art studios and traditional handicraft workshops.

Though many people drive the High Road north from Santa Fe to Taos, taking the Low Road back, you actually get more impressive vistas in both directions if you take the Low Road up and the High Road down. We've presented both High and Low routes from south to north. To follow the High Road from Santa Fe to Taos, take 84/285 to Pojoaque and turn right on Hwy 503, toward Nambé. From Hwy 503, take Hwy 76 to Hwy 75 to Hwy 518.

NAMBÉ PUEBLO

Perhaps because of the isolated location (or inspirational geology), **Nambé Pueblo** has long been a spiritual center for the Tewa-speaking tribes, a distinction that attracted the cruel attentions of Spanish priests intent on conversion by any means necessary. After the Pueblo Revolt and Reconquista wound down, Spanish settlers annexed much of their land.

Nambé's remaining lands have a couple of big attractions off of Hwy 503; the loveliest are two 20-minute hikes to **Nambé Falls** (per car per day $10). The steep upper hike has a photogenic overlook of the falls, while the easier, lower hike along the river takes in ancient petroglyphs. The most popular attraction, however, is **Lake Nambé** (Hwy 101; per car per day $10; camping $25; ☺7am-7pm Apr-Oct), created in 1974 when the US dammed the Rio Nambé, flooding historic ruins but creating a reservoir that attracts boaters (no motors allowed) and trout lovers.

Public events include **San Francisco de Asis Feast Day** (October 4) and the **Catholic Mass and Buffalo Dance** (December 24).

CHIMAYO

Twenty-eight miles north of Santa Fe is the so-called 'Lourdes of America,' **El Santuario de Chimayo** (www.elsantuariodechimayo.us; ☺9am-5pm Oct-Apr, to 6pm May-Sep), one of the most important cultural sites in New Mexico. In 1816, this two-towered adobe chapel was built over a spot of earth said to have miraculous healing properties. Even today, the faithful come to rub the *tierra bendita* – holy dirt – from a small pit inside the church on whatever hurts; some mix it with water and drink it. The walls of the dirt room are covered with crutches, left behind by those healed by the dirt. During Holy Week, about 30,000 pilgrims walk to Chimayo from Santa Fe, Albuquerque and beyond in the largest Catholic pilgrimage in the US. The artwork in the *santuario* is worth a trip on its own.

This village is also famous for the arts and crafts created here. Chimayo has a centuries-old tradition of producing some of the finest weavings in the area and has a handful of family-run galleries. Irvin Trujillo, a seventh-generation weaver, whose carpets are in collections at the Smithsonian in Washington DC and the Museum of Fine Arts in Santa Fe, works out of and runs **Centinela Traditional Arts** (www.chimayoweavers.com; NM 76; ☺9am-6pm Mon-Sat, 10am-5pm Sun). Naturally dyed blankets, vests and pillows are sold, and you can watch the artists weaving on handlooms in the back. Virtually across the road, the Oviedo family has been carving native woods since 1739, and today the **Oviedo Gallery** (www.oviedoart.com; Hwy 76; ☺10am-6pm) is housed in the 270-year-old family farm.

Stay for dinner at **Rancho de Chimayo** (☎505-984-2100; www.ranchodechimayo.com;

County Rd 98; mains $7-15; ☺8:30am-10:30am Sat & Sun, 11:30am-9pm daily, closed Mon Nov-Apr), serving classic New Mexican cuisine, courtesy of the Jaramillo family's famed recipes.

Also highly recommended is the unpretentious **Casa Escondida** (☎505-351-4805; www.casaescondida.com; 64 County Rd 100; r $105-165; ❀🔊), with eight beautiful rooms, a hot tub and big old cat named Griffin.

TRUCHAS

Rural New Mexico at its most sincere is showcased in Truchas, originally settled by the Spaniards in the 18th century. Robert Redford's *The Milagro Beanfield War* was filmed here (but don't bother with the movie – the book it's based on, by John Nichols, is waaaay better). Narrow roads, many unpaved, wend between century-old adobes. Fields of grass and alfalfa spread toward the sheer walls and plunging ridges that define the eastern flank of the Truchas Peaks. Between the run-down homes are some wonderful art galleries, which double as workshops for local weavers, painters, sculptors and other artists. The **Cordovas Handweaving Workshop** (www.la-tierra.com/busyles; Main Truchas Rd; ☺8am-5pm), is run by a friendly fourth-generation weaver named Harry. You can watch him weaving in between browsing his beautiful blankets, placemats and rugs. The **High Road Marketplace** (www.highroadnewmexico.com; 1642 Hwy 76; ☺10am-5pm, to 4pm in winter) is a cooperative art gallery with a huge variety of work by area artists.

Rancho Arriba B&B (☎505-689-2374; www.ranchoarriba.com; Main Truchas Rd; s/d with shared bath $70/90, d $120; @🔊), in a rustic adobe farmhouse on the edge of Pecos Wilderness, has horses and wood stoves, and will cook you dinner with advance notice. It was temporarily closed at the time of research, but there's a good chance it'll be open again by the time you read this.

If you drive through town, rather than taking the left turn for Taos, you'll find yourself heading up a valley at the base of the mountains, where there are trailheads into the Pecos Wilderness.

Six miles north of Truchas, turn left on County Rd 73 and follow the signs to **Ojo Sarco Pottery** (web.mac.com/ojosarco1; County Rd 73; ☺10am-5pm), where you can check out the fine clay creations of master potters Kathy Riggs and Jake Willson. The work of other local artists, from glass-crafters to bell-makers, is also shown here.

LAS TRAMPAS

Completed in 1780 and constantly defended against Apache raids, the **Church of San José de Gracia** (Hwy 76; ☺9am-5pm Fri & Sat) is considered one of the finest surviving 18th-century churches in the USA and is a National Historic Landmark. Original paintings and carvings remain in excellent condition, and self-flagellation bloodstains from Los Hermanos Penitentes (a 19th-century religious order with a strong following in the northern mountains of New Mexico) are still visible.

PICURIS PUEBLO

Located just off the High Road, this was once among the largest and most powerful Pueblos in New Mexico. The Picuris built adobe cities at least seven stories tall and boasted a population approaching 3000. After the Pueblo Revolt and Reconquista, when many retreated to Kansas rather than face De Vargas' wrath, the returning tribe numbered only 500. Between raids by the Spanish and Comanches, that number continued to dwindle.

The **governor's office** (☎505-587-2519; photo/video permits $5/10; ☺8am-5pm Mon-Fri) can, with advance notice, help arrange guided Pueblo tours that include their small buffalo herd, organic gardens, ruins from the old Pueblo site and the exquisite 1770 **San Lorenzo de Picuris Church**. The unique tower kiva is off-limits to visitors but makes an impression even from the outside. The tribe's **Picuris Pueblo Museum** (☎505-587-1099) displays tribal artifacts and local art. The best time to visit the Pueblo is during the popular **San Lorenzo Feast Days** (August 9 and 10), which sees food and craft booths, dances, races and pole climbs.

From Picuris Pueblo, follow Hwy 75 east and go north on Hwy 518 to connect with Hwy 68, the main road to Taos.

PEÑASCO

This scenic village along the Rio Santa Barbara and beneath **Jicarita Peak** (12,835ft) is the gateway to the less crowded northern side of the **Pecos Wilderness**. You'll find trailheads at nearby **Santa Barbara Campground**, which has 22 RV/tent sites (per day $15). From there, it's possible to access the **Skyline Trail**, a multiday backpacking loop that traverses above-treeline

ridges and can easily include ascents of **Truchas Peak** (13,102ft), New Mexico's second-highest, and Jicarita; both are nontechnical walk-ups.

In town, the historic **Peñasco Theatre** (15046 Hwy 75) is part of **Wise Fool** (p269), a collective of performance artists who blend clowning, trapeze, puppetry, music and other forms of storytelling, sometimes to explore complex social issues, other times just to have fun. The Theatre offers myriad programs, concerts, movies and classes throughout the year, including weeklong youth circus camps in summer. Attached to the Theatre is **Sugar Nymphs Bistro** (☎575-587-0311; www.sugarnymphs.com; mains $10-15; ☺11am-2:30pm Wed-Sun, 5:30-7:30pm Thu-Sat), serving gourmet comfort food made mostly from local produce, including a great goat's cheese salad and desserts that often sell out.

Ten miles east of Peñasco, on Hwy 518 towards Mora, is the small, family-oriented **Sipapu Ski Resort** (☎800-587-2240; www.sipapunm.com; lift tickets adult/child/under 7 $39/29/free; ☑). The snow and terrain can't compare to Taos Ski Valley, but lift tickets are cheap and there are lots of special deals, making this a reasonable place to bring the kids. In summer, Sipapu has one of the top-ranked disc (Frisbee) golf courses in the country.

Low Road To Taos

First the bad news about the Low Road: it passes through Española (p284). But then you drive through the Rio Grande Gorge, between towering walls of granite, sculpted volcanic tuff and black basalt. The river tumbles by on your left, carrying tourist-packed white-water rafts downstream. Along the river are numerous pull-off and picnic spots – and **Sugar's BBQ** (1799 Hwy 68; mains $5-12; ☺11am-6pm Thu-Sun), a tin-clad trailer once named one of the top 10 roadside joints in America by *Gourmet* Magazine. Brisket burritos = genius.

Ultimately, you'll emerge from the gorge onto the Taos Plateau. The first vista is truly awesome, with the Sangre de Cristos and the deep river canyon coming suddenly and simultaneously into view. To take the Low Road from Santa Fe, take Hwy 84/285 to Hwy 68. The following places are on the way.

DIXON

While driving through the Rio Grande Gorge, take a slight detour east on Hwy 75 to this small farming and artist community, in the gorgeous Rio Embudo Valley, 24 miles south of Taos. Turn your radio dial to 96.5 FM and tune in to Dixon's own local station, KLDK. And don't miss the original New Mexico **artist studio tour** (p281) if you're in the area on the first weekend of November. While Dixon is famous for its apple orchards, plenty of other crops are grown here too; try to catch the local **farmers market** on Wednesday afternoons in summer and fall, with food fresh from the fields.

At the junction of Hwy 68 and Hwy 75 you'll see **Vivac Winery** (www.vivacwinery.com; ☺10am-6pm Mon-Sat, from noon Sun), run by the genial Padberg brothers, both born and raised in Dixon. Their tasting room features a variety of vintages, including a highly rated Syrah – plus chocolates hand made by Chris's wife, Liliana. Don't drink too much here, though, because 2.5 miles down Hwy 75 you can sample more selections at **La Chiripada Winery** (www.lachiripada.com; NM 75; ☺11am-6pm Mon-Sat, from noon Sun), a frequently award-winning vintner that uses only New Mexican–grown grapes.

Ask at the local food **co-op**, and some kind soul might point you to the **waterfalls**, up a nearby dirt road.

If you're hungry, you're lucky, because **Zuly's Cafe** (www.zulyscafe.org; 234 Hwy 75; mains $5-11; ☺7:30am-3pm Tue-Thu, 7:30am-8pm Fri, 9am-8pm Sat) is here; it's a superfriendly place run by Dixon native Chalako Chilton, who serves some of the best green chile you'll find anywhere. You can even get an espresso! Reduced hours in winter.

For such a small village, there are plenty of great guesthouses, including the charming adobe **La Casita** (☏505-579-4297; www.vrbo .com/79296; casita $90; 🐾), **Rock Pool Gardens** (☏505-579-4602; www.vrbo.com/107806; ste $90; 🛰🐾🐾), with an indoor heated pool, and **Tower Guest House** (☏505-579-4288; www .vrbo.com/118083; cottage $95; 🛰) on a working garlic farm along the Rio Embudo. Rooms must be booked well in advance during the studio tour.

RINCONADA AND PILAR

Grab a pint or a growler at the new **Blue Heron Brewing Co.** (www.blueheronbrews .com; 2214 Hwy 68; ☺11am-6pm Mon-Wed, 10am-8pm Thu-Sat, noon-6pm Sun) in the small community of **Rinconada**, just north of Dixon on Hwy 68, where local brewmasters pour handcrafted ales in an attractive art space

that was once a veterinarian's office. A few more seconds up the road, **Rift Gallery** (www.saxstonecarving.com; Hwy 68; ☺10am-5pm Wed-Sun) showcases the work of sculptor Mark Saxe and Betsy Williams, a potter specializing in the Japanese Karatsu tradition. Each summer, the gallery hosts a highly regarded weeklong stone-carving workshop.

Seven miles further north, tiny **Pilar** is the base for summer white-water rafting on the Rio Grande Racecourse (see p265). Though some outfits are run out of Santa Fe or Taos, others are based right here. **Far Flung Adventures** (☏800-359-2627; www .farflung.com; Pilar Yacht Club), runs full-day and half-day floats ($55 to $96) as well as more thrilling trips down the Taos Box. The **Rio Grande Gorge Visitor Center** (NM 68; ☺9am-4:30pm) has information on campsites and area hikes.

Take a detour on to Hwy 570 at Pilar and visit Stephen Kilborn's **studio** (www.stephen kilborn.com; ☺10am-5pm Mon-Sat, from 11am Sun), whose whimsically painted Southwestern-style pottery puts the 'fun' in functional; sometimes there are great deals on 'factory' seconds.

Keep going on Hwy 570, staying with the river, and you'll soon enter **Orilla Verde Recreation Area** (day-use $3, tent/ RV sites $7/15). This popular stretch of the Rio Grande features flat water appreciated by fishers and inner-tubers who want a relaxing float downstream. For landlubbers, there are sheltered picnic tables and campsites along the river. A couple of trails climb from the river to the rim of the gorge; we like trail Old 570, a dirt road blocked by a landslide, with expansive vistas of the Taos Plateau and the Sangre de Cristos (tip: if you want to hike but others in your group don't, have them drop you off at the trailhead, then drive around and meet you at the top, where Old 570 connects to County Rd 110).

TAOS

Taos is a place undeniably dominated by the power of its landscape: the 12,300-foot snowcapped peaks that rise behind town, a sage-speckled plateau that unrolls to the west before plunging 800 feet straight down into the Rio Grande Gorge. The sky can be a searing sapphire blue or an ominous parade of rumbling thunderheads so big they dwarf the mountains. And then there are the sunsets…

TOP TEN TAOS

Taos Ski Valley (p303) For champagne powder, tree glades and snowboarding!

El Monte Sagrado (p298) For posh high-desert R & R.

Millicent Rogers Museum For a look at one of the best collections of Southwestern jewelry and art anywhere.

La Fonda de Taos (p299) For a peek at DH Lawrence's 'Forbidden Art' and fabulous rooms.

Adobe Bar (p300) For a potent margarita and live music.

Taos Pueblo (p302) For Native American festivals and delicious fry bread

Earthship Rentals (p297) For sleeping off the grid.

Rafting the Taos Box (p296) For sheer white-water thrills.

Rio Grande Gorge Bridge (p294) For the view.

Taos Plaza For wandering.

Taos Pueblo, one of the oldest continuously inhabited communities in the United States and a marvel of adobe architecture, roots the town in a long history with a rich cultural legacy – including conquistadors, Catholicism, and cowboys. Kit Carson – legendary mountain man, soldier, and Indian enemy turned Indian advocate – was the first in a long line of celebrities to settle here, in 1842. His name is still found everywhere, from the main street in the historic district to the surrounding national forest to the local electric company.

A broken wagon wheel stranded a couple of artists in Taos in 1898. They stayed, and their reasons for staying soon got out; before too long an artists' enclave, drawn by light unencumbered by the weight of atmosphere, by colors at once subtle and brilliant, was formed. Today Taos is home to more than 80 galleries, and about 30% of people here call themselves artists.

This little town also became a magnet for writers and creative thinkers of all types. DH Lawrence hoped to build a utopia outside of town; Carl Jung was deeply affected by his visit to Taos Pueblo, which is also where Aldous Huxley found his inspiration for *Brave New World;* Dennis Hopper shot key scenes from *Easy Rider* around Taos, and was so enchanted he moved here. It's not hard to see why.

Taos remains a relaxed and eccentric place, with classic mud-brick buildings, quirky cafes and excellent restaurants. Its 5000 residents include bohemians and hippies, alternative-energy aficionados and old-time Hispanic families. It's both rural and worldly, and a little bit otherworldly.

◉ Sights

The best attraction in the Taos area is **Taos Pueblo.** Built around 1450 and continuously inhabited ever since, it is the largest existing multistoried pueblo structure in the USA and one of the best surviving examples of traditional adobe construction. Otherwise, for a village that gets as much tourist traffic as Taos, there aren't that many actual sights. Wander historic Ledoux St, Taos' art alley. Stop and pose for a picture by the life-size bronzes by Native American artist RC Gorman. Stroll under the verandas of the old adobes surrounding picturesque **Taos Plaza.**

With the Museum Association of Taos, the town's most important museums have united to offer a five-museum pass for $25, saving you $15 if you visit them all. The pass is good for a year and, in the true spirit of Taos, the Association actually encourages you to pass yours off to someone else if you haven't gotten around to each sight yourself! The museums covered include the Millicent Rogers, the Harwood, Taos Historic Museums, and the Art Museum & Fechin Institute.

TOP CHOICE Millicent Rogers Museum   MUSEUM
(Map p292; www.millicentrogers.org; 1504 Millicent Rogers Museum Rd; adult/child $8/6; ⊙10am-5pm, closed Mon Nov-Mar) This museum, about 4 miles from the plaza, is filled with pottery, jewelry, baskets and textiles from the private collection of Millicent Rogers, a model and oil heiress who moved to Taos in 1947 and acquired one of the best collections of Indian and Spanish colonial art in the USA. You want to know what a top-quality squash blossom necklace is supposed to look like? Look no further. Also displayed are contemporary Native American and Hispanic artworks.

Taos Art Museum & Fechin Institute   MUSEUM
(Map p294; www.taosartmuseum.com; 227 Paseo del Pueblo Norte; admission $8; ⊙10am-5pm

Taos Area

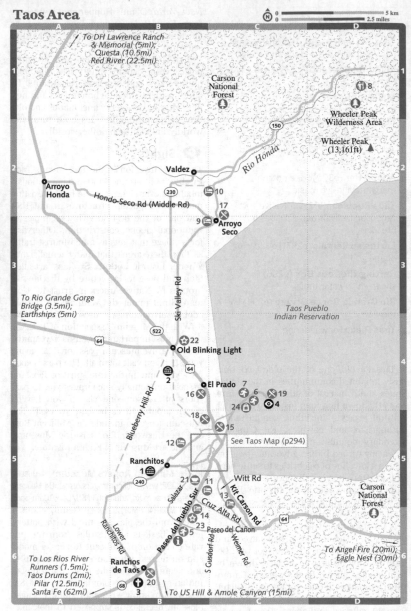

Tue-Sun) This museum was home to Russian artist Nicolai Fechin, who emigrated to New York City in 1922 at age 42 and moved to Taos in 1926. Today his paintings, drawings and sculptures are in museums and collections worldwide. Between 1927 and 1933, Fechin completely reconstructed the interior of his adobe home, adding his own distinctly Russian woodcarvings. The Fechin house exhibits the artist's private collection, including much Asian art, and hosts occasional chamber music events. Five-day

Taos Area

watercolor, sculpture and other arts workshops are offered from May to October at the nearby ranch.

Harwood Foundation Museum   MUSEUM
(Map p294; www.harwoodmuseum.org; 238 Ledoux St; adult/child $8/free; ⊙10am-5pm Tue-Sat, noon 5pm Sun) Housed in a historic mid-19th-century adobe compound, the Harwood Foundation Museum features paintings, drawings, prints, sculpture and photography by northern New Mexican artists, both historical and contemporary. Founded in 1923, the Harwood has been run by the University of New Mexico since 1936 and underwent a major renovation in 1997. It is the second-oldest museum in New Mexico, and one of its most important when it comes to art collections.

Taos Historic Museums   MUSEUM
(www.taoshistoricmuseums.org; adult/child each museum $8/4; ⊙10am-5pm Mon-Sat, noon-5pm Sun) The 1797 **Blumenschein Home & Museum** (Map p294; 222 Ledoux St) was the home of artist Ernest Blumenschein (one of the founding members of the Taos Society of Artists; see p296) in the 1920s. Today it's maintained much as it would have been when the Blumenscheins lived here. The period furniture is interesting, and the art is spectacular. Down the road a bit (you'll

want to drive), the **Martínez Hacienda** (Map p292; 708 Lower Ranchitos Rd), built in 1804, became the end of the line on the northern spur of the Camino Real. With 21 rooms, it's one of the best preserved New Mexican 'Great Houses' from that era. Cultural events are held here regularly.

◢ Earthships   NEIGHBORHOOD
(off Map p292; www.earthship.net; US Hwy 64; tours $5; ⊙10am-4pm) Innovative and off-the-grid, Earthships are self-sustaining, environmentally savvy houses built with recycled materials like used automobile tires and cans. The community is the brainchild of architect Michael Reynolds, whose idea was to develop a building method that 'eliminates stress from both the planet and its inhabitants.' Buried on three sides by earth, the Earthships are designed to heat and cool themselves, make their own electricity and catch their own water. Sewage is decomposed naturally, and dwellers grow their own food. The Earthship 'tour' is a little disappointing – you pay five bucks basically to watch a short dvd and check out the visitor center. It's much more interesting to stay in an Earthship Rental overnight. The tour office is located 1.5 miles past the Rio Grande Gorge Bridge on US Hwy 64 West.

Taos

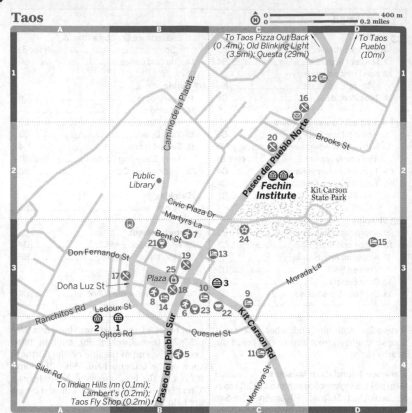

To Taos Pizza Out Back
(0.4mi); Old Blinking Light
(3.5mi); Questa (29mi)

To Taos
Pueblo
(10mi)

Paseo del Pueblo Norte

Brooks St

Fechin
Institute

Kit Carson
State Park

Caminode la Placita

Public
Library

Civic Plaza Dr

Martyrs La

Bent St

Don Fernando St

Doña Luz St

Plaza

Ledoux St

Ranchitos Rd

Ojitos Rd

Siler Rd

To Indian Hills Inn (0.1mi);
Lambert's (0.2mi);
Taos Fly Shop (0.2mi)

Paseo del Pueblo Sur

Quesnel St

Morada La

Kit Carson Rd

Montoya St

San Francisco de Asís Church   CHURCH
(Map p292; St Francis Plaza; ⊘9am-4pm Mon-Fri)
Four miles south of Taos in Ranchos de Taos,
this iconic church was built in the mid-18th century and opened in 1815. Famed for the curves
and angles of its adobe walls, it's been memorialized in Georgia O'Keeffe paintings and
Ansel Adams photographs. Mass is held at 6pm
the first Saturday of the month, and usually at
7am, 9am and 11:30am every Sunday.

Rio Grande Gorge Bridge   BRIDGE, CANYON
On US Hwy 64 about 12 miles northwest of
Taos, the gorge bridge is the second-highest
suspension bridge in the USA. Constructed
in 1965, the vertigo-inducing steel bridge
spans 500ft across the gorge and 650ft
above the river below, and there's a walkway
across it all. The views west over the emptiness of the Taos Plateau and down into the
jagged walls of the Rio Grande will surely
make you gulp as you gape. On the eastern
side of the bridge you'll usually find a motley

array of vendors selling jewelry, sage sticks
and other souvenirs for good prices.

Kit Carson Home & Museum   MUSEUM
(Map p294; www.kitcarsonhomeandmuseum.com;
113 Kit Carson Rd; adult/child $5/3; ⊘11am-5pm)
Kit Carson (1809–68) was the Southwest's
most famous mountain man, guide, trapper, soldier and scout. His home serves as an
excellent introduction to Taos in the mid-
19th century, housing such artifacts as
Carson's rifles, telescope and walking cane.
Built in 1825 with 30in adobe walls and
traditional Territorial architecture, the
home's 12 rooms are today furnished as they
may have been during Carson's day, with
exhibits on all periods of Taos history and
mountain-man lore.

🏃 Activities

Hike, bike, raft, ski, fish...the variety of outdoor activities in the Taos area is exhaustive;

Taos

consult www.taosoutdoorrecreation.com for an online rundown of all your options.

There are a number of well-respected local outfitters who can help you plan and execute your outdoor excursions. **Native Sons Adventures** (Map p292; ☎575 758-9342; www.nativesonsadventures.com; 1033 Paseo del Pueblo Sur; ⊙7am-6pm) is a good one, guiding rafting and mountain-biking trips, renting gear, and running single-track shuttles; if they can't help you, they'll know who can.

If you need to pick up any gear, head to the Plaza for **Taos Mountain Outfitters** (Map p294; www.taosmountainoutfitters.com; 114 S Plaza) or to Bent St for **Mudd-n-Flood** (Map p294; 134 Bent St). Both are well stocked and have substantial sale racks, and the folks behind the counters know what they're talking about.

Winter Sports
In winter it's all about skiing, and most of the action takes place at the **Taos Ski Valley**, which is not actually in the town of Taos; it's about 20 miles away. The ski (and newly minted snowboard) resort has a slew of lodging and eating options, so we've actually given it its own heading in this guide. Check out p303 for more on skiing in Taos.

The best in cross-country skiing is at the Enchanted Forest up by **Red River** (p305), but there's also a great little area in Carson National Forest at **Amole Canyon**, 15 miles south of Taos on Hwy 518.

Just north of Amole Canyon along Hwy 518, **US Hill** – the primo sledding spot in the area – is the most popular place around for kids to get frostbitten and bruised and love every minute of it.

Cottam's Ski & Outdoor (Map p294; www.cottamsskishops.com; 207a Paseo del Pueblo Sur), in town, is a reliable place to rent or buy whatever winter gear you need. They have another location at the ski valley.

Mountain Biking
Where else are you going to find biking this good, this close to the sky? Why bother looking elsewhere when an enormous network of mountain-bike and multi-use trails cover the region of the **Carson National Forest** between Taos, Angel Fire and Picuris Peak?

Standouts include the 9-mile **West Rim Trail** at Orilla Verde Recreation Area, suitable for strong beginners and intermediate cyclists to enjoy views of Rio Grande Gorge; and storied **South Boundary Trail**, considered one of the best mountain-bike trails in the nation – a 28-mile ride for experienced cyclists.

TAOS SOCIETY OF ARTISTS

In 1893 artist Joseph Henry Sharp first visited Taos to produce for publication a group of illustrations depicting the Pueblo. Quite smitten with the scene, Sharp spread the word among his colleagues about his 'discovery,' and shortly afterward relocated here permanently.

Ernest Blumenschein, Bert Phillips and many more of his contemporaries followed, and in 1912 they, along with Oscar Berninghaus, Eanger Irving Couse and Herbert Dunton, established the Taos Society of Artists (TSA). The original six were later joined by other prominent painters, including Lucy Harwood, the only female member, and Juan Mirabol, from Taos Pueblo.

Early TSA paintings were inspired by the backdrop of the Sangre de Cristo Mountains as well as the buildings and people of Taos Pueblo. Set against the tonal shapes and neutral colors of earth, human figures act as flashes of color seen nowhere else in the desert. Pueblo architecture, with clusters of organic and sculptural block shapes reflecting the high desert light, also appealed to the Taos painters' artistic sensibilities.

The artists' styles were as diverse and experimental as the many philosophies of painting that defined the first half of the 20th century. From Sharp's illustrative and realistic approach and Blumenschein's impressionistic treatment of Southwestern themes to the moody art-deco spirit of Dunton's landscapes, the TSA portrayed the same subjects in infinite ways.

Only in later years would the TSA's contribution to contemporary art's development be fully recognized. Historically the paintings of the TSA are seen as a visual documentary of northern New Mexican cultures, which had not yet been so dramatically influenced by the industrial age.

If you want to really challenge yourself, try the 84-mile **Enchanted Circle** loop. It makes a fine regional road-bike circuit once you've acclimatized to the altitude.

There's a surprising amount of information about mountain biking at the Taos Visitor Center. For more advice, talk to the good people at **Gearing Up Bicycle Shop** (Map p294; ☎575-751-0365; www.gearingupbikes.com; 129 Paseo del Pueblo Sur; ☺9am-6:30pm), where you can pick up trail maps, rent bikes (per day from $35) and racks ($7), and set up shuttles.

Hiking & Hot Springs

While there are a number of day-use trails just outside of Taos, particularly on the south side of Hwy 64 east of town, the best day hiking and backpacking is a little ways away, around the Ski Valley, in the Latir Peak Wilderness (p305) plus in and around the Pecos Wilderness (p289).

One popular day hike heads into the Rio Grande Gorge and the **Manby Hot Springs** (aka Stagecoach Hot Springs). A worthy place of pilgrimage – this is where the hot-springs scenes were shot in *Easy Rider* – the quality of the springs depends on the height of the river. To get there, ask a local to draw you a map. The more easily accessible Black Rock Hot Springs along the river are near the John Dunn Bridge, west of Arroyo Hondo, some 9 miles north of Taos.

Rafting

Perched between the Box and Racecourse sections of the Rio Grande, Taos is in a good position for acheiving some white-water satisfaction. Rafting companies run trips to the frothy **Taos Box** when there's enough water to boat it – usually in late spring and early summer. This stretch of river is not for the easily panicked; the rapids can hit Class V (most difficult but still possible, with Class VI being something like 'certain death'), and the remote feeling of the canyon makes it all that much more intense. From spring to fall, the **Racecourse** – downriver at Pilar (p290) – is perpetually popular; it's exciting, but rarely feels death-defying.

Among the best Taos-based river outfits is **Los Rios River Runners** (off Map p292; ☎800-544-1181; 4003 Hwy 68; www.losriosriverrunners.com; Box trips $100-115, Racecourse trips adult/child $50/40, 3-day Chama trips per person $490; ☺8am-6pm) Besides the Box (minimum age 12) and the Racecourse, they also run the scenic Chama. Unique twists include their 'Native Cultures Feast and Float,' which is accompanied by a Native American guide and includes a lunch homemade by a local Pueblo family.

Fishing

The creeks, rivers and lakes around Taos have enough variety to please experts and beginners alike, and scenery ranging from deep rocky canyons to high alpine meadows. Teach the kids at **Eagle Nest Lake** (p306) or **Orilla Verde Recreation Area** (p290); take your fly rod up to the **Red River** or down to the **Rio Santa Barbara**. Don't forget to pick up a one-day/five-day license for $12/24.

For the right flies for these waters, stop by **Taos Fly Shop** (off Map p294; ☑575-751-1312; www.taosflyshop.com; 308c Paseo del Pueblo Sur) and find out what's hatching where. They have expert guides (half-/full day from $250/325) and offer fly-fishing instruction.

Horseback Riding

Rio Grande Stables   HORSEBACK RIDING
(Map p292; ☑575 770 5913, www.lajitasstables .com/taos.htm; ☺mid-May–mid-Sep) Based up by the ski valley, this recommended riding company offers one- to four-hour trips ($50 to $95), all-day rides (including one to the top of Wheeler Peak) and combination horseback/rafting/camping treks they'll customize just for you. Call in advance.

☞ Tours

Historic Taos Trolley Tours   HISTORICAL
(Map p292; ☑575-751-0366; www.taostrolleytours .com; cnr Paseo del Pueblo Sur & Paseo del Cañon; adult/child $33/10; ☺10:30am & 2pm) Offers two different tours aboard red trolleys from the visitor center. One visits Taos Pueblo, San Francisco de Asís and the Plaza (where they'll also pick you up); the other takes in Millicent Rogers Museum and the Martínez Hacienda.

✳✳ Festivals & Events

There are numerous athletic and cultural events all year, as well as visual arts workshops; the visitor center has details. Some of the most memorable and unique are held at Taos Pueblo. Check out p301 for info on the green **Solar Music Festival** in June, which has lately been in a constant state of flux. The **Fiestas de Taos** (www.fiestasdetaos; late July) rock with New Mexican music and dance, and fill the streets with parades. **Christmas holiday** celebrations include mass at San Francisco de Asís Church (p294), plus carolers and *farolitos* everywhere help keep everyone's spirits bright.

🛏 Sleeping

Taos offers a wide variety of accommodations, from free camping in national forests to gourmet B&Bs in historic adobes. Rates can fluctuate wildly depending on what week it is, though June to September and December to February are usually considered high season, with a major spike around Christmas.

Reservation services include the **Taos Association of Bed & Breakfast Inns** (www .taos-bandb-inns.com) and **Taos Vacation Rentals** (☑800-788-8267; www.taosvacation rentals.com).

TOP CHOICE Earthship Rentals   QUIRKY $$
(off Map p292; ☑505-751-0462; www.earthship .net; US Hwy 64; r $120-160) Experience an off-grid night in a boutique-chic, solar-powered dwelling. A cross between organic Gaudí architecture and space-age fantasy, these sustainable dwellings are put together from recycled tires, aluminum cans and sand, with rain-catching and gray-water systems to minimize their footprint. Half buried in a valley surrounding by mountains, they could be hastily camouflaged alien vessels – you never know...

TOP CHOICE Mabel Dodge Luhan House   HISTORIC HOTEL $$
(Map p294; ☑505-751-9686; www.mabeldodge luhan.com; 240 Morada Lane; r $100-195; P)

ANDEAN-ESQUE ADVENTURE

Not everyone who loves to hike and camp has the stamina – or desire – to haul a pack around at 11,000ft above sea level. Around Taos, you don't need to – that's what the llamas are for! **Wild Earth Llama Adventures** (☑800-758-5262; www.llamaadventures.com) runs day hikes and multiday treks in the sweetest spots in the Sangres. They're experts at getting even young kids out into the backcountry, and their lead guide also happens to be a chef. No, no llama riding, but you might be too busy doing your 'Julie Andrews in an alpine meadow' impersonation to care.

Day trips (adult/child $99/69) run year-round; multiday trips (adult/child from $329/119; prices vary with length) run from March to November and can be customized to your needs.

Every inch of this place exudes elegant-meets-rustic beauty. The 'Patroness of Taos,' Mabel Dodge Luhan (by equal measures graceful and grand, scandalous and unbearable) built this fabulous mansion to welcome everyone from Emma Goldman and Margaret Sanger to Carl Jung for a nice chat. You can sleep in rooms where Georgia O'Keeffe, Ansel Adams or Willa Cather once laid their heads, or where DH Lawrence added artful touches. It also runs art workshops.

Doña Luz Inn
INN $$

(Map p294; ✆575-758-9000; www.stayintaos.com; 114 Kit Carson Rd; r $59-229; ❄@🅿🛜) Funky and fun, this inn is a true Taos experience. Rooms, with adobe fireplaces, patios, kitchenettes and hot tubs, range from the cozy La Luz (at $59, the best deal in town) to the three-level Rainbow Room suite with a hot tub on the rooftop sundeck. All are decorated in colorful Spanish colonial style, a cheerful clutter of Native American and Spanish colonial antiques, artifacts and art – lots of it sacred and all of it beautiful.

Historic Taos Inn
HISTORIC HOTEL $$

(Map p294; ✆575-758-2233; www.taosinn.com; 125 Paseo del Pueblo Norte; r $75-275; 🅿❄🛜) Even though it's not the plushest place in town, it's still fabulous, with a cozy lobby, a garden for the restaurant, heavy wooden furniture, a sunken fireplace and lots of live local music at its famed Adobe Bar. Parts of this landmark date to the 1800s – the older rooms are actually the nicest.

American Artists Gallery House B&B
B&B $$

(Map p292; ✆800-532-2041; www.taosbedandbreakfast.com; 132 Frontier Lane; r/ste from $85-190; ❄@🛜) Art flows here in ever-changing shows drawn from local galleries. George the peacock and lots of cats will be your inn-mates, while Jacuzzi suites will blow your mind. All rooms have wood-burning fireplaces. The creative breakfasts are legendary.

Casa Benavides Bed & Breakfast
B&B $$

(Map p294 ✆575-758-1772; www.taos-casabenavides.com; 137 Kit Carson Rd; r $105-300; ❄@🛜) This romantic spot spans five buildings, and has lots of fireplaces, patios, balconies and gardens. Furniture is mostly antique and handmade, and shares space with artful treasures. A couple of the rooms are on the small and dark side, but most are big and bright – see a few if you can. Breakfasts are full and made from scratch.

Old Taos Guesthouse
B&B $$

(Map p292; ✆800-758-5448; www.oldtaos.com; 1028 Witt Rd; r $84-175; ❄@🛜) This atmospheric treasure has spacious, old-world adobe rooms with undulating walls (just try to find a right angle here) and handcarved wood furnishings and doors; the older rooms are nicest. Hidden away in a quiet residential neighborhood, the shady lawn and gardens beckon, with inviting hammocks and 60-mile sunset views. The proprietors are seasoned adventurers and can point you toward great excursions.

Casa Europa
B&B $$

(Map p292; ✆575-758-9798; www.casaeuropanm.com; 840 Upper Ranchitos Rd; r $115-185; 🛜) Cool breezes provide the air-conditioning at this stunning 18th-century estate. Views of pastures and mountains are sublime. Euro-style antiques mix artfully with Southwestern-style pieces. Elaborate breakfast and afternoon treats are offered in summer, evening hors d'oeuvres in winter. Comfort, light and air define this welcoming spot.

El Monte Sagrado
LUXURY HOTEL $$$

(Map p294; ✆800-828-8267; www.elmontesagrado.com; 317 Kit Carson Rd; r $199-499; ❄@🛜🏊) A lush oasis in the high desert, this lavishly decorated ecoresort has bright, luxurious suites whimsically decorated with Native American, Mexican, Moroccan and Egyptian cultures in mind, all arranged around a flourishing courtyard irrigated with a gray-water system. Its Anaconda Bar is exceptionally attractive. There's a full-service on-site spa and plenty of package deals with the ski valley.

Sun God Lodge
MOTEL $

(Map p292; ✆575-758-3162; www.sungodlodge.com; 919 Paseo del Pueblo Sur; r from $55; 🅿❄🛜🐾) The hospitable folks at this well-run two-story motel can fill you in on local history and point you to a restaurant to match your mood. Rooms are clean – if a bit dark – and decorated with low-key Southwestern flair. The highlight is the lush-green courtyard dappled with twinkling lights, a scenic spot for a picnic or enjoying the sunset. Pets stay for $20. Located 1.5 miles south of the Plaza, the Sun God is a great budget choice.

El Pueblo Lodge
HOTEL $

(Map p294; ✆800-433-9612; www.elpueblolodge.com; 412 Paseo del Pueblo Norte; r from $89; 🛜) This standard hotel is right downtown, with big, clean rooms, some with kitchenettes and/or fireplaces, a pool, hot tub and fresh pastries in the morning. Deep discounts are offered in low season or when they're not busy.

La Fonda de Taos
HISTORIC HOTEL $$

(Map p294; ☎800-833-2211; www.lafondataos.com; 108 S Plaza; r $99-259; @🛜) This upscale hotel, formerly owned by notorious playboy Saki Karavas, just can't shake its sexy vibe – even the kiva gas fireplaces in the smallish, sensually angled suites seem like they're illuminating something that's up to no good. Perhaps it's the 'Forbidden Art' collection of DH Lawrence – banned in 1929 Europe and displayed here to consenting adults – depicting, and perhaps inspiring, all sorts of sinful fun. No children under 13.

Indian Hills Inn
HOTEL $

(off Map p292; ☎575-758-4293; www.taosnet.com/indianhillsinn; 233 Paseo del Pueblo Sur; r from $60; 🐾@🛜🐾🐾) This budget hotel close to the Plaza isn't half-bad. The swimming pool is great for kids who've maxed out on art galleries. All rooms were recently recarpeted, but the Deluxe King rooms are noticeably nicer than the Double Queen family rooms. For the location and price, it's a good deal.

✗ Eating

There are some really good restaurants here. A few are even right near the Plaza.

TOP CHOICE Trading Post Cafe
INTERNATIONAL $$$

(Map p292; ☎575-758-5089; www.tradingpostcafe.com; Hwy 68, Ranchos de Taos; lunch mains $8-14, dinner mains $16-32; ⊙11:30am-9:30pm Tue-Sat, 5-9pm Sun) A longtime favorite, the Trading Post is a perfect blend of relaxed and refined. The food, from paella to pork chops, is always great. Portions of some dishes are so big, think about splitting a dish – or, if you want to eat cheap but well, get a small salad and small soup. It'll be plenty!

TOP CHOICE Love Apple
ORGANIC $$

(Map p292; ☎575-751-0050; www.theloveapple.net; 803 Paseo del Pueblo Norte; mains $13-18; ⊙5-9pm Tue-Sun) Housed in the 19th-century adobe Placitas Chapel, the understated rustic-sacred atmosphere is as much a part of this only-in-New-Mexico restaurant as the food. From the posole with shepherd's lamb sausage to the grilled trout with chipotle cream, every dish is made from organic or free-range regional foods. Make reservations!

Dragonfly Café & Bakery
INTERNATIONAL $$

(Map p294; www.dragonflytaos.com; 402 Paseo del Pueblo Norte; lunch mains $4-14, dinner mains $12-21; ⊙11am-9pm Mon-Sat, 9am-3pm Sun; ☑🐾) One of the most charming little places in town, the Dragonfly creates a space that achieves a rustic kind of elegance while remaining comfortable and kid-friendly. Food is delicious and internationally inspired, from Moroccan roast chicken to wild salmon tacos. Monday nights, come for the East Indian menu; every day, come for the fantastic baked goods. Most ingredients are local and/or organic.

Michael's Kitchen
NEW MEXICAN $

(Map p294; 304c Paseo del Pueblo Norte; mains $7-16; ⊙7am-2:30pm; 🐾) Locals and tourists both converge on this old favorite because the menu is long, the food's reliably good, it's an easy place for kids, and the in-house bakery produces goodies that fly out the door. Plus, it serves the best damn breakfast in town. You just may spot a Hollywood celebrity or two digging into a chile-smothered breakfast burrito.

El Gamal
MIDDLE EASTERN $

(Map p294; www.elgamaltaos.com; 12 Doña Luz St; mains $6-10; ⊙9am-5pm; 🛜☑🐾) Vegetarians rejoice! At this casual Middle Eastern place, there's no meat anywhere. We're not sure the falafel quite acheives El Gamal's stated vision to 'promote peace...through evolving people's consciousness and taste buds,' but it's good enough to have as much of a chance as anything else. There's a kids playroom in the back with tons of toys, plus a pool table and free wi-fi.

Taos Pizza Out Back
PIZZA $

(off Map p294; 712 Paseo del Pueblo Norte; slices $4-6, whole pies $13-27; ⊙11am-10pm May-Sep, to 9pm Oct-Apr; ☑🐾) Pizza dreams come true with every possible ingredient under the sun at Taos' top pizza palace; for example, the recommended Vera Cruz has chicken breast and veggies marinated in a honey-chipotle sauce. Slices are enormous, and crusts are made with organic flour. Out Back will also bake dough balls for kids, and has a great back patio.

Doc Martin's
AMERICAN, NEW MEXICAN $$

(Map p294; ☎505-758-1977; Historic Taos Inn, 125 Paseo del Pueblo Norte; breakfast & lunch mains $5-15, dinner mains $12-35; ⊙7:30am-2:30pm, 5pm-9:30pm) Hang out where Bert Philips (the Doc's bro-in-law) and Ernest Blumenschein cooked up the idea of the Taos Society of Artists. Sit by the kiva fireplace, pop a cork on one of the award-winning wines, dive into the *chile rellenos* and you'll be inspired to great things as well. Reservations recommended.

Graham's Grille MODERN AMERICAN $$
(Map p292; 505-751-1350; www.grahamstaos .com; 106 Paseo del Pueblo Norte; mains $7-19; 7:30-10:30am & 11:30am-2:30pm Mon-Fri, 8am-2:30pm Sat & Sun, 5-9pm daily;) Since its opening in 2007, Graham's has consistently been voted one of the best restaurants in Taos. It serves honest, creative food in hip retro-mod environs – think lime-green walls, purple lightbulbs and starched white tablecloths. There's a nice patio out back. The menu features lots of sandwiches and salads, plus seafoods, pasta and an apple-chile-brined pork tenderloin. Yum!

Lambert's MODERN AMERICAN $$$
(off Map p294; 505-758-1009; 309 Paseo del Pueblo Sur; mains $20-35; 5-9pm;) Winner of multiple 'Best of Taos' awards, including best restaurant, Lambert's is a cozy local hangout where patrons sink deeply into sofas and conversation for hours on end. Lace curtains and subtle elegance make this atmospheric eatery a fine experience, whether you're digging into caribou, buffalo or the pepper-crusted lamb loin ($34).

Taos Diner DINER $
(Map p292; www.taosdiner.com; 908 Paseo del Pueblo Norte; mains $4-12; 7am-2:30pm) Diner grub at its finest, prepared with a Southwestern, organic spin. Mountain men, scruffy jocks, solo diners and happy tourists – everyone's welcome here. The breakfast burritos rock.

Orlando's NEW MEXICAN $$
(Map p292; 575-751-1450; www.orlandostaos .com; 1114 Don Juan Valdez Lane; mains $8-12; 10:30am-3pm, 5-9pm;) Hands down the best New Mexican food in Taos, it can get really busy in high season. Just north of town on the main road.

Gorge Bar & Grill AMERICAN $$
(Map p294; 103 E Plaza; mains $9-25; 11am-10:30pm Mon-Thu, to 11:30pm Fri & Sat, to 9pm Sun) Popular with tourists for its hearty American food, margarita menu, and patio overlooking the plaza.

Drinking

Bars
Adobe Bar BAR
(Map p294; Historic Taos Inn, 125 Paseo del Pueblo Norte) There's something about this place. There's something about the chairs, the Taos Inn's history, the casualness, the vibe and the tequila. It's true, the packed streetside patio has some of the state's finest margaritas, along with an eclectic lineup of great live music – and there's almost never a cover.

Anaconda Bar BAR
(Map p294; El Monte Sagrado, 317 Kit Carson Rd) The Anaconda is a work of art, a real feast for the eyes. The bartenders and chefs take care of the other senses, with perfectly made drinks and gourmet pub grub. It is pricey, but it's unique.

Alley Cantina BAR
(Map p294; 121 Terracina Lane) It figures that the oldest building in Taos is a comfy bar, built more than three centuries ago by forward-thinking Native American capitalists as the Taos Pueblo Trading Post. Nowadays you can catch live music ranging from zydeco to rock and jazz almost nightly.

Eske's Brew Pub & Eatery BREWERY
(Map p294; 106 Des Georges Lane) This crowded hangout rotates more than 25 microbrewed ales, from Taos Green Chile to Doobie Rock Heller Bock, to complement hearty bowls of Wanda's green chile stew and sushi on Tuesday. Live local music, from acoustic guitar to jazz, is usually free.

Cafes
Mondo Kultur CAFE
(Map p292; 622 Paseo del Pueblo Sur; snacks $2-4;) Arguably the best coffee in town, with bagels, pastries and other goodies. All ages, from tattooed teens to retirees, gather here. If you've got a laptop, it's hard to beat for getting work done.

Caffe Tazza CAFE
(Map p294; 122 Kit Carson Rd) Not everyone's cup of tea, Tazza caters mostly to the crunchy-hipster-tattooed crowd. Come at night to sample the local literary arts, with open mics, readings and live music.

★ Entertainment

KTAO Solar Center LIVE MUSIC
(Map p292; www.ktao.com; 9 Ski Valley Rd) Taos's best venue for live music. Local, national

GOOD DAY SUNSHINE

Just as the Rio Grande Gorge opens up to engulf US Hwy 68 for the scenic climb into Taos, your radio will start to sputter. Don't put on that tired old CD; flip to KTAO 101.9 FM (www.ktao.com), broadcasting shows like 'Trash and Treasures' (an on-air flea market) and lots of great music.

KTAO has been doing it all with solar power since 1991, when station founder Brad Hockmeyer installed 50,000 watts worth of photovoltaic cells atop Mount Picuris. The station plays whatever the real live DJs feel like playing and features daily horoscope readings (at 10am and 6pm) by local astrologer Josseph the Starwatcher. During 'Licorice Pizza' (10pm weekdays) a whole album – er, CD – is played in its entirety with no commercial interruption. Weekly shows include 'Moccasin Wire' (7:30pm to 10pm Monday), devoted to Native American music, and 'Listen Up' (7pm to 8pm Thursday), a talk show by and for Taos teens.

While this may sound dangerously like small-town schlock, it's anything but. KTAO consistently wins statewide awards for its programming and excellence in journalism.

Attached to the staton is the **KTAO Solar Center**, the best place in town to see concerts. It's family-friendly, and kids under 12 are free. We only hope that they'll be allowed to stage shows out on the back lawn again, like they used to before certain neighbors complained about it. Now, bands play inside a big tentlike structure.

The radio station is no longer associated with the **Taos Solar Music Festival** (www.solarmusicfest.com), which is still held at the end of June and still fun! The festival format and location has been fluid for the past couple of years, so check details. You can probably count on there being a 'solar village,' showcasing anything from the Los Alamos National Laboratory's solar-powered supercomputer to homemade solar cookers. Grab a cup of solar-percolated coffee and chat up alternative-energy lovers pitching straw-bale construction, solar cars, passive solar design ('used at Taos Pueblo for a thousand years!') and of course the Taos Earthships.

and even international acts stop here to rock the house. Even on nights when there are no shows, you can watch the DJs in the booth at the 'world's most powerful solar radio station' while hitting happy hour at the Solar Center's **bar** (⊘from 4pm).

Taos Chamber Music Group   CLASSICAL MUSIC
(www.taoschambermusicgroup.com) For classical and jazz, this group performs at venues throughout the region. See the website for schedules.

Taos Center for the Arts   PERFORMING ARTS
(TCA; Map p294; ✆575-758-2052; www.tcataos.org; 133 Paseo del Pueblo Norte) In a remodeled 1890s adobe mansion, the TCA stages local and international performances of everything from chamber music to belly dancing to theater.

Storyteller Cinema   CINEMA
(Map p292; ✆505-758-9715; 110 Old Talpa Cañon Rd; tickets adult/child $9/6) Catch mainstream flicks at Taos' only movie house, right off Paseo del Pueblo Sur.

 ## Shopping

Taos has historically been a mecca for artists, and the huge number of galleries and studios in and around town are evidence of this. The **John Dunn Shops** (www.johndunnshops.com) pedestrian arcade between the Plaza and Bent St. is lined with indie shops and galleries.

Taos Drums   MUSIC
(off Map p292; www.taosdrums.com; 3956 Hwy 68, Ranchos de Taos) Just south of town you'll find what's touted as the world's largest selection of Native American drums. All are handmade by masters from Taos Pueblo and covered with real hide. Choose from hand drums, log drums, natural-looking drums or ones painted with wildlife or Pueblo motifs.

El Rincón Trading Post   VINTAGE
(Map p294; 114 Kit Carson Rd) This shop dates back to 1909, when German Ralph Meyers, one of the first traders in the area, arrived. Even if you're not looking to buy anything, stop in here to browse through the dusty museum of artifacts, including Indian crafts, jewelry and Old West memorabilia.

Buffalo Dancer JEWELRY
(Map p294; 103a East Plaza) One of the older outlets for Native American jewelry on the Plaza, this store carries Rodney Concha's fine pieces plus other work in silver and semiprecious stones.

ⓘ Information

Holy Cross Hospital (☎575-758-8883; 1397 Weimer Rd)

Police (☎575-758-2216; 107 Civic Plaza Dr)

Post office (Paseo del Pueblo Norte at Brooks St)

Taos Vacation Guide (www.taosvacation guide.com) Good site with sections in French, German and Spanish.

Taos Visitor Center (☎575-758-3873; Paseo del Pueblo Sur at Paseo del Cañon; ⊙9am-5pm; @🛜)

Wired? (705 Felicidad Lane; ⊙8am-6pm Mon-Fri, 8:30am-6pm Sat & Sun) Coffee shop with free wi-fi if you've got a laptop; if not you can log on to their computers (per hour $7).

ⓘ Getting There & Around

One mile north of town, Paseo del Pueblo Norte forks: to the northeast it becomes Camino del Pueblo and heads toward Taos Pueblo, and to the northwest it becomes Hwy 64. The 'old blinking light' north of town is a major landmark for directions (though it now functions as a regular traffic light); from it, Hwy 64 heads west to the Rio Grande Gorge Bridge, Hwy 522 heads northwest to Arroyo Hondo and Questa, and Hwy 150 heads northeast to Arroyo Seco and the Taos Ski Valley.

North Central Regional Transit (www.ncrtd .org) provides free shuttle bus service to Española, where you can transfer to Santa Fe and other destinations; pick-up/drop-off is at the Taos County offices off Paseo del Pueblo Sur, about a mile south of the plaza. **Taos Express** (www .taosexpress.com) has shuttle service to Santa Fe Friday through Sunday ($10). **Twin Hearts Express** (☎800-654-9456) will get you to Santa Fe ($40) and the Albuquerque airport ($50).

The **Chile Line** (www.taosgov.com; one-way 50¢; ⊙7am-5:30pm Mon-Fri) runs north–south along NM 68 between the Rancho de Taos post office and Taos Pueblo every 30 minutes. It also serves the ski valley and Arroyo Seco in winter. All buses are wheelchair-accessible.

AROUND TAOS

The area around Taos has fabulous skiing, cool little towns and some of the best scenery around. Driving the Enchanted Circle makes a fantastic day trip from Taos, while a night in little Arroyo Seco delivers rural New Mexican flavor and crisp high desert air. There's good fly-fishing and cross-country skiing around Red River, and plenty of wilderness to escape to.

Taos Pueblo

Whatever you do, don't miss it. Built around 1450 and continuously inhabited ever since, **Taos Pueblo** (Map p292; ☎505-758-1028; www .taospueblo.com; Taos Pueblo Rd; adult/child $10/5, photography or video permit $5; ⊙8am-4pm) is the largest existing multistoried pueblo structure in the USA and one of the best surviving examples of traditional adobe construction. It's what all that Pueblo Revival architecture in Santa Fe wants to be when it grows up. Note the Pueblo closes for 10 weeks annually, starting in March, for ritual purposes.

Taos Mountain Casino (Map p292; www .taosmountaincasino.com; Taos Pueblo Rd; ⊙8am-1am Sun-Wed, to 2am Thu-Sat) has less razzle-dazzle than some casinos, but you might appreciate its alcohol-and-smoke-free atmosphere.

Taos Indian Horse Ranch (Map p292; ☎505-758-3212, 800-659-3210; 1hr/2hr easy ride $55/95, 2hr experienced ride $125) offers riding trips through Indian land – experienced riders can go fast. It also does an overnight rafting/riding/camping trip; ring for details.

One of New Mexico's largest and most spectacular Indian celebrations, **San Geronimo Day** (September 29 and 30) is celebrated with dancing and food. The huge **Taos Pueblo Pow-Wow** (☎505-758-1028; www .taospueblopowwow.com; Taos Pueblo Rd; admission $5) in the second week of July features Plains and Pueblo Indians gathering for dances and workshops as this centuries-old tradition continues. Of all the Pueblos in northern New Mexico, Taos Pueblo has the most events and celebrations open to the public.

For food, everyone, and we mean everyone, heads to **Tewa Kitchen** (Map p292; Taos Pueblo Rd; mains $6-13; ⊙11am-5pm Wed-Mon Sep-May, to 7pm daily Jun-Aug). It's one of the few places in the state where you can sit down to a plate of Native treats like *phien-ty* (blue-corn fry bread stuffed with buffalo meat), *twa chull* (grilled buffalo) or a bowl of heirloom green chile grown on Pueblo grounds.

You can also grab tacos and the most delicious chewy Indian fry bread ($3 to $5) at the main pueblo.

Just outside the Pueblo, stop at the **Tony Reyna Indian Shop** (Map p292;Taos Pueblo Rd;

⊙8am-noon & 1-6pm), which has a vast collection of arts and crafts from Taos and other tribes.

Several craftspeople sell fine jewelry, micaceous (mica is an aluminum mineral found in local rocks) pottery and other arts and crafts at the main pueblo; you can peruse after touring the place.

Arroyo Seco

For some unprocessed local flavor, a groovy plaza and a growing art scene, Arroyo Seco is the place to be. It's just 10 minutes north of Taos; there's not much to do, but you'll find plenty of ways to do nothing.

Backpackers will find their version of sleeping paradise at the popular, and extremely affordable, **Abominable Snowmansion** (Map p292; ☑575-776-8298; www.snowmansion.com; 476 Hwy 150; campsites $15, dm $20, r with shared/private bath $45/59; P@☎). This HI hostel has a cozy lodge, with clean (if a tad threadbare) private rooms, a wonderful campground with an outdoor kitchen, and simple dorm rooms. For something different – especially if you've got the kids – try sleeping in a tipi ($35)!

The **Adobe and Stars B&B** (Map p292; ☑575-776-2776; www.taosadobe.com; 584 Hwy 150; r incl breakfast $125-190; @☎) has eight large, amazing rooms with working kiva fireplaces, some with Jacuzzi tubs and peaceful mountain views.

Taos Cow (Map p292; mains $5-8; ⊙7am-6pm; ☎) serves sandwiches, breakfast specials, pastries and its much-loved all-natural ice cream in some flavors you'll find nowhere else (like Piñon Caramel).

Taos Ski Valley

People move to New Mexico just to 'ski bum' at Taos for a couple years. Some end up staying longer than they planned. There's just something about the snow, challenging terrain and laid-back atmosphere that makes this mountain a wintery heaven-on-earth – that is, if heaven has a 3275ft vertical drop.

Most visitors come in winter for the skiing and snowboarding. (Once exclusive to skiers, Taos is now open to boarders). Offering some of the most difficult terrain in the USA, it's a fantastic place to zip down steep tree glades and jump cliffs into untouched powder bowls. Summer visitors to the village, which was once the rough-and-tumble gold-mining

town of Twining, find an alpine wilderness with great hiking and cheap lodging.

Seasoned skiers luck out here, with more than half of the 70-plus trails at the **Taos Ski Valley** (Map p292; www.skitaos.org; half-/full-day lift ticket $48/71) ranked expert; the valley has a peak elevation of 11,819ft and gets an average of more than 300in of all-natural powder annually – but some seasons are much better than others. In addition to opening up to snowboarders, the resort added a skier-cross obstacle course to its popular terrain park. Check the resort website for ski-and-stay deals, including weeklong packages with room, board, lessons and lift tickets. At the beginning of the season there are often reduced-rate lift tickets and very good specials on offer.

In summer, several **hiking** trailheads are located along Hwy 150 to Taos Ski Valley and at the northern end of the Ski Valley parking lot, including one to the top of **Wheeler Peak**, New Mexico's highest at 13,161ft.

When it comes to lodging, high season is from Thanksgiving to Easter, but there are dips in March and November and peaks during the holidays. From March to October, many lodges are closed, while those that are open offer excellent discounts.

Probably the best all-round option – with the best specials – is the giant **Snakedance Condominiums & Spa** (☑800-322-9815; www.snakedancecondos.com; 110 Sutton Pl; r $225-575; ✴@☎), which offers ski lodge condo-style digs at the bottom of the lifts. It also has a restaurant, a bar, in-room massages and lots of other amenities, including a hot tub, a sauna and in-room kitchens. Prices vary wildly around the year; those listed here are for the bulk of the ski season (much higher than summer rates but lower than Christmas/spring break).

Famous for its flame-roasted red and green chile, **Tim's Stray Dog Cantina** (☑505-776-2894; 105 Sutton Pl; mains $9-13; ⊙8am-9pm Dec-May; 11am-9pm Jun-Nov) is a ski valley institution. It serves fabulous New Mexican cuisine – the breakfast burritos are perfect fuel-up food – along with fresh margaritas and a big selection of bottled brews. The perfect après-ski or après-hiking hangout.

To reach the valley, take Hwy 64 north out of Taos to the old blinking light (now a regular traffic signal), and veer right on Hwy 150 toward Arroyo Seco. The 20-mile drive winds along a beautiful mountain stream. During the winter, the Chile Line runs several times a day from downtown Taos.

DH Lawrence Ranch & Memorial

In 1924, Mabel Dodge Luhan gave DH Lawrence's wife, Frieda, this 160-acre **ranch** (off Map p292; ☎575-776-2245; www.unm.edu /~taosconf/Taos/DHlawrence.htm; admission free; ◐sunrise-sunset), now administered by the University of New Mexico, where the Lawrence-obsessed can pay their respects to the famed author of such classics as *Lady Chatterley's Lover*.

Lawrence and Frieda lived here for only a few months in 1924–25 along with artist Dorothy Brett, who accepted Lawrence's invitation to create 'Rananim,' a utopian society. Lawrence spent his time repairing the cabins, chopping wood, hiking the trails and (with the help of Frieda) fighting off the attentions of Dorothy and patron Mabel Dodge Luhan. He also managed to complete the novella *St Mawr*, his biblical drama *David*, parts of *The Plumed Serpent* and other works in between. Relax beneath the **Lawrence Tree**, which brings in the O'Keeffe fans (yep, it looks just like her painting) and contemplate what he called 'the greatest experience I ever had from the outside world.'

Lawrence returned to Europe in 1925 and succumbed to tuberculosis in 1930. After Frieda moved back to Taos in 1934, she ordered his body exhumed and cremated, and had the ashes brought here. Luhan and Brett both showed up uninvited to help scatter said ashes, which, according to legend, prompted Frieda to finally dump the remains into a wheelbarrow full of wet cement, saying, 'Let's see them try to steal this!' According to one story, the cement was used to make the memorial's altar – and his personal symbol, the phoenix, rises therefrom.

Ascend the meandering paved walkway to the memorial, designed by Frieda's third husband, where the lump of concrete has been inscribed with Lawrence's initials and green leaves and yellow flowers. It's heartwarming, with a scandalous giggle, just like Lawrence would have wanted.

At the time of research, the ranch had closed for renovations for an indefinite period. Hopefully it will be open by the time you read this, but this is New Mexico, so no guarantees.

Enchanted Circle

Unplug, sit back, unwind and absorb the beauty. You'll understand why they call this 84-mile loop the Enchanted Circle once you start driving – or, to really experience the sublime natural nuances along this stretch of pavement, ride it on your mountain bike. In warm weather, the route is popular with cyclists from around the world for its scenery and challenging altitude and terrain. Comprising NM 522, NM 38 and US 64, the scenic byway is generous with its views – of crystalline lakes, pine forests draped

---

SCENIC DRIVE: VALLE VIDAL LOOP

In the mood for a longer drive through the highlands? Try the 173-mile Valle Vidal Loop, which departs the Enchanted Circle in Questa, heading north past the Wild Rivers Recreation Area on NM 522 and rejoining the road more traveled in Eagle Nest via US 64.

The bulk of the route is impassable during winter, and the washboard gravel road of FR 1950 is no picnic at the best of times – bring a spare tire. The northern gate to FR 1950 is closed April 1 to early June for elk calving season, while the southern gate closes January through March to let them winter in peace. The estimated 1800 elk are a major attraction the rest of the year and are best seen in the morning and evening.

From the small town of Costilla, just below the Colorado border, take NM 196 east. Before long, the road turns to dirt and heads into a wilderness – where elk, wildcats and bears roam – that's sometimes called 'New Mexico's Yellowstone.'

FR 1950 follows stocked Rio Costilla – a fly-fisher's paradise and a great place to relax – and opens on to national forest with unlimited access to multiday backpacking adventures. The road wends through meadows and forest, with outstanding views of granite peaks. Though it's possible to make this drive in a long day trip from Taos, it's much better to stay overnight, either in one of the four developed campgrounds or in the backcountry.

The route becomes blessedly paved again when you make a left onto US 64 for the drive back to Eagle Nest, where you rejoin the Enchanted Circle.

with feldspar, alpine highlands rising to 13,161ft Wheeler Peak, and rolling steppes carpeted with windswept meadows. Welcome to marmot and elk country.

Most towns on the circuit (with the notable exception of Questa) are relatively young, founded in the 1880s gold rush by mostly Anglo settlers looking for the mother lode. It never quite panned out, however, and the abandoned mines and ghost towns are highlights of the trip.

Those settlers who remained turned to tourism, opening ski resorts at Red River and Angel Fire; knickknack shops and adventure tour companies are probably the other two major employers. Just driving through is a pleasant skim of the surface, but take a little time to explore and you may discover one of the highlights of your trip. Folks who've moved here compare their rare world to the Bermuda Triangle; find out why.

The site www.enchantedcircle.org has information about events in towns along the route. **Taos Vacation Guide** (www.taos vacationguide.com) has a quick guide to sights along the way. Fill your gas tank in Taos, where it's cheaper, and allow at least a full day to make the journey.

QUESTA

Primarily a mining town (the last vestige being the nearby molybdenum mine – it's the stuff used to help harden steel), Questa is also a growing enclave of artists, subsistence farmers and other organic types who are choosing to move off the grid.

The town's roots go back more than 400 years. It was once the northernmost settlement in the Americas, when Spain held sway. Its name comes from a typo when the town was founded in 1842: it was meant to be called 'Cuesta,' meaning 'cliff, large hill,' which would fit its looks perfectly, but thanks to a misspelling it became Questa! The **Artesanos de Questa & Visitor Center** (41 Hwy 38; ☺11am-4pm Mon & Thu-Sat) sells work by local artists, can recommend B&Bs, and will point you toward local artists' studios.

Just northeast of town is the **Latir Peak Wilderness**. Scenic alpine trails that climb high above treeline include a loop that ascends 12,708ft Latir Peak. It's one of the sweetest spots around, perfect for a rewarding night or two of backpacking, or an intense day hike.

Southwest of Questa, the **Wild Rivers Recreation Area** offers access to one of the most impressive stretches of the Rio Grande

gorge, where it confluences with the Red River. A few trails plunge 800 feet down into the canyon while others meander along the mesa. The trek back up from river to rim is substantial, so be prepared with water and snacks. If you don't feel like a hike, drive the scenic 13-mile **Wild Rivers Backcountry Byway** loop, which gives some real visual rewards for a minimal amount of effort. La Junta provides the perfect spot for a picnic, overlooking the twin gorges. The **visitor center** (NM 378; tent sites $5-7, day-use $3; ☺10am-6pm Jun-Aug, reduced hours Sep-May) has information about camping. There are five semideveloped tent campgrounds with 22 spaces accessible by car. Four hiking trails lead to another 16 primitive riverside campsites at the bottom of the canyon.

Grab a bite at the **Questa Café** (2422 Hwy 522; mains $4-9; ☺7am-8:30pm Mon-Sat, to 3pm Sun), an expansive diner beloved for its Frito pie, chile cheese fries (go for red) and homemade deserts.

RED RIVER

The cusp of the 19th and 20th centuries saw a pretty wild populace of gold miners and mountain men here, with saloons and brothels lining Red River's muddy thoroughfares. The early years of this century finds mountain men, and women as well, only this time tricked out in Gore-Tex instead of skins, and looking for a whole different kind of extracurricular activity – for the most part. When the hard-drinking miners' hopes were crushed by the difficulty of processing the ore, those who stayed realized that their outdoor paradise might appeal to flatlanders with income. Indeed.

The town appears as a cluster of cheerfully painted shops and chalets, gleaming in the high desert sun. Red River, ski resort for the masses, is decked out in German-peasant style with an Old West theme – you'd think it wouldn't work, but it does.

Six historic buildings and lots of dilapidated mines have been joined by a ski resort, adventure outfitters, ticky-tacky shops galore and, this being New Mexico, art galleries.

The **Red River Chamber of Commerce** (☎800-348-6444; www.redrivernewmex.com; 100 E Main St; ☺8am-5pm Mon-Fri) publishes a comprehensive visitors guide with great information on events and activities. The town virtually shuts down during the off-season, from mid-March to mid-May.

⚡ Activities

TOP CHOICE Enchanted Forest
SKIING

(☏800-966-9381; www.enchantedforestxc.com; NM 38; adult/teen/child $15/12/7; ⊙9am-4:30pm Nov-Mar) Twenty-three miles of groomed cross-country ski trails and another 12 of snowshoe trails wend though aspen and fir forests at New Mexico's premier Nordic ski area. One section is pet-friendly, and a number of trails lead to scenic viewpoints. You can even stay overnight at one of the backcountry yurts ($75). Special events include the illuminated Christmas Luminaria Tour, Moonlight Ski Tours (the Saturday before a full moon) and Just Desserts Eat & Ski (late February), when you'll ski from stand to stand as area restaurants showcase their sweet stuff.

Red River Ski Area
SKIING

(☏800-331-7669; www.redriverskiarea.com; full-/half-day lift ticket $64/49) Red River gets most of its tourism in the wintertime, when folks flock to this ski area. The resort caters to families and newbies, with packages that include lessons and equipment or half-price weekends during the early season (beginning of December). Snowboarders and skiers alike should check out the terrain park complete with boxes and rails, specifically designed to lure you east from Angel Fire.

Frye's Old Town Shootout
WILD WEST

(Main St; admission free; ⊙4pm Tue, Thu & Sat Jun-Sep; ☺) In the summer, the kids won't want to miss downtown Frye's Old Town Shootout. It celebrates the Second Amendment in all its ten-gallon-hat, buckskin-jacket glory, as good guys try to stop the bad guys from robbing a bank and end up in a faux showdown right in the center of town.

Take NM 578 to the edge of the **Wheeler Peak Wilderness** for challenging but oh-so-worth-it hikes. **Horseshoe Lake Trail** leaves the Ditch Cabin Site for a 12-mile round-trip to the 11,950ft-high lake with good camping and fishing. The trailhead is on FR 58A, off Hwy 578, about 8 miles from Red River.

🛏 Sleeping

Red River has more than 50 RV parks, lodges, B&Bs and hotels, many of which offer package deals with local outfitters and the ski area. Discounts on summer room rates are steeper than the slopes here. There are lots of USFS campgrounds along the road between Questa and Red River, open from the end of May until sometime in September.

Copper King Lodge
LODGE $$

(☏800-727-6210; www.copperkinglodge.com; 307 East River St; r $84-200; ❅🐾) Rough-hewn wood, rustic furnishings and a great backyard make these cabin-style apartments and condos with kitchenettes great value. But it's the hot tub next to the river that seals the deal. Rates vary wildly throughout the year.

Lodge at Red River
INN $$

(☏575-754-6280; www.lodgeatredriver.com; 400 E Main St; r from $85; ❅🐾) First built in the 1940s, the Lodge feels historic and quaint but not old. Rooms are small but comfy, and there's an upstairs lounge with couches and books. Downstairs is **Texas Red's Steakhouse** (mains $10-29), Red River's best beef house, which also serves seafood, lamb, chicken and elk.

🍴 Eating & Drinking

Shotgun Willie's
DINER $

(cnr Main St & Pioneer Rd; mains $6-12; ⊙7am-7pm) Locals love this place serving the ultimate hangover sop-up, artery-clogging breakfast specials of fried eggs, meats and potatoes. The true house specialty is the barbecue, served by the pound. Order the brisket combo.

If you prefer a little line dancing with your barbecue, Red River is a favorite stop on the country and western music circuit. Catch live acts on weekends at venues around town, including the **Motherlode Saloon** next to the Lodge at Red River.

EAGLE NEST

This windswept high-meadow hamlet is a better place to explore the great outdoors if you can't take the tourist overkill of Red River. The tiny **chamber of commerce** (☏575-377-2420, 800-494-9117; www.eaglenest.org; Therma Dr; ⊙10am-4pm Tue-Sat) has reams of information. The town sits on the edge of **Eagle Nest Lake State Park** (www.nmparks .com; day-use per vehicle $5; tent/RV sites $8/14), a 2400-acre lake filled with trout and kokanee salmon. Boat rentals are available at **Eagle Nest Marina** (www.cti-excursions.com; Hwy 64; half-day rentals $80).

Three miles east of Eagle Nest on US 64, **Cimarron Canyon State Park** (www.nm parks.com; day-use per vehicle $5; tent/RV sites $8/14) runs alongside a dramatic 8-mile stretch of the scenic Cimarron River, hued in pine greens and volcanic grays. It also encompasses Horseshoe Mine, beaver ponds, lots of wildlife and fishing, and plenty of hikes.

For sleeping, try the **Laguna Vista Lodge** (☑505-377-6522; www.lagunavistalodge.com; 51 Therma Dr; r $125; ✻🐾). It has spacious rooms with amenities galore, including kitchenettes in the family suites and full kitchens in the lake-facing cabins. The on-site country-style restaurant serves lunch and dinner.

ANGEL FIRE

Some love it, others hate it. But regardless, it remains one of New Mexico's more popular ski resorts. In summer a slew of hippie festivals draw baked refugees from lower elevations. No one can question the beauty of the surrounding mountains and valleys, and famous northern New Mexico light – even if the town looks a bit like time-share condo-land.

As if the 2077ft vertical drop and 450 acres of trails weren't enough, **Angel Fire Resort** (☑800-633-7463; www.angelfireresort .com; NM 434; half-/full-day lift ticket $48/64; ✤) allows snowbiking (on bikes with skis) and snowskating (on skateboards without wheels), along with tamer pursuits like snowshoeing. There's a ski park just for kids, making this one serious winter wonderland.

The resort also boasts a Chris Gunnarson-designed, 400ft-long, competition-quality half-pipe with a wicked 26% grade, plus a couple of terrain parks.

In warmer weather golfers can test their skills on one of the highest-altitude **18-hole courses** (green fees from $45; ☺dawn-dusk May–mid-Oct) in the USA.

🛏 Sleeping & Eating

NM 434, or Mountain View Blvd as it is known in town, is the main drag through Angel Fire and has a couple of places to stay not listed here.

Lodge at Angel Fire   LODGE $$
(☑800-633-7463; www.angelfireresort.com; NM 434; r $100-165; ✻@🐾✤) Families will really dig the ski resort's lodging option. The resort organizes loads of children's activities, especially in summertime, and also offers family-oriented packages. If you don't have the kids, it's still a nice place, with a ski-chalet style. The concierge can arrange everything from golf to horseback riding, plus it's big enough to not feel like kid central if you're not traveling with children. Three on-site restaurants mean you won't go hungry. Multinight stays are often required.

Elkhorn Lodge   LODGE $$
(☑575-377-2811; www.elkhornlodgenm.com; 3377 NM 434; r $100-250; ✻🐾) This place has a central location, decks off all rooms, and suites that sleep six and have kitchenettes. The Equestrian Center gives lessons and trail rides. Rates drop in the off-season.

Willie's Smokehouse & Grill   BARBECUE $$
(Pinewood Plaza, 3453 Mountain View Blvd; mains $9-12; ☺11am-8pm Mon-Sat) Head here for barbecued chicken, beef and pork, but if you want to do like the locals, order the burrito grande ($7); it's huge and delicious.

Roasted Clove   MODERN AMERICAN $$$
(☑575-377-0636; www.roastedclove.com; 48 N Angel Fire Rd; mains $17-35; ☺5-9pm Wed-Mon) This long-established restaurant is everyone's favorite for fine dining: from grilled elk tenderloin to the unique Volcano Ahi Stack, and a list of fine wines.

❶ Getting There & Around

Angel Fire is strung out along the northern terminus of NM 434, just south of the intersection with US 64. Continue on US 64 through the Carson National Forest back to Taos.

MORA VALLEY & NORTHEASTERN NEW MEXICO

East of Santa Fe, the lush Sangre de Cristo Mountains give way to high and vast rolling plains. Dusty grasslands stretch to infinity and further – to Texas. Cattle and dinosaur prints dot a landscape punctuated by volcanic cones. Ranching is an economic mainstay, and on many stretches of road you'll see more cattle than cars. You'll probably see herds of bison.

The Santa Fe Trail, along which pioneer settlers rolled in wagon trains, ran from New Mexico to Missouri. You can still see the wagon ruts in some places off I-25 between Santa Fe and Raton. For a bit of the Old West without a patina of consumer hype, this is the place.

Raton & Around

Though Raton isn't a big tourist destination, the well-preserved town will hold your attention for a short stroll. It was founded with the arrival of the railroad in 1879 and quickly grew into an important railway stop

SCENIC DRIVE: CAPULIN VOLCANO & FOLSOM MAN TERRITORY

A 50-mile loop through the high mountain plains above Raton, the Capulin Volcano and Folsom Man Territory Scenic Drive isn't just another stretch of pavement – it's also a history lesson (with volcanoes, which alone should be enticement enough to excite the kids).

America's most important archaeological discovery was made near the tiny town of Folsom, about 40 miles east of Raton. In 1908, George McJunkin, a local cowboy, noticed some strange bones in Wild Horse Arroyo. Cowboy that he was, he knew that these were no ordinary cattle bones. And so he kept them, suspecting correctly that they were bones from an extinct species of bison. McJunkin spoke of his find to various people, but it wasn't until 1926–28 that the site was properly excavated, first by fossil bone expert Jesse Figgins and then by others.

Until that time, scientists thought that humans had inhabited North America for, at most, 4000 years. With this single find, the facts about the continent's ancient inhabitants had to be completely revised. Subsequent excavations found stone arrowheads in association with extinct bison bones dating from 8000 BC, thus proving that people had lived here for at least that long. These Paleo-Indians became known as Folsom Man.

Recent dating techniques suggest that these artifacts are 10,800 years old, among the oldest discovered on the continent, although it is clear that people have lived in the Americas for even longer.

The area is also known for its volcanoes. Rising 1300ft above the surrounding plains, **Capulin Volcano National Monument** is the easiest to visit. From the **visitor center** (www.nps.gov/cavo; per vehicle $5; ⊙8am-4pm), a 2-mile road winds precariously up the mountain to the crater rim (which is at 8182ft). There, a quarter-mile trail drops into the crater and a mile-long trail follows the rim. The entrance is 3 miles north of Capulin, which is 30 miles east of Raton on Hwy 87.

and mining and ranching center. The small **historic district** along 1st, 2nd and 3rd Sts (between Clark and Rio Grande Aves) harbors over two dozen buildings, including the **Shuler Theater** (131 N 2nd St), with an elaborate European rococo interior. Its foyer is graced with eight murals painted during the New Deal (1930s) by Manville Chapman, depicting the region's history from 1845 to 1895.

The **International Bank** (200 S 2nd St) was originally built in 1929 as the Swastika Hotel. Note the reversed swastika signs (a Native American symbol of good luck) on top. During WWII they were covered with tarp and the hotel changed its name in 1943. For more on local history, visit the **Raton Museum** (www.ratonmuseum.org; 108 S 2nd St; admission free; ⊙10am-4pm Wed-Sat Sep-Apr, 9am-5pm Tue-Sat May-Aug).

Locals rave about the **Oasis Restaurant** (1445 S 2nd St; mains $5-15; ⊙6am-8pm, to 8:30 in summer) for breakfast, burgers and burritos. For the best coffee and wi-fi, find **Enchanted Grounds** (111 Park Ave; ⊙7:30am-4:30pm Tue-Sat; to 2pm Mon; 🛜). There are a string of mom-and-pop motels on 2nd St, while the national chain hotels gather on Hwy 64. But the best place to stay is **Sugarite Canyon State Park** (www.nmparks.com; NM 526; tent/

RV sites $8/14), 10 miles northeast of town in the pretty meadows and forests of the Rocky Mountain foothills. In winter, the 7800ft elevation is perfect for cross-country skiing. In summer, 15 miles of hiking trails begin from a half-mile nature trail. To reach it, take Hwy 72 east out of Raton, then turn north onto Hwy 526; it's signposted about 7 miles north of here.

Forty miles west of Raton is the splendidly sprawling **Vermejo Park Ranch** (☎575-445-3097; www.vermejoparkranch.com; Hwy 555; r per person incl meals $550; @🛜), 920 sq miles of forests and meadows and mesas maintained by Ted Turner as a premier fishing and hunting lodge. If you're not into killing things, guests can also take wildlife-watching and photography tours, or ride a horse through classic Western terrain.

ℹ Information

The **visitor center** (www.raton.info; Clayton Rd; ⊙8am-5pm Mon-Fri) has statewide information.

ℹ Getting There & Away

Raton is right on I-25, 8 miles south of the Colorado border. It is best reached by private vehicle. Note that during winter snowstorms,

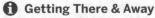

Raton Pass (just north of town) can be shut down, which means you may well be stranded in Raton for a night if you're trying to get to Colorado.

Clayton & Around

Ranches and prairie grasses surround Clayton, a quiet town with a sleepy Western feel on the Texas border. Near the Bravo Dome CO_2 Field (the world's largest natural deposit of carbon dioxide gas), Clayton is where infamous train robber Black Jack Ketchum was caught and hanged in 1901. The **Herzstein Memorial Museum** (☑575-374-2977; Methodist Episcopal Church, 2nd St at Walnut St; admission free; ☺10am-5pm Tue-Sun) tells the story.

If you're moseying about these parts, you'll find over 500 dinosaur footprints of eight different species at **Clayton Lake State Park** (www.nmparks.com; Hwy 370; day-use per vehicle $5, tent/RV sites $8/14), 12 miles northwest of Clayton. The pretty lake is also a good spot for swimming and camping.

Sometimes when you're in the mood for a detour to nowhere, there's nowhere to go. Not true here. Southwest of Clayton, in the most sparsely populated county in New Mexico, the **Kiowa National Grasslands** consist of high-plains ranchland – endless, vast and lonely. Farmed throughout the early 20th century, the soil suffered from poor agricultural techniques and it became useless, essentially blowing away during the dust-bowl years of the 1930s. The most visited section (though visitors are scarce) is **Mills Canyon**, north of Roy (with only a gas station and grocery store). About 10 miles northwest of Roy on Hwy 39, a signposted dirt road heads west another 10 miles to the **Mills Camping Area**, with free primitive camping but no drinking water. The Canadian River forms a small gorge here and the area is quite scenic.

For a meal, a drink, or a good night's sleep you can't do better in these parts than the 1890 **Hotel Eklund** (☑575-374-2551; www.hoteleklund.com; 15 Main St; r from $75; ✾🖨🛜). The new owners, Clayton locals, recently made much needed renovations while staying faithful to the original feel of the inn, including the elegant dining room and the Old West saloon with its beautifully carved bar. Call or check online for rates.

Cimarron

Cimarron has a wild past. It once served as a stop on the Santa Fe Trail, and a hangout for gunslingers, train robbers, desperadoes, lawmen and other Wild West figures like Kit Carson, Buffalo Bill Cody, Annie Oakley, Wyatt Earp, Jesse James and Doc Holliday. The old St James Hotel alone saw the deaths of 26 men within its walls.

Today, Cimarron is a peaceful and serene village with few street signs. Poke around to find what you need, or ask the friendly locals. The town is on Hwy 64, 41 miles southwest of Raton and 54 winding miles east of Taos. The **chamber of commerce** (www.cimarronnm .com; 104 Lincoln St) has an up-to-date website.

Most historic buildings lie south of the Cimarron River on Hwy 21, including the old town plaza, Dold Trading Post, the Santa Fe Trail Inn (which dates to 1854), Schwenk's Gambling Hall, a Wells Fargo Station and the old jail (1872).

Also here is the **St James Hotel** (☑888-376-2664; www.exstjames.com; 617 Collison St; r $70-120; ✾🛜). A saloon since 1873, this well-known place was converted into a hotel in 1880 and renovated 100 years later. It's said to be so haunted that one of the rooms is never rented out. The 10 modern rooms are nice, but it's the authentic period rooms that make this one of the most historic-feeling hotels in New Mexico. Within the hotel, you'll find a decent midrange restaurant and a bar with a pool table.

Get away from it all by booking some time at the **Casa del Gavilan** (☑575-376-2246, 800-428-4526; www.casadelgavilan.com; Hwy 21; r incl breakfast $94-154; 🛜). Set on 225 acres, it's a magnificent Pueblo Revival–style house built around 1908. The four double rooms are decorated with Southwestern antiques and art and come complete with high ceilings, vigas and thick adobe walls; the house is a treat. A two-room guesthouse sleeps up to four people.

Between Cimarron and Casa del Gavilan, Hwy 21 passes through the **Philmont Scout Ranch** (www.philmontscoutranch.org). The largest Boy Scout camp in the country, it spreads out over 137,000 acres along the breathtaking eastern slope of the Sangre de Cristos. While you need to be a Scout to trek the trails, anyone can drop into the **Philmont Museum** (admission free; ☺8am-5pm Mon-Sat) or tour **Villa Philmonte** (☑575-376-1136; suggested donation $5; ☺10:30am & 2:30pm Mon-Fri

MORA VALLEY

This scenic agricultural valley is known throughout northern New Mexico as an enclave where traditional Hispanic ways still remain strong. It was the real-life model for the setting of Frank Waters' novel, *People of the Valley;* it's also one of the poorest nooks in the state, where over 25% of families live below the poverty line. The town of Mora is the hub of the valley, with small communities strung out to the east and west along Hwy 518.

Kids love visiting the **Victory Ranch** (Map p266; ☑575-387-2254; www.victoryranch.com; Hwy 434; adult/child $5/3; ☉10am-4pm, closed Jan-Mar 15; ⊛), 1 mile north of Mora, where you can hand-feed the cute and fluffy herds of alpacas, shop for alpaca wool gifts and even watch a shearing if you time it right (early June).

On Mora's main drag, stop into **Tapetes de Lana Weaving Center** (Map p266; www .tapetesdelana.com; Hwy 518, at Hwy 434; ☉9am-4pm, closed Sat in winter), where you can see handlooms in action, browse for handmade rugs and buy yarns that are spun and dyed on site. In back is one of the few active wool mills in the U.S.; **tours** (per person $5; ☉9am-3pm Mon-Fri) are possible.

Three miles west of Mora on Hwy 518 is the **Cleveland Roller Mill Historical Museum** (Map p266; www.clevelandrollermillmuseum.com; adult/child $2/1; ☉10am-3pm, Sat & Sun summer only), housed in a functional 19th-century flour mill – a beautiful old adobe and stone structure with gears and cogs and pulleys inside.

Six miles east of Mora, the **Salman Ranch** at La Cueva (Map p266; ☑866-281-1515; Hwy 518, at Hwy 442; 10am-4pm Tue-Sun in season; ⊛) is famous for its acres of pesticide-free raspberry fields, where you can pick your own for $5 a pound. Picking season usually runs from mid-August to mid-October (subject to weather). If you're passing by in off-season, you can still stop by the ranch store and take a look at **La Cueva Mill** (Map p266; ☉9am-4pm Thu-Mon Jan-May, to 5pm daily Jun-Dec), a National Historic Site and one of the best-preserved examples of 19th-century industrial adobe buildings.

Getting hungry? Hit **Little Alaska** (Map p266; Hwy 518; mains $5-7; ☉11am-6pm Sun-Thu) in Mora, specializing in barbeque, enchiladas and ice cream. For some of the best tamales ever (plus burgers, burritos and more), served in a friendly local joint, head 6 miles west of Mora to the village of Holman, where you'll find **Casa de Teresa's Tamales** (Map p266; Hwy 518; mains $5-7; ☉8am-5pm Mon-Sat, Sun in summer).

Heading to or from Las Vegas, consider taking Hwy 94, a ridiculously scenic stretch of road, which passes old adobe farmhouses and **Morphy Lake State Park** (Map p266; www.nmparks.com; per vehicle $5, tent/RV sites $8/10), with picnic tables, trout fishing and camping, but no drinking water.

Apr-Oct), the Spanish Mediterranean mansion built in 1927 by Waite Phillips, the oil baron who was Philmont's original benefactor. Pick up outdoor gear and all sorts of Philmont-related souvenirs, some of which are actually pretty cool, at **Tooth of Time Traders** (☉7:30am-6:30pm Jun-Aug, 8am-5pm Sep-May).

Las Vegas & Around

Long before they were discovering carnal pleasures in Las Vegas, NV they were dishing it out in the bordellos of America's original sin city, Las Vegas, NM. Home to the Comanche people for some 10,000 years, the city was established by the Mexican government in 1835, just in time to serve as a stop along the Santa Fe Trail and later the Santa Fe Rail-road. It quickly grew into one of the biggest, baddest boomtowns in the West, and in 1846 the USA took possession of it. Nineteenth-century Las Vegas was a true-blue outlaw town, a place where Billy the Kid held court with his pal Vicente Silva (leader of the Society of Bandits – the roughest, toughest gang in New Mexico) and Doc Holliday owned a saloon (although ultimately his business failed because he kept shooting at the customers).

A century and a half later, there's still the occasional shoot-out, but Las Vegas has grown into a place of faded charm with a lively social swirl (most of it radiating from its two small universities) that feels much more like a small town than New Mexico's third-largest city. More than 900 historic buildings grace its quaint downtown that's served as a Western backdrop for many a Hollywood picture; *Wyatt Earp*, *The Ballad of Gregorio Cortez* and Oscar-winner *No Country for Old Men* are just a few of the movies filmed here. Las Vegas also serves as gateway to the southeastern corner of the Pecos Wilderness (p267) and to Las Vegas National Wildlife Refuge.

◉ Sights & Activities

Hwy 85, or Grand Ave, which runs north–south, parallels the interstate and is the main thoroughfare. The center of the historic district is the Old Town Plaza.

LAS VEGAS

The chamber of commerce publishes walking tours of various historic districts and beautiful neighborhoods surrounding the plaza and Bridge St. Around the historic center, note the lovely Plaza Hotel; it was built in 1880 and is still in use.

FREE City of Las Vegas Museum & Rough Rider Memorial Collection MUSEUM

(727 Grand Ave; ☺10am-4pm Tue-Sat) This small but informative museum chronicles the fabled cavalry unit led by future US president Theodore Roosevelt in the 1808 fight for Cuba. More than one-third of the volunteer force came from New Mexico, and in this museum you'll see their furniture, clothes and military regalia. You can even download stories about the Rough Riders on to your MP3 player.

FREE Santa Fe Trail Interpretive Center MUSEUM

(116 Bridge St; ☺10am-3pm Mon-Sat) At this interpretive center, the local historical society displays an impressive collection of old photos and artifacts from Las Vegas' heyday as a rough-and-tumble trading post on the Santa Fe Trail. Guided tours are available.

AROUND LAS VEGAS

Montezuma HOT SPRING
(Map p266) Five miles northwest of Las Vegas on Hwy 65, this little area is dominated by Montezuma Castle, built in 1886 as a luxury hotel. It's now the United World College of the West. Along the road there, you can soak in a series of natural hot spring pools. Bring a swimsuit and test the water – some are scalding hot! Don't miss the Dwan Light Sanctuary (admission free; ☺6am-10pm) on the school campus, a meditation chamber

where prisms in the walls cast rainbows inside during daylight hours.

Santa Fe National Forest OUTDOORS

(www.fs.fed.us/r3/sfe) Continue past Montezuma, and Hwy 65 will take you to the eastern edge of the forest, where trails lead into the Pecos Wilderness. The most popular day hike in the area starts at El Porvenir campground (tent/RV sites $8, no hookups) and follows trail 223 to the 10,160ft summit of Hermit Peak (Map p266). It's a 10-mile round-trip; sections of the trail switchback steeply and might be a little unnerving if you're prone to vertigo. The peak itself is flat, with amazing views. For more info on hiking, stop into the ranger station, which has topo maps and free trail guides.

FREE Las Vegas National Wildlife Refuge WILDLIFE RESERVE

(Rte 1, ☺dawn-dusk) Five miles southeast of Las Vegas on Hwys 104 and 67, this 14-sq-mile refuge has marshes, woodlands and grasslands to which upwards of 250 bird species have found their way. Visitors can follow a 7-mile drive and walking trails.

Villanueva State Park OUTDOORS

(www.nmparks.com; day-use per vehicle $5, tent/RV sites $8/14) This pretty state park, about 35 miles south of Las Vegas, lies in a red rock canyon on the Rio Pecos valley. A small visitor center and self-guided trails explain the area's history: it was once a main travel route for Native Americans, and in the 1500s, for the Spanish conquistadors. Head south on I-25 for 22 miles, then take Hwy 3 south for 12 miles. A campground is open April to October.

Villanueva & San Miguel HISTORIC SITE

Along Hwy 3 are the Spanish colonial villages of Villanueva and San Miguel (the latter with a fine church built in 1805), surrounded by vineyards belonging to the Madison Winery (www.madisonvineyards.com; Hwy 3; ☺noon-6pm Wed-Sun), which has a tasting room. While here, don't miss La Risa (www.thelarisacafe.com; Hwy 3; mains $8-13; ☺11am-8pm Thu-Sat, 8am-6pm Sun; ☎), a gourmet anomaly in the middle of nowhere, with homemade desserts, breads and pastries.

✹ Festivals & Events

The four-day party surrounding the Fourth of July is a colorful mix of festivities that includes Mexican folk music, dancing and mariachi bands. Other events include the **San Miguel County Fair** on the third weekend in August and a **Harvest Festival**, on the third Saturday of September, with music and food.

🛏 Sleeping

Plaza Hotel   HOTEL $
(☎505-425-3591, 800-328-1882; www.plazahotel-nm.com; 230 Old Town Plaza; r incl breakfast from $79; ❋@🐾) This is Las Vegas' most celebrated and historic lodging, and it's also a decent value. It was opened in 1882 and carefully remodeled a century later; architectural details abound. Recently expanded, it now offers 72 comfortable rooms. Choose between Victorian-style, antique-filled rooms in the original building or bright, monochromatic, kind of sterile rooms in the new adjoining wing.

Sunshine Motel   MOTEL $
(☎505-425-3506; 1201 N Grand Ave; r from $35; ❋) One of the better budget choices on Grand Ave, rooms at this simple motel recently got a fresh coat of paint. It's no-frills but clean, and the owners are friendly.

🍴 Eating

Estella's Café   NEW MEXICAN $
(148 Bridge St; mains $6-12; ⊙11am-3pm Mon-Wed, 11am-8pm Thu-Fri, 10am-3pm Sat) Talk about stepping back in time – this is a classic local diner. Devoted patrons come for the homemade red chile, *menudo* (tripe soup) and scrumptious enchiladas. Owned by the Gonzalez family since 1950, this crowded gem is the best place in town for simple and tasty New Mexican food.

Charlie's Spic & Span Bakery & Café   DINER $
(715 Douglas Ave; mains $7-11; ⊙6:30am-5:30pm Mon-Fri, 7am-5pm Sat, 7am-3pm Sun; 🐾) This Las Vegas institution has listened to the town's gossip for half a century now, and it remains the place for locals to hang out and catch up over a cup of coffee (or vanilla latte) and New Mexican diner fare. Think bean-and-cheese-stuffed *sopaipillas* (fried dough), pancake sandwiches and good old-fashioned hamburgers. Save room for dessert.

World Treasures Traveler's Café   CAFE $
(1814 Plaza St; snacks $3-6; ⊙7am-6:30pm Mon, Tue & Sat, 7am-9pm Wed-Fri, 9am-3pm Sun; 🐾) This coffee-and-sandwich shop housed in a weaving gallery is oriented towards international travelers and locals alike, with wi-fi, a book exchange, board games and couches.

Landmark Grill   AMERICAN $$
(Plaza Hotel; 230 Plaza; mains $7-24; ⊙7am-2pm & 5-9pm) Inside the Plaza Hotel, this is the most upscale restaurant in town, yet it remains down to earth. There's something for almost everyone on the diverse menu, though vegetarians may be limited to salads.

🍷 Drinking & Entertainment

Cafes and coffee shops on Bridge St may have poetry readings or folk music.

Byron T Saloon   BAR
(Plaza Hotel; 230 Old Town Plaza) Within the Plaza Hotel, this bar hosts live jazz, blues and country music on weekends.

Fort Union Drive-In   CINEMA
(☎505-425-9934; 3300 7th St; per car $12; ⊙Fri-Sun May-Sep) One of New Mexico's few remaining drive-in movie theaters lies just north of town and has great views of the surrounding high desert. Call for showtimes.

ℹ Information

Visitor Center (☎800-832-5947; www.lasvegasnewmexico.com; 500 Railroad Ave; ⊙10am-5pm Mon-Fri, 11am-4pm Sat & Sun mid-Oct–Apr, extended hours May–mid-Oct)
Alta Vista Regional Hospital (☎505-426-3500; 104 Legion Dr; ⊙24hr emergency)
Police (☎505-425-7504; 318 Moreno)
Santa Fe National Forest Ranger Station (☎505-425-3534; 1926 7th St; ⊙8am-5pm Mon-Fri)

ℹ Getting There & Around

Las Vegas is located on I-25, 65 miles east of Santa Fe. **Autobuses Americanos** (☎505-425-8387; www.autobusesamericanos.us; 1901 W Grand) stop at Pino's Truck Stop several times a day on their way to Raton and Albuquerque.

Amtrak (☎800-872-7245; www.amtrak.com) operates the *Southwest Chief*, which runs between Chicago and Los Angeles. It stops in Las Vegas daily at 12:40pm westbound, 3:58pm eastbound.

CHACO CANYON & NORTHWESTERN NEW MEXICO

New Mexico's wild northwest is home to wide-open, empty spaces. It is still dubbed 'Indian Country,' and for good reason: huge swaths of land fall under the aegis of the Navajo, Zuni, Acoma, Apache and Laguna tribes. This

313

portion of New Mexico showcases remarkable ancient Indian sites alongside modern, solitary Native American settlements. And when you've had your fill of culture, you can ride a historic narrow-gauge railroad through the mountains, hike around some trippy badlands, or cast for huge trout.

Chama

Eight miles south of the Colorado border, little Chama is tucked into a lush valley that's carved into Rocky Mountain foothills. Native Americans lived and hunted here for centuries, and Spanish farmers settled the Chama River Valley in the mid-1700s, but it was the arrival of the Denver & Rio Grande Railroad in 1880 that really put Chama on the map. Although the railroad closed, the prettiest part still operates as one of the most scenic train trips in the American West.

Sights & Activities

TOP CHOICE **Cumbres & Toltec Scenic Railway**   TRAIN RIDE

(575-756-2151; www.cumbresandtoltec.com; adult/child $91/50; late May–mid-Oct) This railway is both the longest (64 miles) and highest (over the 10,015ft high Cumbres Pass) authentic narrow-gauge steam railroad in the USA. The train runs between Chama and Antonito and is a beautiful trip, through mountains, canyons and high desert. It's at its finest in September and October, when the aspens are ashimmer with golden leaves. Some carriages are fully enclosed, but none are heated, so dress warmly. Whatever you do, make reservations two weeks in advance. There is a snack bar and rest room on board, and the train makes a lunch stop in Osier.

Chama Ski Service   SKIING

(575-756-2492; www.cvn.com/~porters) This place can outfit you with skis and provide information on ski touring. It also provides backcountry touring equipment, including snowshoe rentals.

Cumbres Nordic Adventures   SKIING

(575-756-2746; www.yurtsogood.com) Offers backcountry ski tours in the snowy San Juan Mountains and deluxe backcountry yurt rentals for $109 to $140 per night.

Festivals & Events

Chama has a few events worth dropping in for, including the **Chama Chile Classic Cross-Country Ski Race** (www.chamaski.com; early or mid-February), which attracts hundreds of competitors to 3.1-mile and 6.2-mile races; the **Chama Valley Music Festival** (every Friday and Saturday in July), which features national and international acts; and **Chama Days** (early August), which features a rodeo, firefighters' water fight and chile cook-off.

Sleeping & Eating

Elkhorn Lodge & Café   CABIN $$

(575-756-2105; www.elkhornlodge.net; Hwy 84; r from $80, cabins from $90;) On the banks of the Rio Chama, Elkhorn offers blue-ribbon fly-fishing spots, chuckwagon barbecue dinners and old-time cowboy dances. Choose a simple but spacious motel room in the main log cabin or a freestanding cabin with a kitchenette (especially great for families).

Chama Trails Inn   MOTEL $

(575-756-2156; www.chamatrailsinn.com; 2362 Hwy 17; r from $75;) This is more than another roadside motel, with 16 character-packed rooms with an abundance of

NEW MEXICO CHAMA

SCENIC DRIVE: CHAMA TO TAOS

This nearly 100-mile route makes a fabulous, scenic way to get between Chama and Taos from late May through the first snows in mid-October. The best time for the drive is late September or early October, when the leaves are turning.

From Chama, take Hwy 84/64 about 11 miles south to see the spectacular cliffs in scenic **Brazos Canyon**. Just south of Los Brazos in Los Ojos, don't miss a visit to the famous **Tierra Wools** (575-588-7231, 888-709-0979; www.handweavers.com; 91 Main St; r $65-85), a 100-year-old weaving cooperative in a rustic, century-old building. On weekends, village artisans carry on the Hispanic weaving tradition, with hand-spinning, dyeing and weaving. In addition to a two-bedroom guesthouse, Tierra Wools also offers weaving classes (April to October).

From tiny TA (as Tierra Amarilla is locally know), head east on scenic Hwy 64 over a 10,000ft pass in the Tusas Mountains to Taos, 80 miles away.

handmade Southwestern furniture, local artwork and hand-painted tiles. A few rooms are further warmed with a gas fireplace. A communal hot tub and sauna come in handy after hiking.

Foster Hotel HISTORIC HOTEL $
(☏575-756-2296; www.fosters1881.com; 393 S Terrace Ave; s/d $55/65) If you're looking for local culture, look no further. Built in 1881 as a bordello, the hotel is the only building in Chama that wasn't wiped out by a massive fire in the 1920s. A few of the rooms are said to be so haunted that the doors are locked shut. The others are a bit rough around the edges, so stay for the experience, not for luxury.

**High Country Restaurant
& Saloon** STEAKHOUSE $$
(2289 S Hwy 17; mains $5-23; ◷11am-10pm Mon-Sat, 8am-10pm Sun) This Wild West saloon dishes up burgers, New Mexican food, steak and seafood. It's probably the best all-round eating bet in town.

❶ Getting There & Away

Downtown is 1.5 miles north of the so-called Y-junction of Hwy 84/64 and Hwy 17. Hwy 17 heads north toward Antonito, CO. Hwy 84/64 heads west toward Farmington and Pagosa Springs, CO.

Jicarilla Apache Indian Reservation

The Apache were relatively late arrivals in the Southwest, migrating from the north in the 14th century. This hawkish group was known to use warlike ways to get what they wanted from the more peaceful Pueblo peoples already living here. Indeed, the Zuni Indian word for 'enemy,' *apachu*, led to the Apache's present name. Jicarilla (pronounced hic-a-*ree*-ya) means 'little basket,' reflecting their great skill in basket weaving and other crafts. Apache crafts generally draw visitors to the 1360-sq-mile **reservation** (www.jicarillaonline .com), home to about 3200 people.

Tiny **Dulce**, on Hwy 64 in the northern part of the reservation, is the tribal capital. Unlike at most reservations, alcohol is available. No permits or fees are needed to drive through the reservation, and photography is permitted. The **Little Beaver Celebration**, which includes a rodeo, pow-wow and Spam-carving contest, is held the third weekend of July.

Navajo Dam

Trout are jumpin' and visitors are floating. Navajo Lake, which stretches over 30 miles northeast and across into Colorado, was created by damming the San Juan River. At the base of the dam, there's world-class **trout fishing**. You can fish year-round, but a series of designated zones, each with different regulations, protect the stocks.

The tiny community of Navajo Dam has several outfitters providing equipment, information and guided trips. Talk to the folks at **Born-n-Raised on the San Juan River, Inc** (☏505-632-2194; www.sanjuanriver.com; Hwy 173; half-day/full day from $235/315), based at Abe's Motel & Fly Shop; the guy who started these personalized trips – he now has guides working for him – has been fishing the San Juan since he was a child. The more people in your group, the cheaper the trip.

River floating is also popular around here. Rent boats at the **Navajo Lake Marina** (☏505-632-3245; www.navajomarina.com) or the **Sims Mesa Marina** (☏505-320-0885; www .simsmarina.com) and put in at the Texas Hole parking lot at milepost 12 on Hwy 511. Then lazily float 2.5 miles to Crusher Hole. Ahhh.

The **Enchanted Hideaway Lodge** (☏505-632-2634; www.enchantedhideawaylodge.com; Hwy 173; ste from $65; ✽☏) rents a couple of drift boats ($125 per day). You can also stay the night. It's a friendly and low-key place with several highly recommended and pleasant suites as well as a private house and condos with kitchens and gas grills. The spacious Stone House, with a heavenly outdoor hot tub set in a grove of trees, is particularly nice; fisherfolk on a budget can stay in the cost-effective Fly Room.

Anglers can also try the **Soaring Eagle Lodge** (☏800-866-2719; www.soaringeaglelodge .net; Hwy 173; r incl breakfast from $140; ✽☏), which offers multinight guided fishing tours and half- and full-board options (perfect for those wanting to devote all their waking hours to fishing). Nestled under the cliffs against the river, this beautiful and peaceful place has simple suites with kitchenettes. Try to get one of the units right on the river.

Visit **El Pescador** (Hwy 173; mains $5-12; ◷11am-8pm) for standard, but decent, Mexican and American fare.

There are a few **campgrounds** (www.nm parks.com; tent/RV sites $8/14) along the river. The biggest one is **Pine River**, just past the dam on Hwy 511, with a visitor center and marina. About 10 miles south of the lake, **Cottonwood Campground** (Hwy 511) occupies a lovely spot under the cottonwoods on the river. It has drinking water and toilets but no showers.

Aztec

Although Aztec is primarily on the traveler's map because of the reconstructed Great Kiva at Aztec Ruins, the old downtown has several interesting turn-of-the-19th-century buildings, many on the National Register of Historic Places. The quaint downtown area is along Main St.

An alternative to the bigger and more visited sites like Chaco Culture National Historical Park and Mesa Verde National Park, the 27-acre **Aztec Ruins National Monument** (www.nps.gov /azru; admission $5; ◎8am-5pm Sep-May, to 6pm Jun-Aug) features the largest reconstructed kiva in the country, with an internal diameter of almost 50ft, originally built around AD 1100. Let your imagination wander as you sit inside the Great Kiva. Rangers give early-afternoon talks about ancient architecture, trade routes and astronomy during the summer months.

The small but excellent **Aztec Museum & Pioneer Village** (www.aztecmuseum.org; 125 N Main Ave; admission free; ◎10am-4pm Tue-Sat) features an eclectic collection of historical objects, including telephones, barbershop chairs and a great display of late-19th-century regional photographs. Outside, a small 'pioneer village' has original and replica early buildings, such as a church, jail and bank.

The annual **Aztec Fiesta Days** (first weekend in June) has arts and crafts, food booths and a bonfire during which 'Old Man Gloom' is burned to celebrate the beginning of summer.

If you're into river sports, check out the seconds at **Jack's Plastic Welding** (www .jpwinc.com; 115 S Main Ave) for good deals on slightly imperfect dry bags and Paco Pads (camping mattresses).

Calling itself **Wonderful House** (115 W Aztec Blvd; mains $8-15; ◎11am-9pm Tue-Sun) may be overstating things, but this Chinese restaurant sure is popular. Next door is the best place to stay in Aztec, the **Step Back Inn** (☎505-334-1200; www.stepbackinn.com; 123 W Aztec Blvd; r from $72; ✸☎), with Victorian-style rooms.

If you need more info, try the helpful **visitor center** (☎888-838-9551; www.aztec nm.com; 110 N Ash St; ◎8am-5pm Mon-Fri).

Hwy 516 from Farmington becomes Aztec Blvd in town and continues as Hwy 550, to Durango, Colorado. Turn on to Hwy 173 for Navajo Dam State Park.

Farmington & Around

Well sited for an overnight stay, the region's largest town serves as an OK base for excursions to nearby sites. Farmington itself has nice some parkland on the San Juan River, a quaint downtown and some good trading posts, but most visitors hang around because they're passing through on their way to Monument Valley (on the Arizona–Utah border) or visiting the remote and beautiful Chaco Culture National Historical Park, located about two hours' drive south of Farmington.

◉ Sights & Activities

Shiprock MOUNTAIN
The coolest sight around these parts by far is outside of Farmington proper. Shiprock, a 1700ft-high volcanic plug and a lofty landmark for Anglo pioneers, is also a sacred site to the Navajo. It rises eerily over the landscape west of Farmington. It's certainly visible from Hwy 64, but there are better views from Hwy 491. (Formerly Hwy 666, this stretch of road had a starring role in Oliver Stone's *Natural Born Killers*). Indian Hwy 13, which almost skirts its base, is another good photo-op area.

Salmon Ruin & Heritage Park RUIN
(adult/child $3/1; ◎8am-5pm Mon-Fri, 9am-5pm Sat & Sun) Off of Hwy 64 between Bloomfield and Farmington, the ancient Pueblo that's now a heritage park features a large village built by the Chaco people in the early 1100s. Abandoned, resettled by people from Mesa Verde and again abandoned before 1300, the site also includes the remains of a homestead, petroglyphs, a Navajo hogan and a wickiup (a rough brushwood shelter). Take Hwy 64 east 11 miles toward Bloomfield.

Farmington Museum at Gateway Park MUSEUM
(www.farmingtonmuseum.org; 3041 E Main St; suggested donation $2; ◎8am-5pm Mon-Sat) Farmington itself won't hold your attention for long, but if you need something to do, then this museum is the most worthy pause.

WORTH A TRIP

FINDING NAVAJO RUGS

Sure, Navajo rugs are sold at galleries in a number of New Mexican cities and towns, but why not have a little adventure and look for some near where the best weavers live? About 35 miles south of Shiprock, tucked into the eastern flank of the Chuska Mountains, the villages of Two Grey Hills and Toadlena are renowned as the sources of the finest rugs anywhere in Navajo country. Weavers from this area have largely rejected commercially produced wool and synthetic dyes, preferring the wool of their own sheep in its natural hues. They card white, brown, grey and black hairs together, blending the colors to the desired effect, then they spin and weave the wool – tight – into mesmerizing geometric patterns. The **Toadlena Trading Post** (☑888-420-0005; www.toadlenatradingpost.com), just off Hwy 491 in the town of Newcomb, is the local market where many of these world-class artisans sell their work. Prices range from about $125 to $7000 or more.

Another off-the-beaten-path spot to check out Indian textiles is at the monthly **Crownpoint Navajo Rug Auction** (www.crownpointrugauction.com; Crownpoint), where you can talk to and buy from the weavers directly. Check the website for dates and driving directions.

It mounts national and juried regional art shows, and houses a permanent exhibit on the cultures and history of Farmington.

Bisti Badlands   HIKING
One of the weirdest microenvironments in New Mexico is 38 miles south of Farmington, off Hwy 371. The Bisti Badlands, part of the Bisti/De-Na-Zin Wilderness Area, is an undeveloped realm of multicolored hoodoos, sculpted cliffs and balancing rocks. From the parking area, you have to follow the beaten (but unmaintained) path for at least a mile before getting into the heart of the formations, then just wander as you will, taking care not to damage the fragile geology. The hours just after sunrise and before sunset are most spectacular. Overnight camping is allowed, but you have to haul in all your water. The Farmington **BLM office** (☑505-599-8900; www.nm.blm.gov; 1235 La Plata Hwy; ⊙8am-4:30pm Mon-Fri) has information.

☆ Festivals & Events
Farmington likes to celebrate.

**Invitational Balloon Festival
& Riverfest**   BALLOON
Late May, with music, arts & crafts and food.

Totah Festival   CULTURAL
Labor Day weekend, with juried Native American arts and crafts and a Navajo rug auction.

Northern Navajo Reservation Fair   CULTURAL
Held in Shiprock in early October, featuring a rodeo, powwow and traditional dancing.

This fair is perhaps the most traditional of the large Native American gatherings and begins with the Night Way, a complex Navajo healing ceremony, and the Yei Bei Chei chant, which lasts for several days.

🛏 Sleeping
There's every chain hotel imaginable around the crossroads of Broadway and Scott Ave.

**TOP
CHOICE Kokopelli's Cave**   QUIRKY $$$
(☑505-860-3812; www.bbonline.com/nm/kokopelli; r from $260) For something truly unique, sleep 70ft below the ground in this incredible 1650-sq-ft cave carved from La Plata River sandstone. Equipped with a kitchen stocked for breakfast and lunch, a DVD player with DVDs and a hot tub, this spacious cave dwelling offers magnificent views over the desert and river. The isolation is magnificent. A 3-mile drive on dirt roads and a short hike is required to reach it.

Silver River Adobe Inn B&B   B&B $$
(☑575-325-8219, 800-382-9251; www.silveradobe.com; 3151 W Main St; r $115-175; ❀🐾) Three miles from downtown, this lovely two-room place offers a peaceful respite among the trees on the San Juan River. Fall asleep to the sound of the river, wake to organic blueberry juice and enjoy a morning walk to the prairie-dog village. The additional guesthouse is attractively rustic and is made of adobe and timbers. Advance reservations are required.

✗ Eating & Drinking

Three Rivers Eatery & Brewhouse AMERICAN $$
(101 E Main St; mains $8-26; ⊙11am-10pm;
⊕) Managing to be both trendy *and* kid-friendly, this almost hip spot has good food and its own microbrews. Try the homemade potato skins or artichoke and spinach dip, but keep in mind that the steaks are substantial. Plenty of spiffy sandwiches (like a Thai turkey wrap) and soups (broccoli cheddar) are served at lunchtime.

① Information

Bureau of Land Management (☎505-599-8900; 1235 La Plata Hwy; ⊙7:45am-4pm Mon-Fri) Take Hwy 64 west across La Plata River and head north on La Plata Hwy.

San Juan Regional Medical Center Hospital (☎505-325-5011; 801 W Maple St)

Visitors Bureau (☎505-326-7602; www.farmingtonnm.org; Farmington Museum at Gateway Park, 3041 E Main St; ⊙8am-5pm Mon-Fri)

① Getting There & Away

Greyhound (☎505-325-1009; www.greyhound.com; 126 E Main St) has one or two daily buses to Albuquerque ($53, 3½ hours) and Durango, Colorado ($19, 1½ hours).

Gallup

The mother town on New Mexico's Mother Road seems stuck in time. Settled in 1881, when the railroad came to town, Gallup had her heyday during the road-tripping 1950s, and many of the dilapidated old hotels, pawn shops and billboards, mixed in with today's galleries and Native American

---

DON'T MISS

CHACO CULTURE NATIONAL HISTORICAL PARK & CUBA

Chaco, the center of a culture that extended far beyond the immediate area, was once a carefully engineered network of 30ft-wide roads. Very little of the road system is easily seen today, but about 450 miles have been identified from aerial photos and ground surveys. Clearly, this was a highly organized and integrated culture.

The **park** (per vehicle/bike $8/4; ⊙7am-sunset) contains massive and spectacular Puebloan buildings, evidence of 5000 years of human occupation, set in a remote high desert environment. The largest building, Pueblo Bonito, towers four stories tall and may have had 600 to 800 rooms and kivas. None of Chaco's sites have been reconstructed or restored. If you like isolation and using your imagination, few places compare.

All park routes involve rough and unpaved dirt roads, which can become impassable after heavy rains or snow. Park rangers prefer that visitors enter via Hwy 44/550 on the north side. About 3 miles south of the Nageezi Trading Post on Hwy 44/550 and about 50 miles west of Cuba at mile marker 112.5 on CR 7900, which is paved for 5 miles. Continue on the marked unpaved county road for 16 miles to the park entrance.

Park facilities are minimal – there's no food, gas or supplies. The nearest provisions are along Hwy 44, 21 miles from the **visitor center** (☎505-786-7014; www.nps.gov/chcu; ⊙8am-5pm), where free backcountry hiking permits (no camping) are available. Inquire here about nighttime astronomy programs (April to October).

Ask at the visitor center (where you can also pick up water – it's the only place where water is available) about directions to the **Gallo Campground** (campsites $10), which operates on a first-come, first-served basis. There are no hookups, but toilets, grills and picnic tables are available. Bring your own wood or charcoal.

Mountainous Cuba, about 50 miles from the Chaco turnoff, is your closest hotel bet, with a number of motels catering to Chaco visitors on the town's main street.

For something different try the friendly **Circle A Ranch Hostel** (☎575-289-3350; www.circlearanchhostelry.com; off Hwy 550; dm/r from $25/50; ⊙May–mid-Oct). A real gem, this place is set on 360 beautiful acres in the Nacimiento Mountains. The lovely old adobe lodge, which has exposed beams, grassy grounds, hiking trails and a classic kitchen, is a peaceful and relaxing place to hang out. Choose between private bedrooms (some with quilts and iron bedsteads) and shared bunk rooms. Look for the ranch 5 miles north of Cuba at the end of Los Pinos Rd.

handicraft stores, haven't changed much since the Eisenhower administration.

Just outside the Navajo Reservation, modern-day Gallup is an interesting mix of Anglos and Native Americans; it's not unusual to hear people speaking Navajo on their cell phones while buying groceries at the local Walmart. Gallup's tourism is limited mostly to Route 66 road-trippers and those in search of Native American history. Even with visitors, it's not exactly crowded, and at night it turns downright quiet.

The 'main street of America' (Route 66) runs straight through downtown Gallup's historic district and is lined with pretty, renovated light-red sandstone buildings housing dozens of kitschy souvenir shops and arts and crafts galleries selling Native American wares. Gallup is starting to capitalize on its outdoor attractions, and a growing number of rock climbers and mountain bikers come to challenge their bodies on surrounding sandstone buttes and red mesa tops.

Sights

All roads in downtown Gallup dead-end at Route 66, which runs uninterrupted through town – take Exit 20 or 22 from Hwy 40 to access the best of Route 66 downtown.

Historic District   NEIGHBORHOOD
Gallup's historic district is lined with about 20 structures of historic and architectural interest, built between 1895 and 1938. Most are located along 1st, 2nd and 3rd Sts between Hwy 66 and Hill Ave and are detailed in a brochure found at the visitor center. Among these is the small **Gallup Historical Museum** (📞505-863-1363; 300 W Rte 66; admission by donation; ⊙8:30am-3:30pm Mon-Fri), in the renovated, turn-of-the-19th-century Rex Hotel.

El Morro Theatre   THEATER
(www.elmorrotheatre.com; 207 W Coal Ave; ⊙hours vary). Downtown Gallup's centerpiece is this beautifully restored Spanish Colonial–style theater. Built in 1926 as the town's showcase theatrical house, its renovated interior is comfortably modern. It hosts Saturday movies and children's programs, as well as live theatre, music and dance.

Gallup Cultural Center   CULTURAL BUILDING
(www.southwestindian.com; 218 E Rte 66; ⊙8am-5pm) This cultural center houses a small but well-done museum with Indian art, including excellent collections of both contemporary and old kachina dolls, pottery, sand painting

and weaving. A 10ft-tall bronze sculpture of a Navajo code-talker honors the sacrifices made by many men of the Navajo Reservation in WWII. A tiny theatre screens films about Chaco Canyon and the Four Corners region. In summer, traditional dances are held nightly at 7pm.

Activities

Red Rock Park   OUTDOORS
(⊙8am-4:30pm Mon-Fri, trading post 6:30am-5:30pm) Gallup's gaining a reputation as the kind of outdoors town where you can still get lost on the bike trails should you wish. Read: fewer crowds. Hikers should head 6 miles east of town to beautiful Red Rock State Park. It has a little museum with modern and traditional Indian crafts, a campground and hiking trails. Try the 3-mile round-trip Pyramid Rock trail past amazing rock formations. From the 7487ft summit you can see as far as 50 miles on a clear day.

High Desert Trail System   MOUNTAIN BIKING
Mountain bikers can test their skills on the High Desert Trail System, which offers a variety of terrain for different skill levels, including plenty of sick, slick rock – try the loops off the main trail for the most challenging rides. The trail system is 3 miles north of Gallup on Hwy 491 off the Chico/Gamerco Rd. Pick up maps at the tourist office.

Mentmore Rock Climbing
Area   ROCK CLIMBING
This climbing area lets you challenge yourself with 50 different bolted toprope climbs and some free-climbing areas. Difficulty levels range from 5.0 to 5.13 – grab maps and info at the visitor center. You'll need your own gear and to know what you are doing. Reach the park via Exit 16 off I-40; head north on County Rd 1.

🎉 Festivals & Events

Book accommodations as far ahead as possible during these annual events.

Gallup Inter-Tribal Indian
Ceremonial   CULTURAL
(www.theceremonial.com) Thousands of Native Americans and non-Indian tourists throng the streets of Gallup and the huge amphitheater at Red Rock State Park in early August for the Inter-Tribal Indian Ceremonial Gallup. The 90-year-old tradition includes a professional all-Indian rodeo, beautifully bedecked ceremonial dancers

STRETCH YOUR LEGS: GALLUP MURAL WALK

Home to numerous outdoor murals depicting town life throughout the centuries, Gallup is further proof that New Mexico lives and breathes art. Painted over the last 80 years, the murals grace numerous downtown buildings, including the City Hall. Old and new, they showcase Gallup's tricultural and distinctly Southwestern soul.

Gallup's original murals date back to the 1930s and were created during the Depression as part of President Franklin D Roosevelt's WPA program – an initiative to give out-of-work men jobs building and beautifying towns and parks on railway lines across the country. Some of the original murals can still be seen around town – check out the **McKinley County Courthouse** (213 Coal Ave).

The city takes pride in promoting the outdoor arts, and recently commissioned 12 local artists to paint new murals in central downtown. Nine have been completed and can be viewed on a short mural walk (about 10 blocks total). The murals range from abstract to realist and depict stories of peace and turmoil throughout Gallup's 126-year-old history. Although the murals are large, they don't detract from Gallup's historic aesthetic; rather, they lend a different look to another small, struggling Western town, and take the concept of a public gallery to an entirely different level.

Start your walk at the corner of W Aztec Ave and S 2nd St. The first mural, **Great Gallup** by Paul Newman and Steve Heil, is on the west-facing wall of the City Hall building and uses a variety of media to create a graphic narrative of life in Gallup in panolo. Look for locals on horseback in one, and a blue pick-up truck, so laboriously detailed it resembles an old photograph, in another. The **Gallup Inter-Tribal Indian Ceremonial Mural** by Irving Bahl is our other favorite mural. The last mural on the walk is found on the Ceremonial Building between 2nd and 3rd Sts on Coal Ave. It depicts Native American traditions and sacred Navajo symbols.

from many tribes and a powwow with competitive dancing.

Navajo Nation Fair   CULTURAL
(first weekend in September) While this huge fair is actually just across the Arizona border in nearby Window Rock (p191), it feels like it spills over into Gallup – which is a better place to stay.

Lions Club Rodeo   CULTURAL
In the third week in June, this is the most professional and prestigious of several area rodeos.

Balloon Rally   BALLOON
Almost 200 colorful hot-air balloons take part in demonstrations and competitions at the Balloon Rally at Red Rock State Park in the first weekend in December.

Local Native Americans perform social Indian dances at 7pm nightly from late June to early September at the McKinley County Courthouse.

🛏 Sleeping

Gallup has a number of chain and independent motels just off I-40 – including a Best Western and Holiday Inn. Follow the billboards or Route 66 outside of downtown for a few miles. A number of the motor lodges from the 1950s have gone out of business, but some are still open, a lot of which are pretty dodgy. Rooms cost between $45 and $125, except during Ceremonial week and other big events, when prices can double.

TOP CHOICE El Rancho   HISTORIC HOTEL $$
(☎505-863-9311; www.elranchohotel.com; 1000 E Hwy 66; r from $75; P꩜⊛☺꩜) Hollywood goes Native American–futuristic at Gallup's best, and only, full-service historic lodging option. This town-center hotel with a neon facade was opened in 1937 and quickly became known as the 'home of the movie stars.' Many of the great actors of the '40s and '50s stayed here, including Humphrey Bogart, Katharine Hepburn and John Wayne, when he was filming Westerns in the area. El Rancho features a superb two-story open lobby decorated in rustic old National Park lodge-style. Rooms are big, bright and decorated with eclectic Old West fashions. The hotel has a restaurant and bar, which sometimes hosts bands. If El Rancho is full, the modern motel next door is under the same ownership. It has less interesting rooms that are a bit cheaper.

Red Rock Park Campground CAMPING $
(✆505-722-3839; Churchrock, off Hwy 66; tent/
RV sites $15/18; ☀) Pop your tent up in this
beautiful setting with easy access to tons of
hiking trails. Six miles east of town, it has
showers, flush toilets, drinking water and a
grocery store.

✖ Eating & Drinking

Gallup is a good town to fill up your stomach –
there are a number of restaurants and
watering holes. Many restaurants in Gallup
do not serve liquor, so choose carefully if
having beer with dinner is important.

Coffee House CAFE $
(203 W Coal Ave; mains $4-10; ☉7am-3pm Mon-Fri,
8am-3pm Sat) With local art on the walls and
casual simplicity infusing the space, this is
Gallup's quintessential coffee shop. Soups,
sandwiches and pastries are all good.

El Rancho Restaurant AMERICAN $$
(1000 E Hwy 66; breakfast & lunch mains $6-12, din-
ner mains $8-22; ☉6:30am-10pm; ✦) The menu
here seems to have been created way be-
fore the women's rights movement: most
of the 'leading lady' dishes at the movie-
themed restaurant are of the fruit with
sorbet or cottage cheese variety. Boys, you
can sink your teeth into a hunk of beef –
there are lots of steak and burger choices.
Photos of old-time movie stars plaster the
walls; heavy furniture dots the landscape.
It's straight out of a movie set. The hotel's
49ers Lounge offers drinks in an Old West
setting and live music once a month. Stop
by for the schedule.

Genaro's Café NEW MEXICAN $
(600 W Hill Ave; mains $6-12; ☉10:30am-7:30pm
Tue-Sat) This small, out-of-the-way place
serves large portions of New Mexican food,
but no alcohol. If you like your chile hot,
you'll feel right at home here, just like the
rest of Gallup – this place can get crowded.

Earl's Family Restaurant DINER $$
(1400 E Hwy 66; mains $8-15; ☉6am-9pm Mon-
Sat, 7am-9pm Sun; ✦) The name says it all –
Earl's is a great place to bring the kids.
It has also been serving great green chile
and fried chicken (but no alcohol) since
the late 1940s. And the locals know it; the
fast-food, diner-like place is packed on
weekends. Perhaps you'll even get some
shopping done here: Navajo vendors sell
goods at the eatery to tourists passing
through.

🔒 Shopping

Gallup serves as the Navajo and Zuni
peoples' major trading center, and is arguably the best place in New Mexico for top-
quality goods at fair prices. Many trading
posts are found downtown in the historic
district on Hwy 66.

Just outside of town on the road to Zuni,
seek out **Ellis Tanner Trading Company**
(www.etanner.com; 1980 Hwy 602; ☉8am-7pm
Mon-Sat), run by a fourth-generation local
trader, where you can buy everything from
rugs and jewelry to hardware and groceries.
Be sure to check out the pawn shop.

ℹ Information

Gallup Visitor Information Center (✆505-
727-4440; www.gallupnm.org; 201 E Rt 66;
☉8am-5pm Mon-Fri) Grab a copy of the
full-color, helpful – it has a good map – Gallup
visitors guide, produced annually.
Rehoboth McKinley Christian Hospital
(✆505-863-7000; 1901 Red Rock Dr; ☉24hr
emergency)
Police (✆505-722-2231; 451 State Rd 564)
Post office (950 W Aztec Ave)

ℹ Getting There & Around

The **Greyhound bus station** (✆505-863-3761),
at the Amtrak building next to the cultural
center, has three daily buses to Flagstaff,
AZ ($53, 3½ hours), Albuquerque ($34.50, 2½
hours) and beyond.

Amtrak (✆800-872-7245; www.amtrak.com;
201 E Hwy 66), which has an 'Indian Country
Guide' providing informative narration between
Gallup and Albuquerque, runs an afternoon train
to Albuquerque ($17, 3½ hours) and a daily
evening train to Flagstaff, AZ ($4, 2½ hours).

Zuni Pueblo

This pueblo, 35 miles south of Gallup, is
well known for its jewelry, and you can buy
beautiful pieces at little shops throughout
the town along Hwy 53. If shopping doesn't
interest you, it's still worth driving through
for the sublime sandstone scenery.

In town, past stone houses and beehive-
shaped mud-brick ovens is the massive **Our
Lady of Guadalupe Mission**, featuring
impressive locally painted murals of about
30 life-size kachinas (ancestral spirits). The
church dates from 1629, although it has
been rebuilt twice since then.

The **Ashiwi Awan Museum & Heritage
Center** (Ojo Caliente Rd; admission by donation;

9am-5pm Mon-Fri) displays early photos and other tribal artifacts. The center will also cook traditional meals for groups of 10 or more ($10 per person) with advance reservations. Next door, **Pueblo of Zuni Arts & Crafts** (www.pueblofzuniartsandcrafts.com) sells locally made jewelry, baskets and other crafts.

The most famous ceremony at Zuni is the all-night **Shalak'o ceremonial dance**, held on the last weekend in December. The **Zuni Tribal Fair** (late August) features a powwow, local food, and arts-and-crafts stalls. To participate in any ceremony hosted by the Zuni community, you must attend an orientation; call the tourist office for more information.

The friendly **Inn at Halona** (505-782-4547, 800-752-3278; www.halona.com; Halona Plaza; r from $79), decorated with local Zuni arts and crafts, is the only place to stay on the Pueblo. Since each of the eight pleasant rooms is very different, check out as many as you can to see which fits your fancy. Full breakfasts are served in the flagstone courtyard in the summer. The inn is located behind Halona Plaza, south from Hwy 53 at the only four-way stop in town.

Information is available from the extremely helpful **Zuni Tourism Office** (505-782-7238; www.zunitourism.com; 8am-5.30pm Mon-Fri, 10am-4pm Sat, noon-4pm Sun), which sells photography permits. The office also offers daily tours.

Scenic Route 53

A great alternative way to reach Grants from Gallup is via Scenic Route 53. To get onto Route 53 from I-40 in Gallup, cut south on Hwy 602. Running parallel to I-40, it is home to some of the coolest natural wonders and ancient history in the region. To really experience the out-of-this-world landscape of lava tubes and red arches, traditional old New Mexican towns, volcanic craters and ice caves, you'll need to devote a full day to driving the route and exploring the attractions just off it.

Start your day a half-hour south of Gallup on Hwy 602. Turn east on Hwy 53 to begin. First up is **El Morro National Monument** (www.nps.gov/elmo; adult/child $3/free; 9am-6pm Jun-Aug, 9am-5pm Sep-Oct, 9am-4pm Nov-May), 52 miles southeast of Gallup. Throughout history travelers have left their mark on **Inscription Rock**, which is something like a sandstone guestbook. Well worth a stop, this 200ft outcrop is covered with thousands of carvings, from Pueblo petroglyphs at the top (c 1250) to inscriptions by Spaniard conquistadors and Anglo pioneers. Of the two trails that leave the visitor center, the paved, half-mile loop to Inscription Rock is wheelchair accessible. The unpaved, 2-mile **Mesa Top loop trail** requires a steep climb to the pueblos. Trail access ends one hour before closing.

To camp, visit **El Morro RV Park & Cabins** (505-783-4612; www.elmorro-nm.com; Hwy 53; tent/RV sites $10/25, cabins $79-94;) a mile east of the visitor center with 26 sites and six cabins. Call ahead in the winter since it may be closed from October through April. The on-site **Ancient Way Café** (mains $6-10; 9am-5pm Sun-Thu, 9am-8pm Fri & Sat;) serves home-cooked American, New Mexican and veggie specialties in a rustic dining room. You can wake up in the morning with an espresso and eggs.

Before you reach El Morro, you'll pass through the small town of Ramah. Some of Ramah's Navajo population still practice sheep raising, weaving and other land-based traditions. Most non-Indians are descendents of Mormon settlers. The **Stage Coach Café** (3370 Bond St/Hwy 53; mains $5-15; 7am-9pm Mon-Sat) is a worthy place to eat. It offers great steaks, Mexican food and a giant selection of pies. Service is friendly.

Animal-lovers won't want to miss the **Wild Spirit Wolf Sanctuary** (505-775-3304; www.wildspiritwolfsanctuary.org; 378 Candy Kitchen Rd; tours adult/child $7/4; 10am-4:30pm Tue-Sun;), a 20-mile detour off Hwy 53, southeast of Ramah. Home to rescued captive-born wolves and wolf-dog mixes, the sanctuary offers four interactive walking tours per day, where you walk with the wolves – and get closer than you imagined – that roam the sanctuary's large natural-habitat enclosures. On the quarter-mile walk you'll learn everything you ever wanted to know about wolves – from behavior to what they like to eat to why they make terrible watchdogs. If you want to stay here overnight, primitive **camping** is available for $10 per night, with all the wolf howling you ever wanted to hear included. At the time of research, a newly built guest cabin with two bedrooms, a big loft and full kitchen was about to open; call for rates.

For a few more comforts, head back to Hwy 53 and drive a bit more until you hit **Cimarron Rose** (505-783-4770; www.cimarronrose.com; 689 Oso Ridge Rd; ste $110-185) an eco friendly B&B between Miles 56 and 57. There are three Southwestern-style suites, with tiles, pine walls and hardwood floors (two have kitchens), plus a charming common room. Two goats and a horse organically fertilize Cimarron's perennial gardens, which provide food and shelter for more than 80 species of birds.

Before long, Hwy 53 curves through otherworldly volcanic badlands. **Bandera Ice Cave** (www.icecaves.com; adult/child $10/5; ☺8am-4:30pm), known to Pueblo Indians as Winter Lake, is 25 miles southwest of Grants on Hwy 53. Inside part of a collapsed lava tube, this is a large chunk of ice (tinted green by Arctic algae) that stays frozen year-round – the ice on the cave floor is 20ft thick and temperatures never rise above 31°F (0°C)! Unfortunately, it sounds more interesting than it actually is.

Next up is **El Malpais National Monument** (www.nps.gov/elma). Pronounced el mahl-pie-*ees,* which means 'bad land' in Spanish, the monument consists of almost 200 sq miles of lava flows abutting adjacent sandstone. Five major flows have been identified; the most recent one is pegged at 2000 to 3000 years old. Prehistoric Native Americans may have witnessed the final eruptions since local Indian legends refer to 'rivers of fire.' Scenic Hwy 117 leads modern-day explorers past cinder cones and spatter cones, smooth pahoehoe lava and jagged aa lava, ice caves and a 17-mile-long lava tube system. At the time of research, all lava tube caves were temporarily closed.

El Malpais is a hodgepodge of National Park Service (NPS) land, private land, conservation areas and wilderness areas administered by the Bureau of Land Management (BLM). Each area has different rules and regulations, which change from year to year. The **BLM Ranger Station** (☎505-528-2918; Hwy 117; ☺8:30am-4:30pm), 9 miles south of I-40, has permits and information for the Cibola National Forest. The **El Malpais Information Center** (☎505-783-4774; www.nps.gov/elma; Hwy 53; ☺8:30am-4:30pm), 22 miles southwest of Grants, has permits and information for the lava flows and NPS land. Backcountry camping is allowed, but a free permit is required.

Though the terrain can be difficult, there are several opportunities for hiking through the monument. An interesting but rough hike (wear sturdy footwear) is the 7.5-mile (one way) **Zuni-Acoma Trail**, which leaves

from Hwy 117 about 4 miles south of the ranger station. The trail crosses several lava flows and ends at Hwy 53 on the west side of the monument. Just beyond **La Ventana Natural Arch**, visible from Hwy 117 and 17 miles south of I-40, is the **Narrows Trail**, about 4 miles (one-way). Thirty miles south of I-40 is **Lava Falls**, a 1-mile loop.

County Rd 42 leaves Hwy 117 about 34 miles south of I-40 and meanders for 40 miles through the BLM country on the west side of El Malpais. It passes several craters, caves and lava tubes (reached by signed trails) and emerges at Hwy 53 near Bandera Crater. Since the road is unpaved, you'll want a high-clearance 4WD. Be prepared for poor signage at multiple forks in the road, so drive it during daylight, when you can (hopefully) intuit which turns to make. If you go spelunking, the park service requires each person to carry two sources of light and to wear a hard hat. Take a companion – this is an isolated area.

Grants

Once a booming railway town, and then a booming mining town, today Grants relies on jobs at state prison facilities located nearby. The town seems to be a perpetually shrinking strip on Route 66. There aren't a whole lot of reasons to pull off the interstate, but if you do, check out the **New Mexico Mining Museum** (☎505-287-4802; adult/7-18yr $3/2; ☺9am-4pm Mon-Sat; ♿), which bills itself as the only uranium-mining museum in the world. Hands-on exhibits are made for kids, who will dig descending into the 'Section 26' mine shaft in a metal cage, then exploring the underground mine station.

About 16 miles northeast of Grants looms 11,301ft **Mt Taylor**. Follow Hwy 547 to USFS (US Forestry Service) Rd 239, then USFS Rd 453, to **La Mosca Lookout** at 11,000ft, for views. There are a couple of USFS campgrounds along the way. Otherwise, your best lodging options are the chain hotels around Exit 85 off I-40. For food, go to **El Cafecito** (820 E Santa Fe Ave; mains $3-9; ☺7am-9pm Mon-Fri, to 8pm Sat), easily the most popular place in town.

❶ Information

Cibola National Forest Mount Taylor Ranger Station (☎505-287-8833; 1800 Lobo Canyon Rd; ☺8am-noon & 1-5pm Mon-Fri)

ℹ️ Getting There & Away

Greyhound (✆505-285-6268; www.greyhound
.com) stops at 1700 W Santa Fe Ave and
operates two daily buses to Albuquerque ($25,
1½ hours), Flagstaff, AZ ($58, five hours) and
beyond. Pay the driver in cash or book online.

Acoma Pueblo

Journeying to the top of 'Sky City' is like
journeying into another world. There are
few more dramatic mesa-top locations – the
village sits 7000ft above sea level and 367ft
above the surrounding plateau. It's one of
the oldest continuously inhabited settlements in North America; people have lived
at Acoma since the 11th century. In addition
to a singular history and a dramatic location,
it's also justly famous for its pottery, which is
sold by individual artists on the mesa. There
is a distinction between 'traditional' pottery
(made with clay dug on the reservation) and
'ceramic' pottery (made elsewhere with infe-
rior clay and simply painted by the artist), so
ask the vendor.

Visitors can only go to Sky City on guided
tours, which leave from the **visitor center**
(✆800-747-0181; http://sccc.acomaskycity.org;
tours adult/child $20/12; ☉hourly 10am-3pm
Fri-Sun mid-Oct–mid-Apr, 9am-3:30pm daily mid-
Apr–mid-Oct) at the bottom of the mesa. Note
that between July 10 and July 13 and either
the first or second weekend in October, the
Pueblo is closed to visitors. Though you must
ride the shuttle to the top of the mesa, you
can choose to walk down the rock path to
the visitor center on your own. It's definitely
worth doing this.

Festivals and events include a **Governor's Feast** (February), a harvest dance on
San Esteban Day (September 2) and festivities at the **San Esteban Mission** from December 25 to 28. Photography permits are
included in the ticket price.

The Sky City visitor center is about 13
miles south of I-40 exit 96 (15 miles east of
Grants) or I-40 exit 108 (50 miles west of
Albuquerque).

Sky City Hotel (✆888-759-2489; www.sky
city.com; I-40, exit 102; r from $62; ❋🐾🏊), the
Pueblo's modern casino, has 132 motel-style
rooms and suites dressed up in Southwestern
decor. Amenities include live entertainment,
dining options, room service and a pool.

Laguna Pueblo

From Albuquerque you can zoom along I-40
for 150 miles to the Arizona border in a little
over two hours. But don't. Stop at the Native
American reservation of Laguna, about 40
miles west of Albuquerque or 30 miles east
of Grants. Founded in 1699, it's the youngest of New Mexico's Pueblos and consists of

---

EL CAMINO REAL

El Camino Real de Tierra Adentro – the Royal Road of the Interior Lands – was the Spanish
colonial version of an interstate highway, linking Mexico City to the original capital of New
Mexico at Ohkay Owingeh Pueblo. Later, the trail was extended to Taos. Merchants, soldiers,
missionaries and immigrants followed the route up the Rio Grande Valley, usually covering
about 20 miles a day, stopping at night in *parajes* (inns or campsites) along the way. By
1600, two decades before the Mayflower hit Plymouth Rock, it was already heavily traveled
by Europeans. Along this route, the first horses, sheep, chickens and cows were brought into
what would become the western US. For over 200 years the Camino Real wasn't just the sole
economic and cultural artery connecting it to Colonial Spain – it was the only road into New
Mexico until the Santa Fe Trail reached the area in 1821. This explains why, unlike many other
states with large Latino populations, most Hispanics in New Mexico are and always have
been American citizens. Some families were here before the signing of the Declaration of
Independence, and many were here before New Mexico became part of the US.

Thirty miles south of Socorro at Exit 115 on I-25, **El Camino Real International
Heritage Center** (www.caminorealheritage.org; adult/child $5/free; ☉8:30am-5pm Wed-
Sun) explores the history of the Royal Road with artifacts, bilingual visual displays and
special events. You can drive **El Camino Real de Tierra Adentro National Historic
Trail** through the desolate Jornada del Muerto – the notoriously dry 90-mile stretch that
earned its name by claiming more than a few lives. Coming from the south, start at Exit
32 along I-25; from the north, begin at Exit 139 or 124; see the Heritage Center website
for more details.

six small villages. Since its founders were escaping from the Spaniards and came from many different Pueblos, the Laguna people have diverse ethnic backgrounds.

The imposing stone and adobe **San José Mission** (⊘9am-3pm Mon-Fri), visible from I-40, was completed in 1705 and houses fine examples of early Spanish-influenced religious art. It will beckon you off the interstate.

Main feast days include **San José** (March 19 and September 19), **San Juan** (June 24) and **San Lorenzo** (August 10 and Christmas Eve). Contact **Laguna Pueblo** (☑505-552-6654; www.lagunapueblo.org) for more information.

SILVER CITY & SOUTHWESTERN NEW MEXICO

The Rio Grande Valley unfurls from Albuquerque down to the bubbling hot springs of funky Truth or Consequences and beyond. Before the river hits the Texas line, it feeds one of New Mexico's agricultural treasures: Hatch, the so-called 'chile capital of the world.' East of the river, the desert is so dry it's been known since Spanish times as the Jornada del Muerto – the Journey of Death. Pretty appropriate that this was the area chosen for the Trinity Site, where the first atomic bomb was detonated.

With the exception of Las Cruces, the state's second-largest city, residents in these parts are few and far between. To the west, the rugged Gila National Forest is wild with backcountry adventure, while the Mimbres Valley is rich with archaeological treasures.

Be open to surprises: one of the state's most unique museums is in little Deming, and there are plenty more unexpected finds if you look around.

Socorro

A quiet and amiable layover, Socorro has a downtown with a good mix of buildings dating from the 1800s to the late 20th century. Its standout is a 17th-century mission. Most visitors are birders drawn to the nearby Bosque del Apache refuge.

Socorro means 'help' in Spanish. The town's name supposedly dates to 1598, when Juan de Onate's expedition received help from Pilabo Pueblo (now defunct). The Spaniards built a small church nearby, expanding it into the San Miguel Mission in the 1620s. With the introduction of the railroad in 1880 and the discovery of gold and silver, Socorro became a major mining center and New Mexico's biggest town by the late 1880s. The mining boom went bust in 1893. The New Mexico Institute of Mining and Technology (locally called Tech) offers postgraduate education and advanced research facilities here, and runs a mineral museum.

⊙ Sights & Activities

TOP CHOICE **Bosque Del Apache National Wildlife Refuge** WILDLIFE RESERVE (www.fws.gov/southwest/refuges/newmex/bosque; per vehicle $5; ⊘dawn-dusk) Most travelers flock to Socorro because of its proximity to this refuge. About 8 miles south of town, the refuge protects almost 90 sq miles of fields and marshes, which serve as a major wintering ground for many migratory birds – most notably the very rare and endangered whooping cranes, of which about a dozen winter here. Tens of thousands of snow geese, sandhill cranes and various other waterfowl also roost here, as do bald eagles. The wintering season lasts from late October to early April, but December and January are the peak viewing months and offer the best chance of seeing bald eagles. Upwards of 325 bird species and 135 mammal, reptile and amphibian species have been sighted here. From the **visitor center** (☑575-835-1828; ⊘7:30am-4pm Mon-Fri, 8am-4:30pm Sat & Sun), a 15-mile loop circles the refuge; hiking trails and viewing platforms are easily accessible. To get here leave I-25 at San Antonio (10 miles south of Socorro) and drive 8 miles south on Hwy 1.

San Miguel Mission CHURCH (403 San Miguel Rd) Most of the historic downtown dates to the late 19th century. Pick up the chamber of commerce's walking tour, the highlight of which is the San Miguel Mission, three blocks north of the plaza. Although restored and expanded several times, the mission still retains its colonial feel, and parts of the walls date back to the original building.

✲✲ Festivals & Events

Socorro's **Balloon Rally** in late November is not to be missed; balloonists line up on the street and inflate their balloons prior to a mass ascension. At the **49ers Festival** (third weekend of November), the entire town gets involved in a parade, dancing and gambling, while the **Festival of the Cranes** on the same weekend features special tours of Bosque del Apache, wildlife workshops and arts and crafts.

🛏 Sleeping & Eating

There are budget motels and a few national chains on California St.

Socorro Old Town B&B B&B $$
(📞575-838-2619; www.socorrobandb.com; 114 W Baca St; r $125; 🕸🛜) In the Old Town neighborhood, this B&B has a casual attitude – and entering through the unkempt, screened-in porch, you may wonder if this is just a private home. Inside, that's what it feels like, with easygoing hosts and clean,

comfortable rooms. By the time you read this, they should have wi-fi.

Socorro Springs Brewing Co ITALIAN $$
(www.socorrosprings.com; 1012 N California St; mains $6-24; 🕚11am-9pm) In the mood for a relatively sophisticated experience? Come to this renovated adobe joint for a really good clay-oven pizza, big calzones, decent pasta dishes, lots of salads and homemade soups. At times, the selection of brews can be limited, but whatever they're serving at the moment is smooth and tasty.

Owl Bar Café BURGERS $
(77 Hwy 380; mains $6-15; 🕗8am-8:30pm Mon-Sat) If you can't make it to Hatch (p335) it's worth getting off I-25 at Exit 139 near San

ONLY IN NEW MEXICO: SCENIC ROUTE 60

Highway 60 runs west from Socorro to the Arizona border, cutting past the surreal Sawtooth Mountains, across the vast Plains of San Agustin, and through endless juniper hills. Along the way there are a few spots that are well worth a detour if you've got the time.

About 40 miles west of Socorro, 27 huge antenna dishes (each weighing 230 tons) together comprise a single superpowered telescope – the **Very Large Array Radio Telescope** (VLA; www.nrao.edu; off Hwy 52; admission free; 🕗8:30am-sunset), run by the National Radio Astronomy Observatory. Four miles south of US 60, they move along railroad tracks, reconfiguring the layout as needed to study the outer limits of the known universe. To match the resolving power of the VLA, a regular telescope would have to be 22 miles wide!

The VLA has increased our understanding of black holes, space gases and radio emissions, among other celestial phenomena. And it's had starring and cameo roles in Hollywood films, including *Contact*, *Armageddon* and *Independence Day*. If none of that's enough to interest you, well, they are just unbelievably cool. There's a small museum at the visitor center, where you can take a free, self-guided tour with a window peak into the control building.

Further west on Hwy 60, you'll pass through **Pie Town**. Yes, seriously, a town named after pie. And for good reason. They say you can find the best pies in the universe here (which makes you wonder what they've *really* been doing at the VLA). The **Pie-O-Neer Café** (Hwy 60; 575-772-2711; www.pie-o-neer.com; slices $4.50; 🕗Thu-Mon 11am-4pm summer, Thu-Sun 11am-4pm winter) just might prove their case. The pies are dee-lish, the soups and stews they serve are homemade, and you'll be hard pressed to find another host as welcoming as Kathy Knapp – who advises you to call in advance to make sure they won't run out of pie before you get there! On the 2nd Saturday of September, Pie Town holds its annual **Pie Festival** (www.pietownfestival.com), with baking and eating contests, the crowning of the Pie Queen, wild west gunfight reenactments and horned toad races.

Heading on toward the Arizona border, out in the high desert plains around Quemado, gleams the **Lightning Field** (📞505-898-3336; Quemado; www.diacenter.org/sites/main/lightningfield; adult/child $250/100 Jul-Aug, $150/100 May, Jun, Sep & Oct), an art installation created by Walter de Maria in 1977. Four hundred polished steel poles stand in a giant grid, with each stainless rod about 20ft high – but the actual lengths vary so the tips are all level with each other. During summer monsoons, the poles seem to draw lightning out of hovering thunderheads. The effect is truly electrifying! You can only visit if you stay overnight in the simple on-site cabin, with only six visitors allowed per night. Advance reservations are required. Check out the website for more details.

Hwy 60 can also be reached by heading south along back roads from Zuni Pueblo, Scenic Route 53 and El Malpais.

Antonio for the Owl Bar Café's green chile cheeseburgers. The sandwich is a potent mix of greasy beef, soft bun, sticky cheese, tangy chile, lettuce and tomato. It drips onto the plate in perfect burger fashion.

❶ Information

The **chamber of commerce** (☎575-835-0424; www.socorro-nm.com; 101 Plaza; ☻8am-5pm Mon-Fri, 10am-noon Sat) is helpful.

❶ Getting There & Around

Socorro is on I-25, about 75 miles (a one-hour drive) south of Albuquerque. It is best reached via private vehicle. The historic downtown is small and easily walkable and there is usually plenty of parking.

Truth or Consequences & Around

Home to a growing number of New Age hippies, off-the-grid artists and sustainable-living ecowarriors, kooky Truth or Consequences (T or C) vies for the title of quirkiest little town in New Mexico.

Situated on the banks of the Rio Grande, this high-desert oasis is hot property these days. And we're not just talking about the mineral-rich springs on which it was built and named (T or C was known as Hot Springs until 1950, when the town officially changed its name to match a popular radio game show in an effort to increase tourism). T or C's latest publicity stunt? It's about to become the world's first commercial launch pad to outer space. Yup, you heard us, Richard Branson's Virgin Galactic is set to start blasting tourists off the planet from the nearby spaceport sometime in the near future.

Space travel aside, T or C has also gained a reputation as the place for arty-holistic types to move, drop out and start a different journey – the geothermal energy here is supposedly comparable to Sedona's. The shabby-chic main drag is filled with crystal shops, herbalist offices, yoga studios and a dozen eclectic art galleries and off-the-wall boutiques, the brainchildren of the spiritual seekers, healers, writers and painters who came to find their vision.

❍ Sights & Activities

It won't take you more than an hour, but get your bearings in tiny T or C by strolling down Main St. Each day it seems another art gallery or new herbal-remedy shop opens, and it's fun to just walk and window-shop.

Geronimo Springs Museum   MUSEUM
(211 Main St; adult/student $6/3; ☻9am-5pm Mon-Sat, noon-5pm Sun) An engaging mishmash of exhibits, this museum features minerals, local art and plenty of historical artifacts ranging from prehistoric Mimbres pots to beautifully worked cowboy saddles.

Hot Springs   HOT SPRINGS
For centuries people from these parts, including Geronimo, have bathed in the area's mineral-laden hot springs. Long said to have therapeutic properties, the waters range in temperature from 98°F to 115°F (36°C to 46°C) and have a pH of 7 (neutral).

Most of T or C's hotels and motels double as spas. As there are dozens of places to choose from, have a look at a couple of different spas to find your ideal relaxing spot. Massages and other treatments are usually available. Guests soak free. The swankiest place to take a hot dip by far is **Sierra Grande Lodge & Spa** (☎575-984-6975; www.sierragrande lodge.com; 501 McAdoo St), with mineral baths and a holistic spa offering everything from massage to aromatherapy. The resort charges nonguests $25 for the first person, then $5 for each additional person in the party, to use its mineral springs. For a more casual experience, try **Riverbend Hot Springs**, which offers outdoor tubs by the river. It costs between $10 and $25 per person to soak.

Elephant Butte Lake State Park   LAKE
(www.nmparks.com; I-25; vehicle per day $5, tent/RV sites $8/14). Just 5 miles north of T or C, the state's largest artificial lake (60 sq miles) is an angler's paradise. It's popular with day-trippers from T or C who come for water-skiing, windsurfing and, of course, trophy bass fishing. The nearby **marina** (☎575-744-5567; www.marinadelsur.info) rents tackle and boats (for fishing, pontoon and skiing). Spring and fall are best for fishing; guides will help you get the most out of your time for about $225 to $350 per day (for one to four anglers). Contact professional angler Frank Vilorio, who operates **Fishing Adventures** (☎800-580-8992; www.stripersnewmexico .com) to make sure you take home your fill of striped bass.

✯ Festivals & Events

The **T or C Fiesta**, held the first weekend in May, celebrates the town's 1950 name

SPACEPORT AMERICA: THE ULTIMATE SIDE TRIP

White Sands earned its nickname 'Birthplace of the Race to Space' in 1947, when humanity, courtesy of NASA's Werner von Braun, successfully hurled its first missile out past the stratosphere from among those rolling, pure white dunes. Today, thanks to Virgin Galactic CEO Sir Richard Branson, former Governor Bill Richardson and lots of other pie-in-the-sky visionaries (not to mention state taxpayers who may foot most of the projected $225 million bill), the world's first private spaceport has opened right next door.

Space tourism may well involve a simple 62-mile (straight up) add-on to your New Mexico vacation package. For just $200,000, you can book your flight on *VSS Enterprise* online for a 90-minute ride in a plush cruiser with reclining seats, big windows and a pressurized cabin so you won't need space suits. The vessel is designed by legendary aerospace engineer Bob Rutan, whose *SpaceShipOne* was the first privately funded (by Microsoft cofounder Paul Allen) manned vehicle to reach outer space twice in a row, winning him the $10 million 2004 Ansari X-Prize.

It's not all about tourism, however. Spaceport America has been used by UP Aerospace to launch cheap cargo carriers into low Earth orbit since 2006 and has banked over a million dollars in deposits for future scientific research trips. It's also the new home of the X-Prize competition (the race for private development of reusable spacecraft), as well as other aerospace-themed expositions to be held throughout the year.

Studies estimate that Spaceport America will pump hundreds of millions of dollars annually into the state, particularly in the neighboring towns of Alamogordo and Truth or Consequences. Officials also hope to raise international awareness of New Mexico as a serious high-tech center.

'We might even be able to allow those aliens who landed at Roswell 50 years ago in a UFO a chance to go home,' adds Richard Branson.

change with a rodeo, barbecue, parade and other events. The **Sierra County Fair** (late August) has livestock and agricultural displays, and the **Old Time Fiddlers State Championship** (third weekend in October) features country and western, bluegrass and mariachi music.

🛏️ Sleeping & Eating

When it comes to places to get away, T or C is definitely taking off, but it's still not exactly happening by city standards – it's more of a make-your-own-fun type of place. Don't expect much in the way of nightlife or even lots of eating options. Still, the ones that exist are great. Think about booking ahead in summer.

TOP CHOICE Blackstone

Hotsprings   BOUTIQUE HOTEL **$**
(☎575-894-0894; www.blackstonehotsprings.com; 410 Austin St; r $75-125; ❄🐾) New on the scene, Blackstone embraces the T or C spirit with an upscale wink, decorating each of its seven rooms in the style of a classic TV show, from the *Jetsons* to the *Golden Girls* to *I Love Lucy*. Best part? Each room comes with its own hot spring tub or waterfall. Worst part? If you like sleeping in darkness, a substantial amount of courtyard light seeps into some rooms at night.

Riverbend Hot Springs   BOUTIQUE HOTEL **$**
(☎575-894-7625; www.riverbendhotsprings.com; 100 Austin St; r from $70; ❄🐾) Former hostel Riverbend Hot Springs now offers more traditional motel-style accommodations – no more tipis – from its fantastic perch beside the Rio Grande. Rooms exude a bright, quirky charm, and several units work well for groups. Private hot-spring tubs are available by the hour (guest/nonguest $10/15 for the first hour, then $5/10 per additional hour), as is a public hot spring pool (free for guests; nonguests $10 for the first hour then $5 per hour or $25 per day).

Happy Belly Deli   DELI **$**
(313 N Broadway; mains $2-8; ⏰7am-3pm Mon-Fri, 8am-3pm Sat, 8am-noon Sun) Draws the morning crowd with fresh breakfast burritos.

Café BellaLuca   ITALIAN **$$**
(www.cafebellaluca.com; 303 Jones St; lunch mains $6-15; dinner mains $10-34; ⏰11am-9pm Sun-Thu, to 10pm Fri & Sat) Earns raves for its Italian

WORTH A TRIP

CHLORIDE

In the foothills of the Black Range, tiny Chloride (population 8) was abustle with enough silver miners to support eight saloons at the end of the 19th century. By the end of the 20th century, the town was on the verge of disintegration. Fortunately, the historic buildings are being restored by Don and Dona Edmund, who began renovating the old **Pioneer Store** (☑575-743-2736; www.pioneerstoremuseum.com; ☺10am-4pm) in 1994. Today, this general store from 1880 is a museum with a rich collection of miscellany from Chloride's heyday, including wooden dynamite detonators, farm implements, children's coffins, saddles and explosion-proof telephones used in mines. You can see the **Hanging Tree** to which rowdy drunks were tied until they sobered up; the **Monte Cristo Saloon** (now an artist co-op/gift shop); and a few other buildings in various stages of rehabilitation.

You can stay overnight in the two-bedroom **Harry Pye Cabin** ($100) – Chloride's first building – which has been renovated and modernized. There's even a microwave, since, as Dona puts it, 'I didn't want the women to have to spend their time cooking instead of enjoying the place.' They've got plans to open a cafe during summer.

To get to Chloride from T or C, take I-25 north to exit 83, then take Hwy 52 west.

specialties; pizzas are amazing and the spacious dining room is a pitch-perfect blend of classy and funky.

❶ Information

The **visitor center** (☑575-894-1968; www .truthorconsequenceschamberofcommerce.org; 211 Main St; ☺9am-4:30pm Mon-Fri, 9am-5pm Sat, noon-5pm Sun) and **Gila National Forest Ranger Station** (☑575-894-6677; 1804 N Date St; ☺8am-4:30pm Mon-Fri) have detailed information.

Scenic Route 152

South of T or C, Hwy 152 west leads into mining country and twists over the Black Range to Silver City.

The first community you'll drive through is charming **Hillsboro**, which was revived by local agriculture after mining went bust. Today it's known for its Apple Festival on Labor Day, when fresh-baked apple pies, delicious apple cider, street musicians and arts-and-crafts stalls attract visitors. Grab a bite at the **Hillsboro General Store Café** (100 Main St; mains $8-15; ☺8am-3pm Sun-Fri, 11am-7pm Sat), the historic building that was once the town's dry-goods shop, or at **Lynn Nusom's Kitchen** (602 Main St; mains $5-7; ☺11am-6pm Wed-Sun), run out of a house by an award-winning Southwestern cookbook author. Note that it's cash only. You can stay at the homey **Enchanted Villa B&B** (☑575-895-5686; r from $65; ☎).

Continuing west on Hwy 152, you'll pass the town of **Kingston**, which once had 7000 residents during the silver rush of the 1880s, but today is home to just a handful of folks. The road will soon start to snake around a series of hairpin curves – it's slow going up to 8228ft **Emory Pass**, where a lookout gives expansive views of the Rio Grande basin to the east. Heading down the other side, you'll pass a number of USFS campgrounds.

At **San Lorenzo**, you could turn north on Hwy 35 and head up the Mimbres Valley toward the Gila Cliff Dwellings, or continue west toward Silver City, passing the impossible-to-miss **Santa Rita Chino Open Pit Copper Mine**, which has an observation point on Hwy 152 about 6 miles before it hits Hwy 180. Worked by Indians and Spanish and Anglo settlers, it's the oldest active mine in the Southwest. A staggering 1.5 miles wide, the gaping hole is 1800ft deep and produces 300 million pounds of copper annually.

Silver City & Around

Silver City's streets are dressed with a lovely mishmash of old brick and cast-iron Victorians and thick-walled red adobe buildings, and the place still emits a Wild West air. Billy the Kid spent some of his childhood here, and a few of his haunts can still be found mixed in with the new gourmet coffee shops, quirky galleries and Italian ice-cream parlors gracing its pretty downtown.

Once a rough-and-ready silver hub (and still a copper-mining town), Silver City is now attracting a growing number of adventure addicts who come to work and play in its surrounding great outdoors. With some 15 mountain ranges, four rivers, the cartoonish rock formations in City of Rocks State Parks and the action-packed Gila National Forest all in the vicinity, it's easy to understand the burgeoning love affair between visitors and this classic, Southwestern small town. Plus, as the home to Western New Mexico University, Silver City is infused with a healthy dose of youthful energy.

◉ Sights & Activities

The heart of this gallery-packed Victorian town is encompassed by Bullard, Texas and Arizona Sts between Broadway and 6th St. The former Main St, one block east of Bullard, washed out during a series of massive floods in 1895. Caused by runoff from logged and overgrazed areas north of town, the floods eventually cut 55ft down below the original height of the street. In a stroke of marketing genius, it's now called **Big Ditch Park**.

Western New Mexico University Museum
MUSEUM
(www.wnmu.edu/univ/museum.shtml; 1000 W College Ave; admission free; ⊙9am-4:30pm Mon-Fri, 10am-4pm Sat & Sun) This university museum boasts the world's largest collection of Mimbres pottery, along with exhibits detailing local history, culture and natural history. The gift shop specializes in Mimbres motifs.

Pinos Altos
HISTORIC SITE
Seven miles north of Silver City along Hwy 15 lies Pinos Altos, established in 1859 as a gold-mining town. These days, it's almost a ghost town; its few residents strive to retain the 19th-century flavor of the place. Cruise Main St to see the log-cabin schoolhouse built in 1866, an opera house, a reconstructed fort and an 1870s courthouse. The Buckhorn Saloon is a great place to come for dinner or a beer.

Silver City Museum
MUSEUM
(www.silvercitymuseum.org; 312 W Broadway; suggested donation $3; ⊙9am-4:30pm Tue-Fri, 10am-4pm Sat & Sun) This museum, ensconced in an elegant 1881 Victorian house, displays Mimbres pottery, as well as mining and household artifacts from Silver City's Victorian heyday. Its shop has a good selection of Southwestern books and gifts.

City of Rocks State Park
OUTDOORS
(www.nmparks.com; Hwy 61; day-use $5, tent/RV sites $8/10) Rounded volcanic towers create a cartoonish beauty in nearby City of Rocks State Park. You can camp among the towers in secluded sites with tables and fire pits. A nature trail, drinking water and showers are available. The park is 33 miles southeast of Silver City; take Hwy 180 east to Hwy 61 south.

Gila Hike and Bike
MOUNTAIN BIKING
(☑575-388-3222; www.gilahikeandbike.com; 103 E College Ave; ⊙9am-5:30pm Mon-Fri, 9am-5pm Sat, 10am-4pm Sun) Come here for the scoop on regional single-track routes. Make sure to ask about the gorgeous trail on Signal Peak, a mountain just above the town, with tracks through oaks and ponderosas and views all the way to Mexico. The shop also rents bicycles, snowshoes and camping equipment for exploring the region's outdoor attractions.

🛏 Sleeping

Palace Hotel
HISTORIC HOTEL $
(☑575-388-1811; www.silvercitypalacehotel.com; 106 W Broadway; r from $51; ❄️🀄) This venerable old hotel is the spot to slumber in Silver City. A restored 1882 hostelry, it exudes a low-key, turn-of-the-19th-century charm. The rooms vary from small (with a double bed) to two-room suites (with king- or queen-size beds) outfitted with refrigerators, microwaves, phones and TVs. All have old-fashioned Territorial-style decor.

Gila House Hotel
B&B $$
(☑575-313-7015; www.gilahouse.com; 400 N Arizona St; r from $85; ❄️🀄📶) Housed in an adobe that's over 100 years old, this B&B has preserved its character while upgrading to 21st-century comforts. The common area doubles as one of downtown Silver City's well-regarded art galleries.

KOA
CAMPGROUND $
(☑575-388-3351; www.koa.com; 11824 E Hwy 180; tent/RV sites $24/34, cabins from $47; 📶🀄📶) Five miles east of town, this campground franchise is a clean, child-friendly option with a playground and coin laundry. The 'kamping kabins' are compact but cute and good value, with all the necessities packed into the square wooden rooms. The place fills up in summer, so reserve ahead.

✖ Eating & Drinking

TOP CHOICE **Buckhorn Saloon**   STEAKHOUSE, BAR **$$**
(☑575-538-9911; Main St, Pinos Altos; mains $10-35; ⊙4-10pm Mon-Sat) About 7 miles north of Silver City, this restored adobe eatery offers serious steaks (a house specialty) and seafood amid 1860s Wild West decor – try the buffalo burgers, they're fresh and tasty. Live country music livens up the joint most nights. The crowd ranges from Silver City gallery-owners to hard-core mountain men.

TOP CHOICE **Shevek & Co**   INTERNATIONAL **$$$**
(☑575-534-9168; www.silver-eats.com; 602 N Bullard St; mains $20-30; ⊙5-8:30pm Sun-Tue & Thu, to 9pm Fri & Sat) This delightful eatery is at turns formal, bistro-like and patio-casual – it depends on which room you choose. Sunday brunch is decidedly New York, à la Upper West Side; dinners range from Moroccan to Spanish to Italian, and everything can be ordered tapas-size. Enjoy the excellent selection of beer and wine.

Javalina   CAFE **$**
(201 N Bullard St; pastries from $2; ⊙6am-9pm Mon-Thu, to 10pm Fri & Sat, to 7pm Sun; @ 🛜) This is a great coffee shop, with seating of all sizes and styles, from couches to love seats to wooden chairs. There are board games and reading material and a few computer terminals if you don't have your laptop with you.

Diane's Restaurant & Bakery   AMERICAN **$$**
(☑575-538-8722; 510 N Bullard St; mains $8-25; ⊙11am-2pm & 5-9pm Tue-Fri, 9am-2pm Sat & Sun) Diane's is the local restaurant of choice, especially for weekend breakfasts. If you visit then, order the Hatch Benedict eggs; the house version of the original is doused with the region's beloved chile pepper. Diane's does a busy lunch trade during the week. The romantic appeal is upped at dinner, when there is dim lighting and white linen.

Peace Meal Cooperative   VEGETARIAN **$**
(601 N Bullard St; mains $5-8; ⊙9am-3pm Mon-Sat; ☑) This vegetarian smoothie, sandwich and salad shop is the antidote to the meat overload you might be experiencing by this time on your trip. Try the tofu curry.

ℹ Information

Gila National Forest Ranger Station (☑575-388-8201; www.fs.fed.us/r3/gila; 3005 E Camino Del Bosque; ⊙8am-4:30pm Mon-Fri)
Gila Regional Medical Center (☑575-538-4000; 1313 E 32nd)

Post office (500 N Hudson St)
Visitor center (☑575-538-3785; www.silvercity.org; 201 N Hudson St; ⊙9am-5pm Mon-Fri, 10am-2pm Sat & Sun) Publishes a map with the city's galleries.

ℹ Getting There & Around

Silver City sits just south of the junction of Hwy 180 and Rte 90 and is best reached by private transportation. It's 115 miles from Las Cruces, the closest sizeable junction town. To get here from Las Cruces, head west on US 10 then follow Hwy 180 all the way north to Silver City.

Downtown Silver City is small and walkable and street parking is plentiful. The town also serves as the gateway to the Gila National Forest, just north of town.

Gila National Forest

If you're looking for isolated and undiscovered and a real sense of wildness, 'The Gila' has it in spades. Its 3.3 million acres cover eight mountain ranges, including the Mogollon, Tularosa, Blue and Black. It's here that legendary conservationist Aldo Leopold spearheaded a movement to establish the world's first designated wilderness area, resulting in the creation of the **Gila Wilderness** in 1924; in 1980, the adjacent terrain to the east was also designated as wilderness and named after Leopold.

This is some rugged country, just right for black bears, mountain lions and the reintroduced Mexican grey wolves. Trickling creeks are home to four species of endangered fish, including the Gila trout. In other words, it's ideal for remote and primitive hiking and backpacking. Silver City is the main base for accessing the Gila Wilderness and the interior of the forest, while T or C or Hillsboro are more convenient for reaching the eastern slope of the Black Range.

If you're only up for a day trip, the Gila has a few gems. On the western side of the forest, 65 miles northwest of Silver City off Hwy 180, the **Catwalk** trail follows a suspended metal walkway through narrow Whitewater Canyon. You can see the creek rushing beneath your feet. The catwalk is wheelchair-accessible and great for kids. While some will find it disappointingly short, it offers a painless way to experience a bit of the Gila – and from the end of it you can continue forever into the mountains on dirt trails, if you like. To get here, turn east onto Hwy 174 at Glenwood, where the forest service maintains **Bighorn campground** (admission free; ⊘year-round) with no drinking water or fee.

Just north of Glenwood off of Hwy 180, Hwy 159 twists its way for 9 vertiginous miles on the slowgoing route to **Mogollon**, a semi-ghost town (inaccessible during the winter). Once an important mining town, it's now rather deserted and empty, inhabited by only a few antique and knickknack shops and, as is typical for middle-of-nowhere New Mexico, one proud little restaurant. This one is called the **Purple Onion** (Main St; mains $5-10; ⊘9am-5pm Fri-Sun May-Oct), and it's as good as you'd hope after making the trip.

If you've got a high-clearance 4WD vehicle and a little extra time, you can take one of New Mexico's most scenic roads from the Silver City area right through the heart of the Gila. From Hwy 35 north of Mimbres, **Forest Rd 150** wends through the forest for 60 miles before emerging onto the sweeping Plains of San Agustin. Another option off of Hwy 35 is to drive the rough **Forest Rd 151** to the Aldo Leopold Wilderness boundary, then hike a few miles up to the top of McKnight Mountain, the highest summit in the Black Range.

For serenely comfortable forest slumber, rent one of the five stunningly situated **Casitas de Gila Guesthouse** (☑877-923-4827, www.casitasdegila.com; off Hwy 180, near Cliff; casitas $160-210; ☜), adobe-style casitas set on 90 beautiful acres. Each unit has a fully stocked kitchen, plenty of privacy and one or two bedrooms. Stay a while and the rates drop. There are telescopes, an outdoor hot tub and grills to keep you occupied.

In addition to the Gila National Forest offices in Silver City and T or C, Mimbres' wilderness **ranger station** (☑575-536-2250; Hwy 35; ⊘8am-4:30pm Mon-Fri) is particularly useful.

GILA CLIFF DWELLINGS
Mysterious, relatively isolated and easily accessible, it's easy to imagine how these remarkable cliff dwellings might have looked at the turn of the first century. Here, the influence of the Ancestral Puebloans (p512) on the Mogollon culture is writ large. Take the 1-mile round-trip self-guided trail that climbs 180ft to the dwellings, overlooking a lovely forested canyon. Parts of the trail are steep and involve ladders. The trail begins at the end of Hwy 15, 2 miles beyond the visitor center (www.nps.gov/gicl; admission $3; ⊘8:30am-5pm Jun-Aug, 9am-4pm Sep-May). Between the visitor center and trailhead

are two small **campgrounds** with drinking water, picnic areas and toilets. They're free on a first-come, first-served basis and often fill on summer weekends. A short trail behind the Lower Scorpion Campground leads to pictographs.

GILA HOT SPRINGS
Used by local tribes since ancient times, these springs are 39 miles north of Silver City, within the **Gila Hotsprings Vacation Center** (☑575-536-9551; www.gilahotspringsranch.com; Hwy 15; tent/RV sites $15/20, r from $76; ☒). The pet-friendly resort (dogs can stay for an extra $5 per night) has simple rooms with kitchenettes in a giant red barn-like structure, along with camping sites and an RV park with a spa and showers fed by hot springs. Primitive camping is adjacent to the **hot pools** (hot pools $3, camping & hot pools $4). You can arrange horseback rides, guided fishing and wilderness pack trips and other outfitting services in advance through the center.

Deming & Around
In the least populous of the state's four corners, Deming (founded in 1881 as a railway junction) is popular with retirees. It's surrounded by cotton fields on the northern edge of the Chihuahuan Desert. But if this is a desert, where does all the water come from for the family farms and ranches? It's tapped from the invisible Mimbres River, which disappears underground about 20 miles north of town and emerges in Mexico.

Run by the Luna County Historical Society, the **Deming Luna Mimbres Museum** (☑505-546-2382; 301 S Silver Ave; admission free; ⊘9am-4pm Mon-Sat, 1:30-4pm Sun, closed major holidays) is one of the best regional museums in New Mexico. The display of Mimbres pottery is superb, as is the doll collection – including one rescued from the rubble of Hiroshima. One room is devoted to snapshots of local families, dating back as late as the 1800s. You can see an actual iron lung, and, get this, a braille edition of *Playboy* (maybe someone *was* reading it for the articles).

Fourteen miles southeast of Deming via Hwys 11 and 141, **Rock Hound State Park** (www.nmparks.com; per car $5; tent/RV sites $8/14) is known for the semiprecious or just plain pretty rocks that can be collected here, including jasper, geodes and thunder eggs.

SHAKESPEARE'S GHOSTS

As far as we know, the dusty southwestern corner of New Mexico isn't haunted by any spirits speaking in iambic pentameter, but it is where you'll find **Shakespeare** (www .shakespeareghosttown.com; Hwy 494; 1hr tours adult/child $4/3), 2½ miles south of Lordsburg. One of the best-preserved of any Old West ghost towns (despite having lost its general store in a 1997 fire), it was first established as a stop on the Southern Pacific Mail Line, then grew into a silver mining boom town. Plenty of the West's famous outlaws roosted here at one time or another: 'Curly' Bill Brocius, the killer and rustler, called this home; a young Billy the Kid was a dishwasher at the still-standing Stratford Hotel; Black Jack Ketchum's gang used to come into town to buy supplies.

Shakespeare is open to visitors one weekend a month between July and December, with occasional historical reenactments. Check the website for exact dates.

Don't know what you're looking for? Stop at the **Geolapidary Museum & Rock Shop** (505-546-4021; admission $1; 9am-5pm Thu-Tue), 2 miles before the park entrance. The **Spring Canyon** (8am-4pm Wed-Sun) section of the park has shaded picnic tables and the half-mile Lovers Leap trail.

Kids will like **Lucy's Pasture Donkey Sanctuary** (www.lucyspasture.com; 4745 Franklin Rd; admission free; 10am-5pm), 1.8 miles south of Hwy 549, 17 miles east of Deming on the noninterstate route to Las Cruces. Over 30 donkeys and horses are sheltered here, many after being abused or neglected by their former owners. All are cute and some are talented, like the donkey that can slam dunk a ball through a net. Also on Hwy 549, 3 miles east of Deming, is the tasting room for **St Clair Winery** (www.stclairwinery .com; 9am-6pm Mon-Sat, noon-6pm Sun), New Mexico's largest vintner.

Although it has a good museum and nearby state parks, Deming's big draw is the **Great American Duck Races**, held on the fourth weekend in August. Attracting tens of thousands of visitors, the late summer race is perhaps the most whimsical and popular festival in the state. The main event is the duck races themselves, which offer thousands of dollars in prize money. Anyone can enter for a $10 fee ($5 for kids), which includes 'duck rental.' Other wacky events include the Tortilla Toss (winners toss tortillas over 170ft), Outhouse Races and a Duckling Contest. As if that weren't enough, entertainment ranges from cowboy poets to local musicians, and there's a parade, hot-air balloons and food.

Room rates rise during duck races and the state fair (late September), when you need to make reservations. Probably the best bet in town, the **Grand Motor Inn** (575-546-2632; www.grandmotorinndeming.com; 1721 E Pine St; r from $47;) offers discounts when it's slow. It's a decent spot to sleep, with a grassy inner courtyard and restaurant.

Deming has a handful of good and simple Mexican-American restaurants, along with the brand new **Mimbres Valley Brewery** (www.demingbrew.com; 200 S Gold Ave; mains $6-9; 11am-10pm Sun-Thu, to 11pm Fri & Sat), which does pub food right in a casual local atmosphere.

If you just finished your book, trade it in at **Readers' Cove** (200 S Copper St; 10am-5pm), a fantastic used-book store in a 19th-century adobe house with shelves full of everything from literature to history to pulp.

The **visitor center** (www.demingchamber .com; 800 Pine St; 9am-5pm Mon-Fri, to 3pm Sat;) has tons of local info and wi-fi.

Greyhound (800-231-2222; www.greyhound .com; 300 E Spruce St) runs daily buses to El Paso, TX ($36, 2 hours), Phoenix, AZ ($75, 6 hours), and Las Cruces ($20, 1 hour), along the I-10 corridor.

Las Cruces & Around

At the crossroads of two major highways, I-10 and I-25, Las Cruces makes a great pit stop, once you get past the shock that this rural outpost is actually New Mexico's second-biggest city! Las Cruces and her sister city, Mesilla, sit at the edge of a broad basin beneath the fluted Organ Mountains. There is something special about the combination of bright white sunlight, glassy blue skies, flowering cacti, rippling red mountains and desert lowland landscape found here. The city itself, however, is less than a dream town: sprawling, and beastly hot for a good part of the year.

Las Cruces is an eclectic mix of old and young. The city is home to New Mexico State University (NMSU), whose 15,000-strong student body infuses it with a healthy dose of youthful liveliness, while at the same time its 350 days of sunshine and numerous golf courses are turning it into a popular retirement destination.

Mesilla is the perfect place to lose track of time. Let the centuries slide back as you wander its beautiful historic plaza surrounded by lovely 19th-century buildings adorned with colorful *ristras* (strings of chiles) and shops selling souvenirs ranging from cheap and kitschy to expensive.

◎ Sights

Mesilla NEIGHBORHOOD

(www.oldmesilla.org). Four miles south of Las Cruces is her sister city, Mesilla. Dating back 150 years (and looking pretty much the way it did back then), Mesilla is a charming old adobe town rich in culture and texture. Despite the souvenir shops and tourist-oriented restaurants, the Mesilla Plaza and surrounding blocks remain a step back in time. Wander a few blocks beyond the Plaza to garner the essence of a mid-19th-century Southwestern border town. One highlight of a walk through town is visiting the **San Albino Church** on the plaza. The church, originally built of adobe in 1855, still offers Masses today, both in English and Spanish. Outside the church is a memorial to parishioners who died in combat.

New Mexico Farm & Ranch Heritage Museum MUSEUM

(www.nmfarmandranchmuseum.org; 4100 Dripping Springs Rd; adult/child $5/2; ⊙9am-5pm Mon-Sat, noon-5pm Sun; ⏺) This terrific museum has more than just engaging displays about the agricultural history of the state – it's got livestock! There are daily milking demonstrations and an occasional 'parade of breeds' of cattle, along with stalls of horses, donkeys, sheep and goats. Other demonstrations include blacksmithing (Friday to Sunday), spinning and weaving (Wednesday), and heritage cooking (call for the schedule). You'll understand much more about New Mexican life and culture after a visit here.

Chile Pepper Institute GARDENS

(☎575-646-3028; www.chilepepperinstitute.org; cnr E College Ave & Knox St, Gerald Thomas Hall, room 265; admission by donation; ⊙8am-noon & 1-5pm Mon-Fri) Part of NMSU, the Chile Pepper Institute works with the university's Chile Breeding and Genetics program to promote education and research into New Mexico's flagship food. The institute's office has informative displays (and a chile-themed gift shop), but the real reason to visit is to see the demonstration gardens, filled with a boggling variety of growing chile peppers. The best time to come is just before harvest – July or early August; call in advance to set up a garden tour.

FREE **White Sands Missile Test Center Museum** MUSEUM

(www.wsmr-history.org; Bldg 200, Headquarters Ave; ⊙8am-4pm Mon-Fri, 10am-3pm Sat) Explore New Mexico's military technology history with a visit to this museum, 25 miles east of Las Cruces along Hwy 70. It represents the heart of the White Sands Missile Range, a major military testing site since 1945. There's a missile garden, a real V-2 rocket and a museum with lots of defense-related artifacts. Park outside the Test Center gate and check in at the office before walking to the museum.

Both Mesilla and Las Cruces are home to a burgeoning fine arts and performing arts community, with more than 40 galleries and a number of theatrical and musical production companies scattered around the valley. What's neat about gallery-hopping here is that many of the places double as the artists' studios and most are happy to chat with visitors about their passion. Find out more about arts, theater and dance at the **Branigan Cultural Center** (501 N Main St Mall, Las Cruces; admission free; ⊙9am-4:30pm Mon-Sat). The center also houses the **Museum of Fine Art & Culture** and the **Las Cruces Historical Museum**, with small collections of local art, sculpture, quilts and historic artifacts.

🎉 Festivals & Events

Whole Enchilada Fiesta FOOD

(www.enchiladafiesta.com) In late September, the fiesta is the city's best-known event. It features live music, food booths, arts and crafts, sporting events, a chile cook-off, carnival rides and a parade. It culminates in the cooking of the world's biggest enchilada on Sunday morning.

Southern New Mexico State Fair & Rodeo

CULTURAL

(www.snmstatefair.com) From late September to early October. Features a livestock show, auction, lively rodeo and country-music performances.

International Mariachi Conference

MUSIC

(www.lascrucesmariachi.org) Celebrates this folkloric dance with educational workshops and big-time performances in mid-November.

Fiesta of Our Lady of Guadalupe

RELIGIOUS

This fiesta, held in the nearby Indian village of Tortugas from December 10 to 12, is different. Late into the first night, drummers and masked dancers accompany a statue of Mary in a procession from the church. On the following day, participants climb several miles to Tortugas Mountain for Mass; dancing and ceremonies continue into the night in the village.

🛏 Sleeping

Las Cruces has a dearth of hotel and motel chains. At the cheapest places you can score a room for as little as $45 (plus taxes), the average for a Best Western– or Hampton Inn–style motor lodge with an on-site restaurant and pool is around $80.

TOP CHOICE Lundeen Inn of the Arts

B&B $$

(☑505-526-3326; www.innofthearts.com; 618 S Alameda Blvd, Las Cruces; r incl breakfast $80-125, ste $99-155; P ❄ ⚡) This large, turn-of-the-19th-century Mexican Territorial–style inn is one of the nicest in its genre. The 20 thoughtfully decorated guest rooms are each unique and named for – and decorated in the style of – New Mexico artists. Check out the soaring pressed-tin ceilings in the great room decked out with old-world Jacobean-style furniture and dark wood floors. Owners Linda and Jerry offer the kind of genteel hospitality you don't find much anymore.

Mesón de Mesilla

INN $

(☑575-525-9212; www.mesondemesilla.com; 1803 Ave de Mesilla, Mesilla; r $79-129; ❄ ⚡⚡) This stylish and graceful adobe house has 15 guest rooms with antiques, Southwestern furnishings and modern amenities. A short walk from Mesilla Plaza, the 'boutique-style' house also has a lovely

courtyard; attractive gardens surround the house.

Hotel Encanto de Las Cruces

HOTEL $$

(☑505-522-4300; www.hotelencanto.com; 705 S Telshor Blvd, Las Cruces; r from $99; ❄⚡⚡⚡) This former Hilton is the city's best big hotel. It's got 200 spacious rooms done up in warm Southwestern style. Also on-site is an exercise room, restaurant and lounge.

Royal Host Motel

MOTEL $

(☑575-524-8536; 2146 W Picacho Ave, Las Cruces; r $45-65; ❄⚡⚡⚡⚡) Pets are welcome (extra $10) at this downtown spot with 26 spacious rooms. It's a basic budget motel, but clean and friendly. An on-site restaurant and swimming pool win points.

🍴 Eating

There are two main eating areas: Las Cruces and Mesilla. Located in the heart of the chile capital of the world, this area is home to some of the spiciest Mexican food in the state. Yum.

LAS CRUCES

Nellie's Café

NEW MEXICAN $

(1226 W Hadley Ave; mains $5-8; ⊙8am-2pm Tue-Sun) Without a doubt the favored local Mexican restaurant, Nellie's has been serving homemade burritos, *chile rellenos* and tamales for decades now and has garnered a dedicated following. The slogan here is 'Chile with an Attitude' and the food is deliciously spicy. It's small and humble in decor, but big in taste.

Spirit Winds Coffee Bar

CAFE $

(2260 S Locust; mains $5-15; ⊙7am-7pm Mon-Fri, 7:30am-7pm Sat, 8am-6pm Sun; ⚡) Join the university crowd for excellent cappuccino and gourmet tea, as well as good sandwiches, salads, soups and pastries, and some more substantial dishes come dinner. An eclectic gift and card shop and occasional live entertainment keeps the students, artsy types and business folks coming back.

Cattle Baron

STEAKHOUSE $$

(www.cattlebaron.com; 790 S Telshor Blvd; mains $9-25; ⊙11am-9:30pm Sun-Thu, to 10pm Fri & Sat; ⚡) This small regional chain restaurant serves the best fine steaks in town, cooked to order. If you're not into red meat, don't fear: the Baron offers a wide range of chicken, pasta and seafood options as well as a salad bar and kids' menu. A good spot to bring the tots.

MESILLA

La Posta
NEW MEXICAN $$

(www.laposta-de-mesilla.com; 2410 Calle de San Albino; mains $8-15; ⊙11am-9:30pm) The area's most famous Mexican eatery is housed in an early-19th-century adobe house that predates the founding of Mesilla. A Butterfield stagecoach stop in the 1850s, today's restaurant claims to have the largest collection of tequila in the Southwest (with close to 100 varieties). Order enchiladas or fajitas.

Double Eagle Restaurant
STEAKHOUSE $$$

(✆575-523-6700; www.double-eagle-mesilla.com; 308 Calle de Guadalupe; mains $27-65; ⊙11am-10pm Mon-Sat, noon-9pm Sun) Central courtyards, chandeliers and a 30ft bar are all fabulous assets to this upscale eatery, which serves delicious Continental and Southwestern cuisine in an elegant 19th-century Victorian and Territorial-style setting. The steak is the thing. The restaurant is on the National Register of Historic Places; make sure to walk off lunch with a stroll around the property.

Chope's Bar & Café
NEW MEXICAN $

(Hwy 28, mains $5-10; ⊙11:30am-8:30pm Tue-Sat) About 15 miles south of town and worth every second of the drive, Chope's is a southern New Mexican institution. It isn't anything to look at, but the hot chile will turn you into an addict within minutes. From *chile rellenos* to burritos, you've seen the menu before; you just haven't had it this good. The adjacent bar is loads of fun.

Drinking & Entertainment

The *Bulletin*, is a free weekly published on Thursday, that has up-to-the-minute entertainment information.

El Patio
BAR

(Mesilla Plaza) In an old adobe building, this historic place has been rocking Mesilla since the 1930s. It serves cocktails along with live rock and jazz.

Graham Central Station
THEME BAR

(www.grahamcentralstationlascruces.com; 505 S Main St, Las Cruces; cover $2-20) Join the university students for a night of revelry at this four-in-one club buffet. Listen to big-name country artists, enter a shot-taking contest or dance like you're in Miami at a South Beach–themed lounge under the same roof. It's a bit of a meat market – college kids come here to hook up.

Fountain Theater
CINEMA

(www.mesillavalleyfilm.org; 2469 Calle de Guadalupe, Mesilla; adult/student $7/6) Home of the nonprofit Mesilla Valley Film Society, this theater screens foreign and art films. Check out the website to see what's playing when you're in town.

The American Southwest Theater Company presents plays at the **Hershel Zohn Theater** (http://panam.nmsu.edu/hershelzohn theatre.html; Pan Am Center) on the NMSU campus, while the **Las Cruces Symphony** (www.lascrucessymphony.com) performs at the NMSU Music Center Recital Hall.

ℹ Information

Las Cruces Convention & Visitors Bureau (✆800-343-7827; www.lascrucescvb.org; 211 N Water) Loads of tourist info.

Memorial Medical Center (✆575-522-8641; 2450 S Telshor Blvd, Las Cruces; ⊙24hr emergency)

WORTH A TRIP

HATCH

The town of Hatch, 40 miles north of Las Cruces up I-25, is known as the 'Chile Capital of the World,' sitting at the heart of New Mexico's chile-growing country. New Mexican chiles didn't originate here – most local varieties have centuries-old roots in the northern farming villages around Chimayo and Española – but the earth and irrigation in these parts proved perfect for mass production. Recent harvests have declined sharply, as imported chile is starting to take over the market, but the town still clings to its title. Even if you miss the annual Labor Day Weekend **Chile Festival** (www.hatchchilefest .com; per vehicle $10), just pull off the interstate at Exit 41 and pop into **Sparky's Burgers** (www.sparkysburgers.com; 115 Franklin St; mains $4-10; ⊙10:30am-7pm Thu-Mon, to 7:30 Fri & Sat) for what might be the best green chile cheeseburger in the state (*New Mexico Magazine* thinks so), served with casual pride. Lots of the locals actually order the barbecue – after you smell it, you might too!

Mesilla Visitor Center (☑575-647-9698; www .oldmesilla.org; 2231 Ave de Mesilla; ⊙9:30am-4:30pm Mon-Sat, 11am-3pm Sun)

Police (☑505-526-0795; 217 E Picacho Ave, Las Cruces)

Post office (201 E Las Cruces Ave, Las Cruces)

❶ Getting There & Away

Greyhound (☑575-524-8518; www.greyhound .com; 490 N Valley Dr) has buses traversing the two interstate corridors (I-10 and I-25), as well as buses to Roswell and beyond. **Las Cruces Shuttle Service** (☑800-288-1784; www.lascruces shuttle.com) runs 12 vans daily to the El Paso International Airport ($45 one-way, $15 to $25 for each additional person) and vans to Deming, Silver City and other destinations on request.

CARLSBAD CAVERNS & SOUTHEASTERN NEW MEXICO

Two of New Mexico's greatest natural wonders are tucked down here in the arid southeast: mesmerizing White Sands National Monument and magnificent Carlsbad Caverns National Park. This region also swirls with some of the state's most enduring legends: aliens in Roswell, Billy the Kid in Lincoln, and Smokey Bear in Capitan. Most of the lowlands are covered by hot, rugged Chihuahuan Desert – which once used to be under the ocean – but you can always escape to the cooler climes around the popular forested resort towns of Cloudcroft or Ruidoso.

White Sands National Monument

Undulating through the Tularosa Basin like something straight out of a dream, these ethereal dunes are a highlight of any trip to New Mexico and a must on every landscape photographer's itinerary. Try to time a visit to **White Sands** (www.nps.gov /whsa; adult/under 16yr $3/free; ⊙7am-9pm Jun-Aug, 7am-sunset Sep-May) with sunrise or sunset (or both), when it's at its most magical. From the **visitor center** drive the 16-mile scenic loop into the heart of the dazzlingly white sea of sand that is the world's largest gypsum dune field, covering 275 sq miles. Along the way, get out of the car and romp around a bit. Hike the **Alkali Flat**, a 4.5-mile (round-trip) backcountry trail through the heart of the dunes, or the simple 1-mile loop nature trail. Don't forget your sunglasses – the sand is as bright as snow!

Spring for a $15 plastic saucer at the visitor center gift shop then sled one of the back dunes. It's fun, and you can sell the disc back for $5 at day's end (no rentals to avoid liability). Check the park calendar for sunset strolls and occasional moonlight bicycle rides (adult/child $5/2.50), the latter best reserved in advance.

Backcountry campsites, with no water or toilet facilities, are a mile from the scenic drive. Pick up one of the limited permits ($3, issued first-come, first-served) in person at the visitor center at least one hour before sunset.

Alamogordo & Around

Despite a dearth of amenities, Alamogordo (Spanish for 'fat cottonwood tree') is the center of one of the most historically important space and atomic research programs. Most of the sights in town are kid-oriented, but adults who are young at heart will enjoy them too. You can also check out the tiny art outpost of La Luz or the fine vineyard in equally small Tularosa, both nearby towns.

White Sands Blvd (WSB; also called Hwy 54, 70 or 82) is the main drag through town and runs north–south. Addresses on North White Sands Blvd correspond to numbered cross streets (thus 1310 N WSB is just north of 13th); addresses on South WSB are one block south of 1st.

◉ Sights & Activities

New Mexico Museum of Space History MUSEUM (www.nmspacemuseum.org; Hwy 2001; adult/child $6/4; ⊙9am-5pm; ♿). The most important museum is the four-story New Mexico Museum of Space History. Nicknamed 'the golden cube,' it looms over the town and has excellent exhibits on space research and flight. Its **Tombaugh IMAX Theater & Planetarium** (adult/child $6/4.50; ♿) shows outstanding films on everything from the Grand Canyon to the dark side of the moon, as well as laser shows and multimedia presentations on a huge wraparound screen. If your child has ever been interested in space travel, the museum runs a summer **Space Academy** (per day/week $150/$475; ♿) for kids aged

THREE RIVERS PETROGLYPH NATIONAL RECREATION AREA

The uncrowded **Three Rivers Petroglyph NRA** (☎575-525-4300; County Rd B30, off Hwy 54; per car $2, tent/RV sites $2/10; ⊗8am-7pm Apr-Oct, to 5pm Nov-Mar) showcases over 21,000 petroglyphs inscribed 1000 years ago by the Jornada Mogollon people. The 1-mile hike through mesquite and cacti offers good views of the Sacramento Mountains to the east and White Sands Monument on the horizon. Nearby is a pit house in a partially excavated village. There are six camping shelters with barbecue grills (free), restrooms, water and two hookups for RVs. The **BLM** (☎575-525-4300; Marquess St, off Valley Dr) in Las Cruces has details. Pets are allowed in the campground but are banned from the trails.

The site is 27 miles north of Alamogordo on Hwy 54, and then 5 miles east on a signed road. If you want to rough it for the night, a dirt road continues beyond the petroglyphs for about 10 miles to the Lincoln National Forest, where you'll find **Three Rivers Campground**.

5 through 17. The education-based science program includes some pretty cool features, including flight training in a cockpit simulator, field trips and other hands-on experiments. The week-long sleepover camp is great if you have the time, but even if you're just in town for a few days, it's worth checking out the day camp. So far they plan to keep this running, despite the end of the manned space program...

Toy Train Depot
MUSEUM
(www.toytraindepot.homestead.com; 1991 N White Sands Blvd; admission $4; ⊗noon-4:30pm Wed-Sun; ⛟) Railroad buffs and kids flock to the Toy Train Depot, an 1898 railway depot with five rooms of train memorabilia and toy trains, and a 2.5-mile narrow-gauge minitrain you can ride through Alameda Park.

Alameda Park & Zoo
ZOO
(1021 N White Sands Blvd; adult/3-11yr $2.50/1.50; ⊗9am-5pm; ⛟) Established in 1898 as a diversion for railway travelers, this is the oldest zoo west of the Mississippi. Small but well run, it features exotics from around the world, among them the endangered Mexican gray wolf.

FREE Alamogordo Museum of History
MUSEUM
(www.alamogordohistorymuseum.com; 1301 N White Sands Blvd; ⊗10am-4pm Mon-Fri, 10am-3pm Sat, 1-4pm Sun) This small and thoroughly local museum focuses on Mescalero Indians and the mining, railroad and logging industries. The museum's most cherished holding is a 47-star US flag, one of only a handful that exist because Arizona joined the USA just six weeks after New Mexico did.

La Luz & Tularosa
NEIGHBORHOODS
Alamogordo's most attractive attractions lie outside the city limits. Head 4 miles north on Hwy 54 to the tiny art enclave of La Luz. Home to a motley crew of painters, writers and craftspeople who share a passion for creating artwork and living off the land, this wild outpost remains untouched by commercial tourism and is well worth a browse.

Continue north another 10 miles to the attractive village of Tularosa. It's dominated by the 1869 St Francis de Paula Church, built in a simple New Mexican style. **Tularosa Vineyards** (☎575-585-2260; www.tularosavineyards.com; Hwy 54; ⊗9am-5pm Mon-Sat, noon-5pm Sun) is a friendly and picturesque winery about 2 miles north of Tularosa. It offers daily tastings and tours by appointment

🛏 Sleeping & Eating

This town doesn't have much in the way of creativity; besides the places listed here, there are many other chains scattered along White Sands Blvd. There's free dispersed camping off of Hwy 82, east of Alamogordo on the way to Cloudcroft.

Oliver Lee State Park
CAMPGROUND $
(www.nmparks.com; 409 Dog Canyon Rd; tent/RV sites $8/14) Twelve miles south of Alamogordo, this park is set in a spring-fed canyon where you might see ferns and flowers growing in the desert. From the campground, **Dog Canyon National Recreational Trail** climbs some 2000 feet over 5.5 miles, featuring terrific views of the Tularosa Basin.

THE BLAST HEARD 'ROUND THE WORLD

On just two days a year (the first Saturday in April and October), the public is permitted to tour the **Trinity Site** (per car $25), 35 miles west of Carrizozo, where the first atomic bomb was detonated on July 16, 1945. The eerie tour includes the base camp, the McDonald Ranch house where the plutonium core for the bomb was assembled, and ground zero itself. The test was carried out above ground and resulted in a quarter-mile-wide crater and an 8-mile-high cloud mushrooming above the desert. The radiation level of the site is 'only' 10 times greater than the region's background level; a one-hour visit to ground zero will result in an exposure of one-half to one milliroentgen (mrem) – two to four times the estimated exposure of a typical adult on an average day in the USA. Trinitite, a green, glassy substance resulting from the blast, is still radioactive, still scattered around and still must not be touched. Resist the urge to add it to your road-trip rock collection. This desolate area is fittingly called **Jornada del Muerto** (Journey of Death) and is overshadowed by 8638ft **Oscura Peak** (Darkness Peak on state maps). Travel to Trinity is permitted only as part of an official convoy. Call the **Alamogordo Chamber of Commerce** (☑505-437-6120; www.alamogordo.com) in advance for information.

Best Western Desert Aire Motor Inn
HOTEL **$$**

(☑575-437-2110; www.bestwestern.com; 1021 S White Sands Blvd; r from $78; ☀@☎☒⁂) Recently remodeled, this chain hotel has standard-issue rooms and suites (some with kitchenettes), along with a sauna and whirlpool. In summer, the swimming pool is a cool sanctuary.

Satellite Inn
MOTEL **$**

(☑575-437-8454; www.satelliteinn.com; 2224 N White Sands Blvd; r $44; ☀☎☒) An old-school Alamogordo independent with simple and clean double rooms that have microwave and refrigerator. Rooms are basic, but it's a bit more personal-feeling than your typical roadside motel.

Pizza Patio & Pub
ITALIAN **$$**

(2203 E 1st St; mains $7-15; ⊙11am-8pm Mon-Thu & Sat; til 9pm Fri; ⚐) This is the best something-for-everyone place in Alamogordo, with an outdoor patio and casual indoor dining room. Pizzas and pastas are good, salads are big, and pitchers or pints of beer are on tap.

Margo's
NEW MEXICAN **$**

(504 E 1st St; mains $6-15; ⊙10:30am-9pm Mon-Sat, 11am-8:30pm Sun) There's not much to look at inside, but the New Mexican cuisine is solid and the prices are fair. Family-owned since the early 1980s, Margo's has a robust and tasty combo plate.

Stella Vita
AMERICAN **$$$**

(www.stellavitarestaurant.com; 902 New York St; lunch mains $9-11, dinner mains $20-32; ⊙11am-2pm Mon-Fri, 5-9pm Tue-Sat) This is Alamogordo's most upscale eatery, where you can dine from a meaty menu in an atmosphere of faux elegance under the gaze of a large cow skull. The staff is very friendly, but the light jazz background music is pretty irritating – maybe they'll turn it down for you...

❶ Information

Hospital (☑575-439-6100; 2669 N Scenic Dr; ⊙24hr emergency)

Lincoln USFS National Forest Ranger Station (☑575-434-7200; 1101 New York Ave; ⊙7:30am-4:30pm Mon-Fri)

Police (☑575-439-4300; 700 Virginia Ave)

Post office (30 E 12th St)

Visitor center (☑575-437-6120; www.alamogordo.com; 1301 N White Sands Blvd; ⊙8am-5pm Mon-Fri, 9am-5pm Sat & Sun; ☎)

❶ Getting There & Around

Greyhound (☑800-231-2222; www.greyhound.com; 601 N White Sands Blvd) has daily buses to Albuquerque ($65, 4½ hours), Roswell ($43, 2½ hours), Carlsbad ($77, 4½ hours) and El Paso, TX ($34, 2½ hours). The **Alamo El Paso Shuttle** (☑575-437-1472; Best Western Desert Aire Motor Inn) has four buses daily to the El Paso, TX International Airport ($48, 1½ hours).

Cloudcroft & Around

Nestled high in the mountains, Cloudcroft is pleasant year-round. In winter there's snow tubing and snowmobiling across powder-soaked meadows. In summer, at nearly 2 miles high, Cloudcroft offers refreshing respite from the surrounding desert heat, plus awesome hiking and biking. The town itself is a quaint place to wander, with some early-19th-century buildings, a low-key mountain vibe and one of the top historic resorts in the Southwest. But where Cloudcroft really shines is the great outdoors, and most people visit to play in the surrounding peaks and forests.

◎ Sights

Hwy 82 is the main drag through town; most places are on Hwy 82 or within a few blocks of it.

Sacramento Peak Observatory OBSERVATORY (☑575-434-7000; ⊙visitor center 9am-5pm, closed Feb) One of the world's largest solar observatories is near Sunspot, 20 miles south of Cloudcroft. Though it's primarily for scientists, tourists can take **self-guided tours** (⊙dawn-dusk, year-round) or **guided tours** (adult/child $3/free; ⊙2pm, summer only). The drive to Sunspot, along the Sunspot Scenic Byway, is a high and beautiful one, with the mountains to the east and White Sands National Monument to the west. From Cloudcroft, take Hwy 130 to Hwy 6563. Fill your tank in Cloudcroft before making the drive.

✦ Activities

Hiking

Hiking is popular here from April to November; outings range from short hikes close to town to overnight backpacking trips. Although trails are often fairly flat, the 9000ft elevation can make for some strenuous hiking if you are not acclimatized. The most popular day hike is the 2.6-mile **Osha Loop Trail**, which leaves Hwy 82 from a small parking area 1 mile west of Cloudcroft. The **Willie White/ Wills Canyon Trails** loop through open meadows, with a good chance of seeing elk. The ranger station has tons of info, free trail maps and detailed topo maps for sale.

Golf

The Lodge Resort has a beautiful 18-hole **golf course** (☑575-682-2098; 9/18 holes from $26/46) that is one of the highest and oldest in the USA. In the winter, the course is groomed for cross-country skiing. The Lodge also provides guided snowmobile and horse-drawn sleigh rides.

Mountain Biking

Trails in the Sacramento Mountains offer great mountain biking. **High Altitude** (☑575-682-1229; 310 Burro St; ⊙10am-5:30pm Mon-Thu, to 6pm Fri & Sat; to 5pm Sun) rents bikes and points you in the right direction.

Skiing

In winter, grab the lift up and ski, snowboard or race an inner tube (weekends only) down the hill at **Ski Cloudcroft** (www.skicloudcroft .com; 1920 Hwy 82; all-day ski/tube $35/20; ⊙9am-4pm Nov-Mar). The hill is family oriented, and you can say you've skied the southernmost run in the U.S.

★☆ Festivals & Events

Autumn is celebrated with **Oktoberfest** (first weekend of October) and summer is celebrated with an annual **Cherry Festival** on the third Sunday in June. The nearby hills between Cloudcroft and Alamogordo are rife with cherry orchards.

⊨ Sleeping & Eating

Cloudcroft is blessed with some heavenly choices. There are several USFS campgrounds in the area, open only in summer.

╓TOP╖
║CHOICE║ Lodge Resort & Spa LODGE $$ (☑575-682-2566; www.thelodgeresort.com; 1 Corona Pl; r from $79; @�🕸) One of the best historic hotels in the Southwest, this place is reason enough to visit Cloudcroft. A grand old Lodge built in 1899 as a vacation getaway for railroad employees, today it is a full-scale resort, with a pampering spa with sauna – where treatments are tailored to the customer – a wonderful restaurant, a golf course and beautifully maintained grounds. Try to get a room in the main Bavarian-style hotel; these are furnished with period and Victorian pieces. Pavilion rooms are a few blocks away in a separate, less attractive building.

╓TOP╖
║CHOICE║ Cloudcroft Mountain Park Hostel HOSTEL $ (☑575-682-0555; www.cloudcrofthostel.com; 1049 Hwy 82; dm $17, r with shared bath $30-50; 🕸) Six miles west of Cloudcroft, this hostel is the best lodging deal around. Situated on 28 wooded acres, you can follow deer tracks to views of White Sands and the Tularosa Basin, or just enjoy the forest. Entire families can fit in the large rooms, which are simple but tidy. Shared bathrooms are clean, there's

a fully equipped kitchen, and coffee and tea are provided. The common area is a great place to swap stories with other travelers.

Rebecca's
AMERICAN $$

(⌨575-682-3131; Lodge Resort & Spa, 1 Corona Pl; mains $8-36; ⊙7-10am, 11:30am-2pm & 5:30-9pm) Stop by Rebecca's, at the Lodge, for the long-standing favorite Sunday brunch. It's equally good for other meals – this is by far the best food in Cloudcroft. Kick back on the outside deck, have a beer and check out the spectacular views, then head inside for an elegant meal from a menu that includes everything from steak tenderloin to cheese enchiladas. Hours vary slightly according to season.

Weed Cafe
DINER $

(⌨575-687-3611; 21 Weed Rd, Weed; mains $6-9; ⊙8am-3pm Mon-Thu, 8am-7pm Fri & Sat, 10am-2pm Sun; 🛜) For what might be the most out-of-the-way wi-fi hot spot in New Mexico, mosey on out to the town of Weed, 23 miles southeast of Cloudcroft in the Sacramento Mountains. Aside from internet access, you'll find a friendly local scene, hearty plates of diner food, and live music jam sessions on Friday and Saturday nights.

❶ Information

Stop at the **chamber of commerce** (⌨575-682-2733; www.cloudcroft.net; Hwy 82; ⊙10am-5pm Mon-Sat) or **Sacramento Ranger Station** (⌨575-682-2551; Chipmunk Ave; ⊙7:30am-4:30pm Mon-Fri) for local info.

❶ Getting There & Away

Cloudcroft is about 20 miles east of Alamogordo on Hwy 82 and is best reached via private vehicle.

Ruidoso & Around

You want lively in these parts? You want Ruidoso. Downright bustling in the summer and big with punters at the racetrack, resort-like Ruidoso has an utterly pleasant climate thanks to its lofty and forested perch near the Sierra Blanca (11,981ft). Neighboring Texans and local New Mexicans escaping the summer heat of Alamogordo (46 miles to the southwest) and Roswell (71 miles to the east) are happy campers here (or more precisely, happy cabiners). The lovely Rio Ruidoso, a small creek with good fishing, runs through town. Summertime hiking and wintertime skiing at Ski Apache keep folks busy, as does a smattering of galleries.

◉ Sights

Hwy 48 from the north is the main drag through town. This is called Mechem Dr until the small downtown area, where it becomes Sudderth Dr, heading east to the Y-intersection with Hwy 70. Six miles north on Mechem Dr is the community of Alto, with more accommodations.

Hubbard Museum of the American West
MUSEUM

(www.hubbardmuseum.org; 841 Hwy 70 W; adult/child $6/2; ⊙9am-5pm; 🚸) This fine museum displays more than 10,000 Western-related items including Old West stagecoaches and American Indian pottery, and works by Frederic Remington and Charles M Russell. An impressive collection of horse-related displays, including a collection of saddles and the Racehorse Hall of Fame, lures horse-lovers.

Ruidoso Downs Racetrack
HORSE RACING

(www.raceruidoso.com; Hwy 70; grandstand seats free; ⊙Fri-Mon late May-early Sep) The Ruidoso Downs is one of the major racetracks in the Southwest. The big event is Labor Day's All American Futurity. The world's richest quarter-horse race has a purse of $2.4 million. A track **casino** (⊙10am-midnight Sun-Thu, to 1am Fri & Sat) features an all-you-can eat buffet ($7 to $15).

Mescalero Apache Indian Reservation
INDIAN RESERVATION

About 4000 Apaches live on this 720-sq-mile **reservation** (www.mescaleroapache .com), which lies in attractive country 17 miles southwest of Ruidoso on Hwy 70. The nomadic Apache arrived in this area 800 years ago and soon became enemies with local Pueblo Indians. In the 19th century, under pressure from European settlement and with their mobility greatly increased by the introduction of the horse, the Apache became some of the most feared raiders of the West. Despite the name of the reservation, the Apache here are of three tribes: the Mescalero, the Chiricahua and the Lipan. The **Cultural Center** (⌨575-464-4494; Chiricahua Plaza, off Hwy 70, Mescalero; ⊙hours vary) has an interesting exhibition about the Apache peoples and customs. Of course there's also the Inn of the Mountain Gods, a casino hotel with a champion **golf course** (⌨800-545-9011; guest/nonguest from $60/75) and guided wild-game hunting if you feel like shooting something.

🏃 Activities

The best skiing area south of Albuquerque is **Ski Apache** (snow conditions 575-257-9001; www.skiapache.com; lift ticket adult/child $39/25), 18 miles northwest of Ruidoso on the slopes of beautiful Sierra Blanca Peak. It's not exactly world-class riding, but when it comes to affordability and fun, it's a good choice. Plus, Ski Apache is home to New Mexico's only gondola.

Hiking is popular in warmer months. If you're out for a day, try the 4.6-mile hike from the Ski Apache area to **Sierra Blanca Peak**, an ascent of 2000ft. Take Trail 15 from the small parking area just before the main lot and follow signs west and south along Trails 25 and 78 to Lookout Mountain (11,580ft). From there an obvious trail continues due south for 1.25 miles to Sierra Blanca Peak. For multiday trips, head into the **White Mountains Wilderness**, where 50 miles of trails criss-cross 48,000 scenic acres. The ranger station in Ruidoso has maps and information.

Rio Ruidoso and several national forest lakes offer good fishing. **Flies Etc** (505-257-4968; 2501 Sudderth Dr) has tackle and fishing licenses and runs fly-fishing excursions.

🎣 Festivals & Events

Ruidoso has a lot going on. Some of the highlights:

Apache Maidens' Puberty Ceremony
CULTURAL
Takes place for about four days in early July and features a powwow, rodeo and arts-and-crafts demonstrations.

Ruidoso Art Festival
ART
Attracts thousands of browsing and buying visitors from all over the Southwest on the last weekend of July.

Golden Aspen Motorcycle
MOTORCYCLE RALLY
Draws 30,000 motorcycle-riders the third weekend of September.

Aspenfest
STREET
Held on the first weekend in October, Aspenfest features a chile cook-off and a street festival.

Lincoln County Cowboy Symposium
CULTURAL
The second weekend in October; features cowboy poetry, chuckwagon cooking and horsebreaking.

Oktoberfest
CULTURAL
Bavarian-themed, with German food and beer, along with professional polka dancing and oompah bands. Held the third weekend in October.

🛏 Sleeping

There are lots of area cabin rentals, but some of the ones in town are cramped. Most of the newer cabins are located in the Upper Canyon. Generally, cabins have kitchens and grills, and often fireplaces and decks. The agency **4 Seasons Real Estate** (800-822-7654; www.casasderuidoso.com; 712 Mechem Dr; 8am-5pm) arranges condominium, cabin and lodge rentals. There's plenty of free primitive camping along the forest roads on the way to the ski area.

Shadow Mountain Lodge
LODGE $$
(575-257-4886; www.smlruidoso.com; 107 Main St; r & cabins from $149; ☎) Geared toward couples, these immaculate rooms feature fireplaces and offer romantic allure. A wooden wraparound balcony overlooks the professionally landscaped grounds; the hot tub is tucked away in a gazebo. Individual cabins have Jacuzzi tubs and giant flat-screen TVs. Major discounts are often offered, so check.

Upper Canyon Inn
LODGE $$
(575-257-3005; www.uppercanyoninn.com; 215 Main Rd; r/cabins from $79/119; ☎) The wide variety of rooms and cabins here range from simple good values to rustic-chic luxury. Bigger doesn't necessarily mean more expensive here, so take a look at a few options. The pricier cabins have some fine interior woodwork and Jacuzzi tubs.

Sitzmark Chalet
HOTEL $
(800-658-9694; www.sitzmark-chalet.com; 627 Sudderth Dr; r from $60; ☎) This ski-themed chalet offers 17 simple but nice rooms. Picnic tables, grills and an eight-person hot tub are welcome perks.

Inn of the Mountain Gods
CASINO HOTEL $$
(800-545-9011; www.innofthemountaingods.com; 287 Carrizo Canyon Rd; r $129-299; ☎) This luxury resort hotel on the Mescalero Apache Reservation has surprisingly low rates – online promotions can be even lower. Gamblers can feed slots at the casino, and guided fishing, paddleboat rentals and horseback riding are all just a concierge call away. Several restaurants,

a nightclub, a sports bar and a championship golf course are also on-site. It's fun for a night or two.

High Country Lodge
LODGE $$

(575-336-4321; www.highcountrylodge.net; Hwy 48; r from $89;) Just south of the turnoff to Ski Apache, this funky older place welcomes you with three friendly (wooden) bears. It offers a comfortable selection of rustic and basic two-bedroom cabins, each with kitchen, fireplace and porch. Other facilities include a sauna, hot tub and tennis courts.

Bonito Hollow Campground
CAMPGROUND $

(575-336-4325; tent/RV sites $19/36, r/cabin $45/75; May–mid-Oct) Lots of options on the Bonita River.

Best Western Swiss Chalet
HOTEL $

(575-258-3333; 1451 Mechem Dr; r $69-109;) Convenient to the ski slopes and forest; ask about ski-and-bike packages.

Eating

Rickshaw
ASIAN $$

(575-257-2828; www.rickshawnewmexico.com; 601 Mechmem Dr; lunch mains $7-9, dinner mains $11-22; 11am-9pm Thu-Tue) This is the best Asian food south of Albuquerque, with selections inspired by but not slavish to the cuisine of Thailand, China and India. Order from the menu or be adventurous and sit at the Tanoshimu Table, where you'll dine family-style with strangers on whatever dishes the chef sends out of the kitchen; you pay by the hour and can stay as long as you like. Definitely finish with the ginger-pear crumble over homemade cinnamon ice cream.

Cornerstone Bakery
BREAKFAST $

(359 Sudderth Dr; mains under $10; 7:30am-2pm Mon-Sat, to 1pm Sun;) Stay around long enough and the Cornerstone may become your morning touchstone. Everything on the menu, from omelets to croissant sandwiches, is worthy. Locals are addicted.

Casa Blanca
NEW MEXICAN $$

(575-257-2495; 501 Mechem Dr; mains $9-18; 7am-8:30pm) Dine on Southwestern cuisine in a renovated Spanish-style house or on the pleasant patio in the summer. It's hard to go wrong with the New Mexican plates, but they've also got big burgers and chicken-fried steak. Breakfast gets raves.

Café Rio
PIZZA $

(2547 Sudderth Dr; mains $5-25; 11am-9pm;) Thick-crust pizza, with your choice of toppings, is deservedly popular here, but the stuffed calzones and Greek offerings are also decent for a small-town restaurant. Wash it down with a big selection of international and seasonal beer.

Texas Club
STEAKHOUSE $$$

(575-258-3325; 212 Metz Dr; mains $15-35; 5-9pm Wed-Sun, to 10pm Fri & Sat) One of the busiest and best restaurants in town, and decorated with all the bigness you'd expect in a place that takes its name from Texas (think longhorns and cowboy hats), this place serves big tasty steaks and seafood. There is dancing and live entertainment on the weekends. Call for reservations (it's often packed).

Drinking & Entertainment

Quarters
BAR

(2535 Sudderth Dr) Dance the night away to live blues and rock on the big dance floor, or listen from a barstool or at one of the comfortable tables.

Spencer Theater for the Performing Arts
PERFORMING ARTS

(www.spencertheater.com; 108 Spencer Rd, Alto) In a stunning mountain venue, it hosts theatrical, musical and dance performances. Check the website for what's playing. Take Hwy 220 to Alto.

Flying J Ranch
DINNER SHOW

(505-336-4330; www.flyingjranch.com; Hwy 48; adult/child $24/14; from 5:30 Mon-Sat late May–early Sep;) Families with little ones will love this place, as it delivers a full night of entertainment, not just dinner. Located 1.5 miles north of Alto, this 'Western village' stages gunfights and offers pony rides with their cowboy-style chuckwagon. Western music tops off the evening.

Information

Both the **chamber of commerce** (575-257-7395; www.ruidoso.net; 720 Sudderth Dr; 8am-4:30pm Mon-Fri, 9am-3pm Sat) and the **Smokey Bear Ranger Station** (575-257-4095; 901 Mechem Dr; 7:30am-4:30pm Mon-Fri year-round, plus Sat in summer) are helpful. The chamber's website has Spanish, Italian, German and French translations.

SMOKEY BEAR'S STOMPING GROUNDS

You've seen his likeness in state and national forests everywhere around the region. But did you know that Smokey Bear was also a real black bear? Once upon a time (back in 1950), a little cub was found clinging to a tree, paws charred from a 17,000-acre forest fire in the Capitan Mountains. What better name to give him than that of the famous cartoon bear that had been the symbol of fire prevention since 1944? Nursed back to health, Smokey spent the rest of his days in the National Zoo in Washington, DC, and became a living mascot. At the 3-acre **Smokey Bear Historical State Park** (✆575-354-2748; per day $1), in the village of Capitan, 12 miles west of Lincoln, you can see the bear's grave and learn tons about forest fires. Every Fourth of July, a **Smokey the Bear Stampede** features a parade, a rodeo, cookouts and other festivities. **Smokey the Bear Days**, celebrated the first weekend in May, includes a street dance, wood carving contest, and craft and antique-car shows.

If you're lucky enough to be around on a weekend, make it a point to eat at **Chango's** (✆575-354-1234; 103 Lincoln Ave; mains $10-18; ⊙4-8pm Fri & Sat, 11am-3pm Sun), a seven-table boutique restaurant where the menu changes weekly. The building, over 100 years old, has an interesting history (it's been a fish house, a mink farm and a hotel), and now doubles as an art gallery with fantastical sculptures and avant-garde quills.

❶ Getting There & Around

Greyhound (✆575-257-2660; www.greyhound.com; 138 Service Rd) operates daily service to Alamogordo ($20, one hour), Roswell ($30, 1½ hours), and El Paso, TX ($34, 3½ hours).

Carrizozo

Carrizozo is a little town sitting where the Sacramento Mountains hit the Tularosa Basin. Art galleries and antiques shops line historic 12th St, downtown's main axis. Take a look into **Gallery 408** (408 12th St; www.gallery408.com; ⊙10am-5pm Mon, Fri & Sat, noon-5pm Sun). In addition to the work of a number of regional artists, you can see what remains of the herd of Painted Burros – a Carrizozo concept similar to the Cow Parades of Chicago and New York, but on a slightly smaller scale. Some have pun-tastic names, like The Asstronomer, its body decorated with the night sky. Proceeds from donkey sales benefit the local animal shelter, Miracles Paws for Pets.

For a good breakfast, lunch or caffeine fix, look for **La Brewja Café** (113 Central Ave; mains under $10; ⊙7am-2pm Mon-Fri; @🛜), a funky coffee shop/art space with old-school Formica tables and matching vinyl chairs.

Four miles west of Carrizozo, explore the rocky blackness of a 125-sq-mile lava flow that's 160ft deep in the middle. A 0.6-mile nature trail at **Valley of Fires Recreation Area** (Hwy 380; vehicles $3, tent/RV sites $7/12) is well paved, easy for kids and marked with informative signs describing the geology and biology of the volcanic remains. You're also allowed to hike off-trail, simply cutting cross-country over the flow as you like. There are campsites and shaded picnic tables near the visitor center.

Lincoln

Fans of Western history won't want to miss little Lincoln. Twelve miles east of Capitan along the **Billy the Kid National Scenic Byway** (www.billybyway.com), this is where the gun battle that turned Billy the Kid into a legend took place.

It's hard to believe that in Billy the Kid's era Lincoln had a bustling population of nearly 900. Today it is essentially a ghost town, with only about 50 people living here. Those who do, however, are dedicated to preserving the town's 1880s buildings. Modern influences, such as souvenir stands, are not allowed in town, and the main street has been designated the **Lincoln State Monument**. It's a pretty cool place to get away from this century for a night.

Start at the **Anderson Freeman Visitor Center & Museum** (Hwy 380; adult/child $5/free; ⊙8:30am-4:30pm), where exhibits on the Buffalo soldiers, Apaches and the Lincoln County War explain the town's history. The admission price includes entry to the **Tunstall Store** (with a remarkable display of late 19th-century merchandise), the **courthouse** where the Kid famously shot his way

LEGEND OF BILLY THE KID

So much speculation swirls. Even the most basic information about Billy the Kid tends to cast a shadow larger than the outlaw himself. Here's what we know, or don't. Most historians agree that he was born sometime in 1859, most likely in New York City (or Indiana or Missouri). He *may* be buried in **Old Fort Sumner**, where his skull *may* have been stolen and *possibly* recovered) – that is, unless he colluded with his presumed assassin, Sheriff Pat Garrett, and lived to a ripe, old age...somewhere.

The Kid didn't start out as a murderer. His first known childhood crimes included stealing laundry and fencing butter. In the mid-1870s, about the time the teenage Billy arrived in New Mexico, the 400 residents of **Lincoln** shopped at 'Murphy's,' the only general store in the region. In 1877, though, Englishman John Tunstall arrived and built a competing general store.

Within a year, Tunstall was dead, allegedly shot by Murphy and his boys. The entire region erupted in what became known as the Lincoln County War. Tunstall's most famous follower was a wild teenager named Henry McCarty, alias William Bonney, aka Billy the Kid. Over the next several months the Kid and his gang gunned down any members of the Murphy faction they could find. The Kid was captured or cornered a number of times but managed brazen and lucky escapes before finally being shot by Sheriff Pat Garrett near Fort Sumner in 1881, where he lies in a grave in a barren yard. Maybe.

Enough controversy still dangles over whether he conspired with Sheriff Garrett to fake his death that there is a long-running movement to exhume the body and do a little DNA testing. Brushy Bill Roberts of Hico, Texas, now deceased, claimed that he was actually the elusive outlaw. A man in his 70s claims that Sheriff Garrett's widow told him at the tender age of nine that the conspiracy was, in fact, the truth.

Near the end of his term as governor in 2010, Bill Richardson considered granting the Kid a posthumous pardon, based on historical evidence that he'd been promised one by territorial governor Lew Wallace if he'd give testimony about the murder of Lincoln County Sherriff William Brady in 1878. The Kid testified but, rather than being pardoned, was sentenced to death. After much deliberation, and partly due to protests raised by descendents of Pat Garrett and Lew Wallace, Richardson declined to pardon the Kid.

to freedom, and **Dr Wood's house**, an intact turn-of-the-century doctor's home and office.

During the **Old Lincoln Days** (held the first full weekend in August), now in its sixth decade, musicians and mountain men, doctors and desperadoes wander the streets in period costume, and there are demonstrations of spinning, blacksmithing and other common frontier skills. In the evening there is the folk pageant, 'The Last Escape of Billy the Kid.'

The 19th-century adobe **Ellis Store Country Inn** (☑575-653-4609; www.ellisstore .com; Hwy 380; r incl breakfast $89-$119) offers three antiques-filled rooms (complete with wood stove) in the main house and five additional rooms in a historic mill on the property. The host – once named New Mexico's 'Chef of the Year' – offers a six-course dinner ($75 per person) served in the cozy dining room Thursday to Saturday. Nonguests are welcome with a reservation.

A few miles west on the road to Capitan, **Laughing Sheep Farm and Ranch** (☑575-653-4041; www.laughingsheepfarm.com; mains $11-36; ☺11am-3pm Wed-Sun, 5-8pm Fri & Sat; ⓐ) raises sheep, cows and bison – along with vegetables and fruits – then serves them for lunch and dinner. Food is farm-fresh and delicious. The dining room is comfortable and casual, with live fiddle music on weekend nights plus a play-dough table and an easel to keep the kids happy. At the time of research, comfortable, newly built cabins were just opening to overnight guests; call for rates.

About 14 miles south of Lincoln, **Hurd Ranch Guest Homes** (☑575-653-4331; www .wyethartists.com; 105 La Rinconada, San Patricio; casitas $125-350; ⓐ) is a 2500-acre, very rural place in San Patricio that rents six lovely casitas by an apple orchard. Furnished with style and grace, and lots of original art, some units sleep up to six people. They are outfitted with modern conveniences. Owner and artist Michael Hurd runs the Hurd-La Rinconada Gallery on the premises; he also shows the work of his relatives NC and Andrew Wyeth, his mother Henriette Wyeth and his father Peter Hurd. Pets can stay for $10 (per visit).

Roswell

Whether or not you're a true believer, a visit to Roswell is worth visiting to experience one of America's most enduring, eclectic and fanatical pop-culture phenomena. Sure it's about as cheesy as it gets for some, but conspiracy theorists and *X-Files* fanatics descend from other worlds into Roswell in real seriousness. Oddly famous as both the country's largest producer of wool and its UFO capital, Roswell has built a tourist industry around the alleged July 1947 UFO crash (see p346), after which the military quickly closed the area and allowed no more information to filter out for several decades. Was it a flying

saucer? The local convention and visitors bureau suggest that Roswell's special blend of climate and culture attracted touring space aliens who wanted a closer look! Decide for yourself.

If you're driving east on Hwy 70/380 from the Sacramento Mountains, enjoy the view. Roswell sits on the western edge of the dry plains, and these are the last big mountains you'll see for a while.

The 'Staked Plains' extending east into Texas were once home to millions of buffalo and many nomadic Native American hunters. White settlers and hunters moved in throughout the late 19th century, and killed some 3.5 million buffalo during a two-year period. Within a few years, the region became desolate and empty; only a few groups of Comanche mixed with other tribes roaming the plains, hunting and trying to avoid confinement on reservations. Roswell, founded in 1871, served as a stopping place for cowboys driving cattle.

Roswell

◉ Sights & Activities

The main west-east drag through town is 2nd St and the main north-south thoroughfare is Main St; their intersection is the heart of downtown.

TOP CHOICE International UFO Museum & Research Center
MUSEUM

(Map p345; www.roswellufomuseum.com; 114 N Main St; adult/child $5/$2; ◎9am-5pm) Serious followers of UFO phenomena (not to mention skeptics or the merely curious) will want to check out this museum and research center. Original photographs and witness statements form the 1947 Roswell Incident Timeline and explain the 'great cover-up.'

Roswell

◉ **Sights**
Goddard Planetarium.....................(see 3)
1 Historical Center for Southeast
  New Mexico..A4
2 International UFO Museum &
  Research Center...............................B4
3 Roswell Museum & Art Center...........B3

◉ **Sleeping**
4 Budget Inn..B1

◉ **Eating**
5 Farley's...B2
6 Martin's Capitol Café...........................B4

The library claims to have the most comprehensive UFO-related materials in the world, and we have no reason to be skeptical.

Roswell Museum & Art Center   MUSEUM

(Map p345; www.roswellmuseum.org; 100 W 11th St; admission free; ⊙9am-5pm Mon-Sat, 1-5pm Sun) On a more down-to-earth front, Roswell's excellent museum and art center deserves a visit. Seventeen galleries showcase Southwestern artists including Georgia O'Keeffe, Peter Hurd and Henriette Wyeth, along with an eclectic mix of Native American, Hispanic and Anglo artifacts. A major focus of the museum is space research. The **Goddard Planetarium** is the reconstructed lab of Robert H Goddard, who launched the first successful liquid fuel rocket in 1926. Goddard spent more than a decade carrying out rocket research in Roswell. A variety of early rocketry paraphernalia is also on display.

Historical Center for Southeast New Mexico   MUSEUM

(Map p345; www.hssnm.net; 200 N Lea Ave; admission by donation; ⊙1-4pm) Housed in the 1912 mansion of local rancher James Phelps White, this property is well worth seeing. It's on the National Register of Historic Places, and its interior has been carefully restored to its original early-20th-century decor, with period furnishings, photographs and art.

FREE Bitter Lake National Wildlife Refuge   WILDLIFE RESERVE

(www.fws.gov/southwest; Pine Lodge Rd; ⊙sunrise-sunset) Birders will want to bring their binoculars. Wintering water birds gather at this 38-sq-mile refuge; many birds remain to nest in the summer. To reach the refuge, about 15 miles northeast of Roswell, follow the signed roads from either Hwy 380 or Hwy 285/70.

✯✯ Festivals & Events

As you might imagine, Roswell has a couple of quirky festivals worth checking out.

New Mexico Dairy Day   FOOD

In early June, Dairy Day features the Great Milk Carton Boat Race on Lake Van, 20 miles south of Roswell, as well as cheese-sculpting contests, 36ft-long ice cream sundaes, games and sporting events.

THE TRUTH IS OUT THERE...

It's been more than 60 years now since that heady summer of 1947, when an unidentified flying object fell out of the sky, and crash-landed in the desert near Roswell, and the little New Mexican town is still cashing in on the mystery. Those who believe aliens are out there are convinced it was a UFO that crashed the first week of July in that post-WWII baby-making summer, and that the US government has gone to great lengths to cover up the crash. They certainly have a compelling case with this one.

In a 1947 press release, the government identified the object as a crashed disk. A day later, however, it changed its story: now the disk was really just a weather balloon. The feds then confiscated all the previous press releases, cordoned off the area as they collected all the debris, and posted armed guards to escort curious locals from the site of the 'weather-balloon' crash. A local mortician fielded calls from the mortuary office at the government airfield inquiring after small, hermetically sealed coffins for preventing tissue contamination and degeneration.

Now 60-odd years after the incident, the government is still tight-lipped, and Roswell is the story that will never die. There are frequent eyewitness accounts of flying saucers in the sky, and rumor and misinformation continue to swirl about the original crash, fueling all manner of speculation over what really happened in the desert that day. In the early 2000s, Roswell even spawned its own TV series about alien-mutant hybrid teenagers trying to survive as humans while keeping their alien powers alive and attempting to get home.

Now Roswell celebrates the assertions and denials, the mystery and the speculation surrounding the event in an annual **UFO Festival** (www.roswellufofestival.com). Held on Fourth of July Weekend, it attracts upwards of 20,000 visitors from around the planet – Roswell is now synonymous with UFOs. Interplanetary-travel celebs such as the Duras sisters (known to Trekkies as Klingon warriors from the TV series *Star Trek*), as well as past astronauts, often make appearances. Besides enough lectures, films and workshops to make anyone's ears go pointy, the nighttime parade and alien-costume competitions are not to be missed.

UFO Festival
QUIRKY
Centers around alien-costume competitions and lectures about UFOs.

Eastern New Mexico State Fair
CULTURAL
The main annual event is the State Fair in early October, with rodeo, livestock and agricultural competitions and chile-eating contests.

🛏 Sleeping

There are plenty of chain hotels on the north end of main street, plus independent (sometimes sketchy) budget motels west on 2nd St.

Heritage Inn
HISTORIC HOTEL **$$**
(☑575-748-2552; www.artesiaheritageinn.com; 209 W Main St, Artesia; r incl breakfast from $104; ❄@⑨) The nicest place to stay is actually not in Roswell. If you're traveling between Roswell and Carlsbad and in the mood for slightly upscale digs (this is southeastern New Mexico, don't forget), this turn-of-the-19th century establishment offers 11 Old West–style rooms in Artesia, about 36 miles south of Roswell.

Budget Inn
MOTEL **$**
(Map p345; ☑575-623-6050; 2101 N Main St; r from $35; ❄⑨) Basic but clean digs, with new pillow-top mattresses and continental breakfast. One of the best values in town.

Bottomless Lakes State Park
CAMPGROUND **$**
(www.nmparks.com; Hwy 409; day use per vehicle $5, tent/RV sites $10/14) Seven popular lakes in the area provide welcome relief from summer heat. These primitive campsites are among the best available. To reach them, drive 10 miles east of Roswell on Hwy 380, then 5 miles south on Hwy 409. The Lea Lake site has real bathrooms, showers and the only lake you're allowed to swim in.

🍴 Eating

Wellhead
BREWERY **$$**
(www.thewellhead.com; 332 W Main St, Artesia; mains $8-27; ⊘11am-9pm Mon-Sat) If you're traveling between Roswell and Carlsbad, you'll find some of the region's best food and drink at this modern brewpub restaurant and bar. Housed in a 1905 building and reflecting the town's origins, it's decorated with an oil-drilling theme. Artesia is about 36 miles south of Roswell.

Cowboy Cafe
DINER **$**
(off Map p345; 1120 E 2nd St; mains $4-10; ⊘6am-2pm Mon-Sat) One of the few truly local joints left in town, this is a good option for breakfast before hitting the UFO museum or the road.

Martin's Capitol Café
NEW MEXICAN **$**
(Map p345; 110 W 4th St; mains $7-15; ⊘6am-8:30pm Mon-Sat) Although several inexpensive New Mexican restaurants here are good, this one is homestyle and dependable.

Farley's
AMERICAN **$**
(Map p345; 1315 N Main St; mains $7-13; ⊘11am-11pm Sun-Thu, to 1am Fri & Sat) A boisterous barn-like place that stays open late, Farley's has something for everyone: burgers, pizza, chicken and ribs. It also has a big bar with pool tables and music.

Mama Tucker's
BAKERY **$**
(off Map p345; 3109 N Main St; donuts $1; ⊘5am-5pm Tue-Fri, 5am-1pm Sat-Mon) If you're craving something sweet, head straight here for homemade donuts, cakes and cookies

ⓘ Information

Visitors Bureau (☑575-624-0889; www.roswell mysteries.com; 912 N Main St; ⊘8:30am-5:30pm Mon-Fri, 10am-3pm Sat & Sun; ⑨)
Eastern New Mexico Medical Center (☑575-622-8170; 405 W Country Club Rd; ⊘24hr emergency)
Police (☑575-624-6770; 128 W 2nd St)
Post office (415 N Pennsylvania Ave)

ⓘ Getting There & Around

Greyhound (☑575-622-2510; www.greyhound .com; 1100 N Virginia Ave) has daily buses to Carlsbad ($28, 1½ hours) and Las Cruces ($49, four hours), from where you can transfer to Albuquerque or El Paso, TX.

Carlsbad

When Carlsbad Caverns was declared a national monument in 1923, a trickle of tourists turned into a veritable flash flood. Today, hundreds of thousands of visitors come through annually. Carlsbad is situated on the Pecos River about 30 miles north of the Texas state line, and its main thoroughfare is Hwy 285, which becomes Canal St, then S Canal (south of Mermod St) and then National Parks Hwy at the southern end of town.

⊙ Sights & Activities

Living Desert State Park
ZOO
(www.nmparks.com; 1504 Miehls Dr, off Hwy 285; adult/child $5/3; ⊘8am-8pm Jun-Aug, 9am-5pm

Carlsbad

FREE Carlsbad Museum & Art Center MUSEUM
(Map p348; www.nmculture.org; 418 W Fox St; ⊙10am-5pm Mon-Sat) This museum displays Apache artifacts, pioneer memorabilia and art from the renowned Taos School.

🛏 Sleeping

The nearby national park and mild winters make this a year-round destination; always ask for the best rates. It's mostly chain motels in Carlsbad, plenty of which can be found on Canal St.

TOP CHOICE Trinity Hotel BOUTIQUE HOTEL $$
(Map p348; ☎575-234-9891; www.thetrinityhotel.com; 201 S Canal St; r from $129-199; ❋🕸) This luxurious new place is Carlsbad's best hotel. It's not exactly 'new' – it's in a renovated building that was once the First National Bank. The sitting room of one suite is inside the old vault! Family-run, it's friendly, and the restaurant is easily Carlsbad's classiest.

Stagecoach Inn MOTEL $
(Map p348; ☎575-887-1148; 1819 S Canal St; r from $40; ❋🕸🐾) One of the best values in town, the Stagecoach has clean rooms, a swimming pool and an on-site playground for kids.

Carlsbad KOA CAMPGROUND $
(☎575-457-2000; www.carlsbadkoa.com; 2 Manthei Rd; tent/RV sites from $30/45, cabins $57; 🕸🐾🎱) On Hwy 285 about 12 miles north of Carlsbad, this KOA offers the choice of air-conditioned 'kamping kabins' or grassy tent sites. There's a pool, game room, grocery store, laundry, playground

Sep-May) On the northwestern outskirts of town, this state park is a great place to see and learn about roadrunners, wolves and antelopes, along with desert plants like agave, ocotillo and yucca. The park has a good 1.3-mile trail that showcases different habitats of the Chihuahuan Desert, plus a reptile house.

Lake Carlsbad WATERFRONT
(Map p348) A system of dams and spillways on the Pecos River created the 2-mile Lake Carlsbad, which has a pleasant 4.5-mile trail along its banks. At the north end of Park Dr (or at the east end of Church St), **Carlsbad Riverfront Park** has a beach and swimming area. At nearby **Port Jefferson** (⊙10am-5pm Mon-Sat late May–early Sep, 10am-5pm Sat & Sun early Sep–Oct), you can rent a paddlewheel boat to tour the river.

and showers here. Ask friendly hosts Scott and Susan Bacher about free rides for the kids in a retired fire truck. The KOA is also dog-friendly, with a park especially for your canine companion.

✕ Eating & Drinking

Trinity Restaurant & Wine Bar   AMERICAN $$
(Map p348; www.thetrinityhotel.com; Trinity Hotel, 201 S Canal St; mains breakfast $6-12, lunch $8-12, dinner $10-29; ⊙7-10am, 11am-1:45pm & 5-9pm Mon-Sat, 8am-noon Sun; ⏩) Carlsbad's finest dining features steaks, seafood, and Italian specialties. This is the town's top choice for vegetarians, too, with pastas and salads. Nonkosher carnivores will love the roast pork in a cabernet/green chile reduction. Free wine tastings are held from 3pm to 5pm most days.

Blue House Bakery & Café   BREAKFAST $
(Map p348; 609 N Canyon St; mains $3-9; ⊙6am-2pm Tue-Fri, 6am-noon Mon & Sat) This sweet Queen Anne house perks the best coffee and espresso in this quadrant of New Mexico. Its baked goods are pretty darn good too. At lunchtime, the cheery place has good sandwiches made with fresh breads.

Lucy's   NEW MEXICAN $$
(Map p348; 701 S Canal St; mains $7-16; ⊙11am-9pm Mon-Thu, to 9:30 Fri & Sat) The most popular place in Carlsbad, Lucy's is usually packed with devoted locals *and* visitors. Apart from a great Mexican menu, Lucy's serves up tasty margaritas and a good

selection of microbrews (and admittedly that may be one reason the place is jumpin').

Red Chimney Pit Barbecue   BARBECUE $$
(Map p348; 817 N Canal St; mains $7-15; ⊙11am-2pm, 4:30-8:30pm Mon-Fri) Red Chimney's got quality meats with tasty sauce.

Danny's Place   BARBECUE $
(Map p348; 902 S Canal St; mains $6-12; ⊙11am-9pm) It's not quite as good as Red Chimney, but it is open Sundays (rare in Carlsbad).

❶ Information

Carlsbad Chamber of Commerce (⏩575-887-6516; www.carlsbadchamber.com; 302 S Canal St; ⊙9am-5pm Mon, 8am-5pm Tue-Fri year-round, 9am-3pm Sat May-Sep) Very knowledgeable and helpful with tourist info.

Carlsbad Medical Center (⏩575 887-4100; 2430 W Pierce St; ⊙24hr emergency)

National Parks Information Center (⏩575 885-8884; 3225 National Parks Hwy; ⊙8am-4:30pm Mon-Fri) Information on both Carlsbad Caverns National Park and Guadalupe Mountains National Park. About a mile south of town.

Police (⏩575-885-2111; 405 S Halagueno St)

USFS Ranger Station (⏩575 885-4181; 114 S Halagueno; ⊙7:30am-4:30pm Mon-Fri) Info on Sitting Bull Falls and hiking and backpacking in Lincoln National Forest.

❶ Getting There & Away

Greyhound (off Map p348; ⏩575-887-1108; www.greyhound.com; 1000 Canyon St) buses depart daily for Las Cruces ($65, 6 hours) and

---

WORTH A TRIP

SITTING BULL FALLS

An oasis in the desert, **Sitting Bull Falls** (per vehicle $5; ⊙8:30am-6pm Apr-Sep, to 5pm Oct-Mar) is tucked among the burly canyons of the Guadalupe Mountains, 42 miles southwest of Carlsbad. A spring-fed creek pours 150ft over a limestone cliff, with natural pools below and above the falls that are great for swimming – or at least dunking and cooling off. There are a series of caves behind the waterfalls, which can be explored only with a ranger.

Twenty-six miles of trails around the falls offer the best hiking anywhere near Carlsbad. Though there is no camping in the designated recreation area, backpackers may hike in and camp further up Sitting Bull Canyon, or up Last Chance Canyon, which also usually flows with water. Extended routes from here can take experienced multiday trekkers south all the way into Guadalupe Mountains National Park, in Texas. If you plan on hiking, keep in mind that it gets brutally hot here in summer; it's ideal from late fall to early spring.

Arrange cave walks and pick up trail maps and other info, including a pamphlet about what to do if you encounter a mountain lion, at the Lincoln National Forest office in Carlsbad.

El Paso, TX ($57, 3 hours); the bus stops at the Allsup's gas station a few miles south of town on Hwy 180.

Carlsbad Caverns National Park

Scores of wondrous caves hide under the hills at this unique **national park** (☑575-785-2232, bat info 505-785-3012; www.nps.gov /cave; 3225 National Parks Hwy; adult/child $6/free; ☺caves 8:30am-4pm late May–early Sep, 8:30am-3:30pm early Sep–late May), which covers 73 sq miles. The cavern formations are a weird wonderland of stalactites and fantastical geological features. You can ride an elevator from the visitor center (which descends the length of the Empire State Building in under a minute) or take a 2-mile subterranean walk from the cave mouth to the Big Room, an underground chamber 1800ft long, 255ft high and over 800ft below the surface. If you've got kids (or are just feeling goofy), plastic caving helmets with headlamps are sold in the gift shop.

Guided tours (☑877-444-6777; www .recreation.gov; adult $7-20, child $3.50-10) of additional caves are available, and should be reserved well in advance. Bring long sleeves and closed shoes: it gets chilly.

The cave's other claim to fame is the 300,000-plus Mexican free-tailed bat colony that roosts here from mid-May to mid-October. Be here by sunset, when they cyclone out for an all-evening insect feast.

If you want to scramble to lesser-known areas, ask about Wild Cave tours. The last tickets are sold two to 3½ hours before the visitor center closes. Wilderness backpacking trips into the desert are allowed by permit (free); the visitor center sells topographical maps of the 50-plus miles of hiking trails. November to March is the best time for backpacking – summer temperatures are scorching, and the countless rattlesnakes should be sleeping in winter.

Deep within the park's backcountry is **Lechugilla Cave**. With a depth of 1604ft and a length of some 60 miles, it's the deepest cave and third-longest limestone cave in North America. Sounds incredible – but it's only open to research and exploration teams, with special permission from the park.

I-40 EAST TO TEXAS

It can be pretty tempting to keep the pedal to the metal - or set the cruise-control switch - and power on through the eastern half of I-40 without stopping. But if you've got a little time, there are some interesting historical detours, from the days of the dinosaurs to the worst of the Wild West to some of the best of what remains of classic Route 66 kitsch.

Santa Rosa

Scuba in Santa Rosa? Yup, that's right. Settled in the mid-19th century by Spanish farmers, Santa Rosa's modern claim to fame is, oddly enough, as the scuba diving capital of the Southwest. There's not much else going on here, though.

⊙ Sights & Activities

Take exit 273 from Route 66/I-40 to reach downtown. The main street begins as Coronado St, then becomes Parker Ave through downtown, before becoming Will Rogers Dr when it passes exits 275 and 277.

Blue Hole   DIVING
One of the 10 best spots to dive in the country is, surprisingly, here in li'l ol' Santa Rosa. How could that be? Because of the bell-shaped, 81ft-deep Blue Hole. Fed by a natural spring flowing at 3000 gallons a minute, the water in the hole is both very clear and pretty cool (about 61°F to 64°F, or around 17°C). It's also 80ft in diameter at the surface and 130ft in diameter below the surface. Platforms for diving are suspended about 25ft down. Visit the **Santa Rosa Dive Center** (☑575-472-3763; www.santarosanm.org; Hwy 40/US 66) to set up a dive. The shop is next to the Hole.

Puerto de Luna   HISTORIC SITE
Nine miles south of town along Hwy 91, tiny Puerto de Luna was founded in the 1860s and is one of the oldest settlements in New Mexico. The drive there is pretty, winding through arroyos surrounded by eroded sandstone mesas. In town you'll find an old county courthouse, a village church and a bunch of weathered adobe buildings. It's all quite charming, as long as you're not in a hurry to do something else.

Route 66 Auto Museum   MUSEUM
(www.route66automuseum.com; 2766 Rte 66; adult/child under 5 $5/free; ☺7:30am-6pm Mon-Sat, 10am-5pm Sun Apr-Oct, 8am-5pm Mon-Sat,

10am-5pm Sun Nov-Mar) This museum pays homage to the mother of all roads. It boasts upwards of 35 cars from the 1920s through the 1960s, all in beautiful condition in its exhibit hall, and lots of 1950s memorabilia. It's a fun place; enjoy a milkshake at the '50s-style snack shack. If you're in the market for a beautifully restored old Chevy, the museum doubles as an antique car dealer.

✦ Festivals & Events

Annual Custom Car Show   CAR SHOW
In keeping with the Route 66 theme, this car show, held in August or September, attracts vintage- and classic-car enthusiasts, as well as folks driving strange things on wheels.

Santa Rosa Fiesta   CULTURAL
Homespun, to say the least, the Fiesta has a beauty-queen contest and the bizarre, annual Duck Drop: contestants buy squares and then wait for a duck suspended over the squares to poop – if the poop lands on their square, they win cold cash. Held in the third week of August.

🛏 Sleeping & Eating

The town is home to a number of long-established family-owned diners and roadside cafes, all with historic allure. If you want to stay the night, choose from your favorite chain hotel off of the I-40 exits. Most hotels and restaurants lie along the main thoroughfare, part of the celebrated Route 66.

Silver Moon   DINER $$
(2545 Historic Route 66; mains $9-16; ⊘6am-10pm) A trademark Route 66 eatery that first opened its doors in 1959, Silver Moon serves fantastic homemade *chile rellenos* and other tasty diner grub dressed up with a New Mexican twist. It's popular with travelers following Route 66's old roadhouse trail, as well as locals who come for a morning coffee and a plate of bacon and eggs.

Joseph's Bar & Grill   DINER $$
(865 Historic Route 66; mains $8-20; ⊘7am-10pm Mon-Sat, to 9pm Sun) Route 66 nostalgia lines the walls of this popular place, family-owned since its inception in 1956. Many of the bountiful Mexican and American recipes have been handed down through the generations. Burgers and steaks are as popular as anything smothered in green chile. Joseph's also mixes some serious margaritas.

❶ Information

The **Chamber of Commerce** (☏505-472-3763; www.santarosanm.org; 486 Parker Ave; ⊘8am-5pm Mon-Fri) has tourist information.

❶ Getting There & Away

Santa Rosa's downtown is at exit 273 on Route 66/I-40. The town is about 120 miles east of Albuquerque.

Tucumcari

The biggest town on I-40 between Albuquerque and Amarillo, Tucumcari is a ranching and farming area between the mesas and the plains. It's also home to one of the best-preserved sections of Route 66 in the country. Not surprisingly, it still caters to travelers, with inexpensive motels, several classic pre-interstate buildings and souvenir shops like the Tee Pee Curios.

◎ Sights & Activities

Drive the kids down Tucumcari's main street at night, when dozens of old neon signs cast a blazing glow. The bright, flashing signs are relics of Tucumcari's Route 66 heyday, when they were installed by business owners as a crafty form of marketing to get tired travelers to stop for the night. Tucumcari lies barely north of I-40. The main west-east thoroughfare between these exits is old Route 66, called Tucumcari Blvd through downtown. The principal north-south artery is 1st St.

Mesalands Dinosaur Museum   MUSEUM
(222 E Laughlin St; adult/child $6.50/4; ⊘10am-6pm Tue-Sat Mar-Aug, noon-5pm Tue-Sat Sep Feb; ♿) Well worth a visit is this engaging museum, which showcases real dinosaur bones and has hands-on exhibits for kids. Casts of dinosaur bones are done in bronze (rather than the usual plaster of paris), which not only shows fine detail, but also makes them works of art.

Tucumcari Historical Museum   MUSEUM
(416 S Adams St; adult/child $3/1; ⊘9am-3pm Tue-Sat) Several rooms of the historical museum feature reconstructions of early Western interiors, such as a sheriff's office, a classroom and a hospital room. It's an eclectic collection, to say the least, displaying a barbed-wire collection alongside Indian artifacts.

Art Murals   WALKING TOUR
The town is also home to 31 life-size and larger murals recording Tucumcari's

history throughout the decades. The pieces of art, which adorn buildings on and just north and south of Route 66, are the life work of local painters Doug and Sharon Quarles. Taking the town's mural walk is a great way to stretch your legs and experience Tucumcari's Route 66 legacy. Grab a mural walking map off the website of the **chamber of commerce** (www.tucumcarinm.com/visitors_guide).

🛏 Sleeping

Tucumcari has the usual number of chain motels spread along I-40. It also has a some cool old independent motels on historic Route 66.

⟨TOP CHOICE⟩ Blue Swallow Motel   HISTORIC MOTEL $
(☑575-461-9849; www.blueswallowmotel.com; 815 E Tucumcari Blvd; r from $50; ✱🐾🛜🏊) Spend the night in this beautifully restored Route 66 motel listed on the State and National Registers of Historic Places, and feel the decades melt away. The classic neon sign has been featured in many Route 66 articles and boasts that Blue Swallow offers '100% refrigerated air'. The place has a great lobby, friendly owners and vintage, uniquely decorated rooms.

Historic Route 66 Motel   MOTEL $
(☑575-461-1212; www.tucumcarimotel.com; 1620 E Route 66; r from $30; ✱🛜) When it comes to budget digs, you can't beat this historic motor-court motel with giant plate-glass doors and mesa views. It's nothing splashy, but the 25 rooms are cheap and clean, with comfy beds and quality pillows. Small dogs are welcome, and there's an on-site espresso bar/cafe.

🍴 Eating & Drinking

Del's Restaurant   DINER $$
(www.delsrestaurant.com; 1202 E Tucumcari Blvd; mains $8-15; ⊙11am-9pm) Del's is popular in these here parts simply because it exists. Its New Mexican and American diner fare is mediocre at best and the salad bar is anemic. For breakfast or lunch, try its better sister restaurant, **Kix on 66** (www.kixon66.com; 1102 E Tucumcari Blvd; mains $5-10; ⊙6am-2pm;🛜) with a variety of omelettes and quesadillas, plus an espresso machine.

Pow-Wow Restaurant & Lizard Lounge   NEW MEXICAN $$
(801 W Tucumcari Blvd; mains $8-20; ⊙7am-10pm, bar til late Fri & Sat) Though the menu is a bit

MOVING ON?

For tips, recommendations and reviews, head to shop.lonelyplanet.com to purchase a downloadable PDF of the Texas chapter from Lonely Planet's *USA* guide.

better than Del's, the real draw here is the lounge. Thursdays are karaoke nights, and on some weekends big-name New Mexican bands, like Little Joe y la Familia, drop by to play a few sets.

ⓘ Information

A **chamber of commerce** (☑575-461-1694; www.tucumcarinm.com; 404 W Tucumcari Blvd) keeps sporadic hours.

ⓘ Getting There & Away

Tucumcari is at the crossroads of Historic Route 66, now I-40, and US Hwy 54. It is 110 miles from Amarillo, TX, and 170 miles from Albuquerque.

Fort Sumner

If you have a moment to spare, swing through Fort Sumner. The little village that sprang up around old Fort Sumner gets more than a footnote in the history books for two reasons: the disastrous Bosque Redondo Indian Reservation and Billy the Kid's last showdown with Sheriff Pat Garrett.

⊙ Sights & Activities

Hwy 60 (Sumner Ave) is the main thoroughfare and runs east–west through town; most places of interest lie along it.

Billy the Kid Museum   MUSEUM
(www.billythekidmuseumfortsumner.com; 1601 E Sumner Ave; adult/child $5/3; ⊙8:30am-5pm daily mid-May–Sep, 8:30am-5pm Mon-Sat Oct–mid-May, closed first 2 weeks Jan) With more than 60,000 privately owned items on display, this place is more than just a museum about the famous outlaw. It's a veritable shrine, almost a research institution. Indian artifacts and items from late-19th-century frontier life fill many rooms.

Fort Sumner State Monument   MUSEUM
(www.nmmonuments.org; Hwy 272; adult/child $5/free; ⊙8:30am-5pm) During the 1860s, Fort

Sumner was the heart of the Bosque Redondo Indian Reservation – the destination for Navajos forced from their homeland on the Long Walk (p514), as well as captured Mescalero Apaches. Some 10,000 Native Americans were imprisoned here in terrible conditions, and about one-third of them died. Navajo call Fort Sumner *H'weeldi* – the place of suffering. This is also where the Navajo Treaty was signed in 1868, establishing the Navajo Nation as a sovereign people and creating their reservation in their traditional homeland around the Four Corners. The **Bosque Redondo Memorial** within the Ft. Sumner grounds is informative and worth a visit, but the presentation is a bit sterile, lacking the emotional impact you might expect from an exhibit about such a profound tragedy.

Old Fort Sumner Museum   MUSEUM
(Billy the Kid Rd; admission $5; ☉10am-5pm) This museum, with local history and an emphasis on Billy the Kid, is located near the state monument. Behind the museum you'll find **Billy the Kid's Grave** and that of Lucien Maxwell. The Kid's tombstone is protected by an iron cage because 'souvenir hunters' kept trying to steal it – even in death he's behind bars.

 Festivals & Events

Old Fort Days   CULTURAL
Held on the second weekend in June, this festival features various athletic events. The purse for the winner of the tombstone race, in which contestants must negotiate an obstacle course while lugging an 80lb tombstone, is $2000.

Sleeping & Eating

There are few options in Fort Sumner. If you're looking for a hotel, there's a **Super 8** (☎575-355-7888; www.super8.com; 1559 E Sumner Ave; r from $60) on the east end of town. The best restaurant is **Sadie's** (510 Sumner Ave; mains $5-10; ☉7:30am-2pm & 5-8pm Thu-Mon) where you can pick up a homemade breakfast burrito or other simple but good New Mexican fare.

Information

The **chamber of commerce** (☎575-355-7705; www.ftsumnerchamber.com; 707 N 4th St; ☉9am-4pm Mon-Fri) is helpful.

Getting There & Away

Fort Sumner is on Hwy 60, 84 miles north of Roswell, 45 miles southwest of Santa Rosa and 60 miles west of Clovis. It is best reached by private vehicle.

Southwestern Colorado

Best Places to Stay

- » Willowtail Springs (p364)
- » Kelly Place (p371)
- » Wiesbaden (p379)
- » Jersey Jim Lookout Tower (p364)
- » Ruby of Crested Butte (p384)

Best Places to Eat

- » Kennebec Café (p362)
- » New Sheridan Chop House (p375)
- » Secret Stash (p385)
- » East by Southwest (p362)
- » Absolute Baking & Cafe (p364)

Why Go?

The West at its most rugged, this is a landscape of twisting canyons and ancient ruins, with burly peaks and gusty high desert plateaus. Centuries of boom, bust and boom – from silver to real estate and resorts – tell part of the story. There's also the lingering mystery of its earliest inhabitants, whose relics have been found at the abandoned cliff dwellings in Mesa Verde National Park.

Southwestern Colorado can be a heady place to play. Some of the finest powder skiing in the world melts to reveal winding singletrack and hiking trails in summer. A sense of remove keeps the Old West alive in wooden plank saloons and aboard the chugging Durango railroad.

With all that fresh mountain air, local attitudes – from the ranch hand to the real estate agent – are undoubtedly relaxed. Dally a bit under these ultra-blue skies and you'll know why.

When to Go
Silverton

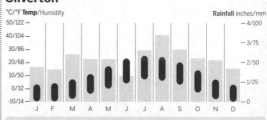

Jun–Aug
Prime time for cycling and hiking the legendary San Juans.

Sep–Nov
Cool days in the high desert and fewer crowds in Mesa Verde.

Dec–Apr
Powder hounds hit the famed slopes of Telluride.

Southwestern Colorado Planning

Summer at high altitude can be chilly – bring warm clothing and sturdy boots. At lower altitudes, the drier desert climate means mild shoulder seasons ideal for camping and mountain biking, while mountain towns like Ouray and Telluride are still buried in snow. In late summer, afternoon mountain thunderstorms are typical, so keep your outings early. Be sure to use caution anywhere above the tree line, and always have plenty of water on hand, since the high-and-dry climate makes it very easy to get dehydrated.

DON'T MISS

In **Mesa Verde National Park**, ranger-led backcountry hikes offer an exclusive peek at America's most mystifying spot. If you're looking to set hearts racing, **San Juan** four-wheeling offers off-path adrenaline with steep cliff drops, hairpin turns and rugged Rockies views.

Powder hounds can grab great late-season deals in the ski town Shangri-la of **Crested Butte**, and foodies can nosh their way through the locavore towns of **Durango**, **Mancos** and **Telluride**.

Tips for Drivers

» US 160, from Durango to Cortez and past Mesa Verde National Park, is the main east–west vein through the region.

» Further north, the fast and convenient US 50 also crosses the state from east to west, linking Montrose with Pueblo, on the north–south I-25 route, a major thoroughfare.

» In winter conditions, chains or snow tires are required on mountain passes.

» For road conditions, call ☎303-639-1111 (recorded message) or visit www.cotrip.org.

Fast Facts

» Colorado population: 5 million

» Area: 104,247 sq miles

» Sales tax: 2.9% state sales tax, plus individual city taxes up to 6%

» Durango to Mesa Verde National Park: 66 miles, one hour

» Telluride to Ouray: 50 miles, one hour

» Durango to Denver: 340 miles, five hours

» Pagosa Springs to Santa Fe: 155 miles, two hours

Powered Up

Thanks to Nikola Tesla, Telluride was the first American city to boast electricity – a key development for the mining that continues today, with the town nesting on the country's biggest uranium belt.

Resources

» Colorado Tourism (☎800-265-6723; www .colorado.com)

» Edible (www.edible communities.com/sanjuan mountains) Local food and farmers markets.

» 14ers (www.14ers.com) Resource for hikers climbing the Rockies' highest summits.

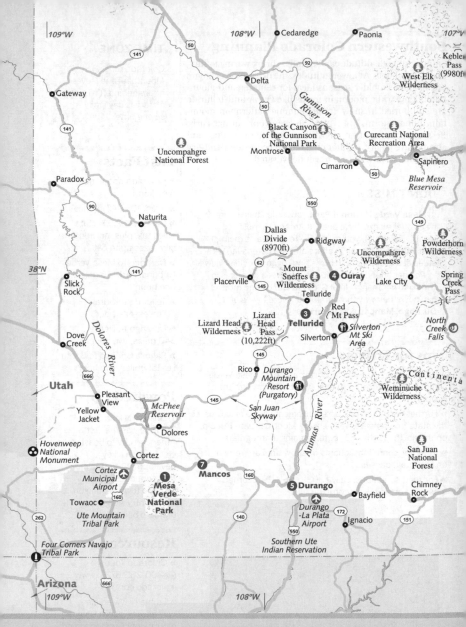

Southwestern Colorado Highlights

① Admiring the ages-old cliff dwellings at **Mesa Verde National Park** (p365)

② Skiing the awesome slopes of spunky **Crested Butte** (p383)

③ Carving the snowbound slopes of **Telluride** (p372)

④ Appreciating the frozen waterfalls and piping hot springs at rugged **Ouray** (p378)

⑤ Tasting the bouquet of local brews at **Durango** (p360)

⑥ Having fun at **Great Sand Dunes National Park**, nature's most stunning sandbox (p383)

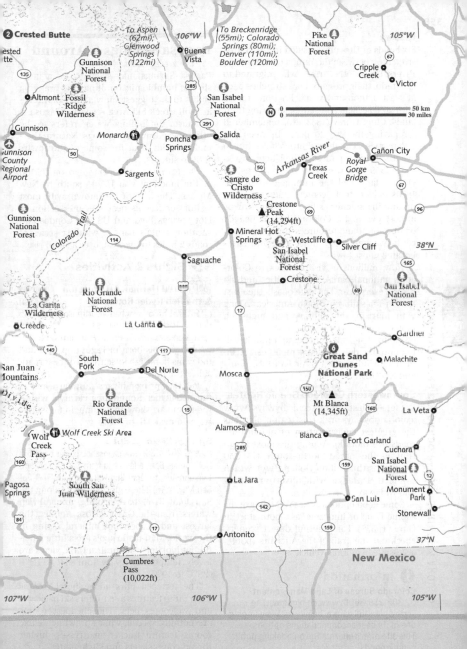

To Aspen (62mi); Glenwood Springs (122mi)

106°W

To Breckenridge (55mi); Colorado Springs (80mi); Denver (110mi); Boulder (120mi)

Pike National Forest

105°W

Buena Vista

Cripple Creek

Victor

67

sted te

135

Altmont

Gunnison National Forest

Fossil Ridge Wilderness

285

San Isabel National Forest

Gunnison

291

Salida

Monarch

50

Poncha Springs

Arkansas River

Royal Gorge Bridge

Cañon City

unnison County Regional Airport

50

Sargents

50

Texas Creek

67

Sangre de Cristo Wilderness

Crestone Peak (14,294ft)

69

96

Gunnison National Forest

114

Mineral Hot Springs

Westcliffe

Silver Cliff

38°N

Saguache

San Isabel National Forest

165

Rio Grande National Forest

888

Crestone

San Isabel National Forest

69

La Garita Wilderness

La Garita

Gardner

Creede

149

112

San Juan Mountains

South Fork

Del Norte

17

Mosca

Great Sand Dunes National Park

6

Malachite

Divide

Rio Grande National Forest

15

150

Mt Blanca (14,345ft)

160

La Veta

Wolf Creek Ski Area

Alamosa

Blanca

Fort Garland

Cuchara

Wolf Creek Pass

285

San Isabel National Forest

160

159

12

Pagosa Springs

South San Juan Wilderness

La Jara

Monument Park

84

142

San Luis

Stonewall

17

159

37°N

Antonito

New Mexico

Cumbres Pass (10,022ft)

107°W

106°W

105°W

0   50 km
0   30 miles

N

7 Poking around friendly and offbeat **Mancos** (p364)

History

Six bands of Utes once resided in a vast area stretching between the Yampa and San Juan Rivers. Unlike other tribes, who migrated to Colorado, their presence here stretches back at least a thousand years. Friction started with gold seekers and settlers entering their lands. Chief Ouray (1833–80), remembered for paving the way to peace between the two parties, actually had little choice but to eventually give up most of the Ute territory.

In 1859, the discovery of gold west of Denver launched the mining era. By the 1870s silver took center stage, making mountain smelter sites thriving towns almost overnight. Colorado relied heavily on its abundant resources until the 20th century, when many mines shut and cities became ghost towns.

Now, millions of visitors flock to Colorado's national parks, historic cities and ski resorts every year. The state boasts the most terrain for skiing in North America. Along with tourism, the military and high-tech industries are major components of the economy. The state is home to a number of high-profile defense-department establishments including the US Air Force Academy and NORAD.

Southwestern Colorado Scenic Routes

Replete with stunning scenic byways (www.coloradobyways.org), this region also has the greatest concentration of old mining roads in Colorado. Among the most beautiful is the paved north–south US 550 (known as the Million Dollar Hwy), which connects Durango with Silverton, Ouray and Ridgway.

Some good options for a 4WD trip are the Alpine Loop or Imogene Pass; both start in Ouray (p378). For beautiful desert scenery, check out the Trail of the Ancients (p369), accessible by normal vehicles.

ℹ Information

Colorado Bureau of Land Management (☎303-239-3600; www.co.blm.gov) The state's plentiful natural beauty makes camping one of its best accommodations options. This site offers information on booking public campgrounds.

Colorado Travel & Tourism Authority (☎800-265-6723; www.colorado.com; PO Box 3524, Englewood, CO 80155) Provides statewide tourism information along with free state highway maps.

Pagosa Springs & Around

POP 1710 / ELEV 7126FT

Pagosa Springs may seem to be a large slice of humble pie, but it has the bragging rights to the biggest snowfall in Colorado – at Wolf Creek Ski Area – nearby. Pagosa, a Ute term for 'boiling water,' refers to the other local draw: hot springs. Natural thermals provide heat for some of the town's 1900 residents.

The town sits east of Durango, on US 160 at the junction with US 84 south to New Mexico. The historic downtown, with most visitor services, is near the intersection of Hot Springs Blvd and US 160. Condos and vacation rentals flank a winding series of roads 2 miles to the west, over a small rise.

◎ Sights & Activities

Fred Harman Art Museum & the Red Ryder Roundup MUSEUM
(☎970-731-5785; www.harmanartmuseum.com; 85 Harman Park Dr; adult/child $4/0.50; ⊙10:30am-5pm Mon-Sat; P 🐾) Fred Harman's comic-book hero was born in Pagosa Springs and today his home is a kitschy and offbeat roadside attraction.

Pagosa Springs' biggest annual event is the Red Ryder Roundup, a carnival with a rodeo and art show and ending in fireworks. It's held near 4th of July.

Springs Resort & Spa SPA
(☎970-264-4168; www.pagosahotsprings.com; 165 Hot Springs Blvd; adult/child from $20/12; ⊙7am-1am Jun-Aug, to 11pm Sun-Thu & to 1am Fri & Sat Sep-May; 🐾🐾) These glorious pools along the San Juan River have healing, mineral-rich waters from the Great Pagosa Aquifer, the largest and deepest hot mineral spring in the world. Man-made pools are a little fanciful but look fairly natural, and the views are lovely. Temperatures vary from 83°F to 111°F (28°C to 49°C).

The terraced pink adobe hotel (rooms from $189) features a spa, offers ski packages and welcomes pets. The cheapest rooms are nothing special, while sprawling deluxe rooms feature thicker mattresses, higher thread-count sheets and kitchenettes.

Pagosa Outside RAFTING
(☎970-264-4202; www.pagosaoutside.com; 350 Pagosa St; rafting from $59; ⊙10am-6pm, reduced hr winter; 🐾) In the springtime, check out this outfitter's white-water trips (Class III) on

LAKE CITY

Whichever road you take to spectacular Lake City, it's worth the drive. Located on two scenic and historic byways – the Silver Thread (Hwy 149) and the 4WD-only Alpine Loop (see p378) – this stress-free mountain community makes the perfect summer day trip or overnight stop. Art galleries and funky shops line the main drag, and there are romantic lodgings and delicious eateries around the Victorian-style historic downtown.

But the weirdness starts every year at the end of June, when the town celebrates **Alferd Packer Days**, a homage to the man who is alleged to have eaten members of his own hiking party in the nearby mountains in 1874. Totally offbeat, the festival includes a mystery-meat cook-off, a bone-throwing contest and coffin races down the main street.

Don't miss one of the most photographed waterfalls in the state. **North Creek Falls** tumble 100 odd feet, crashing through the slot canyon into the Rio Grande River. This booming treasure is hidden south of Lake City in a box canyon off Forest Rd 510, reached via Hwy 149 after crossing Spring Creek Pass.

Lake City is primarily a summer destination. Check the city website (www.lakecity.com) for year-round lodging and services. It's 112 miles north of Pagosa Springs via Hwy 149.

---

the San Juan and Piedra Rivers. The most exciting travels Mesa Canyon, a good spot to sight eagles and other wildlife.

Rivers mellow in summer and the focus turns to river tubing ($15 for two hours, and mountain-biking trips, including a thrilling singletrack route at Turkey Creek, and rentals ($35 per day).

Wolf Creek Ski Area   SNOW SPORTS
(☑970-264-5639; www.wolfcreekski.com; lift ticket adult/child $52/28; ☺Nov–mid-Apr) With more than 450in of snow per year, hitting Wolf Creek on a powder day feels like riding a tidal wave of snow. Located 25 miles north of Pagosa Springs on US 160, this family-owned ski area is one of Colorado's last and best-kept secrets, never crowded and lacking the glitz of larger resorts. Seven lifts service 50 trails, from wide-open bowls to steep tree glades.

**Chimney Rock
Archaeological Area**   ARCHAEOLOGICAL SITE
(☑ visitor cabin 970-883-5359, off-season 970-264-2287; www.chimneyrockco.org; Hwy 151; per vehicle $10, guided tours adult/child $10/5; ☺9am-4:30pm mid-May–late Sep, additional evening hr for special events, tours at 9:30am, 10:30am, 1pm & 2pm; ▣) Like the architects of the elaborate structures in Chaco Canyon – with which this community was connected – the people of the Chimney Rock Archaeological Area were dedicated astronomers and this was a place of spiritual significance. Remains of 100 permanent structures are at the base of two large red-rock buttes.

Today, the rock monuments remain, though the thriving religious and commercial center has been reduced to sketches in stone. The largest pair of buildings, the Great Kiva and Great House, are impressive examples of Chacoan architecture. Designated an Archaeological Area and National Historic Site in 1970, the entire area covers more than 4000 acres of the **San Juan National Forest** land. If the local politicos get their way, Chimney Rock Archaeological Area will soon be designated a National Monument.

🛏 Sleeping & Eating

With the hot springs as a year-round draw, hotels hold rates fairly steady, though are usually cheaper than Durango. Motels and new hotels sprawl out from the city center on US 160. Usually the further away lodging sits from the hot springs, the better the deal.

Fireside Inn Cabins   CABINS $$
TOP CHOICE
(☑888-264-9204; www.firesidecabins.com; 1600 E Hwy 160; cabins from $125, 2-bedroom cabins from $174; ▣❋◉◎▣) Hands down our favorite – each log cabin comes with a Webber grill and planters of wild flowers. Pine interiors have immaculate kitchenettes, quilts, a flat screen TV and wood floors. The San Juan River runs through the back of the property. Equestrians can use the corral, and games available at the central office are great for families.

Pagosa Huts   CABINS $
(www.pagosa-huts.com; San Juan National Forest; cabins $60; ▣) These remote, basic huts are perfect for people trying to get out into the national forest, and they are available to

both hikers and recreational motorists. Getting here is a little rough – the roads can be a mess in the spring – but they offer excellent solitude. Inquire about availability and exact location through the website.

Alpine Inn Motel   MOTEL $

(970-731-4005; www.alpineinnofpagosasprings.com; 8 Solomon Dr; d $69; P❄✳@🐾❄) A converted chain motel, this roadside option is excellent value. The rooms, each with dark carpet and balconies, are a standard size, but the owners are great guides to the local area and there's a deluxe continental breakfast.

Pagosa Brewing Company   BREWPUB $$

(970-731-2739; www.pagosabrewing.com; 118 N Pagosa Blvd; mains $8-12; ☺11am-10pm Mon-Sat; 🍴) Brewmaster Tony Simmons is a professional beer judge, and the Poor Richard's Ale is structured with astute standards – the corn and molasses mix is inspired by the tipple of Ben Franklin. With made-from-scratch pub food (including free-range beef) and picnic tables in a rustic courtyard, it's a fun dinner spot.

JJ's Riverwalk

Restaurant Pub   CONTEMPORARY AMERICAN $$$

(970-264-9100; 356 E Hwy 160; mains $15-40) Overlooking the San Juan River, JJ's has a great vibe, a decent wine list and pleasant service. It can be very spendy, but the menu includes early-bird cheap meals and a nightly happy hour. In summer, patio seating allows you to watch the kayakers paddling by.

ⓘ Information

Pagosa Springs Area Chamber of Commerce (970-264-2360; www.visitpagosasprings.com; 402 San Juan St; ☺9am-5pm Mon-Fri) The Pagosa Springs Area Chamber of Commerce operates a large visitor center located across the bridge from US Hwy 160.

USFS Pagosa Ranger Station (970-264-2268; 180 Pagosa St; ☺8am-4:30pm Mon-Fri)

ⓘ Getting There & Around

Pagosa Springs is at the junction of US 160 and US 84.

Durango

POP 16,700 / ELEV 6580FT

An archetypal old Colorado mining town, Durango is a regional darling nothing short of delightful. Its graceful hotels, Victorian-era saloons and tree-lined streets of sleepy bungalows invite you to pedal around soaking up all the good vibes. There is plenty to do outdoors. Style-wise, Durango is torn between its ragtime past and a cool, cutting-edge future where townie bikes, caffeine and farmers markets rule.

The town's historic central precinct is home to boutiques, bars, restaurants and theater halls. Foodies will revel in the innovative organic and locavore fare that is making it the best place to eat in the state. But there's also interesting galleries and live music that, combined with a relaxed and congenial local populace, make it a great place to visit.

Durango is also an ideal base for exploring the enigmatic ruins at Mesa Verde National Park, 35 miles to the west.

Most visitors' facilities are along Main Ave, including the 1882 Durango & Silverton Narrow Gauge Railroad Depot (at the south end of town). Motels are mostly north of the town center. The compact downtown is easy to walk in a few hours.

◉ Sights & Activities

TOP / **Durango & Silverton**
CHOICE **Narrow Gauge Railroad**   TRAIN RIDE

(970-247-2733, toll-free 877-872-4607; www.durangotrain.com; 479 Main Ave; adult/child return from $83/49; ☺departure at 8am, 8:30am, 9:15am, 10am; 🍴) Riding the Durango & Silverton Narrow Gauge Railroad is a Durango must. These vintage steam locomotives have been making the scenic 45-mile trip north to Silverton (3½ hours each way) for over 125 years. The dazzling journey allows two

---

PEDALING DURANGO

Bike geeks take note: Durango is home to some of the world's best cyclists, who regularly ride the hundreds of local trails ranging from steep singletracks to scenic road rides. Start easy on the **Old Railroad Grade Trail**, a 12.2-mile loop that uses both US Hwy 160 and a dirt road following the old rail tracks. From Durango, take Hwy 160 west through the town of Hesperus. Turn right into the Cherry Creek Picnic Area and the trailhead. For a more technical ride, try **Dry Fork Loop**, accessible from Lightner Creek just west of town. It has some great drops, blind corners and copious vegetation.

hours for exploring Silverton. This trip operates only from May through October. Check online for different winter options.

Big Corral Riding Stable   HORSEBACK RIDING
(970-884-9235; www.vallecitolakeoutfitter.com; 17716 County Rd 501, Bayfield) Highly recommended by locals, this outfitter does day rides and overnight horseback camping for the whole family in the gorgeous Weminiuche Wilderness. If you're short on time, try the two-hour breakfast ride (including sausage, pancakes and cowboy coffee) with views of Vallecito Lake. Located 25 miles northeast of Durango.

Durango Mountain Resort   SNOW SPORTS
(970-247-9000; www.durangomountainresort .com; 1 Skier Pl; lift tickets adult/child from $65/36; midi-Nov–Mar;) Durango Mountain Resort, 25 miles north on US 550, is Durango's winter highlight. The resort, also known as Purgatory, offers 1200 skiable acres of varying difficulty and boasts 260in of snow per year. Two terrain parks offer plenty of opportunities for snowboarders to catch big air

Check local grocery stores and newspapers for promotions and two-for-one lift tickets and other ski season specials before purchasing directly from the ticket window.

**Trimble Spa & Natural
Hot Springs**   HOT SPRINGS
(970-247-0111, toll-free 877-811-7111; www.trimble hotsprings.com; 6475 County Rd 203; day pass adult/child $15/9.50; 10am-9pm Sun-Thu, 10am-10pm Fri & Sat;) For a pampering massage or just a post-hike soak in natural hot springs. Phone or check the website for last-minute specials, which sometimes include two-for-one deals and other discounts. It's 5 miles north of Durango.

Durango Soaring Club   GLIDING
(Val-Air Gliderport; 970-247-9037; www.soar durango.com; 27290 US Hwy 550 North; 20min per person from $100; 9am-6pm mid-May–mid-Oct;) One- and two-person gliding flights highlight the spectacular San Juan scenery. On summer afternoons, when the earth is warmed, the chance of catching rising thermal air currents is best.

Mild to Wild Rafting   RAFTING
(970-247-4789, toll-free 800-567-6745; www.mild 2wildrafting.com; 50 Animas View Dr; trips from $55;) Offers all levels of rafting on the Animas

River; the more adventurous (and experienced) run the upper Animas, which boasts Class III to Class V rapids.

Duranglers   FISHING
(970-385-4081, toll-free 800-347-4346; www .duranglers.com; 923 Main Ave; day trip 1-person/ 2-person $325/350) They won't put the trout on your hook, but Duranglers will do everything to bring you to that gilded moment, serving beginners to experts.

★ Festivals & Events

San Juan Brewfest   BEER
(www.cookmanfood.com/brewfest; Main Ave, btwn 12th & 13th Sts; admission $20; early Sep;) With bands, food and a carnival atmosphere, this event showcases 30-odd specialist brewers from Durango and the region. Attendees (must be aged 21 and over to taste) can vote for the People's Choice award.

Sleeping

**TOP
CHOICE Strater Hotel**   HOTEL $$
(970-247-4431; www.strater.com; 699 Main Ave; d $169-189;) The past lives large in this historical Durango hotel with walnut antiques, hand-stenciled wallpapers and relics ranging from a Stradivarius violin to a gold-plated Winchester. Rooms lean toward the romantic, with comfortable beds amid antiques, crystal and lace. The boastworthy staff goes out of its way to assist with inquiries.

The hot tub is a romantic plus (reserved by the hour), as is the summertime melodrama (theater) the hotel runs. In winter, rates drop by more than 50%, making it a virtual steal. Look online.

Hometown Hostel   HOSTEL $
(970-385-4115; www.durangohometownhostel .com; 736 Goeglein Gulch Rd; dm $30; reception 3:30-8pm;) The bee's knees of hostels, this suburban-style house sits on the winding road up to the college, next to a convenient bike path. A better class of hostel, it's all-inclusive, with linen, towels, lockers and wi-fi. There are two single-sex dorms and a larger mixed dorm, and a great common kitchen and lounge area. Room rates fall with extended stays.

Rochester House   HOTEL $$
(970-385-1920, toll-free 800-664-1920; www .rochesterhotel.com; 721 E 2nd Ave; d $169-219;) Movie posters and marquee lights

adorn the hallways of these two spacious but slightly worn, yet attractive homes. All guests check in at Leland house, across the street. Still, you can't beat the cool townie bikes, available for spins around town. Pet rooms come with direct access outside and some rooms have kitchenettes.

General Palmer Hotel HOTEL $$
(970-247-4747, toll-free 800-523-3358; www .generalpalmer.com; 567 Main Ave; d incl breakfast $105-195; ❀🅿🛜🛗🏊) With turn-of-the-century elegance, this 1898 Victorian has a damsel's taste of floral prints, pewter four-post beds and teddies on every bed. Rooms are small but elegant, and if you tire of TV, there's a collection of board games at the front desk. Check out the cozy library and the relaxing solarium.

Siesta Motel MOTEL $
(970-247-0741; www.durangosiestamotel.com; 3475 N Main Ave; d $58; 🅿❀🛜🛗) This family-owned motel is one of the town's cheaper options, sparkling clean and spacious but admittedly dated. If you're self-catering, there's a little courtyard with a BBQ grill.

✕ Eating

East by Southwest FUSION, SUSHI $$
TOP CHOICE
(970-247-5533; http://eastbysouthwest.com; 160 E College Dr; sushi $4-13, mains $12-24; ⏲11:30am-3pm, 5-10pm Mon-Sat, 5-10pm Sun; 🅿🛗) Low-lit but vibrant, it's packed with locals on date night. Skip the standards for goosebump-good innovations like sashimi with jalapeño or rolls with mango and wasabi honey. Fish is fresh and endangered species are absent from the menu. Fusion plates include Thai, Vietnamese and Indonesian, well matched with creative martinis or sake cocktails. For a deal, grab the happy-hour food specials (5pm to 6:30pm) for around $6.

Randy's MODERN AMERICAN $$$
(970-247-9083; www.randysrestaurant.com; 152 E College Dr; mains $20-25; ⏲5-10pm) Intimate and extremely popular, this upscale spot goes eclectic with seafood and steak, with refreshing lighter fare and specialties like garlic polenta fries. Between 5pm and 6pm, early birds score the same menu for $12 to $14. Happy hour runs from 5pm to 7pm.

Durango Diner DINER $$
(970-247-9889; www.durangodiner.com; 957 Main Ave; mains $7-18; ⏲6am-2pm Mon-Sat, 6am-1pm Sun; 🅿🛗) Enjoy the open view of the griddle at this loveable greasy spoon with button-cute servers and monstrous plates of eggs, smothered burritos or French toast. It's a local institution.

Cyprus Cafe MEDITERRANEAN $$$
(970-385-6884; www.cypruscafe.com; 725 E Second Ave; mains $13-29; ⏲11:30am-2:30pm, 5-9pm, closed Sun; 🛗) Nothing says summer like live jazz on the patio at this little Mediterranean cafe, a favorite of the foodie press. Quality ingredients include locally raised vegetables, wild seafood and natural meats. Favorites include warm duck salad with green olives, oranges and spinach and the Colorado trout with quinoa pilaf. For smaller bites, check out Eno, their wine and coffee bar next door.

Jean Pierre Bakery FRENCH, BAKERY $$$
(970-247-7700; www.jeanpierrebakery.com; 601 Main Ave; mains $15-35; ⏲8am-9pm; 🅿🛗) A charming patisserie serving mouthwatering delicacies made from scratch. Dinner is a much more formal affair. Prices are dear, but at $15, the soup-and-sandwich lunch special with a sumptuous French pastry (we recommend the sticky pecan roll) is a deal.

Olde Tymers Café BURGERS $
(970-259-2990; www.otcdgo.com; 1000 Main Ave; mains $4-10; ⏲11am-10pm; 🅿🛗) Voted as having the best burger in Durango by the local paper, these cozy booths host the college crowd for other American classics too, like fried chicken and mashed potatoes. Ask about the cheap daily specials.

DON'T MISS

KENNEBEC CAFÉ

This countryside romantic **cafe** (970-247-5674; www.kennebeccafe.com; 4 County Rd 124; mains $10-29; ⏲11am-3pm, 5-9pm Tue-Fri, 8am-3pm, 5-9pm Sat & Sun) may flaunt Euro style, but it bares American overtones, with local Ska brews on tap, as well as an extensive wine list. Think tasty and creative – Chef Miguel Carillo serves up Duck Two Ways (seared with a pomegranate glaze) and poblano chiles stuffed with strip steak. Weekend brunch makes playful twists on old favorites, best enjoyed on the patio. It's located in Hesperus, 10 miles west of Durango on Highway 140.

Drinking & Entertainment

Ska Brewing Company BREWERY

(970-247-5792; www.skabrewing.com; 225 Girard St; ⊙11am-3pm Mon-Wed, 11am-3pm & 5-8pm Thu, 11am-8pm Fri) Big on flavor and variety, these are the best beers in town. The small, friendly tasting-room bar, once mainly a production facility, packs with an after-work crowd. Call for dates of weekly BBQs with live music and free food.

Steamworks Brewing BREWERY

(970-259-9200; www.steamworksbrewing.com; 801 E 2nd Ave; mains $10-15; ⊙1pm-midnight Mon-Fri, 11am-2am Sat & Sun) DJs and live music pump up the volume at this industrial microbrewery, with high sloping rafters and metal pipes. College kids fill the large bar area, but there's also a separate dining room with a Cajun-influenced menu.

Durango Brewing Co BREWERY

(970-247-3396; www.durangobrewing.com; 3000 Main Ave; ⊙tap room 9am-5pm) While the ambiance is nothing special, serious beer fans can appreciate that these guys concentrate on the brews. There's taproom tastings and it's open seven days a week.

Diamond Belle Saloon BAR

(970-376-7150; www.strater.com; 699 Main Ave; ⊙11am-late;) A rowdy corner of the historic Strater Hotel, this elegant old-time bar has waitresses flashing Victorian-era fishnets and live ragtime that keeps out-of-town visitors packed in, standing room only, at happy hour. Half-price appetizers and drink specials run from 4pm to 6pm. Also in Strater, The Office serves cocktails in an upscale and much more low-key atmosphere.

Henry Strater Theatre LIVE MUSIC

(970-375-7160; www.henrystratertheatre.com; 699 Main Ave; adult/child from $20/18;) Internationally renown, producing old-world music-hall shows, live bands, comedy, community theatre and more for nearly 50 years.

 Shopping

Durango may be the best place to shop in the region for sporting gear and outdoor fashions (locals will take prAna over Prada any day). There are also delightful boutiques and galleries along Main Ave.

 Pedal the Peaks SPORTING GOODS

(970-259-6880; www.pedalthepeaks.biz; 598b Main Ave; full-suspension rentals $80; ⊙9am-5pm Mon-Sat, 10am-5pm Sun;) This specialist bike store offers the works from mountain- and road-bike sales and rentals, custom-worked cycles, trail maps and accessories. The staff are all hardcore riders, and their friendly advice and local knowledge are second to none.

2nd Avenue Sports SPORTING GOODS

(970-247-4511; www.2ndavesports.com; 600 E 2nd Ave; ⊙9am-6pm Mon-Sat, 10am-5pm Sun) Skiing and extensive cycling and mountain-biking gear for sale and rental.

Maria's Bookshop BOOKS

(970-247-1438; www.mariasbookshop.com; 960 Main Ave; ⊙9am-9pm) A good general bookstore – independently owned and well stocked; does e-reader orders too.

 Information

Durango Area Tourism Office (970-247-3500, toll free 800-525-8855; www.durango.org; 111 S Camino del Rio; ⊙8am-5pm Mon-Fri;) Located south of town, at the Santa Rita exit from US 550.

Mercy Regional Medical Center (970-247-4311; www.mercydurango.org; 1010 Three Springs Ave) Outpatient and 24-hour emergency care.

San Juan–Rio Grande National Forest Headquarters (970-247-4874; www.fs.fed.us/r2/sanjuan; 15 Burnett Ct; ⊙8am-5pm Mon-Sat) Offers camping and hiking information and maps. It's about a half-mile west on US Hwy 160.

Getting There & Away

Durango lies at the junction of US Hwy 160 and US Hwy 550, 42 miles east of Cortez, 49 miles west of Pagosa Springs and 190 miles north of Albuquerque in New Mexico.

AIR Durango–La Plata County Airport (DRO; 970-247-8143; www.flydurango.com; 1000 Airport Rd) Durango–La Plata County Airport is 18 miles southeast of Durango via US Hwy 160 and Hwy 172. Both United and Frontier Airlines have direct flights to Denver; US Airways flies to Phoenix.

BUS Greyhound buses run daily from the Durango Bus Center north to Grand Junction and south to Albuquerque, NM.

Getting Around

Check the website of **Durango Transit** (970-259-5438; www.getarounddurango.com) for local travel information. All Durango buses are fitted with bicycle racks. Free, the bright-red T shuttle bus trundles up and down Main St.

Mancos

POP 1260 / ELEV 7028FT

At 10am, tiny Mancos may feel like another Colorado ghost town, but poke around and you'll find an offbeat and inviting community. Downtown has historic homes, art and crafts cooperatives and landmark buildings, while the countryside offers spacious views and ranch-style B&B options. Mesa Verde National Park is just 7 miles to the west, so if visiting the park is on your itinerary, staying in Mancos makes an appealing alternative to Cortez's rather nondescript motels.

🛏 Sleeping

TOP CHOICE Willowtail Springs LODGE, CABINS $$$

(☎800-698-0603; www.willowtailsprings.com; 10451 County Rd 39; cabins $249-279; 🐾📶) Peggy and Lee, artist and T'ai Chi master, have crafted a setting that inspires and helps you to slow down. Way down, to the pace of the largemouth bass in their pond. Intimate and spectacular, these exquisite camps sit within 60 acres of gardens and ponderosa forest.

Two immaculate cabins and a spacious lake house (sleeping six) feature warm and exotic decor (note the real remnant beehive!) There are also clawfoot tubs, Peggy's fabulous original art and a canoe hitched up to the dock. Kitchens are stocked with organic goodies and extras include candlelight chef dinners, reasonable catered meals and massages. It's also a wildlife sanctuary (raptors are released here) and, for roamers, a little slice of heaven. It's well outside of town; get directions from the website.

TOP CHOICE Jersey Jim Lookout Tower LOOKOUT TOWER $

(☎970-533-7060; www.fs.fed.us/r2/recreation/rentals; r $40; ⏰mid-May–mid-Oct) How about spending the night in a former fire-lookout tower? Standing 55ft above a meadow 14 miles north of Mancos at an elevation of 9800ft, this place is on the National Historic Lookout Register and comes with an Osborne Fire Finder and topographic map.

The tower accommodates up to four adults with a two-night minimum stay. Bring your own bedding and water. There is a functioning kitchen. The reservation office opens on the first workday of March (1pm to 5pm) and the entire season is typically booked within days.

Flagstone Meadows Ranch Bed & Breakfast B&B $$

(☎970-533-9838; www.flagstonemeadows.com; 38080 Rd K-4; d incl breakfast $115-125) A welcoming Western-ranch home with knotty pine walls, quilted beds, cathedral ceilings and a stone fireplace. The Navajo-speaking host offers a wealth of local knowledge, and guests enjoy long views of the snowy La Plata range.

Enchanted Mesa Motel MOTEL $

(☎970-533-7729; www.enchantedmesamotel.com; 862 W Grand Ave; r from $45; 🛏📶) Hipper than most independent motels, this place has shiny lamps, solid wooden furniture and a play area out front for the kids. Best of all, you can shoot pool while waiting for your whites to dry at the laundry room billiards table.

🍴 Eating & Drinking

📋 Absolute Baking & Cafe BREAKFAST, SANDWICHES $

(☎970-533-1200; 110 S Main St; mains $6-8; ⏰7am-2pm; 🐾🛏) The screen door is always swinging open at this town hot spot with giant breakfasts. Try the green chile on eggs—it's made from scratch, as are the organic breads and pastries. Lunch includes salads, big sammies and local, grass-fed beef burgers. Grab a bag for the trail, but don't forgo a square of gooey, fresh carrot cake.

If you're in the market for a new read, the cafe has a decent collection of used books for sale; so grab a cup of coffee, chat with friendly wait staff and just chill out.

Millwood Junction STEAKHOUSE $$

(☎970-533-7338; www.millwoodjunction.com; cnr Main St & Railroad Ave; mains $10-20; ⏰11am-2pm daily, 5:30-10:30pm Mon-Fri; 🛏) A popular steak and seafood dinner joint, though the food isn't always spot on. The restaurant often doubles as a club, showcasing live music.

Fahrenheit Coffee Roasters COFFEE SHOP

(201 W Grand Ave; ⏰7am-5pm Mon-Sat, 7am-2pm Sun; 📶) Surrounded by the aroma of fresh roasted beans, this espresso house also serves slices of homemade pie and breakfast burritos to go.

Arborena WINE BAR

(☎970-533-1381; 114 W Grand Ave; ⏰4-9pm Mon, Thu-Sat) A welcome alternative to another brewery, in this stylish art gallery you can sip wines by the glass, accompanied by cheese plates, baguettes and salads. Thursday is Girls' Night Out – women save a dollar on drinks.

Columbine Bar
BAR

(☎970-533-7397; 123 W Grand Ave; ⊙10am-2am) This smoky old saloon, established in 1903, is one of Colorado's oldest continuously operating bars. Join locals shooting pool over pints of ice-cold local brews.

Mancos Valley Distillery
DISTILLERY

(www.mancosvalleydistillery.com; 116 N Main St; ⊙hours vary) If you're interested in tasting something *really* local, make your way to this alleyway where artisan distiller Ian James crafts delicate rum (and chocolate). With sporadic hours, check the website.

❶ Information

Mancos Valley Visitors Center (☎702-533-7434; www.mancosvalley.com; 101 E Bauer St; ⊙9am-5pm Mon-Fri) Historic displays and a walking-tour map are available at the visitor center. It also has information on outdoor activities and local ranches that offer horseback rides and Western-style overnight trips.

Mesa Verde National Park

More than 700 years after its inhabitants left, the mystery behind **Mesa Verde** (☎970-529 4465; www.nps.gov/meve; 7-day pass private cars/motorcycles $15/8 Jun-Sep, $10/5 low season) remains. This civilization of Ancestral Puebloans (see p512) abandoned the area in 1300. Today their last known home is preserved as Mesa Verde. Amateur anthropologists will love it; the focus on preserving cultural relics makes Mesa Verde unique among American national parks.

Ancestral Puebloan sites are found throughout the canyons and mesas of the park, perched on a high plateau south of Cortez and Mancos, though many remain off-limits to visitors. The NPS strictly enforces the Antiquities Act, which prohibits the removal or destruction of any antiquities and prohibits public access to many of the approximately 4000 known Ancestral Puebloan sites.

If you only have a few hours, the best approach is a stop at the visitor center and a drive around Wetherill Mesa combined with a short walk to the easily accessible Spruce Tree House, the park's best-preserved cliff dwelling. If you have a day or more, take the ranger-led tours of Cliff Palace and Balcony House, explore Wetherill Mesa, linger around the museum or participate in one of the campfire programs run at Morefield Campground.

The park occupies a mesa, with North Rim summit at Park Point (8571ft) towering more than 2000ft above the Montezuma Valley. From Park Point the mesa gently slopes southward to a 6000ft elevation above the Mancos River in the Ute Mountain Tribal Park. Parallel canyons, typically 500ft below the rim, dissect the mesa-top and carry the drainage southward. Mesa Verde National Park occupies 81 sq miles of the northernmost portion of the mesa and contains the largest and most frequented cliff dwellings and surface sites.

Planned for 2012, the new Mesa Verde Visitor and Research Center, located just beyond the park entrance, will replace the Far View Visitor Center. The cutting-edge LEED-certified compound will feature a 7000-sq-ft visitor center featuring exhibits and a repository for the park's 3 million artifacts.

History

A US army lieutenant recorded spectacular cliff dwellings in the canyons of Mesa Verde in 1849-50. The large number of sites on Ute tribal land, and their relative inaccessibility, protected the majority of these antiquities from pothunters.

The first scientific investigation of the sites in 1874 failed to identify Cliff Palace, the largest cliff dwelling in North America. Discovery of this 'magnificent city' occurred only when local cowboys Richard Wetherill and Charlie Mason were searching for stray cattle in 1888. The cowboys exploited their discovery for the next 18 years by guiding both amateur and trained archaeologists to the site, particularly to collect the distinctive black-on-white pottery.

PARK TIPS

The park is busiest over 4th of July, Memorial Day and Labor Day weekends. On busy days, visitors are allowed one tour only. Assure your spot by buying tickets one day in advance (there is often a 45-minute wait in line in summer). The best information can be found in the latest visitor's guide, available online at www.nps.gov/meve/planyourvisit.

Mesa Verde

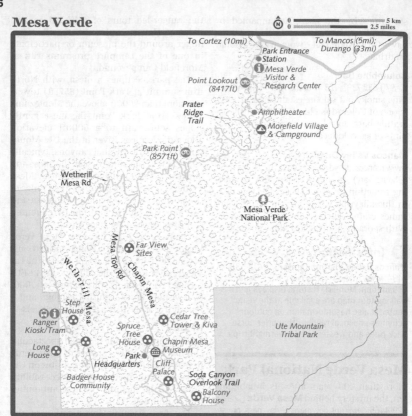

When artifacts started being shipped overseas, Virginia McClurg of Colorado Springs began a long campaign to preserve the site and its contents. McClurg's efforts led Congress to protect artifacts on federal land, with the passage of the Antiquities Act establishing Mesa Verde National Park in 1906.

The park entrance is off US 160, midway between Cortez and Mancos. Near the entrance, the new Mesa Verde Visitor and Research Center opens in 2012. From here it's about 21 miles to park headquarters, Chapin Mesa Museum and Spruce Tree House. Along the way are Morefield Campground (4 miles), the panoramic viewpoint at Park Point (8 miles) and the Far View Lodge – about 11 miles. Towed vehicles are not allowed beyond Morefield Campground.

South from park headquarters, Mesa Top Rd consists of two one-way circuits. Turn left about a quarter mile from the start of Mesa Top Rd to visit Cliff Palace and Balcony House on the east loop. From the junction with the main road at Far View Visitor Center, the 12-mile mountainous Wetherill Mesa Rd snakes along the North Rim, acting as a natural barrier to tour buses and indifferent travelers. The road is open only from Memorial Day in late May to Labor Day in early September.

☉ Sights

PARK POINT

With panoramic views, the fire lookout at Park Point (8571ft) has the highest elevation in the park. To the north are the 14,000ft peaks of the San Juan Mountains; in the northeast is the 12,000ft La Plata range; to the southwest, beyond the southward sloping Mesa Verde plateau, is the distant volcanic plug of Shiprock; and to the west is the prone, humanlike profile of Sleeping Ute Mountain.

CHAPIN MESA

Chapin Mesa features the most dense clusters of remnants of Ancestral Puebloan settlements. It's a unique opportunity to see and compare examples of all phases of construction – from pothouses to Pueblo villages to the elaborate multiroom cities tucked into cliff recesses. Pamphlets describing the most excavated sites are available at either the visitor center or Chapin Mesa Museum.

On the upper portion of Chapin Mesa, the Far View Sites were the most densely settled area in Mesa Verde after AD 1100. The large-walled Pueblo sites at Far View House enclose a central kiva and planned room layout that was originally two stories high. To the north is a small row of rooms and an attached circular tower that likely used to extend just above the adjacent 'pygmy forest' of piñon pine and juniper trees. This tower is one of 57 in Mesa Verde that may once have served as watchtowers, religious structures or astronomical observatories for agricultural schedules.

South from park headquarters, the 6-mile Mesa Top Rd circuit connects 10 excavated mesa-top sites, three accessible cliff dwellings and many vantages of inaccessible cliff dwellings from the mesa rim. It's open 8am to sunset.

Chapin Mesa Museum   MUSEUM
(970-529-4475; www.nps.gov/meve; Chapin Mesa Rd; admission included with park entry; 8am-6:30pm Apr–mid-Oct, 8am-5pm mid-Oct–Apr) A good first stop, with detailed dioramas and exhibits pertaining to the park. When park headquarters are closed on weekends, staff at the museum provide information.

Spruce Tree House   ARCHAEOLOGICAL SITE
(Chapin Mesa Rd; admission included with park entry) The most accessible of the archaeological sites, although the paved half-mile round-trip access path is still a moderately steep climb. Spruce Tree House was once home to 60 or 80 people and its construction began around AD 1210. Like other sites, old walls and houses have been stabilized.

Rangers are on hand to answer questions and offer free guided tours from November to April at 10am, 1pm and 3:30pm.

CLIFF PALACE & MESA TOP LOOPS
This is the most visited part of the park. Access to the major Ancestral Puebloan sites is only by ranger-led tour, and tickets must be pre-purchased in person from the visitor center, Morefield Ranger Station or the Colorado Welcome Center in Cortez. These tours are well-worth it; purchase several days ahead to ensure your spot in high season.

Cliff Palace   ARCHAEOLOGICAL SITE
(Cliff Palace Loop; one-hour guided tour $3) The only way to see the superb Cliff Palace is to take an hour-long ranger-led tour that retraces the steps taken by the Ancestral Puebloans. This grand representative of engineering achievement, with 217 rooms and 23 kivas, provided shelter for 250 or 300 people.

Its inhabitants were without running water. However, springs across the canyon, below Sun Temple, were most likely their primary water sources. The use of small 'chinking' stones between the large blocks is strikingly similar to Ancestral Puebloan construction at distant Chaco Canyon.

Balcony House   ARCHAEOLOGICAL SITE
(Cliff Palace Loop; one-hour guided tour $3) Tickets are required for the one-hour guided tours of Balcony House, on the east side of the Cliff Palace Loop. The tour could prove a challenge for those with a fear of heights or small places. But it includes outstanding views of Soda Canyon, 600ft below the sandstone overhang that once served as the ceiling for 35 to 40 rooms.

Visitors must descend a 100ft-long staircase into the canyon, then climb a 32ft-tall ladder, crawl through a 12ft-long tunnel and climb an additional 60ft of ladders and stone steps to get out. It's not recommended for people with medical problems. The most physical tour in the park, it's also the most rewarding, not to mention fun!

WETHERILL MESA
The less-frequented western portion of Mesa Verde offers a comprehensive display of Ancestral Pueblo relics. The Badger House Community consists of a short trail connecting four excavated surface sites depicting various phases of Ancestral Puebloan development.

Long House   ARCHAEOLOGICAL SITE
(Wetherill Mesa Rd; one-hour guided tour $3) On the Wetherill Mesa side of the canyon is Long House. It's a strenuous place to visit and can only be done as part of a ranger-led guided tour (organized from the visitor center). Access involves climbing three ladders – two at 15ft and one at 4ft – and a

0.75-mile hike, and there's an aggregate 130ft elevation to descend and ascend.

 Step House ARCHAEOLOGICAL SITE
(Wetherill Mesa Rd; admission included with park entry) Step House was initially occupied by Modified Basketmaker peoples residing in pithouses, and later became the site of a Classic Pueblo-period masonry complex with rooms and kivas. The 0.75-mile trail to Step House involves a 100ft descent and ascent.

Activities

Hiking

Hiking is a great way to explore the park, but follow the rules. Backcountry access is specifically forbidden and fines are imposed on anyone caught wandering off designated trails or entering cliff dwellings without a ranger. Please respect these necessary regulations, so that these fragile and irreplaceable archaeological sights and artifacts remain protected for centuries to come.

Always carry water and wear appropriate footwear. Trails – some cliffside – can be muddy and slippery after rain or snow. Most, except the Soda Canyon Trail, are strenuous and involve steep elevation changes. Register at the respective trailheads before venturing out.

The 2.8-mile **Petroglyph Loop Trail** is accessed from Spruce Tree House. It follows a path beneath the edge of a plateau before making a short climb to the top of the mesa, where you'll have good views of the Spruce and Navajo Canyons. This is the only trail in the park where you can view petroglyphs.

The 2.1-mile **Spruce Canyon Loop Trail** also begins at Spruce Tree House and descends to the bottom of Spruce Tree Canyon. It's a great way to see the canyon bottoms of Mesa Verde.

Cycling

Finding convenient parking at the many stops along Mesa Top Rd is no problem for those with bikes. But only the hardy will want to enter the park by bike and immediately face the grueling 4-mile ascent to Morefield Campground, quickly followed by a narrow tunnel ride to reach the North Rim. An easier option is to unlimber your muscles and mount up at Morefield or park headquarters.

Skiing & Snowshoeing

In winter, Mesa Verde's crowds are replaced with blue skies and snows that drape the cliff dwellings. Sometimes there is enough snow to ski or snowshoe after a snowstorm (although Colorado's dry climate and sunshine cause it to melt quickly). Before setting out, check the current conditions by calling park headquarters.

Two park roads have been designated for cross-country skiing and snowshoeing when weather permits. The **Cliff Palace Loop Rd** is a 6-mile relatively flat loop located off the Mesa Top Loop Rd. The road is closed to vehicles after the first snowfall, so you won't have to worry about vehicular traffic. Park at the closed gate and glide 1 mile to the Cliff Palace overlook, continuing on past numerous other scenic stopping points.

The **Morefield Campground Loop Rds** offer multiple miles of relatively flat terrain. The campground is closed in winter, but skiers and snowshoers can park at the gate and explore to their heart's content.

Tours

Park concessionaire **Aramark** (www.visitmesaverde.com; adult/child $35/17.50) offers ranger-led bus tours that depart Far View Lodge at 1pm daily.

DON'T MISS

UTE MOUNTAIN TRIBAL PARK

If Mesa Verde leaves you intrigued but wanting a more intimate experience, this alternative has been getting rave reviews. The **park** (970-749-1452; www.utemountainute.com; Morning Star Lane; half-day/full-day tours per person $28/47; by appointment) features a number of fascinating archaeological sites from both Utes and Ancient Puebloans, including petroglyphs and cliff dwellings, accessed only through tours led by Ute tribal members. While half-day tours are suitable to all, full-day tours are physically demanding; visitors hike 3 miles into the backcountry and up ladders to cliff dwellings. It's best to use transportation provided by the tribal park ($10 per person) to avoid 80 miles of wear and tear on your vehicle.

Book in advance or stop by **Ute Mountain Casino, Hotel & Resort** (hotel reservations 800-258-8007; 3 Weeminuche Dr; d $75-95, sites $30), near Sleeping Ute Mountain, for information. There's also primitive camping and cabin rentals.

SCENIC DRIVE: TRAIL OF THE ANCIENTS

An arid moonscape with cliff dwellings, pottery shreds and rock art, the Trail of the Ancients traces the territory of the Ancestral Puebloans. The 114-mile drive uses Hwy 145, Hwy 184 and US 160. Begin in Cortez and either head northwest toward Hovenweep National Monument on the Utah border (which, like Mesa Verde, contains dense clusters of Ancestral Puebloan dwellings) or southwest toward Four Corners, where Colorado, Utah, Arizona and New Mexico meet. Allow three hours for driving.

Highly recommended, the **Mesa Verde Institute** (www.mesaverdeinstitute.org) runs ranger-led backcountry hikes. The only way to access restricted backcountry, they have proved duly popular, usually selling out. With participants limited to 10 or 12 people, these trips offer a very intimate look at the sites. Tickets may be purchased at the visitor center or online. Also check the website for new or limited-time offerings.

Square House Hiking Tour   HIKING
(per person $20; ⊘8am, Sep–mid-October) The park's most popular ranger-led hike, this strenuous 1-mile hike takes two hours but includes exposure to cliffs, rocky slopes, climbing a 20ft ladder and two shorter ladders. One highlight is seeing one of only two original kiva roofs in the park.

Oak Tree House and Fire Temple   HIKING
(per person $20; ⊘departs 8am late May–early Sep; ♿) This strenuous 1-mile hike takes two hours, features some exposure and requires a 15ft ladder climb. Meet at the Sun Temple (Mesa Top Loop Rd).

Spring House Hiking Tour   HIKING
(per person $40; ⊘8am, May 4-Sep 30) For serious hikers only, this 8-hour, 8-mile round-trip has steep drop-offs, switchbacks and an elevation change of 1500ft. Remote sites are part of the itinerary. Wear hiking boots and bring plenty of water and sunscreen.

✵ Festivals & Events

12 Hours of Mesa Verde   MOUNTAIN-BIKE RACE
(www.12hoursofmesaverde.com; per rider early-bird/regular $65/80; ⊘May) In this popular 12-

hour relay-endurance bike event, teams race against each other over an incredible network of trails across the national park. All proceeds raised go to the Montezuma County Partners – a mentoring program for youths at risk.

🛏 Sleeping

Nearby Cortez, Mancos or Durango (36 miles to the east) have plenty of accommodations. Within the national park, visitors can stay at the lodge or camp. Stay overnight to catch sites during the best viewing hours, participate in evening programs and enjoy the sunset over Sleeping Ute Mountain.

Morefield Campground   CAMPING $
(☑970-529-4465; www.nps.gov/meve; North Rim Rd; campsite $20, canvas tents from $40; ⊘May–mid-Oct) Deluxe campers will dig the big canvas tents kitted out with two cots and a lantern. The park's camping option, located 4 miles from the entrance gate, also has 115 regular tent sites on grassy grounds conveniently located near Morefield Village. The village has a general store, gas station, restaurant, free showers and laundry. Free evening campfire programs take place nightly from Memorial Day (May) to Labor Day (September) at the Morefield Campground Amphitheater.

Far View Lodge   LODGE $$
(☑970-529-4421, toll-free 800-449-2288; www.visitmesaverde.com; North Rim Rd; r from $119; ⊘mid-Apr–Oct; ﭏ❄⊛♿) Perched on a mesatop 15 miles inside the park entrance, this tasteful Pueblo-style lodge has 150 rooms, some with kiva fireplaces. Southwestern-style kiva rooms are a worthy upgrade, with balconies, pounded copper sinks and bright patterned blankets. Don't miss sunset over the mesa from your private balcony. Standard rooms don't have air-con (or TV) and summer daytimes can be hot.

🍴 Eating

Metate Room   CONTEMPORARY AMERICAN $$
(☑800-449-2288; www.visitmesaverde.com; North Rim Rd; mains $15-25; ⊘5-7:30pm year-round, & 7-10am Apr–mid-Oct; ♿♿) With lovely views, this innovative restaurant in the Far View Lodge offers regional flavors with some innovation, with dishes like cinnamon chile pork, elk shepherd's pie and trout crusted in pine nuts. You can also get local Colorado beers.

Far View Terrace Café   CAFE FOOD $
(☑970-529-4421, toll-free 800-449-2288; www.visitmesaverde.com; North Rim Rd; dishes from $5;

⊘7-10am, 11am-3pm & 5-8pm May–mid-Oct; 🖉🖶) In Far View Lodge, a self-service place with reasonably priced meals. Don't miss the house special – the Navajo taco.

ℹ️ Information

MAPS Good maps are issued to visitors at the national park gate on entry. Quality topographical maps can be bought at the visitor center and the museum as well as in stores in Durango and Cortez.

TOURIST INFORMATION Mesa Verde Visitor & Research Center (📞800-305-6053, 970-529-5034; www.nps.gov/meve; North Rim Rd; ⊘8am-7pm daily Jun-early Sep, 8am-5pm early Sep–mid-Oct, closed mid-Oct–May; 🖶) Visitor information and tickets for tours of Cliff Palace, Balcony House or Long House. Note: before the center is completed in 2012, visitors should use the Far View Visitor Center, located 15 miles from the entrance.

Mesa Verde Museum Association (📞970-529-4445, toll-free 800-305-6053; www.mesaverde.org; Chapin Mesa Rd; ⊘8am-6:30pm Apr–mid-Oct, 8am-5pm mid-Oct–Apr; 🖶) Attached to the Chapin Mesa Museum, this nonprofit organization sponsors research activities and exhibits. It has an excellent selection of materials on the Ancestral Puebloans and modern tribes in the American Southwest, and has books, posters and glossy calendars for sale.

Park Headquarters (📞970-529-4465; www.nps.gov/meve; Chapin Mesa Rd; 7-day park entry per vehicle $15, cyclists, hikers & motorcyclists $8; ⊘8am-5pm Mon-Fri; 🖶) The Mesa Verde National Park entrance is off US 160, midway between Cortez and Mancos. From the entrance it is 21 miles to the park headquarters. You can get road information and the word on park closures (many areas are closed in winter).

ℹ️ Getting There & Around

Mesa Verde is best accessed by private vehicle. In the park, a new biodiesel **tram** (free; ⊘9:20am-3:30pm daily, every 30min) shuttles visitors around Wetherill Mesa, starting at the ranger kiosk; park here.

Cortez

POP 8640 / ELEV 6201FT

Cortez fails to beguile, but its location, 10 miles west of Mesa Verde National Park, makes it a logical base, and the surrounding area holds quiet appeal. Mountain bikers will covet the hundreds of great singletrack rides nearby.

Typical of small-town Colorado, downtown Cortez is lined with trinket and rifle shops; family-style restaurants dishing up meat and potatoes; and the requisite microbrewery. The edges of the town are jam-packed with independent motels and fast-food outlets. Far-off mountain vistas complete the picture.

◉ Sights & Activities

FREE **Cultural Park** MUSEUM
(⊘10am-9pm Mon-Sat summer, to 5pm winter) An outdoor space at the Cortez Cultural Center with art, weaving demonstrations and a Navajo hogan. Summer evening programs feature Native American dances six nights a week at 7:30pm, followed at 8:30pm by cultural programs such as Native American storytellers.

FREE **Cortez Cultural Center** MUSEUM
(📞702-565-1151; www.cortezculturalcenter.org; 25 N Market St; ⊘10am-9pm Mon-Sat May-Oct, to 5pm Nov-Apr; 🖶) Exhibits on the Ancestral Puebloans, as well as visiting art displays, make this museum worthy of a visit if you have a few hours to spare.

Crow Canyon Archaeology Center ARCHAEOLOGICAL SITE
(📞970-565-8975, 800-422-8975; www.crowcanyon.org; 23390 Rd K; adult/child $55/30; ⊘9am-5pm Wed & Thu Jun–mid-Sep; 🖶) An excellent way to learn about Ancestral Puebloan culture and the significance of regional artifacts firsthand; daylong programs visit an excavation site west of town. In weeklong sessions, guests share traditional Pueblo hogans and study excavation field and lab techniques. It's 3 miles north of Cortez.

Kokopelli Bike & Board BIKE RENTALS
(📞970-565-4408; www.kokopellibike.com; 30 W Main St; per day $20; ⊘9am-6pm Mon-Fri, to 5pm Sat) The friendly staff at this local bike shop are happy to talk trails, they also rent and repair mountain bikes. For some pre-trip planning, visit the shop's website with great trail descriptions.

🛏️ Sleeping

Budget motels dot the main drag; expect winter discounts around 50%. Sadly, the only campground in town not right next to a highway or dedicated to RVs is the **Cortez-Mesa Verde KOA** (📞970-565-9301; 27432 E Hwy 160; sites $25-32, cabins $50; ⊘Apr-Oct; 📶❄️🖶) at the east end of town.

MOUNTAIN BIKING THE FOUR CORNERS

Cortez offers some epic mountain-bike trails among piñon-juniper woodland and over the otherworldly slickrock mesa. Some ideas include **Sand Canyon**, an 18-mile trail starting at the same-named archaeological site west of Cortez. For advanced riders, the 27-mile **Stoner Mesa Loop** has splendid views. For details, check out *Mountain and Road Bike Routes for the Cortez-Dolores-Mancos Area*. The staff at Kokopelli Bike & Board are helpful.

TOP CHOICE **Kelly Place**   B&B $$

(⌂970-565-3125; www.kellyplace.com; 14663 Montezuma County Rd G; r & cabins $80-155, 2-person campsite/RV site $40/50; ☎⌂) It is pretty rare to find a B&B with archaeological ruins and a network of desert trails with nary another soul in sight. Founded by late botanist George Kelly, this lovely adobe-style guest lodge is situated on 40 acres of orchards, red-rock canyon and Indian ruins abutting Canyon of the Ancients, 15 miles west of Cortez. A pamphlet given to guests helps to locate and understand the ruins, in addition to identifying local plants. Rooms are tasteful and rates (even camping) include an enormous buffet breakfast.

There is a range of cabins, the best sports a private flagstone patio and whirlpool tub. Kelly Place also offers horseback riding, cultural tours and archaeological programs. At night put a DVD on the big-screen TV in the communal lounge and chill with a glass of wine or a tasty microbrew; the lodge serves both.

Tomahawk Lodge   LODGE $

(⌂970-565-8521, 800-643-7705; www.angelfire.com /co2/tomahawk; 728 S Broadway; r from $75; ☎⌂☎) Friendly hosts welcome you at this clean, good-value place. It feels more personable than the average motel with unique Native American art on the walls and a pool out front.

Best Western Turquoise Inn & Suites   HOTEL $$

(⌂970-565-3778; www.bestwestern.com; 535 E Main St; r from $130; P☎⌂☎⌂) With two swimming pools, this is a good choice for families (kids stay free, and the restaurant has a kids' menu). Rooms here are spacious, and bigger families can grab a two-room suite. If you're exploring Mesa Verde all day and just want an affordable and clean, if slightly bland, hotel to crash at night, this central Best Western will do the trick.

🍴 Eating & Drinking

Main Street Brewery & Restaurant   PUB $$

(⌂970-544-9112; 21 E Main St; mains $8-15; ⊙lunch & dinner; ⌂) A cozy spot with German-style house-brewed beers listed on the wall, right next to the hand-painted murals. Beers are excellent and a large menu features everything from southwestern cuisine to Mexican and Italian, with the requisite burgers and pizzas. There's also a downstairs game room with billiards.

Stonefish Sushi & More   JAPANESE $$

(⌂970-565-9244; 16 W Main St; mains $10-16; ⊙4:30-9pm Mon-Thu, to 10pm Sat) With blues on the box and a high tin ceiling, this is southwestern sushi. The rolls are standard fare, but specialties, like the Colorado rancher seared beef and wasabi, liven things up. Cool light fixtures, black tiles and globe shaped fish tanks behind the bar complete the scene.

Nero's Italian Restaurant   ITALIAN $$$

(⌂970-565-7366; 303 W Main St; mains $14-25; ⊙5-9pm Mon-Sat) Though splashed in southwest decor, this local favorite is known for well prepared Italian dishes. Favorites include the half Hudson Valley duckling with garlic and honey glaze and the pecan raviolis. The menu is extensive, with good options for kids.

ℹ Information

Colorado Welcome Center (⌂970-565-4048; 928 E Main St; ⊙9am-5pm Sep-May, to 6pm Jun-Aug) Maps, brochures and some excellent pamphlets on local activities like fishing and mountain biking. Also sells tickets to popular backcountry ranger tours at Mesa Verde National Park.

Southwest Memorial Hospital (⌂970-565-6666; 1311 N Mildred Rd) Provides emergency services.

ℹ Getting There & Around

Cortez is easier to reach by car from Phoenix, AZ, or Albuquerque, NM, than from Denver (379 miles away by the shortest route). East of Cortez, US Hwy 160 passes Mesa Verde National Park on the way to Durango – the largest city in the region.

Cortez Municipal Airport (⌂970-565-7458; 22874 County Rd F) is served by United Express, which offers daily turboprop flights to Denver. The airport is 2 miles south of town off US 160/666.

Dolores

POP 920 / ELEV 6936FT

Scenic Dolores, sandwiched between the walls of a narrow canyon of the same name, has a treasure trove of Native American artifacts and sits near the sublime river of the same name – only rafted in spring. But on a more permanent basis, the McPhee Lake boasts the best angling in the southwest. Food and lodging options here are slim.

◎ Sights & Activities

The Bureau of Land Management manages the **Anasazi Heritage Center** (☑970-882-5600; 27501 Hwy 184; admission $3, free Dec-Feb; ☉9am-5pm Mar-Nov, 10am-4pm Dec-Feb; ℗☝), a must-see for anyone touring the area's archaeological sites. It's 3 miles west of town, with hands-on exhibits including weaving, corn grinding, tree-ring analysis and an introduction to the way in which archaeologists examine potsherds. You can walk through the Dominguez Pueblo, a roofless site from the 1100s that sits in front of the museum, and compare its relative simplicity to the Escalante Pueblo, a Chacoan structure on a nearby hillside.

Dolores is home to **McPhee Lake**, a reservoir that's the second-largest body of water in Colorado. Located in a canyon of the Dolores River, McPhee offers many angling spots accessible only by boat. In skinny, tree-lined side canyons, wakeless boating zones allow for still-water fishing. With the best catch ratio in all of southwest Colorado, it's a great place to teach younger anglers. Make sure you have a valid Colorado fishing license.

⌕ Sleeping & Eating

Find out about nearby campsites in the San Juan National Forest from the **USFS Dolores Ranger Station** (☑970-882-7296; 29211 Hwy 184; ☉8am-5pm Mon-Fri), which has the best options.

Dolores River RV Park   RV PARK $
(☑970-882-7761; www.doloresriverrvparkandcabins.com; 18680 Hwy 145; tent/RV sites $25/35, cabins $45; ☝) Has pleasant though overpriced sites, 1.5 miles east of town.

Rio Grande Southern Hotel   HOTEL $$
(☑866-882-3026; www.rgshotel.com; 101 S 5th St; r incl breakfast $85-110; ☎☝) Norman Rockwell

prints and an old-world front desk beckon guests at this National Historic Landmark which is by far the best sleeping option in town. A cozy library and small, antique-filled guest rooms add to the cluttery charm. It's rumored that Zane Gray stayed in room 4 while writing *Riders of the Purple Sage*.

Rio Grande Southern Restaurant   AMERICAN $$
(☑866-882-3026; www.rgshotel.com; 101 S 5th St; mains $5-15; ☉7am-8pm Wed-Sat; ☝) Downstairs from the historic hotel, is former mayor cooks a standard American menu, with weekly specials including a fish fry and Chicago pizza night.

❶ Getting There & Away

Dolores is 11 miles north of Cortez on Hwy 145, also known as Railroad Ave.

San Juan Mountains

In autumn, yellow aspens dot the San Juans and cool air carries the sharp scent of pine. Day-to-day tensions tend to dissipate into serene, blue-sky days as you amble among towering peaks, picturesque towns and old mines.

The 236-mile **San Juan Skyway** climbs to the top of the world as it twists and turns past a series of 'fourteeners' (peaks exceeding 14,000ft). Places like Telluride, Durango and Silverton have storied pasts of boom and bust. The San Juan Skyway leads you past both churling rapids primed for descent and quiet pockets of the Animas River almost made for fly-fishing. In the summer, there's a rousing, rowdy soundtrack of bluegrass, jazz and folk, when local towns host renowned festivals.

From Ridgway follow US 550 south to Ouray and then over Red Mountain Pass to Silverton. Continue heading south on US 550 until you hit Durango. From here, you can head west on US 160 to the ruins at Mesa Verde, then head north on Rte 145 toward Telluride before following Rte 62 back to Ridgway. To drive the entire byway, allow at least one or two days.

Telluride

POP 2400 / ELEV 8750FT

Surrounded on three sides by mastodon peaks, exclusive Telluride is quite literally cut off from the hubbub of the outside world. Once a rough mining town, today it's dirtbag-meets-diva – mixing the few who can afford the real estate with those scratching out a slope-side living for the sport of it. The town center still has palpable old-time charm, though locals often villainize the recently developed Mountain Village, whose ready-made attractions have a touch of Vegas. Yet idealism remains the Telluride mantra. Shreds of paradise persist with the longtime town free box where you can swap unwanted items (across from the post office), the freedom of luxuriant powder days and bonhomie of its infamous festivals.

Colorado Ave, also known as Main St, has most of the restaurants, bars and shops. You can walk everywhere, so leave your car at the intercept parking lot at the south end of Mahoney Dr (near the visitor center) or at your lodgings.

From town you can reach the ski mountain via two lifts and the gondola. The latter also links Telluride with Mountain Village, the base for the Telluride Ski Resort. Located 7 miles from town along Hwy 145, Mountain Village is a 20-minute drive east, but only 12 minutes away by gondola (free for foot passengers).

Ajax Peak, a glacial headwall, rises up behind the town to form the end of the U-shaped valley. To the right (or south) on Ajax Peak, Colorado's highest waterfall, Bridal Veil Falls, cascades 365ft down; a switchback trail leads to a restored Victorian powerhouse atop the falls. To the south, Mt Wilson reaches 14,246ft among a group of rugged peaks that form the Lizard Head Wilderness Area.

🏃 Activities

Backcountry skiers should look into the incredible San Juan Hut system. In summer, the area has plenty of 4WD routes and some steep but gorgeous hikes.

Telluride Ski Resort
SNOW SPORTS
(☑970-728-7533, 888-288-7360; www.tellurideskiresort.com; 565 Mountain Village Blvd; lift tickets $98) Covering three distinct areas, Telluride Ski Resort is served by 16 lifts. Much of the terrain is for advanced and intermediate skiers, but there's still ample choice for beginners.

Telluride Ski & Snowboarding School
SNOW SPORTS
(☑970-728-7507; www.tellurideskiresort.com; 565 Mountain Village Blvd; full-day adult group lessons $170; ♿) Private and group lessons feature good teachers; there are classes for children and women-only clinics.

Telluride Flyfishers
FISHING
(☑800-294-9269; www.tellurideflyfishers.com; half-day for 2 $280) Housed in Telluride Sports, this outfit offers fishing guides and instruction.

Ride with Roudy
HORSEBACK RIDING
(☑970-728-9611; www.ridewithroudy.com; County Rd 43Zs; 2hr trips adult/child $85/45; ♿) If there ever were a local personality, it's Roudy. On the scene for 30-plus years, he offers all-season trail rides through the surrounding hills with a good dose of hospitality. Call for an appointment and pricing details.

Telluride Nordic Center
SNOW SPORTS
(☑970-728-1144; www.telluridetrails.org; 500 E Colorado Ave) Offers instruction and rentals. Public cross-country trails are in Town Park, along the San Miguel River and the Telluride Valley floor west of town.

Paragon Ski & Sport
SPORTS RENTAL
(☑970-728-4525; www.paragontelluride.com; 213 W Colorado Ave) A one-stop shop for outdoor activities in Telluride, with three town branches and a huge selection of rental bikes.

Easy Rider Bike & Sport
BIKE RENTAL
(☑970-728-4734; 101 W Colorado Ave) A full-service shop with bike rentals, maps and information.

🎉 Festivals & Events

TOP CHOICE Mountainfilm
FILM
(www.mountainfilm.org; ⊙Memorial Day weekend; prices vary) A spirited, four-day screening of outdoor adventure and environmental films that will get you in the mountain mood.

Telluride Bluegrass Festival
MUSIC FESTIVAL
(☑800-624-2422; www.planetbluegrass.com; 4-day pass $185; ⊙late Jun) A wildly rollicking festival attracting thousands for a music-filled weekend. Stalls sell all sorts of food and local microbrews to keep you happy, and acts continue well into the night. Camping out for the four-day festival is very popular. Check out the website for info on sites, shuttle services and combo ticket-and-camping packages – it's all very organized!

Telluride Mushroom Festival
FOOD
(www.tellurideinstitute.org) Fungiphiles sprout up at this festival in late August.

Telluride Film Festival
FILM
(☑603-433-9202; www.telluridefilmfestival.com; entry $25-780) Held in early September, national and international films are premiered throughout town, and the event attracts

SOUTHWESTERN COLORADO TELLURIDE

TELLURIDE CAMPGROUNDS

Right in Telluride Town Park, **Telluride Town Park Campground** (970-728-2173; 500 E Colorado Ave; campsites $20; mid-May–mid-Oct;) offers 42 campsites, showers and swimming and tennis from mid-May to October. Developed campsites cost $20 and are all on a first-come, first-served basis.

Two campgrounds in the Uncompahgre National Forest are within 15 miles of Telluride on Hwy 145 and cost $20. **Sunshine Campground** (970-327-4261; off County Rd 145; sites $20 late May–late Sep) is the nearest and best and offers 15 first-come, first-served campsites; facilities at **Matterhorn Campground** (970-327-4261; Hwy 145; sites $20; May-Sep;), a bit further up the hill, include showers and electrical hookups for some of the 27 campsites.

big-name stars. Some talks and showings are free. For more information visit the film festival website.

Brews & Blues Festival   BEER, MUSIC
(www.tellurideblues.com; mid-Sep) Telluride's festival season comes to a raucous end at this mid-September event, where blues musicians take to the stage and microbrews fill the bellies of fans.

Sleeping

Aside from camping, there are no cheap places to stay in Telluride. During summer, festival times or winter peak seasons, guests pay dearly. Yet, off-season rates drop up to 30%.

Some of the huge properties in Mountain Village can offer a decent rate if you book online, but none have the character of the smaller hotels downtown. Most winter visitors stay in vacation rentals – there are scores of them. To book, contact **Telluride Alpine Lodging** (888-893-0158; www.telluride lodging.com; 324 W Colorado Ave).

TOP CHOICE Hotel Columbia   HOTEL $$$
(970-728-0660, toll-free 800-201-9505; www .columbiatelluride.com; 300 W San Juan Ave; d $350;) Since spendy digs are a given in Telluride, skiers might as well stay right across the street from the gondola. Locally owned and operated, this stylish and

swank hotel pampers. Store your gear in the ski and boot storage and head directly to a room with espresso maker, fireplace and heated tile floors. With shampoo dispensers and recycling, it's also pretty eco-friendly.

Other highlights include a rooftop hot tub and fitness room. Breakfast is included, but food at the connected Cosmopolitan is also excellent – many say it's the best dining room in Telluride.

New Sheridan Hotel   HOTEL $$
(970-728-4351, 800-200-1891; www.newsheridan .com; 231 W Colorado Ave; d from $199;) Elegant and understated, this historic brick hotel (erected in 1895) provides a lovely base camp for exploring Telluride. High-ceiling rooms feature crisp linens and snug flannel throws. Check out the hot-tub deck with mountain views. In the bull's eye of downtown, the location is perfect, but some rooms are small for the price.

Inn at Lost Creek   BOUTIQUE HOTEL $$
(970-728-5678; www.innatlostcreek.com; 119 Lost Creek Lane; r from $189;) Across from Lumière but with a more relaxed decor, this lush boutique-style hotel knows cozy. At the bottom of Telluride's main lift, it's also very convenient. Service is personalized, and impeccable rooms have an alpine style of hardwoods, southwestern designs and molded tin. There are also two rooftop spas. Check the website for packages.

Lumière   HOTEL $$$
(907-369-0400, 866-530-9466; www.lumiere hotels.com; 118 Lost Creek Lane; d from $325, studio from $799;) In Mountain Village, this ski-in, ski-out luxury lodge commands breathtaking views of the San Juans. Think plush and fluff, with seven-layer bedding, Asian-inspired contempo design and suites with top-of-the-line appliances that few probably even use. In the morning, guests enjoy an elegant breakfast reception. But even with the hip sushi bar and luxuriant spa menu, its greatest appeal is the location, which zips you from the slopes to a bubble bath in minutes.

Victorian Inn   LODGE $$
(970-728-6601; www.tellurideinn.com; 401 W Pacific Ave; r from $159;) The smell of fresh cinnamon rolls greets visitors at one of Telluride's better deals, offering comfortable rooms (some with kitchenettes) and a hot tub and dry sauna in a nice garden area. Staff are friendly and guests get lift-ticket discounts.

Kids aged 12 years and under stay free, and you can't beat the downtown location.

Aspen Street Inn BOUTIQUE HOTEL **$$**
(✆970-728-3001, toll-free 800-537-4781; www.telluridehotels.com; 330 W Pacific Ave; d from $195; P❄✿) Near the chairlift, this small hotel has carpeted country-style rooms. Prices are steep for the dog-eared B&B vibe, but loyal visitors rave about the hospitality. Snacks are served in the stone- and wood-lined common room and the back patio is a lovely setting for the hot tub.

✕ Eating

Meals and even groceries can be pricey in Telluride, so check out the hot dog stand or taco truck on Colorado Ave for quick fixes. Gaga for sustainability, many local restaurants offer grass-fed beef or natural meat; we indicate those with the greatest commitment to sustainability.

New Sheridan Chop House MODERN AMERICAN **$$$**
(✆970-728-4531; www.newsheridan.com; 231 W Colorado Ave; mains $19-90; ⏲5pm-2am) With superb service and a chic decor of embroidered velvet benches, this is an easy pick for an intimate dinner. Diners can start with a cheese plate, but from there the menu gets Western. Pasta comes with a creamy wild mushroom and sage sauce. Meat eaters should try the elk shortloin in a hard cider reduction. For a treat, top it off with a flourless dark chocolate cake in fresh caramel sauce.

Cosmopolitan MODERN AMERICAN **$$$**
(✆970-728-0660; www.columbiatelluride.com; 300 W San Juan Ave; mains from $20; ⏲dinner) The on-site restaurant at the Hotel Columbia is one of Telluride's most respected for fine modern dining – can you resist Himalayan yak ribeye or lobster corn dogs? The food is certainly inventive, which makes up for sometimes snooty service.

La Cocina de Luz MEXICAN, ORGANIC **$$**
(www.lacocinatelluride.com; 123 E Colorado Ave; mains $9-19; ⏲9am-9pm; ✿) As they lovingly serve two Colorado favorites (organic + Mexican), it's no wonder that the lunch line is 10 people deep on a slow day at this healthy taquería. There's delicious details too, like handmade tortillas and margaritas with organic lime and agave nectar. With vegan, gluten-free options too.

The Butcher & The Baker CAFE FOOD **$$**
(✆970-728-3334; 217 E Colorado Ave; mains $8-14; ⏲7am-7pm Mon-Sat, 8am-2pm Sun; ✿) Two veterans of upscale catering started this heartbreakingly cute cafe, and no one beats it for breakfast. Hearty sandwiches with local meats are the perfect takeout for the trail and there are heaps of baked goods and fresh sides.

There TAPAS **$**
(✆970-728-1213; http://therebars.com; 627 W Pacific Ave; appetizers from $4; ⏲3pm-late) A popular local caterer opened this hip social alcove for nibbling. East-meets-West in yummy soy paper wraps with asparagus, duck ramen and sashimi tostadas, paired with original cocktails. We liked the jalapeño kiss.

221 South Oak MODERN AMERICAN **$$$**
(✆970-728-9505; www.221southoak.com; 221 S Oak St; mains $19-25; ⏲5-10pm; ✿) A local favorite, with small, seasonal menus playful with world flavors. In a cozy historic home, dine on watermelon, blueberry and feta salad in summer and five-spice short-ribs with sweet potato wontons in winter. Vegetarian menu available upon request.

La Marmotte FRENCH **$$$**
(✆970-728-6232; www.lamarmotte.com; 150 W San Juan Ave; mains from $20; ⏲5pm-late Tue-Sat) Seasonal plates of French cuisine, white linen and candlelit warmth contrast with this rustic 19th-century icehouse. Dishes like the coq au vin with bacon mashed potatoes are both smart and satisfying. There's some organic options and an extensive wine list. Parents should check out their Friday-night winter babysitting options.

Baked in Telluride BAKERY **$**
(✆970-728-4775; www.bakedintelluride.com; 127 S Fir St; mains $6-10; ⏲5:30am-10pm) Back in action after a fire closure, this Telluride institution boasts the West's best bagel, sourdough wheat-crust pizza and some hearty soups and salads. The front deck is a fishbowl of local activity and the vibe is happy casual.

Honga's Lotus Petal ASIAN **$$$**
(✆970-728-5134; www.hongaslotuspetal.com; 135 E Colorado Ave; mains $17-33) For pan-Asian cuisine, beat it to this two-story dining space. Prices are dear but the presentation – ranging from sushi to curries – is lovely. The Korean short ribs just about fall off the bone. So lively and fresh, we can even forgive the pan flutes.

Clark's Market SELF-CATERING
(www.clarksmarket.com; 700 W Colorado Ave; 7am-9pm) The nicest market in town stocks specialty goods and scores of treats, with fresh fruit and deli meats.

Drinking

Smugglers Brewery & Grille PUB
(970-728-0919; www.smugglersbrew.com; 225 S Pine St; 11am-2am;) Beer-lovers will feel right at home at casual Smugglers, a great place to hang out, sample local brew and eat fried stuff.

New Sheridan Bar BAR
(970-728-3911; www.newsheridan.com; 231 W Colorado Ave; 5pm-2am) Well worth a visit in low season for some real local flavor and opinions. At other times, it becomes a rush hour of beautiful ones. But there's old bullet holes in the wall and the plucky survival of the bar itself, even as the adjoining hotel sold off chandeliers and fine furnishings to pay the heating bills during waning mining fortunes.

Last Dollar Saloon BAR
(970-728-4800; www.lastdollarsaloon.com; 100 E Colorado Ave; 3pm-2am) All local color – forget about cocktails and grab a cold can of beer at this longtime late-night favorite, popular when everything else closes. With pool tables and darts.

Entertainment

Fly Me to the Moon Saloon LIVE MUSIC
(970-728-6666; 132 E Colorado Ave; 3pm-2am) Let your hair down and kick up your heels to the tunes of live bands at this saloon, the best place in Telluride to party hard.

Sheridan Opera House THEATER
(970-728-4539; www.sheridanoperahouse.com; 110 N Oak St;) This historic venue has a burlesque charm and is always the center of Telluride's cultural life. It hosts the Telluride Repertory Theater, and frequently has special performances for children.

Shopping

In addition to boutique sporting gear, shoppers will find upscale shops and art galleries (featuring artists of renown) all over town; pick up a local shopping guide.

Telluride Sports SPORTING GOODS
(970-728-4477; www.telluridesports.com; 150 W Colorado Ave; 8am-8pm) With several branches and associated shops in Mountain Village, this main outfitter covers everything outdoors, has topographical and USFS maps, sporting supplies and loads of local information.

Between The Covers BOOKS
(970-728-4504; www.btwn-the-covers.com; 224 W Colorado Ave) With a doting staff, great local reads and creaking floors, this bookstore is a terrific place to browse. For a mean espresso milk shake, go to the coffee counter in back.

Information

Telluride Central Reservations (888-355-8743; 630 W Colorado Ave) Handles accommodations and festival tickets. Located in the same building as the visitor center.

Telluride Library (970-728-4519; www.telluridelibrary.org; 100 W Pacific Ave; 10am-8pm Mon-Thu, 10am-6pm Fri & Sat, 12-5pm Sun;) With free wi-fi, maps, hiking guides and flyers on local happenings, this is a worthy pit stop, especially with kids. In summer they sponsor a free film series in Mountain Village.

Telluride Medical Center (970-728-3848; 500 W Pacific Ave) Handles skiing accidents, medical problems and emergencies.

Telluride Visitor Center (888-353-5473, 970-728-3041; www.telluride.com; 630 W Colorado Ave; 9am-5pm winter, to 7pm summer) This well-stocked visitor center has local info in all seasons. Restrooms and an ATM make it an all-round useful spot.

Getting There & Around

Commuter aircraft serve the mesa-top **Telluride airport** (970-778-5051; www.tellurideairport.com; Last Dollar Rd), 5 miles east of town on Hwy 145. If weather is poor flights may be diverted to Montrose, 65 miles north. For car rental, National and Budget both have airport locations.

In ski season Montrose Regional Airport has direct flights to and from Denver (on United), Houston, Phoenix and limited cities on the East Coast.

Shared shuttles from Telluride airport to town or Mountain Village cost $15. Shuttles between the Montrose airport and Telluride cost $48. Contact **Telluride Express** (970-728-6000; www.tellurideexpress.com).

Ridgway

POP 810 / ELEV 6985FT

Ridgway, with its local quirk, zesty history and scandalous views of Mt Sneffels, is hard to just blow through. Before it got so hip,

COLORADO'S HAUTE ROUTE

An exceptional way to enjoy hundreds of miles of singletrack in summer or virgin powder slopes in winter, **San Juan Hut Systems** (📞970-626-3033; www.sanjuan huts.com; per person $30) continues the European tradition of hut-to-hut adventures with five backcountry mountain huts. Bring just your food, flashlight and sleeping bag – amenities include padded bunks, propane stoves, wood stoves for heating and firewood.

Mountain-biking routes go from Durango or Telluride to Moab, winding through high alpine and desert regions. Or pick one hut as your base for a few days of backcountry skiing or riding. There's terrain for all levels, though skiers should have knowledge of snow and avalanche conditions or go with a guide.

The website has helpful tips and information on rental skis, bikes and (optional) guides based in Ridgway or Ouray.

---

the town also served the backdrop for John Wayne's 1969 cowboy classic, *True Grit*.

It sits at the crossroads of US 550, which goes south to Durango, and Hwy 62, which leads to Telluride, but the downtown is tucked away on the west side of the Uncompahgre River. Through town Hwy 62 is called Sherman and all the perpendicular streets are named for his daughters. Ridgway Area Chamber of Commerce has a lot of information about local activities in the area.

👁 Sights & Activities

TOP CHOICE **Chicks with Picks** CLIMBING INSTRUCTION
(📞970-316-1403, office 970-626-4424; www.chicks withpicks.net; 163 County Rd 12; prices vary) Arming women with ice tools and crampons, this group of renowned women athletes gives excellent instruction for all-comers (beginners included) in rockclimbing, bouldering and ice climbing. Programs are fun and change frequently, with multiday excursions or town-based courses. Clinics also hit the road.

FREE **Ridgway Railroad Museum** MUSEUM
(📞970-626-5181; www.ridgwayrailroadmuseum.org; 150 Racecourse Rd; ⊙10am-6pm May-Sep, reduced

hr Oct-Apr; 🚼) Ridgway's Rio Grande Southern Railroad connected to Durango with the narrow-gauge 'Galloping Goose', a kind of hybrid train and truck that saved the struggling Rio Grand Southern for a number of years, featured here.

Riggs Fly Shop & Guide Service FLY-FISHING
(📞970-626-4460, toll-free 888-626-4460; www.fishrigs.com; Suite 2, 565 Sherman St; half-day fishing tours per person from $225; 🚼) Good guided fly-fishing from half-day beginners' trips to multiday campouts for more experienced fisherfolk. There's also white-water rafting and other regional soft-adventure itineraries.

FREE **Ridgway State Park & Recreation Area** FISHING
(📞970-626-5822; www.parks.state.co.us/parks /ridgway; 28555 US Hwy 550; ⊙dawn-dusk) With a reservoir stocked with loads of rainbow trout, as well as German brown, kokanee, yellow perch and the occasional large-mouth bass. There's also hiking and campsites, 12 miles north of town.

🛏 Sleeping & Eating

Ridgway State Park & Recreation Area CAMPING $
(📞800-678-2267; www.parks.state.co.us/parks /ridgway; 28555 US Hwy 550; tent/RV/yurt sites $16/$20/70; 🚼) With almost 300 available sites, these three campgrounds offer good availability with gorgeous water views, hiking and fishing. If you're tent camping, these 25 sites are 'walk in' but the path is short and a free wheelbarrow is offered to transport your stuff. For a comfortable alternative, check out the cool canvas yurts. Services include rest rooms with coin-op showers and a playground for kids. You can book online or over the phone.

Chipeta Sun Lodge & Spa LODGE $$$
(📞970-626-3737; www.chipeta.com; 304 S Lena St; r $125-235; 🅿) Swank and southwestern, this adobe-style lodge offers a nice upscale getaway. Rooms feature hand-painted Mexican tiles, fireplaces, rough-hewn log beds and decks with a view. In-room magazines invite you to linger and wonderful public areas include a solarium and hot tubs. There's also an on-site spa and yoga classes. Check the website for ski, soak and stay deals.

TOP CHOICE **Kate's Place** BREAKFAST $$
(📞970-626-9800; 615 W Clinton St; mains $9-13; ⊙7am-2pm; 🚼) Consider yourself lucky if the

morning starts with a chorizo-stuffed breakfast burrito and white cheddar grits from Kate's, the best breakfast joint for miles. But the restaurant's dedication to local farmers, warm interior and friendly wait staff seal the deal.

True Grit Cafe AMERICAN **$$**
(☑970-626-5739; 123 N Lena Ave; mains $8-15; ☺lunch & dinner) Scenes from the original *True Grit* were filmed at this loud cafe, but come for the burgers, roast beef, and peach pie. It's friendly, with a crackling fire warming patrons in the winter.

❶ Information

Ridgway Area Chamber of Commerce
(☑970-626-5181, 800-220-4959; www.ridgway colorado.com; 150 Racecourse Rd; ☺9am-5pm Mon-Fri)

Ouray & the Million Dollar Hwy

POP 940 / ELEV 7760FT

With gorgeous icefalls draping the box canyon and soothing hot springs that dot the valley floor, Ouray is one privileged place, even for Colorado. For ice-climbers, it's a world-class destination, but hikers and 4WD fans can also appreciate its rugged and sometimes stunning charms. The town is a well-preserved quarter-mile mining village sandwiched between imposing peaks.

Between Silverton and Ouray, US 550 is known as the Million Dollar Hwy because the roadbed fill contains valuable ore. One of the state's most memorable drives, this breathtaking stretch passes old mine headframes and larger-than-life alpine scenery. Though paved, the road is scary in rain or snow, so take extra care.

◎ Sights

Little Ouray, 'the Switzerland of America,' is very picturesque and littered with old houses and buildings. The visitor center and **museum** (☑970-325-4576; www.ouraycounty historicalsociety.org; 420 6th Ave; adult/child $5/1; ☺1-4:30pm Thu-Sat Apr 14-May 14, 10am-4:30pm Mon-Sat & noon-4:30pm Sun May 15-Sep 30, 10am-4:30pm Thu-Sat Oct 1-30, closed Dec 1-Apr 14; ⬥) issue a free leaflet with details of an excellent walking tour that takes in two-dozen buildings and houses constructed between 1880 and 1904.

Bird-watchers come to Ouray to sight rare birds, including warblers, sparrows and grosbeaks. Box Canyon Falls has the USA's most accessible colony of protected black swifts. The visitor center has resources for bird-watchers, and the excellent **Buckskin Booksellers** (☑970-325-4071; www.buckskin booksellers.com; 505 Main St; ☺9am-5pm Mon-Sat; ⬥) has books and guides.

SCENIC DRIVES: SAN JUAN ROUTES

For the following we suggest a high-clearance 4WD vehicle and some four-wheeling skills.

Alpine Loop

Demanding but fantastic fun, this 63-mile drive into the remote and rugged heart of the San Juan Mountains begins in Ouray and travels east to Lake City before looping back. Along the way you'll cross two 12,000ft mountain passes, with spectacular scenery and abandoned mining haunts. Allow six hours.

Imogene Pass

Every year, runners tackle this rough 16-mile mining road, but you might feel that driving it is enough. Ultra-scenic, it connects Ouray with Telluride. Built in 1880, it's one of the San Juans' highest passes, linking two important mining sites.

In Ouray, head south on Main St and turn right on Bird Camp Rd (City Rd 361). Pass Bird Camp Mine, once one of the San Juans' most prolific, climbing high into the mountains. You will have to cross streams, and at times the road snakes precariously close to sheer cliff drops offering a thrilling adrenaline rush. Eventually the route opens, reaching high alpine meadows before the summit of Imogene Pass (13,114ft). Descending toward Telluride, you'll pass the abandoned Tomboy Mine, which once had a population as large as present-day Ouray. The pass is open only in summer. Allow three hours one way.

🏃 Activities

FREE Ouray Ice Park   ICE CLIMBING
(☎970-325-4061; www.ourayicepark.com; Hwy 361;
⊙7am-5pm mid-Dec–March; 🚼) Enthusiasts
from around the globe come to ice climb at
the world's first public ice park, spanning a
2-mile stretch of the Uncompahgre Gorge.
The sublime (if chilly) experience offers
something for all skill levels.

Ouray Hot Springs   HOT SPRINGS
(☎970-325-7073; www.ourayhotsprings.com; 1220
Main St; adult/child $10/8; ⊙10am-10pm Jun-
Aug, noon-9pm Mon-Fri & 11am-9pm Sat & Sun
Sep-May; 🚼) For a healing soak, try this
crystal-clear natural spring water. It's free
of the sulphur smells plaguing other hot
springs around here, and the giant pool
features a variety of soaking areas at temperatures from 96°F to 106°F (36°C to
41°C). The complex also offers a gym and
massage service.

Ouray Mule Carriage Co   CARRIAGE TOURS
(☎970-708-4946, www.ouraymule.com; 834
Main St; adult/child $15/5; ⊙hourly departures
1-6pm Jun-Aug; 🚼) Clip-clopping along Main
Street, this nine-person dray (been in the
same family since 1944) takes visitors on
interpretive tours of old town.

Ouray Livery   HORSEBACK RIDING
(☎970-708-7051, 970-325-4340; www.ourayllvery
.com; 834 Main St; tour of Ouray 2hr riding $60;
🚼) The Ouray Livery offers short carriage
and stagecoach tours as well as horseback
riding in the mountains. This group has
special-use permits to tour the Grand
Mesa, Uncompahgre and Gunnison
National Forests.

San Juan Scenic Jeep Tours   4WD, FISHING
(☎970-325-0090, 888-624-8403; www.historic
westernhotel.com; 210 7th Ave; adult/child half-
day $54/27, full day $108/54; 🚼) The friendly
folks at the Historic Western Hotel offer off-
road tours of the nearby peaks and valleys.
Hiking, hunting and fishing drop-offs and
pick-ups can be arranged.

San Juan Mountain Guides   CLIMBING, SKIING
(☎970-325-4925, 866-525-4925; www.ourayclimb
ing.com; 474 Main St; 🚼) Ouray's own professional guiding and climbing group is certi-
fied with the International Federation of
Mountain Guides Association (IFMGA).
It specializes in ice and rock climbing and
wilderness backcountry skiing.

✨ Festivals & Events

TOP CHOICE Ouray Ice Festival   ICE CLIMBING
(☎970-325-4288; www.ourayicefestival.com; donation for evening events $15; ⊙Jan; 🚼) The Ouray
Ice Festival features four days of climbing competitions, dinners, slide shows and
clinics in January. There's even a climbing wall set up for kids. You can watch the
competitions for free, but to check out the
various evening events you will need to
make a donation to the ice park. Once inside
you'll get free brews from popular Colorado
microbrewer New Belgium.

🛏 Sleeping

TOP CHOICE Wiesbaden   HOTEL $$
(☎970 325 4347; www.wiesbadenhotsprings.com;
625 5th St; r from $132; 🖥🏊) Quirky, quaint
and new age, Wiesbaden even boasts a natu-
ral indoor vapor cave, which, in another
era, was frequented by Chief Ouray. Rooms
with quilted bedcovers are cozy and roman-
tic, but the sunlit suite with a natural rock
wall tops all. In the morning, guests roam
in thick robes, drinking the free organic
coffee or tea, post-soak, or awaiting their
massage. The on-site Aveda salon also
provides soothing facials to make your
mountain detox complete. Outside, there's
a spacious hot-spring pool (included) and a
private, clothing optional soaking tub with a
waterfall, reserved for $35 per hour.

Beaumont Hotel   HOTEL $$$
(☎970-325-7000; www.beaumonthotel.com; 505
Main St; r $169-259; 🅿) With magnificent
four-post beds, clawfoot tubs and hand-
carved mirrors, this 1886 hotel underwent
extensive renovations to revive the glamour it posed a century ago. Word has it
that Oprah stayed here, and you'll probably
like it too. There's also a spa and boutiques,
but due to the fragile decor, pets and kids
under 16 years old are not allowed.

**🌿 Box Canyon Lodge
& Hot Springs**   LODGE $$
(☎800-327-5080, 970-325-4981; www.boxcanyon
ouray.com; 45 3rd Ave; d $159; 🖥🚼) It's not
every hotel that offers geothermal heat,
and these pineboard rooms prove spa-
cious and fresh. Spring-fed barrel hot
tubs are perfect for a romantic stargazing
soak. With good hospitality that includes
free apples and bottled water, it's popular,
so book ahead.

Amphitheater Forest Service Campground
CAMPING $

(☎877-444-6777; www.ouraycolorado.com/amphi theater; US Hwy 550; tent sites $16; ☺Jun-Aug; ♿) With great tent sites under the trees, this high-altitude campground is a score. On holiday weekends a three-night minimum applies. South of town on Hwy 550, take a signposted left-hand turn.

🏨 St Elmo Hotel
HOTEL $$

(☎970-325-4951, toll-free 866-243-1502; www.st elmohotel.com; 426 Main St; d incl breakfast $139-165; ✱♿) Effusively feminine, this 1897 hotel is a showpiece of the Ouray museum's historic walking tour. Nine unique renovated rooms have floral wallpaper and period furnishings. Guests have access to a hot tub and sauna and there's even some of Ouray's best dining, Bon Ton Restaurant, on-site downstairs.

Ouray Victoria Inn
HOTEL $$

(☎970-325-7222, toll-free 800-846-8729; www .victorianinnouray.com; 50 3rd Ave; d incl breakfast $145; P🛜♿🐾) Refurbished in 2009, 'The Vic' has a terrific setting next to Box Canyon Park on the Uncompahgre riverfront near the Ouray Ice Park. Rooms have cable TV, fridges and coffeemakers, some with balconies and splendid views. Kids will appreciate the deluxe swing set with climbing holds. Rates vary widely by season, but low-season rates are a steal.

Historic Western Hotel, Restaurant & Saloon
HOTEL $

(☎970-325-4645; www.historicwesternhotel.com; 210 7th Ave; r without/with bath $55/95; P♿) Open by reservation in shoulderseason, this somewhat threadbare Wild West boarding-house serves all budgets. The second-floor verandah commands stunning views of the Uncompahgre Gorge, while the saloon serves affordable meals and grog in a timeless setting.

✖ Eating & Drinking

TOP CHOICE Buen Tiempo Mexican Restaurant & Cantina
MEXICAN $$

(☎970-325-4544; 515 Main St; mains $7-19; ☺6-10pm; ♪) Bursting with locals at bar stools and families filling the booths, this is a good-time spot. From the chile-rubbed sirloin to the posole served with warm tortillas, Buen Tiempo delivers. Start with a signature margarita, served with chips and spicy home-made salsa. You can end with a satisfying scoop of deep-fried ice cream. But if you want to find out how the dollars got on the ceiling, it will cost you.

Bulow's Bistro at the Beaumont
MODERN AMERICAN $$

(☎970-325-7000; www.beaumonthotel.com/dine .html; 505 Main St; mains $10-26; ☺closed Sun; ♿) Replacing a more upscale establishment, this popular contemporary bistro offers everything from baguettes to a well-seared rib eye steak, and there's a children's menu as well. Both the restaurant and the outdoor courtyard are lovely and you can choose from the wine cellar's 300 vintages from all over the world.

Bon Ton Restaurant
FRENCH, ITALIAN $$$

(☎970-325-4951; www.stelmohotel.com; 426 Main St; mains $15-36; ☺6-11pm; ♪) Bon Ton has been cooking in a beautiful room under the historic St Elmo Hotel for as long as anyone can remember. In fact, supper has been served at this location for nearly a century. The French-Italian menu includes house specialties of escargot and crawfish tails, and tortellini with bacon and shallots. The wine list is extensive.

Ouray Brewery
BREWERY

(☎970-325-7388; ouraybrewery.com; 607 Main St; ☺11am-9pm) With chairlift bar stools, this pub earns stripes in brews, if not in bar food. Why must so many landlocked menus insist on shrimp?

❶ Information

Ouray Chamber Resort Association (☎970-325-4746, 800-228-1876; www.ouraycolorado .com; 1230 Main St; ☺10am-5pm Mon-Sat, 10am-3pm Sun; ♿) The visitor center is at the Ouray hot-springs pool.

Post office (☎970-325-4302; 620 Main St; ☺9am-4:30pm Mon-Sat)

❶ Getting There & Away

Ouray is on Hwy 550, 70 miles north of Durango, 24 miles north of Silverton and 37 miles south of Montrose. There are no bus services in the area.

Silverton
POP 530 / ELEV 9318FT

Ringed by snowy peaks and steeped in sooty tales of a tawdry mining town, Silverton would seem more at home in Alaska than the lower 48. But here it is. Whether you're into snowmobiling, biking, fly-fishing, beer on tap or just basking in some very high altitude sunshine, Silverton delivers.

It's a two-street town, but only one is paved. Greene St is where you'll find most businesses. Still unpaved, notorious Blair St runs parallel to Greene and is a blast from the past. During the silver rush, Blair St was home to thriving brothels and boozing establishments.

A tourist town by day in summer, once the final Durango-bound steam train departs it reverts to local turf. Visit in winter for a real treat. Snowmobiles become the main means of transportation, and town becomes a playground for intrepid travelers, most of them serious powder hounds.

One of Silverton's highlights is just getting here from Ouray on the Million Dollar Hwy – an awe-inspiring stretch of road that's one of Colorado's best road trips.

☺ Sights & Activities

Silverton Railroad Depot
NARROW GAUGE RAILWAY

(☎970-387-5416; toll-free 877-872-4607; www .durangotrain.com; 12th St; adult/child return from $83/49; ☺departures 2pm, 2:45pm & 3:30pm; ⚑) Buy one-way and return tickets for the brilliant Durango & Silverton Narrow Gauge Railroad at the Silverton terminus or online. A ticket provides admission to the on-site Silverton Freight Yard Museum. The train service offers combination train-bus return trips (with the bus route much quicker). Hikers use the train to access the Durango and Weminuche Wilderness trailheads.

Silverton Museum
MUSEUM

(☎970-387-5838; www.silvertonhistoricsociety.org; 1557 Greene St; adult/child $5/free; ☺10am-4pm Jun-Oct; ℗⚑) Installed in the original 1902 San Juan County Jail, with an interesting collection of local artifacts and ephemera.

⎍TOP CHOICE⎍ Silverton Mountain Ski Area
SKIING

(☎970-387-5706; www.silvertonmountain.com; State Hwy 110; daily lift ticket $49, all-day guide & lift ticket $99) Not for newbies, this is one of the most interesting and innovative ski mountains in the US – a single lift takes advanced and expert backcountry skiers up to the summit of an area of ungroomed ski runs. Numbers are limited and the mountain designates unguided and the more exclusive guided days.

The lift rises from the 10,400ft base to 12,300ft. Imagine heli-skiing *sans* helicopter. You really need to know your stuff – the easiest terrain here is comparable to skiing double blacks at other resorts.

Kendall Mountain Recreation Area
SKIING

(☎970-387-5522; www.skikendall.com; Kendall Pl; daily lift tickets adult/child $15/10; ☺11am-4pm Fri & Sat Dec-Feb; ⚑) Managed by the town, with just one double 1050ft chairlift and four runs, all suitable for beginners. People goof around on sleds and tubes, and it's cheap and family-friendly. Rent gear from the Kendall Mountain Community Center.

⚑ San Juan Backcountry
TOURS

(☎970-387-5565; toll-free 800-494-8687; www .sanjuanbackcountry.com; 1119 Greene St; 2hr tours adult/child $60/40; ☺May-Oct) Offering both 4WD tours and rentals, these folks get you out and into the brilliant San Juan Mountain wilderness areas around Silverton, often in modified open-top Chevy Suburbans.

⎽ Sleeping

Wyman Hotel & Inn
B&B $$$

(☎970-387-5372; www.thewyman.com; 1371 Greene St; d incl breakfast $125-230; ☎) A handsome sandstone on the National Register of Historic Places, this 1902 building brims with personality. Local memorabilia lines long halls with room after room of canopy beds, Victorian-era wallpaper and chandelier lamps. Every room is distinct, none more so than the caboose that you can rent out back. Includes a full breakfast plus afternoon wine and cheese tasting.

Inn of the Rockies at the Historic Alma House
B&B $$

(☎970-387-5336; toll-free 800-267-5336; www .innoftherockies.com; 220 E 10th St; r incl breakfast from $110; ℗❈⚑) Opened by a local named Alma in 1898, this inn has nine unique rooms furnished with Victorian antiques. You can't beat the hospitality or the New Orleans-inspired breakfasts, served in a chandelier-lit dining room. There's also a garden hot tub.

Bent Elbow
HOTEL $$

(☎970-387-5775; toll-free 877-387-5775; www.the bent.com; 1114 Blair St; d $100-145; ℗☎⚑) Located on notorious Blair St, these creaky rooms once served as a bordello. For what you get these days, prices are a little steep, but the decoration is pleasingly quaint and Western.

Locals say the restaurant (mains $6 to $12) has the best cooking in town. It's a cheerful dining room with a gorgeous old wood shotgun bar that serves Western American fare.

Silver Summit RV Park
CAMPING $

(☑970-387-0240, toll-free 800-352-1637; www.silversummitrvpark.com; 640 Mineral St; RV sites $36 plus electricity $3; ☺May 15-Oct 15; P🌐📶🐾) A mixed business running rental Jeeps out of the RV park headquarters (two-/four-door Jeep Wranglers $155/185). The park has good facilities including a laundry, hot tub, fire pit and free wi-fi.

Red Mountain Motel & RV Park
MOTEL, CAMPING $

(☑970-382-5512, toll-free 800-970-5512; www.redmtmotelrvpk.com; 664 Greene St; motel r from $78, cabins from $70, RV/tent sites $38/20; ☺year-round; P🌐📶🐾🐕) Standard, with warm and tiny log cabins fully outfitted with little kitchenettes. The managers seem keen to make sure guests and customers have a good time. The river, with good fishing, is just a few minutes' walk away. Jeep and ATV rental are available, as well as guided tours, snowmobiling, fishing and hunting.

✗ Eating & Drinking

Stellar Bakery & Pizzeria
CAFE $$

(☑970-387-9940; 1260 Blair St; mains $8-15; ☺11am-10pm; 🐾) Great for lunch or dinner, with signature stellar pizzas, friendly service and an easy atmosphere. Beers by the bottle are available and there's also a selection of fresh baked quiches, pastas and salads.

Handlebars
AMERICAN $$

(☑970-387-5395; www.handlebarssilverton.com; 117 13th St; mains $10-20; ☺lunch & dinner, May-Oct; 🐾) Steeped in Wild West kitsch, this place still serves worthy baby-back ribs basted in a secret BBQ sauce and other Western fare. The decor, a mishmash of old mining artifacts, mounted animal heads and cowboy memorabilia, gives this place a ramshackle museum-meets-garage-sale feel.

After dinner, kick it up on the dance floor to the sounds of live rock and country music.

TOP CHOICE Montanya Distillers
BAR

(www.montanyadistillers.com; 1332 Blair St; mains $8-20; ☺11:30am-7pm) Finding handcrafted rum in the Rockies is like digging up a nugget of gold. This smart and inviting shoebox is run by hip female bartenders with a lazy pour. They're known to invite you for the first shot and talk you into organic tamales, free popcorn and exotic cocktails handmade with homemade syrups and award-winning rum. It's worth it just for the cozy, fun atmosphere. Note: low season hours change.

Silverton Brewery & Restaurant
BREWERY

(☑970-387-5033; www.silvertonbrewing.com; 1333 Greene St; ☺11:30am-10pm) This hugely popular brewery consistently wins a thumbs-up for its brews, food and atmosphere. The food (mains $7 to $19) is a clever mix of comfort favorites. The beer bratwurst with homemade sauerkraut is a house specialty.

❶ Information

Silverton Chamber of Commerce & Visitor Center
(☑970-387-5654, toll-free 800-752-4494; www.silvertoncolorado.com; 414 Greene St; ☺9am-5pm; 🐾) The Silverton Chamber of Commerce & Visitor Center provides information about the town and surrounds. It's staffed by friendly volunteers and you can buy tickets for the Durango & Silverton Narrow Gauge Railroad here.

❶ Getting There & Away

Silverton is on Hwy 550 midway between Montrose, about 60 miles to the north, and Durango, some 48 miles to the south. Other than private car, the only way to get to and from Silverton is by using the Durango & Silverton Narrow Gauge Railroad or the private buses that run its return journeys.

Black Canyon of the Gunnison National Park

The Colorado Rockies are most famous for their mountains, but the **Black Canyon of the Gunnison National Park** (☑970-249-1915, 800-873-0244; www.nps.gov/blca; 7-day admission per vehicle $15; ☺8am-6pm summer, 8:30am-4pm fall, winter & spring; P🐾) is the inverse of this geographic feature – a massive yawning chasm etched out over millions of years by volcanic uplift and the flow of the Gunnison River.

A dark, narrow gash above the Gunnison River leads down a 2000ft chasm that's as eerie as it is spectacular. Sheer, deep and narrow, it earned its name because sunlight only touches the canyon floor when the sun is directly overhead. No other canyon in America combines the narrow openings, sheer walls and dizzying depths of the Black Canyon, and a peek over the edge evokes a sense of awe (and vertigo) for most.

Two miles past the park entrance on South Rim Drive, **South Rim Visitor Center** (☑970-249-1915, 800-873-0244; www.nps.gov /blca; ☺8:30am-4pm fall, winter & spring, 8am-6pm summer) is well stocked with books and maps, and enthusiastic National Parks Service staff offer a wealth of information on hiking, fishing and rock climbing.

The park spans 32,950 acres. Head to the 6 mile-long South Rim Rd, which takes you to 11 overlooks at the edge of the canyon, some reached via short trails up to 1.5 miles long (round-trip). At the narrowest part of Black Canyon, Chasm View is 1100ft across yet 1800ft deep. Rock climbers are frequently seen on the opposing North Wall. Colorado's highest cliff face is the 2300ft **Painted Wall**. To challenge your senses, cycle along the smooth pavement running parallel to the rim's 2000ft drop-off. You definitely get a better feel for the place than when trapped in a car.

In summer the East Portal Rd is open. This steep, winding hairpin route takes you into the canyon and down to the river level where there are picnic shelters and superb views up the gorge and the craggy cliff faces. This area is popular with fly-fishers.

For a surreal experience, visit Black Canyon's South Rim in winter. The stillness of the snow-drenched plateau is broken only by the icy roar of the river at the bottom of the canyon, far, far below.

The park has three campgrounds although only one is open all year round. Water is trucked into the park and only the **East Portal Campground** (☑970-249-1915; www .nps.gov/blca; sites $12; ☺spring to fall) has river-water access. Firewood is not provided and may not be collected in the national park – campers must bring their own firewood into the campgrounds. Rangers at the visitor center can issue a backcountry permit, if you want to descend one of the South Rim's three unmarked routes to the infrequently visited riverside campsites.

The park is 12 miles east of the US Hwy 550 Junction with US Hwy 50. Exit at Hwy 347 – well marked with a big brown sign for the national park – and head north for 7 miles.

GREAT SAND DUNES NATIONAL PARK

A strange sight, the country's youngest national park features 55 miles of towering Sahara-like dunes tucked against the looming peaks of the Sangre de Cristo range. Sandboarding, or just running down them full speed, is heaps of fun. The **visitor center** (☑719 378 6399; www.nps.gov/grsa; 11999 Hwy 150; adult $3; ☺8:30am-6:30pm summer, 9am-4:30pm winter, to 5pm spring & fall) provides information. Camp in **Pinyon Flats Campground** (www.recreation .gov; Great Sand Dunes National Park; sites $14; ☺year-round; 🐾).

The park is 164 miles (approximately 3¼ hrs) from Crested Butte and 114 miles (2¼ hours) from Pagosa Springs, Colorado. From Crested Butte, take CO-135 to CO-114 south, then head east toward Mosca and follow the signs to the park. The visitors center is 3 miles north of the park entrance; access to the dunes is another mile along the road.

Crested Butte

POP 1680 / ELEV 8885FT

Powder bound Crested Butte has retained its rural character better than most Colorado ski resorts. Ringed by three wilderness areas, this remote former mining village is counted among Colorado's best ski resorts (some say *the* best). The old town center features beautifully preserved Victorian-era buildings refitted with hip shops and businesses. Strolling two-wheel traffic matches the laid-back, happy attitude.

In winter, the scene centers around Mt Crested Butte, the conical ski mountain emerging from the valley floor. But come summer, these rolling hills become the state wildflower capital (according to the Colorado State Senate), and many mountain-bikers' fave for sweet alpine singletrack.

◉ Sights & Activities

TOP CHOICE **Crested Butte Mountain Heritage Museum**   MUSEUM

(☑970-349-1880; www.crestedbuttemuseum.com; 331 Elk Ave; adult/child $3/free; ☺10am-8pm summer, noon-6pm winter; P🐾) In one of the oldest buildings in Crested Butte, a worthwhile visit for the Mountain Bike Hall of Fame or to see a terrific model railway. Exhibits range from geology to mining and early home life.

Crested Butte Center for the Arts
PERFORMANCE SPACE

(☑970-349-7487; www.crestedbuttearts.org; 606 6th St; prices vary; ☺10am-6pm; P⚡) With shifting exhibitions of local artists and a stellar schedule of live music and performance pieces, there's always something lively and interesting happening here.

TOP CHOICE Crested Butte Mountain Resort
SKIING

(☑970-349-2222; www.skicb.com; 12 Snowmass Rd; lift ticket adult/child $87/44; ⚡) Catering mostly to intermediates and experts, Crested Butte Mountain Resort sits 2 miles north of the town at the base of the impressive mountain of the same name. Surrounded by forests, rugged mountain peaks, and the West Elk, Raggeds and Maroon Bells-Snowmass Wilderness Areas, the scenery is breathtaking. It's comprised of several hotels and apartment buildings, with variable accommodations rates.

Crested Butte Nordic Center
CROSS-COUNTRY SKIING

(☑970-349-1707; www.cbnordic.org; 620 2nd St; day passes adult/child $15/10; ☺8:30am-5pm; ⚡) With 50km of groomed cross-country ski trails around Crested Butte, this center issues day and season passes, manages hut rental and organizes events and races. Ski rentals and lessons are available, in addition to ice-skating, snowshoeing and guided tours of the alpine region.

Adaptive Sports Center
OUTDOOR ACTIVITIES

(☑970-349-2296; www.adaptivesports.org; 10 Crested Butte Way; ⚡) This nonprofit group helps people with disabilities participate in outdoors activities and adventure sports.

Fantasy Ranch
HORSEBACK RIDING

(☑970-349-5425, toll-free 888-688-3488; www.fantasyranchoutfitters.com; 935 Gothic Rd; 1½hr/3hr/day rides $55/85/120; ⚡) Offers short trail rides (guests over seven years and under 240lbs), wilderness day rides and multiday pack trips. One highlight is a stunning ride from Crested Butte to Aspen round-trip.

MOVING ON?

For tips, recommendations and reviews, head to shop.lonelyplanet.com to purchase a downloadable PDF of the Rocky Mountains chapter from Lonely Planet's USA guide.

Alpineer
MOUNTAIN BIKING

(☑970-349-5210; www.alpineer.com; 419 6th St; bike rental per day $20-50; ⚡) Serves the mountain-biking mecca with maps, information and rentals. It also rents out skis and hiking and camping equipment.

Crested Butte Guides
OUTDOOR ACTIVITIES

(☑970-349-5430; www.crestedbutteguides.com; off Elk Ave) Guide service for hardcore backcountry skiing, ice climbing or mountaineering. With over a decade of experience, these guys can get you into (and out of) some seriously remote wilderness. They can also provide equipment.

Black Tie Ski Rentals
SNOW SPORTS

(☑970-349-0722, toll-free 888-349-0722; www.blacktieskis.com; Unit A/719 4th St; ☺7:30am-10pm winter; ⚡) Black Tie rents skis, skiing equipment and snowboards.

🛏 Sleeping

Visitors to Crested Butte can stay either in the main town, better for restaurants and nightlife, or in one of the many options at the mountain resort. Some of the Crested Butte Mountain Resort hotels and apartment buildings close over the shoulder seasons in spring and fall, but others offer great discounts and longer-stay incentives – check websites, compare prices and bargain. If you've come for the hiking, mountain biking or to enjoy the wildflowers, you can do very well at these times.

TOP CHOICE Ruby of Crested Butte
B&B $$$

(☑800-390-1338; www.therubyofcrestedbutte.com; 624 Gothic Ave; d $129-249, suite $199-349; P✳🛜⚡) Thoughtfully outfitted, down to the bowls of jellybeans and nuts in the stylish communal lounge. Rooms are brilliant, with heated floors, high-definition flat-screen TVs with DVD players (and a library), iPod docks and deluxe linens. There's also a Jacuzzi, library, ski-gear drying room, free wi-fi and use of retro townie bikes. Hosts help with dinner reservations and other services. Pets get a first-class treatment that includes their own bed, bowls and treats.

Crested Butte International Hostel
HOSTEL $

(☑970-349-0588, toll-free 888-389-0588; www.crestedbuttehostel.com; 615 Teocalli Ave; dm $25-31, r $65-110; 🛜⚡) For the privacy of a hotel with the lively ambience of a hostel, grab a room here. One of Colorado's nicest hostels, the best private rooms have their own baths. Dorm bunks come with reading lamps and lockable drawers, and the communal area has a stone fireplace and comfortable couches. Rates vary with the season, with winter being high season. Extended stays attract discounts.

Inn at Crested Butte
BOUTIQUE HOTEL $$

(970-349-2111, toll-free 877-343-211; www.innatcrestedbutte.net; 510 Whiterock Ave; d $130-200; P❄️✳️📶🐕🏊) This recently refurbished hotel offers smart, modern rooms. Some have balcony views over Mt Crested Butte, and all feature antiques, flat-screen TVs, coffeemakers and minibars. Especially if you get a king-sized bed, space can seem cramped.

Elevation Hotel & Spa
HOTEL $$$

(970-349-2222; www.skicb.com; 500 Gothic Rd; r from $200; P🐕) At the base of Crested Butte Mountain Resort and just steps from a major chairlift, this swank address offers oversized luxury rooms ready for first call on powder days. Check online for specials, particularly at the start or end of the season.

The Atmosphere Restaurant is a trendy place for dining, while the hotel's slope-side deck is the spot for a beer by the fire pit while you watch snowboarders whizz by.

Crested Butte Mountain Resort Properties
RENTAL AGENCY

(CBMR Properties; 888-223-2631; www.skicb.com) This property-management group, part of the Crested Butte Mountain Resort, handles reservations for dozens of the lodges, hotels and apartment buildings at the resort.

✗ Eating & Drinking

TOP CHOICE **Secret Stash**
PIZZA $$

(970-349-6245; www.thesecretstash.com; 21 Elk Ave; mains $8-20; ⏰5-10pm; 🚗🐕) A locals go-to place, this pizza and calzone joint has phenomenal food and a hip interior where you can sit on the floor upstairs or park yourself in a velvety chair on the lower level and catch up on the gossip. The Notorious Fig pizza (with Asiago, fresh figs, prosciutto and truffle oil) won a pizza world championship. We think you'd like it too. Exotic cocktails are also a house specialty.

🍴 Soupçon
FRENCH $$$

(970-349-5448; www.soupconcrestedbutte.com; 127 Elk Ave; mains $17-32; ⏰6-10:30pm; 🐕) Specializing in seduction, this petite French bistro occupies an ambient old mining cabin with just a few tables. Chef Jason has worked with big New York City names and keeps it fresh with local meat and organic produce. Reserve ahead.

Avalanche Bar & Grill
PUB $$

(www.avalanchebarandgrill.com; off Gothic Rd; mains $7-19; ⏰7:30am-9pm winter, from 11:30am summer; 🚗🐕) One of the favorite *après ski* venues, Avalanche is right on the slopes. Test your hunger against their encyclopedic menu of American comfort foods (tuna melts, burgers, club sandwiches, pizzas) as well as an impressive lineup of desserts and beverages. There's a kids menu too.

Camp 4 Coffee
COFFEE SHOP $

(www.camp4coffee.com; 402 1/2 Elk Ave) Grab your caffeine fix at this serious local roaster, the cutest cabin in town, shingled with license plates (just as local miners once did when they couldn't afford to patch their roofs).

Princess Wine Bar
WINE BAR $

(970-349-0210; 218 Elk St; ⏰6am-midnight; 📶) Intimate and perfect for conversation over some sampling of the select regional wine list. There's regular live acoustic music featuring local singer-songwriters. A popular *après ski* spot.

☆ Entertainment

On CB's lively music scene, most bands play **Eldo Brewery** (970-349-6125; www.eldoBrewery.com; 215 Elk Ave; cover charge varies; ⏰3pm-late, music from 10:30pm; 🐕), a popular microbrewery. Nightclub/sushi-bar **Lobar** (970-349-0480; www.thelobar.com; 303 Elk Ave; occasional cover charge) goes disco late-night, complete with mirror balls DJs and sometimes live music.

The best community theatre is **Crested Butte Mountain Theatre** (970-349-0366; www.cbmountaintheatre.org; 403 2nd St; prices vary; ⏰vary; 🐕), for bargains check out a dress rehearsal show.

ℹ️ Information

Crested Butte Visitor Center (970-349-6438; www.cbchamber.com; 601 Elk Ave; ⏰9am-3pm) Crested Butte's visitor center is packed with information and staffed by helpful people.

Post office (970-349-5568; www.usps.com; 217 Elk Ave; ⏰7:30am-4:30pm Mon-Fri, 10am-1pm Sat)

ℹ️ Getting There & Away

Crested Butte is a 30-minute drive from Gunnison. The trip from Ouray to Crested Butte takes a little less than three hours.

Utah

Includes »

Why Go?

Though not everyone knows it, Utah is one of nature's most perfect playgrounds. The state's rocky terrain comes ready-made for hiking, biking, rafting, rappelling, rock climbing, skiing, snowmobile riding, horseback pack-tripping, four-wheel driving... Need we go on? More than 65% of the lands are public, including 12 national parks and monuments.

Southern Utah is defined by red-rock cliffs, sorbet-colored spindles and seemingly endless sandstone desert. The forest- and snow-covered peaks of the Wasatch Mountains dominate northern Utah. Interspersed you'll find old pioneer buildings, ancient rock art and ruins, and traces of dinosaurs.

Mormon-influenced rural towns can be quiet and con-servative, but the rugged beauty has attracted outdoorsy progressives as well. Salt Lake City (SLC) and Park City es-pecially, have vibrant nightlife and foodie scenes. So pull on your boots or rent a jeep: Utah's wild and scenic hinterlands await. We'll meet you later at the nearest boho coffeehouse.

Best Places to Stay

» Sundance Resort (p499)
» Torrey Schoolhouse B&B (p426)
» Quail Park Lodge (p445)
» Under the Eaves Inn (p454)
» Sorrel River Ranch (p411)

Best Places to Eat

» Café Diablo (p427)
» Hell's Backbone Grill (p429)
» Parallel 88 (p456)
» Love Muffin (p412)
» Talisker (p493)

When to Go
Salt Lake City

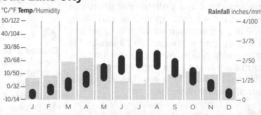

May	Oct	Jan–Mar
The mild weather makes this an excellent time to hike, especially in southern Utah.	Colorful autumn leaves come out, but a welcome touch of warmth lingers.	Powder hounds gear up for the skiing at SLC and Park City mountain resorts.

Utah Planning

Utah is not a large state, but it is largely rural. That means unless you are staying in Salt Lake City or Park City, you'll need a car. If you're headed to the parks in southern Utah, your cheapest bet may be to fly into Las Vegas and rent a ride there.

DON'T MISS

Sure, some of Utah's rugged beauty can be seen roadside. But one of the great things about the state is how much of it is set aside for public use. You'll gain a whole new perspective – and appreciation – of the terrain if you delve deeper. Not-to-be-missed outdoor adventures are available for all skill levels, and outfitters are there to help. Challenge yourself by rappelling into the narrow canyons around **Zion National Park** or mountain biking on the steep and sinister **Slick Rock Trail** in Moab. Or take it easy on your body (though not your vehicle) by going off-pavement along one of the state's many 4WD roads. Whether you're rafting on the **Colorado River** or skiing fresh powder in the **Wasatch Mountains**, you'll see the state in a whole new way.

Tips for Drivers

» Driving between major cities can be quite a speedy affair. The three interstate freeways have a 75mph limit.

» Cruising in from Denver on I-70? Make sure you get gas in Green River (345 miles, 5¼ hours). The 104 miles between there and Salina is the largest stretch of US interstate without services.

» When traveling between Las Vegas and SLC, consider a scenic detour east on Hwy 9 at St George to Hwy 89 north. It's longer (365 miles, seven hours, St George to SLC; compared with 303 miles and 4¼ hours on the I-15), but you'll pass through some stunning red-rock country.

» In general, plan to take your time on smaller roads and byways. The state has some daunting geographic features. Switchbacks, steep inclines, reduced speed limits – and stunning views – are all part of the experience.

TIME ZONE

Utah is on Mountain Standard Time (generally seven hours behind GMT), but does follow daylight saving time from mid-March to early November. Note that if you're traveling into Arizona, there's an hour's difference spring to fall.

Fast Facts

» Population: 2.9 million
» Area: 84,900 sq miles
» Time Zone: Mountain Standard Time
» Sales Tax: 4.7%
» SLC to Moab: 235 miles, 4 hours
» St George to SLC: 304 miles, 4¼ hours
» Zion to Moab: 359 miles, 5½ hours

Liquor Laws

Although a few unusual liquor laws remain, regulations have relaxed recently. For more information, see p393.

Resources

» Utah Office of Tourism (☎800-200-1160; www .utah.com) Free Utah Travel Guide; website in six languages.

» Utah State Parks & Recreation Department (☎877-887-2757; www .stateparks.utah.gov) Info about the 40-plus state parks.

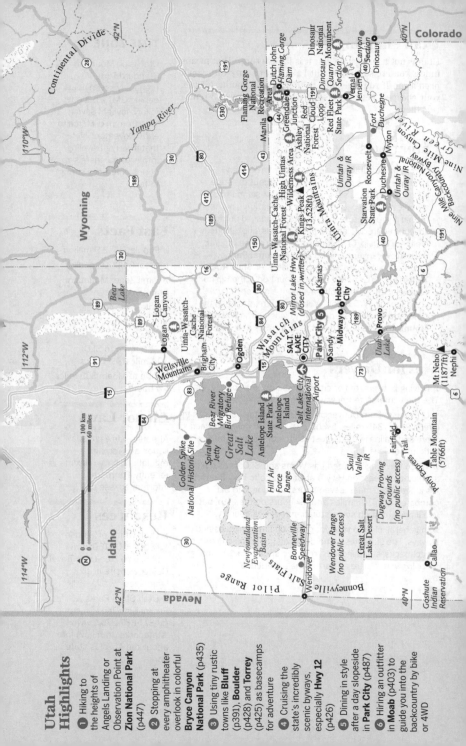

Utah Highlights

❶ Hiking to the heights of Angels Landing or Observation Point at **Zion National Park** (p447)

❷ Stopping at every amphitheater overlook in colorful **Bryce Canyon National Park** (p435)

❸ Using tiny rustic towns like **Bluff** (p391), **Boulder** (p428) and **Torrey** (p425) as basecamps for adventure

❹ Cruising the state's incredibly scenic byways, especially **Hwy 12** (p426)

❺ Dining in style after a day slopeside in **Park City** (p487)

❻ Hiring an outfitter in **Moab** (p403) to guide you into the backcountry by bike or 4WD

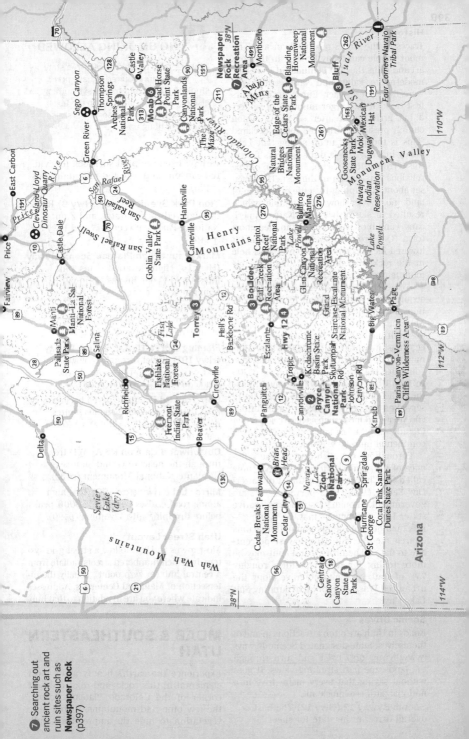

7 Searching out ancient rock art and ruin sites such as **Newspaper Rock** (p397)

MOAB & SOUTHEASTERN UTAH

History

Traces of the Ancestral Puebloan and Fremont people can today be seen in the rock art and ruins they left behind. But it was the modern Ute, Paiute and Navajo tribes who were living here when European explorers first trickled in. Larger numbers of settlers didn't arrive until after second Mormon church president Brigham Young declared 'This is the place!' upon seeing Salt Lake Valley in 1847. The faithful pioneers fled to this territory, then part of Mexico, to escape religious persecution in the east. They then set about attempting to settle every inch of land, no matter how inhospitable, which resulted in skirmishes with Native Americans – and more than one abandoned ghost town. (One group was so determined that it lowered its wagons by rope through a hole in the rock to continue on an impassible mountain trail; see p433.)

For nearly 50 years after the United States acquired the land, the Utah Territory's petitions for statehood were rejected due to the Mormon practice of polygamy, or the taking of multiple wives. Tensions and prosecutions mounted until 1890 when Mormon leader Wilford Woodruff officially discontinued the practice. (For more, see p520.) In 1896 Utah became the 45th state. About the same time, Utah's remote backcountry served as the perfect hideout for notorious Old West 'bad men', such as native son Butch Cassidy, and the last spike of the first intercontinental railroad was driven here.

Throughout the 20th century the influence of the modern Mormon church, now called the Church of Jesus Christ of Latter-Day Saints (LDS), was pervasive in state government. Though it's still a conservative state, LDS supremacy may be waning – less than 60% of today's population claims church membership (the lowest percentage to date). The urban/rural split may be more telling for future politics: roughly 75% of state residents now live along the urbanized Wasatch Front surrounding Salt Lake City.

Scenic Drives

Roads in Utah are often attractions in and of themselves. State-designated Scenic Byways (www.byways.org) twist and turn through the landscape past stunning views. It goes without saying that every main drive in a national park is a knock-out.

Scenic Byway 12 (Hwy 12) The best overall drive in the state for sheer

NO SMOKING ALLOWED

Utah is pretty much a smoke-free state. All lodgings are required to have non-smoking rooms, but most have nothing else (exceptions are noted in the text). Restaurants, and even some bars, also prohibit lighting up.

variety: from sculpted slickrock to vivid red canyons and forested mountain tops (p426).

Zion Park Scenic Byway (Hwy 9) Runs through red-rock country, and Zion National Park, between I-15 and Hwy 89 (p449).

Markagaunt High Plateau Scenic Byway (Hwy 14) High elevation vistas, pine forests and Cedar Breaks National Monument are en route (p460).

Nine Mile Canyon Rd A rough and rugged back road leads to a virtual gallery of ancient rock art and ruins (p504).

Flaming Gorge-Uintas Scenic Byway (Hwy 191) Travel through geologic time on this road; as you head north, the roadside rocks get older (p503).

Burr Trail Rd Dramatic paved backcountry road that skirts cliffs, canyons, buttes, mesas and monoliths on its way to the Waterpocket Fold (p433).

Cottonwood Canyon Rd A 4WD trek through the heart of Grand Staircase-Escalante National Monument (p433).

Mirror Lake Hwy (Rte 150) This high-alpine road cruises beneath 12,000ft peaks before dropping into Wyoming (p490).

Utah Street Layout

Most towns in Utah follow a street grid system, in which numbered streets radiate from a central hub (or zero point), usually the intersection of Main and Center Sts. Addresses indicate where you are in relation to that hub.

MOAB & SOUTHEASTERN UTAH

Experience the earth's beauty at its most elemental in this rocky-and-rugged desert corner of the Colorado Plateau. Beyond the few pine-clad mountains, there's little vegetation to hide the impressive handi-

Utah Street Layout

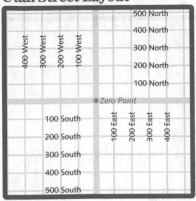

work of time, water and wind: the thousands of red-rock spans in Arches National Park, the sheer walled river gorges from Canyonlands to Lake Powell, and the stunning buttes and mesas of Monument Valley. The town of Moab is the best base for adventure, with as much four-wheeling, white-knuckle rafting, outfitter-guided fun as you can handle. Or you can lose the crowd while looking for Ancestral Puebloan rock art and dwellings in miles of isolated and undeveloped lands.

Note that many regional restaurants and shops – some motels even – close or have variable hours after the May to late October high season.

Bluff

Tiny tot Bluff isn't much more than a spot in the road. But a few great motels and a handful of restaurants, surrounded by stunning red rock, make it a cool little base for exploring the far southwestern corner of the state. From here you can easily reach Moki Dugway (30 miles), Hovenweep National Monument (40 miles), Monument Valley (47 miles) and Natural Bridges National Monument (61 miles), just to mention a few area sights, as well as explore the surrounding Bureau of Land Management (BLM) wilderness.

There's no visitor center here at the crossroads of Hwys 191 N and 163. You can log onto www.bluff-utah.org, but local business owners and staff are your best resource (they know the hikes betterthan an office worker could, anyway). To preserve the night sky, Bluff has no streetlights.

◉ Sights & Activities

The BLM field office in Monticello has information about the public lands surrounding Bluff. Local motel Recapture Lodge also sells topographic maps for hiking; a public trail leads down from the lodging to the San Juan River.

Bluff Fort
HISTORIC SITE
(www.hirf.org/bluff.asp; 5 E Hwy 191; admission by donation; ⊙9am-6pm Mon-Sat) Descendants of the original pioneers have re-created the original log cabin settlement near the few remaining historic buildings in Bluff.

Sand Island Petroglyphs
ARCHAEOLOGICAL SITE
(www.blm.gov; Sand Island Rd, off Hwy 163) On BLM land 3 miles west of Bluff, these freely accessible petroglyphs were created between 800 and 2500 years ago. The nearby campground boat launch is the starting point for San Juan River adventures

Far Out Expeditions
ADVENTURE TOUR
(☑435-672-2294; www.faroutexpeditions.com; full-day from $165) Interested in remote ruins and rock art? Vaughn Hadenfeldt leads much sought after single- and multiday hikes into the desert surrounds.

Wild Rivers Expeditions
RAFTING
(☑800-422-7654; www.riversandruins.com; day trip adult/child $165/120) Float through the San Juan River canyons with this history- and geology-minded outfitter; you'll also get to stop and see petroglyphs.

Buckhorn Llama
ADVENTURE TOUR
(☑435-672 2466; www.llamapack.com; per day from $300) Llama-supported multiday pack trips into hard-to-reach wilderness.

🛏 Sleeping

Recapture Lodge
MOTEL $
(☑435-672-2281; www.recapturelodge.com; Hwy 191; r incl breakfast $70; ❄🐾@🛜🏊) This locally owned, rustic motel makes the best base for area adventures. Super-knowledgeable

---

PUBLIC LANDS

Public lands – national and state parks and monuments, national forests and Bureau of Land Management (BLM) lands – are Utah's most precious natural resource for visitors. Check out www.publiclands.org.

Southeastern Utah

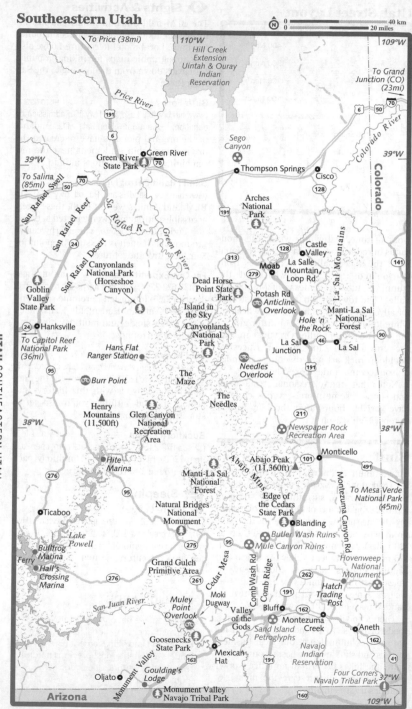

0 — 40 km
0 — 20 miles

To Price (38mi)
110°W
Hill Creek Extension Uintah & Ouray Indian Reservation
109°W
To Grand Junction (CO) (23mi)

Price River
191
6

Sego Canyon

Green River State Park
Green River
70
Thompson Springs
Cisco
39°W
39°W
128

To Salina (85mi)
70
50

San Rafael Swell

Arches National Park
191

San Rafael Reef
San Rafael R
Sa Rafael R
Green River

Castle Valley
128
La Salle Mountain Loop Rd
Moab
279
313
141

24
San Rafael Desert
Canyonlands National Park (Horseshoe Canyon)
Dead Horse Point State Park
Potash Rd
Anticline Overlook
Manti-La Sal National Forest
La Sal Mountains

Goblin Valley State Park
Island in the Sky
Hole 'n the Rock
90

24 Hanksville
Canyonlands National Park
La Sal Junction
46
La Sal
191

To Capitol Reef National Park (36mi)
Hans Flat Ranger Station
Needles Overlook

95
Burr Point
The Maze
The Needles
38°W
38°W

Henry Mountains (11,500ft)
Glen Canyon National Recreation Area
211
Newspaper Rock Recreation Area

Hite Marina
Abajo Peak (11,360ft)
Monticello
101
491

276
Manti-La Sal National Forest
Edge of the Cedars State Park
To Mesa Verde National Park (45mi)

Ticaboo
Natural Bridges National Monument
Blanding
Montezuma Canyon Rd

Lake Powell
Butler Wash Ruins
Mule Canyon Ruins
262
Hovenweep National Monument

Bullfrog Marina
Ferry
Hall's Crossing Marina
275
95
Cedar Mesa Rd
Comb Wash Rd
Comb Ridge

Grand Gulch Primitive Area
261
Hatch Trading Post

San Juan River
276
Moki Dugway
191
162

Muley Point Overlook
Valley of the Gods
Bluff
Montezuma Creek
Aneth

Goosenecks State Park
Sand Island Petroglyphs
162

163
Mexican Hat
191
Navajo Indian Reservation
41

Oljato
Goulding's Lodge
Monument Valley
37°W
Four Corners Navajo Tribal Park

Arizona
Monument Valley Navajo Tribal Park
160
109°W

CAN I GET A DRINK IN UTAH?

Absolutely. You always could, it's just gotten easier in recent years. Private club memberships are no more: a bar is now a bar (no minors allowed), and you don't have to order food to consume alcohol in one of them. As far as restaurants go, few have full liquor licenses, and most places that serve dinner also have beer and wine only. Either way, if you're in a restaurant, you have to order food to drink there. Some rules to remember:

» Mixed drinks and wine are available only after midday; 3.2% alcohol beer can be served starting at 10am.

» Mixed drinks cannot contain more than 1.5 ounces of a primary liquor, or 2.5 ounces total including secondary alcohol. Sorry, no Long Island Iced Teas or double shots.

» Packaged liquor can only be sold at state-run liquor stores; grocery and convenience stores can sell 3.2% alcohol beer and malt beverages. Both are open Monday through Saturday only.

staff help out with trip planning and present educational slide shows in season. Thankfully there's plenty of shade around the pool and on the property's 3½ miles of walking trails.

Desert Rose Inn MOTEL $$
(☑435-672-2303, 888-475-7673; www.desertrose inn.com; Hwy 191; r $99-110, cabins $129-159, ❄⊚☑) Wood porches wrap completely around a dramatic, two-story log building at the edge of town. Quilts on pine beds add to the comfort of extra large rooms and cabins.

Sand Island Campground CAMPGROUND $
(☑435-587-1500; www.blm.gov; Sand Island Rd; tent & RV sites $10; ❂May-Oct) The San Juan River location helps cool things off at these 27 first-come, first-served sites. Pit toilets and drinking water only; no hookups, no showers.

Far Out Bunkhouse GUESTHOUSE $
(☑435-672-2294; www.faroutexpeditions.com; cnr 7th East & Mulberry Sts; 1 or 2 in room $90) Two private six-bunk rooms available in a guesthouse run by the eponymous hiking outfitter.

Kokopelli Inn MOTEL $
(☑435-672-2322, 877-342-6099; www.kokoinn .com; Hwy 191; r $62-72; ❄❈☑) Basic, 26-room motel.

✖ Eating

San Juan River Kitchen NEW MEXICAN $$
(75 E Main St; lunch $8-13, dinner $9-20; ❂11am-9pm Tue-Sun) The inventive, regionally-sourced Mexican-American dishes here use organic ingredients whenever possible. Don't skip the homemade chipotle chocolate ice cream for desert.

Comb Ridge Coffee CAFE $
(Hwy 191; baked goods $2-6; ❂7am-3pm Wed-Sun, varies Nov-Feb; ☑) Grab an espresso, muffin or stack of blue-corn pancakes inside this arty adobe cafe-gallery.

Twin Rocks Cafe NATIVE AMERICAN $-$$
(913 E Navajo Twins Dr; mains $6-14; ❂7am-9pm) At Twin Rocks you can try fry bread (deep-fried dough) with any of your three daily meals: as part of a breakfast sandwich, wrapped up as a Navajo taco at lunch or accompanying stew with dinner.

Cottonwood Steakhouse STEAKHOUSE $$-$$$
(cnr Main & 4th West Sts; mains $18-25; ❂5-10pm Mar-Nov) Yee-haw! Sure it's pricey, but you're paying for Wild West-style fun to go with your outdoor-grilled rib-eye steak, pardner.

Hovenweep National Monument

This area straddling the Utah-Colorado state line was home to a sizeable Ancestral Puebloan population before abandonment in the late 1200s (perhaps because of drought and deforestation). Since 1923, six sets of sites have been protected as a **national monument** (www.nps.gov/hove; 7-day per vehicle $6; ❂trails sunrise-sunset, visitor center 8am-5pm).

The **Square Tower Group** near the visitor center is what people are generally referring to when speaking of Hovenweep. Pick up the interpretive guide ($1), essential for understanding the unexcavated ruins. **Stronghold House** is reachable from a paved, wheelchair-accessible path and from there you overlook the rest of the ruins.

To get a closer look, you'll have to hike down into the canyon (and back up); follow the trail clockwise to best see the ruins unfold around every corner. Most of the eight brick towers and unit houses were constructed between 1230 and 1275. The masonry skills it took to piece together such tall structures on such little ledges definitely inspires admiration.

The other sections of the park require 4WD and/or lengthy hikes. Ask for a map at the visitor center, where there's also a nice 30-site **campground** (tent & RV sites $10) with water and toilets; no hookups. Otherwise, there's a whole lotta nothin' else out here. The closest store is the **Hatch Trading Post** (County Rd 414), an atmospheric white-brick building that sells a few sundries and some Native American crafts. Other than that, supplies are in Blanding (45 miles), Bluff (40 miles) and Cortez, Colorado (43 miles).

The best route to the park is paved Hwy 262. From the turnoff east at Hwy 191 follow the signs; it's a 28-mile drive to the main entrance (past Hatch Trading Post). Use caution traveling on any unpaved roads here: all become treacherous in wet weather. From Hovenweep, Mesa Verde National Park (p365) is 75 miles east in Colorado.

Valley of the Gods

Up and over, through and around: the 17-mile unpaved road that leads through Valley of the Gods is like a do-it-yourself roller coaster – amid some mind-blowing scenery. In other states, this incredible butte-filled valley would be a national park, but such are the riches of Utah that here it is merely a BLM-administered area (www.blm.gov). Locals call it 'mini-Monument Valley'. The field office in Monticello puts out a BLM pamphlet, available online, identifying a few of the sandstone monoliths and pinnacles that have been named over the years, including **Seven Sailors, Lady on a Tub** and **Rooster Butte.**

IN SEARCH OF ANCIENT AMERICA

Cliff dwellings, centuries-old rock art and artifacts – the southern part of the state is a great place to explore the ancient, Ancestral Puebloan cultures. Top sites include:

» **Hovenweep National Monument** (p393)

» **Anasazi State Park Museum** (p429)

» **Edge of the Cedars State Park** (p397)

» **Great Gallery, Canyonlands – Horseshoe Canyon** (p402)

» **Newspaper Rock** (p397)

» **Grand Gulch Primitive Area** (p396)

But there's far more than that to explore: small ruins and petroglyphs are to be found all across BLM lands. We recommend you hire an outfitter in Bluff, Moab, Torrey, Boulder or Escalante – especially if you're an inexperienced backcountry hiker or don't have a 4WD. Their experience and knowledge will take you far.

If you're well aware that you need at least a gallon of water per person per day, know how to negotiate rock and sand in your high-clearance SUV and can read a topographic map, you may want to explore on your own. Ask locals for tips (hint: you can also suss out the ruin symbols on the *Delorme Utah Atlas & Gazetteer*). In the far southeast, a good place to start is off Comb Wash Rd (linking Hwys 95 and 163) near Bluff, as is Montezuma Canyon Rd, north of Hovenweep.

A few things to keep in mind:

» Take only pictures – do not remove any artifacts you find, it's against the law. Not only will touching or moving items contaminate future study, you'll ruin the amazing experience for the next visitor.

» Tread lightly – though sandstone structures seem sturdy, climbing on building walls causes irreparable damage. Don't do it.

» Respect the spiritual and historical value of these places – they are sacred to many Native Americans.

» Leave no trace – pack out anything you pack in. You leave the least effect on the area's ecology if you walk on slickrock or in dry washes.

Free, dispersed camping among the rock giants is a dramatic – if shade-free – prospect. In such an isolated, uninhabited place, the night sky is incredible. Or you could spend a secluded night at one of the very few pioneer ranches in the area, now the **Valley of the Gods B&B** (970-749-1164; www.valley ofthegods.cjb.net; off Hwy 261; r incl breakfast $85-115), 6.5 miles north of Hwy 163. Simple, rustic beds feel right at home in exposed wood-and-stone rooms. Water is trucked in and solar power is harnessed out of necessity (leave your hair dryer at home).

A high-clearance vehicle is advised for driving the Valley of the Gods (County Rd 242). This author's little Volkswagen GTI made it on a very dry day, but don't try it without a 4WD if it has rained recently. Allow an hour for the 17-mile loop connecting Hwys 261 and 163. The nearest services are in Mexican Hat, 7 miles southwest of the Hwy 163 turnoff.

Mexican Hat

The settlement of Mexican Hat is named after a sombrero-shaped rock off Hwy 163. The town is little more than a handful of simple lodgings, a couple of places to eat and a store or two on the north bank of the San Juan River. The south bank marks the edge of the Navajo Reservation. Monument Valley is 20 miles to the south; Bluff 27 miles to the east. The cliffside **San Juan Inn** (435-683-2220, 800-447-2022; www.sanjuaninn .net; Hwy 163; r $85; ✸) perches high above the river. The motel rooms are pretty basic, but they're the nicest in town. You can buy Navajo crafts, books and beer on site at the **trading post** (7am-9pm). **Old River Grille** (mains $7-15; 7am-8pm) has southwestern home-cooking and the only full liquor license for at least 50 miles.

Monument Valley

From Mexican Hat, Hwy 163 winds southwest and enters the Navajo Reservation and (after 22 miles) Monument Valley, on the Arizona state line. Though you'll recognize it instantly from TV commercials and Hollywood movies (remember where Forrest Gump stopped his cross-country run?), nothing compares with seeing the sheer chocolate-red buttes and colossal mesas for real. To get close, you must visit the **Monument Valley Navajo**

Tribal Park. For details about the park and places to stay, such as Goulding's Lodge (a motel-lodge restaurant-grocery trading-post museum-tour operator), see p189.

Goosenecks State Park

If instead of heading south to Medicine Hat you turn north on Hwy 261, you'll come to a 4-mile paved road that turns west to Goosenecks State Park. The attraction here is the mesmerizing view of the San Juan River. From above, the serpentine path carved by years of running water is dramatically evident. You can see how the river snaked back on its course, leaving gooseneck-shaped spits of land untouched. The park itself doesn't have much to speak of: there are pit toilets, picnic tables and free campsites, but frequent high winds discourage staying long.

Moki Dugway & Around

Ready for a ride? Eleven miles north of Goosenecks, Moki Dugway is a roughly paved, hairpin-turn filled section of Hwy 261 that ascends 1100ft in just 3 miles (you descend traveling south). Miners dug out the extreme switchbacks in the 1950s to transport uranium ore. Today it's a way to Lake Powell, and to some hair-raising fun. Wide pullouts allow a few overviews, but for most of the time you cannot see what's around the sharp corners. The dugway is not for anyone who's height sensitive (or for those in a vehicle more than 28ft long).

LOCAL PASSPORTS

Southeastern Utah national parks sell a **local passport** (per vehicle $25) that's good for a year's entry to Arches and Canyonlands National Parks, plus Hovenweep and Natural Bridges National Monuments. **Federal park passes** (www.nps.gov/findapark/passes. htm; per vehicle adult/senior $80/10), available online and at parks, allow year-long access to all federal recreation lands in Utah and beyond – and are a great way to support the Southwest's amazing parks.

BUTLER WASH & MULE CANYON RUINS

The drive along Hwy 95 between Blanding and Natural Bridges provides an excellent opportunity to see isolated Ancestral Puebloan ruins. No need to be a backcountry trekker here: it's only a half-mile hike to **Butler Wash Ruins** (14 miles west of Blanding), a 20-room cliff dwelling. Scramble over the slickrock boulders (follow the cairns) and you're rewarded with an overlook of the sacred kivas, habitation and storage rooms that were used c 1300.

Though not as well preserved, the base of the tower, kiva and 12-room **Mule Canyon Ruins** (20 miles west of Blanding) are more easily accessed. Follow the signs to the parking lot just steps from the masonry remains. The pottery found here links the population (c 1000 to 1150) to the Mesa Verde group in southern Colorado; Butler Wash relates to the Kayenta group of northern Arizona. Both are on freely accessible BLM-administered land.

Past the northern end of the dugway, take the first western-traveling road to **Muley Point Overlook**. This sweeping cliff-edge viewpoint looks south to Monument Valley and other stunning landmarks in Arizona. Pay attention, the unsigned turnoff is easy to miss.

Follow Hwy 261 further north to the wild and twisting canyons of **Cedar Mesa** and **Grand Gulch Primitive Area** (www.blm .gov), both hugely popular with backcountry hikers. The BLM-administered area also contains hundreds of Ancestral Puebloan sites, many of which have been vandalized by pot hunters. (It bears repeating that all prehistoric sites are protected by law, and authorities are cracking down on offenders.) The 4-mile one-way **Kane Gulch** (600ft elevation change) leads to a great view of the **Junction Ruin** cliff dwelling. To hike in most canyons you need a $2 day-use permit ($8 overnight). In season (March to June 15, September and October) some walk-in permits are available at the **Kane Gulch Ranger Station** (Hwy 261, 4 miles south of Hwy 95; ⊙8am-noon Mar–mid-Nov), but the number is strictly limited so make advance reservations by calling the **Monticello Field Office** (☑435-587-1510). Off season, self-serve permits are available at trailheads. Know that this is difficult country with primitive trails; the nearest water is 10 miles away at Natural Bridges National Monument.

Natural Bridges National Monument

In 1908 **Natural Bridges National Monument** (www.nps.gov/nabr; Hwy 275; 7-day per vehicle $6; ⊙24hr, visitor center 8am-6pm Apr-Sep, 8am-5pm Oct-Mar) became Utah's first National Park Service (NPS) land. The highlight is a dark-stained, white sandstone canyon with three giant natural bridges.

The oldest – beautifully delicate **Owachomo Bridge** – spans 180ft and rises over 100ft above ground, but is only 9ft thick. **Kachina Bridge** is the youngest and spans 204ft. The 268ft span of **Sipapu Bridge** makes the top five of any 'largest in the US' list (the other four are in Utah, too). All three bridges are visible from a 9-mile winding loop road with easy-access overlooks. Most visitors never venture below the canyon rim, but they should. Descents may be a little steep, but distances are short; the longest is just over half a mile one-way. Enthusiastic hikers can take a longer trail that joins all three bridges (8 miles). Don't skip the 0.3-mile trail to the **Horsecollar Ruin** cliff dwelling overlook. The elevation here is 6500ft; trails are open all year, but steeper sections may be closed after heavy rains or snow.

The 12 first-come, first-served sites at the campground (tent & RV sites $10), almost half a mile past the visitor center, are fairly sheltered among scraggly trees and red sand. The stars are a real attraction here – this has been designated an International Dark Sky Park and is one of the darkest in the country. There are pit toilets and grills, but water is available only at the visitor center; no hookups. The campground fills on summer afternoons, after which you are directed to camp in a designated area along Hwy 275. No backcountry camping is allowed. Towed trailers are not suitable for the loop drive.

The nearest services are in Blanding, 47 miles to the east. If you continue west on Hwy 95 from Natural Bridges, and follow Hwy 276, the services of Lake Powell's Bullfrog Marina are 140 miles away.

Blanding

Two specialized museums elevate small, agriculturally-oriented Blanding a little above its totally dull name. Still, it's best to visit as a day trip, or en route between Bluff (22 miles) and Moab (75 miles). Both the motels and the (alcohol-free) restaurants are, well...bland.

Blanding Visitor Center (☎435-678-3662; www.blandingutah.org; cnr Hwy 191 N & 200 East; ⌚8am-7pm Mon-Sat) has some areawide information. If you're here, the small pioneer artifact collection is worth a look.

Edge of the Cedars State Park Museum (www.stateparks.utah.gov; 660 W 400 N; admission $5; ⌚9am-5pm Mon-Sat) houses a treasure trove of ancient Native American artifacts and pottery gathered from across southeastern Utah. Informative displays provide a good overview of area cultures. Outside, you can climb down into a preserved ceremonial kiva built by the Ancestral Puebloans c 1100. The encroaching subdivision makes you wonder what other sites remain hidden under neighborhood houses.

Born of a private owner's personal collection, the **Dinosaur Museum** (www.dinosaur-museum.org; 754 S 200 West; adult/child $3/1.50; ⌚9am-5pm Mon-Sat mid-Apr–mid-Oct) is actually quite large. Mummified remains and fossils come from around the world, but most interesting is the collection of old dinosaur-movie-related exhibits.

Fatboyz Grillin (164 N Hwy 191; mains $10-16; ⌚11am-9pm Mon-Sat, noon-9pm Sun) has blue-plate specials, like lasagna and pot roast, in addition to good barbecue. For a sweet treat with a side of novelty, head to **Old Bank Creamery** (30 W 100 S; ⌚11-7pm Jun-Aug) in a tiny 100-year-old stone bank. Innovative flavors include cotton candy and peanut-butter cup.

Monticello

Monticello (mon-ti-*sell*-o) sits up in the foothills of the Abajo (or Blue) Mountains, and is a bit cooler than other towns in the region. As the seat of San Juan County, it is the place to get information about the far southeast corner of Utah. Here you're midway between Moab (54 miles) and Bluff (47 miles); both have better places to stay but this is the closest town to the Canyonlands' Needles District.

Just west of town, **Manti–La Sal National Forest** (www.fs.fed.us/r4/mantilasal) rises to 11,360ft at Abajo Peak. Hundreds of trail miles crisscross the 1.4-million-acre park. Here, spruce- and fir-covered slopes offer respite from the heat (expect about a 10°F, or 6°C, drop in temperature for every 1000ft you ascend), and spring wildflowers and fall color are a novelty in the arid canyonlands.

Talking Stones (☎435-587-2881; www.talkingstonestours.com; full-day from $150) leads rock-art tours and excursions into the Abajo Mountains. **Abajo Haven Guest Ranch** (☎435-979-3126; www.abajohaven.com; 5440 N Cedar Edge Ln; cabins $70) is already up in the mountains; guest cabin rental includes a free tour to private Native American sites.

Other places to stay include **Canyonlands Lodge at Blue Mountain** (☎435-220-1050; www.canyonlandslodge.com; Hwy 191; r $89-119, cabins $119-179; ❄📶), a giant log lodge adjacent to the national forest 10 miles south of town, and **Inn at the Canyons** (☎435-587-2458; www.monticellocanyonlandsinn.com; 533 N Main St; r $75-85; ❄📶🏊), with modernized motel rooms on the main drag.

Peace Tree Juice Café (516 N Main St; mains $5-14; ⌚7.30am-4pm daily, plus 5-9pm May-Sep) is a great place for full breakfasts, organic espresso, smoothies, lunch wraps or healthy, flavorful dinners (in season). Slow service hasn't stopped **Lamplight Restaurant** (655 E Central St; mains $7-18; ⌚5-10pm Mon-Sat) from being the local choice for pasta, steaks and seafood for eons.

San Juan Visitor Center (☎435-587-3235, 800-574-4386; www.southeastutah.com; 117 S Main St; ⌚10am-4pm Mon-Fri Nov–mid-Mar, 8am-5pm daily mid-Mar–Oct) has general information on attractions, forest service and other public

DON'T MISS

NEWSPAPER ROCK RECREATION AREA

This small, free recreation area showcases a single large sandstone rock panel packed with more than 300 **petroglyphs** attributed to Ute and Ancestral Puebloan groups during a 2000-year period. The many red-rock figures etched out of a black 'desert varnish' surface make for great photos (evening sidelight is best). The site, about 12 miles along Hwy 211 from Hwy 191, is usually visited as a short stop on the way to the Needles section of Canyonlands National Park (8 miles further).

lands in the region. (Many of its brochures are available online, too.) The **BLM Monticello Field Office** (☎435-587-1510; 435 N Main St; ◷7:45am-noon & 1-4:30pm Mon-Fri) is the place to inquire about area backcountry BLM hiking, driving, camping and permits. Buy topographic maps here. And if you like to get way, way off the beaten path on multi-day hikes, ask about the brilliantly empty Dark Canyon Primitive Area.

From Monticello there's a shortcut to Canyonlands National Park – Needles District (22 miles instead of the main route's 34 miles). Take County Rd 101 (Abajo Dr) west to Harts Draw Rd (closed in winter); after 17 scenic miles you join Hwy 211 near Newspaper Rock Recreation Area. Befitting the region's religiousness, Hwy 666, which goes to Colorado, was officially renamed Hwy 491 in 2003.

Canyonlands National Park

A 527-sq-mile vision of ancient earth, Canyonlands is Utah's largest national park. Vast serpentine canyons tipped with white cliffs loom high over the Colorado and Green Rivers, their waters a stunning 1000ft below the rim rock. Skyward-jutting needles and spires, deep craters, blue-hued mesas and majestic buttes dot the landscape. Overlooks are easy enough to reach. To explore further you'll need to contend with difficult dirt roads, great distances and limited water resources.

The Colorado and Green Rivers form a Y that divides the park into three separate districts, inaccessible to one another from within the park. Cradled atop the Y is the most developed and visited district, **Island in the Sky** (30 miles/45 minutes from Moab). Think of this as the overview section of the park, where you look down from viewpoints into the incredible canyons that make up the other sections. The thin hoodoos, sculpted sandstone and epic 4WD trails of the **Needles District** are 75 miles/90 minutes south of Moab. Serious skill is required to traverse the 4WD-only roads of the most inaccessible section, the **Maze** (130 miles/3½ hours from Moab).

Fees & Permits

In addition to the **park entrance fee** (Island & Needles sections only, 7-day per vehicle $10), permits are required for overnight backpacking, mountain biking, 4WD trips and river trips.

Designated camp areas abut most trails; open-zone camping is permitted in some places. Horses are allowed on all 4WD trails. Permits are valid for 14 days and are issued at the visitor center or ranger station where your trip begins. Reservations are available by fax or mail from the **NPS Reservations Office** (☎435-259-4351; fax 435-259-4285; www.nps.gov/cany/planyourvisit/back countrypermits.htm; 2282 SW Resource Blvd, Moab, UT 84532; ◷8:30am-noon Mon-Fri) up to two weeks ahead. A few space-available permits may be available same-day, but advanced reservations are essential for spring and fall trips. Costs are as follows:

Backpackers $15 per group

General mountain bike or 4WD day-use $30 for up to three vehicles

Needles Area 4WD day-use $5 per vehicle

River trips $30 per group in Cataract Canyon, $20 elsewhere; plus $20 per person fee

Regulations

Canyonlands follows most of the national park hiking and backcountry use regulations. A few rules to note:

» No ATVs allowed. Other four-wheel-drive vehicles, mountain bikes and street-legal motorbikes are permitted on dirt roads.
» Backcountry campfires are allowed only along river corridors; use a fire pan, burn only driftwood or downed tamarisk, and pack out unburnt debris.
» Free or clean-aid rock climbing is allowed, except at archaeological sites or on most named features marked on US Geological Survey (USGS) maps. Check with rangers.

❶ Information

Island in the Sky and the Needles District have visitor centers, listed in the respective sections below. Many of the brochures from the **Canyonlands NPS** (www.nps.gov/cany/planyourvisit/brochures.htm) are available online. The information center in Moab also covers the park.

❶ Getting Around

The easiest way to tour Canyonlands is by car. Traveling between districts takes two to six hours, so plan to visit no more than one per day. Speed limits vary but are generally between 25mph and 40mph. Outfitters in Moab have hiker shuttles and guide rafting, hiking, biking and 4WD tours in the park.

Canyonlands National Park

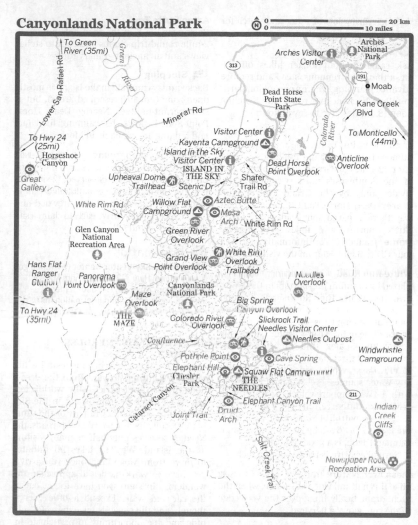

CANYONLANDS – ISLAND IN THE SKY

You'll comprehend space in new ways atop the appropriately named Island in the Sky. This 6000ft-high flat-topped mesa drops precipitously on all sides, providing some of the longest, most enthralling vistas of any park in southern Utah. The 11,500ft Henry Mountains bookend panoramic views in the west, and the 12,700ft La Sal Mountains are to the east. Here you can stand beneath a sparkling blue sky and watch thunderheads inundating far-off regions while you contemplate

applying more sunscreen. The island sits atop a sandstone bench called the White Rim, which indeed forms a white border 1200ft below the red mesa top and 1500ft above the river canyon bottom. An impressive 4WD road descends from the overlook level.

The complimentary video at the visitor center provides great insight into the nature of the park. And a reminder to keep your park entry receipt – admission to Island in the Sky includes entry to Needles, too.

Overlooks and trails line each road. Most trails at least partially follow cairns over slickrock. Bring lots of water and watch for cliff edges!

👁 Sights & Activities

Ask rangers about longer hikes off the mesa that are strenuous, steep and require advance planning. There's one major, hard-to-follow backpacking route: the Syncline Loop (8.3 miles, five to seven hours).

Scenic Drive   DRIVING TOUR

From the visitor center the road leads past numerous overlooks and trailheads, ending after 12 miles at **Grand View Point** – one of the Southwest's most sweeping views, rivaled only by the Grand Canyon and nearby Dead Horse Point State Park. Halfway there, a paved spur leads (past **Aztec Butte**) northwest 5 miles to **Upheaval Dome** trailhead. An informative driving tour CD rents for $5 from the visitor center.

White Rim Road   MOUNTAIN BIKING, DRIVING TOUR

Blazed by uranium prospectors in the 1950s, primitive White Rim Rd encircling Island in the Sky is the top choice for 4WD and mountain-biking trips. This 70-mile route is accessed near the visitor center via steeply descending Shafer Trail Rd. It generally takes two to three days in a vehicle or three to four days by bike. Since the route lacks any water sources, cyclists should team up with a 4WD support vehicle or travel with a Moab outfitter. Permits are required and rangers do patrol. *A Naturalist's Guide to the White Rim Trail*, by David Williams and Damian Fagon, is a good resource.

Several easy trails pack a lot of punch:

Mesa Arch Nature Trail   HIKING

Hike this half-mile loop at sunrise, when the arch, dramatically hung over the very edge of the rim, glows a fiery red.

Upheaval Dome   HIKING

Here, a half-mile spur leads to an overlook of a geological wonder that was possibly the result of a meteorite strike 60 million years ago.

White Rim Overlook Trail   HIKING

A mile before Grand View Point, this is a good spot for a picnic and a 1.8-mile round-trip hike.

Grand View Trail   HIKING

At the end of the road, the trail follows a 2-mile round-trip course at rim's edge. Even if you don't hike, **Grand View Point Overlook** is a must-see.

Aztec Butte Trail   HIKING

Back near the Y in the road, this moderate 2-mile round-trip climbs slickrock to stellar views and an ancient granary ruin.

🛏 Sleeping

Backcountry camping in the Island is mostly open-zone (not in prescribed areas), but is still permit-limited. Nearby Dead Horse Point State Park also has camping; food, fuel and lodging are available in Moab.

Willow Flat Campground   CAMPGROUND $

(tent & RV sites $10) Seven miles from the visitor center, the first-come, first-served, 12-site Willow Flat Campground has vault toilets but no water, and no hookups. Bring firewood and don't expect shade. Arrive early to claim a site during spring and fall.

ℹ Information

Island in the Sky Visitor Center (www.nps.gov /cany/island; Hwy 313; ⊘8am-6pm Mar-Oct, 9am-4:30pm Nov-Feb) Get books, maps, permits and campground information here. Schedules are posted daily for ranger-led lectures and hikes.

CANYONLANDS – NEEDLES DISTRICT

Named for the spires of orange-and-white sandstone jutting skyward from the desert floor, the Needles District's otherworldly terrain is so different from Island in the Sky, it's hard to believe they're part of the same park. Despite having paved access roads, the Needles receives only half as many visitors as the Island. Why? It takes 90 minutes to drive from Moab, and once you arrive, you have to work harder to appreciate the wonders – in short, you have to get out of the car and walk. Expend a little energy, though, and the payoff is huge: peaceful solitude and the opportunity to participate in, not just observe, the vastness of canyon country. Morning light is best for viewing the rock spires.

Needles Visitor Center lies 2.5 miles inside park boundaries and provides drinking water. Hold on to your receipt, admission (7-day per vehicle $10) includes entry to Island in the Sky.

👁 Sights & Activities

Needles has a couple of short trails (none wheelchair accessible), but getting off the beaten path is this section's premier attraction. Many challenging day-hikes connect in a series of loops, some requiring route-finding skills. And 50 miles of 4WD and mountain-biking roads (permit required, see p398) crisscross the park. Know what you're doing, or risk damaging your vehicle and endangering yourself. Towing fees run from $1000 to $2000 – really. If you're renting a 4WD vehicle, check the insurance policy; you might not be covered here.

Scenic Drive   DRIVING TOUR

Though not much of a drive-by park, the paved road continues almost 7 miles from the visitor center to **Big Spring Canyon Overlook**. Parking areas along the way access several short trails to sights, including arches, **Pothole Point**, Ancestral Puebloan ruins and petroglyphs. All trails listed are off this drive; use the park map you receive on entry to navigate.

Cave Spring Trail   HIKING

Especially popular with kids, the Cave Spring Trail (0.6-mile loop, easy to moderate) leads up ladders and over slickrock to an abandoned cowboy camp. The hand-print pictographs on the last cave's walls are haunting.

Slickrock Trail   HIKING

Scamper across slickrock to fabulous views of the canyon; on the return route, you face the district's needles and spires in the distance (2.4-mile loop, moderate).

Chesler Park/Joint Trail Loop   HIKING

Get among the namesake needles formations. An awesome 11-mile route loops across desert grasslands, past towering red-and-white-striped pinnacles and between deep, narrow slot canyons, some only 2ft across. Elevation changes are mild, but the distance makes it an advanced day hike.

DON'T MISS

INDIAN CREEK

About 16.5 miles along Hwy 211, driving into the Needles District, look up. Even if you don't rock climb, it's fascinating to watch the experts scaling the narrow cliffside fissures near **Indian Creek** (www.friendsofindiancreek.org). There's a small parking lot from where you can cross the freely accessible Nature Conservancy and BLM grazing land.

Elephant Canyon Trail   HIKING

For gorgeous scenery, the Elephant Canyon Trail (11-mile loop) to Druid Arch is hard to beat. The *National Geographic Trails Illustrated* Canyonlands map should suffice, but if you're inclined to wander, pick up a 7.5-minute quadrangle USGS map at the visitor center.

Elephant Hill   MOUNTAIN BIKING, FOUR-WHEEL DRIVING

This 32-mile round-trip is the most well-known and technically challenging route in the state, with steep grades and tight turns (smell the burning brakes and clutches). If you've always wanted to rock climb on wheels, you've found the right trail. Don't try this as your first 4WD or mountain-bike adventure.

Colorado River Overlook   MOUNTAIN BIKING, DRIVING TOUR

The route to the Colorado River Overlook is easy in a vehicle and moderately easy on a mountain bike. Park and walk the final, steep 1.5-mile descent to the overlook.

Salt Creek Canyon Trail   MOUNTAIN BIKING, DRIVING TOUR

Following the district's main drainage, archaeology junkies love the rock art along this 27-mile loop; moderately easy for vehicles and moderate for bikes.

🛏 Sleeping & Eating

Backcountry camping, in prescribed areas only, is quite popular, so it's hard to secure an overnight permit (p398) without advance reservation. Monticello (34 miles) and Moab (75 miles) are the nearest full-service towns.

Squaw Flat Campground   CAMPGROUND $

(www.nps.gov/cany; tent & RV sites $15) This first-come, first-served, 27-site campground 3 miles west of the visitor center fills up every day – spring to fall. It has flush toilets and running water, but no showers, and no hookups. Opt for side A, where many sites (12 and 14, for example) are shaded by juniper trees and cliffs. Maximum allowable RV length is 28ft.

Needles Outpost   CAMPGROUND $

(☑435-979-4007; www.canyonlandsneedlesoutpost.com; Hwy 211; tent & RV sites $15; ☺Apr-Nov) If Squaw Flat is full, the dusty private campground at Needles Outpost is an alternative. Shower facilities are $3 for campers, $7 for noncampers. An on-site store sells limited camping supplies, gasoline and propane.

UTAH CANYONLANDS NATIONAL PARK

127 HOURS: BETWEEN A ROCK AND A HARD PLACE

What started out as a day's adventure turned into a harrowing ordeal for one outdoorsman exploring some spectacular slots near Canyonlands National Park in the spring of 2003. Canyoneering southeast of the remote Horseshoe Canyon section in Bluejohn Canyon, Aron Ralston became trapped when a crashing boulder pinned his hand and wrist. The story of how he cut himself out of the situation (literally, he cut off his arm with a pocketknife) was first turned into a compelling book, and then the 2010 Oscar-nominated movie *127 Hours*. The film showcases both the amazing beauty of Utah's canyonlands, and the brutal reality of its risks.

The lunch counter and grill (open 8:30am to 4:30pm) serves sandwiches and burgers.

❶ Information

Needles Visitor Center (www.nps.gov/cany /needles; Hwy 211; ☺8am-6pm Mar-Oct, 9am-4:30pm Nov-Feb) Smaller, but has similar books and guidance to Islands in the Sky.

CANYONLANDS – HORSESHOE CANYON

Way far west of Island in the Sky, **Horseshoe Canyon** (admission free) shelters one of the most impressive collections of millennia-old rock art in the Southwest. The centerpiece is the **Great Gallery** and its haunting Barrier Canyon-style pictographs from between 2000 BC and AD 500. The heroic, bigger-than-life-size figures are magnificent. Artifacts recovered here date back as far as 9000 BC. That said, it's not easy to get to. The gallery lies at the end of a 6.5-mile round-trip hiking trail descending 750ft from a dirt road. Plan on six hours. Rangers lead hikes here on Saturday and Sunday from April through October; contact the **Hans Flat Ranger Station** (☎435-259-2652; www.nps.gov/cany /horseshoe; Hwy 24; ☺9am-4:30pm) for times.

You can camp on BLM land at the trailhead, though it's really a parking lot. There is a single vault toilet, but no water. From Moab the trip is about 120 miles/2¾ hours. Take Hwy 191 north to I-70 west, then Hwy 24 south. About 25 miles south of I-70, past the turnoff for Goblin Valley State Park, turn east and follow the gravel road 30 miles. Hanksville is 45 miles/1½ hours.

CANYONLANDS – THE MAZE

A 30-sq-mile jumble of high-walled canyons, the **Maze** (admission free) is a rare preserve of true wilderness for hardy backcountry veterans. The colorful canyons are rugged, deep and sometimes completely inaccessible. Many of them look alike and it's easy to get turned around – hence the district's name.

(Think topographic maps and GPS.) Rocky roads absolutely necessitate reliable, high-clearance 4WD vehicles. Plan on spending at least three days, though a week is ideal. If you're at all inexperienced with four-wheel driving, stay away. Be prepared to repair your jeep and, at times, the road. There may not be enough money on the planet to get you towed out of here. Most wreckers won't even try.

Predeparture, always contact the **Hans Flat Ranger Station** (☎435-259-2652; www .nps.gov/cany/maze; ☺9am-4:30pm) for conditions and advice. The station is 136 miles (3½ hours) from Moab, and has a few books and maps, but no other services. Take Hwy 191 north, I-70 west, and then Hwy 24 south. Hans Flat is 16 miles south of Horseshoe Canyon. The few roads into the district are poor and often closed with rain or snow; bring tire chains from October to April.

Around Canyonlands

The BLM **Canyon Rims Recreation Area** (www.blm.gov/utah/moab; Needles Overlook Rd; admission free) to the east of the national park has two interesting overlooks, undeveloped hiking and backcountry driving. Turn west off Hwy 191 (32 miles south of Moab, 27 miles north of Monticello); a paved road leads 22 miles to **Needles Overlook** and a panorama of the park. Two-thirds of the way to the overlook, the gravel **Anticline Overlook Rd** stretches 16 miles north to a promontory with awesome views of the Colorado River.

Three miles after the Hwy 191 turnoff is **Windwhistle Campground** (tent & RV sites $12; ☺Mar-Oct). The 20 well-spaced, first-served sites have fire rings and scenic vistas. Pit toilets; water available May through September.

Dead Horse Point State Park

The views at **Dead Horse Point** (www.state parks.utah.gov; off Hwy 313; day-use per vehicle $10; ⊙6am-10pm) pack a wallop, extending 2000ft down to the winding Colorado River, up to La Sal Mountains' 12,700ft peaks and out 100 miles across Canyonlands' mesmerizing stair-step landscape. (You might remember it from the final scene of *Thelma & Louise*, where they drove off into the abyss.) If you thrive on rare, epic views, you're gonna love Dead Horse.

Drive Hwy 313 south from Hwy 191, 30 miles northwest of Moab, following the road as it turns left into the park (if you go straight you'll reach Island in the Sky). Toward the end of the drive, the road traverses a narrow ridge just 90ft across. Around the turn of the 20th century, cowboys used the mesa top as a sort of natural corral by driving wild horses onto it and blocking the ridge. The story goes that ranch hands forgot to release the horses they didn't cull, and the stranded equines supposedly died with a great view of the Colorado River...

The **visitor center** (⊙8am-6pm mid-Mar–mid-Oct, 9am-5pm mid-Oct–mid-Mar) has exhibits, shows on-demand videos and sells books and maps. Rangers lead walks and talks in summer. To escape the small (but sometimes chatty) crowds, take a walk around the mesa rim. Visit at dawn or dusk for the best lighting. South of the vistor center, the 21-site **Kayenta Campground** (☑800-322-3770; www.stateparks.utah.gov; tent & RV sites $20) provides limited water and a dump station, but no hookups. Reservations are accepted from March to October, but you can often secure same-day sites by arriving early. Fill RVs with water in Moab.

Moab

An island of civilization in a sea of stunning wilderness, Moab serves as a terrific base camp for area excursions. Hike in Arches or Canyonlands National Parks during the day, then come back to a comfy bed, a hot tub and your selection of surprisingly good restaurants at night. Here you can browse the shelves at an indie bookstore, shop for groceries till midnight, sit down for dinner at 9pm and still find several places open for a beer afterward. There's a distinct sense of fun here in 'Utah's Recreation Capital'. Dozens of rafting and riding outfitters (moun-

tain bike, jeep, ATV, horse...) based here take forays into national parks and onto public lands.

It was miners in search of 'radioactive gold', ie uranium, starting in the 1950s that blazed a network of back roads, laying the groundwork for Moab to become a 4WD mecca. But neither mining nor the hundreds of Hollywood films shot here had as much influence on the character of Moab as the influx of youth-culture, fat-tire, mountain-bike enthusiasts. Development does come at a price though: chain motels, fast-food joints and T-shirt shops line the main drag. The town gets overrun March through October, and the impact of all those feet, bikes and 4WDs on the fragile desert is a serious concern (use existing trails). People here love the land, even if they don't always agree about how to protect it. If the traffic irritates you, just remember – you can disappear into the vast desert in no time.

⊙ Sights

Between breakfast and dinner there's not much going on in Moab; most people get out of town for activities.

Museum of Moab   MUSEUM
(Map p404; www.moabmuseum.org; 118 E Center St; adult/child $5/free; ⊙10am-5pm Mon-Sat, noon-5pm Sun Mar-Oct; noon-5pm Mon-Sat Nov-Apr) On a rainy day you might want to check out the regional exhibits – on everything from paleontology and geology to uranium mining and Native American art.

FREE **Red Cliffs Adventure Lodge**   MUSEUM
(Mile 14, Hwy 128; ⊙8am-10pm) This lodge, 15 miles northeast of town, hosts the Moab Museum of Film & Western Heritage, showing Hollywood memorabilia and posters

---

ⓘ WATER REFILLING STATIONS

In addition to the water stations at area national park visitor centers, you can refill your jugs for free at **Gear Heads** (471 S Main St; ⊙7am-9pm May-Oct, off-season hours vary) outdoor store. Alternatively go to the natural, outdoor tap at **Matrimony Springs** (Hwy 128, 100yd east of Hwy 191 on the right).

Moab

0 — 200 m
0 — 0.1 miles

To Tag-A-Long Expeditions &
Moab Desert Adventures (0.1mi);
Poison Spider Bicycles & Adventure
Inn (0.1mi); Moab Rafting & Canoe
Co & Inca Inn (0.2mi)

City Park

100 West

Main St

300 North

200 North

Walnut La

100 North

Center St

Williams Way

100 West

Main St

100 East

200 East

300 East

100 South

200 South

300 South

Pack Creek

Mill Creek

Grand St

191

Uranium Ave

Kane Creek Blvd

Huntridge Dr

Aspen Ave

Main St

To Chile Pepper
Bike Shop (0.1mi);
Moab Brewery &
Paradox Pizza (0.1mi);
Rim Tours (1mi)

2
25
12
8
10
3
27
16
28
13
26
30
38
39
29
40
1
4
14
5
32 33
31
24
35
36
34
37
17
19
9
22
6
11
23
7
15
20
18
21

Moab

UTAH MOAB

from all the films shot in the area. There's also a tasting and sales room for its on-site winery.

Spanish Valley Winery   WINERY
(www.moab-utah.com/spanishvalleywinery; Zimmerman Lane, off Stocks Dr; ◷noon-7pm Mon-Sat Mar-Oct) For some no-frills wine tasting, visit the surprisingly good Spanish Valley Winery, 6 miles south of Moab on Hwy 191.

🏃 Activities

The visitor center has a helpful collection of free brochures highlighting near-town rock art, movie locations, driving tours, and 4WD and hiking trails. Moab abounds in outfitters for mountain biking, whitewater rafting, hiking, and backcountry ATV and jeep tours. Can't choose just one activity? No worries. Many operators, such as Moab Adventure Company and Canyon Voyages Adventure Co, will help you plan multisport or multiday adventures. The visitor center has a complete list of all outfitters, way too numerous to include here.

Mountain Biking

Moab's mountain biking is world-famous. Challenging trails ascend steep slickrock and wind through woods and up 4WD roads. People come from everywhere to ride the famous Slickrock Bike Trail and other challenging routes. If you're a die-hard, ask about trips to the Maze. Bike shop websites and www.discovermoab .com/biking.htm are good trail resources, or pick up *Above & Beyond Slickrock*, by Todd Campbell, and *Rider Mel's Mountain Bike Guide to Moab*. In recent years, the BLM has opened several new loops and temporarily closed others. Follow BLM guidelines, avoid all off-trail riding and pack everything out (including cigarette butts). Spring and fall are the busiest seasons. In summer you'd better start by 7am, otherwise it gets too hot.

For rentals, be sure to reserve in advance. Road and full-suspension bikes run $40 to $65 per day. Shops are generally open from 8am to 7pm from March through October, and 9am to 6pm November through February. Full-day tours run from

TOP MOAB MOUNTAIN-BIKING TRAILS

Slickrock Trail Moab's legendary trail will kick your ass. The 12.7-mile round-trip, half-day route is for experts only (as is the practice loop).

White Rim Trail Canyonlands National Park's 70-mile, three- to four-day journey around a canyon mesa-top is epic.

Bar-M Loop Bring the kids on this easy 8-mile loop skirting the boundary of Arches, with great views and short slickrock stretches.

Gemini Bridges A moderate, full-day downhill ride past spectacular rock formations, this 13.5-mile one-way trail follows dirt, sand and slickrock.

Klondike Bluffs Trail Intermediates can learn to ride slickrock on this 15.6-mile round-trip trail, past dinosaur tracks to Arches National Park.

Moonlight Meadow Trail Beat the heat by ascending La Sal Mountains to 10,600ft on this moderate 10-mile loop among aspens and pines (take it easy; you *will* get winded).

Park to Park Trail A new paved-road bike path travels one-way from Moab into Arches National Park (30 miles), or you can turn off and follow the Hwy 313 bike lane to the end of Canyonlands' Island in the Sky park (35 miles).

$115 to $225 per person including lunch and rental.

Rim Cyclery MOUNTAIN BIKING
(Map p404; ☑435-259-5333; www.rimcyclery.com; 94 W 100 N) Moab's longest-running family-owned bike shop not only does rentals and repairs, it also has a museum of mountain-bike technology.

Poison Spider Bicycles MOUNTAIN BIKING
(☑435-259-7882, 800-635-1792; www.poisonspider bicycles.com; 497 N Main St) Friendly staff are always busy helping wheel jockeys map out their routes. Well-maintained road and suspension rigs for rent; private guided trips organized in conjunction with Magpie Adventures.

Rim Tours TOUR
(☑435-259-5223, 800-626-7335; www.rimtours .com; 1233 S Hwy 191) Well-organized multi-day trips cover territory all across southern Utah; day tours are available for top local trails, including Canyonlands. The 18-mile downhill sunrise ride is all adrenaline.

Moab Cyclery MOUNTAIN BIKING
(Map p404; ☑435-259-7423, 800-451-1133; www .moabcyclery.com; 391 S Main St) Good half-, full-, multiday – and multisport – tours. Rental and sales; biker shuttles available.

Chile Pepper Bike Shop MOUNTAIN BIKING
(☑435-259-4688, 888-677-4688; www.chilebikes .com; 720 S Main St) Rentals and repairs, plus helpful trail maps. Used bikes for sale.

Western Spirit Cycling Adventures TOUR
(☑435-259-8732, 800-845-2453; www.western spirit.com; 478 Mill Creek Dr) Canyonlands White Rim, Utah and nationwide multiday tours.

White-Water Rafting
Whatever your interest, be it bashing through rapids or gentle floats studying canyon geology, rafting may prove the highlight of your vacation. Rafting season runs from April to September; jet-boating season lasts longer. Water levels crest in May and June.

Most local rafting is on the Colorado River, northeast of town, including the Class III to IV rapids of **Westwater Canyon**, near Colorado; the wildlife-rich 7-mile Class I float from **Dewey Bridge to Hittle Bottom** (no permit required); and the Class I to II **Moab Daily**, the most popular stretch near town (no permit required; expect a short stretch of Class III rapids).

Rafters also launch north of Moab to get to the legendary Class V rapids of **Cataract Canyon** (NPS permit required). This Colorado River canyon south of town and the Confluence is one of North America's most intense stretches of white water. If you book anything less than a five-day outfitter trip to get here, know that some of the time downstream will be spent in a powered boat. Advanced do-it-yourself rafters wanting to run it will have to book a jet-boat shuttle or flight return.

North of Moab is a Class I float along the **Green River** that's ideal for canoes. From there you can follow John Wesley Powell's

UTAH MOAB

1869 route. (Note that additional outfitters operate out of the town of Green River itself.)

Full-day float trips cost $65 to $90; white-water trips start at $155. Multiday excursions run $350 to $800, while jet-boat trips cost about $70. Day trips are often available on short notice, but book overnight trips well ahead. Know the boat you want: an oar rig is a rubber raft that a guide rows; a paddleboat is steered by the guide and paddled by passengers; motor rigs are large boats driven by a guide (such as jet boats). For more on rapids classification, see p46.

Do-it-yourselfers can rent canoes, inflatable kayaks or rafts. Canoes and kayaks run $35 to $45 per day, rafts $65 to $130 per day, depending on size. Without permits, you'll be restricted to mellow stretches of the Colorado and Green Rivers; if you want to run Westwater Canyon or enter Canyonlands on either river, you'll need a permit. Contact the BLM (☏435-259-2100; www.blm.gov/utah/moab) or NPS (☏435-259-4351; www.nps.gov/cany/permits.htm), respectively. Reserve equipment, permits (p398) and shuttles way in advance.

Sheri Griffith Expeditions
RAFTING
(☏435-259-8229, 800-332-2439; www.griffithexp.com; 2231 S Hwy 191) Operating since 1971, this rafting specialist has a great selection of river trips on the Colorado, Green and San Juan Rivers – from family floats to Cataract Canyon rapids, from a couple hours to a couple weeks.

Canyon Voyages Adventure Co
RAFTING
(Map p404; ☏435-259-6007, 800-733-6007; www.canyonvoyages.com; 211 N Main St) In addition to half- to five-day mild white-water and kayaking trips, Canyon organizes multisport excursions that include options like hiking, biking and canyoneering. Kayak, canoe and outdoor equipment rental available.

Tex's Riverways
KAYAKING
(☏435-259-5101; www.texsriverways.com; 691 N 500 West) Full-service independent adventure support: Tex's rents complete kayak and canoe outfits (with required portable toilets), offers land-transport boat shuttles and jet-boat hiker shuttles, and provides thorough advice.

Tag-A-Long Expeditions
ADVENTURE SPORTS
(☏435-259-8946, 800-453-3292; www.tagalong.com; 452 N Main St) This rafting outfitter offers a little of everything: flat-water jet boat rides, white water rafting, land safaris, horseback riding, scenic flights, skydiving,

Nordic skiing and more. Ask about jet boat return support for Cataract Canyon trips.

Canyonlands by Night and Day
BOAT TOUR
(☏435-259-2628, 800-394-9978; www.canyonlandsbynight.com; 1861 N Hwy 191) Daytime and sunset group jet boat tours are the primary attraction at this riverfront operator, but they also offer packages that include dinner, scenic flights and land tours.

Moab Rafting & Canoe Co
KAYAKING
(☏435-259-7722, 800-753-8216; www.moab-rafting.com; 805 N Main St) Small company with guided and self-guided canoe and raft trips.

Navtec Expeditions
ADVENTURE SPORTS
(Map p404; ☏435-259-7983, 800-833-1278; www.navtec.com; 321 N Main St) Comprehensive rafting excursions, combo hiking and 4WD trips.

Adrift Adventures
ADVENTURE SPORTS
(Map p404; ☏435-259-8594, 800-874-4483; www.adrift.net; 378 N Main St) Rafting, jet boat rides, sport boat rides, 4WD land excursions and multisport packages, plus Arches National Park bus tours.

Slickrock Air Guides
SCENIC FLIGHTS
(☏435-259-6216, 866-259-1626; www.slickrockairguides.com) Air shuttles for Cataract Canyon trips.

Splore
RAFTING
(☏801-484-4128; www.splore.org) If traveling with someone with a physical or mental disability book a raft trip with this operator, based in Salt Lake City.

Hiking
Don't limit yourself to the national parks, there's hiking on surrounding public lands as well.

Corona Arch Trail
HIKING
(trailhead 6 miles north, Potash Rd) To see petroglyphs and two spectacular arches, hike the moderately easy 3-mile, two-hour walk. You may recognize Corona from a well-known photograph showing an airplane flying through it – this is one big arch.

Negro Bill Canyon Trail
HIKING
(Map p416; trailhead 3 miles north of Moab, Hwy 128) The moderately easy trail includes a 2.5-mile walk along a stream. (The totally politically incorrect canyon name refers to a prospector who grazed his cows here in the 1800s.) Scoot down a shaded side canyon to find petroglyphs, then continue to the 243ft-wide **Morning Glory Natural**

Bridge, at a box canyon. Plan on three to four hours.

La Sal Mountains HIKING
(www.fs.usda.gov; La Sal Mountain Loop) To escape summer's heat, head up Hwy 128 to the Manti–La Sal National Forest lands in the mountains east of Moab and hike through white-barked aspens and ponderosa pines.

Canyonlands Field Institute TOUR
(☑435-259-7750, 800-860-5262; http://canyon landsfieldinst.org; 1320 S Hwy 191) All-ages interpretive hikes and canoe trips – a wonderful introduction to the parks and the area.

Deep Desert Expeditions HIKING
(☑435-260-1696; www.deepdesert.com; full-day $175-220) Archaeological hikes, photo treks, multiday guided backpacking, catered camping and Fiery Furnace walks – in winter, too!

Four-Wheel Driving
The area's primitive backroads are made for 4WD enthusiasts. But if you don't bring or rent ($150 to $200 per day) your own Jeep, you still have options. Several outfitters offer group 4WD tours, or 'land safaris', in multipassenger-modified, six to eight person Humvee-like vehicles (two hours from $65 to $90). Note that rafting companies may have combination land/river trips. You can also bring your own ATV, or rent off-road utility vehicles like Rhinos and Mules (seating two to four), or four-wheelers (straddled like a bicycle), from $129 to $169 per day. Personal 4WD vehicles and ATVs require an off-highway vehicle (OHV) permit, available at the visitor center. Outfitter hours are generally 7:30am to 7pm March through October, 8am to 5pm November through February.

Moab Information Center has tons of free route info, as well as *Moab Utah Backroads & 4WD Trails* by Charles Wells, and other books for sale. Canyonlands National Park also has some epic 4WD tracks. If you go four-wheeling, stay on established routes. The desert looks barren, but it's a fragile landscape of complex ecosystems. Biological soil crusts (see p531) may take a century to regenerate after one tire track (really).

Hell's Revenge FOUR-WHEEL DRIVING
(www.discovermoab.com/sandflats.htm; Sand Flats Recreation Area, Sand Flats Rd) For experienced drivers only, the best-known 4WD road in Moab is in the BLM-administered area east of town, which follows an 8.2-mile route up and down shockingly steep slickrock.

Moab Adventure Center ADVENTURE SPORTS
(Map p404; ☑435-259-7019, 866-904-1163; www .moabadventurecenter.com; 225 S Main St) The open-air, canopy-topped land safaris offered here are popular. This megacenter also arranges, alone or in combination, rafting trips, Jeep rental, horseback riding, rock climbing, guided hikes, scenic flights and even Arches National Park bus tours.

High Point Hummer & ATV Tours ADVENTURE SPORTS
(Map p404; ☑435-259-2972, 877-486-6833; www .highpointhummer.com; 281 N Main St) Take a two- to four-hour thrill ride up the slickrock on a group Hummer tour, follow a guide as you drive yourself on a four-wheeler or utility vehicle tour, or rent an ATV yourself.

Dan Mick's Jeep Tours DRIVING TOUR
(☑435-259-4567; www.danmick.com) Private Jeep tours and guided drive-your-own-4WD trips with good ol' boy Dan Mick.

Elite Motorcycle Tours DRIVING TOUR
(☑435-259-7621, 888-778-0358; www.elitemotor cycletours.com; 1310 Murphy Lane) Dirt bike and street-legal motorcycle rental and tours.

Farabee's Outlaw Jeep Tours DRIVING TOUR
(Map p404; ☑435-259-7494; www.farabeesjeep rentals.com; 35 Grand St) Customized Jeep rental and off-road ride-along or guide-led tours.

Cliffhanger Jeep Rental DRIVING TOUR
(Map p404; ☑435-259-0889; www.cliffhangerjeep rental.com; 40 W Center St) TeraFlex suspension Jeeps, Rhino two-seaters and four-wheelers for rent.

Coyote Land Tours DRIVING TOUR
(☑435-259-6649; www.coyotelandtours.com) Daily tours in a bright-yellow Mercedes Benz Unimog off-road vehicle (seats 12); call ahead.

Rock Climbing & Canyoneering
Climb up cliffsides, rappel into rivers and hike through slot canyons. Half-day canyoneering or climbing adventures run from around $99 to $165 per person.

Wall Street ROCK CLIMBING
(Potash Rd) Rock climbers in town gravitate toward Wall Street; it's Moab's El Ca̠ .tan, so it gets crowded.

SEGO CANYON

It's rare to see the rock art of three different ancient cultures on display all in one canyon, but that's precisely what you can do at Sego. The canyon itself is 4 miles north of I-70 at Thompson Springs (41 miles north of Moab, 26 miles east of Green River). On the south-facing wall, the Barrier Culture pictographs are the oldest (at least 2000 years old); the wide-eyed anthropomorphic creatures take on a haunted, ghostlike appearance to modern eyes. The Fremont petroglyphs were carved about 1000 years ago. Many of the line-art figures are wearing chunky ornamentation and headdresses (or is it antennae?). The third panel is from the 19th-century Native American Ute tribe; look for the horses and buffalo.

If you drive half a mile further north up the canyon, you come to a little ghost town. The few buildings here were deserted when a mining camp was abandoned in the 1950s.

Gear Heads Outdoor Store ADVENTURE SPORTS
(Map p404; ☑435 259 4327; www.gearheads outdoorstore.com; 471 S Main St; ⊙7am-9pm) Stock up on all the outdoor gear you need, including climbing ropes, route guides, books and water-jug refills. The knowledgeable staff are quite helpful.

Moab Desert Adventures ADVENTURE SPORTS
(☑435-260-2404, 877 765-6622; www.moabdesert adventures.com; 415 N Main St) Top-notch climbing tours scale area towers and walls; the 140ft arch rappel is especially exciting. Canyoneering and multisport packages available.

Desert Highlights ADVENTURE SPORTS
(Map p404; ☑435-259-4433, 800-747-1342; www .deserthighlights.com; 50 E Center St) Canyoneering and combo raft trips here are big on personal attention. Regulations are being reviewed, but in the past they've had canyoneering permission for Fiery Furnace and other Arches National Park trips.

Moab Cliffs & Canyons ADVENTURE SPORTS
(Map p404; ☑435-259-3317, 877-641-5271; www .cliffsandcanyons.com; 231 N Main St) Canyoneering, climbing and scenic hiking trips. Ask about Fiery Furnace hikes.

Windgate Adventures ADVENTURE SPORTS
(☑435-260-9802; www.windgateadventures.com) Private guide Eric Odenthal leads guided climbing, canyoneering, arch-rappelling and photo trips.

Air Adventures
Moab's airport is 16 miles north of town on Hwy 191. Small-plane scenic flights run about $150 per hour.

Redtail Aviation SCENIC FLIGHTS
(☑435-259-7421; www.redtailaviation.com) Fly high above Arches, Canyonlands, Lake Powell, San Rafael Swell, Monument Valley and more.

Slickrock Air Guides SCENIC FLIGHTS
(☑435 259 6216; www.slickrockairguides.com) 'Flightseeing' over Canyonlands National Park and around greater southern Utah.

Skydive Moab EXTREME SPORTS
(☑435 259-5867, www.skydivemoab.com; tandem jump $189-229) Skydiving and base-jumping.

Canyonlands Ballooning BALLOONING
(☑435-655-1389, 877-478 3544; www.canyonlands ballooning.com; 4 hours $250) Soar over canyon country and Manti–La Sal Mountains.

Skiing & Snowshoeing
It's a local secret that La Sal Mountains, which lord over Moab off Hwy 128, receive tons of powder, just perfect for cross-country skiing – and there's a hut-to-hut ski system ($35 per person, per night).

Tag-A-Long Expeditions SKIING
(☑435-259-8946, 800-453-3292; www.tagalong .com; 452 N Main St) Book self-guided cross-country ski packages, snowmobile transfers and hut lodging here.

Rim Cyclery SKIING
(Map p404; ☑435-259-5333; www.rimcyclery.com; 94 W 100 N) Rents skis and provides trail maps.

Gear Heads Outdoor Store SNOW SPORTS
(Map p404; ☑435-259-4327, 888-740-4327; www .gearheadsoutdoorstore.com; 471 S Main St) Rents snowshoes and provides trail maps.

UTAH MOAB

UTAH, YOU OUGHTA BE IN PICTURES

The movie industry has known about the rugged wilds of southern Utah since the early days – in the 1920s, film adaptations of Zane Grey novels were shot here. All told, more than 700 films (and many TV shows) have been shot on location across the state. Iconic movies with Utah cameos include:

» *Thelma & Louise* – Remember where they drive off the cliff? That was outside Canyonlands National Park at Dead Horse Point (p403). Scenes were also filmed in Arches National Park (p415).

» *Forrest Gump* stopped his cross-country run in front of Monument Valley (p395), which straddles the Utah-Arizona line. *Easy Rider* motorcycled through, too; *2001: A Space Odyssey* used the monoliths to represent outer space.

» *Con Air* and *Independence Day* both have landing scenes shot on the super-smooth Bonneville Salt Flats (p480).

» In *High School Musical*, Zac Efron danced his way through East High School in Salt Lake City (p466), just like Kevin Bacon had done at Payson High School, south of Provo (p500) in *Footloose*.

» Kanab (p443) was the shooting location for heaps of Western movies, with stars such as John Wayne and Clint Eastwood.

Other Activities

Red Cliffs Lodge HORSEBACK RIDING
(☑435-259-2002, 866-812-2002; www.redcliffs lodge.com; Mile 14, Hwy 128; half-day $100) In Castle Valley, 14 miles north of town, Red Cliffs Lodge provides the only area horseback trail rides (March to November). If you book a multisport rafting trip that includes horseback riding, you'll still be coming here.

Matheson Wetlands Preserve BIRDWATCHING
(☑435-259-4629; www.nature.org; 934 W Kane Creek Blvd; admission free; ⊘dawn-dusk) The Nature Conservancy oversees the 890-acre preserve just west of town. At the time of research, a wildfire had closed sections of the park indefinitely. Check for updates before heading out with your binoculars.

Moab Photo Tours PHOTOGRAPHY
(☑435-259-4700; www.moabphototours.com) Area photo workshops and tours by local photographers.

★ Festivals & Events

Moab loves a party, and throws them regularly. For a full calendar, log onto www.discovermoab.com.

Skinny Tire Festival SPORTS
(www.skinnytirefestival.com) Road cycling festival; first weekend in March.

Jeep Safari SPORTS
(www.rr4w.com) The week before Easter, about 2000 Jeeps (and thousands more people) overrun the town in the year's biggest event. Register early; trails are assigned.

Moab Fat Tire Festival SPORTS
(www.moabfattirefest.com) One of Utah's biggest mountain-biking events, with tours, workshops, lessons, competitions and plenty of music; in October.

Moab Folk Festival MUSIC
(www.moabfolkfestival.com) Folk music and environmental consciousness combine. This November festival is 100% wind powered, venues are easily walkable and recycling is encouraged.

🛏 Sleeping

Rates given here are for March to October; prices drop by as much as 50% outside those months. Some smaller places close November through March. Most lodgings have hot tubs for aching muscles and mini-refrigerators to store snacks; motels have laundry facilities to clean up the trail dirt. Cyclists should ask whether a property provides *secure* bike storage, not just an unlocked closet.

Though Moab has a huge number of motels, there's often no room at the inn. Reserve as far ahead as possible in season. For a full town lodging list, see www.discovermoab.com.

In addition to local campgrounds listed below, there's also camping in nearby national and state parks. Rafting outfitter Canyon Voyages rents tents and sleeping bags.

Sorrel River Ranch
TOP CHOICE
LODGE $$$

(☑435-259-4642, 877-359-2715; www.sorrelriver .com; Mile 17, Hwy 128; r $340-530; ❋@≋) Southeast Utah's only full-service luxury resort and gourmet restaurant was originally an 1803 homestead. The lodge and log cabins sit on 240 acres along the banks of the Colorado River. Ride horses past the alfalfa fields, or just soak in the fabulous spa with river views.

Cali Cochitta
B&B $

(Map p404; ☑435-259-4961, 888-429-8112; www .moabdreaminn.com; 110 S 200 East; cottages incl breakfast $125-160; ❋⛛) Make yourself at home in one of the charming brick cottages a short walk from downtown. A long wooden table on the patio provides a welcome setting for community breakfasts. The vibe is warm but the innkeepers live off-site, giving you your privacy.

Up the Creek Campground
CAMPGROUND $

(Map p404; ☑435-260-1888; www.moabupthe creek.com; 210 E 300 South; tent sites 1/2 people $25/25; ⛲Mar-Oct) There's something about this shady, tent-only grove that fosters a sense of community, and it's a plus that the 20 sites are within walking distance of downtown. Showers are included, but are also available to nonguests for $6; no fires.

Castle Valley Inn
B&B $$

(☑435-259-6012; www.castlevalleyinn.com; 424 Amber Ln, off La Sal Mountain Loop; r & cabins incl breakfast $135-225; ❋) For tranquility – or cycling – it's hard to beat this Castle Valley location, 15 miles north of Moab. Rooms (in the main house, or new cabins with kitchens) sit amid orchards of apples, plums and apricots. Cozy quilts add to the warm welcome and there's an outdoor hot tub.

Red Cliffs Lodge
LODGE $$-$$$

(☑435-259-2002, 866-812-2002; www.redcliffs lodge.com; Mile 14, Hwy 128; ste $159-319; ❋≋⛛) Part dude ranch, part luxury motel, Red Cliffs has comfy suites with vaulted ceilings, kitchenettes and private-if-cramped patios (some overlook the river). Taste the wines made at the on-site winery, go for a trail ride or arrange a rafting trip or ATV rental with the activities desk.

Redstone Inn
MOTEL $

(☑435-259-3500, 800-772-1972; www.moabred stone.com; 535 S Main St; r $75-99; ❋⛛🐾) You get a lot for your budget buck here: simple, pine-paneled rooms with refrigerators, microwaves, coffee makers and free wired internet access. There's a bike wash area and storage, guest laundry, on-site hot tub and pool privileges across the street. Thin walls, though.

Aarchway Inn
MOTEL $$

(☑435-259-2599, 800-341-9359; www.aarchway inn.com; 1151 N Hwy 191; r incl breakfast $129-169; ❋⛛🐾) Space sets this 75-room motel apart. You could have a conga line in the giant standard bedrooms and family suites. Aarchway has the town's biggest swimming pool and there's a humongous parking lot next door for your all-terrain toys. Hike nature trails directly from here, at the northern end of town.

Goose Island Campground
CAMPGROUND $

(www.blm.gov/utah/moab; Hwy 128; campsites $12) Ten no-reservation riverside BLM campgrounds lie along a 28-mile stretch of Hwy 128 that parallels the Colorado River northwest of town. The 18-site Goose Island, just 1.4 miles from Moab, is the closest. Pit toilets, no water.

Big Horn Lodge
MOTEL $-$$

(Map p404; ☑435-259-6171, 800-325-6171; www .moabbighorn.com; 550 S Main St; r $79-119; ⛛≋) OK, so the exterior is kitschy Southwestern Indian-style, c 1970, but the knotty-pine paneled interiors are cozy, service is taken seriously and there are loads of extras (including heated swimming pool and hot tub, refrigerators and coffee makers).

Adventure Inn
MOTEL $

(☑435-259-6122, 866-662-2466; www.adventure innmoab.com; 512 N Main St; s/d incl breakfast $65/80; ⛲Mar-Oct; ❋⛛) A great little indie motel, the Adventure Inn has spotless rooms (some with refrigerators) and decent linens, as well as laundry facilities. There's a picnic area on site; no hot tub.

Inca Inn
MOTEL $

(☑435-259-7261, 866-462-2466; www.incainn.com; 570 N Main St; r incl breakfast $59-99; ⛲Feb-Nov; ❋⛛≋) Who expects a pool at these prices? This small mom-and-pop motel has older but spick-and-span rooms, plus a place to take a dip. Breakfast is light and snacky.

Gonzo Inn
MOTEL $$

(Map p404; ☑435-259-2515, 800-791-4044; www .gonzoinn.com; 100 W 200 South; r $159, ste $205-339, both incl breakfast Apr-Oct; ❋@⛛≋🐾) Brushed metal-and-wood headboards, concrete shower stalls and '50s retro patio furniture spruce up this standard motel. Bicycle wash-and-repair station on site.

Sunflower Hill INN $$
(Map p404; ☑435-259-2974, 800-662-2786; www .sunflowerhill.com; 185 N 300 East; r incl breakfast $165-225; ✳🐾🛜🌊) Kick back in an Adirondack chair amid the manicured gardens of two inviting buildings: a rambling 100-year-old farmhouse and an early 20th-century home. All 12 guest quarters have a sophisticated country sensibility.

Desert Hills B&B $$
(☑435-259-3568; www.deserthillsbnb.com; 1989 S Desert Hills Ln; r incl breakfast $119-138; ✳🛜) Get away from the traffic in town at this homey B&B in a suburban neighborhood. The four simple rooms have log beds, pillow-top mattresses and minifridges – and come with friendly, personal service.

Pack Creek Ranch LODGE $$-$$$
(☑888-879-6622; www.packcreekranch.com; off La Sal Mountain Loop; cabins $175-275; 🛜) Stay in one of 11 log cabins on a working ranch in the mountains, 2000ft above – but only 15 miles south – of Moab. No TVs; two-night minimum.

Mayor's House B&B $$
(☑435-259-6015, 888-791-2345; www.mayorshouse .com; 505 Rose Tree Ln; r incl breakfast $100-140; ✳@🌊) A modern brick house with spacious, quiet rooms; near downtown. Has a heated pool and hot tub.

Bowen Motel MOTEL $
(Map p404; ☑435-259-7132, 800-874-5439; www .bowenmotel.com; 169 N Main St; r incl breakfast $79-89; ✳🛜🐾🌊) Basic motel steps from shops and restaurants. The two-story building has been updated; the single-story is scheduled to be.

Best Western Canyonlands Inn MOTEL $$
(Map p404; ☑435-259-2300, 800-649-5191; www .canyonlandsinn.com; 16 S Main St; r $150-190; ✳🌊) A comfortable, chain choice at the central crossroads of downtown. Features a fitness room, laundry, playground and outdoor pool.

Holiday Inn Express HOTEL $$
(☑435-259-1150, 800-465-4229; www.hiexpress .com/moabut; 1653 Hwy 191 N; r $141-169; ✳🌊) Some of the newest, upper midrange rooms in town.

Lazy Lizard Hostel HOSTEL $
(☑435-259-6057; www.lazylizardhostel.com; 1213 S Hwy 191; dm/s/d $9/24/28, cabins $32-42; ✳@) Hippie hangout with frayed couches, worn bunks and small kitchen.

Canyonlands Campground CAMPGROUND $
(Map p404; ☑435-259-6848; www.canyonlandsrv .com; 555 S Main St; tent sites $25-29, RV sites with hookups $35-39, camping cabins $58; ✳🛜🌊) Old-growth tree-shaded sites, right in town but still quiet. Includes showers, laundry, store, small pool and playground.

Portal RV Resort CAMPGROUND $
(☑435-259-6108; www.portalrvresort.com; 1261 N Hwy 191; tent sites $21, RV sites with hookups $30-55; 🛜🌊) The best place for luxury RVers, with long pull-throughs. Has showers, spa, laundry, store and dog run.

Slickrock Campground CAMPGROUND $
(☑435-259-7660, 800-448-8873; www.slickrock campground.com; 1301 1/2 N Hwy 191; tent sites $23-29, RV sites with hookups $31-38, cabins $49; ⊙Mar-Nov; ✳🛜🐾🌊) North of town. Tent sites have canopies; RV sites have 30-amp hookups only. Nonguest showers $3; also has hot tubs, heated pool and a store.

Sand Flats Recreation Area CAMPGROUND $
(www.discovermoab.com/sandflats.htm; Sand Flats Rd; tent & RV sites $10) At the Slickrock Bike trailhead, this mountain-biker special has 120 nonreservable sites, fire rings and pit toilets, but no water and no hookups.

✗ Eating

There's no shortage of places to fuel up in Moab, from backpacker coffeehouses to gourmet dining rooms. Pick up the *Moab Menu Guide* (www.moabmenuguide.com) at area lodgings. Some restaurants close earlier, or on variable days, from December through March.

TOP CHOICE Love Muffin CAFE $
(Map p404; 139 N Main St; mains $6-8; ⊙7am-2pm; 🛜) Early-rising locals buy up many of the daily muffins – like the 'breakfast' with bacon and blueberries. Not to worry, the largely organic menu at this vibrant cafe also includes creative sandwiches, breakfast burritos and inventive egg dishes like 'verde', with brisket and slow-roasted salsa.

Jeffrey's Steakhouse STEAKHOUSE $$$
(Map p404; ☑435-259-3588; 218 N 100 West; mains $22-40; ⊙5-10pm) A historic sandstone building serves as home to one of the latest

UTAH MOAB

HOLE 'N THE ROCK

An unabashed tourist trap 12 miles south of Moab, **Hole 'n the Rock** (www.moab-utah .com/holeintherock; 11037 S Hwy 191; adult/child $5/3; ⊙9am-5pm; 🚻) is a 5000-sq-ft home-cum-cave carved into sandstone and decorated in knockout 1950s kitsch. What *weren't* owners Albert and Gladys Christensen into? He was a barber, a painter, an amateur engineer and a taxidermist; she was a cook (the cave once housed a restaurant) and lapidary jeweler, and they lived in the blasted-out home until 1974. The hodgepodge of metal art, old signs, small petting zoo and stores make it worth the stop, but you have to tour the surprisingly light-filled home to believe it.

stars on the local dining scene. Jeffrey's is serious about beef, which comes grain-fed, wagyu-style and in generous cuts. If the night is too good to end, head upstairs to the upscale Ghost Bar. Reservations advised.

Moab Brewery AMERICAN $$
(686 S Main St; mains $8-18; ⊙11:30am-10pm Mon-Thu, 11:30am-11pm Fri & Sat) A good bet for a group with diverse tastes. Choosing from the list of microbrews made in the vats just behind the bar area may be easier than deciding what to eat off the vast and varied menu.

Milt's BURGERS $
(356 Mill Creek Dr; mains $3-6; ⊙11am-8pm Mon-Sat) Pull up one of only a handful of stools at this tiny 1954 burger stand, or order through the screen window and eat under the tree. Locals love the chili cheeseburgers, hand-cut fries and oh-so-thick milkshakes (try butterscotch-banana).

Buck's Grill House MODERN SOUTHWESTERN $$-$$$
(1394 N Hwy 191; mains $15-36; ⊙5:30-9:30pm) Contemporary Southwestern specialties, such as duck tamales with adobo and elk stew with horseradish cream, are what Buck's does best (there are veggie options, too). Opt for white tablecloth service in the restaurant, or a more casual evening in the bar.

EklectiCafé ORGANIC $
(352 N Main St; breakfast & sandwiches $5-7; ⊙7am-2:30pm Mon-Sat, to 1pm Sun; 🛜🐾) Soy-ginger-seaweed scrambled eggs anyone? This wonderfully quirky cafe lives up to its eclectic name in food choice and decor. Come for organic coffee, curried wraps and vegetarian salads. Dinner served some weekend evenings.

Sorrel River Grill MODERN AMERICAN $$$
(☏435-259-4642; Sorrel River Ranch, Mile 17, Hwy 128; breakfast $10-12, lunch $12-15, dinner

$24-40; ⊙7am-3pm & 5-10pm Mar-Oct, 8-10am & 5:30-7:30pm Nov-Feb) For romance, it's hard to beat the wraparound verandah overlooking red-rock canyons outside Moab. The New American menu changes seasonally, but expect seared steaks, succulent rack of lamb and the freshest seafood flown in.

Desert Bistro MODERN SOUTHWESTERN $$$
(☏435-259-0756; 1266 N Hwy 191; mains $20-50; ⊙5:30-10pm Mar-Oct) Stylized preparations of game and seafood are the specialty at this welcoming white-tablecloth restaurant inside an old house. Everything is made on site, from freshly baked bread to delicious pastries. Great wine list, too

Miguel's Baja Grill MEXICAN $$
(Map p404; 51 N Main St; mains $12-20; ⊙5-10pm) Dine on Baja fish tacos and margaritas in the sky-lit breezeway patio lined with brightly painted walls. Fajitas, *chile rellenos* (stuffed peppers) and seafood mains are all ample sized.

Singha Thai THAI $$
(Map p404; 92 E Center St; mains $13-18; ⊙11am-9:30pm Mon-Sat, 5-9pm Sun) Ethnic food is rare as rain in these parts, so locals pile into this authentic Thai cafe for curries and organic basil chicken. No bar.

Sabuku Sushi FUSION $$
(Map p404; 101 N Main St; breakfast $7-15; ⊙11am-2pm & 5-10pm) Newcomer Sabuku impresses with fresh sushi, inventive vegetarian rolls and small plates such as elk *tataki* (like carpaccio, with an Asian twist).

Paradox Pizza PIZZERIA $$
(☏435-259-9999; 729 S Main St; pizzas $12-22; ⊙shop 11am-10pm, delivery 4-10pm) You may want to order your scrumptious locally-sourced and organically-oriented pizzas to go; the dining area is kinda small and generic. Our favorite? The 'fun guy', with

UTAH MOAB

whole-milk mozzarella and ricotta, plus portabellas.

Eddie McStiff's AMERICAN $$
(Map p404; 59 S Main St; mains $10-20; ⏰11:30am-midnight, until 1am Fri & Sat) Though it's as much microbrewery-bar as restaurant, the burgers and pizzas (gluten-free available) are almost as popular as the beer here.

Zax AMERICAN $-$$
(Map p404; 96 S Main St; breakfast $5-9, sandwiches $8-10, mains $16-22; ⏰7am-10pm) Dining out in Moab can get expensive, so locals load up at the all-you-can-devour soup, pizza and salad bar ($12) in this semi-generic American eatery.

Jailhouse Café BREAKFAST $$
(Map p404; 101 N Main St; breakfast $11-14; ⏰11am-noon Mar-Oct) The eggs benedict here is hard to beat but it ain't cheap. You're paying for the cute former-jailhouse and patio setting.

Peace Tree Café AMERICAN $
(Map p404; 20 S Main St; wraps $4-8, mains $16-24; ⏰8am-6pm Nov-Feb, 8am-8pm Mar-Oct) Fresh fruit smoothies, sandwich wraps and healthy mains to take out or eat in.

Moonflower Market HEALTH FOOD $
(Map p404; 39 E 100 N; ⏰9am-8pm Mon-Sat, 10am-3pm Sun) Nonprofit health food store with loads of community info.

Moab Farmers Market MARKET $
(400 N 100 West; ⏰8am-noon Sat May-Oct) Local farms vend their summer produce in Swanny City Park.

City Market & Pharmacy MARKET $
(Map p404; 425 S Main St; ⏰6am-midnight) Moab's largest grocery store, with sandwiches and salad bar to go.

🍷 Drinking

The two local brewpub restaurants, Moab Brewery and Eddie McStiff's, are good places to drink as well as eat, and the latter often has live music.

Wake & Bake CAFE
(Map p404; McStiffs Plaza, 59 S Main St; ⏰7am-7pm; 🛜) Great vibe at this groovy cafe next to a bookstore; ice cream and sandwiches available.

Dave's Corner Market COFFEE SHOP
(401 Mill Creek Dr; ⏰6am-10pm) Sip shade-grown espresso with locals at the corner convenience store.

Woody's Tavern BAR
(Map p404; 221 S Main St) Full bar with great outdoor patio; live music Friday and Saturday in season.

Ghost Bar BAR
(Map p404; 218 N 100 West; ⏰7-11pm) A loungey, dime-sized jazz nook serving wine and a full list of cocktails; upstairs at Jeffrey's Steakhouse.

Red Rock Bakery & Cafe CAFE
(Map p404; 74 Main St; internet per ½hr $2; ⏰7am-6pm; @🛜) This tiny coffeehouse has tasty baked goods - and three internet terminals for web surfing.

⭐ Entertainment

Bar-M Chuckwagon DINNER SHOW
(📞435-259-2276, 800-214-2085; www.barmchuckwagon.com; Hwy 191; adult/child $25/12.50; ⏰Apr-Oct; 🎫) Reserve ahead for a night of unapologetic tourist fun, 7 miles north of Moab. The evening starts with a gunfight in a faux Western town, followed by a cowboy Dutch-oven dinner and Western music show.

Canyonlands by Night & Day DINNER SHOW
(📞435-259-5261, 800-394-9978; www.canyonlandsbynight.com; 1861 N Hwy 191; adult/child $65/55; ⏰Apr-Oct; 🎫) Start with dinner riverside, then take an after-dark boat ride on the Colorado with an old-fashioned light show complete with historical narration.

Moab Arts & Recreation Center CONCERT VENUE
(Map p404; www.moabcity.state.ut.us/marc; 111 E 100 N) The rec center hosts everything from yoga classes to contra dance parties and poetry gatherings.

🔒 Shopping

Every few feet along downtown's Main St, there's a shop selling T-shirts and Native American-esque knickknacks, but there are good galleries among the mix. Every second Saturday in spring and fall there's an evening artwalk that includes artist's receptions; contact the **Moab Arts Council** (www.moabartscouncil.org) for more information. Note that from March to October most stores stay open until 9pm.

Desert Thread ARTS & CRAFTS
(29 E Center St) Pick up a gorgeous hand-knitted scarf or bag, or buy supplies to do it yourself.

Arches Book Company &
Back of Beyond
BOOKS

(83 N Main St; 🕾) Excellent, adjacent indie bookstores with extensive regional selection. Coffee shop on site.

❶ Information

Emergency

Cell phones work in town, but not in canyons or the parks.

Grand County Emergency Coordinator (☑435-259-8115) Search and rescue.

Police (☑911)

Medical Services

Moab Regional Hospital (☑435-259-7191; 719 W 400 N) For 24-hour emergency medical care.

Tourist Information

BLM (☑435-259-2100; www.blm.gov/utah /moab) Phone and internet info only.

Moab Information Center (cnr Main & Center Sts; ☺8am-8pm) Excellent source of information on area parks, trails, activities, camping and weather. Extensive bookstore and knowledgeable staff. Walk-in only.

Websites

Moab Area Travel Council (www.discovermoab .com) Comprehensive online resource.

Moab Happenings (www.moabhappenings .com) Events listings.

❶ Getting There & Around

Moab is 235 miles southeast of Salt Lake City, 150 miles northeast of Capitol Reef National Park, and 115 miles southwest of Grand Junction, CO.

Great Lakes Airlines (☑800-554-5111; www flygreatlakes.com) has regularly scheduled flights from **Canyonlands Airport** (CNY, www.moab airport.com; off Hwy 191), 16 miles north of town, to Denver, CO, Las Vegas, NV, and Page, AZ. Major car-rental agencies have representatives at the airport. **Roadrunner Shuttle** (☑435-259-9402; www.roadrunnershuttle.com) and **Coyote Shuttle** (☑435-260-2097; www.coyoteshuttle.com) offer

SHOWERING ESSENTIALS

Area BLM, national and state park campgrounds do not have showers. You can wash up at several in in-town campgrounds, and at biking outfitter Poison Spider Bicycles, for a small fee ($3 to $6).

on-demand Canyonland Airport, hiker-biker and river shuttles.

Moab Luxury Coach (☑435-940-4212; www .moabluxurycoach.com) operates a scheduled van service to and from SLC (4¾ hours, $149 one-way) and Green River (one hour, $119 one-way).

A private vehicle is pretty much a requirement to get around Moab and the parks. But on week-day evenings and weekends, **Moab Pedicab Company** (☑435-210-1382) runs a luxury bike taxi – hail it on the street or call dispatch.

Arches National Park

Giant sweeping arcs of chunky sandstone frame snowy peaks and desert landscapes at Arches National Park, 5 miles north of Moab. The park boasts the highest density of rock arches anywhere on Earth: more than 2500 in a 116-sq-mile area. You'll lose all perspective on size at some, such as the thin and graceful Landscape Arch, which stretches more than 290ft across (one of the largest in the world). Others are tiny, the smallest only 3ft across. Once you train your eye, you'll spot them everywhere (like a giant game of *Where's Waldo?*) An easy drive makes the spectacular arches accessible to all. Fiery Furnace is a not-to-be-missed area of the park, though a guided tour is required to reach it.

❍ Sights & Activities

The **park** (admission 7-day, per vehicle $10) has many short hikes; the most popular stops lie closest to the visitor center. Crowds are often unavoidable, and parking areas overflow on weekends, spring to fall. In summer arrive by 9am, when crowds are sparse and temperatures bearable, or visit after 7pm and enjoy a moonlight stroll. July highs average 100°F (38°C); carry at least one gallon of water per person if hiking. Two rugged backroads lead into semi-solitude, but 4WD is recommended – ask at the visitor center.

Rock climbing is allowed only on un-named features. Routes require advanced techniques. No permits are necessary, but ask rangers about current regulations and route closures. For guided canyoneering into the Fiery Furnace, contact an outfitter in Moab.

There are also some fairly easy hikes here, too. Many quick walks lead to named formations, such as **Sand Dune Arch** (0.4-mile round-trip) and **Broken Arch** (1-mile round-trip).

UTAH ARCHES NATIONAL PARK

Arches National Park

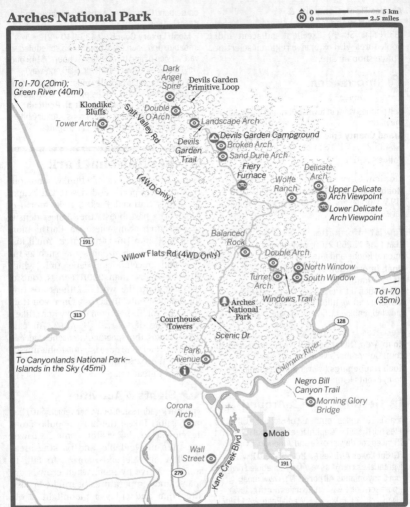

To I-70 (20mi);
Green River (40mi)

Dark Angel Spire

Devils Garden Primitive Loop

Klondike Bluffs

Double O Arch

Salt Valley Rd

Tower Arch

Landscape Arch

Devils Garden Campground

Devils Garden Trail

Broken Arch

Sand Dune Arch

(4WD Only)

Fiery Furnace

Wolfe Ranch

Delicate Arch

Upper Delicate Arch Viewpoint

Lower Delicate Arch Viewpoint

Balanced Rock

Willow Flats Rd (4WD Only)

Double Arch

North Window

Turret Arch

South Window

Windows Trail

Arches National Park

To I-70 (35mi)

Courthouse Towers

Scenic Dr

Park Avenue

To Canyonlands National Park– Islands in the Sky (45mi)

Colorado River

Negro Bill Canyon Trail

Morning Glory Bridge

Corona Arch

Moab

Wall Street

Kane Creek Blvd

UTAH ARCHES NATIONAL PARK

Scenic Drive

DRIVING TOUR

The park's one main road snakes up ancient Navajo sandstone, past many trailheads and incredible formations, such as **Park Avenue**, a mile-long trail past a giant fin of rock reminiscent of a New York skyline, and **Balanced Rock**, a 3577-ton boulder sitting atop a spindly pedestal, like a fist shooting out of the earth. Don't miss the two small spur roads that veer off to the west (43 miles round-trip total). Sights listed here are all along this drive; use the park map received on entry to navigate.

Delicate Arch

HIKING

You've seen this arch before: it's the unofficial state symbol and is pictured on what seems like every piece of Utah tourist literature ever printed. The best way to experience the arch is from beneath it. Park near **Wolfe Ranch**, a well-preserved 1908 pioneer cabin. From there a footbridge crosses **Salt Wash** (near Native American rock art) and marks the beginning of the moderate-to-strenuous, 3-mile round-trip trail to the arch itself. The trail ascends slickrock, culminating in a wall-hugging ledge before reaching the arch. Tip: ditch the crowds by passing beneath the arch and continuing down the rock by several yards to where there's a great view, but fewer folks (bring a picnic). If instead you drive past the ranch to the end of the spur road, there's a 50yd paved path (wheelchair accessible) to the **Lower Delicate Arch Viewpoint**.

Windows Trail   HIKING

Tight on time? Do part or all of the easy 1-mile round-trip, which brings you up to **North Window**, where you can look out to the canyon beyond. Continue on to **South Window** and castle-like **Turret Arch**. Don't forget to see **Double Arch**, just across the parking lot.

Fiery Furnace   HIKING

Advance reservation is usually necessary for the three-hour ranger-led **Fiery Furnace hikes** (adult/child $10/5; ☉Mar-Oct) that explore the maze of spectacularly narrow canyons and giant fins. This is no walk in the park. (Well, it is, but...) Be prepared to scramble up and over boulders, chimney down between rocks and navigate narrow ledges. The effort is rewarded with a surprising view – an incredibly thin arch or soaring slot – around every turn. The ranger stops plenty of times to talk (and let hikers rest).

If you're an accomplished route finder and want to go it alone, you must pay a fee, watch a video and discuss with rangers how to negotiate this confusing jumble of canyons before they'll grant you a permit. A few outfitters in Moab have permits to lead hikes here as well.

Devils Garden Trail   HIKING

At the end of the paved road, 19 miles from the visitor center, Devils Garden trailhead marks the beginning of a 2- to 7.7-mile round-trip hike that passes at least eight arches. Most people only go the relatively easy 1.3 miles to **Landscape Arch**, a gravity-defying 290ft-long behemoth. Further along the trail gets less crowded, and grows rougher and steeper toward **Double O Arch** and **Dark Angel Spire**. The optional, difficult **Devils Garden Primitive Loop** has narrow-ledge walking and serious slickrock hiking. Ask rangers about conditions before attempting.

🛏 Sleeping & Eating

Devils Garden Campground   CAMPGROUND **$**
(☑877-444-6777; www.recreation.gov; tent & RV sites $20) Don't expect much shade, just red rock and scrubby piñon trees at the park's only campground, 19 miles from the visitor center. A few of the sites at the top have La Sal Mountain views. From March to October only, half the sites are available by reservation. Otherwise, it's first-come, first-served. For same-day availability check at the visitor center, not the campground. Facilities include drinking water, picnic tables, grills and toilets, but no showers (available in Moab). RVs up to 30ft are welcome, but generator hours are limited; no hookups.

No food is available in the park. Again, Moab is the place to stock up or dine out.

ℹ Information

Cell phones do not work in most of the park.
Canyonlands Natural History Association (www.cnha.org) Sells area-interest books and maps online, and at national park visitor centers.
Grand County Emergency Coordinator (☑435-259-8115) Search and rescue coordinator.

ROCK FORMATIONS 101

The magnificent formations you see throughout southern Utah are created by the varying erosion of sandstone, mudstone, limestone and other sedimentary layers. When water freezes and expands in cracks it forms **fins**: thin, soaring, wall-like features like those in the Fiery Furnace at Arches. When portions of the rock break away underneath, an **arch** results. A **bridge** forms when water passes beneath sandstone, causing its erosion. But rivers dry up or change course, so it can sometimes become difficult to tell a bridge from an arch. **Hoodoos** are freestanding pinnacles that have developed from side-eroding fins; layers disintegrate at different rates, creating an irregular profile (often likened to a totem-pole shape). Though they look stable, rock formations are forever in flux, and eventually they all break and disappear. As you stroll beneath these monuments to nature's power, listen carefully, especially in winter, and you may hear spontaneous popping noises in distant rocks – it's the sound of the future forming. (If you hear popping noises *overhead*, however, run like heck!)

Visitor center (www.nps.gov/arch; 7-day per vehicle $10; ⊙24hr, visitor center 7:30am-6:30pm Apr-Oct, 8am-4:30pm Nov-Mar) Watch the informative video, check ranger-led activity schedules and pick up your Fiery Furnace tickets here.

ⓘ Getting There & Around

One may be instituted eventually, but as yet the park has no shuttle system and no public buses. So you pretty much need your own wheels. Several outfitters in Moab run motorized park tours: Moab Adventure Center and Adrift Adventures have scenic drive van tours; Tag-A-Long Expeditions ventures into the backcountry.

Green River

This laid-back little town is primarily useful as a base for river running on – guess where? The Green River, go figure. The Colorado and Green Rivers were first explored in 1869 and 1871 by the legendary one-armed Civil War veteran, geologist and ethnologist John Wesley Powell. The town was settled in 1878, and now mainly relies on the limited tourism for income. Accommodations may be slightly cheaper here than in Moab, 53 miles southeast, but there are far fewer services. If you're passing through the third weekend in September, be sure to attend the Melon Days festival; this is, after all, the 'world's watermelon capital'.

⊙ Sights

Outside of town there is an unpredictable geyser, and fossil track sites; ask at the visitor center for directions.

John Wesley Powell River History Museum MUSEUM
(www.jwprhm.com; 885 E Main St; adult/child $3/1; ⊙8am-7pm Apr-Oct, 9am-5pm Tue-Sat Nov-Mar) Learn about John Wesley Powell's amazing travels at this comprehensive museum, with a 20-minute film based on his diaries. It has good exhibits on the Fremont Indians, geology and local history.

Green River State Park PARK
(www.stateparks.utah.gov; Green River Blvd; per car $5; ⊙7am-10pm Mar-Oct, 8am-5pm Nov-Feb) Shady Green River State Park has picnic tables, a boat launch and a nine-hole golf course, but no trails.

☆ Activities

White-water rafting trips are the most popular, but the Green River is flat between the town and the confluence of the Colorado River, making it good for floats and do-it-yourself canoeing. But the current is deceptively strong – swim only with a life jacket.

Moki Mac River Expeditions RAFTING
(☎435-564-3361, 800-284-7280; www.mokimac.com; 220 E 700 South) Rent a canoe ($25 per day), take an easy day-float (per adult/child $69/55), or book a single- to multiday white-water raft (from $100 per person, per day).

Holiday Expeditions RAFTING
(☎435-564-3273, 800-624-6323; www.holidayexpeditions.com; 10 Holiday River St) Multiday rafting tours; themed trips (naturalist, women-only, mountain biking) available.

Colorado River & Trail RAFTING
(☎801-261-1789, 800-253-7328; www.crateinc.com) Though based in Salt Lake City, this outfitter offers several Green River-launched rafting trips.

⨀ Sleeping

Midrange chain motels are surprisingly well represented along Business 70 (Main St).

Green River State Park CAMPGROUND $
(☎800-322-3770; http://utahstateparks.reserveamerica.com; tent & RV sites $16) Though the 42 green and shady campsites in this riverfront park are open year-round, the restrooms are closed December through February. Water, showers and boat launch on site; no hookups.

Robbers Roost Motel MOTEL $
(☎435-564-3452; www.rrmotel.com; 325 W Main St; s $31-38, d $40-45; ✱❀ ≋) What a great mini motorcourt motel. Staff are super accommodating and small-and-simple budget rooms are well cared for.

River Terrace Inn MOTEL $$
(☎435-564-3401, 877-564-3401; www.river-terrace.com; 1880 E Main St; r incl breakfast $110-106; ✱❀ ≋) Ask for a riverfront room, with a terrace overlooking the water. There's a full-service restaurant, and the free breakfast bar includes omelets.

Shady Acres RV Park CAMPGROUND $
(☎435-564-8290, 800-537-8674; www.shadyacresrv.com; 350 E Main St; tent sites $20-27, RV sites

$33-36, camping cabins $42; @🛜📱🍴🏊) 16-acre campground with lots of facilities: playground, dog run, associated laundromat, internet cafe and sandwich shop.

✕ Eating & Drinking

Roadside stands sell fresh watermelons in summer.

Ray's Tavern   BURGERS $$
(25 S Broadway; mains $8-26; ⊙11am-10pm) Residents and rafters alike flock to this local beer joint for the best hamburgers and fresh-cut French fries around. The steaks aren't bad either. Pass the time reading the displayed T-shirts donated by river runners from around the world, or have a game of pool with a Utah microbrew in hand.

Green River Coffee Co   CAFE $
(115 W Main St; breakfast & lunch sandwiches $5-8; ⊙7am-5pm; @🛜) As the sign says, 'We're open when we're here.' Drop in and discuss politics with the local coffee circle, grab a sandwich or catch up on your used-book reading at this super-relaxed coffeehouse.

Desert Flavors   ICE CREAM $
(cnr Main St & Broadway; treats $2-6; ⊙8am-4pm Apr-Oct) Homemade ice cream flavors may include watermelon or 'Green River mud', their own version of rocky road.

Melon Vine Food Store   MARKET $
(76 S Broadway; ⊙8am-7pm Mon-Sat) Grocery store; deli sandwiches available.

ⓘ Information

Emery County Visitor Center (☎435-564-3600, 888-564-3600; www.emerycounty.com/travel; 885 E Main St; ⊙8am-8pm Mar-Oct, 8am-4pm Tue-Sun Nov-Feb) Attached to the local museum, pick up info and river guide books and maps here.

ⓘ Getting There & Around

Green River is 182 miles southeast of SLC and 53 miles northwest of Moab. It is the only town of note along I-70 between Salina, UT (108 miles west), and Grand Junction, CO (102 miles east) – so fuel up.

Amtrak (☎800-872-7245; www.amtrak.com; 250 S Broadway) Green River is the only stop on the daily California Zephyr train run in southeastern Utah. Next stop east is Denver, CO ($85, 10¾ hours).

Greyhound (☎435-564-3421, 800-231-2222; www.greyhound.com; Rodeway Inn, 525 E Main St) Buses go to Grand Junction, CO ($36, one hour and 40 minutes).

Moab Luxury Coach (☎435-940-4212; www.moabluxurycoach.com; Rodeway Inn, 525 E Main St) Operates a scheduled van service to and from SLC ($149 one-way, 3½ hours) and Moab ($119 one-way, one hour).

Goblin Valley State Park & Around

A Salvador Dali-esque melted-rock fantasy, a valley of giant stone mushrooms, an otherworldly alien landscape or the results of an acid trip the creator went on? No matter what you think the stadium-like valley of stunted hoodoos resembles, one thing's for sure: the 3654-acre **Goblin Valley State Park** (www.stateparks.utah.gov; Goblin Valley Rd, off Hwy 24; per car $7; ⊙park 6am-10pm, visitor center 8am-5pm) is just plain fun. A few trails lead down from the overlooks to the valley floor, but after that there's no path to follow. You can climb down, around and even over the evocative 'goblins' (2ft to 20ft-tall formations). Kids,

---

WORTH A TRIP

HENRY MOUNTAINS

Southwest of Hanksville, the majestic **Henry Mountains** (11,500ft) was the last range to be named and explored in the lower 48. It's so remote that the area was famous as a hiding place for outlaws such as Butch Cassidy. The range is home to one of the country's remaining free-roaming (and elusive) wild bison herds; you can expect pronghorn antelopes, mule deer and bighorn sheep as well. Exploring here is for serious adventurers only.

There are two main access roads: from Hanksville, follow 1100 East Street to the south, which becomes Sawmill Basin Rd; from Hwy 95, about 20 miles south of Hanksville, follow the Bull Mountain Scenic Backway west. Both are very rough and rocky dirt roads; flat tires are common and 4WD vehicles are highly recommended. Rangers patrol infrequently. Contact the BLM Field Office in Hanksville for more information.

photographers and Lonely Planet writers especially love it. The park is 46 miles southwest of Green River.

A 19-site **campground** (☎800-322-3770; http://utahstateparks.reserveamerica.com; tent & RV sites $16) has little shade; nevertheless it books up on most weekends. Water and showers, but no hookups. West of the park off Goblin Valley Rd is BLM land – free dispersed camping, no services (stay on designated roads).

Twenty miles further south on Hwy 24 is **Hanksville** (population 350, elevation 4300ft). If you don't need gas, there's little reason to stop. It's better to stay in Green River, Torrey or at Lake Powell, depending on where you're headed. The **BLM Field Office** (☎435-542-3461; 380 S 100 West; ⌚8:30am-4:30pm Mon-Fri) has maps and information for surrounding lands, particularly the Henry Mountains. If you have to stay, **Whispering Sands Motel** (☎435-542-3238; www.whisperingsandsmotel.com; 90 S Hwy 95; r $70-90; @) is the town's nicest lodging, though that's not saying much. Before continuing south, fill up your car and carry your own food and water. There are no more services until you get to Bullfrog Marina (70 miles) or Mexican Hat (130 miles).

Glen Canyon National Recreation Area & Lake Powell

In the 1960s construction of a massive dam flooded Glen Canyon, forming Lake Powell, a recreational playground. Almost 50 years later this is still an environmental hot-button topic, but generations of Western families have grown up boating here. Water laps against stunning, multihued cliffs that rise hundreds of feet; narrow channels and tributary canyons twist off in every direction.

Lake Powell stretches for more than 185 miles, surrounded by millions of acres of desert incorporated into the **Glen Canyon National Recreation Area** (7-day per vehicle $15). Most of the watery way lies within Utah. However, Glen Canyon Dam itself, the main Glen Canyon National Recreation Area visitor center, the largest and most developed marina (Wahweap) and the biggest town on the lake (Page) are all in Arizona. For more on services, and sights such as Rainbow Bridge, see p183.

In Utah, primary access is 70 miles south of Hanksville; check in at the **Bullfrog Visitor Center** (☎435-684-7423; ⌚9am-5pm Mar-Oct) for general info. At the end of the road, **Bullfrog Marina** (☎435-684-3000; www.lakepowell.com; Hwy 276; ⌚9am-4pm Mar-Oct) rents out boats – 19ft runabouts ($400) and personal watercraft ($335) – by the day, but houseboats are its big business. You can rent a 46ft boat that sleeps 12 for between $2500 and $4000 per week. Invest in the waterproof *Lake Powell Photomap* ($11) so you can pilot your craft to some great canyon hikes.

Landlubbers can spend the night at the marina's waterfront **Defiance House Lodge** (☎435-684-3000; www.lakepowell.com; Hwy 276; r $140-175; ⌚Mar-Oct) and eat at **Anasazi Restaurant** (Hwy 276; breakfast $8-12, mains $10-28; ⌚7am-10pm Mar-Oct). The restaurant serves pretty standard all-American fare, but it does try to use local produce and sustainable practices. Also on site: a small convenience store, marine fuel and trailer parking. The 24-space **campground** (☎435-684-3000; www.lakepowell.com; Hwy 276; tent & RV sites $34-38; ⌚Mar-Oct;), with showers, is just up the road. The pavement is wide (50ft pull-throughs), but there's little ground cover.

Inland, 12 miles or so from the marina, there are a couple of marine-service/gas-station/convenience-store/deli complexes. **Ticaboo Lodge** (☎435-788-2110; www.ticaboo.com; Hwy 276; r $70-90; ⌚May-Sep;) is a sleeping alternative with a three-meal-a-day restaurant and bar attached.

To continue south along Hwy 276 you have to take the **ferry** (☎435- 684-3088; www.lakepowell.com; per car $25; ⌚closed Dec-Feb) to Hall's Crossing. The trip takes about 30 minutes. There are four crossings a day between 9am and 4pm, June to August; only two boats run between 9am and 2pm, March through May and between 10am and 3pm September through November.

The **Hall's Crossing** (☎435-684-7000; www.lakepowell.com; ⌚8am-4pm Mar-Oct) marina has a store, boat launch, great kid's playground and **campground** (tent & RV sites $34-38; ⌚Mar-Oct;). At the time of writing Hite Marina remained closed due to low water levels.

ZION & SOUTHWESTERN UTAH

Wonder at the deep-crimson canyons of Zion National Park, hike among the delicate pink-and-orange minarets at Bryce Canyon, drive past the swirling grey-white-and-purple mounds of Capitol Reef. Southwestern Utah is so spectacular that the vast majority of the territory has been preserved as national park or forest, state park or BLM wilderness. Rugged and remote Grand Staircase-Escalante National Monument (GSENM) is larger than Rhode Island and Delaware put together. The whole area is ripe for outdoor exploration, with narrow slot canyons to shoulder through, pink sand dunes to scale and wavelike sandstone formations to seek out.

Several small towns, including artsy Springdale, service these parks. But do note that getting to some of the most noteworthy sites can be quite an uphill hike. Elevation changes in the region – mountainous highs to desert lows – pose an additional weather challenge. In the end, any effort you make usually more than pays off with a stunning view of our eroding and ever-changing Earth.

(Note that you'll average no more than 35mph to 50mph on scenic highways in the area.)

Capitol Reef National Park

Native Americans once called this colorful landscape of tilted buttes, jumbled rocks and sedimentary canyons the Land of the Sleeping Rainbow. The park's centerpiece is Waterpocket Fold, a 100-mile-long monocline (a buckle in the Earth's crust) that blocked explorers' westward migration like a reef blocks a ship's passage. Known also for its enormous domes – one of which kinda sorta resembles Washington DC's Capitol Dome – Capitol Reef harbors fantastic hiking trails, rugged 4WD roads and 1000-year-old Fremont petroglyph panels. At the park's heart grow the shady orchards of Fruita, a Mormon settlement dating back to the 1870s.

The narrow park runs north-south following the Waterpocket Fold. A little over 100 miles southwest of Green River, Hwy 24 traverses the park. Capitol Reef's central region is the Fruita Historic District. To the far north lies Cathedral Valley, the least-visited section, and toward the south you can cross over into Grand Staircase-Escalante National Monument on the Burr Trail Rd. Most services, including food, gas and medical aid, are in the town of Torrey, 11 miles west.

MESA FARM MARKET

About 23 miles east of Capitol Reef's visitor center, near Mile 102, is **Mesa Farm Market** (435-487-9711; Hwy 24, Caineville; 7am-7pm Mar-Oct). Stop here for straight-from-the-garden organic salads, freshly baked artisan bread and cinnamon rolls, homemade cheeses, homegrown organic coffee and fresh-squeezed juices. Note that hours do vary.

Sights & Activities

There's no fee to enter or traverse the park in general, but the Scenic Drive has an admission fee. Remember that Capitol Reef has little shade. Drink at least one quart of water for every two hours of hiking and wear a hat. Distances listed for hiking are one-way. For backcountry hikes, ask for the information pamphlets at the visitor center or check online. Ranger Rick Stinchfield's *Capitol Reef National Park: The Complete Hiking and Touring Guide* is also a great reference.

Technical rock climbing is allowed without permits. Note that Wingate Sandstone can flake unpredictably. Follow clean-climbing guidelines, and take all safety precautions. For details, check with rangers or see www.nps.gov/care.

Petroglyphs
ARCHAEOLOGICAL SITE

(Map p424) Just east of the visitor center on Hwy 24, look for the parking lot for freely accessible **petroglyphs**; these are the rock-art carvings that convinced archaeologists the Fremont Indians were a group distinct from the Ancestral Puebloan. Follow the roadside boardwalk to see several panels.

Panorama Point & Gooseneck Overlook
LOOKOUT

(Map p424) Two miles west of the visitor center off Hwy 24, a short unpaved road heads to Panorama Point and Gooseneck Overlook. The dizzying 800ft-high viewpoints above serpentine Sulphur Creek are worth a stop. Afternoon light is best for photography.

Fruita Historic District
HISTORIC SITE

(Map p424) Fruita (*froo*-tuh) is a cool green oasis, where shade-giving cottonwoods and fruit-bearing trees line the Fremont River's banks. The first Mormon homesteaders arrived here in 1880; Fruita's final resident left in 1969. Among the historic buildings, the

Southwestern Utah

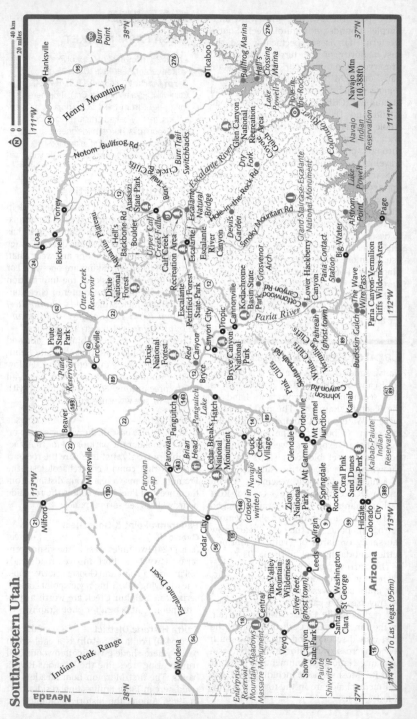

NPS maintains 2700 cherry, apricot, peach, pear and apple trees planted by early settlers. Visit between June and October and pluck ripe fruit from the trees, for free, from any unlocked orchard. For availability, ask rangers or call the **fruit hotline** (☏435-425-3791). Pick only mature fruit; leave the rest to ripen. Near the orchards is a wonderful **picnic area**, with roaming deer and birds in the trees – a desert rarity.

Across the road from the blacksmith shop (just a shed with period equipment) is the **Ripple Rock Nature Center** (⊙noon-5pm daily Jun, 10am-3pm Tue-Sat Jul-Aug; 🐾), a family-oriented learning center. The **Gifford Homestead** (⊙8am-5pm Mar-Oct) is an old homestead museum where you can also buy fruit-filled minipies and jams.

Scenic Dr

SCENIC DRIVE

(Map p424; per week, per vehicle $7; ⊙24hr) Pay admission at the visitor center or self service kiosk to go beyond Fruita Campground on the 9-mile-long, paved Scenic Dr. Numbered roadside markers correspond to an interpretive driving tour available at the visitor center or online. The best part is the last 2 miles between the narrow sandstone walls of Capitol Gorge – it'll knock your socks off. To continue south past Pleasant Creek, a 4WD vehicle is advised.

Capitol Gorge Trail

HIKING

(Map p424) At the end of Scenic Dr is Capitol Gorge Trail (1 mile, easy), which leads past petroglyphs. Spur trails lead to **Pioneer Register**, where names carved in the rock date back to 1871, and the **Tanks**, giant water pockets. Look for the spur to the **Golden Throne** formation off Capitol Gorge Trail (another mile).

Grand Wash Trail

HIKING

(Map p424) Also along Scenic Dr, a good dirt road leads to Grand Wash Trail (2.25 miles, easy), a flat hike between canyon walls that, at one point, tower 80 stories high but are only 15ft apart. You can follow an offshoot to **Cassidy Arch** (2 miles).

Hickman Bridge Trail

HIKING

(Map p424) This popular walk (1 mile, moderate) includes a canyon stretch, a stunning natural bridge and wildflowers in spring. Mornings are coolest; it starts about 2 miles east of the visitor center off Hwy 24.

Notom-Bullfrog Rd

SCENIC DRIVE

(Map p424) This is a rough, rough road that heads south from Hwy 24 (5 miles east of the visitor center) paralleling Waterpocket Fold. Thirty-two miles south, you can turn west toward Hwy 12 and Burr Trail Rd (p426) in Grand Staircase-Escalante National Monument. Along the way, **Strike Valley Overlook** has one of the best comprehensive views of the Waterpocket Fold itself. If you instead continue south, you're on the way to Lake Powell and Bullfrog Marina in Glen Canyon National Recreation Area, another 35 miles away.

Cathedral Valley Loop

MOUNTAIN BIKING, SCENIC DRIVE

(Map p424; Caineville Wash Rd) Long-distance mountain bikers and 4WDers love this 58-mile route through Cathedral Valley, starting 18.6 miles east of the visitor center. The bumpy, roughshod backcountry road explores the remote northern area of the park and its alien desert landscapes, pierced by giant sandstone monoliths eroded into fantastic shapes. Before starting, check conditions at the visitor center and purchase an interpretive route guide.

🛏 Sleeping & Eating

The nearest motel lodging and dining are, again, in Torrey.

Fruita Campground

CAMPGROUND $

(Map p424; Scenic Dr; campsites $10) The terrific 71-site Fruita Campground sits under mature cottonwood trees alongside the Fremont River, surrounded by orchards. First-come, first-served sites have access to water, but no showers. Spring through fall, sites fill up early.

Free primitive camping is possible year round at **Cathedral Valley Campground** at the end of River Ford Rd, and at **Cedar Mesa Campground**, about 23 miles south along Notom-Bullfrog Rd.

ℹ Information

Occasional summer thunderstorms pose a serious risk of flash flooding. Always check weather with rangers at the visitor center. Bugs bite in May and June. Summer temperatures can exceed 100°F (38°C) at the visitor center (5400ft), but it's cooler than Moab. If it's too hot, ascend to Torrey (10°F, or 6°C, cooler) or Boulder Mountain (30°F, or 17°C, cooler).

Visitor center (☏435-425-3791; www.nps.gov /care; cnr Hwy 24 & Scenic Dr; ⊙8am-6pm Jun-Aug, 8am-4:30pm Sep-May) Inquire about ranger-led programs, watch the short film, then ooh and aah over the 64-sq-ft park relief map,

Capitol Reef National Park

N

0 ——————— 20 km
0 ——————— 10 miles

9 ▲

Upper Cathedral Valley Overlook 📷

Cathedral Valley

Caineville Wash Rd

Hartnet Rd

Cathedral Valley Loop

Waterpocket Fold

Caineville ○

Fremont R

24

To Torrey (7mi)

Gooseneck Overlook 📷 **4**
ⓘ
5 ◎ **8**
2 ◎ **1**
11 ▲

Grand Wash Trail

Scenic Dr

3 ◎ **7**

Capitol Gorge Trail

6

Notom-Bullfrog Rd

Pleasant Cr

Capitol Reef National Park 🏛

Dixie National Forest 🏛

10 ▲

● Bitter Creek Divide (5650ft)

Henry Mountains

Anasazi State Park 🏛

Boulder ○

12

Burr Trail Rd

Strike Valley Overlook 📷

Burr Trail Switchbacks 📷

Calf Creek Recreation Area 🏛

Waterpocket Fold

To Bryce Canyon National Park (40mi)

Escalante River

Hole-in-the-Rock Rd

Grand Staircase-Escalante National Monument 🏛

Glen Canyon National Recreation Area 🏛

Capitol Reef National Park

carved with dental instruments. The bookstore sells several interpretive trail and driving tour maps (50¢-$2) as well as area-interest books and guides.

ℹ Getting Around

Capitol Reef has no public transportation system. Aside from Hwy 24 and Scenic Dr, park routes are dirt roads bladed only a few times a year. In summer you may be able to drive Notom-Bullfrog Rd and the Burr Trail in a regular passenger car. Remote regions like Cathedral Valley will likely require a high-clearance 4WD vehicle. Check weather and road conditions with rangers before heading out.

Bicycles are allowed on all park roads but not trails. Cyclists and hikers can arrange drop-off/pick-up shuttle services (from $25) with **Hondoo Rivers & Trails** (☑435-425-3519, 800-332-2696; www.hondoo.com; 90 E Main St, Torrey).

Torrey

Old pioneer homestead buildings line the main street of this quiet town and, in the distance, stunning red-rock cliffs and mountains catch the light. Torrey's primary industry has long since shifted from logging and ranching to outdoor tourism. Capitol Reef National Park is only 11 miles east, Grand Staircase-Escalante National Monument is 40 miles south and national forests surround the town. In summer there's a whiff of countercultural sophistication in the air – and great dining – but from November to February the town shuts down.

◎ Sights & Activities

Capitol Reef is the major area attraction, but there are other freely-accessible public lands nearby. Many of the main street lodgings have Native American arts and crafts for sale in their 'trading posts'.

Fishlake National Forest PARK
More than 300 miles of trails cover the mountainous forest; four-wheel drive roads lead north of town around **Thousand Lake Mountain** (11,306ft). Hwy 72, 17 miles west of town in Loa, is a paved route through the same area. **Fish Lake**, a giant trout fishery, is 21 miles northwest of Loa, off Hwy 25. Check with the **Fremont River/Loa Ranger District Office** (☑435-836-2811; www.fs.fed.us /r4/fishlake; 138 S Main St, Loa; ⊙9am-5pm Mon-Fri) for info.

Dixie National Forest PARK
(www.fs.fed.us/dxnf) The expansive Dixie National Forest contains **Boulder Mountain** (11,317ft) to the south of Torrey. Nearby are numerous fishable lakes and streams, as well as campgrounds, hiking, biking and ATV trails. **Teasdale Ranger Station** (☑435-425-3702; 138 E Main St, Teasdale; ⊙9am-5pm Mon-Fri), 4 miles southwest, is the nearest source of information.

⊙ Tours & Outfitters

Guides and outfitters cover the surrounding area well (Capitol Reef, national forest lands, Grand Staircase-Escalante National Monument and beyond). A half-day excursion runs from $90 to $225 per person.

Hondoo Rivers & Trails ADVENTURE SPORTS
(☑435-425-3519, 800-332-2696; www.hondoo.com) One of southern Utah's longest-operating backcountry guides has half- and full-day hiking and driving tours that cover slot canyons and rock art, multiday horseback trail rides, and raft-and-ride combo trips.

Capitol Reef Backcountry Outfitters ADVENTURE SPORTS
(☑435-425-2010, 866-747-3972; www.backcountry outfitters.com; 875 E Hwy) In addition to 4WD and hiking packages, Backcountry Outfitters also rents bicycles ($40 per day) and ATVs ($150 per day). Shuttles and guided bike, ATV and horseback rides available, too.

Thousand Lakes RV Park FOUR-WHEEL DRIVING
(☑435-425-3500, 800-355-8995; www.thousand lakesrvpark.com; 1110 W Hwy 24) Rents 4WD vehicles from $95 per day.

UTAH TORREY

DON'T MISS

HWY 12

Arguably Utah's most diverse and stunning route, **Hwy 12 Scenic Byway** (http://scenic byway12.com) winds through rugged canyonland, linking several national parks on a 124-mile journey from near Capitol Reef southeast past Bryce Canyon. See how quickly and dramatically the land changes from wooded plateau to red-rock canyon, from slickrock desert to alpine forest, as it climbs over an 11,000ft mountain. Many consider the best section of the road to be the switchbacks and petrified sand dunes between Torrey and Boulder. Then again, the razor-thin Hogback Ridge between Escalante and Boulder is pretty stunning, too.

Pretty much everything in this chapter between Torrey and Panguitch is on or near Hwy 12. Highlights include foodie-oriented eateries in tiny tot Boulder, Lower Calf Creek Falls recreation area for a picnic, a hike in GSENM, and an incredible drive through arches and technicolor red rock in Red Canyon. Take time to stop at the many viewpoints and pullouts, especially at Mile 70, where the Aquarius Plateau lords over giant mesas, towering domes, deep canyons and undulating slickrock, all unfurling in an explosion of color.

Boulder Mountain Adventures & Alpine Angler's Flyshop FISHING
(☑435-425-3660; www.alpineadventuresutah.com; 310 W Main St) Guided fishing trips and multi-day excursions that include both horseback riding and fishing.

★ Festivals

If you're here on the third weekend in July, don't miss the **Bicknell International Film Festival** (www.thebiff.org), just a couple miles up Hwy 24 in Bicknell. This wacky B-movie spoof on Sundance includes films, parties, a swap meet and the 'fastest parade in America'.

🛏 Sleeping

Camping is available in Capitol Reef National Park and in Dixie and Fishlake National Forests.

TOP CHOICE **Torrey Schoolhouse B&B** B&B $$
(☑435-633-4643; www.torreyschoolhouse.com; 150 N Center St; r incl breakfast $110-140; ☺Apr-Oct; ❀✿❀) Ty Markham has done an exquisite job of bringing a spacious, 1914 schoolhouse back to life as a B&B. Dressed-down in country elegance, each airy room has light colors, high ceilings and well-chosen antiques. After consuming the full gourmet breakfast you might need to laze in the garden a while before you head out hiking.

Austin's Chuckwagon Motel MOTEL $
(☑435-425-3335; www.austinschuckwagonmotel .com; 12 W Main St; r $75-85, cabins $135; ☺Mar-Oct; ❀✿❀❀) Rustic wood buildings ring the pool and shady grounds here at the town center. Good value-for-money motel rooms have sturdy, basic furnishings; cabins also have kitchens. The on-site general store, deli and laundromat are a bonus.

Thousand Lakes RV Park CAMPGROUND $
(☑435-425-3500, 800-355-8995; www.thousand lakesrvpark.com; Hwy 24; tent/RV sites $18/28, camping cabins $35-95; ☺Apr-Oct; ❀✿❀) Twenty-two acres filled with facilities and services, including a heated swimming pool, playground, trading post gift shop, 4WD rental and evening cook-out dinners ($15 to $23). Morning muffins and hot coffee included.

Lodge at Red River Ranch INN $$-$$$
(☑435-425-3322, 800-205-6343; www.redriver ranch.com; 2900 W Hwy 24, Teasdale; r incl breakfast $160-245; @❀) In the grand old tradition of Western ranches, the great room here has a three-story open-beam ceiling, timber walls and Navajo rugs. Details are flawless – from the country quilts on high-thread-count sheets to the cowboy bric-a-brac decorating the lodge's fine-dining room. Wander the more than 2000 private acres, or enjoy the star-filled sky from the outdoor hot tub. No room TVs.

Rim Rock Inn MOTEL $
(☑435-425-3398, 888-447-4676; www.therimrock .net; 2523 E Hwy 24; r $69-89; ☺Mar-Nov; ❀❀❀) Among the red-rock cliffs east of town near Capitol Reef, this family-owned hilltop place offers basic, standard-issue motel rooms – with superb sunset vistas. Two good on-site restaurants share the views.

Muley Twist Inn B&B B&B $$
(☑435-425-3640, 800-530-1038; www.muleytwist
inn.com; 249 W 125 South Teasdale; r incl breakfast
$99-140; ☺Apr-Oct; ❄☎) Set against a tower-
ing red sandstone dome in a Teasdale neigh-
borhood, the big wooden farmhouse with a
wraparound verandah looks small. It isn't.
Casual rooms at the down-to-earth inn are
spacious and bright.

Pine Shadows Cabins BUNGALOW $$
(☑435-425-3939, 800-708-1223; www.pineshadow
cabins.net; 195 W 125 South, Teasdale; cabins
$76-99; ❄☎) Spacious, modern cabins (two
beds and kitchenette) sheltered among
piñon pines at the end of the road, near
trails.

Sandcreek RV Park CAMPGROUND $
(☑435-425-3577; www.sandcreekrv.com; 540
Hwy 24; tent sites/RV sites/cabins $15/23/30; ☎)
Friendly little campground with horseshoe pit, horse pasture ($5 per night) and
laundry. Nonguest showers $3.

Torrey Trading Post MOTEL $
(☑435-425-3716; www.torreytradingpost.com;
75 W Main St; cabins $35) Bare-bones but dirt-
cheap cabins with shared bathroom.

Best Western Capitol Reef Resort MOTEL $$
(☑435-425-3761, 888-610-9600; www.bestwestern
utah.com; 2600 E Hwy 24; r $76-129; ❄☎❄) Plain-
Jane chain, with stunning red-cliff balcony
views.

Skyridge Inn MOTEL $
(☑435-425-3222, 877-824-1508; www.skyridge
inn.com; 950 E Hwy 24; r incl breakfast $109-
142; ❄☎) Country farmhouse B&B near
town.

🍴 Eating & Drinking

The nearest supermarket is 16 miles west,
in Loa.

TOP CHOICE Café Diablo MODERN SOUTHWESTERN $$$
(☑435-425-3070; 599 W Main St; mains $25-
40; ☺11:30am-10pm mid-Apr–Oct; ☎) One of
southern Utah's best, Café Diablo serves
outstanding, highly stylized Southwestern
cooking – including succulent vegetarian
dishes – bursting with flavor and towering
on the plate. Think turkey *chimole* (a spicy
stew), Mayan tamales and fire-roasted
pork tenderloin on a cilantro waffle. Book
ahead, you don't want to miss this one.

UTAH TORREY

ON BUTCH CASSIDY'S TRAIL

Nearly every town in southern Utah claims a connection to Butch Cassidy (1866-?), the Old West's most famous bank and train robber. As part of the Wild Bunch, Cassidy (né Robert LeRoy Parker) pulled 19 heists from 1896 to 1901. Accounts usually describe him with a breathless romanticism, likening him to a kind of Robin Hood. Bring up the subject in these parts and you'll likely be surprised at how many folks' grandfathers had en-counters. The robber may even have attended a dance in the old **Torrey Schoolhouse** (p426), now a B&B. And many a dilapidated shack or a canyon, just over yonder, served as his hideout. The most credible claim for the location of the famous Robbers' Roost hideout is in the **Henry Mountains** (p419).

In the wee town of **Circleville**, located 28 miles north of Panguitch, stands the honest-to-goodness boyhood home of the gun-slingin' bandit. The cabin is partially renovated but uninhabited, and is situated 2 miles south of town on the west side of Hwy 89. When reporters arrived after the release of the film *Butch Cassidy and the Sundance Kid* (1969), they met the outlaw's youngest sister, who claimed that Butch did in fact not die in South America in 1908, but returned for a visit after that. Writers have been digging for the truth to no avail ever since. You can see where they filmed Robert Redford's famous bicycle scene at the **Grafton ghost town** (p457), outside Rockville.

Local lore holds that Cassidy didn't steal much in Utah because this is where his bread was buttered. Whatever the reason, the Wild Bunch's only big heist in the state was in April 1897, when the gang stole more than $8000 from Pleasant Valley Coal Company in Castle Gate, 4 miles north of Helper on Hwy 191. The little **Western Mining & Railroad Museum** (296 S Main St, Helper; adult/child $2/1; ☺10am-5pm Mon-Sat May-Aug, 11am-4pm Tue-Sat Sep-Apr), 8 miles north of Price, has exhibits on the outlaws, including photos, in the basement. For more, check out *The Outlaw Trail*, by Charles Kelly.

KIVA KOFFEEHOUSE

Just past the Aquarius Plateau at Mile 73 on Hwy 12, you reach the singular **Kiva Koffeehouse** (☎435-826-4550; www.kivakoffeehouse.com; soups & pastries $2-6; ☺8am-4:30pm Wed-Mon Apr-Nov). This round structure was built directly into the cliffside. Floor-to-ceiling glass windows, separated by giant timber beams, overlook the expansive canyons beyond. Besides serving barista coffee and yummy baked goods, Kiva also rents two cushy hideaway cottage rooms (r $170; 🐾) with whirlpool tubs, fireplaces – and the same stellar views.

Slacker's Burger Joint   BURGERS $
(165 E Main St; burgers $6-8; ☺11am-9pm Fri & Sat, 11am-8pm Mon-Thu, 11am-5pm Sun Mar-Oct) Order an old-fashioned burger (beef, chicken, pastrami or veggie), hand-cut fries (the sweet-potato version is delish) and thick milkshake (in a rainbow of cool flavors like cherry cordial), then enjoy – inside, or out at the picnic tables.

Rim Rock Patio   PIZZERIA $
(2523 E Hwy 24; mains $6-10; ☺lunch & dinner Apr-Oct, dinner Nov-Mar) The best place in Torrey to drink beer also serves up good pizzas, salads, sandwiches and ice cream. Families and friends play darts or disc golf, listen to live bands and hangout.

Rim Rock Restaurant   AMERICAN $$-$$$
(2523 E Hwy 24; mains $18-29; ☺5-9:30pm Mar-Dec) Grilled steaks, pastas and fish come with a million-dollar view of red-rock cliffs. Arrive before sunset for the best show. Full bar.

Robber's Roost Books & Beverages CAFE $
(185 W Main St; baked goods $1.50-3; ☺8am-4pm Mon-Sat, 1-4pm Sun May-Oct; @🐾) Linger over a latte and a scone on comfy couches by the fire at this peaceful cafe-bookstore with bohemian bonhomie. Sells local-interest books and maps; also has three computer terminals (internet access per hour $5) and free wi-fi.

Castle Rock Coffee & Candy   CAFE $
(cnr Hwys 12 & 24; breakfast & sandwiches $4-8; ☺7am-5pm Mar-Oct; @🐾) The coffeehouse that serves Utah-roast brews, bakes its own candy and banana bread, and blends up fruit smoothies, now also serves breakfast and lunch. Try the Reuben sandwich.

Austin's Chuckwagon General Store
                        MARKET $
(12 W Main St; ☺7am-10pm Apr-Oct) Sells camping supplies, groceries, beer and deli sandwiches to go.

☆ Entertainment

Support the local arts scene by attending an **Entrada Institute** (www.entradainstitute.org; ☺Sat Jun-Aug) event, such as an author reading or evening of cowboy music and poetry, at Robber's Roost Books & Beverages.

❶ Information

Austin's Chuckwagon General Store has an ATM.
Sevier Valley Hospital (☎435-896-8271; 1000 N Main St, Richfield) The closest full hospital is 60 miles west on I-70.
Wayne County Travel Council (☎435-425-3365, 800-858-7951; www.capitolreef.org; cnr Hwys 24 & 12; ☺noon-7pm Apr-Oct) Friendly source of area-wide information.

❶ Getting There & Around

Rural and remote, Torrey has no public transportation. Activity outfitters can provide hiker shuttles to the national park.

Boulder

Though the tiny town of Boulder is only 32 miles south of Torrey on Hwy 12, you have to traverse 11,317ft-high Boulder Mountain to get there. Until 1940, this isolated outpost received its mail by mule. It's still so remote that the federal government classifies it as a 'frontier community'. Nevertheless, Boulder has a diverse population of down-to-earth folks that range from artists and ecologists to farmers and cowboys. It's a great little place, and well worth a stop. Stay longer and use it as a base to explore surrounding public lands. Note that pretty much all services shut down November through March.

◉ Sights & Activities

Hikes in the northern area of Grand Staircase-Escalante National Monument are near here, but the national forest and

BLM lands in the area are also good for hiking and backcountry driving. Burr Trail Rd (p433) is the most scenic drive, but Hell's Backbone (p438) has its thrills, too.

Anasazi State Park Museum MUSEUM
(www.stateparks.utah.gov; Main St/Hwy 12; admission $5; ⊙8am-6pm Jun-Aug, 9am-5pm Sep-May) The pieced-back-together jars and jugs on display are just a few of the thousands and thousands of pottery shards excavated. Today the petite museum protects the Coomb's Site, excavated in the 1950s and inhabited from AD 1130 to 1175. The minimal ruins aren't as evocative as some in southeastern Utah, but the museum is well worth seeing for the re-created six-room pueblo and excellent exhibits about the Ancestral Puebloan peoples. Inside, there's a seasonal information desk where you can talk to rangers and get backcountry road updates.

Box-Death Hollow Wilderness Area HIKING
(www.blm.gov) This ruggedly beautiful wilderness area surrounds Hell's Backbone Rd. A 16-mile backpack, **Boulder Mail Trail** follows the mule route the post used to take.

Dixie National Forest HIKING
(www.fs.fed.us/dxnf) North of Boulder, the Escalante District of this 2 million-square-acre forest has trails and campgrounds, including a few up on Boulder Mountain.

Earth Tours HIKING
(☑435-691-1241; www.earth-tours.com; trips per person from $150; ⊙Mar-Oct; ✤) Founder, and main guide, PhD geologist Keith Watt has an enthusiasm for the area that is catching. Choose from among the numerous half- and full-day area hikes offered or take a 4WD trip into the backcountry.

Escalante Canyon Outfitters HIKING
(ECO; ☑435-691-3037, 888-326-4453; www.ecohike.com; 2520 S Lower Deer Creek Rd; ⊙Mar-Nov) Started by cofounder of the Southern Utah Wilderness Alliance Grant Johnson, ECO hikes has well-regarded multiday treks with canyonland or archaeological-site focus.

Hell's Backbone Ranch & Trails HORSEBACK RIDING
(☑435-335-7581; www.bouldermountaintrails.com; off Hell's Backbone Rd; half-day $80-95) Head across the slickrock plateau, into Box-Death Hollow Wilderness or up the forested mountain on two-hour to full-day area horseback rides. Or maybe you prefer a multiday camping trip or cattle drive?

Red Rock 'n Llamas HIKING
(☑435-616-7421, 877-955-2627; www.redrocknllamas.com) Yes, these multiday treks are actually llama-supported (kids love it). Drop-camp service, camping gear rental and hiker shuttles also available.

Sleeping

Boulder Mountain Lodge LODGE $$
(☑435-335-7460; www.boulder-utah.com; 20 N Hwy 12; r $110-175; ✤@🐾) Watch the birds flit by on the adjacent 15-acre wildlife sanctuary and stroll through the organic garden – Boulder Mountain Lodge has a strong eco-aesthetic. It's an ideal place for dayhikers who want to return to high-thread-count sheets, plush terry robes and an outdoor hot tub. Hell's Backbone Grill, on site, is a southern Utah must-eat.

Boulder Mountain Ranch LODGE $-$$
(☑435-335-7480; http://bouldermountainguestranch.com; off Hell's Backbone Rd; r $70-105, cabins $95-115; 🐾) Enjoy a peaceful 160-acre wilderness setting with outfitter-led hikes and activities available. Bunk and queen rooms in the giant log lodge enjoy a communal atmosphere; rustic out-cabins are more private. The dining room has chef-cooked meals at breakfast and dinner.

Pole's Place MOTEL $
(☑435-335-7422, 800-730-7422; www.boulderutah.com/polesplace; r $50-75; ⊙Mar-Oct; ✤) Small and simple, this mom-and-pop motel is lovingly maintained. Limited TV.

✖ Eating

TOP CHOICE **Hell's Backbone Grill** MODERN SOUTHWESTERN $$-$$$
(☑435-335-7464; Boulder Mountain Lodge, 20 N Hwy 12; breakfast $8-10, dinner $16-34; ⊙7am-11:30am & 5:30-9:30pm Mar-Oct) Soulful, earthy preparations of Southwestern dishes include locally-raised meats and organically grown produce from their garden. Zen Buddhist owners Jen Castle and Blake Spalding not only feed the stomach, they feed the community, training staff in mindfulness and inviting the whole town to a 4th of July ice cream social and talent show. Dinner reservations are a must. Save room for the Chimayo-chile ginger cake with butterscotch sauce.

TOP CHOICE **Burr Trail Grill & Outpost** MODERN SOUTHWESTERN $-$$
(cnr Hwy 12 & Burr Trail Rd; mains $7-18; ⊙grill 11am-2:30pm & 5-9:30pm, outpost 7:30am-8pm

Mar-Oct; 🛜) The organic vegetable tarts and eclectic burgers (plus scrumptious home-made cookies and cakes) at the Grill rival the more famous restaurant next door. We like the homey vibe here, where locals come to chat-and-chew or celebrate friends' birthdays. The Outpost is a wonderfully artsy gallery as much as it is gift shop and coffeehouse.

Hills & Hollows Country Store MARKET $
(Hwy 12; ⊙9am-7pm, gas 24hr) Groceries and organic snacks available year-round, though hours may be limited November through February.

ℹ️ Information
The tiny town has no visitor center, but info is available online at www.boulderutah.com.

Boulder Interagency Desk (☎435-335-7382; Anasazi State Park Museum, Hwy 12; ⊙9am-5pm mid-Mar–mid-Nov) BLM and other public-land trail and camping information.

Escalante

With a population of just under one thousand, Escalante is the largest settlement on the north side of the GSENM. Folks here are an interesting mix of ranchers, old-timers, artists and post-monument-creation outdoors lovers. The town itself doesn't have tons of character, but there are lodgings and restaurants. Numerous outfitters make this their base for hiking excursions, and you could too. Lying at the head of several park backroads, not far from the most popular GSENM hikes, the location is good. Escalante is 28 miles south of Boulder, roughly halfway between Capitol Reef (76 miles) and Bryce Canyon (50 miles).

⊙ Sights & Activities
The Monument provides most of the attraction for the area; hikes off Hwy 12 and Hole-in-the-Rock Rd are within 12 to 30 miles drive.

Escalante Petrified Forest State Park PARK (www.stateparks.utah.gov; day use $6; ⊙day use 8am-10pm) Two miles west of town, the centerpiece of this state park is a 130-acre lake. Hike uphill about a mile on an interpretive route to see pieces of colorful millions-of-years-old petrified wood. Follow another short interpretive trail past further examples of the mineralized wood. The sites at the **campground** (☎800-322-3770; http://

utahstateparks.reserveamerica.com; tent & RV sites with/without hookups $16/20; 🚐🏕) are reserveable; showers available.

Escalante Outfitters ADVENTURE SPORTS
(☎435-826-4266; www.escalanteoutfitters.com; 310 W Main St; ⊙8am-9pm Mar-Oct, 9am-6pm Tue-Sat Nov-Feb; 🛜) A traveler's oasis: this store and cafe sells area books, topographic maps, camping and hiking gear, liquor, espresso, breakfasts and pizza. Guided fly-fishing trips and natural-history tours are available (from $45 per person). It also rents out tiny, rustic cabins ($45) and mountain bikes (from $35 per day).

Excursions of Escalante HIKING
(☎800-839-7567; www.excursionsofescalante.com; 125 E Main St; full-day from $145) For area canyoneering and climbing trips, Excursions is the best; it does hiker shuttles and guided photo hikes, too. At the time of writing, its outfitter store and cafe was under reconstruction.

Escape Goats ADVENTURE SPORTS
(☎435-826-4652; http://escapegoats.us; full-day $80-150) Take an evening tour or day-hike to dinosaur tracks, slot-canyons and ancient sites. Supplies for multiday catered pack-trips are carried by goats. Yes, goats.

Utah Canyons ADVENTURE SPORTS
(☎435-826-4967; www.utahcanyons.com; 325 W Main St) Guided day hikes, multiday supported treks, hiker shuttles and a small outdoors store.

Escalante Jeep Rental ADVENTURE SPORTS
(☎435-616-4144; www.escalantejeeprentals.com; 495 W Main St; ⊙10am-5pm) Jeeps, ATVs and 4WD utility vehicles for rent; from $180 per day.

Gallery Escalante GALLERY
(http://galleryescalante.com; 425 W Main St; ⊙9am-5pm) This artist-owned local art gallery with multiday Photoshop workshops sends students out into the field 'on assignment'.

🛏 Sleeping
For a full list of area motels, B&Bs and rentals, check out www.escalante-cc.com.

Canyons Bed & Breakfast B&B $$
(☎435-826-4747, 866-526-9667; www.canyonsbnb.com; 120 E Main St; r incl breakfast $125-135; ❄🛜) Upscale cabin-rooms with porches surround a shaded terrace and gardens where

you can enjoy your gourmet breakfast each morning. Except for a small dining area, the wooden 1905 ranch house on-site is private.

Rainbow Country Bed & Breakfast B&B $-$$
(☑435-826-4567, 800-252-8824; www.bnbescalante.com; 586 E 300 S; r incl breakfast $69-109; ❈🛜) You couldn't ask for better trail advice than what you receive over big home-cooked breakfasts here. The split-level house on the edge of town is not flashy, just comfortable and homey – with a big TV lounge (no room TVs), guest refrigerator and outdoor hot tub.

Circle D Motel MOTEL $
(☑435-826-4297; www.escalantecircledmotel.com; 475 W Main St; r $65-75; ❈🛜❈) It's just an updated, older motel, but the friendly proprietor goes out of his way to accommodate guests. Room microwaves and minifridges are standard.

✗ Eating

Esca-Latte Cafe & Pizza PIZZERIA $-$$
(310 W Main St; breakfast $3-6, pizza $10-18; ⊙8am-9pm Mar-Oct; 🛜) For granola and quiche at breakfast, and tasty homemade pizza and beer for lunch and dinner, visit Escalante Outfitters' eatery.

Cowboy Blues AMERICAN $$
(530 W Main St; sandwiches & mains $9-20; ⊙11am-10pm) Family-friendly meals here include BBQ ribs, steaks and daily specials like burritos or meatloaf. Plus this is the only place in town with a full bar.

Circle D Eatery AMERICAN $$
(475 W Main St; breakfast & sandwiches $5-9, mains $9-16; ⊙7am-9:30pm, limited hours Nov-Feb) Smoked meats, pastas, burgers and hearty breakfasts.

Griffin Grocery MARKET $
(30 W Main St; ⊙8am-7pm Mon-Sat) The only grocery in town.

❶ Information

There's no town visitor center; check out www.escalante-cc.com. The nearest hospital is 65 miles west in Panguitch.
Escalante Interagency Office (☑435-826-5499; www.ut.blm.gov/monument; 775 W Main St; ⊙7am-5:30pm mid-Mar–mid-Nov, 8am-4:30pm mid-Nov–mid-Mar) The source for information about area public lands; jointly operated by the BLM, the USFS and NPS.

Grand Staircase-Escalante National Monument

Nearly twice the size of Rhode Island, the 1.9-million-acre Grand Staircase-Escalante National Monument (GSENM) is the largest park in the Southwest and has some of the least visited yet most spectacular scenery. Its name refers to the 150-mile-long geological strata that begins at the bottom of the Grand Canyon and rises, in stair steps, 3500ft to Bryce Canyon and Escalante River Canyon. Together the layers of rock reveal 260 million years of history in a riot of colors. Sections of the GSENM have so much red rock that the reflected light casts a pink hue onto the bottom of clouds above.

Established amid some local controversy by President Bill Clinton in 1996, the monument is unique in that it allows some uses that would be banned in a national park (such as hunting and grazing, by permit), but allows fewer uses than other public lands to maintain its 'remote frontier' quality. Tourist infrastructure is minimal and limited to towns on the park's edges. Hwy 12 skirts the northern boundaries between Boulder, Escalante and Tropic. Hwy 89 arcs east of Kanab into the monument's southwestern reaches.

The park encompasses three major geological areas. The Grand Staircase is in the westernmost region, south of Bryce Canyon and west of Cottonwood Canyon Rd. The Kaiparowits Plateau runs north-south in the center of the monument, east of Cottonwood Canyon Rd and west of Smoky Mountain Rd. Canyons of the Escalante lie at the easternmost sections, east of Hole-in-the-Rock Rd and south of the Burr Trail, adjacent to Glen Canyon National Recreational Area.

◉ Sights & Activities

The BLM puts out handy one-page summaries of the most-used day trails. GSENM is also filled with hard-core backcountry treks. Ask rangers about Coyote Gulch, off Hole-in-the-Rock Rd; Escalante River Canyon; Boulder Mail Trail; and the Gulch, off the Burr Trail. Falcon Guide's *Hiking Grand Staircase-Escalante* is the most thorough park-hiking handbook, but we like the more opinionated *Hiking From Here to Wow: Utah Canyon Country* – it has great details and snazzy color pics, too. The waterproof Trails Illustrated/National Geographic map *No 710 Canyons of the Escalante* is good, but to hike the backcountry you'll need

READ ALL ABOUT IT

The otherworldly beauty of Utah has moved many to words almost as eloquent as the nature itself.

Edward Abbey (1927-89) Abbey became intimate with Arches National Monument when he worked there in the 1950s as a seasonal ranger, pre-national park. Environmentalist? Anarchist? It's hard to pin Abbey down. Many of his essay collections are set (in part) in Utah. Start with *Desert Solitaire: A Season in the Wilderness*.

Everett Ruess (1914-34) Artist, poet, writer and adventurer, Everett Ruess set out on his burro into the desert near the Escalante River Canyon at 20 years old, never to be seen again. He left behind scores of letters that paint a vivid portrait of life in canyon country before humans and machines. Pick up a copy of *Everett Ruess: A Vagabond for Beauty*, which includes his letters and an afterword by Edward Abbey.

Craig Childs (1967-) You'll never see a slot canyon in the same light again after reading the heart-thumping account of flash floods in *Secret Knowledge of Water*, a travelogue that follows naturalist Childs' Utah desert hikes. His *House of Rain* explores ancient ruins in the Four Corners area.

Terry Tempest Williams (1955-) Born and raised in Utah, Tempest Williams has been both poet and political advocate for the wilderness she loves. In addition to *Red*, an essay collection focused on southeastern Utah, check out *Refuge*, a lyrical elegy for her mother and the Great Salt Lake.

Wallace Stegner (1909-93) A graduate of the University of Utah, Stegner became one of the classic writers of the American West. *Mormon Country* provides an evocative account of the land the Mormons settled and their history; *Big Rock Candy Mountain* is historical fiction that follows a couple's prosperity-seeking moves to Utah.

Tony Hillerman (1925-2008) Many of Hillerman's whodunits take place on Navajo tribal lands similar to those in Utah and New Mexico around Monument Valley. Landscape and lore are always woven into his mysteries.

USGS 7.5-minute quadrangle maps. Pick these up at any visitor center.

Heading off-trail requires significant route-finding skills; GPS proficiency isn't enough. Know how to use a compass and a topographical map, or risk getting lost. Always check with rangers about weather and road conditions before driving or hiking. After heavy rain or snow roads may be impassable, even with a 4WD. Slot canyons and washes are flash-flood prone. If it starts to rain while you're driving, *stop*. Storms pass and roads dry quickly, sometimes even within 30 minutes. Never park in a wash. Carry a gallon of water per person, wear a hat and sunscreen, and carry food, maps and a compass. Help in case of an emergency will be hard to find. Avoid walking on biological soil crusts (p531), the chunky black soil that looks like burnt hamburger meat; it fixes nitrogen into the ground, changing sand to soil.

There are no entrance fees for the 24-hour-accessible GSENM.

Devils Garden   HIKING

(Mile 12, Hole-in-the-Rock Rd; ⚫) Easy hikes are scarce in the monument – the closest thing is a foray into Devils Garden, where rock fists, orbs, spires and fingers rise 40ft above the desert floor. A short walk from the car leads to giant sandstone swirls and slabs. From there you have to either walk in the sand or over, among and under the sandstone – like in a giant natural playground.

Lower Calf Creek Falls Trail   HIKING

(Mile 75, Hwy 12; admission $2) The most popular and accessible hike lies halfway between Torrey and Boulder. This sandy, 6-mile round-trip track skirts a year-round running creek through a spectacular canyon before arriving at a 126ft waterfall – a joy on a hot day. Pick up the interpretive brochure to help spot ancient granary ruins and pioneer relics.

Escalante Natural Bridge Trail   HIKING

(15 miles east of Escalante, Hwy 12) Be ready to get your feet wet. You'll crisscross a stream seven times before reaching a 130ft-high,

100ft-long natural bridge and arch beyond (4.4 miles round-trip).

Upper Calf Creek Falls Trail HIKING
(btwn Mile 81 & 82, Hwy 12) A short (2.2 miles round-trip) but steep and strenuous trail leads down slickrock, through a desert moonscape, to two sets of pools and waterfalls that appear like a mirage at hike's end.

Dry Fork Slot Canyons HIKING
(Mile 26, Hole-in-the-Rock Rd) A remote but popular Hole-in-the-Rock Rd hike leads to four different slot canyons, complete with serpentine walls, incredible narrows and bouldering obstacles. **Dry Fork** is often overlooked as not tight or physically challenging enough, but it's our favorite. You can walk for miles between undulating orange walls, with only a few small boulder step-ups. To get into dramatic **Peekaboo**, you have to climb up a 12ft handhold-carved wall (much easier if you're tall or not alone). Even narrower **Spooky Gulch** may be too small for some hikers. The farthest, **Brimstone Gulch**, is also the least interesting. Ask rangers for directions and always return the way you came. Climbing up and out of slots, then jumping down the other side, may trap you below the smooth face you've descended.

Cottonwood Canyon Rd SCENIC DRIVE
(off Hwys 12 & 89) This 46-mile scenic backway heads east, then south, from Kodachrome Basin State Park, emerging at Hwy 89 near Paria Canyon-Vermilion Cliffs Wilderness Area. It's the closest entry into GSENM from Bryce and an easy though sometimes rough drive, passable for 2WD vehicles (RVs not recommended). Twenty miles south of Hwy 12 you'll reach **Grosvenor Arch**, a yellow-limestone double arch, with picnic tables and restrooms.

The road continues south along the west side of the **Cockscomb**, a long, narrow monocline in the Earth's crust. The Cockscomb divides the Grand Staircase from Kaiparowits Plateau to the east; there are superb views. The most scenic stretch lies between Grosvenor Arch and **Lower Hackberry Canyon**, good for hiking. The road then follows the desolate Paria River valley toward Hwy 89.

Hole-in-the-Rock Rd SCENIC DRIVE
(off Hwy 12) From 1879 to 1880, more than 200 pioneering Mormons followed this route on their way to settle southeastern Utah. When the precipitous walls of Glen Canyon on the Colorado River blocked their path, they blasted and hammered through the cliff, creating a hole wide enough to lower their 80 wagons through – a feat that is honored by the road's name today. The final part of their trail lies submerged beneath Lake Powell. History buffs should pick up Stewart Aitchison's *Hole-in-the-Rock Trail* for a detailed account.

The history is often wilder than the scenery along much of this 57-mile, dusty washboard of a road, but it does have several sights and trailheads. The road is passable to ordinary passenger cars when dry, except for the last, extremely rugged 7 miles, which always require 4WD. The road stops short of the actual **Hole-in-the-Rock**, but hikers can trek out and scramble

---

WORTH A TRIP

BURR TRAIL RD

The region's most immediately gratifying, dramatic backcountry drive is a comprehensive introduction to southern Utah's geology. You pass cliffs, canyons, buttes, mesas and monoliths – in colors from sandy white to deep coral red. Sweeping curves and steep up-and-downs add to the attraction. Just past the **Deer Creek trailhead** look for the towering vertical red-rock slabs of **Long Canyon**. Stop at the crest for views of the sheer **Circle Cliffs**, which hang like curtains above the undulating valley floor. Still snowcapped in summer, the **Henry Mountains** rise above 11,000ft on the horizon.

After 30 paved miles (1½ hours), the road becomes loose gravel as it reaches Capitol Reef National Park and the giant, angled buttes of hundred-mile-long **Waterpocket Fold**. The dramatic **Burr Trail Switchbacks** follow an original wagon route through this monocline. Be sure to see the switchbacks before returning to Boulder. Another option is to turn onto Notom-Bullfrog Rd and continue north to Hwy 24 (32 miles) near Torrey, or south to Glen Canyon and Lake Powell (35 miles). Note that this part of the route is rough, and not generally suited to 2WD.

down past the 'hole' to **Lake Powell** in less than an hour. Sorry, no elevators for the climb back up.

Skutumpah & Johnson
Canyon Rds   SCENIC DRIVE

The most westerly route through the monument, the unpaved Skutumpah Rd (*scoot-em-paw*) heads southwest from Cottonwood Canyon Rd near Kodachrome Basin State Park. First views are of the southern end of Bryce Canyon's **Pink Cliffs**. A great little slot-canyon hike, accessible to young and old, is 6.5 miles south of the turnoff at **Willis Creek**. After 35 miles (two hours), Skutumpah Rd intersects with the 16-mile paved Johnson Canyon Rd, and passes the **White Cliffs** and **Vermilion Cliffs** areas en route to Hwy 89 and Kanab. Four-wheel drive is recommended; ask GSENM rangers about conditions

☞ Tours & Outfitters

Outfitters and guide services that operate in GSENM are based in Boulder, Escalante, Torrey and Kanab.

🛏 Sleeping & Eating

Most sleeping and eating is done in Escalante, Boulder or Kanab. The GSENM website (www.ut.blm.gov/monument) lists suggested areas for free dispersed camping. Pick up the required permit at a visitor center. Remember: water sources must be treated or boiled, campfires are permitted only in certain areas (use a stove instead), and biting insects are a problem in spring and early summer. Watch for scorpions and rattlesnakes.

There are two developed campgrounds in the northern part of the monument:

Calf Creek Campground   CAMPGROUND $
(www.ut.blm.gov; Hwy 12; tent & RV sites $7) Beside a year-round creek, Calf Creek Campground is surrounded by red-rock canyons (hot in summer) and has 14 incredibly popular, nonreserveable sites and drinking water available; no hookups. The campground is near the trailhead to Lower Calf Creek Falls, 15 miles east of Escalante.

Deer Creek Campground   CAMPGROUND $
(Map p424; www.ut.blm.gov; Burr Trail Rd; tent & RV sites $5; ☺mid-May–mid-Sep) This campground, 6 miles southeast of Boulder, has few sites and no water, but sits beside a year-round creek beneath tall trees.

ℹ Information

Food, gas, lodging and other services are available in Boulder, Escalante, Torrey and Kanab.

Big Water Visitor Center (☏435-675-3200; 100 Upper Revolution Way, Big Water; ☺9am-6pm Apr-Oct, 8am-5pm Nov-Mar) Near Lake Powell.

Cannonville Visitor Center (☏435-826-5640; 10 Center St, Cannonville; ☺8am-4:30pm Apr-Oct) Five miles east of Tropic.

Escalante Interagency Office (☏435-826-5499; 775 W Main St, Escalante; ☺7am-5:30pm mid-Mar–mid-Nov, 8am-4:30pm mid-Nov–mid-Mar)

Grand Staircase-Escalante National Monument (☏435-826-5499; www.ut.blm.gov /monument; PO Box 225, Escalante, UT 84726) For advance information.

Grand Staircase-Escalante Partners (http:// gsenm.org) Volunteer opportunities.

Kanab Visitor Center (☏435-644-4680; 745 E Hwy 89, Kanab; ☺7:30am-5:30pm) Southwestern section; park headquarters.

ℹ Getting Around

There is no public transportation in the park. High-clearance 4WD vehicles allow you the most access, since many roads are unpaved and only occasionally bladed. (Most off-the-lot SUVs and light trucks are *not* high-clearance vehicles.) Heed all warnings about road conditions. Remember to buy gasoline whenever you see it.

Some outfitters in towns around the park have hiker shuttles or 4WD rentals. However, if you plan to do a lot of backroad exploring and are arriving via Las Vegas, it may be cheaper overall to rent from there.

Kodachrome Basin State Park

Petrified geysers and dozens of red, pink and white sandstone chimneys – some nearly 170ft tall – resemble everything from a sphinx to a snowmobile at **Kodachrome Basin** (☏435-679-8562; www.stateparks.utah.gov; per vehicle $6; ☺day use 6am-10pm) The park lies off Hwy 12, 9 miles south of Cannonville and 26 miles southeast of Bryce Canyon National Park. Visit in the morning or afternoon, when shadows play on the red rock. Most sights are along hiking and mountain-biking trails. The moderately easy, 3-mile round-trip **Panorama Trail** gives the best overview. Be sure to take the side trails to **Indian Cave**, where you can check out the handprints on the wall (cowboys' or

Indians'?), and **Secret Passage**, a short hike through a narrow slot canyon. **Angel Palace Trail** (1-mile loop, moderate) has great desert views from on high.

Red Canyon Trail Rides (☑435-834-5441, 800-892-7923; www.redcanyontrailrides.com; 1-hr ride $30; ☉Mar-Nov), based near Bryce, offers horseback rides here in the state park.

The 26 well-spaced sites at the reservable park service **campground** (☑800-322-3770; http://utahstateparks.reserveamerica.com; tent/RV sites with hookups $16/20) get some shade from juniper trees. Big showers, too.

The four **Red Stone Cabins** (☑435-679-8536; www.redstonecabins.com; Kodachrome Basin State Park; cabin $90; ☉Mar-Nov, by prearrangement Dec-Feb; ❄️❄️) are simple, but cozy, with all the essentials (linens, microwave, mini-fridge and coffee maker) and either a king bed or two queens. The same family runs a little **camp store** (☉8am-6:30pm Sun-Thu, to 8pm Fri & Sat Apr-Oct).

Bryce Canyon National Park & Around

The sorbet-colored, sandcastle-like spires and hoodoos of Bryce Canyon look like something straight out of Dr Seuss' imagination. Though the smallest of southern Utah's national parks, this is perhaps the most immediately visually stunning, particularly at sunrise and sunset when an orange wash sets the otherworldly rock formations ablaze. Steep trails descend from the rim into the 1000ft amphitheaters of pastel daggers, then continue through a maze of fragrant juniper and undulating high-mountain desert. The location, 77 miles east of Zion and 39 miles west of Escalante, helps make this a must-stop on any southern Utah park itinerary.

Shaped somewhat like a seahorse, the narrow, 56-mile-long park is an extension of the sloping Paunsaugunt Plateau which rises from 7894ft at the visitor center to 9115ft at Rainbow Point, the plateau's southernmost tip. The high altitude means cooler temperatures here than at other Utah parks (80°F, or 27°C, average in July). Crowds arrive in force from May to September, clogging the park's main road (shuttle optional). For solitude, explore trails on the canyon floor. Weather-wise, June and September are ideal; in July and August be prepared for thunderstorms and mosquitoes. In winter, snow blankets the park, but the snowcaps on formations

are stunning. Most roads are plowed; others are designated for cross-country skiing and snowshoeing.

You can't enter the park without passing through the townlike sleep-shop-eat-outfit complex, Ruby's Inn, immediately north. The motel has been part of the landscape since 1919 when it was located at the canyon's rim. After the area was declared a national monument in 1923, owner Rueben Syrett moved his business north to his ranch, its current location. In 2007 the 2300-acre resort was officially incorporated as Bryce Canyon City.

◉ Sights & Activities

Park admission is $25 per week, per car. The NPS newspaper, *Hoodoo*, lists hikes, activities and ranger-led programs. The views from the overlooks are amazing, but the best thing about Bryce is that you can also experience the weirdly eroding hoodoos up close. Descents and ascents can be long and steep, and the altitude makes them extra strenuous. Take your time; most trails skirt exposed drop-offs.

Additional activities, including mountain-biking trails, are available nearby in Red Canyon, 13 miles west, and Kodachrome Basin State Park, 22 miles east, on Hwy 12.

Rim Road Scenic Drive   SCENIC DRIVE
(Map p436) The lookout views along along the park's 18-mile-long main road are amazing; navigate using the park brochure you receive at the entrance. **Bryce Amphitheater** – where hoodoos stand like melting sandcastles in shades of coral, magenta, ocher and white, set against a deep-green pine forest – stretches from **Sunrise Point** to **Bryce Point**. For full effect, be sure to walk all the way out to the end of any of the viewpoints; a shaft of sunlight suddenly breaking through clouds as you watch can transform the scene from grand to breathtaking.

Note that the scenic overlooks lie on the road's east side. You can avoid left turns on the very busy road by driving all the way south to **Rainbow Point**, then turning around and working your way back, stopping at the pullouts on your right. From late May to early September a free bus shuttle goes as far as Bryce Amphitheater, the most congested area. You can hop off and back on at viewpoints. The free Rainbow Point bus tour hits the highlights daily at 9am and 1pm; inquire at the visitor center.

Bryce Canyon National Park

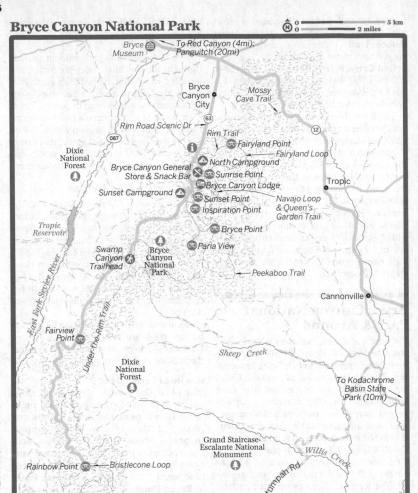

Rim Trail

HIKING

(Map p436) The easiest hike, this 0.5- to 5.5-mile-long (one-way) trail outlines Bryce Amphitheater from Fairyland Point to Bryce Point. Several sections are paved and wheelchair accessible, the most level being the half mile between Sunrise and Sunset Points. In the summer, you could easily take the shuttle to any one point and return from another instead of backtracking to a car.

Navajo Loop

HIKING

(Map p436) Many moderate trails descend below the rim, but this is one of the most popular. The 1.4-mile trail descends 521ft from Sunset Point and passes through the famous narrow canyon **Wall Street**. Combine part of the Navajo with the **Queen's Garden Trail** for an easier ascent. Once you hike the 320ft to Sunrise Point, follow the Rim Trail back to your car (2.9-mile round-trip).

Fairyland Loop

HIKING

(Map p436) With a trailhead at Fairyland Point north of the visitor center, the 8-mile round-trip makes for a good half-day hike (four to five hours). The tall hoodoos and bridges unfold best if you go in a clockwise direction. On the trail there's a 700ft elevation change, plus many additional ups and downs.

Bristlecone Loop
HIKING

(Map p436) The 1-mile Bristlecone Loop, at road's end near Rainbow Point, is an easy walk past 1600-year-old bristlecone pines, with 100-mile vistas.

Mossy Cave Trail
HIKING

(Map p436) Outside main park boundaries (east of the entrance), off Hwy 12 at Mile 17, take the easy half-mile one-way walk to the year-round waterfall off Mossy Cave Trail, a summertime treat and frozen winter spectacle.

Peekaboo Trail
HIKING

(Map p436) The fairly level 7-mile-long Peekaboo Trail, which leaves from Bryce Point, allows dogs and horses. Not recommended in high summer – it doesn't always smell the best.

Ranger-Led Activities
HIKING

During summer and early fall, rangers lead canyon-rim walks, hoodoo hikes, geology lectures, campfire programs and kids' ecology walks. If you're here when skies are clear and the moon's full, don't miss the two-hour Moonlight Hike among the hoodoos. Register same-day at the **visitor center** (Map p436), but do so early.

Backcountry Hikes
HIKING

Only 1% of all visitors venture onto the backcountry hikes. You won't walk among many hoodoo formations here, but you will pass through forest and meadows with distant views of rock formations. And oh, the quiet. The 23-mile **Under-the-Rim Trail**, south of Bryce Amphitheater, can be broken into several athletic day hikes. The 11-mile stretch between Bryce Point and **Swamp Canyon** is one of the hardest and best. Get backcountry permits ($5 to $15) and trail info from rangers at the visitor center.

Bryce Museum
MUSEUM

(Map p436; www.brycewildlifeadventure.com; 1945 W Hwy 12; admission $8; ⊙9am-7pm Apr-Oct) Visit this barnlike natural history museum – with more than 400 taxidermied animals, butterflies, and Native American artifacts – then feed the feral deer and other animals in the yards surrounding. West of the park.

☞ Tours & Outfitters

Canyon Trail Rides
HORSEBACK RIDING

(☑435-679-8665; www.canyonrides.com; Bryce Canyon Lodge) The national park's only licensed outfitter operates out of the park lodge. You can take a short, two-hour trip to the canyon floor ($50) or giddy-up for a half day ($75) through the dramatic hoodoos on Peekaboo Trail.

Ruby's Inn
ADVENTURE SPORTS

(☑435-834-5341, 866-866-6616; www.rubysinn .com; 1000 S Hwy 63) Just outside the park, Ruby's offers guided horseback rides (half-day $75), ATV tours (three hours $100) and mountain-bike rental (half-day $35) – not to mention the rodeo performances, helicopter rides and snowmobiling. Inquire at the inn.

Red Canyon Trail Rides
HORSEBACK RIDING

(☑435-834-5441, 800-892-7923; www.redcanyon trailrides.com; Bryce Canyon Pines, Hwy 12; half-day $65; ⊙Mar-Nov) Ride for as little as a half hour or as long as a whole day on private and public lands outside the park, including Red Canyon.

Bryce Wildlife Adventures
ADVENTURE SPORTS

(☑435-834-5555; www.brycewildlifeadventure .com; Bryce Museum, 1945 W Hwy 12; ⊙9am-7pm Apr-Oct) ATV (from $105 for three hours) and mountain-bike ($12.50 per hour) rentals, near public land trails outside the park.

Mecham Outfitters
HORSEBACK RIDING

(☑435-679-8823; www.mechamoutfitters.com; half-day $75) Based in Tropic, leads half- and full day rides in nearby Dixie National Forest and on GSENM lands.

Cycling

Several companies lead four- to six-day, Bryce to Zion road cycling tours:

Rim Tours
CYCLING

(☑435-259-5223, 800-626-7335; www.rimtours .com)

Western Spirit Cyclery
CYCLING

(☑435-259-8732, 800-845-2453; www.western spirit.com)

Backroads Bicycle Adventures
CYCLING

(☑800-462-2848; www.backroads.com)

✸ Festivals & Events

The park doesn't host any events, but Ruby's Inn does.

SCENIC DRIVES: SOUTHERN UTAH

People come from around the world to drive in southern Utah, and Hwy 12 (p426) and Burr Trail (p433) may be the biggest draws. But from paved desert highways for RV-cruisers to rugged backcountry trails for Jeepsters, there are drives for every taste.

Comb Wash Rd (near Bluff) Straddling Comb Ridge, Comb Wash Rd (or CR 235) is a dirt track that runs for about 20 miles between Hwys 163 and 95 (parallel to Hwy 191) west of Blanding and Bluff. Views are fantastic (bring binoculars) and the ridge contains numerous ancient cliff dwellings. High-clearance 4WD vehicles recommended; in wet weather, this road is impassable.

Colorado River Byway (near Moab) Hwy 128 follows the river northeast to Cisco, 44 miles away just off I-70. Highlights are Castle Rock, the 900ft-tall Fisher Towers, the 1916 Dewey Bridge (one of the first across the Colorado) and sightings of white-water rafters.

La Sal Mountain Loop Rd (near Moab) This road heads south into the Manti–La Sal forest from 15 miles north of Moab, ascending switchbacks (long RVs not recommended) into the refreshingly cool forest, with fantastic views. Connects with Hwy 191, 8 miles south of Moab. The 67-mile (three to four hour) paved loop closes in winter.

Loop-the-Fold (near Torrey) This 100-mile loop links several top drives; roughly half is on dirt roads generally accessible to 2WD passenger vehicles. Pick up a driving guide ($2) at the Capitol Reef National Park visitor center. West of the park, there are the rocky valleys of Hwy 12. It only gets better after turning east along Burr Trail Rd to Strike Valley Overlook. Then take the rough Notom-Bullfrog Rd north to finish the loop at Hwy 24.

Caineville Wash Rd (near Torrey) Just west of Capitol Reef National Park, turn north off Hwy 24 to the otherworldly monoliths like Temple of the Sun and Temple of the Moon on Caineville Wash Rd. Continue on into the northern part of the park and Glass Mountain, a 20ft mound of fused selenite. Two-wheel drive is usually fine for the first 15.5 miles. With a 4WD you can make this a 58-mile Cathedral Valley loop along Hartnet Rd, which fords the Fremont River just before rejoining Hwy 24.

Hell's Backbone Rd (near Boulder) The gravel-strewn 48 miles from Hwy 12 along Hell's Backbone Rd to Torrey is far from a shortcut. You'll twist, you'll turn, you'll ascend and descend hills, but the highlight is a single-lane bridge atop an impossibly narrow ridge called Hell's Backbone.

Hwy 14 (near Cedar City) This paved scenic route leads 42 miles over the Markagunt Plateau, ending in Long Valley Junction at Hwy 89. The road rises to 10,000ft, with splendid views of Zion National Park to the south. Make sure you detour at Cedar Breaks National Monument.

Bryce Canyon Winterfest　　SPORTS
In early February; includes everything from cross-country skiing and snowmobiling to archery and snow sculpting.

Bryce Canyon Rim Run　　SPORTS
Held in August, the run follows a 6-mile course partially along the Bryce Canyon rim outside the park.

🛏 Sleeping

The park has one lodge and two campgrounds. Most travelers stay just north of the park in Bryce Canyon City, near the Hwy 12/63 junction or 11 miles east in Tropic. Other lodgings are available along Hwy 12,

and 24 miles west in Panguitch. Red Canyon and Kodachrome Basin State Park also have campgrounds.

INSIDE THE PARK

Trailers are allowed only as far as Sunset Campground, 3 miles south of the entrance. Backcountry camping permits ($5) are available at the visitor center.

Bryce Canyon Lodge　　LODGE $$-$$$
(Map p436; ✆435-834-8700, 877-386-4383; www.brycecanyonforever.com; Hwy 63; r & cabins $130-175; ⊗Apr-Oct; ⊛) Built in the 1920s, the main lodge exudes rustic mountain charm, with a large stone fireplace and

exposed roof timbers. Most rooms are in two-story wooden satellite buildings with private balconies. A variety of older and newer cabins all have inherent charm, with creaky porches and woodsy settings. Be warned: the walls prove thin if the neighbors decide to get noisy. Furnishings are decidedly dated througout. No TVs.

North Campground
CAMPGROUND $
(Map p436; ☏877-444-6777; www.recreation.gov; Bryce Canyon Rd; tent & RV sites $15) The 100-plus NPS campground near the visitor center has a camp store, laundry, showers, flush toilets and water. Loop C is the closest to the rim (sites 59 and 60 have great views, but little privacy). Reservations are accepted early May through late September. No hookups.

Sunset Campground
CAMPGROUND $
(Map p436; ☏877-444-6777; www.recreation.gov; Bryce Canyon Rd; tent & RV sites $15; ☉Apr-Sep) Though more wooded than North Campground, Sunset has few amenities beyond flush toilets and water available. (For laundry, showers and groceries, visit North.) Twenty of the tent sites are reservable early May to late August.

OUTSIDE THE PARK
A full list of area motels is available at www.brycecanyoncountry.com.

Best Western Ruby's Inn
MOTEL $-$$$
(☏435-834-5341, 866-866-6616; www.rubysinn.com; 1000 S Hwy 63; r $135-180; ❊@☏≋) Watch a rodeo, admire Western art, buy cowboy souvenirs, wash laundry, seriously grocery shop, fill up with gas, log on to the internet, dine at restaurants and then post a letter about it all. At Ruby's complex you can even buy bottles of wine and spirits – maybe the rarest service of all. The main inn motel rooms are thoroughly up-to-date. Subsidiary **Bryce View Lodge** (☏435-834-5180, 888-279-2304; www.bryceviewlodge.com; r $70-110; ☉Apr-Oct) has smaller, less spiffy rooms, geared toward budget travelers. **Best Western Plus Bryce Grand Canyon Lodge** (☏435-834-5700, 866-866-6634; www.brycecanyongrand.com; r $135-199; ☉Apr-Oct; ❊@☏≋) is the newest of the options, with cushy rooms, lodgey decor and additional guest-only amenities, such as a private pool, laundry and fitness center.

Stone Canyon Inn
INN $$-$$$
(☏435-679-8611, 866-489-4680; www.stonecanyoninn.com; 1220 Stone Canyon Lane, Tropic; r incl

breakfast $135-190, cabins $330; ❊☏) Backed by natural hills and technicolor sunsets adjoining backcountry parklands, this stately stone and-wood inn offers adventure out the back door. New cabins are spacious and luxuriously private, though they're trumped by the charm of the main house rooms, with hot breakfasts with homemade pastries and breads included.

Bryce Country Cabins
BUNGALOW $-$$
(☏435-679-8643, 888-679-8643; www.brycecountrycabins.com; 320 N Main St, Tropic; cabins $75-195; ☉Feb-Oct; ❊☏) Knotty-pine walls and log beds add lots of charm to the roomy one- and two-bedroom cabins here; some with kitchens, some with microwaves and minifridges. Though the cabins line the main street, rear-facing swings have great views of farm fields and far-off cliffs.

Bullberry Inn
B&B $$
(☏435-679-8820, 800-249-8126; www.bullberryinn.com; 412 S Hwy 12, Tropic; r incl breakfast $95-125) Built in 1998 this purpose-built, farmhouse-style B&B at the far edge of town has spacious, spotless rooms. The welcoming owners make the bullberry jam served with home-baked goodies at the full country breakfast.

Bryce Canyon Resort
MOTEL $$
(☏435-834-5351, 800-834-0043; www.brycecanyonresort.com; cnr Hwys 12 & 63; r $99-189, cabins $159-210; ❊☏≋≋) Four miles from the park, this is the less-chaotic alternative to Ruby's Inn. Deluxe rooms include newer furnishings and extra amenities; cabins and cottages have kitchenettes and sleep up to six. Outfitter packages and smoking rooms available.

Bryce Canyon Pines
MOTEL $-$$
(☏435-834-5441, 800-892-7923; www.brycecanyonmotel.com; Hwy 12; tent/RV sites $20/30, r & cottages $75-130; ☉Apr-Nov; ≋) This old, rambling white clapboard motel has been in the same family for ages. Cottages have the most character; dated standard rooms have simple beds with simple spreads. There's is a homey restaurant, horseback riding and basic campground on site, 8 miles northwest of the park entrance.

Ruby's RV Park & Campground
CAMPGROUND $
(☏435-834-5301, 866-866-6616; www.rubysinn.com; 1000 S Hwy 63; tent sites $24, tipis $34-46, RV sites with partial/full hookups $35/42, cabins

$55-59; ⊙Apr-Oct; 🛜🏊) The 200 sites, camping cabins (no linens) and tipis (bring your own sleeping bag and cot) adjacent to all those services at Ruby's Inn are in a fairly forestlike, if commercial, setting.

Buffalo Sage B&B
B&B **$-$$**

(📞435-679-8443, 866-232-5711; www.buffalosage.com; 980 N Hwy 12, Tropic; r incl breakfast $80-110; ❄🛜) Up on a bluff west of town, three exterior-access rooms lead out to an expansive, upper-level deck or ground-level patio with great views. The owner's background in art is evident in the decor. Do note that the communal living area is shared by cats and dog.

🍴 Eating & Entertainment

Nobody comes to Bryce for the cuisine. Expect so-so Western fare, such as grilled pork chops and chicken-fried steaks. If you're vegetarian, BYOV or subsist on salad and fries.

INSIDE THE PARK
Bryce Canyon Lodge
MODERN AMERICAN **$$$**

(Map p436; 📞435-834-5361; Bryce Canyon Rd; breakfast & sandwiches $8-15, dinner $26-42; ⊙7am-10pm Apr-Oct) By far the best, and priciest, place to eat. Meats are perfectly grilled and sauces caringly prepared. Though upscale, the rustic, white tablecloth-clad dining room is more family-friendly than romantically refined – or quiet, even.

Bryce Canyon General Store & Snack Bar
MARKET **$**

(Map p436; Bryce Canyon Rd, nr Sunrise Point; dishes $3-7; ⊙noon-10pm) Sells basic supplies, sandwiches and pizza in season.

OUTSIDE THE PARK
Most of the area motels have so-so eateries on site.

Pizza Place
PIZZERIA **$$**

(21 N Main St, Tropic; pizzas & sandwiches $5-18; ⊙noon-9pm Apr-Oct, 5-8:30pm Thu-Sat Nov-Mar) Think wood-fired flatbread piled high with fresh ingredients. When locals eat out, they come to this family-owned joint. Serves pizzas, salads and sandwiches.

Ebenezer's Bar & Grill
DINNER SHOW **$$$**

(📞800-468-8660; www.rubysinn.com; 1000 S Hwy 63; dinner show $26-32; ⊙7pm nightly mid-May–Sep) Kitschy but good-natured fun, an evening at Ebenezer's includes live country-and-western music served up beside a big BBQ dinner: steak, pulled pork, chicken or salmon. It's probably the best meal served at the Ruby's complex and is wildly popular, so book ahead.

Bryce Canyon Pines
AMERICAN **$-$$**

(📞435-834-5441; Bryce Canyon Pines, Hwy 12; breakfast & lunch $5-12, dinner $10-19; ⊙6:30am-9:30pm Apr-Nov) A classic, rural Utah, meat-and-potatoes kind of place. Homemade pies baked here are so good, they're also served in Tropic.

Clarke's Restaurant
AMERICAN **$$**

(121 N Main St, Tropic; breakfast & lunch $4-15, dinner $12-22; ⊙7:30am-9pm Mon-Sat, variably shortened hours Nov-Mar; 🛜) Beer and wine are available at this full-service, three-meal-a-day option.

Clarke's Grocery
MARKET **$**

(121 N Main St, Tropic; sandwiches $4-6; ⊙7:30am-7pm Mon-Sat) Tropic's only grocery store has a deli sandwich counter and homemade baked goods.

ℹ Information

Some services are just north of the park boundaries on Hwy 63. The nearest town is Tropic, 11 miles northeast on Hwy 12; the nearest hospital is 25 miles northwest in Panguitch.

Bryce Canyon National Park Visitor Center (📞435-834-5322; www.nps.gov/brca; Hwy 63; ⊙8am-8pm May-Sep, to 6pm Oct & Apr, to 4:30pm Nov-Mar) Get information on weather, trails, ranger-led activities and campsite availability; the introductory film is worth seeing. Good selection of maps and books.

Bryce Canyon Natural History Association (📞435-834-4600; www.brycecanyon.org) Pre-trip online book shopping.

Garfield County Travel Council (📞435-676-1160, 800-444-6689; www.brycecanyoncountry.com) There's no town visitor center, so plan ahead online or by phone.

Ruby's Inn (www.rubysinn.com; 1000 S Hwy 63) Post office, grocery store, showers ($6), free wi-fi and computer terminals ($1 for five minutes).

ℹ Getting Around

A private vehicle is the only way around from fall through spring. If you're traveling in summer, ride the voluntary **shuttle** (ride free; ⊙9am-6pm late May-Sep), lest you find yourself stuck without a parking spot. (Note: the park's visitor center parking lot fills up, too.) Leave your car at the Ruby's Inn or Ruby's Campground stops, and ride the bus into the park. The shuttle goes as far as Bryce Point; buses come roughly every

15 minutes, 8am to 8pm. A round-trip without exiting takes 50 minutes. Tune in to 1610AM as you approach Bryce to learn about current shuttle operations. The *Hoodoo* newspaper shows routes.

No trailers are permitted south of Sunset Point. If you're towing, leave your load at your campsite or in the trailer turnaround lot at the visitor center.

Red Canyon

Impressive, deep-ocher-red monoliths rise up roadside as you drive along Hwy 12, 10 miles west of the Hwy 63-Bryce Canyon turnoff. The aptly named **Red Canyon** (www .fs.fed.us/dxnf; Dixie National Forest) provides super-easy access to these eerie, intensely colored formations. In fact, you have to cross under two blasted-rock arches to continue on the highway. A network of trails leads hikers, bikers and horseback riders deeper into these national-forest-service lands.

Check out the excellent geologic displays and pick up trail maps at the **visitor center** (435-676-2676; Hwy 12; 9am-6pm Jun-Aug, 10am-4pm May & Sep). Several moderately easy hiking trails begin near the center: the 0.7-mile **Arches Trail** passes 15 arches as it winds through a canyon; the 1-mile **Pink Ledges Trail** winds through red rock formations. For a harder hike, try the 2.8-mile, two- to four-hour **Golden Wall Trail**. Legend has it that outlaw Butch Cassidy once rode here; a tough 8.9-mile hiking route, **Cassidy Trail**, bears his name.

There are also excellent mountain-biking trails in the area; the best is 7.8-mile **Thunder Mountain Trail**, which cuts through pine forest and red rock. Outfitters near Bryce Canyon National Park rent mountain bikes and offer horseback rides through Red Canyon.

Surrounded by limestone formations and ponderosa pines, the 37 no-reservation sites at **Red Canyon Campground** (www.fs.fed .us/dxnf; tent & RV sites $15; mid-May–Sep) are quite scenic. Quiet-use trails (no ATVs) lead off from here, making this a good alternative to Bryce Canyon National Park camping. There are showers and a dump station, but no hookups.

If you prefer a roof over your head, continue west. The rooms and log cabins at family-run **Harold's Place** (435-676-2350; www.haroldsplace.net; Hwy 12; r $55-70, cabins $65-75; Mar-Oct;), just before the intersection of Hwys 12 and 89, are cozy and

spotless. Locals recommend the above-average **restaurant** (breakfast $5-10, dinner $12-20; 7-11am & 5-10pm Mar-Nov) for favorites like balsamic chicken and pecan-crusted trout. More food and lodging choices are available in nearby Panguitch and Hatch.

Panguitch

Founded in 1864, historically Panguitch was a profitable pioneer ranching and lumber community. Since the 1920s inception of the national park, the town has had a can't-live-with-or-without-it relationship with Bryce Canyon, 24 miles east. Lodging long ago became the number-one industry, as it's also used as an overnight stop halfway between Las Vegas (234 miles) and Salt Lake City (245 miles). Other than some interesting turn-of-the-20th-century brick homes and buildings, there aren't a lot of attractions in town. The small downtown main street has an antique store or two, but mostly people fill up with food and fuel, rest up, and then move on. In a pinch you could use it as a base for seeing Bryce, Zion and Cedar Breaks.

Panguitch is the seat of Garfield County and hosts numerous festivals. Two of the best are in June: the **Quilt Walk Festival** celebrates pioneer history and **Chariots in the Sky** is a huge hot-air balloon festival.

🛏 Sleeping

Red Brick Inn B&B $$
(435-676-2141, 866-732-2745; www.redbrickinn utah.com; 11161 N 100 West; r incl breakfast $99-199; May-Oct;) One of the town's beloved red-bricks, this 1920s Dutch colonial was once the town's hospital. Be sure to ask warm and welcoming proprietor Peggy to share some of its history. Comfy room styles here vary from country gingham and Victorian frill to a fun, faux-lakefront cabin room. Beverage center and outdoor hot tub on site.

Crum Cottage B&B $
(435-676-2574; www.crumcottage.com; 259 E Center St; r incl breakfast $85;) Nicely simple new B&B rooms in this renovated red-brick home are an excellent alternative to a motel. The price is more than right; friendly hosts provide a big breakfast and advice on area adventures.

Grandma's Cottage RENTAL $$
(435-690-9495; www.aperfectplacetostay.net; 90 N 100 West; rentals $85-145; Mar-Nov;) A renovated studio, cottage and home in

central Panguitch now serve as vacation rentals; great for families.

Marianna Inn Motel
MOTEL $-$$
(435-676-8844, 800-598-9190; www.marianna inn.com; r $75-105; ✴✦✧✴) Rooms in the dollhouse-like, pink-and-lavender motel with the large shaded swing deck are standard. But the newest additions – deluxe log-style rooms – are worth splurging on. BBQ grill available for guests.

Hitch-N-Post
CAMPGROUND $
(435-676-2436; www.hitchnpostrv.com; 420 N Main St; tent/RV sites with hookups $15/25; ✦✴) Small lawns and trees divide RV spaces; tent sites are in a grassy field, but still have barbecue grills. RV wash and heavy-duty laundry on site.

Canyon Lodge
MOTEL $
(435-676-8292, 800-440-8292; www.colorcountry .net/~cache; 210 N Main St; r $59-69; ✴✦) Thoroughly clean, older 10-room motel, with classic neon sign and helpful hosts. Hot tub on site.

Color Country Motel
MOTEL $
(435-676-2386, 800-225-6518; www.colorcountry motel.com; 526 N Main St; r $50-80; ✴) An economical, standard motel with perks – a pool and outdoor hot tub. Smoking rooms available.

✖ Eating & Drinking

Remember that eateries in Hatch, and Harold's Place in Red Canyon, are also close by.

Cowboy's Smokehouse BBQ
BARBECUE $$
(95 N Main St; breakfast & lunch $5-12, dinner $15-28; ✧7am-9pm Mar-Oct) The best barbecue in Garfield County draws 'em in from all over, including Bryce. Good steaks, too. The old main street storefront is a perfect setting for live country music some summer weekends.

Henrie's Drive-in
BURGERS $
(154 N Main St; burgers $3-6; ✧11am-9pm Mar-Oct) Craving a deliciously greasy burger and fries? Look no further. (Don't forget the milkshake.)

Joe's Main Street Market
MARKET $
(10 S Main St) The town's main grocery store.

ℹ Information

Garfield County Travel Council (435-676-1102, 800-444-6689; www.brycecanyon country.com) Town and county information.

Garfield Memorial Hospital (435-676-8811; 224 N 400 East; ✧24hr)

Powell Ranger Station (435-676-9300; www.fs.fed.us/dxnf; 225 E Center St; ✧8am-4:30pm Mon-Fri) Dixie National Forest camping and hiking info.

Hwy 89 – Panguitch To Kanab

Most people pass through this stretch of Hwy 89 as quickly as possible en route from Zion to Bryce national parks. All the better for you – the tiny old towns along the way have a few restaurant and lodging gems hidden within. (Note that businesses' seasonal closings change with weather and whim.) Remember when reading distances that you'll average between 35mph and 50mph along these roads.

Independent motels and a few eateries line Hwy 89 in **Hatch**, 25 miles southwest of Bryce Canyon and 15 miles south of Panguitch. **Café Adobe** (16 N Main St, Hatch; mains $7-15; ✧10:30am-7pm Mar–mid-Nov) has long been the residents' fave for gourmet hamburgers, creative sandwiches and tasty Mexican food. And 'locals' here live in Panguitch or Tropic. Don't pass up the homemade tortilla chips and chunky salsa.

A locally-retired Las Vegas developer and his family have single-handedly breathed new life into sleepy Hatch with several seasonal lodgings and eateries. **Galaxy Diner** (177 S Main St; mains $5-10; ✧6:30am-2pm mid-Mar–late Oct) is a pseudo-typical 1950s diner and ice cream parlor, next to a Harley Davidson shop. **Hatch Station Dining Car** (177 S Main St; mains $15-23; ✧5-9:30pm mid-Mar–late Oct) serves the best prime rib around, in fun, knickknacky surrounds. Next door, there's a convenience store and bargain rooms at **Hatch Station Motel** (177 S Main St; r $48-56; ✧mid-Mar–late Oct; ✴). Even better are the **Hatch Has Cabin Fever** (177 S Main St; cabins $65; ✧mid-Mar–late Oct; ✴) king and double-queen log cabins with lots of room, microwaves, little refrigerators and coffee makers.

If you're looking for more of an escape, turn off the highway and head toward **Cottonwood Meadow Lodge** (435-676-8950; www.panguitchanglers.com; Mile 123, Hwy 89; cabins & houses $205-360; ✦) on the Sevier River. The restored pioneer farmhouse has three bedrooms; 1860s log-and-mortar cabins evoke rustic romanticism; and upscale

Western decor makes it hard to imagine that the one-bedroom building was ever a barn. Fly-fish on the property in the day, then hang out by the fire pit at night.

Further south, 50 miles from Bryce and 26 miles to Zion, **Glendale** is a historic little Mormon town founded in 1871. Today it's an access point for Grand Staircase-Escalante National Monument (p431). From Hwy 89, turn onto 300 North at the faded sign for GSENM; from there it turns into Glendale Bench Rd, which leads to scenic **Johnson Canyon** and **Skutumpah Rds**.

The seven-room **Historic Smith Hotel** (435-648-2156, 800-528-3558; www.historic smithhotel.com; 295 N Main St, Glendale; r incl breakfast $47-84;) is more comfortable than a favorite old sweater. Don't let the small rooms turn you off. The proprietors are a great help in planning your day and the big breakfast tables are a perfect place to meet other intrepid travelers from around the globe. Great back decks and garden, too. Next door, **Buffalo Bistro** (305 N Main St; burgers & mains $8-24; 4-9:30pm Thu-Sun mid-Mar–mid-Oct) conjures a laid-back Western spirit with a breezy porch, sizzling grill and eclectic menu. Try buffalo steaks, wild boar ribs, rabbit and rattlesnake sausages – or pasta. The gregarious owner chef has a great sense of humor; he sometimes hosts music and events, and sometimes closes early.

In Mt Carmel, the **Thunderbird Foundation for the Arts** (435-648-2653, www.thunder birdfoundation.com; Mile 84, Hwy 89, Mt Carmel) runs exhibits and artist retreats in adjacent spaces. The beautiful **Maynard Dixon Home & Studio** (self-guided tour $10; 10am-5pm May-Oct) is where renowned Western painter Maynard Dixon (1875-1946) lived and worked in the 1930s and '40s. Look, too, for a couple other galleries, arts-and-crafts and rock shops along the way.

At the turnoff for Hwy 9, Mt Carmel Junction has two gas stations (one with a sandwich counter) and a couple of decent sleeping options about 15 slow-and-scenic miles from the east entrance of Zion and 18 miles north of Kanab. The Navajo lookout on the outside of the **Best Western East Zion Thunderbird Lodge** (435-648-2203, 800-780-7234; www.bestwesternutah.com; cnr Hwys 9 & 89, Mt Carmel Junction; r $85-109;) is just a facade; the rooms within are standard Best Western.

The quilt-covered four-poster beds sure are comfy at **Arrowhead Country Inn &**

Cabins (435-648-2569, 888-821-1670; www .arrowheadbb.com; 2155 S State St, Mt Carmel Junction; r $79-129, cabins $129-269, both incl breakfast;). The east fork of the Virgin River meanders behind the inn and a trail leads from here to the base of the white cliffs.

Kanab

Vast expanses of rugged desert extend in each direction from the remote outpost of Kanab. Don't be surprised if it all looks familiar: hundreds of Western movies were shot here. Founded by Mormon pioneers in 1874, John Wayne and other gun-slingin' celebs really put Kanab on the map in the 1940s and '50s. Just about every resident had something to do with the movies from the 1930s up until the '70s. You can still see a couple of movie sets in the area and hear old-timers talk about their roles. In August, the **Western Legends Roundup** celebrates 'Utah's little Hollywood'.

Kanab sits at a major crossroads: GSENM is 20 miles, Zion 40 miles, Bryce Canyon 80 miles, Grand Canyon's North Rim 81 miles and Lake Powell 74 miles. It makes a good base for exploring the southern side of GSENM and Paria Canyon-Vermilion Cliffs Wilderness formations such as the Wave. Coral Pink Sand Dunes State Park is a big rompin' playground to the northwest.

Note that local opening hours are often altered by mood and demand, especially off season.

Sights

Though the town itself isn't the main attraction, there are false-front facades and store names such as Denny's Wig Wam, so just looking around can be kitschy fun. The visitor center has an exhibit of area-made movie posters and knowledge about sites.

Best Friends Animal Sanctuary RESCUE CENTER (435-644-2001; www.bestfriends.org; Angel Canyon, Hwy 89; admission free; 9:30am-5:30pm;) Kanab's most famous attraction is outside of town. Surrounded by more than 33,000 mostly private acres of red-rock desert 5.5 miles north of Kanab, Best Friends is the largest no-kill animal rescue center in the country. The center shows films and gives facility tours four times a day; call ahead for times and reservations.

The 1½-hour tours let you meet some of the more than 1700 horses, pigs, dogs, cats, birds and other critters on site. Volunteers come from around the country to work here. Spending the night in one of eight one-bedroom cottages with kitchenettes ($140) or in a one-room cabin ($92) and volunteering for at least a half-day allows visitors to borrow a dog, cat or pot-bellied pig for the night.

The sanctuary is located in Angel Canyon (Kanab Canyon to locals) where scores of movies and TV shows were filmed during Kanab's Hollywood heyday. The cliff ridge about the sanctuary is where the Lone Ranger reared up and shouted 'Hi-yo Silver!' at the end of every episode.

FREE Frontier Movie Town & Trading Post
FILM LOCATION

(297 W Center St; ⊙7:30am-11pm Apr-Oct, 10am-5pm Nov-Mar) Wander through a bunkhouse, saloon and other buildings used in Western movies filmed locally, including *The Outlaw Josey Wales*, and brush up on such tricks of the trade as short doorways (to make movie stars seem taller). This classic roadside attraction sells all the Western duds and doodads you could care to round up. Lists of movies shot here, and some of the DVDs of the films themselves, are available.

FREE Parry Lodge
HISTORIC SITE

(www.parrylodge.com; 89 E Center St; ⊙8pm Sat Jun-Aug) Parry Lodge became movie central when it was built in the 1930s. Stars stayed here and owner Whit Parry provided horses, cattle and catering for the sets. There are nostalgic photos on lobby and dining room walls, and on summer Saturday nights the hotel shows the old Westerns in a barn out back.

Johnson Canyon
DRIVING TOUR

Heading into GSENM, the paved scenic drive into Johnson Canyon is popular. More movies were filmed here, and 6 miles along you can see in the distance the Western set where the long-time TV classic *Bonanza* was filmed (on private land). Turn north off Hwy 89, 9 miles east of Kanab.

Paria movie set
DRIVING TOUR

The Paria movie set (pa-*ree*-uh), where many Westerns were filmed, was burnt down during the 2007 Western Legends Roundup. A 5-mile dirt road leads to a picnic area and an interpretive sign that shows what the set looked like. A mile further north, on the other side of the river, it's a hike to look for the little that's left of **Pahreah ghost town**. Floods in the 1880s rang the death knell for the 130-strong farming community. Since then, time and fire have taken the buildings and all but the most rudimentary signs of settlement. But the valley is a pretty introduction to GSENM. The signed turnoff for Paria Valley is 33 miles from Kanab on Hwy 89.

Moqui Cave
MUSEUM

(www.moquicave.com; adult/child $4/2; ⊙9am-7pm Mon-Sat Mar-Nov) Another interesting tourist trap, Moqui Cave, 5 miles north of town, is an oddball collection of genuine dinosaur tracks, real cowboy and Indian artifacts, and other flotsam and jetsam that the football-star father of the owner collected in the 1950s – all inside a giant cave.

👉 Tours & Outfitters

Half-day outfitter tours start at $120.

Paria Outpost
ADVENTURE TOUR

(☎928-691-1047; www.paria.com) Friendly, flexible and knowledgeable; 4WD tours and guided hikes through the rocks and sand of GSENM and Paria Canyon-Vermillion Cliffs.

Lit'l Bit Ranch
HORSEBACK RIDING

(☎435-899-9655; http://litlbitranch.org; 2550 E Hwy 89) Horseback rides (from $60 for two hours) and horse boarding by arrangement; lodging available also.

Windows of the West Hummer Tours
ADVENTURE TOUR

(☎888-687-3006; www.wowhummertours.com) Personalizable backcountry excursions (two hours to full-day) to slot canyons, petroglyphs and spectacular red-rock country.

Terry's Camera
PHOTO TOUR

(☎435-644-5981; www.utahcameras.com) Customized area photo tours and workshops.

🎆 Festivals & Events

Western Legends Roundup
FILM

(☎800-733-5263; www.westernlegendsroundup.com) The town lives for the annual Western Legends Roundup in late August. There are concerts, gunfights, cowboy poetry, dances, quilt shows, a film festival and more. Take a bus tour to all the film sites, or sign up for a Dutch-oven cooking lesson.

🛏 Sleeping

Kanab has a proliferation of old, indie budget motels and some house rentals. For a full list, see www.kaneutah.com.

TOP CHOICE **Quail Park Lodge** MOTEL $$
(☑435-215-1447; www.quailparklodge.com; 125 N 300 W; r $100-130; ❋@❋❋❋) Schwinn Cruiser bicycles stand near vibrant beach balls bobbing in the postage-stamp-size pool and yellow clamshell chairs wait outside surprisingly plush rooms. A colorful retro style pervades all 13 rooms at the refurbished 1963 motel. Mod cons include free phone calls, microwaves, minifridges and complimentary gourmet coffee.

Purple Sage Inn B&B $$
(☑435-644-5377, 877-644-5377; www.purplesage inn.com; r incl breakfast $120-150; ❋❋) From a cabinet-encased, fold-down bathtub to brass push-button light switches, the antique details are exquisite. In the 1880s this was a Mormon polygamist's home, then in the 1900s it became a hotel where Western author Zane Grey stayed. As a B&B, Zane's namesake room – with its quilt-covered wood bed, sitting room and balcony access – is our favorite.

Parry Lodge MOTEL $-$$
(☑435-644-2601, 888-289-1722; www.parrylodge .com; 89 E Center St; r 70-125; ❋❋❋❋❋) The aura of Western movie-days gone by is more special than many of the rooms at the town's classic, rambling old motel. Some bear the names of movie stars who stayed here, like Gregory Peck or Lana Turner. If quality is your concern, opt for the L-shaped double queens, nicely refurbished in cottage decor.

Bob Bon Inn Motel MOTEL $
(☑435-644-3069, 800-644-5094; www.bobbon .com; 236 N 300 West; r $40-60, ❋❋❋❋) The small-but-spotless 16 log-cabin rooms here are a great deal. Owner Bonnie Riding knows a lot about local movies; every inch of every reception room wall is covered with old Western stars' autographed photos.

Victorian Charm Inn HOTEL $$
(☑435-644-8660, 800-738-9643; www.kanab victoriainn.com; 190 N 300 West; r incl hot breakfast $119-130; ❋❋❋) From the architecture to appointments, the inn is a modern-day interpretation of period Victoriana. Ethan Allen furnishings, gas fireplaces and jetted tubs grace every room.

Holiday Inn Express HOTEL $$
(☑435-644-3100, 800-315-2621; www.hiexpress /kanabut.com; 217 S 100 E; r/ste $129/149; ❋@ ❋❋❋) Newest and nicest chain property.

Treasure Trail Motel MOTEL $
(☑435-577-2645, 800-603-2687; www.treasure trailmotel.net; 150 W Center St; r $66-85; ❋❋ ❋❋) Friendly little independent motel; microwaves and mini-refrigerator standard.

Hitch'n Post Campground CAMPGROUND $
(☑435-644-2142, 800-458-3516; www.hitchnpost rvpark.com; 196 E 300 South; tent/RV sites with hookups $16/27, camping cabins $28-32; ❋❋) Friendly 17-site campground near the town center; laundry and showers.

✖ Eating & Drinking

Numerous themed restaurants, ice cream parlors and such line Center St.

Rocking V Café MODERN AMERICAN $$
(97 W Center St; mains $12-25; ⊙5-10pm; ☑) Fresh ingredients star in dishes like hand-cut buffalo tenderloin and chargrilled zucchini with curried quinoa. Local artwork decorating the 1892 brick storefront is as creative as the food.

Houston's Trail's End Restaurant AMERICAN $$
(☑435-644-2488; 32 E Center St; breakfast $5-10, mains $7-21; ⊙7am-10pm) The food must be good if locals frequent a place where the waitresses wear cowboy boots and play six-shooters. Order up chicken-fried steak and gravy for down-home goodness. No alcohol.

Calvin T's Smoking Gun BARBECUE $$
(78 E Center St; mains $12-24; ⊙11:30am-10pm; ❋) Excellent barbecue, including pulled pork and slabs of ribs, served cafeteria style. In the back courtyard there's a kitschy replica of an Old West movie backdrop, with a pioneer wagon, a saloon and a jail to play on.

Jakey Leighs CAFE $
(4 E Center St; sandwiches $4-8; ⊙7am-10pm Tue-Sat, to 3pm Sun & Mon; ❋) Come here for tasty quiche and OK coffee on the pleasant patio, or grab a sandwich for the road.

Laid Back Larry's HEALTH FOOD $
(98 S 100 East; ⊙7:30am-3pm, off-season hours vary; ☑) Pick up fresh smoothies, egg sandwiches on spelt English muffin or healthy lunch specials at this tiny stop. A few health-food and vegetarian goodies are for sale, too.

Luo's CHINESE $$
(365 S 100 E; mains $10-18; ⊙11am-10pm) For a change. Surprisingly good Chinese food; great vegetable selection.

Honey's Marketplace
MARKET $

(260 E 300 S; ⊘7am-10pm) Full grocery store with deli; look for the 1950s truck inside.

☆ Entertainment

Crescent Moon Theater
THEATER

(☑435-644-2350; www.crescentmoontheater.com; 150 S 100 East; ⊘May-Sep) Cowboy poetry, bluegrass music and comedic plays are just some of what is staged here. Monday is $2 Western movie night.

🔒 Shopping

Western clothing and bric-a-brac are sold, along with Native American knickknacks, at shops all along Center St.

Willow Canyon
Outdoor Co
OUTDOOR EQUIPMENT

(263 S 100 East; ⊘7:30am-8pm, off-season hours vary) It's easy to spend hours sipping espresso and perusing the eclectic books here. Before you leave, outfit yourself with field guides, camping gear, USGS maps and hiking clothes.

ℹ️ Information

As the biggest town around the GSENM, Kanab has several grocery stores, ATMs, banks and services.

BLM Kanab Field Office (☑435-644-4600; 318 N 100 East; ⊘8am-4pm Mon-Fri) Provides information and, November 16 through March 14, issues permits for hiking the Wave in Paria Canyon-Vermilion Cliffs Wilderness Area.

GSENM Visitor Center (☑435-644-4680; www.ut.blm.gov/monument; 745 E Hwy 89; ⊘7:30am-5:30pm) Provides road, trail and weather updates for the Monument.

Kane County Hospital (☑435-644-5811; 355 N Main St; ⊘24hr)

Kane County Office of Tourism (☑435-644-5033, 800-733-5263; www.kaneutah.com; 78 S 100 East; ⊘9am-7pm Mon-Fri, to 5pm Sat) The main source for area information; great old Western movie posters and artifacts on display.

Local police (☑435-644-5807; 140 E 100 South)

Visit Kanab (www.visitkanab.com)

ℹ️ Getting There & Around

There is no public transportation to or around Kanab.

Xpress Rent-a-Car (☑435-644-3408; www.xpressrentalcarofkanab.com; 1530 S Alt 89) Car and 4WD rental.

Around Kanab

CORAL PINK SAND DUNES STATE PARK

Coral-colored sand is not especially strange in the southern half of GSENM, but seeing it gathered as giant dunes in a 3700-acre **state park** (☑435-648-2800; Sand Dunes Rd; day-use $6; ⊘day-use dawn-dusk, visitor center 9am-9pm Mar-Oct, to 4pm Nov-Feb) is quite novel. The pinkish hue results from the eroding red Navajo sandstone in the area. Note that 1200 acres of the park are devoted to off-highway vehicles, so it's not necessarily a peaceful experience unless you're here during quiet hours (10pm to 9am), though a 0.5-mile interpretive dune-hike does lead to a 265-acre, ATV-free conservation area.

The same winds that shift the dunes can make tent camping unpleasant at the 22-site **campground** (☑800-322-3770; http://utahstateparks.reserveamerica.com; tent & RV sites $16), with toilets and hot showers; no hookups. Reservations are essential on weekends when off-roaders come to play.

PARIA CANYON-VERMILION CLIFFS WILDERNESS AREA

With miles of weathered, swirling slickrock and slot-canyon systems that can be hiked for days without seeing a soul, it's no wonder that this wilderness area is such a popular destination for hearty trekkers, canyoneers and photographers. Day-hike permits cost $5 to $7 and several are very tough to get. General information and reservations are available at www.blm.gov/az/st/en/arolrsmain/paria/coyote_buttes.html. In-season info and permits are picked up at **Paria Contact Station** (www.blm.gov/az; Mile 21, Hwy 89; ⊘8:30am-4pm Mar 15-Nov 15), 44 miles east of Kanab. Rangers at the BLM Kanab Field Office are in charge of permits from November 16 through March 14. Remember that summer is scorching; spring and fall are best – and busiest. Beware of flash floods.

Day hikers fight like dogs to get a **North Coyote Buttes** permit. This trail-less expanse of slickrock includes one of the Southwest's most famous formations – the **Wave**. The nearly magical sight of the slickrock that appears to be seething and swirling in waves is well worth the 6-mile, four- to five-hour round-trip hike. Go online to request advance permits four months ahead. Otherwise you can hope for one of the handful of next-day walk-in permits available. Line up for the lottery by 7am in spring and fall.

As an alternative, take the 3.4-mile round-trip hike starting at **Wire Pass** trailhead, a popular slot-canyon day-hike with self-service trailhead permits. The pass dead-ends where Buckskin Gulch narrows into some thrillingly slight slots. Another option is to start at the Buckskin Gulch trailhead and hike 0 miles one-way to its narrow section.

All trailheads listed lie along House Rock Valley Rd (4.7 miles west of the contact station); it's a dirt road that may require 4WD. Inquire with rangers.

Two miles south of the contact station along a different dirt road, you come to primitive **White House Campground** (tent sites $5). The five walk-in sites have pit toilets, but no water and few trees. Overnight backcountry camping permits are easier to get than day-hike ones, and can be reserved online and in person. Use of human-waste carryout bags is encouraged; the contact station provides them for free.

Paria Outpost & Outfitters (928-691-1047; www.paria.com; Mile 21, Hwy 89; r incl breakfast $65, tent/RV sites $16/20;) has spare B&B rooms at its kicked-back lodge and campground (no hookups) between Kanab and the wilderness area. Outfitter trips and hiker shuttles available.

East Zion

Eighteen miles north of Kanab, the turnoff for Hwy 89 leads about 15 miles to the east entrance of Zion National Park.

Families love activity-rich **Zion Ponderosa Ranch Resort** (435-648-2700, 800-293-5444; www.zionponderosa.com; N Fork Rd, off Hwy 9; tent & RV sites with hookups $10/47, cabins without bath/deluxe ste $65/159;), occupying 4000 acres on Zion's eastern, up-country side. Several great backcountry trails lead from 4WD roads here into the national park. But you may never leave the property since you can hike, bike, canyoneer, climb, swim, play sports, ride four-wheelers and horses, and eat three meals a day here (packages available). Wi-fi-enabled camping sites and cabins (linens included), served by huge showers/bathrooms, are real bargains. The fancier cabin suites are the only lodgings with air-con, but it's less essential up here above 6000ft. North Fork Rd is about 2.5 miles from the park's East Entrance; continue 5 miles north of Hwy 9 from there.

Closer to the highway, **Zion Mountain Resort** (435-688-1039, 866-648-2555; http://zionmountainresort.com; Hwy 9; cabins $159-199, ste $225-300;) has a similar adventure and lodging set-up, though it's a bit fancier. Buffalo roam (and appear on the dinner menu) at this 6000-acre resort. In season it runs a restaurant, pizza place and primitive campground (sites $10) too. Registration is 2.5 miles east of the Zion park entrance.

Zion National Park

The soaring red-and-white cliffs of Zion Canyon, one of southern Utah's most dramatic natural wonders, rise high over the Virgin River. Hiking downriver through the Narrows or peering beyond Angels Landing after a 1400ft ascent is indeed amazing. But, for all its awe-inspiring majesty, the park also holds more delicate beauties: weeping rocks, tiny grottoes, hanging gardens and meadows of mesa-top wildflowers. Lush vegetation and low elevation give the magnificent rock formations here a whole different feel from the barren parks in the east.

Most of the 2.7 million annual visitors enter the park along Zion Canyon floor; even

Zion National Park

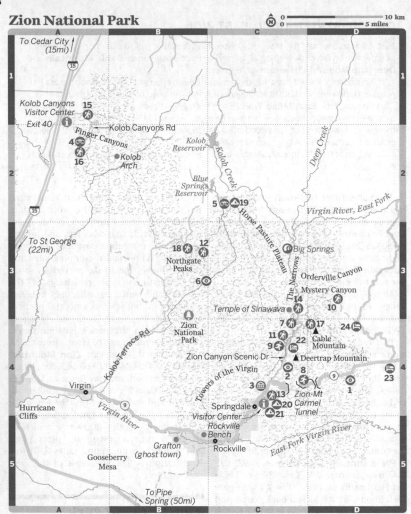

the most challenging hikes become congested May through September (shuttle required). But you have other options. Up-country, on the mesa tops (7000ft), it's easy to escape the crowds – and the heat. And the Kolob Canyons section, 40 miles northwest by car, sees one-tenth of the visitors year-round.

Summers are hot (100°F, or 38°C, is common); summer nighttime temperatures drop into the 70s (low 20s in Celsius). Beware of sudden cloudbursts from July to September. Winter brings some snow, but daytime temperatures can reach up to 50°F

(10°C). Wildflowers bloom in May, as do the bugs; bring repellant.

Fees & Permits

Park admission is $25 per week, per vehicle, and an annual Zion Pass is $50. Note that you have to pay to drive through the park on Hwy 9, whether you plan to stop or not. Keep your receipt, it's good for both the main and Kolob Canyons sections.

Backcountry permits (☎435-772-0170; www.nps.gov) are required for all overnight trips (including camping and rock climbs with bivouacs), all through-hikes of the

Zion National Park

Virgin River (including the Narrows top hike) and any canyoneering hikes requiring ropes for descent. Use limits are in effect on some routes to protect the environment Online permit reservations ($5 reservation fee) are available for many trips, up until 5pm the preceding day. For busy routes there may be a lottery. Twenty-five percent of available permits remain reserved for walk-in visitors the day before or day of a trip. Trying to get a next-day walk-in permit on a busy weekend is like trying to get tickets to a rock concert; lines form at the Backcountry Desk by 6am or earlier.

Permit fees (which are in addition to the reservation fee) are $10 for one to two hikers, $15 for three to seven hikers, and $20 for eight to twelve hikers.

⊙ Sights & Activities

The park occupies 147,000 acres. Driving in from east Zion, Hwy 9 undulates past yellow sandstone before getting to tighter turns and redder rock after the Zion-Mt Carmel Tunnel. Zion Canyon – with most of the trailheads and activities – lies on Hwy 9 near the south entrance, and the town of Springdale. No roads within the park directly connect this main section with the Kolob Canyons section in the northwest. Unless you hike, you'll have to drive the 40 miles (an hour) between the two, via Hwy 9, Rte 17 and I-15.

SCENIC DRIVES

Zion Canyon Scenic Dr
SCENIC DRIVE

The premier drive in the park leads between towering cliffs of an incredible red-rock canyon and accesses all the major front-country trailheads. A shuttle bus ride is required April through October. If you've time for only one activity: this is it. Your first stop should be the **Human History Museum** (☎435-772-0168; admission free; ⊙9am-7pm late May-early Sep, 10am-5pm early Mar-late May & early Sep-Nov, closed Dec-early Mar), the excellent exhibits and 22-minute film are a great introduction to the park. There are shuttle stops, and turn-outs, at viewpoints like the **Court of the Patriarchs**, at the **Zion Lodge**, and the end point, the **Temple of Sinawava**. Use the map you receive at the entrance to navigate. The shuttle takes 45 minutes round-trip; we'd suggest allowing at least two hours with stops.

Hwy 9
SCENIC DRIVE

East of the main park entrance, Hwy 9 rises in a series of six tight switchbacks before the 1.1-mile Zion-Mt Carmel Tunnel, an engineering marvel constructed in the late 1920s. It then leads quickly into dramatically different terrain – a landscape of etched multicolor slickrock, culminating at the mountainous **Checkerboard Mesa**.

Kolob Canyons Rd
SCENIC DRIVE

The less-visited, higher-elevation alternative to Zion Canyon Scenic Dr. Sweeping vistas of cliffs, mountains and finger canyons dominate the stunning 5-mile overlook-rich red-rock route. The scenic road, off I-15, lies 40 miles from the main visitor center.

HIKING

Distances for hikes listed below are one-way. Trails can be slippery; check weather conditions before you depart. Flash floods occur

UTAH ZION NATIONAL PARK

DON'T MISS

ANGELS LANDING TRAIL

Among harder trails, the 2.5-mile **Angels Landing Trail** (1490ft ascent) is the one everyone's heard of – and fears. At times the trail is no more than 5ft wide, with 1500ft drop-offs to the canyon floor on both sides. Follow the sandy flood plain until you start ascending sharply. After Walter's Wiggles, the set of 21 stonework zigzags that take you up a cleft in the rock, there's a wide area (with pit toilet) which offers vistas and a place to gather strength. Acrophobes may stop here, before the chain-assist rock climb and the 5ft-wide ridge – with 1000ft-plus drop-offs – that you have to cross. The final push to the top is even steeper, and requires some rock scrambling – but oh, the views from the top...

year-round, particularly in July and August. Check weather and water conditions with rangers before hiking in river canyons. If you hear thunder, if water rises suddenly or goes muddy, or if you feel sudden wind accompanied by a roar, immediately seek higher ground. Climbing a few feet can save your life; if you can't, get behind a rock fin. There's no outrunning a flash flood.

Zion Canyon   HIKING
Spring to fall, the mandatory shuttle stops at all major trailheads along Zion Canyon Scenic Dr, allowing one-way hikes. In low season you can park at these stops, but you'll have to hike back to your car.

Of the easy-to-moderate trails, the paved, mile-long **Riverside Walk** (1 mile) at the end of the road is a good place to start. When the trail ends, you can continue along in the Virgin River for 5 miles to **Big Springs**; this is the bottom portion of the **Narrows** – a difficult backpacking trip. Yes, you'll be hiking in the water (June through October), so be prepared.

A steep, but paved, half-mile trail leads to the lower of the **Emerald Pools**. Here water tumbles from above a steep overhang, creating a desert varnish that resembles rock art. It's worth your while to hike a mile further up the gravel to the more secluded Upper Pool. Note: you will have to scramble up (and back down) some stairlike rocks. The quarter-mile-long

Weeping Rock Trail climbs 100ft to hanging gardens.

Hidden Canyon Trail has sheer drop-offs and an 850ft elevation change in just over a mile before you reach the narrow, shady canyon. Think of it as an easier test of your fear of heights.

The most work (2150ft elevation change) is rewarded with the best views – at the top of **Observation Point Trail** (4 miles). From here you look down on Angels Landing – heck, the whole park really. A backcountry shortcut leads here with much less legwork – the East Mesa Trail, see p447.

The paved **Pa'rus Trail** parallels the scenic drive from Watchman Campground to the main park junction (about 2 miles). It's the only trail that allows bicycles and dogs.

The only marked trail along Hwy 9 in east Zion is **Canyon Overlook Trail**, a moderately easy half-mile walk, yielding thrilling views 1000ft down into Zion Canyon. But you can also stop at Hwy 9 pullouts where there are some interesting narrow canyon hikes and slickrock scrabbles. In summer, locals park at one turnout, climb down, cross under the road and follow a wash to the river for a cool dip...happy searching. Just be aware of your surroundings, and stay in the wash or on the rock to avoid damaging the desert ecology.

Kolob Terrace Road   HIKING
Fourteen miles west of Springdale, Kolob Terrace Rd takes off north from Hwy 9, weaving in and out of BLM and national park highlands. (The road is closed due to snow from at least November to March.) **Wildcat Canyon Trailhead** lies about 28 miles north, after a hairpin turn. From here, follow the Wildcat Canyon Trail till you get to the turnoff for **Northgate Peaks Trail**. You'll traipse through meadows, filled with wildflowers in spring, and pine forests before you descend to the viewpoint overlooking the peaks. It's a whole different – and much less visited – side of Zion. Wildcat Canyon to Northgate Peaks overlook is 2.2 miles one-way. About 5 miles north of Wildcat Canyon is the gravel road to **Lava Point**, where there's a lookout and a campground.

Kolob Canyons Road   HIKING
In the northwestern section of the park, the easiest trail is at the end of the road: **Timber Creek Trail** (0.5 miles) follows a 100ft ascent to a small peak with great views. The main hike is the 2.7-mile-long

Taylor Creek Trail, which passes pioneer ruins and crisscrosses the creek. The 7-mile one-way hike to **Kolob Arch** has a big payoff: this arch competes with Landscape Arch in Arches National Park in terms of being one of the biggest in the world. Fit hikers can manage it in a day, or continue on to make it a multiday backcountry trans-park connector.

Backcountry   HIKING
Zion has hundreds of miles of backcountry hiking trails, wilderness camping and enough quiet to hear the whoosh of soaring ravens overhead. The most famous route is the unforgettable **Narrows**, a 16-mile journey into skinny canyons along the Virgin River's north fork (June through October). Plan on getting wet: at least 50% of the hike is in the river. The trip takes 12 hours; split it into two days, spending the night at one of the designated campsites you reserved or finish the hike in time to catch the last park shuttle. The trail ends among the throngs of day hikers on Riverside Walk at the north end of Zion Canyon. A trailhead shuttle is necessary for this and other one-way trips.

Ask rangers about weather conditions and other trails. If you hike the entirety of Zion, north to south, it's a four day traverse of 50-plus miles. All backcountry hiking and camping requires a permit.

CYCLING
Zion Canyon Scenic Drive is a great road ride when cars are forbidden in shuttle season. You can even carry your bicycle up to the end of the road on the shuttle and cruise back down. Bikes are only allowed on the scenic drive and on the 2 mile Pa'rus Trail. Mountain biking is prohibited in the park, but there are other public land trails nearby. Rentals and advice are available in Springdale.

CLIMBING & CANYONEERING
If there's one sport that makes Zion special, it's canyoneering. Rappel over the lip of a sandstone bowl, swim icy pools, trace a slot canyon's curves – canyoneering is beautiful, dangerous and sublime all at once. Zion's slot canyons are the park's most sought-after backcountry experience; reserve far in advance.

Zion Canyon also has some of the most famous big-wall rock climbs in America. However, there's not much for beginners or those who like bolted routes. Permits are required for all canyoneering and climbing.

Get information at the Backcountry Desk at the Zion Canyon Visitor Center, which also has route descriptions written by climbers.

Guided trips are prohibited in the park. Outfitters in Springdale hold courses outside Zion, after which students can try out their newfound skills in the park.

Subway   CANYONEERING
This incredibly popular route (9.5 miles, 1850ft elevation change) has four or five rappels of 20ft or less, and the namesake tube-looking slickrock formation. Start at the Wildcat Canyon trailhead off Kolob Terrace Rd. Hiker shuttle required.

Mystery Canyon   CANYONEERING
Mystery Canyon lets you be a rock star: the last rappel drops into the Virgin River before admiring crowds hiking the Narrows. It's accessed off Zion Ponderosa Ranch roads in East Zion; ask rangers for more information. Backcountry permit required; hiker shuttle necessary.

Pine Creek Canyon   CANYONEERING
A popular route with moderate challenges and rappels of 50ft to 100ft, Pine Creek has easy access from near the Canyon Overlook Trail. A backcountry permit is required.

OTHER ACTIVITIES
Canyon Trail Rides   HORSEBACK RIDING
(Map p448; ☑435-679-8665, 435-772-3810; www .canyonrides.com; ☺Mar-Nov) Zion's official horseback-riding concessionaire operates across from Zion Lodge. Take a one-hour ($40) or three-hour ($75) ride on the Sand Bench Trail along the Virgin River.

☞ Tours & Outfitters
Cycling, rock-climbing, canyoneering and driving-tour outfitters from Springdale operate outside the park.

Zion Canyon Field Institute   TOUR
(☑435-772-3264, 800-635-3959; www.zionpark .org; half-day from $50) Explore Zion by moonlight, take a wildflower photography class, investigate Kolob Canyon's geology or help clean up the Narrows. All courses and tours include some hiking.

FREE Ride Along With A
Ranger   DRIVING TOUR
(☑435-772-3256; www.nps.gov/zion; Zion Canyon Visitor Center; ☺May Oct) Reservations are usually required for the entertaining 90-minute, ranger-led Zion Canyon shuttle

UTAH ZION NATIONAL PARK

tour that makes stops not on the regular route. It's a great non-hiking alternative for those with limited mobility.

Red Rock Shuttle & Tours   DRIVING TOUR
(☑435-635-9104; www.redrockshuttle.com) Private van tours of Zion, $100 per person for six hours.

🛏 Sleeping

Both of the park's large, established campgrounds are near the Zion Canyon Visitor Center. For wilderness camping at designated areas along the West Rim, La Verkin Creek, Hop Valley and the Narrows you'll need a permit (p448). More lodging and camping is available in Springdale.

Zion Lodge   LODGE **$$-$$$**
(Map p448; ☑435-772-7700, 888-297-2757; www .zionlodge.com; Zion Canyon Scenic Dr; r $150-170, cabins $165-180, ste $185; 🏵@🛜) Stunning red-rock cliffs surround you on all sides, and that coveted location in the middle of Zion Canyon (and the red permit that allows you to drive to the lodge in shuttle season) is what you're paying for. The lodge was first built in the 1920s, but it burnt down in 1966. The reconstructed lodge is not as grand as those in other states. Although they're in wooden buildings with balconies, the motel rooms are just motel rooms: nothing fancy. Carved headboards, wood floors and gas fireplaces do give 'Western cabins' more charm, but be warned that paper-thin walls separate you from neighbors. There are two eateries and a big lawn for lounging outside. No room TVs.

Watchman Campground   CAMPGROUND **$**
(Map p448; ☑435-772-3256, 877-444-6777 for reservations; www.recreation.gov; Hwy 9; tent sites $16, RV sites with hookups $18-20) Towering cottonwoods provide fairly good shade for the 165 well-spaced sites at Watchman (95 have electricity). Reservations are available May through October; book as far in advance as possible to request a riverside site. Fire grates, drinking water and flush toilets; no showers. Note that there is sometimes construction works happening during the winter season.

South Campground   CAMPGROUND **$**
(Map p448; ☑435-772-3256; Hwy 9; tent & RV sites $16; ⊘mid-Mar–Oct) The South Campground has very similar scenery and the same basic facilities as Watchman, except that here limited generator use is allowed because there are no hookups. The 116 first-come,

first-served tent sites often fill up by 10am. Note that this ground sits beside the busy Pa'rus Trail.

Lava Point Campground   CAMPGROUND **$**
(Map p448; Lava Point Rd; ⊘Jun-Sep) Six first-come, first-served park sites 35 miles up Kolob Terrace Rd at 7900ft. Pit toilets, no water.

🍴 Eating

The lodge has the only in-park dining; otherwise head to Springdale.

Red Rock Grill   AMERICAN **$$-$$$**
(Map p448; ☑435-772-7760; Zion Lodge, Zion Canyon Scenic Dr; breakfast $6-11, lunch sandwiches $7-12, dinner $16-28; ⊘6:30-10:30am, 11:30am-3pm & 5-10pm Mar-Oct, hours vary Nov-Feb) Settle into your log-replica chair and peer out of the window-lined dining room or relax on the big deck with magnificent canyon views. Though the dinner menu touts its sustainable-cuisine stance for dishes like roast pork loin and flatiron steak, the results are hit-or-miss. Dinner reservations recommended. Full bar.

Castle Dome Café   CAFE **$**
(Map p448; Zion Lodge, Zion Canyon Scenic Dr; mains $4-8; ⊘11am-5pm Apr-Oct) This counter-service cafe serves sandwiches, pizza, salads, soups, Asian-ish rice bowls and ice cream.

ℹ Information

Visitor center hours vary slightly month to month. We list the minimums for each season.

Kolob Canyons Visitor Center (☑435-586-0895; Kolob Canyons Rd, off I-15; ⊘8am-6pm May-Sep, 8am-4:30pm Oct-Apr) Small, secondary visitor center in the northwest section of the park.

Lonely Planet (www.lonelyplanet.com/usa /southwest/zion-national-park) Planning advice, author recommendations, traveler reviews and insider tips.

National Park Rangers Emergency (☑435-772-3322)

Zion Canyon Backcountry Desk (☑435-772-0170; www.nps.gov/zion/planyourvisit; Zion Canyon Visitor Center; ⊘7am-6pm May-Sep, 8am-4:30pm Oct-Apr) Provides backcountry trail and camping information and permits. Some permits available online.

Zion Canyon Visitor Center (☑435-772-3256; www.nps.gov/zion; ⊘8am-6pm May-Sep, 8am-4:30pm Oct-Apr) Several rangers are on hand to answer questions at the main visitor center; ask to see the picture binder of hikes to know what you're getting into. The large number of ranger-led activities are listed here.

Zion Lodge (☑435-772-3213; Zion Canyon Scenic Dr) Free wi-fi and two free internet terminals in the lobby.

Zion Natural History Association (☑435-772-3264, 800-635-3959; www.zionpark.org) Runs visitor center bookstores; great online book selection for advance planning.

Getting There & Around

Bus

There is no public transportation to the park.

St George Express (☑435-652-1100; www .stgeorgeexpress.com) Shared van service to St George ($75, one hour) and Las Vegas ($100, three hours).

Private Vehicle

Arriving from the east on Hwy 9, you have to pass through the free **Zion-Mt Carmel Tunnel**. If your RV or trailer is 7ft 10in wide or 11ft 4in high or larger, it must be escorted through, since vehicles this big need both lanes. Motorists requiring an escort pay $15 over the entrance fee, good for two trips. Between April and October, rangers are stationed at the tunnel from 8am to 8pm daily; at other times, ask at the entrance stations. Vehicles prohibited at all times include those more than 13ft 1in tall or more than 40ft long.

Park Shuttle

How you get around Zion depends on the season. Between April and October, passenger vehicles are not allowed on Zion Canyon Scenic Dr. The park operates two free, linked shuttle loops. The **Zion Park Shuttle** makes nine stops along the canyon, from the main visitor center to the Temple of Sinawava (a 45-minute round-trip). The **Springdale Shuttle** makes six regular stops and three flag stops along Hwy 9 between the park's south entrance and the Majestic View Lodge in Springdale, the hotel furthest from the park. You can ride the Springdale Shuttle to Zion Canyon Giant Screen Theatre and walk across a footbridge into the park. The visitor center and the first Zion shuttle stop lie on the other side of the kiosk.

The propane-burning park shuttle busses are wheelchair-accessible, can accommodate large backpacks and carry up to two bicycles or one baby stroller. Schedules change, but generally shuttles operate from at least 6:45am to 10pm, every 15 minutes on average.

HIKER SHUTTLE Outfitters that offer hiker shuttles (from $25 to $35 per person, two-person minimum, reservation required) to backcountry and canyoneering trailheads include:

Red Rock Shuttle & Tours (☑435-635-9104; www.redrockshuttle.com) Picks up from Zion Canyon Visitor Center.

Zion Adventure Company (☑435-772-1001; www.zionadventures.com)

Zion Rock & Mountain Guides (☑435-772-3303; www.zionrockguides.com)

Springdale

Positioned at the entrance to Zion National Park, Springdale is a perfect little resort town. Stunning red cliffs form the backdrop to eclectic cafes and restaurants big on local produce and organic ingredients. Galleries and shops line the long main drag, interspersed with indie motels and B&Bs. Many of the outdoorsy folk who live here moved from somewhere less beautiful, but you will occasionally run into a life-long local who thinks 'they're just rocks.'

◉ Sights & Activities

Hiking trails in Zion are the area's biggest attraction. There are also some awesome single-track, slickrock mountain-bike trails as good as Moab's. Ask local outfitters about **Gooseberry Mesa**, **Hurricane Cliffs** and **Rockville Bench**.

The Virgin River is swift, rocky and only about knee-deep: more of a bumpy adventure ride than a leisurely float, but tubing (outside the park only) is popular in the summer. Note that from June to August, the water warms to only 55°F to 65°F (13°C to 18°C). Zion Canyon Campground and some other riverside lodgings have good water-play access.

Zion Adventure Company WATER SPORTS (☑435-772-1001; www.zionadventures.com; 36 Lion Blvd; ⊙tubing 10am-4pm May-Sep) River-tubing packages include tube and water-sock rental, drop-off and pick-up. The float stretches about 2.5 miles, and lasts from 90 minutes to two hours depending on water flow. There's much faster, high-adventure tubing (including safety gear) on offer during spring run-off in May.

Deep Canyon Adventure Spa DAY SPA (☑435-772-3244; www.deepcanyonspa.com; Flanigan's Inn, 428 Zion Park Blvd; 1hr treatments from $89) After a hard day's hike, the river-stone massage will be your muscles' new best friend.

Zion Canyon Elk Ranch FARM (☑435-619-2424; 792 Zion Park Blvd; by donation; ⊙dawn to dusk; 🐾) You can't miss this ranch right in the middle of town. It offers kids of all ages the chance to pet and feed the elk and buffalo. The property has been in the owner's family for more than 100 years.

☞ Tours & Outfitters

The towns two main outfitters, Zion Rock & Mountain Guides and Zion Adventure Company, lead hiking, biking, climbing, rappelling and multisport trips on the every-bit-as-beautiful BLM lands near the park (half-days from $150). We highly recommend canyoneering as a quintessential area experience. Both outfitters are also one-stop shops for adventure needs: they sell ropes and maps, have classes, provide advice and suit you up with rental gear (harnesses, helmets, canyoneering shoes, dry suits, fleece layers, waterproof packs and more). The hiker shuttles and gear rental are especially handy for one-way slot-canyon routes and Narrows hikes. Both companies have excellent reputations and tons of experience around Zion.

Bike rentals range from $25 to $40 per half day.

Zion Rock & Mountain Guides
ADVENTURE SPORTS

(☎435-772-3303; www.zionrockguides.com; 1458 Zion Park Blvd; ⊗8am-8pm Mar-Oct, hours vary Nov-Feb) More down-to-business than other outfitters, and especially good for sporty types. All classes and trips are private. Static rope line rental available.

Bike Zion
MOUNTAIN BIKING

(☎435-772-0320; www.bikingzion.com; Zion Rock & Mountain Guides) Zion Rock's on-site sister cycle shop; does rentals and tours. Showers available.

Zion Adventure Company
ADVENTURE SPORTS

(☎435-772-1001; www.zionadventures.com; 36 Lion Blvd; ⊗8am-8pm Mar-Oct; 9am-noon & 4-7pm Nov-Feb) Slick videos and diagrams help put the tentative at ease; good for young families. Winter snowshoes and crampon rentals available.

Zion Cycles
MOUNTAIN BIKING

(☎435-772-0400; www.zioncycles.com; 868 Zion Park Blvd; ⊗9am-7pm Feb-Nov) Tandem, road and mountain-bike rentals and sales. No tours.

Red Desert Adventures
ADVENTURE SPORTS

(☎435-668 2888; www.reddesertadventures.com) A small company; provides private guided hiking, biking and canyoneering.

Zion Outback Safaris
ADVENTURE TOUR

(☎866-946-6494; www.zionjeeptours.com; 3hr adult/child $64/46) Backroad 4WD tours in a 12-seat modified truck.

✵ Festivals & Events

Springdale celebrates quite often, contact the Zion Canyon Visitor Bureau for specifics.

St Patrick's Day
PARADE

St Patrick's Day (March 17) parade and celebration includes a green Jell-O sculpture competition.

Zion Canyon Music Festival
MUSIC

(www.zioncanyonmusicfestival.com) Folk (and other music) filled weekend in late September.

🛏 Sleeping

Prices listed here are for March through October – rates plummet in the off-season. The lower the address number on Zion Park Blvd, the closer the park entrance; all lodgings are near shuttle stops. Look for slightly less expensive B&Bs around Zion, eg in Rockville.

TOP CHOICE Under the Eaves Inn
B&B $$

(☎435-772-3457, 866-261-2655; www.under-the-eaves.com; 980 Zion Park Blvd; r incl breakfast $95-125, ste $185; ✹🐾) From colorful tractor reflectors to angel art, the owners' collections enliven every corner of this quaint 1930s bungalow. The fireplace suite is huge; other character-filled rooms are snug. Hang out in the arts-and-crafts living room or on Adirondack chairs and swings in the gorgeous gardens. Local restaurant coupon for breakfast.

Canyon Ranch Motel
MOTEL $-$$

(☎435-772-3357, 866-946-6276; www.canyonranchmotel.com; 668 Zion Park Blvd; r $89-119, apt $109-139; ✹🐾🏊) Small, cottage-like buildings surround a shaded lawn with redwood swings, picnic tables and a small pool at this 1930s motor-court motel. Inside, rooms are thoroughly modern; apartments have kitchenettes.

Driftwood Lodge
LODGE $$-$$$

(☎435-772-3262, 888-801-8811; www.driftwoodlodge.net; 1515 Zion Park Blvd; r $129-159, ste $199-299; ✹🐾🏊🍴) Rich material and dark leathers define the upscale style of thoroughly remodeled rooms at this eco-minded lodging. Some of the contemporary suites have pastoral sunset views of field, river and mountain beyond. An expansive pool and the town's top restaurant, Parallel 88, are on the grounds.

Zion Canyon Campground & RV Resort

CAMPGROUND **$**

(📞435-772-3237; www.zioncamp.com; 479 Zion Park Blvd; tent/RV sites with hookups $30/25; @🏊🐾🍴) Water and tubing access at this 200-site campground are just across the Virgin River from the national park. Attached to the Quality Inn Motel, shared amenities include: heated pool, laundry, camp store, playground and restaurant. Not all sites have shade.

Cliffrose Lodge

MOTEL **$$-$$$**

(📞435-772-3234, 800-243-8824; www.cliffrose lodge.com; 281 Zion Park Blvd; r $159-189; 🏊🐾🌐) Kick back in a lounge chair or take a picnic lunch to enjoy on the five gorgeous acres of lawn and flower gardens leading down to the river. High-thread-count bedding and pillow-top mattresses are among upscale touches.

Canyon Vista Suites B&B

B&B **$$**

(📞435-772-3801; www.canyonvistabandb.com; 897 Zion Park Blvd; ste incl breakfast $129-159; 🏊🌐) All the homey comfort of a B&B, coupled with the privacy of a hotel. Individual entrances lead out from Southwestern or Old World-esque rooms onto a wooden porch or a sprawling patio and lawn with river access. Breakfast coupons; hot tub on-site.

Red Rock Inn

B&B **$$**

(📞435-772-3139; www.redrockinn.com; 998 Zion Park Blvd; cottages incl breakfast $127-132; 🏊🌐) Five romantic country-contemporary cottages spill down the desert hillside, backed by incredible red rock. Enjoy the full hot breakfast (egg dish and pastries) that appears at the door either on the hilltop terrace or your private patio.

Zion Canyon Bed & Breakfast

B&B **$$-$$$**

(📞435-772-9466; www.zioncanyonbandb.com; 101 Kokopelli Circle; r incl breakfast $135-185; 🏊🌐) Deep canyon colors – magenta, eggplant, burnt sienna – complement not only the scenery, but the rustic Southwestern styling. Everywhere you turn there's another gorgeous red-rock view framed perfectly in an oversized window. Full gourmet breakfasts.

Desert Pearl Inn

HOTEL **$$-$$$**

(📞435-772-8888, 888-828-0898; www.desert pearl.com; 707 Zion Park Blvd; r $158-188, ste $300; 🌐@🏊) How naturally stylish: twig sculptures decorate the walls and molded metal headboards resemble art. Opt for a spacious riverside king suite to get a waterfront patio.

Novel House Inn

B&B **$$$**

(📞435-772-3650, 800-711-8400; www.novelhouse .com; 73 Paradise Rd; r $139-159; 🏊) Incredible detail has gone into each of the author-themed rooms: Rudyard Kipling has animal prints and mosquito netting, and a pillow in the Victorian Dickens room reads 'Bah humbug'... Breakfast coupons; hot tub.

Pioneer Lodge

MOTEL **$$**

(📞435-772-3233, 888-772-3233; www.pioneer lodge.com; 838 Zion Park Blvd; r $134-149; 🏊@🌐🍴) In the absolute center of town; pine-bed rooms have a rustic feel.

Harvest House

B&B **$$**

(📞435-772-3880; www.harvesthouse.net; 29 Canyon View Dr; r incl breakfast $120-150; 🏊🌐) Modern B&B alternative with full breakfast.

Best Western Zion Park Inn

MOTEL **$$**

(📞435-772-3200, 800-934-7275; www.zionparkinn .com; 1215 Zion Park Blvd; r $115-119; 🏊@🌐🍴🐾) Rambling lodge complex includes a great room, putting green, badminton court, two pools, two restaurants and a liquor store.

Terrace Brook Lodge

MOTEL **$**

(📞435-772-3932, 800-342-6779; 990 Zion Park Blvd; s & d $85-109; 🏊🐾🌐) Bare-bones basic motel. The two-bed rooms are newer than the singles.

LIKE A VIRGIN

Fourteen miles west of Springdale, you can't help but pass a Virgin. The town, named after the river (what else?), has an odd claim to fame – in 2000 the council passed a law requiring every resident to own a gun. Locals are fined $500 if they don't. Kolob Terrace Rd takes off north from here to Lava Point in Zion National Park. The huge store at the **Virgin Trading Post** (1000 W Hwy 9; ⏱9am-7pm) sells homemade fudge, ice cream and every Western knickknack known to the world. But it's the hard-to-miss **Old West Village** (admission $1; 🐾) that's the real reason to stop. Have your picture taken inside the 'Virgin Jail' or 'Wild Ass Saloon' before you feed the deer, donkey and llama in the petting zoo. It's pure, kitschy fun.

✖️ Eating

Note that many places in town limit hours variably – or close entirely – off season. Those listed as serving dinner have beer and wine only, unless otherwise noted. The saloon at Bit & Spur and the wine bar within Parallel 88 are fine places to drink as well as eat. Springdale is not big on nightlife.

TOP CHOICE Parallel 88   MODERN AMERICAN $$$

(✓435-772-3588; Driftwood Lodge, 1515 Zion Park Blvd; breakfast $10-16, dinner $20-48; ⊘7-10:30am & 5-10pm Mar-Oct, off-season hours vary) Chef Jeff Crosland has mastered 'casually elegant' with a top-notch seasonal menu and friendly, approachable service. Most nights he can be seen chatting with guests on the patio as they nosh on impossibly tender green-apple pork loin surrounded by impossibly gorgeous red-cliff views. Full bar.

Whiptail Grill   SOUTHWESTERN $$

(✓435-772-0283; 445 Zion Park Blvd; mains $10-16; ⊘11am-7pm Apr-Oct; ✐) The old gas-station building isn't much to look at, but man, you can't beat the fresh tastes here: pan-seared tilapia tacos, chipotle chicken enchiladas, organic beef Mexican pizza... Outdoor patio tables fill up quick.

Oscar's Café   MODERN SOUTHWESTERN $$

(948 Zion Park Blvd; breakfast & burgers $9-14, dinner $16-28; ⊘8am-10pm) From green-chile laden omelets to pork *verde* burritos (with a green salsa), Oscar's has the Southwestern spice going on. But it also does smoky ribs, shrimp and garlic burgers well. The living-room-like, Mexican-tiled patio with twinkly lights (and heaters) is a favorite hang-out in the evening.

Bit & Spur Restaurant
& Saloon   MODERN SOUTHWESTERN $$

(1212 Zion Park Blvd; mains $14-28; ⊘5-10pm daily Mar-Oct, 5-10pm Thu-Sat Nov-Feb) Sweet-potato tamales and chile-rubbed rib-eyes are two of the classics at this local institution. Inside, the walls are wild with local art; outside on the deck it's all about the red-rock sunset. Full bar.

Café Soleil   CAFE $

(205 Zion Park Blvd; breakfast & mains $5-10; ⊘6:30am-7pm; 🛜) The food is every bit as good as the free trade coffee. Try the Mediterranean hummus wrap or giant vegetable frittata; pizza and salads, too. Breakfast served till noon.

Park House Cafe   CAFE $

(1880 Zion Park Blvd; breakfast & sandwiches $5-10; ⊘7:30am-3:30pm Mar-Oct) Wake up as late as you like: Park House Cafe serves their Asiago bagel with egg and avocado – along with other breakfast items – until 2pm. Burgers, sandwiches and salads are all made from the freshest ingredients. Great little walled patio, too. Barbecue is served some summer evenings.

Flying Monkey   PIZZERIA $$

(975 Zion Park Blvd; mains $10-16; ⊘11am-9:30pm) Wood-fired goodness at great prices. Expect interesting ingredients like fennel and yellow squash on your roast veggie pizza or Italian sausage with the prosciutto on your oven-baked sandwich. Burgers, salads and pastas, too.

Mean Bean Coffee House   CAFE $

(932 Zion Park Blvd; sandwiches $3-6; ⊘7am-5pm Jun-Aug, 7am-2pm Sep-May; 🛜) Probably the town's best brew. This great local hangout attracts outdoorsy types for their first cup of organic java, soy latte or chai of the day. Take your breakfast burrito or panini up to the roof deck.

Springdale Fruit Company Market   MARKET $

(2491 Zion Park Blvd; sandwiches $8; ⊘8am-8pm Apr-Oct, ✐) On-site orchards produce summertime fruit, for sale along with organic, vegan and gluten-free foodstuffs beginning in summer. Enjoy made-to-order focaccia sandwiches and fruit smoothies at picnic tables in the parklike surrounds.

Thai Sapa   ASIAN $$

(145 Zion Park Blvd; mains $10-20; ⊘noon-9:30pm Apr-Oct, hours vary Nov-Mar) This mix of Thai, Chinese and Vietnamese cuisine is your only ethnic option in town; service can be spotty.

Orange Star   DESSERTS $

(✓435-772-0255; 868 Zion Park Blvd; sandwiches & smoothies $3-7; ⊘11am-8pm Mar-Oct) Fresh fro-yo smoothies like the 'Angels Landing', with Ghirardelli chocolate and toffee chips.

Sol Foods Downtown Supermarket   MARKET

(✓435-772-3100; 995 Zion Park Blvd; ⊘7am-11pm Apr-Oct, 9am-8pm Nov-Mar) The 'big' supermarket in Springdale.

Switchback Trading Co   MARKET

(1149 Zion Park Blvd; ⊘noon-9pm Mon-Sat) The only liquor store is part of the Best Western complex.

☆ Entertainment

OC Tanner Amphitheater   THEATER
(☑435-652-7994; www.dixie.edu/tanner; 300 Lion Blvd; ⊙mid-May–Aug) Outdoor amphitheater surrounded by red rock; stages classical, bluegrass, country and other concerts and performances.

Zion Canyon Giant Screen Theatre   THEATER
(www.zioncanyontheatre.com; 145 Zion Park Blvd) Catch the 40-minute *Zion Canyon: Treasure of the Gods* on a six-story screen – it's light on substance but long on beauty.

🔒 Shopping

Eclectic boutiques and outdoorsy T-shirt shops are scattered the length of Zion Park Blvd. Stunning photography is particularly well represented among area galleries – not surprising given Zion's beauty. Look, too, for the three dimensional oil paintings of Anna Weiler Brown and the colorful multimedia works of Deb Durban, both locals. Hours vary off season.

David Petit Gallery   ARTS & CRAFTS
(975 Zion Park Blvd; ⊙10:30am-8pm Wed-Sat, 3-8pm Tue) Our favorite intrepid outdoorsman-photographer. His rock art and ruin photos are unlike any others.

David J West Gallery   ARTS & CRAFTS
(801 Zion Park Blvd; ⊙10am-9pm Tue-Sun Mar-Oct, to 8pm Nov-Feb) Iconic local-landscape photography; sells some photo gear.

Fatali Gallery   ARTS & CRAFTS
(105 Zion Park Blvd; ⊙11am-7pm Mar-Nov) Otherworldly colors, sensation-causing national-park photography.

De Zion Gallery   ARTS & CRAFTS
(1051 Zion Park Blvd; ⊙noon-6pm Mar-Oct) Large studio, with many Utah artists represented.

Sundancer Books   BOOKS
(975 Zion Park Blvd; ⊙10am-7pm Mar-Oct, off-season hours vary) Great selection of area-related interest books.

Redrock Jewelry   JEWELERY
(998 Zion Park Blvd; ⊙10am-6pm Mar-Oct, off-season hours vary) Gorgeous, local artist-made jewelry.

❶ Information

There's no town information office; go online to www.zionpark.com and www.zionnationalpark .com. The nearest full service hospital is in St George.

Doggy Dude Ranch (☑435-772-3105; www .doggyduderanch.com; 800 Hwy 9) Most local lodgings don't accept pets; board your pampered pooch 3.7 miles west of the park boundary.

Pioneer Lodge Internet Café (Zion Park Blvd; per 25min $3.50; ⊙6:30am-9pm) Two internet terminals.

Zion Canyon Medical Clinic (☑435-772-3226; 120 Lion Blvd; ⊙9am-5pm Tue-Sat Mar-Oct, 9am-5pm Tue Nov-Feb) Walk-in urgent-care clinic.

❶ Getting Around

There's no public transportation to the town, but from April through October the free Springdale Shuttle operates between stops in town and Zion National Park. For more information, see p453.

Around Zion National Park

Just five miles west of Zion National Park, **Rockville** (no services) seems like a neighborhood extension of Springdale. There are a few old buildings, but otherwise it's mostly housing. B&Bs here can be a slightly cheaper alternative to those nearer the park.

The bicycle scene in *Butch Cassidy and the Sundance Kid* was filmed in the nearby **Grafton ghost town**. You can wander freely around the restored 1886 brick meeting house and general store, and a nearby pioneer cemetery. A few pioneer log homes stand on private property. Getting to Grafton can be tricky. Turn south on Bridge Rd, cross the one-lane bridge and turn right. Bear right at the fork and follow signs for 2 miles to the ghost town.

A big backyard pool, gardens leading down to the river and a terrace for breakfast make **Desert Thistle Bed & Breakfast** (☑435-772-0251; www.thedesertthistle.com; 37 W Main St; r incl breakfast $110-145; ❂🛜❂) the top choice, for summer especially. Rooms are posh. **Bunk House at Zion** (☑435-772-3393; www.bunkhouseatzion.com; 149 E Main St; r incl breakfast $55-80) is a bit more down-to-earth. The thoroughly green two-bedroom B&B serves organic breakfasts with ingredients from their orchard and uses 100% renewable energy, even employing an antique wood-fired stove and push-powered lawnmower.

Other alternatives include country farmhouse-like **Rockville Rose** (☑435-772-0800; www.rockvilleroseinn.com; 125 E Main St;

r incl breakfast $95-115; ✴🛜), floral-but-modern **Dream Catcher Inn** (☑435-772-3600, 800-953-7326; www.dreamcatcherinnzion .com; 225 E Main St; r incl breakfast $80-110; ✴🛜) and the simple rooms at older **Amber Inn** (☑435 772 9597; www.amber-inn.com; 244 W Main St; r $100-115; ✴🛜).

Fourteen miles west of Springdale, the next little community is Virgin; the turnoff to Kolob Terrace Rd and a couple of trading posts are here. **Red Coyote Cafe** (239 W Hwy 9; breakfast & sandwiches $4-9; ⊙7:30am-4:30pm Mar-Oct, off-season hours vary; 🛜) is a local hangout that often has live music on Saturday afternoons. Wine and beer available.

West of town, a 1.5-mile gravel-and-dirt road leads south to **La Verkin Overlook**. Stop for a fantastic 360-degree view of the surrounding 40 sq miles, from Zion to the Pine Valley Mountains.

Hurricane, 22 miles from Springdale, has the nearest full-size supermarkets and other services, including a couple of much-needed-after-dusty-backroads car washes.

Cedar City

POP 27,800 / ELEV 5800FT

This sleepy college town comes to life every summer when the Shakespeare festival takes over. Associated events, plays and tours continue into fall. Year-round you can make one of the many B&Bs a quiet homebase for exploring the Kolob Canyons section of Zion National Park or Cedar Breaks National Monument. At roughly 6000ft, cooler temperatures prevail here as compared to Springdale (60 miles away) or St George (55 miles); there's even the occasional snow in May.

⊙ Sights & Activities

The play's the thing for most people visiting Cedar City. See relevant park sections for the best nearby hiking.

**Frontier Homestead State
Park Museum** MUSEUM
(http://stateparks.utah.gov; 635 N Main St; admission $3; ⊙9am-5pm Mon-Sat; 👪) Kids love the cabins and the brightly painted 19th-century buggies, as well as the garden full of old farm equipment to run through. Living history demos take place June through August.

Cedar Cycle CYCLING
(☑435-586-5210; www.cedarcycle.com; 38 E 200 South; ⊙9am-5pm Mon-Fri, 9am-2pm Sat)

PAROWAN GAP

People have been passing this way for millennia, and the **Parowan Gap** (www .blm.gov; freely accessible) petroglyphs prove it. Look closely as you continue walking along the road to find panels additional to those signed. Archeoastronomers believe that the gap in the rocks opposite the petroglyphs may have been used as part of an ancient, astronomically-based calendar. The Cedar City & Brian Head Tourism & Convention Bureau, in Cedar City, has colorful interpretive brochures explaining site details.

After you rent a bike (from $30 per day) the knowledgeable staff can point you to local trails.

✯ Festivals & Events

Cedar City is known for its year-round festivities. For a full schedule, see www .cedarcity.org.

Utah Shakespearean Festival CULTURAL
(☑435-586-7878, 800-752-9849; www.bard.org; Southern Utah University, 351 W Center St) Southern Utah University has been hosting Cedar City's main event since 1962. From late June into September, three of the bard's plays and three contemporary dramas take the stage. From mid-September into late October three more plays are presented – one Shakespearean, one dramatic and one musical. Productions are well regarded, but you also shouldn't miss the extras: 'greenshows' with Elizabethan minstrels, literary seminars discussing the plays and costume classes are all free. Backstage and scene-changing tours cost extra. Note that children under six are not allowed at performances, but free childcare is available.

The venues are the open-air **Adams Shakespearean Theatre**, an 819-seat reproduction of London's Globe Theater; the modern 769-seat **Randall L Jones Theatre**, where backstage tours are held; and the less noteworthy **Auditorium Theatre** used for matinees and rainy days. Make reservations at least a few weeks in advance. At 10am on the day of the show, obscured-view gallery seats for the Adams performance go on sale at the walk-up **ticket office** (cnr 300 W & W Center Sts; ⊘10am-7pm late Jun-Aug & mid-Sep–Oct).

Groove Fest
MUSIC
(www.groovefestutah.com) A late September weekend grooves with folksy and funky sound.

Neil Simon Festival
CULTURAL
(www.simonfest.org) American plays staged mid-July to mid-August.

Cedar City Skyfest
SPORTS
(www.cedarcityskyfest.org) Hot-air balloons, kites and model rockets go off in September.

🛏 Sleeping

The following rates are for the high season (March through October), but weekends during the Shakespearean Festival may cost more.

Anniversary House
B&B $$
(☑435-865-1266, 800-778-5109; http://the anniversaryhouse.com; 133 S 100 W; r incl breakfast $99-119; ✳🛜✳) Remarkably comfortable rooms, a great-to-talk-to-host and thoughtful extras make this one of our faves. Savor freshly baked cake and complimentary beverages in the mission-style dining room or lounge around in the landscaped backyard. Outdoor kennel available.

Garden Cottage B&B
B&B $$
(☑435-586-4919, 866-586-4919; www.thegarden cottagebnb.com; 16 N 200 W; r incl breakfast $119-129; ✳🛜✳) Romantic vines climb up the steep-roofed cottage walls, and in season a fantasia of blooms grow in encompassing gardens. If you like antiques and quilts, you're going to love Garden Cottage. The owner has done an amazing job displaying family treasures. No room TVs.

Big Yellow Inn
B&B $$-$$$
(☑435-586-0960; www.bigyellowinn.com; 234 S 300 W; r incl breakfast $99-199; ✳@🛜) A purpose-built Georgian Revival inn with room to roam: a dining room, a library, a den and many porches. Upstairs rooms are elegantly ornate. Downstairs, the ground-floor walk-out rooms are simpler and a bit more 'country'. The owners also oversee several adjunct B&B properties and vacation rentals around town.

Amid Summer's Inn
B&B $$
(☑435-586-2600, 888-586-2601; www.amid summersinn.com; 140 S 100 W; r incl breakfast

$109-179; ✳@🛜) Tasteful additions have brought the guestroom count to 10 at this 1930s home-based B&B. Common areas and some rooms have a Victorian feel; others are more over-the-top trompe l'oeil fantasies. Accommodating hosts; great breakfasts.

Iron Gate Inn
B&B $$
(☑435-867-0603, 800-808-4599; www.theiron gateinn.com; 100 N 200 West; r incl breakfast $119-179; ✳@🛜) Rambling porches and a big yard surround the distinct 1897 Second Empire Victorian house with large, modern-luxury guest rooms. Enjoy your breakfast on the large shady patio.

Best Western Town & Country
MOTEL $$
(☑435-586-9900, 800-780-7234; 189 N Main St; r incl breakfast $86-109; ✳@🛜✳) Rooms are giant and rates are right at this well-cared-for Best Western.

🍴 Eating

How wonderful it would be if Cedar City had dining on a par with its B&Bs and top-notch theater. But alas, poor Yorick, it doth not. Hours are usually extended variably during Shakespeare weekends.

Sonny Boy's BBQ
BARBECUE $
(126 N Main St; mains $6-14; ⊘11am-9pm Mon-Thu, 11am-10pm Fri & Sat) Locals love the piles of slow-smoked meat and fun side dishes such as fried pickles. Eat in or take out.

Grind Coffeehouse
CAFE $
(19 N Main St; sandwiches $7-10; ⊘7am-7pm Mon-Sat, 8am-5pm Sun; @🛜) Hang out with the locals and have a barista-made brew, a great hot sandwich or a big salad. Sometimes there's music on the menu.

Garden House
AMERICAN $-$$
(164 S 100 West; lunch $8-12, dinner $14-22; ⊘11am-9:30pm Mon-Sat) Homemade soups, sandwiches, pastas and seafood dishes top the menu at this house-turned-rambling restaurant. A senior-citizen fave.

Two popular and unpretentious Western steakhouses lie just outside town in rustic red-rock settings:

Rusty's Ranch House
STEAKHOUSE $$
(Hwy 14; mains $15-28; ⊘5-9pm Mon-Sat) Two miles east of Cedar City.

Milt's Stage Stop
STEAKHOUSE $$
(Hwy 14; mains $16-30; ⊘5-9pm) Five miles east of town.

UTAH CEDAR CITY

Shopping

Groovacious Music Store   MUSIC
(www.groovacious.com; 171 N 100 West; ⊙10am-
9pm Mon-Sat) The local music store (with
awesome vinyl) hosts concerts and other
events.

Information

**Cedar City & Brian Head Tourism &
Convention Bureau** (⊘435-586-5124, 800-
354-4849; www.scenicsouthernutah.com; 581
N Main St; ⊙8am-5pm Mon-Fri, 9am-1pm Sat)
Area-wide info and free internet use.

Cedar City Ranger Station (⊘435-865-3200;
www.fs.fed.us/r4/dixie; 1789 N Wedgewood Ln;
⊙8am-5pm Mon-Fri) Provides Dixie National
Forest information.

Valley View Medical Center (⊘435-868-
5000; http://intermountainhealthcare.org;
1303 N Main St; ⊙24hrs) Hospital.

Zions Bank (3 S Main St) Currency exchange
& ATM.

Getting There & Around

You'll need private transportation to get to and
around Cedar City.

Hwy 14

As scenic drives go, **Hwy 14** is awesome. It
leads 42 miles over the Markagunt Plateau,
cresting at 10,000ft for stunning vistas of
Zion National Park and Arizona. The surrounding area is part of **Dixie National
Forest** (www.fs.fed.us/r4/dixie). For information, check in with Cedar City Ranger
Station. Though Hwy 14 remains open all
winter, snow tires or chains are required between November and April.

Hiking and biking trails, past the Cedar
Breaks National Monument turnoff on Hwy
14, have tremendous views; particularly at
sunset. They include the short (less than a
mile one-way) **Cascade Falls** and **Bristlecone Pine Trail** and the 32-mile **Virgin River
Rim Trail**. A signed turnoff 24.5 miles from
Cedar City leads to jumbled **lava beds**.

Boating and fishing are the activities
of choice at **Navajo Lake**, 25 miles east of
Cedar City. You can rent a motorboat ($75
to $120 per day) or stay over in a historic
1920s cabin at **Navajo Lake Lodge** (⊘702-
646-4197; www.navajolakelodge.com; cabins $70-
120; ⊙May-Oct). The rustic lodgings include
bedding, but no refrigerators.

Five miles further east, **Duck Creek
Visitor Center** (⊘435-682-2432; Hwy 14;

⊙9am-4:30pm late May-early Sep) provides
information for nearby trails and fishing in
the adjacent pond and stream. Here at
8400ft, the 87 pine-shaded **Duck Creek
Campground** (⊘877-444-6777; www.recreation
.gov; Hwy 14; tent & RV sites without hookups $10-
30; ⊙late May-early Sep) sites are blissfully
cool in summer. The ever-expanding log-
cabin town **Duck Creek Village** (www.duck
creekvillage.com) has more services, including a couple of restaurants, realty offices,
cabin rental outfits, a laundromat and an
internet cafe. The village area is big with
off-road enthusiasts – ATVs in summer and
snowmobiles in winter.

About 7 miles east of Duck Creek, a
signed, passable dirt road leads the 10
miles to **Strawberry Point**, an incredibly
scenic overview of red-rock formations and
forest lands.

Cedar Breaks National Monument

Sculpted cliffs and towering hoodoos glow
like neon tie-dye in a wildly eroded natural amphitheater encompassed by **Cedar
Breaks National Monument** (www.nps.gov
/cebr; per person $4). The majestic kaleido-
scope of magenta, salmon, plum, rust and
ocher rises to a height of 10,450ft atop the
Markagunt Plateau. The compact park lies
22 miles east and north of Cedar City, off
Hwy 14. There are no cedar trees here, by the
way: early pioneers mistook the evergreen
junipers for cedars.

This altitude gets more than a little snow,
and the monument's one road, Hwy 148, is
closed from sometime in November through
to at least May. Summer temperatures range
from only 40°F to 70°F (4°C to 21°C); brief
storms drop rain, hail and even powdery
white snow. In season, rangers hold geology
talks and star parties at the small **visitor
center** (⊘435-586-9451; Hwy 148; ⊙8am-6pm
Jun–mid-Oct).

No established trails descend into the
breaks, but the park has five viewpoints off
Hwy 148 and there are rim trails. **Ramparts
Trail** – one of southern Utah's most magnificent trails – leaves from the visitor center. The
elevation change on the 3-mile round-trip is
only 400ft, but it can be tiring because of the
overall high elevation. **Alpine Pond Trail** is a
lovely, though less dramatic, 4-mile loop.

The first-come, first-served **Point
Supreme Campground** (tent & RV sites

without hookups $14; ☺late Jun-Sep) has water and restrooms, but no showers; its 28 sites rarely fill.

Brian Head

The highest town in Utah, Brian Head towers over Cedar City, 35 miles southwest. 'Town' is a bit of an overstatement though; this is basically a big resort. From Thanksgiving through April, snow bunnies come to test the closest slopes to Las Vegas (200 miles). Snowmobiling in winter and mountain-biking in summer are also popular. The tiny **Brian Head Visitor Center** (☑435-677-2810; www .brianheadutah.com; Hwy 148; 9am-4:30pm Mon-Fri; ☎) leaves pamphlets out after hours. Cedar City & Brian Head Tourism & Convention Bureau in Cedar City has more info.

Advanced skiers might grow impatient with the short trails (except on a powder day), but there's lots to love for beginners, intermediates and free-riders at **Brian Head Resort** (☑435-677-2035; www.brianhead.com; Hwy 143; day lift ticket adult/child $45/32). Lines are usually short and it's the only resort in Utah within sight of the red-rock desert. Here's the lowdown: 1320ft vertical drop, base elevation 9600ft, 640 acres and seven high-speed triple lifts. A ski bridge connects all the lifts. A highlight is the kickin' six-lane snow-tubing area (with surface lift), and there's a mini-terrain park for snowboarders. Forty-two miles of cross-country trails surround Brian Head, including semi-groomed trails to Cedar Breaks National Monument.

During July and August the elevation keeps temperatures deliciously cool. Ride the **summer chair-lift** (day lift ticket $10; ☺9:30am-4:30pm Fri-Sun Jul-Sep) up to 11,000ft for an alpine hike or mountain biking. The visitor center puts out a list of area trails.

The resort's lodges and town's sports shops, such as **Georg's Ski & Bike Shop** (☑435-677-2013; www.georgsskishop.com; Hwy 143), rent skis and snowboards ($27 to $32 per day), mountain bikes ($35 to $45) and more. Rent an ATV or a guided snowmobile tour with **Thunder Mountain Sports** (☑435-677-2288; www.brianheadthunder.com; 539 N Hwy 143; ☺8:30am-5:30pm); half-days for each run are $99 to $150.

Check the ski resort website for lodging and skiing packages – two nights in Vegas, two nights in Brian Head can be quite reasonable. A long list of condo rentals is available on the visitor center website. But for our mountain-lodging buck, what could be better than warming by an outdoor fireplace or dining under giant timber-frame trusses like those at the **Grand Lodge** (☑888-282-3327, 435-677-4242; www.grandlodgebrianhead .com; 314 Hunter Ridge Rd; r $119-195; @☎☀☀). Villa apartments at **Cedar Breaks Lodge & Spa** (☑435-677-900, 877-505-6343; www .cedarbreakslodge.com; 222 Hunter Ridge Rd; apt $95-275; @☎☀☀) sleep four to eight and have kitchens – great for families. Both lodgings have indulgence-worthy spas.

Apple Annie's Country Store (The Mall, 259 S Hwy 143; ☎) is the local grocery store, post office and state liquor store. The Tex-Mex menu at **Mi Pueblo** (406 S Hwy 143; mains $9-20; ☺11am-9pm) has a long list of beef and

---

WORTH A TRIP

FREMONT INDIAN STATE PARK

Sixty miles northwest of Cedar City, off I-70, **Fremont Indian State Park & Museum** (☑435-527-4631; http://stateparks.utah.gov; 3820 W Clear Creek Canyon Rd; admission $5; ☺9am-5pm) is a great introduction to one of the state's other ancient peoples. Fremont Indians inhabited more northerly areas than the well-known ancient group known as the Anasazi, or Ancestral Puebloans. Indications are that the Fremont were fairly sedentary agriculturalists who tended to settle in small groups. Though much is still up for debate, many sites were probably plowed-under on Mormon pioneer-settled ground (farmers do tend to like the same areas).

The park contains one of the largest collections of Fremont Indian rock art in the state: more than 500 panels on 14 interpretive trails. There's also a reconstructed kiva you can climb down into. Be sure to watch the visitor center film and pick up an interpretive brochure for the trails. If you want to learn more about the culture, *Traces of Fremont* by Steven Simms is an excellent resource. Other Fremont sites include those in Dinosaur National Monument, Nine Mile Canyon and Sego Canyon.

seafood dishes. **Bump & Grind Café** (☎435-677-3111; 259 S Hwy 143; mains $4-11; ☺11am-9pm) serves a variety of pastas and sandwiches regularly, plus breakfast on some weekends.

From December through April there's a free ski shuttle that travels around town.

St George

Nicknamed 'Dixie' for its warm weather and southern location, St George has long been attracting winter residents and retirees. Brigham Young, second president of the Mormon church, was one of the first snowbirds in the one-time farming community. An interesting-if-small historic downtown core, area state parks and a dinosaur-tracks museum hold some attraction. But for travelers, the abundant and affordable lodging are what make this an oft-used stop between Las Vegas and Salt Lake City – or en route to Zion National Park after a late-night flight.

The town lies about 41 miles (up to an hour) from Zion National Park's south entrance, 30 miles (25 minutes) from the Kolob Canyons' entrance on I-15, and 57 miles (45 minutes) from Cedar City to the north.

◉ Sights

Pick up a free, full-color, historic-building walking tour brochure at the visitor center. The intersection of Temple and Main Sts is at the heart of the old town center.

Dinosaur Discovery Site　　　MUSEUM
(www.dinotrax.com; 2200 E Riverside Dr; adult/child $6/3; ☺10am-6pm Mon-Sat) St George's oldest residents aren't retirees from Idaho, but Jurassic-era dinosaurs. Entry gets you an interpretive tour of the huge collection of tracks, beginning with a video. The casts were first unearthed by a farm plow in 2000 and rare paleontology discoveries, such as dinosaur swim tracks, continue to be made.

Mormon Sites　　　RELIGIOUS
The soaring 1877 **Mormon Temple** (440 S 300 East; ☺visitor center 9am-9pm) was Utah's first. It has a visitor center, but is otherwise closed to the general public. Built concurrently, the red-brick **Mormon Tabernacle** (cnr Tabernacle & Main Sts; ☺9am-5pm) occasionally hosts free music programs and is open to touring.

FREE **Brigham Young Winter Home**　　MUSEUM
(67 W 200 N; ☺9am-5pm) A tour of the Mormon leader's seasonal home and headquarters illuminates a lot about early town and experimental-farming history.

FREE **Jacob Hamblin Home**　　　MUSEUM
(Santa Clara Dr; ☺9am-5pm) For another evocative picture of the Mormon pioneer experience, head 5 miles north of town to Santa Clara and the 1863 Jacob Hamblin Home, where orchards still grow.

FREE **Daughters of Utah Pioneers Museum**　　　MUSEUM
(DUP; www.dupinternational.org; 145 N 100 East; ☺10am-5pm Mon-Sat) Two floors packed full with pioneer artifacts, furniture, photographs, quilts, guns and so on.

🏃 Activities

Trails crisscross St George. Eventually they'll be connected and the trail along the Virgin River will extend to Zion; get a map at the visitor center. Mountain-bike rental costs $30 to 45 per day. A handful of local golf courses are open to the public (many more are private). Reserve up to two weeks in advance at www.sgcity.org/golf. And don't forget that Snow Canyon State Park is quite close.

Green Valley Trail　　　MOUNTAIN BIKING
(off Sunbrook Rd) Also called Bearclaw Poppy, this 6-mile trail offers first-rate, playground-like mountain biking on slickrock.

Paragon Climbing　　　ROCK CLIMBING
(☎435-673-1709; www.paragonclimbing.com) Paragon Climbing runs excellent introductory rock-climbing courses ($120 for 2½ hours) and guided mountain-biking excursions ($35 to $50 per hour).

Paragon Adventures　　ADVENTURE SPORTS
(☎435-673-1709; www.paragonadventure.com) Book ahead for road or mountain-bike tours with Paragon Adventures. It also offers local rock-climbing lessons and tours, small-group canyoneering, interpretive hikes, zipline courses – and babysitting. Trips from $55 per hour.

Red Rock Bicycle Company　　MOUNTAIN BIKING
(☎435-674-3185; www.redrockbicycle.com; 446 W 100 S; ☺9am-7pm Mon-Fri, 9am-6pm Sat, 9am-3pm Sun) Rentals available.

Bicycles Unlimited MOUNTAIN BIKING
(435-673-4492; www.bicyclesunlimited.com; 90 S 100 East; 9am-6pm Mon-Sat) Rentals available.

Tours & Outfitters

Meet Dixie's Famous Pioneers Tour WALKING
(436-627-4525; cnr 200 North & Main Sts; tour $3; 10am Tue-Sat Jun-Aug) Brigham Young and Jacob Hamblin are just two of the costumed characters you'll meet on this pleasant ramble through the old-town core.

Festivals & Events

A full festival list is available at www.st georgechamber.com.

Dixie Roundup SPORTS
(435-628-8282) A mid-September weekend full of Western fun, including a parade and rodeo.

St George Marathon SPORTS
(www.stgeorgemarathon.com) This October event takes over the town, attracting runners from all 50 states.

Sleeping

Around about Eastertime, St George becomes Utah's spring-break capital. Head to St George Blvd and Bluff St near I-15 for chain motels. Pretty much every lodging offers a golf package. Tent campers will do best on nearby public lands; see p464.

Seven Wives Inn B&B $$
(435-628-3737, 800-600-3737; www.seven wivesinn.com; 217 N 100 West; r & ste incl breakfast $95-185;) Two 1800s homes lovely bedrooms and suites surround well-tended gardens and a small pool at this charming inn. Yes, as you can guess from the name, one of the owners harbored fugitive polygamists there in the 1880s.

Green Gate Village INN $$
(435-628-6999, 800-350-6999; www.greengate villageinn.com; 76 W Tabernacle St; r incl breakfast $119-159;) Book a room or a whole house from among nine historic buildings brought together to make a historic village of sorts, complete with a general store. Antiques such as white-iron beds and ornate carved vanities figure prominently in all the lodgings.

Red Mountain Resort & Spa RESORT $$$
(435-673-4905, 877-246-4453; http://red mountainspa.com; 1275 E Red Mountain Circle;

r from $230;) A Zen-chic sensibility pervades the low-profile adobe resort, right down to the silk pillows that echo the copper color of surrounding cliffs. Full meals, guided hikes, spa services and fitness classes are all included to varying degrees.

Temple View RV Resort CAMPGROUND $
(435-673-6400, 800-776-6410; www.temple viewrv.com; 975 S Main St; tent/RV sites without hookups $31/42;) The 260 sites at this mega resort mostly accommodate (up to 45ft) RVs, but there are a few tent spots. Amenities include a rec room, business center, swimming pool, gym, putting green and cable hookups.

Best Western Coral Hills MOTEL $-$$
(435-673-4844; www.coralhills.com; 125 E St George Blvd; r incl breakfast $71-108;) You can't beat being a block or two from downtown restaurants and historic sights. Waterfalls and spiffed-up decor set this locally owned franchise apart.

Dixie Palm Motel MOTEL $
(435-673-3531, 866-651-3997; www.dixiepalms motel.com; 185 E St George Blvd; r $39-67;) It may not look like much outside, but regular maintenance and TLC put the Dixie Palm at the head of the low-budget pack. The 15 rooms have minifridges and microwaves.

America's Best Inn & Suites MOTEL $
(435-652-3030, 800-718-0297; www.stgeorge innsuites.com; 245 N Red Cliffs Dr; r incl breakfast $49-89;) Well positioned off I-15, with good facilities.

Green Valley Spa RESORT $$$
(435-628-8060, 800-237-1068; www.greenvalley spa.com; 1871 W Canyon View Dr; r $169-399;) Luxury sports resort: 4000-sq-ft golf center, 14 tennis courts and six swimming pools.

Eating & Drinking

All the big chain restaurants and megamarts you'd expect line up along I-15.

Twenty-Five on Main CAFE $$
(25 N Main St; mains $6-12; 8am-9pm Mon-Thu, to 10pm Fri & Sat) Homemade cupcakes are not all this bakery-cafe does well. We also like the breakfast panini, the warm salmon salad and the pasta primavera, overflowing with veggies.

Painted Pony MODERN AMERICAN $$-$$$
(435-634-1700; 2 W St George Blvd, Ancestor Sq; sandwiches $9-12, dinner $24-35; 11am-10pm)

UTAH ST GEORGE

Think gourmet comfort food. At dinner you might choose a juniper-brined pork chop, at lunch, meatloaf with a port wine reduction and rosemary mashed potatoes.

Xetava Gardens
Cafe MODERN SOUTHWESTERN **$$-$$$**
(☑435-656-0165; 815 Coyote Gulch Ct, Ivins; breakfast & sandwiches $6-12, dinner $15-32; ☺8am-4pm daily, plus 5:30-9pm Thu-Sat; ☑) We'd drive much further than 8 miles for the creative Southwestern cuisine served here in a stunning red-rock setting. Try dishes like organic blue-corn waffles and chile-rubbed lamb. Dinner reservations recommended.

Benja Thai & Sushi
ASIAN **$$**
(W St George Blvd, Ancestor Sq; mains $12-15; ☺11:30am-10pm Mon-Sat, 5-9pm Sun) A pan-Asian menu is certainly more diverse than most offerings in St George. Eclectic specialty rolls share a menu with pad thai and teriyaki chicken.

Bear Paw Café
CAFE **$**
(75 N Main St; mains $5-9; ☺7am-3pm Mon-Sat) Homey cafe with big breakfasts.

Thomas Judd's General Store
ICE CREAM **$**
(76 Tabernacle St; ice cream $1.50-3; ☺11am-9pm Mon-Sat) Stop for a sweet scoop of ice cream or piece of nostalgic candy in Green Gate Village.

Anasazi Steakhouse
STEAKHOUSE **$$-$$$**
(☑435-674-0095; 1234 W Sunset Blvd; mains $15-33; ☺5-10pm) Grill your steak (or shrimp, or portabella mushroom...) yourself on a hot volcanic rock.

☆ Entertainment
St George gets pretty quiet after dark. For any area music or events, check listings in free monthly newspaper the *Independent* (www.suindependent.com).

Tuacahn Amphitheater
THEATER
(☑435-652-3300, 800-746-9882; www.tuacahn .org) Ten miles northwest in Ivins; hosts musicals in summer and other performances year-round.

St George Musical Theater
THEATER
(☑435-628-8755; www.sgmt.org; 37 S 100 West) Puts on musicals year-round.

ℹ Information
Additional information is available at www .utahsdixie.com and www.sgcity.org.

Chamber of Commerce (☑435-628-1658; www.stgeorgechamber.com; 97 E St George Blvd; ☺9am-5pm Mon-Fri) The visitor center caters to relocating retirees, and has loads of city info.

Dixie Regional Medical Center (☑435-251-1000; http://intermountainhealthcare.org; 1380 E Medical Center Dr; ☺24hr) Hospital.

St George Field Office (☑435-688-3200; 345 E Riverside Dr; ☺8am-4pm Mon-Fri) Get interagency information on surrounding public lands: USFS, BLM and state parks. Topographic maps and guides available.

Utah Welcome Center (☑435-673-4542; http://travel.utah.gov; Dixie Convention Center, I-15; ☺8:30am-5:30pm) Statewide information 2 miles south of St George. There's a wildlife museum (think taxidermy) onsite with the same hours.

ℹ Getting There & Around
St George is on I-15 just north of the Arizona border, 120 miles from Las Vegas and 305 miles from SLC.

Air
Taxis (to downtown $15) and all the standard chain car-rental companies are represented at the St George airport. Note that Las Vegas McCarran International Airport, 120 miles south, often has better flight and car-rental deals than Utah airports.

St George Municipal Airport (SGU; www .flysgu.com; 4550 S Airport Parkway) A new airport with expanded service.

Delta (☑800-221-1212; www.delta.com) Connects SLC and St George several times daily.

United Express (☑800-864-8331; www .united.com) Has four weekly flights to and from Los Angeles, CA.

Bus
Greyhound (☑435-673-2933, 800-231-2222; www.greyhound.com; 1235 S Bluff St) Buses depart from the local McDonald's en route to SLC ($65, 5½ hours) and Las Vegas, NV ($29, two hours).

St George Express (☑435-652-1100; www .stgeorgeexpress.com; 1040 S Main St) Shuttle service to Las Vegas, NV ($35, two hours) and Zion National Park ($25, 40 minutes).

Around St George
Follow Hwy 18 northwest out of St George and you'll come to a series of parks and attractions before reaching higher elevations and Dixie National Forest. Go northeast of town on I-15 for more parks and a small ghost town.

SNOW CANYON STATE PARK

Red and white swirls of sandstone flow like lava, and actual lava lies broken like sheets of smashed marble in this small, accessible park. **Snow Canyon** (☑435-628-2255; http://stateparks.utah.gov; 1002 Snow Canyon Dr, Ivins; per vehicle $6; ☺day use 6am-10pm; ♿) is a 7400-acre sampler of southwest Utah's famous land features, 11 miles northwest of St George. Easy trails, perfect for kids, lead to tiny slot canyons, cinder cones, lava tubes and fields of undulating slickrock. Summers are blazing hot: visit in early morning or come in spring or fall. The park was named after prominent Utah pioneers, not frozen precipitation, but for the record it does very occasionally snow here.

Hiking trails loop off the main road. **Jenny's Canyon Trail** is an easy 1-mile round-trip to a short slot canyon. Wind through a cottonwood-filled field, past ancient lava flows to a 200ft arch on **Johnson Canyon Trail** (2-mile round-trip). A 1000ft stretch of vegetation-free **sand dunes** serves as a playground for the kiddies, old and young, near a picnic area.

Cycling is popular on the main road through the park: a 17-mile loop from St George, where you can rent bikes. There's also great **rock climbing** in-park, particularly for beginners, with over 150 bolted and sport routes, plus top roping.

Apart from during the unrelenting summer, the 35-site **campground** (☑800-322-3770; http://utahstateparks.reserveamerica.com; tent/RV sites without hookups $20/16) is great, and so scenic. You can reserve any of the 30 sites (14 with electrical and water hookups) up to four months in advance. Showers and dump station available.

VEYO

The tiny village of Veyo lies 17 miles north of St George on Hwy 18. A warm spring-fed swimming pool (about 80°F, or 27°C) on the Santa Clara River is the main attraction at **Veyo Pool & Crawdad Canyon Climbing Park** (☑435-574-2300; www.veyo pool.com; Veyo Pool Resort Rd; adult/child swim $6/4; ☺11am-8pm May-Aug). But there's also a cafe, picnicking area and sun deck. Eighty-foot high basalt walls in Crawdad Canyon are perfect for rock climbing and have been equipped with more than 100 bolted routes ($5 per day).

Back on the highway there are competing stores that sell homemade mini-pies.

MOUNTAIN MEADOWS MASSACRE MONUMENT

About 10 miles north of Veyo on Hwy 18 stands a remote monument to one of the darkest incidents in the Mormon settlement of Utah. In 1857, for reasons that remain unclear, Mormons and local Indians killed about 120 non-Mormon pioneers – including women and children – who were migrating through the area. The simple, freely-accessible monument, maintained by the LDS, is well-kept but provides little information. On September 11, 2011 it was declared a national historic landmark, so this may change. In the meantime, if you're interested in finding out more, the book *Massacre at Mountain Meadows* by Ronald Walker and documentaries such as *Burying The Past: Legacy of the Mountain Meadows Massacre* fully illuminate the subject. Honestly, the story is a lot more compelling than the sight.

PINE VALLEY MOUNTAIN WILDERNESS

Mountains rise sharply in the 70 sq mile **Pine Valley Wilderness Area** (www.fs.fed.us/r4/dixie) in the Dixie National Forest, 32 miles northwest of St George off Hwy 18. The highest point, **Signal Peak** (10,365ft), remains snow-capped till July and rushing streams lace the mountainous area. The St George Field Office provides information and free backcountry permits.

When the desert heat blurs your vision, Pine Valley offers cool respite. Most hikes here begin as strenuous climbs. The 5-mile round-trip **Mill Canyon Trail** and the 6-mile **Whipple Trail** are most popular, each linking with the 35-mile **Summit Trail**.

Pine Valley Recreation Complex (☑877-444-6777; www.recreation.gov; tent & RV sites $12, day-use $2; ☺May-Sep), 3 miles east of Pine Valley, has a couple of pine-shaded campgrounds at 6800ft. They all have water but no showers or hookups; bring mosquito repellent.

SILVER REEF GHOST TOWN

A few of the old stone buildings are inhabited, others are crumbling at this 19th-century silver-mining ghost town. The restored **Wells Fargo building** (admission free; ☺10am-4pm Mon-Sat) houses a museum and art gallery. Diagrams of the rough-and-tumble town and mine give a feel of what it was like back in the day. You do need them because it's hard to imagine, giving the encroaching subdivision. Take exit 23 off I-15, 13 miles northeast of St George (past Leeds).

HILDALE-COLORADO CITY

Just 42 miles southeast of St George on Hwy 9, straddling the Utah-Arizona border, sit the twin towns of Hildale-Colorado City. Though the official Mormon church eschewed plural marriage in 1890, there are those that still believe it is a divinely decreed practice. The majority of the approximately 7000 residents here belong to the polygamy-practicing Fundamentalist Church of Jesus Christ of Latter-Day Saints (FLDS). The spotlight focused on this religious community when leader Warren Jeffs was convicted of being an accomplice to rape here in 2007. After that, many of the FLDS faithful, including Jeffs, moved to a fenced compound in Texas. There he was convicted of child sexual assault, for 'spiritual marriages' resulting in the pregnancies of underage girls, and sentenced to life in a Texas prison in 2011.

Other than residents' old-fashioned clothing and a proliferation of really large houses (for multiple wives and even more multiple children), these look like any other American towns. We recommend you respect their privacy. However, if you walk into a Wal-Mart in Washington or Hurricane and see several varying-age females shopping together wearing pastel-colored, prairie-style dresses and lengthy braids or elaborate up-dos, it's a pretty safe guess that they are sister wives. Other, less conspicuous sects are active in the state as well.

SALT LAKE REGION

The vast Salt Lake Valley is what Brigham Young referred to when he announced 'this is the place!' to his pioneering followers in 1847. Today almost 80% of the state's population, nearly 2 million people, live along the eastern edge of the Wasatch Mountains from Ogden to Provo. Salt Lake City (SLC) sits smack in the middle of this concentration, but you'd never know it from the small size of the city. To the north and west is the Great Salt Lake and 100 miles of salt flats stretching into Nevada.

Salt Lake City

Utah's capital city, and the only one with an international airport, has a surprisingly small-town feel. Downtown is easy to get around and, outside entertainment enclaves, come evening it's fairly quiet. You'd never know 1.2 million people live in the metro area. Yes, this is the Mormon equivalent of Vatican City, and the LDS owns a lot of land, but less than half the town's population are church members. The university and the great outdoors-at-your-doorstep have attracted a wide range of residents. A liberal spirit is evident everywhere from the coffee-houses to the yoga classes, where elaborate tattoos are the norm. Foodies will find much to love among the multitude of international and organic dining options (think Himalayan and East African). And when the trail beckons, you're a scant 45 minutes from the Wasatch Mountains' brilliant hiking and skiing. Friendly people, great food and outdoor adventure – what could be better?

⊙ Sights

Mormon Church-related sights mostly cluster near the down centerpoint for SLC addresses: the intersection of Main and South Temple St. (Streets are so wide – 132ft – because they were originally built so that four oxen pulling a wagon could turn around.) The downtown hub expects to experience a renaissance with the development of City Creek. To the west, the University Foothills District has most of the museums and kid-friendly attractions. For more tips, check out p475.

TEMPLE SQUARE & AROUND

FREE **Temple Square** PLAZA
(Map p472; www.visittemplesquare.com; ☺visitor centers 9am-9pm) The city's most famous sight occupies a 10-acre block surrounded by 15ft-high walls. LDS docents give free, 30-minute tours continually, leaving from the visitor centers at the two entrances on South and North Temple Sts. Sisters, brothers and elders are stationed every 20ft or so to answer questions. (Don't worry, no one is going to try to convert you – unless you express interest.) In addition to the noteworthy sights, there are administrative buildings and two theater venues.

Salt Lake Temple RELIGIOUS
(Map p472; Temple Sq) Lording over the square is the impressive 210ft-tall Salt Lake Temple. Atop the tallest spire stands a statue of the angel Moroni who appeared to LDS founder Joseph Smith. Rumor has it that when the place was renovated, cleaners found old bullet marks in the gold-plated surface. The temple and ceremonies are private, open only to LDS in good standing.

Greater Salt Lake City

FREE Tabernacle RELIGIOUS

(Map p472; Temple Sq; ☉9am-9pm) The domed, 1867 auditorium – with a massive 11,000-pipe organ – has incredible acoustics. A pin dropped in the front can be heard in the back, almost 200ft away. Free daily organ recitals are held at noon Monday through Saturday, and at 2pm Sunday. For more on Mormon Tabernacle Choir performances, which are not all held here, see p476.

Family History Library LIBRARY

(Map p472; www.familysearch.org; 35 N West Temple St; ☉8am-5pm Mon, 8am-9pm Tue-Sat) Thousands of people come to Salt Lake City every year to research their family history at the largest genealogical resource on Earth, the Family History Library. Because the LDS believes you must pray on your ancestors' behalf to help them along their celestial path, it has acquired a mind-boggling amount of genealogical information to help identify relatives. Volunteers scour the globe microfilming records in the tiniest of villages and then make them freely available here, and through libraries across the country.

FREE Joseph Smith Memorial Building BUILDING

(Map p472; 15 E South Temple St; ☉9am-9pm Mon-Sat) East of the Brigham Young Monument is the Joseph Smith Memorial Building, which was, until 1987, the elegant Hotel Utah. Inside, there's a large-screen theater with eight daily screenings of the 65-minute *Joseph Smith: The Prophet of the Restoration*, about Mormon beliefs.

FREE Beehive House HOUSE

(Map p472; ☎801-240-2671; 67 E South Temple St; ☉9am-8:30pm Mon-Sat) Brigham Young lived with one of his wives and families in the Beehive House during much of his tenure as governor and church president in Utah. The required tours, which begin on your arrival, vary in the amount of historic house detail provided versus religious education offered, depending on the particular LDS docent. The attached 1855 **Lion House**, which was home to a number of Young's other wives, has a self-service restaurant in the basement. Feel free to look around the dining rooms during mealtimes.

Brigham Young Monument MONUMENT
(Map p472) On Main St at South Temple St the Brigham Young Monument marks the zero point for the city.

FREE **Museum of Church History & Art** MUSEUM
(Map p472; www.churchhistorymuseum.org; 45 N West Temple St; ☉9am-9pm Mon-Fri, 10am-7pm Sat & Sun) Adjoining Temple Square, this museum has impressive exhibits of pioneer history and fine art.

City Creek PLAZA
(Map p472; Social Hall Ave, btwn Regent & Richards Sts) An LDS-funded, 20-acre pedestrian plaza with fountains, restaurants and retail along City Creek was under construction at time of research.

GREATER DOWNTOWN

Salt Lake City Main Library LIBRARY
(Map p472; www.slcpl.org; 210 E 400 South; ☉9am-9pm Mon-Thu, 9am-6pm Fri & Sat, 1-5pm Sun) You can do more than read a book at this library. Meander past dramatic glass-walled architecture, stroll through the roof garden or stop by the ground-floor shops (from gardening to comic-book publishing). Occasional concerts are held here too.

FREE **Utah State Capitol** HISTORIC BUILDING
(Map p472; www.utahstatecapitol.utah.gov; ☉8am-8pm Mon-Fri, 8am-6pm Sat & Sun) The 1916 Utah State Capitol, modeled after the US capitol, cost an amazing $2.7 million to build back in the day. After six years, and 500 cherry trees, a full renovation of the building and grounds was completed in 2007. Look for colorful Works Progress Administration (WPA) murals of pioneers, trappers and missionaries adorning part of the building's dome. Free hourly tours (from 9am to 4pm) start at the 1st-floor visitor center.

Other Historic Buildings HISTORIC SITE
(www.utahheritagefoundation.com) The Utah Heritage Foundation puts out a free self-guided downtown walking tour brochure available from the visitor center and online. It also has brochures for several other neighborhoods, and an MP3 downloadable audio tour of the Gateway and Warehouse district.

FREE **Pioneer Memorial Museum** MUSEUM
(Map p472; www.dupinternational.org; 300 N Main St; ☉9am-5pm Mon-Sat year-round, plus 1-5pm Sun Jun-Aug) You'll find relics from the early days at Daughters of Utah Pioneers (DUP) museums throughout Utah, but the Pioneer Memorial Museum is by far the biggest. The vast, four-story treasure trove is like Utah's attic, with a taxidermy two-headed lamb and human-hair artwork in addition to more predictable artifacts.

Clark Planetarium MUSEUM
(Map p472; ☎801-456-7827; www.clarkplanetarium.org; 110 S 400 West; tickets adult/child $8/6; ☉10:30am-10pm Sun-Thu, 10:30am-11pm Fri & Sat) You'll be seeing stars at Clark Planetarium, home to the latest and greatest 3-D sky shows and Utah's only IMAX theater. There are free science exhibits, too. The planetarium is on the edge of the Gateway, a combination indoor-outdoor shopping complex anchored by the old railway depot.

FREE **Gilgal Garden** GARDENS
(Map p472; www.gilgalgarden.org; 749 E 500 South; ☉8am-8pm Apr-Sep, 9am-5pm Oct-Mar) Talk about obscure. Gilgal Garden is a quirky little green space hidden in a home-filled neighborhood. Most notably, this tiny sculpture garden contains a giant stone

---

WORTH A TRIP

KENNECOTT'S BINGHAM CANYON COPPER MINE

The view into the century-old **mine** (www.kennecott.com; Hwy 111; per vehicle $5; ☉8am-8pm Apr-Oct), 20 miles southwest of SLC, is slightly unreal. Massive dump trucks (some more than 12ft tall) look no larger than toys as they wind up and down the world's largest excavation. The 2.5-mile-wide and 0.75-mile-deep gash, which is still growing, is visible from space – and there's a picture from Apollo 11 inside the museum to prove it. Overall, it's a fascinating stop.

sphinx wearing Mormon founder Joseph Smith's face.

UNIVERSITY FOOTHILLS DISTRICT

Utah Museum of Natural History MUSEUM
(Map p470; http://umnh.utah.edu; 200 Wakara Way; adult/child $7/5; ☺10am-5pm Mon-Sat) The massive Rio Tinto Center makes a suitable home for the museum's prize Huntington Mammoth, one of the most complete fossils of its kind in the world. After taking a hiatus, it and other Utah-found objects and fossils are once again on display – in a shiny new museum building.

This is the Place Heritage Park HISTORIC SITE
(Map p470; www.thisistheplace.org; 2601 E Sunny side Ave; park admission free, village adult/child $10/7 Jun-Aug; ☺9am-5pm Mon-Fri, 10am-5pm Sat; 🚻) Dedicated to the 1847 arrival of the Mormons, the heritage park covers 450 acres. The centerpiece is a living-history village where, June through August, costumed docents depict mid-19th-century life. Admission includes a tourist-train ride and activities. The rest of the year, access is limited to varying degrees at varyingly reduced prices; you'll at least be able to wander around the exterior of the 41 buildings. Some are replicas, some are originals, such as Brigham Young's farmhouse.

Red Butte Garden GARDEN
(Map p470; www.redbuttegarden.org; 300 Wakara Way; adult/child $8/6; ☺9am-9pm May-Aug, 9am-5pm Sep-Apr) Both landscaped and natural gardens cover a lovely 150 acres, all accessible by trail, here in the Wasatch foothills. Check online to see who's playing at their popular outdoor summer concert series.

Utah Museum of Fine Arts MUSEUM
(Map p470; ☎801-581-7332; www.umfa.utah.edu; 410 Campus Center Dr; adult/child $7/5; ☺10am-5pm Tue, Thu & Fri, 10am-8pm Wed, 11am-5pm Sat & Sun) Soaring galleries showcase permanent collections of tribal, Western and modern art at the Utah Museum of Fine Arts.

FREE **Olympic Legacy Cauldron Park** PARK
(Map p470; www.utah.edu; Rice-Eccles Stadium, 451 S 1400 East; ☺10am-6pm Mon-Sat) The University of Utah, or 'U of U', was the site of the Olympic Village in 2002. This small on-site park has giant panels detailing the games and contains the torch. A 10-minute dramatic but heartfelt film booms with artificial fog and sound effects.

🏃 Activities

The best of SLC's outdoor activities are 30 to 50 miles away in the Wasatch Mountains (p481), but gear is available in town. Bicycle rental ranges from $35 to $50 per day. In winter, public transportation links the town with resorts.

Church Fork Trail HIKING
(Millcreek Canyon, off Wasatch Blvd; day-use $3) Looking for the nearest workout with big views? Hike the 6-mile round-trip, pet-friendly trail up to Grandeur Peak (8299ft). Millcreek Canyon is 13.5 miles southwest of downtown.

Utah Olympic Oval SKATING
(☎801-968-6825; www.olyparks.com; 5662 S 4800 West; adult/child $6/4) You can learn to curl as well as skate at Utah Olympic Oval, the site of speed-skating events in the 2002 Winter Olympics. Check ahead for public hours, which vary.

Miller Motorsports Park EXTREME SPORTS
(☎435-277-7223; http://millermotorsportspark.com; 2901 N Sheep Lane, Tooele) Feel the need for speed? Head 30 miles west of town, where you can take a lesson and get behind the wheel of a 325 horsepower Mustang GT race model (reservations required), kart race or do a zip line. Book ahead. Utah Jazz' late Larry Miller built the raceway.

Outfitters

REI OUTDOORS
(off Map p470; ☎801-486-2100; www.rei.com; 3285 E 3300 South; ☺10am-9pm Mon-Fri, 9am-7pm Sat, 11am-7pm Sun) Rents and sells camping equipment, climbing shoes, kayaks and most winter-sports gear. It also stocks a great selection of maps and activity guides, and has an interagency public-lands help desk inside.

Wasatch Touring ADVENTURE SPORTS
(Map p472; ☎801-359-9361; www.wasatchtouring.com; 702 E 100 South) Rents bikes, kayaks, climbing shoes and ski equipment.

Black Diamond Equipment ADVENTURE SPORTS
(off Map p470; www.bdel.com; 2092 E 3900 South; ☺10am-7pm, Mon–Sat 11am-5pm Sun) Retail store for leading manufacturer of climbing and ski gear that headquarters here in SLC.

🎊 Festivals & Events

Utah Pride Festival CULTURAL
(http://utahpridefestival.org) June gay pride festival with outdoor concerts, parade and 5km run.

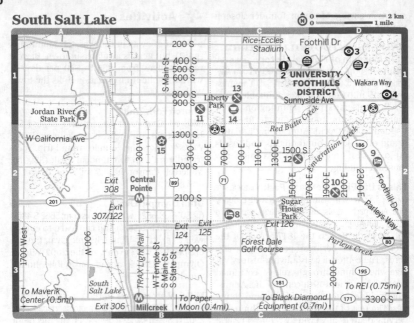

South Salt Lake

Utah Arts Festival CULTURAL
(www.uaf.org) Concerts, exhibitions and craft workshops during three days; late June.

Days of '47 CULTURAL
(www.daysof47.com) A pioneer parade, rodeo and re-enacted encampment are all part of the July-long festival celebrating the city's first settlers.

🛏 Sleeping

Downtown chain properties cluster around S 200 West near 500 South and 600 South; there are more in Mid-Valley (off I-215) and near the airport. At high-end hotels rates are lowest on weekends. Look for camping and alternative lodging in the Wasatch Mountains.

Parrish Place Bed & Breakfast B&B **$$**
(Map p470; ☎801-832-0970, 855-832-0970; www.parrishplace.com; 720 E Ashton Ave; r incl breakfast $99-139; P❀🛜) 'Comfortably antique' describes SLC's most reasonable, 19th-century mansion B&B. Rooms have both elegant and eclectic details – like a commode that is behind a decorative screen instead of a door. Continental breakfast arrives in a basket at your door daily. Hot tub and complimentary beverage center on site.

Peery Hotel HOTEL **$-$$**
(Map p472; ☎801-521-4300, 800-331-0073; www.peeryhotel.com; 110 W 300 South; r $90-130; P❀@🛜) Egyptian-cotton robes and sheets, carved dark-wood furnishings, individually decorated rooms – prepare to be charmed by the 1910 Peery. Small but impeccable bathrooms have pedestal sinks and aromatherapy jams and jellies. This stately hotel stands smack in the center of the Broadway Ave entertainment district, walking distance to restaurants, bars and theaters. Parking $10 per day.

Hotel Monaco HOTEL **$$-$$$**
(Map p472; ☎801-595-0000, 877-294-9710; www.monaco-saltlakecity.com; 15 W 200 South; r $139-249; P❀@🛜🐾) Rich colors, sleek stripes and plush prints create a whimsical mix at this sassy boutique chain. Here, pampered guest pets receive special treatment, and the front desk will loan you a goldfish if you need company. Evening wine receptions are free; parking ($15) and internet access ($10) are extra.

Inn on the Hill B&B **$$**
(Map p472; ☎801-328-1466; www.inn-on-the-hill.com; 225 N State St; r incl breakfast $120-180; P❀@🛜) Maxfield Parrish Tiffany glass adorns the entryway of this stunning 1906

South Salt Lake

Renaissance Revival mansion high above Temple Sq. Play billiards or read by the fire in one of three parlors.

Anniversary Inn B&B $$-$$$
(Map p472; ☎801-363 4953, 800-324-4152; www.anniversaryinn.com; 678 E South Temple St; ste incl breakfast $129-249; P✳@☎) Sleep among the tree trunks of an enchanted forest or inside an Egyptian pyramid: these 3-D themed suites are nothing if not over the top. The quiet location is near a few good restaurants, and not far from Temple Sq.

Grand America HOTEL $$$
(Map p472; ☎801-258-6000, 800-621-4505; www.grandamerica.com; 555 S Main St; r $189-289; P✳@☎≈) Rooms in SLC's only true luxury hotel are decked out with Italian marble bathrooms, English wool carpeting, tasseled damask draperies and other cushy details. If that's not enough to spoil you, there's always afternoon high tea or the lavish Sunday brunch. Paid parking ($15).

Crystal Inn & Suites MOTEL $-$$
(Map p472; ☎801-328-4466, 800-366-4466; www.crystalinnsaltlake.com; 230 W 500 South; r incl breakfast $75-95; P✳@☎≈) Restaurants and Temple Sq are within walking distance of the downtown, multistory branch of Crystal

Inns, a Utah-owned chain. Smiling staff here are genuinely helpful and there are lots of amenities for this price point (including a huge, hot breakfast).

Skyline Inn MOTEL $
(Map p470; ☎801-582-5350; www.skylineinn.com; 2475 E 1700 South; r $53-70; ✳@☎≈) A good choice for bargain-hunting skiers and hikers. This indie motel is only 30 minutes from the slopes, and has a hot tub, too. Rooms could use some refurbishment, though.

Ellerbeck Mansion B&B B&B $$
(Map p472; ☎801-355-2500, 800-966-8364; www.ellerbeckbedandbreakfast.com; 140 North B St; r incl breakfast $119-159) Rambling red-brick mansion with homey, eclectic decor. Walking distance to downtown.

Rodeway Inn MOTEL $
(Map p472; ☎801-534-0808, 877-424-6423; www.rodewayinn.com; 616 S 200 West; r incl breakfast $59-109; P✳@☎≈) Solid budget choice, within walking distance of downtown.

Avenues Hostel HOSTEL $
(Map p472; ☎801-359-3855, 801-539-8888; www.saltlakehostel.com; 107 F St; dm $18, s/d with shared bath $30/40, with private bath $40/50; ✳@☎) Well-worn hostel; a bit halfway house-like with long-term residents, but a convenient location.

✖ Eating

Foodies may be surprised to learn how well you can eat in SLC. Many of Salt Lake City's bountiful assortment of ethnic and organically-minded restaurants are within the downtown core. There are also small enclaves in atmospheric neighborhoods 9th and 9th and 15th and 15th (near the intersection of 900 East and 900 South, 1500 East and 1500 South). Up in the foothills southeast of downtown are a few canyons options.

TOP CHOICE Copper Onion MODERN AMERICAN $$
(Map p472; 111 E Broadway; brunch $7-13, small plates $5-13, dinner $15-18; ☺11:30am-10pm Mon-Fri, 10:30am-10pm Sat & Sun) Locals can't stop raving about the farm-to-table fresh food at the Copper Onion. And for good reason: small plates like ricotta dumplings and pork belly salad have an earthy realness that calls out to be shared. Even the pastas are perfectly al dente. Design-driven rustic decor provides a convivial place to enjoy it all. Full bar available.

Downtown Salt Lake City

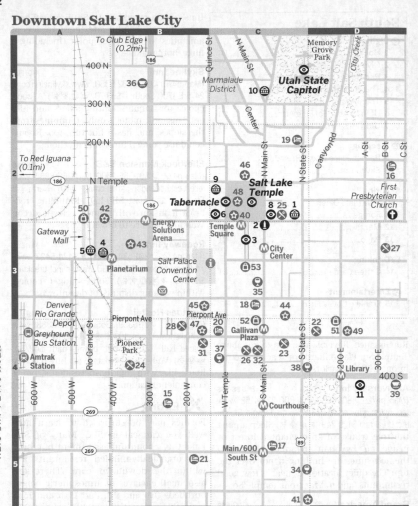

Red Iguana MEXICAN **$$**
(off Map p472; 736 W North Temple; mains $10-16; ⏰11am-10pm Mon-Thu, 11am-11pm Fri, 10am-11pm Sat, 10am-9pm Sun) Ask for a plate of sample mole if you can't decide which of the seven chile- and chocolate-based sauces sounds best. Really, you can't go wrong with any of the thoughtfully-flavored Mexican food at this always-packed, family-run restaurant.

Mazza MIDDLE EASTERN **$$**
(Map p470; 1515 S 1500 East; sandwiches $7-10, dinner $15-21; ⏰11am-10pm Mon-Sat; 🖉) Well-known items such as kebabs, schwarma and hummus are, of course, on the menu. But

so are more regional specialties, many from Lebanon. Love what they do with lamb and eggplant. Great upscale-casual atmosphere, too.

Pago ORGANIC **$$-$$$**
(Map p470; ✆801-532-0777; 878 S 900 East; mains $18-27; ⏰11am-3pm & 5-10pm Tue-Sat) Seasonal eclectic mains include dishes like a Moroccan fried chicken with frisée or a truffle burger. Sit outside at the few sidewalk tables and you'll feel like part of the chummy neighborhood. Dinner reservations recommended.

American casual dishes well. The lively pub atmosphere is always fun.

Lion House Pantry Restaurant
AMERICAN **$**

(Map p472; 63 E South Temple St; meals $7-12; ☺11am-8pm Mon-Sat) Down-home, carb-rich cookin' just like your Mormon grandmother used to make – only it's served cafeteria-style in the basement of an historic house. Several of Brigham Young's wives used to live here (including this author's great-great-great grandmother).

Takashi
JAPANESE **$$-$$$**

(Map p472; 18 W Market St; rolls $8-14, mains $15-25; ☺11:30am-2pm & 5:30-10pm Mon-Sat) The best of a number of surprisingly good sushi restaurants here in landlocked Salt Lake. Even LA restaurant snobs rave about the excellent rolls at ever-so-chic Takashi.

Forage
MODERN AMERICAN **$$$**

(Map p470; ☎801-708-7834; 370 E 900 South; mains $25-45; ☺5:30-10pm Tue-Sat) Food as art. The minimalist creative flourishes here attract both gourmets and awards; its five-course tasting menu is an event. Reserve ahead.

Ruth's Diner
DINER **$-$$**

(4160 Emigration Canyon Rd; mains $6-16; ☺8am-10pm) Once a railcar diner, Ruth's has expanded into a sprawling institution. We love the canyon surrounds – and the eggs benedict. Summer concerts sometimes accompany dinner.

🌿 One World Everybody Eats
ORGANIC **$**

(Map p472; 41 S 300 East; ☺11am-9pm Mon-Sat, 9am-5pm Sun; ☑) At this eco-conscious, community-oriented eatery, you decide what you pay and your portion size (they will provide suggestions). Daily-changing dishes include salads, stir-fries, pastas, Indian curries and the like.

Curryer
INDIAN **$**

(Map p472; 300 South, btwn S State & S Main Sts; dishes $4-6; ☺11am-2pm) This former hot-dog cart, modified with a tandoori oven, serves up a tasty range of regional Indian food from butter chicken to vegan-friendly *aloo matar* (spiced potatoes and peas).

Blue Plate Diner
DINER **$-$$**

(Map p470; 2041 S 2100 East; breakfast & burgers $4-8, mains $8-10; ☺7am-9pm Sun-Thu, 7am-10pm Fri & Sat) A hip, retro diner with a soda

Wild Grape
MODERN AMERICAN **$$-$$$**

(Map p472; 481 E South Temple; breakfast & lunch $6-15, dinner $18-24; ☺8am-10pm Mon-Fri, 9am-10pm Sat & Sun) Billing itself as a 'new West' bistro, Wild Grape creates modern versions of country classics. We like the weekend brunch dishes best.

Squatters Pub Brewery
AMERICAN **$$**

(Map p472; 147 W Broadway; mains $9-15; ☺11am-midnight Sun-Thu, until 1am Fri & Sat) Come for an Emigration Pale Ale, stay for the blackened tilapia salad. In addition to great microbrews, Squatters does a wide range of

Downtown Salt Lake City

fountain, colorful patio and postcards from around the country as decoration.

Sage's Cafe   VEGETARIAN $$
(Map p472; 473 E Broadway; sandwiches $7-10, mains $13-16; ⊙11am-2pm & 5-10pm Mon-Fri, 10am-10pm Sat & Sun; ⊿) Creative, mostly vegan, mostly organic meals in a comfy former house.

Log Haven   MODERN AMERICAN $$$
(⊉801-272-8255; Mill Creek Canyon Rd; mains $24-32; ⊙5-10pm) Romantic log cabin restaurant in the hills.

Market Street Grill   SEAFOOD $$-$$$
(Map p472; ⊉801-322-4668; 48 W Market St; breakfast $5-10, lunch specials $13, mains $19-28;

⊙breakfast, lunch & dinner) SLC's favorite seafood served at a cosmopolitan fish house.

Sawadee   THAI $$
(Map p472; 754 E South Temple St; mains $9-11; ⊙11am-2:30pm & 5-10pm Mon-Sat) Decent Thai food, fabulous dark-wood-and-bubbling-fountain decor.

Red Rock Brewing Company   PUB $$
(Map p472; ⊉801-521-7446; 254 S 200 West; sandwiches $7-10, mains $14-18; ⊙11am-11pm) So-so service, but this brewpub still attracts a crowd.

Downtown Farmers Market   MARKET $
(Map p472; Pioneer Park, cnr 300 South & 300 West; ⊙8am-1pm Sat mid-Jun–late Oct, 4pm-

SALT LAKE CITY FOR CHILDREN

Salt Lake is a kiddie-friendly city if there ever was one. In addition to some of the sights already listed, the wonderful hands-on exhibits at the **Discovery Gateway** (Map p472; www.childmuseum.org; 444 W 100 South; admission $8.50; ⊙10am-6pm Mon-Thu, 10am-8pm Fri & Sat, noon-6pm Sun; ⊞) stimulate imaginations and senses.

Kids can help farmhands milk cows, churn butter and feed animals at **Wheeler Historic Farm** (www.wheelerfarm.com; South Cottonwood Regional Park, 6351 S 900 East; admission free, hay ride $2; ⊙9:30am-5:30pm; ⊞), which dates from 1886. There's also blacksmithing, quilting and hay rides in summer.

More than 800 animals inhabit zones such as the Asian Highlands on the landscaped 42-acre grounds at **Hogle Zoo** (Map p470; www.hoglezoo.org; University Foothills District, 2600 East Sunnyside Ave; adult/child $9/7; ⊙9am-5pm; ⊞). Daily animal encounter programs help kids learn more about their favorite species.

Tracy Aviary (Map p470; www.tracyaviary.org; 589 E 1300 South; adult/child $7/5; ⊙9am-5pm; ⊞) lets little ones toss fish to the pelicans as one of its interactive programs and performances. More than 400 winged creatures from around the world call this bird park home.

With 55 acres of gardens, full-scale working-petting farm, golf course, giant movie theater, museum, dining, shopping and ice cream parlor: what doesn't the **Thanksgiving Point** (3003 N Thanksgiving Way, Lehi; all-attraction pass adult/child $25/19; ⊙10am-8pm Mon-Sat; ⊞) have? The on-site **Museum of Ancient Life** (museum only adult/child $10/8) is one of the highest-tech and most hands-on dinosaur museums in the state. Kids can dig for their own bones, dress up a dinosaur, play in a watery Silurian reef... To get here take exit 287 off I 15; Lehi is 28 miles south of downtown SLC.

dusk Tue Aug-Sep) Regionally-grown produce, ready to eat baked goodies and local crafts.

🍷 Drinking

Pubs and bars that also serve food are mainstays of SLC's nightlife, and no one minds if you mainly drink and nibble. In addition to those listed here, see Squatters and Red Rock breweries under Eating. A complete schedule of local bar music is available in the *City Weekly* (www.cityweekly.net).

Gracie's
BAR
(Map p472; 326 S West Temple; ⊙11am-2am) Even with two levels and four bars, Gracie's trendy bar-restaurant still gets crowded. The two sprawling patios are the best place to kick back. Live music or DJs most nights.

Green Pig
BAR
(Map p472; 31 E 400 South; ⊙11am-2am) Your friendly neighborhood watering hole hosts poker tournaments, has live jam sessions and plays sporting events on big screens. The roof patio is tops.

Bayou
PUB
(Map p472; 645 S State St; ⊙noon-1am) Known almost as much for its Cajun specialties and pub grub as for its vast selection of beer; by

day office workers dine, by night they party. Live music weekends.

Beerhive Pub
PUB
(Map p472; 128 S Main St; ⊙noon-1am) More than 200 beer choices, including many Utah-local microbrews, are wedged into this downtown storefront bar. Good for drinking and conversation.

Coffee Garden
COFFEE SHOP
(Map p470; 895 E 900 South; ⊙6am-11pm Sun-Thu, 6am-midnight Fri & Sat; 🛜) Our favorite coffeehouse has a great laid-back vibe at the heart of the eclectic 9th and 9th neighborhood. A multitude of tasty homebaked goods come with and without the sin (gluten and fat-free available).

Salt Lake Roasting Co
COFFEE SHOP
(SLRC; Map p472; 320 E 400 South; ⊙7am-midnight; 🛜) It's all about the beans here – from 100% Kona to Gayo Mountain shade-grown Sumatran. There's an SLRC branch cafe in the SLC Library.

☆ Entertainment

We wouldn't say the nightlife is all that hot; major dance clubs change frequently and few are open more than a couple nights a

WHAT THE...?

The beer you get in many a restaurant, and all grocery stores, doesn't exceed 3.2% alcohol content by weight. Whoa...how am I ever going to get buzzed, you ask? Well it may be easier than you think. The alcohol content for beers sold in the US is generally measured by volume, not weight. So a '3.2' beer is actually closer to a 4% beer by volume (a typical Budweiser is 5% by volume). So there's really not that big a difference.

week. See the *City Weekly* (www.cityweekly .net) for listings. Classical entertainment options, especially around Temple Sq, are plentiful.

Nightclubs

Tavernacle Social Club　　　　CLUB
(Map p472; 201 E Broadway; ☺5pm-1am Tue-Sat, 8pm-midnight Sun) Dueling pianos or karaoke nightly.

Hotel/Elevate　　　　　　　　CLUB
(Map p472; 155 W 200 South; 9pm-2am Thu-Sat) Top DJs spin house music and more; live music includes R&B and jazz.

Burt's Tiki Lounge　　　　　CLUB
(Map p472; 726 S State St; ☺9pm-2am Thu-Sat) More divey club than tiki lounge; music may be punk, funk or ska – anything loud.

Live Music & Theater

In addition to venues listed below, there are also concerts on Temple Sq, at the Library and in Red Butte Gardens in the summertime. The Salt Lake City Arts Council provides a complete cultural events calendar on its website (www.slcgov.com /arts/calendar.pdf). Unless otherwise noted, reserve through **ArtTix** (☑801-355-2787, 888-451-2787; www.arttix.org).

Mormon Tabernacle Choir　　LIVE MUSIC
(☑435-570-0080 for tickets; www.mormon tabernaclechoir.org) Hearing the world-renowned Mormon Tabernacle Choir is a must-do on any SLC bucket list. A live choir broadcast goes out every Sunday at 9:30am. September through November, and January through May, attend in person at the **Tabernacle** (Map p472; Temple Sq). Free public rehearsals are held here from 8pm to 9pm Thursday. From June to August and in December – to accommodate larger crowds – choir broadcasts and rehearsals are held at the 21,000-seat **LDS Conference Center** (Map p472; cnr N Temple & Main St). Performance times stay the same, except that an extra Monday-to-Saturday organ recital takes place at 2pm.

Gallivan Center　　　　　CONCERT VENUE
(Map p472; www.thegallivancenter.com; 200 South, btwn State & Main Sts) Bring a picnic to the outdoor concert and movie series at the Gallivan Center, an amphitheater in a garden; runs in summer.

Assembly Hall　　　　　CONCERT VENUE
(Map p472; www.visittemplesquare.com; Temple Sq) A lovely 1877 Gothic building in Temple Sq; hosts concerts big and small.

Rose Wagner Performing Arts Center　　　　　　　THEATER
(Map p472; 138 W 300 South) Many of SLC Arts Council's dramatic and musical theater performances are staged here.

Depot　　　　　　　CONCERT VENUE
(Map p472; ☑801-355-5522; 400 W South Temple; www.smithstix.com) Primary concert venue for rock acts.

Sports

Utah Jazz　　　　　　　BASKETBALL
(☑801-325-2500; www.nba.com/jazz) Utah Jazz, the men's professional basketball team, plays at the **Energy Solutions Arena** (Map p472; www.energysolutionsarena.com; 301 W South Temple St), where concerts are also held.

Utah Grizzlies　　　　　ICE HOCKEY
(☑801-988-7825; www.utahgrizzlies.com) The International Hockey League's Utah Grizzlies plays at the **Maverik Center** (www.maverik center.com; 3200 S Decker Lake Dr, West Valley City), which hosted most of the men's ice-hockey competitions during the Olympics.

Salt Lake Bees　　　　　BASEBALL
(☑801-325-2273 for tickets; www.slbees.com) The AAA minor-league affiliate of the Anaheim Angels plays at **Franklin Covey Field** (Map p470; 77 W 1300 South).

 Shopping

An interesting array of boutiques, antiques and cafes line up along Broadway Ave (300 South), between 100 and 300 East. Drawing on Utah pioneer heritage, SLC has quite a few crafty shops and galleries scattered around. A few can be found on the 300 block of W Pierpont Ave. Many participate in the one-day **Craft Salt Lake** (www.craft lakecity.com) expo in August.

Sam Weller Books BOOKS
(Map p472; ☏801-328-2586; 254 S Main; ☺10am-7pm Mon-Sat) The city's biggest and best independent bookstore also has a praise-worthy local rare book selection. Note that at press time, Weller's was looking for a new downtown location.

Utah Artist Hands ARTS & CRAFTS
(Map p472; 61 W 100 South) Local artists' work, all made in-state.

Sewing Parlor ARTS & CRAFTS
(339 W Pierpont; ☺11:30am-6pm Wed-Fri, 1-6pm Tue & Sat) Pick up the supplies to create your own clothing, or have something custom made here.

Ken Sanders Rare Books BOOKS
(Map p472; www.kensandersbooks.com; 268 S 200 East) Specializes in Western authors.

Gateway MALL
(Map p472; 200 South to 50 N, 400 West to 500 West) Major-label shopping mall right downtown.

❶ Information

Emergency
Local police (☏801-799-3000; 315 E 200 South)

Media
City Weekly (www.cityweekly.net) Free alternative weekly with good restaurant and entertainment listings; twice annually it publishes the free *City Guide*.

Deseret News (www.desnews.com) Ultraconservative, church-owned paper.

Salt Lake Magazine (www.saltlakemagazine .com) Lifestyle and food.

Salt Lake Tribune (www.sltrib.com) Utah's largest-circulation daily paper.

Medical Services
University Hospital (☏801-581-2121; 50 N Medical Dr) For emergencies, 24/7.

Money
Note that it can be difficult to change currency in Utah outside SLC.

Wells Fargo (79 S Main St) Convenient currency exchange and ATM.

Post
Post office (www.usps.com; 230 W 200 South)

Tourist Information
Public Lands Information Center (☏801-466-6411; www.publiclands.org; REI Store, 3285 E 3300 South; ☺10:30am-5:30pm Mon-Fri, 9am-1pm Sat) Recreation information for nearby public lands (state parks, BLM, USFS), including the Wasatch-Cache National Forest.

Visitor Information Center (☏801-534-4900; Salt Palace Convention Center, 90 S West Temple; ☺9am-6pm Mon-Fri, 9am-5pm Sat & Sun) Publishes free visitor-guide booklet; large gift shop on site.

Websites
Downtown SLC (www.downtownslc.org) Arts, entertainment and business information about the downtown core.

Lonely Planet (www.lonelyplanet.com/usa /southwest/salt-lake-city) Planning advice, author recommendations, traveler reviews and insider tips.

Salt Lake Convention & Visitors Bureau (www.visitsaltlake.com) SLC's official information website.

GAY & LESBIAN SLC

Salt Lake City has Utah's only gay scene, however limited. Pick up the free *Q Salt Lake* (www.qsaltlake.com) for listings. Utah Pride Festival, one weekend in June, is a big party and parade. The town's closest thing to a gay-ish neighborhood is 9th and 9th (900 South and 900 East), where Coffee Garden is the neighborhood cafe. An upbeat coffee shop inside the Utah Pride Center, **Café Marmalade** (www.utahpridecenter.com; 361 N 300 West; ☺7am-9pm Mon-Fri, 8am-9pm Sat, 10am-9pm Sun) has open-mike nights, weekend BBQs and concerts, and the largest GLBT library in the state.

GLBT-friendly entertainment venues include:

Club Edge (off Map p472; 615 N 400 West) Large dancefloor and DJs; Sunday is Latin gay night.

Paper Moon (off Map p470; 3737 S State St) Nightclub boasting a big tube of lipstick and stripper poles; had a lesbian orientation, now attracts a mixed community.

THE BOOK OF MORMON, THE MUSICAL

Singing and dancing Mormon missionaries? You betcha...at least on Broadway. In the spring of 2011 *The Book of Mormon*, the musical, opened to critical acclaim at the Eugene O'Neill Theatre in New York. The light-hearted satire about missionaries in Uganda came out of the comic minds that also created the *Avenue Q* musical and the animated TV series *South Park*. No wonder people laughed them all the way to nine Tony Awards. The LDS church's official response? Actually quite measured, avoiding any direct criticism. Though it was made clear that their belief is that while the Book the musical can entertain you, the Book the scripture can change your life.

❶ Getting There & Away

Springdale and Zion National Park are 308 miles to the south; Moab and Arches are 234 miles south and east.

Air

Five miles northwest of downtown, **Salt Lake City International Airport** (SLC; www.slcairport .com; 776 N Terminal Dr) has mostly domestic flights, though you can fly direct to Canada and Mexico. **Delta** (www.delta.com) is the main SLC carrier.

Bus

Greyhound (☑800-231-2222; www.greyhound .com; 300 S 600 West) connects SLC with southwestern towns, including St George, UT ($55, six hours); Las Vegas, NV ($62, eight hours); and Denver, CO ($86, 10 hours).

Train

Traveling between Chicago and Oakland/Emeryville, the California Zephyr from **Amtrak** (☑801-322-3510, 800-872-7245; www.amtrak .com) stops daily at **Union Pacific Rail Depot** (340 S 600 West). Southwest destinations include Denver, CO, ($115, 15 hours) and Reno, NV ($64, 10 hours). Schedule delays can be substantial.

❶ Getting Around

Two major interstates cross at SLC: I-15 runs north-south, I-80 east-west. I-215 loops the city.

CONNECT PASS

Salt Lake City Visitors Bureau (www .visitsaltlake.com) sells one- to three-day discounted attraction passes (one day, adult/child $24/20) online and at the visitor center. But unless you plan to visit every child-friendly attraction in the town – and some outside of town – it probably isn't worth your while.

The area around Temple Square is easily walkable, and free public transportation covers much of the downtown core, but to go beyond you will need your own vehicle.

To/From the Airport

Express Shuttle (☑800-397-0773; www .xpressshuttleutah.com) Shared van service, $16 to downtown.

Yellow Cab (☑801-521-2100) Private taxi; from $25 to downtown.

Utah Transit Authority (UTA; www.rideuta .com; one-way $2) Bus 550 travels downtown from the parking structure between terminals 1 and 2.

Car & Motorcycle

National rental agencies have SLC airport offices.

Rugged Rental (☑801-977-9111, 800-977-9111; www.ruggedrental.com; 2740 W California Ave; ⊙8am-6pm Mon-Sat) Rents 4WDs, SUVs and passenger cars. Rates are often better here than at the majors.

Public Transportation

UTA (www.rideuta.com) Trax, UTA's light-rail system, runs from Central Station (600 W 250 South) west to the University of Utah and south past Sandy. The center of downtown SLC is a free-fare zone. During ski season UTA buses serve the local ski resorts ($7 round-trip).

Antelope Island State Park

The Great Salt Lake is the largest body of water west of the Great Lakes, but it's hard to say just exactly how big it is. Since 1873 the lake has varied from 900 to 2500 sq miles. Maximum depths have ranged from 24ft to 45ft – it's wide and shallow, like a plate. Spring runoff raises levels; summer's sweltering heat lowers them. Evaporation is why the lake is so salty, but its salinity varies drastically, from 6% to 27% (compared with only 3.5% for seawater), depending on location and weather.

The lake is recognized as a Unesco World Heritage Site for its importance for migratory routes. During fall (September to November) and spring (March to May) migrations, the hundreds of thousands of birds descend on the park to feast on tiny brine shrimp along the lakeshore en route to distant lands. The best place to experience the lake (and see the birds) is at **Antelope Island State Park** (☎801-773-2941; http://stateparks.utah.gov; Antelope Dr; day use per vehicle $9; ⊘7am-10pm May-Sep, off-season hours vary), 25 miles north of SLC. White-sand beaches, birds – and buffalo – are what attract people to the pretty, 15-mile-long park. That's right: the largest island in the Great Salt Lake is home to a 500-strong herd of American bison, or buffalo. The **fall roundup**, for veterinary examination, is a thrilling spectacle. Also making their year-round home here are burrowing owls and raptors as well as namesake antelope, bighorn sheep and deer.

Inquire about the many ranger-led activities, watch an introductory video and pick up a map at the **visitor center** (⊘9am-5pm). Nineteen miles of **hiking trails** provide many opportunities to view wildlife; however, some trails are closed during mating and birthing seasons. There is an 8-mile driving loop and a dirt-road spur that leads 11 miles to **Fielding Garr Ranch** (⊘9am-5pm). Take a look around what was a working farm from 1848 until 1981, back when the state park was created.

North of the visitor center there's a small marina and simple **Buffalo Island Grill** (mains $6-14; ⊘11am-8pm May-Sep). The white, sandy **beach** to the south on Bridger Bay has showers and flushing toilets that both swimmers (more like floaters with all that salt) and campers use. The 18-site **Bridger Bay Campground** (☎800-322-3770 for reservations; http://utah stateparks.reserveamerica.com; tent & RV sites $13) has shelters for shade, water and pit toilets, but no hookups.

To get to the park, head west from I-15 exit 335 and follow the signs; a 7-mile causeway leads to the island.

Brigham City & Around

POP 17,100 / ELEV 4315 FT

Drive north on I-15 from Salt Lake City, past Ogden (p495), the gateway to the Wasatch Mountains ski resorts, and after 50 miles you'll get to the turnoff for Brigham City. The town is pretty small, with a few natural attractions, and one famous restaurant. The stretch of Hwy 89 south of town is known as the 'Golden Spike Fruitway' – from July through September it is crowded with fruit stands vending the abundant local harvest. One week in September Brigham City celebrates 'Peach Days'. Contact **Box Elder County Tourism** (☎435-734-2634; www.box elder.org) for area information.

West of town, the **Bear River Migratory Bird Refuge** (www.fws.gov/bearriver; W Forest St; admission free; ⊘dawn-dusk) engulfs almost 74,000 acres of marshes on the northeastern shores of the Great Salt Lake. The best time for bird-watchers is during fall (September to November) and spring (March to May) migrations. Birds banded here have been recovered as far away as Siberia and Colombia. Cruising along the 12-mile, barely elevated touring road feels like you're driving on water. You can hear the replicated migratory calls and find out more year round at the **Wildlife Education Center** (☎435-734-6426; 2155 W Forest St; admission free; ⊘10am-5pm Mon-Fri, 10am-4pm Sat). The center is just after the I-15 intersection; the driving tour is 16 miles west. Free bird-watching tours leave from here twice daily; reserve ahead.

Get into hot water year-round at **Crystal Hot Springs** (☎435-279-8104; www .crystalhotsprings.net; 8215 N Hwy 38; pool adult/child $6.50/4.50, slides $10; ⊘noon-10pm Mon-Fri, 10am-10pm Sat, 11am-7pm Sun), 10 miles north in Honeyville. Adults float in different

---

SCENIC DRIVE: PONY EXPRESS TRAIL

Follow more than 130 miles of the original route that horse-and-rider mail delivery took on the **Pony Express Trail Backcountry Byway** (www.byways.org) from Fairfield to Callao. The trail begins at one of the former stops, in **Camp Floyd/Stagecoach Inn State Park** (http://stateparks.utah.gov; adult/child $2/free; ⊘9am-5pm Mon-Sat), 25 miles southwest of I-15 along Hwy 73. Most of the road is maintained gravel or dirt and is passable to ordinary cars in good weather. In winter, snow may close the route; watch for flash floods in summer.

SETTING SPEED RECORDS: BONNEVILLE SALT FLATS

Millennia ago, ancient Lake Bonneville covered northern Utah and beyond. Today, all that remains is the Great Salt Lake and 46 sq miles of shimmering white salt. The surface you see is mostly made up of sodium chloride (common table salt) and is 12ft deep in spots, though officials are worried about shrinkage and have started salt reclamation efforts. The Bonneville Salt Flats are now public lands managed by the **BLM** (☑801-977-4300; www.blm.gov/ut/st/en/fo/salt_lake/recreation/bonneville_salt_flats.html), and are best known for racing. The flat, hard salt makes speeds possible here that aren't possible anywhere else.

On October 15, 1997, Englishman Andy Green caused a sonic boom on the salt flats by driving the jet-car *ThrustSSC* to 763.035mph, setting the first ever supersonic world land-speed record. Several clubs hold racing events throughout the year; for a complete list, check the BLM website. Driving up to the flats is a singular optical experience. The vast whiteness tricks the eye into believing it's snowed in August, and the inexpressible flatness allows many to see the Earth's curvature. You may recognize the scene from movies, such as *Con Air* and *Independence Day*, that filmed scenes here.

The flats are about 100 miles west of SLC on I-80. Take exit 4, Bonneville Speedway, and follow the paved road to the viewing area parking lot (no services). From here you can drive on the hard-packed salt during late summer and fall (it's too wet otherwise). Obey posted signs: parts of the flats are thin and can trap vehicles. Remember, salt is insanely corrosive. If you drive on the flats, wash your car – especially the undercarriage – afterward. If you're traveling west, there's a rest stop where you can walk on the sand (and wash off your shoes in the bathroom). The nearest town is Wendover on the Utah–Nevada state line.

temperature soaking pools while kids zip down the water slides, which are open shorter hours than the pools from September through May. The log lodge and pools are well taken care of. There's also a small **campground** (tent/RV sites with hookup $15/25).

Brigham City is an easy day trip from Salt Lake, and there are a few motels, including a decent **Days Inn** (☑435-723-3500, 888-440-2021; www.daysinn.com; 1033 S 1600 West; r incl breakfast $75-90; ☏☒).

Utahans have been known to travel for hours to eat at **Maddox Ranch House** (☑435-723-8545; 1900 S Hwy 89; mains $17-25; ☺11:30am-9:30pm Tue-Sat), where they've been cutting thick beef steaks, cut from locally raised livestock, since 1949. You can still see the ranch out back where they originally started in the cattle business. Fried chicken and bison steaks are popular here, too. Don't expect anything fancy. This is a family-owned place used to serving families. No reservations accepted; expect to wait even if you go early. Out back at **Maddox Drive-In** (1900 S Hwy 89; mains $4-10; ☺11am-8:30pm Tue-Sat), carhop waiters deliver the famous fried chicken and bison burgers to your car window. Don't miss the homemade sarsaparilla soda.

Logan & Around

POP 42,700 / ELEV 4775FT

Logan is a quintessential old-fashioned American community with strong Mormon roots and a long downtown core. It's situated 80 miles north of Salt Lake City in bucolic Cache Valley, which offers year-round outdoor activities. Ask about the possibilities at **Cache Valley Visitor Bureau** (☑435-752-2161, 800-882-4433; www.tourcachevalley.com; 199 N Main St; ☺9am-5pm Mon-Fri).

The 19th-century frontier comes to life with hands-on living history activities at a Shoshone Indian camp and a pioneer settlement at the **American West Heritage Center** (www.awhc.org; 4025 S Hwy 89; adult/child $7/5; ☺11am-4pm Tue-Sat Jun-Aug, off-season hours vary; ☒), south of town. The center hosts many popular festivals, including weeklong **Festival of the American West** in July.

There are a couple of B&Bs around town, and midrange chain motels are well represented on Hwy 89. The comfy **Best Western Weston Inn** (☑435-752-5700, 800-532-5055; http://westoninn.com; 250 N Main; r incl breakfast $75-99; ☏☒) is right downtown. Twenty-five miles east in Logan Canyon, **Beaver Creek Lodge** (☑435-946-3400, 800-946-4485; www

.beavercreeklodge.com; Mile 487, Hwy 89; r $109-149) is a great getaway, with horseback riding, snowmobiling, skiing and other activities. No room phones.

For all-round American food, **Angie's Restaurant** (690 N Main St; mains $5-12; ☉6am-10pm) is very popular. The old bungalows along 100 East are home to a couple of interesting eateries, including the **Crepery** (130 N 100 East; mains $3-10; ☉9am-9pm Mon-Sat), where inventive crepe-stuffings include savory egg dishes and sweet s'mores (with marshmallow, chocolate and graham crackers).

WASATCH MOUNTAINS

Giant saw-toothed peaks stand guard along the eastern edge of Utah's urban centers. When the crush of civilization gets too much, locals escape to the forested slopes. The Wasatch Mountain Range is nature's playground all year long, but in winter a fabulous low-density, low-moisture snow – 300in to 500in of it a year – blankets the terrain. Perfect snow and thousands of acres of high-altitude slopes helped earn Utah the honor of hosting the 2002 Winter Olympics. The skiing in the Wasatch range is some of the best in North America.

Resort towns cluster near the peaks; Park City, on the eastern slopes, is the most well known and quasi-cosmopolitan of the bunch. Salt Lake City resorts, on the western side, are easiest for townies to reach. Ogden is the sleeper of the bunch and Sundance is known as much for its film festival as its ski trails. Most areas lie within 45 to 60 minutes of the SLC airport, so you can leave New York or Los Angeles in the morning and be skiing by noon.

 Information

Season

Ski season runs mid-November to mid-April – only Snowbird stays open much past Easter. However, snow varies: the 2010-11 winter set an all-time record, and deep powder hung around until June. Saturday is busiest; Sunday ticket sales drop by a third because LDS members are in church. Summer season is from late June until early September.

Hours

Day lifts usually run from 9am to 4pm.

Prices

Children's prices are good for ages six to 12; under sixes usually ski free. All resorts rent equipment (about $30 per day for ski or snowboard packages, $35 per day for a mountain bike). You may save a few bucks by renting off-mountain, but if there's a problem with the equipment, you're stuck. Ski schools are available at all resorts.

Conditions

Most resorts have jumped into the digital age and have powder reports, blogs and weather condition updates you can sign up to receive on their websites.

Rules

No pets are allowed at resorts and four-night minimum stays may be required December through March.

Ski Utah (☎800-754-8724; www.skiutah.com) Puts out excellent annual winter vacation guides – in paper and online.

THE REMOTE NORTHWEST

On May 10, 1869, the westward Union Pacific Railroad and eastward Central Pacific Railroad met at Promontory Summit. With the completion of the transcontinental railroad, the face of the American West changed forever. **Golden Spike National Historic Site** (www.nps.gov/gosp; per vehicle $7; ☉9am-5pm), 32 miles northwest of Brigham City on Hwy 83, has an interesting museum and films, auto tours and several interpretive trails. Steam-engine demonstrations take place June through August. Aside from Golden Spike National Historic Site, few people visit Utah's desolate northwest corner. But while you're here...

At the end of a dirt road (4WD recommended but not required), 15 miles west of the Golden Spike visitor center, there's a wonderfully unique outdoor art installation, the **Spiral Jetty** (www.spiraljetty.org). Created by Robert Smithson in 1970, it's a 1500ft coil of rock and earth spinning out into the water. It's a little hard to find; get directions from the visitor center.

WORTH A TRIP

LOGAN CANYON SCENIC BYWAY

Pick up a free interpretive trail guide at the Cache Valley Visitor Bureau in Logan before you head off on the 40-mile riverside drive through **Logan Canyon Scenic Byway** (http://logancanyon.com; Hwy 89 btwn Logan & Garden City). Wind your way up through the Bear River Mountains, past Beaver Mountain, before descending to the 20-mile-long Bear Lake, a summer water-sports playground. Along the way there are numerous signposted hiking and biking trails and campgrounds, which are all part of the **Uinta-Wasatch-Cache National Forest** (www.fs.usda.gov). It's beautiful year-round, but July wildflowers and October foliage are particularly brilliant. Note that parts of the route may be closed to snow December through May and campgrounds may not open until late June. Check conditions with the **Logan Ranger District Office** (☏435-755-3620; 1500 East Hwy 89; ☺8:30am-4:30pm).

Dangers & Annoyances

Backcountry enthusiasts: heed avalanche warnings! Take a course at a resort, carry proper equipment and check conditions. Drink plenty of fluids: dehydrated muscles injure easily.

Utah Avalanche Center (☏888-999-4019; http://utahavalanchecenter.org)

Road conditions (☏511)

Getting Around

Buses and shuttles are widely available, so you don't need to rent a car to reach most resorts. Advanced skiers looking for knock-your-socks-off adventure should definitely consider a backcountry tour.

Ski Utah Interconnect Adventure Tour (☏801-534-1907; www.skiutah.com/interconnect; ☺mid-Dec–mid-Apr) Six resorts in one day; $295 price tag includes lunch, lift tickets and all transportation.

Salt Lake City Resorts

Because of Great Salt Lake-affected snow, SLC resorts receive almost twice as much snow as Park City. The four resorts east of Salt Lake City sit 30 to 45 miles from the downtown core at the end of two canyons. Follow Hwy 190 up to family-oriented Solitude and skier fave Brighton in Big Cottonwood Canyon. In summer you can continue over the mountain from to Heber and Park Cities. To the south, Little Cottonwood Canyon is home to the seriously challenging terrain at Snowbird and the all-round ski-purist special, Alta. Numerous summer hiking and biking trails lead off from both canyons.

ℹ Information

For lodging-skiing package deals, see www.visitsaltlake.com or contact resorts directly.

Cottonwood Canyons Foundation (☏801-947-8263; www.cottonwoodcanyons.org) USFS ranger-led programs available at Alta, Brighton and Snowbird.

Ski Salt Lake Super Pass (www.visitsaltlake.com/ski_salt_lake; 4-day pass adult/child $208/120) Pass includes one day's lift ticket for each of the four resorts and all your transportation on UTA ski buses and light rail in town.

Getting Around

December through April, reach the resorts for $7 round-trip via SLC's public transit system, UTA. Bus route 951 goes from the downtown core to Snowbird and Alta. Six ski-service park-and-ride lots are available around town. The most convenient is Wasatch, from where you can take bus 960 to Solitude and Brighton or bus 951 or 990 to Snowbird and Alta. Buses also run between resorts in the same valley.

Alta Shuttle (☏435-274-0225, 866-274-0225; www.altashuttle.com) Shared van service between SLC and Snowbird or Alta.

Canyon Transportation (☏801 255-1841, 800-255-1841; www.canyontransport.com) Shared van service between SLC and Solitude, Brighton, Snowbird or Alta; from $38 one-way. Private service available to other destinations.

UTA (☏801-743-3882; www.rideuta.com)

Wasatch Park & Ride Lot (6200 S Wasatch Blvd)

SNOWBIRD SKI & SUMMER RESORT

If you can see it, you can ski it at **Snowbird** (☏801-933-2222, 800-232-9542; www.snowbird.com; Little Cottonwood Canyon; day lift ticket adult/child $74/40), the industrial-strength resort with extreme steeps, long groomers, wide-open bowls (one of them an incredible 500 acres across) and a kick-ass terrain park. The challenging slopes are particularly popular with speed demons and testosterone-driven snowboarders. The 125-passenger **aerial**

Wasatch Mountains

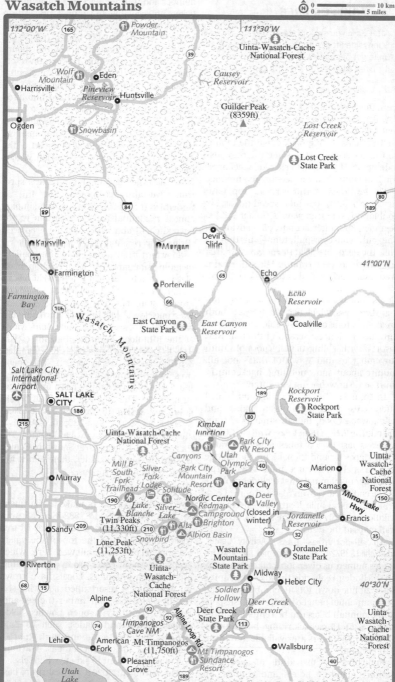

SKI FOR FREE

After 3pm you ski for free on the Sunnyside lift at Alta. The program is set up to get beginners, or those for whom it's been a while, back on the slopes.

tram (tram only round-trip $14; ⊘9am-4pm Dec-May, 11am-8pm Jun-Aug, 11am-5pm Sep-Nov) ascends 2900ft in only 10 minutes; die-hards do 'tram laps', racing back down the mountain to re-ascend in the same car they just rode up on. If you like to ski like a teenager, you'll flip out when you see this mountain.

The lowdown: 3240ft vertical drop, base elevation 7760ft; four high-speed quads, six double lifts, one tramway; 2500 acres, 27% beginner, 38% intermediate, 35% advanced. The only conveyor-pull tunnel in the US links the need-for-speed **Peruvian Gulf** area and intermediate terrain in **Mineral Basin**. Wednesday, Friday and Saturday, one lift remains open until 8:30pm for night skiing. Skiers (not boarders) can get an $88 Alta-Snowbird pass, which permits access to both areas, for a total of 4700 skiable acres. Snowbird has the longest season of the four SLC resorts, with skiing usually possible mid-November to mid-May. But that's not all, inquire about snowmobiling, backcountry tours and snowshoeing in winter.

In summer, the Peruvian lift and tunnel offer access to Mineral Basin **hiking** and wildflowers. Good, though strenuous, trails include the **White Pine Lake Trail** (10,000ft), which is just over 3 miles one-way. Watch rocky slopes around the lake for the unique pika – a small, short-eared, tailless lagomorph (the order of mammals that includes rabbits). At the end of the canyon road is **Cecret Lake Trail**, an easy 1-mile loop with spectacular wildflowers (July and August). Pick up basic trail maps at the resort.

An **all-activities pass** (Activity Center; adult/child $39/24; ⊘11am-8pm mid-Jun–Aug) includes numerous diversions: take a tramway up to Hidden Peak, ride the luge-like Alpine Slide, zipline down 1000ft, climb a rock wall or trampoline bungee jump. Full suspension mountain bikes can be rented for three hours ($35). Horseback riding, backcountry 4WD and ATV tours are available, too (from $40 per hour).

Snowbird has five kinds of accommodation, including hotels and condos, all booked through the resort's central phone number and website; packages including lift tickets are available. In summer, prices drop precipitously. The splashy black-glass-and-concrete 500-room **Cliff Lodge** (r $450-611; @🛜🏊) is like a cruise ship in the mountains, with every possible destination-resort amenity – from flat-screen TVs to a recently-remodeled, luxurious full-service spa. Request a 'spa level' room to have unlimited access to the rooftop pool. Otherwise check out the dramatic 10th-story glass-walled bar and settle for the level-three swimming pool with ski run views. Right at the heart of the resort's Snowbird Center pedestrian village, this lodge always bustles.

At the other end of the quietness spectrum, we also recommend the **Inn at Snowbird** (r $315-500; 🛜🏊), with a simpler, almost residential feel to it. Studio rooms have kitchens and wood-burning fireplaces. (Bring groceries and you'll save a bundle.)

Snowbird resort has 15 eating outlets, including standards like a coffee shop, pizza place, steakhouse and aprés-ski bars. **General Gritts** (Snowbird Center; ⊘11am-6pm) grocery store has a deli and liquor sales. Everyone loves looking out through 15ft windows to spectacular mountain views at the 10th-floor **Aerie Restaurant** (☎801-933-2160; Cliff Lodge; mains $24-38; ⊘7am-11am & 5-10pm Dec-Feb, 6-9pm Apr-Oct). The menu lives up to the fine prices; reservations are a must. The adjacent lounge has a full bar and sushi menu. The 3000-sq-ft deck at **Creekside Café & Grill** (Gadzoom lift base; breakfast & sandwiches $6-10; ⊘9am-2:30pm Dec-Apr) is a great place to grab a sandwich slopeside. The **Plaza Deck**, a huge patio at Snowbird Center, is a favorite place to gather; there's often live music weekend afternoons.

ALTA

Dyed-in-the-wool skiers make a pilgrimage to **Alta** (☎801-359-1078, 888-782-9258; www.alta.com; Little Cottonwood Canyon; day lift pass adult/child $69/36), at the top of the valley. No snowboarders are allowed here, which keeps the snow cover from deteriorating, especially on groomers. Locals have grown up with Alta, a resort filled not with see-and-be-seen types, but rather the see-and-say-hello crowd. Wide-open powder fields, gullies, chutes and glades, such as **East Greeley**, **Devil's Castle** and **High Rustler**, have helped make Alta famous. Warning: you may never want to ski anywhere else.

The lowdown: 2020ft vertical drop, base elevation 8530ft; 2200 skiable acres, 25%

beginner, 40% intermediate, 35% advanced; three high-speed chairs, four fixed-grip chairs. You can ski from the Sunnyside lift for free after 3pm, which is great for families with little ones who tire easily (lifts close at 4:30pm). Get the $88 Alta-Snowbird pass, which permits access to both areas for a stunning 4700 acres of skiing. Expert powder hounds, ask about off-piste snow-cat skiing in **Grizzly Gulch** ($325 for five runs).

No lifts run in summer, but there are 10 miles of local trails. From July to August, **Albion Basin** (www.fs.fed.us/wildflowers/regions /intermountain/AlbionBasin) is abloom with wildflowers. July, when an annual wildflower festival is held, is usually peak season.

The lodging options at Alta are like the ski area: simple and just as it's been for decades. Every place here has ski-in, ski-out access and a hot tub. Winter rates, as listed, include breakfast and dinner and require a four-night minimum stay. Lodge restaurants and snack bars are seasonal (December through March) and open to the public.

Alta Lodge (☎801-742-3500, 800-707-2852; www.altalodge.com; dm $146, d $320-590, d without bath $275-378; ✖️⚓️@🛜) is a mid-century modernist interpretation of a cozy mountain lodge. The attic bar (open to nonguests) is frequented by intellectuals playing backgammon. Expect to make friends there and at family-style dinners in this classical comfortable Alta lodge.

Granite-block-built **Snowpine Lodge** (☎801-742-2000; www.thesnowpine.com; male dm $109, r per person with private bath $169-239, with shared bath $125), Alta's most basic, is the die-hard skier's first choice. An eight-room expansion overlooks Eagle's Nest and Albion Basin.

You'll likely see families with teenagers embarrassed by their parents at the always-fun **Alta Peruvian** (☎801-742-3000, 800-453-8488; www.altaperuvian.com; dm $132, r per person with/without bath $204/158; @🛜✖️). Spacious knotty-pine common areas (movies shown nightly) make up for the tiny rooms. The bar here is Alta's après-ski scene. None of the previous two lodges have room TVs.

Enjoy all the creature comforts of a city hotel at **Rustler Lodge** (☎801-742-2200, 888-532-2582; www.rustlerlodge.com; dm $200, d $625-950, d without bath $380; @🛜✖️). Take an early morning stretch class before you hit the slopes and refresh in the eucalyptus sauna afterwards.

Sleep surrounded by July and August wildflowers at **Albion Basin Campground**

(☎800-322-3770; www.reserveamerica.com; Little Cottonwood Canyon Rd; campsites $17; ☺Jul-Sep). The 19 sites sit at 9500ft, among meadows and pine trees, 11 miles up the canyon. Drinking water; no showers, no hookups.

Chef Curtis Kraus uses locally produced ingredients whenever possible on his seasonally-changing, ingredient-driven menu at **Shallow Shaft Restaurant** (10199 E Hwy 210, Alta Town; mains $12-28; ☺5-10pm Dec-April, 6-9pm Thu-Sat Jul-early Sep). Mid-mountain, try **Collin's Grill** (Watson's Shelter, Wildcat Base; mains $11-22; ☺11am-2:30pm Dec-Apr) for homemade artisanal soups and French Country mains (make reservations) and **Alf's** (Cecret lift base; sandwiches $6-10; ☺9:30am-4pm) for a self-service burger and a look at the antique skis on the walls.

For more general information, see www .discoveralta.com.

SOLITUDE

Though less undiscovered than it once was, you can feel sometimes as if you've got the mountain to yourself at **Solitude** (☎801-534-1400, 800-748-4754; www.skisolitude.com; Big Cottonwood Canyon Rd; day lift ticket adult/child $68/42). It's still something of a local secret, so there's room to learn plus lots of speedy, roller-coaster-like corduroy to look forward to once you've gotten your ski legs. They added three new quads in recent years. If you're an expert, you'll dig the 400 acres of lift-assist cliff bands, gullies, over-the-head powder drifts and super-steeps at off-piste **Honeycomb Canyon**. Everything here, including the expert grooming, is first class. Some facilities, such as the **ice skating rink** (Village; admission free 3-8pm Jan-Mar), are only open to overnight guests.

The lowdown: 2047ft vertical drop, base elevation 7988ft; 1200 acres, 20% beginner, 50% intermediate, 30% advanced; eight lifts. Ask about helicopter skiing with **Wasatch Powderbird Guides** (☎801-742-2800; www .powderbird.com; per day from $1120); scenic flights, too.

North of the resort's lodges, Solitude's **Nordic Center** (day pass adult/child $17/free; ☺8:30am-4:40pm Dec-Mar & Jun-Aug) has 12 miles of groomed classic and skating lanes and 6 miles of snowshoeing tracks through enchanting forests of aspen and pine. In summer the Nordic Center becomes a visitor center and the boardwalk encircling **Silver Lake** becomes the easiest nature trail around, great for children and the mobility-impaired. Ask about guided owl-watching walks and other activities. No swimming, no dogs allowed; this is SLC's watershed.

June through August, the **Sunrise lift** (day pass $15) opens for chair-assist mountain-biking and hiking from Wednesday through Sunday. You can also rent mountain bikes and motorized mountain scooters, and play disc (Frisbee) golf at the resort.

Many hiking trails leave from various trail-heads outside the resorts along Hwy 190. Look for trailhead signs. One of the most attractive hikes is the 2-mile round-trip **Lake Blanche Trail**, beginning at the **Mill B South Fork trailhead**, about 5 miles into the canyon.

Most of the 'Village' lodgings at Solitude are atmospheric, Alpine-esque condos. **Central reservations** (800-748-4754; www.skisolitude.com) often has packages that cut room rates by as much as 50%. Of the four full-kitchen properties, we prefer the wood-and-stone rooms at **Creekside Lodge** (apt $270-425; 🐾🏠), with working fireplaces and balconies. The **Inn at Solitude** (r $269-299; @🐾🏠) is the only hotel-style lodging, with an on-site spa and hot tub; no balconies. All accommodations share Club Solitude's heat-ed outdoor pool, sauna, fitness room, games room and movie theater.

Cozy up fireside at **St Bernard's** (801-535-4120; Inn at Solitude; breakfast buffet $14, mains $28-32; ⊗7:30-11am & 5-10pm Dec-Mar) for an unexpectedly good French dinner with wine pairing. The foodie's fave is **Kimi's Mountainside Bistro** (Village; mains $18-25; ⊗11am-10pm Dec-Mar; Wed-Fri 5-9pm, 10am-2pm & 5-9pm Sat & Sun late-May–mid-Oct), which serves down-to-earth artisanal American meals much of the year. You can tip a pint at the **Thirsty Squirrel** (Village; ⊗2-9pm Dec-Mar) – though Big Cottonwood Canyon's best après-ski and bar scene is at Brighton.

For an adventurous treat, hike or snow-shoe a mile into the woods for a sumptu-ous, but unpretentious, five-course meal in a bona-fide canvas **Yurt** (801-536-5709; www.skisolitude.com/yurt.cfm; dinner winter/summer $100/65; ⊗5:30pm Tue-Sun Dec-Mar, 6:30pm Wed-Sun Jul-Sep). Be sure to reserve way ahead, and bring your own wine; corkage is included in price. (There's another yurt dinner at the Canyons in Park City, but this is the original and the best.)

A great alternative to resort or city sleep-ing, eating and drinking is the classic moun-tain roadhouse, **Silver Fork Lodge** (801-533-9977, 888-649-9551; www.silverforklodge.com; 11332 E Big Cottonwood Canyon; breakfast & sand-wiches $6-10, dinner $15-26, r incl breakfast $145;

⊗8am-9pm Sun-Thu, 8am-9:30pm Fri & Sat), a mile west of Solitude. Creative comfort food is served in the rustic dining room, which feels like a cozy log cabin with its crackling fireplace. Western furnishings outfit the twin, queen and bunk-bed rooms simply; the creaking floors only add character. In summer, sit outside and watch humming-birds buzz across gorgeous alpine scenery. All year, warm up in the hot tub.

BRIGHTON

Slackers, truants and bad-ass boarders rule at **Brighton** (801-532-4731, 800-873-5512; www.brightonresort.com; Big Cottonwood Canyon Rd; day lift ticket adult/child $62/29). But don't be intimidated: the low-key resort where many Salt Lake residents first learned to ski remains a good first-timers' spot, especially if you want to snowboard. Thick stands of pines line sweeping groomed trails and wide boulevards, and from the top, the views are gorgeous. The whole place is a throwback: come for the ski-shack appeal coupled with high-tech slope improvements and modernized lodge.

The lowdown: 1745ft vertical drop, base elevation 8755ft; 1050 acres, 21% beginner, 40% intermediate, 39% advanced; six chair lifts. One hundred percent of Brighton's terrain is accessible by high-speed quads. There's a half-pipe and terrain park and a lib-eral open-boundary policy on non-avalanche-prone days. The park has some of the best area **night skiing** (200 acres, 22 runs) until 9pm, Monday to Saturday. A magic carpet slope lift means beginners can just step on and go, or you can leave the kiddies behind at the day-care center.

No lifts operate during summer months, but locals still come up to go hiking in the alpine meadows and to picnic by area lakes.

The 20 basic rooms at **Brighton Lodge** (801-532-4731, 800-873-5512; www.brightonresort.com; dm $102, r $225-275) go quick; they're retro, but a good deal within spitting distance of the lifts. No room TVs, but there are more than 200 movies you can watch in the common room, or just sit by the fireplace after you've hot-tubbed it. Room prices are crazy low in summer (from $38 including breakfast).

The **Milley Chalet** (⊗8:30am-4:30pm) is the modern ski-lodge base, with various self-service food options. For après-ski drinks and pub grub, you gotta go to the A-frame right on the hill. **Molly Green's** (Brighton Manor; pizza $8-18, mains $7-13; ⊗11am-10pm Mon-Sat, 10am-10pm Sun Dec-Mar) has a roaring fire, a gregarious old-school vibe and great slopeside views. Sunday brunch is always a big hit, too. **Brighton Store & Cafe** (11491 Big Cottonwood Canyon Rd; breakfast & sandwiches $6-8; ☺8am-3pm) serves year-round.

Lands near the top of Big Cottonwood Canyon are part of the **Uinta-Wasatch-Cache National Forest** (www.fs.usda.gov). Camp at 44-site, first-come, first-served **Redman Campground** (Solitude Service Rd; campsites $17; ☺late Jun-Sep) and you'll be sleeping under tall pines at a high-elevation creekside ground (8300ft) near the top of the canyon. Several trails lead off from here and Silver Lake is nearby. Water available; no showers, no hookups.

Park City

POP 8100 / ELEV 6900FT

Century-old buildings line the one main street, looking particularly charming after a new dusting of snow, or at nightfall when the twinkling lights outlining the eaves have been turned on. It's hard to imagine that this one-time silver boomtown ever went bust. Condos and multimillion-dollar houses abut the valleys and center at Utah's premier ski village. Fabulous restaurants abound, and the skiing is truly world class.

Park City skyrocketed to international fame when it hosted the downhill, jumping and sledding events at the 2002 Winter Olympics. Today it's the permanent home base for the US Ski Team; at one time or another most US winter Olympians train at the three ski resorts and Olympic Park here. Though the eastern front gets fewer inches per year than the western front of the Wasatch Mountains, there's usually snow from late November through mid-April. Winter is the busy high season.

Come summer, more residents than visitors gear up for hiking and mountain biking among the nearby peaks. June to August, temperatures average in the 70s (low 20s in Celsius); nights are chilly. Spring and fall can be wet and boring; resort services, limited in summer compared with winter, shut down entirely between seasons. Even some restaurants take extended breaks, in May especially.

◎ Sights & Activities

Skiing is the big area attraction, but there are activities enough to keep you more than busy in both summer and winter. Most are based out of the three resorts: Canyons, Park City Mountain and Deer Valley.

Utah Olympic Park ADVENTURE SPORTS
(☑435-658-4200; www.olyparks.com/uop; 3419 Olympic Pkwy; admission free; ☺10am-6pm) Visit the site of the 2002 Olympic ski jumping, bobsledding, skeleton, Nordic combined and luge events, which continues to host national competitions. There are 10m, 20m, 40m, 64m, 90m and 120m Nordic ski-jumping hills as well as a bobsled-luge run. The US Ski Team practices here year round – in summer, the freestyle jumpers land in a bubble-filled jetted pool, and the Nordic jumpers on a hillside covered in plastic. Call for a schedule; it's free to observe. The engaging and interactive **Alf Engen Ski Museum**, also on-site, traces local skiing history and details the 2002 Olympic events. Experts offer 45-minute guided **tours** (adult/child $7/5; ☺11am-4pm) on the hour.

Not content to just watch the action? No problem. Reserve ahead and you adults can take a 70mph to 80mph **bobsled ride** (summer/winter $60/200) with up to an incredible 4 to 5Gs of centrifugal force. The summer **Quicksilver Alpine Slide** (driver/rider $60/200) is suitable for drivers over eight years old and riders who are three to seven. Clip on a harness and ride the 50mph **Extreme Zipline** (100-250lbs, per ride $20) or the shorter **Ultra Zipline** (50-275lbs, per ride $15). Saturday in summer there is a **Freestyle Show** (admission $10) that takes off at 1pm. Inquire about bobsled, skeleton, free-jump and free-style lessons year round.

Skiing, Snowboarding & Sledding

All three resorts and in-town sports shops have equipment rental (day ski rental adult/child from $36/25) and ski lessons. Plan ahead online and you can use the **Quick Start Program** (www.parkcityinfo.com/quickstart) to trade your airline boarding pass for a free same-day afternoon lift ticket at Park City's three resorts.

Canyons SNOW SPORTS
(☑435-649-5400, 888-604-4169; www.thecanyons.com; 4000 Canyons Resort Dr; two-day lift ticket adult/child $170/102) Nearly $60 million is scheduled to be invested in Canyons in the coming years. With it, the resort's identity is evolving, and it is poised to compete with the country's best. Phase one has introduced the first North American 'bubble' lift, with an enclosed, climate-controlled top, along with 300 new acres of advanced skiable

Park City

N

0 — 200 m
0 — 0.1 miles

9th St

Main St

Park Ave

8th St

14

To Old Town
Guest House
(0.1mi)

Town Lift

Silver Creek

Heber Ave

17

13

6

2

21

8

Deer Valley Dr

6th St

Swede Al

Park Ave

11

10

9

4

Transit
Center

5th St

Deer Valley Dr

Marsac Ave

15

16

5

1

4th St

P

P

Woodside Ave

Main
Street
Mall

18

20

Swede Al

7

19

3rd St

Park Ave

Norfolk Ave

2nd St

3

12

Ontario Canyon

Park City

🌐 Activities, Courses & Tours
1 Aura Spa..C5

🛏 Sleeping
2 Sky Lodge...B3
3 Treasure Mountain Inn........................C6
4 Washington School House...................B4

🍴 Eating
5 Bistro 412..C5
6 Easy Street Steak & Seafood B3
7 Eating Establishment...........................C6
8 Jean Louis Restaurant.........................B3
Shabu ....(see 18)
9 Talisker..B4
10 Taste of Saigon....................................B4
Uptown Fare...................................(see 3)
11 Wahso...B4
12 Wasatch Brew Pub...............................C6
13 Zoom B3

🍸 Drinking
14 High West Distillery & Saloon A2
15 No Name Saloon & Grill.......................B6
16 O'Shucks...C5
17 Park City Roasters...............................B3
18 Sidecar Bar...C5
19 Spur..C6

🎭 Entertainment
20 Egyptian Theatre Company..................C5
21 Park City Box Office.............................B3

acreage and an increased snow-making capability. So far six lodging properties are on site and new restaurants are being added. The resort currently sprawls across nine aspen-covered peaks 4 miles outside of town, near the freeway.

The lowdown: 3190ft vertical drop, base elevation 6800ft; 4000 acres, 10% beginner, 44% intermediate, 46% advanced; 19 lifts, including a gondola. Varied terrain on 176 trails means there's something for all levels, with wide groomers for beginners and intermediates and lots of freshies on a powder day. Experts: head to **Ninety-Nine 90**. There's a liberal open-boundary policy (heed avalanche warnings) as well as six natural half-pipes, one of them a whopping mile long, perfect for boarding. **Cross-country skiing** and **sleigh rides**, for pleasure or to dinner, are also available. You can even ride along on (two hours, $95) or drive (eight hours, $395) a state-of-the-art **Snow Cat groomer**. Sightseers could take the recently

relocated **gondola** (round-trip $20) up for not only views, but for Belgian waffles or lunch in the **Red Pine** area.

Park City Mountain Resort SNOW SPORTS
(☎435-649-8111, 800-222-7275; www.parkcity mountainresort.com; 1310 Lowell Ave; two-day lift ticket adult/child $178/112; 🚠) From boarder dudes to parents with tots, everyone skis Park City Mountain Resort, host of the Olympic snowboarding and giant slalom events. The awesome terrain couldn't be more family-friendly – or more accessible, rising right over downtown.

The lowdown: 3100ft vertical drop, base elevation 6900ft; 3300 acres, 17% beginner, 52% intermediate, 31% advanced; seven high-speed lifts, eight fixed-grip chairs, one magic carpet. Park City's skiable area covers nine peaks, ranging from groomers to wide-open bowls (750 acres of them!) to cotton mouth-inducing super steeps and the nation's only superpipe. Experts: make a beeline to **Mount Jupiter**; the best open trees are in the **Black Forest**. For untracked powder, take the **Eagle** lift up to **Vista**. Test your aerial technique on an Olympic-worthy boarding and freestyle course at three amazing terrain parks. Kids' trails are marked with snowbug statues near the magic carpet lift and the resort will hook teens up with area locals who provide the lay of the land. Check out the online activity planner at www mymountainplanner.com. To avoid crowds, stay out late: **night skiing** lasts until 9pm. In winter there's open-air **ice skating** (admission $9; ⏰1am-5pm) at the Resort Center.

Though the resort has no affiliated hotels, it does offer package lodging-skiing deals with nearby properties, and restaurants and après-ski are on site. The fact that **Town Lift** takes you right from Main St up to the village area makes all downtown accommodations accessible.

Gorgoza Park SNOW SPORTS
(3863 West Kilby Rd, at I-80; 4hr adult/child 6 & under $30/15; ⏰1-8pm Mon-Fri, noon-8pm Sat & Sun mid-Dec–Mar; 🚠) Lift-served snow tubing takes place at Park City Mountain's Gorgoza Park, 8 miles north of town, off I-80. Plunge down three beginner or four advanced lanes; for kids under 12 there's a **miniature snowmobile track** (per ride $9), and for littler ones the **Fort Frost play area** (admission $6) with carousel. The Park City Mountain Resort-wide **shuttle** (☎435-645-9388) will take you out there directly if you reserve.

Deer Valley　　　SNOW SPORTS
(☎435-649-1000, 800-424-3337; www.deervalley
.com; Deer Valley Dr; day lift ticket adult/child
$90/56, round-trip gondola ride $15) Want to be
pampered? Deer Valley, a resort of superlatives, has thought of everything from tissue
boxes at the base of slopes to ski valets. Sla-
lom, mogul and freestyle-aerial competitions
in the 2002 Olympics were held here, but the
resort is as famous for superb dining, white-
glove service and uncrowded slopes as metic-
ulously groomed as the gardens of Versailles.
Note that there's no snowboarding allowed.

The lowdown: 3000ft vertical drop, base
elevation 6570ft; 2026 acres, 27% beginner,
41% intermediate, 32% advanced; one
high-speed gondola, 11 high-speed quads,
nine fixed-grip chairs. Every trail follows
the fall line perfectly, which means you'll
never skate a single cat-track. **Lady Morgan** has 200 acres of new terrain (65 acres
of which is gladed), well separated from the
Jordanelle Gondola area. Only a prescribed
number of daily lift tickets are sold, so
powder hounds can find hundreds of acres
of untracked glades and steeps, days after
a storm.

Resort-owned **snowmobiling** (☎435-
645-7669; 1-hr $99; ◷9am-5pm) takes place
5 miles down the road on Garff Ranch;
reserve ahead.

White Pine Touring　　　SKIING
(☎435-649-8710; www.whitepinetouring.com;
1790 Bonanza Dr; 3-hr tour $175) Guided cross-
country ski trips take you 20 minutes
away from Park City and can include yurt
camping accommodations. In town, the
associated **Nordic Center** (cnr Park Ave &
Thames Canyon Dr; day pass adult/child $18/10;
◷9am-6pm) grooms a 12-mile cross-country
course (rental available) with 2-, 3- and
6-mile loops of classic and skating lanes.
Skate skiing lessons available.

Wasatch Powderbird　　　SKIING
(☎801-742-2800, 800-974-4354; www.powderbird
.com; full-day $1050) Advanced skiers can
arrange area heli-skiing packages that
include six to seven runs.

Other Snow Sports
Activity pick-up service is available from
most resorts. Reservations are always a must.

All Seasons Adventures　　　SNOW SPORTS
(☎435-649-9619; www.allseasonsadventures.com;
per hr $35-250) Dog sledding, sleigh riding,
cross-country skiing, snowshoe tours and
geocaching treasure hunts offered.

**Rocky Mountain Recreation
of Utah**　　　SNOW SPORTS
(☎435-645-7256, 800-303-7256; www.rockymtn
rec.com; per hr $70-300) Snowmobile tours,
horse-drawn sleigh rides (to dinner or
around) and dog sledding.

Hiking
You'll feel on top of the world in the peaks
over Park City, where over 300 miles of trails
crisscross the mountains. Pick up a summer
trail map at the visitor center.

Mountain Vista Touring　　　HIKING
(☎435-640-2979; www.parkcityhiking.com; half-
day $85; ◷mid-Apr–mid-Nov) Guided trips
include hot springs and moonlight hikes.

Mountain Biking
Park City's big secret is its amazing mountain biking. The visitor center has trail maps
and you can rent bikes (from $40 per day)
from sports shops in town and at all the
resorts; some even have lift-assist riding.

Mid-Mountain Trail　　　MOUNTAIN BIKING
One of the best for mountain biking is this
15-mile one-way trail, which follows the
topography at 8000ft, connecting Deer
Valley to Olympic Park. You could also
start at Park City Mountain, bike the steep
Spiro Trail up to Mid-Mountain, then
return on roads for a 22-mile loop.

Historic Union Pacific Rail Trail　　　TRAIL
(http://stateparks.utah.gov; admission free; ◷24hr)
A 28-mile multiuse trail that's also a state

SCENIC DRIVE: MIRROR LAKE HWY

This alpine route, also known as Hwy 150, begins about 12 miles east of Park City in
Kamas and climbs to elevations of more than 10,000ft as it covers the 65 miles into
Wyoming. The highway provides breathtaking mountain vistas, passing by scores of
lakes, campgrounds and trailheads in the **Uinta-Wasatch-Cache National Forest**
(www.fs.fed.us). Note that sections may be closed to traffic well into spring due to heavy
snowfall; check online.

park. Pick it up at Bonanza Dr just south of Kearns Blvd.

White Pine Touring
CYCLING

(☑435-649-8710; www.whitepinetouring.com; 1790 Bonanza Dr; 3-hr tour for 2 people $170) Bike rentals and guided biking tours

Other Summer Activities

Park City Mountain Resort
ADVENTURE SPORTS

(www.parkcitymountainresort.com; 1310 Lowell Ave; ⊙10:30am-5pm Jun-Aug) We love the **Town Lift**-served hiking and mountain biking (day pass $20). Park City Mountain also operates a 3000ft-long **alpine slide** (per ride $10), where a wheeled sled flies down 550ft along a cement track, as well as a super-long **zipline ride** (2300ft long, 550ft vertical; $20). Kids not tired yet? Check out the **adventure zone** (admission $20) with its climbing wall, spiderweb climb, boulder climb and slide. Note that hours vary depending on the activity and the month.

Canyons
ADVENTURE SPORTS

(www.thecanyons.com; 4000 Canyons Resort Dr; ⊙10am-5pm Jun-Aug) A scenic ride on the **gondola** (round-trip $15) is great for sightseers, but hiking trails also lead off from here. Mountain bikers should head over to the **Gravity Bike Park** (day pass $25), which has varied trails accessed by the High Meadow Lift. Other activities include disc golf, miniature golf, lake pedal boats and hot-air balloon rides. On weekends in summer and winter live-music concerts rock the base area.

Deer Valley
ADVENTURE SPORTS

(www.deervalley.com; Deer Valley Dr; day lift pass $20, ⊙10am-5pm mid-Jun–early Sep) In summer, Deer Valley has more than 50 miles of hiking and mountain-biking trails served by its three operating lifts. Horseback riding and free guided hikes are available by request.

Rocky Mountain Recreation of Utah
HORSEBACK RIDING

(☑435-645-7256, 800-303-7256; www.rockymtnrec .com; Stillman Ranch, Weber Canyon Rd) Horseback rides ($70 per hour), wagon rides with dinner ($75) and guided pack and fly-fishing trips ($295 per day).

All Seasons Adventures
HORSEBACK RIDING

(☑435-649-9619; www.allseasonsadventures.com; half day $60-150) Area guided kayaking, hiking, mountain biking, horseback riding, ATV riding and geocaching scavenger races.

National Ability Center
ADVENTURE SPORTS

(NAC; ☑435-649-3991; www.nac1985.org; 1000 Ability Way) Year-round adapted sports program for people with disabilities and their families: horseback riding, rafting, climbing and biking.

Wellness & Massage

When you've overdone it on the slopes, a spa treatment may be just what the doctor ordered. Deer Valley and the Canyons both have swanky spas.

Aura Spa
SPA

(Map p488; ☑435-658-2872; 405 Main St; 1hr from $85) Schedule energy-balancing chakra work after your rubdown at in-town Aura Spa.

The Shop
YOGA

(www.parkcityyoga.com; 1167 Woodside Ave; by donation) Stretch out the kinks with an Anusara yoga class at this amazing warehouse space. Walk-ins welcome.

★☆ Festivals & Events

Sundance Film Festival
FILM

(www.sundance.org) Independent films and their makers, movie stars and their fans fill the town to bursting for 10 days in late January. Passes, ticket packages and the few individual tickets sell out well in advance; plan ahead.

🛏 Sleeping

Prices in this section are for high winter season (mid-December through mid-April, minimum stays required); during Christmas, New Year's and Sundance it costs more. There's a dearth of budget lodging in Park City in winter. Consider staying down in Salt Lake or Heber Valley. Also check the ski resorts' websites for packages that combine condo or hotel accommodations and lift tickets, which can be a good deal. All three ski resorts have condo rentals that can be booked directly. Resort lodging has ski-in advantages, but staying near nightlife in the old town can be more fun. Note that off-season, rates drop 50% – or more. For a complete list of the more than 100 condos, hotels and resorts in Park City, log onto www.visitparkcity.com.

Sky Lodge
LUXURY HOTEL $$$

(Map p488; ☑435-658-2500, 888-876-2525; www .theskylodge.com; 201 Heber Ave; ste $285-495; ❈@🛜❄) The urban loft-like architecture containing the chic Sky Lodge suites both complements and contrasts the three

UTAH PARK CITY

GETTING INTO SUNDANCE FILM FESTIVAL

In late January, this two-week festival takes over both Park City and Sundance Resort completely. Films screen not just there but at venues in Salt Lake City and Ogden as well. Room rates soar across the Wasatch front, yet rooms are snapped up months in advance. Passes ($300 to $3000), ticket packages ($300 to $1000) and individual tickets ($15) are similarly difficult to get. You reserve a timeslot to purchase online at www.sundance.org /festival, starting in December (sign up for text-message announcements). You then call during your appointed hour to reserve, but there are no guarantees. Note that seats may be a little easier to secure during week two (week one is generally for the industry). Any remaining tickets are sold a few days ahead online and at the main **Park City Box Office** (Gateway Center, 136 Heber Ave; ⊘8am-7pm mid-Jan–late Jan). If you don't succeed, do like the locals and go skiing. The slopes are remarkably empty during this two-week period.

historic buildings which house the property's restaurants. You can't be more stylish, or more central, if you stay here.

Washington School House BOUTIQUE HOTEL $$$
(Map p488; ☑435-649-3800, 800-824-1672; http://washingtonschoolhouse.com; 543 Park Ave; ste incl breakfast $700; ❋❂❤❄) Architect Trip Bennett oversaw the restoration that turned an 1898 limestone schoolhouse on a hill into a luxurious boutique hotel with 12 suites. How did the children ever concentrate when they could gaze out at the mountains through 9ft-tall windows instead?

Old Town Guest House B&B $$
(off Map p488; ☑435-649-2642, 800-290-6423; www.oldtownguesthouse.com; 1011 Empire Ave; r incl breakfast $99-199; ❋❤) Grab the flannel robe, pick a paperback off the shelf and snuggle under a quilt on your lodgepole bed or kick back on the large deck at this comfy in-town B&B. The host will gladly give you the lowdown on the great outdoors, guided ski tours, mountain biking, and the rest.

Woodside Inn B&B $$
(☑435-649-3494, 888-241-5890; 1469 Woodside Ave; r $159-299, ste $299-399, both incl breakfast; ❋❤) A contemporary take on the B&B; this purpose-built, condo-looking inn has eight guest quarters (most with whirlpool tubs) and a dining room and den to share. Having hosts that will help with everything, including airport transfers, is a great advantage.

St Regis Deer Valley LUXURY HOTEL $$$
(☑435-940-5700, 877-787-3447; 2300 Deer Valley Dr East; r $500-1000; ❋@❤❄❂) You have to ride a private funicular just to get up to the St Regis. So whether you're lounging by the outdoor fire pits, dining on an expansive terrace or peering out over your room's balcony rail, the views are sublime. The studied elegant-rusticity here is the height of Deer Valley's luxury lodging.

Treasure Mountain Inn HOTEL $$$
(Map p488; ☑435-655-4501, 800-344-2460; www .treasuremountaininn.com; 255 Main St; ste $235-295; ❋❤) Park City's first member of the Green Hotel Association utilizes wind energy and serves organic food in its breakfast restaurant. Some of the upscale condos have fireplaces, all have kitchens, and they're decorated in earthy tones.

Hyatt Escala Lodge HOTEL $$$
(☑435-940-1234, 888-591-1234; 3551 North Escala Court; r $269-299, ste $309-419; ❋❤❄) Finished in 2011, the upscale lodge rooms are all meant to have a residential feel. Indeed, suites have full kitchens and a personal grocery shopping service is available throughout. From here you're not more than a few ski strides away from the Canyons resort lifts.

Park City Crash Pads CONDO $-$$
(☑435-901-9119, 877-711-0921; www.parkcitycrash pads.com; r $119-170) Take advantage of the condo market through this reasonable consolidator. Buildings and facilities may not be the newest, but all rooms have 300-thread-count duvets, iPod clock radios, and many have kitchens.

Chateau Après Lodge MOTEL $-$$
(☑435-649-9372, 800-357-3556; www.chateau apres.com; 1299 Norfolk Ave; dm $40, d/q $105/155; ❤) The only budget-oriented accommodation in town is this basic, 1963 lodge – with a 1st-floor dorm – near the town ski lift. Reserve ahead.

Park City Peaks HOTEL **$$**

(✔435-649-5000, 800-333-3333; www.parkcity
peaks.com; 2121 Park Ave; r $149-249; ❄@🌐☂)
Comfortable, contemporary rooms include
access to heated outdoor pool, hot tub,
restaurant and bar. Great deals off sea-
son. December through April, breakfast
is included.

Goldener Hirsch LUXURY HOTEL **$$$**

(✔435-649-7770, 800-252-3373; www.goldener
hirschinn.com; Deer Valley, 7570 Royal St; r incl
breakfast $299-639; 🌐) You can tell the Gold-
ener was fashioned after a lodge in Salzburg
by the hand-painted Austrian furniture,
feather-light duvets and European stone
fireplaces. 'Stay & Ski Deer Valley' packages
available.

Park City RV Resort CAMPGROUND **$**

(✔435-649-8935; www.parkcityrvresort.com; 2200
Rasmussen Rd; tent sites $21, RV sites with hookups
$30-45; @🌐☂👫) Amenities galore (games
room, playground, laundry, hot tub, fishing
pond, kids' climbing wall), 6 miles north
of town at I-80.

Holiday Inn Express HOTEL **$-$$**

(✔435-658-1600, 888-465-4329; www.holidayinn
express.com; 1501 W Ute Blvd; r incl breakfast $170-
207; ❄🌐) Save money by staying outside
downtown, near Kimball Junction stores
and restaurants.

Shadow Ridge Resort Center HOTEL **$$-$$$**

(✔435-649-4300, 800-451-3031; www.shadow
ridgeresort.com; 50 Shadow Ridge Rd; r $189-
299; 🌐☂) A hundred yards from Park City
Mountain lifts.

Waldorf Astoria LUXURY HOTEL **$$$**

(✔435-647-5500; www.parkcitywaldorfastoria.com;
2100 Frostwood Dr; r $729-1500; @🌐☂) Top
luxury property at the Canyons.

✖ Eating

Park City is well known for exceptional up-
scale eating – a reasonable meal is harder
to find. In the spring and summer, look
for half-off main-dish coupons in the *Park
Record* newspaper. *Park City Magazine*
puts out a full menu guide. In addition to
the places listed here, the three ski resorts
have numerous other eating options in
season. Assume dinner reservations are
required at all top-tier places in winter. Note
that from April through November restaur-
ants reduce open hours variably, and may
take extended breaks.

TOP CHOICE **Talisker** MODERN AMERICAN **$$$**

(Map p488; ✔435-658-5479; 515 Main St; mains
$21-42; ◐5:30-10pm) Talisker elevates
superb food to the sublime: lobster hush
puppies, anyone? Settle into one of the four
individually-designed dining rooms and
see what long-time resident and chef Jeff
Murcko has to offer on his daily changing
menu. The chef also oversees the menus at
Canyons resort restaurants.

J&G Grill INTERNATIONAL **$$$**

(✔425-940-5760; St Regis Deer Valley, 2300 Deer
Valley Dr E; mains $20-32; ◐7am-2pm & 6-9pm)
Excellent meat and fish here might have
a sublimely simple grill treatment or a
Malaysian-Thai influence. Either way, we
prefer to enjoy it at the convivial commu-
nal table, where you can mingle with 20
other discriminating diners.

Jean Louis Restaurant INTERNATIONAL **$$$**

(Map p488; ✔435-200-0602; 136 Heber Ave;
mains $27-40; ◐dinner) Renowned restaur-
ateur, chef and quite the character, Jean
Louis has created an upscale, world-cuisine
restaurant that still manages to feel
warm and welcoming. Here, it's all about
good food.

**Easy Street Steak
& Seafood** STEAKHOUSE **$$-$$$**

(Map p488; ✔435-658-9425; 201 Heber Ave; breakfast & brunch $10-16, burgers $15, mains $25-40;
◐9am-10pm Dec-Mar; 5-10pm Mon-Fri, 9am-2pm &
5-10pm Sat & Sun Apr-Nov) The high ceilings and
tall windows of the old Utah Coal & Lumber
building are perfect for a fine steakhouse.
Or you could have the wild-mushroom
bruschetta and succulent rib-eye served in
the more casual bar downstairs.

Wahso ASIAN **$$$**

(Map p488; ✔435-615-0300; 577 Main St; mains
$29-40; ◐5-10pm) Park City's cognoscenti
flock to this modern pan-Asian phenom-
enon whose fine-dining dishes may include
lamb vindaloo or Malaysian snapper. Expect
to see and be seen.

Maxwell's PIZZERIA **$-$$**

(1456 New Park Blvd; pizza slices $3, mains $10-
20; ◐11am-9pm Sun-Thu, 11am-10pm Fri & Sat)
Eat with the locals at the pizza, pasta and
beer joint tucked in a back corner of the
stylish outdoor Redstone Mall, north of
town. Huge, crispy-crusted 'Fat Boy' pizzas
never linger long on the tables.

Bistro 412 FRENCH $$
(Map p488; 412 Main St; mains $12-26; ⊘11am-2:30pm & 5-10pm) The cozy dining room and French bistro fare here, including beef *Bourguignonne* and *cassoulet* (a hearty bean stew made with elk, sausage and lamb bacon), will keep you warm in winter. During summer months, steak *frites* on the outdoor deck might be more appropriate.

🗹**Good Karma** FUSION $-$$
(1782 Prospector Ave; breakfast $7-12, mains $10-20; ⊘7am-10pm) Whenever possible, local and organic ingredients are used in the Indo-Persian meals with an Asian accent at Good Karma. You'll recognize the place by the Tibetan prayer flags flapping out front.

Squatters Roadhouse Grill PUB $-$$
(1900 Park Ave; burgers $9-12, mains $10-19; ⊘8am-10pm Sun-Thu, 8am-11pm Fri & Sat) The better of the town brewpubs, as far as food goes. We love the Asiago, cheddar and Havarti mac-and-cheese. Breakfast is served until 2pm daily.

Windy Ridge Cafe AMERICAN $$
(1250 Iron Horse Dr; lunch $10-15, dinner $15-20; ⊘11am-3pm & 5-10pm) Escape the Main St mayhem at this out-of-the-way American cafe. Across the parking lot, the **bakery** (⊘8am-6pm) makes many of the tasty treats. Both are part of the Bill White restaurant group, which also counts Grappa (taverna Italian), Chimayo (Southwest) and Ghidotti's (fine Italian) among its numbers.

Uptown Fare CAFE $
(Map p488; 227 Main St; sandwiches $5-11; ⊘11am-3pm) Comforting house-roasted turkey sandwiches and homemade soups at the hole-in-the-wall hidden below the Treasure Mountain Inn.

Lookout Cabin MODERN AMERICAN $$
(Canyons, 4000 Canyons Resort Dr; mains $10-20; ⊘11:30am-3:30pm Dec-Mar) Gourmet lunch and après ski mid-mountain. Think kirsch cherry fondue and Kobe beef-turned-burger.

Zoom AMERICAN $$$
(Map p488; ☑435-649-9108; 660 Main St; mains $20-36; ⊘11:30am-2:30pm & 5-10pm) Robert Redford-owned restaurant in a rehabbed train depot.

Shabu FUSION $$$
(Map p488; ☑435-645-7253; 442 Main St; small plates & rolls $10-17, mains $24-34; ⊘11am-2:30pm, 5-11pm Thu-Tue) Hip, inventive Asian small plates and namesake *shabu shabu* (a hotpot of flavorful broth with meat or veggies).

Wasatch Brew Pub PUB $-$$
(Map p488; 250 Main St; lunch & sandwiches $7-12, dinner $10-17; ⊘11am-10pm) Pub grub at the top of Main St.

Taste of Saigon VIETNAMESE $$
(Map p488; 580 Main St; mains $10-15; ⊘11am-3pm & 5-10pm) Reasonably priced Vietnamese dishes, even better lunch specials.

Eating Establishment AMERICAN $-$$
(Map p488; 317 Main St; breakfast & sandwiches $9-12, dinner $15-20; ⊘8am-10pm) Local institution; service can be hit-or-miss.

🍷 Drinking

Main St is where it's at. In winter there's action nightly; weekends are most lively off-season. For listings, see www.thisweekinparkcity.com. Several restaurants, such as Bistro 412, Easy Street, Squatters and Wasatch Brew Pub, also have good bars.

TOP CHOICE **High West Distillery & Saloon** BAR
(Map p488; 703 Park St; ⊘2pm-1am daily, closed Sun & Mon Apr-Jun & Sep-Dec) A former livery and Model A-era garage is now home to Park City's most happenin' nightspot. You can ski in for homemade rye whiskey at this micro distillery. What could be cooler?

Spur BAR
(Map p488; 352 Main St; ⊘5pm-1am) What an upscale Western bar should be: rustic walls, leather couches, roaring fire. Good grub, too. Live-music weekends.

Sidecar Bar BAR
(Map p488; 333 Main St, 2nd fl; ⊘5pm-1am) Local and regional bands (rock, funk, swing) play to a 20-something crowd.

No Name Saloon & Grill BAR
(Map p488; 447 Main St; ⊘11am-1am) There's a motorcycle hanging from the ceiling and Johnny Cash's 'Jackson' playing on the stereo at this memorabilia-filled bar.

O'Shucks PUB
(Map p488; 427 Main St; ⊘10am-2am) The floor crunches with peanut shells at this hard-drinkin' bar for snowboarders and skiers. Tuesdays see $3 schooners (32 ounces) of beer.

Park City Roasters CAFE
(638 Main St; ⊘6:30am-6pm; 🛜) This cyber coffeehouse is a cool place to hang out, sip

a shade-grown brew and catch up on your news reading – online or on paper.

☆ Entertainment

Symphony, chamber music, bluegrass, jazz and other musical events happen throughout summer and winter; pick up the free *This Week in Park City* (www.parkcityweek.com).

Egyptian Theatre Company THEATER
(Map p488; www.egyptiantheatrecompany.org; 328 Main St) The restored 1926 theater is a primary venue for Sundance; the rest of the year it hosts plays, musicals and concerts.

🛍 Shopping

The quality of stores along Main St has improved in recent years. In addition to the typical tourist 'is and schlocky souvenirs, you'll find upscale galleries and outdoor clothing brands. **Park City Gallery Association** (www.parkcitygalleryassociation.com) puts out a gallery guide and sponsors art walks.

Tanger Outlet MALL
(Kimball Junction, Hwy 224) Dozens of outlet and other outdoor mall shops at the junction with I-80 (exit 145).

ℹ Information

Main Street Visitor Center (☑435-649-7457; 528 Main St; ☺11am-6pm Mon-Sat, noon-6pm Sun) Small desk inside the Park City Museum downtown.

Park City Clinic (☑435-649-7640; 1665 Bonanza Dr) Urgent care and 24-hour emergency room.

Park City Magazine (www.parkcitymagazine.com) Glossy magazine with some events listings.

Park Record (www.parkrecord.com) The community newspaper for more than 130 years.

Visitor Information Center (☑435-649-6100, 800-453-1360; www.parkcityinfo.com; cnr Hwy 224 & Olympic Blvd; ☺9am-7pm Mon-Sat, 11am-4pm Sun Jun-Sep; hours vary Oct-May) Large office in the northern Kimball Junction area.

ℹ Getting There & Away

Downtown is 5 miles south of I-80 exit 145, 32 miles east of SLC and 40 miles from the airport. Hwy 190 (closed October through March) crosses over Guardsman Pass between Big Cottonwood Canyon and Park City.

Park City Transportation (☑435-649-8567, 800-637-3803; www.parkcitytransportation.com), **All Resort Express** (☑435-649-3999, 800-457-9457; www.allresort.com) and **Powder for the People** (☑435-649-6648, 888-482-7547; www.powderforthepeople.com) all run shared van service ($39 one-way) and private-charter vans (from $99 for one to three people) from Salt Lake City International Airport. The latter also has Powder Chaser ski shuttles (from $45 round-trip) that will take you from Park City to Salt Lake City resorts.

ℹ Getting Around

Traffic can slow you down, especially on weekends; bypass Main St by driving on Park Ave. Parking can also be challenging and meter regulations are strictly enforced. Free lots are available in Swede Alley; those by 4th and 5th Sts are especially convenient.

Better still, forgo the rental and take a shuttle from the airport. The excellent public transit system covers most of Park City, including the three ski resorts, and makes it easy not to need a car.

Park City Transit (www.parkcity.org/city departments/transportation) Free trolleybuses run one to six times an hour from 8am to 11pm (reduced frequency in summer). There's a downloadable route map online.

Ogden & Around

During its heyday, historic 25th St was lined with brothels and raucous saloons; today the restored buildings house restaurants, galleries, bakeries and bars. The old town is atmospheric, but the main attraction here is 20 miles east in the Wasatch Mountains of Ogden Valley. Since skiing here is more than an hour's drive from Salt Lake City, most metro area residents head to Park City or the SLC resorts, leaving Snowbasin and Powder Mountain luxuriously empty. The villages of Huntsville and Eden, halfway between town and mountains, are nearest to the resorts.

⦿ Sights

Ogden Eccles Dinosaur Park MUSEUM
(www.dinosaurpark.org; 1544 E Park Blvd; adult/child $7/6; ☺10am-5pm Mon-Sat, noon-5pm Sun, closed Sun Nov-Mar; 🐾) Prepare for your children to squeal as a couple of animatronic dinosaurs roar to life inside the museum at Ogden Eccles Dinosaur Park. Outside, it's like a giant playground where you can run around, under and over life-size plaster-of-Paris dinosaurs.

Motor-Vu Drive-In THEATER
(http://motorvu.com; 5368 S 1050 West; ☺dusk Fri-Sun Mar-Nov) Kids also love piling in the car to catch a flick at this old time drive-in movie theater. There's a swap meet here on Saturday at 8am.

Union Station MUSEUM
(2501 Wall Ave; adult/child $6/4; ☺10am-5pm Mon-Sat) This old train houses three small museums dedicated to antique autos, natural history and firearms.

🏃 Activities

Snowbasin SNOW SPORTS
(☑801-620-1100, 888-437-5488; www.snowbasin .com; 3925 E Snowbasin Rd, Huntsville; day lift ticket adult/child $66/40) Snowbasin hosted the 2002 Olympic downhill, and it continues to be a competitive venue today. Snowhounds are attracted to everything from gentle slow-skiing zones to wide-open groomers and boulevards, jaw-dropping steeps to gulp-and-go chutes. Snowbasin also has four terrain parks and a dedicated **snow tubing** lift and hill. They groom 26 miles of **cross-country skiing**, both classic and skating; ask about yurt camping.

The lowdown: 3000ft vertical drop, base elevation 6400ft; 3000 acres, 20% beginner, 50% intermediate, 30% expert; one tram, two gondolas, two high-speed quads, four fixed-grip chairs. The lift system is one of the most advanced in the Southwest, but for now Snowbasin remains a hidden gem with fantastic skiing, top-flight service and nary a lift line. The exposed-timber-and-glass **Summit Day Lodge** (accessible to non-skiers) has a massive four-sided fireplace and a deck overlooking daredevil steeps, in addition to good restaurants.

In summer, the **gondola** (day pass $18; ☺9am-6pm Sat & Sun) takes you up to Needles restaurant and hiking and mountain-biking trails; bike rentals available for $50 per day. Check online for the Sunday afternoon outdoor concert series line-up.

Powder Mountain SNOW SPORTS
(☑801-745-3772; www.powdermountain.com; Rte 158, Eden; day lift ticket adult/child $59/32) If you're someone who likes to don a backpack and spend the day alone, you'll groove on Powder Mountain. They've had banner years of late, and you'll have plenty of room to roam with more than 7000 skiable acres. More than 3000 acres are lift-served by four chairs (one high speed) and three rope

tows. There are two terrain parks and night skiing till 10pm. Best of all, two weeks after a storm, you'll still find powder.

The **Snow Cat Safari** (per day $395) accesses 3000 acres of exclusive bowls, glades and chutes for a day gliding on powder. A **Lightning Ridge** single Snow Cat ride-and-run costs $15. Inquire about **backcountry guided tours** and **snow-kiting lessons**. The rest of the lowdown: 3005ft vertical drop, base elevation 6895ft, 7000 skiable acres; 25% beginner, 40% intermediate, 35% advanced.

Wolf Mountain SNOW SPORTS
(☑801-745-3511; www.wolfmountaineden.com; 3567 Nordic Valley Way, Eden; day lift ticket adult/child $35/22; ♿) The old-fashioned mom-and-pop mountain. At only 1600 skiable acres and with a 1604ft vertical drop, who'd think Wolf Mountain would garner any superlatives? But since all five lifts are lit until 9pm, Wolf Mountain has some of the largest night skiing terrain in Utah. The magic carpet lifts provide good access for young'uns; 25% beginner, 50% intermediate, 25% advanced runs.

iFly EXTREME SPORTS
(☑801-528-5348; http://iflyutah.com; 2261 Kiesel Ave; per flight $49; ☺noon-10pm Mon-Sat) Take off on an indoor skydiving adventure at iFly; reservations required.

🛏 Sleeping

Cradled by mountains, Ogden Valley is the preferred place to stay. If you choose to stay in town, you'll have more eating and drinking options.

OGDEN TOWN

Of the standard chain motels near I-15, the Comfort Inn is among the newest.

Ben Lomond Historic Suite Hotel HOTEL $-$$
(☑801-627-1900, 877-627-1900; www.benlomond suites.com; 2510 Washington Blvd; r incl breakfast $79-119; ❋@🖵🛜🏊) Traditional rooms in this 1927 downtown hotel could use an update, but you can't beat the local history connection.

Hampton Inn & Suites HOTEL $$
(☑801-394-9400, 800-426-7866; 2401 Washington Blvd; r $92-159; ❋@🛜) Contemporary rooms; short walk to restaurants.

OGDEN VALLEY

There are no accommodations owned by the ski resorts, but all three have condo partners that offer ski packages; check their websites. The town of Eden is closest to Powder and Wolf Mountains; Huntsville is closest to Snowbasin. For a full lodging list, see www.ovba.org.

Jackson Fork Inn   B&B $-$$
(☎801-745-0051,800-255-0672;www.jacksonfork inn.com; 7345 E 900 South, Huntsville; r/ste incl breakfast $85/150) A big ol' white barn has been turned into a simple, seven-room B&B. Downstairs there's a homey restaurant serving dinner and Sunday brunch.

Red Moose Lodge   LODGE $$
(☎801-745-6667, 866-996-6673; http://thered mooselodge.com; 2547 N Valley Junction Dr, Eden; r $99-129; @🗧🗖🗖) This 27-room log lodge is especially kid friendly, with a game room, climbing fort, ball courts and heated pool, plus an on-site spa. In winter, take the free shuttle to ski resorts.

Atomic Chalet B&B   B&B $$
(☎801-745-0538; www.atomicchalet.com; 1st St, Huntsville; r incl breakfast $85-125; 🗧) Down-to-earth and comfy, this cedar-shake cottage makes an excellent home away from home. After a day spent skiing or hiking, relax in the hot tub, watch a film from the video collection or play a game of billiards.

Snowberry Inn   B&B $$
(☎801-745-2634, 888-746-2634, 1315 N Hwy 158, Eden; r incl breakfast $109-238; 🗷) Family-owned log cabin B&B with game room; no room TVs. Ski packages available.

Alaskan Inn   INN $$-$$$
(☎801-621-8600; 435 Ogden Canyon Rd, Ogden; cabins & ste incl breakfast $139-194; 🗷) Luxury Western-themed suites and cabins in the picturesque canyon, just outside Ogden Valley.

✖ Eating & Drinking

Look for restaurants and a handful of bars in Ogden town on historic 25th St between Union Station and Grant Ave.

OGDEN TOWN
Roosters 25th Street Brewing Co   PUB $-$$
(253 25th St; brunch & sandwiches $8-10, mains $10-20; ⊗11am-10pm Mon-Fri, 10am-10pm Sat & Sun) Once a house of ill repute, this great old town building is now an upscale gastro brewpub. It has a sister restaurant in Union Station, at the end of the street.

Grounds for Coffee   CAFE $
(126 25th St; dishes $2-6; ⊗6:30am-8pm Mon-Thu, 6:30am-10pm Friday & Sat, 8am-6pm Sun) Full coffee-drink menu, plus baked goods and some sandwiches, in an artsy 1800s store-front setting.

Brewski's   BAR $
(244 25th St; ⊗10am-1am) More than 20 beers on tap; live-music weekends.

OGDEN VALLEY
Shooting Star Saloon   PUB $
(7350 E 200 South, Huntsville; burgers $5-8; ⊗noon-9pm Wed-Sat, 2-9pm Sun) Open since 1879, tiny Shooting Star is Utah's oldest con-tinuously operating saloon. Seek this place out: the cheeseburgers – and cheap beer – are justly famous.

Eats of Eden   ITALIAN $$
(2529 N Hwy 162, Eden; mains $10-16; ⊗11:30am-9pm Tue-Sat) Munch on pizza or pasta inside the rustic restaurant, or surrounded by val-ley on the small patio.

Grey Cliff Lodge Restaurant   AMERICAN $$-$$$
(508 Ogden Canyon, Ogden; brunch $16.50, dinner $18-30; ⊗5-10pm Tue-Sat, 10am-2pm & 3-8pm Sun) An old-fashioned resort restaurant, it's an institution in Ogden Canyon.

Carlos & Harley's   TEX-MEX $$
(5510 E 2200, Eden; mains $11-16; ⊗11am-9pm) A lively Mexican cantina inside the old Eden General Store.

ⓘ Information

Ogden Valley Business Association (www .ovba.org) The online lowdown on Valley activities, eateries and lodging.

Ogden Visitors Bureau (☎866-867-8824; www.ogdencvb.org; 2501 Wall Ave; ⊗9am-5pm Mon-Fri) Town and area info.

Outdoor Information Center (☎801-625-5306; Union Station, 2501 Wall Ave ⊗9am-5pm Mon-Fri year-round, plus 9am-5pm Sat Jun-Sep) Handles USFS and other public lands trail and campground info.

ⓘ Getting There & Away

Greyhound (☎801-394-5573, 800-231-2222; www.greyhound.com; 2393 Wall Ave) has daily buses traveling between Ogden town and SLC ($18.50, 45 minutes), but you really need a car to get around anywhere in the Valley.

Heber City & Midway

Twenty miles south of Park City, Heber City (population 9780) and its vast valley make an alternative base for exploring the surrounding mountains. A popular steam-powered railway runs from here. A scant 3 miles east, Midway (population 2130) is modeled after an Alpine town, with hand-painted buildings set against the slopes. Here you'll find activity-laden resorts, great for families, and a thermal crater you can swim in. Resort activities are open to all, and cross-country skiing and is close to both towns.

◉ Sights & Activities

Much of the forested mountains east of the towns have hiking, biking, cross-country skiing, ATV and snowmobile trails that are part of the **Uinta-Wasatch-Cache National Forest** (www.fs.usda.gov).

Heber Valley Historic Railroad　　TRAIN RIDE
(☑435-654-5601; www.hebervalleyrr.org; 450 S 600 West, Heber; 3hr adult $30-89, child $25-74) The 1904 Heber Valley Historic Railroad chugs along on scenic trips through the steep-walled Provo Canyon, as well as taking numerous themed trips.

Homestead Crater　　SWIMMING
(☑435-654-1102; www.homesteadresort.com; Homestead Resort, 700 N Homestead Dr, Midway; admission $16; ◎noon-8pm Mon-Thu, 10am-8pm Fri & Sat, 10am-6pm Sun) Swim in a 65ft-deep geothermal pool (90°F, or 32°C, year-round) beneath the 50ft-high walls of a limestone cone open to the sky. This is way cool. Reservations required.

Soldier Hollow　　ADVENTURE SPORTS
(☑435-654-2002; www.soldierhollow.com; off Hwy 113; day pass adult/child $18/9; ◎9am-4:30pm) A must-ski for cross-country aficionados, Soldier Hollow, 2 miles south of Midway, was the Nordic course used in the Olympics. Its 19 miles of stride-skiing and skating lanes are also open to snowshoeing. For nonskiers, there's a 1201ft-long **snow-tubing hill** (adult/child 3-6 $18/8; ◎noon-8pm Mon-Sat, noon-4pm Sun); book in advance on weekends, since ticket sales are capped. Snow season is December through March. May through October, the resort's gorgeous 36-hole **golf course**, **mountain biking** trails and **horseback riding** are popular. (Equipment rentals $19 to $35 per day.)

⛭ Sleeping

The standard chain gang of motels are available on Main St in Heber City.

Swiss Alps Inn　　MOTEL $
(☑435-654-0722; www.swissalpsinn.com; 167 S Main St; r $65-85; ☜☒) This independent Heber City Main St motel has huge rooms with hand-painted doors, and you get a free milkshake from the associated restaurant next door.

Homestead Resort　　RESORT $$
(☑435-654-1102, 800-327-7220; www.homestead resort.com; 700 N Homestead Dr, Midway; r $135-190; ﹫☜☒☒) Most destination family resorts of this caliber faded into obscurity a generation ago. A collection of homey buildings and cottages gathers around the resort's village green. Activities include 18-hole golf, cycling, horseback riding, hot-spring swimming, spa-going, volleyball, shuffle board and croquet. The restaurants are good, too; some of the packages include meals.

Blue Boar Inn　　INN $$$
(☑435-654-1400, 800-650-1400; www.theblueboar inn.com; 1235 Warm Springs Rd, Midway; r incl breakfast $175-225; ﹫) It's as if an ornate Bavarian inn had been teleported to Utah. Everything from the hand-painted exterior to the ornately carved wooden furniture screams Teutonic.

Zermatt Resort & Spa　　RESORT $$$
(☑866-627-1684; www.zermattresort.com; 784 West Resort Dr, Midway; r incl breakfast $175-295; ﹫☜☒) The 'Adventure Haus' at this upscale resort not only has mountain-bike rentals; they'll arrange scenic dare-devil flights, fly-fishing lessons and boat rental on a nearby lake. Complimentary ski and golf shuttles head to Park City and Sundance.

✖ Eating

Dairy Keen　　BURGERS $
(☑435-654-5336; 199 S Main St, Heber City; burgers $3-6; ◎11am-9pm) Look for the miniature train that travels overhead at this local play on Dairy Queen. The ice-cream sundaes and shakes can't be beat (try boysenberry).

Snake Creek Grill　　AMERICAN $$
(650 W 100 South/Hwy 113, Heber City; mains $16-20; ◎5-10pm Thu-Sun) One of northern Utah's best restaurants looks like a saloon from an old Western. The all-American Southwest-style menu features blue-cornmeal crusted

MT TIMPANOGOS

On the north side of Provo Canyon, take the paved, 16-mile **Alpine Loop Rd** (Hwy 92) – an incredibly scenic, twisting road past 11,750ft Mt Timpanogos. At 6800ft, stay overnight at the **Mount Timpanogos Campground** (☎877-444-6777; www.reserveamerica .com; tent & RV sites $16; ☺May-Oct). Pit toilets, water; no hookups. A trailhead leads from here into the surrounding fir tree-filled wilderness.

Spectacular, star-like helictite formations are on view at three mid-mountain caverns in **Timpanogos Cave National Monument** (☎801-756-5238; www.nps.gov/tica; off Hwy 92; 3 days per vehicle $6; ☺7am-5:30pm Jun-Aug, 8am-5pm Sep & Oct). Book ahead or get there early for a 1½-hour ranger-led tour (adult/child $7/5); they fill up. To get to the caves, you have an uphill hike that can't be done more than an hour before your tour time. Hwy 92 is closed December through March.

trout and finger-lickin' ribs. Halfway between downtown Heber City and Midway.

Blue Boar Inn　　　　INTERNATIONAL $$-$$$
(☎435-654-1400, 800-650-1400; www.theblue boarinn.com; 1235 Warm Springs Rd, Midway; breakfast & sandwiches $8-11, dinner $24-28; ☺7am-10pm) The European-inspired experience at this inn's dining room, open to nonguests, is worth the reservation you need to make.

Mountain House Grill　　　　AMERICAN $$
(☎435-654-5370; 70 E Main St, Midway; mains $9-19; ☺7am-2:30pm) For casual all-American.

❶ Information

Most of the services are in Heber City.
Heber Ranger Station (☎435-654-0470; 2460 S Hwy 40; ☺8am-4pm Mon-Fr) Uinta-Cache-Wasatch National Forest info.
Heber Valley Chamber of Commerce (☎435-654-3666; www.hebervalleycc.org; 475 N Main St; ☺8am-5pm) Pick up information about both towns here.
Sidetrack Café (☎435-654-0563; 94 S Main St; ☺6:30am-5pm Mon-Fri, 7:30am-5pm Sat & Sun) Log onto the internet (free with purchase) over coffee and sandwiches.

❶ Getting There & Around

Hwy 190 continues over Guardsman Pass to Big Cottonwood Canyon and SLC (closed in winter).
Greyhound (☎801-394-5573, 800-231-2222; www.greyhound.com; 2393 Wall Ave) Daily buses from Ogden to SLC ($11.50, 55 minutes).
UTA (☎801-743-3882, 888-743-3882; www .rideuta.com; cnr Wall & 23rd Sts) Runs express bus service to SLC ($4, 50 minutes), with diminished frequency on weekends.

⬆ Sundance Resort

Art and nature blend seamlessly at **Sundance** (☎801-225-4107, 800-892-1600; www.sundanceresort.com; 9521 Alpine Loop Rd, Provo; r $225-319 @☺), a magical resort-cum-artist-colony founded by Robert Redford, where bedraggled urbanites connect with the land and rediscover their creative spirits. Participate in snow sports, ride horseback, fly-fish, write, do yoga, indulge in spa treatments, climb or hike Mt Timpanogos, nosh at several wonderful eateries and then spend the night in rustic luxury. Day-trippers should ask for trail maps and activity guides at the **general store** (☺9am-9pm), which shoppers love for the artisan handicrafts, home furnishings and jewelry (catalog available).

Mount Timpanogos, the second-highest peak in the Wasatch, lords over the **ski resort** (☎801-223-4849 for reservations; day lift ticket adult/child $49/27), which is family- and newbie-friendly. The 500-skiable-acre hill is primarily an amenity for the resort, but experienced snow riders will groove on the super-steeps. The **Cross Country Center** (☺9am-5pm Dec-Apr) has 16 miles of groomed classic and skating lanes on all-natural snow. You can also snowshoe 6 miles of trails past frozen waterfalls (ask about nighttime owl-watching walks). The woods are a veritable fairyland.

May through September, there's lift-assist **hiking** and **mountain biking**; rental available (from $35). Sundance hosts numerous year-round **cultural events**, from its namesake film festival (p492) and screenwriting and directing labs, to writers' workshops and music seminars. In summer there are outdoor films, plays, author readings and great music series at the **amphitheater**. Don't miss the **art shack** (☺10am-5pm), where you can throw pottery and make jewelry.

Lucky enough to be staying over? Rough-hewn cottage rooms are secluded, tucked among the trees on the grounds; the perfect place to honeymoon or write your next novel. Decor differs but they've all got pine walls and ever-so-comfy furnishings, plus quilts, paperback books and board games; some have kitchens. Two- to four-bedroom houses (from $1025) are also available.

Sundance's top-flight restaurant, **Tree Room** (☎801-223-4200; mains $25-41; ☺5-9pm Tue-Thu, 5-10pm Fri & Sat) is a study in rustic-mountain chic – with a big tree trunk in the middle of the room. Here the modern American menu items are as artfully presented as the chichi clientele. You'll be hard-pressed to find a better meal this side of San Francisco. For something lighter, pick up a turkey and cranberry relish panini to-go at the **Deli** (sandwiches $7-10; ☺7am-9pm) and then enjoy it on the grounds. The **Foundry Grill** (breakfast & sandwiches $8-16, dinner $16-31; ☺8-11am, 11:30am-4pm & 5-9pm Mon-Sat, 9am-2pm & 5-9pm Sun) is also available for most meals.

Built of cast-off barn wood, the centerpiece of the **Owl Bar** (☺5pm-11am Mon-Thu, 5pm-1am Fri, noon-1am Sat, noon-11pm Sun) is a century-old bar where the real Butch Cassidy once drank. The place looks like a Wild West roadhouse, but it's full of art freaks, mountain hipsters and local cowboys imbibing by a roaring fireplace.On Friday and Saturday there's often live music.

Provo

The third-largest city in Utah is a conservative town with a strong Mormon influence. The most compelling reason to visit is to see Brigham Young University (BYU) on a day trip from Salt Lake City, 45 miles north. University Ave, Provo's main thoroughfare, intersects Center St in the small old downtown core. Note that the whole place pretty much shuts down on Sunday

The **BYU campus** (www.byu.edu) is enormous and known for its squeaky-clean student dress codes. Drive 450 East north toward the **Hinckley Alumni & Visitor Center** (☎801-422-4678; cnr W Campus & N Campus Drs; ☺8am-6pm Mon-Sat) where tours begin, by appointment. The university's what's-this-doing-here **Museum of Art** (☎801-378-2787; admission free; ☺10am-6pm Tue, Wed & Fri, 10am-9pm Mon & Thu, noon-5pm Sat) is one of the biggest in the Southwest, with a concentration on American art. Temporary exhibits are top notch. BYU sporting events take place at **Lavell Edwards Stadium** (☎801-422-2981; www.byutickets.com; 1700 N Canyon Rd).

You can ice skate in town at **Peaks Ice Arena** (☎801-377-8777; www.peaksarena.com; 100 N Seven Peaks Blvd; adult/child $6/4; ☺Mon-Sat), where the Olympic hockey teams faced off in 2002. Free-skate hours vary.

Provo is close enough to SLC that you can easily make it in a day. If you stay over, we recommend the 1895 **Hines Mansion B&B** (☎801-374-8400, 800-428-5636; www.hinesmansion.com; 383 W 100 South; r incl breakfast $129-199; @☻). The 'Library' guest room has a 'secret passage' door to the bathroom.

The historic downtown has numerous little independent, ethnic restaurants; many around the intersection of Center St and University Ave. **Guru's** (45 E Center St; mains

DONNY & MARIE

Well-known Mormon family the Osmonds have long called Provo, Utah, home. Seven of the nine children born to George and Olive ('Mother') Osmond participated in the family singing group 'The Osmonds' that was a sensation in the '70s. Most of the Osmond offspring have spawned large families of their own (totaling 120 descendants at last count). Pop icons Donny and Marie branched out musically, singing and hosting a live variety show. Remember 'A Little Bit Country, A Little Bit Rock 'n' Roll'?

Marie's 2007 runner-up success on the TV hit *Dancing with the Stars* helped reignite interest in the entertaining family. Two years later, Donny trumped his sister's achievement by winning the mirror-ball trophy on the same show. In 2011 the duo celebrated the 500th performance of the new Donny & Marie show staged at the Flamingo hotel in Las Vegas.

DINOSAUR DIAMOND

Some darn clever marketing people came up with a dual-state national scenic byway. **Dinosaur Diamond** (www.dinosaurdiamond.org), which aims to give Dino his due by promoting and protecting paleontology along its 512-mile suggested route in Colorado and Utah. Following their lead, here are our fossilized favorites in Utah:

Dinosaur National Monument (Vernal) Touch 150-million-year-old bones still in the ground!

Dinosaur Discovery Site (St George; p462) Some of the most amazing dinosaur trackways ever found.

Utah Museum of Natural History (SLC; p469) The new home for the Huntington mammoth.

Utah Field House of Natural History State Park Museum (Vernal) Still growing, but an amazing, kid-friendly Utah dinosaur museum.

Museum of Ancient Life (Lehi; p475) Interactive exhibits provide an overview of world dinosaurs.

Cleveland-Lloyd Dinosaur Quarry (Price; p504) Watch 'em digging up new discoveries daily.

Red Fleet State Park (Vernal) More 200-milllion-year-old footprints.

And just for fun:

Dinosaur Museum (Blanding; p397) Dino movie memorabilia and models.

Ogden Eccles Dinosaur Park (Ogden; p495) Jurassic-era playground for kids.

$6-11; ⊙11am-9pm Mon-Sat) has an eclectic café menu, including rice bowls, and **Gloria's Little Italy** (1 E Center St; lunch $10-12.50, mains $15-19; ⊙11am-9pm Mon-Thu, until 10pm Fri & Sat) is always popular.

Get information at the **Utah Valley Visitors Bureau** (☑801-851-2100; www.utahvalley.org/cvb; 111 S University Ave; ⊙8:30am-5pm Mon-Fri, 9am-3pm Sat), inside the beautiful courthouse.

UTA (☑801-743-3882, 888-743-3882; www.rideuta.com) runs frequent express buses to SLC ($5), with diminished service Sunday.

NORTHEASTERN UTAH

A remote and rural area, Northeastern Utah is high wilderness terrain (much of which is more than a mile above sea level) that has traditionally attracted farmers and miners. Rising oil prices spurred oil and gas development in the rocky valleys, which in turn has led to increased services in towns like Vernal. Most travelers come to see Dinosaur National Monument, but you'll also find other dino dig sites and museums, as well as Fremont Indian rock art and ruins in

the area. Up near the Wyoming border, the Uinta Mountains and Flaming Gorge attract trout fishers and wildlife lovers alike.

Vernal & Around

The capital of self-dubbed 'Dinoland', Vernal is the closest town to Dinosaur National Monument (20 miles east). You'd never know it from the big pink allosaurus that welcomes you to town. Don't miss the great natural history museum in town.

There are a number of great drives in the area, through public lands and parks, including the road up to the gorgeous rivers and lake of Flaming Gorge, just 35 miles north. The **Dinosaurland Travel Board** (☑800-477-5558; www.dinoland.com; 134 W Main; ⊙8am-5pm Mon-Fri) provides information on the entire region; pick up driving-tour brochures for area rock art and dino tracks here. The **Vernal Ranger Station** (☑435-789-1181; www.fs.usda.gov/ashley; 355 N Vernal Ave; ⊙8am-5pm Mon-Fri) has details on camping and hiking in Ashley National Forest, to the north.

The informative film at the **Utah Field House of Natural History State Park**

SCENIC DRIVE: RED CLOUD LOOP

After you see the dinosaur tracks at Red Fleet State Park, continue on Hwy 191 for 21 miles north of Vernal, then take off west on **Red Cloud Scenic Backway**. The road starts out tame, then rises sharply up to 10,000ft in twists and turns. The one-and-a-half lane road has steep drop-offs and dramatic pine scenery amid the eastern Uinta peaks. Allow three hours to return the full 74 miles back to Vernal via Dry Fork Canyon Rd, where you can stop at the McConkie Ranch Petroglyphs.

Museum (http://stateparks.utah.gov; 496 E Main St; ⊙9am-5pm Mon-Sat; 🚸) is the best all-round introduction to Utah's dinosaurs. Interactive exhibits, video clips and, of course, giant fossils are wonderfully relevant to the area. There's loads to keep the kids entertained, and the museum is still growing.

Ten miles northeast of Vernal on Hwy 191, check out hundreds of fossilized dinosaur tracks at **Red Fleet State Park** (📞435-789-4432; http://stateparks.utah.gov; admission $7; ⊙6am-10pm Apr-Oct, 8am-5pm Nov & Dec). Eleven miles northwest, the 200ft of **McConkie Ranch Petroglyphs** (Dry Fork Canyon Rd; by donation; ⊙dawn-dusk) are well worth checking out. Generous ranch owners built a little self-serve info shack with posted messages and a map, but be advised that the 800-year-old Fremont Indian art require some rock-scrambling to see. Being on private land has really helped; these alien-looking anthropomorphs are in much better shape than the many that have been desecrated by vandals on public lands. Follow 3000 West to the north out of Vernal. You can visit both as part of the 74-mile Red Cloud Loop. For even more rock art and ruins, we recommend the nearby Nine Mile Canyon drive.

The Green and Yampa Rivers are the main waterways in the area; both have some rapids and more genteel floats. Trips (May through September) run from $85 to $800 for one to five days. Check with **Don Hatch River Expeditions** (📞435-789-4316, 800-342-8243; www.donhatchrivertrips.com, 221 N 400 East) or **Dinosaur Expeditions** (📞800-345-7238; www.dinoadv.com).

Contemporary comforts like deluxe mattresses and flat-screen TVs come standard both in the hotel rooms at **Landmark Inn & Suites** (📞435-781-1800, 888-738-1800; Rte 149; r incl breakfast $69-109; 🛜), and at the much more reasonable B&B rooms in a purpose-built house across the street. The latter is a bargain, though walls can be thin. Guests all share the buffet breakfast and fitness room at the main building. A number of new motels have popped up west of town in recent years, including **Marriott Springhill Suites** (📞435-781-9000, 888-287-9400; www.marriott.com; 1205 W Hwy 40; r $109-139; ✳@🛜), with supersized rooms, an indoor pool and outdoor sundeck. Flaming Gorge and Dinosaur National Monument both have camping.

For homemade soup, a tasty panini and a good read, stop into **Backdoor Grille** (87 W Main St; mains $5-8; ⊙11am-8pm), at the rear of Bitter Creek Books. **Dinosaur Brew Haus** (550 E Main St; burgers $5-10; ⊙5-10pm) serves up burgers and microbrews on tap. The hearty down-home grub at **Naples Country Café** (1010 E Hwy 40; breakfast & sandwiches $4-8, mains $9-15; ⊙7am-10pm), east of town, includes mile-high meringue pies.

Vernal is 145 miles west of Park City and 112 miles north of Price.

Dinosaur National Monument

Earl Douglass discovered one of the largest dinosaur fossil beds in North America here in 1909. He camped out and tenaciously protected the site until it was made a national park in 1915.

Driving in from Vernal, after about 13 miles, turn left at the **Utah Welcome Center** (📞800-200-1160; Hwy 40, Jensen; ⊙9am-5pm), which can provide information on the region and the state. A further 7 miles down the road, you enter the **Dinosaur Quarry** (www.nps.gov/dino; per vehicle $10; ⊙9am-5pm) section of the park.

In the early 1900s, hundreds of tons of rock was blasted away to expose the quarry. Many of the bones were only partially excavated, left half in the rock so that visitors could see how they were found – then the quarry was enclosed in a glass-sided building. Unfortunately the soil was unstable and the structure eventually became unsafe. Reopened after being closed for many years, you can once again see this marvelous site. You can also hike up to touch still-embedded, 150 million-year-old fossils on the trail. Take the free ranger-led interpretive hike, if available; you'll spot more than can easily be found on your own.

Pick up a brochure for the scenic driving tour that continues south for 13 miles past Fremont Indian rock art, ending at homesteader Josie Bassett's cabin and several trailheads. The monument straddles the Utah-Colorado state line. The Utah portion of the park contains all the fossils, but the **Canyon Section Visitor Center** (☑970-374-3000; www.nps.gov/dino; Dinosaur, CO; per car $10; ☺9am-4pm Jun-Aug, 8am-4:30pm Wed-Sun Sep & May) shows a good movie and there are pretty hikes.

Staying over? Pitch your tent at the waterfront **Green River Campground** (Dinosaur Quarry; campsites $12; ☺mid-Apr–Oct); first-come, first-served. The 88 sites have access to running water (indoor plumbing and the river), but no showers. Ask about primitive camping.

If you'd rather a roof over your head, book at the comfy-cozy **Jensen Inn** (☑435-789-590; 5056 S 9500 East, Jensen; r incl breakfast $95-150; @☎), 3 miles north of the Hwy 40 turnoff on Hwy 149. Sleep in a tipi ($95) or camp ($55) on the grounds and you can still get the scrumptious home-cooked breakfast.

Flaming Gorge National Recreation Area

Named for its fiery red sandstone canyon, Flaming Gorge provides 375 miles of shoreline around Flaming Gorge Reservoir, which straddles the Utah-Wyoming state line. As with many artificial lakes, fishing and boating are prime attractions. Various records for giant lake trout and Kokanee salmon have been set here. The area also provides plenty of hiking and camping in summer, and cross-country skiing and snowmobiling

in winter. Keep an eye out for common wildlife such as moose, elk, pronghorn antelope and mule deer; you may also see bighorn sheep, black bears and mountain lions. The lake's 6040ft elevation ensures pleasantly warm but not desperately hot summers – daytime highs average about 80°F (27°C).

Information is available from www.flaminggorgecountry.com, the **USFS Flaming Gorge Headquarters** (☑435-784-3445; www.fs.fed.us/r4/ashley; 25 W Hwy 43, Manila; ☺8am-5pm Mon-Fri) and at the **Flaming Gorge Dam Visitor Center** (☑435-885-3135; Hwy 191; ☺9am-5pm May-Sep). Day use of some Flaming Gorge areas costs $5 at self-pay stations.

In Dutch John, rent a fishing, pontoon or ski boat ($110 to $280 per day) from **Cedar Springs Marina** (☑435-889-3795; www.cedarspringsmarina.com; off Hwy 191; ☺Apr-Oct), 2 miles east of Flaming Gorge Dam. The best fishing is found with a guide; ask at the marina or contact **Trout Creek Flies** (☑435-885-3355; www.fishgreenriver.com; cnr Hwy 191 & Little Hole Rd). A guided half-day trip will cost you about $325 for two people. Aim to fly-fish late June to early July, before the river is flooded with fun floaters. Trout Creek also rents rafts and kayaks ($60 to $80 per day) and runs a floater shuttle.

Ashley National Forest (www.fc.fod.us/r4/ashley) runs more than two dozen May-to-September campgrounds in the area. The 7400ft elevation, ponderosa pine forest location and excellent clifftop overlook views of the reservoir make **Canyon Rim** (☑877-444-6777; www.recreation.gov; Red Canyon Rd, off Hwy 44; tent & RV sites $15) a top choice. Keep an eye out for bighorn sheep. Water; no showers or hookups.

Activities at **Red Canyon Lodge** (☑435-889-3759; www.redcanyonlodge.com; 790 Red Canyon Rd, Dutch John; cabins $110; ☺closed Mon-Thu Nov-Mar) include fishing, rowing, rafting and horseback riding, among others. Its pleasantly rustic cabins have no TVs. **Flaming Gorge Resort** (☑435-889-3773; www.flaminggorgeresort.com; 155 Greendale/Hwy 191,

---

SCENIC DRIVE: FLAMING GORGE-UINTAS SCENIC BYWAY

Heading north from Vernal, 80 miles into the northeastern Uintas Mountains, Flaming Gorge-Uintas Scenic Byway (Hwy 191) is a drive and a geology lesson all in one. As you climb up switchbacks to 8100ft, the up-tilted sedimentary layers you see represent one billion years of history. Interpretive signs explain what different colors and rock compositions indicate about the prehistoric climate in which they were laid down. It's a great route for fall color and wildlife-watching, too.

Dutch John; r $110, ste $150) has similar water-based fun, and rents decent motel rooms and suites. Both have decent restaurants. Convenience stores in Dutch John have deli counters.

High Uintas Wilderness Area

The Uinta Mountains are unusual in that they run east-west, unlike all other major mountain ranges in the lower 48. Several peaks rise to more than 13,000ft, including Kings (13,528ft), which is the highest point in the Southwest. The central summits lie within the **High Uintas Wilderness Area** (www.fs.fed.us/r4/ashley), part of Ashley National Forest, which provides 800 sq miles of hiking and horseback riding opportunities. No roads, no mountain biking and no off-road driving permitted. The reward? An incredible, remote mountain experience, one without snack bars or lodges.

Price & San Rafael Swell

Though not the world's most interesting town in itself, Price can serve as a base for exploring backcountry dinosaur and ancient rock-art sites in the San Rafael Swell and beyond. It's en route from Green River (65 miles) to Vernal (112 miles), so a stopover is also possible. The staff at the **Castle Country Travel Desk** (☎800-842-0789; www.castlecountry.com; 155 E Main St; ☺8am-5pm Apr-Sep, 9am-5pm Mon-Sat Oct-Mar) can help you plan out your regional routes. In the same building (same hours),

the **College of Eastern Utah Prehistoric Museum** (www.museum.ceu.edu; adult/child $5/2; ☺9am-5pm Mon-Sat) exhibits fossils that were discovered within two hours of the museum. Look for the Utah raptor, first identified in this part of the world.

Thirty miles south of Price you can visit an actual dinosaur dig site. More than 12,000 bones have been taken from the ground at **Cleveland-Lloyd Dinosaur Quarry** (☎435-636-3600; adult/child $6/2; ☺10am-5pm Fri & Sat, noon-5pm Sun late Mar-Oct). A dozen species of dinosaur were buried here 150 million years ago, but the large concentration of meat-eating allosaurus has helped scientists around the world draw new conclusions. Two excavations are on display and the visitor center's exhibits are quite informative. Several hikes lead off from there. Take Rte 10 south to the Elmo/Cleveland turnoff and follow signs on the dirt road.

These southern lands between Hwys 10 and 6/24 are the canyons, arches and cliffs of the **San Rafael Swell**. Look for the purples, grays and greens that indicate ancient seabeds, in addition to the oxygenated oranges and reds of this anticline. The area is all BLM land where free dispersed camping and some four-wheeling is allowed. Sights include a 1200ft canyon drop at **Wedge Overlook**, Barrier Canyon-style pictographs at **Buckhorn Wash**, and a suspension **footbridge**. Ask for a basic map at the town visitor center or the quarry site. For more details contact the **BLM Price Field Office** (☎435-636-3600; www.blm.gov; 125 S 600 West; ☺9am-4:30pm Mon-Fri) or go online to www.emerycounty.com/travel.

SCENIC DRIVE: NINE MILE CANYON

Abundant rock art is the attraction on the **Nine Mile Canyon National Backcountry Byway** (www.byways.org), billed as the 'longest art gallery in the world'. You can also spot Fremont granaries and structures along the canyon walls (bring binoculars). Many of the petroglyphs are easy to miss; some are on private property. Pick up a free guide at area restaurants or at the Castle Country Travel Desk in Price or the Utah Welcome Center outside Dinosaur National Monument. Allow at least three to five hours for the 70-mile unpaved ride from Wellington (on Hwy 6) to Myton (on Hwy 40). Get gas before you go: there are no services.

About 23 miles northeast along Nine Mile Canyon Byway from the Hwy 6/191 turnoff, you can stay at the simple **Nine Mile Bunk & Breakfast** (☎435-637-2572; www.ninemilecanyon.com; r with shared bath $70, camping cabins $55, both incl breakfast), with two big ranch house rooms on spacious grounds; plus you can stay in old pioneer cabin or pitch a tent on site ($10). The rustic accommodations are run by a 'retired' ranching couple who are the nicest folks you'd ever want to meet. They run canyon tours (half-day from $155), too.

STARVATION STATE PARK

No one is quite sure who did the stealing, but either trappers in the area stashed some winter stores in the mountains, or Native Americans did, and then the other group took the food. Advance planners starved when they found no tasty treats buried under the snow, or so the story goes. In all likelihood bears were to blame for the theft and the name of **Starvation State Park** (http://stateparks.utah.gov; Hwy 40, Duchesne; day-use $7, ⊙6am-10pm Jun-Aug, 8am-5pm Sep-May).

Subsequent homesteaders tried to make a go of it here on the Strawberry River, but with a short growing season and frozen ground they had no better luck fending off hunger. Today the park contains a 3500-acre reservoir as well as plenty of picnickers. The 60-site **Lower Beach Campground** (☏800-322-3770; http://utahstateparks .reserveamerica.com; tent & RV sites with hookups $16-25; ⊙Jun-Sep) has showers and features a sandy beach. Primitive camping is also available here – don't forget to bring food!.

The well-preserved ancient archaeological sites protected by Wilcox Ranch are now part of **Range Creek Wildlife Management Area** (www.wildlife.utah.gov/range_creek), east of East Carbon (25 miles southeast of Price). Since the family turned the property over to the government, the public has been allowed limited access. The best way to explore is with a full-day 4WD tour ($125 per person) run by **Tavaputs Ranch** (☏435-637-1236; www.tavaputs ranch.com; per person incl meals $200; ⊙mid-Jun–mid-Sep) Included in the lodging price are three meals, backcountry hikes, scenic drives and wildlife tours on the 15,000-acre spread; horseback riding is $50 extra.

Free camping is allowed off established roads on the San Rafael Swell BLM lands. The motels off Hwy 6/191 and on Main St aren't exactly exciting, but they are plentiful. **Super 8** (☏435-637-8088, 888-288-5081; www .super8.com; 180 N Hospital Dr; r $60-80; ❋☎) has fine, basic rooms. Thirty miles south in Castle Dale, **San Rafeal Swell Bed & Breakfast** (☏435-381-5689; www.sanrafael bedandbreakfast.com; 15 E 100 N; r incl breakfast $65-110; ❋☎) has more of a personal touch. Less expensive rooms share a bath; some are a bit themey.

The best place to eat in town, isn't themey. Though barely out of Price, **Grogg's Pinnacle Brewing Company** (1653 N Carbonville, Helper; burgers $6-10, mains $12-18; ⊙11am-10pm) is technically in Helper. Friendly staff, tasty casual-American fare and microbrews on tap make this the place to be. Look for other eateries along Main St.

Understand
❯Southwest USA

Southwest USA Today

It's All Politics...

Tourism officials in Arizona are surely not pleased by headlines in recent years. One of the biggest issues facing the state is illegal immigration. About 250,000 people crossed illegally into Arizona from Mexico in 2009. Although that was a 50% decline from a few years earlier, the state passed law SB 1070 in 2010, requiring police officers to ask for identification from anyone they suspect of being in the country illegally.

What's happening on the ground? Across the Southwest, the number of arrests for illegal border crossings has dropped. Is the ongoing recession making the US less attractive? Perhaps it's the beefed up US Border Patrol. The number of border patrol agents jumped from 10,000 in 2004 to more than 20,700 in 2010. Agents have a very visible presence in southern Arizona: there are checkpoints, and you'll likely see their green-and-white SUVs whizzing down two-lane backroads.

Fiscal woes are the other political hot potato. States are slashing spending, and in Arizona and Utah state park budgets have gone under the knife. Many in Arizona are operating on a five-day schedule, closing on Tuesday and Wednesday; in Utah, state parks have cut the number of rangers. In May 2011, Nevada's unemployment rate was 12%, which was higher than the national average. Luxury condominiums in Vegas sit empty and mountain resort properties in Colorado are experiencing declines in business.

Despite state park budget woes, the Southwest's national parks are faring OK. Attendance was up in Grand Canyon National Park in 2010, and the park welcomed 4.38 million recreational visitors, making it the second-most-visited national park in the US (behind Great Smoky Mountains). Zion National Park ranked eighth.

» Population of AZ, NM, UT, NV & CO: 19 million

» Regional unemployment rate June 2011: 8.9%

» US unemployment rate June 2011: 9.2%

» Cost of marriage license in Nevada: $60

» Sprinting speed of a roadrunner: 15mph

Dos and Don'ts

» Do tip everyone in Vegas.

» Don't smoke inside a building without asking first. Non-smoking laws are increasingly common, and many people are strongly against secondhand smoke in their homes.

» Do leave a 15-20% tip for your waiter when served a meal.

» Don't take pictures on Native American land without first asking permission.

» Do make sure you know what time zone you're in when crossing states.

Top Movies

127 Hours (2010) Aron Ralston's harrowing experience in Utah's red-rock country. **Thelma & Louise** (1991) Dead in Dead Horse State Park? Pshaw. The duo lives to celebrate the movie's 20th anniversary in 2011.

belief systems
(% of population)

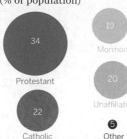

34
Protestant

10
Mormon

20
Unaffiliated

22
Catholic

5
Other

if the Southwest was 100 people

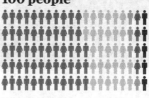

58 would be Caucasian
29 would be Hispanic
4 would be Native American

4 would be African American
5 would be other

...or the Weather

Although the exact causes are unclear – climate change, residential development, government policy – the Southwest has been particularly hard-hit by forest fires in recent years. The 2011 Wallow Fire was the worst in Arizona's history, burning about 538,000 acres. At about the same time, the Las Conchas Fire burned more than 244 sq miles near Los Alamos, NM. The good news? A record snowpack in western mountain ranges in early 2011 spelled w-a-t-e-r (after melting) for Nevada and Arizona, where water levels have been dropping the last 10 years. Lake Mead might swell by 40ft.

On the Bright Side

NASA may have wrapped up the shuttle program, but entrepreneurs like Richard Branson are looking to the stars – and taking action. Branson's Virgin Galactic is on course to send civilian 'astronauts' into space from the new Spaceport in New Mexico in the next few years. Tickets are $200,000, with a $20,000 deposit; about 430 people have signed up for a flight.

Not all advancements require a spaceport. On the south rim of the Grand Canyon, finishing touches have been added to the impressive new visitor center. Ecofriendly initiatives in the national park are gaining traction, including a park-and-ride shuttle from Tusayan and a bicycle rental service. Environmentally, Colorado is leading the way with its extremely progressive clean-energy standards, with legislated incentives for residents to use clean energy and significant growth in solar energy jobs.

Last but not least, New Mexico and Arizona are both celebrating 100 years of statehood in 2012.

» Number of pueblos in New Mexico: 19

» Grand Canyon's widest chasm: 18 miles

» Percentage of land that is public in Utah: 70%

» Miles of railroad track on Durango to Silverton line: 45

The hottest recorded temperature in Arizona was 128°F (53.5°C) at Lake Havasu City.

Greeting People

» 'Hi, how are you?' is expected to receive a cheerful, 'Thanks. I'm fine.' Actual complaints are frowned upon.

» Don't be overly physical. Some Americans will hug, but many more will just shake hands. Big kisses will likely get you slapped.

How to Speak Southwestern

adobe – building style using straw and mud (traditional) or sand and clay (modern)
farolitos – Hispanic Christmas tradition; made by placing a candle inside a waxed bag lined with sand

hacienda – old Spanish colonial mansion
kiva – round-fronted adobe fireplace; once used for worship, today it's used for warmth
portales – covered porches
ristra – string of dried red chiles, often seen hanging from porches

History

History is a hands-on experience in the Southwest. Museums? Save 'em for later. First you'll want to explore the scruffy OK Corral, or climb into a lofty cliff dwelling, or simply join the congregation inside a 1700s Spanish mission. Historic spots like these are what make the region so fascinating. The land, with its mineral-rich hills and stubborn inaccessibility, is intricately tied to the regional history. Settlers were lured here for a variety of reasons: rumors of gold and copper, the possibility of religious freedom and the likelihood of unfettered adventure and self-determination.

In sun-baked Phoenix today, travelers can see the remains of canals built by the ancient Hohokam people to transport water to their fields. An ascent into Ancestral Puebloan cliff dwellings in Arizona, New Mexico or Colorado reveals the sweep of the land and the advantages of building a home far above the ground. Native American tribes eventually moved in from other regions, learning the symbols and stories of their predecessors and weaving them into their own cultural narrative.

The Spanish conquistadors, seeking the Seven Cities of Gold, left their mark on the landscape too. Their expeditions in the 1500s led to the construction of the missions, which opened the door for regional development and Western civilization – with a lot of bloodshed along the way. The Mormons arrived in 1847, building temples, orderly streets and religious outposts throughout Utah. Prospectors started towns, too, in the 19th century, and their mine shafts and old buildings are still visible in boom-and-bust towns across the region. These mining towns and the surrounding ranchland lured families seeking a better life, as well as cowboys, sheriffs and outlaws – restless, free-range men who kept upsetting the balance between chaos and civilization. Their spirit lives on today.

In the 1900s, the Southwest made its mark scientifically. The world's first atomic bomb was developed under top-secret conditions at Los Alamos: southern New Mexico was a launch pad for rockets, and the desert served as a blasting ground for the first atomic bomb in 1945

TIMELINE	AD 100	1300s	1598
	The region's dominant indigenous cultures emerge. The Hohokam settle in the desert, the Mogollon in the mountains and valleys and Ancestral Puebloans build cliff dwellings around the Four Corners.	The entire civilization of Ancestral Puebloans living in Mesa Verde, CO, leaves behind a sophisticated city of cliff dwellings, creating one of history's most enduring unsolved mysteries.	A large force of Spanish explorers, led by Don Juan de Onate, stops near present-day El Paso, TX, and declares the land to the north New Mexico for Spain.

PETROGLYPHS: WRITTEN ON THE LAND

Petroglyphs can be found etched into desert-varnished boulders across the Southwest. This rock art is simple yet mysterious and always leaves us wondering: who did this, and why? What were they trying to say?

Dating from at least 4000 BC to as late as the 19th century, rock art in the Southwest has been attributed to every known ancestral and modern people. In fact, one way archaeologists track the spread of ancestral cultures is by studying their distinctive rock art styles, which tend to be either abstract or representational and anthropomorphic. Representational rock art is almost always more recent, while abstract designs appear in all ages.

We can only speculate about what it means. This symbolic writing becomes obscure the moment the cultural context for the symbols is lost. Archaeologists believe much of the art was likely the work of shamans or elders communicating with the divine. Some of the earliest abstract designs may have been created in trance states. Certain figures and motifs seem to reflect a heavenly pantheon, while other rock art may tell stories – real or mythical – of successful hunts or battles. Some etchings may have served as simple agricultural calendars, marking the start of harvest season, for example, by the way a shadow falls across a picture.

Other images may have marked tribal territory, and some may have been nothing more than idle doodling. But no matter what the meaning, each rock-art site – whether a petroglyph (inscribed or pecked into the stone) or pictograph (painted figure) – is irreplaceable, whether as a valuable part of the human archaeological record or the continuing religious traditions and cultural patrimony of contemporary tribes.

Preserve rock-art sites for future generations by observing these rules of etiquette:

» Do not disturb or remove any artifacts or features of the site.

» Do not trace, repaint, remove graffiti or otherwise touch or apply any materials to the rock art.

» Stay back at least 10ft from all rock-art panels, using binoculars or a zoom lens for better views.

More recently, the Southwest gained fame for two historic firsts. In 1981 Sandra Day O'Connor, who grew up on an Arizona ranch, was the first woman appointed to the United States Supreme Court. In 2008, New Mexico's Bill Richardson was the first Hispanic to seek the office of President of the United States.

The First Americans

Archaeologists believe that the region's first inhabitants were hunters – descendants of those hardy souls who crossed the Bering Strait into North America 25,000 years ago. The population grew, however, and wild game became extinct, forcing hunters to augment their diets with

1609	1682	1846-48	1847
Santa Fe, America's oldest capital city, is founded. The Palace of Governors is the only remaining 17th-century structure; the rest of Santa Fe was destroyed by a 1914 fire.	During the Pueblo Revolt, northern New Mexico Pueblos drive out the Spanish after the latter's bloody campaign to destroy Puebloan kivas and ceremonial objects.	The battle for the West is waged with the Mexican–American War. The Treaty of Guadalupe ends the fighting, and the US annexes most of Arizona and New Mexico.	Mormons fleeing religious persecution arrive in Salt Lake City by wagon train; over the next 20 years more than 70,000 Mormons will escape to Utah via the Mormon Pioneer Trail.

Cliff Dwellings

» Mesa Verde National Park, CO

» Bandelier National Monument, NM

» Gila Cliff Dwellings National Monument, NM

» Montezuma Castle National Monument, AZ

» Walnut Canyon National Monument, AZ

» Navajo Nation National Monument, AZ

berries, seeds, roots and fruits. After 3000 BC, contact with farmers in what is now central Mexico led to the beginnings of agriculture in the Southwest. Primitive corn was grown, and by 500 BC beans and squash were also cultivated. Between 300 BC and AD 100, distinct groups began to settle in villages in the Southwest.

The Hohokam, Mogollon & Ancestral Puebloans

By about AD 100, three dominant cultures were emerging in the Southwest: the Hohokam of the desert, the Mogollon of the central mountains and valleys, and the Ancestral Puebloans. Archaeologists originally called the Ancestral Puebloans the Anasazi, which comes from a Navajo term meaning 'ancient enemy' and has fallen out of favor.

The Hohokam lived in the deserts of Arizona from 300 BC to AD 1400, adapting to desert life by creating an incredible river-fed irrigation system. They also developed low earthen pyramids and sunken ball courts with sloped earthern walls. These oval-shaped courts, which varied in size, may have been used for organized games as well as for markets and community gatherings.

The Mogollon culture settled near the Mexican border from 200 BC to AD 1400. They lived in small communities, often elevated on isolated mesas or ridge tops, and built pit dwellings, which were simple structures of wood, shrubs and mud built over a small depression in the ground. Although they farmed, they depended more on hunting and foraging for food. Growing villages featured the kiva – a circular, underground chamber used for ceremonies and other communal purposes.

Around the 13th or 14th century, the Mogollon were likely being peacefully assimilated by the Ancestral Puebloan groups from the north. One indication of this is the beautiful black-on-white Mimbres pottery with its distinctive animal and human figures executed in a geometric style reminiscent of Puebloan ware. (The Mimbres were Mogollons who lived in a remote valley area in southwestern New Mexico between 1100 and 1150AD.) The Gila Cliff Dwellings in New Mexico are a late-Mogollon site with Puebloan features.

The Ancestral Puebloans inhabited the Colorado Plateau, also called the Four Corners area, which comprises parts of northeastern Arizona, northwestern New Mexico, southwestern Colorado and southeastern Utah. This culture left the Southwest's richest archaeological sites and ancient settlements, some of which are still inhabited.

Today, descendants of the Ancestral Puebloans live in Pueblo Indian communities along New Mexico's Rio Grande, and in the Acoma, Zuni and Laguna Pueblos in northwest New Mexico. The oldest links with

» Mural, Santa Fe Trail

1849
A regular stagecoach service starts along the Santa Fe Trail. The 900-mile trail will serve as the country's main shipping route until the arrival of the railroad 60 years later.

1864
Kit Carson captures 9000 Navajo and forces them to walk 400 miles to a camp near Fort Sumner. Hundreds of Native Americans die along 'The Long Walk.'

1869
One-armed Civil War veteran John Wesley Powell leads the first Colorado River descent, a grueling 1000-mile expedition through the Grand Canyon's rapids that kills half of his men.

the Ancestral Puebloans are found among the Hopi tribe of northern Arizona. The mesa-top village of Old Oraibi has been inhabited since the 1100s, making it the oldest continuously inhabited settlement in North America.

By about 1400, the Hohokam had abandoned their villages. There are many theories on this tribe's disappearance, but the most likely explanation involves a combination of factors, including drought, overhunting, conflict among groups and disease. The Mogollon people were more or less incorporated into the Ancestral Puebloans, who also all but disappeared from their ancestral cliff dwellings at Mesa Verde in southwestern Colorado by the 1400s – their mass exodus began in the 1300s.

For more about the Native American peoples of the Southwest, see p522.

The Spaniards Arrive

Francisco Vasquez de Coronado led the first major expedition into North America in 1540. It included 300 soldiers, hundreds of Native American guides and herds of livestock. It also marked the first major violence between Spanish explorers and the native people.

Those Who Came Before, by Robert H and Florence C Lister, is an excellent source of information about the prehistory of the Southwest and the archaeological sites of the national parks and monuments of this area.

The expedition's goal was the fabled, immensely rich Seven Cities of Cibola. For two years, they traveled through what is now Arizona, New Mexico and as far east as Kansas, but instead of gold and precious gems, the expedition found adobe pueblos, which they violently commandeered. During the Spaniards' first few years in northern New Mexico, they tried to subdue the Pueblos, resulting in much bloodshed. The fighting started in Acoma Pueblo, in today's New Mexico, when a Spanish contingent of 30 men led by one of Onate's nephews demanded tax payment in the form of food. The Acoma Indians responded by killing him and about half of his force. Onate retaliated with greater severity. Relations with the Native Americans, poor harvests, harsh weather and accusations of Onate's cruelty led to many desertions among the colonizers. By 1608, Onate had been recalled to Mexico. A new governor, Pedro de Peralta, was sent north to found a new capital in 1609 – Santa Fe remains the capital of New Mexico today, the oldest capital in what is now the USA.

In an attempt to link Santa Fe with the newly established port of San Francisco and to avoid Native American raids, small groups of explorers pressed into what is now Utah but were turned back by the rugged and arid terrain. The 1776 Dominguez-Escalante expedition was the first to survey Utah, but no attempt was made to settle there until the arrival of the Mormons in the 19th century.

In addition to armed conflict, Europeans introduced smallpox,

1881	1919	1931	1938
In 1881, Wyatt Earp, along with his brothers Virgil and Morgan, and Doc Holliday, kill Billy Clanton and the McLaury brothers during the OK Corral shootout in Tombstone, AZ.	The Grand Canyon becomes the USA's 15th national park. Only 44,173 people visit the park that year, compared to 4.4 million in 2010.	Nevada legalizes gambling and drops the divorce residency requirement to six weeks; this, along with legalized prostitution and championship boxing, carries the state through the Great Depression.	Route 66 becomes the first cross-country highway to be completely paved, including more than 750 miles across Arizona and New Mexico.

measles and typhus, to which the Native Americans had no resistance, into the Southwest. Upward of half of the Pueblo populations were decimated by these diseases, shattering cultures and trade routes and proving a destructive force that far outstripped combat.

The Long Walk & Apache Conflicts

For decades, US forces pushed west across the continent, killing or forcibly moving whole tribes of Native Americans who were in their way. The most widely known incident is the forceful relocation of many Navajo in 1864. US forces, led by Kit Carson, destroyed Navajo fields, orchards and houses, and forced the people into surrendering or withdrawing into remote parts of Canyon de Chelly in modern-day Arizona. Eventually starvation forced them out. About 9000 Navajo were rounded up and marched 400 miles east to a camp at Bosque Redondo, near Fort Sumner in New Mexico. Hundreds of Native Americans died from sickness, starvation or gunshot wounds along the way. The Navajo call this 'The Long Walk.'

The last serious conflicts were between US troops and the Apache. This was partly because raiding was the essential path to manhood for the Apache. As US forces and settlers moved into Apache land, they became obvious targets for the raids that were part of the Apache way of life. These continued under the leadership of Mangas Coloradas, Cochise, Victorio and, finally, Geronimo, who surrendered in 1886 after being promised that he and the Apache would be imprisoned for two years and then allowed to return to their homeland. As with many promises made during these years, this one, too, was broken.

Even after the wars were over, Native Americans continued to be treated like second-class citizens for many decades. Non–Native Americans used legal loopholes and technicalities to take over reservation land. Many children were removed from reservations and shipped off to boarding schools where they were taught in English and punished for speaking their own languages or behaving 'like Indians' – this practice continued into the 1930s.

Westward Ho

Nineteenth-century Southwest history is strongly linked to transportation development. During early territorial days, movement of goods and people from the East to the Southwest was very slow. Horses, mule trains and stagecoaches represented state-of-the-art transportation at the time. Major routes included the Santa Fe Trail and the Old Spanish Trail, which ran from Santa Fe into central Utah and across Nevada to Los Angeles, CA. Regular stagecoach services along the

1943	1945	1946	1947
High in the northern New Mexican desert, Los Alamos is chosen as the headquarters of the Manhattan Project, the code name for the research and development of the atomic bomb.	The first atomic bomb is detonated in a desolate desert area in southern New Mexico that is now part of the White Sands Missile Range.	The opening of the glitzy Flamingo casino in Vegas kicks off a building spree. Sin City reaches its first golden peak in the '50s.	An unidentified object falls in the desert near Roswell. The government first calls it a crashed disk, but the next day calls it a weather balloon and closes off the area.

Santa Fe Trail began in 1849; the Mormon Trail reached Salt Lake City in 1847.

The arrival of more people and resources via the railroad led to further land exploration and the frequent discovery of mineral deposits. Many mining towns were founded in the 1870s and 1880s; some are now ghost towns, while others, like Tombstone, Arizona, and Silver City, New Mexico, remain active.

The Wild West

Romanticized tales of gunslingers, cattle rustlers, outlaws and train robbers fuel Wild West legends. Good and bad guys were designations in flux –a tough outlaw in one state became a popular sheriff in another. And gunfights were more frequently the result of mundane political struggles in emerging towns than storied blood feuds. New mining towns mushroomed overnight, playing host to rowdy saloons and bordellos where miners would come to brawl, drink, gamble and be fleeced.

Legendary figures Billy the Kid and Sheriff Pat Garrett, both involved in the infamous Lincoln County War (p344), were active in the late 1870s. Billy the Kid reputedly shot and killed more than 20 men in a brief career as a gunslinger – he himself was shot and killed by Garrett at the tender age of 21. In 1881, Wyatt Earp, along with his brothers Virgil and Morgan, and Doc Holliday, shot dead Billy Clanton and the McLaury brothers in a blazing gunfight at the OK Corral in Tombstone, Arizona – the showdown took less than a minute. Both sides accused the other of cattle rustling, but the real story will never be known.

Butch Cassidy and the Sundance Kid (p427) once roamed much of Utah. Cassidy, a Mormon, robbed banks and trains with his Wild Bunch gang during the 1890s but never killed anyone.

The cry 'Geronimo!' became popular for skydivers after a group of US Army paratroopers training in 1940 saw the movie *Geronimo* (1939) one night, then began shouting the great warrior's name for courage during their jumps.

HISTORY THE WILD WEST

TOP FIVE OLD WEST SITES

» **OK Corral, Tombstone, AZ** Home of the famous 1881 gunfight, with the Earps and Doc Holliday facing Billy Clanton and the McLaury brothers.

» **Lincoln, NM** Shooting grounds of Billy the Kid; he left a still-visible bullet hole in the courthouse wall during a successful escape.

» **Jerome, AZ** Once known as the 'wickedest town in the old West,' it brimmed with brothels and saloons; now known for ghosts.

» **Virginia City, NV** Where the silver-laden Comstock Lode was struck; it's now a national historic landmark.

» **Silverton, CO** Old miners' spirit and railroad history with a historical downtown.

1950	1957	1963	1973
A radio game show host challenges any town to name itself after the show. Tiny Hot Springs, NM accepts the challenge and renames itself Truth or Consequences.	Los Alamos opens its doors to ordinary people for the first time. The city was first exposed to the public after the atomic bomb was dropped on Japan.	The controversial Glen Canyon Dam is finished and Lake Powell begins, eventually covering ancestral Indian sites and rock formations but creating 1960 miles of shoreline and a boater fantasyland.	The debut of the MGM Grand in 1973 signals the dawn of the era of corporate-owned 'megaresorts' and sparks a building bonanza along the Strip that's still going on today.

Depression, War & Recovery

While the first half of the 20th century saw much of the USA in a major depression, the Southwest remained relatively prosperous during the Dust Bowl days.

Las Vegas came on to the scene after the completion of a railroad linking Salt Lake City and Los Angeles in 1902. It grew during the despair of the '20s and reached its first golden peak (the second came at the turn of the century) during the fabulous '50s, when mob money ran the city and all that glittered really was gold.

During the Depression, the region benefited from a number of federal employment projects, and WWII rejuvenated a demand for metals mined in the Southwest. In addition, production facilities were located in New Mexico and Arizona to protect those states from the vulnerability

The late environmentalist and essayist Edward Abbey wrote that the canyon country of the Colorado Plateau once had a 'living heart' – Glen Canyon, now drowned beneath Lake Powell.

GUNFIGHT AT THE OK CORRAL

Considering it's the most famous shoot-out in the history of the Wild West, we know pitifully little of what really happened on October 26, 1881. We know that Ike and Billy Clanton and their cohorts Frank and Tom McLaury belonged to a loose association of rustlers and thieves called the Cowboys. Wyatt Earp was an on-again-off-again lawman with one heck of a mustache, who was serving as a temporary deputy to his brother Virgil, Tombstone's city marshal. Their other brother, Morgan, was also a deputy. Doc Holliday, a dentist, was their good buddy. Neither Wyatt nor Doc was squeaky-clean.

Long-simmering bad blood between the Earp group and the Cowboys began to boil over just before the shoot-out. Earlier that month, Frank McLaury had threatened to kill all of the Earps. On the day of the shoot-out, the Cowboys had come to Tombstone and were apparently in violation of the law requiring them to check their weapons. Virgil was the only one of these gunslingers who wasn't itching for a showdown, preferring to keep the peace. But the situation got out of hand. As the men confronted each other on the street, shots rang out. According to lore, Wyatt shot Frank McLaury at the same time Billy Clanton shot at Wyatt. During this first exchange, Frank was hit but didn't go down and Wyatt escaped unscathed. After about 30 seconds, it was all over. Tom had been felled by the sawn-off shotgun wielded by Doc, Frank was hit again, and Billy Clanton was dropped by a shot to the chest. All three were dead. Doc had been grazed in the hip, Virgil in the calf and Morgan was hit in the back. Wyatt was untouched.

Wyatt and Doc were charged with murder but exonerated, although questions remained about who was really guilty. Soon after, a full-scale vendetta broke out between the Earps and Cowboys. Morgan was shot and killed; Virgil was attacked, lost the use of his left arm, and fled to Tucson. Wyatt and Doc, after doing some damage of their own to the Cowboy clan, moved up to Colorado, each going his own way.

1996

President Bill Clinton establishes Utah's Grand Staircase-Escalante National Monument, which is unique in allowing some uses (such as hunting and grazing by permit) usually banned in national parks.

2002

Salt Lake City hosts the Winter Olympics and becomes the most populated place to ever hold the winter games, as well as the first place women competed in bobsled racing.

» Olympic banner, SLC

2004

Sin City is back! Las Vegas enters its second golden heyday, hosting 37.5 million visitors, starting work on its latest 'megaresort' and becoming the number-one party destination.

of attack. Migrating defense workers precipitated population booms and urbanization, which was mirrored elsewhere in the Southwest.

The struggle for an adequate supply of water for the growing desert population marked the early years of the 20th century, resulting in federally funded dam projects such as the 1936 Hoover Dam and, in 1963, Arizona's Glen Canyon Dam and Lake Powell. Water supply continues to be a key challenge to life in this region, with 2001-02 the driest year on record. For more information, see p531.

The Atomic Age

In 1943, Los Alamos, then a boys school perched on a 7400ft mesa, was chosen as the top-secret headquarters of the Manhattan Project, the code name for the research and development of the atomic bomb. The 772-acre site, accessed by two dirt roads, had no gas or oil lines and only one wire service, and it was surrounded by forest.

Isolation and security marked every aspect of life on 'the hill.' Scientists, their spouses, army members providing security, and locals serving as domestic help and manual laborers lived together in a makeshift community. They were surrounded by guards and barbed wire and unknown even to nearby Santa Fe; the residents' postal address was simply 'Box 1663, Santa Fe.'

Not only was resident movement restricted and mail censored, there was no outside contact by radio or telephone. Perhaps even more unsettling, most employee-residents had no idea why they were living in Los Alamos. Knowledge was on a 'need to know' basis; everyone knew only as much as their job required.

In just under two years, Los Alamos scientists successfully detonated the first atomic bomb at New Mexico's Trinity site, now White Sands Missile Range.

After the US detonated the atomic bomb in Japan, the secret city of Los Alamos was exposed to the public and its residents finally understood why they were there. The city continued to be clothed in secrecy, however, until 1957 when restrictions on visiting were lifted. Today, the lab is still the town's backbone, and a tourist industry embraces the town's atomic history by selling T-shirts featuring exploding bombs and bottles of La Bomba wine.

Some of the original scientists disagreed with the use of the bomb in warfare and signed a petition against it – beginning the love/hate relationship with nuclear development still in evidence in the Southwest today. Controversies continue over the locations of nuclear power plants and transportation, and disposal of nuclear waste, notably at Yucca Mountain, 90 miles from Las Vegas.

ANASAZI

Anasazi, a Navajo word meaning 'ancient enemy,' is a term to which many modern Pueblo Indians object; it's no longer used.

2006	2010	2011	2012
Warren Jeffs, leader of the Fundamentalist Church of the Latter Day Saints (FLDS) is charged with aggravated assaults of two under-age girls. He is serving a life-plus-20 years sentence.	Arizona passes controversial legislation requiring police officers to request identification from anyone they suspect of being in the US illegally. Immigration-rights activists call for a boycott of the state.	Jared Loughner is charged with shooting Arizona Congresswoman Gabrielle Giffords outside a Tucson grocery store. Giffords suffers a critical brain injury, six others are killed.	New Mexico and Arizona celebrate 100 years of statehood with special events and commemorative stamps. Arizona is the last territory in the lower 48 to earn statehood.

The Way of Life

Individuality is the cultural idiom of the Southwest. The identities of this region, centered on a trio of tribes – Anglo, Hispanic and Native American – are as vast and varied as the land that has shaped them. Whether your personal religion involves aliens, nuclear fission, slot machines, art or peyote, there's plenty of room for you in this harsh and ruggedly beautiful chunk of America.

Although the region's culture as a whole is united by the psychology, mythology and spirituality of its harsh, arid desert landscape, the people here are a sundry assortment of characters not so easily branded. The Southwest has long drawn stout-hearted pioneers pursuing slightly different agendas than those of the average American. Mormons arrived in the mid-1800s seeking religious freedom. Cattle barons staked their claims with barbed wire and lonely ranches, luring cowboys in the process. Old mining towns like Jerome and Bisbee in Arizona were founded by fierce individualists – gamblers, mining-company executives, storekeepers and madams. When the mining industry went bust in the 20th century, boomtowns became ghost towns for a while, before a new generation of idealistic entrepreneurs transformed them into New Age art enclaves and Old West tourist towns. Scientists flocked to the empty spaces to develop and test atomic bombs and soaring rockets.

Today, these places attract folk similar to the original white pioneers – solitary, focused and self-reliant. Artists are drawn to the Southwest's clear light, cheap housing and wide, open spaces. Collectors, in turn, follow artists and gentrify towns like Santa Fe and Taos in New Mexico, Prescott in Arizona and Durango in Colorado. Near Truth or Consequences, NM, global entrepreneur Richard Branson of Virgin Galactic is fine-tuning a commercial spacecraft that will launch paying customers into space from the scrubby desert. But not all new arrivals are Type A. There are, thank goodness, the mainstream outcasts still coming to the Southwest to 'turn on, tune in and drop out.'

For years, these disparate individuals managed to get along with little strife. In recent years, however, the state and federal governments' very visible efforts to stop illegal immigration have destroyed the kumbaya vibe, at least in Southern Arizona. These efforts include Arizona's controversial SB 1070 – a law that requires police officers to ask for ID from anyone they suspect of being in the country illegally – and a simultaneous surge in federal border patrol agents and checkpoints. The anti-immigration rhetoric isn't common in day-to-day conversation, but heightened press coverage of the most vitriolic comments, coupled with the checkpoints and ever-present border patrol vehicles, do cast a pall over the otherwise sunny landscape. Fortunately, outside southern Arizona, other regions of the Southwest have retained the live-and-let-live philosophy.

PROTEST

The Phoenix Suns protested Arizona's new immigration law in 2010 by changing the team's name on their jerseys to 'Los Suns' (that's Spanglish) for one game.

Regional Identity

For the most part, residents of the Southwest are more easygoing than their counterparts on the East and West Coasts. They tend to be friendlier too. Even at glitzy restaurants in the biggest cities (with the exception of Las Vegas), you'll see more jeans and cowboy boots than haute couture. Chat with a local at a low-key pub in Arizona or Colorado, and they'll likely tell you they're from somewhere else. They moved out here for the scenery, unpolluted air and slower pace of life. Folks in this region consider themselves environmentally friendly. Living a healthy lifestyle is important, and many residents like to hike, mountain bike, ski and ride the rapids. They might have money, but you won't necessarily know it. It's sort of a faux pas to flaunt your wealth.

Las Vegas is a different story. But a place where you can go from Paris to Egypt in less than 10 minutes can't possibly play by the rules. This is a town that's hot and knows it. The blockbuster comedy *The Hangover* stoked its image as party central. The identity here is also a little different – there's an energy to Sin City not found elsewhere in the region. People from Vegas don't say they're from the Southwest, or even from Nevada. They say they're from Las Vegas, dammit.

If Vegas is all about flaunting one's youthful beauty, then Arizona may just be its polar opposite. In the last decade, Arizona has done a great job at competing with Florida for the retiree-paradise award – the warm weather, dry air, abundant sunshine and lots and lots of space draw more seniors with each year. You'll see villages of RV parks surrounding Phoenix and Tucson and early-bird specials are the plat du jour at many restaurants.

Colorado, Arizona and New Mexico all have large Native American and Hispanic populations, and these residents take pride in maintaining

For first-person accounts and opinion pieces about key events in Native American history, visit www .digitalhistory .uh.edu, an online 'digital' textbook compiled by the University of Houston.

THE WAY OF LIFE REGIONAL IDENTITY

WHAT'S IN A NAME?

Though the stereotypes that too often accompany racial labels are largely ignored in the Southwest, it's still a challenge for publishers to figure out the most accurate (and politically correct) term for various ethnic groups. Here's the rundown on our terminology:

» **Native American** After introducing themselves to one very confused Christopher Columbus, the original Americans were labeled 'Indians.' The name stuck, and 500 years later folks from Mumbai are still trying to explain that no, they don't speak a word of Tewa. 'Native American' is recommended by every major news organization, but in the Southwest most tribal members remain comfortable with the term 'Indian.' Both terms are used in this book. However, the best term to use is always each tribe's specific name, though this can also get complicated. The name 'Navajo,' for instance, was bestowed by the Spanish; in Athabascan, Navajo refer to themselves as Diné. What to do? Simply try your best, and if corrected, respect each person's preference.

» **Anglo** Though 'Caucasian' is the preferred moniker (even if their ancestors hailed from nowhere near the Caucuses) and 'white' is the broadest and most useful word for European Americans, in this region the label for non-Iberian Europeans is 'Anglo' ('of England'). Even English speakers of Norwegian-Polish ancestry are Anglo around here, so get used to it.

» **Hispanic** The Associated Press prefers hyphens: 'Mexican-American,' 'Venezuelan-American' – and are Spanish-speaking US citizens more properly 'American-Americans'? Obviously, it's easier, if less precise, to use 'Latino' to describe people hailing from the Spanish-speaking Americas. Then add to that list 'Chicano,' 'Raza' and 'Hispano,' a de-anglicized term currently gaining popularity, and everyone's confused. But, because this region was part of Spain for 225 years and Mexico for only 25, and many folks can trace an unbroken ancestry back to Spain, 'Hispanic' ('of Spain') is the term used throughout this state and book, sprinkled with 'Spanish' and all the rest.

POLYGAMY & THE MORMON CHURCH *LISA DUNFORD*

Throughout its history, Utah has been a predominately Mormon state; more than 60% of the current population has church affiliation. But as late church president Gordon Hinckley was fond of saying, the Church of Jesus Christ of Latter-Day Saints (or LDS, as the modern Mormon faith is known) has nothing to do with those practicing polygamy today.

Members of the LDS believe the Bible is the Word of God and that the *Book of Mormon* is 'another testament of Jesus Christ,' as revealed to LDS church founder Joseph Smith. It was in the 1820s that the angel Moroni is said to have led Smith to the golden plates containing the story of a family's exodus from Jerusalem in 600 BC, and their subsequent lives, prophesies, trials, wars and visitations by Jesus Christ in the new world (Central America). Throughout his life he is said to have received revelations from God, including the 1843 visitation that revealed the righteous path of plural marriage to the prophet. Polygamy was formally established as church doctrine in 1852 by the second president, Brigham Young.

For all the impact plural marriage has had, it seems odd that the practice was officially endorsed for less than 40 years. By the 1880s US federal laws had made polygamy a crime. With the threatened seizure of church assets looming, president Wilford Woodruff received spiritual guidance and abdicated polygamy in 1890.

Today the church has more than 14 million members and a missionary outreach that spans the globe. But what happened to polygamy? Well, fundamentalist sects broke off to form their own churches almost immediately; they continue to practice today. The official Mormon church disavows any relationship to these fundamentalists, and shows every evidence of being embarrassed by the past.

Estimates for the number of people still practicing polygamy range as high as 50,000 in Utah. Some you'd never recognize; they're just large families. Others belong to isolated, cultlike groups such as the FLDS in Hildale-Colorado City on the Utah-Arizona border, which have distinct styles of dress and hair. Some of these sects have become notorious for crimes committed by some of their members.

Though polygamy itself is illegal, prosecution is rare. Without a confession or videotaped evidence, the case is hard to prove. Men typically marry only their first wife legally (subsequent wives are considered single mothers by the state, and are therefore entitled to more welfare). The larger Utah populace is deeply ambivalent about polygamy. Tens, maybe hundreds, of thousands of them wouldn't exist but for the historic practice, including me. My great-great-great grandmother, Lucy Bigelow, was a wife of Brigham Young.

their cultural identities through preserved traditions and oral history lessons.

Lifestyle

In a region of such diversity and size, it's impossible to describe the 'typical' Southwestern home or family. What lifestyle commonalities, after all, can be seen in the New Age mystics of Sedona, the businesspeople, lounge singers and casino workers of Las Vegas and the Mormon faithful of Salt Lake City? Half the fun of touring the Southwest is comparing and contrasting all these different identities.

Utah's heavily Mormon population stresses traditional family values; drinking, smoking and premarital sex are frowned upon. You won't see much fast fashion or hear much cursing here.

Family and religion are also core values for Native Americans and Hispanics throughout the region. For the Hopi, tribal dances are such sacred events they are mostly closed to outsiders. And although many Native Americans and Hispanics are now living in urban areas, working as professionals, large family gatherings and traditional customs are still important facets of daily life. See p522 for more on contemporary Native American life.

Because of its favorable weather and boundless possibilities for outdoor adventures, much of the Southwest is popular with transplants from the East and West Coasts. In cities like Santa Fe, Telluride, Las Vegas, Tucson and Flagstaff, you'll find a blend of students, artists, wealthy retirees, celebrity wannabes and adventure junkies. In urban centers throughout the region (with the exception of Utah) many people consider themselves 'spiritual' rather than religious, and forgo church for Sunday brunch. Women work the same hours as men, and many children attend daycare.

With the exception of Mormon Utah, attitudes toward gays and lesbians in the Southwest are generally open, especially in major cities like Las Vegas, Santa Fe and Phoenix.

The book *Bringing Down the House* is a fascinating (and true) story of MIT students who broke the bank in Vegas by counting cards in the mid-'90s. The book was then made into the film *21* (2008).

Sports

Professional sports teams are based in Phoenix and Salt Lake City. The Arizona Diamondbacks of Phoenix play major league baseball from April through September; the only Southwestern major league football team, the Arizona Cardinals, play from September through December. Basketball (men play November through April) is more competitive; you can watch hoops with Salt Lake City's Utah Jazz (men) or the Phoenix Suns (men). The women's pro basketball team, Phoenix Mercury, plays June through early September.

Because pro tickets are hard to get, you'll have a better rim shot with college sports. Albuquerque teams across the board are quite popular. The University of Arizona Wildcats consistently place among the best basketball teams in the nation.

Several major league baseball teams (like the Chicago White Sox) migrate from the cold, wintry north every February and March for training seasons in warmer Arizona. They play in what is aptly referred to as the Cactus League.

THE WAY OF LIFE SPORTS

Native American Southwest Jeff Campbell

The Southwest is sometimes called 'Indian Country,' but this nickname fails to capture the diversity of the tribes that make the region their home. From the Apache to the Zuni, each tribe maintains distinctions of law, language, religion, history and custom that turn the Southwest's incomparable, seemingly borderless painted desert into a kaleidoscopic league of nations.

The People

The cultural traditions and fundamental belief systems of the Southwest's tribes reflect their age-old relationship to the land, the water, the sky and the creatures that inhabit those elements. This relationship is reflected in their crafts, their dances and their architecture.

Native Americans today live incredibly diverse lives, as they inherit a legacy left by both their ancestors and the cultures that invaded from outside. Culturally, tribes grapple with dilemmas about how to prosper in contemporary America while protecting their traditions from erosion and their lands from further exploitation, and how to lift their people from poverty while maintaining their sense of identity and the sacred.

Apache

The Southwest has three major Apache reservations: New Mexico's Jicarilla Apache Reservation and Arizona's San Carlos Apache Reservation and Fort Apache Reservation, home to the White Mountain Apache Tribe. All the Apache tribes descend from Athabascans who migrated from Canada around 1400. They were nomadic hunter-gatherers who became warlike raiders, particularly of Pueblo tribes and European settlements, and they fiercely resisted relocation to reservations.

The most famous Apache is Geronimo, a Chiricahua Apache who resisted the American takeover of Indian lands until he was finally subdued by the US Army with the help of White Mountain Apache scouts.

Havasupai

The Havasupai Reservation abuts Arizona's Grand Canyon National Park beneath the Canyon's south rim. The tribe's one village, Supai, can only be reached by an 8-mile hike or a mule or helicopter ride from road's end at Hualapai Hilltop.

Havasupai (hah-vah-*soo*-pie) means 'people of the blue-green water,' and tribal life has always been dominated by the Havasu Creek tributary of the Colorado River. Reliable water meant the ability to irrigate fields, which led to a season-based village lifestyle. The deep Havasu Canyon also protected them from others; this extremely peaceful people basically avoided Western contact until the 1800s. Today, the tribe relies on tourism, and

Native American Reservations

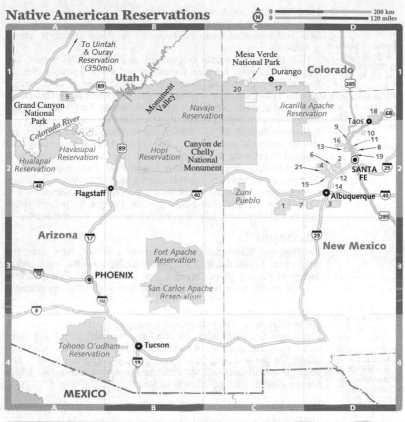

Native American Reservations

Reservations

1 Acoma Pueblo	C2
2 Cochiti Pueblo	D2
3 Isleta Pueblo	D2
4 Jemez Pueblo	D2
5 Kaibab-Paiute Reservation	A1
6 Kewa Pueblo	D2
7 Laguna Pueblo	C2
8 Nambé Pueblo	D2
9 Ohkay Owingeh (San Juan) Pueblo	D2
10 Picuris Pueblo	D2
11 Pojoaque Pueblo	D2
12 San Felipe Pueblo	D2
13 San Ildefonso Pueblo	D2
14 Sandia Pueblo	D2
15 Santa Ana Pueblo	D2
16 Santa Clara Pueblo	D2
17 Southern Ute Reservation	C1
18 Taos Pueblo	D1
19 Tesuque Pueblo	D2
20 Ute Mountain Reservation	C1
21 Zia Pueblo	D2

Havasu Canyon's gorgeous waterfalls draw a steady stream of visitors. The tribe is related to the Hualapai.

Hopi

The Hopi Reservation occupies more than 1.5 million acres in the middle of the Navajo Reservation. Most Hopi live in 11 villages at the base and on top of three mesas jutting from the main Black Mesa; Old Oraibi, on

Third Mesa, is considered (along with Acoma Pueblo) the continent's oldest continuously inhabited settlement. Like all Pueblo peoples, the Hopi are descended from the Ancestral Puebloans (formerly known as Anasazi).

Hopi (*ho*-pee) translates as 'peaceful ones' or 'peaceful person.' The Hopi are renowned for their traditional and deeply spiritual lifestyle. They practice an unusual, near-miraculous technique of 'dry farming'; they don't plow, but plant seeds in 'wind breaks', which protect the plants from blowing sand, and natural water catchments. Their main crop has always been corn (which is central to their creation story).

Hopi ceremonial life is complex and intensely private, and extends into all aspects of daily living. Following the 'Hopi Way' is considered essential to bringing the life-giving rains, but the Hopi also believe it fosters the well-being of the entire human race. Each person's role is determined by their clan, which is matrilineal. Even among themselves, the Hopi keep certain traditions of their individual clans private.

The Hopi are skilled artisans; they are famous for pottery, coiled baskets and silverwork, as well as for their ceremonial kachina dolls.

The US population in 2010 was 309 million. Native Americans/Native Alaskans represent 0.9% of the total, which is about 2.78 million people.

Hualapai

The Hualapai Reservation occupies around a million acres along 108 miles of the Grand Canyon's south rim. Hualapai (*wah*-lah-pie) means 'people of the tall pines'; because this section of the Grand Canyon was not readily farmable, the Hualapai were originally seminomadic, gathering wild plants and hunting small game.

Today, forestry, cattle ranching, farming and tourism are the economic mainstays. The tribal headquarters are in Peach Springs, AZ, which was the inspiration for 'Radiator Springs' in the animated movie *Cars*. Hunting, fishing and rafting are the reservation's prime draws, but the Hualapai have recently added a unique tourist attraction: the Grand Canyon's Skywalk glass bridge that juts over a side canyon 4000ft (1,220m) below your feet.

The People by Stephen Trimble is as comprehensive and intimate a portrait of Southwest native peoples as you'd hope to find, bursting with Native American voices and beautiful photos.

Navajo

The Navajo Reservation, also called the Navajo Nation, is by far the largest and most populous in the US, covering 17.5 million acres (over 27,000 sq miles) in Arizona and parts of New Mexico and Utah. Using a Tewa word, the Spanish dubbed them 'Navajos' to distinguish them from their kin the

HOPI KACHINAS

In the Hopi religion, maintaining balance and harmony between the spirit world and our 'fourth world' is crucial, and the spirit messengers called kachinas (also spelled katsinas) play a central role. These supernatural beings are spirits of deities, animals and even deceased clan members, and they can bring rain, influence the weather, help in daily tasks and punish violators of tribal laws. They are said to live atop Southwest mountains; on the winter solstice they travel to the Hopi Pueblos, where they reside until the summer solstice.

In a series of kachina ceremonies and festivals, masked dancers impersonate the kachinas; during these rituals, it is believed the dancers are inhabited by and become the kachinas. There are hundreds of kachina spirits: some are kindly, some fearsome and dangerous, and the elaborate, fantastical costumes dancers wear evoke the mystery and religious awe of these beings. In the 1990s, to keep these sacred ceremonies from becoming trivialized as tourist spectacles, the Hopi closed most to the public.

Kachina dolls (*tithu* in Hopi) are brightly painted, carved wooden figures traditionally given to young Hopi girls during certain kachina festivals. The religious icons become treasured family heirlooms. The Hopi now carve some as art meant for the general public.

Apache, but Navajo (*nah*-vuh-ho) call themselves the Diné (dee-*nay;* 'the people') and their land Dinétah.

Nationwide, there are about 300,000 Navajo, making it the USA's second-largest tribe (after the Cherokee), and the Navajo's Athabascan tongue is the most spoken Native American language, despite its notorious complexity. In the Pacific Theater during WWII, Navajo 'code talkers' sent and received military messages in Navajo; Japan never broke the code, and the code talkers were considered essential to US victory.

Like the Apache, the Navajo were feared nomads and warriors who both traded with and raided the Pueblos and who fought settlers and the US military. They also borrowed generously from other traditions: they acquired sheep and horses from the Spanish, learned pottery and weaving from the Pueblos and picked up silversmithing from Mexico. For more details about Navajo history, see p514. Today, the Navajo are renowned for their woven rugs, pottery and inlaid silver jewelry. Their intricate sandpainting is used in healing ceremonies.

The reservation has significant mineral reserves – Black Mesa, for instance, contains the USA's largest coal deposit, perhaps 21 billion tons – and modern-day mining of coal, oil, gas and uranium has been an important, and controversial, economic resource. Mining has depleted the region's aquifer, contaminated water supplies (leading, some claim, to high cancer rates), and impacted sacred places.

Tribal headquarters are in Window Rock, AZ, and the reservation boasts numerous cultural and natural attractions, including Monument Valley, Canyon de Chelly National Monument, Navajo National Monument and Antelope Canyon.

Pueblo

New Mexico contains 19 Pueblo reservations. Four reservations lead west from Albuquerque – Isleta, Laguna, Acoma and Zuni – and 15 Pueblos fill the Rio Grande Valley between Albuquerque and Taos: Sandia, San Felipe, Santa Ana, Zia, Jemez, Kewa Pueblo (or Santo Domingo), Cochiti, San Ildefonso, Pojoaque, Nambé, Tesuque, Santa Clara, Ohkay Owingeh (or San Juan), Picuris and Taos. For more information about the Pueblos, see www.indianpueblo.org.

These tribes are as different as they are alike. Nevertheless, the term 'Pueblo' (Spanish for 'village') is a convenient shorthand for what these tribes share: all are believed to be descended from the Ancestral Puebloans and to have inherited their architectural style and their agrarian, village-based life – often atop mesas.

Pueblos are unique among American Indians. These adobe structures can have up to five levels, connected by ladders, and are built with varying combinations of mud bricks, stones, logs and plaster. In the central plaza of each pueblo is a kiva, an underground ceremonial chamber that connects to the spirit world.

With a legacy of missionary activity, Pueblos tend to have Catholic churches, and many Pueblo Indians now hold both Christian and native religious beliefs. This unmerged, unconflicted duality is a hallmark of much of Pueblo modern life.

Other Tribes: Paiute, Ute & Tohono O'odham

Paiute

The Kaibab-Paiute Reservation is on the Arizona–Utah border. The Kaibab (*cay*-bob) are a band of Southern Paiute (*pie*-oot) who migrated to the Colorado Plateau around 1100. They were peaceful hunter-gatherers who moved frequently across the arid, remote region, basing their movements on seasonal agricultural needs and animal migrations.

NATIVE AMERICAN SOUTHWEST THE PEOPLE

For decades, traditional Navajo and Hopi have successfully thwarted US industry efforts to strip-mine sacred Big Mountain, but the fight continues. Black Mesa Indigenous Support (www .blackmesais.org) tells their story.

N Scott Momaday's Pulitzer Prize–winning *House Made of Dawn* (1968), about a Pueblo youth, launched a wave of Native American literature.

The tribe's lifestyle changed drastically in the 1850s when Mormons began settling the region, overtaking the land for their farms and livestock. The Kaibab-Paiute Reservation, located on the Arizona Strip west of Fredonia, is next to a vitally important regional spring, one that was also important to the Mormons. Today, near the spring, their reservation runs a public campground and contains Pipe Spring National Monument; the Kaibab-Paiute worked with the National Park Service to create rich displays about Native American life. The tribe is renowned for its basketmaking.

Ute

Along with the Navajo and Apache tribes, Utes helped drive the Ancestral Puebloans from the region in the 1200s. By the time of European contact, seven Ute tribes occupied most of present-day Colorado and Utah (named for the Utes). In the 16th century, Utes eagerly adopted the horse and became nomadic buffalo hunters and livestock raiders.

There are three main Ute reservations. With over 4.5 million acres, the Uintah and Ouray Reservation in northeastern Utah is the second largest in the US. Ranching and oil and gas mining are the tribe's main industries. The Ute Mountain Utes (who call themselves the Weeminuche) lead guided tours of Mancos Canyon in Ute Mountain Tribal Park; their reservation abuts Mesa Verde National Park in southwestern Colorado. The Southern Ute Reservation relies in part on casinos for income.

Tohono O'odham

The Tohono O'odham Reservation is the largest of four reservations that make up the Tohono O'odham Nation in the Sonoran Desert in southern Arizona. Tohono O'odham (to-ho-no oh-oh-dum) means 'desert people.' The tribe was originally seminomadic, moving between the desert and the mountains seasonally. They were famous for their calendar sticks, which were carved to mark important dates and events, and they remain well known for their baskets and pottery. Today, the tribe runs two casinos and the Mission San Xavier del Bac in southern Arizona.

Arts

Native American art nearly always contains ceremonial purpose and religious significance; the patterns and symbols are woven with spiritual meaning that provides an intimate window into the heart of

The Indian Arts and Crafts Board (www.doi.gov /iacb) publishes a directory of Native American–owned businesses, certifies expensive craft items (always ask to see a certificate) and punishes deceptive merchants.

LEGAL STATUS

Although Arizona's major tribes are 'sovereign nations' and have significant powers to run their reservations as they like, their authority – and its limitations – is granted by Congress. While they can make many of their own laws, plenty of federal laws apply on reservations, too. The tribes don't legally own their reservations – it's public land held in trust by the federal government, which has a responsibility to administer it in a way that's beneficial for the tribes. Enter the Bureau of Indian Affairs.

While Indians living on reservations have officially been American citizens since 1924, can vote in state and national elections, and serve heroically in the armed forces, they are not covered by the Bill of Rights. Instead, there's the Indian Civil Rights Act of 1968, which does grant reservation dwellers many of the same protections found in the Constitution, but not all. This is not an entirely bad thing. In some ways, it allows tribal governments to do things that federal and state government can't, which helps them create a system more attuned to their culture.

Southwest people. By purchasing arts from Native Americans themselves, visitors have a direct, positive impact on tribal economies,
which depend in part on tourist dollars.

Pottery & Basketry

Pretty much every Southwest tribe has pottery and/or basketry traditions. Originally, each tribe and even individual families maintained
distinct styles, but modern potters and basketmakers readily mix,
borrow and reinterpret classic designs and methods.

Pueblo pottery is perhaps most acclaimed of all. Typically, local clay
determines the color, so that Zia pottery is red, Acoma white, Hopi
yellow, Cochiti black and so on. Santa Clara is famous for its carved
relief designs, and San Ildefonso for its black-on-black style, which
was revived by world-famous potter Maria Martinez. The Navajo and
Ute Mountain Utes also produce well-regarded pottery.

Pottery is nearly synonymous with village life, while more portable
baskets were often preferred by nomadic peoples. Among the tribes who
stand out for their exquisite basketry are the Jicarilla Apache (whose
name means basketmaker), the Kaibab-Paiute, the Hualapai and the
Tohono O'odham. Hopi coiled baskets, with their vivid patterns and
kachina iconography, are also notable.

To learn about Navajo rugs, visit www.gonavajo .com. To see traditional weaving demonstrations, visit the Hubbell Trading Post in Ganado, AZ.

Navajo Weaving

According to Navajo legend, Spider Woman taught humans how to
weave, and she seems embodied today in the iconic sight of Navajo
women patiently shuttling handspun wool on weblike looms, creating
the Navajo's legendary rugs (originally blankets), so tight they held water.
Preparation of the wool and sometimes the dyes is still done by hand,
and finishing a rug takes months (occasionally years).

Authentic Navajo rugs are expensive, and justifiably so, ranging from
hundreds to thousands of dollars. They are not average souvenirs but
artworks that will last a lifetime, whether displayed on the wall or the
floor. Take time to research, even a little, so you recognize when quality
matches price.

Silver & Turquoise Jewelry

Jewelry using stones and shells has always been a native tradition;
silverwork did not arrive until the 1800s, along with Anglo and Mexican contact. In particular, Navajo, Hopi and Zuni became renowned
for combining these materials with inlaid-turquoise silver jewelry.
In addition to turquoise, jewelry often features lapis, onyx, coral,
carnelian and shells.

Authentic jewelry is often stamped or marked by the artisan, and
items may come with an Indian Arts and Crafts Board certificate; always
ask. Price may also be an indicator: a high tab doesn't guarantee authenticity, but an absurdly low one probably signals trickery. A crash course
can be had at the August Santa Fe Indian Market.

Etiquette

When visiting a reservation, ask about and follow any specific rules.
Almost all tribes ban alcohol, and some ban pets and restrict cameras.
All require permits for camping, fishing and other activities. Tribal rules
may be posted at the reservation entrance, or visit the tribal office or the
reservation's website (most are listed in this book).

The other thing is attitude and manner. When you visit a reservation,
you are visiting a unique culture with perhaps unfamiliar customs. Be
courteous, respectful and open-minded, and don't expect locals to share
every detail of their lives.

To donate to a cause, consider Black Mesa Weavers for Life and Land (www .migrations. com), which aids traditional Diné women on the Navajo Reservation to sell and market their handmade weavings.

WEAVING

Ask First, Document Later Some tribes restrict cameras and sketching entirely; others may charge a fee, or restrict them at ceremonies or in certain areas. If you want to photograph a person or their property, ask permission; a tip may or may not be expected.

Pueblos Are Not Museums At Pueblos, the incredible adobe structures are homes. Public buildings will be signed; if a building isn't signed, assume it's private. Don't climb around. Kivas are nearly always off-limits.

Ceremonies Are Not Performances Treat ceremonies like church services; watch silently and respectfully, without talking, clapping or taking pictures, and wear modest clothing. Powwows are more informal, but remember: unless they're billed as theater, ceremonies and dances are for the tribe, not you.

Privacy and Communication Many Native Americans are happy to describe their tribe's general religious beliefs, but not always or to the same degree, and details about rituals and ceremonies are often considered private. Always ask before discussing religion and respect each person's boundaries. Also, Native Americans consider it polite to listen without comment; silent listening, given and received, is another sign of respect.

Geology & the Land David Lukas

In the Santa Catalina Mountains outside Tucson, you can ascend from searing desert to snow-blanketed fir forests within 30 miles, the ecological equivalent of driving 2000 miles from southern Arizona to Canada. Contrasts like these, often in close proximity, make the Southwest a fascinating place to explore. While everyone thinks immediately of deserts and cacti, alpine tundra and verdant marshes are also part of the landscape.

The desert itself is anything but monotonous; look closely and you will discover everything from fleet-footed lizards to jewel-like wildflowers. As Southwest ecowarrior Edward Abbey wrote in *Desert Solitaire: A Season in the Wilderness*, 'The desert is a vast world, an oceanic world, as deep in its way and complex and various as the sea.' The Southwest's four distinct desert zones, each with its own unique mix of plants and animals, are superimposed on an astonishing complex of hidden canyons and towering mountains.

The Land

Geologic History

It may be hard to imagine now, but the Southwest was once inundated by a succession of seas. There is geological evidence today of deep bays, shallow mud flats and coastal dunes. During this time North America was a young continent on the move, evolving slowly and migrating northward from the southern hemisphere over millions of years. Extremely ancient rocks (among the oldest on the planet) exposed in the deep heart of the Grand Canyon show that the region was under water two billion years ago, and younger layers of rocks in southern Utah reveal that this region was continuously or periodically under water until about 60 million years ago.

At the end of the Paleozoic era (about 245 million years ago), a collision of continents into a massive landmass known as Pangaea deformed the Earth's crust and produced pressures that uplifted an ancestral Rocky Mountains. Though this early mountain range lay to the east, it formed rivers and sediment deposits that began to shape the Southwest. In fact, erosion leveled the range by 240 million years ago, with much of the sediment draining westward into what we now call Utah. Around the same time, a shallow tropical sea teeming with life, including a barrier reef that would later be sculpted into Carlsbad Caverns, covered much of southern New Mexico.

For long periods of time (between episodes of being under water), much of the Southwest may have looked like northern Egypt today: floodplains and deltas surrounded by expanses of desert. A rising chain

On the evening of July 5, 2011, a mile-high dust storm with an estimated 100-mile width enveloped Phoenix after reaching speeds between 50 and 60mph. Visibility dropped to between zero and a quarter mile. There were power outages, and Phoenix International Airport temporarily closed.

Visit www .publiclands .org for a one-stop summary of recreational opportunities on government-owned land in the Southwest, regardless of managing agency. The site also has maps, a book index, links to relevant agencies and updates on current restrictions and conditions.

of island mountains to the west apparently blocked the supply of wet storms, creating a desert and sand dunes that piled up thousands of feet high. Now preserved as sandstone, these dunes can be seen today in the famous Navajo sandstone cliffs of Zion National Park.

Pages of Stone: Geology of the Grand Canyon & Plateau Country National Parks & Monuments, by Halka and Lucy Chronic, is an excellent way to understand the Southwest's diverse landscape.

Mountains & Basins

This sequence of oceans and sand ended around 60 million years ago as North America underwent a dramatic separation from Europe, sliding westward over a piece of the Earth's crust known as the East Pacific plate and leaving behind an ever-widening gulf that became the Atlantic Ocean. This East Pacific plate collided with, and pushed down, the North American plate. This collision, named the Laramide Orogeny, resulted in the birth of the modern Rocky Mountains and uplifted an old basin into a highland known today as the Colorado Plateau. Fragments of the East Pacific plate also attached themselves to the leading edge of the North American plate, transforming the Southwest from a coastal area to an interior region increasingly detached from the ocean.

In contrast to the compression and collision that characterized earlier events, the Earth's crust began stretching in an east–west direction about 30 million years ago. The thinner, stretched crust of New Mexico and Texas cracked along zones of weakness called faults, resulting in a rift valley where New Mexico's Rio Grande now flows. These same forces created the stepped plateaus of northern Arizona and southern Utah.

Increased pulling in the Earth's crust between 15 and eight million years ago created a much larger region of north–south cracks in western Utah, Arizona and Nevada known as the Basin and Range province. Here, parallel cracks formed hundreds of miles of valleys and mountain ranges that fill the entire region between the Sierra Nevada and the Rocky Mountains.

During the Pleistocene glacial period, large bodies of water accumulated throughout the Southwest. Utah's Great Salt Lake is the most famous remnant of these mighty Ice Age lakes. Basins with now completely dry, salt-crusted lakebeds are especially conspicuous on a drive across Nevada.

For the past several million years the dominant force in the Southwest has probably been erosion. Not only do torrential rainstorms readily tear through soft sedimentary rocks, but the rise of the Rocky Mountains also generates large powerful rivers that wind throughout the Southwest, carving mighty canyons in their wake. Nearly all of the contemporary features in the Southwest, from arches to hoodoos, are the result of weathering and erosion.

Geographic Make Up of the Land

The Colorado Plateau is an impressive and nearly impenetrable 130,000-sq-mile tableland lurking in the corner where Colorado, Utah, Arizona and New Mexico join. Formed in an ancient basin as a remarkably coherent body of neatly layered sedimentary rocks, the plateau has remained relatively unchanged even as the lands around it were compressed, stretched and deformed by powerful forces.

The most powerful indicators of the plateau's long-term stability are the distinct and unique layers of sedimentary rock stacked on top of each other, with the oldest dating back two billion years. In fact, the science of stratigraphy – the reading of Earth history through its rock layers – stemmed from work at the Grand Canyon, where an astonishing set of layers have been laid bare by the Colorado River cutting across them. Throughout the Southwest, and on the Colorado Plateau in particular, layers of sedimentary rock detail a rich history of ancient oceans, coastal mudflats and arid dunes.

SLICKROCK

The often-used term 'slickrock' refers to the fossilized surfaces of ancient sand dunes. Pioneers named it slickrock because their metal-shoed horses and iron-wheeled wagons would slip on the surface.

All other geographic features of the Southwest seem to radiate out from the plateau. To the east, running in a north–south line from Canada to Mexico, are the Rocky Mountains, the source of the mighty Colorado River, which gathers on the mountains' high slopes and cascades across the Southwest to its mouth in the Gulf of California. East of the Rocky Mountains, the eastern third of New Mexico grades into the Llano Estacado – a local version of the vast grasslands of the Great Plains.

In Utah, a line of mountains known collectively as the Wasatch Line bisects the state nearly in half, with the eastern half on the Colorado Plateau, and the western half in the Basin and Range province. Northern Arizona is highlighted by a spectacular set of cliffs called the Mogollon Rim that run several hundred miles to form a boundary between the Colorado Plateau to the north and the highland region of central Arizona. The mountains of central Arizona decrease in elevation as you travel into the deserts of southern Arizona.

Landscape Features
Red Rock Formations

The Southwest is jam-packed with one of the world's greatest concentrations of remarkable rock formations. One reason for this is that the region's many sedimentary layers are so soft that rain and erosion readily carve them into fantastic shapes. But not any old rain. It has to be hard rain that is fairly sporadic because frequent rain would wash the formations away. Between rains there have to be long arid spells that keep the eroding landmarks intact.

The range of colors on rocky landscapes in the Southwest derive from the unique mineral composition of each rock type, but most visitors to the parks are content to stand on the rim of Grand Canyon or Bryce Canyon and simply watch the breathtaking play of light on the orange and red rocks.

This combination of color and soft rock is best seen in badlands, where the rock crumbles so easily you can actually hear the hillsides sloughing away. The result is an otherworldly landscape of rounded knolls, spires and folds painted in outrageous colors. Excellent examples can be found in Arizona's Painted Desert of Petrified Forest National Park, at Utah's Capitol Reef National Park or in the Bisti Badlands south of Farmington, New Mexico.

More-elegantly sculptured and durable versions are called hoodoos. These towering, narrow pillars of rock can be found throughout the Southwest, but are magnificently showcased at Utah's Bryce Canyon

For an insight into how indigenous peoples used this landscape, read *Wild Plants and Native Peoples of the Four Corners,* by William Dunmire and Gail Tierney.

A summer thunderstorm in 1998 increased the flow of Zion's Virgin River from 200 cubic ft per second to 4500, scouring out canyon walls 40ft high at its peak flow.

Arches National Park has more than 2500 sandstone arches. The opening in a rock has to measure at least 3ft in order for the formation to qualify as an arch.

CRYPTOBIOTIC CRUSTS: WATCH YOUR STEP!

Cryptobiotic crusts, also known as biological soil crusts, are living crusts that cover and protect desert soils, literally gluing sand particles together so they don't blow away. Cyanobacteria, one of the Earth's oldest life forms, start the process by extending mucous-covered filaments into dry soil. Over time these filaments and the sand particles adhering to them form a thin crust that is colonized by algae, lichen, fungi and mosses. This crust plays a significant role in desert food chains, and also stores rainwater and reduces erosion.

Unfortunately, the thin crust is easily fragmented under heavy-soled boots and tires. Once broken, the crust takes 50 to 250 years to repair itself. In its absence, winds and rains erode desert soils, and much of the water that would nourish desert plants is lost. Many sites in Utah, in particular, have cryptobiotic crusts. Protect these crusts by staying on established trails.

National Park. Although formed in soft rock, these precarious spires differ from badlands because parallel joints in the rock create deeply divided ridges that weather into rows of pillars. Under special circumstances, sandstone may form fins and arches. Utah's Arches National Park has a remarkable concentration of these features, thought to have resulted from a massive salt deposit that was laid down by a sea 300 million years ago. Squeezed by the pressure of overlying layers, this salt body apparently domed up then collapsed, creating a matrix of rock cracked along parallel lines. Erosion along deep vertical cracks left behind fins and narrow walls of sandstone that sometimes partially collapse to create freestanding arches.

Streams cutting through resistant sandstone layers form natural bridges, which are similar in appearance to arches. Three examples of natural bridges can be found in Utah's Natural Bridges National Monument. These formations are the result of meandering streams that double back on themselves to cut at both sides of a rock barrier. At an early stage of development these streams could be called goosenecks as they loop across the landscape. A famous example can be found at the Goosenecks State Park in Utah.

Edward Abbey shares his desert philosophy and insights in his classic *Desert Solitaire: A Season in the Wilderness*, a must-read for desert enthusiasts and conservationists.

Sandstone Effects

Many of the Southwest's characteristic features are sculpted in sandstone. Laid down in distinct horizontal layers, like a stack of pancakes, these rocks erode into unique formations, like flat-topped mesas. Surrounded by sheer cliffs, mesas represent a fairly advanced stage of erosion in which all of the original landscape has been stripped away except for a few scattered outposts that tower over everything else. The eerie skyline at Monument Valley on the Arizona–Utah border is a classic example.

Where sandstone layers remain fairly intact, it's possible to see details of the ancient dunes that created the sandstone. As sand dunes were blown across the landscape millions of years ago they formed fine layers of cross-bedding that can still be seen in the rocks at Zion National Park. Wind-blown ripple marks and tracks of animals that once walked the dunes are also preserved. Modern sand dunes include the spectacular dunes at White Sands National Monument in New Mexico, where shimmering white gypsum crystals thickly blanket 275 sq miles.

Looking beneath the surface, the 85-plus caves at Carlsbad Caverns National Park in southern New Mexico are chiseled deep into a massive 240-million-year-old limestone formation that was part of a 400-mile-long reef similar to the modern Great Barrier Reef of Australia.

Geology of the Grand Canyon

Arizona's Grand Canyon is the best-known geologic feature in the Southwest and for good reason: not only does its immensity dwarf the imagination, but it also records two billion years of geologic history – a huge amount of time considering the Earth is just 4.6 billion years old. The Canyon itself, however, is young – a mere five to six million years old. Carved out by the powerful Colorado River as the land bulged upward, the 277-mile-long canyon reflects the differing hardness of the 10-plus layers of rocks in its walls. Shales, for instance, crumble easily and form slopes, while resistant limestones and sandstones form distinctive cliffs.

The North Rim of the Grand Canyon is 1200ft higher than the South Rim. The altitude of the North Rim ranges from 8000ft to 8800ft.

The layers making up the bulk of the canyon walls were laid during the Paleozoic era, 570 to 245 million years ago. These formations perch atop a group of one- to two-billion-year-old rocks lying at the bottom of the inner gorge of the canyon. Between these two distinct sets of rock is the Great Unconformity, a several-hundred-million-year gap in the geologic record where erosion erased 12,000ft of rock and left a huge mystery.

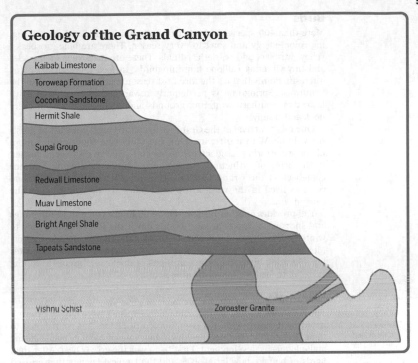

Geology of the Grand Canyon

Kaibab Limestone

Toroweap Formation

Coconino Sandstone

Hermit Shale

Supai Group

Redwall Limestone

Muav Limestone

Bright Angel Shale

Tapeats Sandstone

Vishnu Schist

Zoroaster Granite

Wildlife

The Southwest's desolate landscape doesn't mean it lacks wildlife — on the contrary. However, the plants and animals of North America's deserts are a subtle group and it takes patience to see them, so many visitors will drive through without noticing any at all. While a number of species are widespread, others have adapted to the particular requirements of their local environment and live nowhere else in the world. Deep canyons and waterless wastes limit travel and dispersal opportunities for animals and plants as well as for humans, and all life has to hunker down and plan carefully to survive.

Animals

Reptiles & Amphibians

While most people expect to see snakes and lizards in a desert, it's less obvious that frogs and toads find a comfortable home here as well. But on a spring evening, many of the canyons of the Southwest reverberate with the calls of canyon tree frogs or red-spotted toads. With the rising sun, these are replaced by several dozen species of lizards and snakes that roam among rocks and shrubs. Blue-bellied fence lizards are particularly abundant in the region's parks, but visitors can always hope to encounter a rarity such as the strange and venomous 'Gila monster' lizard. Equally fascinating, if you're willing to hang around and watch for a while (but never touch or bother), are the Southwest's many colorful rattlesnakes. Quick to anger and able to deliver a painful or toxic bite, rattlesnakes are placid and retiring if left alone.

Birds

More than 400 species of birds can be found in the Southwest, bringing color, energy and song to every season. There are blue grosbeaks, yellow warblers and scarlet cardinals. There are massive golden eagles and tiny vibrating calliope hummingbirds. In fact, there are so many interesting birds that it's the foremost reason many people travel to the Southwest. Springtime is particularly rewarding, as songbirds arrive from their southern wintering grounds and begin singing from every nook and cranny.

One recent arrival at the Grand Canyon tops everyone's list of must-see wildlife. With a 9ft wingspan, the California condor looks more like a prehistoric pterodactyl than any bird you've ever seen. Pushed to the brink of extinction, these unusual birds are staging a minor comeback at the Grand Canyon. After several decades in which no condors lived in the wild, a few wild pairs are now nesting on the canyon rim.

Fall provides another bird-watching highlight when sandhill cranes and snow geese travel in long skeins down the Rio Grande Valley to winter at the Bosque del Apache National Wildlife Refuge in New Mexico. The Great Salt Lake is one of North America's premier sites for migrating birds, including millions of ducks and grebes stopping each fall to feed before continuing south.

Mammals

The Southwest's most charismatic wildlife species were largely exterminated by the early 1900s. A combination of factors has contributed to their decline over the decades, including loss of habitat, over-hunting and oil-and-gas development. First to go was the grizzly bear. After that, herds of buffalo, howling wolves and the tropical jaguars that crossed the border out of Mexico also disappeared from the region. Prairie dogs (actually small rodents) vanished with hardly a trace, even though they once numbered in the billions.

Like the California condor, however, some species are being reintroduced. A small group of Utah prairie dogs were successfully released in Bryce Canyon National Park in 1974. Mexican wolves were released in the midst of public controversy into the wilds of eastern Arizona in 1998.

Mule deer still roam as widely as ever, and coyote are seen and heard nearly everywhere. Small numbers of elk, pronghorn antelope and bighorn sheep dwell in their favorite habitats (forests for elk, open grasslands for pronghorns and rocky cliffs for bighorns), but it takes a lot of luck or some sharp eyes to spot them. Even fewer people will observe a mountain lion, one of the wildest and most elusive animals in North America.

An estimated nine million free-tailed bats once roosted in Carlsbad Caverns. Though reduced in recent years, the evening flight is still one of the premier wildlife spectacles in North America.

WHAT'S THE BLM?

The Bureau of Land Management (www.blm.gov) is a Department of Energy agency that oversees more than 245 million surface acres of public land, much of it in the West. It manages its resources for a variety of uses, from energy production to cattle grazing to recreational oversight. What does that mean for you? All kinds of outdoor fun.

You'll also find both developed camping and dispersed camping. Generally, when it comes to dispersed camping on BLM land, you can camp where you want as long as your campsite is at least 900ft from a water source used by wildlife or livestock. You cannot camp in one spot for more than 14 days. Pack out what you pack in and don't leave campfires unattended. Some regions may have more specific rules, so check the state's camping requirements on the BLM website and call the appropriate district office for specifics. For developed campground information, you can also visit www.recreation.gov.

DESERT FLOWERS

Some of the Southwest's biggest wildlife surprises are the incredibly diverse flowers that appear each year in the region's deserts and mountains. These include desert flowers that start blooming in February, and late summer flowers that fill mountain meadows after the snow melts or pop out after summer thunderstorms wet the soil. Some of the largest and grandest flowers belong to the Southwest's 100 or so species of cacti; these flowers are one of the reasons collectors seek out cacti for gardens and homes. The claret-cup cacti is composed of small cylindrical segments that produce brilliant red flowers in profusion from all sides of their prickly stems. Even a 50ft-tall giant saguaro, standing like a massive column in the desert, has prolific displays of fragrant yellow flowers that grow high on the stem and can be reached only by bats.

Plants

Although the Southwest is largely a desert region, the presence of many large mountain ranges creates a remarkable diversity of niches for plants. One way to understand the plants of this region is to understand life zones and the ways each plant thrives in its favored zone.

At the lowest elevations, generally below 4000ft, high temperatures and lack of water create a desert zone where drought-tolerant plants such as cacti, sagebrush and agave survive. Many of these species have greatly reduced leaves to reduce water loss, or they hold water (cacti, for example) to survive long hot spells.

At mid-elevations, from 4000ft to 7000ft, conditions cool a bit and more moisture is available for woody shrubs and small trees. In much of Nevada, Utah, northern Arizona and New Mexico, piñon pines and junipers blanket vast areas of low mountain slopes and hills. Both trees are short and stout to help conserve water.

Nearly pure stands of stately, fragrant ponderosa pine are the dominant tree at 7000ft on many of the West's mountain ranges. In fact, this single tree best defines the Western landscape and many animals rely on it for food and shelter; timber companies also consider it their most profitable tree. High mountain, or boreal, forests composed of spruce, fir, quaking aspen and a few other conifers are found on the highest peaks in the Southwest. This is a land of cool, moist forests and lush meadows with brilliant wildflower displays.

There are more than 100 species of cacti in the Southwest. The iconic saguaro can grow up to 50ft tall, and a fully hydrated giant saguaro can store more than a ton of water.

Environmental Issues

In an arid landscape like the Southwest, many of the region's most important environmental issues revolve around water. Drought has so severely impacted the region that researchers were warning that 110-mile long Lake Mead has a 50% chance of running dry by 2021, leaving an estimated 12 to 36 million people in cities from Las Vegas to Los Angeles and San Diego in need of water. On the bright side, the melting of a record snowpack in western mountain ranges in 2011 pumped up water supplies in the Southwest.

Construction of dams and human-made water features throughout the Southwest has radically altered the delicate balance of water that sustained life for countless millennia. Dams, for example, halt the flow of warm waters and force them to drop their rich loads of life-giving nutrients. These sediments once rebuilt floodplains, nourished myriad aquatic and riparian food chains, and sustained the life of ancient endemic fish that now flounder on the edge of extinction. In place of rich annual floods, dams now release cold waters in steady flows that favor the introduced fish and weedy plants that have overtaken the West's rivers.

Many of the Southwest's most common flowers can be found in *Canyon Country Wildflowers*, by Damian Fagan. Chapters are arranged by the color of the flowers, including white, yellow and blue.

In other areas, the steady draining of aquifers to provide drinking water for cows and sprawling cities is shrinking the water table and drying up unique desert springs and wetlands that countless animals once depended on during the dry season. Cows further destroy the fragile desert crust with their heavy hooves, and also graze on native grasses and herbs that are soon replaced by introduced weeds. Development is increasingly having the largest impact, as uniquely adapted habitats are bulldozed to make room for more houses.

Read Marc Reisner's *Cadillac Desert: The American West and Its Disappearing Water* for a thorough account of how exploding populations in the West have utilized every drop of available water.

The region's stately pine and fir forests have largely become thickets of scrawny little trees. The cutting of trees and building of roads in these environments can further dry the soil and make it harder for young trees and native flowers to thrive. Injuries to an ecosystem in an arid environment take a very long time to heal.

In the Grand Canyon in 2007 there were an estimated 70,000 commercial sightseeing flights, mostly during the summer months. Responding to a high level of visitor complaints, not to mention the fact that federal law mandates 'natural quiet' within the national-park boundaries, the park released a draft environmental impact statement (EIS) in early 2011, with public comments due at press time. A copy of the draft EIS is currently on the park's website. As drafted, the EIS allows for *more* flights, but requires quiet technology and a move away from many sensitive cultural, natural and tourist areas.

Southwest Cuisine

Whoever advised 'moderation in all things' has clearly never enjoyed a streetside Sonoran dog in Tucson. A Sonoran dog 'moderated' is not a Sonoran dog at all. Same goes for a messy plate of *huevo rancheros* at a small-town Arizona diner. Or a green chile cheeseburger at the Owl Bar Café near Socorro, NM. Food in the Southwest is a tricultural celebration not well suited for the gastronomically timid, or anyone on a diet. One or two dainty bites? Impossible! But c'mon, admit it, isn't the food part of the reason you're here?

Three ethnic groups – Mexican, cattle country Anglo and Native American – influence Southwestern food culture. Spain and Mexico controlled territories from Texas to California well into the 19th century, and when they officially packed up, they left behind their cooking style and many of their best chefs. The American pioneers who claimed these states also contributed to the Southwest style of cooking. Much of the Southwest is cattle country, and whether you are in Phoenix, Flagstaff or Las Vegas you can expect a good steak. Native American cuisine – which goes beyond fry bread – is gaining exposure as locally grown, traditional plants and seasonings are appearing on more menus across the region.

Staples & Specialties

Huevos rancheros is the quintessential Southwestern breakfast; eggs prepared to order are served on top of two fried corn tortillas, loaded with beans and potatoes, sprinkled with cheese, and served swimming in chile. Breakfast burritos are built by stuffing a flour tortilla with eggs, bacon or chorizo, cheese, chile and sometimes beans.

A Southwestern lunch or dinner will probably start with a big bowl of corn chips and salsa. Almost everything comes with beans, rice and your choice of warm flour or corn tortillas, topped with chile, cheese and sometimes sour cream. Blue-corn tortillas are one colorful New Mexican contribution to the art of cooking. Guacamole is also a staple, and many

---

EATING GREEN IN THE SOUTHWEST

Numerous restaurants throughout the five-state region are dedicated to serving only organic, and when possible buying local, which helps their community self-sustain. One of the most unique, ecofriendly and wholesome eating experiences in the Four Corners can be enjoyed at Hell's Backbone Grill in Boulder, UT. It takes four hours on a lonely, potholed stretch of road to reach this super-remote foodie outpost, but those who make the drive will be rewarded. The restaurant is sustainable, growing most of its bounty on its 2-acre organic farm – the vegetables are divine. Owner Jen Spalding says her goal for the restaurant is to evoke a little bit of provincial France in off-the-grid Utah.

restaurants will mix the avocado, lime, cilantro (coriander), tomato and onion creation right at your table!

Steak & Potatoes

Home, home on the range, where the ranches and the steakhouses reign supreme. Have a deep hankerin' for a juicy slab of beef with a salad, baked potato and beans? Look no further than the Southwest, where there's a steakhouse for every type of traveler. In Phoenix alone choices range from the old-school Durant's to the outdoor Greasewood Flat to the family-friendly Rawhide Western Town & Steakhouse. In Utah, the large Mormon population influences culinary options – good, old-fashioned American food like chicken, steak, potatoes, vegetables, homemade pies and ice cream prevail.

Mexican & New Mexican Food

Mexican food is often hot and spicy, but it doesn't have to be. If you don't like spicy food, go easy on the salsa. There are some distinct regional variations in the Southwest. In Arizona, Mexican food is of the Sonoran type, with specialties such as *carne seca* (dried beef). Meals are usually served with refried beans, rice, and flour or corn tortillas; chiles are relatively mild. Tucsonans refer to their city as the 'Mexican food capital of the universe,' which, although hotly contested by a few other places, carries a ring of truth. Colorado restaurants serve Mexican food, but they don't insist on any accolades for it.

New Mexico's food is different from, but reminiscent of, Mexican food. Pinto beans are served whole instead of refried; posole (a corn stew) may replace rice. Chiles aren't used so much as a condiment (like salsa) but more as an essential ingredient in almost every dish. *Carne adobada* (marinated pork chunks) is a specialty.

If a restaurant references red or green chile or chile sauces on the menu, it probably serves New Mexican style dishes. The state is famous for its chile-enhanced Mexican standards. The town of Hatch, NM, is particularly known for its green chiles.

Native American Food

Modern Native American cuisine bears little resemblance to that eaten before the Spanish conquest, but it is distinct from Southwestern cuisine. Navajo and Indian tacos – fried bread usually topped with beans, meat, tomatoes, chile and lettuce – are the most readily available. Chewy *horno* bread is baked in the beehive-shape outdoor adobe ovens *(hornos)* using remnant heat from a fire built inside the oven, then cleared out before cooking.

Most other Native American cooking is game-based and usually involves squash and locally harvested ingredients like berries and piñon nuts. Though becoming better known, it can be difficult to find, especially in Southwestern Colorado, Utah and Las Vegas. Your best bets are festival food stands, powwows, rodeos, Pueblo feast days, casino restaurants or people's homes at the different pueblos.

Exceptions include Albuquerque's Indian Pueblo Cultural Center, the Metate Room in Southwestern Colorado, Tewa Kitchen near Taos Pueblo and the Hopi Cultural Center Restaurant & Inn on the Hopi Reservation.

Fruit & Vegetables

Beyond the chile pepper, Southwestern food is characterized by its use of posole, *sopaipillas* (deep-fried puff pastry) and blue corn. Posole, Spanish for hominy, is dried or frozen kernels of corn processed in a lime solution to remove the hulls. It's served plain, along with pinto beans, as a side dish. Blue-corn tortillas have a heartier flavor than the

---

Eat Your Words

carne seca – beef that is sun-dried before cooking

fry bread – deep-fried, doughy Native American bread

mole – slightly spicy chocolate-flavored chile sauce

sopaipilla – deep-fried puff pastry with honey

tamale – slightly sweet corn dough wrapped in a corn husk then steamed. Often stuffed with meat

---

John Middelkoop's documentary *Beans from God: the History of Navajo Cooking* examines the significant role that food plays in Navajo spiritual life.

more common yellow corn tortillas. Pinto beans, served either whole or refried, are a basic element of most New Mexican dishes.

Beans, long the staple protein of New Mexicans, come in many colors, shapes and preparations. They are usually stewed with onions, chiles and spices and served somewhat intact or refried to a creamy consistency. Avocados are a delightful staple, made into zesty guacamole. 'Guac' recipes are as closely guarded and vaunted by cooks as their bean recipes.

Nouvelle Southwestern Cuisine

An eclectic mix of Mexican and Continental (especially French) traditions began to flourish in the late 1970s and continues to grow. Try innovative combinations such as chiles stuffed with lobster or barbecued duck tacos. But don't expect any bargains here. Southwestern food is usually inexpensive, but as soon as the chef tacks on a 'nouvelle' tag, the tab soars as high as a crested butte.

Generally speaking, cities such as Phoenix, Tucson, Santa Fe and Albuquerque have the most nouvelle Southwestern restaurants.

Wine, Beer & Margaritas

In the Southwest it's all about the tequila. Margaritas are the alcoholic drink of choice, and synonymous with this region, especially in heavily Hispanic New Mexico, Arizona and Southwestern Colorado. Margaritas vary in taste depending on the quality of the ingredients used, but all are made from tequila, a citrus liquor (Grand Marnier, Triple Sec or Cointreau) and either fresh squeezed lime or premixed Sweet & Sour.

Our perfect margarita includes fresh squeezed lime (say no to the ultra-sugary and high-carb packaged mix), a high-end tequila (skip the gold and go straight to silver or pure agave – we like Patron or Herrendura Silver) and Grand Marnier liquor (better than sickly sweet Triple Sec). Ask the bartender to add a splash of orange juice if your drink is too bitter or strong.

Margaritas are either served frozen, on the rocks (over ice) or straight up. Most people order them with salt. Traditional margaritas are lime flavored, but these days the popular drink comes in a rainbow of flavors – best ordered frozen.

Locally brewed beers are also popular in this region, and people like to gather after work for a drink at their local microbrewery – a pub where beer is produced in-house. Microbreweries are abundant throughout the Southwest, and many of the beers are also sold in local grocery and liquor stores. Many microbrews are considered 'big beers' – meaning they have a high alcohol content.

There are three things a good wine grape needs: lousy soil, lots of sunshine and dedicated caretakers, all of which can be found in New Mexico and Arizona. For a full run-down of New Mexico's 40+ producers, visit the New Mexico Wine Growers Association at www.nmwine.com. La Chiripada Winery, with a shop on the Taos plaza, is our choice for regional vineyards, serving a fabulous Riesling and Cabernet Sauvignon.

In Arizona, the best-known wine region is in the southern part of the state near Patagonia. The Verde Valley between Phoenix and Flagstaff is close on Patagonia's heels in terms of quality and publicity. Tool lead singer and Jerome resident Maynard James Keenan is actively involved in producing Arizona wines, and he owns or co-owns three wineries and vineyards across the state. The Arizona Wine Growers Association (www.arizonawine.org) lists the state's wine producers.

For something nonalcoholic, you'll find delicious espresso shops in the bigger cities and sophisticated small towns; in rural Arizona or Nevada you're likely to get nothing better than stale, weak diner

SOUTHWEST CUISINE WINE, BEER & MARGARITAS

The folks behind the much-lauded cookies at the Jacob Lake Inn, on the road to the Grand Canyon's North Rim, say the lemon-zucchini cookies have a passionate following (www.jacoblake.com).

FRITO PIE

You can't visit Albuquerque without ordering a Frito pie – a messy concoction of corn chips, beef chile, cheese and sour cream. You can find it in restaurants and it's always served at city festivals.

coffee, however. Santa Fe, Phoenix, Durango, Truth or Consequences and Tucson all have excellent coffee shops with comfortable couches for reading or studying. Basically, if the Southwestern town has a college, it will have a good coffee shop. That's a regional given.

Vegetarians & Vegans

Most metro area eateries offer at least one veggie dish, although few are devoted solely to meatless menus. These days, fortunately, almost every larger town has a natural-food grocer. You may go wanting in smaller hinterland towns, however, where beef still rules. In that case, your best bet is to assemble a picnic from the local grocery store.

'Veggie-heads' will be happiest in New Mexico and Arizona; go nuts (or more specifically, go piñon). Thanks to the area's long-standing appeal for hippie types, vegetarians and vegans will have no problem finding something delicious on most menus, even at drive-throughs and tiny dives. One potential pitfall? Traditional Southwestern cuisine uses lard in beans, tamales, *sopaipillas* (deep-fried puff pastry) and flour (but not corn) tortillas, among other things. Be sure to ask – often, even the most authentic places have a pot of pintos simmering for vegetarians.

Arts & Architecture

Art has always been a major part of Southwest culture and one of the most compelling ways for its people to express their heritage and ideologies. The rich history and cultural texture of the Southwest is a fertile source of inspiration for artists, filmmakers, writers, photographers and musicians.

For more on the rich Native American culture, see p526.

Literature

From the classic Western novels of Zane Grey, Louis L'Amour and Larry McMurtry to contemporary writers like ecosavvy Barbara Kingsolver and Native American Louise Erdrich, authors imbue their work with the scenery and sensibility of the Southwest. Drawing from the mystical reality that is so infused in Latin literature, Southwestern style can sometimes be fantastical and absurdist, yet poignantly astute.

DH Lawrence moved to Taos in the 1920s for health reasons, and went on to write the essay 'Indians and Englishmen' and the novel *St Mawr*. Through his association with artists like Georgia O'Keeffe, he found some of the freedoms from puritanical society that he'd long sought.

Tony Hillerman, an enormously popular author from Albuquerque, wrote *Skinwalkers*, *People of Darkness*, *Skeleton Man* and *The Sinister Pig*. His award-winning mystery novels take place on the Navajo, Hopi and Zuni Reservations.

Hunter S Thompson, who committed suicide in early 2005, wrote *Fear and Loathing in Las Vegas*, set in the temple of American excess in the desert; it's the ultimate road-trip novel, in every sense of the word.

Edward Abbey, a curmudgeonly eco-warrior who loved the Southwest, created the thought-provoking and seminal works *Desert Solitaire* and *The Journey Home: Some Words in Defense of the American West*. His classic *Monkey Wrench Gang* is a fictional and comical account of real people who plan to blow up Glen Canyon Dam before it floods Glen Canyon.

John Nichols wrote *The Milagro Beanfield War*, part of his New Mexico trilogy. It's a tale of a Western town's struggle to take back its fate from the Anglo land barons and developers. Robert Redford's movie of the novel was filmed in Truchas, NM.

Barbara Kingsolver lived for a decade in Tucson before publishing *The Bean Trees* in 1988. Echoing her own life, it's about a young woman from rural Kentucky who moves to Tucson. Her 1990 novel, *Animal Dreams*, gives wonderful insights into the lives of people from a small Hispanic village near the Arizona–New Mexico border and from an Indian Pueblo.

For chick lit that gives you a feel for the land, adventures and people of the Southwest, read Pam Houston's books. Her collection *Cowboys Are*

Top Places for Art & Culture

» Phoenix, AZ

» Santa Fe, NM

» Taos, NM

» Indian Pueblo Cultural Center, Albuquerque, NM

» Salt Lake City, UT

My Weakness is filled with funny, sometimes sad, stories about love in the great outdoors.

Cinema & Television

New Mexico's Green Filmmaking Initiative encourages producers to think about sustainability when creating movies and TV shows here. Visit www.nmfilm.com for resources on creating ecofriendly shoots, and the opportunity to win grants for creating green films.

The movie business is enjoying a renaissance in the Southwest, with New Mexico as the star player. During his two terms as governor (2002–2010), Bill Richardson wooed Hollywood producers and their production teams to the state. The bait? A 25% tax rebate on production expenditures. His efforts helped inject more than $3 billion into the economy. On television, the critically acclaimed American TV series *Breaking Bad* is set and filmed in and around Albuquerque. Joel and Ethan Coen shot the 2007 Oscar winner *No Country for Old Men* almost entirely around Las Vegas, NM (doubling for 1980s west Texas). The Coen brothers returned in 2010 to shoot their remake of *True Grit*, basing their production headquarters in Santa Fe and filming on several New Mexico ranches.

Las Vegas, NV, had a starring role in 2009's blockbuster comedy *The Hangover*, an R-rated buddy film that earned more than $467 million worldwide. A town just outside of Las Vegas is the new home of Kody Brown, his four wives and their 16 children, a polygamous family profiled in TLC's reality show *Sister Wives*. The family is currently under criminal investigation in Utah, their former home, where bigamy is a third-degree felony.

A few places have doubled as film and TV sets so often that they have come to define the American West. In addition to Utah's Monument Valley, popular destinations include Moab, for *Thelma and Louise* (1991), Dead Horse Point State Park, also in Utah, for *Mission Impossible: 2* (2000), Lake Powell, Arizona, for *Planet of the Apes* (1968) and Tombstone for the eponymous *Tombstone* (1993). Scenes in *127 Hours*, about Aron Ralston's harrowing experience trapped in Blue John Canyon in Utah's Canyonlands National Park, were shot in and around the canyon.

The region also specializes in specific location shots. Snippets of *Casablanca* (1942) were actually filmed in Flagstaff's Hotel Monte Vista, *Butch Cassidy and the Sundance Kid* (1969) was shot at the Utah ghost town of Grafton, and *City Slickers* (1991) was set at Ghost Ranch in Abiquiú, NM.

Music

The larger cities of the Southwest are the best options for classical music. Choose among Phoenix's Symphony Hall, which houses the ArizonaOpera and the Phoenix Symphony Orchestra, the famed Santa

---

EARTHSHIP ARCHITECTURE

Is that Mos Eisley Spaceport about 2 miles past the Rio Grande Gorge? No, it's the world's premier sustainable, self-sufficient community of Earthships. This environmentally friendly architectural form, pioneered in northern New Mexico, consists of auto tires packed with earth, stacked with rebar and turned into livable dwellings (http://earthship.org).

The brainchild of architect Mike Reynolds, Earthships are a form of biotecture (biology plus architecture: buildings based on biological systems of resource use and conservation) that maximizes available resources so you'll never have to be on the grid again.

Walls made of old tires are laid out for appropriate passive solar use, packed with tamped earth, and then buried on three sides for maximum insulation. The structures are outfitted with photovoltaic cells and an elaborate gray-water system that collects rain and snow, which filters through several cycles that begin in the kitchen and end in the garden.

Though the Southwest is their home, Earthships have landed in Japan, Bolivia, Scotland, Mexico and beyond, and are often organized into communities.

Fe Opera, the New Mexico Symphony Orchestra in Albuquerque, and the Arizona Opera Company in Tucson and Phoenix.

Nearly every major town attracts country, bluegrass and rock groups. A notable major venue is Flagstaff's Museum Club, with a lively roster of talent. Surprisingly, Provo, UT, has a thriving indie rock scene, which offers a stark contrast to the Osmond-family image that Utah often conjures. A fabulous festival offering is Colorado's Telluride Bluegrass Festival.

Las Vegas is a mecca for entertainers of every stripe; current headliners include popular icons like Celine Dion and Barry Manilow, but for a little gritty goodness head to the Joint.

Try to catch a mariachi ensemble (they're typically dressed in ornately sequined, body-hugging costumes) at southern New Mexico's International Mariachi Festival.

Acoma Pueblo's new 40,000-sq-ft Sky City Cultural Center and Haak'u Museum (http://museum .acomaskycity .org) showcases vibrant tribal culture ongoing since the 12th century.

Architecture

Not surprisingly, architecture has three major cultural regional influences in the Southwest. First and foremost are the ruins of the Ancestral Puebloans – most majestically their cliff communities and Taos Pueblo. These traditional designs and examples are echoed in the Pueblo Revival style of Santa Fe's New Mexico Museum of Art and are speckled across the city and the region today.

The most traditional structures are adobe – mud mixed with straw, formed into bricks, mortared with mud and smoothed with another layer of mud. This style dominates many New Mexico cityscapes and landscapes.

Mission-style architecture of the 17th and 18th centuries, seen in religious and municipal buildings like Santa Fe's State Capitol, is characterized by red-tile roofs, ironwork and stucco walls. The domed roof and intricate designs of Arizona's Mission San Xavier del Bac embody the Spanish Colonial style.

In the 1800s Anglo settlers brought many new building techniques and developed Territorial-style architecture, which often includes porches, wood trimmed doorways and other Victorian influences.

Master architect Frank Lloyd Wright was also a presence in the Southwest, most specifically at Taliesin West in Scottsdale, AZ. More recently, architectural monuments along Route 66 include kitschy motels lit by neon signs that have forever transformed the concept of an American road trip.

Painting, Sculpture & Visual Arts

The region's most famous artist is Georgia O'Keeffe (1887–1986; see p286), whose Southwestern landscapes are seen in museums throughout the world. The minimalist paintings of Agnes Martin (1912–2004) began to be suffused with light after she moved to New Mexico. Also highly regarded is Navajo artist RC Gorman (1932–2005), known for sculptures and paintings of Navajo women. Gorman lived in Taos for many years.

Both Taos and Santa Fe, NM, have large and active artist communities considered seminal to the development of Southwestern art. Santa Fe is a particularly good stop for those looking to browse and buy art and native crafts. More than 100 galleries line the city's Canyon Rd, and Native American vendors sell high-quality jewelry and crafts beside the plaza.

The vast landscapes of the region have long appealed to large-format black-and-white photographers like Ansel Adams, whose archives are housed at the Center for Creative Photography at the University of Arizona.

For something different, pop into art galleries and museums in Las Vegas, specifically the Bellagio, which partners with museums and foundations around the world for knock-out exhibitions, and the new City Center, which hosts art by internationally renowned artists like Jenny Holzer, Maya Lin and Claes Oldenburg.

The National Cowboy Poetry Gathering – the bronco of cowboy poetry events – is held in January in Elko, Nevada. Ropers and wranglers have waxed lyrical here for more than 25 years (www .westernfolklife .org).

Jewelry & Crafts

Hispanic and Native American aesthetic influences are evident in the region's pottery, paintings, weavings, jewelry, sculpture, woodcarving and leatherworking. See p527 for a discussion of Navajo rugs and p524 for Hopi kachina dolls. Excellent examples of Southwestern Native American art are displayed in many museums, most notably in Phoenix's Heard Museum and Santa Fe's Museum of Contemporary Native Arts. Contemporary and traditional Native American art is readily available in hundreds of galleries. For tips on buying Native American jewelry and crafts, see p278.

Kitsch & Folk Art

The Southwest is a repository for kitsch and folk art. In addition to the predictable Native American knockoffs and beaded everything (perhaps made anywhere but there), you'll find invariable UFO humor in Roswell and unexpected nuclear souvenirs at Los Alamos, both in New Mexico. Pick up an Atomic City T-shirt, emblazoned with a red and yellow exploding bomb, or a bottle of La Bomba wine.

More serious cultural artifacts fill the Museum of International Folk Art in Santa Fe.

Dance & Theater

Native Americans have a long tradition of performing sacred dances throughout the year. Ceremonial or ritual religious dances are spiritual, reverential community occasions, and many are closed to the public. When these ceremonies are open to the public, some tribes (like the Zuni) require visitors to attend an orientation; always contact the tribes to confirm arrangements.

Social dances are typically cultural, as opposed to religious, events. They are much more relaxed and often open to the public. They occur during powwows, festivals, rodeos and other times, both on and off the reservation. Intertribal dance competitions (the lively 'powwow trail') are quite popular; the dancing may tell a story or be just for fun, to celebrate a tribe or clan gathering. The public may even be invited to join the dance.

Native Americans also perform dances strictly for the public as theater or art. Though these may lack community flavor, they are authentic and wonderful.

Classical dance options include Ballet West in Salt Lake City and Ballet Arizona in Phoenix. Dance and theater productions are flashy and elaborate in Las Vegas, where they have always been a staple of the city's entertainment platform. In Utah, Park City's George S and Dolores Doré Eccles Center for the Performing Arts hosts varied events.

NAMPEYO

Hopi cultural expression as we think of it today owes much to a woman named Nampeyo. Born on First Mesa in 1859 or '60 to a Hopi father and Tewa mother, she learned how to work clay from her paternal grandmother. A natural, she earned the reputation as a master as a young woman, and was known for her inspired designs. Influenced by the patterns on shards of ancient pots that her husband brought to her from the ruins at Sikyatki, where he was helping with an archaeological dig, Nampeyo created a style that blended past motifs with her own artistic instincts.

At the time, pottery was a dying craft, as contact with traders enabled the Hopi to buy pre-made goods. But as Nampeyo's work began to fetch high prices and draw worldwide attention, a renaissance of Hopi arts was sparked, not only in pottery, but also in silver, woodcarving and textiles. Thanks to her influence, the tradition more than lives on – it's been taken to higher levels of artistry than at any time in the tribe's past.

Survival Guide

Directory A–Z

Accommodations

From barebones to luxurious to truly offbeat, the Southwest offers a vast array of lodging options. Cookie-cutter chains line the interstates, providing a nice safety net for the less adventurous, but it's the indie-owned places that really shine. Where else but the Southwest can you sleep in a concrete wigwam or a cavern 21 stories underground? For road-trippers, the most comfortable accommodations for the lowest price are usually found in that great American invention, the mom-and-pop roadside motel.

For last-minute deals, check www.hotels.com, www.kayak.com, www.expedia.com, www.travelocity.com, www.orbitz.com, www.hotwire.com and www.priceline.com. For more on discounts, see p549.

Accommodations listings in this book are ordered by preference. Rates are based on standard double-occupancy in high season:

» $ less than $100
» $$ $100–200
» $$$ more than $200

Unless otherwise noted, breakfast is *not* included, bathrooms are private and all lodging is open year-round. Rates generally don't include taxes, which vary considerably between towns and states. Most places are non-smoking although some national chains and local budget motels may offer smoking rooms. Ask beforehand; many places charge a fee, which can be hefty, for smoking in a non-smoking room.

As for icons, a parking icon is only used in the biggest cities. The internet icon appears where a place has computers available for public use or where an innkeeper is OK with people briefly using their personal computer. If you're carrying a laptop, look for the wi-fi icon. Child-friendly hotels now have their own icon, as do pet-friendly lodgings. The Top Choice icon indicates those accommodations that truly stand out.

High season varies depending on the region within the Southwest. In general, the peak travel season runs June through August, except in the hottest parts of Arizona, when some places slash their prices in half because it's just too darn hot.

The peak travel season for southern Arizona and the ski areas of northern Utah (for different reasons) and other mountainous areas are mid-December to mid-April. Generally, we only list high-season rates. For more seasonal discussions, see p18.

Holidays (p550) command premium prices. When demand peaks, and during special events no matter the time of year, book lodgings well in advance.

Note cancellation policies when booking. Many accommodations will charge a cancellation fee, or the amount of your first night's stay (in some cases the full stay), if you cancel after the stated date.

Some resorts and B&Bs have age restrictions. If you're traveling with children, inquire before making reservations.

B&Bs & Inns

B&Bs are a good choice for travelers looking for more personal attention and a friendly home base for regional exploration. B&Bs may not work as well for longer stays, especially if you want to cook your own meals. In smaller towns, simple guesthouses may charge $60 to $130 a night for rooms with a shared bathroom, breakfast included. Some have more charming features, such as kiva fireplaces, courtyards or lounge areas. These fancier B&Bs typically charge $125 to $195 per night with a private bathroom, although the nicest could cost more than $250 per night. Most B&Bs have fewer than 10 rooms, and many don't allow pets or young children.

Camping

Free dispersed camping (independent camping at non-established sites) is permitted in many backcountry areas including national forests and Bureau of Land Management (BLM) lands, and less often in national and state parks. This can be particularly helpful in the summer when every motel within 50 miles of the Grand Canyon is full. If that's the case, try Kaibab National Forest beside the southern and northern boundaries of the national park. Stake your spot among the ponderosas, taking care not to camp within a quarter-mile of any watering hole or within a mile of any developed campgrounds or administrative or recreational sites. For the latest information about how far you're allowed to drive from the nearest road to pitch camp, see the Travel Management Rule updates for Kaibab National Forest at www.fs.fed.us.

For more information about dispersed camping on BLM land see p530. The more developed areas (especially national parks) usually require reservations in advance. To reserve a campsite on federal lands, book through **Recreation gov** (☑877-444-6777, 518-885-3639; www.recreation.gov).

Many state parks and federal lands allow camping, sometimes free, on a first-come, first-served basis. Developed camping areas usually have toilets, water spouts, fire pits, picnic tables and even wireless internet. Some don't have access to drinking water. It is always a good idea to have a few gallons of water in your vehicle when you're out on the road. Some camping areas are open year-round, while others are open only from May through to the first snowfall – check in advance if you're planning to slumber outdoors in winter.

Basic tenting usually costs $12 to $25 a night and cabins and teepees are sometimes available too. More developed campgrounds may be geared to RV travel and cost $25 to $45 a night. For information on renting an RV, see p561. **Kampgrounds**

of America (KOA; ☑406-248-7444; www.koa.com) is a national network of private campgrounds with tent sites averaging $30 to $32 per night plus taxes.

Hostels

Staying in a private double at a hostel can be a great way to save money and still have privacy (although you'll usually have to share a bathroom), while a dorm bed allows those in search of the ultimate bargain to sleep cheap under a roof. Dorms cost between $18 and $23, depending on the city and whether or not you are a Hostelling International (HI) member. A private room in a Southwestern hostel costs between $25 and $50.

Most hostels in the Southwest are run independently and are not part of **Hostelling International USA** (☑301-495-1240, www.hiusa.org) They often have private or single rooms, sometimes with their own bathrooms. Kitchen, laundry, notice board and TV facilities are also typically available. **Hostels.com** (www.hostels.com) lists hostels throughout the world.

Hotels

Prices vary tremendously from season to season, and they are only an approximate guideline in this book. Rates also don't include state and local occupancy taxes, which can be as high as 14% combined. High seasons and special events (when prices may rise) are indicated in the text, but you never know when a convention may take over several hundred rooms and make beds hard to find – and raise prices. Members of the American Association of Retired Persons

(AARP) and the American Automobile Association (AAA) often qualify for discounts.

Lodges

Normally situated within national parks, lodges are often rustic looking but are usually quite comfy inside. Rooms generally start at $100 but can easily be double that in high season. Since they represent the only option if you want to stay inside the park without camping, many are fully booked well in advance. Want a room today? Call anyway – you might be lucky and hit on a cancellation. In addition to on-site restaurants, they also offer touring services.

Motels

Budget motels are prevalent throughout the Southwest. In smaller towns, they will often be your only option. Many motels have at-the-door parking, with exterior room doors. These are convenient, though some folks, especially single women, may prefer the more expensive places with safer interior corridors.

Prices advertised by motels are called rack rates and are not written in stone. You may find rates as low as $35, but expect most to fall into the $50 to $75 range. If you simply ask about any specials or a reduced rate, you can often save quite a bit of money. Children are often allowed to stay free with their parents.

Motel 6 is usually the cheapest of the chains.

Resorts & Guest Ranches

Luxury resorts and guest ranches (often called 'dude ranches') really require a stay of several days to be

---

BOOK YOUR STAY ONLINE

For more accommodations reviews by Lonely Planet authors, check out hotels.lonelyplanet.com. You'll find independent reviews, as well as recommendations on the best places to stay. Best of all, you can book online.

appreciated and are often destinations in themselves. Start the day with a round of golf or a tennis match, then luxuriate with a massage, swimming, sunbathing and drinking. Guest ranches are even more like 'whole vacations,' with active schedules of horseback riding and maybe cattle roundups, rodeo lessons, cookouts and other Western activities like, um, hot-tubbing. When planning, be aware that ranches in the desert lowlands may close in summer, while those in the mountains may close in winter or convert into skiing centers. See the website of the **Arizona Dude Ranch Association** (www.azdra.com) for a helpful dude ranch comparison chart for the Grand Canyon State.

Business Hours

Generally speaking, business hours are from 10am to 6pm. In large cities a few supermarkets and restaurants are open 24 hours a day. In Utah many restaurants are closed on Sunday. Unless there are variances of more than half an hour in either direction, the following are 'normal' opening hours for places reviewed in this book:

Banks 8:30am-4:40pm Mon-Thu, to 5:30pm Fridays, some open 9am-12:30pm Sat.

Bars 5pm-midnight Sun-Thu, to 2am Fri & Sat.

Government offices 9am-5pm Mon-Fri.

Post offices 9am-5pm Mon-Fri, some open 9am-noon Sat.

Restaurants Breakfast 7am-10:30am Mon-Fri; brunch 9am-2pm Sat & Sun; lunch 11:30am-2:30pm Mon-Fri; dinner 5pm-9:30pm Sun-Thu, later Fri & Sat. In larger cities and resort towns many restaurants serve at least a limited menu from open to close; in Vegas restaurants can stay open 24 hours.

Shops 10am-6pm Mon-Sat, noon-5pm Sun. Shopping malls may keep extended hours.

Dangers & Annoyances

Southwestern cities generally have lower levels of violent crime than larger cities like New York, Los Angeles and Washington, DC. Nevertheless, violent crime is certainly present.

Take these usual precautions:

» Lock your car doors and don't leave any valuables visible. Smash-and-grab thefts can be a problem at trailhead parking lots.

» Avoid walking alone on empty streets or in parks at night.

» Avoid being in the open, especially on canyon rims or hilltops, during lightning storms.

» Avoid riverbeds and canyons when storm clouds gather in the distance; flash floods are deadly.

» When dust storms brew, pull off to the side of the road, turn off your lights and wait it out. They don't usually last long.

» Drivers should watch for livestock on highways and in American Indian reservations and areas marked 'Open Rangelands.'

» When camping where bears are present, place your food inside a food box (one is often provided by the campground).

» Watch where you step when you hike – particularly on hot summer afternoons and evenings, when rattlesnakes like to bask on the trail.

» Scorpions spend their days under rocks and woodpiles; use caution.

THE SWARM

Africanized 'killer' bees have made it to southern Arizona. They've moved into the cliff dwellings at Tonto National Monument and have attacked hikers in Saguaro National Park. They're in the Phoenix area, and around Tucson, too. Each Africanized bee actually has less venom than your average honeybee, but they have very short tempers, and the real danger is the swarm factor. One sting by itself is no big deal, unless you're allergic. But because the whole swarm is easily provoked, victims may be stung a hundred times or more, which could be life-threatening to even healthy, non-bee-allergic people.

Chances are you won't run into any killer-bee colonies, but here are a few things to know. Bees are attracted to dark colors, so hike in something light. Forget the perfume, and if a bee starts 'bumping' you, it could be its way of warning you that you're getting too close to the hive. Your best move is to get away from there.

If you do attract the angry attention of a colony, RUN! Cover your face and head with your clothing, your hands, or whatever you can, and keep running. Don't flail or swat, as this will only agitate them. They should stop following you before you make it half a mile. If you can't get that far, take shelter in a building or a car or under a blanket. Don't go into the water unless you happen to have a straw in your pocket – the swarm will just hover above and wait for you to come up for air. If you do get stung by lots of bees, get medical help – and if you try to get the stingers out, scrape them away, don't pull, which will unintentionally inject more venom.

Discount Cards & Coupons

From printable internet coupons to coupons found in tourist magazines, there are price reductions aplenty. For lodging, pick up one of the coupon books stacked outside highway visitor centers. These typically offer some of the cheapest rates out there.

Senior Cards

Travelers aged 50 and older can receive rate cuts and benefits at many places. Inquire about discounts at hotels, museums and restaurants before you make your reservation. US citizens aged 62 and older are eligible for the $10 **Senior Pass** (http://store.usgs.gov/pass), which allows lifetime entry into all national parks and discounts on some services (Golden Age Passports are still valid).

A good resource for travel bargains is the **American Association of Retired Persons** (AARP; ☎888-687-2277; www.aarp.org), an advocacy group for Americans aged 50 years and older.

Electricity

120V/60Hz

120V/60Hz

Food

Eating sections are broken down into three price categories. These price estimates do not include taxes, tips or beverages.
» $ less than $10
» $$ $10–$20
» $$$ more than $20

Note that many Utah restaurants are closed on Sunday; when you find one open (even if it's not your first choice), consider yourself among the fortunate.

For details about Southwestern specialties and delicacies, see p537.

Gay & Lesbian Travelers

The most visible gay communities are in major cities. Utah and southern Arizona are typically not as freewheeling as San Francisco. Gay travelers should be careful in predominantly rural areas – simply holding hands might get you assaulted.

The most active gay community in the Southwest is in Phoenix. Santa Fe and Albuquerque have active gay communities, and Las Vegas has an active gay scene. Conservative Utah has almost no visible gay life outside Salt Lake City.

Damron (www.damron.com) publishes the classic gay travel guides. **OutTraveler** (www.outtraveler.com) and **PlanetOut** (http://PlanetOut.com/travel) publish downloadable gay travel guides and articles. Another good resource is the **Gay Yellow Network** (www.gayyellow.com), which has listings for numerous US cities including Phoenix.

National resource numbers include the **National Gay and Lesbian Task Force** (☎202-393-5177 in Washington, DC; www.thetaskforce.org) and the **Lambda Legal Defense Fund** (☎213-382-7600 in Los Angeles; www.lambdalegal.org).

Health

Altitude Sickness

Visitors from lower elevations undergo rather dramatic physiological changes as they adapt to high altitudes. Symptoms, which tend to manifest during the first day after reaching altitude, may include headache, fatigue, loss of appetite, nausea, sleeplessness, increased urination and hyperventilation due to overexertion. Symptoms normally resolve within 24 to 48 hours. The rule of thumb is, don't ascend until the symptoms descend. More severe cases may display extreme disorientation, ataxia (loss of coordination and balance), breathing problems (especially a persistent cough) and vomiting. People afflicted should descend immediately and get to a hospital.

To avoid the discomfort characterizing the milder symptoms, drink plenty of water and take it easy – at 7000ft, a pleasant walk around Santa Fe can wear you out faster than a steep hike at sea level.

Dehydration

Visitors to the desert may not realize how much water they're losing, as sweat evaporates almost immediately and increased urination (to help the blood process oxygen more efficiently) can go unnoticed. The prudent tourist will make sure to drink more water than usual – think a gallon (about 4L) a day if you're active. Parents can carry fruit and fruit juices to help keep kids hydrated.

Severe dehydration can easily cause disorientation and confusion, and even day hikers have got lost and died because they ignored their thirst. So bring plenty of water, even on short hikes, and drink it!

Heat Exhaustion & Heatstroke

Dehydration or salt deficiency can cause heat exhaustion. Take time to acclimatize to high temperatures and make sure you get enough liquids. Salt deficiency is characterized by fatigue, lethargy, headaches, giddiness and muscle cramps. Salt tablets may help. Vomiting or diarrhea can also deplete your liquid and salt levels. Anhydrotic heat exhaustion, caused by the inability to sweat, is quite rare. Unlike other forms of heat exhaustion, it may strike people who have been in a hot climate for some time, rather than newcomers. Always use water bottles on long trips. One gallon of water per person per day is recommended if hiking.

Long, continuous exposure to high temperatures can lead to the sometimes-fatal condition heatstroke, which occurs when the body's heat-regulating mechanism breaks down and the body temperature rises to dangerous levels. Hospitalization is essential for extreme cases, but meanwhile get out of the sun, remove clothing, cover the body with a wet sheet or towel and fan continually.

Holidays

New Year's Day January 1
Martin Luther King Jr Day 3rd Monday of January
Presidents Day 3rd Monday of February
Easter March or April
Memorial Day Last Monday of May
Independence Day July 4
Labor Day 1st Monday of September
Columbus Day 2nd Monday of October
Veterans Day November 11
Thanksgiving 4th Thursday of November
Christmas Day December 25

Insurance

It's expensive to get sick, crash a car or have things stolen from you in the US. When it comes to health care, the US has some of the finest in the world. The problem? Unless you have good insurance, it can be prohibitively expensive. It's essential to purchase travel health insurance if your regular policy doesn't cover you when you're abroad.

If your health insurance does not cover you for medical expenses abroad, consider supplemental insurance. Find out in advance if your insurance plan will make payments directly to providers or reimburse you later for overseas health expenditures.

To insure yourself from theft of items in your car, consult your homeowner's (or renter's) insurance policy before leaving home.

Worldwide travel insurance is available at www.lonelyplanet.com/travel_services. You can buy, extend and claim online anytime – even if you're already on the road.

International Visitors

US entry requirements continue to change as the country fine-tunes its national security guidelines. All travelers should double-check current visa and passport regulations *before* coming to the USA.

Entering the Country

Getting into the US can be complicated. Plan ahead. For up-to-date information about visas and immigration, check with the **US State Department** (☎202-663-1225; www.travel.state.gov).

Apart from most Canadian citizens and those entering under the Visa Waiver Program (VWP), all foreign visitors to the US need a visa. Pursuant to VWP requirements, citizens of certain countries may enter the US for stays of 90 days or fewer without a US visa. This list is subject to continual reexamination and bureaucratic rejigging. At press time these countries included Andorra, Australia, Austria, Belgium, Brunei, Czech Republic, Denmark, Estonia, Finland, France, Germany, Greece, Hungary, Iceland, Ireland, Italy, Japan, Latvia, Liechtenstein, Lithuania, Luxembourg, Malta, Monaco, the Netherlands, New Zealand, Norway, Portugal, San Marino, Singapore, Slovakia, Slovenia, South Korea, Spain, Sweden, Switzerland and the UK.

If you are a citizen of a VWP country you do not need a visa *only if* you have a passport that meets current US standards *and* you get approval from the Electronic System for Travel Authorization (ESTA) in advance. Register online with the Department of Homeland Security at https://esta.cbp.dhs.gov at least 72 hours before arrival. Canadians are currently exempt from ESTA.

Because the Department of Homeland Security is

continually modifying its requirements, even travelers with visa waivers may be subject to enrollment in the US-Visit program. For most visitors (excluding, for now, most Canadian and some Mexican citizens) registration consists of having a digital photo and electronic (inkless) finger-prints taken. Contact the **Department of Homeland Security** (www.dhs.gov/US-visit) for current requirements.

Every foreign visitor entering the USA from abroad needs a passport. In most cases, your passport must be valid for at least another six months after you are due to leave the USA. If your passport doesn't meet current US standards you'll be turned back at the border.

If your passport was issued before October 26, 2005, it must be machine readable (with two lines of letters, numbers and the repeated symbol <<< at the bottom); if it was issued between October 26, 2005 and October 25, 2006, it must be machine readable and include a digital photo on the data page or integrated chip with information from the data page; and if it was issued on or after October 26, 2006, it must be an e-Passport with a digital photo and an integrated chip containing information from the data page. Nationals from the Czech Republic, Estonia, Greece, Hungary, Latvia, Lithuania, Malta, Slovakia and South Korea must have an e-Passport.

Money

The dollar (commonly called a buck) is divided into 100 cents. Coins come in denominations of one cent (penny), five cents (nickel), 10 cents (dime), 25 cents (quarter) and the rare 50-cent piece (half dollar). Notes come in one-, five-, 10-, 20-, 50- and 100-dollar denominations.

See the inside front cover for exchange rates and p18 for information on costs.

ATMS & CASH

ATMs are great for quick cash influxes and can negate the need for traveler's checks entirely, but watch out for ATM surcharges as they may charge $2 to $3 per withdrawal. Some ATMs in Vegas may charge $5 for withdrawing cash – read before you click enter.

The Cirrus and Plus systems both have extensive ATM networks that will give cash advances on major credit cards and allow cash withdrawals with affiliated ATM cards. Look for ATMs outside banks and in large grocery stores, shopping centers, convenience stores and gas stations.

To avoid possible bank holds for sums larger than the transaction, or account-draining scams, consider paying with cash at gas stations instead of using your debit card at the pump.

CREDIT CARDS

Major credit cards are widely accepted throughout the Southwest, including at car-rental agencies and most hotels, restaurants, gas stations, grocery stores and tour operators.

American Express (800-528-4800; www.americanexpress.com)

Diners Club (800-234-6377; www.dinersclub.com)

Discover (800-347-2683; www.discover.com)

MasterCard (800-627-8372; www.mastercard.com)

Visa (800-847-2911; www.visa.com)

SOUTHWEST WITH PETS

When it comes to pet-friendly travel destinations, the Southwest is one of the best. More and more hotels accept pets these days, although some charge extra per night, others make you leave a deposit and still others have weight restrictions – less than 35lb is usually the standard. To not get hit with an extra $50 in dog-room fees, call the hotel in advance. One of the most unique pet-friendly options in the Southwest is in Santa Fe: head to the swank **Ten Thousand Waves Japanese Resort & Spa** (p272).

At national parks, check first before you let your pet off the leash – many forests and park lands have restrictions on dogs. If you're planning a long day in the car, vets recommend stopping at least every two hours to let your dog pee, stretch their legs and have a long drink of water. If your dog gets nervous or nauseated in the car, it is safe and effective to give her Benadryl (or its generic equivalent) to calm her down. The vet-recommended dosage is 1mg per pound.

When stopping to eat during a downtown stroll, don't immediately tie your dog up outside the restaurant. Instead ask about the local laws.

In this guide, look for the pet-friendly icon [🐾] if you're traveling with Fido and need a pet-friendly lodging.

The following websites have helpful pet-travel tips:
Humane Society (www.humanesociety.org/animals/resources/tips/travelling_tips_pets_cars.html) Tips on travel with pets.

Best Friends Animal Society (www.bestfriends.org) May have you driving to Kanab just to adopt a pet, but also has a wealth of general info.

CURRENCY EXCHANGE

Banks are usually the best places to exchange currency. Most large city banks offer currency exchange, but banks in rural areas do not. Currency-exchange counters at the airports and in tourist centers typically have the worst rates; ask about fees and surcharges first. **Travelex** (☏877-414-6359; www.travelex.com) is a major currency-exchange company but **American Express** (☏800-297-2977; www.american express.com) travel offices may offer better rates.

TRAVELER'S CHECKS

With the advent of ATMs, traveler's checks are becoming obsolete, except as a trustworthy backup. If you carry them, buy them in US dollars; local businesses may not cash them in a foreign currency. Keeping a record of the check numbers and those you have used is vital for replacing lost checks, so keep this information separate from the checks themselves. For refunds on lost or stolen checks call **American Express** (☏800-221-7282) or **Visa** (☏800-227-6811).

TIPPING

Taxi drivers expect a 15% tip. Waiters and bartenders rely on tips for their livelihoods: tip $1 per drink to bartenders and 15% to 20% to waiters and waitresses unless the service is terrible (in which case a complaint to the manager is warranted) or about 20% if the service is great. Don't tip in fast-food, takeout or buffet-style restaurants where you serve yourself. Baggage carriers in airports and hotels should get $2 per bag or $5 per cart minimum. In hotels with daily housekeeping, leave a few dollars in the room for the staff for each day of your stay when you check out. In budget hotels, tips are not expected but are always appreciated.

Post

The **US Postal Service** (USPS; ☏800-275-8777; www .usps.gov) provides great service for the price. For 1st-class mail sent and delivered within the US, postage rates are 44¢ for letters up to 1oz (20¢ for each additional ounce) and 29¢ for standard-size postcards. If you have the correct postage, drop your mail into any blue mailbox. To send a package weighing 13oz or more, go to a post office.

International airmail rates for letters up to 1oz and postcards are 80¢ to Canada or Mexico, and 98¢ to other countries. You can have mail sent to you care of General Delivery at most big post offices in the Southwest. When you pick up your mail, bring some photo identification. General delivery mail is usually held for up to 30 days. Most hotels will also hold mail for incoming guests.

Call private shippers such as **United Parcel Service** (UPS; ☏800-742-5877; www .ups.com) and **Federal Express** (FedEx; ☏800-463-3339; www.fedex.com) to send more important or larger items.

Telephone

Always dial '1' before toll-free (800, 888 etc) and domestic long-distance numbers. Remember that some toll-free numbers may only work within the region or from the US mainland, for instance. But you'll only know if it works by making the call.

All phone numbers in the US consist of a three-digit area code followed by a seven-digit local number. All five Southwestern states require you to dial the full 10-digit number for all phone calls because each state has more than one area code. You will not be charged for long-distance fees when dialing locally. When calling a cell phone anywhere in the USA you need to always dial the 10-digit number; however, you do not need to dial the country code (☏1) when calling from within the United States.

Pay phones aren't as readily found at shopping centers, gas stations and other public places now that cell phones are more prevalent. But keep your eyes peeled and you'll find them. If you don't have change, you can use a calling card.

To make international calls direct, dial ☏011 + country code + area code + number. (An exception is to Canada, where you dial ☏1 + area code + number. International rates apply for Canada.)

For international operator assistance, dial ☏0. The operator can provide specific rate information and tell you which time periods are the cheapest for calling.

If you're calling the Southwest from abroad, the international country code for the US is ☏1. All calls to the Southwest are then followed by the area code and the seven-digit local number.

CELL PHONES

In the USA, cell phones use GSM 1900 or CDMA 800, operating on different frequencies than systems in other countries. The only foreign phones that will work in the US are tri- or quad-band models. If you have one of these phones, check with your service provider about using it in the US. Make sure to ask if roaming charges apply; these will turn even local US calls into pricey international calls.

If your phone is unlocked, however, you may be able to buy a prepaid SIM card for the USA, which you can insert into your international cell phone to get a local number and voicemail.

Even though the Southwest has an extensive cellular network, you'll still find a lot of coverage holes when you're driving in the middle of nowhere. Don't take undue risks thinking you'll be able to call for help from anywhere.

Once you get up into the mountains or in isolated areas, cell phone reception can be sketchy at best.

PHONECARDS

Private prepaid phonecards are available from convenience stores, supermarkets and pharmacies. Cards sold by major telecommunications companies such as AT&T may offer better deals than start-up companies.

Internet Access

Public libraries in most cities and towns offer free internet access, either at computer terminals or through a wireless connection, usually for 15 minutes to an hour (a few may charge a small fee). In some cases you may need to obtain a guest pass or register. Most towns have at least one shop that offers a computer to get online, and in big cities like Phoenix, Las Vegas and Salt Lake City you'll find dozens. It generally costs $10 and up to log on, which isn't cheap – if you can bring your laptop do so, as most places that serve coffee also offer free wi-fi as long as you order a drink. Several national companies – McDonald's, Panera Bread, Barnes & Noble – are now providing free wi-fi.

When places reviewed in this book have computers available for public use, it's noted with an @ icon. If you're traveling with a laptop, look for the wi-fi icon.

Besides coffee shops, airports and campgrounds often offer laptop owners a chance to get online for free or a small fee. You're most likely to be charged for wi-fi usage in hotels – some places charge up to $20 per day. Check the following websites for lists of free and fee-based wi-fi hot spots nationwide: www.wififreespot.com and www.wi-fihotspotlist.com.

For a selection of useful websites about Southwest USA, see p19.

Legal Matters

If you are arrested for a serious offense in the US, you are allowed to remain silent, entitled to have an attorney present during any interrogation and presumed innocent until proven guilty. You have the right to an attorney from the very first moment you are arrested. If you can't afford one, the state must provide one for free. All persons who are arrested are legally allowed to make one phone call. If you don't have a lawyer or family member to help you, call your embassy or consulate.

The minimum age for drinking alcoholic beverages in the US is 21; you'll need a government-issued photo ID to prove it (such as a passport or a US driver's license). Stiff fines, jail time and penalties can be incurred if you are caught driving under the influence of alcohol or providing alcohol to minors.

The legal ages for certain activities around the Southwest vary by state. For information about speed limits and other road rules, see p560.

National & State Parks

Before visiting any national park, check out its website, using the navigation search tool on the National Park Service (NPS) home page (www.nps.gov). On the Grand Canyon's website (www.nps .gov/grca), you can download the seasonal newspaper, *The Guide*, for the latest information on prices, hours and ranger tours. There is a separate edition for both the North and South Rims.

At the entrance of a national or state park, be ready to hand over cash (credit cards may not always be accepted). Costs range from nothing at all to $25 per vehicle for a seven-day pass. If you're visiting several parks

EMERGENCIES

If you need any kind of emergency assistance, such as police, ambulance or firefighters, call 911. A few rural phones might not have this service, in which case dial 0 for the operator and ask for emergency assistance.

in the Southwest, you may save money by purchasing the **America the Beautiful** (http://store.usgs.gov/pass; pass $80) annual pass. It admits four adults and their children under 16 for no additional cost to all national parks and federal recreational lands for one year. US citizens and permanent residents aged 62 and older are eligible for a lifetime Senior Pass. US citizens and permanent residents with a permanent disability may qualify for a free Access Pass.

Due to ongoing fiscal woes, many state governments across the West and Southwest are slashing their budgets for state parks. State parks in Arizona and Utah have been particularly hard hit, and it's not yet clear which ones will ultimately survive. In Utah, funding has been cut from $12.2 million to $6.8 million in the last few years. Some state parks in Arizona are operating on a five-day schedule, closed Tuesdays and Wednesdays. Before visiting a state park, check its website to confirm its status.

Photography

Print film can be found in drugstores and at specialty camera shops. Digital camera memory cards are available at chain retailers such as Best Buy and Target.

Furthermore, almost every town of any size has a photo

shop that stocks cameras and accessories. With little effort you should be able to find a shop to develop your color print film in one hour, or at least on the same day. Expect to pay about $7 to process a roll of 24 color prints. One-hour processing is more expensive, usually around $12. FedEx Office is a major chain of copy shops with one-stop digital photo printing and CD-burning stations.

For information on photographing reservations and pueblos, see p527.

Tours

For travelers with a limited amount of time or specialized interests, tours may be the best option. Always read the fine print; tour prices may or may not include airfare, meals, taxes and tips. Well-run **Backroads, Inc** (✆800-462-2848; www.backroads.com) offers hiking and cycling trips for all ages across Arizona, New Mexico and southern Utah.

The sophisticated Washington, DC, **Smithsonian Journeys** (✆887-338-8687; www.smithsonianjourneys.org)

organizes academically inclined, upscale tours such as Santa Fe Opera and Astronomy in Arizona.

Road Scholar (✆877-4254-5768; www.roadscholar.org), created by Elderhostel, Inc, offers a whole host of educational programs.

For an alternative to pure tourism, look into **Global Citizens Network** (GCN; ✆612-436-8270, 800-644-9292; www.globalcitizens.org) where socially-conscious visitors can work with the Navajo Nation in both Arizona and New Mexico.

Information about smaller site- or town-specific tour companies is sprinkled throughout the individual chapters of this guidebook.

Travelers with Disabilities

Travel within the Southwest is getting better for people with disabilities, but it's still not easy. Public buildings are required to be wheelchair accessible and to have appropriate rest-room facilities. Public transportation services must be made accessible to all, and telephone

companies have to provide relay operators for the hearing impaired. Many banks provide ATM instructions in braille, curb ramps are common, many busy intersections have audible crossing signals, and most chain hotels have suites for guests with disabilities. Still, it's best to call ahead to check.

Disabled US residents and permanent residents may be eligible for the lifetime Access Pass, a free pass to national parks and 2000 recreation areas managed by the federal government. Visit http://store.usgs.gov/pass/access.html.

For up-to-date information about wheelchair-accessible activities in Arizona, visit **Accessing Arizona** (www.accessingarizona.com). You'll find up-to-the-minute information about travel and accessibility issues at **Rolling Rains Report** (www.rollingrains.com).

Wheelchair Getaways (✆main office 800-642-2042, Arizona 888-824-7413, New Mexico 505-247-2526, Las Vegas 602-494-8257; www.wheelchairgetaways.com) rents accessible vans in Phoenix, Tucson, Albuquerque, Las Vegas and Reno.

A number of organizations specialize in the needs of travelers with disabilities:

Disabled Sports USA (✆301-217-0960; www.dsusa.org) Offers sports and recreation programs for those with disabilities and publishes *Challenge* magazine.

Mobility International USA (✆541-343-1284; www.miusa.org) Advises on mobility issues, but primarily runs an educational exchange program.

Society for Accessible Travel & Hospitality (SATH; ✆212-447-7284; www.sath.org) Advocacy group provides general information for travelers with disabilities.

Splore (✆801-484-4128; www.splore.org) Offers accessible outdoor adventure trips in Utah.

TIPS FOR SHUTTERBUGS

» Morning and evening are the best times to shoot. The same sandstone bluff can turn four or five different hues throughout the day, and the warmest hues will be at sunset. Underexposing the shot slightly (by a half-stop or more) can bring out richer details in red tones.

» When shooting red rocks, a warming filter added to an SLR lens can enhance the colors of the rocks and reduce the blues of overcast or flat-light days. Achieve the same effect on any digital camera by adjusting the white balance to the automatic 'cloudy' setting (or by reducing the color temperature).

» Don't shoot into the sun or include it in the frame; shoot what the sunlight is hitting. On bright days, move your subjects into shade for close-up portraits.

» A zoom lens is extremely useful; most SLR cameras have one. Use it to isolate the central subject of your photos. A common composition mistake is to include too much landscape around the person or feature that's your main focus.

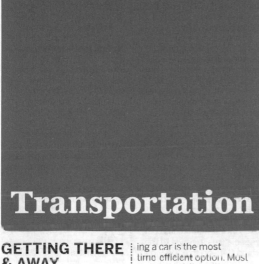

Transportation

GETTING THERE & AWAY

Most travelers to the Southwest arrive by air and car, with bus running a distant third place. The train service is little used but available. Major regional hubs include Las Vegas (p87), Phoenix (p127), Albuquerque (p250) and Salt Lake City (p478).

Flights, tours and rail tickets can be booked online at www.lonelyplanet.com/bookings. For information about entering the USA from overseas, see p550.

Air

Unless you live in or near the Southwest, flying in and rent-ing a car is the most time efficient option. Most domestic visitors fly into Phoenix, Las Vegas or Albuquerque. International visitors, however, usually first touch down in Los Angeles, New York, Miami, Denver or Dallas/Fort Worth before catching an onward flight to any number of destinations.

Airports & Airlines

International visitors might consider flying into Los Angeles and driving. **Los Angeles Airport** (LAX; ☎310-646-5252; www.lawa.org/welcomeLAX.aspx) is an easy day's drive from western Arizona or southwestern Utah, via Las Vegas. The following airports are located in the Southwest.

Albuquerque International Sunport (ABQ; ☎505-244-7700; www.cabq.gov/airport; ☎) Serving Albuquerque and all of New Mexico, this is a small and friendly airport that's easy to navigate.

Denver International Airport (DEN; ☎303-342-2000; www.flydenver.com; ☎) Serving southern Colorado, Denver is only four hours from northeastern New Mexico by car.

McCarran International Airport (LAS; ☎702-261-5211; www.mccarran.com; ☎) Serves Las Vegas and southern Utah. Las Vegas is 290 miles from the South Rim of the Grand Canyon and 277 miles from the North Rim.

Salt Lake City International Airport (SLC; ☎801-575-2400; www.slcairport.com; ☎) Serving Salt Lake City and northern Utah, it's a good choice if you're headed to the North Rim of the Grand Canyon and the Arizona Strip.

Sky Harbor International Airport (PHX; ☎602-273-3300; www.skyharbor.com; ☎) Located in Phoenix, this busy airport is 220 miles from the South Rim of the Grand Canyon and 335 miles from the North Rim.

Tucson International Airport (TUS; ☎520 573 8100; www.tucsonairport.org; ☎) Serving Tucson and southern Arizona, this is a small and easily navigated airport.

CLIMATE CHANGE & TRAVEL

Every form of transport that relies on carbon-based fuel generates CO_2, the main cause of human-induced climate change. Modern travel is dependent on aeroplanes, which might use less fuel per kilometer per person than most cars but travel much greater distances. The altitude at which aircraft emit gases (including CO_2) and particles also contributes to their climate change impact. Many websites offer 'carbon calculators' that allow people to estimate the carbon emissions generated by their journey and, for those who wish to do so, to offset the impact of the greenhouse gases emitted with contributions to portfolios of climate-friendly initiatives throughout the world. Lonely Planet offsets the carbon footprint of all staff and author travel.

Land

Border Crossings

From Yuma, AZ (p202), you can cross into Baja California and Mexico. Nogales, AZ, is also a prime border town. For more information about traveling south of the Southwest, pick up Lonely Planet's *Baja & Los Cabos* and *Mexico* guides. The biggest gateway if you're traveling in New Mexico is El Paso, TX, to reach Ciudad Juarez.

Don't forget your passport if you are crossing the border.

For information on visas, see p550.

Bus

Long-distance buses can get you to major points within the region, but then you will need to rent a car (see p560), as public transportation to the national parks, including the Grand Canyon, is nonexistent. Bus lines also don't serve many of the smaller towns, including important tourist hubs like Moab. Additionally, bus terminals are often in more dangerous areas of town. Having said that, **Greyhound** (☑800-231-2222; www.greyhound.com) is the main US bus system.

To save money on bus travel, plan seven days in advance, travel on weekdays, travel with a companion and avoid holiday travel. Search the internet for special deals. Students, military personnel and seniors receive discounts.

When you've graduated from **Green Tortoise** (☑800-867-8647; www.greentortoise .com), a rolling mosh pit of youthful sightseers, but you still want to sleep on a bus and hang with like-minded adventurers, look into **Adventure Bus** (☑888-737-5263; www.adventurebus.com). It specializes in travel to the Grand Canyon and the Moab area and recently added an Arizona Desert Explorer trip.

Car & Motorcycle

As mentioned, while the quickest way to get to the Southwest is by plane, the best way to get around is by car. Many places can only be reached by car, and it's nearly impossible to explore the national parks by bus.

Then there's the small matter of driving. If you love driving, you'll be in heaven. Of the 160,000 or so miles in the national highway system, the Southwest has more stunning miles than any other part of the country – just look at all the scenic byway signs!

Long-distance motorcycle driving is dangerous because of the fatigue factor that sets in. Please use caution during long hauls.

For more details about getting around the region by car or motorcycle, including road rules, see p560.

Train

Three **Amtrak** (☑800-872-7245; www.amtrak.com) trains cut a swath through the Southwest, but they are not connected to one another. Use them to reach the region but not for touring around. The Southwest Chief offers

---

CROSSING THE MEXICAN BORDER

At the time of research, the issue of crime-related violence in Mexico was front and center in the international press. Nogales, AZ, for example, is safe for travelers, but Nogales, Mexico was a major locus for the drug trade and its associated violence. As such, we cannot safely recommend crossing the border for an extended period until the security situation changes. Day trips are OK, but anything past that may be risky.

The US State Department recommends that travelers visit its website before traveling to Mexico (http://travel.state.gov/travel/cis_pa_tw/cis/cis_970.html). Here you can check for travel updates and warnings and confirm the latest border crossing requirements. Before leaving, US citizens can sign up for the Smart Traveler Enrollment Program (STEP; http://travel.state.gov/travel/tips/registration/registration_4789.html) to receive email updates prior to departure.

US and Canadian citizens returning from Mexico must present a US passport or passport card, and Enhanced Driver's License or a Trusted Traveler Card (either NEXUS, SENTRI or FAST cards). US and Canadian children under the age of 16 can also enter using their birth certificate, a Consular Report of Birth Abroad, naturalization certificate or Canadian citizenship card. All other nationals must carry their passport and, if needed, visas for entering Mexico and reentering the US. Regulations change frequently, so get the latest scoop at www.cbp.gov.

Driving across the border is a serious hassle. At the border or at the checkpoint 13 miles south of it, you need to pick up a free Mexican tourist card. US or other nations' auto insurance is not valid in Mexico and we strongly suggest you buy Mexican insurance on the US side of the border. Rates range from $19 to $26 per day, depending on coverage and your car's age and model.

a daily service between Chicago and Los Angeles, via Kansas City. Significant stations include Albuquerque, NM, and Flagstaff and Williams, AZ. As an added value, on-board guides provide commentary through national parks and Native American regions. The California Zephyr offers a daily service between Chicago and San Francisco (Emeryville) via Denver, with stops in Reno, NV and Salt Lake City, UT. The Sunset Limited runs thrice weekly from Los Angeles to New Orleans and stops in Tucson, AZ.

Book tickets in advance and look for plenty of available deals. Children, seniors and military personnel receive good discounts. Amtrak's USA Rail Pass offers coach class travel for 15 ($389), 30 ($579) and 45 ($749) days, with travel limited to 8, 12 or 18 one-way segments. Changing trains or buses completes one segment. In other words, every time you step off the train to either visit a city or to get on another Amtrak train or vehicle, you use up one of your allotted segments. Plan carefully.

It's not unusual for Amtrak trains, especially on longer routes, to run late.

GETTING TO THE SOUTHWEST

By Bus

FROM	TO	FARE ($)*	DURATION (HR)
Chicago, IL	Las Vegas, NV	330-425	38-40
Dallas, TX	Albuquerque, NM	188-259	13-15
Los Angeles, CA	Las Vegas, NV	84-129	6
Portland, OR	Salt Lake City, UT	194-267	18

*Round-trip prices

By Car or Motorcycle

FROM	TO	VIA	DURATION (HR)
Dallas, TX	Albuquerque, NM	I-35 & I-40	11½
Denver, CO	Santa Fe, NM	I-25	6½
Los Angeles, CA	Las Vegas, NV	I-15	5
San Diego, CA	Phoenix, AZ	I-8	7
San Francisco, CA	Santa Fe, NM	I-5 & I-40	19

By Train

FROM	TO	FARE ($)*	DURATION (HR)
Chicago, IL	Albuquerque, NM	280	26
Chicago, IL	Salt Lake City, UT	363	35
Los Angeles, CA	Flagstaff, AZ	148	11
Los Angeles, CA	Tucson, AZ	78	10
San Francisco, CA	Salt Lake City, UT	180	18

*Round-trip prices

GETTING AROUND

Once you reach the Southwest, traveling by car is the best way to get around and allows you to reach rural areas not served by public transportation. If you do not relish long drives, you can always take buses and trains between a limited number of major destinations and then rent a car. But that's both time-consuming and more expensive than driving yourself and stopping everywhere along the way.

Air

Because distances between places in the Southwest are so great, regional airports are located in a number of smaller towns such as Yuma and Flagstaff (both in Arizona), and Carlsbad and Taos (both in New Mexico). But since these airports primarily serve residents and business people, and because flying

ROAD DISTANCES (miles)

	Albuquerque, NM	Bryce Canyon NP, UT	Cortez (Mesa Verde NP), CO	Grand Canyon (North Rim), AZ	Grand Canyon (South Rim), AZ	Las Cruces, NM	Las Vegas, NV	Phoenix, AZ	Salt Lake City, UT	Santa Fe, NM
Bryce Canyon NP, UT	620									
Cortez (Mesa Verde NP), CO	280	390								
Grand Canyon (North Rim), AZ	470	130	340							
Grand Canyon (South Rim), AZ	410	290	370	210						
Las Cruces, NM	230	820	500	710	530					
Las Vegas, NV	580	250	570	270	280	670				
Phoenix, AZ	420	430	400	340	220	390	290			
Salt Lake City, UT	620	260	350	390	520	1030	420	710		
Santa Fe, NM	60	660	280	530	470	280	640	520	630	
Tucson, AZ	500	540	470	470	350	280	410	120	820	560

between these places is quite expensive and impractical, we have focused on the major air gateways (see p555). Still, you can find information about these smaller airports scattered throughout the regional chapters.

Airlines in the Southwest

Great Lakes (☎307-433-2899; www.greatlakesav.com) Direct flights between Prescott, AZ, and Los Angeles, CA, and between Farmington, CO (near Durango), and Denver, CO.

Southwest Airlines (☎800-435-9792; www.southwest.com) Major regional and budget carrier; flies to Albuquerque, NM, Tucson, AZ, Phoenix, AZ, Las Vegas, NV, Salt Lake City, UT, and El Paso, TX.

United Express (☎800-864-8331; www.united.com) Flies between Los Angeles International Airport (LAX) and Yuma, AZ.

US Airways (☎800-428-4322; www.usairways.com) Flies between Flagstaff, AZ, and Sky Harbor International Airport in Phoenix.

Bicycle

Cycling is a cheap, convenient, healthy, environmentally sound and, above all, fun way of traveling. In the Southwest – because of altitude, distance and heat – it's also a good workout. Cyclists should carry at least a gallon of water and refill bottles at every opportunity since dehydration (p550) is a major problem in the arid Southwest.

Airlines accept bicycles as checked luggage, but since each airline has specific requirements, it's best to contact them for details. Bicycle rentals are listed throughout this guide whenever there's a desirable place to cycle that also offers rentals. Expect to spend $25 to $50 a day for a beach cruiser or basic mountain bike. For more on cycling, see p41. Moab (p406) is generally considered the mountain-biking capital of the Southwest. The countryside around Sedona (p143) is great for biking.

Cyclists are permitted on some interstates in all five Southwestern states, but typically not in urban areas or where there's no alternative route or frontage road. Check the laws and maps for each state before hopping on an interstate and, where possible, ride adjacent frontage roads instead of the freeway. On the road, cyclists are generally treated courteously by motorists. In New Mexico and in certain counties and localities in Nevada and Arizona (including Flagstaff and Tucson), helmets are required by law for those under 18. There are no requirements in Colorado and Utah, but in any case, they should be worn to reduce the risk of head injury.

Cycling has increased in popularity so much in recent years that concerns have risen over damage to the environment, especially from unchecked mountain biking. Know your environment and regulations before you ride. Bikes are restricted from entering wilderness areas and some designated trails but may be used in Bureau of Land Management (BLM) singletrack trails and National

Park Service (NPS) sites, state parks, national and state forests.

Bus

Greyhound (☎800-231-2222; www.greyhound.com) is the main carrier to and within the Southwest, operating buses several times a day along major highways between large towns. Greyhound only stops at smaller towns that happen to be along the way, in which case the 'bus terminal' is likely to be a grocery-store parking lot or something similar. In this scenario, boarding passengers usually pay the driver with exact change. To see if Greyhound serves a town, look for the blue and red Greyhound symbol. The best schedules often involve overnight routes; the best fares often require seven days' advance notice.

Greyhound no longer offers service to Santa Fe, NM. Your best bet is to ride to Albuquerque, NM, then hop onto the adjacent Rail Runner train (p250), which takes 90 minutes to get to Santa Fe.

Car & Motorcycle

The Interstate system is thriving in the Southwest, but smaller state roads and fine scenic byways (see the regional chapters for these beauties) offer unparalleled opportunities for exploration. As for the former, I-10 runs east–west through southern Arizona, I-40 runs east–west through Arizona and central New Mexico, I-70 runs east–west through central Utah and I-80 runs east–west through northern Utah. In the north–south direction, I-15 links Las Vegas to Salt Lake City and I-25 runs through central New Mexico to Denver, CO. The oh-so-classic Route 66 more or less follows the modern-day I-40 through Arizona and New Mexico.

Automobile Associations

The **American Automobile Association** (AAA; ☎800-874-7532; www.aaa.com) provides members with maps and other information. Members also get discounts on car rentals, air tickets and some hotels and sightseeing attractions, as well as emergency road service and towing (☎800-222-4357). AAA has reciprocal agreements with automobile associations in other countries. Be sure to bring your membership card from your home country.

Emergency breakdown services are available 24 hours a day.

Driver's Licenses

Foreign visitors can legally drive a car in the USA for up to 12 months using their home country's driver's license. However, an IDP (International Driving Permit) will have more credibility with US traffic police, especially if your normal license doesn't have a photo or isn't in English. Your home country's automobile association can issue an IDP, valid for one year. Always carry your license together with the IDP.

Fuel

Gas stations are common and many are open 24 hours a day. Small-town stations may be open only from 7am to 8pm or 9pm.

At most stations, you must pay before you pump. The more modern pumps have credit/debit card terminals built into them, so you can pay right at the pump. At more expensive, 'full service' stations, an attendant will pump your gas for you; no tip is expected.

Insurance

Liability insurance covers people and property that you might hit. For damage to the actual rental vehicle, a collision damage waiver (CDW) is available for about $26 to $28 per day. If you have collision coverage on your vehicle at home, it might cover damages to rental cars; inquire before departing. Additionally, some credit cards offer reimbursement coverage for collision damages when you use the card to rent a car; again, check before departing. There may be exceptions for rentals of more than 15 days or for exotic models, jeeps, vans and 4WD vehicles. Check your policy.

Note that many rental agencies stipulate that damage a car suffers while being driven on unpaved roads is not covered by the insurance they offer. Check with the agent when you make your reservation.

BUSES AROUND THE SOUTHWEST

FROM	TO	FARE ($)*	DURATION (HR)
Albuquerque, NM	Salt Lake City, UT	125-176	19
Las Vegas, NV	Phoenix, AZ	45-65	8-9
Phoenix, AZ	Tucson, AZ	21-28	2
Tucson, AZ	Albuquerque, NM	99-140	9-14

*One-way prices

Rental

Rental cars are readily available at all airports and many downtown city locations. With advance reservations for a small car, the daily rate with unlimited mileage is about $30 to $46, though you might find lower rates. Larger companies don't require a credit card deposit, which means you can cancel without a penalty if you find a better rate. Midsize cars are often only a tad more expensive. Since deals abound and the business is competitive, it pays to shop around. Aggregator sites like www .kayak.com can provide a good cross-section of options. You can often snag great last-minute deals via the internet; rental reservations made in conjunction with an airplane ticket often yield better rates too.

Most companies require that you have a major credit card, are at least 25 years old and have a valid driver's license. Some national agencies may rent to drivers between the ages of 21 and 25 but may charge a daily fee.

If you decide to fly into one city and out of another, you may incur drop-off charges. Check the amount before finalizing your plans. Bidding for cars on **Priceline** (www .priceline.com) is one of the cheapest ways to rent a vehicle – you can pick the city, but not the rental company. Priceline even allows you to pick up a car in one city and drop it off in another. However, dropping off the car in another state may raise the rate.

Road Conditions & Hazards

Be extra defensive while driving in the Southwest. Everything from dust storms to snow to roaming livestock can make conditions dangerous. Near Flagstaff, watch for elk at sunset on I-17. The animals apparently like to soak up warmth from the blacktop (or so we've heard). You don't want to hit an elk, which can weigh between 500 and 900 pounds.

Distances are great in the Southwest and there are long stretches of road without gas stations. Running out of gas on a hot and desolate stretch of highway is no fun, so pay attention to signs that caution 'Next Gas 98 Miles.'

For updates on road conditions within a state, call ☑511. From outside a state, try one of the following:

Arizona (☑888-411-7623; www.az511.com)

Nevada (☑877-687-6237; www.safetravelusa.com/nv)

New Mexico (☑800-432-4269; http://m.nmroads.com)

Southern Colorado (☑303-639-1111; www.cotrip.org)

Utah (☑866-511-8824; www .commuterlink.utah.gov)

Road Rules

Driving laws are slightly different in each state, but all require the use of safety belts. In every state, children under five years of age must be placed in a child safety seat secured by proper restraints. For more details about seat belt laws for children see (p48).

The maximum speed limit on all rural interstates is 75mph, but that drops to 65mph in urban areas in Colorado, Nevada and Utah. New Mexico allows urban interstate drivers to barrel through at 75mph. The limit for Arizona drivers in urban areas is 65mph, but lawmakers require cars to crawl through high-density areas at 55mph. On undivided highways, the speed limit range will vary from 30mph in populated

---

I'M JUST WORKING FOR THE BORDER PATROL...

Officers of the federal United States Border Patrol (USBP) are ubiquitous in southern Arizona. Border patrol officers are law enforcement personnel who have the ability to pull you over, ask for ID and search your car if they have reasonable cause. Be aware that there's a good chance they'll flash you to the side of the road if you're driving down back roads in a rental or out-of-state car. This is because said roads have been used to smuggle both people and drugs north from Mexico. As a result we advise you to always carry ID, including a valid tourist visa if you're a foreign citizen, and car registration (if it's a rental car, your rental contract should suffice). Be polite and they should be polite to you. Agents may ask to see inside your trunk (boot) and backseat; it's probably best to let them do so (assuming you have nothing illegal to hide).

It's almost guaranteed that you'll drive through checkpoints down here. If you've never done so before, the 'stop side' of the checkpoints is the route going from south (Mexico) to north (USA). There's a chance you'll just be waved through the checkpoint; otherwise slow down, stop, answer a few questions (regarding your citizenship and the nature of your visit) and possibly pop your trunk and roll down your windows so officers can peek inside your car. Visitors may consider the above intrusive; all we can say is grin and bear it. For better or worse, this is a reality of traveling in southern Arizona.

INSPECTION STATIONS

When entering California, agricultural inspection stations at the Arizona–California border may ask you to surrender fruit in an attempt to stop the spread of pests associated with produce.

areas to between 65mph and 70mph on stretches where tumbleweeds keep pace with wily coyotes.

Motor Home (RV)

Rentals range from ultra-efficient VW campers to plush land yachts. After the size of the vehicle, consider the impact of gas prices, gas mileage, additional mileage costs, insurance and refundable deposits; these can add up quickly. It pays to shop around and read the fine print. Given the myriad permutations in rental choices, it's incredibly hard to generalize, but to get you started, you might expect a base rate for a four-person vehicle to run $1050 to $1300 weekly in the summer, plus 32¢ for each additional mile. Get out a good map and a calculator to determine if it's practical.

Before heading out, consult www.rvtravel.com for tips galore then purchase a campground guide from **Woodall's** (www.woodalls.com), which also has a great all-round website, or **Kampgrounds of America** (KOA; ☎406-248-7444; www.koa .com), and hit the road.

For RV rentals contact the following:

Adventure Touring RV Rentals (☎866-457-7997; www.adventuretouring.com) Serving Los Angeles, Las Vegas, Phoenix and Salt Lake City.

Adventure on Wheels (☎800 943-3579; http:// wheels9.com) Located in Las Vegas.

Cruise America (☎800-671-8042; www.cruiseamerica .com) Locations nationwide, including Las Vegas, Phoenix, Flagstaff, Tucson, Salt Lake City, Albuquerque and Colorado Springs.

Train

Several train lines provide services using historic steam trains. Although they are mainly for sightseeing, the Williams to Grand Canyon (p174) run is a destination in itself. More scenic train rides are located in Clarkdale, AZ (p141), Chama, NM (p313), Santa Fe, NM (p269), and Durango, CO (p359).

For info on Amtrak trains, see p556.

behind the scenes

SEND US YOUR FEEDBACK

We love to hear from travelers – your comments keep us on our toes and help make our books better. Our well-traveled team reads every word on what you loved or loathed about this book. Although we cannot reply individually to postal submissions, we always guarantee that your feedback goes straight to the appropriate authors, in time for the next edition. Each person who sends us information is thanked in the next edition – and the most useful submissions are rewarded with a free book.

Visit **lonelyplanet.com/contact** to submit your updates and suggestions or to ask for help. Our award-winning website also features inspirational travel stories, news and discussions.

Note: We may edit, reproduce and incorporate your comments in Lonely Planet products such as guidebooks, websites and digital products, so let us know if you don't want your comments reproduced or your name acknowledged. For a copy of our privacy policy visit lonelyplanet.com/privacy.

OUR READERS

Many thanks to the travelers who used the last edition and wrote to us with helpful hints, useful advice and interesting anecdotes:

Melissa Bazley, John Bennett, Eleanor Butler, Kim Dorin, Tony Fox, Jaclyn Gingrich, Giovanni Govoni, Duncan Grant, Mandeep Gulati, Arnaud Kaelbel, Marijn Kastelein, Tamara Kozak, Michael McMillan, Carsten Menke, Leah Moore, Janét Moyle, Michael Nicholas, Melanie Nisbet, Dale Parriott, Francesca Pittoni, Charlotte Pothuizen, Ulrich Raich, Ann & Bill Stoughton, Emanuela Tasinato, Silke Warmer, Madeleine Wasser

AUTHOR THANKS

Amy C Balfour

Thank you Suki and the Southwest team for top-notch editing and mapping. Big cheers to my super-helpful co-authors Lisa, Michael, Sarah and Carolyn. Many thanks to Deb Corcoran, Tucson's greatest docent, and Judy Hellmich-Bryan, who provided the latest news for Grand Canyon National Park. A special shout out to Lucy, Michael, Madeline, Claire and Clay Gordon for their hospitality and Phoenix insights, thanks Rob Hill and a toast to Mark Baker and Bisbee's

in-the-know barflies. Ninette Crunkleton and Melissa Peeler, thanks for the Arizona leads!

Michael Benanav

Thank you, Whitney George, in Ruidoso, for a great story about one Mike the Midget and a mysterious village beneath Bonita Lake. This summer, a huge thanks goes to the firefighters around the state. And to Kelly and Luke, thanks for always letting me go – and for always welcoming me back!

Sarah Chandler

My trusty co-pilot, the intrepid Jennifer Christensen, deserves serious props for remaining calm during flat tires, blizzards and a losing streak in the smoky blackjack room of the Hotel Nevada. Vek Neal and Todd Rice, thanks for being my partners in crime as we rocked out from the Double Down to the Bellagio: having that much fun is probably illegal, even in Nevada. Finally, to Jack and everyone at the Hard Rock, thanks for showing me how the locals brave Vegas nightlife (fearlessly, of course).

Lisa Dunford

I always meet so many kindred spirits on the Utah road. Thanks go to Nan Johnson, Peggy Egan, Trista Rayner, Nicole Muraro, David Belz, Jessica Kunzer, Lisa Varga and Ty Markham, among others. I very much enjoyed talking to you all. Thanks, too, to the many park rangers I met, for the ever-helpful job they do.

Carolyn McCarthy

Sincere gratitude goes out to all those who contributed to this book. An exceptionally snowy spring made it a challenge. Thanks also to Louise, Conan, Anne and the Cameron Johns family for their thoughtful hospitality. Richard proved adept at attacking the snowy passes and the all-American breakfasts. Finally, virtual microbrews go out to Melissa and the Fruita crowd for shoring me up in the home stretch.

ACKNOWLEDGMENTS

Climate map data adapted from Peel MC, Finlayson BL & McMahon TA (2007) 'Updated World Map of the Köppen-Geiger Climate Classification', *Hydrology and Earth System Sciences*, 11, 163344.

Cover photograph: Balanced Rock, Arches National Park, Utah, Andrew Marshall & Leanne Walker/LPI.
Many of the images in this guide are available for licensing from Lonely Planet Images: www.lonelyplanetimages.com.

THIS BOOK

This 6th edition of Southwest USA was researched and written by a fabulous author team (see Our Writers), with Amy C Balfour coordinating. Wendy Yanagihara and Jennifer Denniston contributed to the Grand Canyon section. Beth Kohn wrote the Reno text. The Native American chapter was based on text by Jeff Campbell. The Travel with Children was based on text by Jennifer Denniston.

This guidebook was commissioned in Lonely Planet's Oakland office, laid out by Cambridge Publishing Management, UK, and produced by the following:

Commissioning Editor Suki Gear

Coordinating Editors Karen Beaulah, Asha loculari
Coordinating Cartographer Eve Kelly
Coordinating Layout Designer Paul Queripel
Managing Editors Helen Christinis, Kirsten Rawlings
Managing Cartographers Alison Lyall, Shahara Ahmed
Senior Cartographer Anita Banh
Managing Layout Designer Chris Girdler
Assisting Editors Elin Berglund, Kathryn Glendenning, Michala Green, Briohny Hooper, Amy Karafin, Hazel Meek, Emma Sangster, Ceinwen Sinclair, Helen Yeates

Assisting Cartographers Ildiko Bogdanovits, Julie Dodkins, Joelene Kowalski, Sophie Reed, Brendan Streager
Assisting Layout Designer Julie Crane
Cover Research Naomi Parker
Internal Image Research Sabrina Dalbesio
Color Designer Tim Newton
Indexer Marie Lorimer

Thanks to Lucy Birchley, Seviora Citra, Ryan Evans, Jane Hart, Yvonne Kirk, Susan Paterson, Trent Paton, Angela Tinson, Gerard Walker

NOTES

index

000 Map pages
000 Photo pages

how to use this book

These symbols will help you find the listings you want:

- 👁 Sights
- 🏊 Beaches
- 🏃 Activities
- 🎓 Courses

- 👉 Tours
- 🎊 Festivals & Events
- 🛏 Sleeping
- ✕ Eating

- 🍸 Drinking
- ☆ Entertainment
- 🛍 Shopping
- ℹ Information/Transport

Look out for these icons:

TOP CHOICE	Our author's recommendation
FREE	No payment required
🌿	A green or sustainable option

Our authors have nominated these places as demonstrating a strong commitment to sustainability – for example by supporting local communities and producers, operating in an environmentally friendly way, or supporting conservation projects.

These symbols give you the vital information for each listing:

- ☎ Telephone Numbers
- ◷ Opening Hours
- Ⓟ Parking
- ⊖ Nonsmoking
- ✳ Air-Conditioning
- @ Internet Access

- 📶 Wi-Fi Access
- 🏊 Swimming Pool
- 🥗 Vegetarian Selection
- 📖 English-Language Menu
- 👪 Family-Friendly
- 🐾 Pet-Friendly

- 🚌 Bus
- ⛴ Ferry
- Ⓜ Metro
- Ⓢ Subway
- ⊖ London Tube
- 🚊 Tram
- 🚆 Train

Reviews are organised by author preference.

Map Legend

Sights
- 🏖 Beach
- 🛕 Buddhist
- 🏰 Castle
- ✝ Christian
- 🕉 Hindu
- ☪ Islamic
- ✡ Jewish
- ❶ Monument
- 🏛 Museum/Gallery
- ⊗ Ruin
- 🍷 Winery/Vineyard
- 🐒 Zoo
- ⊙ Other Sight

Activities, Courses & Tours
- 🤿 Diving/Snorkelling
- 🛶 Canoeing/Kayaking
- ⛷ Skiing
- 🏄 Surfing
- 🏊 Swimming/Pool
- 🚶 Walking
- 🏄 Windsurfing
- ⊕ Other Activity/Course/Tour

Sleeping
- 🛏 Sleeping
- ⛺ Camping

Eating
- ✕ Eating

Drinking
- ☕ Drinking
- ☕ Cafe

Entertainment
- ✪ Entertainment

Shopping
- 🛍 Shopping

Information
- ☑ Post Office
- ❶ Tourist Information

Transport
- ✈ Airport
- ⊗ Border Crossing
- 🚌 Bus
- 🚡 Cable Car/Funicular
- 🚲 Cycling
- ⛴ Ferry
- Ⓜ Metro
- 🚝 Monorail
- Ⓟ Parking
- Ⓢ S-Bahn
- 🚕 Taxi
- 🚉 Train/Railway
- 🚊 Tram
- ⊖ Tube Station
- Ⓤ U-Bahn
- • Other Transport

Routes
- Tollway
- Freeway
- Primary
- Secondary
- Tertiary
- Lane
- Unsealed Road
- Plaza/Mall
- Steps
-)≡≡(Tunnel
- Pedestrian Overpass
- Walking Tour
- Walking Tour Detour
- Path

Boundaries
- International
- State/Province
- Disputed
- Regional/Suburb
- Marine Park
- Cliff
- Wall

Population
- ✪ Capital (National)
- ◉ Capital (State/Province)
- ● City/Large Town
- • Town/Village

Geographic
- 🏠 Hut/Shelter
- 🏮 Lighthouse
- 👁 Lookout
- ▲ Mountain/Volcano
- 🌴 Oasis
- ❶ Park
-)(Pass
- 🌳 Picnic Area
- 💧 Waterfall

Hydrography
- River/Creek
- Intermittent River
- Swamp/Mangrove
- Reef
- Canal
- Water
- Dry/Salt/Intermittent Lake
- Glacier

Areas
- Beach/Desert
- +++ Cemetery (Christian)
- ××× Cemetery (Other)
- Park/Forest
- Sportsground
- Sight (Building)
- Top Sight (Building)

Carolyn McCarthy

Author Carolyn McCarthy was introduced to southern Colorado as a university freshman, when a freak blizzard stranded her orientation group in tents at 12,000ft in the Sangre de Cristo range. With sagebrush, powdery peaks and Spanish lore, the region soon became a favorite. In the last seven years she has contributed to more than a dozen Lonely Planet titles. She has also written for *National Geographic*, *Outside* and *Lonely Planet Magazine*, among other publications. You can follow her Americas blog at www.carolynswildblueyonder.blogspot.com.

Read more about Carolyn at:
lonelyplanet.com/members/carolynmccarthy

Contributing Authors

Jeff Campbell has been a travel writer for Lonely Planet since 2000. He was the coordinating author of three editions of *USA*, as well as editions of *Southwest USA*, *Zion & Bryce National Parks*, *Hawaii*, *Florida*, and *Mid-Atlantic Trips*, and he's been a contributor on other titles. He wishes that he called the Southwest home, but next best is meeting and writing about those who do.

David Lukas is a professional naturalist whose travels and writing take him around the American West and further afield. He has contributed environment and wildlife chapters to about 20 Lonely Planet guides. David's favorite Southwest moment was getting up to watch sunrise on the magnificent hoodoos at Bryce Canyon (don't miss it!).

OUR STORY

A beat-up old car, a few dollars in the pocket and a sense of adventure. In 1972 that's all Tony and Maureen Wheeler needed for the trip of a lifetime – across Europe and Asia overland to Australia. It took several months, and at the end – broke but inspired – they sat at their kitchen table writing and stapling together their first travel guide, *Across Asia on the Cheap*. Within a week they'd sold 1500 copies. Lonely Planet was born.

Today, Lonely Planet has offices in Melbourne, London and Oakland, with more than 600 staff and writers. We share Tony's belief that 'a great guidebook should do three things: inform, educate and amuse.'

OUR WRITERS

Amy C Balfour

Amy has hiked, biked, skied and gambled her way across the Southwest, finding herself returning again and again to Flagstaff, Monument Valley and, always, the Grand Canyon. On this trip she fell hard for Bisbee and Chiricahua National Monument. When she's not daydreaming about red rocks and green chile cheeseburgers, she's writing about food, travel and the outdoors. Amy has authored or co-authored 11 guidebooks for Lonely Planet, including *Los Angeles Encounter*, *California*, *Hawaii* and *Arizona*.

Read more about Amy at:
lonelyplanet.com/members/amycbalfour

Michael Benanav

Michael came to New Mexico in 1992 and quickly fell under its spell; soon after, he moved to a rural village in the Sangre de Cristo foothills, where he still lives. A veteran international traveler, he can't imagine a better place to come home to after a trip. Aside from his work for LP, he's authored two non-fiction books and writes and photographs for magazines and newspapers. His website is www .michaelbenanav.com.

Read more about Michael at:
lonelyplanet.com/members/michaelbenanav

Sarah Chandler

Long enamored of Sin City's gritty enchantments, Sarah jumped at the chance to sharpen her blackjack skills while delving into the atomic and alien mysteries of rural Nevada. In Vegas, Sarah learned the secret art of bypassing velvet ropes, bounced from buffets to pool parties, and explored the seedy vintage glamour of downtown. Sarah is currently based between the US and Amsterdam, where she works as a writer, actor, and lecturer at Amsterdam University College. When in doubt, she always doubles down.

Read more about Sarah at:
lonelyplanet.com/members/sarahchandler

Lisa Dunford

As one of the possibly thousands of descendants of Brigham Young, Lisa was first drawn to Utah by ancestry. But it's the incredible red rocks that keep her coming back. Driving the remote backroads outside Bluff, she was once again reminded how here the earth seems at its most elemental. Before becoming a freelance Lonely Planet author 10 years ago, Lisa was a newspaper editor and writer in South Texas. Lisa co-authored Lonely Planet's *Zion & Bryce Canyon National Parks*.

Read more about Lisa at:
lonelyplanet.com/members/lisadunford

MORE WRITERS

Published by Lonely Planet Publications Pty Ltd
ABN 36 005 607 983
6th edition – March 2012
ISBN 978 1 74179 466 3
© Lonely Planet 2012   Photographs © as indicated 2012
10 9 8 7 6 5 4 3 2 1
Printed in China

Although the authors and Lonely Planet have taken all reasonable care in preparing this book, we make no warranty about the accuracy or completeness of its content and, to the maximum extent permitted, disclaim all liability arising from its use.